G-MAN

G-MAN

J. EDGAR HOOVER

AND THE

MAKING

OF THE

AMERICAN CENTURY

BEVERLY GAGE

VIKING

VIKING
An imprint of Penguin Random House LLC
penguinrandomhouse.com

LIBRARY OF CONGRESS CATALOGING-IN-PUBLICATION DATA
Names: Gage, Beverly, author.
Title: G-man : J. Edgar Hoover and the making of the American century / Beverly Gage.
Description: New York : Viking, [2022] | Includes bibliographical references and index.
Identifiers: LCCN 2022021309 (print) | LCCN 2022021310 (ebook) |
ISBN 9780670025374 (hardcover) | ISBN 9780593492611 (ebook)
Subjects: LCSH: Hoover, J. Edgar (John Edgar), 1895-1972, |
United States. Federal Bureau of Investigation—Officials and employees—Biography. |
Government executives—United States—Biography. | United States—History—20th century.
Classification: LCC HV7911.H66 G34 2022 (print) | LCC HV7911.H66 (ebook) |
DDC 363.25092 [B]—dc23/eng/20220902
LC record available at https://lccn.loc.gov/2022021309
LC ebook record available at https://lccn.loc.gov/2022021310

Printed in the United States of America
4th Printing

Book design by Daniel Lagin

For Nick

CONTENTS

Part III

POWER AND POLITICS

(1945–1959)

Part IV
THE WAR AT HOME
(1960–1972)

INTRODUCTION

In 1959, FBI director J. Edgar Hoover arrived at a government screening room to watch the story of his life. At the age of sixty-four, he had long ago gone thick around the middle (though FBI weight codes forbade his employees from doing the same). The press said he looked like a bulldog—squat frame, bulging wide-set eyes, fearsome jowls—but this had not always been the case. Thirty-five years earlier, when he became director of the FBI, he had been the trim, dazzling wunderkind of the administrative state, buzzing with physical energy and big ideas for reform. At the time, the Bureau of Investigation had been a law enforcement backwater, riddled with scandal and failure and controversy. In the three and a half decades that followed, Hoover rebuilt it and then rebuilt it again, according to his own priorities and in his own image.

Some found the result frightening to behold—a political surveillance force without precedent in American life. Hoover always insisted that his creation was thoroughly American. Born and bred in Washington, D.C., he believed in the power of the federal government to do great things and fight great battles on behalf of the nation's citizens. He also believed that there were certain groups—communists and racial minorities, above all—who threatened that project. His career reflected both themes: a faith in progressive, expert-driven government and a commitment to an avenging social conservatism. His genius came in amassing enough power to promote and enforce those ideas as he saw fit.

Now he had a chance to discover what Hollywood thought of it all. *The FBI Story* followed the life of an organization rather than a man. But as everyone knew, Hoover *was* the FBI, its driving force and animating spirit. The film starred Jimmy Stewart as FBI agent Chip Hardesty, the embodiment of all that Hoover wanted his employees to be. Since taking over the Bureau in 1924, Hoover had cultivated a particular type of man as his ideal agent: tall, white, conservative, athletic, always in a dark suit and spit-shined shoes, either a lawyer or an accountant by training. In the 1930s, the newspapers had started describing this figure as a G-Man—or "Government Man"—the front-line soldier in the country's War on Crime. As one of the federal government's longest-serving and most prominent officials, Hoover became known as the ultimate G-Man, a political legend whose life and career were inextricable from the growth of federal bureaus and agencies and departments, and from the fraught public debate over how they were supposed to use their powers.

Colleagues liked to say Hoover was "married" to his Bureau, a policeman with neither time nor inclination for anything beyond the job. This was not quite true. If he was married to anyone, it was to Clyde Tolson, his famously loyal associate director. Tolson had joined the Bureau in the late 1920s, when Hoover was still working out his law enforcement vision. Since then, Tolson had been a model employee, but he had become something more as well. Where Hoover went, Tolson went too: not only to the office, but to the nightclub and the racetrack, on vacations and out for weeknight dinners, to family events and White House receptions. They were, in essence, a couple, though almost nobody—especially Hoover—referred to them that way.

Tolson attended the screening with Hoover. He also appeared with Hoover for a brief cameo in the film: Hoover seated at his mahogany desk, poring over serious investigative papers, with Tolson standing to his right. The rest of the film tracked Stewart's character but the stories were all Hoover's, the greatest hits of his three-decades-plus career. As Agent Hardesty, Stewart solved the gruesome Osage Indian murders of the mid-1920s. From there, the film broadened out into the kidnappings and gangster shoot-outs of the 1930s, the German sabotage and espionage cases of the war years, and, most recently, the FBI's investigations of communists. Those cases, along with the Bureau's attendant public relations campaigns, had made Hoover into one of the most widely admired men in American politics, championed by Republicans and Democrats, conservatives and liberals alike. They had also earned him a small but incisive group of critics, who warned that his methods and thirst for power endangered American democracy.

The FBI Story director Mervyn LeRoy counted himself among Hoover's admirers. He had allowed Hoover to review and approve the film's script. Still, he confessed to being nervous about what the FBI director would think. If Hoover was most famous as a lawman, he was also known as a ruthless political warrior, unyielding to those who criticized him or tarnished his Bureau's reputation. To LeRoy's relief, Hoover looked pleased as the lights came up. "Mervyn, that's one of the greatest jobs I've ever seen," he declared after two and a half hours of watching his life story unfold. One aide thought he saw tears in Hoover's eyes, the first time he had ever seen the indomitable FBI director show a human side.[1]

IF HOOVER HAD DECIDED TO STEP DOWN AT THAT MOMENT IN 1959, AFTER thirty-five years at the FBI's helm, we might remember him differently: as a popular and well-respected government official, often cruel and controversial but a hero to more Americans than not. Instead, he stayed on through the 1960s and emerged as one of history's great villains, perhaps the most universally reviled American political figure of the twentieth century. His abuses and excesses, from the secret manipulations of COINTELPRO to his deep-seated racism, offer a troubling case study in unaccountable government power.

G-Man is the first major biography of Hoover to be published in nearly three decades. One of its goals is to document those abuses and then some, drawing upon recently released files to show how Hoover rose to power and then stayed there, decade after decade, using the tools of the administrative state to create a personal fiefdom unrivaled in U.S. history. But Hoover was more than a one-dimensional tyrant and backroom schemer who strong-armed the rest of the country into submission. As FBI director from 1924 until his death in 1972, he was the most influential federal appointee of the twentieth century, a confidant, counselor, and adversary to eight U.S. presidents. He also embodied conservative values ranging from anticommunism to white supremacy to a crusading and politicized interpretation of Christianity. Far from making him a public scourge, these two aspects of his life garnered him the admiration of millions of Americans, including many of the country's leading politicians, for most of his career.[2]

Hoover's network of supporters began at the very top, with the eight presidents—four Republicans, four Democrats—who kept him in office and then hoped that he would do their bidding. They did not always agree with his methods and ideas. But they relied on him, respected him, and, in most cases, feared him. The presidents who did the most to empower Hoover were the two great liberal titans of the twentieth century: Franklin Roosevelt and Lyndon Johnson. Hoover's closest friend among the eight was Richard Nixon, an ally and fellow anticommunist warrior of more than three decades' standing. Popular legend suggests that Hoover held on to power as long as he did through blackmail and intimidation—and it is true that he was skilled in such arts. But no public servant could survive for forty-eight years without support from both above and below. The truth is that Hoover stayed in office for so long because many people, from the highest reaches of government down to the grassroots, wanted him there and supported what he was doing.

After more than a decade of study, I do not count myself among Hoover's admirers. But this book is less about judging him than about understanding him—and thus understanding ourselves and our national political past. As a biographer, I have tried to keep Hoover's humanity in view (a consideration he did not always extend to others). I have also tried to avoid slipping into timeworn stereotypes of him as a single-minded Machiavellian operator—or, worse yet, as an unblemished national hero. Over the course of his forty-eight years as FBI director, Hoover got to know nearly everyone who mattered in Washington and helped to influence an astonishing range of national events, from the New Deal "War on Crime" on up through World War II, McCarthyism, the Rosenberg and Hiss cases, the Kennedy and King assassinations, the civil rights and anti-war struggles, and the political machinations that led to Watergate. *G-Man* places Hoover back where he once stood in American political history—not at the fringes, but at the center.

The pages that follow use Hoover's story to explain the trajectories of governance, policing, race, ideology, political culture, and federal power as they evolved over the course of the twentieth century. In particular, the book situates Hoover within two political traditions now often seen to be at odds. As an appointed civil servant, Hoover championed professionalism, scientific authority, and apolitical expertise. At the same time, he saw himself as part of a vanguard force protecting key conservative principles. Today, when the Republican Party regularly denounces both federal authority and nonpartisan expertise, it can be hard to imagine these ideas fitting together. But Hoover made it work for almost half a century, a conservative state-builder throughout the heyday of American liberalism.

G-MAN EXPLORES THE FULL SWEEP OF HOOVER'S LIFE AND CAREER, FROM HIS birth in 1895 to a modest civil-service family through his death in 1972 as one of the most famous and controversial political men in America. Hoover lived his entire life in Washington, D.C. His biography is also the story of his hometown as it transformed from a sleepy parochial city into a center of global power. Of the many ambitious men who descended on Washington during Hoover's lifetime—the Wilson-era progressives, the brash New Dealers, the military-industrial architects of the early Cold War—few matched Hoover's bureaucratic genius and political skill. When Hoover arrived at the Justice Department during World War I, the Bureau of Investigation was a tiny, obscure pseudo-agency, composed of a few dozen detectives chasing a hodgepodge of minor offenders. By the time he died in office, the FBI employed thousands of special agents and presided over investigations of federal crimes including interstate auto theft, kidnapping, bank robbery, and civil rights violations in addition to domestic "subversion" and espionage. During his lifetime, Hoover supervised countless political investigations, criminal inquiries, and counterespionage operations. He also made hundreds of speeches and published hundreds of articles on matters ranging from to law and order to communism to the virtues of the Christian family. We need not admire his agenda or applaud his methods to appreciate the sweeping nature of his influence.

G-Man shows how Hoover built the FBI into one of the most storied institutions in American government. It also seeks to restore the sense of uncertainty, experimentation, and genuine risk that went into that process. Hoover's popular image suggests that exercising power is a simple task: press a few buttons, whisper in a few ears, twist a few arms, and presto, the world opens up. The truth is that power does not simply arrive. It has to be created, policy by policy, law by law, step by excruciating step.

For Hoover, this happened slowly. His first decade as Bureau chief mostly involved paperwork and internal reforms. Only with the New Deal and its flexing of federal muscle did the FBI begin to resemble the agency we know today. It may seem odd, given Hoover's legendary contempt for liberals, to think of the FBI as a New Deal initiative. And yet the tools of New Deal liberalism—professionalization, centralization, administrative expansion—are what enabled his rise. Schooled as small-*d* democrats, Americans tend to narrate our national politics as a series of election cycles. Less often noted, but at least as important, are the stories of appointed officials like Hoover, those unelected (and sometimes unaccountable) bureaucrats who find a path to power outside of electoral processes.

Hoover's fundamental views changed little over the course of his career—one part high-minded administration, one part narrow-minded reaction. Yet he knew how to be flexible and adapt quickly to changing circumstances. Federal jurisdiction determined which laws he was bound to enforce, but that category shifted constantly, as Congress enacted new legislation and president after president looked to the FBI to carry out new duties. Every few years, Hoover found himself forced to master a new field of law enforcement—kidnapping and bank robbery, foreign espionage, lynching, organized crime, political surveillance, civil and voting rights. Often, he had to do it in just a few months' time and in the midst of crisis. That he managed such challenges as effectively as he did can be attributed to a surprising degree of nimbleness and creativity, traits not often associated with career bureaucrats, much less with Hoover. It can also be chalked up to self-interest. Above all, Hoover sought to protect his own autonomy and acclaim, judging each new circumstance by what it would or would not do for his career and his Bureau.

As an appointed official, Hoover sometimes found his professional obligations at odds with his personal views. His greatest abuses of power tended to occur in just such situations. When Hoover wanted to target a particular group or individual but did not necessarily have the law on his side, he turned to the tried-and-true method of secrecy. He created COINTELPRO, now the most notorious program of his career, in order to continue attacking the Communist Party once the Supreme Court ruled other techniques unconstitutional. He justified bugging Martin Luther King's hotel rooms as a vital national-security imperative, though he acknowledged that the FBI would be subjected to ferocious criticism if caught. During Hoover's lifetime, there were no congressional intelligence committees to hold the Bureau to account. Even his ostensible boss, the attorney general, did not necessarily have access to Bureau files. With good reason, Hoover expected that everything the FBI did would remain secret unless he dictated otherwise. Partly as a result, FBI files are filled with remarkably candid discussions of his strategies, priorities, and prejudices.

If Hoover's outsize faith in his own judgment often pushed the FBI into questionable and even illegal territory, on occasion it also led him to take enlightened positions and to ally with unlikely bedfellows. During World War II, he opposed Japanese internment on grounds that it was unconstitutional and likely to disrupt the FBI's home-front policing. He built working relationships with the NAACP and the ACLU, activist organizations whose leaders would later view those collaborations with dismay. During the 1940s, he faced down white Southern opposition in order to investigate racial lynchings, convinced that the FBI's legitimacy was at stake. In the 1950s, he quietly helped to destroy Senator Joseph McCarthy, whom he viewed as a friend but also as a loose-cannon threat to the anticommunist cause. In the years that followed, he initiated famously vicious campaigns against civil rights and New Left activists, including King. To a lesser degree, he also went after the Ku Klux Klan and white supremacist groups, viewing them as dangerous vigilantes. When Nixon became president, Hoover was thrilled to have a close friend in office but opposed Nixon's attempts to undermine FBI independence and use its agents as a personal dirty-tricks squad.

While Hoover occasionally made common cause with liberals and civil libertarians, he found his deepest affinities among conservatives, men and women who shared his views on race, religion, and Reds, the three volatile R's of mid-century politics. Anticommunism defined Hoover's outlook, the first principle of a worldview that extended from weighty matters of foreign policy and political surveillance down to the advice he regularly doled out to American parents. Seeking to understand the rise of modern conservatism, historians have often emphasized a postwar trajectory leading from William F. Buckley through Republican presidential candidate Barry Goldwater and on up to Ronald Reagan. Hoover's story suggests a different genealogy: he formed his worldview during the Progressive Era, and changed it little in the ensuing years. His career also underscores the importance of examining those conservatives who exercised real state power throughout the middle of the twentieth century, years supposedly dominated by an entrenched liberal consensus.[3]

Measured by what he accomplished—not just by what he said—Hoover was among the most powerful conservative political figures of the twentieth century, able to steer the ship of state in his direction even when electoral politics and White House sentiment might have dictated otherwise. He never allied himself with a political party. As a Washington resident, he never even cast a vote. That nonpartisan identity helped him to survive in office as other Washington power brokers fell by the wayside. It also gave him a platform from which to opine as a seemingly objective expert about those groups and individuals he deemed to be dangerous to the country at large. Most of those groups came from the left—not just the Communist Party but also the full array of civil rights, anti-war, New Left, labor, gay rights, and socialist organizations that sprang up over the course of his career to challenge the status quo. But Hoover was never entirely comfortable with his far-right supporters either, viewing many of them as irresponsible conspiracy theorists who detracted from rather than reinforced FBI authority. In choosing which groups to disrupt and which to ignore, Hoover altered the trajectory of American history, turning the FBI into an enforcement arm for his personal vision of national virtue.

How he balanced the competing priorities of his job changed over the course of his half century in office. Hoover came to government work in the chaos of World War I and the first Red Scare, trained early on in the art of political surveillance. When the public turned against such activities, he refashioned himself as a good-government reformer and devotee of civil liberties, dominant features of his image well into the 1940s. Hoover built the FBI while insisting that he opposed the creation of a national police force, positioning himself as a champion of local law enforcement. Once the FBI was firmly established, he turned back to the themes of his early years, proclaiming his Bureau to be the nation's great bulwark against communism. The 1950s marked the height of Hoover's popularity. That decade was also the period in which his institutional and ideological agendas most closely aligned. During the 1960s, the FBI slipped into crisis, as Hoover increasingly abandoned the professional, apolitical ethos supposedly at the heart of Bureau operations in favor of crusades against his political and ideological enemies.

Hoover's determination to forge his own path through American politics does not mean that he ignored popular sentiment; far from it. No modern official better understood how crucial public opinion was to the accomplishment of bureaucratic goals—and to the legitimacy of federal power. As early as the 1930s, polls ranked Hoover as one of the most admired men in America. Even in the 1960s and early 1970s, by far his most controversial years, he was a consistently popular figure. Some of that popularity rested on his ability to keep secrets, to hide from the public what the FBI was really doing. In many cases, though, Hoover was perfectly open about his opinions and priorities. Though many Americans were shocked to learn about COINTELPRO, it is now clear that Hoover informed Congress, the president, and the attorney general about the program in the late 1950s—and none of them registered any objection. And when he revealed his own biases and agenda to the broader public, Americans by and large approved. After he denounced Martin Luther King in 1964 as the country's "most notorious liar," polls showed that 50 percent of Americans supported Hoover, while just 16 percent sided with King. The fact that these two men have since exchanged places in our preferred national narrative should not obscure the less palatable historical realities.[4]

If there is a tragic element to Hoover's story, it is that he failed to abide by his own best principles. And his tragedy, in turn, became our own. Hoover did not invent most of the ideas he espoused. But he legitimated them and knew how to put them into action. His emphasis on professionalism and apolitical expertise insulated him from critics who said he was nothing but a far-right ideologue. Conversely, his declamations on the perils of communism, atheism, social disorder, and defiance of the law gave him a passionate grassroots base all but unheard-of among bureaucrats. It was this combination of factors—openness and secrecy, liberalism and conservatism, hard and soft power—that gave Hoover his extraordinary staying power.

ONE CHALLENGE OF WRITING ABOUT A FIGURE LIKE HOOVER IS THE SHEER wealth of material: nearly every chapter in this biography could be a book. Indeed, the most famous episodes in the pages that follow—the Palmer Raids, the capture of John Dillinger, Pearl Harbor, the Hiss case, the Rosenberg trial, COINTELPRO, the Kennedy assassination, the Mississippi Burning murders, the FBI's surveillance of King and the Black Panthers (just to name a few)—have been the subjects of entire literatures in their own right. The FBI produced paper and then more paper, Hoover's favorite measure of bureaucratic productivity. And Hoover was an obsessive chronicler of his own history, amassing more than two hundred archival boxes of press clippings over his forty-eight years as director.

In researching Hoover's life, I have examined hundreds of thousands if not millions of pages of records, ranging from FBI case files to Hoover's childhood diaries to his correspondence with presidents, celebrities, and friends. Along the way, I have benefited enormously from the work of other scholars and journalists, whose research and writing are discussed in a Note on Sources section at the back of the book. *G-Man* contains a vast array of new archival material; one thrill of working on a subject like the FBI is that never-before-seen archives and files open on a regular basis. Over the past decade, I have filed dozens of Freedom of Information Act requests, yielding thousands of pages of documents never before studied by historians. I have also taken advantage of important files released by the FBI and other government agencies since the early 1990s, when the last major Hoover biographies were published.[5]

Out of these releases have come many discoveries, archival and interpretive alike. Some pertain to Hoover's childhood; though he often described an idyllic upbringing, newly available documents show that he grappled with a family legacy of suicide, scandal, mental illness, even violent crime. Others reveal the forces that shaped his early consciousness—most notably, his college membership in Kappa Alpha, a reactionary Southern fraternity that championed racial segregation and Lost Cause culture. Still others offer glimpses into Hoover's internal life. Understanding his sexuality poses daunting challenges for a biographer—but here, too, new sources (and older sources, now reinterpreted) have helped to make a hidden story more visible. A guarded and secretive man, Hoover could be surprisingly open in correspondence with friends and family. Through these materials, *G-Man* presents glimpses of his emotional reactions to events ranging from the Kennedy assassination to his own mother's death. It also offers a reassessment of his relationship with Tolson, by far the most important of his adult life.

When it comes to Hoover's leadership of the FBI, the new material released, acquired, requested, and discovered since the last major Hoover biographies is nothing short of staggering. Some of it tends to vindicate Hoover, or at least to provide a more accurate understanding of why he behaved as he did. Other new documents show Hoover at his worst, fueled by a toxic blend of defensiveness, racism, and personal rage. Many of my own Freedom of Information Act requests have focused on far-right and white supremacist groups, an area of FBI work far less studied than its repression of the American left. There, it turns out that Hoover did more than he has been given credit for, though not nearly as much as the situation often warranted.

The bulk of Hoover's energies went into crime fighting, law enforcement, and domestic intelligence, and here there is much new to reveal as well. Chapter 40 takes up one of most oft-cited myths about Hoover—the idea that he denied the existence of organized crime and the Mafia—and shows how the FBI initiated its own secret campaigns against organized crime in the 1950s. Other chapters describe how he developed the FBI's political surveillance capacities, looking to World War II as well as the postwar Red Scare as crucial years of growth and experimentation.

For better or worse, Hoover had a hand in nearly every event of national significance from the moment he became FBI director in 1924 to the day he died in that post in 1972. His career was made possible not only by his political and bureaucratic genius, but by a transformation in American governance that concentrated power and attention and money at the federal level, and that gave unelected officials like Hoover a critical new role to play. The pages that follow tell that story through the life of a single—and singular—political figure, the twentieth century's quintessential Government Man. To look at him is also to look at ourselves, at what Americans valued and fought over during those years, what we tolerated and what we refused to see.

G-MAN

Part I

THE FEDERAL CITY

(1895–1924)

CHAPTER 1

The Oldest Inhabitants

(1800–1895)

Hoover with his parents
Annie and Dickerson
around 1900. He was born
and raised in Washington,
D.C. He lived there for
the rest of his life.

NATIONAL ARCHIVES AND
RECORDS ADMINISTRATION

When J. Edgar Hoover told the story of his life, he began with a childhood parable. Even as a little boy, he sought out lessons and morals: "1. Eat slowly. 2. Eat regularly. 3. Do not eat between meals," he wrote in a childhood newspaper, composed at age eleven. As an adult, he tended to describe his early years as a series of edifying adventures, each building upon the last to make him a decent, God-fearing man. He particularly liked the story of his first job, delivering groceries at Washington's Eastern Market, when he discovered that running faster and working harder than all the other boys meant bigger tips.[1]

Hoover did work hard as a boy, earning near-perfect grades and a spotless record as a Sunday school teacher. All the same, his childhood—even more than most—was messy and uncertain, shaped by family tragedies that began well before his birth. In 1880, fifteen years before Hoover was born, his maternal grandfather drowned himself in the Anacostia River, leaving behind a note despairing of the "hypocritical and false-swearing people" who had driven him to the act. Four decades later, Hoover's own father died of "melancholia" and "inanition" (what we today might describe as severe depression), disappearing first into sadness and rage and, later, losing the desire to eat or live. In between, there were other births and deaths, and even a murder scandalous enough to make the front page.[2]

As an adult, Hoover never spoke publicly of these difficulties. It would have been anathema for him to do so, a confession of pain and weakness from a man who valued certitude and control. There are connections nonetheless: between the emotional chaos of childhood and the emotional challenges of adulthood; between the teenager forced to keep secrets about his father and the government servant for whom secrets became a way of life. As a young man, Hoover was driven to succeed, first as high school valedictorian, then as a law-school standout, and finally in the Justice Department, where he went to work at the age of twenty-two. Some of these early accomplishments flowed from genuine talent and ambition. Even in high school, students knew him as a boy on his way up. But fear and necessity drove him during those years as well, a pressure to earn money and to do all that his father (and his grandfathers before that) had failed to do. By the time he reached his late twenties, he had acquired the two essential elements of his professional outlook: first, a passionate commitment to the idea of nonpartisan, expert-driven career government service; second, a deep-seated conservatism on matters of race, religion, and left-wing threats to the political status quo. These themes would define his career, but as a boy he was still learning, absorbing stern lessons and cautionary tales from his family, schools, and hometown.

The closest Hoover ever came to acknowledging a less than perfect childhood was in 1938, a few months after his mother's death, when he published an unusually personal article speculating about what might happen "If I Had a Son." In that article, he noted that boys want to worship their fathers "as head of the house, a repository of all knowledge, the universal provider, the righteous Judge." Such admiration became impossible when parents relied on "half-truths" to lull their children into a false sense of security. "If I had a son, I'd swear to do one thing: I'd tell him the truth," Hoover wrote. "No matter how difficult it might be, I'd tell my boy the truth." The advice is surprising, coming from a man who spent his adult life avoiding the exposure of uncomfortable truths about himself and the institution he created. As a guiding principle for telling his story, though, it seems like a fine place to begin.[3]

FROM HIS GRANDPARENTS AND GREAT-GRANDPARENTS, MEN AND WOMEN HE mostly never knew, Hoover inherited two important legacies. The first was a set of roots in the federal city of Washington, D.C., where traditions of government service and social hierarchy existed side by side. The second was a history of violence and breakdown among the family's men, including the premature deaths of his grandfathers more than a decade before his birth. From his Washington roots he gained both his professional mission and his political worldview. From his family's difficulties he took a merciless anxiety about the world, and a desire to control what happened around him.

As a clan, the Hoovers seem to have hailed from German stock, but so far back that it hardly mattered. During the eighteenth century, the family lived in Pennsylvania before migrating south to Washington in the early nineteenth century. The city was brand-new in those years, an artificial creation carved from muck and swamp after the states failed to settle on Philadelphia or New York for their national capital. The initial vision had been grandiose: wide avenues and breathtaking public buildings testifying to the promise of the American republic. It lost something in the execution. When the federal government arrived to set up shop in 1800, one congressman pronounced Washington "a city in ruins," its grand avenues thick with mud and its public buildings little more than clapboard planks nailed up against the cold. Fourteen years later, the British burned the city and local residents started over again. Hoover's ancestors arrived in the midst of this rebuilding, forever linking the Hoover family to the ups and downs of the federal government.[4]

Hoover's great-grandfather William, a butcher, became a true Washington patriarch, fathering eleven children. By the middle of the nineteenth century, those children, and their children's children, occupied a dusty stretch of Sixth Street between M and N Streets, near what was then the outer perimeter of habitation. The Hoovers were a close-knit, well-established Washington family, if just outside the downtown corridors of power.[5]

Some of the early family men were slave owners, though of a distinctly Washington sort. To the north and south, Maryland and Virginia maintained flourishing plantation economies, and thus large concentrations of men and women held in bondage. In Washington, a political and commercial city, even prominent slaveholders claimed at best a handful of enslaved persons. One early Hoover claimed ownership over two human beings: a boy under fourteen and a slightly older woman, who presumably provided household help. Hoover's paternal great-grandfather, Dickerson Naylor, owned at least one enslaved person, freed only with the abolition of slavery in the district in 1862. Antebellum Washington was a Southern town, committed to the practice of slavery and to the racial order it entailed.[6]

This Southern legacy would become an important part of Hoover's upbringing and worldview. And yet there was another side to Washington's racial history and this, too, shaped Hoover's family inheritance. As a federal city in the midst of the plantation South, antebellum Washington often served as a refuge for Black men and women. Long-standing rumors suggest that at least one of Hoover's ancestors hailed from this population. For decades after his appointment as FBI director, there were rumors that Hoover came from a "passing" family—that he was, under the one-drop rule governing racial classifications, actually Black. Circumstantial evidence makes the idea plausible:

Hoover's family lived in a multiracial city and engaged in the sorts of work often per-formed by Black men and women. Still, census and genealogical documents suggest that the Hoovers were mostly what they said they were: a tight-knit clan of small shop-keepers and tradesmen, among the oldest white families in the city.[7]

From the outside, visiting writers often mocked nineteenth-century Washington as a backwater—a "City of Magnificent Intentions" dismally lacking in worthwhile "houses, roads, and inhabitants," in the words of Charles Dickens. Families like the Hoovers thought differently, and they organized a distinct local culture to prove it. The most committed of them joined the Association of the Oldest Inhabitants of the District of Columbia, open only to families present long before Washington became a center of national power. But for all the insistence upon the distinction between locals and politicians, between residents and government transients, nobody lived in Wash-ington for long without being drawn into the federal orbit. The Hoovers were no ex-ception. Around 1853, Hoover's great-grandfather took a job as a messenger for the post office, among the lowest rungs of the federal hierarchy. That same year, his grand-father, John Thomas Hoover, signed on as a clerk with the U.S. Coast and Geodetic Survey, the first scientific agency to be endorsed and funded by the federal government. Between them, they began a family tradition of government service that would con-tinue almost unbroken for the next 120 years.[8]

OF ALL HIS PATERNAL ANCESTORS, INCLUDING HIS OWN FATHER, HOOVER turned out most like his grandfather John Thomas, the man who introduced the fam-ily to professional government work. They shared a name: "John Edgar" was, in part, a tribute to John Thomas. But the affinity seems to have gone much deeper, a common-ality of ideas, ambition, and temperament that reached across generations. As a young man, John Thomas was relentlessly driven and efficient, determined to secure a foot-hold in the emerging federal bureaucracy. He was the first family member to show how diligence, organization, and a knack for file keeping could yield a successful govern-ment career. Socially, too, he set the template that his grandson would later follow: membership in the Presbyterian Church, along with active participation in the Ma-sonic order and its fraternal Washington networks.

As a boy, John Thomas grew up fast, the oldest of his parents' eleven children. Ac-cording to family lore, at age fifteen he turned down offers to attend West Point and the Naval Academy in order to remain in Washington and seek his fortune. Whether or not the story was true, it pointed to something important about Hoover family tradition: staying in Washington was the expected thing. In 1853, at the age of eigh-teen, John Thomas accepted a clerkship at the Coast Survey, a turning point that brought the Hoover clan into white-collar government employment. Two years later, he married Cecilia Naylor, the daughter of a prosperous grocer and small slaveholder.

And two years after that, Cecilia gave birth to Hoover's father, Dickerson, a thin, gentle boy who would grow up surrounded by boisterous aunts, uncles, and cousins, and who would eventually follow his father into the Coast Survey.[9]

Congress had created the survey to map the coastline of the Louisiana Purchase. By the time John Thomas went to work there in the 1850s, it had acquired a reputation as one of the few well-established professional agencies in Washington, an early progenitor of the modern civil service. Its chief was Alexander Dallas Bache, a dashing West Point graduate (and great-grandson of Benjamin Franklin) who viewed the survey as a means to promote scientific enterprise using the purse strings of the federal government. Bache was both a visionary and a bureaucrat, an early example of the sort of independent administrator Hoover himself would later become.[10]

Hoover's grandfather was unusually close to Bache, something between a personal assistant and surrogate son. John Thomas originally signed on to work in the survey's computing division, which calculated map coordinates and double-checked the work of human "computers" in the field. Several years into his work, he was promoted to the post of field secretary. In that role, he began to write Bache's correspondence, plan his schedule, and accompany his boss on official expeditions. This swift rise suggests that John Thomas shared another of his future grandson's talents: the ability to please older men in positions of power. Bache praised John Thomas for his "zeal and fidelity."

Coast Survey men shared a distinctive approach. Though they worked for the government, survey employees considered themselves scientific professionals, set apart from the Sturm und Drang of electoral politics. As such, they were among the first bona fide members of the modern administrative state, men who believed that their value lay in expertise and bureaucratic skill rather than in partisan loyalty. But politics had a way of intruding in Washington. When the Civil War broke out in 1861, the survey was put to work building fortifications on League Island near Philadelphia in preparation for a Southern attack that never came. While working on the project, John Thomas contracted tuberculosis, the beginning of a long, slow decline that altered the family's plans for the future.[11]

He returned home to Washington to find the city transformed, its slave system shattered, its population doubled, its oldest residents bewildered by the change. He, too, had changed, no longer the energetic, forward-looking man he had once been. After a brief convalescence, he returned to survey work as head of its Division of Charts and Instruments. He survived more than a decade in the post and even recruited his oldest son, Dickerson—Hoover's father—to join him. The son brought little of the "zeal" and vision that had been the father's trademark. An early photo of Dickerson shows a sallow man with a receding chin and wide-set eyes, gazing distantly off-camera, hardly the heir to his father's once-robust energies.[12]

Dickerson joined the survey in 1876, at the age of twenty. Over the next few years, his father entered a final decline, slowly giving up on church and charitable activities as his lung infection returned. The end came suddenly on May 25, 1878. "Within the fortnight preceding that date he was at the office as usual, efficiently discharging duties to which he had been long accustomed," recalled a Coast Survey publication. Then his lungs gave out.[13]

His government obituary mourned the loss of "one of the most useful members of the Coast Survey" at the age of forty-three. It made no mention of his eldest son, Dickerson, just twenty years old and now the head of the family.[14]

JOHN THOMAS'S PREMATURE DEATH WAS ONE MAJOR RUPTURE IN HOOVER'S family past—a jarring moment of loss that forever altered his father's prospects and put the family under deep financial constraints. Another came from his mother's side and was the more dramatic of the two, not a protracted, helpless decline but a concentrated few years of devastation and betrayal.

Hoover's mother, Annie, descended from the Hitz line—the most prominent family of nineteenth-century Swiss Washington, several rungs up from the Hoovers on the city's class ladder. Its local patriarch was John, or Hans, Hitz (another inspiration for Hoover's first name). Raised as a mining engineer in the meticulous Swiss tradition, Hans had arrived in Washington during the 1830s with his wife, parents, and several children. He worked closely with the Coast Survey but made his real money off of private ventures, managing gold and zinc mines while helping to run an odd assortment of local businesses. In recognition of this success, he earned an appointment as the first Swiss consul general to the United States, the highest post available for a Swiss citizen living in America.[15]

By today's standards, being a Washington diplomat in the 1850s was not glamorous. Nor was there much for a Swiss consul to do in a city where foreign-born residents made up just 20 percent of the population, and only a tiny fraction of those foreign-born residents were Swiss. Switzerland itself was a relatively new nation, its central government cobbled together in the wake of the 1848 revolutions that swept through Europe. As its consul general, Hitz was a largely symbolic figure. In local circles, however, he had real status as a civic leader and man of wealth. By the time Hans died in 1864, he had become a significant enough personage to attract the attention of Abraham Lincoln, who allegedly attended his funeral. Lincoln's Secretary of State, William Seward, also found Hitz a "most estimable and worthy character."[16]

The Swiss government soon appointed Hans's oldest son and namesake, John, as its new consul general. Over the next decade, John carried on his father's good works, presiding over Swiss cultural festivals, spearheading local efforts to assist the "deserving poor," even helping to coordinate the creation of a Swiss farming colony in Tennessee. In 1872, he also helped to establish the German-American Bank, devoted to serving the financial needs of Washington's German-speaking population.[17]

Thanks to this family lineage, Hoover's mother, Annie, grew up in relative splendor. Childhood portraits show a plump, rosy-cheeked princess, adorned in velvet, satin, and ribbons, her auburn hair arranged in tidy ringlets. Annie attended a local Catholic high school, then a convent finishing school in Switzerland, both rare privileges in the late nineteenth century. Annie's father, a machinist and technical draftsman named Jacob Scheitlin, earned far less than his illustrious in-laws, but he managed to provide for his family and to carve out his own place of respect within Washington's Swiss society.[18]

In 1878, everything fell apart. The precipitating event was the collapse of John Hitz's German-American Bank, a family secret so shameful and so well-kept that it has never appeared in any account of Hoover's past. On October 31, 1878, depositors showed up at the German-American Bank only to find a sign on the front door announcing, "This bank is suspended." In a time before federal deposit insurance, this news meant that their money was simply gone, squandered on bad debt and poor investments in the midst of a bitter nationwide recession. The bank held the savings of Washington's German-Swiss community. When it collapsed, so did the networks of kinship, respect, and prosperity that had given the Hitz family its luster.

The months that followed seem to have been a time of soul-searching for the entire family, as they struggled to cope with the practical and personal consequences of the bank collapse. John Hitz came out swinging; his diplomatic status, he argued, ought to prevent him from being prosecuted in American courts. Hoover's grandfather Jacob proved less resilient, almost certainly among the depositors wiped out that year. In early April 1880, a year and a half after the bank collapse, Jacob went missing. On April 10, a passerby found his body in the Anacostia River, near a spot known as Devil's Elbow. Jacob had tied himself to a stake so that he would be unable to resist when the tide washed over him—"Suicide by Drowning," in the words of a local headline.[19]

Before his death, Jacob composed a note lamenting that his most intimate acquaintances had betrayed him, and that his life had become a failure through no fault of his own. "My wish is that I have Christian burial in some spot, and that after my death I do not come in contact with hypocritical and false-swearing people," he wrote, perhaps a reference to John Hitz and his fellow bank officials. Like John Thomas Hoover two years earlier, Jacob Scheitlin left behind a wife and three children. His daughter, Annie—Hoover's mother—had just turned nineteen.[20]

HOOVER'S PARENTS MET AND MARRIED EACH OTHER DURING THIS PERIOD OF turmoil, two wounded young people reeling from the collapse of their families. Acquaintances may have puzzled over what drew them together, noting that Annie came from the illustrious Hitz family while Dickerson came from far less. And yet as individuals, more than the sum of their family backgrounds, they had a surprising amount in common, at least in the hazy early months of romance. Their marriage cannot be separated from the context of family loss—for Dickerson, the death of his father; for Annie, the bank collapse and her father's mental decline. Like Dickerson, Annie found herself left with a grieving mother and two younger siblings to care for. Surely she hoped that her young husband—gainfully employed at the Coast Survey, still mourning his own father—would be a balm and source of stability. But Dickerson had his own demons and, like her father's, they would only grow more insistent in the years that followed.

First, though, there were the good times. John Hitz's legal troubles eventually settled down; he resigned as consul general and served only a brief time in jail. During the interim, Annie and Dickerson began their own family. Dickerson Jr., or "Dick," was born in September 1880, five months after his grandfather's suicide. Sister Lillian came along two years later. The young couple moved into a modest house just a few hundred feet from where Annie grew up, perhaps hoping to provide ballast for her widowed mother. In 1890, at the age of twenty-nine, Annie gave birth to a third child, a baby girl named Sadie Marguerite, the adored pet of two much older siblings. When Dickerson lost his job at the Coast Survey a few years later, he managed to recover by taking up work at a family-owned shoe shop. The store was nothing glamorous, but it was enough to keep everyone afloat: Dickerson at the shoe shop, Annie caring for the baby, Dick and Lillian at Brent Elementary School, a few blocks away.[21]

Had events gone differently, Hoover might have been born into this world—a family successfully knit together, its difficult past managed if not forgotten. But the Hoovers were not yet free from family tragedy. During a vacation in Atlantic City in the summer of 1893, three-year-old Sadie Marguerite fell ill with a sore throat and fever. Within a few days, she was dead of diphtheria, one of the most feared childhood diseases of the nineteenth century. The family brought her little body back to Washington. "She is buried," Hoover noted in an adolescent journal, "in Congressional Graveyard, Wash. D.C." His own birth came seventeen months later, carrying the promise of a new beginning but also the weight of his family's history.[22]

CHAPTER 2

Little Edgar

(1895–1905)

Hoover as a little boy in
Washington, D.C. He was
the pampered baby of the
family. His sister Sadie died
as a toddler less than two
years before he was born.

NATIONAL ARCHIVES AND
RECORDS ADMINISTRATION

On the same page of the teenage journal where he noted his sister Sadie's death, Hoover composed an account of his own birth. "On Sunday Jan 1, 1895 at 7:30 A.M. I, Edgar Hoover was born to my father + mother," he wrote. "The day was cold + snowy but clear. The Doctor was Mallan. I was born at 413 Seward Sq S.E. , Wash. DC." He recorded these details in a brown rectangular notebook, small enough to be tucked away in a front coat pocket. On the cover of the notebook, in careful cursive script, he wrote his name as he then conceived of it: "Mr. Edgar Hoover." He also marked the cover with one of the words that would later become a hallmark of his career. "PRIVATE," he wrote in large capital letters, warning off anyone inclined to pry into his teenage affairs.

Inside, there were no great secrets—no confessions of youthful passion, no quiet hopes about what the future might hold for "Mr. Edgar Hoover." The notebook's pages mainly contain spare accounts of his family history. This style suggests that certain aspects of the man were already present in the child. Even as a boy, Hoover ordered his world through dates, facts, and figures. But it is worth being cautious about imposing too much of the stern, guarded Bureau director back onto the little boy. Hoover grew up in a home far more loving and less sterile than the one he later created for himself. And he liked to do little boy things, floating along the Tidal Basin in summer, sleighing across the city when there was snow on the ground.[1]

Despite his parents' early difficulties, Hoover grew up in a caring household, where he was taught—and came to believe—that great things could happen through hard work and self-discipline. As early as elementary school, he proved to be an ambitious, hardworking child, eager to please his teachers and parents alike. There was some pressure, especially from Annie, but much of it seems to have come from within. Born in the wake of his sister's death, Hoover tried hard to be the redemptive child, to do things right and replace the child his parents had lost. Though as an adult he insisted that others conform to his ideals, as a boy he sought to be what everyone wanted him to be.

ONE OF THE EARLIEST SURVIVING PHOTOS OF HOOVER COMES FROM THE YEAR of his birth, a conventional Victorian portrait of a baby boy seated cheerily on an Oriental chaise longue, his white lace gown hanging down just so, his black leather shoes buffed to a shine. The photo is the work of a professional, and in that sense a testament to his parents' pride in their new arrival. Despite (or perhaps because of) their grief over Sadie, they cherished the new baby enough to hire a photographer to capture his earliest months. A second photo, commissioned two or three years later, evokes this impression even more powerfully. There, Hoover grasps the scroll of a small ornate bench, a toddler with waxed-down hair neatly parted on the left, dressed in a dark, gold-buttoned suit with a high-necked white collar. He has the hint of a smile on his face, a rarity for the era's somber portraiture. It is the photo of a well-loved child, of whom much would be expected.[2]

Hoover was a New Year's baby, born early on the morning of January 1. The date gave his birthday a charge of significance: New Year's was a moment of hope and renewal, of casting off old burdens and embracing the new. The city of Washington took this mission seriously, enacting elaborate annual rituals to refresh its democratic energies. Each January 1, the president threw open the doors to the White House for a public reception. Anyone could walk in, shake his hand, and pretend to be part of the governing elite. On the day Hoover was born, Grover Cleveland hosted the "most picturesque gathering" in years, with foreign dignitaries in national regalia lined up alongside local mothers and toddlers awaiting their chance to be ushered in past the Marine Band. Once he was old enough, Hoover liked to join the annual procession. On January 1, 1910, the day he turned fifteen, he waited in line to shake hands with

President William Howard Taft ("but was late," he chastised himself) before heading off to celebrate at a local church reception. The Washington of Hoover's youth was at once a small town and a seat of federal power.[3]

The city looked different from the one Hoover's parents had known as children. In a single generation, a guidebook noted, Washington had expanded from a "shabby, overgrown village" into a first-rate "modern metropolis." In 1861, the year of Annie's birth, the city had claimed some seventy-five thousand residents. By the time Hoover was born in 1895, its population had doubled and then almost doubled again, reaching a quarter million people. With this expansion came technological marvels: electric lights and apartment buildings; streetcars and telephones; rolling parks and pillared government buildings. In 1900, when Hoover was five, the city celebrated its one hundredth anniversary with a light show and parade emphasizing the "theme of miraculous change." And to Hoover's parents, even his older brother and sister, it *was* miraculous—change on a scale unthinkable even a few decades earlier. To Hoover, it was all perfectly ordinary, part of his modern childhood world.[4]

There were other aspects of life in Washington that might have seemed ordinary to a boy of Hoover's generation but were in fact extraordinary and of surprisingly recent vintage. First among them was the city's lack of democracy. As residents of a federal district rather than a state, Washingtonians could not vote and claimed no representation in Congress. For a brief time during Reconstruction, however, the city had allowed both Black and white men to cast ballots in municipal elections, a nod to the war's democratic promise. When the resulting government found itself mired in fiscal challenges, white citizens did what they did throughout the South: they blamed Black voters and officeholders. In 1878, rather than tolerate the discomforts of interracial democracy, Congress did away with *all* voting—by white and Black men, in federal and local elections. Hoover never saw his parents participate in an election and grew up with the assumption that he himself would never vote. He was taught instead that he was part of a special population: those Americans who made the government run but who stood outside of electoral politics, freed from its turmoil and temptations.[5]

The man who dominated Washington's political culture during Hoover's childhood was nonetheless an elected official: big, boisterous, unpredictable Theodore Roosevelt, the youngest president ever. As New York's police commissioner, Roosevelt had championed police reform and professionalization, later two of Hoover's signature issues. In Washington, Roosevelt branched out, first as civil service commissioner, then as a Rough Rider and war booster, then as vice president and finally as president, elevated to the White House by William McKinley's assassination in 1901. McKinley's murder set in motion political shifts that would prove critical to Hoover's career, launching a nationwide panic over political revolutionaries and anarchist radicals. As a six-year-old boy, though, Hoover must have been far more interested in the menagerie of animals that Roosevelt kept at the White House, including a bear, a lizard, a hyena,

a blue macaw, guinea pigs, and a pony. The president had six children, from little Quentin, two years younger than Hoover, on up through blustery Alice, two years younger
than Hoover's sister Lillian.[6]

Hoover paid attention to what went on at the Roosevelt White House. Around age
eleven, briefly inspired to mount a childhood newspaper, he wrote an item on Alice's
impending marriage to Speaker of the House Nicholas Longworth. Like his diary
entries, the article consisted mainly of dates and details, including a verbatim transcript of the couple's marriage license. Hoover's paper also noted the more mundane
features of Washington life: retirement parties for government servants; teachers' bids
to increase their wages; receptions sponsored by local civic and church clubs. In southeast Washington, neighborhood news was government news, and government news,
in turn, was intimate and local.[7]

THE HOUSE WHERE HOOVER GREW UP WAS TYPICAL OF ITS BLOCK, A NEAT TWO-
story structure with a shaded front porch and a quick run of stairs down to the sidewalk. Dickerson and Annie had purchased the home in 1892, the same year as Sadie
Marguerite's death, perhaps hoping to start anew. The address was 413 C Street SE,
just one digit off from Annie's childhood home at 414, though the numbers made the
two places sound closer than they were. In between stood a nice green park, two blocks
long and about a block wide—effectively, Hoover's front yard. In 1903, when Hoover
was eight, the city named the park after former secretary of state William Seward. Thus
emerged the childhood address listed in Hoover's notebook: 413 Seward Square.[8]

By suburban standards, the Hoover household was not quite big enough for three
children. On the first floor, the house featured a front parlor and back kitchen, bright-
ened by tall breezy windows that ran nearly floor to ceiling. Upstairs, there were three
bedrooms linked by a narrow hallway—one for the parents, and one each for Hoover's
older siblings, Dick and Lillian. Dick was fifteen when Hoover was born, a strapping
high school freshman on his way to an impressive run as a football player and class
president. Lillian was fourteen and she, too, was in school, laboring toward a career as
a public school teacher. As the baby of the family, Hoover slept downstairs in a back
room that might otherwise have housed a domestic servant. The Hoover family had
daytime help, but could not afford a live-in cook or housekeeper.[9]

Many of their neighbors lived similarly modest lives, working- and middle-class
people who earned their money as clerks, draftsmen, and laborers. Of the eight households on their block, none employed a live-in servant, and most had more than one
working family member. Several lacked a father or male head of household. Next door
at 411 C Street was a single mother who lived with her adult son, a machinist, and adult
daughter, a skilled laborer, along with two teenage sons employed as clerks. On the
other side were two middle-aged sisters getting by on schoolteacher wages. Nearly

every household on the street offered its own variation: a divorced woman living with her adult children; two sisters and two brothers living in a combined household; a widowed dressmaker and her adult daughter, a clerk. By the standards of their neighborhood, the Hoovers were the exception rather than the rule, one of only two families on the block consisting of a working father and a mother at home raising children.[10]

Those families were white, privileged occupants of a desirable park block. Step a few feet away, though, and the neighborhood was far more diverse, less a tidy assemblage of the white middle class than a multiracial enclave as yet unsure of its identity or social order. Washington has often been described as a citadel of segregation, with white blocks neatly separated from Black. But segregation was a process rather than a social fact in the late nineteenth century, and during Hoover's childhood that process was still underway. By the time he was born, the city boasted one of the largest Black populations of any city in the U.S. It also laid claim to many of the nation's most prominent Black institutions. Hoover's backyard, where Annie tended her garden, looked out onto Ebenezer Methodist Episcopal Church, one of the oldest Black congregations in the city. And while Washington's schools and churches tended to be segregated, many other aspects of city life were not. Hoover was born into in a city where Black and white residents sat side by side in libraries and on streetcars, in federal offices and cafeterias (though that would change as he came of age). Far from inhabiting a static white enclave, he began to learn about race in a city where Jim Crow was just becoming the law of the land, and where racial separation was a matter of frequent dispute.[11]

Seward Square provided Hoover with a choice vantage point from which to view the city's spectacles as well as its conflicts. From the park, he could look straight up Pennsylvania Avenue to the Capitol, just a few blocks away. If he turned around, he faced the grungy neighborhood of Pipetown, home to hundreds of sailors from the navy yard. Washington was a construction boomtown during Hoover's youth, and he saw that, too: the Senate and House office buildings, rising in Beaux Arts magnificence along the flanks of the Capitol; the twenty-three-karat-gold-plated dome of the new Greco-Roman Library of Congress, peeking out above the trees. His neighborhood also contained more boyish delights, including a penny-candy store, a bakery, and an ice cream shop. Hoover took advantage of nearby Eastern Market, the grand bazaar where everyone in southeast Washington, society matrons and servants alike, came to purchase foodstuffs hauled in from the farms of Maryland and Virginia. At the age of twelve, he began to linger outside the market in search of gainful employment. When he saw a customer particularly weighted down with goods—vegetables and game hens, pastries and cheeses—he offered to carry the items home for a small fee.[12]

His delivery-boy experience became one of his favorite childhood memories, an example of how even a boy born to a government city could showcase the American entrepreneurial spirit. "His first customer paid him ten cents for lugging two well-laden baskets of groceries to her home, nearly a mile away; and by the end of the day he had a handful of nickels and dimes which he had earned," read an official FBI account of his first job. "After converting a part of his earnings into a dollar bill, he ran home to share the pride of his accomplishment with his mother." Hoover later claimed that he worked nearly every day after school and from seven a.m. to seven p.m. on Saturdays, seeking to best the other boys. Like many of his memories, this one appears to be exaggerated; his teenage diary shows a more fitful level of activity and inconsistent wages. But the emotional thrust of the tale—his ambition, his devotion to his mother, his neighborhood know-how—rings true enough. From an early age, Hoover was a student of Washington, running errands in its dusty streets.[13]

AROUND THE HOOVER HOUSEHOLD, IT WAS ANNIE, NOT DICKERSON, WHO SET expectations. Some have described her as a "martinet," a controlling mother whose rigid ways squelched whatever gentleness might have been part of her son's nature. It is true that Annie liked to keep the house tidy; she was, after all, the granddaughter of the Swiss consul. The characterization nonetheless smacks of a timeworn stereotype, in which assertive mothers have long been dismissed as shrews and nags. To the degree that Annie sought control over her household and children, it may have been because the men in her life proved unreliable—a matter of necessity as much as desire. Her few surviving letters to Hoover are full of affection, addressed to "Dear Little Edgar," signed "with lots of love + kisses" from "Mama." So are the notes from his father, written on occasional trips out of town for the Coast Survey. "It makes me somewhat homesick so will write a few lines to you which will bring me closer to home," Dickerson wrote to his son during one extended journey. Hoover grew up in a loving if troubled household, with parents who did their best.[14]

Dickerson had been struggling financially when Hoover was born, still trying (but failing) to succeed in the shoe business. Then, in a stroke of fortune that may well have saved the family finances, the Coast Survey's printing foreman fell ill. In June 1895, after three years of exile, Dickerson returned to the Survey to take over the printing foreman's position. He held the job for the next twenty-two years, the entirety of Hoover's childhood. Unlike his own father, John Thomas, who had ventured into the field and suffered for it, Dickerson was rarely required to travel. He mostly spent his days close to home printing maps of the country and its new imperial territories: Hawaii, Guam, Puerto Rico, the Philippines. He was never quite the success at the Coast Survey that his father had been. The most the annual report ever noted was that Dickerson did his job "ably" and performed a "satisfactory amount of work." The job nonetheless became the family's financial bedrock. From the age of six months, Hoover grew up in a federal household and relied on a government paycheck.[15]

His older brother, Dick, initially seemed destined for greater things. Fifteen years old when Hoover was born, Dick was already everything his father was not: motivated, confident, popular. As a teenager, Dick attended Eastern High School, just down the street from the Hoover home, where he led the cadet corps, played quarterback on the championship football team, and won election as the 1899 senior class president. He went to work for the Coast Survey after graduation, spending a summer at a field survey in Havre de Grace, Maryland. But he had bigger dreams—instilled, perhaps, by Annie—and soon left his father's work behind. Dick lived at home while attending law school at the Columbian University (soon to become the George Washington University), a step up from his parents' high school educations. While in school he took a job as stenographer for a senator and then for the district's chief of police, providing his little brother an early contact with the world of crime and law enforcement.[16]

Dick later recalled pushing Hoover "thousands of miles" in a rickety old baby carriage during these years, a dutiful if reluctant teenager trudging the streets of Capitol Hill. Undoubtedly, though, their sister Lillian did much of the work—perhaps a source of her later estrangement from and resentment of her younger brother. Lillian graduated from high school in 1901, two years behind Dick. Instead of going to university, she enrolled at the Washington Normal School, a two-year training academy for teachers. In 1904, when *The Washington Post* offered to pay for thirteen local teachers to visit the Saint Louis World's Fair, she got herself elected as the most popular first-grade teacher in Washington though she had been on the job for only a few months.[17]

The World's Fair turned out to be Hoover's first big trip as well, thanks not to Lillian but to Dickerson, who was sent there by the Coast Survey, most likely as a mapmaker for displays in the U.S. government building. The fair paid tribute to the Louisiana Purchase and to Lewis and Clark, pioneers in the arts of land survey and geodetic mapping. It also featured actual "primitive" peoples from newly acquired U.S. territories such as the Philippines, putting human beings on display both as curiosities and as supposed proof of the superiority of Western civilization. Hoover and Annie took it in, visiting the fair by day and holing up with Dickerson at night. After his wife and son left, Dickerson wrote home to say that he missed the small rituals of their life together. "It is cold here and if you was here that big overcoat would just be right to keep you warm," he told nine-year-old Hoover. "I sleep in your little bed and I wish you were here so that I could fight you in the morning. Mama might think you ain't strong but just let her try to fight you and she will find out." Dickerson's letters show certain limits to his schooling, but they also reveal a warm and unmistakable affection for his youngest son.[18]

Annie's voice was loving, too, if a bit more prescriptive, inclined toward instruction as well as praise. When Hoover was about ten years old, Annie and Dickerson took a trip to Boston, leaving him behind with his brother and sister. Both parents wrote to "little Edgar" to describe the strangeness of the places they were seeing: the elevated train rushing "right by the window" in New York, the "fairyland" of ritzy Brookline, the ways that Boston was "a big place but not anything like New York . . . more on the order of Washington." Annie, though, took care to urge her son to be good and obedient. "Was so glad to hear you were perfect in your spelling and Arithmetic," she wrote. "Study hard at your lessons and your music, and try to be a very good boy."[19]

So he did. At age six, he began attending Brent Elementary, a segregated public school a few blocks east of Seward Square. He took pride in pleasing his teachers, and in fulfilling their expectations of courteous behavior. "Never kept back once," he later wrote in his "PRIVATE" notebook. "Had a clean character & high standing in every grade." Even as a child, Hoover had a talent for ingratiating himself with authority figures, happily running errands for his teachers and composing charming notes of appreciation.[20]

At home, he appears to have been no less cooperative and eager to please. He referred to his parents as "Mamma" and "Papa," childish names that he preserved until his high school years. For fun, he took shopping trips downtown or to the navy yard, sometimes in Annie's company. In the backyard garden, he helped to tend the rose beds and to gather late-summer tomatoes. On vacations, he threw himself into family activities. On one memorable trip to the shore, Hoover recalled a grand time battling the Atlantic undertow, attending concerts, and watching "the moon rise out of the water," content to be in his parents' company. When big events came to Washington, his parents made a point of taking him to see them. In 1909, Orville and Wilbur Wright staged a series of flight demonstrations in northern Virginia, and Hoover visited three days in a row. "Wright flew to Alexander [*sic*] and back in 14.20 min," he noted on the third day. "I first outsider to shake Orville's hand."[21]

All of this was testament to Annie's and Dickerson's resilience, their ability to put the difficulties of their early experiences to rest. But history was not done with them, and there were other tragedies in their future.

CHAPTER 3

The Boy Problem

(1905–1909)

Hoover and bicycle, around age ten. He worked as a grocery delivery boy, among other odd jobs. For fun, he preferred indoor pursuits.

On October 23, 1905, Hoover's aunt Mary was shot and killed in a "modest little house" on Ninth Street SE, less than a mile from his childhood home. Mary was the second wife of Rudolph Scheitlin, Annie's younger brother (and Hoover's uncle), a man for whom adulthood had proved to be one long string of difficulties. Just a teenager when his father committed suicide, Rudy had spent his adult life wandering and searching—running off to the navy and then returning to get married, only to see his first wife die, another major loss before the age of thirty. On the day Mary was killed, he had been working the day shift at the navy yard in Anacostia. He returned home to find her slumped in the parlor, shot twice in the head by her drunken lover, who then turned the gun on himself. According to news reports, a few days before the murder Rudy had warned the other man "that he would have to cease his visits, and that if he did not I would seek the law to prevent him from coming to my home." At that point Mary had run off. "That was the last I saw of either of them until I entered the house this afternoon and found both of them dead on the floor," he told *The Washington Post*.[1]

The crime made headlines across the city. "Slayer a Suicide," the *Post* announced. "Bodies Found by Husband Who Had Resented Attentions to Wife." The articles that followed revealed a sordid tale at odds with the Hoover family's settled life. Mary was an alcoholic—"a good woman, save at those times when she would indulge in liquor," Rudy insisted. About two years earlier, she had taken up with a "trifling fellow," an alcoholic barroom singer who worked only occasionally (and then as a bartender). The two "had been intimate for some time," one article noted, "and this intimacy . . . caused many quarrels between her and Mr. Scheitlin." The murder was a vicious surprise but there was a long history of violence, addiction, and adultery behind it.[2]

For a future lawman like Hoover, this might have made for a convenient origin story, the moment when crime and sin first barreled into his childhood world. He never mentioned it, though, filing it away as a family secret alongside his grandfather's suicide and, later, his own father's mental collapse. There are signs that his aunt's murder affected him nonetheless, the beginning of a reckoning with issues of manhood, crime, and personal virtue that would continue for the rest of his life. In the weeks after the murder, Hoover's grades dropped. Not long after that, he created his little childhood newspaper, a boy's imitation of the sensational headlines around him.[3]

Over the next four years, as he transitioned from childhood into adolescence, Hoover began to think more seriously about matters of life and death, about what might make for a virtuous identity and a secure existence. He also began to struggle for the first time with the pressures of manhood and the social expectations that accompanied it. The early twentieth century was in the throes of what historians have described as a masculinity crisis, a set of deep and pressing cultural anxieties about whether American men would be able to meet the challenges of the modern world. The crisis trickled down to the nation's boys and adolescents, who found themselves barraged with prescriptions about how to be the right sort of man. At the age of ten, Hoover may have understood his aunt's murder as a dramatic example of what could happen if he strayed off that righteous path. For decades to come, he would warn about the dangers of women who drank and violated the sanctity of the home, and about the weak men who allowed such activities to occur. It was in early adolescence—in those years after his aunt's murder—that he began to consider such matters, and to sort out some of his own answers.

AMERICANS IN 1905 HAD LITTLE BUT CONTEMPT FOR A MAN LIKE RUDY SCHEITlin. According to the era's conventional wisdom, American men were fast abandoning the Victorian attributes of discipline, duty, and self-restraint in favor of debauchery and self-indulgence. As a result, the nation was awash in lost souls like Rudy, who

disappointed their families and generated chaos wherever they went. Reformers agonized over the rise of sedentary desk jobs, the temptations of city life, the decline of
frontier conquest—all alleged sources of enervation among American men. They prescribed a variety of solutions, from vigorous daily exercise to spiritual awakening to
masculine "rebirth" through military conflict. In particular, they sought to intervene
in the lives of adolescent boys like Hoover, to teach them how to be proper men.[4]

This pressure was acute in Washington, where Theodore Roosevelt set a high bar
for what he described as "the strenuous life." As a child, Roosevelt had been weak and
asthmatic, more than once at death's door. By his own account, he willed himself out
of this sickly state into a robust existence filled with hunting, boxing, and "manly
vigor." He urged all boys to do the same, and not just for their own sakes. According
to Roosevelt, the nation's ability to rule its new imperial possessions depended upon
cultivating young men who would "not shrink from danger." So did the future of the
white race, allegedly in peril both at home and abroad.[5]

A raft of books sprang up to explain how boys might live up to the president's
charge. One was *The Boy Problem,* a psychological exegesis of the need for discipline,
self-control, and physical activity among the boys of Hoover's generation. Published in
1902, *The Boy Problem* described children as small creatures who needed to be taught
how to eat and behave properly, and how to control their wilder selves. Failure to do so
could be catastrophic, the book declared, and many new organizations sprang up to
ward off this danger. The Boy Scouts, founded in 1910, promised to end "degeneracy"
by transforming American boys from "flat-chested cigarette-smokers, with shaky
nerves and doubtful vitality" into "robust, manly, self-reliant" men. Boys needed exercise, outdoor activity, camaraderie, and discipline, all agreed, along with a strict set of
rules to follow. [6]

Hoover absorbed these ideas as he approached adolescence, composing lists of good
habits and proverbs to stave off sloth and decline. His homegrown "Weekly Review"
featured instructions on how to grow from a selfish, lazy boy into a self-disciplined
man. He liked to cite Ben Franklin: "Eat not to dullness; drink not to elevation";
"What is worth doing is worth doing well"; "One to-day is worth two tomorrows." In
the surviving issues of the paper, neatly typewritten in blue or black ink, Hoover comes
across as a boy trying to become an adult as soon as possible.[7]

The newspapers document an emerging focus on crime, violence, and death. Perhaps in reaction to his aunt's murder, eleven-year-old Hoover went out of his way to
note all manner of violent occurrences throughout his neighborhood, including heart
attacks, suicides, explosions, and even a near miss when his mother's hair caught fire in
the kitchen. He seemed particularly interested in sudden death. "Mr. Jones, the purser
of the Anne Arundel, dropped dead on board the boat Tuesday night," noted one
entry. "Fritz Reuter committed suicide in the parlor of his hotel on Monday about 11
o'clock," read another. The writing shows the peculiar lack of affect that so many peo-

ple would comment upon later in life; according to "Editor J.E. Hoover," the people of Washington "dropped dead" or "committed suicide in the parlor" without so much as a fond goodbye. But he also liked jokes and funny little ditties, especially those that seemed to evoke the secret world of adult men. "Keep your eyes wide open before marriage, half shut afterwards," he instructed his readers, citing Franklin.

The main feature of each paper usually focused on the tale of a great man who had overcome laziness, indifference, or temptation to forge a life of masculine virtue. In one edition, Hoover described an odd incident in which a young Abraham Lincoln allegedly showed up late to court, covered in filth, because he had stopped to rescue a pig stuck in the mud. Another article presented a tribute to George Washington, blaming "George's cousin, Ike" for the infamous chopping down of the cherry tree (which Hoover worried might actually have been a persimmon tree). Hoover's reading habits showed a fascination with tales of adventurous men: *Robinson Crusoe*, James Fenimore Cooper's Leatherstocking Tales, Theodore Roosevelt's *The Winning of the West*. His reading reinforced the same message he heard all around him: to become a man, a boy had to show both vigorous physicality and the ability to discipline himself at all moments.[8]

Hoover had a hard time living up to these prescriptions. On January 1, 1908, near the end of his time at the Brent School, he began to keep a diary, documenting a growing seriousness about his identity as a young man but also a record of some of the ways he fell short. He made note of his physical characteristics: At the age of fourteen, Hoover was just over five feet tall and weighed 88.5 pounds—a skinny, even scrawny boy of below-average height. As a rule, he preferred to be indoors, immersed in books or magazines, or attending to a mysterious duty described as "routine clerical work." He seems to have been concerned about his health—perhaps a result of his parents' fear of losing another child, perhaps an inborn aspect of his temperament. He noted various ailments: "Went to bed with grip"; "Cloudy. Sick. Cool. Read magazines." He also endorsed the prescriptions of the Brent School's Good Health Club: "Don't eat adulterated food. Don't eat too much. Don't eat between meals. Clean your teeth." He would maintain these preoccupations—with food and weight, germs and cleanliness—into adulthood, even as he learned, like Teddy Roosevelt before him, how to project "vigor."[9]

And when he did encounter sickness or disability, Hoover took pains to hide it. He grew up with a stutter, all too easily classified as a sign of nervousness or lack of verve. There is no evidence that he ever received professional treatment for the problem. Instead, he seems to have overcome the challenge by experimenting with various speech patterns, then practicing hour after hour in front of a mirror. The result was a rapid-fire, clipped speaking style that would emerge as one of the remarked-upon features of his adult bearing. As with many aspects of his early life, Hoover never spoke publicly about his stutter. But his style of speech earned him the nickname "Speed"—and that, too, stuck into adulthood. In later years, he attributed the nickname to his speed in delivering groceries to Washington society ladies, and the press by and large accepted this idea. Born of a childhood struggle, his fast talk became a symbol of efficiency and manly determination, as if he operated at a swifter pace and on a higher plane than everyone else in Washington.[10]

THERE WAS ANOTHER, MORE POTENT SECRET THAT HOOVER BEGAN TO KEEP AS he moved into the complications of adolescence: his father, Dickerson, the man who should have been his role model and guide, was not at all well. Dickerson had never quite fit the mold of the vigorous man. He was too gentle, too content with his modest job at the Coast Survey. But what Hoover witnessed as he moved into his early teenage years was something altogether different, a level of emotional instability and mental anguish that went far beyond a mere personality quirk. Details are hard to come by. "All's I ever heard was it was probably depression," one relative recalled. Another thought that Dickerson had "a nervous breakdown," though precisely why or what sort was never entirely clear. For a boy of Hoover's temperament and anxieties, the timing could hardly have been worse. As he struggled with what it meant to become a man, his own father was fading.[11]

The idea of depression as a disease barely existed at the turn of the twentieth century. Instead, most Americans understood the problem as a failure of the will and a dismal reflection on an individual's character. Popular medical writers often suggested that patients simply buck up. "The lesson to be learned from this is as follows," read one neurologist's treatise. "Lead an active but varied life." The advice made sense within the cultural conversation about manhood: living vigorously was both a prescription and a cure. It also may help to explain Hoover's growing lists of proverbs and good-living rules. By gaining control of his body and health at an early age, perhaps he hoped to protect himself from the disease that afflicted his father. Dickerson managed to hold on to his job at the Coast Survey, trudging back and forth each day to the print shop. At home, though, he was apparently prone to mood swings and periods of fierce, immobile sadness.[12]

What must it have been like for Hoover to spend his early adolescence in the shadow of his father's depression? Today's medical literature is unswerving in at least part of the answer: coping with a depressed parent becomes one of the defining facts of a child's life. Some children respond by becoming depressed themselves, carried down by the weight of example, circumstance, and heredity. Others show a surprising resilience, pushing back with a determination not to allow the same thing to happen to them. Hoover fit into the latter category, but it is difficult to imagine that he escaped entirely unscathed. At the very least, Dickerson's illness must have accentuated Hoover's worries about his own health and mental fitness.[13]

Annie's guidance may have helped her son. She, too, had witnessed her father's mental collapse, then suicide, and had come through all right. But her brothers had not fared nearly so well, and continued to provide disturbing evidence of how a father's troubles might be passed down through the generations. Her brother Rudy remarried a year after Mary's murder but soon found himself divorced again, scraping together a living as a naval-yard laborer. Annie's youngest brother, Johnny, who had been just eight years old when his father committed suicide, seems to have led a life of chaos and frustration as well, fueled by alcohol abuse and financial woes. For money, he worked as a laborer, carpenter, painter, and clerk. He married and had several children, but the family never quite achieved stability. In southeast Washington, Johnny was well known for his "drunken escapades" and for drinking up his family's wages.[14]

The one man from Annie's family who managed to provide a redemptive example turned out to be her uncle John Hitz, whose poor stewardship of the German-American Bank had made headlines so long before. After serving his sentence, Hitz had worked his way back into the good graces of the local Swiss elite. He eventually assumed a charitable role as superintendent of the Volta Bureau, an experimental organization for the deaf founded by Alexander Graham Bell. There, Hitz built friendships with celebrities such as Helen Keller and Clara Barton, even doubling as Barton's personal secretary in his final years. Hoover grew up knowing his great-uncle as a figure of renewed esteem, an imposing old man with a long white beard who liked to read from the Bible. Then, on March 25, 1908, when Hoover was thirteen, Hitz collapsed and died at Union Station, eliminating yet another source of strength and guidance. The funeral preparations kept Hoover home from school. The funeral itself attracted dignitaries including Bell, Keller, and Barton—Hoover's first close-up glimpse of a Washington power gathering.[15]

WITH DICKERSON NOW AN ON-AGAIN, OFF-AGAIN FATHER, AND WITH FEW VIable role models among the family's other men, Hoover turned to his brother, Dick, who became an independent man just as his little brother entered adolescence. After graduating from law school, Dick went to work at the federal Steamboat Inspection Service, where he set a good example for his brother by advancing rapidly. What may have mattered most to Hoover, though, was the way Dick negotiated through the thickets of temptation and lassitude that had felled other men in the family. Far more directly than other Hoover relatives, Dick forged the path that Hoover would follow: high school stardom, then George Washington University law school, then a dedicated rise through a government agency. Dick also laid the foundations of Hoover's emerging religious faith. In addition to his schoolwork and professional commitments, Dick developed a reputation as a successful lay preacher and Protestant missionary. He brought his little brother along with him.

Like nearly every other institution in American life, the Protestant church was experiencing its own "masculinity crisis" in the early twentieth century, a worry that men had left the pews, never to return. According to a 1910 study commissioned by the Young Men's Christian Association, women outnumbered men at Protestant churches by almost two to one. The imbalance was particularly acute at Sunday school, where female teachers dominated the ranks, and where women allegedly spent their time instructing boys in a "goody-goody, wishy-washy, sissy, soft conception of religion," in the words of one scornful critic. Hoover's childhood years saw an outpouring of books on so-called Muscular Christianity: *The Masculine in Religion, The Manhood of the Master, Manly Songs for Christian Men.* Psychologist G. Stanley Hall, one of the movement's leaders, recommended that Christ himself be buffed up as a way of increasing Protestantism's appeal. In a public opinion survey, Hall discovered that most viewers turned to words like "sick, unwashed, sissy, ugly, feeble" when presented with a standard painting of Christ on the cross. Hall advocated a Jesus with muscles and bulk, fighting back against his persecutors rather than succumbing meekly to crucifixion.[16]

Dick embraced this form of Christianity. He seems to have enjoyed the evangelist's challenge, working the Anacostia waterfront and the local jail as a missionary to hard men. By the time Hoover was old enough to join him on such outings, Dick had acquired experience preaching not only at missions and soup kitchens but also to church groups. Though he started out as a Presbyterian, Dick switched his allegiance to the Lutheran Church of the Reformation on Pennsylvania Avenue, helmed by an "energetic and magnetic" young pastor named John Weidley. Under Rev. Weidley's authority, Dick became superintendent of the Sunday school and a leader of its youth outreach.[17]

Hoover followed along. Under Dick's tutelage, he became a dedicated Bible student and boy soprano. He even won a prize—his own copy of the New Testament—for memorizing catechism verses. Hoover followed his brother into leadership roles as well, winning election as secretary of his Sunday school class just a few days after his thirteenth birthday. Of all the events mentioned in his adolescent diary, few are recorded as consistently as his church activities. Hoover also made careful note of his brother's attention: "Took a walk with Dick cross the bridge"; "Dick took supper in here."[18]

Dick's teachings reinforced what Hoover was learning elsewhere: that self-discipline and adherence to the proper rules made for a godly and manly life. "As a youth, I was taught basic beliefs," Hoover recalled. "For instance, I was taught that no book was ever to be placed above the Bible." While Dick may have led his brother into the church, Hoover made an active decision to stay, concluding that what he heard at prayer meetings and church services spoke to something important within. From the pulpit, Rev. Weidley stressed positive thinking, the ability to rise above adversity and "to accomplish your task." "In this life there are many dark clouds to limit the horizon of our vision," he explained, "but the joys set before us, and the brightness illuminating our pathway are far more numerous." It is not hard to see why such a message might have appealed to Hoover, newly confronted with family troubles. A few days before his fourteenth birthday, Rev. Weidley baptized him in a private ceremony. Dick was there to watch and support his younger brother in the transition from a boy into a man.[19]

ULTIMATELY, THOUGH, DICK HAD HIS OWN LIFE TO LEAD. IN SEPTEMBER 1907, he married a fellow churchgoer named Theodora Hanft, the daughter of a clerk at the Bureau of Engraving and Printing. ("The day was unsettled in the morning but cleared up in the evening," Hoover noted in his journal. "Dr. Weidly [*sic*] officiated.") The following June, his sister Lillian married a high school acquaintance named Fred Robinette, who worked with Dickerson at the Coast Survey. Her wedding took place at the Hoover home, which had been spruced up with palms and white flowers. Annie wore black for the occasion, still in mourning for her uncle John. A few weeks after that, on "a cool beautiful evening with a full moon" (in Hoover's description), Dick's wife gave birth to a daughter and Hoover became an uncle for the first time.[20]

By any reasonable standard, Dick and Lillian stayed close to home and remained involved in their brother's life. Dick bought the house next door to his parents, and they fenced in the two backyards together. Lillian moved a few blocks away, but came back frequently and even gave birth to her first child in the family home. There was no mistaking the change in Hoover's life, however, as he went from being the pampered youngest son to the only child in the house. With Lillian's wedding, Hoover became the sole daily witness to his parents' domestic joys and struggles, the child most responsible for their happiness and well-being. In later years, he would come to resent his brother and sister for abandoning him just as their parents began to grow older and (though he did not say it quite so explicitly) as their father was starting to flounder and fail. At the time, though, it may have looked more promising, less a moment of abandonment than a coming-of-age.[21]

CHAPTER 4

Jump High and Leap Quick

(1909–1913)

Hoover in his high school
cadet uniform, around
1912. At Washington's
Central High School, he
was a stand-out student:
valedictorian, debate star,
captain of the cadets.

COLLECTION OF THE NATIONAL
LAW ENFORCEMENT MUSEUM

If Hoover had followed Dick's example down to the last detail, he would have attended Eastern High School, just a short walk from Seward Square. Instead, in
September 1909 he enrolled at Central High, several miles away in the heart of the
Northwest. Both Lillian and Dick had attended Eastern. Central was a step up, widely
recognized as the most competitive and desirable of the city's white public high
schools. Family connections helped to ease the transition. Hoover's uncle Halsted,
Dickerson's youngest brother, ran Central's music department, conducted the glee
club, and helped to supervise the dramatic association. Though Hoover preferred to
think of himself as a boy who rose through merit alone, he started at Central with an
important advantage.[1]

He made the most of it. For Hoover, the high school years turned out to be "formative," in his later description, a time when he acquired lasting ideas about discipline

and success, about how to win political arguments and how to behave as a Christian man. Central High also gave him his first taste of real-world accomplishment and success. During his time there, Hoover emerged as an undisputed class star: valedictorian, debate champion, cadet captain. On this small stage, he also began to test his capacity as a leader of men.[2]

CENTRAL HIGH WAS THE PRODUCT OF A CIVIC DREAM. CONCEIVED IN THE 1880s at a moment of great hope for public education, the school established itself as the crown jewel in the city's network of free high schools. Like most local institutions, Central was segregated. Black students attended their own high school (later renamed for the poet Paul Laurence Dunbar) several blocks away. For its white students, the city provided facilities unimaginable during Annie's and Dickerson's childhoods, when most Americans had considered high school an elite privilege. Central's first building, a three-story brick structure, featured more than a dozen classrooms, a military exercise space, an exhibition hall, a library, scientific laboratories, and a teachers' lounge—thirty rooms all told. By the time Hoover entered in 1909, a push was on to relocate to a bigger and better building, with updated lighting and sewage systems, a larger auditorium, and better science labs. "The school has been continually advancing in rank among the preparatory schools of the country," the Central yearbook reported in the spring before Hoover's freshman year.[3]

Central's curriculum reflected its aim to compete with the best. Students learned not only the three R's but also German, French, Latin, and Greek; chemistry and biology; drawing, music, and history. Outside the classroom, they participated in football, track, baseball, tennis, and basketball; debate and student government; the cadet and rifle corps; theater and glee club. The culture of the school emphasized discipline in all aspects of student life, including strict silence in the hallways. The students seemed to have absorbed and accepted this striving ethos. In the fall of 1909, as Hoover began his first year, the school newspaper featured a poem urging the new crop of freshman to "jump high and leap quick" as they faced the challenges of high school life.[4]

Hoover embraced Central's culture of achievement. During the first few weeks, he observed with relief that he seemed capable of meeting the school's demands. "Did fine in studies at school," he wrote on September 22. Things also went "fine" on September 24 and 26. One classmate remembered Hoover as a focused, unsmiling teacher's pet, determined to prove himself in the classroom. "John Edgar would enter Miss (or is it Mrs.?) Farr's math class, speak no word to anyone, circle the back of the class, and seat himself directly in front of that most excellent teacher and drink in every word she uttered." He was the same boy at Central that he had been at Brent Elementary: attentive to teachers, eager to please, and even more eager to demonstrate his abilities. His grades bore this out. During his first year, Hoover achieved grades of E (for "excellent") in all his classes, except for one G ("good") in Latin and another in spelling. In his sophomore year, he received E's in everything but spelling. As a junior, he earned an E in "neatness," as well as in his academic subjects, with his only end-of-semester G coming in French. In a school renowned for its high academic standards, his grades helped earn him a reputation as the "Perfect Student," according to a classmate's description.[5]

As a matter of social standing, however, good grades got him only so far. Like the rest of the country, Central High believed that it had a "boy problem," simultaneously identified as a lack of heft among its brainy male students and as an excess of disruptive behavior among the rest. Girls outnumbered boys two to one (in school as in church). But even the most talented female students were expected to play cheerleading roles while their male counterparts engaged in "active battle," as one girl wrote in the school paper. In late 1908, the year before Hoover enrolled, Central established a study hall specifically for third-year boys, led by a male teacher, in hopes that "the boys under his direction shall become more manly, of greater self-reliance, and better able to uphold the reputation of Old Central as it should be upheld," according to a student account. Outside the classroom, the school's principal urged boys to pour their energies into sports and physical conflict. To encourage them, Central organized an assembly with Harvard president Charles Eliot, who emphasized physical as well as mental education, thus transforming the typical Harvard student "from a stooping, weak and sickly youth into one well-formed, robust, and healthy." Even more than most boys at Central, Hoover was under pressure to demonstrate that he fit into the latter category, that his academic prowess would not undermine his success beyond the classroom.[6]

Hoover's closest relative at Central, his uncle Halsted, was not much help in this area. An artistically minded man, Halsted was Dickerson's youngest brother by some fourteen years; he had been just eight years old when their father died. Halsted grew up with his mother, Cecilia, as sole parent, and stayed on with her after he reached adulthood, a harbinger of Hoover's own future. She died at the start of Hoover's freshman year, leaving Halsted alone in the family house, a personal loss that elicited expressions of "sincere sympathy" in the Central High paper. Halsted was popular with the students, who called him "Pop Hoover" and regularly praised his singing. But his subject—music and choral performance—hardly offered a solution to Hoover's "boy problem." Instead of following his uncle's example, Hoover chose to follow his brother, Dick, and try out for the football team.[7]

DICK HAD PLAYED AT EASTERN, A STAR IN THE MOST IMPORTANT SPORT THE school had to offer. At Central, Hoover went to freshman tryouts and was immediately cut from the team, one of the few blows he encountered during his high school years. He turned instead to the cadet corps, and there he found his social home. The cadets offered junior military training (something like a high school version of today's

ROTC). At Central, the corps practiced regularly throughout the year, culminating in a citywide regimental competition. The final drills often took place on the White House Ellipse, with the secretary of war or the secretary of the navy presiding. In the spring of 1909, just before Hoover's freshman year, President William Howard Taft himself had attended the proceedings, offering a "highly complimentary" review of what he saw.[8]

Hoover never expressed any interest in a military career, either as a teenager or as an adult. But in high school the cadet corps was a major point of pride. "There is not the slightest doubt that the drill is beneficial to schoolboys," declared Hoover's company captain in his junior year. "It is a form of athletics—one of the best forms—and the discipline and training develops those traits in a young man's character which he will need most in after life." Unlike football, where Hoover was considered small and weak, the cadet corps demanded relatively little coordination or strength. What mattered among cadets was the ability to walk a straight line, to execute drills in rain and snow, to submit to discipline and hierarchy, to put up with shouldering a rifle for hours on end.[9]

Most Central boys found such conditions hard to tolerate. Hoover did not. Even as a freshman, he gloried in the discipline of the corps, noting cadet practices in his diary, only occasionally—and then only in the dead of winter—giving any hint that drill practice might be less than ideal. He was especially fond of the cadet uniform, with its high collar and gold epaulets. A photo of Hoover in cadet dress shows a thin, frowning teenager, the visor of his boxy cap pulled low over his eyes, his shoulders thrown back in an approximation of soldierly style. It is the photo of someone who takes himself seriously and who is trying, despite protruding ears and a youthful countenance, to be taken seriously in turn.[10]

In his junior year, he earned promotion to second sergeant of Company B, ranked just below Company A in the school hierarchy. In that position, he became known as an enthusiastic drillmaster. "Is that a lion roaring, or is it an approaching thunderstorm?" ran a joke in the student paper. "O' no sir; it is just Hoover counting cadence for Company B." Though still in high school, Hoover was beginning to think through many of the ideas that he would later pass on to his employees: organizational loyalty, exhaustive discipline, attention to hierarchy, the need to "fight" in order to succeed. He was also starting to learn about the importance of community support for maintaining morale within the ranks. Despite their best efforts, Company B often failed to attract much of an audience among fellow students, who vastly preferred football games to drill competitions. Company officers found themselves begging for "loyal support from the school, in order to produce a drill of which every supporter will be proud."[11]

All of this conveys an image of Hoover as a stern young man, beholden to duty, honor, and accomplishment. Yet it is clear from his diary, and from scattered evidence in the school paper, that he enjoyed the corps and viewed it as a source of camaraderie and good times. During freshman year, his corps meetings evoked one of the few expressions of genuine enthusiasm—indeed, of any emotion—in his personal diary. "Went to squad meeting…," he recorded on January 7, 1910, "corporal. Capt. Lieunt + serg all there. Had a great time." Later, as an officer, he reveled in weekly strategy meetings that lasted well into the night, "convening early in the evening and often adjourning early in the morning," by his own account.[12]

The one area of cadet life where Hoover seems to have stumbled was in the annual dances with members of the opposite sex. For many students, these events marked the high point of their social lives. School publications were packed with gossip about which boys looked best in uniform, and about who might be accompanying whom to the big events. Hoover is curiously missing from all such gossip, and from any other speculation about dating or sexual experimentation. The chief evidence that he even attended such events is a 1913 dance card that he saved for many years. Under "partners," the lineup is blank.[13]

Hoover preferred to spend his time with other boys—especially with Lawrence Jones, better known as "Biff." Jones was everything Hoover's brother, Dick, had been: "Big, brawny, intelligent," in the words of Central's yearbook, not only a football star but also class president. Hoover seems to have regarded Jones with the same giddy admiration that infected the rest of the school. "Biff Jones and I buddied around together all the time," he later recalled, "and it always drew a laugh from our friends to see the big, powerful Biff accompanied by a youngster half his size." Jones joined the cadet corps, where he and Hoover forged a friendship, spending hours side by side at drill practice and strategy meetings. As the cadet corps drew to a close during senior year, Jones expressed the fervent adolescent wish that it might go on forever. "Now that the guns of our men are in their racks, our sabres sheathed for the last time, and no more cadet life is left for us," he wrote, "we feel the loss of it all very keenly." Ultimately, he would organize his adult life around the pillars of his high school success, going on to lead the West Point football team, first as a player and later as head coach.[14]

Hoover, too, held on to certain patterns from high school. He would always reserve his greatest affection for other men, a fact readily ascribed to boyish camaraderie during high school but one that would raise difficulties and questions in years to come. Mostly, he chose men with whom he shared an institutional bond, as in the cadet corps, where he and Jones labored side by side together in a clear hierarchy and common purpose. When he could hire his own employees, he proved partial to men like Jones as well: big, amiable football players, models of what American men were supposed to be.

HOOVER'S FINAL AREA OF ACHIEVEMENT AT CENTRAL WAS THE DEBATE TEAM, a sphere that fortuitously involved brains rather than brawn. For a boy who had once struggled with a stutter, competitive public speaking may have been the ultimate proving ground, showing how he had prevailed over supposed weakness and disability. The debate team contained both boys and girls. Like so many activities at Central, however, it was prized most for its ability to turn ill-formed young men into self-disciplined, powerful leaders. "Public men are unceasing in their expression of the true value of good instruction in public speaking," noted one student essay. Given the school's location and ties to the political world, Central students assumed that boys who succeeded there would go on to public service, and that growing up in Washington would give them an edge. "In our city we have the Congress of the American people—a body of men whose political existence depends on their ability to debate," explained the school paper. "We also have the Congressional Library, an institution which offers opportunity for unlimited study on any subject under the sun." With these tools at his disposal, Hoover learned how to craft an argument, how to conduct in-depth research, and how to claim a political voice in the wider world.[15]

Central's debate team was wildly successful, with an undefeated record stretching back several years. Even so, Hoover emerged as a star: energetic, meticulous, and showing little tolerance for those who preferred to goof off. Before major competitions, he hunkered down at the Library of Congress along with his teammates "for weeks, into the small hours, sometimes all night long," according to the school paper, all for "the thrill" of bringing a victory back to Central. During his junior year, the debate team achieved eleven consecutive victories, a string of triumphs that put them in first place citywide. Hoover organized and then won the junior class debate, in which he argued that the United States ought to annex Cuba. At other competitions, the team explored political issues ranging from toll-taking at the Panama Canal to women's suffrage to the question of whether "the attitude of organized labor toward free speech and free press is a menace to American civilization." As a debater, Hoover constructed arguments that did not necessarily reflect the political positions he would develop later in life, but the debate experience, like the cadet corps, gave him a confidence he might otherwise have lacked.[16]

HOOVER SEEMS TO HAVE LIKED ALMOST EVERYTHING ABOUT HIGH SCHOOL: the late-night conversations, the mental and physical challenges, the relentless push toward success. But he also still loved the church, and he deepened his religious commitments throughout his high school years. Around 1909, just as Hoover was getting started at Central, both he and Dick switched their allegiance from Lutheran Reformation to the First Presbyterian Church, where a pastor named Donald Campbell MacLeod had recently come to prominence. Born just after the Civil War, Rev. MacLeod was known throughout Washington as a "brilliant young divine," with a special talent for bringing boys and men back to religious faith. Another disciple of Muscular Christianity, MacLeod presented Christ as a man of "mighty achievements" who "set himself apart" through discipline and an unwavering commitment to purpose above and beyond the self.[17]

As at Lutheran Reformation, Hoover did his best to emulate this example of manhood, appearing regularly in cadet garb to drill younger children in their Bible verses. While at Sunday school, he may also have encountered early experiments in church-based sexual education. In 1911, at the start of Hoover's junior year, the National Sunday School Association established a Department of Purity to address an issue "shunned all too long by the home, the school, the press and the church": adolescent sexuality. The lessons echoed broader social concerns about masculinity and self-discipline. "Sexual excitement during the period of adolescence means undermining of nerves, ruin to health, and, by and by, sickly, peevish and stupid offspring," one pious reformer explained. Such descriptions alluded to the peril of venereal disease, with the attendant possibility of mental illness. The virtuous paths consisted of abstinence or heterosexual marriage, preferably in that order, with all other forms of experimentation deemed "uncontrollable, incorrect, and degrading." Like the church's other prescriptions for manhood, the purity doctrine emphasized self-control as a surefire way to stay out of trouble. For an adolescent like Hoover, whose father and uncles provided such troubling examples of moral and mental failure, it may have seemed like an appealing option.[18]

Church was not all doom and gloom, however. In fall, before the opening of Sunday school, MacLeod helped to lead a Rally Day to drum up the children's enthusiasm for their coming religious devotions. Hoover particularly remembered MacLeod's willingness to spend time with the boys in his congregation. "He made it a practice every Saturday to visit with the children in the neighborhood. And, after he had become acquainted with the boys, he began suggesting baseball games, hikes, sporting activities, and other events," Hoover later wrote. "Because of his understanding and guidance, we came to look forward from Saturday to Saturday to being with Dr. MacLeod and to baseball games which he organized on our neighborhood sand-lot."[19]

Hoover would look back upon MacLeod as his model parent. "I am convinced that today if more adults would devote a little more time to playing with their sons or with the children in the neighborhood and spending a little more time with them," he wrote in the 1940s, "much could be accomplished in the development of better citizens." While he may have played the role of surrogate father, MacLeod was above all a passionate evangelical who believed that the workings of Christ had to be made present in the everyday. He taught Hoover to believe that, too. "One of the outstanding sins of the Christian church today is the flagrant disregard of the word of Jesus," MacLeod informed his congregation in 1909. "Does not this indicate something wrong with our hearts, something wrong with our love?" Only after Americans underwent a "spiritual awakening," he argued, could the nation's social and political ills be solved.[20]

MacLeod rejected the Social Gospel favored by many progressives, who believed that good works and the right legislation could be expressions of God's will. In his view, conversion came first, and all else was irrelevant. "Sin is the paramount issue," he declared in the midst of a nationwide coal strike in 1902, adding that "legislation will not solve the real problems of humanity." MacLeod's insistence on personal sin as the root of social evil provided Hoover with ideas he would later apply to the study of crime. As an adult, Hoover would insist that criminality came from within, and that tweaking legislation would always fall short absent the redemption of the soul.[21]

Far more than the artifice of debate club, MacLeod shaped Hoover's emerging political consciousness, especially his budding conservatism on social issues. MacLeod scoffed at labor unions. He urged congregants to "make Washington a city of God" rather than seek the right to vote. He supported the fierce temperance crusade of the Anti-Saloon League, instructing his young congregants to avoid alcohol consumption at all costs. He also actively enforced racial segregation, more and more a matter of conflict within the district. In 1903, MacLeod told the press that he had made a mistake in marrying a light-skinned Black man to a white woman. "I would not have married them had I known that he was a negro," MacLeod explained. In 1910, while Hoover was one of his young parishioners, MacLeod led the effort to exclude Black children from the city's grand Sunday school parade. He also refused to recognize Black delegates to the global Sunday school convention.[22]

Hoover accepted all of this without question. "Dr. MacLeod made a profound impression upon every member of the group that came in contact with him," he wrote decades later, "and as I came to know him better I arrived at the conclusion that if preachers were men like this then I wanted to enter the ministry."[23]

WHEN ASKED IN LATER YEARS TO EXPLAIN WHY HE DECIDED TO BECOME A LAWyer rather than a preacher, Hoover pointed not to his own desires or any sort of professional calling, but to "matters over which I had no control." Those "matters" likely involved his father's mental illness, the one continuing blight upon an otherwise smooth and successful high school journey. We have only a handful of facts about what happened to Dickerson during this time, but those few hint at unacknowledged depths of family pain and regret. Sometime around Hoover's senior year of high school, Dickerson was committed to Laurel Sanitarium, a private hospital specializing in "nervous and mental diseases, alcoholic and drug addiction," according to a directory of psychiatric facilities. The departure must have been jarring for Hoover—a father sent away, quietly and secretively, after years of uncertain health.[24]

By the standards of early-twentieth-century mental institutions, Laurel was nice enough—a private asylum rather than a state-run hospital, perched on a grassy expanse in the Maryland countryside. Dickerson's treatment was undoubtedly more harrowing. When he entered Laurel, a favored, state-of-the-art cure for all manner of mental illness was known as "hydrotherapy," in which a patient might be wrapped in tight wet-sheet packs or immobilized in a "continuous tub bath" in hopes that the water might provide a shock to the system. Laurel's founders believed in hydrotherapy and made the construction of the proper facilities, including "hot air cabinets" and "shower baths," a top priority. [25]

Annie may have tried to shield Hoover from the severity of Dickerson's condition. In the summer of 1912, just after his junior year, Hoover went off to spend several weeks with relatives in Wytheville, Virginia, far out in the state's western countryside. Annie's correspondence was chatty and solicitous, betraying no serious crisis at home. Dickerson sent at least one letter, too, noting explicitly that he was "on the front porch, Sunday morning," and reporting on recent visits to the theater despite the "awful hot weather since you left." Without better documentation, we cannot be sure that the dates line up with Dickerson's time at Laurel, or that Hoover was sent to Virginia as insulation from his father's illness. It seems likely, however, that he *was* sent away deliberately. Despite Hoover's pleas for a visit, Annie insisted that he stay on his own: "Enjoy yourself and have a good time and get a good long rest."[26]

Fragmentary accounts suggest that Dickerson came back from Laurel a different man—"very changed, short-tempered and irritable," in the words of one relative. Perhaps Hoover responded with compassion and sadness. More likely, he viewed his father's difficulties as he had been taught to view them: as signs of weakness and failure. Hoover's niece remembered that he seemed to be enraged by his father's illness. "My mother used to say Uncle Edgar wasn't very nice to his father when he was ill. He was ashamed of him. He couldn't tolerate the fact that granddaddy had mental illness. He never could tolerate anything that was imperfect." In the early twentieth century, a teenager like Hoover had no way to talk about this fury and resentment. Instead, he seems to have pretended that nothing was happening, and moved on with his own life.[27]

HOOVER'S FINAL YEAR AT CENTRAL WAS A MARVEL OF ACCOMPLISHMENT. HIS near-perfect grades won him the title of class valedictorian. He pushed the debate team to another successful season, earning further accolades as one of Central's most outstanding public speakers. In the cadet corps, he leapt over Biff Jones to earn the coveted position of captain in Company A, Central's top slot, while Jones took the captaincy of Company B. In March 1913, Hoover helped to lead the Central cadets down Pennsylvania Avenue for Woodrow Wilson's inaugural parade, his first official role in the nation's political pageantry. In May, he marched in dress parade on the White House Ellipse and led his company in the citywide drill competition.[28]

Given the difficulties of his home life, these are remarkable feats, early examples of the resilience under adversity that Hoover would exhibit for much of his career. But his voice during these years has a tightly wound quality, as if the slightest deviation from perfect grades and proper living might bring his impressive forward march to a sudden halt. As captain of Company A, he wrote a column for the school paper. He chose the slogan "Fight" to capture his unswerving commitment to the task at hand. "Men, it can be shown in numerous ways, by attendance, by setups, by detail and last but not least by concentration," he wrote. "Concentration is shown by cutting out all 'kidding,' by putting your mind on the drill and forgetting everything else." His reflections on debate showed an equally grim focus on discipline and self-improvement. "It teaches one to control his temper and free himself from sarcasm; it gives self-possession and mental control," he wrote of training for debate. By senior year, Hoover had apparently accepted the idea that "self-possession and mental control" were man's highest calling, the best hope for keeping tragedy and failure at bay.[29]

His fellow students responded to this record of accomplishment much as his government colleagues later would—with respect and admiration, but not necessarily with affection and love. In the school's 1913 yearbook, portraits of fellow cadets and debaters emphasized their physical dynamism or personal charm; one was a "tall, good-looking, brilliant exhibit," another "a 'fighty' soldier, and one of the best friends anyone could have." Hoover gained recognition for his seriousness of purpose and fondness for political moralizing, described stiffly as "a gentleman of dauntless courage and stainless honor."[30]

Whether Hoover understood the distinction between affection and admiration is hard to say. His adolescent identity hints at the man he would later become: the scolding FBI chief, writing blistering missives to his men and to the country at large. All the same, he had some fun, and he reveled in a sense of belonging. "The year has been a most enjoyable one, for there is nothing more pleasant than to be associated with a company composed of officers and men whom you feel are behind you heart and soul," he wrote of the cadet corps. "The saddest moment of the year was . . . when I realized that I must part with a group of fellows who had become a part of my life." Hoover would not entirely leave these men behind. He held on to what he had discovered at Central, including many of his friendships, for decades to come. But there was indeed some loss in the experience of leaving high school. Upon graduation, many of the boys Hoover had competed with and grown to admire set off for new adventures around the country. Hoover stayed in Washington, like his brother and father and grandfathers before him.[31]

CHAPTER 5

Dieu et les Dames

(1913–1917)

Hoover (back row, far right) with the George Washington University chapter of Kappa Alpha, his college fraternity. Founded in 1865 to preserve the cause of the white South, Kappa Alpha became a model for the FBI's institutional culture. *KAPPA ALPHA JOURNAL*

For Hoover, college life began as a disappointment. Biff Jones was off to West Point, the beginning of an illustrious football career. Other Central graduates headed for schools such as Columbia, Harvard, the University of Michigan, and Cornell. Hoover had been the best among them—valedictorian, debate star, cadet captain—yet he was forced to stay home, working during the day and attending night classes. In the fall of 1913, he enrolled in the evening law program at George Washington University, the same college his brother, Dick, had attended fifteen years earlier. He also began his first government job, a clerk's position at the Library of Congress. These were the least adventurous and most predictable options available, the same choices that had been made by generations of Hoover men before him.[1]

Hoover may have blamed his family (especially his father) for his stunted prospects. Dick was little help. By 1915, Dick was a father of three and the chief clerk of the Steamboat Inspection Service, wrapped up in his own responsibilities. Lillian soon moved into a sprawling old house in Maryland with her husband and children, battling health issues that would come to resemble her father's. Even Rev. MacLeod departed for other climes, accepting a pastorate in Springfield, Illinois, during the summer after Hoover's high school graduation. That left Hoover at home alone with Annie and Dickerson, whose illness must have dominated the family's rhythms. Despite his star turn in high school, Hoover had run up against his family's emotional and financial limits. His choices—to stay in Washington and work for the government—may not have felt much like choices at all.[2]

Hoover was never quite the success at GW that he had been at Central, but he managed to stay near the top of his class and to acquire some basic legal knowledge. He also began to refine the inchoate cleverness of high school debate into a more focused set of ideological commitments. One important force behind this evolution was Kappa Alpha, the Southern fraternity Hoover joined as a freshman and rose to lead as its chapter president in his final year. With Kappa Alpha, Hoover gained entrée to Washington's political elite, hobnobbing with the fraternity's network of conservative Southerners in Congress. He also received an explicit education in segregationist politics and the cultural defense of white supremacy. Founded in 1865 to honor the defeated Confederate general Robert E. Lee, Kappa Alpha actively promoted the Lost Cause myth, in which a noble South had been defeated by Yankee interlopers and Black agitators who misunderstood its way of life. During Hoover's college years, that story served to justify the hardening of racial lines not only throughout the South but in Washington itself, where Woodrow Wilson, the first Southern-born president since the Civil War, sanctioned the segregation of federal employment. Though Hoover had grown up in a segregating city, it was through his fraternity that he first formalized his racial outlook, adopting a Southern ideology that linked segregation with order and virtue and the "gentleman's" way of life.

Together, GW, Kappa Alpha, and the Library of Congress introduced several of the basic concepts Hoover would put into practice once he left college and entered full-time government work as a lawyer and, later, as FBI director. If high school had encouraged Hoover's ambitions, it was during college that he honed his worldview. From the library he took essential lessons in how to run a bureaucracy and manage vast amounts of information. At his college and fraternity, he found the social world and racial values that would define much of his adult life. For decades to come, Hoover would look back to his college years for the kind of men he hoped to employ at the Bureau and for the few intimate companions he kept at his side.

WHEN PRESIDENT WILSON ARRIVED IN 1913, WASHINGTON STILL RETAINED some of its small-town feel, but the level of conflict was picking up fast. "We are in a period of clamor, of bewilderment, of an almost tremulous unrest," social commentator Walter Weyl had noted the previous year. The presidential contest had reflected this sense of urgency. All of the 1912 candidates expressed concern about the growing inequality between the nation's rich and poor, and about its pernicious effect on Amer-

ican democracy. All agreed, too, that only the federal government could hope to counterbalance the economic might of gargantuan corporations like Standard Oil and U.S.
Steel. Washington would now have to be a place not only to administer the government but also, in their shared progressive vision, to transform the nation.[3]

Wilson brought a polite but hopeful tone to that discussion and to the city of
Washington itself. A former president of Princeton, he looked upon the capital as a
place chock-full of potential but in need of serious help. Theodore Roosevelt had
treated the city as a playground, to be enlivened with fistfights, exotic animals, and
boyish spectacle. Wilson showcased the college man's reserve and authority, a thin-
faced, paled-eyed patrician with narrow wire spectacles and an air of constant surprise.
His presence made Washington a professional man's city, in which books and expertise
could be prized over masculine showiness. Perhaps this intellectual environment provided consolation for Hoover: if he could not go off to Princeton, at least some of
Princeton had come to him.

As a scholar of government, Wilson specialized in the study of public administration, an emerging field in which his work exerted a pioneering influence. He believed
in the value of a nonpartisan, professional civil service, the area of government in
which the Hoover men had long worked and, sometimes, thrived. Wilson had also
tackled the problem of partisanship among elected officials. He had concluded that it
was possible, under the right leadership, for everyone to work together on the public's
behalf. During his first few years in office, he attempted to show how the administrative state ought to work, rallying a Democratic-majority Congress to create new
executive-branch institutions including the Federal Trade Commission and Federal
Reserve. He also helped to push through the nation's first income tax, aimed at the
colossal fortunes of men like J. P. Morgan and John D. Rockefeller. While these laws
hardly touched middle-class families like the Hoovers, they set an example of what a
determined, progressive leader might accomplish under the right conditions.

Wilson embraced segregationist politics along with his tributes to experts and administration, a combination not at all unusual among the era's progressives. Though
he had lived for decades in New Jersey, he was a Southern man by birth, a proud son of
Virginia. Like most white Southerners, Wilson felt that Reconstruction had been an
unmitigated disaster, its damage contained only once white Southerners pushed Black
men out of political office and established Jim Crow. When he came to Washington,
he brought with him a generation of Southern-born appointees raised on this story.
Fully half of his cabinet consisted of Southern men, a situation not seen since before
the Civil War. They in turn brought what they had learned as "redeemers," white Democrats who had spent the past few decades creating and enforcing segregation in their
home states.

Wilson licensed these men to carry out a similar program within the federal government, where generations of both Black and white public servants—including the

Hoovers—had managed to carry on their work side by side. Under the Wilson admin-istration, many government departments built walls between their Black and white employees, forcing Black clerks into separate bathrooms and out of government cafete-rias. Others fired their Black employees rather than bother with the effort of segrega-tion. The result of Wilson's initiatives was a sudden reordering of Washington's social geography, the drawing of clear racial lines where things had been blurry before. As a boy, Hoover had always attended segregated schools and churches. Now, just as he prepared to enter the more egalitarian realm of federal employment, that world be-came segregated, too.[4]

HOOVER KNEW THE LIBRARY OF CONGRESS WELL BY THE TIME HE BEGAN WORK-ing there in 1913. As a boy, he had taken in the building's grandeur, with its triple-arched entrance, vast flights of exterior stairs, and greenish dome and cupola—all just a few blocks up Pennsylvania Avenue from Seward Square. As a high school student, he had studied there in preparation for key debates, an earnest researcher in white shirt and dark pants, dwarfed by the library's brilliant-colored murals depicting the finest achievements the world of arts and letters had to offer. The library shared the values that had once animated the Coast Survey—reason, order, knowledge, and expertise. These were carved into its stonework, a "gorgeous and palatial monument," in the words of one guidebook, "to its National sympathy and appreciation of Literature, Science and Art." In more than one way, the Library was a familiar place to Hoover.[5]

He got his job there in the usual Washington fashion, through a combination of merit and personal pull. It was not unusual for a Central boy to work at the library; the 1912 class president, a year ahead of Hoover, was already there, earning his way through Georgetown. Hoover had the extra advantage of an uncle who belonged to the Cosmos Club, where the library's chief administrator, Herbert Putnam, happened to be a mem-ber. An opinionated red-haired Boston man, Putnam had come to the library in 1899 hoping to do what William Bache had done at the Coast Survey a generation earlier: turn a government body into a center of professionalism, science, and intellect.[6]

Hoover began his job in October 1913 at a salary of $360 per year, his first govern-ment paycheck. He worked in the "order division," acquiring and sorting the endless run of materials that arrived at the library each day. During his first year on the job, the library processed more than 125,000 new books and pamphlets. Its accessions in-cluded not only books published in the U.S., but obscure and priceless works from nearly every world civilization: a Hebrew-language "Semitica" collection donated by philanthropist Jacob Schiff; Chinese, French, and Italian literature; a compendium of pamphlets and books on "the social revolutionary movement in Europe," including early German-language editions of Marx and Engels. Hoover helped to track these works as they made their way onto the library's shelves.[7]

After the excitement of high school, there was no avoiding the fact that this was drudge work: sorting and filing, hour after hour, for low pay. At Putnam's library, though, the challenge of processing information came with a certain frisson. One of Putnam's great innovations had been the creation of a card index (known, appropriately, as the Library of Congress system) through which the library's enormous archive of books and information could be retrieved at a moment's notice. Until Putnam's arrival, there had been no reliable method of searching and sorting the library's collections. In that sense, his new classification system was nothing short of revolutionary, the Google of its day.

Looking back, Hoover complained that other clerks urged him to slow down with his sorting and classifying. He ignored them. By the time he left his library job in 1917, he had more than doubled his starting salary, and he had acquired skills that put him at the cutting edge of the era's information technology. One of his great selling points when he arrived at the Justice Department was his ability to sort immense amounts of data and to find it when needed.[8]

He learned other things from his time at the library as well, practical lessons in how to manage people and how to make a government bureaucracy function. Of all the men Hoover encountered during his early years in government, it was Putnam who first showed him how to run an effective agency. Putnam believed in the library's identity as a nonpartisan professional organization; he went to Congress for money because he had to, not because politicians knew best. He nurtured a powerful institutional identification among the library's employees, insisting that clerks and librarians subordinate their desires to "the personality of the institution itself." He also demanded unflinching loyalty.

As a public figure, Putnam was extraordinarily sensitive to the library's image, developing elaborate codes of behavior for how employees ought to interact with congressmen and citizens alike. He enforced these rules through a blizzard of "General Orders," infamous memos outlining everything from proper cataloging procedure to how to greet patrons. Meticulous to a fault, he exercised personal control over staff, budgets, communications, and ordering for the library collections—in short, everything that mattered. When he found even the slightest error by a clerk or librarian, he was famous for tirades of such "precision and eloquence" that they "would arrest circulation and scar the flesh" of his employees. To the degree he was willing to delegate, he insisted on being able to choose his own staff and fought to keep them outside civil service rules, established in the 1880s to reduce partisan influence over government staffing. The civil service merit-testing system, in which bosses were supposed to accept all eligible comers, reduced employers' hiring discretion—presumably the reason Putnam rejected it.

Putnam's methods yielded a mixed reputation in Washington. Some viewed him as a truly inspiring leader, brimming with "the energy and nerve that could ensure success." Others saw him as a tyrant and megalomaniac. Hoover went on to replicate many of Putnam's best and worst qualities.[9]

AFTER A FULL DAY'S WORK AT THE LIBRARY OF CONGRESS, HOOVER SET OFF across town for the GW law school, located in the second floor of the Masonic Temple, an imposing limestone monolith in the heart of the Northwest. As a university, GW was something of an oddity, at least compared to more tradition-bound schools such as Harvard and Yale. Founded in 1821 as Columbian College (and renamed in 1904), the school was supposed to have been the premier national university, an institution that would draw culture, science, and intellect to the capital, like the Coast Survey and the Library of Congress. Over the years, it had instead become a profession-oriented night school for local students like Hoover.

Students and faculty alike took pride in the idea that GW might yet prove itself against the odds. "The history of the George Washington University has been that of the struggle of perseverance and determination," the student yearbook noted in 1914, at the conclusion of Hoover's first year. For students from Central High—and there were many of them at GW—it was another familiar culture, at once striving and defensive, deeply rooted in local government culture. As one professor noted during Hoover's freshman year, up to 75 percent of GW students worked during the day, usually for the government. The school specialized in two- and three-year night programs; students graduated with degrees in dentistry, medicine, library work, teaching, engineering, or law. From there, with the possible exception of the doctors and dentists, the vast majority returned to government work, theoretically with a brighter future and higher salary.[10]

When Hoover started, there were about two hundred students enrolled at the law school. Many of them came from Washington, either because they grew up there or because they had migrated as young adults seeking federal work. Like Central, GW included both men and women, but they tended to be divided by professional program: men mostly became doctors, lawyers, dentists, and engineers; women became teachers, nurses, and librarians. GW had no Black students, a policy of segregation that it would maintain well into the 1950s.[11]

Hoover's course schedule offered little flexibility, a plod through Corporations, Contracts, Equity, Property, Domestic Relations, Torts, and Evidence. Like most turn-of-the-century law schools, GW ascribed to the case-law system; students spent hours poring over individual cases and puzzling out the application of legal principles. Hoover thrived in this sort of detail-oriented environment. He saved all of his law school notebooks, filling them with rules, regulations, and exceptions. Some of the classes provided a foundation for his later work. He studied federal procedure as well as "brief-making," two areas where he would soon excel. There were also some notable absences. Apparently Hoover the future crime fighter never took a class in criminal procedure. Nor did he ever formally study constitutional law. Many of the questions that would come to dominate his career—about free speech and civil liberties, federal criminal jurisdiction and civil rights—barely existed during his time in law school.[12]

Even for district residents like Hoover, GW's greatest selling point was not its classroom instruction but its access to the rest of Washington. By catering to federal employees, the law school developed a network of students and alumni connected to nearly every conceivable form of government and political work. During his first year, Hoover attended a law school banquet featuring Maryland senator Blair Lee and speaker of the house Champ Clark, whose son, Bennett, attended GW. In his third year, it was Virginia attorney general John Garland Pollard and "Uncle Joe" Cannon, the famed Republican congressman who had preceded Clark as house speaker. The dynamic eighty-year-old Cannon, who got his start under Abraham Lincoln, warned GW's students that their generation "will be up against a new order of things." Like many GW students—ambitious but practical, well connected but not quite elite—Hoover planned to be in the thick of it.[13]

THE LIBRARY OF CONGRESS AND GW LAW SCHOOL EQUIPPED HOOVER WITH THE technical and professional skills to successfully navigate a government career. But there was a third institution that came into his life during these years, and it mattered as much as the other two. This was Kappa Alpha, the Southern fraternity Hoover joined during his first months on campus. In a college life constrained in so many ways, Kappa Alpha became Hoover's chief source of sustenance and friendship. It also solidified the conservative racial outlook he would preserve, with minor variations, for the rest of his life. Kappa Alpha described itself as the nation's most influential Southern fraternity, a gathering place for "the Southland's favored sons." When Hoover joined, the national fraternity included sitting congressmen and senators from many Southern states, including Texas, Alabama, Florida, and South Carolina. These men shaped how Hoover thought about the essential questions of the day—racial segregation first among them.[14]

Established just months after the end of the Civil War, Kappa Alpha dedicated itself to carrying on the legacy of the "incomparable flower of Southern knighthood" known as Robert E. Lee. According to fraternity legend, its early members also helped to create the first Ku Klux Klan, founded around the same time. Both Kappa Alpha and the Klan traced certain origins to Kuklos Adelphon, a defunct prewar Southern fraternal order known as "old Kappa Alpha." When Hoover joined half a century later, at least one national Kappa Alpha leader was still insisting that "we started the Ku Klux Klan and should claim our part in its work." The fraternity's official journal neither confirmed nor denied the claim.[15]

Kappa Alpha promoted an exclusive regional identity. Members boasted that they belonged to "the single fraternity which has confined itself to Southern territory or to soil where Southern sentiment prevails." They also described themselves as knightly "gentlemen" modeled after Lee's style and principles. They took as their motto "Dieu et les Dames" ("God and the Ladies"), a phrase intended to evoke a tradition of white masculine chivalry tarnished by Confederate defeat. To those in the know, the phrase was shorthand for all the values of the Old South, including the idea that white women needed to be protected from the supposedly dire threat of Black sexual violence. The Mississippi legislature inscribed "Dieu et les Dames" on the ceiling of its new state-house, built in 1903—a sign of Kappa Alpha's political reach and regional influence.[16]

One of the most prominent Kappa Alphas around Washington was John Temple Graves, a Southern newspaper editor and early Kappa Alpha member who rose to fame as a passionate defender of both segregation and lynching. Born before the Civil War, Graves had come of age with the fraternity, joining as a member in 1871 and rising to Knight Commander, the fraternity's highest national post, a decade later. In the years since, he had emerged as an outspoken believer in "separation" as the only possible solution to the "serious, menacing, and supreme" racial problem bedeviling the South. Graves called for deporting Black people to the Pacific Islands, some "untaken and undeveloped" Western territory, or even "the dark continent" itself, as a possible alternative to segregation. He also argued for the repeal of the Fifteenth Amendment, which allowed Black men the right to vote, labeling it "the American mistake of the century." In 1906, he helped to spark the Atlanta race riot by encouraging white violence to stem an alleged epidemic of crime and sexual violence at the hands of Black men. Black leaders identified Graves as the most influential voice—"South or North, white or black"—in support of the riot, which saw dozens of Black residents shot, hanged, and beaten to death. Kappa Alpha took a more positive view of his actions. In 1907, just a year after the riot, the fraternity's Atlanta chapter held a banquet in his honor.[17]

Another of Kappa Alpha's favored sons was Thomas Dixon, famed for his admiring trilogy of novels about the Reconstruction-era Ku Klux Klan. Born and raised in North Carolina, Dixon had joined Kappa Alpha at Wake Forest before moving on to a gadfly career as a lawyer, actor, journalist, and minister. By the time Hoover enrolled at GW, Dixon was best known as a fiction author and playwright—in effect, the nation's bard of white supremacy. His novels portrayed the Klan as an avenging, godly force, sent to save Southern white women (and civilization itself) from rape and pillage at the hands of debauched former slaves. Dixon believed the men of KA had a special role to play in carrying on this legacy. "God ordained the southern white man to teach the lessons of Aryan supremacy," he maintained, and he considered Kappa Alpha one of God's best vehicles. He also wrote widely on the evils of socialism. One novel, published during Hoover's Central High years, depicted a California commune's descent into starvation, tyranny, and violence as a result of its socialistic experiments.

Dixon shared some of Graves's ability to stir up violent racial conflict, with black-face stagings of his novel *The Clansman* sparking near riots in several cities. As with Graves, Kappa Alpha stood by Dixon even as Black leaders accused him of making "'blood' money" off of their pain. In 1910, in one such gesture of support, fraternity members turned out for performances of Dixon's new play, *The Sins of the Father*, which depicted a segregationist politician driven to murder-suicide as a result of mis-cegenation.[18]

When Hoover joined Kappa Alpha in 1913, both Dixon and Graves were still deeply involved in fraternity life. Indeed, Graves lived in Washington and made a point of showing up to local events. In October 1913, Hoover's first fall at GW, Graves appeared at the Kappa Alpha house for an alumni reception, where he urged young recruits to embrace "the high ideals of the order," in the words of *The Washington Post*. A few months later, he appeared at another local fraternity banquet, delivering a speech titled "Kappa Alpha" as alumni yelled and cheered and tossed their napkins in favor of his message. Hoover's first year at GW happened to be the fiftieth anniversary of the Battle of Gettysburg and the Emancipation Proclamation, a coincidence of timing that gave Kappa Alpha's Old South mythology and white supremacist politics a special resonance within national debate. In the summer of 1914, between Hoover's first and second years at law school, Graves proposed to preserve such sentiments in a "great memorial" to Robert E. Lee, to be carved into the granite face of Stone Mountain, Georgia. Kappa Alpha members plunged into raising money for the effort, just as they would for "any other movement which has as its object the perpetuation of the glory of the Old South," as their journal explained.[19]

Though the carving began in 1915, it would take decades for the memorial to be completed, a granite reminder of slavery and white supremacy looming over the pic-nickers below. In the meantime, Thomas Dixon came up with his own ideas for promoting the Kappa Alpha cause. Around the same time that Hoover joined the fraternity, Dixon began collaborating with director D. W. Griffith on *The Birth of a Nation*, a three-hour silent-film adaptation of Dixon's novel *The Clansman*. In February 1915, during Hoover's second year of law school, Woodrow Wilson screened the film at the White House, a major public relations triumph for the filmmakers. He purportedly loved its heroic depiction of Klansmen riding to the rescue of a belea-guered white South. Elsewhere, the film met with a more mixed response, as millions of white citizens thrilled to its racial demagoguery while Black organizations and their sympathizers fought to have the film banned. Among the film's greatest admirers was a Southern preacher named William Simmons, who chose Stone Mountain as the site for a midnight ceremony reestablishing the Klan, thus blending the visions of Dixon and Graves.[20]

At Hoover's local KA chapter, the response to the film was more muted but no less enthusiastic. In 1916, the fraternity's Washington alumni sponsored a screening of the film, which Hoover almost certainly attended. His later career suggests that he accepted much (though not all) of what the film had to say.[21]

IF FIGURES SUCH AS GRAVES AND DIXON MAY HAVE DOMINATED THE FRATERNITY's national profile, it was through the local chapter that Hoover saw how their ideas might be translated into political action. Thanks to its Washington location, the local alumni chapter boasted an array of powerful politicians among its members. Many of them took an interest in the activities and future careers of the GW boys. Texas senator Morris Sheppard, a prominent voice in the campaign to segregate federal employment, regularly attended dinners and alumni events. Judge John Thornton, a Confederate veteran and senator from Louisiana, made a practice of inviting Kappa Alphas to dinner at the Senate restaurant. Other alums actually lived at the fraternity's Washington chapter house, an unusual arrangement that gave the younger members direct access to aspiring mentors and role models.[22]

The GW chapter was explicit about its networking goals: as members boasted in the fraternity's national journal, they wanted to be "known and recognized as the producer of leaders." Members regarded the chapter house as a sanctified place. "It is a home for my soul," one wrote, "an altar for my devotion, a hearth for my faith, a center for my affections, and a foretaste of heaven." For Hoover, whose family could be a source of strife and pain, the fraternity also provided a place of escape. Though he could never afford to live at the grand fraternity house, he spent hundreds of hours there, usually after his evening classes and often well into the night. He likely spent some holidays there as well, one of the local boys who stayed behind when the out-of-towners dispersed.[23]

As in high school, Hoover threw himself into the task of impressing his peers. In his third year at GW, he volunteered to serve as delegate to the campus interfraternity council. In his final year, he became chapter president and took it upon himself to ingratiate the fraternity with the university's top men. That fall, he hosted a private fraternity tea and reception to honor Rear Admiral Charles Stockton, the renowned naval officer and president of GW. A few months later, he presided over a Christmas reception at the chapter house, with Congressman Samuel Nicholls of South Carolina as a featured speaker and guest. At the 1916 alumni gathering, held at the historic Ebbitt hotel, the audience was packed with important Southerners, including Nicholls, Texas congressman Robert Lee Henry, former Missouri governor Joseph Folk, and John Abercrombie, newly elected to the House from Alabama. Abercrombie in particular proved to be an important connection whose presence in government would help to protect and support Hoover during his earliest years as a federal official.[24]

———

IT WOULD BE HARD TO OVERSTATE THE IMPORTANCE OF SUCH CONNECTIONS for Hoover's future career. And yet the fraternity was more than a networking opportunity. It was also an experience that yielded enduring friendships. "Kappa Alpha is not a fraternity," one speaker explained to the national convention in 1914. "It is a philosophy of life." Kappa Alpha offered many of the same qualities that had attracted Hoover to the cadet corps: it was all male, sociable yet hierarchical, oriented toward a set of common rituals and principles. Hoover's closest friends in college were Kappa Alpha brothers, and they did nearly everything together, from hunting and fishing to parties and overnight trips. They swore their undying loyalty to each other, pledging to think of their chapter house as "the place where the sacrament of Brotherhood is administered, the Word of Brotherhood is preached, the Power of Brotherhood is felt, the Spirit of Brotherhood is manifested, the Love of Brotherhood is revealed." For most college boys, fraternity membership turned out to be a passing phase, a carefree stop on the road to marriage and family. For Hoover, Kappa Alpha would become a way of life, a touchstone for the FBI's internal values, and a shorthand way to measure the character, loyalty, and political sympathies of the men he hired to work for him.[25]

Hoover's closest friend in Kappa Alpha was Thomas Frank Baughman, a law student one year his junior. Like Hoover, Baughman lived at home and worked throughout his time in college, first as a telephone operator and later as a Senate page or clerk. Baughman also became a committed Kappa Alpha and absorbed most of the same lessons Hoover did. In the spring of 1916, Baughman signed on as a delegate to the national fraternity convention and received a full-immersion weekend in the culture and lore of the Lost Cause. The convention was held in Richmond, the former Confederate capital, where the delegates took time out for a silent march and wreath-laying at the city's new monument to Robert E. Lee. Back in Washington, Baughman attended alumni events, listening to Graves and other distinguished alumni alongside Hoover.[26]

Hoover's closeness with Baughman raises a question that would persist throughout his adult life: Was this just a friendship? Or was it a romantic, even sexual, relationship? Same-sex relationships were not unheard of at GW, where interested students occasionally staged clandestine dances and social events in out-of-the-way spots. Indeed, fraternities themselves often became places of quiet same-sex experimentation. It would hardly have been remarkable for Hoover to explore these possibilities, especially at a moment when he was experimenting with so many other aspects of his adult identity. Still, to view Hoover's bonds with other men primarily in romantic or sexual terms is to misunderstand how a fraternity like Kappa Alpha operated. The whole point of joining was to build deep bonds of affection with other men, to find companions who could be loved and trusted throughout the vicissitudes of life. "When I became a member," one Kappa Alpha recalled to his brothers in 1915, "I promised to take you into my confidence, to share with you my secrets, and, in brief, to treat you with more respect and courtesy than one ordinarily pays a blood relation." Far from hiding the love that members might develop for each other, the fraternity sought to encourage it, within the proper bounds of "knightly" behavior.[27]

If there was anything unusual about Hoover, it was perhaps that he threw himself so wholeheartedly into this effort, to the exclusion of most other social interests. For all their soaring rhetoric about the bonds between men, Kappa Alpha members spent a great deal of time trying to attract women, sponsoring dances and receptions intended to lure in members of the opposite sex. Hoover presumably attended these events, but there is no evidence that he showed any interest in heterosexual dating or marriage. In a lifetime of fulfilling expectations, his romantic life was one place where Hoover refused to conform.[28]

His fraternity brothers, like his high school classmates, seem to have viewed him with some bemusement—at once impressed by his talents and taken aback by his fervor. His nickname in the 1916 yearbook was "Josephus," after the imposing and mercurial warrior-scholar who wrote the first histories of Jews in Rome. As in the cadet corps, Hoover saw his fraternity brothers not merely as beloved friends, but as men to be improved, disciplined, and taught. In return, they regarded him with not only affection and admiration but also a touch of fear.[29]

HOOVER WALKED THROUGH HIS GRADUATION IN JUNE 1916, LISTENING AS President Stockton urged the students to aim high in their future endeavors. Then, for reasons never entirely explained, he decided to stay at GW for an extra year. He enrolled in the university's small Master of Law program, one of only four students his year working toward that unusual and unnecessary degree. Perhaps he simply wanted the extra credential, a way to set himself apart from the ordinary law student. Or perhaps he was not yet ready to leave his college friends and fraternity. Whatever the cause, it turned out to be a crucial decision. If Hoover had left school in 1916, he would have entered a world of government employment thoroughly familiar to his father and grandfather. By the time he finished a year later, nearly everything had changed. In the spring of 1917, two months before Hoover's graduation, the United States declared war on Germany. His hometown of Washington became the center of a war machine.[30]

CHAPTER 6

The Great Adventure

(1917–1918)

An army recruitment poster, 1917. Hoover graduated from law school just as the U.S. was entering World War I. He did not enlist. Instead, he went to work for the Justice Department and stayed there for the rest of his career.

HUNTINGTON LIBRARY

On the evening of April 2, 1917, two months before Hoover's law school graduation, President Woodrow Wilson made his way through a gentle rain to the U.S. Capitol, where he asked Congress for a declaration of war. Three days later, Dickerson Hoover resigned from his job at the Coast Survey, bringing a sputtering end to his thirty-seven-year government career. These two events—one of global-historical significance, one intensely private and personal—provide the backdrop for Hoover's transition from college man into full-time government servant. The war promised unknown peril but also boundless opportunity. Dickerson's resignation was a reminder of old limits and pressures. Two months after Wilson's address, Hoover finally left GW with his master's degree, ready to throw in his lot with the wartime government but also urgently in need of a steady job. This confluence of events helps to explain how Hoover so quickly ended up in the Justice Department and at least a bit about why he stayed for so long.[1]

At another moment, Hoover's career might have veered in a different direction, toward tax law, trade regulation, or, like his brother Dick, steamboat inspection. But the months following Hoover's graduation marked the birth of a vast new experiment in federal surveillance of political dissidents and "alien enemies," so that was where Hoover got his start. World War I marked a turning point in the history of civil liberties, the moment that the federal government began to watch its citizens and residents on a mass scale, and to keep files on their political activities. Hoover happened to be present at the creation, an accident of timing that forever altered his ambitions and his professional path.[2]

His introduction came through the German internment program, a haphazard effort aimed at detaining noncitizens alleged to pose a danger to the home front. Today, it is widely known that the United States sent more than a hundred thousand Japanese Americans to internment camps during World War II. Less recognized is that policy's anti-German precedent, the program in which Hoover first began to experiment with administering and enforcing the law. Hoover took from his wartime experience a budding vision of how federal power could be expanded and multiplied—not only through coercion but also through coordination with local and state governments, and through direct alliances with citizen groups. He also learned how propaganda could shift public opinion, and how willing certain sorts of Americans could be to offer up their services to a cause. He began to think about the limits of federal power, too—what could be done publicly, what had to be done secretly, what should never be attempted at all. He would later oppose Japanese internment based on what he learned during World War I. But during these early years he was a student of wartime processes, not a critic.

WHEN HOOVER ARRIVED AT LAW SCHOOL, DOMESTIC ISSUES LIKE WOMEN'S suffrage and socialism had dominated political talk on campus. Slowly, though, the war had begun to crowd out everything else, to become *the* issue rather than one of many. Events drove that shift: the 1915 sinking of the British merchant boat *Lusitania*, with more than a hundred Americans aboard; the stalemated battles at the Somme and Verdun in 1916, with their unspeakable death tolls; the calls in many sectors of American society—finance, especially—for more active aid to suffering Britain; the insistence by others that the war was a capitalist conspiracy and a soulless charnel house, with nothing to offer the American people. Hoover did not play much of a role in these campus debates. He focused on grades, fraternity affairs, and his day job ordering books. Like everyone else, though, he eventually found the war impossible to avoid.[3]

For GW students, the turning point came in the spring of 1916, when the city of Washington began a buildup of National Guard volunteers. The war was controversial at the time; President Wilson ran for reelection on the platform that "He kept us out of war!" On campus, though, war supporters began to recruit for "student military camps," where interested young men could receive training in cavalry exercises, field surveys, and infantry maneuvers. They were aided in this effort by a long list of military alumni and faculty enthused about what Theodore Roosevelt described as the "Great Adventure" of war. Wilson himself came around to that position in early 1917, as the Germans resumed unrestricted submarine warfare and made a secret bid to bring Mexico into a war against the United States. On April 2, 1917, in the hours before his war message, thousands of protesters had descended on the Capitol, begging him not to lead the nation's men into the European carnage. But Congress ultimately agreed with Wilson, declaring war in an overwhelming if not unanimous vote.[4]

Over the next several weeks, the pressure to volunteer for military service intensified at GW, especially among fraternity men. On April 19, two weeks after the declaration of war, Kappa Alpha hosted a banquet where former Missouri governor (and fraternity alum) Joseph Folk emphasized the "spiritualizing influence" bound to result "if every man and woman above 17 wore a uniform of khaki." The push grew still more intense by May, after Congress approved the president's request for a nationwide military draft. The draft would apply to all men between the ages of twenty-one and thirty, precisely Hoover's peer group, and many college men rushed to volunteer, thus avoiding the ignominy and loss of control that might come with conscription. Draft registration was slated to begin on June 5, 1917, one day before Hoover's graduation.[5]

All of which raises an obvious question: Why didn't Hoover join up? He was the right age, with stellar cadet-corps training, about to be finished with law school. He was healthy, capable, and, even at the age of twenty-two, an experienced leader of men. By one estimate, some 80 percent of his Kappa Alpha chapter left for either the army or navy. Hoover continued his life in Washington. As graduation loomed, he reached out to his network of relatives and local contacts, seeking not an officer's commission (as his training in Company A might have indicated) but a home-front government post. Thanks to their help, in the summer of 1917 he landed a job with the Justice Department at $990 per year. His salary was just $150 more than what he had been earning at the Library of Congress, but it came with a draft exemption.[6]

Hoover was no doubt relieved to avoid the war. But his decision not to enlist probably had less to do with his temperament or preferences than with the same problem that had constrained his choices after high school: the situation at home. Dickerson experienced no miraculous recovery during Hoover's law school years. If anything, he appears to have grown worse, unable to maintain even the rudiments of a daily routine. With his resignation from the Coast Survey, Annie and Dickerson lost their income and became dependent on their youngest son. And so Hoover, once again, stayed at home with them.

———

AFTER HIGH SCHOOL, THERE HAD BEEN SOMETHING DISAPPOINTING ABOUT remaining in Washington while other men set out to explore the world. This time, the world came to Washington. During the spring and summer of 1917, while Hoover was wrapping up his classes at GW and poking around for employment, some forty thousand war workers poured into the district, each of them hoping to secure a government job. A few were famous and accomplished, "dollar-a-year men" who volunteered their services running the new war agencies. Many more were young and anonymous and spent their days toiling away in "tempos," the drab temporary office buildings that sprang up along the mall. Later generations would mythologize other moments of intensified federal activity—the imaginative fervor of the New Deal, the vast organizational triumphs of World War II—as among the most vital periods of their lives. For Hoover's generation, it was the Great War that mattered and that brought the federal government to life on a grand scale.[7]

Countless "firsts" were rushed into being during those early months of war: the first mass draft, the first widespread use of the income tax, the first significant experiments in federal propaganda and surveillance. The swiftness and scale of these changes have led historians to identify 1917 as the moment the American state began to acquire its truly modern form, the one in which men like Hoover would make their careers. In Washington, the lived experience of the wartime bureaucracy was not quite so tidy. What stood out to many federal employees was not how powerful the government was but how weak it seemed, and how little anyone appeared to know what they were doing.

The anxieties bubbled up everywhere: Who would pay for the war? Who would fight in it? Would the American people support it? Could the war indeed be won? Wilson had a simple answer to most of these questions: a democratic people would fight a war for democracy through democratic means. What he meant in theory was that all forms of mobilization, from the draft to war finance, would be voluntary rather than coercive. In practice, this approach had a darker side, an insistence on conformity that tended to fuel both vigilante violence and a new regime of speech codes and legal restrictions. Going to war had never been popular: German Americans did not want to fight against Germany; Irish Americans did not want to fight on behalf of England; workers, socialists, and Westerners showed little interest in fighting to make good on New York bankers' overseas loans. The war effort thus began amid cries to squelch "disloyalty," root out spies, and silence internal critics. Like many war workers, Hoover found himself pushed and pulled between competing imperatives—to build new structures while maintaining traditional limits, to suppress dissent while fighting a democratic war.[8]

This combination of ambition and anxiety, of liberation and repression, could be found nearly everywhere in Washington. With the influx of war workers, housing suddenly became a precious commodity. Boarders began to crowd into homes that had once housed single families. Annie and Dickerson took in a man named Roy Plympton, a twenty-nine-year-old postal worker who, like Hoover, seems to have avoided the draft. There were soldiers around the city, too: a total of 130,000 men in uniform within a twenty-five-mile radius. Perhaps most visible of all were the single young women, arriving from small towns across the country to take up secretarial work. Late in life, one of Hoover's confidants would spread the story that Hoover had fallen in love with one of these war workers in 1917, a woman named Alice who broke his heart by taking up with a soldier fighting in France. If true (and the evidence is meager), it would mark an important moment in Hoover's coming-of-age, his first serious flirtation with a member of the opposite sex.[9]

More likely, Hoover was simply part of the wartime social whirl, with its tendency to push back against the strictures he had absorbed as a church boy and perfect student. The presence of so many young, transient people gave Washington a new energy but also a sense of social chaos and disorder. The city went dry in the fall of 1917, a morals measure promoted by Texas senator (and loyal Kappa Alpha brother) Morris Sheppard. But such restrictions did not prevent the development of an energetic underground social scene. Despite its martial atmosphere, Washington was an exciting, even wild place to be as the war began. "The one invariable rule seemed to be that every individual was found doing something he or she had never dreamed of doing before," a local writer observed. That insight turned out to be one of the open secrets of the war: If you were headed to the battlefields of France, you were in serious trouble. If you were in Washington, you were indeed embarking upon a "Great Adventure."[10]

HOOVER BEGAN HIS JOB AT THE JUSTICE DEPARTMENT ON JULY 26, 1917, SIX DAYS after the national draft lottery. In later years, July 26 would emerge as a storied date in FBI lore, celebrated with flowers, parties, and letters of congratulation. In 1917, though, very little about the Justice Department seemed especially promising. Created by Congress during Reconstruction, the department had spent the past half century dealing mostly with issues of trade and taxation and cleaning up after botched elections. Until 1917, the department was insignificant enough to fit into a limestone mansion that had once been a stand-alone private residence. Hoover's arrival coincided with the move to an eight-story office building, a sign not only of the department's growing size and status but also of the mounting wartime chaos.[11]

The man in charge at Justice was an antitrust lawyer named Thomas Gregory, the first of many attorneys general who would come and go over the course of Hoover's career. To a Kappa Alpha like Hoover, Gregory was a familiar type. Born in Mississippi, the son of a Confederate doctor, he had come of age in the turmoil of Reconstruction and emerged as a passionate Texas Democrat. Once in Washington, he stayed loyal to the Southern Society, home to many influential Kappa Alphas. He had accepted the post of attorney general on the assumption that he would continue his antitrust work while helping Wilson solidify Democratic power. When war broke out, he found himself grappling with "activities wholly different in character."

Among those activities, three stood out as major sources of controversy and challenge. The first was draft enforcement, a duty that required the Justice Department to police the compliance of millions of American men. The second came under the auspices of the Espionage Act of 1917, passed in June as a tool for suppressing not only bona fide foreign espionage but also any act that might "willfully cause or attempt to cause insubordination, disloyalty, mutiny, or refusal of duty, in the military or naval forces of the United States." Finally, there was the "alien enemy" problem—the issue of what to do about noncitizens born in belligerent countries but currently living in the United States, where they were now suspected of danger or disloyalty. As Gregory noted, all three of these duties fundamentally altered the Justice Department's "relationship to the daily life and habits of our citizens." From his first day on the job, Hoover was thrown into negotiating this new relationship between the government and its citizens and finding his own place within it.[12]

Out of the war came his first experiences in surveillance, detection, and law enforcement. And there were other lessons as well, in governance and bureaucracy, in managing an organization that suddenly found itself under tremendous pressure to deliver. Like Herbert Putnam at the Library of Congress, Gregory provided Hoover with a model of institutional leadership, and one much closer to Hoover's future profession. The attorney general could be venomous toward "disloyal" Americans. "May God have mercy on them, for they need expect none from an outraged people and an avenging Government," he declared in one oft-cited speech. At the same time, Gregory cautioned against mob violence and prejudging German-born residents. He showed a similarly mixed approach when it came to federal power, expanding the Justice Department bureaucracy while also warning against creating bureaucracies that might be impossible to dismantle when the war ended. Gregory worked to build the wartime government, but he did so with one eye on conservative states' rights principles and another on the dangerous passions that could be unleashed by "100 percent Americanism."[13]

IN THE FIRST DOCUMENT HE SIGNED AS A JUSTICE DEPARTMENT EMPLOYEE, Hoover promised to "support and defend the Constitution of the United States against all enemies, foreign and domestic." In 1917, that meant dealing with one of the new facets of the department's war work: the internment and registration of German "alien enemies." Most of this work took place within the War Emergency Division, created to serve as a clearinghouse for home-front intelligence. Hoover also came into contact during these first few months with the organization to which he would dedicate his life: the Justice Department's little-known Bureau of Investigation. Just nine years old in 1917, the Bureau functioned as the department's detective wing, investigating violations of federal law. Hoover's first encounters with Bureau agents came through his German internment work: they performed the on-the-ground field inquiries while he processed the cases from Washington. He must have liked what he saw. For the rest of his life, he would champion the investigative process as one of the government's highest callings.[14]

During his war address in April, Wilson had delivered a warning to foreign-born residents who had neglected to become American citizens, vowing to use the "firm hand of stern repression" in all cases of "disloyalty." Millions of Americans had responded to his call by purging their communities of all things German: no more Beethoven or Wagner, no more German-language instruction, no more "sauerkraut" or "hamburgers" (instead, Americans ate "liberty cabbage" and "liberty sandwiches"). Some citizens went even further, engaging in acts of group violence to police patriotism by force. On the same day as Wilson's speech, a mob in Wyoming seized a pro-German loyalist and hung him from a tree; they cut him down before he could choke to death and forced him to kiss the American flag in gratitude. On August 1, just days after Hoover started his job, another vigilante group abducted anti-war labor radical Frank Little in Butte, Montana, tied him to the back of a car, and hauled him through the town before hanging him from a railroad trestle.[15]

Americans justified such actions by pointing not only to wartime atrocities, but to the menace of home-front sabotage. As early as 1915, military authorities had begun to warn that German agents were behind mysterious explosions of ships and defense facilities along the East Coast. The worst episode occurred at Black Tom Island, just off the tip of Manhattan. There, saboteurs blew up a federal munitions depot and produced a massive explosion that killed several people and rattled the entire city. It would take two decades for the government to prove definitively that Black Tom was, indeed, an act of German sabotage. But many Americans needed no convincing about the potential for Germany teachery. According to one study, more than seventy people in the United States died at the hands of home-front mobs during 1917 and 1918.[16]

The Department of Justice responded to anti-German sentiment with both alarm and encouragement. Attorney General Gregory urged Americans to exercise restraint despite the passions of war, and to respect the rights of both German citizens and anti-war dissenters. At the same time, he licensed the creation of a volunteer brigade known as the American Protective League, soliciting some 250,000 men to sign up as deputies of the Justice Department to provide extra manpower in enforcing wartime laws. Though Gregory had hoped that the organization might constrain certain mob tendencies, APL members soon became vigilantes in their own right, zealously seeking out immigrants and flashing badges that identified them as "secret service" operatives despite a near-total lack of screening or training.[17]

Wartime restrictions reinforced their sense of righteousness. By executive order, all German-born men over the age of fourteen who had not become U.S. citizens were automatically considered "alien enemies," a category that meant they had to register with the federal government and could be "apprehended, restrained, secured, and removed" at any moment. Those who remained at large were forbidden to live within half a mile of any military facility and could not own guns or other "implements of war." They were also not permitted to live anywhere within Washington, D.C., making the national capital the only American city to purge itself entirely of noncitizen Germans. Those who resisted were subject to arrest and imprisonment in an army-run internment camp, surrounded by barbed wire.[18]

Hoover's earliest duties at the Justice Department seem to have focused on "questions relating to the parole of men in detention," especially German seamen who had been captured in American waters. By December, he moved on to offering preliminary assessments of internment cases themselves. Most of the alleged violations were procedural rather than overtly dangerous: living too close to the waterfront, failing to register as an alien enemy. It was up to Hoover not to gather evidence but to render judgment. There were no hearings or trials, just a few sheets of paper outlining the known facts. If the department so decided, the accused could be sent without further question to a military internment facility and forced to stay there, potentially for the duration of the war.

These were subjective decisions, often made in haste. "I have a feeling of suspicion about this fellow and recommend permanent detention as the safest course," wrote one Justice Department lawyer, reviewing the case of a Southern Pacific railroad employee whose route took him near wartime facilities. Hoover relied on similarly vague instincts to render his decisions. In one case, he recommended internment for a man who had denounced President Wilson as a "cock-sucker and a thief"; the man, Hoover concluded, used "various vulgar and obscene remarks" in the service of "the most pronounced pro-German expressions." Hoover felt similarly alarmed about the case of a German teenager who had fought beside Pancho Villa in Mexico, then snuck back across the U.S. border. In yet another case, he identified a man's "lying about his social standing and connections" as a reason for internment, despite the fact that allegations of spying and direct contact with German agents "have not been able to be substantiated by evidence."[19]

But Hoover could also show compassion and a willingness to give accused men a second chance. In one case, he reviewed the arrest of German citizen Max Schachman, accused of selling whiskey to men in uniform and "soliciting men for immoral women." These were clear violations of wartime statutes. Hoover recommended that Schachman nonetheless be paroled, perhaps since the man was the sole support for a wife and three children. In a similar case, Hoover argued for mercy toward a German-born sailor who had snuck back into maritime employment (forbidden by wartime regulations) after failing to find a job on dry land. Hoover even suggested parole for the Southern Pacific employee who engendered the "feeling of suspicion" in his Justice Department colleague. In all three instances, Hoover acknowledged that the men had broken the law but declined to see them as dangers to the war effort. But in all three cases he was overruled by superiors.[20]

He may have concluded from this experience that compassion and restraint were unlikely to be rewarded, especially in moments of national emergency. By the attorney general's estimate, more than six thousand "suspected enemy aliens" were interned or detained under presidential warrants for the duration of the war, along with "several thousand" more held for shorter periods. The salutary effects of the program, he boasted, were even more widespread. "The summary character and severe penalty of internment has acted throughout the country as a powerful deterrent against alien-enemy activity," Gregory wrote in 1918. What mattered, in this view, was not that the program doled out perfect justice, but that it taught a lesson about the power and reach of the wartime government.[21]

THOUGH HOOVER WAS ASSIGNED TO GERMAN CASES, HE ALSO WITNESSED A second—and ultimately more influential—campaign of surveillance and prosecution during those first months of war. This one targeted men and women of the American left, self-admitted revolutionaries who held the war in open contempt as a needless bloodbath and an act of imperial folly. They came in a variety of affiliations: disciples of the Midwestern socialist Eugene Debs; militant unionists from the Industrial Workers of the World; anarchists who appealed for an end to both capitalism and organized government; Black activists who opposed the war as an exercise in democratic hypocrisy. During Wilson's first term, they had all spoken out vociferously against the "hell of slaughter" propagated "by the ruling class to rob and kill and enslave the working class," in Debs's words. Until the spring of 1917, those sentiments had been reasonably popular, attracting thousands of followers to rallies and protests. Once Congress entered the war and approved the Espionage Act, however, popular sentiment shifted, and the few remaining dissenters found themselves isolated and vulnerable. The Bolshevik Revolution, which erupted in November 1917, added to the sense that revolutionary socialism could be a dangerous force, especially during the instability of wartime.[22]

There is no evidence that Hoover had thought systematically about socialism, anarchism, or other forms of left-wing politics before his arrival at the Justice Department in 1917. During high school, the debate team had taken on questions of free speech and labor activism, but it gave equal time to both sides. At the Library of Congress, he had processed books on European socialists and revolutionaries, but had little time to read them or think about how they applied to American life. From Kappa Alpha and the Presbyterian Church he picked up general suspicions about immigrants and radicals and racial minorities, but those views were hardly exceptional, even in progressive circles. Though Hoover had been taught to be wary of such groups, he appeared to have no fixed ideas about what lay behind left-wing sentiment or what the nation might do about it.

The wartime Justice Department provided his education. Hoover's first day of work occurred just as the department closed its headline-grabbing trial against the famed anarchists Emma Goldman and Alexander Berkman, two of the first political dissenters to be prosecuted under the wartime laws. Beginning in May 1917, Goldman and Berkman had hosted several meetings of their hastily formed No-Conscription League, designed to foment resistance to the federal draft. Both had previously spent time in jail: Goldman for incitement to riot and defiance of laws forbidding public discussion of birth control; Berkman for his 1892 assassination attempt on the industrialist Henry Clay Frick. Now they were being prosecuted for violating the new draft laws. In July 1917, a federal jury convicted them of conspiracy to disrupt the war effort, and a judge sentenced them each to two years in prison, plus a ten-thousand-dollar fine.[23]

In the months that followed, Hoover saw cases mounted against dozens, then hundreds, then thousands of other men and women, most of them war dissenters and radicals. The Department of Justice made a special effort to rein in the Industrial Workers of the World, the only major labor organization to continue speaking out against Wilson's war effort. On September 5, 1917, six weeks into Hoover's new job, federal agents and local police raided IWW offices throughout the country, seizing membership rolls and arresting the organization's leadership. That summer, after a spectacular mass trial, a Chicago federal judge sentenced nearly a hundred Wobbly leaders to prison for violations of the Espionage and Selective Service Acts. The organization's figurehead, the one-eyed former miner Bill Haywood, received a draconian sentence of twenty years in federal prison.[24]

The list of prosecutions went on and on, ranging from pacifists to brash revolutionaries to those who simply happened to say the wrong thing at the wrong time. Among the groups targeted were Black editors and activists, who tended to focus their commentary not on the foreign conflict, but on the vicious racial war brewing at home. Skeptical of Wilson's democratic language, they did not hesitate to point out that lynching, economic repression, Jim Crow, and denials of voting rights hardly made the U.S. a model for the world. If anything, the war seemed to be making things worse at home. In East Saint Louis, Illinois, white residents responded to an influx of Black defense workers with a weeklong riot that left dozens of Black residents dead and hundreds more fleeing for their lives. Justice officials responded not by attempting to stem the violence, but by prosecuting dissenters who dared to suggest that Black men should not fight "to make the world safe for a democracy that you can't enjoy."[25]

These early raids and speech laws would have a profound influence on Hoover's postwar life, his first encounter with the political questions and surveillance techniques that would ultimately define his career. In 1917, though, he was just beginning to figure out what it all meant, a student of men who believed that mere criticism of the government necessitated a "firm hand of stern repression."

IN NOVEMBER, AS HOOVER APPROACHED HIS TWENTY-THIRD BIRTHDAY, PRESIdent Wilson announced another major task for the Justice Department. Beginning in February, all German-born men who were not citizens of the United States would be expected to register with the federal government. The logistical challenge was tailormade for the skills Hoover had acquired at the Library of Congress. Under the registration program, almost half a million names would be gathered, filed, cataloged, and processed. It was here, in the realm of bureaucracy and administration, that Hoover truly made his mark.[26]

The registration campaign opened nationwide on February 4. Hoover was assigned to coordinate the effort in New York, where local police gathered the initial forms before passing them along to the Justice Department. The assignment was itself a small vote of confidence; New York was the nation's largest city and boasted its highest concentration of Germans. He excelled at the work. Throughout the spring and into the summer, his office maintained a relentless focus on registration: forms and lists needed in triplicate, affidavits to be signed, "indistinct" photographs to be retaken. Hoover seemed to have boundless energy for counting and recounting, then seeking out additional files. In May, his office complained that they had received only 15,146 enemy alien affidavits, wondering where the other 24,216 might be. As time went on, the numbers of missing files grew smaller but Hoover's attention to detail did not. To the 94th Precinct in Brooklyn he protested that he had received 626 names of registered aliens, but only 624 affidavits. The affidavits themselves he scrutinized page by page, noting whether all questions had been answered properly and whether the registration officer had signed each statement. When the president ordered that German-born women, too, should register, Hoover took on the extra paperwork, supervising thousands of new registrations throughout New York City. His dedication would have been impressive under any circumstances, the sort of devotion and efficiency that bosses tend to notice. At the Justice Department in the spring of 1918, it made him nothing short of invaluable.[27]

Soon enough, Hoover's bosses began to reward his success. Within a year, he earned a promotion to the position of "attorney." His salary nearly doubled as well, from $990 to $1,800. This followed the pattern he had established at the Library of Congress— hard work and quick promotion, accompanied by monetary reward. It also fulfilled one of the great unspoken hopes of his childhood: that he would someday surpass his father. After little more than a year, Hoover was making almost as much as Dickerson had earned after a lifetime of work at the Coast Survey.[28]

AND THEN THE WHOLE THING WAS OVER, ALMOST AS SUDDENLY AS IT HAD begun. Socially, the whirl of wartime activity began to slow in September 1918, when the global flu pandemic hit Washington. City authorities shut down public schools, movie theaters, stores, churches, restaurants—anything that was not essential war work, in anyplace residents might be at risk of contracting the virus. The toll was vicious nonetheless: thirty-five thousand flu cases and thirty-five hundred deaths in just six weeks. By the time Washington began to recover, the war itself was drawing to a close. On November 5, the Republicans retook Congress in the midterm elections, a pitiless rejection of Wilson's plea for Democratic support to negotiate a "democratic peace." Still, peace was coming. With it would come the dismantling of the wartime bureaucracy.[29]

Hoover anticipated these events and set out to secure himself a peacetime government job. In early November, he drummed up a letter of recommendation for a post in the Labor Department, where former Alabama congressman (and prominent Kappa Alpha) John Abercrombie was now the solicitor. He also sought out a permanent position within the Justice Department, securing a memo that testified to his "exceptional ability" in alien registration matters. Both documents stressed the qualities that had made him a standout in high school and college: "He works hard and industriously, putting in much overtime work"; "He is thorough, dependable and diligent in all that he undertakes." Neither one described him as especially brilliant or creative. Rather, they emphasized his capacity and willingness to complete high volumes of tedious work.[30]

When the armistice finally took effect on November 11, Washington citizens lit bonfires on the White House Ellipse—symbols of victory, but also pyres to mark the death of their wartime city. Two days later, Hoover signed an oath vowing to "support and defend the Constitution of the United States" once again, this time as an employee of the peacetime Department of Justice.[31]

CHAPTER 7

The Radical Division

(1919)

Cartoon depicting the deportation of 249 alleged anarchists, including the famed Emma Goldman, in December 1919. As the twenty-four-year-old head of the Justice Department's new Radical Division, Hoover orchestrated the deportation effort.

NEW YORK TIMES

In most lives, there are years when things move faster than usual, when change finally arrives with an unmistakable thump. For Hoover, 1919 was one of those years. During a few short months, as the war receded and the postwar world took shape, he found his life's mission. In 1919, he began to engage directly with the "radical problem," to confront the constellation of anarchists, socialists, communists, and Black activists that he would seek to contain for the rest of his life. He also earned what was arguably the most important promotion of his career. He started the year as a nobody, a mid-ranking ex–war worker at a shrinking government agency. By late summer, he had become the wunderkind head of the Justice Department's new Radical Division, located in the organization to which he would devote his life: the Bureau of Investigation.

What Hoover accomplished during his first months at the Radical Division forever changed the nature of American politics, launching an unprecedented experiment in peacetime political surveillance. And yet Hoover was as much a servant as a leader during 1919, still following the dictates and priorities of older, more powerful men. His own ideas about radicalism were not terribly unique; in the turmoil of 1919, with millions of workers on strike and enthusiasm for socialist revolution sweeping through Europe, plenty of Americans shared a basic desire to suppress revolutionary thought and social disorder. As during the war, Hoover's strength lay in his ability to make the mechanisms of government work productively toward a widely shared (if controversial) political goal. He lacked—and would never quite acquire—any real understanding of radicals themselves, of why men and women might think that the United States and its capitalist system should be transformed in the name of social justice. But he had a quick mind and an enthusiasm for organization that made him valuable to the postwar government. At the age of twenty-four, Hoover already knew things about bureaucracy and government that helped him stand out as a man capable beyond his years. In other ways, though, he was remarkably young and parochial, still sleeping in his childhood bedroom, still part of the same conservative tight-knit Washington society in which he had come of age.

Looking back, Hoover would speak only selectively about what happened in 1919, claiming that he played little role in that year's so-called Red Scare or in the Palmer Raids, its most infamous feature. In truth, he was a critical part of the effort, and his experiences that year provided another lasting element of his political education.

THAT 1919 WOULD BE A TURNING POINT FOR HOOVER WAS NOT AT ALL EVIDENT when the year began. On January 1, his twenty-fourth birthday, his family life looked much as it had for years. There was Annie and there was Dickerson, and they lived with a lengthening shadow over their home. Retirement had not eased Dickerson's mental distress. If anything, it seems to have made his depression worse, removing what little structure had once held his life together.

For Hoover, work became a great escape, but opportunities for advancement dried up fast in the first months after the war. By early 1919, high-level appointees were flooding back out of the capital, off to resume the more profitable ventures of private life. Many lower-level workers stayed at first, hoping to make a go of their new careers. They found to their dismay that federal employment was now an uncertain business. Nearly all the colleagues who would later form Hoover's inner circle shared this disconcerting experience, spending the war in Washington and then holding on against the odds when others gave up and retreated.

Hoover spent much of that time trying to recapture the routines of his prewar life. He once again took a leadership role at Kappa Alpha, now as one of the older men who liked to hang around the chapter house. Elected treasurer of the local alumni association, in early 1919 he helped to lead the hunt for a headquarters worthy of the fraternity's self-image: "a big national club in Washington City, with a big n—— at the front door in long coat and brass buttons to greet you with 'Yassah, Boss,'" as the KA journal put it, using openly racist language. For social activities, the Washington alumni held discussions on "the origins and development of the Ku Klux Klan" while the nearby Maryland chapter pioneered a racially degrading blackface tradition known as the Cotton Pickers' Minstrel. When the new Washington headquarters opened, the fraternity journal celebrated the fulfillment of its original vision. "The big n—— in a long coat and brass buttons was at the front door," the journal reported. Hoover was one of the men who made it happen.[1]

On the professional side, though, there was not much to do except watch and wait. With Wilson away at the Paris Peace Conference, Hoover seems to have spent the end of 1918 and the beginning of 1919 wrapping up wartime duties at the Justice Department, unsure about what to do next. That sense of uncertainty was only fueled by what was happening in the rest of the country, where 1919 was shaping up to be one of the most dramatic years on record. On February 6, union workers shut down the city of Seattle in a spectacular general strike, holding out for five days before the threat of federal troops forced them back to work. Meanwhile congressional committees were starting to turn away from the European war to investigate a "class war" potentially brewing at home. That same month, North Carolina senator Lee Overman announced that his Senate subcommittee, originally convened to combat German propaganda, would now investigate labor unrest and Soviet-inspired revolutionary activity.

He found plenty to go on. In March 1919, Lenin announced the creation of the Third International, or Comintern, a central organizing body intended to foment global revolution. He acknowledged in a public letter to American workers that "it may take a long time before help can come from you." But for many Americans, including Hoover, the possibility of revolution did not look so remote. Ultimately, 1919 turned out to be one of the most strike-prone years in U.S. history; more than four million workers—20 percent of the workforce—walked off their jobs. While many were seeking primarily to keep up with a sharp spike in the postwar cost of living, there was enough revolutionary language, and real revolutionary sentiment, to heighten concerns in Washington. At the War Department, officials came up with War Plan White, a secret program for suppressing a nationwide insurrection. At the Justice Department, the challenge of figuring out what to do fell to A. Mitchell Palmer, Wilson's next appointee as attorney general—and Hoover's next boss.[2]

FOR MORE THAN A CENTURY, PALMER HAS OCCUPIED "AN UNENVIABLE PLACE in history as the leading symbol of the great Red Scare of 1919–20," in the words of his biographer. That was not his goal when he became attorney general in 1919. The son of Pennsylvania Quakers, Palmer had started his political career as a dutiful party servant and congressional hopeful, an ambitious Democrat in a dauntingly Republican state.

Against the odds, he won election to Congress in 1908. Against even greater odds, he helped Woodrow Wilson achieve a respectable showing in Pennsylvania in 1912. As attorney general, he assumed office with broad support, especially among Wilson Democrats. From there, he hoped for a smooth ride all the way to the White House as the next Democratic presidential nominee. That this did not happen owes a great deal to the work he and Hoover began performing together in the summer of 1919.[3]

War laws such as the Espionage Act were still in effect when Palmer took office, since the Great Powers had yet to settle upon a treaty in Paris. But nobody at Justice seemed sure about what to do with those laws now that the country was—practically, if not technically—at peace. Once in office, Palmer ordered thousands of German alien enemies released from parole and imprisonment. But when it came to the question of what to do about political radicals—the department's other chief target of wartime suspicions—he hesitated, unsure about both the limits and possibilities of the attorney general's prosecutive power.

As an alternative to criminal prosecution, he turned to an area of law where federal authority seemed more certain. In October 1918, just weeks before the end of the war, Congress passed an immigration bill allowing for the deportation of all noncitizens "who are members of, or affiliated with, any organization, association, society, or group, that writes, circulates, distributes, prints, publishes, or displays" material calling for "sabotage," "the unlawful assaulting or killing of any office or officers of the Government," or "the overthrow by force or violence of the Government of the United States." The law specifically targeted "aliens who are members of the anarchistic and similar classes," aiming to provide the Justice Department with wide latitude to go after the country's small but energetic anarchist movement. That movement contained a wide range of adherents, from utopian pacifists to figures such as Luigi Galleani, an Italian-born anarchist who openly advocated terrorism and assassination as tools of revolution. In November 1918, less than a month after the law's passage, the government had begun to issue deportation warrants for Galleani and his followers.[4]

Even a deportation campaign was not the sort of thing that Palmer planned to do immediately, however. In order to carry out deportations, the Justice Department required the cooperation of the Labor Department, which had jurisdiction over all immigration matters. Palmer, in turn, needed someone familiar with the surveillance and deportation process, preferably someone already well connected at Labor. In March 1919, he promoted Hoover to the position of special assistant to the attorney general, charged with answering queries about immigration and deportation law. A month later, the issue acquired a new sense of urgency.[5]

ON APRIL 28, 1919, A NOVELTY PACKAGE FROM GIMBELS DEPARTMENT STORE arrived at the office of Seattle mayor Ole Hanson. The box came sheathed in the official

Gimbels wrapping paper. Inside, the package contained a thin glass vial, topped by a cap that seemed to be leaking some sort of liquid. Called in to examine the contents, police determined that the "novelty sample" was actually a bomb, the liquid was nitric acid, and someone was trying to kill the mayor.[6]

The story of Hanson's close call barely made the Washington, D.C., papers. The following day, however, another Gimbels bomb showed up, this time at the home of Senator Thomas Hardwick in Georgia. Assuming the shipment contained a pencil sample, Hardwick's wife instructed a maid to open it. The bomb blew off the maid's hands at the wrist and burned through one of her eyes, leaving her "fighting against odds for her life," in the words of an Atlanta paper. At this point, Washington began to pay attention. Both Hardwick and Hanson had taken a hard line against radical "agitators": Hanson as the mayor who had crushed the Seattle general strike; Hardwick as the chief sponsor of the Immigration Act of 1918. It was not much of a leap to conclude that their antiradical positions and their status as bombing targets might be connected.[7]

In New York, a postal clerk reading about the Hardwick bomb had an even more alarming thought. A few days earlier, he had set aside a pile of Gimbels packages for lack of postage. When he rushed back to the central post office, he found sixteen bombs sitting in the postage-due area, addressed to some of the most prominent men in American life. All told, the authorities uncovered thirty bombs scattered throughout the postal system, most likely "an anarchist plot to spread terror throughout the country," in the words of the Associated Press. Among those targeted were more than a dozen Washington officials, including Supreme Court justice Oliver Wendell Holmes Jr., immigration commissioner Anthony Caminetti, labor secretary William B. Wilson— and attorney general A. Mitchell Palmer.[8]

At first, Palmer urged calm in response to the mail bombs—which, after all, had largely failed (if due mostly to the bombers' incompetence). Other would-be victims were not so sanguine. "I trust Washington will buck up and clean up and either hang or incarcerate for life all the anarchists in the country," Mayor Hanson declared. "If the government doesn't clean them up I will." As if in response to Hanson's call, on May Day—the international workers' day of revolution—groups of soldiers and sailors smashed their way into left-wing meeting halls throughout New York, ransacking literature, beating peaceful demonstrators, and throwing members out onto the streets. In Cleveland, a police detective shot and killed a man during May Day demonstrations, while the downtown turned into "a seething mass of socialists, police, civilians, and soldiers" subdued only after at least one rolled in. Washington itself escaped largely untouched by the May Day episodes, but the local papers told of the escalating violence: first the general strike, then the bombs, then the near riots across the country. "May Day has come and gone, leaving in its trail a record of bloody clashes between anarchy and law," *The Washington Post* reported. "Over the scene was the terrible shadow of a dastardly bomb plot aimed at the lives of prominent citizens who had been marked for slaughter by secret assassins."[9]

And then came an event so extraordinary—and so well coordinated in its violence—that even those inclined to dismiss such worries had to take notice. On the evening of June 2, Palmer had just retired for the night when he heard a loud thump. Moments later came a roar, then the whoosh of shattering glass, as the walls of the house trembled around him. Someone had thrown a bomb at the front door, decimating the downstairs parlor. Assistant secretary of the navy Franklin Roosevelt came running from his house across the street and found Palmer "theeing" and "thouing" on the lawn, the shock of the blast having summoned forth his childhood Quakerisms. Human limbs and bits of flesh covered the yard, the remains of the man who had transported the bomb. Scattered across the lawn was a series of pink paper pamphlets titled "Plain Words" and signed by "The Anarchist Fighters."

The missives complained of the repression visited upon dissenters during the war. "We have been dreaming of freedom, we have talked of liberty, we have aspired to a better world, and you jailed us, you clubbed us, you deported us, you murdered us whenever you could." The so-called Anarchist Fighters also foretold a coming war against the American ruling class. "There will have to be bloodshed; we will not dodge; there will have to be murder: we will kill, because it is necessary." Later that night, Palmer learned that similar flyers had been found outside midnight bomb explosions in six other cities, including Cleveland, Boston, and New York. Though only one person had been killed, there was no mistaking either the bombers' intent or their sophisticated level of coordination.[10]

HOOVER AWOKE THE NEXT MORNING TO A CITY SUDDENLY BACK AT WAR, ITS public buildings under heavy guard and its public men braced for attack. At the Capitol, congressmen spoke loudly of new legislation "to deal with acts of violence designed to overthrow the government." Palmer welcomed several of them into his wrecked library, where they encouraged him to "ask for what you want" to address the radical threat. When Palmer appeared at Justice offices later that day, he shuttered himself in a conference room with top federal and police officials to decide just what that might be. He emerged with a statement labeling the bombs the work of the country's "anarchistic element," aimed at nothing less than the destruction of the government. To curb this threat, he soon announced a plan to reorganize the Justice Department's antiradical and investigative operations.[11]

Palmer had already identified a top candidate to take over the Bureau of Investigation: William J. Flynn, a New York cop and federal investigator turned national celebrity and private eye. It would be Flynn's job to solve the two major bomb plots, to sift through the human flesh and singed flyers left on Palmer's lawn. But Palmer's reorganization had another aim as well: "a drastic policy of deporting all alien radicals," as *The Washington Post* described it. That policy reflected Palmer's assumption that his attackers had been immigrants, carrying out forms of violent revolt alien to the American people. To coordinate a deportation campaign, though, he would need men with skills different from Flynn's: lawyers who knew how to manage large amounts of information, make immigration cases, and see those cases through the federal bureaucracy.[12]

It is surely no coincidence that Hoover sent his first known memo on the subject of radicalism on June 14, the day after Palmer appeared before Congress. Any ambitious man might have read the situation this way, seeing in the reorganization a surge of new funds and opportunities for advancement. Hoover also happened to be well qualified for the work, one of the few Justice employees already skilled in "alien" matters. Yet what finally brought him into Palmer's inner circle may have had less to do with particular skills than with his Kappa Alpha connections—specifically, his connection to John Abercrombie, the former Alabama congressman and stalwart KA who was now serving as the solicitor of labor. In order to carry out large-scale deportation, Palmer needed the cooperation of the Labor Department, which maintained jurisdiction over all immigration matters. When labor secretary William B. Wilson left Washington for several months to attend to his dying wife, he placed the department and its immigration matters in Abercrombie's care.

Hoover never acknowledged the role his fraternity connections may have played in his rising status at the Justice Department. Whatever the cause, in the summer of 1919 he found himself plucked from obscurity to become the point man between Labor and Justice—and thus one of the key players in the emerging deportation campaign. On July 1, less than a month after the bombing of his house, Palmer gave Hoover a 50 percent raise. He also put Hoover in charge of the Justice Department's new "Radical Division."[13]

ON JULY 19, 1919, LESS THAN THREE WEEKS AFTER HOOVER'S APPOINTMENT, Washington exploded again. The instigators this time were not anarchists but U.S. soldiers and sailors. Rumors had circulated that a Black man had attempted to rape a white woman, the wife of a naval officer. In retaliation, a mob of white servicemen set off down Pennsylvania Avenue armed with makeshift weapons, including wooden planks and lead pipes. Like so many other cities that summer, Washington soon erupted into mass violence, with armed white residents attacking Black neighborhoods and Black residents defending their homes and families with whatever weapons they could find. By the time President Wilson called in the army to restore order on July 22, more than a dozen men and women lay dead, both white and Black. Hoover blamed the violence on Black intellectuals and agitators. "Something must be done to the editors of [Black] publications as they are beyond doubt exciting the negro elements of this country to riot," he wrote. He modeled his approach on what he had seen at the Justice Department during the war, when Black editors had been targeted for surveillance and prosecution. Now gathering information on such matters fell under the umbrella of his new Radical Division, scheduled to open its doors on August 1.[14]

Officially, the Radical Division fell within the Bureau of Investigation, the Justice Department's detective body. But Hoover was not identified as a Bureau agent, and there was no expectation that he would perform the field investigations in which agents specialized. As Flynn noted in an August 12 memo, the Radical Division existed primarily for research and coordination, tasked with sorting evidence gathered by other men and orchestrating the mechanisms of deportation. Hoover's duties included building up detailed files on members of "anarchistic and similar classes," documenting their citizenship status and political affiliations. It also required analytic research of the sort Hoover had first engaged in as a high school debater, distilling tangled arguments about "Bolshevism and kindred agitations" into a persuasive legal case for deportation.[15]

With these instructions in place, Hoover began an experiment unprecedented in federal history: the first systematic peacetime attempt to track the political opinions of noncitizens and to deport them en masse. He also began to collect information on native-born and naturalized citizens, assuming that the federal government would soon enact a peacetime sedition statute allowing for the prosecution and jailing of U.S. radicals. That initiative encompassed potentially hundreds of thousands, if not millions, of Americans, anyone whose "kindred agitations" might bring them under federal scrutiny. To carry out this gargantuan task, Hoover was assigned a Washington staff of thirty-one men and women (mostly clerks and typists), along with sixty-one field agents rerouted from traditional Bureau duties.[16]

While Hoover played little role in selecting most of his field employees, like the Library of Congress's Herbert Putnam he went out of his way to recruit a tight circle of assistants. Most of his field employees were much older and more experienced, seasoned investigators reallocated to the new division. For his own assistants, Hoover chose men who were as young and inexperienced as he was—and who were, not incidentally, already his friends. He recruited Frank Baughman, his old Kappa Alpha pal, now returned from the war. He also hired George Ruch, a Central High and GW law school graduate.

Hoover began his first months as a federal administrator with a surprising degree of autonomy. Contrary to later myth, he did not come up with the idea of deportation raids or set high-level strategy in 1919. He did, however, exercise some control over how information was sorted, collated, and interpreted. His first triumph was the file system. "When the Radical Division was formed," he wrote that fall, "the files of the Bureau of Investigation were found to be in such shape as to be of practically little or no use in the preparation of cases for deportation." According to Hoover's assessment, finding a single case file could take up to three or four hours. Locating the files of everyone who belonged to a given organization was nearly impossible. Hoover thus set out to do for the Radical Division what Putnam had done for the Library of Congress: to make its vast stores of information accessible at a moment's notice.

He called his process the Editorial File System, placing himself at its core. All reports coming from the field were to be routed directly through his office, marked "Attn. Mr. Hoover." From there, he passed the documents on to an editorial room, where his small staff drew up separate index cards classifying each report by subject name, state, city, organization, ideological orientation, periodical, and event. Once the index cards existed, clerks filed the reports according to a numbered classification system modeled on Putnam's Library of Congress catalog. By early fall, Hoover boasted that the Division's cabinets held fifty thousand index cards. By end of his first year, that number had reached more than one hundred thousand. The time necessary to find any given document shrank accordingly, down to "at the maximum within two minutes." Hoover insisted on reading as much of the material as possible, then writing out meticulous instructions to field agents. He doubted the competence of his inherited employees, who "had little or no knowledge of the requirements of the immigration law," and who turned in reports riddled with errors and inconsistencies. At the same time, he was anxious to establish his authority, and to make sure that his employees took him seriously. As one of the youngest men among them, he showed remarkable confidence, certain that he and only he knew what to do in the midst of this ambitious new federal experiment.[17]

The documents that poured into the Radical Division that fall provided an almost unlimited array of targets for Hoover's staff. By early September the division had amassed extensive information on IWW and "anarchistic" activities, with particular attention to their respective roles in the nation's strike wave. "Alien negro agitators" earned their own files—most notably Marcus Garvey, founder of the Universal Negro Improvement Association and a recent immigrant from Jamaica. As Flynn suggested, the division also gathered information about U.S. citizens in hopes of future prosecution under yet-to-be-created federal law. A summary report released in November warned of "a well concerted movement among a certain class of negro leaders" to promote "race consciousness" on matters such as lynching, voting rights, and social equality. The report also analyzed the rising tide of poetry, criticism, radical political writing coming out of Harlem and other major cities, much of it "defiantly assertive" on issues of race. Hoover built dossiers on dozens of organizations and individuals involved in such activities, while the Justice Department awaited new legislation.[18]

Many of Hoover's characterizations in such reports utterly missed their mark, lumping together anarchists and socialists, reformers and revolutionaries, intellectuals and organizers, as violent threats to the social order. But merely gathering the information through a central mechanism was a feat of its own. At a time when few men in the federal government knew much about radical politics, Hoover's files gave him the appearance of mastery.

IN THOSE THOUSANDS OF PAGES, ONE NAME STOOD OUT: EMMA GOLDMAN, THE most famous anarchist in the nation, the woman whose ringing opposition to the draft had made her one of the Justice Department's first wartime targets. Goldman was still in federal prison when Hoover stumbled across her case in August 1919. As he pored over the reports at the Radical Division, he noticed that Goldman was about to be released from prison—and that nobody had made any preparations for what would happen next. Under her wartime sentence, she was supposed to be deported after serving out her prison term, but there was no plan to acquire a deportation warrant. In one of his most significant early actions as head of the Radical Division, Hoover decided to take action.

The federal authorities had tried and failed to deport Goldman before, always stumbling over technicalities. Hoover plunged into her case on the assumption that this time would be different, that the new deportation law, combined with public sentiment against anarchists, would overwhelm any past hesitation. In a late August memo, he singled out Goldman as one of "the most dangerous anarchists in this country," warning that her "return to the community" would cause "undue harm" if the Justice Department failed to act. On September 8, he dispatched an emergency wire to the federal penitentiary where Goldman was being held, begging the warden to hold her until the immigrant authorities could acquire a warrant. He gained a few days' reprieve, enough time to arrange for Goldman to be arrested once again. "Immediately upon this subject's release from the penitentiary she was taken into custody by the immigration authorities upon a deportation warrant," Hoover wrote in a summary report for his new division, "with excellent prospects of her early deportation from this country."[19]

At some point during this set of exchanges, Hoover seems to have made a crucial decision: he would personally take control of the evidence in Goldman's case. On the day of her scheduled release, he sat down with the immigration commissioner to talk about assigning one of the Labor Department's "best field agents" to Goldman "in order that there may be no flaw in the evidence." Hoover transported that evidence to Atlanta in late September for the immigration hearing of Goldman's ally and former lover Alexander Berkman, taking "particular precaution to see that each exhibit was introduced in whole," as he later noted. Upon his return, he met with a group of senators to discuss deportation policy, one of his first high-level sessions on Capitol Hill. A few days later, he took the train to New York "for the purpose of going over certain phases of evidence to be used in the Goldman deportation proceedings." While there, he dashed from appointment to appointment, meeting with private detectives downtown, poring over newspaper archives near city hall, even going off to a Bronx warehouse to locate copies of Goldman's magazine, *Mother Earth*.[20]

Hoover's political worldview developed and hardened in the process, transforming what had been a general anxiety into a new set of antiradical certitudes. During his trip to New York, Hoover experienced his first direct encounter with flesh-and-blood "radicals," and his response testified to how quickly he came to view them as imminent threats to the nation. On the night Hoover arrived, Bureau agents escorted him to an opera house where some three thousand people, "mostly of foreign extraction," had gathered to raise money for the imprisoned labor activist Tom Mooney, who had been convicted three years earlier of throwing a bomb into a military parade in San Francisco. The crowd was especially worked up because the New York police had allegedly attacked a parade in support of the Russian Revolution that very afternoon. With Hoover watching, outraged speakers denounced the attack, drumming up some three hundred dollars on behalf of "the babies who had been killed on the afternoon parade," as Hoover wrote in a report to Palmer.

Hoover came away disgusted—not by the beatings, but by the speakers' exaggerations and distortions of what the police had done. "As a matter of fact . . . , no one had been killed," he wrote testily, "but the audience readily believed the violent statements which were made by the speakers." He also disapproved of the crowd's fury and unrestrained emotion, the ways that "some of the persons in the audience . . . became over-enthusiastic" upon hearing descriptions of the police crackdown. He expressed surprise that none of them said anything that "over-stepped the line prescribed by law": there were no calls for bombings, assassinations, or the violent overthrow of the government. But Hoover viewed even this restraint as a sign of the speakers' craftiness and ill intent, their desire to stay out of jail while stirring up the masses. "It is quite obvious that a law should be passed whereby the subjects advocating such methods as they did could be reached at the present time," he concluded.[21]

DESPITE HOOVER'S MEMO WRITING AND FILE PROCESSING, DESPITE PALMER'S grandiose promises, by October 1919 there were no deportations, the bomb plots remained unsolved, and Emma Goldman had been released on bail. If anything, the forces of "unrest" appeared to be gaining that fall, with fractious strikes erupting in the steel industry, coal mines, and even the Boston police force. The president himself had succumbed to the stress of the moment, collapsing of a stroke in early October and retreating to his White House bedroom, where he remained in isolation from the public for several months. On Capitol Hill, Senator Miles Poindexter went after Palmer, introducing a resolution in which Congress demanded to know "the reason for the failure of the Department of Justice to take legal proceedings for the arrest, punishment, and deportation" of those who "have preached anarchy and sedition." In response, Hoover offered a display of the bureaucratic virtuosity that would become a hallmark of his career. On October 18, four days after Poindexter's speech, Hoover reported that he was ready to act in the Goldman deportation. Later that month, he rushed back to New York to attend Goldman's hearing, and to present the reams of evidence that his office had amassed. Of the half-dozen government lawyers in the room, Hoover was by far the most junior. But it was his evidence—carefully gathered, collated, and transported personally to the city—that defined the day's proceedings. Goldman recalled being shocked at the sheer number of pages stacked against her. "I found the inquisitors sitting at a desk piled high with my dossier," she later wrote. "The documents, classified, tabulated, and numbered, were passed on to me for inspection." Her lawyer asked for a delay in proceedings in order to have time to look through the bewildering stack of material.[22]

So Hoover headed back to Washington, this time to reengage the long-anticipated deportation raids. For their first target, he and Palmer chose the Union of Russian Workers, an obscure anarchist group whose few thousand members hailed almost exclusively from the former Russian Empire. On October 30, three days after the Goldman hearing, Hoover confirmed that he would begin to request deportation warrants from the Labor Department. Four days later, he produced the first thirty-four affidavits against URW members, sworn statements by federal agents. By November 7, the date designated for the raid, that number increased more than tenfold, each new warrant vetted by Hoover and signed by Abercrombie, his fellow Kappa Alpha.

The raids began that night. Over several hours, federal agents and local deputies forced their way into meeting halls and private homes in eighteen cities, arresting everyone on the premises and seizing literature, banners, accounts books, weapons, and membership lists. Hoover stayed in Washington, processing and collating reports as they came in from the field. It was not a gentle operation; agents and policemen broke furniture, pushed people down stairs, and wrenched several men and women out of bed. Nor did things go wholly according to plan. Of the 1,182 men and women arrested that night, Hoover had secured warrants for only four hundred. These factors would later come back to haunt the Bureau, symbols of bureaucracy gone awry. That night, though, what stood out was everything that had *not* gone wrong: The secrecy had not been blown, agents had not missed their cues, bombs had not gone off.

Before dawn, Palmer claimed credit, issuing a press release boasting that the Justice Department had broken the back of a group "even more radical than the Bolsheviki." Lest anyone miss the significance, the attorney general soon delivered a full report to Congress, in direct rebuttal to Poindexter's accusations that Palmer had been too soft on radicals. Much of his information came from Hoover, the first time Hoover would shape a major congressional inquiry. Palmer emphasized the critical role of the Radical Division in planning for the raids, and in helping to define the extent and urgency of the anarchist threat. He then asked for the same peacetime sedition law that Hoover had contemplated in the wake of the Central Opera House gathering—something that would enable the Justice Department to cast a wider net over not only immigrants but also U.S.-born radicals.[23]

And at that moment he seemed likely to get it. Despite grumblings on the left, Palmer's appeal met with near-universal enthusiasm in the major papers. "If enacted into law the government would have a powerful weapon against offenses and offenders against whom it is now helpless," *The Washington Post* reported. Even the president, still largely incapacitated, wrote in to Congress with a few words of support. Just twenty-four years old, in his position for less than half a year, Hoover had already made a mark on national politics.[24]

AFTER PALMER'S STATEMENT, THINGS MOVED QUICKLY. ON DECEMBER 5, GOLD-man turned herself in at Ellis Island, having exhausted her efforts to quash the deportation order. Three days later, Hoover revisited New York for another hearing on her case in federal court. News reports described "J.E. Hoover, special assistant to the attorney general" as one of "half a dozen attorneys" critical to the Goldman case, the first time his name had been mentioned in the press as a Justice Department representative. Hoover marked an even greater achievement two days later, on December 10, when Goldman's lawyer insisted on convening once more—this time before the Supreme Court. For the rest of his life, Hoover would note proudly that he had appeared in front of the legendary Louis Brandeis, albeit as a largely silent junior attorney. In the end, it was Brandeis, with his impeccable moral authority among progressives, who sealed Goldman's fate. On December 11, the Supreme Court ruled that Berkman should be deported immediately, while granting Goldman another week to get organized. Rather than fight the ruling and risk separation from Berkman, Goldman surrendered.[25]

Her acquiescence brought to fruition five months of Hoover's work, success in the biggest case he had yet taken on. There is no mistaking his glee during the final days of preparation for her departure from the country. On December 16, he ordered up maps of Russia, Latvia, Estonia, and Finland—the better to view "the proposed vacation which a few of our anarchist friends will shortly take to Northern Russia." The deportees would depart on the *Buford*, an old steel troopship that would take them as far as Finland. From there, they would make their way by land into Soviet Russia. All these plans, as one paper noted, occurred under "a thick veil of official secrecy."[26]

When the veil lifted on December 20, Hoover went to New York to supervise the deportations in person. At Ellis Island, the deportees received no advance notice of their impending departure. Down at the Battery, meanwhile, an official delegation of politicians and appointed officials was already assembling for the big event. Hoover stood out for his nervous excitement, a "slender bundle of high-charged electric wire," in the description of one congressman.

At three thirty, the deportations began. The prisoners—246 men and three women—marched single file up the gangplank onto the tug, flanked by guards with rifles and automatic pistols. On board, Hoover spoke briefly with Goldman, who declared the government's repressive policies "the beginning of the end of the United States." One congressman, watching the exchange, found Goldman "quite bitter against Mr. Hoover," not least for the lack of notice about the time of deportation. Hoover ignored her complaints, wandering the *Buford*'s decks, corridors, and barracks until around six a.m., when the tug pulled up once again to remove anyone not bound for Finland. "Shortly after 6 o'clock," the *New York Herald* reported, "splashing and rasping in the silence of the empty bay, the anchors came up to the bow, the Buford's prow swung lazily eastward, a patch of foam slipped from the stern and 249 persons who didn't like America left it." For Hoover, it was a stunning public triumph, the peak moment of a year already filled with so much change, drama, and success. Though he could hardly have imagined it that cold December morning, it also marked the beginning of the end of his first Red Scare.[27]

CHAPTER 8

New Elements

(1920)

Headline from *The Boston Globe,* April 1920. Less than three years out of law school, Hoover presented himself as the federal government's first great expert on communism.   BOSTON GLOBE

Hoover reveled in the praise that came his way in the wake of the *Buford*'s sailing, not only from Palmer, Flynn, and Abercrombie but also from the press at large. With this backing, he began to envision new raids that would bring yet more success. This time, as he and Palmer pictured it, the raids would target not a small, obscure anarchist organization but two of the country's newest and most audacious left-wing groups: the Communist Party and the Communist Labor Party. The decision to pursue the communist parties marked a major shift in Bureau priorities. From now on, communists—not anarchists—would be the focus of the deportation effort. It also launched a new period in Hoover's career, in which he came face-to-face with the "communist menace" that would ultimately consume so much of his professional energy.

During the November raids, Hoover had mostly been a facilitator. Other men had chosen the targets, decided the policy and the law. Now he intended to play a more active role in setting the agenda, planning the strategy, and laying out the scope of the threat. The communists were "new elements in the political life of this country," he noted in an October 1919 memo, but who exactly were they—reformers or revolutionaries? Socialists or Bolsheviks? Americans or Russians? In December 1919, with the *Buford* launched and Goldman exiled, Hoover began to think through his answers to these questions.[1]

He initially assumed the Justice Department would have an easy rout—a repeat of the November raids, only bigger and better. As it turned out, the 1920 raids did not call forth the same near-universal praise. Instead, they produced Hoover's first major embarrassment in the national arena. Some of his critics came from within the federal government itself, administrators and bureaucrats well positioned to weigh in on new plans for arrests, deportations, and raids. Others came from outside, lawyers and professors from such rarefied environs as the Harvard Liberal Club. What they shared was a sense that something dangerous was afoot in the Justice Department's effort to suppress radical groups, that the United States had abandoned essential principles of due process and free speech. Today, we would refer to them as "civil libertarians," but in 1920 that phrase—and the worldview it evoked—was just beginning to take shape.

For Hoover, the criticism that erupted in the spring of 1920 came as a genuine shock—the first time in his life, outside of the brief showdown with Poindexter, that he was forced to contend with serious disapproval. Until this point, he had always been a star, the boy who knew how to please his elders and win respect. His moments of difficulty had been private and internal, family secrets kept secret. The criticism brought out an ugly, vindictive side to Hoover's personality—one that had always been there, perhaps, but had been controlled by a steady diet of praise and success. Rather than pause and consider what the department's critics had to say, Hoover struck back, putting Justice agents to work digging into his critics' backgrounds and personal foibles. His aggressive response to criticism would become a lifelong practice and ultimately a source of scandal, though nobody at the Justice Department in 1920 suggested the approach might be unbecoming of a government servant.

Ultimately, Hoover framed the backlash of 1920 not as a genuine political conflict, but as an outrageous conspiracy between the "radical elements" and their elite defenders, who were softheaded, misguided progressives duped into serving the revolutionary cause. His interpretation of events left him with a bitter sense of righteousness, the self-pitying assurance that he had been horribly wronged. At the same time, he retained the ability to learn from his surroundings and figure out new ways to get ahead. From the bitter contests of 1920 came important lessons about how to manage bureaucratic allies and enemies, about the press and its fickleness, about when to make certain actions public and keep others secret. But these were lessons learned the hard way. In 1920, for the first time in his life, Hoover failed at something he set out to do.

———

WHEN HOOVER WROTE THAT THE COMMUNISTS PRESENTED "NEW ELEMENTS" in the nation's political life, he meant the phrase literally. For decades, the Socialist Party had been a major force on the American left, a big-tent party flexible enough to welcome both reformers and revolutionaries. The war split the socialists just as it cleaved through so much else in American life, with those opposed to the war on one side and those who argued that the war might provide a spur for reform on the other. The Bolshevik Revolution cracked open another divide. Though most socialists supported its spirit, they argued bitterly over if, how, and when such a revolution might occur in the United States. In late August 1919, party leaders convened an emergency meeting in Chicago to work through these factional differences. After a series of walkouts, expulsions, and vicious accusations, the party split into three groups: the old Socialists, the new Communist Party, and the slightly newer Communist Labor Party of America. Federal informants reported back from the meeting that the difference between the two splinter groups was minuscule. The parties drew up almost identical platforms, calling for "the overthrow of capitalist rule and the conquest of political power by the workers," in the words of the Communist Labor Party's version.[2]

At the moment of the split, Hoover was just a month into his job at the Radical Division. He recognized from the first that his professional reputation would depend in part upon how he addressed the challenge of the new communist groups. Their membership numbers were small: a total of about forty thousand, many of them Russian-speaking immigrants. But as the parties themselves were eager to point out, numbers alone did not measure influence. Seizing upon Lenin's example, each party positioned itself as the one true American vanguard, a small, highly mobilized band of militants destined to lead the working class into revolution. Though this was more fantasy than reality, Hoover took them at their word. From the first, he shared with the communists an interest in exaggerating their influence, and thus positioning himself as an indispensable public servant who might hold them at bay.[3]

His first imperative was research and surveillance, bringing the new parties into his growing collection of files. He also viewed the communist parties as excellent candidates for deportation, just the sort of unapologetic revolutionaries that the attorney general hoped to target. In mid-December, as he prepared to send the *Buford* off with its first batch of deportees, he composed a formal brief arguing that Communist Party members openly advocated force and violence, just like the anarchists, and were similarly deportable en masse. On Christmas Eve, he sent along a second, shorter brief showing that the Communist Labor Party was indistinguishable from its rival, that the two had separated due to interpersonal rather than ideological disputes. By the end of the year, he had become the Justice Department's leading expert on American communism, the author of the first federal briefs ever written on the subject.[4]

As literary works, Hoover's briefs bore the same tone as his arguments against Goldman and Berkman: incredulous, conspiratorial, convinced that manifestos and texts alone could provide proof of individual beliefs and guilt. The documents also showed evidence of careful research, conducted on a near-Olympian scale. Hoover spent the Christmas season familiarizing himself with some of the more extravagant texts of the American left. Many foretold the coming destruction of capitalism, though they differed widely on the question of violence. "No lives need be lost, not one drop of blood need be shed, if the working class will rally to the I.W.W. with its program of peaceful evolvement," promised *The Red Dawn,* one of the books on Hoover's reading list. Hoover sought to persuade his superiors that communists actually embraced violence, however cagey their writings might be. By virtue of joining one of the two parties, he argued, members committed themselves to the armed overthrow of the government and the capitalist system.[5]

To make his case, Hoover needed to establish a plausible narrative of the Bolshevik Revolution, an event still poorly understood in the West. He saw the revolution in conspiratorial terms—not as a revolt against an unjust, tyrannical czar but as a gathering of criminals intent on promoting bloodshed and murder. He went back to the works of Karl Marx, "wherein it is specifically stated that not only will the class struggle manifest itself on the industrial field but that it will also direct its energies towards struggle for Government control and for the capture and destruction of the capitalist state," as he wrote in one brief. American communists he presented the same way, as individuals actively plotting the violent overthrow of the U.S. government. Hoover saw little distinction between the social theories of a nineteenth-century German philosopher, the actions of an embattled Russian revolutionary government, and the moment-to-moment proclivities of American radicals. All were part of the same criminal plot.[6]

Hoover's studying and writing had a single aim: the deportation of foreign-born communists in another spectacular round of raids. Through the Radical Division's informants, Hoover had gained access to a hodgepodge of party membership and subscription lists, supplemented by public statements and local agent reports. From these, he compiled his own lists of foreign-born alleged communists to be targeted during the next campaign. On December 22, Hoover sent the Labor Department a breakdown of the warrants needed for each major city, with more than two thousand all told. Over the next several days, the number ballooned to some three thousand, more than ten times the number of people deported on the *Buford.* Hoover maintained that "the interests of the country and the investigations made by this office demand immediate attention," and requested that all warrants be issued by December 27.[7]

That left the Labor Department just five days—including Christmas Eve and Christmas—to complete a gargantuan task. In order for the raids to be carried out, the Secretary of Labor would have to rule on whether or not the two organizations fit within the limits of deportation law. Hoover also requested a review of what was known as Rule 22, an internal Labor Department policy allowing anyone arrested on deportation charges to consult with a lawyer. During the November raids, Hoover had discovered that lawyers usually advised their clients not to disclose their place of birth, political ideas, or organizational affiliations, a practice known as the "talk strike." For this next round, he hoped to avoid that problem by interviewing prisoners *before* they consulted with their lawyers—a small but significant change in the wording of Rule 22.[8]

Coming from a twenty-four-year-old assistant to the attorney general, these were astonishing requests: Hoover wanted an unprecedented number of warrants, targeting two entirely new organizations, along with a major revision of Labor Department policy, and he wanted it all done in a matter of days. What made him think it all might be possible may have been the fact that John Abercrombie, his Kappa Alpha brother, was still in charge at Labor. On December 27, after consulting with his superiors, Abercrombie spent the day signing the three-thousand-plus arrest warrants requested by Hoover. A few days later, he quietly changed the department's policy on legal counsel, instructing agents to mention the possibility of a lawyer not at the start of a hearing, but "as soon as such hearing has proceeded sufficiently in the development of the facts to protect the Government interests." Hoover got everything he had asked for, a vote of confidence in his ability to pull off the impossible. And so, on the day after his twenty-fifth birthday, with the full backing of his superiors at the Justice and Labor Departments, he set out to commit the greatest blunder of his young life.[9]

THE RAIDS OF JANUARY 2 ARE ONE OF THE MOST MYTHOLOGIZED EVENTS OF their age—a symbol of government abuse and lawless policing, of mindless hysteria and blind repression. So it is worth clearing up a few misconceptions. The first is the idea that the government swept up mainly innocent, apolitical naïfs during the raids, befuddled immigrants who happened to be in the wrong place at the wrong time. There were some cases of mistaken arrests and mistaken identities. But most of those arrested were indeed "radicals," enmeshed in a world of impassioned anti-capitalist agitation. Their revolutionary leanings do not mean that they deserved what happened to them; there were countless cases of brutality and incompetence, abuse of due process, and sheer ignorance of the law. It does mean, however, that the raids hit their intended targets. Just four months after their founding, the communist parties found themselves under siege by the federal government, the beginning of a wrenching struggle that would last for decades.

The second important myth—one propagated by Hoover himself, once the tide of public opinion turned against him—is that Palmer was the driving force behind the raids, while Hoover was merely the cautious, obedient subordinate. This had been true during the November raids. By December, though, Hoover was indisputably in charge of coordinating the operation, even as Palmer remained the boss and figurehead. "On the evening of the arrests, this office will be open the entire night, and I desire that you communicate by long distance to Mr. Hoover any matters of vital importance or interest which may arise during the course of the arrests," a leading Bureau official wrote on December 27. Hoover would occupy similar positions many times in the future—seated at his desk in Washington, hundreds of miles away from the drama in the field, but still overseeing the flow of events. In late 1919, he was not yet the boss but he was one of the central figures: selecting the targets, managing the warrants, keeping the lists.[10]

The final misconception is that the raids provoked an immediate backlash, as if the injustice of an ever-expanding campaign against noncitizens, with limited legal representation, was self-evident to Americans from the start. In truth, it took almost two months for the backlash to build, and it was bureaucratic resistance, not public outrage, that finally brought an end to what one key player described as "the deportations delirium." At first, nearly everyone—at Justice, at Labor, in the newspapers—supported the idea of mass deportation, and they thought for many weeks that Hoover had made another brilliant success.[11]

On Friday, January 2, Hoover arrived at the Justice Department bundled in his winter gear and prepared to stay the night. "There will be made this evening throughout the entire country arrests totaling over 3,000 of persons charged with being communists who will be held for deportation," he wrote in a confidential memo, brimming with excitement. The raids were scheduled for nine o'clock, but that was just the beginning. Throughout the night, there would be questions from agents, new demands for warrants, and—if all went well—arrest reports from the field. Friday was a regular communist meeting night, and the Bureau had instructed its employees to "arrange with your under-cover informants to have meetings of the Communist Party and Communist Labor Party held on the night set."[12]

Around nine p.m., local police and federal agents began banging on doors in New York, Philadelphia, Detroit, and dozens of other cities. Hoover later admitted that there were "clear cases of brutality" and that many arrested were not necessarily party members. That night, however, he was pleased with what he learned. Agents had been instructed to look for anything that might help document the parties' inner workings: "All literature, books, papers, and anything hanging on the walls should be gathered up; the ceilings and partitions should be sounded for hiding places." But it was the numbers that really mattered. Arrest counts poured in from the field: 82 in Buffalo, 76 in Saint Louis, 90 in Trenton. Agents lacked warrants in hundreds of individual cases; in Saint Louis alone, fully 42 of the 76 people arrested had been seized without warrants. But warrantless arrests had been expected, and Hoover had the machinery in place to address the problem. Throughout the night and into the next day he cabled request after request to the Labor Department, where officials had promised to release "telegraphic warrants" on demand.[13]

Even for a man as meticulous as Hoover, the sheer scale of the effort made firm numbers hard to come by. In overnight reports to the press, the Justice Department estimated that more than fifteen hundred "alleged radicals" had been arrested, with "twice that number" expected before dawn. Historians now suspect the number may have been higher, with as many as seventy-three hundred arrests. The exact number will likely never be known and is somewhat beside the point. What is indisputable, as the Associated Press noted, is that Hoover helped to pull off "the greatest round-up of radicals in the nation's history."[14]

NEWSPAPERS RECOGNIZED THE ACHIEVEMENT. "IF SOME OR ANY OF US . . . HAVE ever questioned the alacrity, resolute will, and fruitful, intelligent vigor of the Department of Justice in hunting down those enemies of the United States," *The New York Times* declared on January 5, "the questioners and doubters have now cause to approve and applaud." And while Palmer received the lion's share of credit, Hoover increasingly earned mention by name. "Mr. Hoover made a thorough investigation of the principles and manifestos of the two parties," the *World* reported, "and submitted many exhibits of the literature and propaganda on which the claims of law violations are based." In just a few months, he had moved from obscurity to public notice, from relative ignorance to acknowledged expertise.[15]

Within the federal bureaucracy, Hoover found himself accorded a new level of deference. As recently as December, he had been a junior player at the Goldman and Berkman hearings. Now he was anointed to make the government's case against its communist defendants. In mid-January, when Labor Secretary Wilson decided to review the Communist Party's status under deportation laws, it was Hoover who represented the Justice Department. At the hearing, Hoover denounced the party as "an integral part of an international conspiracy," firing off quotes from Communist Party publications calling for "destruction," "annihilation," and "violence." The communists sent four lawyers to defend them, all experienced men from big cities like Chicago, New York, and Boston. The debate came down to the meaning of words, with the communists' attorneys contending that references to "force" were simply metaphors, while Hoover insisted that the words meant just what they said. Within forty-eight hours, Labor Secretary Wilson sided with Hoover.

Palmer seized upon this decision as a personal victory, a sign that he had been right to launch his crusade and to put so much faith in his young assistant. He rewarded Hoover with a raise, this time from three thousand to four thousand dollars per year. As the praise continued to roll in, Hoover believed he had hit upon a magic formula, one that might be endlessly repeated. "The raids . . . certainly met with unusual success," he wrote in a late February memo, boasting that they had been "conducted so far as I know with no adverse criticism." As it turned out, he simply wasn't paying attention.[16]

———

THERE HAD BEEN HINTS ALL ALONG, SMALL BURSTS OF RESISTANCE THAT TO A more experienced man might have signaled the greater eruption to come. As early as January 12, just ten days after the communist raids, Pennsylvania U.S. attorney Francis Fisher Kane resigned in protest. The following day, a group of lawyers in Boston filed habeas corpus proceedings on behalf of prisoners being held at Deer Island, just off the New England coast. Conditions on the island were abysmal, with six hundred men jammed into barracks planned for three hundred, with no heat and dwindling food. One man had already committed suicide, and at least two more were sick with pneumonia. Still others had arrived humiliated, having been frog-marched in chains and handcuffs through the streets of Boston while bystanders showered them with trash and spit. Things were little better in places like Ellis Island, where hundreds of men were forced to sleep on steel slabs without mattresses. In Detroit, eight hundred prisoners had been stuffed into a windowless corridor with only one working bathroom and no beds.[17]

Hoover privately acknowledged that "unsanitary conditions and much congestion" racked the facilities where potential deportees waited. But he failed to see how the Justice Department could be at fault. Running the detention facilities was a problem for the Labor Department, not the Justice Department, he insisted. Overconfident and blind to political consequences that would hurt him over the next several months, he also failed to account for his comfort with paper rather than people. Understanding communism was, for Hoover, a matter of reading texts and writing memos. His bookish approach had gotten him far with the Justice Department, but it did not prepare him well for the political fight to come. In early March, Abercrombie decided to leave Washington to run for the Senate from Alabama. With that, Hoover lost his most important ally at the Labor Department, and the delicate bureaucratic machinery he had built for Palmer began to collapse.[18]

The man in line behind Abercrombie was Louis Post, the assistant secretary of labor and an official with whom, until 1920, Hoover had maintained relatively congenial relations. Post styled himself a workingman's bureaucrat, an intellectual and reformer who had spent his life advocating egalitarian policies such as women's suffrage and the single tax. His leftist proclivities might have signaled some sort of impassable difference with Hoover, but until 1920 the two men had been remarkably cooperative. From his position at Labor, Post had approved Goldman's deportation warrant. He had also participated in some of the critical meetings in which the communist raids had been planned. Looking back, Post claimed that he had always felt the raids were "oppressive, unlawful and un-American." It was not until early March, though, that he showed any overt sign of discontent. With Secretary Wilson gone on sick leave, and with Abercrombie now off to campaign, Post effectively became the top man at Labor.[19]

What followed was a case study in bureaucratic politics, in the ability of a man positioned in the right place at the right time to exercise power far beyond his job description. Post had been listening for months to complaints from his left-leaning friends, who warned that the federal government had crossed the line into tyranny. Now, suddenly elevated to a key position, he decided to put a stop to the Justice Department's arbitrary exercise of power. The mechanism he chose was laughably simple. Rather than process Hoover's deportation cases en masse, in the spring of 1920 Post began to review each case individually, applying his own standard. First, he required evidence that any given Communist or Communist Labor Party member actually knew what was written in the party's manifesto. Second, he required that the member truly believed it. Like Hoover's change to Rule 22, these were legalistic tweaks, but ones with powerful implications. Under Post's standard, each person would have to be judged as an independent thinker, with his or her own ambivalences and distinct interpretations of the revolutionary cause.

Hoover found this approach preposterous, arguing that the law "does not require that the alien who is a member of such organization . . . also actually believe in the principles advocated by the organization." But neither he nor Palmer could do much to stop it. Over the next few weeks, Post proceeded to dismiss cases he viewed as having insufficient evidence for deportation. Meanwhile, others were beginning to protest the raids and pursue relief in the courts. In early April, Hoover rushed to Boston, where an alarmed federal judge had agreed to hear the case of the men imprisoned on Deer Island. The local press welcomed Hoover as one of Palmer's rising stars, despite his "extreme youth" and "boyish looks." But once in the courtroom, Hoover discovered that his growing reputation counted for little without a sympathetic ear at the bench. Lawyers from the Harvard Liberal Club—including future Supreme Court justice Felix Frankfurter—depicted their clients as innocents swept up in a government vendetta. The judge seemed to share their perspective, badgering subpoenaed Bureau agents, scoffing openly at the government's botched warrant process. Hoover said little during the hearings, outside of some whispered counsel to the U.S. attorney. After a few days of misery, with the hearing still underway, he boarded the train back to Washington.[20]

What Hoover experienced upon his return would stay with him for years. On April 9, Post released a scorching public statement denouncing the raids and exposing the details of what he had witnessed from the inside. He declared the raids the shame of the nation, "drastic proceedings on flimsy proof to deport aliens who are not conspiring against our laws, and do not intend to." Despite the vast number of cases sent his way, Post charged, he had run across only a handful of men and women who posed any danger to society. "As a rule the hearings show the aliens arrested to be working men of good character," he declared. Post's words reflected the human sympathy missing from Hoover's late nights checking lists, reading manifestos, and assembling affidavits.

"It is pitiful to consider the hardship to which they and their families have been sub-jected," Post mourned, all "for nothing more dangerous than affiliating with friends of their own race, country and language."[21]

ANOTHER MAN MIGHT HAVE LISTENED TO WHAT POST SAID, TAKING A MOMENT to reflect upon his own actions and examine what it meant to introduce mass raids—indeed, an entire new system of political surveillance—into the peacetime body poli-tic. Hoover had been trained throughout high school and college to do just that: to respond with discipline, fortitude, clear analysis, and good sportsmanship to the many challenges that life was bound to present. Instead he viewed Post's challenge as a per-sonal affront, to be crushed as swiftly and firmly as possible. For the first time, Hoover helped to mobilize federal agents to gather intelligence on his critics, a practice that would later become routine at his Bureau. He also withdrew bureaucratic support from the Labor Department, the beginning of a lifelong practice of rescinding co-operation from other institutions at moments of conflict—and a lifelong effort to dis-tance himself from the Palmer Raids. Almost immediately, men at Labor began to note that Hoover seemed to be available only for "brief, hurried conferences." Even then, the young man who had once supplied such endless lists and elaborate statistical rundowns suddenly seemed to have little to offer.[22]

Palmer had declared his candidacy for the Democratic presidential nomination on March 1, so Post's attack posed a political as well as a bureaucratic problem. On April 14, Palmer took the case straight to President Wilson in the first cabinet meeting con-vened in more than seven months. Wilson was out of bed, but barely, his jaw still drooping from the stroke, too weak to stand when other men entered the room. De-spite the president's fragile state, the meeting soon devolved into a shouting match between Palmer and the secretary of labor, who had also returned to Washington and, like Palmer, had decided to dig in his heels in support of his subordinate. According to the diary of one cabinet official, the president had little to say on the matter, beyond a single sphinxlike sentence, in which he "told Palmer not to let the country see red."[23]

What did Wilson mean by those cryptic instructions? Did the president intend to restrain Palmer, to instruct his attorney general that enough was, at last, enough? Or was it a gesture of support, a plea to prevent the rise of Bolshevism and its attendant ills? Whatever the president intended, he had little capacity to impose his will. Later that afternoon, speaking with reporters, Palmer denounced the latest rail strike as a harbinger of revolution. "Some people thought in January when I made my statement about the 'Red' activities and began the raids that I was seeing red," he noted, perhaps in a nod to the president. "I have no earthly doubt that the same sort of a thing which has happened to the railroads is being planned for other industries." The following day, in a gesture of support for Palmer, a Kansas congressman introduced a resolution of impeachment against Post. Then, taking Post's side, Secretary of Labor Wilson decided to consider the case of the Communist Labor Party, and to render a new ruling about whether its members ought to be deported.[24]

This hearing convened on April 24 in a bland Labor conference room not much different from the one where Hoover had pleaded his case in January. Called upon to deliver opening remarks, Hoover took his by-now standard approach, throwing down a stack of "voluminous communist literature," in the words of the Associated Press, then plunging into a recitation of outlandish revolutionary quotes. This time, however, the men in the room were less inclined to be patient. Hoover had barely stopped speaking before the communists' lawyer hit back with questions about the Justice Department's own activities: How many informants were in the party? What role did they play in setting up the meetings for the night of January 2? He accused Hoover of deliberately stretching the law and violating the First Amendment, and cited by name at least one party member alleged to be a Bureau informant. Hoover seems to have been unprepared for the attack. "The man who will say that . . . has uttered a deliberate and malicious falsehood, and the man who makes such a statement is a liar," he burst out, using at least one "ugly word," according to newspaper reports. For a young lawyer schooled in the virtues of self-control, this was a rare display of public emotion, and a sign of how quickly principle could fall away under pressure. Far from redeeming his cause, Hoover's breakdown at the Labor hearings seemed to suggest that the raiding effort was out of control.[25]

That impression only increased over the next few days, as Palmer attempted—and failed—to regain mastery of the situation. In late April, he issued warnings of a violent conspiracy that would dwarf the bombings of 1919 and lead to a full-blown uprising on May Day, 1920. When the day arrived, he barricaded himself in his office, protected by four bodyguards, while the capital police fanned out in a security lockdown "unequalled in the history of Washington." In New York, thousands of police officers went on high alert, assigned to protect banks, government buildings, and prominent men. Then nothing happened. "Palmer's Riot Predictions Fail," noted one paper. "Nobody Murdered Yet."[26]

And then Louis Post was back yet again, this time to testify in front of Congress, a full three hours on May 7 and another five hours on May 8. Post was a remarkable spokesman in his own defense, in full command of the technocratic and legal details, able to laugh and tell jokes where Hoover had only been able to level accusations and throw fits. Hoover was there for all eight bitter hours, watching and taking notes as Post systematically picked apart the deportation system. Post openly disagreed with Hoover's legal strategies, describing the entire raiding campaign as a violation of due process. Where he differed from Hoover most fundamentally, however, was in his view of the men being held for deportation. To Hoover, they had always been abstractions, names and numbers on a list, all one and the same in their political sentiments. To

Post, they were human beings—"simple-minded, hard-working men, who have joined an organization that they thought was legitimate, and did not know it was illegitimate until they got arrested in the raids." Far from being revolutionary communists, Post alleged, most were simply befuddled immigrants who showed up in the wrong place at the wrong time.[27]

Neither Post nor Hoover got it quite right. As Hoover insisted, many party members *were* genuine revolutionaries, inspired and transformed by the Bolshevik example (if nowhere near being able to replicate it). At the same time, the parties were small and weak and highly factionalized—hardly an immediate danger, as Post pointed out. Many committee members entered the hearing room suspicious of Post's claims but came away convinced that he had a point. Hoover found the episode thoroughly discouraging, especially since Post blamed the Justice Department for nearly everything that had gone wrong since the January raids. "I was present during the entire time that he was before the committee," Hoover wrote in a memo to Palmer, "and the charges made by him, as well as the innuendo given by him could lead one to but one conclusion, namely that the Department of Justice had broken all rules of law in its activities against the Reds."[28]

WITH THAT, HOOVER BEGAN TO TURN HIS ATTENTION TO ASSESSING THE DAMage. He spent a gloomy few weeks running the numbers, composing memo after memo showing how Post had let bona fide communists slip away. The count looked dismal: of the 6,350 deportation cases sent to immigration authorities by late April, the Labor Department had ordered 762 deportations, but had canceled 1,293 warrants, with the rest of the cases still pending. Only 263 men and women had actually been deported thus far, the vast majority on the *Buford*, alongside Emma Goldman.[29]

With Palmer's approval, Hoover tried to get out of the deportation business, instructing agents to slough off the "weak cases" and make sure the others were "speedily disposed." But new problems continued to pop up. In early May, Hoover learned that a group called the National Popular Government League planned to issue a report denouncing the Justice Department. "The issue is, shall the spy system be set up in America? Shall the Government respect the law?" read the group's promotional materials. Hoover recognized the handiwork of the same lawyers who had gone after him in Boston—the Harvard liberals—and he decided to use the investigative bureaucracy under his control to gather information about his critics. In May, he launched "a discreet and thorough investigation" of the organization and its major figures, including Harvard law professors Felix Frankfurter and Zechariah Chafee. A wealth of details came in, from his adversaries' weight and height ("45 years old; about 5 feet, 9 inches tall . . . dark complexion, hair and eyes; clean shaven and careless of dress") to their reputation and character ("below the average in physical energy and endurance, judgment, common sense, attention to duty, professional knowledge, leadership, force, initiative, military neatness and bearing"). Hoover even sent agents to steal documents from the National Civil Liberties Bureau, soon to be renamed the American Civil Liberties Union (ACLU), fast emerging as one of the country's most influential voices on issues of free speech and constitutional rights.[30]

Before he could sort out what to do with all this material, Congress invited Palmer to testify on Capitol Hill, so Hoover switched his attention to preparing his boss for the occasion. In late May, Hoover composed a strategy memo for the hearing, advising Palmer to make nice with the committee but not to "mince words" about Post. "Tell the committee and the country the real story of the Red menace," he suggested, and of "the efforts of the Department of Justice to specifically curb the spread of Bolshevism." In Hoover's view that "story" was a tale of a virtuous government crusade brought down by a conspiracy between intellectuals, lawyers, and radicals.[31]

Palmer followed Hoover's script. On June 1, the attorney general took his seat before the judiciary committee and launched into 209 pages of testimony and exhibits, including a lengthy statement prepared by the Radical Division. Hoover sat at Palmer's side the whole time, the fidgety son beside the gray-haired rock of a father. He spoke just six words over the course of Palmer's two-day appearance: "No, sir; it has not," and then, much later, "Yes." But his imprint was everywhere—in the words Palmer uttered, in the exhibits submitted for review, and in the policies under scrutiny.

Most of all, it was there in the attorney general's righteous claim that the good men of the Justice Department had done their best, only to be betrayed by "our so-called 'liberal' press" and its allies within the courts and government. "I wish you to understand that the body of these people is the favorable culture into which the revolutionary agitators place their germs of social treason," Palmer said, "and that it is here they grow most rapidly and from here that they are able to do a great deal of damage." Hoover would hold on to that conviction for the rest of his life: the Bolshevist menace was still out there, preparing to come back stronger than ever. In the spring of 1920, however, Congress no longer seemed especially alarmed. Soon after Palmer's testimony, they quietly shuffled off to recess, without declaring either Palmer or Post the victor.[32]

FOR A MAN UNDER SO MUCH SCRUTINY, PALMER DID SURPRISINGLY WELL AT the Democratic convention a few weeks later, a contender until the thirty-ninth ballot. Hoover followed his boss out to San Francisco for the convention, but later claimed he had spent only a few hours there, glancing in at the red-white-and-blue bunting before departing to visit local Bureau field offices. Within a few weeks of arriving home, Hoover found his trip under question by a congressional committee investigating Palmer's alleged use of government funds and Justice Department staff to support his presidential campaign. Hoover denied any wrongdoing. "I was engaged wholly in conference with officials of the department on strictly departmental work in connection with the investigation of Red activities while in the West and in San Francisco," he told *The New York Times*. But even that work was fast losing its currency. Thanks to postwar budget cuts, Hoover spent the summer of 1920 pruning back rather than expanding his work for the first time since taking over the Radical Division. Hoping to distance himself from the recent scandals, he also adopted a bland new name for his organization, to be known thereafter as the General Intelligence Division.[33]

For a moment that fall, Hoover briefly thought his fortunes might be reversed once again. On September 16, 1920, a bomb exploded on Wall Street, killing thirty-eight bystanders and reviving calls for "drastic action with relation to the deportations of alien criminal anarchists," in Palmer's words. But even such a horrific crime—the deadliest terrorist bombing the country had yet seen—failed to shift the political equation. Hoover helped to supervise the federal inquiry, to no avail. Like the earlier bombings, the Wall Street explosion went unsolved. By early 1921, even Palmer was no longer in a forgiving mood. Called to testify before a Senate committee, he named Hoover as the man most responsible for planning the deportation raids—and, by implication, for screwing them up. "If you would like to ask Mr. Hoover, who was in charge of this matter, he can tell you," Palmer told the senators when queried about what had gone wrong, and Hoover was forced to answer their questions about why lawyers had been banned from the interrogation rooms and about the lack of immigration warrants. The hearings trailed off inconclusively on March 3, Palmer's last full day in office, but the record was now clear. Though he would spend the rest of his career attempting to distance himself from the fact, Hoover had been "in charge" of one of the most disastrous, most criticized, and worst-run operations ever undertaken by the Department of Justice.[34]

CHAPTER 9

No. 2

(1921–1924)

Hoover in 1924. During the early 1920s, despite serious missteps, he developed a reputation as a good-government reformer in the midst of Justice Department corruption scandals.

In the winter of 1921, as Palmer and Wilson slunk from office, Hoover encountered another challenge: the White House was changing hands, and a new group of men was coming to power. The last time this happened, Hoover had been in high school. Now, eight years later, he had made good on his Central High ambitions, but it looked as if his once-promising career might be coming to an end. As a Washington native— therefore a nonvoter—he claimed no party allegiance. Informally, though, he appeared to be identified with Palmer and the Democrats, and with their most spectacular missteps. Hence the problem. In 1921, Republican Warren Harding was moving into the White House, prepared to make a clean sweep of federal appointments after eight years of Democratic rule.

Hoover's family life—difficult even at the best of times—only compounded his worries. As winter wore on, his father could no longer muster the energy to eat or drink. On March 30, less than a month after Hoover's congressional testimony, Dickerson died at home on Seward Square. Hoover provided the family details for the death certificate: Dickerson was sixty-four years, four months, and nine days old, the eldest son of John Thomas and Cecilia Naylor Hoover. The doctor listed the cause of death as "melancholia," with a secondary diagnosis of "inanition," or exhaustion of the will. The family laid Dickerson's body to rest in Congressional Cemetery next to little Sadie, apparently without a public funeral. To the end, Hoover seems to have viewed his father as an embarrassment, a failed man unable to live up to prevailing ideals of virtue and success. In the spring of 1921, he faced the disturbing possibility that he might be a failure too.[1]

What happened instead must be seen as a testament to both his personal resolve and his professional adaptability. Even as his superiors in the Justice Department departed, even as his father slipped away, Hoover decided to stay on and fight for his career. But remaining in government proved to be no easy task. During the Harding years, Hoover was forced to rebuild his political network almost from scratch, ingratiating himself with a new generation of Republican politicians and officials. These friends, in turn, produced their own scandals and problems. By all accounts—Hoover's included—the period between 1921 and 1924 ranked as the most chaotic, dishonest, and disgraceful in the history of the Justice Department. During these years, as the focus on radicalism receded, Justice became known as the "Department of Easy Virtue," where poker games, whiskey peddling, and the baldest forms of graft prevailed. Trying to put the ignominy of the deportation raids behind him, Hoover found himself negotiating back-office patronage and political rivalry, struggling against the odds to save not only his job, but his career.[2]

He learned a great deal during the Harding years, as formative in their own way as his time at Central, GW, and the Wilson-era Justice Department. Those earlier experiences had taught him about ambition and discipline, bureaucracy and leadership, race and radicalism. But none had forced him to confront the seamier side of Washington life, the wheeling and dealing that made up the raw stuff of political power. Hoover began to discover that aspect of government in 1921, under the tutelage of men who had come of age in the infamous Ohio political machine. If he harbored certain qualms about their behavior, as he later claimed, he never registered an objection powerful enough to imperil his job. Instead, he survived by adapting his principles and strategies to new circumstances, trying to please the men above him and control the men below.

HARDING'S INAUGURATION ON MARCH 4 LIFTED THE PALL THAT HAD HUNG over Washington since Wilson's stroke. A tall, square-jawed man with dark eyebrows and a full head of dignified gray hair, Harding was known for looking presidential, and he did his best to keep up appearances. Policy was not his strong suit. He enjoyed meeting the public and making ordinary citizens feel appreciated; for a few minutes before lunch each day, anyone could come to the White House and shake the president's hand. In contrast to Wilson's self-serious passion, Harding brought a cheerful demeanor to the White House. With it came some of the less savory traditions he had acquired through a lifetime in Ohio politics.

Prohibition had taken effect nationwide in early 1920, a grand experiment in enforcing virtue through law. At the White House, though, alcohol continued to flow freely. "The study was filled with cronies," recalled Washington doyenne Alice Roosevelt Longworth, whose wedding had so fascinated Hoover as a boy. "Trays with bottles containing every imaginable brand of whiskey stood about, cards and poker chips ready at hand—a general atmosphere of waistcoats unbuttoned, feet on the desk, and spittoons alongside." The party often continued in the "Little House on H Street" owned by Harding's friend, millionaire playboy and *Washington Post* publisher Ned McLean (who was in turn given a "complimentary" appointment as a Bureau agent). The stories of what went on in there, as well as in a "Little Green House on K Street," would later spark national outrage: truckloads of liquor delivered straight from federal storehouses, poker games running late into the night, judgeships and pardons auctioned off to the highest bidder. During the election, though, millions of people thought that Harding was just what the nation needed, a dose of "normalcy" after the anguish and strain of the war, the Red Scare, the strikes, and the flu pandemic.[3]

Hoover remained cautious, watching and waiting to see what the new attorney general, Harding's friend and campaign manager, Harry Daugherty, might have in mind. Ohio-born and bred, Daugherty styled himself a big-city dandy. His signature look was a formfitting three-piece suit with a pearl stickpin in the necktie. At age sixty-one, he had started to overflow that getup, with fleshy folds of skin settling around his collar. His hair was thinning and his paunch was growing, and many people said there was something shifty about his looks—an impression perhaps inspired by his one blue eye and one brown eye, perhaps from deeper knowledge of his political practices. He exuded the confidence of a man who usually got his way. "I felt that he lived by a code of his own," the journalist Mark Sullivan wrote years later. "If this code did not happen to be identical with the world's conventions, so much the worse for the world's conventions."

Daugherty's insouciance extended to his personal life—and here Hoover may have found the attorney general's example intriguing. Though technically still married, Daugherty lived, worked, and traveled in the near-constant company of a man named Jess Smith, an Ohio dress salesman eleven years his junior. Smith operated as something like Daugherty's personal assistant—"a secretary, greeter, go-between, valet, odd-job man, and foil," in the summary of one historian. It was clear to most acquaintances, though, that their relationship went beyond official business. Back in Ohio they regularly spent days together in a run-down cabin out in the woods, their "bachelor's shack." In Washington, they took up the social roles usually reserved for spouses.

When Daugherty went to the White House for dinner, or out on a yacht with the president, Smith was invariably at his side. For a time, they even lived together, first at the H Street house, later at a suite in the tony Wardman Park Hotel. Washington society seemed to accept their partnership. Smith's ex-wife described Daugherty as her ex-husband's "intimate friend." Newspapers chose similar words: Smith was Daugherty's "intimate associate" or "constant companion." Hoover's own relationships would eventually be described the same way, reflecting some of the same characteristics.

Like many Harding appointees, Daugherty was a product of the Ohio Republican machine at its most formidable. Including Harding, five of the previous ten presidents had been Ohio Republicans. Daugherty was also a "boss" in the least flattering and most corruptible sense, a man who viewed politics as a game and government as a chance to get his hands on the public till. It was he who had put Harding over the top at the 1920 Republican convention. In the standard formulation, he took a "dark horse" candidate and made him president by twisting arms in the convention's "smoke-filled" back rooms. His appointment as attorney general occasioned cries of outrage, but Harding never wavered. When they arrived in Washington, Harding gave special orders to install a direct phone line between the White House and Justice Department. The two men spoke several times a day. Daugherty made no secret of Harding's dependence and loyalty. "When I met him, he was a like a turtle sitting on a log," Daugherty liked to say. "I pushed him in the water."[4]

DAUGHERTY MADE ANOTHER PUSH IN LATE MARCH, AROUND THE TIME OF Dickerson's death. According to news reports, Daugherty planned to hire a new director for the Bureau of Investigation, replacing the "anarchist chaser" William J. Flynn with the famed private detective William J. Burns. Like Flynn, Burns was a red-haired Irishman, with the same unruly mustache and imposing girth, but with the distinction of being an Ohio Republican. Hoover had met Burns in 1919 through the Emma Goldman case, when Burns had offered his agency's assistance in securing her deportation. The two men came across each other again in the fall of 1920, during the hectic days immediately after the Wall Street bombing, when Burns vowed to use his private detective agency to solve the case. Once rumors of the Burns appointment began to circulate, Hoover made use of these contacts to assist the Burns agency in its bombing investigation, helping to perform the sorts of tasks—filing and paperwork, interagency coordination, passport and deportation proceedings—at which he had come to excel. His gamble, undertaken without Flynn's knowledge or approval, soon paid off. On August 18, 1921, the attorney general announced that Burns would be taking over as director of the Bureau of Investigation. Four days later, in a move that went unnoticed in the national press, Burns appointed Hoover to be his number two man: the Bureau's assistant director.[5]

In future years, Hoover would have nothing kind to say about his time working for Burns, a man who came to stand for everything the nation despised about the detective profession. The stories were legion: paying informers to lie and set up innocent men for high-profile crimes; buying off juries and intimidating jurors when they couldn't be bought. Burns's worst misstep, in Hoover's later telling, was the appointment of Gaston Means, a North Carolina con man, to a Bureau post. Hoover would describe Means as the swindler par excellence—"the most amazing figure in contemporary criminal history" and "the greatest faker of all time." That Burns would have appointed such a creature proved irrevocably the corruption and poor judgment that once reigned at the Bureau, according to Hoover's later account.[6]

Much of what he said was true, but there was an element of betrayal and distortion in Hoover's accusations. Burns was actually quite popular when appointed, a hero detective not yet fallen from grace. Given Hoover's mixed record on the deportation raids, Burns was remarkably kind and generous toward his young subordinate, one in a long succession of higher-ups who stepped in at crucial moments to sustain Hoover's career. Despite the recent criticism and controversy, despite the failure of the raids and bombing investigations, Burns seems to have recognized in Hoover the same qualities that had first impressed the men of the War Emergency Division: his dogged work ethic; his willingness to flatter and aid his superiors; his skills in record keeping and cataloging; his apparently indefatigable enthusiasm for bureaucratic life. What Burns needed was not a visionary or a great investigator but a competent administrator, a second-in-command who knew the ins and outs of the Bureau.

Hoover understood that he had been hired as the paperwork man, an unobtrusive subordinate skilled at filing and organization. At the same time, he moved to secure a group of assistants whose primary loyalty would be to him and not to Burns. His friends Frank Baughman and George Ruch stayed on, having proven their loyalty through GW, the war, the raids, and now the uncertainty of partisan transition. Hoover also reached out to a "very bright + intelligent girl" named Helen Gandy, who had been hired at the Justice Department during the war. Two years younger than Hoover, Gandy had worked with him at the wartime department, and then moved up as his personal secretary when he went to the Radical Division. According to office gossip, the two had engaged in a minor romance along the way—a bumbling, overserious Hoover cultivating the vulnerable new girl, who let him down easy. Whether or not Hoover ever expressed any romantic interest, by 1921 he had come to regard Gandy mostly as a competent secretary and a reliable ally within the tangled Justice bureaucracy. "Kindly arrange to return to Washington soon as possible," he cabled to her on the day of his appointment.[7]

Hoover later claimed that his team functioned as outliers during the Burns years, an upright band in a den of thieves. At the start, though, Hoover and Burns seem to have gotten along perfectly well. Physically, they were a study in contrasts: the expansive, theatrical detective, with his bowler hats and fat cigars, versus the wiry, anxious twenty-six-year-old. But they shared a deeper sympathy of outlook and a common set of professional goals. Burns had once been a government protégé himself, breaking up major counterfeiting rings and shady land deals as a young Secret Service agent. Those achievements had made him a darling of good-government progressives, an icon of efficiency and professionalism. Many of the reforms and innovations for which Hoover later claimed credit emerged during his few years of collaboration with Burns.

AT THE RADICAL DIVISION, HOOVER HAD BEEN ENGAGED PRIMARILY IN POLITI-cal surveillance: gathering, analyzing, and coordinating information about allegedly dangerous groups. Under Burns, he got his first real taste of law enforcement. Founded in 1908, the Bureau of Investigation had never been intended to compete with local police. Instead, it was supposed perform whatever investigative duties the Justice De-partment might require under federal law. Several members of Congress had expressed concern that the Bureau might evolve into "a central police or spy system in the Federal Government," in the words of one representative—a prediction that many felt had been fulfilled under Palmer. But even at the height of the Palmer Raids, much of the Bureau's work had little to do with policing political opinion. At its core, the Bureau was a lot like any other detective force; it existed to gather evidence that prosecutors could use in court. But rather than investigate the usual run of criminal activity— murders and thefts and assaults—its activity was restricted to violations of federal law. And what ended up in that category was a matter of historical contingency rather than common sense.[8]

At the time the Bureau was created, the biggest issues had been taxation and anti-trust work. Then, just a few years in, Congress enacted the 1910 White Slave Traffic Act (better known as the Mann Act), vague legislation that criminalized the transpor-tation of women across state lines for "prostitution or debauchery, or for any other immoral purpose." The law sent Bureau agents and their deputies into nearly every vice district in America, a situation tailor-made for corruption and exploitation. It also demanded that they engage in tasks for which they had little formal training. Partly as a consequence, the Bureau became something of a dumping ground for well-connected, if not especially well-qualified, young constituents of influential congressmen. The war years further expanded the Bureau's duties and thus the issues of quality control, with inexperienced detectives scrambling to figure out the intricacies of home-front espio-nage, antiradical surveillance, and draft enforcement. After the war the Bureau's scope increased still further—not only into antiradical activities but also into interstate car theft, designated by Congress in 1919 as a federal crime. Hoover became assistant di-rector without ever working directly in such areas of criminal investigation, the Bu-reau's true bread and butter. He soon found he still had a lot to learn.[9]

One of Burns's assignments for Hoover was the establishment and coordination of a national system for organizing criminal fingerprints, an area of forensic science just beginning to gain authority as a reliable tool of identification. When Burns assumed office, fingerprints were still a haphazard business—routine procedure in some police departments, unheard of and unthinkable in others. Where fingerprints did exist they were often compiled and contained at the local level. Burns's idea was to bring all the prints to Washington, centralizing them in a single filing and identification system accessible to police throughout the country. If an officer needed to find out who was in his custody, he would wire prints to the Identification Division in Washington, which in turn would respond with the relevant information. Hoover knew the file system, he knew how to organize paper, and he had the energy to do it.[10]

Aside from the fingerprint system, Hoover concentrated his energies on internal policy, working to bring the Bureau in line with the ideals of professionalism and government efficiency he had absorbed throughout his Washington upbringing. With Burns's guidance, Hoover orchestrated a daunting series of internal reforms during the final months of 1921. Most of the orders to execute these changes went out under Burns's signature, but Hoover played a key role in writing and distributing them. Three reforms in particular would later become inviolate principles of Hoover's FBI, though he would never acknowledge their origins in the scandalous Burns era. In 1922, the Bureau began training schools for newly hired agents, instructing them in "the fundamentals of investigative work." The following year, an order went out to clean up "the appearance and conduct of the offices" in order to make a favorable impression on the public. Finally, the Bureau revised its press policy, forbidding low-level agents from being identified by or speaking with reporters. "I desire that wherever conditions arise that the press becomes informed of certain achievements or arrests effected by agents of this Bureau that the name of the agent not be used in giving the information to the local representatives of the press," read Burns's order, sent under Hoover's initials. As director, Hoover would coin his own name for this impersonal approach: He would call the FBI a "we" organization rather than an "I" organization, though he himself rarely seemed to be above taking credit.[11]

The Burns years also gave Hoover a chance to experiment in areas of investigation that had thus far figured only marginally in his official work. As assistant director, he oversaw the Bureau's ongoing work under the Mann Act, which the Supreme Court now interpreted to cover not only prostitution and other commercial activity but also adultery and underage or interracial sex. Hoover did not investigate cases directly. But he gained quite an education by reading his agents' reports of teenage girls seduced by older men, of unmarried couples living as "man and wife," and of the profit-seeking sale of sex.[12]

He also deepened his engagement with the Bureau's racial politics, encountering cases that both affirmed and challenged what he had learned at Kappa Alpha. Faced with calls for the federal government to begin investigating lynchings, Hoover tended to look the other way, attributing most such violence to "a Negro who assailed a white girl," as he wrote of one Omaha lynching. By contrast, he actively pursued cases involving Black leaders and activists. One of Burns's most high-profile targets was Marcus Garvey, the Jamaican immigrant and founder of the Universal Negro Improvement Association, who had gained a widespread following for his calls to Black self-determination and communion with Africa. Hoover initially tried to fit Garvey into the ethos of the Palmer Raids, seeking evidence of radical affiliations before concluding that "he has not yet violated any federal law." With that line of investigation foreclosed, the Bureau turned instead to accusations of dubious fundraising for Garvey's Black Star transatlantic steamer line. In 1923, after considerable prodding from Hoover, federal prosecutors convicted Garvey on mail fraud charges, sending him to the Atlanta federal penitentiary for two years, followed by deportation to Jamaica. To Hoover, the deportation was a hard-won victory, his biggest immigration case since Emma Goldman. It was also his first experience of success against a high-profile Black leader.[13]

The Garvey case fit easily with what Hoover had been taught by Kappa Alpha's leadership: that Black men were dangerous, a force to be controlled by dedicated white knights. But there was at least one instance in which his new duties seemed to conflict what he had learned at the fraternity—and this experience, too, would have lasting consequences. In 1922, the governor of Louisiana contacted the federal government to plead for help in combatting a resurgent Ku Klux Klan. At Kappa Alpha, Hoover had been schooled in the virtues of the Reconstruction-era Klan, absorbing the *Birth of a Nation* myth that portrayed the Klan as the guardians of social purity and order. What the governor described in Louisiana was different, however, a wholesale campaign of murder and intimidation directed at the Klan's political enemies. Murder was not a federal crime, but the state's most prominent Klansman, or "Kleagle," happened to be keeping a mistress and traveling across state lines with her in violation of the Mann Act. And so, after consulting with the attorney general, Burns and Hoover dispatched Bureau agents to Louisiana to gather the necessary evidence.

The decision does not suggest that Hoover was beginning to question white supremacy. Instead, as a newly minted law enforcement official, he was starting to see the Klan as a force of lawlessness, the sort of group that fomented violence, social disorder, and contempt for law enforcement if left unchecked. On March 10, 1924, the imperial Kleagle pleaded guilty in federal court to violating the Mann Act, Hoover's first victory in what would become a lifetime of trying to contain an organization he had once been taught to revere.[14]

WHAT MOST PEOPLE LATER REMEMBERED ABOUT THE BURNS ERA, HOWEVER, were not the reforms and putative successes but the failures—the string of high-profile embarrassments and scandals that began almost immediately and did not stop until both Burns and Daugherty had been driven from office. In late 1921, Burns announced that he was ready to "clean up the whole case" of the Wall Street bombing, only to backpedal just days later, admitting he had been taken in by a con man working for his own agency. The following summer, Hoover and Burns orchestrated a raid on a secret Communist Party meeting in Bridgman, Michigan, but found the Bureau humiliated once again. After a mad dash through the woods, agents netted some two dozen top party officials, along with a cache of manifestos, membership lists, and direct communications with Moscow. When the time came to use these materials in court, however, the case collapsed. In the run-up to the trial of party leader William Z. Foster, an undercover operative came forth to testify that Burns had instructed him to lie in order to frame Foster as a dangerous subversive. The trial ended with a hung jury, yet another sputtering, inconclusive finish to another major communist case.[15]

Added to all of this were the problems besetting the larger Justice Department, as Daugherty initiated his own brand of countersubversive warfare. In the summer of 1922, some four hundred thousand rail workers walked out on strike, the most ambitious labor action since the steel strike of 1919. Daugherty labeled the strike "a conspiracy worthy of Lenin" and went after the strikers with a vengeance, securing an injunction that directed them not to picket or congregate anywhere near the rail yards and not to communicate about the strike. The injunction provoked a backlash from congressmen alarmed at such a harsh anti-labor stance. In December 1922, less than two years into his tenure, a House committee voted to hear impeachment charges against Daugherty, a far more aggressive challenge than Palmer had encountered even at the height of his infamy.

The impeachment case never amounted to much more than political theater, and Congress soon absolved Daugherty. After that, though, the Justice Department entered a period of social and institutional free fall. Daugherty became ill, taking to bed for six weeks, followed by months recuperating in a wheelchair. Then, just as he seemed about to regain his strength, his "intimate friend" Jess Smith shot himself, committing suicide in the apartment the two men had shared at the Wardman Park. Burns lived one floor down, and he rushed upstairs to tidy the scene before the police appeared. According to friends, Smith had been depressed for weeks before the suicide, fearful that Daugherty no longer needed or wanted him.[16]

To outsiders, the whole affair looked suspicious from beginning to end; friends and family speculated that Smith had been murdered, or had killed himself to protect Daugherty's secrets. To Hoover, Smith's death may have carried a different meaning. If he had ever looked to Smith and Daugherty as a model for how two men might live as "intimate friends" and nonetheless maintain political influence and public legitimacy, he may have seen this ending—so graphic, violent, and public—as a bleak omen.

———

THEN THE REAL SCANDALS BEGAN. ON AUGUST 2, 1923, PRESIDENT HARDING collapsed and died at the Palace Hotel in San Francisco. Almost immediately, chaos engulfed what remained of his administration. The most infamous episode involved the Teapot Dome naval oil reserve in Wyoming, where leases had been parceled out to prominent businessmen through a complicated series of bribes and back-office deals. What mattered most to Hoover's career was not so much the oil scandal itself, but the secondary drama it provoked within the Justice Department. In February 1924, Montana senator Burton Wheeler accused Daugherty of gross negligence in failing to go after the oilmen more assertively. "We find the Department of Justice, instead of trying to detect the greatest crooks and those guilty of the greatest crimes against the nation that have ever been perpetrated, we find the Department of Justice protecting them all during this time," Wheeler complained. In early March, the Senate launched another investigation into corruption within Daugherty's Justice Department, with the possibility of more impeachment proceedings.[17]

The evidence that came out over the next few months went well beyond Teapot Dome, showing how Daugherty and Burns—and by implication, the entire Justice Department—had abused the public trust in order to reap personal gain. On March 12, 1924, Jess Smith's former wife appeared before the Senate committee to reveal that Smith had returned to Ohio every two or three weeks with tales of Washington "intrigue" and lucrative financial scams cooked up by the attorney general. Gaston Means, the con-man detective who would loom so large in Hoover's imagination, followed with even more incredible stories about the hundreds of thousands of dollars raked in by Smith, Daugherty, and their so-called Ohio Gang. Though Means was hardly a credible witness (and he later tried to retract his statement), other people followed with similar stories, day after day of some of the most jaw-dropping testimony ever delivered to a Senate committee.[18]

Hoover's name rarely came up at the hearings, and then it was in only the most cursory fashion. An obvious question remains nonetheless: How much did he know about what was going on, and to what degree did he participate? In later years, he claimed to have been a babe in the woods, surrounded by evil and danger but largely oblivious to it. Given his position in the Justice Department, however, his naive posture does not quite ring true. Burns and Daugherty were remarkably close to each other. And Hoover was Burns's second-in-command, in touch daily with his boss about a wide range of issues. Many of the key figures in the scandals worked out of the Justice Department, with access to department files and manpower to assist in private transactions. Smith even carried Bureau credentials, though he was not officially employed at the department.[19]

Hoover was probably not directly involved in the corruption and bribery, but he surely knew more than he admitted. As one senator noted, it was impossible to survive in the Justice Department during those years without knowing something about what was going on. "The Department of Justice and the Bureau of Investigation are hand-picked by Daugherty," he explained, "and rotten to the core." But Hoover did survive, as he would survive scandal after scandal, attorney general after attorney general, over the next half century. Even as he helped Burns in reorganizing the Bureau and running down the Communist Party, he seems to have been aware of the political danger inher-ent in the more sordid aspects of departmental affairs. He tried to make sure that his name was kept out of them. Unlike during the Palmer years, when he had been forced to answer for his boss's missteps, he held back from too close a personal identification with his Republican bosses. And when the political winds began to shift in the spring of 1924, Hoover shifted with them—no longer the loyal subordinate to men like Daugherty and Burns, but instead one of their most indignant critics.[20]

Even then, he paid attention to what Daugherty and Burns had to teach about fac-ing down political enemies, and making sure those enemies suffered for their political attacks. Daugherty blasted the investigating senators as tools of the communists, "re-ceived in the inner Soviet circles as comrades." He also sent Bureau agents after the senators directly, ransacking their offices and tapping their phone lines to uncover incriminating information. Hoover had experimented with both techniques after the Palmer Raids, when the Harvard liberals had tried so hard to make an example of him. Daugherty took things further. "Harry Daugherty was a defiant and vengeful man who was ready to strike back with all the considerable resources of the Department of Justice," reflected Senator Wheeler, one of Daugherty's chief critics (and therefore one of his targets). In Montana, Wheeler found his home district swarming with federal agents, then learned he would be charged with defrauding the government in a series of low-level land deals. Wheeler was later found innocent, but plenty of damage was already done. [21]

In years to come, Hoover would employ both of Daugherty's techniques—red-baiting his enemies and using the Bureau to intimidate them—as basic mechanisms for protecting his power. What he largely avoided—and what finally brought down both Daugherty and Burns—was the overt corruption, the willingness to sell the power of his office for immediate monetary gain. In late March 1924, at the peak of the scandals, President Calvin Coolidge asked for Daugherty's resignation. Burns stepped down six weeks later, neither the first nor last time that other men's losses proved to be Hoover's gain. Instead of marking the end of what was already a shock-ingly controversial career for a twenty-nine-year-old man, the scandals of the Harding era brought another new beginning.

Part II

BUILDING THE BUREAU

(1924–1945)

Preface

For all of their ups and downs, Hoover's first years of government service left him with a powerful sense of who he was and what he stood for. As a career professional, he took great pride in his administrative skill, a true believer in the progressive virtues of efficiency, order, and expertise. As a political thinker, he leaned conservative, committed to racial and social hierarchy, with his greatest ire reserved for the communists, anarchists, and other self-proclaimed revolutionaries who sought to upend it. These two aspects of his identity would define the rest of his career, sometimes in concert and sometimes in tension, as he sought to be an apolitical administrator and a political crusader to varying degrees. Hoover's early bids for success had been a mixed story, with swift and transcendent victories but also plunging humiliations, all on a scale unthinkable to most men in their twenties. His timing had been fortuitous but also challenging. As the federal government grew to meet the exigencies of war, it brought once-in-a-generation opportunities but also a loss of certainty. His early years were above all a time of experimentation, as the administrative state expanded around him, and as he studied and learned from the examples of other men.

In 1924, he earned the chance to put his own ideas into action as head of the institution to which he would devote the rest of his life. Over the next two decades, Hoover rebuilt the Bureau of Investigation as the organization he wanted it to be, sloughing off the controversies of the Palmer and Burns years, refashioning it into a model government agency under the acronym FBI. The letters stood for Federal Bureau of Investigation, but Hoover liked to say they really meant "Fidelity, Bravery, and Integrity," the supposed hallmarks of an FBI culture crafted in his exacting image. Between 1924 and 1945, he created many of the initiatives that would become synonymous with the FBI: its forensic lab and crime statistics, its training school at Quantico, its public relations division, its National Academy intended to "professionalize" the local police. He also acquired new duties that would define and then redefine his agents' identity: first as squeaky-clean lawyers and accountants; then as crime-fighting federal avengers; and finally as spies and counterspies, returning to the job of political surveillance. Between

1924 and 1945, the number of FBI agents grew from 381 to 4,900, part of an unprecedented expansion of federal employment that began with the New Deal and exploded during World War II. Hoover's thousands of agents would come to occupy a special place in that story of American state-building as the ultimate "G-Men," or "Government Men": the lived embodiment of the nation's sudden and awesome increase in federal authority.

Hoover sought throughout these decades to avoid the sort of backlash that had brought down his predecessors, to show everyone—especially the nation's liberals and progressives—that he was different from the Bureau directors who had come before. His chief strategy for doing that was to cultivate a reputation as an apolitical, bipartisan administrator, equally at home in budget-conscious Republican administrations and in the sprawling energies of Franklin Roosevelt's New Deal. The strategy worked well, winning him praise not only from the century's greatest liberal president but also from vast swaths of the public, liberals and conservatives alike, who thrilled to his promises of integrity in high office, of government service wedded to a noble public ideal. That Hoover did not always live up to the exacting standards he set for himself went without saying (nobody, in truth, could). When crises came, he showed himself to be a ruthless political operator, determined to protect his bureaucratic prerogatives and autonomy.

His government celebrity won him entrée into a glamorous social world, in which he began to explore new aspects of his sexuality and identity for the first time. With him in much of that journey was Clyde Tolson, a fellow GW graduate whom he met in the late 1920s and forged into both a professional and personal companion. By the mid-1930s, Hoover and Tolson could be found hobnobbing together not just in Washington but in New York and California, where they carved out something of a private life, a social pair if never quite an acknowledged couple. Hoover never made much of a distinction between the personal and the professional, however. During these years, Tolson became the associate director of the FBI as well.

Hoover's determination to move beyond the difficulties of his early years came to a climax during World War II, when he fought off accusations that he was still, in spirit as well as policy, the troubled heir to Palmer and Daugherty and Flynn and Burns. To prove otherwise, he made common cause with the civil libertarians who had once been his greatest critics. The war years would be the high point of his reputation as a professional, apolitical administrator, divorced from politics and ideology and the bitter struggles that both entailed. Even as Hoover remade himself as a paragon of the administrative state, though, he never forgot the other part of his early political education: the sense of threat and disorder lurking just beneath the surface, the need for conservative warriors to defend the status quo.

CHAPTER 10

The New Sleuth

(1924–1925)

An early publicity shot of the Bureau of Investigation under Hoover's leadership. He emphasized files (and filing cabinets), not guns and drama.

NATIONAL ARCHIVES AND RECORDS ADMINISTRATION

As Hoover later told it, May 10, 1924, marked the day of the Bureau's rebirth. That morning, Burns stopped by the Justice building to bid farewell, his once imposing frame now stooped in defeat. A few hours later, Hoover received a summons from the attorney general appointed to replace Harry Daugherty, a stern New York law professor named Harlan Fiske Stone. Hoover arrived at Stone's office prepared to denounce Burns and plead his own case. He knew, though, that his fate was uncertain. At the age of twenty-nine, Hoover already carried the taint of two major Justice scandals: first the Palmer Raids, then the spiraling corruptions of Teapot Dome. The obvious thing would be to fire him, and to cleanse the department of the men who had participated in its greatest humiliations and failures.

Stone did little to put Hoover at ease. More than six feet tall, with broad shoulders and a famously penetrating stare, the attorney general had made a career of intimidating young lawyers, recently as dean of Columbia Law School. Born to a well-off New Hampshire family, he came from a world of financial ease and intellectual combat far removed from the striving, penny-pinching culture of Hoover's civil service Washington. Stone had criticized the Palmer Raids as a cruel and outrageous abuse of federal power. In demeanor and reputation, he was the antithesis of Daugherty—incorruptible, deeply intellectual, politically cautious. He made no secret of his desire for a Bureau director who would be the antithesis of Burns.

Hoover remembered the attorney general "scowling" over his reading glasses as he delivered some surprising news. "Young man," Stone said, "I want you to be acting director of the Bureau of Investigation." With those words, the meeting with Stone became the most important professional encounter of Hoover's life. Even in the moment, Hoover recognized an opportunity that would not come around again. He also supposedly recognized that a slate of major reforms would have to be enacted quickly, lest the legacies of his predecessors pull him down. "I'll take the job, Mr. Stone, on certain conditions," he replied, according to his own version of the encounter. "The Bureau must be divorced from politics and not be a catch-all for political hacks. Appointments must be based on merit. Second, promotions will be made on proved ability and the Bureau will be responsible only to the attorney general."

Stone uttered a few gruff words in response. "I wouldn't give it to you under any other conditions. That's all. Good day."[1]

This tale—of youth meeting experience, of merit winning out over connections—would become Hoover's founding myth, separating *his* Bureau from the iniquity and incompetence that had come before. Hoover's description of his appointment accentuated how his past as a son of Washington, educated and disciplined in government culture, pushed him inexorably into leadership of the Bureau. It downplayed other aspects of his history: the racism of Kappa Alpha, his early training in wartime surveillance, his bitter struggles with communists and anarchists, his immersion in Washington's backroom politics. It also erased his connections with his notorious former bosses. Stone provided a laudable professional genealogy: at last Hoover had a direct superior who would not be forced to resign amid scandal and controversy.

For decades to come, Hoover would identify Stone—not Gregory, Palmer, or Flynn, and certainly not Daugherty or Burns—as "my ideal of what a public-servant should be." Long after Stone had left the Justice Department, Hoover clung to the story of the reform-minded law professor and the battered young public servant joining forces at the Bureau's darkest hour. The episode captured everything Hoover wanted to convey about the "new" Bureau that emerged in 1924: under his leadership, it would be efficient, apolitical, meritocratic, and brimming with the energy that only a young, ambitious director could provide.[2]

Alas, Hoover's account of his confidence in those first crucial minutes with Stone is almost certainly exaggerated. Far from being the quick-thinking young man ready to dictate terms, Hoover was anxious and tentative in his first months as acting director, constantly seeking Stone's approval. The ideas that Hoover allegedly punched out on

May 10—hiring by merit, insulation from patronage politics, clear lines of command—
were already on Stone's mind. And they were not, for that matter, original ideas, but
part of the emerging repertoire of progressive-minded Washington. It is true that
Hoover became director with the zeal of a bona fide reformer, convinced that the ideals of technocratic prowess and official expertise would cure the ailing Bureau. At the
same time, he harbored a deep suspicion of movements proposing to use the levers of
government to enact significant social change. Throughout his career, he would show
a remarkable ability to juggle these two traditions—to be an enthusiastic federal bureaucrat but also a great skeptic about what an empowered federal government would
be called upon to do.

IT WAS STONE, NOT HOOVER, WHO TOOK CHARGE OF EVENTS THAT SPRING. ON
May 13, three days after their initial meeting, he outlined his agenda in a memo addressed to Hoover. The memo adhered closely to the principles articulated during that
first encounter: the Bureau was to become a model meritocracy, setting aside its history
of political surveillance and corruption. Stone demanded the immediate firing of partisan hangers-on and "incompetent or unreliable" agents, including Burns loyalists
such as Gaston Means. Constructing an effective bureaucracy would be a matter of
finding the right men, he instructed, not simply of crafting the right policies. The attorney general did not yet trust Hoover to make such judgments, so he insisted that his
office, not Hoover's, approve all hiring and firing decisions.[3]

Stone assured reporters that the Bureau rejected all forms of political and personal
surveillance. "There is always a possibility that a secret police may be a menace to free
government and free institutions," he noted in what would turn out to be an oft-cited
interview, "because it carries with it the possibility of abuses of power which are not
always quickly apprehended or understood." Henceforth the Bureau would stick to the
letter of the law, Stone maintained, eschewing all interest in "political or other opinions." He proceeded to shut down the General Intelligence Division (formerly the
Radical Division), where Hoover had made such an indelible mark just a few years
earlier.[4]

Though he would later depart from certain aspects of his boss's vision, there is little
in Hoover's record during these first uneasy months to suggest that he viewed himself
as anything other than Stone's loyal disciple. He knew that Stone had appointed him
as *acting* director, a placeholder while the attorney general searched for a more competent and experienced man. Under the circumstances, Hoover projected a frantic, eager-
to-please quality, the scramble of an energetic subordinate rather than a self-possessed
executive. The weeks after his appointment brought a display of bureaucratic energy
that rivaled anything Hoover had undertaken during the war or even at the peak of
the Palmer Raids.

Hoover had come of age in an era of federal expansion, when the war and then postwar crisis had necessitated flexibility and invention on an unprecedented scale. By 1924, he seemed to assume that a major office reorganization could be effected in a matter of weeks. His most important move was restructuring the accountability and inspection systems that linked the director with his far-flung agents in the field. Beginning in May, Hoover divided the Bureau into six divisions, including an inspection unit that would conduct regular reviews of each local field office. He also mandated that recruits arrive with some form of accounting or legal training—preferably a law degree. This combination of new standards and regular reviews promised to give Hoover, at least temporarily, what no director before had ever experienced: control over a group of dependable, professional men who knew both the requirements and limits of their jobs. It also had the potential to deliver the prize he coveted: appointment not as the acting boss, but as Bureau director.[5]

HIS OLD COMMUNIST FOES WERE NOT IMPRESSED. "DESPITE THE PROTESTA-tions of Attorney General Stone . . . , the expected has happened . . . ," the *Daily Worker* newspaper, the house organ of the Communist Party, grumbled in late 1924. "Now that the excitement is over, we find J H Hoover [*sic*] slipping his feet in Burns' shoes." Members of the emerging civil liberties movement, with its subset of moderate, well-heeled citizens, expressed similar concerns. These were Stone's people, the law professors and Ivy League attorneys whose wartime stance on behalf of dissenters had begun to transform the legal landscape. Many had retreated to private life since the Palmer days, content to ascribe Bureau excesses to the hysteria of war. Others continued to voice doubts that the department's "illegal practices," once established, could be so easily unlearned and contained. In the spring of 1924, Harvard law professor Felix Frankfurter warned Stone of the "Herculean" effort needed to improve the "unsavory atmosphere" and "professional demoralization" at "the fountain-head of the Federal administration of justice." Unlike Palmer, who had denounced Frankfurter as a personal enemy and national traitor, Stone welcomed the gesture. "I need all the help I can get," he admitted.[6]

For Hoover, Stone's sympathy with Frankfurter posed a formidable obstacle. During the dark days of 1920, Hoover had engaged in open combat with Frankfurter and his allies, denouncing them as liars and dupes. Now Stone demanded that Hoover make nice with his former enemies—indeed, that he persuade them personally of his goodwill and sincerity. Just weeks after his appointment, Hoover spoke with Roger Baldwin, founder of the American Civil Liberties Union and one of the nation's most outspoken opponents of wartime internment, speech laws, and deportation raids. In the summer and fall of 1924, Hoover and Baldwin met in a series of one-on-one conferences, instigated by Stone, to reach an accord about the proper limits and uses of

Bureau power. And for a while, that accord largely held. Especially in those tentative early months, under the tight watch of the attorney general, Hoover wanted little more than to distance himself from past Bureau practices. Baldwin's faith was not misplaced when he wrote to Stone that Hoover's approach "meets every suggestion which any of us could possibly make." Stone, delighted to see past conflicts defused, sent the letter along to Hoover. "This may be embarrassing praise," he noted, "but I suppose we will have to endure it like the hot weather."[7]

Hoover had more months of endurance ahead. Over the course of the summer, he purged the Bureau's most notorious agents, reordered its bureaucracy, and charmed some of its greatest critics. He also launched a program of favors and ingratiation aimed at the attorney general, instructing agents in far-flung cities to extend "every courtesy and attention" during Stone's official visits. Still, as of September, Hoover showed no great confidence that his efforts would be rewarded. "When I relinquish the duties of Acting Director," he wrote to a Bureau colleague, "I want to leave, if possible, a service that is as perfect as is physically human to establish." The letter hinted at the grueling perfectionism that had driven Hoover to accomplish so much in so little time and that would soon define the culture of his Bureau.[8]

THE UNCERTAINTY AND POLITICAL TURMOIL OF 1924 TOOK A TOLL ON HOOVER'S health. Since childhood, he had favored order and predictability, placing himself in situations that offered a clear hierarchy and defined set of rules. Now, with his appointment in limbo and his onetime patrons exiled, the old strategies broke down. On a doctor's advice, he took up smoking cigarettes, hoping to relax the growing tightness in his gut and restore proper digestion. When he found himself too tense to eat, he slipped his food to Spee Dee Bozo, his frisky Airedale puppy. According to his niece Margaret, who moved in with Hoover and Annie in 1926, Hoover still indulged in occasional trips to the ice cream parlor, joining her for a streetcar ride and then treating them each to a chocolate or pistachio cone as they strolled back to Seward Square.[9]

These are curiously childish images: Hoover with his puppy, Hoover with his ice cream cone. At work, he acted older than his years, a twenty-nine-year-old bossing around men twice his age. At home, he still slept in his childhood bedroom and bid his mother good night. He held on to other aspects of his youth as well, seeking to replicate in adulthood some of the masculine camaraderie he had found first in the cadet corps and then at Kappa Alpha. He joined the University Club, founded twenty years earlier by then–secretary of war William Howard Taft to unite the city's college-educated men. For outdoor pursuits, he signed up with the Columbia Country Club in Chevy Chase, a favorite among political men. He also joined the Scottish Rite Order of Freemasonry, better known as the Masons, an all-male Protestant fraternal order well suited to Hoover's love of ritual, secrecy, and hierarchy.[10]

Through these institutions, he continued his education in the social rituals of Washington's elite: how to mix dinner and politics, how to shore up secret alliances, how to play a decent game of golf. Hoover was still a junior figure, a supplicant rather than a provider of favors. But his memberships marked him as an up-and-comer, a young man whose reputation, social skills, and financial resources had put him on the fast track to influence and success. On December 10, 1924, as if to affirm this narrative, Stone finally promoted Hoover to the position of Bureau director—no longer acting, but now the real boss. It was exactly seven months since their first meeting and three weeks shy of Hoover's thirtieth birthday.

WHEN HOOVER HAD BEEN APPOINTED ACTING DIRECTOR ON MAY 10, NOBODY outside official circles had taken much notice. This time, the press paid attention. The articles on his appointment were mostly back-page write-ups, often little more than a photo and caption. They made little mention of his complicated past under Palmer, portraying him instead as a pleasant young bureaucrat on the rise.

Observing this rush of approval, Felix Frankfurter once again wrote to Stone from Harvard to warn that "Hoover was too actively associated with the Mitchell Palmer deportation proceedings" to reform the Bureau effectively. In deference to the attorney general, Frankfurter acknowledged that Hoover "might be a very effective and zealous instrument of the realization of the 'liberal ideas' which you had in mind" as long as Stone remained in office. Frankfurter worried, though, that Hoover might revert to old ways under a less liberal and "energizing" boss. Stone argued that they would have to take "the fat with the lean"—and that for now, Hoover would do fine. Over the long term, though, it was Frankfurter who proved the more prescient of the two. Throughout his career, Hoover would often defer to his "liberal" bosses at the White House and the Justice Department, accommodating political reality as necessary and often earning their wholehearted support. But he would also build independent forms of power that insulated him from political pressure and allowed him to carry out his own agenda.

Calvin Coolidge, the first president of Hoover's long career as director, showed no great interest in the appointment one way or another. A thin-lipped Massachusetts native, Coolidge was most often described in the negative: dour, silent, inaccessible. His political outlook, too, tended toward a single word: no. A proud conservative even in the prewar heyday of progressivism, Coolidge viewed his role as president to restrain the federal government, to spend taxpayer dollars as infrequently and efficiently as possible. He boasted, in an unusual but successful campaign speech, that the American people would hardly notice "if the Federal Government should go out of existence." Coolidge admired the creative power and stern realism of American industry, promising to ape corporate efficiency while keeping the government out of the business of business.[11]

Hoover paid homage to these views in his earliest public statements, vowing to bring to the Bureau a height of efficiency and smooth management never before seen in American law enforcement. Echoing Coolidge, he tried to define his mission in negative terms, as an attempt to rein in an unruly and overweening site of federal sprawl. Building upon Stone's reforms, Hoover promised to shrink the Bureau's size still further, fire still more inefficient agents, and remain true to Coolidge-style penny-pinching. And yet this fealty to Coolidge's "business methods," the impulse to hold back and say no, captured only part of Hoover's worldview. To an admiring press, he also seemed to be at the vanguard of the modernizing state, where ambitious young bureaucrats were determined to throw off the orthodoxies of the past to meet the exigencies of the future.

The standard-bearer of that outlook was not Coolidge but his commerce secretary, the engineer and wartime food administrator Herbert Hoover, no relation to the eager young director of the Bureau of Investigation. Like Coolidge, the commerce secretary believed that personal character, far more than social conditions or government policy, formed the bedrock of a virtuous republic. Where he differed from the president was in his faith that federal action, carried out in appropriate and limited ways, could nonetheless bring about progress.[12]

As Bureau director, Hoover adopted this mindset, stressing expertise over tradition, order over chaos, human intelligence over superstition. He presented himself as an individualist for whom character and morals were as important as any paper credential. Though ostensibly a member of the law enforcement profession, he went out of his way to separate himself from ordinary policemen, whom he depicted as a cabal of corrupt, undereducated, easy-to-deceive thugs. A variety of police practices came in for special criticism, each said to embody the underhanded and unscientific approach that dominated the law enforcement profession. One was the so-called third degree, in which police relied on beatings, threats, and torture to extract confessions from unwilling suspects. Another was the use of "promises" and "inducements," especially monetary payments, to get witnesses and informants to talk. Finally, there was the wiretapping of telephone calls, which Hoover derided as a form of "entrapment" and deception better suited to gangsters than to government officials. He advocated adopting the latest in science, forensics, and psychology, modern forms of knowledge that would make such old-fashioned strong-arm techniques obsolete. He described this approach as a way to make the police more professional, a theme that would last for decades, even as Hoover retreated from some of his early reform ideas.[13]

In order to enact "professionalism," Hoover needed professionals. As he boasted to the papers, after 1924 he required all new agents to possess either a legal or accounting degree, markers of professional training and white-collar success. He also sought out men who would uphold the highest ideals of citizenship, refusing the temptations of alcohol, womanizing, bribery, even run-of-the-mill sloth. "I want the public to look upon the Bureau of Investigation of the Department of Justice as a group of gentle-men," he informed a national magazine, "and if the men here engaged can't conduct themselves in office as such, I will dismiss them." It was both a statement of principles and a reminder that Hoover was at last in charge.[14]

SUCH CLAIMS WERE FAIRLY TYPICAL OF 1920S WASHINGTON, PART OF A DECADES-long trend toward professionalizing the civil service. What made the sentiment nota-ble was the fact that Hoover was a detective, a line of work hardly known for its high standards and clean living. Nearly every news report on his appointment stressed the contrast between "the old-fashioned sleuth," with his "gum shoes," "false whiskers," and "'roughneck' methods," and the new law enforcement type epitomized by Hoover: a "lawyer" and "trained investigator" attuned to a well-defined "philosophy of the pro-fession." Hoover sought to enhance this distinction, posing for photos seated with paperwork at his desk rather than out on the prowl with his derby hat and magnifying lens. His demeanor exuded both modesty and professional efficiency; he would rather speak of index cards, fingerprints, and personnel reforms than of Sherlock Holmes–style theatrics. More than one reporter noted his white-collar charm and lack of blus-ter. "There is about him none of the hard-boiled detective which Burns was so fond of affecting. You are instantly pleased by him, drawn to him." Lest such descriptions sound overly feminine, Hoover was quick to insist that brains rather than brawn would define the police work of the future. "There is nothing mushy or soft or senti-mental about Mr. Hoover," the same reporter wrote. "He can be just as forceful and hard-hitting in his dealings with criminals as the toughest of his profession."[15]

While the celebration of the "new detective" reflected certain genuine changes, it also drew upon a more reactionary strain of 1920s politics. The image of expert and gentleman rested on some of the same nativist assumptions that had produced the Immigration Act of 1924, which codified preferences for the Protestants of Western Europe over the Catholics and Jews of the East, and which effectively excluded African and Asian immigrants altogether. Hoover's appointment brought out some of these same prejudices. "For the first time in many years a Protestant and member of the Masonic fraternity has been appointed director of the Bureau of Investigation . . . ," a Masonic magazine cheered. "William J. Burns, an ardent Roman Catholic, preceded Mr. Hoover in the position, and before Mr. Burns another Romanist, W.J. Flynn, held the office." The assumption was there in the physical comparisons—fat vs. slim, red hair vs. brown—as well as in discussions of Hoover's personal habits. Burns had chomped on cigars and reveled in the New York limelight. Hoover enjoyed playing golf when he was not bur-ied under paperwork.[16]

When the press praised Hoover's appointment, the implication was clear: reform-ing the Bureau meant replacing its urban Catholic leadership with superior Protestant men. Efficiency, modesty, merit, and golf—these would be the bywords of Hoover's more refined and distinctly more Protestant Bureau.

HOOVER'S BID TO DEFINE THE BUREAU AS A WHITE-COLLAR SANCTUARY MADE a certain amount of practical sense. Bureau agents in 1924 *were* more like lawyers than bona fide policemen, at least as far as their official duties were concerned. Despite their Burns-era reputation as spy-hunters and strikebreakers, agents had no formal authority to carry weapons and often did their work unarmed. They were not even supposed to make arrests; embarrassing as it might be, when a federal agent sought to apprehend a suspect, he often had to turn to local authorities to complete the official capture. Political surveillance had always been a stretch for the Bureau, conducted at the edges of the law. But with such activities now banned by the attorney general, they were left with an odd array of duties and obligations. Bureau agents performed a variety of antitrust and anti-corruption work. They also investigated auto theft and prostitution, but only when the perpetrators crossed state lines. Other than that, most law enforcement still occurred at the local level.

By far the trickiest of area of federal jurisdiction was Prohibition, which had evolved by late 1924 from a moral experiment into a full-blown law enforcement crisis. From the first, there had been far too few federal agents to enforce a law of such scope. Rather than fostering civic peace, Prohibition emboldened an influential underworld determined to apply the time-tested lessons of American capitalism to the illegal liquor trade. Of equal concern, from the perspective of police administrators, was Prohibition's effect on the very men charged with its enforcement. Far from purifying police ranks, Prohibition was fast proving an irresistible temptation for local and federal police alike, who often could earn more in bribes than they received in their salary checks. Hoover counted himself lucky that primary federal responsibility for Prohibition enforcement lay with the Treasury Department, not with Justice.[17]

He still had to contend with Prohibition in other ways, though. Hoover vowed to fire any agent caught drinking—not because he was "a fanatic" on the question, he insisted, but because "when a man becomes a part of this Bureau he must so conduct himself, both officially and unofficially, as to eliminate the slightest possibility of criticism." He also launched a moral crusade against corrupt public officials elsewhere in government who took advantage of Prohibition's rewards and temptations. While Treasury agents attempted to restrain the likes of Al Capone, Bureau agents began to go after local sheriffs, politicians, prison wardens, and federal judges, whose taste for the finer things in life had put them in cahoots with the very gangsters they were supposed to be policing. In Savannah, Georgia, evidence gathered by Bureau agents helped to convict 142 people on charges of corruption and bribery. In Cleveland, the Bureau exposed a corrupt federal prohibition director and his multiyear record of government fraud. In Cincinnati, Bureau efforts resulted in the indictment of seventy-one individuals as part of a "conspiracy" between local police and Prohibition agents, in Hoover's words, "to defeat the enforcement of the prohibition law."[18]

In that sense, Prohibition was actually a gift to Hoover, a chance to prove that his agents were different from the dissolute, cynical, and easily bribed local police. It also allowed him to distinguish the Bureau from other federal agencies, which despite occasional successes proved largely incapable of handling the challenges of Prohibition. "I do not want this bureau to be referred to in terms I have frequently heard used against other governmental agencies," he warned subordinates in his May 1925 letter. The Bureau, he hoped, would be a model for other, lesser agencies, where inefficiency, corruption, and machine politics ruled.[19]

IN CONTRAST TO THE MORASS OF PROHIBITION ENFORCEMENT, HOOVER HELD up the Bureau's new Identification Division as the embodiment of all that he hoped to achieve as director. Launched in July 1924, just a few months into his temporary appointment, the division aimed to consolidate the nation's criminal fingerprints into a central Washington clearinghouse under Bureau authority. That effort had begun under Burns, but never quite gathered steam. For Hoover, it became a matter of pride as well as necessity. As a law enforcement professional, he viewed fingerprints as a chance to use modern scientific techniques in the service of catching criminals. As a bureaucrat, he also saw an opportunity to exercise federal authority in a strategic but limited way. To guide the division's work, he adopted Herbert Hoover's "associational" principle, which dictated cooperation between the local and federal authorities. In this vision, local police departments would voluntarily hand over fingerprints taken after felony arrests. In return, they would gain access to a set of national files and well-educated experts.

But launching the fingerprint division was easier said than done. Most police departments did not collect fingerprints on any routine or systematized basis. Those that did often failed to send them to the two national identification centers that had existed before 1924. The first, maintained by the International Association of Chiefs of Police, was already located in Washington, though understaffed and disorganized. The second, at the federal government's Leavenworth penitentiary, was in worse shape still. There, federal prisoners processed the fingerprints of their fellow convicts, the proverbial wolves guarding the henhouse.[20]

Hoover pictured something different: a flawless paperwork machine in which each criminal would have a set of fingerprints, each set of fingerprints would have a file, and each file would have dozens of clerks available to decipher its meaning. By bringing the nation's fingerprints under Bureau control, he would gain a point of contact with every police department in the country, and potentially with every American citizen. He would also play a role in solving high-profile crimes across the nation. The Identification Division hearkened back to his dream of building a file on every radical and subversive, but where that effort reeked of subjectivity and political bias, this one carried the imprimatur of science. Modern identification would be clean and efficient, infallible and necessary, and it would help rid the nation of crime and disorder. This vision of cooperation, not coercion, would long serve as Hoover's model for how relations between local and federal law enforcement were supposed to work. He could say, without exaggeration, that the identification files were a voluntary effort, not a federal power grab—thoroughly in keeping with a conservative vision of how to grow the modern state.

High praise came his way. "Since crime has grown beyond the bounds of local interest, this is the method by which the crime preventive agencies operate from a centralized point," Washington's *Evening Star* wrote in May 1925. "Like the center of a spider's web stands the National Identification Bureau." It was not the last time that Hoover's Bureau would be compared to a spider's web, with a single vital creature at its center. Hoover did not feel terribly powerful, though, at least not yet. He knew that the world had a way of disrupting order and efficiency. He saw, too, that countless bureaucratic challenges remained. First among them was finding the men who could live up to his standards, and who would join him in building his Bureau.[21]

CHAPTER 11

Kappa Alpha Bureau

(1925–1928)

Clyde Tolson in 1930.
The inscription identifies
Hoover as "my best
friend."

On the surface, nothing much happened at the Bureau after Hoover's initial spurt of reforms. He began with 606 employees in late 1924; three years later, he had 581. His appropriation hardly budged during the same period, hovering just above $2 million. By the numbers, the Bureau presented a picture of stasis and lassitude, a corps of men dutifully abiding by the letter of the law. "They do their work quietly and efficiently," one congressman noted in late 1928, "and you never hear any account given of it until they come here to report."[1]

Scratch the surface, though, and Hoover was changing nearly every aspect of the Bureau experience, with an eye toward achieving administrative perfection. During his first years as director, he reshaped what it meant to be an agent, dictating the Bureau's first personnel manuals, establishing a rigid training system, and expanding his system of regular field office inspections. He also recruited a tight-knit team of young executives, many of them straight from George Washington University law school, who would lead the Bureau well into the 1940s. One of those men, Clyde Tolson, would go on to become Hoover's most intimate friend and lifetime companion. During these first years, though, Tolson was just one of many.

Hoover's transformation of the Bureau during these years was not simply a flexing of bureaucratic power. It was also a cultural project, shaped by the conservative principles—about race and religion, about gender and social hierarchy—that he had absorbed as a young man. Before Hoover's appointment, the Bureau had regularly hired Black agents, if not in great numbers. Hoover put an end to that practice, and instead placed Black men in servant roles such as chauffeur and greeter. Jewish employees fared slightly better, though they, too, came in for extra scrutiny under Hoover. As he built his new Bureau, Hoover sought to enforce the vision of white Christian masculinity imparted to him through the institutions of his youth.

He ultimately accomplished far more. As FBI director, Hoover would take advantage of the influence acquired through his federal office to attempt to reshape the nation's political culture as a whole. The men he recruited in the 1920s served as both models of his ideal citizen and as aides in bringing this project to fruition. Together, they endured episodes of real darkness and violence, including the murder of a Bureau agent just ten months into Hoover's term as director. Hoover's employees also experienced what his fraternity brothers and cadet corps had complained about years earlier: his tendency to scold, preach, and browbeat when things did not go his way. To the papers, he said that he sought agents who possessed the qualities of "honesty, loyalty, and common sense." His actual practice was somewhat less exalted. To help him manage and build his new Bureau, Hoover sought men as much like himself as possible.[2]

ON JANUARY 5, 1925, LESS THAN A MONTH INTO HOOVER'S TERM AS DIRECTOR, Coolidge nominated Harlan Stone to the Supreme Court. As his mentor departed, Hoover began to search for an assistant director at the Bureau, someone who could do for his regime what he had done for Burns's. The position required a delicate balance between executive authority and subordinate humility, between the self-possession to think quickly and the temperament to obey orders. With Stone departing, Hoover may also have recognized the need for an older, more experienced man to help carry out the reform process. He found his candidate in Harold Nathan, a previously undistinguished, forty-four-year-old agent languishing in the Pittsburgh office.

At just over five feet eight and 165 pounds, slightly stooped and bespectacled, Nathan hardly fit Hoover's idealized image of the gentleman lawyer. Born in New York to a Jewish family, he had attended City College and graduated with decent marks, followed by two years of law school. Nathan spoke five languages (French, German, Italian, Spanish, and Yiddish) in addition to English, the first three more or less fluently. He read widely in ancient literature, attended the opera, and liked to compose classical poetry with a smutty, modernist edge. Nathan could be biting about Hoover's youth, ribbing his boss for appearing so "young + boyish." But he was also funny and self-effacing. Hoover, oddly, seemed to tolerate and even admire Nathan's jokey side. Only Nathan could suggest that "the trouble with many of our offices is that our Agents in Charge are somewhat foggy mentally" and get away with it.[3]

Hoover came into contact with Nathan in early May 1924, when the agent worked briefly at Washington headquarters. Over the next several months, Hoover began to promote Nathan with a speed that rivaled his own precocious rise. The turning point seems to have come with a memo composed by Nathan in January 1925, responding to Hoover's plea for suggestions from the field about how to reform the internal bureaucracy. In the memo, Nathan recommended annual efficiency reports for each Bureau employee, in which they would be rated, ranked, and stacked against each other. Hoover wrote to Nathan a week later, announcing that the idea was already being put into effect. Within two months, he asked Nathan to review all Bureau applications. By May 1, 1925, Nathan was assistant Bureau director, charged with supervising all personnel matters, coordinating investigations, and running the Bureau in Hoover's absence—in short, "carrying out and effecting all directions and orders of the Director."[4]

WITH HIS ASSISTANT DIRECTOR IN PLACE, HOOVER TURNED TO IDENTIFYING recruits. He looked mainly in the places he knew. His most important recruiting ground was GW law school, where he could be assured of finding young men trained to both his legal and cultural specifications. Since Hoover's freshman year, the law school population had doubled twice over, rising from fewer than three hundred students in 1913 to 1,050 by the spring of 1925. As the status and possibilities of federal employment changed, so did the law school's reputation. No longer a quick run around college, the law school now required that entering students complete at least some undergraduate education before starting their legal studies. The university's goals for its young men reflected Hoover's own: not simply to create useful civil servants, but to fashion a serious corps of government gentlemen.[5]

Hoover's old Kappa Alpha chapter had grown during these years as well, rising from twenty-eight members when Hoover graduated to forty-three by 1928. Along the way, it became one of the most potent networks through which Hoover recruited Bureau leadership material. As future Bureau inspector Hugh Clegg recalled, by the mid-1920s it was almost impossible to get through three years at the GW chapter of Kappa Alpha without at least considering Bureau employment. Though scattered at field offices throughout the country, KAs-turned-Bureau-agents often stopped by the fraternity house during visits to Washington, extolling the excitement of investigative work and assuring the younger men that a job could be had for the asking. Clegg, a pudgy, snub-nosed transplant from Mississippi, must have seemed like a particularly valuable prospect. In addition to being fraternity president, he had worked at the Library of Congress, where Hoover, too, got his start. A few days before graduation, a Kappa Alpha alum offered to set up an interview at the Bureau. On the morning of his commencement exercises, Clegg met with Hoover. That same day, he submitted his Bureau application.[6]

Other campus organizations served a similar function, attracting recruits through both deliberate effort and word of mouth. Out of the network around the Utah Legal Club, a pseudo-fraternity for campus Mormons, came agents Samuel Cowley, and Reed Vetterli—both destined to be major Bureau figures in the 1930s. To this lineup Hoover added a rush of other recruits plucked from the GW ranks. D. Milton (Mickey) Ladd, son of a North Dakota senator, managed the GW football team before joining the Bureau and eventually rising to the post of domestic intelligence chief. Future FBI technical expert John Edwards, a recruit from Coal Creek, Tennessee, had been a Kappa Alpha a few years before Hugh Clegg. Hoover's college friend Frank Baughman stayed on at the Bureau as well, rising to be the number three man under Nathan and the elder statesmen of the GW generation. Like Hoover, these men came to the Bureau already imbued with a professional ethos, but also with conservative ideas on race and religion and the ideal social order. Whatever their individual talents, their outstanding characteristic as a group was sheer monotony of outlook and background.[7]

BY FAR THE MOST IMPORTANT OF THESE RECRUITS WAS CLYDE TOLSON, HIRED as a special agent in March 1928. By the time he applied to the Bureau, Tolson had already spent almost a decade working for the government. He had also joined the Masons, attended GW, and pledged a fraternity—the three pillars of Hoover's ideal Bureau man. Tolson was not a star, either on campus or at the War Department, where he worked. But he was capable and discreet and seemed to be on his way up—just what Hoover wanted.[8]

Born in Laredo, Missouri, Tolson had grown up imbued with the small-town morals Mark Twain once described as both the region's blessing and its curse. His father worked as a special agent for the Chicago, Milwaukee, and St. Paul Railroad, lashed to the rhythms of the rail. That professional status exempted Tolson from the sort of grinding farm labor that extracted most Missouri boys from school at an early age. Five years Hoover's junior, Tolson graduated from the Laredo high school in 1915, just as the European war began its descent into the trenches. Two years later, he moved with his parents to Cedar Rapids, Iowa, where he enrolled in a local business college. Though his performance was "O.K. in every way," in the assessment of a former teacher, Tolson was restless and isolated in Iowa. In 1918, with the war bureaucracy booming, he moved to Washington in search of an independent future.[9]

Tolson's story fit a generational narrative: strapping young boy, recently come of age, heads off to save the world for democracy. But there was a hitch. Once in Washington, he became a stenographer, not a soldier. As one Bureau official later noted, Tolson was "physically fitted" for "rugged work," a tall, thin man whose clean-cut good looks made him the picture of Midwestern health. Like Hoover, though, he seemed to prefer the quiet and orderly nature of office life. In 1919, after the end of the war, Tolson earned a ranking of 291 out of 3,099 War Department clerks. In 1920, he rose to 177 among the 2,779 clerks still employed. Even as postwar attrition accelerated, Tolson decided to stay in Washington as a junior member of the federal ranks. By the end of 1920, he had secured a job as confidential clerk to Wilson's outgoing secretary of war, Newton D. Baker. He held the position for seven years, serving under two more presidential administrations and three successive secretaries of war.[10]

By the time Tolson joined the Bureau at age twenty-seven, he had already spent almost a decade immersed in a government culture that prized secrecy and discretion. At the War Department, Tolson honed the very qualities Hoover sought in his new agents: personal charm, ease in social situations, and front-office efficiency, in addition to his skills in stenography, touch typing, and dictation. He also learned how to be an effective confidant to powerful men, how to keep their secrets and flatter their vanity. As former Secretary Baker assured the attorney general, "he was a boy of fine presence, serious attention to his duties, and excellent intelligence."[11]

But Tolson had never intended to devote himself to what amounted to a glorified stenographer's life. In 1920, even as he accepted the confidential clerk's position, he enrolled at GW to begin work toward his legal degree. He built a respectable record as a member of the track team and a decent if not spectacular student. His brother, Hillory, was the real campus star; he led pep rallies, won major awards, and ran the GW athletic association. Both brothers joined Sigma Nu, a popular fraternity for athletes and a major center of GW's social whirl. Clyde lived at the fraternity house on N Street for seven years, three of them as Sigma Nu's president. Among his fellow residents was Guy Hottel, the brash young campus football captain. Tolson also got to know Stanley Tracy: yearbook editor, Utah Legal Club stalwart, and track team manager. Like Tolson, both Hottel and Tracy eventually joined the Bureau, rising to high positions under Hoover's favor. But it was Tolson who would enjoy the greatest success there, as well as the most intimate relationship with its director.[12]

HOOVER WAS NOT A KIND BOSS. NOR DID HE WISH TO BE. ALL SUCCESSFUL INvestigations, he believed, rested on a foundation of accurate paperwork; the better the bureaucracy, the better the outcome. His assumption did not always hold up, given the often intuitive and spontaneous nature of detective work. But Hoover was a lawyer and organizer, not an investigator, so the rules came first. He spent hours each day dictating memos on such matters as typographical errors, office cleanliness, and the proper stamps to be affixed on Bureau forms. He understood any deviation from policy as a personal insult, a sign of insufficient devotion to the job, and, worse, insufficient loyalty to the director. When Nathan happened to be late producing a background memo, for instance, Hoover interpreted it not as human error but as "another indication of the apathetic attitude that seems to be manifested at times in the Bureau on important matters."[13]

All the same, if he liked you he brought you up fast, with the accompanying rise in salary, power, and prestige. Nathan's salary more than doubled during his first few years as assistant director. Clegg's took off as well, rising from a recruit's pittance to an inspector's executive salary in just five years. Tolson's rose the fastest of all; within less than three years of his appointment, he was an assistant director, making almost as much as Nathan. "It is my belief that it is better to pay large salaries to a comparatively small group of efficient men than to have on the job a lot of poor men who are likely to blunder," Hoover explained to *The Evening Star*. The swift promotions, like the initial screening, were part of Hoover's trademark approach, an effort to create a loyal insider elite whose actions and interests would reflect his own. Fortunately, if he tended to criticize, he also tended to move on quickly once the requisite apologies had been offered.[14]

The key to securing his favor was not only having the right background; that simply got you in the door. Bureau up-and-comers also had to learn Hoover's desires and policies, and to enforce them ruthlessly. At the head of each field office was a special agent in charge (SAC), the chief point of contact between Hoover and his corps of clerks and agents. Washington boasted two offices: a regular field office for carrying out investigations, and Hoover's own headquarters, filled not with investigative personnel but with supervisors, inspectors, and administrators. Agents referred to Hoover's office either as "HQ" or as "SOG," short for "Seat of Government." During these early years, the Bureau was small enough that Hoover knew most of his employees. As time went on, though, SOG became a fearsome and distant specter, the site of Hoover's mysterious and often mercurial authority.

In 1927, Hoover codified his policies in a manual, soon to be known as the bible of Bureau employment. Like its namesake, the manual consisted of dos and don'ts for the faithful: do dress smartly and report in frequently; don't drink alcohol, engage in political campaigning, or speak to the press. Many instructions concerned the proper routing and content of paperwork. Abstracts were to be filed in triplicate (blue, green, and white); administrative reports were to be filed monthly; all letters were to "cover only one subject matter, the title of which shall be set forth at the right of the salutation or in the first paragraph." Of particular concern was any "indecent" material that agents might encounter in the course of investigation. This was to be placed in a "sealed container" and labeled an "Obscene Matter." Hoover feared a moral or procedural slipup that would discredit the Bureau. Accordingly, he instructed agents to keep track of "clippings from any publications which relate to the Bureau, its personnel or activities." To avoid even the hint of scandal, he also demanded that agents pay their debts promptly and "patronize hotels of the better class."[15]

Bureau employment, the manual made clear, was a total life experience, a job that stretched far beyond what one did between the hours of nine and five. Indeed, few Bureau employees worked such limited hours. Hoover came to expect and receive voluntary overtime, in which "voluntary" meant "unpaid." He also expected agents to transfer offices without complaint, packing up on short notice and often paying for the moves themselves. Especially for new agents, frequent and unpredictable transfers became one of the dominant facts of Bureau life. Hoover refused to post recruits to their hometowns or even their home states, reasoning that they might abuse local connections for personal gain. Such instability gave the Bureau a heavy bias toward young, unattached men, who often moved in and out of temporary group apartments as they bounced from city to city.

Hoover viewed his employees as interchangeable parts. "By using the new system," he explained, "it is possible to transfer an agent from Philadelphia to San Francisco and have him perfectly at home the next day." Within the Bureau, this system gave him an almost cultish control over his employees' personal and social lives. Agents plunked down in a strange city naturally turned to their Bureau comrades for friendship and emotional support. As they settled in, whether for weeks or years, the intensity of their work militated against developing many outside contacts. The enforced isolation included single and married men alike. "Our poor wives!" one agent later reflected. "Theirs was a lonely and narrow world."[16]

Hoover tracked all hirings, firings, and transfers on a national map that hung in his office, with each man represented by a tag affixed to a pin indicating his current location. He also received regular reports on each agent's investigative competence, office talents, and overall character—the so-called efficiency reports that Nathan had introduced in 1925. Every few months, the head of each field office filed a standard form rating his men on attributes ranging from "health" and "loyalty" to "aggressiveness," "tact," "personal appearance," and "executive ability." Youth and charm earned high marks, while the worst one could say of a Bureau man was that he was "old looking" or "disloyal." Each agent's strengths and weaknesses were combined into a numerical "efficiency rating," between 1 and 100, that became the basis for hiring, firing, and promotion. In his first assessment, even Tolson earned only an 86.[17]

Agents rarely knew their own efficiency ratings; that, too, had been Nathan's suggestion. Nor did they know in advance when they might run up against the most fearsome of all Bureau procedures: the field office inspection. At least twice a year, a team of inspectors from the Washington headquarters descended upon each field office, a pile of manuals and efficiency forms in tow. While there, they pored over every aspect of office life, noting the contents and appearance of each employee's desk, the amount of backlogged paperwork, the contents and condition of the supply closet, the number of long-distance telephone calls. They also recorded their impressions of individual clerks, secretaries, and agents, sending detailed and highly personalized reports back to Washington. As Clegg later noted, the inspections were Hoover's most powerful tool for enforcing internal discipline among his employees—"one of the real right arms of Mr. Hoover."[18]

When inspectors found room for improvement, as they always did, field agents could expect stern letters of reprimand, lodged forever in their personnel files. Hoover's handpicked favorites were not immune. If anything, Hoover seemed to focus his greatest outrage on the men he trusted most. When Nathan overlooked several typos in one edition of the manual, Hoover pronounced himself "astounded at not only the inexcusably poor phraseology, misspellings, but ridiculous expressions which appeared therein." Officials who relaxed their supervision of the stenographic pool came in for similar disdain. "I cannot believe that these memorandums and letters have been scrutinized before being sent to me," Hoover wrote to his division chiefs in 1928, after noticing minor errors in the outgoing mail. "I am at a loss to understand how correspondence, if it is checked by the stenographer, by the supervisor, and by the Division Head can reach my desk for action in the condition it frequently does."[19]

Such over-the-top language was typical of Hoover's approach. He thrived as an office man, eager to refine his rule book and create a perfect self-sustaining bureaucracy. Far from viewing the office as a place of drudgery and repetition, he experienced it as a site of high emotional drama. Inefficiency showed a lack of loyalty, improper stamps were signs of sloth, typos were personal insults. Messy offices were not only unsightly, but violated his Swiss-bred devotion to cleanliness and order. "I do not believe that I have ever noted an office in a more untidy and chaotic condition than existed in Division Six at the close of business yesterday," he wrote after one visit to the identification facilities. Improperly stored office supplies were "a disgrace." Consumption of food in the office tempted "vermin." Hoover believed in the connection between appearance and reality, organization and outcome: If his agents couldn't keep their offices clean, how on earth would they ever complete investigations?[20]

AFTER ALL, INVESTIGATIONS—NOT PAPERWORK, NOT OFFICE SANITATION— were the Bureau's raison d'être. The rest of Hoover's efforts would have been for naught if the Bureau failed to solve crimes and conduct effective inquiries. Many of their duties, such as investigating antitrust violations and filing fingerprints, conformed nicely to Hoover's preferred white-collar image. Sometimes, though, his agents were still forced to act as street-level lawmen, and then they could run into real danger. On October 11, 1925, a day that Hoover would later identify as a watershed for his Bureau, veteran agent Ed Shanahan was shot in the chest during an attempt to arrest a career auto thief named Martin Durkin. As Hoover noted, Durkin's bullets made Shanahan "the first one in the service ever killed."

To the public, Hoover put forth a show of detective confidence, filtering the posturing of a Flynn or Burns through his instinctive formality and reserve. "We'll get Durkin. It won't do not to get him," he vowed, adding, "It is most salutary to have criminals know that once an agent of the government, of this bureau, gets on his trail, he is there to stick to the end." Behind the scenes, though, Hoover was less certain, questioning whether his green corps of college men would be up to the task. To lead the investigation, he turned to San Antonio agent Gus Jones, a grizzled holdover from the Burns and Flynn years. Partial to cowboy hats and unvarnished honesty, Jones was nobody's model of the educated gentleman. But he had experience and authority, two qualities in short supply at Washington headquarters. Over the next three months, Jones led a nationwide search for Durkin, finally tracking him down on a train in Saint Louis.[21]

The Durkin case went down as a triumph for Hoover. All the same, it underscored the weakness of the institution he had inherited. Shanahan had been unarmed, a casualty of the Bureau's haphazard policy on carrying weapons. Even if he had survived the confrontation, he had no formal authority to arrest Durkin. Shanahan's murder itself fell outside federal jurisdiction, a local case prosecuted in the Illinois state courts. The Bureau could launch a manhunt only because Durkin happened to be a fugitive in the auto-theft case. As Hoover pointed out to Congress in 1927, "Under the Federal statutes it is not a crime to kill a Government officer." When Congress failed to act on his complaint, Hoover added the problem to the list of things he hoped to change about the Bureau.[22]

THERE WERE OTHER TRIUMPHS DURING HOOVER'S FIRST YEARS AS WELL, SENsational and gruesome cases tossed up from the Bureau's grab bag of jurisdictions. In Oklahoma, agents broke a brazen murder-and-theft ring on the Osage Indian reservation. In Pittsburgh, Bureau experts identified the fingerprints of a would-be bank robber who had blown himself up—along with "quite a number of people"—when the teller refused to hand over cash. Hoover recited these triumphs in his annual appearances before the House Appropriations Committee. In a ritual that would be repeated for decades, he deployed a dizzying array of charts and statistics to prove that while the Bureau's work was increasing, its efficiency and cost savings were growing even faster. He also boasted of the ways in which his strict rules and personnel policies had remade the Bureau as a model government agency.[23]

His corps of insiders largely accepted these claims, writing off his memos and occasional cruelties as the price of institutional success. "He was reputed to be a strict disciplinarian and had he not been I would not have stayed," Clegg recalled. For some, though, his rigidity and insistence on bureaucratic perfection bordered on the intolerable, if not the inhumane. Employees complained about his personal viciousness and punitive mindset. They also remarked upon some of his stranger policies, such as the insistence that all windows be left open during the winter to prevent any hint of heat-induced sloth. According to one employee, Hoover forbade clerks in the fingerprint division to speak or "attend to their personal needs" without permission. And some of these complaints went public, subjecting his internal policies to the disdainful scrutiny of Washington scandal sheets. "Almost unbelievable charges of slave-driving in the Department of Justice, charges that clerks in the division of investigation, under Edgar J. Hoover [sic], are made uncomfortable so that they will do more work," a local tabloid noted.[24]

In 1929, agent Joseph Bayliss, a seven-year veteran, went even further, filing a complaint with the Justice Department about the innumerable ways in which Hoover sought to control his employees, from quixotic transfers to punitive demotions to seemingly random shifts in inspection standards. His effort seems to have yielded no serious consequences for Hoover, perhaps because Bayliss came off in the document as an unstable ex-employee. But the complaint accurately identified some of the contradictions in Hoover's emerging Bureau culture, with its distinctive blend of by-the-books discipline and personal favoritism. "Since Hoover took charge in May, 1924, practically all instructions issued by him have been repressive and directed against the personnel rather than against the criminal," Bayliss wrote. "He has destroyed the individual initiative in men whose work requires initiative and resourcefulness." Bayliss estimated that some 75 percent of Bureau personnel secretly loathed Hoover, despite their outward cooperation and flattery. The few exceptions, he said, were the director's hand-picked lackeys and internal enforcers. According to Bayliss, men who lived in Washington, D.C., and attended college with Hoover were "particularly favored" at the Bureau, where "personal loyalty to the Director" was now among the highest forms of achievement.[25]

CHAPTER 12

Depression Days

(1929–1932)

November 24, 1932
Laboratory established

A page from a book prepared by Bureau officials in honor of Hoover's thirtieth anniversary as director. The book depicts career highlights, including the establishment of the FBI's famed forensic laboratory, built on Hoover's ideas of "scientific policing."

COLLECTION OF THE NATIONAL LAW ENFORCEMENT MUSEUM

Hoover's first five years as director had been remarkably scandal-free: no oil deals or liquor payoffs, no questionable roundups or major abuses of civil liberties. By 1929, with the initial work of remaking the Bureau now complete, Hoover could take a deep breath. The rest of the country was not so fortunate. Over the next four years, ten million people lost their jobs, the stock market fell by 90 percent, and breadlines became a regular feature of the national landscape. For Hoover, though, the dawn of the Great Depression was a time of good fortune and rising status—in some ways the happiest years he would ever know.

During those years, he continued to build the Bureau but at a less frantic pace, establishing carefully circumscribed programs that would refine the Bureau's law enforcement role. These strategic choices, in turn, set him on a path toward what today's political scientists describe as "bureaucratic autonomy." Despite its cumbersome name, bureaucratic autonomy is a simple concept: autonomous bureaucrats can do what they want, regardless of politicians' needs or desires. As one scholar has noted, successful bureaucrats need at least three attributes to achieve true independence: a clear vision, a loyal popular constituency, and a reputation for attaining genuine results. Hoover had begun to create all three during his early years as director. In the early 1930s, he accelerated the process.[1]

He did not simply grab whatever chances came his way. Contrary to his later reputation for self-aggrandizement, Hoover mostly said no to new duties in the early 1930s: no to Prohibition enforcement; no to investigating organized crime; no to wiretapping, raiding communists, and intervening in violent clashes on the street. He said yes only in areas where he believed his white-collar agents could excel, such as collecting crime statistics and performing scientific lab work. His careful approach put the Bureau in a comfortable position as the Great Depression took hold—secure in its institutional culture, but not yet forced to contend with the greater problems of the age.

CRIME WAS ON THE COUNTRY'S MIND IN THE LATE 1920S, AND FOR GOOD REASON. While Hoover was busy refining his internal policies, the American murder rate had risen sharply, with Prohibition providing the soil in which violent organized crime syndicates could take root and grow. That trend continued between 1929 and 1933; while the nation's economy slumped, the murder rate rose to new peaks. Other forms of crime seemed to be on the rise as well, though as Hoover would soon point out, the nation had few dependable statistics by which to measure what was taking place. Certainly the country *believed* that it was experiencing a crime wave. "Few subjects occupy more space in contemporary literature . . . than analyses of the crime wave, its extent, causes and possible remedies," one criminologist noted. Prohibition, undertaken as an effort to legislate virtue, seemed to be producing violence and lawbreaking of historic proportions. And criminals were now aided by the best modern technology, from machine guns to bulletproof vests to the speediest of getaway cars.[2]

So it came as no great surprise when Herbert Hoover, the newly elected Republican president, mentioned the subject of crime in his inaugural speech. What was surprising was that he considered it a matter for federal action. As all lawmen knew, most policing and prosecution happened at the local and state levels. Outside certain limited areas of jurisdiction—auto theft, white slavery, crime on Indian reservations, antitrust work—the federal government was among the least important players in the criminal justice system. The new president wanted to change that. Speaking to a rain-soaked audience on March 4, 1929, he identified "the failure of our system of criminal justice" as one of the top concerns of his administration. Two months later, he appointed an eleven-member commission under the leadership of former attorney general George Wickersham to investigate the criminal justice system in its entirety, ranging from parole and prisons to police procedure and liquor enforcement.[3]

Over the next year, the Wickersham Commission heard witness after witness describe the horrors of Prohibition, including the bribery of police, the rise of organized crime, and the "third degree" meted out by frustrated law enforcement officers. Hoover played a limited role in those proceedings, just as he had played a limited role in Prohibition enforcement itself. In the single biggest case of 1929—the federal prosecution of Chicago gangster Al Capone—he did little, aside from sending agents to prove that Capone was alive and well in Miami, hardly too sick to appear before a grand jury. The Bureau had limited jurisdiction over figures like Capone, a situation that may have come as a relief to Hoover but that left the Bureau without a clearly defined role to play in the nation's roiling crime debate. Hoover's challenge under the new administration was to articulate a mission that would keep the Bureau out of controversy while giving it a useful mission.[4]

He settled on the issue of crime statistics, arguing that the nation could not hope to fight crime without knowing how much of it actually existed. "It is impossible to ascertain whether there is a crime wave for the very reason that there have been no accurate records from which a proper conclusion could be drawn," he explained. Hoover also had other, more self-interested reasons to seek out this particular task. Like the gathering of fingerprints, the collection of statistics would keep his men in the realm of scientific, white-collar work while simultaneously putting them at the center of the law enforcement profession. To do the job effectively, the Bureau would have to maintain ties with each of the nation's thousands of police departments, developing valuable contacts and giving each of those departments a reason to support the Bureau. Even more important, the agency that took charge of statistical information would determine how to count the numbers, and would be able to cast its own interpretation of the causes of and solution to the crime problem. By taking control of crime statistics, Hoover could expand the Bureau's influence with relatively little effort, risk, or expenditure of manpower.[5]

The Wickersham Commission recognized that statistics could be an art as well as a science, and thus could be manipulated in the service of a particular cause. Police departments hoping to increase their appropriations might inflate their statistics. Conversely, they might undercount crime to show how effective their methods could be. Federal lawmen such as Hoover had their own potential conflicts of interest. A nationwide crime spike might bring added funding at the federal level, offering an incentive to exaggerate what was happening. Statistics could also be nudged one way or another to prove some political point: about alcohol consumption, about urban governance, about race or immigration or gender or the sort of person most likely to become a criminal. The Bureau depended on the cooperation of local police not only to gather statistics, but to carry out nearly all of its carefully enumerated duties. A man like Hoover might want to produce statistics that pleased the local authorities, thus enhancing his influence and power.

To avoid such conflicts of interest, many commission members supported the Census Bureau—not the Bureau of Investigation—as the ideal body to gather national crime statistics. Unlike a law enforcement agency, the Census Bureau would have no reason to manipulate crime statistics "as a basis for requesting appropriations or for justifying the existence of or urging expanded powers and equipment for the agency in question," the commission noted. In response, Hoover positioned himself as the defender of the nation's police, outraged on their behalf at the suggestion that they might do such a thing. There was considerable irony in this stance, since Hoover himself had never done much criminal police work, long identifying himself as the antithesis of flat-footed, bumbling patrolmen. As he matured, though, he began to recognize the value of the police constituency, and to promote himself as its Washington advocate.[6]

The strategy succeeded. As Hoover began to talk about assuming control of statistics, he received the backing of the powerful International Association of Chiefs of Police, which had collaborated with him in establishing the Identification Division several years before. He had been showing his appreciation for the group ever since, speaking at annual meetings and cooperating on initiatives of mutual concern. Now their support proved crucial. Before the Wickersham Commission could issue its report, the IACP began working with Hoover to create a national system for compiling crime statistics that would operate under his personal control.[7]

Their actions made the question of who would be in charge of receiving and interpreting the nation's crime statistics a fait accompli. As Hoover and the IACP pointed out to the commission, police officials *wanted* to work with the Bureau and would resist sharing their numbers with any rival agency. Under the circumstances, the rest of Washington had little choice but to go along. In June 1930, Congress passed a bill authorizing the Bureau to collect the statistics, and the president signed the bill into law. A few months later, Hoover issued his first Uniform Crime Report, launching what remains the central clearinghouse for national crime statistics today.[8]

When the Wickersham Commission delivered its final recommendations the following spring, it once again argued for moving authority over crime statistics into the Census Bureau as a way to prevent "serious abuse" and manipulation of the numbers by law enforcement officials. At the same time, the commission acknowledged that it had been outfoxed, and that the Bureau of Investigation was likely to remain in charge of statistics for the immediate future. Their concession hinted at what would soon become one of Hoover's most famous attributes: for the first time, he showed that he could not only control what happened inside the Bureau but also persuade the rest of Washington to do what he wanted.[9]

PERHAPS THE GREATEST DISAPPOINTMENT OF THE WICKERSHAM COMMISSION was how little anybody seemed to care about the final report by the time it was released in 1931. Two years earlier, crime had been the issue of the hour. By the early 1930s, the country's economic collapse was the only thing that mattered. The wallop of the Great Depression came with a precipitous fall in national morale. On January 1, 1930, as Hoover celebrated his thirty-fifth birthday, *The Washington Post* reported that "Business Leaders Face 1930 Confidently." A year later, confidence was harder to muster; "Business Leaders Face 1931 with Courage," the *Post* noted. By the time 1932 rolled around, the best the paper could come up with was the lukewarm assurance that "2 Cabinet Officials Optimistic for 1932."[10]

Within this broader economic crisis, the city of Washington had two things going for it. The first and most important was a stable government payroll of some $175 million, ladled out annually. The second, as one local columnist delicately phrased it, was its status as "a place of personal wealth," populated by men and women willing to fund their own way to live near the seat of power. These attributes meant that the city got along nicely in the first years of the Depression; it saw no major real estate bust, no wave of bank closings, no sharp spike in unemployment. If anything, the Depression brought good times to Washington. As the rest of the nation's economy shrank, the government payroll grew, from 59,800 employees in 1927 to 71,252 by the dawn of 1932. So did the city's physical capacity. Over six years, federal authorities funneled more than $125 million into a downtown beautification and construction program, most of it targeted at providing new homes for government agencies along the National Mall. The jewel of the construction program was Federal Triangle, a massive neoclassical complex on the rise along the demolition-strewn blocks between the White House and the Capitol. The Department of Justice was slated for its own labyrinth at Pennsylvania and Ninth, a move that would place Hoover and his men closer to the center of political power.[11]

Even in prosperous Washington, though, there were thousands of people in need. As early as January 1930, *The Washington Post* described a family of three put out on the street in Hoover's Southeast neighborhood, surrounded by their knockabout furniture. Over the next several years, the city attracted increasing numbers of "transients or drifters," in the *Post*'s description, drawn in by rumors of construction jobs and government handouts. In 1932, the so-called Bonus Expeditionary Force arrived, first a few hundred men, then a few thousand, then women and children, too, setting up camps in abandoned government buildings and along the Potomac. They were seeking an early release of the government bonuses promised to Great War veterans, a modest supplement that might mean the difference between starvation and stability. Instead, they were met with intransigence from the White House, which viewed the Bonus marchers as the vanguard of a dangerous underclass.[12]

In July, in one of the least popular decisions of his increasingly unpopular tenure, the president sent in armed troops who proceeded to set fire to the camps, tear gas the protesters, and drive them out of the city. The smoke from burning pup tents and tin sheeting floated for miles over Washington, reaching even the finest neighborhoods.[13]

AT THE BUREAU, HOOVER DID NOT WORRY MUCH ABOUT THE DEPRESSION, OR about most of the pressing economic and political questions of the day. He was enjoying his job and taking pleasure in the perks that came with it. Even as much of the country retreated into stunned silence, Hoover was establishing a vibrant social life for the first time in his adult existence. During his earliest years as director, he had been too overwhelmed to do much beyond go to work and come home, with perhaps a Masonic meeting or fraternity dinner in between. In subsequent decades, he would be too famous—and too aware of public scrutiny—to move freely within Washington's gossipy, high-stakes social scene. The early Depression years were unique in Hoover's life, the one moment in which he felt secure professionally but had not fully entered the public eye. He was content in a way he had not been since his days at Kappa Alpha, and in a way that he would never quite experience again.

The Bureau itself became his prime social outlet, the center of a busy calendar that included frequent trips, dances, and sporting events. During the early 1930s, Hoover traveled often with Bureau subordinates, combining business trips with outings to national parks and afternoons on the links. He also began to sponsor athletic teams and celebratory balls for his employees, attending them devotedly as both a boss and participant. His plans reflected a trend toward "welfare capitalism," in which company-sponsored leisure activities were thought to substitute for higher wages or unionization. While Hoover was busy changing the Bureau, the Bureau was changing him, too, making him more worldly and thoughtful, less the precocious youngster and somewhat more the seasoned boss. As director, he took on pressures and obligations, but he also gained rare opportunities for adventure and for expanding the scope of his personal experience. Chief among these was the chance to travel and see the country—to move beyond the Washington radius where he had been born, attended school, and spent the first decade of his professional career.

His work took him all over the country: to Yellowstone and Seattle and Los Angeles, to Florida, Duluth, Chicago, and Detroit. The trips had great personal meaning, encounters with the wild and expansive nation he had been assigned to police. After a visit to Glacier National Park, he wrote to Stone of the landscape's mystical grandeur. "I think the ruggedness of it and its isolation cannot be equaled by any one of our great National Parks. Particularly does it appeal, I believe, to one around Washington, because there one can really commune with Nature." For an urban boy, raised in the cobblestone gray of Washington, America's open spaces and wide peaks were a marvel.[14]

Still, Washington was home. When Herbert Hoover entered the White House, newspapers had started to joke about the growing number of Hoovers in government service, from the White House doorkeeper "Ike" Hoover to Edgar's older brother, Dick (now inspector general of the Steamboat Inspection Service), to Hoover himself. As the Depression wore on, bearing the president's name became less amusing. By 1932, nearly every symptom of Depression suffering bore the Hoover moniker. Shantytowns were "Hoovervilles"; empty, turned-out pockets were "Hoover flags"; dead jackrabbits, shot by starving farmers, were "Hoover hogs." At one congressional hearing, Hoover the Bureau director was forced to explain that the headline "Hoover Declares War on Workers" referred to the man in the White House, not to himself. Indeed, he expressed a certain amount of sympathy for men struggling to find jobs. "The unemployment situation in the United States is one of the reasons for some of the crime committed today," he wrote to the Wickersham Commission, summarizing the views of a fellow law enforcement official.[15]

Outside of direct questioning, though, Hoover offered few opinions on the country's perilous economic situation. With no serious financial worries, he could indulge in pastimes that had been off-limits in his younger, more frugal years. He had always enjoyed antiques, with an eye for Chinese bronzes. Now he began to haunt the city's auction houses, where he became known as "Mr. H." He dined out frequently as well, usually lunch at the Mayflower Hotel, followed by dinner at the famed Harvey's Restaurant. Both establishments were pillars of Washington society, relatively untouched by the Depression's poverty and despair. Hoover did not move in the most elite Washington circles, but he was on the edges of them, part of the prosperous strata of mid-level government employees with enough spare cash to keep the city's restaurants, hotels, and theaters afloat.[16]

With him on such occasions was a rotating cast of Bureau executives, encouraged by unwritten rules to join the same clubs, eat at the same restaurants, and participate in the same social activities as their boss. The Bureau itself also provided a range of social outlets. In 1926, Hoover helped to create a Masonic lodge affiliated with the Justice Department, with himself as master. Five years later, he created a Bureau athletic league "to promote and encourage athletics as a means to better health, to stimulate fair play, and to create a better understanding of each other." To run the league, Hoover appointed GW graduate Stan Tracy, who had helped to coordinate athletic activities on campus. By the mid-1930s four out of five Bureau employees were participating in the league, with swimming the most popular sport, followed by horseback riding and baseball. Their victories and failures were dutifully reported in two Bureau newsletters, the weekly *Reporter*, dedicated to sports updates, and the monthly *Investigator*, designed "to enhance the mission of the FBI and to boost morale by showing cohesiveness of employees working as a team."[17]

Hoover built an entire social world around such events, going from baseball games to Masonic meetings like a young Bureau grandee. That this intensity of commitment blurred the lines between professional and private conduct seemed to be of little concern to anyone. Throughout his life, Hoover remained blind to the coercive nature of his social relationships, in which he inevitably occupied a position of power. Or perhaps he simply liked it that way. For a man who sought control in many aspects of his life, combining the roles of friend and subordinate may have brought a measure of comfort.

Eventually, this pattern would leave Hoover with a yes-men problem, his employees obsequious and desperate to anticipate his personal whims. During these early years, though, the blend of social and professional duties seems to have created a sense of camaraderie not unlike what he had experienced at Kappa Alpha. Outside of the identification and statistics divisions, there were just seventy-six employees at Bureau headquarters in 1932. Each one knew Hoover personally.[18]

HOOVER WAS ABLE TO BUILD SUCH A HOMOGENEOUS, TIGHT-KNIT CORPS PARTLY due to a quirk of federal policy: Bureau agents did not fall under civil service regulation. Their exemption was a product of happenstance rather than policy design, but the oversight benefited Hoover immensely. Under civil service rules, he would have been required to accept any employee who passed certain tests and met certain requirements. Without civil service requirements, he could pick and choose the men he wanted, hiring and firing them at will, just as Herbert Putnam had done at the Library of Congress. The exemption gave Hoover unique power over his employees, and it was one of the great secrets of his success—the procedural oversight that allowed his Bureau, in contrast to so many other agencies, to acquire its distinctive identity.

Hoover lavished attention on personnel policies during his first decade as director. In December 1929, during his annual appropriations testimony, he described in detail an agent's hiring and training, implying that his own high standards outdid anything dreamed of by the civil service. He did not mention his unofficial favoritism: the GW degree, the fraternity background he liked his agents to have. Instead, he emphasized the Bureau's superiority to other government agencies in nearly every aspect of its professional screening. Bureau employees "are not appointed under civil service," he noted. Rather, they were chosen for their educational qualifications and then subjected to a battery of social and technical tests, including a written exam, screenings for "proper personality" and "proper personal appearance," and a full physical workup. If approved, the agent hired on for a six-week training school, another exam, and finally a two-month probationary period. "If his services are satisfactory," Hoover concluded, "he receives a permanent assignment in the field service."

Hoover's testimony was partly defensive. In the late 1920s, Congress passed the Welch Bill, which attempted to restructure the pay system of federal agencies. Rumors suggested that a more uniform imposition of civil service rules might be next, folding

Hoover's men into the system. Seeking to head off this possibility, Hoover pointed out that his agents already adhered to prohibitions on political advocacy, and that he rejected all pressure by politicians to hire hacks and favored sons. If anything, he insisted that civil service standards were too lenient for his taste. Bureau men were professionals, as one Justice employee noted in a 1928 memo, engaged in "highly specialized" and "unique" work that "defies classification." They could not possibly be drawn from a pool that also fed the Labor, Commerce, and Agriculture Departments.[19]

There were two problems with this claim. First, other agencies operated under civil service regulation and did just fine. Second, an entire section of the Bureau, Hoover's prized Identification Division, already worked under civil service rules as well. Hoover often lauded the division as a paragon of efficiency—"the most vitally necessary organization for law enforcement in this country to-day," as he informed the Appropriations Committee in February 1931. When it came to the civil service question, though, he regularly bemoaned identification employees' incompetence and lack of professional demeanor. A month after praising the division before Congress, he ordered Bureau officials to draw up a list of problems they had encountered at the hands of their own civil service employees.[20]

As he had with crime statistics, Hoover ultimately prevailed. Despite the rumors, he kept his agents under his control, while the identification clerks continued to operate under the civil service. Some agents cited Hoover's direct authority as a source of loyalty and esprit de corps. He "handled, or approved, all appointments originally and they knew that," Clegg recalled. "He, consequently, was rewarded by a very faithful service, and hard work and successful work." Others saw something less benevolent in Hoover's exercise of internal discretion. "If you have any backbone or independence and do not fit into the so-called 'Super Efficiency' machine . . . you are given the boot," one critic complained in 1933. "The director could not be the petty tsar and get away with these injustices if there was a court of appeals or if his men were under the Civil Service."[21]

HOOVER'S HOMAGE TO SCIENCE AND PROFESSIONALISM WAS NOT ALL TALK. AS he gained confidence, he began to accelerate the development of programs based on these principles, hoping to give the Bureau a clear role to play within the president's anti-crime agenda. The Identification Division and the crime statistics program had set the template: both required technical expertise and enabled the Bureau to coordinate the work of local police departments. In 1932, Hoover introduced two other projects that fit this model.

The first was a publication known as "Fugitives Wanted by Police," launched in the fall of 1932. As the title suggested, the earliest issues focused narrowly on escaped prisoners and other fugitives from justice, providing police across the country with profiles and fingerprints through which they might assist each other in apprehension. With the increasing number of automobiles, fugitives could more easily cross from one municipality into another to avoid detection. Hoover's proposed solution was to make information about their crimes and identities more widely available. In its earliest incarnations, the top-secret publication went out only to chiefs of police. Over time, though, Hoover began to use the magazine to convey other forms of technical information: how to dust for the most detailed fingerprints, how to handle explosives. In 1935, the publication acquired a new name—a general *Law Enforcement Bulletin*, no longer restricted to fugitives, now Hoover's house organ for communicating with local police.[22]

The second initiative was more ambitious. In 1932, during the worst months of the Great Depression, Hoover set out to create the world's most spectacular forensic laboratory, and despite his limited budget he invested heavily. The equipment alone necessitated a major appropriation. The lab needed ultraviolet lamps, specialized cameras, and at least three different kinds of microscope. It also required moulage facilities, where agents could reconstruct "parts of the human body," especially wounds and missing limbs, in cast form. Hoover aspired to build the nation's most extensive collection of bullets, guns, cartridges, typewriters, tire treads, and paper watermarks, to assist local police in identifying scattered bits of evidence. He approved equipment for hair and fiber analysis, as well as a "chemical apparatus for the examination of blood stains." He provided these high-skill services free of charge to local police departments, who sent in evidence for testing just as they submitted criminal statistics and fingerprints. To run the facility, he appointed Charles Appel, a thirty-seven-year-old college graduate and Washington, D.C., native.[23]

WHILE HOOVER EMBRACED CERTAIN NEW DUTIES IN THE EARLY 1930S, HE avoided many more, and these choices, too, mattered for the Bureau's future. Asked before a congressional committee about the ethics of wiretapping, Hoover swore that the Bureau had never engaged such "unethical" methods. Asked by the president to investigate the Bonus Army debacle, he did his best to limit the Bureau's role to checking fingerprints and passing along left-leaning pamphlets. Asked by another congressional committee about the activities of the Communist Party, he spoke at length about the party's "dangerous" revolutionary outlook but insisted that "since 1924 to date there has been no investigation conducted by the Department of Justice of communistic activities."[24]

He also played little initial role in 1932's most sensational and heavily publicized crime: the kidnapping of aviator Charles Lindbergh's twenty-month-old baby boy. In the case's early weeks, as the frantic family assembled the fifty-thousand-dollar ransom and begged for their son's return, the Bureau tested fingerprints and circulated state police circulars but remained far from the center of action. As in many high-profile crimes, Hoover pointed to a lack of jurisdiction. He could provide advice and coordination and technical support but he was not in charge.[25]

Only after New Jersey authorities located the baby's body—mostly decomposed, left to rot in a shallow grave a few miles from the Lindbergh estate—did he begin to develop a more active role. The New Jersey and New York police would always be the lead agencies, the ones who hunted down clues, conducted most of the interviews, and performed the grunt work. But by late spring of 1932 the public demand to find the kidnapper was too great for the federal authorities to ignore. On May 13, the day after the baby's body was found, President Hoover instructed the Bureau to serve as a clearinghouse for federal efforts concerning the case—"the first time such a drastic move has been made except in time of war," in *The Evening Star*'s overblown description. The following month, Congress went still further, voting to make interstate kidnapping a federal crime. The law was a logical outcome of the president's commitment to bringing the federal government into the battle against crime. It also marked the start of a disturbing new era at the Bureau, and the end of Hoover's Depression idyll.[26]

CHAPTER 13

Chairman of the Moral Uplift Squad

(1927–1932)

Hoover (right) with agent Melvin Purvis around 1934. Their surviving correspondence allows unique glimpses of Hoover's inner life and sexual attitudes.

NATIONAL ARCHIVES AND RECORDS ADMINISTRATION

One other feature of Hoover's life became more noticeable as he settled into the comfortable patterns of adulthood. Now well into his thirties, he still showed no interest in women and no signs of getting married. In his younger years, his single status had been unremarkable, easily explained by the need to buckle down and make a living. Then, too, it was perfectly ordinary for young men to spend their time with each other, passing seamlessly from the cadet corps to the fraternity to the University Club and the Masons. The structure of American manhood often separated men from women, providing clubs, fraternities, offices, saloons—even entire professions—where they could hold themselves apart from female influence. Still, at a certain point men were supposed to step forward, propose marriage, and begin a family. By the early 1930s, Hoover was the proper age, earning a decent salary, with no serious obligations or debts beyond the care of his aging mother. Getting married was the next obvious thing.

Other Bureau men understood this imperative, peeling off one by one from Hoover's social circle to assume the trappings of married life. Frank Baughman—the Kappa Alpha brother who had seen Hoover through so much of college and the early Justice years—married in 1932, with Hoover by his side as best man. Hoover, by contrast, grew increasingly removed from the entire prospect of marriage. He expressed little interest in women either inside or outside of the Bureau, where he spent the vast majority of his time. Though only men could be appointed as agents, the Bureau employed its fair share of young women: clerks and secretaries hired to file reports, take dictation, and identify fingerprints. The most important of these was Helen Gandy, who had stayed with Hoover after his promotion to director, and who continued to take his calls, greet his visitors, and keep track of his confidential files. Gandy remained single, even as other women at the Bureau married and moved on from paying work. Hoover did not prohibit dating between male and female employees. His own social outings and expressions of intimacy nonetheless occurred almost exclusively with other men.[1]

Americans had a name for this sort of figure: he was a "bachelor," a label that would be applied to Hoover repeatedly as he aged into definitive single status. The bachelor was an established type in the early twentieth century, when the rise of office jobs and city living meant that more men could entertain the possibility of a single life. Hoover's domestic arrangements fit one of the best-known stereotypes: that of the bachelor who lived at home in order to care for his widowed mother. But there were other, less virtuous forms of life associated with bachelorhood as well. According to conventional wisdom, bachelors came in a variety of suspect variations: playboys and bon vivants; weak-willed or degenerate "sissies"; career men too serious to tolerate feminine flightiness; nebbishes too awkward to relax in female company.[2]

Hoover was certainly a career man. "He married the Bureau of Investigation," admirers would later explain. The women around him saw something else, an inability to forge deep emotional relationships of any sort at all. His niece Margaret acknowledged that his devotion to work left little time or patience for dating. "I think he regarded women as a kind of hindrance," she said. "You know, they sort of got in your way when you were going places." At the same time, she argued, he was trapped by a larger failing, an abiding "fear of becoming too personally involved with people." Doris Rogers, who joined the Bureau's Chicago office as a secretary in the early 1930s, saw a similar insecurity. "The perception of Hoover at the Bureau was that he was not a whole person. He needed someone else to buoy him. That was why he always had to have a man follow him around."[3]

These ideas fit with the reigning stereotypes of bachelorhood, alternately seen as a benign social phenomenon and a deep cultural threat. Today, another explanation seems far more obvious: Hoover had settled into adulthood as a gay man—perfectly capable of intimacy and sex, just not with women. As during his college years, the contours of Hoover's social life in the early 1930s fit with this proposition. If anything, it is the most straightforward explanation for the life he chose. Few people reach their midthirties without having some sort of sexual experience. While we have no detailed record of what transpired behind closed doors, it seems safe to say that Hoover was not having sex with women.

But merely applying a label does not get us very far toward understanding his interior life—how he himself thought about his most intimate relationships. The fact is that we know very little about Hoover's innermost thoughts and feelings on the subjects of sexuality and desire. There is one great exception, however—an extraordinary cache of letters between Hoover and Bureau agent Melvin Purvis, one of Hoover's closest friends and ultimately one of the most famous Bureau employees of the 1930s. It was Purvis who saved the letters, providing a rare glimpse into his boss's personal longings and foibles. Hoover was by turns funny, tender, solicitous, and flirtatious in his correspondence with Purvis. He could also be stern and sometimes punitive. He lavished attention on Purvis's physical attributes: the agent's fine features, his swooning effect on women, a certain insouciance that made Purvis, in Hoover's view, one of "the Clark Gables of the service." At the same time, he insisted that Purvis reply promptly to all his letters, address him by his nickname, even acquire films and antiques on his behalf.[4]

His banter with Purvis presented one of the few documented instances in which Hoover was willing to laugh at himself. "Of course my interest is solely as a censor or as Chairman of the Moral Uplift Squad," he joked upon receiving a set of films he had requested, apparently some sort of erotic footage distributed by the Tru-Vue company. He also used humor to mask more overt admiration. "It was some night + I am still looking forward to you producing a set," he wrote after viewing the films, thanking Purvis for his "sassy note" and suggesting that the agent create his own erotic oeuvre. The correspondence contains nothing that would reveal a sexual relationship between the two men. But their emotions and flirtations went beyond the ordinary run of club-and-work friendship. The Purvis letters show that Hoover actively sought out the affections of other Bureau men, and used his position as director to push the boundaries of his relationships.[5]

BEFORE HE WAS A BUREAU AGENT, PURVIS WAS A MODEL SOUTHERN BOY, A SON of middling privilege in low-country South Carolina. Born in 1903 in Timmonsville, a segregated tobacco town, he followed a Hooveresque path, serving as captain of his high school cadet corps and later joining Kappa Alpha. After studying law, he accepted a position with the only decent firm in the region, but earned no salary and racked up only limited fees. His employers "doubted that Applicant would make any great success in the practice of law as he was not aggressive enough in going after the dollars," one Bureau report noted of Purvis's lackluster law career. After twenty months of frustration, Purvis applied for a job at the State Department but received a prompt rejection. His congressman suggested that Purvis apply to the Bureau, where young, legally trained Kappa Alphas were in short supply but great demand.[6]

Purvis was just twenty-three years old when he applied, two years shy of Hoover's minimum for agents. And it showed. Slight and boyish, with a teenager's cautious gait and self-conscious smile, Purvis could easily be mistaken for a college student. During their first interview, Nathan found him absurdly young and naive, "pretty much like a kid." He doubted Purvis's tales of global travel and sophistication ("probably all over the state of South Carolina"). But Nathan thought him pleasant and healthy enough, if not, according to his legal colleagues, "exceptionally brilliant," and decided to hire him.[7]

Like all new agents, Purvis was required to move anywhere in the country without complaint. A week after signing on, he found himself in Dallas, where he set to work studying the Bureau manual and running down auto thefts. From there, he moved on to various other field offices, including New York, Cincinnati, Butte, and Chicago. He traveled between postings with an entourage: not only his Black "valet," who worked as maid, chauffeur, and butler, but also his palomino mare. Even his means of transportation was fabulous, an eight-cylinder Pierce-Arrow automobile that could outrun all but the most fortified government vehicles. He presented himself as a man of style, even if neither his salary nor his age had yet grown to meet his aristocratic tastes.[8]

Perhaps it was this personal flair that caught Hoover's eye. By late 1927, less than a year into Purvis's career, Hoover ordered the twenty-four-year-old back to Washington to be groomed for executive assignment. Bureau supervisors recognized Purvis's personal charm and rock-solid loyalty, but they noted several troubling qualities that seemed to mesh uneasily with Hoover's hierarchical culture. Purvis often showed up late—just a minute or two, but enough to earn official censure. According to one supervisor, he also suffered from "being over-confident," a Napoleonic trait perhaps intended to make up for his slight stature, reedy voice, and relative youth. Purvis was not the sort of boy who had been held up to Hoover during childhood as the masculine ideal. Nor did he live up to Hoover's recent vision of the model Bureau agent. "He is not the rugged type who impressed one as being a forceful character," one report noted.[9]

Purvis compensated for his lack of vigor, another supervisor observed, with inflated self-regard. "In my opinion, this agent has one major fault, the existence of which he is aware, and which he is striving to correct. It is, that he is possessed of great confidence in himself." His trajectory at the Bureau seemed designed to slow him down. In contrast to the rocketing careers of favorites like Tolson and Clegg, Purvis lagged in the lower ranks for his first few years. Throughout that period, he knew Hoover mostly as other agents did: as an inspiring but mercurial, punitive, and highly disciplined boss.

Their main form of communication was the Bureau memo, in which Hoover reminded Purvis "to take immediate steps to see that my orders . . . are carried out at once" and came down hard if and when he failed to do so.[10]

Like most savvy agents, Purvis knew how to soothe Hoover in such circumstances. "I am not unmindful of my responsibility in connection with matters of this nature," he wrote in April 1929, apologizing for submitting a late expense voucher. "I assure you that every effort will be put forth to see that no derelictions of this nature occur in the future." It also appears to be Purvis, not Hoover, who made the first move to introduce a more intimate note into their relationship. In late 1929, he asked to consult with Hoover "about matters of a personal nature." Hoover responded positively, inviting Purvis for a one-on-one meeting in Washington. Precisely what they discussed during that meeting remains unclear, but Purvis returned to his field office pleased and relieved. In early January 1930, he sent Hoover a decorous but enthusiastic letter of thanks for listening to his travails.[11]

His Bureau career soon began to take off. Not long after his conference with Hoover, he received a small but significant raise, followed by a transfer to the Cincinnati office. After that, the largesse came regularly, including several more raises and a rare week of vacation in October. Finally, in November, he received yet another raise and a major promotion to special agent in charge at Cincinnati. The posting made him, at the age of twenty-seven, the youngest man ever known to have led a Bureau field office. It also launched a far more intimate, if never entirely transparent, phase of his relationship with Hoover.[12]

THE CHANGE APPEARS TO HAVE STARTED IN FEBRUARY 1931, WHEN HOOVER arrived in Cincinnati to deliver a speech before the local Lawyers Club. Despite the importance Hoover attached to proper facilities, the Cincinnati field office was just one big room, with twelve identical wooden desks for the agents and a handful more for the stenographers and accountants. Hoover did not conduct a full inspection. Instead, he delivered his speech, praising the GW professors who taught him about the law and boasting about his early triumph over Emma Goldman. Other than that, he spent his time talking with Purvis about relations with the area's U.S. attorney, who was under investigation. The conversation apparently veered into more private terrain as well, perhaps a rehashing of the "personal" matters that Purvis had introduced the previous year.[13]

When he returned to Washington, Hoover adopted a tone rarely seen in his official correspondence with other agents. In his initial letter, he sent instructions to avoid involvement in the local scandal, but then he sought an update on Purvis's romantic life. "I am still holding my breath waiting your announcement of embarkation upon the matrimonial sea," Hoover wrote. "If I hold it much longer I am going to die from exhaustion so please relieve the strain and let me know what you are planning to do, are doing or have done about this all momentous problem."[14]

Nothing in the letter explicitly indicates anything other than fraternity-style teasing, one Kappa Alpha ribbing another. And yet the urgent, even gushing tone—"I am going to *die* from exhaustion"—suggests something more personal. Hoover's expressions give the correspondence an almost juvenile aspect, as if he were inquiring about the status of his schoolboy crush. Purvis played along. He quickly wrote back to assure Hoover, "I have not done anything about it and right now I am not doing anything. It has been postponed indefinitely, and may yet receive the pocket veto." He addressed the letter to "Mr. Hoover" (Hoover had written to "Melvin"), an indication that Bureau hierarchy held sway even as the two men began making plans to see each other outside of official auspices.[15]

Purvis's rejection of marriage (at least for the moment) did not end the conversation about his romantic life. If anything, it piqued Hoover's interest. On March 16, four days after receiving Purvis's letter, Hoover responded that he was both "interested and amused" by the sudden change of heart. He sought more detail about Purvis's reasoning and priorities on the marital front. "I don't know which saying applies to you in connection with this matter," he wrote, "that is to say 'Faint heart never won fair lady' or 'Soft in love, soft in head'." Over the next few weeks, these sayings became the basis for an elaborate but cryptic exchange that danced around questions of marriage, desire, and perhaps even sexual orientation. On March 20, Purvis noted that "those sayings you mentioned recently do not apply to me. There may be a saying, though that does apply." Hoover, further intrigued, wrote back three days later. "Your Postscript starts me guessing again," he informed Purvis. "I would like to know what saying you had in mind so I can properly catalogue you."[16]

How to catalog him, indeed. Their banter is elusive, the precise nature of their mutual interest in such matters obscured beneath layers of propriety and evasive code. Though these early letters still mostly concerned Bureau business, none of them were placed in Purvis's official Bureau file, an indication that Hoover considered them to be personal correspondence. In one letter, Hoover admitted to Purvis that he had trouble expressing affection: "Usually when I am greatly moved I become tongue-tied and cannot express my sentiments." But he did just fine in these letters, showing concern and caring if never explicitly addressing what their evolving relationship meant. Ten years Purvis's senior, Hoover adopted a solicitous, almost fatherly tone, inquiring after the young agent's health, urging him to get more sleep, even insisting that he take a day or two off. "To be at the office all day and all night is a thing that you cannot stand," he wrote, contradicting the perception that he wanted every agent working at every moment.[17]

For professionals who claimed to work at all hours, the two men spent a surprising amount of time discussing domestic affairs, from ear infections to the collection of music boxes. Both adored their pets. "I do not know of anything that has given me more pleasure and happiness than my own dog and I know exactly what the puppy will mean to you," Hoover wrote in 1932, celebrating Purvis's acquisition of a rambunctious fox terrier. Purvis also shared Hoover's love of antiques, trading tips about the best stores in cities where the Bureau maintained a significant presence. In June 1931, Hoover sent Purvis the catalog for Mermod & Co., one of his favorite New York shops. Beyond catalogs, they often traded gifts, some mildly illicit in nature. "You have my curiosity aroused as to the package which you have been deliberating sending me," Hoover wrote to Purvis in September 1932. "I am somewhat concerned as to whether it would be safe for my secretary to open it. You better indicate that when you send it forward."[18]

It is difficult to say what Purvis thought of this burgeoning intimacy with his boss. At moments, he appears to encourage Hoover, returning wink for wink, joke for joke. At other times, he seems awkward and self-conscious, unsure about the line between professional and personal relations. Nowhere was this more notable than in his back-and-forth with Hoover about how to address his letters. In official mail, there was no question: Hoover was "Mr. Hoover" or "The Director"; Purvis was "Mr. Purvis" or "Sir." For their private correspondence, read only by the two of them, Hoover found such titles too constraining. In October 1931, he began urging Purvis to make his notes "less formal and stop using 'MISTER.'"[19]

Purvis responded with confusion and nervousness about this shift in protocol. "How am I to address you if I am not to use the 'MISTER.'?" he wanted to know. He experimented with "Chairman" as a possible substitute. Hoover merely took the title as a chance to push further. "'Chairman'—of what, I don't know, unless it is the Moral Uplift Squad," he joked, repeating one of his favorite phrases. Purvis's "Chairman" reference may have been an inside joke, since he noted that Hoover was truly the "ex-chairman" of the squad, a man hopelessly fallen from grace. The teasing captured something rarely revealed in Hoover's official correspondence: an admission that his position of rectitude and squeaky-clean public morality was partly a false front.[20]

They experimented with "Mel" and "Jayee," one of Hoover's many nicknames among friends. On occasion, though, Purvis reverted to the slightly more formal "JEH," which became Hoover's sometime signature as well. When a newspaper mistakenly referred to Purvis as the Bureau's director, Hoover briefly took to calling him "director," noting in jest that the Washington office could use another set of eyes and ears. "On the other hand, I am, as I have said, somewhat concerned because of your well-known proclivities along certain lines," he added. "I fear that my good reputation as Chairman of the Moral Uplift Squad may become seriously affected by reason of confusing your activities with those of mine, the latter always being above any reproach." He was referring to Purvis's reputation as a ladies' man, but the question of their respective "proclivities" continued to weave through their correspondence.[21]

Of all their shared interests, few received as much attention as the topic of women—specifically, of Purvis's alleged prowess with and swooning effect upon members of the opposite sex. Hoover spent pages extolling Purvis's physical beauty and magnetic powers of attraction, as well as his heartlessness toward his legions of female admirers. Much of his writing focused on Purvis's alleged romances with Helen Gandy and the other Bureau secretaries, though there is no evidence that Purvis actually dated or took much interest in the agency "girls." When Purvis sent along a photo of himself, Hoover complained that Gandy stopped working and spent the afternoon "floating around in the air," gushing about "how 'SWEET' you look." A year and a half later, after sending another photo, Purvis learned that "Miss Gandy has been practically useless since its arrival and has now asked for several days' leave in order to fully recuperate from the debilitating effects of viewing your sheik-like appearance." On yet another occasion, Purvis received a note over Hoover's signature praising the mysterious "power" of a recent photograph. In the postscript, Hoover claimed, "The fact Mel is that Miss Gandy actually prepared this letter."[22]

It is possible that Gandy was romantically interested in Purvis, and that she openly shared this information with her boss. It seems as likely that she served as a stand-in for Hoover's own difficult-to-express affections. Hoover was not above using his position as Bureau director to promote the alleged romance between Gandy and Purvis, bringing Purvis to Washington for official business but also, as one letter noted, "just to take a look at you." In the fall of 1932, he went so far as to order Purvis to escort Gandy to the Bureau's Halloween masquerade ball. For weeks before the ball, both Purvis and Gandy were subject to widespread mockery around the office, with Hoover joking that "Miss Gandy has promised she will wear a cellophane gown." That prospect, in turn, fueled widespread comment among Bureau executives. Harold Nathan composed a poem on the subject. To Purvis himself, Nathan issued a direct order: "Please don't apply a match to her cellophane garment."[23]

For all the joking, Hoover's heightened attention to Purvis's private life had the potential to turn serious and even threatening. They were friends and intimates, but Hoover was still the boss, able to exact punishment if things did not go his way. Purvis clearly feared this prospect, responding swiftly at the merest hint of displeasure or misunderstanding. On one occasion, his secretary mistakenly noted on a personnel form that Purvis was now "married" rather than "single." Hoover's reply, delivered just days later, demanded to know why Purvis had not notified the Bureau of his sudden change in status. Alarmed, Purvis wrote back to assure Hoover that he had no desire to get married: "In fact, I doubt my ability to even get married." His secretary, he added, had made the mistake due to a terrible headache.[24]

Hoover, apparently mollified, noted that the confusion had given him "an awful headache" as well, then returned to his standard teasing about Purvis's sexual escapades. "Everyone seems to pretty well have your number so that there is little use of your trying now to cover up the situation," he wrote. "My advice to you, however, is that you watch your step and not be guilty of committing bigamy."[25]

What was Purvis's "number"? It is possible that Hoover himself never quite knew. Perhaps Purvis felt genuine affection, even desire, for Hoover. Or perhaps he was simply making his best guess about what his boss wanted to hear. Whatever else he may have thought or felt, Purvis had mastered the one skill that assured Bureau success: pleasing J. Edgar Hoover.

WHAT WAS BEING NEGOTIATED IN THEIR CORRESPONDENCE WAS NOT JUST A friendship or even a romance. It was also a power relationship, a question of how far Hoover could push and how far Purvis might push back. Desire and affection, humor and concern—all of these were present and, presumably, genuine. But they were never far removed from the knowledge that Hoover was Purvis's boss, and that he could enforce his will through Bureau policy. If Hoover had one great personal failing, it was perhaps not his inability to love, but his inability to establish relationships outside of formal and controlling hierarchies.

Hoover's fondness for Purvis enhanced the young agent's career. Whether or not it served the Bureau is another question. As they grew closer, Hoover accelerated Purvis's rise through the ranks, offering extra trips to Washington, holding out plum jobs in return for an affectionate letter, or as a reward for a moment of charm. This was not special treatment, exactly. It was simply how the Bureau worked, with Hoover's personal and professional interests enmeshed. Along the way, he often ignored the warnings of other Bureau executives, who found Purvis capable but still overconfident and too green for a leadership position.

There is no mistaking the fact that Purvis's career took off only after he began the more personal phase of his correspondence with Hoover. In the spring of 1931, as they traded jokes about their marital hesitations, "Mr. Hoover" informed "Mr. Purvis" in a formal Bureau notice that he was being transferred to Washington, D.C. Hoover may have been trying to bring Purvis more tightly into his personal orbit. If so, the effort largely failed. Purvis spent the spring and summer of 1931 as head of the Washington field office, but the time did not go well. Accustomed to the more laid-back atmosphere of distant field offices, Purvis paid insufficient attention to storeroom supplies, press etiquette, and other oft-scrutinized Bureau policies.

His track record did not improve after a transfer in August to run the fingerprint division. It was a laughably bad choice, playing to all of Purvis's weaknesses and none of his strengths. In September, Hoover reprimanded Purvis for smoking cigarettes inside the division building, professing to be "amazed" at the indiscretion. Less than a month later, he transferred Purvis to the Bureau's most rough-and-tumble field office: Oklahoma City. Hoover often used Oklahoma as a proving ground. "What we usually do is to send a new man to Oklahoma, where things are still in the raw," he explained in 1926. "If he's got any yellow about him, it will come out and we get rid of him. But if he's got the courage and the determination and isn't afraid to work hard, he won't have to stay there long."[26]

Purvis made it through. But he was lonely throughout, writing mournful letters to Hoover describing his isolation and his determination to succeed at Bureau business. The two men did not see each other much during 1932, though Hoover warned, "I may surprise you some of these days and give you a ring at your apartment." Meanwhile their correspondence continued to deepen, as did Hoover's faith in his young agent. One sign of this trust was Purvis's transfer, after only four months, to head the field office in Birmingham, Alabama—relief from his Oklahoma banishment and a post closer to his heart and upbringing. Even more significant was an increase in "special" assignments channeled to Purvis outside of official Bureau procedures. These were personal favors for Hoover, negotiated in private letters rather than in official Bureau memos. By the summer of 1932, even as he rhapsodized about Gandy's affections and "cellophane gown," Hoover began to rely on Purvis to carry out a variety of secret tasks. "There is a very confidential matter that I may call you to Washington to take care of for me shortly," Hoover wrote in July, as Purvis settled in at Birmingham. "There is certain information which I want to either prove or disprove and I believe that you possibly are the only one who could handle it for me if you are willing to do so."[27]

The letter did not indicate what that "certain information" might be. Purvis, however, was eager to help out. "I sincerely hope that you will let me handle that matter for you because I will be more than glad to do it," he wrote. It was both the reassurance of a friend and the plea of a supplicant in exile. And it seemed to work. Other Bureau executives continued to question Purvis's temperament and leadership abilities. "He is a little impatient for things to happen," Clegg noted in 1932, even as he praised Purvis's "loyalty." Hoover, though, had already made up his mind to give Purvis the biggest reward yet. In October 1932, he appointed Purvis special agent in charge at Chicago, one of the Bureau's largest and most important field offices.[28]

Looking back, Purvis remembered his journey north to Chicago as a time of triumph and promise—a validation of all that he had accomplished during his first five years at the Bureau. "The date of my appointment as a special agent in charge of the Bureau of Investigation in Chicago coincides roughly with the beginning of the federal government's intensive war on crime," he would write in his autobiography. "Hell started popping immediately."[29]

CHAPTER 14

Government Men

(1933)

President Franklin Roosevelt signs bills expanding federal law enforcement power, May 18, 1934. Standing, from left: Attorney General Homer Cummings, Hoover, Arizona senator Henry Ashurst, and Assistant Attorney General Joseph Keenan.

NATIONAL ARCHIVES AND RECORDS ADMINISTRATION

In March 1933, not long after Purvis arrived in Chicago, Franklin Delano Roosevelt swept into Washington with his own band of energetic young advisers. Three months later, a vicious crime out of Kansas City drew their attention to issues of crime and law enforcement, Hoover's supposed area of expertise. These two events pushed Hoover out of his comfortable bureaucratic tinkering and into a law enforcement challenge he could never have imagined. After 1933, employees like Purvis were no longer merely gentlemen agents, interested in accounting, science, and law. They also became "G-Men," or "Government Men," symbols of all that federal workers could do and be in Roosevelt's brash new age of government activism.

The legend of the Bureau during this era—of the showdown with John Dillinger and Pretty Boy Floyd, Machine Gun Kelly and the Barker gang—has been told many times. In the mythic version, Hoover is cast as the indispensable man, the one figure without whom none of the epic drama would have occurred. According to that narrative,

Hoover in 1933 emerged as a hero and visionary, facing down the worst America had to offer. To outsiders, keen to debunk this triumphal image, he has often looked more like an opportunist and manipulator.[1]

Both of these stories rest on flawed assumptions: that Hoover intended this transformation to happen, that he sought his crime-fighting power eagerly, that he experienced the early New Deal as a period of triumph and fulfillment. The truth is that Hoover was nervous about getting involved in the problem of violent crime, and about managing such duties within a Democratic administration. Only when federal involvement became unavoidable did he send his agents into the fray against gangsters armed with machine guns, stolen cars, and bulletproof vests. Even then, it was with trepidation and a deep awareness of how little any of them knew about what to do. To Hoover's grief, some of his men learned the hard way what it meant to fight crime in this new age of federal power. In just seventeen months, between June 1933 and November 1934, four Bureau agents were shot to death, a gut-wrenching loss for such a small and tight-knit agency.

As a result, the Bureau (or the Division of Investigation, as it was temporarily renamed in 1933) became a far more grim and serious place than it had been during the previous decade. Roosevelt's "War on Crime" made the modern FBI, but it also made the Bureau into something Hoover never intended it to be. The high-minded principles he had stood for in the 1920s—restraint and integrity, brains over brawn—proved hard to maintain under the pressures of solving violent, heavily publicized crimes. Bowing to the exigencies of the moment, Hoover's gentleman agents began to act more like ordinary cops: paying off informants, setting up wiretaps, intimidating suspects to obtain dubious confessions—in short, doing many things that Hoover had promised they would never do.

They also became killers. The shootings of arch-criminals such as Dillinger have often been described in heroic terms: a face-off between good and evil, between the law and the outlaw. But for Hoover these moments of triumph came with a difficult and fundamental shift in identity. By the middle of 1934, he was running an organization of lawyers and accountants who had become gunmen. Some of them shot to kill.

FOR MUCH OF THE COUNTRY, ROOSEVELT'S ELECTION CAME AS A WELCOME RE-lief. For Hoover, it presented a problem of the first order. Though he had gotten his start under the Democratic administration of Woodrow Wilson, since 1921 Hoover had labored exclusively within Republican regimes. As a result he was seen as a Republican loyalist, his innate conservatism and emphasis on federal-local cooperation the embodiment of all that the party of the 1920s held dear. Now, for the first time in fourteen years, Democrats controlled the White House as well as both chambers of Congress. Roosevelt promised a clean sweep of Washington's stagnant Republican ranks.

If the partisan landscape looked daunting, Hoover may have seen signs of hope in other aspects of Roosevelt's character. A son of wealth and a former governor of New York, Roosevelt came to office not as an ideologue with fixed ideas but as a man of "direct, vigorous action," as he promised the country in his inaugural address. The president was no stranger to Washington, having served as assistant secretary of the navy (like his fifth cousin, Theodore Roosevelt). He had also encountered his share of tribulation and disappointment, nominated as vice president on the 1920 Democratic ticket only to lose the election and then succumb to polio, a disease that destroyed his ability to walk unaided. Few Americans understood the extent of Roosevelt's disability. Nor did they understand the scale of the federal transformation that they were about to experience. What they saw when they voted for Roosevelt was an optimistic and confident aristocrat, his face lit up by a mischievous grin, cigarette dangling from the end of an impossibly long black filter, promising that government could be used to improve the lot of ordinary Americans.[2]

Hoover believed he could make peace with this way of thinking. Indeed, by certain measures, he already thought that way himself. Despite his fealty to Coolidge-era limits, Hoover maintained a powerful faith in the project of government and in what a well-administered agency, attentive to efficiency and good policy, could accomplish. He also knew how to work with politicians, even as he understood that the Bureau's fate rested in large part on its reputation as an apolitical, professional agency. As part of the Justice Department, the Bureau was already positioned to take advantage of the expansion of executive-branch agencies, bureaus, and departments that would become a hallmark of the New Deal. And Hoover was ready to do what he had done in the past: use his energy and charm to persuade his superiors to keep him on in government when other men were leaving.

The challenge was in the execution. That February, as he prepared for the presidential inauguration, Roosevelt announced the appointment of Montana senator Thomas Walsh as attorney general, a sop to the Democrats' progressive wing but a disastrous choice for Hoover. Walsh had led the Senate inquiries into the Palmer Raids in 1921. Now he made no secret of his plans to fire the Republican holdovers at Justice and replace them with Democrats. First, though, the seventy-three-year-old Walsh dashed off to Havana to seal his wedding vows with a wealthy Cuban widow. On the train back to Washington, he experienced what appeared to be a heart attack, tumbling from his lower berth onto the floor, where his wife found him dead. Hoover met the train at Union Station, his manner stiff and official amid the crush of mourning friends and sympathetic Cuban expats. Then he returned to Bureau headquarters and began to speculate about the attorney general's replacement.[3]

The events following Walsh's death highlighted the single most outstanding feature of Hoover's career: his ability to survive in Washington, outlasting president after president and pleasing both Democrats and Republicans. That this would be the case

was not yet clear in the spring of 1933, however. On March 4, another rainy inauguration day, Hoover gathered Bureau executives around the radio to hear Roosevelt assure Americans that "fear itself" was their greatest enemy. Then he sat back to wait for
his future to be determined. Roosevelt called an emergency session of Congress to
begin on March 9, charged with stanching a flood of bank closings that threatened to
engulf the financial system. To ensure that legislators focused on the task at hand and
not on the scramble of patronage politics, he decided to delay as many as a hundred
thousand appointments. The result, as one adviser later noted, was that the administration began its first hundred days in "hostile territory," encamped within a federal
city still staffed by Republicans. Some of those appointees, including Hoover, would
have to wait for months to learn whether they would have a role to play in the Roosevelt
administration.[4]

Hoover spent that time doing what he had done in 1924, when Harlan Stone was
weighing his appointment, and again in 1930, when the Wickersham Commission
was pondering crime statistics: he mobilized his own supporters. Within the legal profession, Stone, still at the Supreme Court, wrote to Felix Frankfurter, now a key Roosevelt adviser, to certify Hoover's good works and respect for civil liberties. From
Congress, Southern Democrats (the key constituency of Kappa Alpha) sent letters of
support to the president as well. Seeking to repeat his triumph at Wickersham, Hoover
also turned to the International Association of Chiefs of Police, whose members testified to his popularity among law enforcement officials. "It would be very gratifying if
it could be announced . . . that the Honorable J. Edgar Hoover, Director of the Bureau
of Investigation and Identification of the Department of Justice had been retained in
his position," the president of the IACP wrote to the White House in advance of the
group's upcoming convention, praising the "wonderful cooperation" that Hoover had
fostered with local police.[5]

Roosevelt paid little attention, at least initially. During his first hundred days, he
rebuilt the banking system, legalized beer, and transformed the nation's approach to
agricultural policy, unemployment relief, and mortgage financing—fifteen major bills
in all. For Hoover, so far down the ladder of priorities as to be nearly invisible, that
same period brought little activity. The neglect worried him. It also gave his detractors
a chance to enact a mobilization of their own. Even as he marshaled his supporters, his
critics reminded the president of Hoover's rigid personality and inflated sense of importance. They raised questions about his personal life as well. "In relation to J. Edgar
Hoover, will say I have heard some disquieting rumors," one congressman noted in a
letter to the White House, asking to meet personally with the president "to discuss the
matter." If that was a reference to Hoover's sexuality, though, the congressman apparently need not have bothered. Roosevelt had heard the "many rumors of Hoover's homosexuality," according to his son Elliott, but didn't give them much thought. "These

were not grounds for removing him, as Father saw it, so long as his abilities were not impaired."[6]

Far more dangerous were the articles, small in number but alarming in their implications, that noted Hoover's imperfect fit with the buoyant reformers and liberal attorneys of the New Deal. Journalist Ray Tucker would accuse Hoover of using his "boy detectives" to shadow New Deal officials, especially those with the temerity to offer criticism of Hoover's reign. Tucker's article suggested that Hoover did not put much faith in the liberalizing impulses of Roosevelt's so-called Brain Trust, the inner circle of social scientists and law professors who served as the president's closest advisers. "Mr. Hoover, whose first important post was in the 'radical division,' has always been obsessed with a complex against liberals and advanced thinkers," Tucker wrote. Left to his own devices, the article suggested, Hoover would be more likely to investigate Roosevelt's cabinet members than to approve their experiments in social welfare, labor rights, or even criminology.[7]

At another moment, this swirl of innuendo might have inflicted serious damage on the career of a mid-level bureaucrat. Hoover was saved once again not only by his record of accomplishment and network of support, but by events beyond his control. On June 17, as Roosevelt finished out his first hundred days, armed gangsters shot and killed four law enforcement officials in an early-morning gun battle at Kansas City's Union Station. The killers were identified as Vernon C. Miller, "Pretty Boy" Floyd, and Adam Richetti. One of the murdered men was Ray Caffrey, a thirty-one-year-old Nebraska lawyer and Bureau agent.[8]

HOOVER RECEIVED NEWS OF THE MURDERS IN A CRACKLING PHONE CALL TO his emergency line at Seward Square, just after seven o'clock on Saturday morning. "It was a massacre, Mr. Hoover," the Kansas City field office supervisor Reed Vetterli panted into the phone. "Ray Caffrey is dead. Joe Lackey may not pull through. Two Kansas City detectives and the chief of police for McAlester, Oklahoma, were killed. So was Frank Nash." Both Caffrey and Lackey were Bureau agents, assigned to escort the fugitive Nash back to Leavenworth, from which he had escaped while on an errand for the warden three years earlier. Vetterli himself was a recent GW graduate, campus Mormon leader, and fraternity man who had run on the track team along with Tolson. Hoover had promised all three agents a challenging but safe and distinguished job, akin to what they might have found in any law office. Now he told Vetterli to head for the hospital, where doctors could attend to a gunshot wound in the agent's right arm. He dispatched another agent to Caffrey's apartment to inform his wife that her husband had been shot to death in the Union Station parking lot.[9]

Hoover's impulse as he absorbed the news was to think not of the future but of the past. As a model of action—his only model, really—he turned to the 1925 killing of Ed Shanahan by the auto thief Martin Durkin, the one incident during his tenure that had provoked a similar crisis. As in that case, Hoover promised to hunt his agent's murderer to the ends of the earth. But how to do it? And whom to put in charge? Hoover contemplated these questions for five long hours before deciding that his new breed of agent was not quite right for the job. He turned instead to Gus Jones, the San Antonio gunslinger who had led the Durkin manhunt. Jones commandeered an emergency flight and arrived in Kansas City in the middle of the night. Harold Nathan soon followed, dispatched from Washington not as a gunslinger himself, but as Hoover's eyes and ears on the ground. In the meantime, Hoover instructed Vetterli to make the massacre his top priority. "I cannot too strongly emphasize the imperative necessity of concentrating upon this matter, without any let-up in the same until the parties are taken," he wrote. As a sign of his intentions, he acquired two submachine guns for the Kansas City office.[10]

That decision would have important consequences for the Bureau, the first of many shifts away from the genteel white-collar ethic that had dominated Hoover's first decade as director. But Hoover was not sure on June 17 whether he would be with the Bureau another week or several years. That afternoon, as the nation's headlines demanded answers about the massacre at Kansas City, he was not a visionary but a frightened and unsettled man, faced with a violent situation that he was not at all sure his gentleman agents could handle.

IT WAS ATTORNEY GENERAL HOMER CUMMINGS WHO SAW SOMETHING ELSE: A chance to promote federal laws on "gangsterism" and "racketeering," and to define the crime problem as a crisis worthy of the New Deal's energies. Commandeered as a last-minute replacement for the unfortunate Walsh, Cummings had thrown himself into his new job with the same ambition and enthusiasm Hoover had exhibited in his first tenuous months as director. A Yale graduate and former mayor of Stamford, Connecticut, Cummings came across as an eastern patrician: several inches taller than Hoover, with a balding pate and mild, Puritan eyes. In 1920, as temporary head of the Democratic National Committee, he had supported Roosevelt's bid for the vice presidency. A decade later, he was one of the first party men to seize upon Roosevelt as a presidential candidate. When the president-elect learned of Walsh's death, Cummings happened to be right nearby, preparing to head south for the inauguration.[11]

During his early months in office, he followed Roosevelt's lead, hunting down gold hoarders, firing Republican patronage appointees, promising to root out the alleged corruption that had toppled the American financial system. Included in this lineup was the final, gasping end of Prohibition, given Roosevelt's imprimatur in March and expected to be ratified by the states forthwith. To prepare for the law's repeal, on June

10 the president signed an executive order to reorganize various government detective agencies into a new Division of Investigation, slated to include the Bureau, the finger-print division, and the Treasury Department's remaining Prohibition agents. Roos-evelt and Cummings concluded that Hoover would be the best man to run it, but exactly how it would all work was still an open question when the guns went off in Kansas City on June 17.[12]

To the press, Cummings declared the Kansas City murders a "challenge to Ameri-can civilization" and vowed, with Hoover, to find the guilty parties. But he was not entirely sure they had the right to enter what appeared to be an ordinary, if dramatic, murder case. Cummings decided to solve that problem with rhetoric rather than law, at least for the moment. On July 29, building on what Herbert Hoover had done with the Wickersham Commission, Cummings declared a federal "war" on crime and called for the empowerment of a federal army to fight it. Lest local police chiefs complain of a power grab, he also announced the reappointment of the man so many of them had written in to support, the thirty-eight-year-old Bureau of Investigation chief, J. Edgar Hoover.[13]

HOOVER WANTED THE JOB, OF COURSE. BUT SOME PART OF HIM MAY HAVE BEEN tempted to run the other way. For all the attorney general's bravado and "bellicist" language, Hoover was under no illusion that fulfilling his ambitions was going to be easy. The Kansas City inquiry was already stalling, amid much recrimination. The Lindbergh kidnapping case was in even worse shape. Though Hoover had avoided the early phases of that crime, in recent months the Bureau had been involved in tracking the ransom money delivered to the baby's kidnapper. His technicians were well suited to the task, which mainly involved tracking serial numbers and processing finger-prints. Thus far, though, they had come up with nothing.[14]

Then there was the Urschel case, the latest terrifying crime to make national head-lines. On July 22, a week before Hoover's reappointment, oilman Charles Urschel had been snatched from the screened porch of his Oklahoma City mansion while engrossed in an evening bridge game. Hoover himself supposedly spoke with Mrs. Urschel when she called the division's new federal kidnapping hotline (National 8-7117), a sign both of the Bureau's small size in 1933 and of Hoover's belief that he alone could handle things properly at crisis moments. Urschel's return home the following week, after a ransom payment of two hundred thousand dollars, coincided almost exactly with Hoover's appointment as division director, making that case, too, into a test of the division's competence.

To Hoover's relief, his agents managed to track Urschel's train of half-remembered clues to a remote Texas farm owned by the family of George "Machine Gun Kelly" Barnes, a Tennessee gangster whose nickname reflected his reputation for inchoate violence. In late September, they located Kelly himself, along with his wife, Kathryn, in a run-down Memphis bungalow. According to legend, upon seeing the armed agents Kelly raised his hands in alarm and shouted, "Don't shoot, G-men!"—supposedly the first time any Bureau agent had heard the slang term for themselves as the New Deal's "Government Men."

Evidence suggests that it may have been Kathryn, not George, who uttered the famous phrase (itself not necessarily new to Hoover's men). "Honey, I guess it's all up for us," she supposedly said. "The 'g' men won't ever give us a break." Whatever the truth of the incident, Hoover did not embrace the term at first. Though headlines began to trumpet the exploits of crime-fighting "Federal 'G' Men," Hoover continued to hold on to a more sedate and limited view of his job. "This was not done with any story book detective hocus pocus," he explained to *The Washington Herald*. "It was a plain job of coordinating the efforts of Federal, State and local authorities and above all getting the public to help us."[15]

EVEN HOOVER COULD SEE THAT THINGS WERE CHANGING IN 1933, THOUGH, whether he liked it or not. At his December appearance before the House Appropriations Committee, he outlined the range of investigative duties acquired during Roosevelt's first six months in office, from investigations into gold hoarding and racketeering to income tax evasion and the supervision of machine gun sales. Cummings had still bigger and better plans in mind. In the weeks after Hoover's appointment, Cummings took it upon himself to identify the nation's top "public enemies"—not just the Kellys, but an entire slate of small-time bank robbers, kidnappers, and murderers who, according to the attorney general, constituted a threat to the nation. Cultural mythmakers soon made this string of young delinquents into legends: Charles Arthur "Pretty Boy" Floyd, who stole foreclosure papers along with bankers' cash; the Barker gang, supposedly led by its aged, machine-gun-wielding matriarch "Ma Barker"; Bonnie and Clyde Barrow, sufficiently self-promoting to compose their own "ballad" of outlaw life; the insouciant bank robber John Dillinger, who would eventually become known as "public enemy No. 1."[16]

Many of their crimes did not necessarily fall under federal jurisdiction, a fact to which Hoover clung as he tried to regain his bearings under the onslaught of events. But Cummings saw their theatrical potential. To house this new breed of supervillains, he declared, the government would open an isolated, escape-proof federal prison on San Francisco's Alcatraz Island, reserved for "criminals of the vicious and irredeemable type." He also laid plans to transform Hoover's men into a "superpolice force," in the phrasing of *The New York Times*, equipped with the latest in scientific inventions and high-power weaponry.[17]

Of everything that happened in this federalizing process, it was Cummings's decision to arm the Bureau's agents that brought the deepest and most lasting change to Hoover's carefully constructed institutional culture. Agents had long been permitted to carry guns for self-defense; at Kansas City, Caffrey had been wielding a pistol, and Lackey was armed as well. Hoover's early manuals had discouraged the idea, however, emphasizing that "it is not desired that each Agent shall carry arms as a general practice." Now, at Cummings's insistence, all agents began to master an array of firearms skills, including short- and long-range marksmanship with the Thompson submachine gun, the 12-gauge automatic shotgun, and both bolt-action and Monitor automatic rifles. In addition, they were expected to learn how to handle tear gas guns and grenades, and how to protect themselves with gas masks and bulletproof vests.[18]

This proved to be a tricky process. Hoover had selected his men for their personal charm and paperwork skills; some had never held a gun. Moreover, many did not want to, urging Hoover to preserve the strategies that had thus far set Bureau men apart from the thuggish police. "If we stick to the intelligent investigations that Agents of this Bureau are well-qualified to pursue," a Saint Paul, Minnesota, supervisor argued to Hoover, "it will always be the best and most convincing manner in which to perform our work." In Washington, some of Hoover's GW-trained officials dragged their feet, avoiding the firing range. Out in the field, agents practiced shooting at pumpkins and glass bottles, and often missed. Sometimes they even asked for training from the local police.

It is not clear how well Hoover himself ever learned to shoot a weapon. Bureau photographers would later take numerous publicity shots of him brandishing a tommy gun. But there are few records of his marksmanship or his participation in the nitty-gritty of firearms training. He had never shown any inclination to seek out violence or war. Nor did he apparently find much enthusiasm for potential shoot-'em-ups with armed outlaws. As Bonnie and Clyde continued to dodge the authorities throughout late 1933, Hoover authorized agents to stay abreast of what was happening but kept the case a low priority. And when the Indiana authorities sought help in finding John Dillinger, Hoover held back as well.[19]

He explained that the Bureau lacked jurisdiction in such cases—that to jump on the bandwagon without explicit authority from Congress was to repeat the mistakes of his predecessors, who had seized power that was not theirs, with disastrous results. Perhaps he also knew that once he took such steps, there would be no turning back. To fully engage the nation's "public enemies" would be to leave behind the sanctuary of his gentleman's Bureau and to enter a different and darker world.

CHAPTER 15

The Black Chamber

(1934)

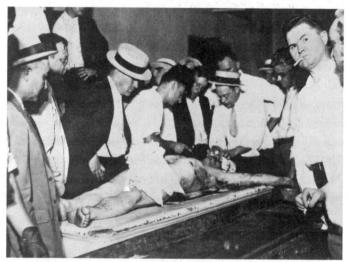

The body of bank robber John Dillinger at the Chicago morgue. Hoover's
agents shot Dillinger in a famous gun battle outside the city's Biograph
Theater on July 22, 1934.

NATIONAL ARCHIVES AND RECORDS ADMINISTRATION

On March 3, 1934, events forced Hoover's hand. That morning, John Dillinger
broke out of a local jail in Crown Point, Indiana. He had been there less than
six weeks, flown in under heavy guard after an arrest in Tucson, Arizona, photographers and reporters in tow to record his saucy smile and his promises to best the police
once again. Already a folk legend, Dillinger was wanted for crimes throughout the
Midwest, including a string of armed robberies and jailhouse escapes. At Crown Point
he was being held for the murder of a police officer, gunned down during a January
bank heist that netted the Dillinger gang twenty thousand dollars.

The Indiana authorities had begged for federal assistance after that shoot-out, noting that Dillinger's supply of machine guns, fast cars, bulletproof vests, and quick-
change disguises made him all but impervious to local authorities. As in so many other
cases, Hoover said he lacked jurisdiction, offering to coordinate the fingerprint analysis while declining to involve his men directly. Dillinger, Hoover claimed, was a local

problem—daunting, ambitious, and well traveled, but not a federal criminal. Nothing about the Dillinger case appealed to Hoover, least of all Dillinger's record of embarrassing police adversaries. At Crown Point, the gangster ultimately used a fake wooden gun (allegedly whittled in his cell) to subdue several guards, sauntered out the door, and made off in a stolen car.

That last act turned him into Hoover's problem. Everyone presumed Dillinger was headed for Chicago, the Midwest's first city for gangsters and fugitives. In the process, he would cross state lines in possession of a stolen car—a federal crime that brought him under Hoover's jurisdiction.[1]

The manhunt that ensued over the next four months has often been depicted as Hoover's greatest law enforcement victory, an epic battle in which his federal agents finally ginned up the courage to face a violent enemy—and won. In truth, even after months of firearms training, they were woefully unprepared for this sort of work, a group of lawyers and accountants who suddenly found themselves involved in street battles and machine-gun fire. Between March and November 1934, three more Bureau agents died at the hands of armed fugitives. Many others sustained serious wounds or witnessed graphic violence, and came to know what it was like to live under the daily threat of death. As special agent in charge at Chicago, the epicenter of so much of the era's brutality, Melvin Purvis bore a special burden. All three of the men who died came out of the Chicago office, and Purvis held himself responsible, the "hell" that he later described in his memoir.

The arrival of intense and repeated violence fundamentally changed what it meant to be a Bureau agent. In the summer of 1934, Roosevelt pushed through legislation formally authorizing Bureau agents to carry guns and make arrests. Other laws created new roles for federal authorities in cases of kidnapping, bank robbery, and the hunting of fugitive felons. This led to shifts in power, culture, and tactics within the Bureau itself. During 1934, Hoover's agents became men who not only endured but also inflicted violence, adopting methods such as "third-degree" intimidation that Hoover had once vowed to purge from police practice. They also experimented with the use of wiretaps and began to pay out large sums of money for "underworld" information. By the middle of 1934, that "underworld" had begun to pay homage to Hoover's shift in tactics, whispering of the Bureau as a "Black Chamber" in which the old rules—even the law itself—no longer applied.[2]

THE CHICAGO OFFICE STOOD AT THE CENTER OF THIS TRANSFORMATION, THE place where changes occurred most quickly and under the greatest duress. When Melvin Purvis motored north in the fall of 1932, his pup beside him and the rest of his entourage en route, he had been brimming with confidence, the youngest Bureau man ever appointed to head a major field office. By the end of his first year there, he "discovered that I still had a great deal to learn" about the pitfalls and challenges of the big city. At the age of twenty-nine, he had already served the Bureau in a half-dozen locales. But none of them were like Chicago, still Al Capone's city in spirit if no longer in fact.[3]

Few colleagues were especially surprised that Purvis's experiences in community theater and accounting fraud left him ill equipped to deal with these complications. "Here was this genteel attorney from the South who looked like he was fresh out of college," his secretary recalled, "and Hoover put him in the toughest spot there was." Purvis went out of his way to assure Hoover that he could handle whatever happened. "Please be advised that I have recently had a good deal of practice with revolver, machine gun, shotgun, and other types of arms," he wrote as the push for such training began. Purvis later described his two years in Chicago as a coming-of-age experience, when he cast off his dilettantish ways in favor of manhood's serious mien. But there was a darker side to what he experienced during those years. As special agent in charge, Purvis learned how long to hold a prisoner without food, water, or sleep, how to organize a tear gas raid, how to shoot to kill. And he taught these skills to other men, his own inner circle of GW graduates and Kappa Alphas. By the time it was over, his Chicago agents would be known throughout the Bureau as men unafraid of "police work," that nebulous realm where the gentlemanly arts of law crossed over into brutality and coercion.[4]

Under these pressures, Purvis began to develop new aspects to his personality, no longer just the charmer of his early Bureau years. In February 1934, after the Chicago office arrested a man suspected of involvement in the Lindbergh kidnapping, Purvis hauled the prisoner to his private office and proceeded to conduct "relentless grilling" and "constant bombardment of questions" for the next forty-eight hours. What else the interrogation entailed went unrecorded, but it apparently came at great cost. Though the prisoner failed to confess any crimes, he hung himself in jail less than a week later, knotting two neckties together and jumping from a chair while the guards were off searching for an aspirin.[5]

Hoover expressed sympathy for Purvis, even as the press came looking for an explanation. In the way of guidance, he sent along a column from the Christian self-help author Bruce Barton, whose writings he had long admired. Barton suggested that true gentlemen responded to criticism with a stoic and dignified "silence"—the "unanswerable answer" in a carping and ungrateful world.[6]

Hoover also urged Purvis to respond with action. "Keep a stiff lip + get Dillinger for me," he wrote in early April, "+ the world is yours."[7]

PURVIS TRIED. ON APRIL 9, HE ARRESTED DILLINGER'S GIRLFRIEND, BILLIE Frechette. The occasion was a major coup, except that Dillinger himself had been sitting outside the bar where the arrest took place. Upon seeing a bevy of dark-suited, anxious-looking federal agents milling around, he drove away. Embarrassed at the mistake, Purvis transported Frechette back to the field office for the sort of "vigorous" interview that was becoming standard Chicago practice. Over the next forty-eight hours, agents interrogated her under blazing lights, offering little in the way of food, drink, or sleep. After she refused to give them what they wanted, Purvis sent her to St. Paul for trial.

Things went downhill from there. Hoping for a break, Purvis dispatched agents across the state of Indiana and as far south as Louisville, Kentucky, following underworld tips about Dillinger's whereabouts. A few days later, a tip informed the Bureau that their target was actually in Sault Sainte Marie, but by the time agents arrived Dillinger was long gone. From Washington, Hoover continued to express understanding, but only to a point. In mid-April, he demanded that Purvis systematize methods for analyzing leads and conducting surveillance, and that Purvis stay in the office to supervise and coordinate rather than follow his agents into the field. That same month, he dispatched Hugh Clegg to St. Paul, a Washington disciplinarian sent to bring the Midwestern field agents under control.

On April 22, Purvis called with a breakthrough. According to a reliable informant, Dillinger and several other members of his gang were holed up at a Wisconsin resort known as Little Bohemia, dining, gambling, and drinking, and would stay at least through the following morning. Hoover understood the significance of this report: the moment had come for the Chicago office to take up arms against the fugitives who had so often humiliated the local police. Acting on Hoover's orders, Purvis dashed to the Chicago office half-dressed and chartered two rickety planes to Rhinelander, Wisconsin. A few hours later, his team landed and commandeered several cars for the frigid hour-long drive from the airfield.[8]

Hoover's role was largely passive, a matter of waiting, wondering, and pacing the floor back in Washington. Contact was spotty, especially once his agents left the town of Rhinelander for the Little Bohemia lodge. Still, Hoover was hopeful—confident, even—about their chances to bring the case to a close. Sometime between 2:15 and 3:50 a.m., he decided to alert the Washington papers that the Bureau had Dillinger surrounded and would soon be announcing either his death or arrest.

Like Purvis, Hoover later blamed the dogs for the disaster that came next. As Purvis and the other agents snuck up toward the resort through the woods, the owner's pet hounds heard them coming and started to bark, warning the men inside. When drunken figures began stumbling out of the resort moments later, agents shouted a few panicked warnings and then began to fire. Their bullets struck a local federal workcamp employee, killing him instantly. They also injured two other innocent men. It was the first time in Bureau history that agents had killed civilians. Far from being the avenging warriors of the federal government, they showed themselves to be inept, poorly trained, and at least as dangerous as the gangsters inside the lodge.

Afterward, agent W. Carter Baum, a twenty-nine-year-old GW law graduate, sat shell-shocked in one of the borrowed cars, certain that he was the one responsible for the federal worker's death. "I can never shoot this gun again," he told a fellow agent. Meanwhile, Dillinger and his compatriots were sneaking out the back of the lodge, scurrying along an incline by the beach. When the agents finally bombarded the lodge with tear gas, the only people left inside were the gang's wives and girlfriends.[9]

In the confusion that followed, Baum and a second agent, Jay Newman, managed to catch up with a member of the Dillinger gang, the youthful-looking Baby Face Nelson, just down the road. Nelson had used his pistol to force his way into a local farmer's car. When the two agents arrived, he jumped out of the back seat. "I know you bastards are wearing bulletproof vests," he informed them, aiming his machine gun at their car, "so I will give it to you high and low." Newman leaned back so that Baum could get a clear shot from the passenger's seat. But the young GW lawyer never raised his weapon. Instead, when Nelson began to fire, Baum tumbled out the passenger's side door and attempted to run. Nelson shot him in the neck, the bullets traveling smoothly past the agent's twenty-five-pound steel vest and striking his heart.[10]

HOOVER RECOGNIZED THE BLOODBATH AT LITTLE BOHEMIA AS A CRISIS OF major proportions. Once again, an agent was dead, a GW man shot down before the age of thirty. This time, though, his men had also killed a civilian, severely wounded two innocent bystanders, and blown their chance to do the one thing that the president and attorney general had demanded above all else: get John Dillinger. At best, Little Bohemia might be seen as a nightmarish series of mistakes. At worst, it could be interpreted as an indictment of Hoover's entire system—proof that scientific detectives and managerial efficiency were no match for ambitious and violent outlaws. A phone call at 3:50 on Monday morning informed him of Baum's death. Around seven a.m., he learned "that the three women with the Dillinger gang at the hotel had been taken into custody," and that everyone else had escaped. By the time he conceded the need for a public statement at noon on Monday, Hoover still knew little about what had happened, and had to admit that fact to the press.

Cummings tried to make the best of things, smoothly incorporating the Little Bohemia disaster into his campaign to expand federal police powers. "If we had had an armored car up there in Wisconsin," he informed the House Judiciary Committee on the day after the shootings, "our men could have driven up to the house where Dillinger was. The terrible tragedy would not have happened." In Cummings's view, Hoover's men were the true victims—not only of the Dillinger gang but also of a lazy and timid Congress that failed to provide them with the proper jurisdiction, training, and equipment. Most commentators saw something different. The problem in Wisconsin, the cowboy humorist Will Rogers pointed out, was not that Hoover's men lacked sufficient weaponry; it was that they shot the wrong people. "Well, they had John Dillinger surrounded and was all ready to shoot him when he come out," Rogers quipped in a widely quoted column. "But another bunch of folks came out ahead, so they just shot them instead."[11]

Given the circumstances, Hoover's response over the next few days was surprisingly measured. On April 26, he attended Carter Baum's funeral in Silver Spring, Maryland, where the casket was borne by six Bureau agents. Back at headquarters, he designated Harold Nathan to investigate what had gone wrong. Despite calls for Purvis's resignation, Hoover did not make any immediate moves. Instead, he promised to wait until the facts were in and to adjust his strategy accordingly. Three days after the shooting, he wrote to the attorney general in defense of his men on the ground. "I do not believe . . . that there can be any criticism leveled at the Agents for the action which they took in this matter," he wrote. "They were approaching a known gangsters' hide-out, and they saw three men leaving this hide-out. These three men were called upon to halt, but instead of doing so, they entered an automobile and proceeded to drive away, and consequently, the Agents fired." The letter was especially generous toward Purvis, noting that as head of the Chicago office he was not, technically, in charge at Little Bohemia, which was all the way off in Wisconsin.[12]

Hoover's personal relationship with Purvis undoubtedly influenced his approach to the crisis. But Hoover also must have seen a certain self-interest in defending his men; to admit their errors was to admit his own, and to call into question his system of administration and governance. His defensive tone suggests that he felt a genuine responsibility for what had gone wrong in Wisconsin: he, not Congress, had sent those men into the most dangerous situation they had ever faced. Despite his bravado, Little Bohemia seems to have been a moment of self-doubt, his sober confidence in administration and proper procedure buckling under the weight of grief and uncertainty.

He did not admit this publicly. Within the division, however, his actions reflected a new level of commitment to the grim reality at hand. Even as he absolved Purvis and Clegg of wrongdoing, Hoover began to scour his files for qualified sharpshooters, transferring several men to a reconstructed "Dillinger Squad" that would, in Cummings's words, "shoot to kill." He also lent official sanction to tactics he had long derided as crutches for the weak and unscientific police, authorizing wiretaps on gangland associates and offering to pay informants good money for their tips. To carry out these assignments, he turned not to Purvis or Nathan but to several rough-and-tumble Burns holdovers. In a retreat from his much-touted personnel policies, he urged special agents in charge to seek out recruits "who, while possibly not possessed of legal or accounting training, might be of use in connection with our work because of their knowledge and participation in law enforcement work."[13]

The shift in tone was striking, Purvis's secretary recalled, and it resonated through-out the division. "After Little Bohemia I realized the mood in the office had changed," she said. "It was much more real now."[14]

ASTONISHINGLY, LITTLE BOHEMIA REDOUNDED TO HOOVER'S POLITICAL BEN-efit. Over the next two months, prodded by Cummings, the Democratic Congress pushed through bill after bill designed to increase federal law enforcement power, all predicated on the idea that Hoover's men needed such laws to combat the likes of Dillinger. On May 18, Hoover attended his first bill-signing ceremony at the White House, standing behind Franklin Roosevelt as the president signed six bills expanding federal jurisdiction in areas such as bank robbery, kidnapping, and the apprehension of fugitive felons. Among the new laws was authorization to offer cash rewards for the capture of the nation's most wanted federal criminals.[15]

Many of the laws relied on the interstate commerce clause, the constitutional bul-wark of so many other New Deal reforms, to justify federal intervention in the local arena of crime. Others built on the edifice of the New Deal's own reforms, authorizing federal involvement in bank robberies, for instance, based on the banks' membership in an emboldened Federal Reserve system and a newly created FDIC. Under the new laws, Hoover's agents were officially authorized to carry weapons and make arrests, codifying into law what had already become widespread in practice. In a nod to Carter Baum and Ray Caffrey, Congress also designated the murder of a federal agent as a federal crime. Hoover had hoped for such legislation after the June 1919 bombings, which had wrecked Palmer's home and almost killed the attorney general, and again after Ed Shanahan's murder in 1925. Now, however, the law carried an air of fore-boding. More agents were likely to die, everyone agreed, before the War on Crime was over.[16]

AND STILL, THERE WAS DILLINGER. AFTER LITTLE BOHEMIA, HIS EVERY MOVE became a press sensation, and a point of humiliation for Hoover. In late April, Dill-inger and two accomplices shot it out with Saint Paul–area police. A few weeks later, he robbed the First National Bank in Fostoria, Ohio, escaping with more than $17,000. In June, his gang added almost $30,000 to the take, killing a policeman while ripping off the Merchants National Bank in South Bend, Indiana. These exploits made him America's "public enemy No. 1," according to Cummings, an official designation that carried up to a $10,000 reward for his capture. But there was no capture—nothing even close to it. Facing the possibility of another failed case, Hoover ceased his banter with Purvis in favor of frustrated instruction. "It is imperative that every resource of this Division be utilized to bring about an apprehension, and an early apprehension, of the members of the Dillinger gang," he wrote, "and I cannot continue to tolerate action of investigators who permit leads to remain uncovered, or at least improperly covered."[17]

To sort out the situation, Hoover sent yet another GW man, the straitlaced Sam Cowley, to supervise matters in Chicago. As Hoover later told the story, it was Cowley who finally brought Dillinger to heel. In reality, what pushed the case to its dramatic conclusion was old-fashioned, in-the-gutter police work. In late July, Purvis received a call from two local police officers offering to put him in touch with a local madam named Ana Sage. When Purvis and Cowley met with Sage later that day, she informed them that she knew John Dillinger and his girlfriend. In fact, all three were scheduled to go to the movies together sometime soon. Sage promised to tip off the Bureau once the plans were set. In return, she wanted help with her impending deportation case.

Like the story of Little Bohemia, the tale of the shoot-out in Chicago on July 22 would go down as national legend—though this time, it was Hoover's men who came out victorious. For months, newspapers lingered on the sensational details: how the federal men lay in wait outside the Biograph Theater; how Dillinger sat inside, unsuspecting, through the full run of *Manhattan Melodrama,* starring Clark Gable; how Purvis lit a cigar when Dillinger emerged from the theater, a secret signal to other agents to ready their weapons; how they saw Dillinger reach for his pistol, then gunned him down in the street, the crowd first fleeing and screaming in fear and then rushing back to dip their handkerchiefs in his blood. As at Little Bohemia, Hoover played no active part, granting his approval by phone and then sitting back in Washington to await the news. He was at Seward Square when the call came through announcing that Dillinger was dead. Armed with good news at last, he returned to the office to hold a press conference.

The newspapers seized upon Dillinger's death as a national turning point, proof that federal power would in the end triumph over the forces of disorder and aggression. "The erasure of John Dillinger in a Chicago alleyway means more than the end of a desperado at bay," declared the *New York Herald Tribune,* "it symbolizes the twilight of the gangster era." Hoover claimed credit, praising his men for their brave work and denouncing Dillinger as "just a yellow rat," but he showed far less joy and swagger than the press might have expected. Perhaps he was too aware of the many "gangsters" still at large: Baby Face Nelson, Pretty Boy Floyd, the Barker gang, Alvin Karpis, the Lindbergh kidnapper. Or perhaps he simply recognized that bloodshed was now a regular feature of life at the Bureau.[18]

HOOVER SOUNDED AS IF HE WANTED THE DILLINGER CASE TO DISAPPEAR. "IF I'D had my way about the whole thing," he told the Associated Press, "I'd have issued a simple one-sentence statement: 'John Dillinger was shot and killed by federal agents

in Chicago last night at 10:40 p.m.' and then rung the curtain down and forgotten it."
But there would be no forgetting Dillinger, whose name would be forever tied to
Hoover's. In the fall of 1934, there was also no forgetting the Kansas City Massacre,
which remained unsolved despite Hoover's public vows of justice. Hoover seemed to
interpret the public's enthusiasm for the Dillinger shooting as license to let go of restraint in the Kansas City investigation. As summer gave way to fall, he began encouraging his men to step up the use of the "good vigorous physical interview," and to use
their newly approved weapons to save the government from the expense of a trial.[19]

The Chicago office once again led the way. Purvis was still nominally in charge,
now known as the national hero who got John Dillinger. But it was Hoover and Cowley, the two Washington heavyweights, who planned and authorized the escalation of
force. Purvis's secretary watched the Chicago men adopt a "swashbuckling" physicality as their expectations of "comfortable careers in the more polite forms of investigation" began to evaporate. By the fall of 1934, agents were openly displaying "bruised
knuckles" acquired from deploying "more primitive arguments with refractory prisoners." They took pride in instilling fear—even terror—in the prisoners under their charge.
Several days after Dillinger's shooting at the Biograph, a small-time grifter and Dillinger associate named James Probasco threw himself out the window of a nineteenth-
floor conference room of the federal building rather than face interrogation by the
Chicago office, another suicide under Purvis's leadership.[20]

Hoover expressed few regrets about the prisoner's death, noting only that it was an
act of "extreme carelessness" on the part of supervising agents. He showed a similar
disdain toward Vivian Mathias, a gun moll detained in September for questioning in
the Kansas City case, upon her release from prison. Agents persuaded the warden to
drop her outside the penitentiary gates without advance notice. They then snatched
her up and drove her to a rental apartment in Detroit, where she was held "incommu-
nicado" for the next twelve days. Hoover approved the pseudo-kidnapping, including
her transfer to Chicago at the end of the month, where, in Cowley's words, agents
knew an established method for "breaking down [women's] mental resistance." Within
twenty-four hours of her arrival in Chicago, Mathias began "talking considerably,"
according to official reports, "although she was apparently frightened to death."[21]

What happened to Vivian Mathias during her two weeks in federal custody? Official records offer euphemism rather than detail, but scattered reports in other cases
suggest the range of new methods adopted by Hoover's men. More than once, internal
documents noted Hoover's desire to keep the prisoners from contacting lawyers or
family members, a method revived from the Palmer days. They also discussed plans to
spirit prisoners across state lines in the event of habeas corpus proceedings, counting
on judges in states like Texas to offer decisions "favorable to the Government." Most
of all, the files depicted a world of physical abuse, sleep deprivation, and other forms of

approved intimidation—a grab bag of tactics denoted, in official parlance, as "good vigorous physical interviews." Hoover rarely interfered with such techniques. "We need a substantially built agent in New Orleans for a few days," one aide noted in a memo to the director, making no secret of the interrogation plans. Such men were needed, a second memo added, not to "ask detailed technical questions" but to "work on those people for the persuasive part." As one headquarters executive noted, suspects often refused to talk despite their "yellow" hearts—"and, of course, there is a way to deal with people like that." One prisoner offered a nightmarish description of what such words meant, claiming that Chicago agents beat and starved him, threatened him with guns, and bragged that they could shoot him down in the street anytime they pleased and nobody would dare ask questions.[22]

Though Hoover continued to speak out against the "third degree," he tacitly approved the use of force by his own men as an unfortunate necessity. Sometimes, under pressure to deliver results, he went so far as to encourage his agents to shoot first and ask questions later. He made it clear, for instance, that he hoped to assassinate Pretty Boy Floyd, the chief suspect in the Kansas City case. "Orders are out to kill Floyd on sight," he wrote in June, "and if he doesn't surrender in short time, he will no doubt be killed by our men."[23]

Agents did as they were told. In late October, police in Wellsville, Ohio, happened upon Floyd lounging in a local farmer's field. Though they seized his companion, Floyd disappeared into the woods. Two days later, Chicago agents, working in conjunction with the local police, tracked him to a remote farmhouse several miles away. Spotting Floyd behind the corncrib, the lawmen used their new weapons to shoot the suspect as he fled. He died within minutes, sixteen months after the death of federal agent Ray Caffrey in Kansas City. As the on-site supervisor, "Melvin H. Purvis, youthful attorney who turned sleuth, marked another notch on his gun" that day, the Associated Press reported.[24]

WAS THIS JUSTICE? THE NEWSPAPERS CERTAINLY SEEMED TO THINK SO, CELEbrating each arrest and shoot-out as a triumph of law over chaos, good over evil. What Hoover thought is somewhat less clear. Certainly he did not experience the gunfights and murders as unambiguous progress. In the wake of the Dillinger case, Hoover lost one of his most cherished friendships, coming to view Purvis as a disloyal grandstander rather than an affectionate confidant. He also lost part of what he had built as a young man, leaving behind the fraternal atmosphere of the early Bureau years in favor of the more serious, violent, and ambitious mien of the New Deal state. Perhaps most important, he lost men—young agents whose fumbles with their pistols and machine guns were at least partly his fault. The history of what happened in 1934—of his sudden willingness to authorize assassination and strong-arm tactics—might be read as an effort to make up for the failings that ended Ray Caffrey's life in Kansas City and Carter Baum's at Little Bohemia.

There were more deaths to come. The worst was the murder of Sam Cowley, the pudgy GW lawyer and cheerful Mormon whom Hoover had sent to reorganize the Chicago office. In late November, Cowley caught a tip that Baby Face Nelson—one of the last holdouts from the Dillinger gang, the man who had murdered Carter Baum at Little Bohemia—might be leaving his hideaway and heading for the open road. Despite Cowley's status as a longtime "desk man," he grabbed a submachine gun and, with fellow agent Herman Hollis, rushed off to look for Nelson's car. They lasted only a few seconds under fire. From the side of the highway, Hollis was shot in the head and died instantly. Cowley sustained wounds to the abdomen and chest, lingering on at the hospital for several hours. Hoover spoke with Cowley's family and assured them that the agent "had a chance to pull through." A few hours later, Cowley died. The young agent had not been wearing his bulletproof vest. Nor had he been officially certified in the use of firearms.[25]

The gangster Nelson also died in the shoot-out, a bloody climax to the Bureau's months-long engagement with the Dillinger gang. Hoover expressed little joy over the news. "Yes, we got the guy," he said, "but he killed two of our men. It was two lives for one." An Associated Press reporter noted that Hoover seemed to be bearing up well under the strain, "still the well-dressed modern detective," but that there was no mistaking his grief. As another newspaper pointed out, Cowley had started out as one of Hoover's "night-school lawyers," a professional man who never expected to wield a gun. After the Dillinger case, that sort of agent was no more. Working for the Bureau now meant being a crack shot as well as a scientist and gentleman.[26]

CHAPTER 16

It's FBI Now

(1934–1935)

The new image of Hoover's "G-Men": tommy guns and tough-guy poses. From left: Hoover, *American Magazine* editor Sumner Blossom, and author Courtney Ryley Cooper, one of Hoover's favorite newspaper collaborators. December 31, 1935.

NATIONAL ARCHIVES AND RECORDS ADMINISTRATION

O n December 10, 1934, two weeks after Sam Cowley's death, Franklin Roosevelt laid out another task for Hoover and the law enforcement profession. "I ask you . . . to do all in your power to interpret the problem of crime to the people of this country," the president urged at a conference of criminal justice officials, and to "build up a body of public opinion" to support federal leadership on the issue. The speech marked a subtle shift in the president's thinking, the end of one approach to the War on Crime and the beginning of another. During his first two years in office, Roosevelt had merely hoped to get the emergency under control. Now, with John Dillinger, Pretty Boy Floyd, and Baby Face Nelson all secure in their graves, he recognized a different opportunity. Rather than simply battle crime, Roosevelt wanted men like Hoover to sell their work to the public, to show how the federal government could play an active and forward-thinking role in Americans' everyday experiences. "I want the backing of every man, every woman and every adolescent child in every state of the United States and in every county of every state—their backing for what the officers of law and order are trying to accomplish," Roosevelt declared.

He delivered this exhortation on the opening night of the attorney general's National Conference on Crime, a jam-packed, four-day affair at the capital's Memorial Convention Hall. While Hoover's men had been stumbling through the last stages of the Dillinger and Kansas City cases, Homer Cummings had invited roughly six hundred of the nation's law enforcement experts to Washington for an end-of-year policy extravaganza. Since then, Roosevelt's Democrats had trounced their Republican adversaries in the midterm elections, evidence to both the attorney general and the president that "a sweeping change in public psychology" was now possible.[1]

This promising circumstance made what Roosevelt said doubly important—not just a statement about crime policy, but a sign of what he wanted from those who would help to shape the next phase of the New Deal. The president acknowledged that crime was only one of the major challenges facing the nation. "The problems of feeding and clothing the destitute, making secure the foundations of our agricultural, industrial and financial structures" had occupied much of his time. Now, however, he urged the conference-goers to imagine how they might capture the public imagination and thus play a more prominent role in remaking citizens' relationship with the police. Roosevelt expressed admiration for the principles enacted by reformers like Hoover: scientific policing, administrative efficiency, local/federal cooperation. But he also suggested that such reforms could no longer stand alone. "An administrative structure that is perfect will still be ineffective in its results unless the people of the United States understand the larger purposes and cooperate with these purposes."[2]

Hoover had always grasped the importance of public support, but viewed this more explicit approach with some skepticism. Though he welcomed interest from trusted reporters, he worried that most newsmen who covered the crime war were out to sensationalize events and publish lurid stories. The increasingly powerful Hollywood film industry was still worse, with its love of gore and bloodshed, and its tendency to glamorize the romantic outlaw. But even Hoover could see Roosevelt's point: despite the Bureau's monopoly on statistics, it was newspapers, radio, and film that shaped how most Americans thought about crime. And so—reluctantly, under pressure from the president and attorney general—he began to entertain new ways to think about the art of publicity, and about Roosevelt's charge to "interpret" crime for the masses. He would eventually be proclaimed a "genius of public relations." At first, though, he followed more than he led. His strengths lay not in any great instinct for media manipulation or press management, but in the areas that had always served him well: the ability to learn quickly, to adapt to new situations, and to deliver what he believed his bosses wanted.[3]

———

ROOSEVELT HAD ARRIVED IN OFFICE WITH CERTAIN FIXED IDEAS ABOUT THE press, and about the potential for molding public opinion to his administration's ends. The best line of his inaugural speech—"We have nothing to fear but fear itself"— linked lawmaking with mass opinion and emotion. He knew that even the president would be powerless without the backing of the public will. The fight against "fear," as he framed it, was a battle of belief; Americans would have to decide that their problems could be solved, and that the federal government was the right vehicle for doing it. Herbert Hoover had held the press at arm's length, viewing reporters as little more than reprobates out to undermine the national morale. Beginning in March 1933, Roosevelt invited the press back into the White House, holding regular conferences in which he identified reporters by name and encouraged them to ask questions. In situations where the press could not be cajoled and flattered into reflecting his message, Roosevelt took his case straight to the people. His first "fireside chat," delivered by radio on March 12, 1933, asked Americans to "unite in banishing fear" while Washington reorganized the banking system.[4]

As Roosevelt acknowledged at the crime conference, law enforcement matters had never been much of a priority in these settings; his fireside chats took on labor and unemployment, banking and finance as the most pressing emergencies. The men at Justice had fumbled their way through the early crime war on their own, without any formal press policy or specific plan of engagement. Hoover's only press strategy—if it could be called a strategy—consisted of building relationships with a few carefully selected Washington reporters. His favorite was an ex–circus performer named Courtney Ryley Cooper, usually not the sort of man he was inclined to trust. Cooper never went to college, knew little about the law, and ran off at sixteen to join the carnival circuit rather than a fraternity. He was also tainted by an association with Hoover's old boss William J. Flynn. In 1919, while Hoover was busy organizing the Radical Division, Cooper had collaborated with Flynn on a salacious book about the German "spies and intrigues" of the Great War.[5]

In requesting his first interview with Hoover in April 1933, Cooper emphasized the need to highlight "a few contrasts with older days," promising to depict Hoover as a different sort of leader. At that point, Hoover still thought of himself as Cummings's loyal subordinate, so he insisted on approval from the attorney general. As their relationship developed, though, Cooper had pushed Hoover to think of himself in more independent terms. In early 1934, the two men worked together on a magazine series under Hoover's byline, with articles such as "Brains Against Bullets" illustrating how Hoover's administrative and scientific reforms helped to solve major crimes. At a time when other reporters were glorifying shoot-outs and car chases, Cooper stuck with

Hoover's preferred subjects of fingerprints and microscopes, and submitted every article for fact-checking and approval. [6]

This cozy arrangement might have continued indefinitely if not for Dillinger, whose case brought a wave of press interest on an entirely different scale. In August 1934, a few weeks after Dillinger's death, Cummings hired a reporter named Henry Suydam to serve as the Justice Department's press agent, responsible for fielding the deluge of inquiries about Dillinger and other high-profile cases as well as for developing a long-term public relations strategy. Suydam found Hoover a challenging student, suspicious of reporters' motives and locked in his own narratives about what should and should not be said. Objecting to melodramatic prose, the future public relations "genius" complained that most press coverage, "aside from the lack of good taste involved, is harmful to the prestige of the Division and may militate against the successful consummation of the work under its jurisdiction."[7]

IF NEWSPAPERS WERE BAD, FILM WAS EVEN WORSE. SINCE THE FIRST COMMERCIAL release of a talking film in 1927, sun-dappled Hollywood had come to represent everything that Hoover disliked about the nation's "melodramatic" approach to crime. Where Hoover sought to project institutional integrity, Hollywood loved the rule-breaking, lone-wolf policeman. Where Hoover preferred microscopes and filing cabinets, filmmakers wanted car chases and guns. To Hoover's initial dismay, the kidnappings and bank robberies of the early 1930s turned out to be ready-made for the film medium, packed with romance, violence, and human drama. Even more alarming, some of the earliest talking films lavished their attention and sympathies not on police, but criminals. *The Public Enemy*, one of the great blockbusters of 1931, depicted the evolution of a golden-hearted street kid into a hardened criminal, celebrating the antihero who managed to outwit the police and gun down his rivals.[8]

Hoover worried that this sort of story undermined law enforcement, teaching children that the lawbreaker might be right and the police wrong. "I often wonder just what effect their glorification of the criminal has upon the mind and actions of the youth of today," he confessed to the American Bar Association in the summer of 1934. Talking films glamorized all manner of illicit activity, from forbidden eroticism (adultery, homosexuality, miscegenation) to narcotics use and prison life. The economic crisis ratcheted up the stakes, creating added pressure for ever more sensational subjects to lure in a paying crowd. The film industry had tried to place limits on these pressures by developing a "film production code" under the leadership of former Republican postmaster William Hays, but those rules had proved tricky to enforce.[9]

In 1934, Roosevelt began to push for more concerted action. Early in the year, he sent a representative out to Hollywood to discuss creating a government censorship board, charged with regulating films just as the New Deal government had begun to regulate so many other industries. A few days later, the Motion Picture Producers suddenly announced a revival of the voluntary code they had devised years earlier—a last-ditch attempt to avoid federal censorship by censoring themselves. This time, the film industry empowered Hays not only to review major-studio scripts but to censor them accordingly. At the same moment that Hoover acquired new enforcement powers in the realm of criminal law, the Hays office gained the right to dictate what could and could not be portrayed in American films.[10]

The Hays Code took effect in July 1934, the same month as John Dillinger's death, a coincidence of timing that would soon push Hoover and Hollywood into an awkward embrace. Under the codes, pictures that poked fun at the authorities or sought to cast aspersions on religion were banned. In their place films would now adhere to a conservative moral formula: "The sanctity of the institution of marriage and the home shall be upheld"; "Sex perversion or any inference to it is forbidden"; "Miscegenation (sex relationship between the white and black races) is forbidden." At the top of this list were strictures for dealing with "crimes against the law," the category most important to Hoover. Under the code, filmmakers would no longer portray methods of theft, murder, robbery, arson, drug trafficking, safecracking, dynamiting, liquor consumption, or "use of firearms" in detail. Most important, the code forbade filmmakers to portray criminal activity "in such a way as to throw sympathy with the crime as against law and justice or to inspire others with a desire for imitation." If American directors wanted to make movies about crime, the policemen now had to be the heroes.[11]

HOOVER'S OWN SPEECH AT THE DECEMBER CRIME CONFERENCE EMPHASIZED "cooperation" between federal and local law enforcement, along with the need for "honesty, integrity, ability, education and courage" among the nation's police—all the old reform themes. Later that week, he more or less collapsed. Hoover spent his fortieth birthday sick in bed with "the grippe," writing thank-you notes for Christmas presents and attempting to catch up on sleep. Even as he lay in his sickbed, though, there were hints that 1935 was going to allow for little rest. For the first time, the Washington papers featured his birthday as a significant local event. "Hoover, Nemesis of Crime, Passes Milestone No. 40," *The Washington Herald* noted. Despite his exhaustion, Hoover also managed to do something he had never done before: at the request of local papers, he delivered a New Year's message. "We of the Division of Investigation feel a degree of pride in the success which attended its work in 1934," he informed *The Washington Times*. Looking ahead, he warned, "We must exercise every precaution, however, to prevent any pride in past achievements from militating against our earnest, tireless efforts to make the accomplishments of the future excel in every way those of the past." The statement sounded like nothing so much as the good-hearted boosterism of Central High, as if none of the trauma and bloodshed of the previous year had taken place.[12]

Hoover looked different at forty than he had a decade ago, when he bounded into the office as the trim young director. He was thickening, his waist a few inches wider and softer, his face starting to acquire the heavy jowls that would eventually lead so many reporters to compare him to a bulldog. Those same newsmen had trouble characterizing his physique at forty. He was described alternately as a "quiet, heavy set man," "a long-legged lawyer with a booming voice," and a boss who "looks like a muscle-man [but] is shy as a momma's boy." He had acquired a pair of round, dark-framed eyeglasses (another sign of aging) but he rarely wore them in public.[13]

He also acquired a new office. The previous fall, while Hoover's men were busy running down Nelson and Floyd, the Justice Department had begun the daunting task of moving into its building on Pennsylvania Avenue, one of the last and most grandiose of the federal structures commissioned during the recent boom. Reporters ticked off the most extravagant statistics: two miles of corridors, twenty-nine elevators, twenty-three acres of floor space. Descriptions teetered between admiration and terror, as mere mortals were swallowed up by the "long, long corridors—so long that they must be broken at intervals with doors that would seem unnecessary . . . ; office after office, nameless, merely numbered, with numbers that run into the thousands." To educate the public in American history, the architects commissioned no less than sixty-eight murals. To illustrate legal principles, they ordered fifty-seven sculptures. Even the front doors seemed designed both to inspire and to dwarf the ambitions of ordinary men. Made of solid aluminum, they stood some twenty feet high.[14]

The Bureau occupied much of the building's top three floors, about a third of the total office space, another sign of Hoover's growing stature. Administrators and top executives shared the fifth floor with the communications division, alongside top Justice officials and investigative personnel. The sixth floor housed the Bureau's growing file collection, and the staff who attended to it. Above that was the identification division—"these millions of cards with their black smudges"—along with the high-tech lab. The Bureau claimed part of the basement for a soundproofed pistol range and a gym where agents trained in jujitsu and boxing, symbols of the Bureau's new tough-guy image.[15]

Hoover's oak-paneled office projected a different impression, less the oomph of the fistfight and more the coolness of a royal visitation hall. Furnishings were sparse: a plum-colored rug, a freestanding bronze ashtray, two guest chairs, an American flag. The only item of significant size was Hoover's mahogany desk, transferred from his old office and placed on a small riser so that Hoover sat a few inches above his guests. He displayed a few smaller personal items, mementos and little showpieces left out for public consumption. The most eye-catching was a bronze statuette of Hercules holding aloft a club, poised to take on more than could be asked of ordinary mortals. Asked by a reporter about the item's origin and meaning, Hoover explained that "it was a present" from a friend who "thought it symbolized the work of the division." His desk featured a framed photo of the late Spee Dee Bozo, his loyal Airedale. Hoover also displayed a copy of the poem "If—", Rudyard Kipling's ode to the glories and challenges of manhood. Like the statue of Hercules, the poem portrayed a figure burdened by impossible tasks, but with the strength to "never breathe a word about your loss." Hoover knew the words by heart.[16]

What most guests recalled, though, were not the desktop trinkets or dog photos, or even the vast expanse of the office itself. Instead, they remembered the carefully staged exhibit located just outside Hoover's office doors. There, he jettisoned the subtle cues of his formal office in favor of a gruesome tribute to the Bureau's crime-fighting prowess. On display in an oblong, glass-topped case were relics drawn from the Bureau's biggest cases: John Dillinger's gold-rimmed eyeglasses, cigar, and bloodstained straw boater; Kathryn Kelly's tousled red wig; a jug that once held the ransom note in the Urschel kidnapping. Alongside them lay a veritable arsenal of weapons, including "machine guns, shotguns, revolvers and knives taken from criminals." Each was duly identified by owner, from Dillinger's bulletproof vest to Clyde Barrow's Browning automatic. The exhibit identified a ghostly white face set among the guns and evidence as Dillinger's death mask, a clay rendering of the bank robber's tortured features after agents gunned him down at the Biograph.[17]

THE DISPLAY CASE OUTSIDE HOOVER'S OFFICE WAS NOT NECESSARILY WHAT Roosevelt had in mind when he called upon law enforcement to "interpret" the problem of crime. But it was a start, a hint that Hoover was taking notice of the public interest in crime narratives and adjusting his self-presentation accordingly. Another clue came when Hoover began to push for a new name to replace the "Division of Investigation." Since the end of Prohibition, he had longed to break away from what remained of the Prohibition Bureau—technically a separate entity, but still under the roof of his division. He had also advocated for a renaming, pointing out that other government agencies maintained their own "divisions" of investigation, a source of frequent confusion. In March 1935, just after completing the move into his new office, he got his wish.[18]

For all its later significance, the adoption of the name Federal Bureau of Investigation—FBI—occurred with little fanfare. Many other bureaus went through similar shifts during the 1930s, losing an initial here, gaining another there. As a reconfigured "alphabet agency," the FBI was little different from the Civilian Conservation Corps (CCC), Works Progress Administration (WPA), or Securities and Exchange Commission (SEC), three-letter agencies born of early New Deal planning.

Still, the name meant a great deal to Hoover and his inner circle, who had toiled for more than a decade to prove themselves different from the tainted Bureau of the past. To them, the name "FBI" provided a long-desired opportunity to draw a line with the past and redefine itself for the dawning age of government public relations. "Those initials also represent the three things for which the Bureau and its representatives always stand: 'Fidelity-Bravery-Integrity,'" an inspector declared in the Bureau's in-house magazine.[19]

The press liked the change. "It's F.B.I. Now," declared one of Hoover's favorite reporters, labeling the three-initial formula a "godsend to headline writers." A new name and a new office only went so far, however. Roosevelt's larger questions remained: How would the FBI interpret the issue of crime? To come up with an answer, Hoover turned not to Henry Suydam, the Justice Department's press agent, but to Courtney Ryley Cooper, the circus man turned news reporter who had worked so closely with Hoover in the early 1930s. In the fall of 1934, just before the crime conference, Cooper had proposed to Hoover that they collaborate on a book: Cooper would write the text and Hoover would write the foreword. Together, they would produce just what the moment called for: a "crime book" that "book-sellers all over America . . . can get behind and push to the limit."[20]

Coming from anyone else, the offer would certainly have been rejected. Since it came from Cooper, Hoover took a chance and said yes. In contrast to press conferences, where he offered statements and reporters wrote whatever they wanted, the book provided an opportunity for him to put his own stamp on the crime-war narrative, to go on record about what had happened and why. Cooper agreed to abide by Hoover's suggestions and allowed him to approve the book's title, *Ten Thousand Public Enemies*. In return, Hoover furnished Cooper with Bureau files and case summaries, and designated agents to fact-check the book. Suydam warned that opening up Bureau materials might anger other reporters, and "might lead the readers to believe that the Department had not used much discretion in the matter." Hoover ignored these instructions and treated Cooper as a special confidant.[21]

Cooper found Hoover's attention to be a mixed blessing. While he depended upon Hoover for access and gravitas, he also expressed frustration at the Bureau's painstaking attention to detail and at Hoover's hesitation about engaging the true drama of what had taken place over the past few years. As the weeks went on and the publication date neared, Cooper was forced to remind his Bureau friends that "time is getting a little short in setting this stuff up and making corrections." Agents nonetheless continued to churn out fact-checking memos, fixing dates, name spellings, phrasings, and technicalities of criminal law. In mid-January, Hoover balked when an agent noted that Cooper's writing contained "considerable criticism, directly and by innuendo, of local police departments as well as of the Bureau of Prisons." Despite Cooper's impatience, Hoover ordered another vetting of the book.[22]

When the book finally emerged, reviewers had no trouble identifying it "as a mouthpiece of the director of that interesting bureau, John Edgar Hoover," in the words of *The Washington Post*. As Hoover's first effort to live up to Roosevelt's dictum, *Ten Thousand Public Enemies* attempted to combine scientific management and white-collar integrity with gangsters and guns. The result encompassed an odd range of attributes, in which Hoover came across both as a "friendly, businesslike" sort of fellow and as the righteous scourge of "'sob sisters,' 'morons' and 'smug citizens' who ... either do nothing to prevent crime or display an active sympathy for the criminal."[23]

The title promised more than the book delivered. "Ten thousand public enemies" referred to the hard core of violent criminals who had necessitated the federal government's turn to "machine guns, automatic rifles and perhaps tear-gas guns in order to be properly armed." And yet the book itself took some two hundred pages to arrive at the Kansas City Massacre and another hundred before plunging into the Dillinger case—leaving fewer than sixty pages to get through all the really exciting stuff. The bulk of the early chapters focused on Hoover's transformation of the Bureau. "A vast power ... slowly has been building, to a great degree in comparative secrecy," Cooper wrote, "until it now can take its place as a stanchion to strengthen the local law enforcement agencies of the nation." To the degree that Cooper engaged specific crimes or actual criminals, he did so by way of illustrating the value of Hoover's scientific techniques and the importance of national uniformity and coordination. The book served as a rollout for Hoover's new FBI, fitting the latest headlines into his preferred narrative.[24]

TEN THOUSAND PUBLIC ENEMIES SOLD TOLERABLY WELL. BUT IT WAS THE FILM industry, not the staid world of publishing, that made Hoover into a national legend. In making the transition to the code system, the film studios had granted themselves a brief adjustment period, in which they would be permitted to make violent, graphic crime films—as long as the authorities won. The result was a gold rush on shoot-outs and bloodshed, as filmmakers tried to cash in on their last few moments of opportunity. "Moviegoers are in for a siege of gunfire ..." one columnist predicted in the spring of 1935. "But now, the head-line conscious cinema, alert as ever to maintain its standing as a lusty, topical form of theatre, has discovered ... those cool, efficient and daring public benefactors, the Department of Justice men."[25]

The siege began with *G-Men*, released by Warner Brothers in April 1935, around the same time as the publication of *Ten Thousand Public Enemies*. Like Hoover's book, the film featured a heroic corps of detective-lawyers hell-bent on stemming the nation's violent crime epidemic. Given those similarities, many observers assumed that Hoover had played some role in film's creation. In truth, *G-Men* came about as a Hollywood effort from start to finish: written by commercial screenwriters and produced by a major studio, without either the help or sanction of the FBI. "The Department has approved no motion picture scenario or production purporting to deal with its work," Cummings said on March 23, just as the film was due to be released. According to *Motion Picture Daily*, Hoover ordered his agents to stay away from all preview showings and "to refuse any statements whatsoever regarding them." He made an exception for himself, though, venturing to Baltimore in early May to view one of the first local screenings.[26]

To his surprise, Hoover liked at least some of what he saw. *G-Men* starred James Cagney as a scrappy attorney turned federal agent, transferring onto the lawman the same reckless charisma that had been so alluring in *The Public Enemy*. As its title suggests, the film lavishes attention upon the "Government Men" of the Bureau, and hits upon most of Hoover's favorite themes: the importance of college-educated agents, the rigor of the Bureau's firearms training, the scientific revolution within law enforcement, the need to insulate policing from politics. Characters pause frequently to deliver stock praise for federal crime fighting. "It's a great department . . . and a great bunch of fellas," one character says. "When they tackle a job they stick to it 'til they're finished, with no fat-faced politician standing around telling 'em what to do." *G-Men* put the Bureau's facilities on-screen for the first time, offering glamour shots of a gym, a bustling lab, and a fingerprint division. A character named Bruce Gregory stands in for Hoover, doling out stern personnel orders and delivering speeches to Congress in favor of greater power for his agents. Faced with the prospect of battling "Gregory's" men, the film's leading crime-boss character decides to get out of the rackets, explaining to skeptical underworld confidants that crime would no longer pay now that the "G-Men" had stepped up their game.[27]

This was precisely what the code hoped to accomplish: The agents came across as heroes; the gangsters appeared repentant or incompetent. And yet there was much about the picture that also infuriated Hoover. *G-Men* was essentially a gangster picture flipped on its head—"an old type in a new garment," as one pro-censorship group put it. Far from being one of Hoover's clean-cut college boys, Cagney's character Brick Davis grows up as an urban street tough mentored by a Capone-esque boss. While Hoover prided himself on obedience from subordinates, the rookie Davis is a go-it-alone maverick, always pushing the limits of government rules. Despite his law school education, Davis manages to solve the crime and get the girl only by drawing on insider tips from his underworld contacts. FBI agents had in fact used such methods in the Dillinger case, but Hoover still preferred a brainier, more scientific image. He argued for dispassionate policing, removed from all personal and political considerations; Brick Davis mostly wants to avenge the murder of fellow agents.

By those standards, the real surprise about *G-Men* was that Hoover did not react more aggressively against it. He instructed field offices to respond to fan mail with a statement denying both the Bureau's cooperation and its approval. But in a reversal of his previous stance, he also embraced the film's title and accepted that he was now a G-Man, fully immersed in American public relations and culture. [28]

LOOKING BACK, HUGH CLEGG RECALLED WITH AMUSEMENT JUST HOW LITTLE the men of the Bureau initially understood the movie's import. "When the *G-Men* picture came out it was the biggest propaganda help we ever had in our lives: We just didn't know it was going to be." Over the next five months, Hollywood released several more "G-Man" films, under such dukes-up titles as *Show Them No Mercy!* and *Let 'Em Have It.* In the process, they transformed the crime-fighting federal agent into a staple of popular culture—and turned "J. Edgar Hoover" into a household name. "Whether it is in anybody's conscious intention or not, and I suspect it is, this string of G-men melodramas is very likely to have an important by-product," wrote columnist Heywood Broun. "A vast mass of propaganda is being loosed to convince the American public that the agents of the Justice Department are invariably brave, never corruptible and always right." Though he did not control this "vast mass of propaganda," Hoover ended up as its prime beneficiary.[29]

It was not just Hollywood that came calling: comic books and radio, newspapers and magazines, all wanted a piece of the action. Faced with this deluge of interest, Hoover finally committed himself to a long-term public relations initiative. When he did, it was with the same single-minded determination and grand ambition that he had applied to nearly every other endeavor since Central High School. In July 1935, he welcomed NBC radio for a live tour of Bureau offices, with the broadcast hosted by none other than Courtney Ryley Cooper. That same month, Hoover began to work with NBC producer Phillips Lord on a thirteen-episode series titled *G-Men*, based on major cases from Bureau files. In October came the rollout of a pulp magazine called *G-Men*, featuring the "Famous Cases of J. Edgar Hoover" along with a Hoover speech in every issue. Not long after that, a rival magazine known as *The Feds* entered circulation, touting Hoover as "America's popular Public Hero No. 1." Hoover still complained about sensationalism and distortion (Lord's follow-up radio show, *Gangbusters,* earned special ire), but he no longer believed that he could stand apart or look away.[30]

At the FBI itself, Hoover flung the doors open to the public, organizing a free daily tour for visitors, hosted by specially trained clerks and agents. In its first iteration, he offered one daily tour for approximately twelve tourists. By early 1936, the tours had become so popular that Hoover expanded them to include at least three rounds per day, accommodating up to a thousand visitors. When even that expansion proved to be inadequate, he arranged with Universal to produce yet another G-Man film, this one in collaboration with the FBI, under the title *You Can't Get Away With It!* The film was an FBI tour writ large, "made up of interesting, dramatic, and authentic facts," in Hoover's words. In a stilted letter of endorsement for the film poster, he linked the movie with the need to change public opinion on the subject of crime, echoing Roosevelt's exhortations. "I feel that it will serve a most useful purpose in impressing upon millions of minds—especially those of the youth of this country—the fact that a life of crime is a sordid one," Hoover wrote. He hoped, too, that it would rally the nation behind the cause of law enforcement.[31]

Perhaps most important, Hoover concluded that public relations—like crime statistics and fingerprints, lab facilities and office inspections—would thereafter become a permanent feature of FBI work, one of the tasks to which men would be dedicated and assigned. Toward the end of 1935, he ordered the establishment of an FBI public relations unit, soon to be known as the Crime Records Section. To lead it, he designated the one man he had come to rely upon above all others, Clyde Tolson.[32]

CHAPTER 17

Right-Hand Man

(1935–1936)

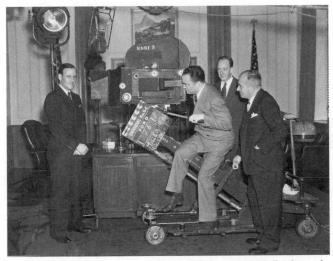

Hoover turning the camera on Tolson, October 14, 1936. By the mid-1930s, Tolson was the most important relationship in Hoover's life. With film director Charles Ford (far right) and William Miller, inside Hoover's office.

NATIONAL ARCHIVES AND RECORDS ADMINISTRATION

I f asked to identify Hoover's favorite agent, many Americans in 1935 would have summoned a single name: Melvin Purvis, Hoover's onetime protégé and correspondent, now the star of the Dillinger drama. During the case's difficult early months, Purvis had been an object of mockery, not only from Hoover but from a hostile press. After the shoot-out at the Biograph, he became a public hero, second only to Hoover as the nation's most famous G-Man. When Baby Face Nelson gunned down Sam Cowley, Purvis rushed to Cowley's hospital bed and vowed, "If it's the last thing I do, I'll get Baby Face Nelson—dead or alive." When Hollywood came calling, hoping to make a film of Purvis's life story, he entertained that possibility, too. Apparently he did not anticipate, or perhaps did not care, what such activities would mean for his relationship with Hoover. Far from embracing the fame and success of his most "sheik-like" and charming of young agents, Hoover grew jealous in 1935. Before the year was over, he forced Purvis out of the Bureau.[1]

The split did not happen quickly or easily. As late as Christmas 1934, Hoover was still sending letters filled with the old flirtation and banter. And yet he understood that something had changed, that Purvis was now his rival rather than his subordinate. In November, an inspection team noted that Purvis was flouting Hoover's rules, sauntering in late, allowing stenographers to smoke on the premises, and treating the office as a personal hangout, with "dirty underwear and shirts" scattered throughout. "[Purvis] is extremely temperamental, egotistical," Hoover's inspection team warned. "He had been giving more time to his own personal interests and to his social activities than he had been giving to the office which he represents." In March 1935, rumors around Chicago said Purvis had been spotted drunk at a party, brandishing a gun and shouting incoherently.[2]

At that point Hoover undertook a campaign of harassment so petty and vindictive that it can be explained only in personal terms. He transferred Purvis to Charlotte, North Carolina, stripping him of his authority at the famed Chicago office. Along the way, he began to second-guess nearly everything Purvis did. When Purvis authorized the use of a Bureau car to deliver a fugitive to Alcatraz, for instance, Hoover sent an indignant memo about the proper use of official vehicles. The message could hardly have been more clear: Hoover was hoping to restore their relationship to its old ingratiating boss-and-subordinate dynamics. But the ultimatums—no speaking with the press, no contact with the film industry, no questioning orders—proved untenable to Purvis. Though the public still knew him as Hoover's G-Man par excellence, he resigned from the Bureau in early July 1935, explaining to the press that his decision was "purely personal."[3]

Hoover never spoke with Purvis again, an act of banishment that suggested not indifference but an ongoing intensity of emotion. With Purvis safely off in exile, he turned his attention instead to another emerging favorite.

WHEN HE JOINED THE BUREAU IN 1928, CLYDE TOLSON HAD BEEN ONE AMONG many, an attractive young lawyer and GW fraternity man. Slowly, though, over the course of late nights and shared crises, he had begun to emerge as something unique: Hoover's most intimate colleague, social partner, and confidant. His swift promotions told part of the story: inspector in 1929, assistant director in 1930. So did his record of special privileges. Tolson and Hoover began to travel together as early as July 1930, when they embarked on a golf trip to Summit, Pennsylvania. Hoover wanted Tolson by his side at official Washington functions, growing petulant when the White House resisted adding another name to its official list. "It is my opinion that he should be included with the names of the other officials of the department whose names are placed upon the list for the White House invitations," Hoover wrote. Unlike Purvis, who got to know Hoover from afar, Tolson was right in Washington, a daily part of

Hoover's existence. And Tolson wanted to be there. In the fall of 1930, not long after his promotion to assistant director, he sent Hoover a professional headshot of himself looking young and handsome and ready to take on the world. "To my best friend 'Speed,'" Tolson inscribed the photo, evoking Hoover's childhood nickname.[4]

Their relationship intensified in 1935, and not just because of Purvis's fall from grace. In the midst of the G-Man craze, Hoover's social life took off, and he wanted someone along for the ride. Together, they plunged into a whirl of nightclubs, film premieres, and star-studded parties. In doing so, they subjected themselves to a new level of public scrutiny. For the first time, Hoover's relationships were out in the open, a matter for the news columns and gossip sheets rather than merely a fact of life at the Bureau. He kept certain aspects of his relationship with Tolson private, hidden from public view. And yet what is most striking about their budding relationship is not its furtive quality but its openness, vitality, and broad social acceptance. Far from hiding their affection, Hoover and Tolson moved freely together during the 1930s. When Edgar received an invitation, so did Clyde.

Some of those outings still centered around Bureau life. Increasingly, though, they began to venture beyond the confines of Washington, building new social circles in New York, Florida, and California. They were seen together at the best nightclubs and Broadway theaters, at the top racetracks and boxing arenas. They were also spotted side by side on more somber occasions, including the funerals of close family members and friends.

Newspapers usually described Tolson in official terms, as Hoover's "aide" or "right hand man." Friends and Bureau colleagues stuck with a similar story, insisting for decades that both men were too "masculine" to have been anything other than solid friends, reflecting a standard mid-century view of male homosexuality as something for "sissies" and outliers. There were at least a few friends and acquaintances who saw something else in their relationship, however. "Everybody knew about J. Edgar Hoover . . . ," Broadway star Ethel Merman recalled decades later. "A lot of people have always been homosexual. To each his own." The Stork Club, their favorite watering hole, welcomed patrons with "blue noses, white ermines, striped trousers, and checkered lives," one customer recalled. These were the sorts of terms their sophisticated new friends used to describe, and to accept, unconventional relationships like the one developing between Hoover and Tolson.[5]

TOLSON'S PROMOTION TO ASSISTANT DIRECTOR IN 1930 HAD PLACED HIM ON par with the acerbic and entertaining Harold Nathan, but the actual division of responsibility put Tolson much closer to Hoover. Nathan ran the investigative side of things, orchestrating the police-work triumphs that won the Bureau its headlines. Tolson was the institution man—assistant director for personnel and administration—charged with making sure that the machine ran smoothly from his Washington post. Hoover put him in charge of inspections, recruitment, employee activities, and personnel reviews—matters close to Hoover's heart. He relied on Tolson to be available at all times, a desire that only increased with the crime wave and the FBI's personnel expansion. While Nathan rushed out to Kansas City after the Union Station shootings, Tolson had managed what needed to be done from Washington, ordering guns for the Midwestern offices and then sitting down to compose letters of condolence to the victims' families.[6]

Within the Bureau, Tolson became known for his attention to detail, his inexhaustible knowledge of Bureau policy, and above all his loyalty to Hoover. He had a way of maintaining order in the midst of chaos, Hugh Clegg remembered—"just a well-qualified and stabilizing sort of a person." Tolson showed a talent for guessing Hoover's preferences and adjusting his own views accordingly. In 1934, charged with investigating allegations that agents had mutinied against Purvis at Little Bohemia, Tolson dismissed the claims as the product of an agent's "disordered and possibly hysterical state of mind," a nod to Hoover's then-fond attitude toward Purvis. When Hoover changed his mind about Purvis a few years later, Tolson followed suit. It was Tolson who alerted Hoover to the rumors that Purvis had gotten drunk and brandished his weapon at the Chicago party.[7]

Some of Tolson's disdain for Purvis may have stemmed from personal or professional jealousy. But it was also his job to hold the line on agents' behavior, ensuring that everyone at the Bureau met Hoover's exacting standards. "I think it is imperative, with the growing size of our Division, that strict discipline be maintained and that the new men particularly realize that we mean business," Hoover wrote in a memo to Tolson in late 1934. Tolson acted as the internal watchdog, testing and measuring other employees' honesty and loyalty to Hoover.[8]

As head of the Crime Records Section, he also helped Hoover communicate with the outside world and manage the growing challenge of public relations. As early as 1932, Tolson had taken charge of the circular "Fugitives Wanted by Police," soon to become the *Law Enforcement Bulletin*. In 1933, he began serving as point man for Courtney Ryley Cooper and other favored reporters, answering queries when needed and fending off those he deemed unnecessary. Tolson's duties as the Bureau's publicity man expanded more swiftly in the months after *Ten Thousand Public Enemies* and *G-Men*, as requests poured in from reporters and film directors. In July 1935, he helped to coordinate with Cooper as the FBI made the leap into radio. In a nod to Tolson's special status, Cooper signed his notes to Hoover with "best regards to you and Clyde."[9]

THERE WAS ANOTHER FIGURE WHOSE PRESENCE AT THE BUREAU TESTIFIED TO Tolson's increasing significance in Hoover's life. Like Tolson himself, this man was a perfect FBI specimen: five feet nine and strikingly handsome, with a well-defined jaw, a broad flat nose, and a muscular build. He also happened to be Tolson's longtime roommate, the GW alum and Sigma Nu fraternity brother Guy Hottel. Publicly, Hoover described Hottel as a just another Bureau agent, one of hundreds of men in his employ. And yet it is clear that Hottel played a unique role in Hoover and Tolson's relationship, the one man invited along on vacations and nights out, turning their partnership into three instead of two. He also received special privileges at the Bureau. From the moment Hottel accepted the job in 1934, Hoover bent and even broke the rules for him. Hottel's sudden arrival at the FBI in 1934 raises provocative questions: Was he there as a favor to Tolson or as a genuinely qualified recruit? What role did he play in mediating the relationship between Hoover and Tolson? And once welcomed into that relationship, what did he see and know?[10]

Hottel had been a star at GW: captain of the football team, inducted into the top honor societies, the most popular man on campus and in Tolson's fraternity, where he got to know some of the Bureau's future top men. His only flaw as a recruit was his academic record. As an undergraduate, he ended up on academic probation a whopping three times. Eventually he enrolled in the law school but failed to take a single exam or finish a course. Perhaps for this reason, he initially went into insurance rather than government service.

He remained tied to the Bureau nonetheless, both through his friendship with Tolson and through his broader circle of acquaintances. In 1928, forced to abandon the Sigma Nu house in the wake of graduation, Hottel and Tolson moved into a flat near the fraternity. A few years after that, they relocated to the Westchester Apartments on Cathedral Avenue, where, according to the rental manager, Hottel cultivated "many friends" and ended up "very well-liked by everyone." Hoover was among those friends, frequently stopping by the apartment with Tolson as part of their weeknight routine. In 1934, when Hottel quit his insurance job rather than accept a transfer to Chicago, Hoover suggested the obvious: "Well, why don't you come with us?"[11]

There was never much question about whether Hottel's Bureau application would be approved. Tolson's brother (now an assistant director of the National Park Service) gave a glowing reference, assuring the interviewing agent that "he has never heard anything derogatory to applicant and has never heard of him ever getting in any trouble whatsoever." FBI official Stan Tracy testified that Hottel had been a "popular student" at GW, "exceptionally active in athletics" and admired "by both students and professors." Tolson personally signed off on the application. "Recommend appointment Guy Hottel as Sp Agt Caf 8 for Sept school," he jotted in a memo, "address Apt 431B Westchester Apts." At no point did Tolson acknowledge in writing what everyone at the Bureau knew: 431B of the Westchester was his own apartment.[12]

This tendency to overlook the rules for Hottel, to simply pass him along, held for years to come, as he rose to become a top Bureau official as well as a key member of

Hoover's social world. Hoover whisked him through training, then assigned him to the usual run of distant offices. Once in the field, Hottel promptly crashed a Bureau car. While Hoover demanded that he pay for the damage, two months later he gave the agent a raise, based on Tolson's recommendation. In July 1935, Hottel endured a head injury when another agent ran their car into a telephone pole. The following month, he got a raise of three hundred dollars, personally approved by both Hoover and Tolson. By the end of 1935, Hottel had earned a third raise as well as a transfer back to D.C. Despite his weak record, Hoover decided to place Hottel at the important Washington field office, where he could resume living with Tolson.[13]

Hottel later described his treatment as typical Bureau policy. "You got quick promotion in those days." Others have suggested a more complicated narrative: that Hoover went out of his way for Hottel because Hottel knew his secrets. In later years Hottel allegedly boasted that he had seen Hoover and Tolson involved in "sex parties at Hoover's house, you know, with the boys"—indeed, that Hoover coerced his Bureau subordinates into attending these gatherings as a rite of passage. Such claims by themselves do not amount to much. The policeman who described Hottel's confession offered no documentation beyond his own memory, and Hottel allegedly revealed such stories while stupendously drunk. The most that can be said is that the stories fit with Hoover's pattern of using his status as FBI director to develop intimate relationships with his subordinates. His right to do so was baked into Bureau culture: homosocial intensity, strict hierarchy, the need for employees always to please and placate the boss. At the very least, Hottel's status as a close friend and social favorite helps to explain his own peculiar FBI record. In 1936 alone, he earned reprimands for offending the Colombian ambassador, playing golf while on call, and failing to restrain drunken companions at the Congressional Country Club. The following year, Hoover appointed him special agent in charge of the Washington field office.[14]

HOOVER HAD A LONG PRACTICE OF HIRING MEN HE LIKED AND RESPECTED, then developing greater friendship and intimacy through their work together. Beginning in 1935, his job also began to provide him another social outlet. With both Hollywood and Washington backing him as "America's popular Public Hero No.1," Hoover suddenly discovered he was the kind of man other people wanted to meet. After four decades of plugging along in Washington, he entered a glittering, cosmopolitan world populated by film stars, socialites, athletes, and wisecracking reporters. And he welcomed the change. Despite his faith in self-discipline and serious-minded work, Hoover finally let loose a little bit in 1935. Tolson (and sometimes Hottel) joined him, in the background but attentively present and ready to support their director.[15]

As *The Washington Herald* noted, in the wake of the Dillinger case and the *G-Men* film, everyone who was anyone wanted a chance to peek inside the FBI. "Competing with the Lincoln Memorial, the Washington Monument and the cherry blossoms is a display with a distinctly modern lure," the paper wrote. "It presents 'gats,' 'rods,' bullets, sawed-off shotguns, the gun used by 'Baby Face' Nelson when he killed Inspector Cowley, the bullet-proof vest worn by John Dillinger." If it was convenient, Hoover might occasionally greet public tours. For truly important people, though, he went out of his way. Their tours included visits to his office, where they could peruse the weapons stash and strange trinkets left over from the crime war. They also made their way to the basement shooting range, where special guests were permitted to shoot live ammunition from a tommy gun, then pose for pictures. In the standard photo, visitors faced directly into the camera, the barrels of their guns pointed out.[16]

Hoover joined in countless photos of this sort, whether with the manager of the Detroit Tigers or the editor of *The American Magazine*. Tolson's office was responsible for organizing the tours, and Hoover could be vicious when they made a mistake. On one occasion, agents failed to notify him that a baron and baroness would be passing through, yielding a cutting memo from Hoover to Tolson. "I believe it would be entirely possible for Mrs. Franklin Roosevelt to come down, casually join one of the tours, give her name and be shown through, and the Director's office not even be informed," Hoover wrote. When Mrs. Roosevelt did show up a few months later, escorting a group of schoolgirls, Tolson made sure that Hoover was her tour guide.[17]

The roster of men and women who traipsed through the FBI in the late 1930s included a who's who of American celebrity: film stars Jean Harlow and James Cagney, stage duo Victor Moore and Billy Gaxton, bandleader Guy Lombardo and screen legend Walter Pidgeon. Even "America's little darling," child actress Shirley Temple, showed up for a series of photos in which she peered into a big black microscope and rode the iron horse in the training gym. Other occasions brought radio stars, Boy Scouts, professional athletes, Shriners, and Jewish boys on educational junkets from the Lower East Side.[18]

Washington itself treated Hoover as a hometown hero. In January 1935, GW alumni hosted a luncheon for him and his brother, Dick, now fifty-five and also making news, as an investigator of steamboat accidents. In June, GW presented Hoover with an honorary doctoral degree, eighteen years after he had graduated into the tumult of the Great War. Kappa Alpha put him on the cover of its monthly journal, boasting of his success at developing "a law enforcement unit second to none in the world." Even the Roosevelt administration paid homage. In the spring of 1935, the government requisitioned two bulletproof Pierce-Arrow limousines capable of reaching 110 miles per hour, polished off with dark blue paint and a chromium finish. One was for Roosevelt, who had survived an assassination attempt in 1933. The other was for Hoover.[19]

The Washington press recognized Hoover's status as a favored son of the executive branch. "Edgar Hoover and Harry Hopkins Called Chief Personalities of Young New

Deal," one paper noted, pairing Hoover with one of Roosevelt's closest personal advisers. Now, though, it was not just the reflected glory of the president or attorney general that brought Hoover's name into the papers. Reporters massaged the available tidbits about his own life: his fondness for antiques, the fact that he lived alone with his "handsome mother," his preference for "bachelor solitude." In August, *Time* even put him on the cover, one of the highest honors the national magazine world could bestow. The article addressed the usual themes of crime detection and federal administration. But it also paid attention to his life outside the office, noting that "he is a bachelor, living with his semi-invalid mother in the pleasant frame house where he was born" and that his "friends . . . are few and include no women." The article mentioned just three men who seemed personally important to Hoover: his college friend Frank Baughman, his coauthor, Courtney Ryley Cooper, and his "assistant" Clyde Tolson.[20]

Like many other onlookers that year, the *Time* reporter gained only a dim comprehension of Hoover's true affections. Though Baughman, Cooper, and Hottel appeared on occasion, smiling and mugging for group photos, it was Tolson who showed up everywhere, sitting with Hoover at the theater, smiling and laughing on the sidelines of baseball games and ringside at fights. When Hoover went back to the Bureau around two o'clock one morning, responding to a false alarm, Tolson came along. When Hoover celebrated his twentieth anniversary at the Justice Department, Tolson posed with him for photos: two men shaking hands in matching white summer suits, surrounded by a sea of flowers. They made little effort to hide from the press, and joked openly about their adventures together. When they got stuck in shallow water on a Potomac fishing expedition, Tolson quipped to a reporter, "I'm not supposed to know how to row. I'm supposed to see that others do it—and I always do my duty."[21]

One of Tolson's "duties" was to help Hoover navigate this choppy new world of celebrity, to be at his side when the publicity men, filmmakers, and famous guests came to call. Tolson and Hoover perfected their own pose for the cameras. In a typical shot, Hoover sat at his desk while Tolson stood to his right, peering down at important papers on the blotter. Even in the office, though, they could still have fun. When a Hollywood director showed up to shoot some footage at the Bureau in 1936, Hoover commandeered the equipment and turned the lens on Tolson. A Bureau photographer captured the scene in a still picture: Hoover sitting astride the metal arm of the bulky film camera, controlling the angle and suppressing a grin, while an amused but self-conscious Tolson holds still for his gaze.[22]

OF ALL THE INVITATIONS THAT CAME THEIR WAY IN 1935, NONE WAS MORE IM-portant than the one from Walter Winchell, the nation's premier gossip columnist. The son of Russian Jewish immigrants in New York, Winchell had clawed his way from vaudeville to media stardom by cultivating a distinctive "slanguage" that conveyed both a winking insider status and street savvy. By the time he met Hoover in August 1934, Winchell dominated the gossip press, handing out dollops of publicity and notoriety to the nation's fame seekers through his syndicated column and wildly popular radio show. The truly favored could earn an invitation to join Winchell at his table inside the Stork Club, the most fashionable and sought-after fixture of New York nightlife. Winchell issued this invitation to Hoover in the fall of 1934. Always attuned to social cues and hierarchy, he made sure to extend the welcome for two. "He was also quite impressed with Mr. Tolson," an FBI memo noted.[23]

Like so many of Hoover's relationships, his friendship with Winchell depended upon an exchange of professional benefit: Hoover provided tips and legitimacy, while Winchell provided sympathetic publicity and a touch of glamour. During early 1935, as Hoover began to entertain the possibility of a more robust public relations effort, Winchell became one of his first points of contact, as dependable as Cooper but with the ability to deliver far more influence far more quickly. As a sign of his favor, Hoover began to provide Winchell with Bureau protection in cities where the columnist's penchant for writing about corrupt politicians and underworld "banditti" got him into hot water. He also passed along information and rumors of benefit to the Bureau. By the fall of 1935, the information exchange had grown so obvious that "considerable talk is heard of late in New York City implying that Winchell has some connection within the Bureau with a Bureau official which permits him to secure these news items before other reporters," the New York field office noted.[24]

What set Winchell apart from other reporters—what gave him his special cachet in Hoover's life—was his status as a cultural tycoon and social arbiter, the biggest man in New York's café society. Winchell's domain encompassed everything about the city that transcended the Depression: heiresses and starlets, highballs and big bands, Cole Porter's Broadway and Dorothy Parker's bon mots. At the center of it all was the Stork Club, the most glittering of the former speakeasies now operating as legitimate taxpaying businesses. Even in 1935, two years after the end of Prohibition, the Club gave off an aura of decadence and illicit activity, the sort of place where, in Porter's famous phrase, "anything goes." Winchell had helped to make the Stork Club's reputation, declaring it "New York's New Yorkiest place," and he enjoyed privileges unheard of for other guests, including near-exclusive rights to dine and entertain at his own specially reserved Table 50. Film stars and debutantes came to see and be seen. So did politicians and grand dukes and tycoons and former bootleggers. Out front, the club hung a gold chain to separate the throngs of the curious from the truly desirable. Winchell ushered Hoover and Tolson beyond the chain and into the strange, liminal world inside.[25]

Given his upbringing, Hoover might have declined the invitation, rejecting the club's smoke-hazed world in favor of the clean living of the Presbyterian Church. Instead, both he and Tolson seemed drawn to the club's manic late-night culture, in which lines of propriety, identity, and social hierarchy could be crossed with impunity.

After years of being the rule follower and fussbudget amid charming football stars, Hoover reveled in his new identity as the celebrity of the hour. His activities reflect a giddy, almost bottomless desire for attention, along with an adolescent wonder that he, too, was now feted by the biggest names and invited to the best parties.

The Stork maintained certain limits: no Black patrons, no women unaccompanied by a man after six p.m. Within those limits, however, the club catered to experimentation and excess. On one New Year's Eve, Hoover and Tolson joined fashion model Luisa Stuart and heavyweight boxer James Braddock for an all-night bacchanal. They dressed up silly, with Hoover donning an extravagantly plumed fez and Tolson a tall shiny cap. All of them played to the cameras, present to record the party of all parties on the night of all nights. In one photo, Hoover points a fake rifle at Braddock, who's pretending to wind up for a knockout punch. In another, Stuart turns the gun on Hoover, who puts his hands in the air in mock surrender.[26]

By the middle of 1935, the duo of "J. Edgar Hoover, the boss of the 'G-Men'... and Clyde Tolson, Hoover's right hand man" had become a fixture of the Broadway scene. Not only Winchell but rivals such as Leonard Lyons proclaimed proudly that "J. Edgar Hoover, head G-Man, now talks the Broadway lingo as a result of his night-club visits." The Stork Club's owner, Sherman Billingsley, even introduced a new drink in their honor: the FBI Fizz.[27]

Many nights sent Hoover and Tolson hopping from the Stork to other clubs such as Toots Shor's and 21, where they were greeted as crime-fighting celebrities and plied with favors and drinks. On one particularly exhausting evening, they accompanied Winchell to a party for Ernest Hemingway, where the writer attempted to display his tough-guy prowess by sparring with the host. While Winchell's column regularly contained references to their café-society adventures, he moved carefully when it came to describing the relationship between Hoover and Tolson. After Hoover appeared on the cover of *Time*, Winchell fumed in his column that the magazine had misrepresented the FBI director. "If Time's intent was to make Mr. Hoover appear like a sissy, let it be recorded now that he isn't at all," Winchell wrote. "As a matter of fact, Mr. Hoover and his assistant, Clyde Tolson, are concrete examples of what the well-dressed lads should wear."[28]

Winchell treated them as a social couple, invariably signing his personal notes with "my best to Clyde and yourself." He also invited them for regular Sunday brunches at his Manhattan apartment, one duo among many. Luisa Stuart, the budding model who spent New Year's Eve with them, recalled that Hoover once showed up alone, claiming that Tolson was sick. "After he left, people said Clyde wasn't really sick," she later recalled. "They'd had a big fight. The word was that Hoover had found Clyde in bed with another man." The point of the story was not how scandalous the revelation was, but how ordinary such situations were in Stork Club circles. Stuart claimed that she once overheard Tolson wishing drunkenly that he could dance cheek to cheek with

Hoover, and even saw the two men hold hands on occasion. She found the sight confusing until someone "told me they were queers or fairies."[29]

Throughout New York, police targeted clubs and acts catering explicitly to a gay clientele. But "queers" and "fairies" quietly thrived in the Broadway scene of the early 1930s, from the wildly popular composer Cole Porter on down through the artistic ranks. Hoover and Tolson forged an especially close relationship with singing sensation Ethel Merman, star of Porter's musical *Anything Goes* and, not incidentally, the mistress of married Stork Club owner Sherman Billingsley. They attended her 1936 opening night in Porter's *Red, Hot and Blue!*, then gushed to the papers about her performance. When they missed another opening night, they sent a joint telegram of apology. "We're sorry we can't be in the front row to hiss—no kiss you," read the note. "Tenderest regards. John Edgar Hoover. Clyde Tolson."[30]

IN ALL THESE ENCOUNTERS—THE LATE NIGHTS AT THE STORK, THE LONG DAYS at the office—Tolson and Hoover were building a life together, sharing work and a sense of mission, and along the way having some fun. But how did they actually feel about each other? And how did they conceive of their relationship, outside of office formalities and polite terms such as "right-hand man"? Here the evidence is more sparse, and must be interpreted rather than quoted. But the evidence is there nonetheless: of an erotic intimacy as well as a hierarchical dynamic, a supportive social partnership as well as a deliberately obscured affection.

Take a single episode: Miami, Florida, February 1936. At Winchell's suggestion, Hoover and Tolson traveled south together for a vacation in Miami Beach, a respite from the cold that would soon become an annual winter ritual. Hottel came along, too, the third man on fishing trips, beach outings, visits to the track, and nights on the town. Hottel described such trips as run-of-the-mill bachelor adventures, filled with jai alai, horse racing, and lazy afternoons on the beach. Hoover could be funny and relaxed outside the office, Hottel recalled, less the tyrannical boss than the egalitarian friend. But there were moments of discomfort, especially when Hoover called upon Hottel to mollify or police Tolson. On one occasion, Hottel canceled a double date with Tolson and two women after Hoover refused to spend the evening on his own. Hottel described Hoover's pressure less as sexual jealousy and more as Hoover's need for control. "Mr. Hoover had ways of getting his own way, you know," Hottel recalled decades later. "Mr. Hoover was a little selfish in that respect—looking out for his own interests. He wasn't going to get married. So he liked it the way it was."[31]

Hoover's private vacation photographs suggest a slightly different story—an experience of mutual attraction and intimacy between Hoover and Tolson that made Hottel all but irrelevant. Unlike official FBI shots, with their stiff, carefully contained poses, these more personal photos showcase the physical dynamism of Tolson, a remarkably handsome thirty-six-year-old man with a dazzling smile. Hoover had photos of Tolson on the beach, his hair tousled in the wind and his chest bare above rumpled swim trunks. He also kept a photo of Tolson asleep in a beach chair, arms and legs crossed in front of him. In some pictures, Hoover and Tolson are together, standing along the shore in bathing suits. In most, Hoover looks older and thicker than Tolson but also happy, his face alight with the sort of big, broad grin that would never appear in Bureau files. Occasionally the two men are touching, with Hoover's arm slung across Tolson's shoulders. More often, they are close but decorously apart. The most intimate photos are the ones taken in secret: Hoover looking out to sea from the prow of a fishing boat; Hoover in his striped robe on the hotel deck; Hoover walking, shirt-less, through an open doorway. Sometimes they took matching photos, each man framed in silhouette with the ocean as background.[32]

Were these the photographs of friends or lovers, coworkers or coconspirators—or perhaps all at once? Even as Hoover's job made it possible for him to hire men whose company he enjoyed, it also provided a logical explanation for those relationships, keeping them at once inside and outside the public eye. This fusion of worlds—of the public and the private, of work and intimacy—remained at the heart of his relationship with Tolson for decades to come. On July 1, 1936, a few months after their return from Florida, Hoover promoted Tolson to a newly created position known as "assistant to the director," vaulting him over Harold Nathan into the Bureau's number two spot. Tolson responded with an extraordinary display of commitment: he stayed on the job for the rest of Hoover's life.[33]

CHAPTER 18

Sob Sisters and Convict Lovers

(1935–1938)

"EVERY AGENT OF THIS DEPARTMENT KILLED ON DUTY WAS SHOT BY A **PAROLED CRIMINAL**"
J. EDGAR HOOVER

SOBSISTER

SUPERSENTIMENTALIST

Think THAT Over!

In the mid-1930s, Hoover began to hone a moralistic law-and-order message. Cartoon from the *Omaha World-Herald*, May 1936.

© 1936 OMAHA WORLD-HERALD

If Hoover's new social life allowed for some libertine indulgence, his public messaging did not. As a private citizen, he lived at the edge of social convention, staying up late at glittering clubs and dinner parties, moving through town in the company of a handsome man. As a federal law enforcement official, however, he held tight to the strictures of his Presbyterian youth—and in 1935, even as he reveled in the grand experiments of Broadway and the Stork Club, he began to speak out in the stern, moralizing voice he had first cultivated as a young man. To promote his message, he called upon the Bureau's press apparatus as well as his own newfound celebrity, taking advantage of the public's growing interest in his views to articulate the law-and-order themes that would become another key element of his public identity. His emerging political voice sounded different from the one he had adopted during his first decade as director, when establishing his bona fides as a good-government reformer and efficient administrator drove Bureau priorities. Now, as a crime-fighting celebrity and political figure in his own right, he began to share his thoughts about "the home, the church, and the school," and the nation began to listen.[1]

In Hoover's formulation, crime was more than a law enforcement challenge; it constituted an epic struggle between good and evil. According to Hoover, that struggle took place within each individual, and drew upon the virtues—discipline, self-control, resistance to temptation—that he had been taught as a child. It occurred within families as well, as parents tried (and too often failed) to instill such virtues through instruction and example. It required schools and churches to do their part, teaching young people not just the necessity of self-control, but the need to defer to higher authorities such as law, government, and God. Perhaps most of all, it necessitated vigilance by the nation *as* a nation. Though most enforcement was local, Hoover explained, the behavior of young people was a measure of national unity and strength of purpose. Beginning in 1935, he presented himself as an arbiter of these essential virtues, not merely a law enforcement expert but, increasingly, a judge of the nation's soul.

Millions lauded him as a hero for taking a stand. In one 1936 poll, boys between the ages of eight and eighteen ranked Hoover as the nation's second most admired man, just behind Robert Ripley, of the radio serial *Ripley's Believe It or Not*. Others saw something dangerous in his outlook, a tendency to reduce the complexities of human existence to a few inflammatory phrases. Hoover's first instinct when faced with such criticism was to strike back, just as Palmer had taught him to do in 1920. And yet the later stereotype of Hoover as a bully and purveyor of gossip only begins to capture the range of methods he developed during these first years of fame to promote and enforce his views. In the 1930s, he also discovered the power of fostering a mass constituency, recognizing the potential inherent in the millions of ordinary citizens who thrilled to the G-Men movies and who showed up by the hundreds each day to tour the Bureau.[2]

Like Winchell, who balanced his celebrity club-hopping with an image as the champion of "Mr. and Mrs. America," Hoover learned to play the part of the self-made, populist bureaucrat, taking to the road in a grueling schedule of speeches about the decline of American society and the loss of the nation's moral compass. He also began to use the Bureau itself as an engine of social persuasion, launching anti-vice crusades aimed at prostitutes, gamblers, and "sex criminals," people who posed a moral as well as physical danger to the nation's women and children. These efforts brought a certain amount of criticism. But they helped to solidify his identity as a social conservative among the New Deal liberals and as a distinctive national voice.

FOR HIS FIRST INTERVENTION, HOOVER CHOSE AN ISSUE THAT HAD BEEN AGI-tating police for more than a decade: the use and abuse of the nation's parole system. Penologists had invented parole in the late nineteenth century as a spur to rehabilitation, reasoning that the possibility of early release for good behavior might incentivize prisoners to change. In Hoover's view, parole had since come to stand for all the ills of modern criminal justice: local corruption, sympathy for gangsters, the nation's inability to confront the crime problem as a civic menace. As Hoover pointed out, nearly every "public enemy" who shot or killed a federal agent in the early 1930s was out on parole. The policy encouraged contempt for law enforcement among would-be criminals, according to Hoover, assuring them of brief stays in prison no matter how grave their offenses.[3]

During the early months of Roosevelt's crime war, Hoover had viewed parole as a matter beyond his purview, "under the jurisdiction of another branch of the Department of Justice." Over the following year, however, his growing celebrity boosted his confidence in speaking out. "Yes, I have strong opinions on parole," he admitted to a reporter. "I have a right to have them. This division has had men slaughtered by brutes out on parole." According to the reporter, Hoover seemed to come alive as he spoke the words. "There's a gleam in the eyes of Edgar Hoover when he speaks of the 'paroled brutes' who slaughtered his men; and there's real bitterness in his voice." After years of suppressing his opinions, of deferring to men higher up in Washington, Hoover used his fame to articulate his own worldview.[4]

The public responded well. In July 1935, Hoover traveled with Tolson to Atlantic City, New Jersey, to deliver his annual speech at the convention of the International Association of Chiefs of Police. Usually, it was a humdrum affair, focused on personnel reform and forensic technique. This time, the press was paying attention, and Hoover catered to their presence. Adopting the pose of an outraged general, he lashed into the "sentimentalists, crooks, sob sisters and convict lovers" whose tender "mercy" for the "foul body-snatcher" had helped to kill his men. "This is a time when law enforcement must fight for its right to conquer the criminal world," he maintained. "It must combat the aids by which crime flourishes—easy parole, easy commutation, easy probation from sob sister judges, and above all, that monumental fake which has too long been perpetrated upon the American public, the prison sentence which says one thing and means another." The world he described had two sides: the law and the forces of lawlessness. The struggle was to determine which side the American public would be on.[5]

In depicting the coming showdown, Hoover drew upon the same imagery he had once used to characterize political radicals: criminals were vicious animals, their sympathizers feminized weaklings or deluded eggheads. One observer labeled his speech "the bluntest talk on crime ever delivered by a public official." Another saw a rallying cry for ordinary Americans who had been waiting for someone to deliver a bit of common sense about crime. "Every decent man and woman in America is cheering for J. Edgar Hoover, for he is a scrapper," wrote one columnist. "He shoots from the hip and, God bless him, let us hope every bullet hits its mark." Hoover seemed to be a New Dealer who despised social workers and bleeding hearts, a white-collar reformer who held both criminologists and professors in contempt. With his Atlantic City speech, he put himself on record as a law-and-order conservative in an administration of social policy liberals.[6]

While much of the press delighted in Hoover's belligerent stance, penologists and reformers responded with befuddlement, taken aback by the ferocity of his words. They had known him for years as a respectful and serious man. Suddenly, he was denouncing them as fiends incarnate, blowing up disagreements over policy into a divine struggle for the American soul. Sing Sing warden Lewis Lawes, the nation's most prominent penal reformer, dismissed Hoover's speech as "one showing a very narrow viewpoint." Hoover focused on policing, investigation, and the drama of the manhunt. Lawes emphasized rehabilitation and penal policy, convinced that so-called criminals could be returned to society as law-abiding men and women. Lawes thought Hoover's approach revealed a fundamental lack of empathy—not only toward those convicted of crimes but also toward men and women struggling to help them change. "It is not a matter of being soft or coddling," he explained. "We are dealing with human beings." For reformers such as Lawes, Hoover's outlook was too rigid to account for the messiness of real life or the complexities of human nature.[7]

The critiques had little effect. If anything, Hoover's rhetoric escalated throughout the summer of 1935, even as he and Tolson spent more time at places like the Stork and 21. He seemed to thrive on the attention accorded his remarks, growing ever more outspoken in his denunciations of "human rats" and the "gutter scum" who helped them. To assist the public in making sense of this more aggressive Bureau director, in the summer of 1935 the Associated Press put together a mini-dictionary of his "sizzling" crime-related terms. In the Hoover lexicon, criminal defense attorneys were henceforth to be identified as "shyster lawyers" and "legal vermin," while parole advocates were "sob sisters," "intruders," "convict lovers," and "fuss-budget busybodies." "J. Edgar Hoover, chief of the 'G-men,'" the AP concluded, "has entered the front rank of Capital phrasemakers with a bang."[8]

HOOVER'S BID FOR LEADERSHIP ON THE CRIME ISSUE WAS MORE THAN RHE- torical. In the summer of 1935, making use of the institution-building skills that remained his hallmark and greatest strength, he announced the creation of a training school—soon to be known as the FBI National Academy—for the edification of the nation's policemen. The academy followed the same model as the Identification Division and the crime lab, with the FBI serving as the professional vanguard for the nation's supposedly under-equipped and ill-trained police. In this case, though, it was the policemen themselves who were the objects of reform, recruited to Washington for twelve weeks of classes and indoctrination in Hoover's ideas. Roosevelt himself had approved the plan after deciding, in the attorney general's words, that "public psychology is good today, Congress is friendly, and law enforcement agencies throughout the country are in a cooperative mood." Under Hoover's plan, the nation's policemen would receive the same training as FBI agents, and would therein be converted to his ideas.[9]

The academy started small, with officers invited from twenty-five carefully selected local police departments. Most of what they learned involved technical matters ranging from forensic lab work and interrogation technique to the preparation of accurate and legible reports. With such instructions came a crash course in Hoover's preferred culture of technical skill, professionalism, and nonpartisan administration—a "scientific college of crime detection," in one reporter's description. Despite the academy's small size, Hoover anticipated that its graduates would bring his ideas back to their hometowns, thus spreading the FBI's influence and creating a national network of police officials loyal to the Bureau. "Under this project there will ultimately be at least one man in each city who speaks the language of the Federal Bureau of Investigation," Hoover explained to Congress, thus eliminating sources of friction and misunderstanding between local and federal authorities. Within a few years, he expanded this vision to include police officials from outside the United States on the logic that they, too, could benefit from FBI training while fostering cooperation across borders. Over the long term, it was expected that many of the academy candidates would not only rejoin their local departments, but would go on to lead them—and to transform them in Hoover's image.

Classes met inside the Justice building, where the local officers could gaze in wonder upon the array of microscopes, tire treads, chemicals, handwriting samples, fiber scraps, and high-tech cameras used in the FBI's work. The policemen turned students also gained access to FBI shooting ranges, where they were taught "to manipulate all the high powered weapons needed to cope with hoodlums," in one newspaper's description. Most of all, they learned about the FBI's internal culture, with its emphasis on no-typo paperwork, efficiency in filing, and white-collar demeanor. Homer Cummings likened it to a West Point for law enforcement, charged with training the elite future officers of the police profession. Others preferred a different term. Though Hoover could not require college degrees for the nation's tens of thousands of policemen, one paper explained, he could educate them in his ideas and methods at the new "G-Men's University."[10]

EVEN AS THE NATIONAL ACADEMY TAUGHT POLICEMEN HOW TO BEHAVE LIKE G-Men, Hoover sought to impart a different set of lessons to the American public— not about the duties of government to address the crime problem, but about what Rev. MacLeod had taught him as a boy: that crime was above all a matter of sin and personal responsibility. Expanding upon the "boy problem" of his childhood, he focused much of his attention on "America's youth problem," a catchall term for everything from an alleged rise in juvenile crime to the vague sense that young people no longer lived up to their parents' moral standards. He did not, in truth, possess reliable statistics about minor crimes committed by children, which were notoriously difficult to count and classify. But evidence of worries over their moral slippage were all too easy to find. As the sociologists Robert and Helen Lynd pointed out in their classic 1929 study, *Middletown*, technologies such as the automobile and the talking picture meant that young people were spending their leisure time far away from home—and therefore away from parental supervision. Since then, the Depression had produced millions of down-and-out young people, unemployed and rootless and riding the rails in search of jobs. Hoover tended to underplay such social factors, describing crime as an individual problem to be solved through self-control, discipline, and resistance to temptation.[11]

Unlike those in the "cream-puff school of criminology," Hoover presented criminal activity first and foremost as a test of character. Even the most innocuous activities could present hidden temptations. "Crime often plays bridge with you," he warned. "Crime dances with your sons and daughters." Only through personal vigilance could the ordinary citizen hope to remain on the side of right and good. If Hoover believed in self-improvement, however, he also understood that boys—and girls, too— could not be expected to maintain such high standards alone. It was up to parents to set the right example and to mete out punishment when children fell short. In speeches and columns, Hoover blamed criminal activity among youth on their parents' failure to enforce household decorum. "It is time for America to resurrect that standard of discipline which did much to give this country its rugged, stalwart honesty of purpose, its determination, its achievements," Hoover explained. He did not mention the difficulties he had encountered within his own family: his aunt's murder, his father's descent into mental illness. But some of the ways that he described the difference between the edifying and troubled home seemed to reflect the values of his mother's household. He often distinguished between the "clean" life of the upright family and the germ-ridden environment of the criminal, likening crime to "a highly dangerous epidemic of disease" requiring "every possible sanitary measure" in response. "The problem of crime is the problem of the family," he concluded, urging parents to look beyond their own needs and desires.[12]

The school and church, too, had important roles to play in molding young men and women into decent citizens. Beginning in 1935, Hoover emerged as one of the nation's great champions of Sunday school, wistfully recalling his own days as a prizewinning Bible student and instructor. "In these complex times, the task of the church has become infinitely more difficult and, correspondingly, the need for its teachings more pronounced," he explained to *Baptist Student* magazine. He prescribed Bible verses as guides to fighting crime, testifying to the ways in which they had helped him through periods of trial and tribulation. After years as the apolitical bureaucrat, he began to speak openly of his Presbyterian upbringing and to present himself as a man of faith.[13]

———

IF HOOVER HAD ATTEMPTED TO DELIVER THIS MORAL INSTRUCTION ALONE, HE would only have gotten so far. But he had an entire federal bureaucracy at his disposal. As he refashioned his public image, he demanded that his agents conform to and embody his ideas, an intensification of the ideological training that had long been part of Bureau life. Beginning in 1938, Hoover required employees to adopt the FBI Pledge for Law Enforcement Officers, a dense one-page statement that combined good-government professionalism with vows to root out cultural and moral rot. Under the pledge, they promised "to testify without bias or display of emotion," but also "to eliminate the criminal parasite which preys upon our social order." The two messages—one of dispassionate restraint, the other of total moral conviction—reflected the ongoing contradictions in Hoover's persona.[14]

At the center of this ideological work was Crime Records, the division that had been founded to crunch statistics and prepare annual reports but now functioned as Hoover's public relations division. As Hoover became more outspoken, his public relations unit followed suit, churning out speeches, editorials, and advice columns to promote his message, then offering them free to any interested newspaper. Upon publication, Crime Records sent personal notes from the director even to the smallest of small-town newspapers, thanking them for supporting Hoover's anti-crime efforts. That practice, in turn, produced still more adulatory press. Small-town editors could hardly believe that the "Chief of America's Heroic G-Men," in the words of the Shelbyville, Kentucky, *Sentinel*, would take the time to acknowledge their efforts. Prompt response to citizen inquiries had long been a Hoover policy, but now such letters entailed a brush with celebrity, the thrilling idea that a man as busy and famous as J. Edgar Hoover still cared about the little people of America.[15]

Speaking invitations poured in—from civic groups and churches, schools and businesses, each seeking to learn how to create a generation of "law-abiding, successful, and forward looking citizens." Hoover accepted an astonishing number of those invitations, but there were hundreds more he could not. To address this demand, Crime Records organized a speaker's bureau populated by agents of good appearance and verbal competence who traveled and made speeches "with the zeal of old missionaries" on Hoover's behalf. The most important of them was Louis Nichols, a GW law graduate hired in 1934 and transferred to the publications section in the fall of 1935, just as the G-Man craze was seizing the nation. Six feet tall and "rather handsome," in the observation of a fellow agent, Nichols quickly became known for his "unusual interest and intense enthusiasm" for Bureau work. A veteran of the YMCA's public relations office, he did almost anything that Crime Records needed, from writing about parole policy to directing tours. Indeed, he worked too hard even for Hoover's taste. In July 1936, after less than a year at Crime Records, Nichols collapsed at his home, plagued by convulsions, and Hoover insisted he take a break. After recovering, Nichols went on to become the single most important Bureau official other than Hoover or Tolson, charged with managing the FBI's public image and press relations over the next two decades.[16]

One cornerstone of his strategy was the ongoing cultivation of a grassroots constituency. Among the first groups to sign up were men's professional organizations, institutions to which Hoover had always been drawn, and that now warmed to his message of self-discipline and masculine righteousness. Hoover was still a Mason, but his status did not stop rival groups such as Kiwanis International from inviting him to speak. Businessmen's organizations showed a similar interest. In 1935, Hoover spoke before the annual meeting of the New York State Chamber of Commerce. The following year he lectured to the Junior Chamber in Memphis. He warned its young members against succumbing to "the idiotic idolatry of cowardly outlaws" or listening to the "sentimental yammerheads" who viewed crime as something other than a battle between good and evil.[17]

Hoover paid special attention to boys' organizations, perhaps recalling his own struggles as a teenager to find mentors who could serve as models of a successful and productive life. Many of the groups that reached out to him had themselves been founded in response to the "boy problem" of the early twentieth century, including the Boy Scouts of America. Now these groups welcomed Hoover as a moral instructor, his message of hard work and spiritual rigor in line with their institutional missions. "I would rather be received into the hearts of a group of young men like this than by an adult assembly," he told the students of Philadelphia's Northeast High School, a message he would repeat before countless teenage boys over the next several decades. He expressed particular fondness for youth baseball leagues, recalling the excitement of meeting Rev. MacLeod for weekend games in the neighborhood sandlot.[18]

To women's organizations—and especially to mothers—Hoover's message was far more frightening. "Federal Agent Paints Dark Picture of Crime in Address Before D.A.R.," one newspaper noted, describing his speech to the Daughters of the American Revolution. In that appearance, Hoover laid out a fearsome vision of a society under siege by an army of violent criminals, leaving behind "miles upon miles of stiffened corpses," including three hundred thousand Americans "who today are walking the streets, not realizing they are doomed to die by the foul hand of the murderer." To prevent this outcome, he called upon the women of America to mount their own army and fight back. In 1937, the General Federation of Women's Clubs heeded his call with an initiative to mobilize its members behind Hoover's anti-crime agenda. In Cleveland alone, some twenty thousand club women began to organize discussions about crime, establish local classes for underprivileged boys, and advocate for citizenship instruction in public schools—all, as the federation boasted, with the endorsement and "cooperation of J. Edgar Hoover."[19]

That same year, the American Legion came calling, the start of the most important popular alliance of Hoover's career. Formed in 1919 to serve veterans, the Legion had posed early problems for the Bureau, with its members carrying out vigilante attacks against political radicals and labor organizers during the run-up to the Palmer Raids. By 1937, though, Hoover came to see the Legion as a possible base of support. That year, the Legion's Washington leadership approached the FBI with an offer to sponsor Bureau speakers in local public schools, part of a national outreach initiative that included the founding of Boys State, a civics-and-citizenship camp for young men. With Hoover's approval, Nichols began dispatching Bureau agents to school assemblies to speak on "Law Enforcement as a Profession" and to screen films such as *You Can't Get Away with It* and *Crime Does Not Pay*. In 1938, the Washington branch proposed to take the program nationwide, with the aim of providing every schoolchild in America a few moments in the presence of a live G-Man. Hoover loved the idea. "I feel that your organization has been of tremendous assistance to the FBI in the handling of the vexing juvenile delinquency problem," he wrote to the group's executives, praising them as a "bulwark of protection" against the decline of national morals.[20]

FOR ALL HIS SUCCESS IN CULTIVATING A NATIONAL AUDIENCE, HOOVER STILL had to make his way in Washington. And there his situation was growing more complicated by the minute. Outside the Capitol, things were going swimmingly well, with friends and supporters and hangers-on popping up each day. Inside, not everyone appreciated the blustery new FBI director. In 1936, one senator decided to call Hoover's bluff, the first time since the Palmer days that Hoover was forced to endure a hostile encounter in front of Congress. In response, he showed that he was no longer the nervous junior official he had once been. He was now a man with a national reputation, a popular constituency, and a growing sense of how to use his political power.

The episode began in early 1936, when the House Appropriations Committee welcomed him to testify. "The committee is always delighted to have you with us Mr. Hoover," the chair announced, "to hear you in the presentation of your justifications for the Bureau." Hoover was seeking a $5.8 million budget—the largest in Bureau history, more than twice what he had started with in 1924. To his surprise, the committee not only agreed to the sum but also added $225,000, explaining that "the activities of the G-Man have caught the public fancy." Later that month, a friendly senator introduced a bill raising Hoover's salary from $9,000 to $10,000 per year.[21]

The problem came from Senator Kenneth McKellar, a gruff Tennessee Democrat and member of the Senate Appropriations Committee. McKellar had opposed Hoover's reappointment in 1933, convinced that Bureau agents had once rifled his Senate office in search of political secrets. But none of McKellar's previous grumbling about the Bureau had amounted to much, in part because Hoover had never been important enough to warrant persistent attention. In 1936, that calculation changed, and McKellar saw a chance to go after him.

On April 10, Hoover showed up with Tolson to testify before McKellar's committee, expecting the same treatment from the Senate that he had received before the House two months earlier. Less than a minute into Hoover's appearance, however, McKellar interrupted to object that $6.025 million "seems to be a tremendous sum of money." For the next half hour, and in a second session on April 11, he proceeded not just to denounce Bureau policy, but to scoff at Hoover's identity as the nation's most important straight-shooting lawman. He noted that Hoover was actually a lawyer who spent most of his time behind a desk, and thus had no right to lecture policemen about how to do their jobs. "How many arrests have you made," McKellar demanded, "and who were they?" Hoover noted weakly that he'd "handled the investigations" of Emma Goldman and Alexander Berkman twenty years earlier, implicitly admitting that he had not, in fact, ever made an arrest. A few days later, at McKellar's suggestion, the Appropriations Committee scaled back the Bureau's budget to $5.8 million, eliminating the $225,000 approved by the House as a tribute to Hoover.[22]

In purely monetary terms, this was hardly worth worrying about—a trim of less than 4 percent in a Depression year when efficiency in government was already a bipartisan battle cry. But Hoover saw something critical at stake—not just money but pride and autonomy, the right to speak out on matters of national import. McKellar's attack called into question Hoover's crime-fighting prowess as well as his rising status as a law-and-order spokesman. "The Senate did its worst in connection with our appropriation," Hoover wrote a few days after his testimony. "I have not, however, given up the fight."[23]

Hoover's fight to prove McKellar wrong showed his increasing sophistication in organizing his supporters to put pressure on Congress. After the vote, a Mississippi-born FBI agent called on his state's senator, Theodore Bilbo, who promised to talk to "the Old Boy, meaning Senator McKellar" in return for a Bureau tour. That same day, one of Hoover's FBI speakers happened to be lecturing at the Contemporary Club, an organization composed of wealthy and influential New Yorkers. "All of them stated voluntarily that they would immediately 'get busy'," the agent assured Hoover, "and contact various Senators and Representatives in Washington who, they felt, would give every assistance possible." Since the Senate would have to approve the committee's decision, that gave Hoover just under a week to drum up votes from senators inclined to support the Bureau, and to change the minds of those who didn't. In the meantime, he ordered agents in Tennessee to round up support for the Bureau, and to let McKellar know that he was being watched.[24]

Hoover's public relations apparatus played a critical role in the campaign. Some newsmen attempted to contact him directly, promising to rustle up positive stories to counteract the "rather nasty" coverage of McKellar's interrogation. In other cases, Hoover's men took it upon themselves to contact local editors and radio stations. From

Philadelphia, a veteran of the Kansas City investigation wrote to say that he had spoken with three area papers, each of which agreed to publish editorials in support of restoring the $225,000. Similar sentiments poured in from papers enthusiastic about Hoover's law-and-order message. All made roughly the same point, championing Hoover as a uniquely effective public servant in a Washington establishment riddled with corruption and inefficiency.[25]

When the day of the vote arrived, the task of defending Hoover fell to Republican Senator Arthur Vandenberg, a dedicated Bureau ally. Like many Republicans, Vandenberg viewed Hoover as the great exception to New Deal profligacy—a Republican holdover who still knew what to do with government appropriations. Now Vandenberg declared his support of the Bureau's extra $225,000. "It does not make the slightest difference what the Senator from Tennessee has to say about relative arithmetic," Vandenberg said. "This happens to be a problem in the realm of grim reality. It is a problem which involves the basic protection of life and property in the United States against major crime; and upon that subject the most expert witness in America is J. Edgar Hoover, head of the Bureau of Investigation. I stand with him to the last necessity which he may require. So do the American people."[26]

So, to Hoover's relief, did a majority of the Senate. Just after three p.m., senators began calling with the good news: the Senate had agreed to restore the $225,000. "I am told," Hoover wrote a few days later, "it was actually the first time a Committee Chairman was so completely repudiated as McKellar was." Bureau staff noted each caller, as well as each senator who voted in favor of the Bureau, so that Hoover could send notes of thanks.[27]

Hoover had a message for McKellar as well. While in New York on the afternoon of April 30, Hoover received word that his agents had finally located Alvin Karpis, the last great figure of the Barker gang, at a hideout in New Orleans. Hoover and Tolson flew out the next morning, chartering a transport plane for a grueling journey south. The purpose of this mad dash was to refute McKellar's accusation that Hoover could not make an arrest. Karpis later said that low-level agents did all the dangerous work, capturing him and confiscating his rifle, then calling out to Hoover once the coast was clear. Hoover told a different story. Karpis "was scared to death when we closed in on him," he claimed. "He shook all over—his voice, his hands, and his knees." Both parties agreed that Hoover made the final arrest, grabbing Karpis inside a getaway vehicle, then instructing an agent to tie a necktie around the prisoner's wrists. In all the excitement, nobody remembered to bring a set of handcuffs, a picturesque touch that would become a staple of the Hoover legend.[28]

News accounts recognized the significance of what had taken place. "Karpis Arrest Hoover's First," cheered the *Milwaukee Sentinel*. So, apparently, did Senator McKellar. With no advance warning, he showed up at the FBI Academy graduation, sliding quietly into a chair proffered by Hoover's deputy Hugh Clegg. Toward the end of the ceremony, Clegg recalled, McKellar stood up to say something—a moment of trepidation for everyone in the room. "I surrender!" McKellar declared, in Clegg's recollection. "J. Edgar Hoover is the greatest American we have today. I was mistaken."[29]

"From that time on," Clegg explained, "he was a close friend and would argue strongly for the appropriation."[30]

HOOVER WAS NOT THE ONLY LAW ENFORCEMENT OFFICIAL ENGAGED IN THIS sort of politics, in which apocalyptic warnings of youth crime and moral laxity could produce both headlines and funds. In New York, District Attorney Thomas Dewey showed some of Hoover's talent for grabbing the spotlight. In Washington, Harry Anslinger, the young chief of the Federal Bureau of Narcotics, warned of a violence-ridden marijuana epidemic about to seize the country and began to conduct arrests accordingly. Hoover, too, soon went beyond words and stagy arrests to order his Bureau into action. In 1936, he "dusted off" the Mann Act, in one agent's words, launching a nationwide anti-vice and anti-prostitution campaign that served to reinforce his moral bromides with concerted federal action. Unlike the War on Crime, instigated by the attorney general and the White House, the vice raids were a campaign of choice for Hoover. They put the Bureau in the position of protecting not only life and property but also national virtue. By focusing on prostitution, Hoover could act as both a conservative moral arbiter and an efficient law enforcement administrator.[31]

He defined the Mann Act broadly, insisting that any contact across state lines—including by phone or telegraph—provided justification for Bureau action. Under this interpretation, each local brothel owner and sex worker was potentially committing a federal crime. In February 1936, Hoover justified the arrest of New York madam Mae Scheible, identified in the press as the "millionaire queen of the prostitution industry," on charges of trafficking women across state lines to supply her high-end brothels. Several months later, in the wake of the McKellar showdown, he extended the raids to Connecticut, where a network of brothel owners allegedly traded women up and down the Eastern Seaboard. As one agent later recalled, the Connecticut raids put Hoover in touch with all manner of "sexual abnormality," from "homosexuals" and "lesbians" to "sadists, masochists, and fetishists" and "mass orgies." But what Hoover emphasized publicly was the trafficking and victimization of young women, the area where the Bureau's jurisdiction was strongest. He used the Connecticut raids to introduce a campaign "against white slave rings everywhere in the country," approving raids on houses of prostitution in Cleveland, Boston, Chicago, Baltimore, Corpus Christi, even Hawaii.[32]

As the campaign intensified, Hoover continued to approve techniques he had once banned as cheap police work, to be used only for the most heinous of crimes. In preparation for the raids, he authorized multiple wiretaps. He also pressured his men to recruit confidential informants, including working prostitutes, who agreed to spy on illegal activities and provide client lists. When the moment of arrest finally came, Hoover made a point of being on the ground with his men—again refuting McKellar's accusation that he was no more than a desk man. In Atlantic City, he snuck into town with Tolson, hiding out in his hotel room until the final moment. Then, in a single coordinated burst of action, his agents descended on local brothels, resulting in the arraignment of 137 people. The *New York Herald Tribune* identified the raiding spree as "the biggest vice haul of recent years," the culmination of Hoover's yearlong effort to set the nation on a virtuous track.[33]

Like his earlier showboating, the prostitution raids produced their fair share of critics. The famed writer H. L. Mencken, for one, informed a grand jury that only "morons and idiots" believed in Hoover's approach to enforcing morality. But the raids' overall effect was to secure Hoover's place in the pantheon of moral crusaders—a major figure able not only to articulate his ideas, but to conduct his own anti-crime campaigns and make the mechanisms of government work according to his agenda. In September 1937, a month after the Atlantic City raids, he expanded that agenda again, calling for a "War on the Sex Criminal!" in the words of one headline. Like "white slavery," "sex criminal" could encompass a vast range of behavior, from rape, murder, and child molestation to acts of consensual "perversion" like the ones they had found in Connecticut. Hoover promised to eliminate them all, arguing that "the 'harmless' pervert of today can be and often is the loathsome mutilator and murderer of tomorrow." He viewed his role as one of public exhortation, a national Cassandra warning of the perils ahead.[34]

ALL THIS LEFT HOOVER WITH A PARADOXICAL PUBLIC IMAGE. FROM ONE VANtage point, he was the same firm apolitical administrator he had always been, moving soberly between partisan factions. From another, he was a cosmopolitan socialite and celebrity, at home in the latest of late-night New York gatherings. From still a third, he was a national scold and moralist, unflinching in his demands that all Americans— including politicians—live up to a strict code of personal virtue. In the fall of 1937, *The New Yorker* assigned writer Jack Alexander to make sense of it all in a multipart feature profile. The first sentence captured Hoover's role as the country's self-serious moral champion, "a dynamic, high-strung, fidgety man, to whom a mere suggestion of crime is a call to arms." The article also described Hoover's personal life, in which "night clubs are his favorite form of relaxation" and "the hilarity of an early-morning table group" at the Stork Club or 21 served as a relief from his self-imposed discipline. It likened Hoover to Benito Mussolini, with his fondness for brass eagles, national flags, and masculine posturing, while noting Hoover's "wry amusement" at the comparison, his insistence that he was simply a modest, middle-class American boy. Alexander made no attempt to resolve these contradictions. Rather, he portrayed Hoover as a man struggling to figure it all out himself.[35]

CHAPTER 19

The Gathering Storm

(1936–1938)

Fritz Kuhn, leader of the German-American Bund, reviews a pro-Nazi parade at a Bund camp in New Jersey. May 1, 1938. With Roosevelt's approval, Hoover and the FBI began investigating Nazi, communist, and other "subversive" organizations in the mid-1930s.

LIBRARY OF CONGRESS

Even as he wrestled with his few critics in Congress and the press, Hoover retained the loyalty of the one man who really mattered in Washington: Franklin Roosevelt. It had been Roosevelt who made it possible for Hoover to become a crime fighter, to take on bank robbers and gangsters, to have his men carry guns and make arrests. And it had been Roosevelt who lent Hoover crucial support during the promotional burst of 1935, when Hoover became a national celebrity and a practitioner of public relations. In August 1936, even as Hoover barnstormed the country denouncing New Deal social workers and softhearted liberals, Roosevelt secretly handed over a third significant gift, one that would allow Hoover's power to expand and flourish long after the president left office. In a confidential meeting, he asked Hoover to begin investigating "Fascism and Communism," the two great ideological forces threatening to upend the global order of the 1930s and to challenge the status quo at home. And he wanted it all done quietly, without the speeches, editorials, and public relations he had encouraged in the crime arena.[1]

The inspiration for Roosevelt's request came from a wave of social turbulence unlike anything since 1919, when Hoover had launched the Radical Division. Little more than a year into Roosevelt's presidency, San Francisco dockworkers pulled off the first general strike since the 1919 strike in Seattle—but unlike the Seattle workers, they won, securing union members and improved working conditions at ports up and down the West Coast. The following year, Roosevelt signed the National Labor Relations Act, establishing federal protection for union organizing and bargaining in another landmark victory for labor. Rather than calming domestic affairs, the law had helped to inspire a revolt within the American Federation of Labor, as the bushy-browed firebrand John L. Lewis led a walkout of the country's most militant industrial unions. As president of the United Mine Workers of America, Lewis had helped to lead the great coal strike of 1919. Now he was not only winning strikes but also forging a new Congress of Industrial Organizations (CIO) to bring the miners' organizing tactics and social-democratic vision into steel, auto, and other major industries.[2]

The growing conflict gave the 1936 election season a charge of uncertainty: Roosevelt seemed likely to win, but under what conditions? His Republican opponent, the millionaire Kansas governor Alf Landon, was a weak candidate. But there were other influential men, many of them with movements behind them, who ripped into Roosevelt's record. From Detroit, the "radio priest" Charles Coughlin complained that the president was too close to Jews and communists. Senator Huey Long, the "Kingfish" of Louisiana, had offered his own variation on Coughlin's populist economics and hinted that he might seize the Democratic nomination from Roosevelt, until an assassin's bullet kept him from making good on his promise. From Europe came news of a rising fascist threat: Adolf Hitler in Germany, Benito Mussolini in Italy, the outbreak of civil war in Spain. And each of these developments seemed to be producing its own strange offspring in the United States, with a revived Communist Party gearing up to fight fascism while a homegrown Nazi movement sought to implant fascism on American soil.[3]

Even for a president as confident and broad-minded as Roosevelt, it was impossible to keep track of everything: the strikes and plots, the shifting sands of a hundred impassioned ideological and political debates. Roosevelt also believed that staying on top of the domestic situation would be crucial to his reelection campaign. So he reached out to Hoover for help. On the morning of August 24, Hoover arrived at the White House, where he found the president "desirous of discussing the question of the subversive activities in the United States, particularly Fascism and Communism," as he noted in a "confidential memorandum" about the meeting. Roosevelt confessed that "he had been considerably concerned" about both phenomena, and about what they might mean for the stability of American society. He wanted Hoover's help not in investigating particular crimes, but in "obtaining a broad picture of the general movement and its activities as may affect the economic and political life of the country as a whole." In other words, he wanted Hoover to start spying on political dissidents again.

Hoover did not try to assuage the president's concerns. Instead, he confessed his own worries that the nation was beset by "subversive" political forces, many of them locked in a secret conspiracy to undermine both the presidency and the social order. He singled out a few key leaders: the miners' John Lewis; the Australian-born Harry Bridges, head of the San Francisco dockworkers; even Heywood Broun, a New York newsman and founder of the American Newspaper Guild. Together, Hoover warned, "they would be able at any time to paralyze the country in that they could stop all shipping in and out through the Bridges organization; stop the operation of industry through the Mining Union of Lewis; and stop publication of any newspapers of the country through the Newspaper Guild." Understandably concerned, Roosevelt asked Hoover what to do.

Hoover suggested something that would transform the work of the FBI yet again, just two years after his men began carrying weapons and hunting down gangsters. In response to Roosevelt's query, Hoover raised the possibility of reviving the "general intelligence" function that Harlan Stone had banned in 1924—in essence, moving the FBI back into political surveillance work. The proposal implied a historical analogy: With the return of the social conflicts that had plagued the country in 1919, the FBI would reengage in the political work it had performed in that earlier era. And yet there was no forgetting what had happened in between: the outcry against the Palmer Raids, the rise of a new civil liberties consciousness, the establishment of Stone's directive.

To get around those obstacles, Hoover offered Roosevelt a strategy for getting started in secret, without going to Congress. As Hoover acknowledged, the FBI appropriation contained no money for "general intelligence" activities. However, it did allow for investigations undertaken at the behest of the State Department—and "if the State Department should ask for us to conduct such an investigation we could do so under our present authority," Hoover explained to the president. In that way, nobody outside of the executive branch would need to know what the FBI was doing: not Congress, not the ACLU, and certainly not the press and public.

Roosevelt appreciated the canny nature of the suggestion, and asked that Hoover come back for a follow-up meeting when Secretary of State Cordell Hull could be present. On August 25 or September 1 (Hoover later offered conflicting dates), Hoover slipped back into the White House for that meeting, "at which time the Secretary of State, at the President's suggestion, requested of me . . . to have investigation made of the subversive activities in this country." According to Hoover, Roosevelt had entertained the idea of a written order, to be kept secure in a White House safe. The president decided against it, though, and the entire exchange—Hoover's official reentry into the world of "general intelligence"—took place quietly.[4]

After twelve years of tweaking administrative policies and learning to fight crime, Hoover was suddenly back where he had started: investigating subversives, communists, and German sympathizers. This time, though, he planned to move cautiously, with as little public attention as possible. In contrast to his anti-vice campaigns, nobody would know the full scale of what Hoover had initiated for many years to come. "It has been kept very secret and has not been generally known as being in existence," he explained to Roosevelt in 1938, "for obvious reasons."[5]

ONE OF ROOSEVELT'S MOST PRESSING CONCERNS WAS DOMESTIC FASCISM, IN-cluding activities being conducted or supported by the Nazi government on American soil. As early as 1933, just after Hitler's seizure of power in Germany, the president had requested that Hoover investigate "Nazi propaganda in this country." The following May, even as Hoover was reeling from the Little Bohemia disaster, Roosevelt had reached out again with a request to keep an eye on "the Nazi movement" within the U.S., espe-cially its "anti-racial" (or anti-Semitic) and "anti-American" activities. These had been isolated queries rather than any major shift in policy, but they had entailed departures from Stone's instructions, hints of what was to come.[6]

Roosevelt's 1936 directive licensed a broader inquiry. It also allowed Hoover consid-erable discretion to decide who would and would not be investigated under the "fascist" label. In the summer of 1936, "fascist" was among the most widely deployed epithets in American politics. Its boundaries, though, were far from self-evident. There were a small number of self-proclaimed "fascist" organizations, mainly populated by German and Italian immigrants enamored of Hitler and Mussolini. Beyond that, vast swaths of the public embraced what might be considered fascist ideas: anti-Semitism, corpo-ratism, the belief that democratic capitalism was too weak and decadent to survive. In electoral politics, the term was often used to criticize strongman posturing and con-centrated power—"demagoguery," to use another popular word. At other times, *fascist* suggested a commitment to racial scapegoating. Critics of Jim Crow segregation, in particular, used the fascist label to highlight similarities between the American South and Hitler's Germany, two societies that maintained strict racial hierarchies through a combination of law and violence.[7]

Hoover chose a narrower definition, interpreting Roosevelt's directive to refer in the main to pro-Nazi groups that expressed outright admiration for Hitler. The most obvious target was the German-American Bund, by far the largest and most prominent of the pro-Nazi organizations operating within the U.S. Created in 1933 under the name Friends of New Germany, the Bund had quickly come under pressure for its open allegiance to the Third Reich. In the spring of 1936, a few months before Hoover's meeting with Roosevelt, its leaders had reorganized around a more American name and theme, adopting a platform that affirmed "the right to cherish the German language and German customs" and "to oppose all racial intermixture" but also "to honor and defend the Constitution, the flag and institutions of the United States."

Its Americanization effort only went so far. At the Bund's first public meeting, in April 1936, "American Fuehrer" Fritz Kuhn had addressed an audience of some fifteen hundred followers while dressed in a Nazi military uniform, urging them toward full-throated support of the Third Reich. A few months later, Kuhn traveled to Germany and ended up in a surprise meeting with Hitler, who urged him to "continue the fight." After his return, the Bund opened several summer camps modeled on Hitler Youth, designed to turn impressionable American boys into stalwart Nazis. The camps became the focus of Hoover's investigation.[8]

Even in this clear instance of "fascist" sympathies, Hoover moved cautiously, willing to investigate but wary of pressing his case too hard, or of speaking too openly about what the FBI was doing. No doubt he hoped to be effective. But above all he wanted to keep his activities hidden, for fear of provoking the same backlash that had once followed the Palmer Raids. Throughout 1936 and into 1937, he said little about fascism or the Bund, even as he traveled the country railing against the "gutter scum" of the crime world and the "sob sisters" who sympathized with them. He said nothing when the Bund marched through the German neighborhood of Yorkville in Manhattan, clashing with anti-Nazi and Jewish protesters. And he said nothing after the FBI completed a thousand-page report on the Bund's summer camps, delivered to the White House and the Justice Department in the first days of 1938. According to press accounts, the report described a highly disturbing Nazi culture being promoted at the camps: "parading in grey and black uniforms," "displaying the swastika," "use of the Nazi salute." The FBI concluded, however, that these activities were not part of any plan for an armed revolutionary uprising, and that they fell within the bounds of protected political speech. According to one account, Bund headquarters "rocked with jubilation" at the news. Given a mandate to act on domestic fascism, Hoover chose to hold back, sanctioning the Bund to proceed with business as usual.[9]

Why did Hoover act with such caution, especially against a group so widely reviled? Certainly he feared the sort of criticism that had resulted from the Palmer Raids, when the Bureau had been accused of overstepping its bounds. Perhaps he also felt a measure of sympathy toward the Bund, with its devotion to racial hierarchy and its passionate opposition to "Jewish Marxism and Communism," in Kuhn's words. Over the next several decades, Hoover would go on to apply a similar standard to other far-right groups: investigating them, but without the same enthusiasm and commitment that he applied to groups on the left. The secret investigations of the 1930s provided a chance to experiment and establish patterns while few Americans were yet paying attention.[10]

———

HOOVER ADOPTED A MORE EXPANSIVE APPROACH WHEN IT CAME TO COMMU-
nism, but here, too, he proceeded in fits and starts, with a high degree of secrecy. What
began in 1936 was less a rush back to the days of the Radical Division and more a
chance to reengage with the subject that had once been his chief area of expertise. Some
of the same adversaries were still around. William Z. Foster, who had led the 1919 steel
strike, was now a leading communist figure; he ran for president on the party ticket in
1924, 1928, and 1932. So was Elizabeth Gurley Flynn, the fearless IWW "rebel girl,"
second only to Emma Goldman in 1919 as the most famous female radical in the nation. They brought with them a small but devoted cohort of men and women who
weathered the tribulations of the 1920s and lived to see global capitalism nearly collapse, just as Marx had predicted.

There were new elements within communism as well, developments that began to
move the party from the revolutionary fringes into a thriving liberal-left mainstream.
In 1933, Roosevelt formally recognized the Soviet Union, establishing diplomatic relations after a decade and a half of stalemate. Two years later, Stalin called for the creation of an international anti-facist front, in which party members around the world
would set aside old animosities in the service of unity against a growing global threat.
In the United States, communist leaders began reaching out to groups they had once
considered hopelessly retrograde: trade unions, socialists, even New Deal reformers.
All were to be part of the so-called Popular Front, a coalition that would punch back
against the fascist threat while advancing revolutionary ideals.

By 1936, the Popular Front strategy had produced a level of unprecedented popularity and legitimacy for the Communist Party within the United States. Formal membership never rose above a hundred thousand, but the communists' willingness to work
with other groups made the party one of the practical and ideological centers of the
Depression-era left. "Communism is the Americanism of the 20th century," party leader
Earl Browder proclaimed, and thousands of Americans seemed to think it was true.
Most party members joined up openly, signing party cards and paying dues and marching in demonstrations. Others joined in secret, fearful that communist affiliation
might damage their professional reputations or foreclose opportunities that might someday be useful to the cause. The party would later accuse its enemies of conjuring up
fantastical allegations about who was and was not a secret member. But the policy of
secret membership itself was real enough, if applied only selectively. So was the category of "fellow traveler," used to identify left-leaning activists, workers, and professionals who sympathized with communist ideals and moved in a far-left circles but who
never formally joined the party. To accommodate this extended circle, the party created a network of "front" organizations, such as the National Negro Congress and the

American League Against War and Fascism. Front groups were communist in spirit and organization but not in name.

Millions of people fell into one or another of these categories in the 1930s. They came from nearly every walk of life, including government, Hollywood, journalism, and the labor movement. A few were famous: composer Aaron Copland, singer Paul Robeson, writers John Dos Passos and John Steinbeck and Richard Wright, folk troubadour Woody Guthrie. Most lived far more modest lives, balancing gainful employment with time spent on party activities. Communists were legendary for their militant work ethic; they showed up more often and stayed longer than everyone else. They were also known for their ideological rigidity, a problem only partly solved by the Popular Front dictum to cooperate with socialists and liberals.

Though inspired by urgent concerns over European fascism, the Popular Front party nudged members into struggles over unemployment, social welfare, and labor rights at a moment when such issues had real political momentum. They also engaged the cause of Black civil rights, on the premise that race was a pernicious social construct developed to divide the working class. At a time when few white-run organizations took any interest in civil rights issues, communists invested time and energy—and often risked their lives—in emerging fights against lynching, Jim Crow segregation, and the economic oppression of Southern sharecroppers. As a result, the party gained a small but significant Black membership in places such as New York and Alabama, where the party's defense of the Scottsboro Boys, nine Black youths accused of raping a white woman, attracted international attention. In 1932, the party ran a Black man, James Ford, as its vice presidential candidate, with Foster at the top of the ticket. They won far less than 1 percent of the total but their support was rising.[11]

All of which worried Hoover. From the first, it was clear that communism—not fascism—occupied the greater part of his imagination, and that he viewed the party's engagement with labor unions, civil rights, and reform politics as a growing internal threat. After his meetings with Roosevelt, Hoover set about demarcating the categories of dangerous activity most pressing for the Bureau to track, outlining a system for filing, sorting, and retrieving the information received from field offices much like the one he had created under Palmer. Only two of Hoover's categories explicitly addressed the "Nazi" and "Fascisti" problems. All the rest—almost a dozen additional classifications—targeted areas of political life where communists were thought to play a significant or potentially significant role. One of these was the federal government, which by Hoover's estimate now employed 2,850 open and secret CP members, especially in left-leaning bodies like the National Labor Relations Board. Another area was civil rights organizing—or as Hoover categorized it, "Negroes"—with agents sent south to investigate sharecropper organizing, among other activities. They found no evidence that Southern landlords violated federal law by throwing tenants off the land and onto government relief rolls, a conclusion that the head of the Southern Tenant Farmers Union characterized as "unfair, inaccurate and incomplete."[12]

Of all the areas of concern identified in Hoover's emerging intelligence system, none was more significant than organized labor, the sphere of political life to which communists devoted the lion's share of their energies, and in which they therefore exercised the greatest influence. And no group loomed larger than the Congress of Industrial Organizations (CIO), the industrial-organizing powerhouse founded by the miners' John Lewis. Though communists had once despised the idiosyncratic Lewis as a "Bosses' Agent" and "Scab-Head," under the aegis of the Popular Front they began to cooperate, with hundreds of experienced party hands signing on as CIO organizers. By one estimate, in the late 1930s some 40 percent of CIO unions were "either led by Communists and their close allies or significantly influenced by them," a record that gave Hoover ample reason to investigate.[13]

Beyond the sprawling categories of "industry," "general strike," and "organized labor," Hoover paid special attention to employment sectors in which the Communist Party or the CIO exerted some measure of power and influence. The designation "newspaper field" referred not only to general press coverage, but to the American Newspaper Guild, singled out by Hoover during his meeting with Roosevelt as a union "which has strong Communistic leanings." The category of "maritime" included the National Maritime Union, an interracial seamen's union affiliated with the CIO, as well as the International Longshoremen's Association, which had helped to carry out the 1934 San Francisco strike under the leadership of Harry Bridges, whose membership in the Communist Party was widely alleged. At their August 1936 meeting, Hoover had warned Roosevelt that "the Bridges organization," like the newspaper guild, "was practically controlled by Communists." Over the next few years, the FBI began not only to watch the maritime situation but also to assist in deportation efforts against the Australian-born Bridges.[14]

Hoover also kept an eye on major industries, which despite Depression trauma still made up the lifeblood of the American economy. In a memo to Roosevelt, he singled out the steel industry as a special area of concern—for reasons that needed no explanation to the president. In 1935, party leader Earl Browder had committed the CP to "enter with all its forces and resources in the campaign of organizing the unorganized" in the steel industry. The following year, a newly created Steel Workers Organizing Committee within the CIO had taken them up on the offer, hiring dozens of party members to organize steel employees into a national union. For Foster, the CIO's success fulfilled a dream that had begun a generation earlier, when he led the failed steel strike of 1919. For Hoover, who had been watching Foster during those early years, the confrontations that erupted once again in 1937—this time resulting in victory for the steelworkers—merely confirmed the need for increased surveillance.[15]

Dramatic events were also taking place in the auto and mining industries, similarly identified by Hoover as key areas of Bureau concern. In February 1937, workers at a General Motors plant in Flint, Michigan, staged what came to be known as the great "sit-down strike," occupying the factory and refusing to move until their bosses agreed to negotiate with the union. As in steel, several of the chief organizers at Flint were Communist Party members. So were some of the officials at the United Auto Workers, the confident new union empowered in the wake of the strike. Finally, there was Lewis's own union, the United Mine Workers, where according to Hoover, "the Communists had now decided to make very definite plans to get control." Like other union leaders, Lewis grudgingly worked with party members throughout the Popular Front era, despite his public disdain for communism. None of this made the UMW, UAW, or United Steelworkers into Communist-run or even Communist-dominated organizations, but it did mean that under Roosevelt's directive, Hoover had permission to look into what they were doing.[16]

MOST OF THE FBI'S GENERAL INTELLIGENCE WORK BETWEEN 1936 AND 1938 WAS just that: a matter of gathering intelligence and developing the "broad picture" that Roosevelt had requested, of compiling information rather than acting upon it. Despite Hoover's evident alarm over the CIO and its potential to "paralyze" the country, there are few substantive reports of FBI interference with strikes during these years, or of direct intervention in employer-employee relations. The one great exception came in the workplace closest to Hoover's heart. In 1936, just as Hoover was beginning to investigate the national labor situation, his own employees attempted to form a union under the auspices of the American Federation of Government Employees (AFGE), bringing the passions of the age into the pristine confines of the FBI itself.

The situation burst into public view in mid-July, just before Hoover's meeting with Roosevelt, when the union sent a six-page brief to the attorney general accusing Hoover of running a white-collar "sweatshop" and engaging in anti-union activity. The letter focused on conditions within the fingerprint division—still Hoover's pride and joy but also the one area of the Bureau formally protected by civil service rules. Hoover had always considered its civil service protection a weak spot in his employment structure, and 1936 reminded him why. Unlike his agents, his fingerprint clerks had some outside recourse in matters of hiring and firing, the ability to appeal to something more than the director's whims and policies.[17]

His employees' basic complaints were nothing new, echoes of what the dissident agent Joseph Bayliss had alleged during Hoover's first years as director. Workers in the fingerprint division complained that they were required to stand nearly all day, for fear that stools might make them appear lazy or sloppy when tours came by. All window shades had to be kept at precisely the same level, no matter the angle of the sun, to provide a tidy, uniform impression for outside visitors. Employees who showed up to work without a belt were required to wear their coats for the entire day, regardless of temperature, to hide their slovenly appearance. And the list went on, one bewildering rule after another, all designed to display a perfect picture of institutional order. According to the union complaint, Hoover's rigidity had created an attrition crisis at the fingerprint division, where some thirty-five of 150 identification experts quit their jobs in the first six months of 1936 alone. Those who remained met with swift retaliatory action when they expressed discontent or tried to form a union.[18]

Under federal labor law, retaliatory firing for labor organizing was now supposed to be illegal; employers could not get rid of workers who wanted to unionize any more than politicians could ban voters who liked the other candidate—a principle of workplace democracy. Hoover either did not understand the new law or did not care. He interpreted his employees' actions as an attempt by subversives to undermine confidence in American institutions and to bring the functioning of the nation's government to a halt. Rather than negotiate further, he fired the main organizers.[19]

Cummings backed Hoover in his resistance to the union, refusing to entertain the employees' complaints. In response, the fired men took to the streets, picketing and chanting outside Justice headquarters while handing out pamphlets describing the many small cruelties of FBI life. Their demands were hardly revolutionary but their language was vicious, charging Hoover with "spying on the men, overtime, inadequate pay, harsh enforcement of petty regulations and the speed-up resulting from an undermanned force." For a boss accustomed to praise and fawning obedience from his employees, the protests came as a shock. "Mr. Hoover's life has been made a little more uncomfortable in the last few days by public charges that his highly-publicized fingerprint section is, in reality, a sweatshop," the left-wing *Nation* magazine declared with satisfaction.[20]

And it might have gotten more uncomfortable still, if not for the fact that the AFGE's leadership actually sided with Hoover. Though often presented as a monolithic front, the labor movement of the late 1930s was deeply divided between liberals and radicals, and between those who preferred negotiation and those who sought direct action or even revolution in the streets. As one article pointed out, the union struggle at the FBI not only pitted clerks against bosses; it also marked "a battle between conservative, old-line majority factions of the [labor] organization and the idealistic members, ranging from pale pink liberals to vivid red radicals."[21]

Hoover's own role in the showdown came to a climax in August, when the AFGE called an emergency meeting at a Washington labor temple. As proceedings began, a black-hooded figure arose and identified himself as "the spirit of J. Edgar Hoover." When the presiding chairman expressed tongue-in-cheek surprise at Hoover's death, the "spirit" clarified the situation. "I am the spirit of John Edgar Hoover's better self, which has died long since from the subtle poison of excessive authority. I can return to his body only once that better self is resurrected." Behind him, union members lined up to denounce Hoover as a "social criminal," in violation of the nation's labor laws. "If Hoover is not checked now," they insisted, "he will be encouraged to launch an open campaign against the entire labor movement." It was a prescient warning, but the AFGE leadership saw things differently. Citing unauthorized picketing, they voted to expel the offending lodge from the national union.[22]

That brought an end to Hoover's battle with the fingerprint division—indeed, to the only labor struggle ever waged within the confines of his Bureau. Happy to dismiss the whole affair as a subversive rebellion, he did little to address the substance of his employees' claims. He did, however, institute two minor changes to ensure that such a situation never occurred again. In the fall of 1936, he accepted the resignation of Identification Division chief John Edwards, once a trusted member of the Bureau's GW-and-Kappa-Alpha-bred inner circle, informing Edwards that "if he had maintained harmony in his division among the employees . . . they would have had no desire to join a union." His second change was less punitive, an extension of the public relations techniques that had proved so successful in recent years. Rather than blackball the entire union, Hoover invited its sympathetic leaders to visit the Bureau, promising an exclusive tour.[23]

IF THE CHALLENGE FROM HIS OWN EMPLOYEES WAS EASILY DISPATCHED, THE same could not be said of a more serious problem that arose in the late 1930s, and that would ultimately test the limits of the Bureau's renewed intelligence initiatives. In mid-February 1938, amid fears about a coming German invasion of Austria, the FBI took custody of a German immigrant and former U.S. Army enlistee named Guenther Rumrich, arrested by New York police in a bumbling passport theft scheme. Hoover did not want the case, especially because his agents had not made the initial arrest. But Rumrich had done something that made Hoover's wishes all but impossible to fulfill. Under questioning by the New York police, he confessed to being a German spy and ardent Nazi, stealing passports in order to facilitate the movement of Hitler's spies around the world. At the time there was no federal agency specifically tasked with handling foreign espionage on American soil. So the case fell to the FBI, under the logic that its recent involvement in the Bund investigations made it best equipped to handle such a situation.

Hoover was not at all ready, however—just as he had not been ready when the War on Crime fell in his lap. Things started reasonably well, with Rumrich naming names, identifying locations, and describing the elaborate espionage ring he had helped to run. FBI agents then rounded up the suspects and proceeded to gather further evidence. Hoover approached it all as he had approached big cases like Dillinger and the Barker gang: suspects would be identified, evidence scientifically gathered, and a grand jury convened. He failed to recognize that these were spies, not ordinary criminals. The German government had a powerful interest in making sure that they did not testify or rot in American prisons. After being released in advance of grand jury proceedings, most of the key plotters slipped out of the country one by one. To Hoover's horror, when agents went back to find them, only four of the eighteen original suspects were still in the United States.[24]

Unlike most of the FBI's political intelligence work, this colossal error did not remain a secret. Hoover blamed the lead agent in the case, Leon Turrou, and promptly fired him, just as he had fired the responsible parties at the fingerprint division. According to Hoover, Turrou had erred by leaking news of the arrests, then doubled down on the mistake by trying to sell his own story—based on proprietary government information—to the highest press bidder. The real problems ran deeper. As Turrou admitted, the FBI simply did not know how to conduct espionage investigations. Indeed, nobody else in the government knew how to do it either. Questioned about the spy case during an October 1938 press conference, Roosevelt emphasized a "very definite responsibility" on the part of the federal government to get a handle on the situation, and even suggested he might consider the creation of a new espionage agency.[25]

Initial reports assured the public that any "central spy-control bureau" would not fall under FBI auspices. "There is no intention to enhance the power—and publicity—of F.B.I. director J. Edgar Hoover," wrote one columnist. But Roosevelt had a long history of turning to Hoover in such situations, and despite the FBI's missteps, he did so once again. During a cabinet meeting in mid-October, Roosevelt raised the idea of assembling a committee to survey the state of intelligence operations and "make definite recommendations as to how to proceed." Cummings brought the information back to Hoover, and asked him to propose something that might ease the president's concerns.[26]

In response, Hoover did something brash: despite the FBI's obvious failures in the Rumrich case, he made a bid for the Bureau to become the nation's chief counterespionage agency—in essence, for Roosevelt to expand its power yet again. To make his case, Hoover cited all that the Bureau had done, quietly and without controversy, since Roosevelt's secret 1936 directive. According to Hoover, by late 1938 the FBI had amassed some twenty-five hundred names of individuals "engaged in activities of Communism, Nazism, and various types of foreign espionage," including maritime and industrial workers, labor organizers, "youth," and "Negroes." It was also actively collecting sixty-five "daily, weekly and monthly publications," and gathering further information from contacts in "professional, business and law enforcement fields." Hoover's numbers no doubt sounded better than they were, a mishmash of CIO organizers, Black activists, and perhaps the occasional Nazi spy. But he believed that they were enough to legitimize another quiet "expansion." He gave a rough estimate of what it would cost: $39,000 for naval intelligence, $35,000 for the army, and $300,000 for the FBI. Lest the White House encounter criticism over the plan, he urged that it all take place "with the utmost degree of secrecy" and without attempting to pass new legislation or form any new committee.[27]

In early November, Hoover received a request to join Roosevelt aboard a secure presidential train when it stopped in New York en route to the family estate in Hyde Park. The two men sat inside the train car for several minutes, as the president's advisers and security detail milled about. When he emerged, Hoover had most of what he wanted. Though Roosevelt did not approve the full $300,000, he gave the FBI $150,000, apportioned from a discretionary fund, to build up its counterespionage ranks. Another $100,000 went to naval and military intelligence, to be divided between them. According to Hoover's memo of the meeting, the president "approved the plan which I had prepared," authorizing the FBI to take the federal lead in efforts to combat espionage, sabotage, and subversion on American soil.[28]

Other than that memo, there was no record of the meeting: no request to Congress or the State Department, no official signature for the records. It was just another handshake deal between Hoover and the president who had already given him so much. With a global war looming on the horizon, Roosevelt's decision would license a level of domestic spying and surveillance as yet unimagined in 1938. For the moment, though, Hoover had other problems to address, and on these the president could be of little help.

CHAPTER 20

Mothers and Sons

(1938–1939)

Hoover (left) and Tolson (right) with Tolson's mother at the Stork Club in New York, October 1939. Tolson's father died in August; his mother is in mourning dress. Jack Entratter, daytime manager of the Stork Club, is standing.

NATIONAL ARCHIVES AND RECORDS ADMINISTRATION

Hoover referred to cancer as the "gangster disease": it preyed upon innocent victims, draining them of life and joy before delivering its final blow. His mother, Annie, received her diagnosis sometime around 1935, just as Hoover's fame began to hit its Dillinger peak. She was seventy-five years old, a widow for a decade and a half, still living in the same house her husband had bought for her in 1892. Both of her sons were making headlines. Her daughter had three healthy children, now almost grown. So perhaps the diagnosis was something that Annie simply accepted, a good life's work done. She took to her bed, too exhausted to maintain her usual hard-scrubbing rigor.[1]

Hoover did his best to care for her, hiring a round-the-clock nurse. Her decline accompanied her son's rise, and some of Hoover's grief and worry made its way into his public commentary. "When we look upon the gnarled, tired hands of an old woman they remind us of the tired hands of some one we worship above all other early things"; he mourned "the hands which labored so faithfully for us; the hands which grew so tired and weary in our service during the years of our childhood." The death of their much-adored dog, Spee Dee Bozo, only enhanced the sense of homebound gloom. Hoover said that the Airedale's final hours marked "one of the saddest days of my life." He buried Spee Dee in a white shroud at the pricey Aspin Hill Pet Cemetery, where Washington's elite marked the passing of their beloved pets. A few months later, he gave Annie a little black terrier named Scottie in an attempt to fill the void.[2]

Hoover complained that his brother and sister abandoned him during these years, too wrapped up in their own families to step forward and help ease their mother's way. And he resented their absence, the final indignity in a lifetime of being cast as a mama's boy. Years later, he would point out bitterly that Annie had failed to change her will, distributing her possessions among all three children despite the fact that he alone took charge of caring for her.[3]

For daily support, Hoover looked not to his family, but to Tolson, the one person who remained by his side even as Annie slipped into the final stages of decline. On Valentine's Day 1938, Tolson sent Annie a floral bouquet. "Mother was quite pleased with the beautiful Valentine flowers which you sent her," Hoover wrote in a formal thank-you note, "and asked me to tell you how much she appreciates your remembrance of her on this occasion." Over the next few weeks, Hoover prepared to say goodbye to the mother to whom he had dedicated so much of his adult life. Annie died at home on the night of February 22. Hoover buried her two days later in the family plot at Congressional Cemetery, next to his father, Dickerson, and tiny Sadie Marguerite.[4]

ANNIE'S DEATH LEFT HOOVER REELING. "I HAVE BEEN RESTING . . . TRYING TO readjust to what at present seems like a completely shattered life," he wrote to a friend after the funeral. "Mother was such a part of my life that I feel so utterly alone." He found normal activities rendered strange and "overwhelming." Still, he saw little choice other than to forge ahead. "One must carry on somehow and the support which I have from a few real friends has been most sustaining," he wrote. Hottel recalled that Hoover seemed to accept Annie's death but rarely spoke of it. Like mental illness, cancer was often kept secret in the 1930s, a source of shame, confusion, and regret. Her death came and went without public discussion, another chapter of Hoover's family life consigned to shadows and silence.[5]

In response, Hoover did what he had done more and more since the start of Annie's illness: he fled Washington. It was likely no coincidence that his first Florida vacation with Hottel and Tolson seems to have occurred as Annie fell ill. While Florida had the pull of sunshine, there was also the push of Annie's sickness, the desire to escape a bleak winter house smelling of illness and decay. In mid-March 1938, after a hard winter of witnessing his mother's decline and death, he and Tolson left once again to Miami, where a young photographer snapped a picture of Hoover "snoozing in the sunshine" outside their private hotel cabana.[6]

New York remained another refuge. On weekends, according to the gossip sheets, Hoover and Tolson frequently returned to the Stork Club, the Paradise, or 21, often to meet with Winchell. It was a peak year for café society, with the harshest conditions of the Depression lifted and the trials of war still to come. In the months after Annie's death, Hoover and Tolson dined alongside literary legend Dorothy Parker at the Stork Club and watched champion boxer Joe Louis pummel his German-born rival Max Schmeling at Yankee Stadium. Beyond the tabloid excitement, they continued to live the lives they had built for themselves in New York, an accepted duo within the world of "Broadwayites" and nightclub devotees.[7]

Hoover's travel schedule throughout 1938 and 1939 suggests a kind of restlessness, as if simply being on the road allowed him to avoid the questions and silences that awaited him at Seward Square. He and Tolson often attempted to travel in secret, for professional reasons but also perhaps for personal ones. During a trip to Kansas City in May, they registered incognito at their hotel and swore the front-desk staff to secrecy—all to no avail. Reporters sniffed them out in the penthouse suite, a three-bedroom extravaganza featuring a grand piano, a walnut-lined dining room, a butler's pantry, and "ankle-deep carpets." An enterprising newsman went so far as to knock on the door, which was reportedly opened by a tall, handsome man in "a Hollywood *café au lait* lounging robe." This was presumably Tolson (officially registered in the room next door) playing his usual role as both intimate companion and press liaison for his overextended boss. Upon returning east, Hoover spent the weekend not in Washington but in New York, where Winchell spotted him at Yankee Stadium surrounded by "a trio of G-lamour Men," the closest thing Hoover now had to a family.[8]

DESPITE HOOVER'S ATTEMPTS TO CARRY ON AS USUAL, ANNIE'S DEATH RAISED a vexing social dilemma: Since he no longer lived with his mother, how would he explain his "bachelor" status? The press wasted little time in calling the question. Less than two months after Annie's death, Washington columnist Evelyn Peyton Gordon declared Hoover the new "pet" of "capital society." "Until his mother's death a few weeks ago," Gordon wrote, "the famous G-Man lived with her, and was known as something of a 'woman hater.' Now that he is alone tongues are beginning to wag and surmises to be made as to just how long J. Edgar will remain in unwedded bliss." If it was really his mother who had been holding him back, he was now free to pursue his own agenda.

Just what that agenda might be was a subject of intense speculation. In late March, Hoover and Tolson appeared at the Mayflower for their customary lunch. Rather than heading straight to their table, however, they paused at the elevator bank. When the doors slid open, two women—a petite blonde and a "willowy" brunette—conspicuously sallied forth, joining Hoover and Tolson for a "secluded" luncheon. The sight was extraordinary enough to make headlines in Los Angeles, where the *Times* published a three-paragraph story recounting the date in detail. "Loungers in the lobby of one of the capital's swankest hotels rubbed their eyes with amazement the other noon. Washington's best-known bachelor and most confirmed woman-dodger was lunching with two gorgeous out-of-town damsels." The reporter noted that the press was watching eagerly to find out what would happen next.[9]

Hoover was cagey when asked directly. In 1939, in a widely syndicated interview with a society reporter, he described his lifelong search for an "old-fashioned girl," someone whose virtues and modesty would make him a suitable wife. About his dating record he commented only that "the girls men take out to make whoopee with are not the girls they want as the mother of their children," lamenting that he mostly met the former type in his profession. He claimed to harbor a deep fear of marriage, and of the rejection it might bring. "If I ever marry and the girl fails me, ceases to love me, and our marriage is dissolved," he explained, "it would ruin me. I couldn't take it, and I would not be responsible for my actions." The problem was not that he was uninterested in women, his words implied, but that he cared about them too deeply.

As a practical matter, Hoover made little effort to meet the sort of "old-fashioned girl" he professed to want. Throughout the spring of 1938, as he traveled the country with Tolson, gossip columns began to attach him to various models and actresses—"socalled glamor girls," in Hoover's words—from his Stork Club circle. In April, Winchell revealed Hoover's supposed romance with Lela Rogers, a forty-six-year-old aspiring Broadway writer and producer best known as the stage mother of film star Ginger Rogers. Hoover may have met Lela in 1937, when the FBI investigated a series of threats against Ginger. But only in 1938, after media began to speculate about his bachelor status, did he offer any hint of romantic interest. On paper, she was an excellent choice: more or less the proper age, the proper social status, even the proper political ideology. She was also skilled in public relations, one of the few women trained by the Marines to serve as an ambassador to the public. In mid-June, during a press interview, she mentioned that Hoover had telephoned at three o'clock in the morning. When the reporter asked if they were involved, Rogers played coy, joking that "Congress cut down the bureau's appropriations" and therefore she would have to wait awhile for her engagement ring. The reporter interpreted her quip to mean that "Ginger Rogers' Mother May Wed J. Edgar Hoover, G-man Chief."[10]

By all accounts, this was pure fantasy; no questions had been popped, no rings exchanged. Rogers herself insisted that she had been horribly misunderstood. "Oh. Now I don't know what to say," she complained to another reporter. "We're very good friends, it's true. But this is a horrible spot to put me in. I wish you'd move me off it." Hoover took a more equivocal stance. "I don't think my personal affairs are of interest to the public," he said. "That's not saying yes nor no." It is difficult to imagine that Rogers—a skilled public relations professional, with long-standing ties to both Winchell and Courtney Ryley Cooper—went into the whole episode unsuspecting. Nor does it seem plausible that Hoover would have tolerated an unplanned burst of gossip with such good humor. More likely, they joined forces to create a useful myth.[11]

COLUMNS EXPRESSING DOUBT ABOUT HOOVER'S DATING RECORD IMPLIED that Tolson, too, was a "woman hater" and "woman-dodger" who had deliberately chosen life with his charismatic male boss. Melvin Purvis—still the country's most famous G-Man, aside from Hoover—provided a convenient point of contrast, as rumors in the spring of 1938 suggested that he planned to marry his childhood sweetheart. Of more immediate consequence for Tolson was the impending marriage of Guy Hottel. Tolson and Hottel had lived together off and on since college, fraternity brothers playing out an extended adolescence. Hottel's departure left Tolson, like Hoover, more alone than he had been in years, the routine commitments of his life thrown into flux.[12]

Tolson also had his share of family problems. His brother, Hillory, the golden boy of GW, was in the midst of a wrenching divorce. Back in Iowa, Tolson's father was dying, raising questions about who would now care for his aged mother. Hoover flew out to Iowa for the funeral, posing for family photos with Tolson's country relatives. A few months later, they brought Tolson's mother back to New York for a distraction. A photo from the Stork Club shows a tiny Midwestern matron in mourning dress, her half smile, wire-rimmed glasses, and veiled black hat decidedly out of sync with café society glamour. Seated at her right, Hoover glances bemusedly at Tolson, while Tolson stares straight into the camera, grinning and laughing. This was what spouses did: tend to aging parents, attend family funerals, sit by patiently while out-of-town relatives sampled big-city wares.[13]

In that sense, Tolson and Hoover already had the affectionate, supportive marriage they were supposed to want. Still, this was not what the columnists meant when they speculated about the marriage prospects of "handsome Clyde Tolson!" Like Hoover, Tolson responded to the gossip in the logical way: he began to date women. His most serious girlfriend seems to have been a Miami divorcee named Frances Baswell, alleged to be "wedding-bell shopping" with him in early 1939. Though her name came and went quickly, the possibility that Tolson might indeed get married seemed to weigh on Hoover. Decades later, Hottel said that Hoover once begged him to intervene when Tolson seemed too interested in one of his dates. "I didn't say, 'Dump her,'" Hottel recalled. "I said 'Forget her.'" Hottel claimed that Hoover's stance was less a matter of romantic jealousy than of wanting things his own way, loath to share Tolson's time and attention.[14]

———

HOOVER DID INITIATE ONE SIGNIFICANT CHANGE IN HIS RELATIONSHIP WITH
Tolson after Annie's death: rather than pulling away, he moved closer. In the spring of
1938, Tolson moved to an apartment at the Marlyn complex on Cathedral Avenue,
initially with Hottel, but soon on his own. Around the same time, Hoover began preparations to move out of Seward Square for the first time in his life. He no longer fit in
along his childhood streets, a national celebrity living well below his means. Always
tenuous, the neighborhood's middle-class identity seemed to be slipping, as the local
real estate market succumbed to Depression brutalities and what would soon be known
as "white flight." Hoover wanted a home of his own in a neighborhood better suited to
a man of his station. A few months after Annie's death, he brought in a Bureau photographer to capture his childhood home as it looked during his final months of residence. Then he put the house up for sale, ready to begin a new life across town, closer
to Tolson.[15]

Hoover purchased a house at Thirtieth Place, a secluded single-block street in the
bucolic Northwest neighborhood of Forest Hills. The builder's ad emphasized the area's racial exclusivity: "Safely restricted to assure a permanently desirable environment," it read, code for the "covenants" that bound white homeowners to sell only to
white buyers. In contrast to Seward Square's close-packed rowhouses, Forest Hills offered yards and trees, its newly constructed homes spaced far apart. Hoover chose a
brick house toward the end of the block, priced at twenty-five thousand dollars. From
his new home, some seven miles from the seat of government, Hoover could no longer
walk to work. But he now lived just three miles from Tolson, an easy drive along Nebraska Avenue through the segregated Northwest.[16]

The house itself had been built for a family "on a generous scale," with a screened
porch looking out onto a walled-in shaded yard. "In planning the lovely garden, special
thought was given to creating privacy," the house ad explained—presumably a major
selling point for Hoover. He adopted his mother's dog, Scottie, suddenly free to roam
in the backyard. To keep Scottie company, Hoover acquired a little cairn terrier named
G-Boy, one of a succession of cairns that he would dote upon for the rest of his life.
Hoover later said that he liked dogs better than people. "They're great company to me,"
he told a reporter. "The less I think of some people, the more I think of my dogs. I can
leave in the morning and be in a bad mood, and when I come home at night they'll
jump all over me." It was in the months after Annie's death that his dogs began to take
on this increased importance—no longer merely pets, but the primary members of his
near-suburban family.[17]

Hoover held on to other sentimental bits of his life with Annie, including a series
of framed family portraits. For the first time, however, he was free of his mother's tastes
and restrictions, and able to decorate his own home as he wished. He had always loved

to collect antiques and other objets d'art: stone carvings, etched glass, Western statuary. Now he put them out on display, covering nearly every available surface. The house came to contain hundreds of items—vases and ashtrays, silverware and candelabra, landscape paintings and quirky miniatures. The effect was less clutter than curation; each object carried its own story, and visitors were supposed to ask. There was nonetheless something incongruous about Hoover's form of domesticity: America's toughest crime fighter surrounded by delicate porcelain and artful trinkets. Many guests were struck by the fussy decor—"like drifting into a Victorian home," one neighbor commented, still Annie's domain in spirit if not in fact.[18]

Some of what Hoover displayed would surely not have been tolerated at his mother's house. In addition to the vases, tchotchkes, and flatware, Hoover decorated his home with an array of nude statuary, mostly of the male variety. In one of its earliest iterations, his living room decor featured a naked boy, sculpted in marble, slumped on an end table. A second male nude, frozen in runner's form, stood across the room. Built-in shelves presented variations on the godly Greek ideal—Cupid and Hercules, Apollo and Zeus, often naked, rendered in stone or bronze. What could not fit in the living room ended up downstairs in the basement, the most personal of Hoover's "public" rooms. He chose a western motif: Native American throw rugs on the floor, cowboy hats on the walls, a deer's head above the fireplace. Certain items fit uneasily with the western theme, however. On the walls he hung autographed pictures of friends and celebrities, along with a gilt-framed photo of a naked woman in profile. Outside in the yard, a life-size statue of a boy stood perched atop a fountain pedestal, clad only in his boots.[19]

What did all this mean to Hoover? He left no written record of his aesthetic choices, and the objects do not speak for themselves. But he did keep a few items in his personal collections that attempted to put words to images, and perhaps they explain some of what he thought and felt. One was a photograph of a bronze sculpture titled *Friendship*, by the San Francisco artist Haig Patigian: two nude men standing back-to-back, honed from the same metal slab but separated by a rough-hewn head-to-toe barrier. In the sculpture, the men touch longingly but just barely, their fingers brushing together below waist level. During the 1920s, the YMCA had used the *Friendship* sculpture to teach boys about proper behavior—how to love each other without acting upon "lustful" thoughts. "Let this man burn with a fierce desire toward that man," the YMCA had instructed, "but let him not evidence that desire except by the actions of his eyes, his hands, and his heart."

Shot in black-and-white, the photo of the statue in Hoover's possession came accompanied by a poem titled "A Song of Men." It told the painful story of "that rare, quiet friendship of men": "Something strange there. Beautiful, but a little terrible too." It interpreted the statue as a display of anguish but also of love and solidarity—two men at once "linked" but forever apart. The poem talked of "coming out" from loneliness and despair into "the lust and vigor of manhood." It told of "everything shared," but "always something withheld"—"each man coming out and finding the hand of his friend yet never quite coming out." More than any other memento in Hoover's home, the poem and photograph seem to offer a meditation on his relationship with Tolson, at once open and secret.[20]

Tolson came often to Thirtieth Place. Photographs show him thoroughly at home there: smoking a cigarette in an Adirondack chair out back, buttoning his suit coat on the half-lit screened porch. There are shots of Hoover alone during these years as well, a suburban breadwinner just returned from work, playing with his dogs in the backyard. Without a family of his own, he relied on a fleet of Black servants to care for the house and gardens, beginning with his housekeeper, Annie Fields, who was responsible for cooking and cleaning. In a neighborhood where only white people owned homes, Fields's skin color marked her as a servant, able to work in Hoover's home and maintain her own room there but not to purchase property. She took care of Hoover in ways large and small, a second "Annie" devoting her life to his tastes and needs. She also, by default, tended to Tolson. According to her sister, Fields understood that "there was something between" the two men, but she was discreet and loyal, the qualities Hoover most prized in his employees.[21]

The other essential figure in the life of Thirtieth Place was James Crawford, the chauffeur tasked with shuttling Hoover back and forth between home and office. Unlike Fields, Crawford was a Bureau employee, having worked his way up from warehouse laborer to office messenger before being appointed as Tolson's chauffeur in 1934 and then, the following year, as Hoover's personal driver. Before Thirtieth Place, Crawford recalled, Hoover and Tolson went to work in separate cars, coming from opposite directions. After the move, they developed a new routine, with Crawford arriving in the morning to pick up Hoover, then stopping along the way to collect Tolson. Crawford usually dropped them off a bit east of the Justice Department, around the White House. Hoover and Tolson liked to walk the last six or seven blocks together, a transition from one part of their shared life to another.[22]

BECAUSE THERE WAS ALWAYS WORK TO DO, SOME OF IT AS WRENCHING AS THE personal events that rocked Hoover and Tolson during these years. In early 1938, Little, Brown publishers released *Persons in Hiding*, a compendium of crime stories published under Hoover's byline. The book reflected Hoover's preoccupation with mothers and children, men and women, social norms and the criminals who violated them. Like Hoover's speeches, it affirmed what he had been taught in childhood: that the difference between virtue and vice came down to self-control, and that for every young man who succumbed to the temptations of crime and deviance, there was another "who had the 'will-power to resist.'" He dedicated the book to Cooper and Cooper's wife—and to his Bureau staff and "my Assistant, Clyde A. Tolson," whose "untiring efforts" made it possible for the book to exist.[23]

Cooper would go on to write one more book with Hoover's cooperation. Published in 1939, *Designs in Scarlet* took the reader into the netherworld of prostitutes, pimps, and the outlaw life, a tour rife with both thrills and moralizing. Cooper concluded from his research that "evil" was alive and well in the land, creeping ever closer to the middle-class American home. The following year, perhaps unable to make his peace with what he had seen, he hanged himself in his hotel room, one more loss for Hoover in a season of difficulty.[24]

Hoover's work, too, took him to dark places in the late 1930s, an unending run of the worst that humanity had to offer. In the winter of 1938, Hoover and Tolson flew out west to lead the search for the body of a seventy-two-year-old Chicago millionaire who had been kidnapped at gunpoint several months earlier. The Bureau tracked the ransom money to a career criminal placing bets at a racetrack in California. Hoover and Tolson accompanied the suspect on the chartered plane from Los Angeles to Minneapolis, then on a rumbling car trip into snowy northern Wisconsin. Over the course of several hours of travel on foot and by sleigh, their manacled prisoner identified the underground dugout where he'd first held his victim and led the search party to a branch-covered pit where he had buried two bodies.[25]

Hoover later expressed pride in this adventure, another installment in his effort to prove that he could, indeed, make arrests. "It was a new experience for us, because we are big town boys," he said of the trek through the woods, "but we could do it because we keep in excellent physical condition." He nonetheless admitted to being unsettled by such close contact with human evil, in which the kidnapper apparently let his elderly victim starve for several days before delivering a final, skull-shattering blow. Hoover's voice "was heavy at times with the anger he felt over the enormity and horror of the double crime," *The Washington Times* reported, noting how weary and worn down he seemed after "days of relentless effort."[26]

Other cases that year brought similar cycles of triumph and despair, with Hoover and Tolson experiencing almost all of it together. In early June, they flew to Miami to oversee the case of little Skeegie Cash, a five-year-old boy abducted from his bedroom in a small Florida town. News photos show them striding along Miami's commercial boulevards, brows knitted in a near parody of G-Man determination. But they were doing genuinely hard work—conducting "the greatest man hunt ever seen in Florida," in Hoover's words. In the final stages, Hoover stayed up for forty-eight hours straight. He went to view the boy's decomposing body when agents located it just after midnight on June 9, hidden away in a palmetto thicket, still clad in striped pajamas. Hoover announced the terrible discovery at 1:25 a.m., describing the tiny body concealed in "almost impenetrable" underbrush. He then begged forgiveness for ending the press conference. "That will be all tonight," he declared. "I have been up two nights and am very tired."[27]

Despite his exhaustion, a few days later he and Tolson headed off to New York, where the body of a missing twelve-year-old boy had recently washed up on a beach off of Long Island Sound, headless and trussed with copper wire. In late October, they went back to the city to supervise another kidnap-murder case. By the time Hoover announced arrests in that case on November 1, the papers noted, he looked "weary and unshaven," awake for thirty-nine straight hours. Sometimes work and personal affairs collided directly. In Iowa for Tolson's father's funeral, Hoover insisted that they return to New York to carry out the arrest of an accused murderer named Louis "Lepke" Buchalter, a top organized crime figure. Winchell arranged the arrest, negotiating with Buchalter and persuading the culprit to turn himself in. Hoover arrived just in time to take Buchalter into custody.[28]

Perhaps unsurprisingly, this pace of events, combined with all the other pressures that difficult year, brought on a bout of illness. In early 1939, Hoover began to complain of laryngitis and throat pain. A medical examination showed some minor congestion, along with wear and tear on the vocal cords "not unexpected in one who uses the voice excessively." The doctor recommended that Hoover restrict himself to "an ordinary conversational tone" at all times—in other words, that Hoover should stop yelling at everyone. Hoover does not appear to have taken the advice.[29]

He may have been more partial to the suggestions of an acquaintance who knew of his recent travails and wrote in February 1939 to offer a bit of solace. The note included a poem with "some thoughts in it which are very striking," the friend wrote, and which might, by implication, help Hoover sort through some of his recent difficulties and dilemmas. The poem depicted Christ as a living man, describing his perseverance in the face of "suspicion, heckling, condemnation," his belief in himself though he "was not quite understood even by His mother." It also described a man wearied by humanity and by the demands it placed upon him. During his time on earth, the poem mourned, "Jesus was worn to death by labor, Now by excessive loneliness, Now by the pressure of the crowd." He was forced to walk alone, despite the "sententious and wise friends" who sought to ease his burden.

The letter spoke to Hoover's self-pitying side, his penchant for seeing himself as the lone savior in a sinners' world. It may also have reflected some of his weariness about the events of 1938 and 1939: his mother's death, the murders and kidnappings, the social pressure to conform. The advice Hoover may have appreciated most came in the poem's title, a single phrase repeated after each stanza: "Yet He went on," no matter what the world sent his way.[30]

CHAPTER 21

Terror by Index Card

(1939–1940)

HOOVER SHOWS 'EM

Hoover's wartime crackdowns on communist and fascist groups led to criticism on civil liberties grounds. The cartoon depicts him vanquishing his foes. Cartoon by Leo Joseph Roche, *Buffalo Courier-Express*, March 23, 1940.

BUFFALO COURIER-EXPRESS/
NATIONAL ARCHIVES AND
RECORDS ADMINISTRATION

Hoover was off sunning in California when the next great chapter in world events began: on September 1, 1939, Germany invaded Poland and within days another European war was afoot. The situation had been darkening for weeks, first with stalled negotiations between the Great Powers and then, on August 23, with the surprise announcement of a nonaggression pact between Germany and the Soviet Union. Still, when Hoover left Washington in late August the papers seemed hopeful that Hitler wanted peace. The invasion made that expectation moot. "An era began yesterday," *The Washington Post* declared on September 4 as England and France entered the war, already adopting the cool remove of historical distance. "What lay ahead as Europe plunged into the second World War nobody could know or guess."[1]

Hoover did not rush back to Washington to find out. Hottel's impending marriage made the California sojourn a last hurrah for the trio. The fact that Hoover remained out west does not mean that he ignored the war, however. It merely suggests his confidence in what he had already done to prepare. Roosevelt's 1936 general intelligence directive, followed by the 1938 expansion, meant that the Bureau already possessed extensive files on those groups most likely to come under wartime scrutiny, including the Communist Party and German-American Bund. Indeed, since 1938 Hoover had deepened the Bureau's commitment to this secret work. That year, the House of Representatives had created the Un-American Activities Committee (HUAC) under the leadership of Martin Dies, a conservative Texas Democrat who vowed to make the Roosevelt administration take action against internal threats. In January 1939, responding to Dies's pressure, Roosevelt had announced an FBI effort to investigate communist and fascist groups—"the most sweeping ever undertaken into subversive movements," in one paper's view. He failed to mention that Hoover had already been doing this work since at least 1936, under secret presidential directive.[2]

In later years, Hoover would build a complicated alliance with HUAC, working both for and against the committee as his relations with Roosevelt's successors frayed. In 1939, though, he was still the president's man. The arrival of a new attorney general—the first since Homer Cummings's appointment in 1933—only underscored the need to remain on the president's side. Just five years Hoover's senior, former Michigan governor Frank Murphy arrived in office known as something of a civil liberties advocate, the leader who had refused to call in troops on the sit-down strikers. Among his first acts at the Justice Department was the creation of a civil liberties unit based on the principle that "where there is social unrest . . . we ought to be most anxious and vigilant in protecting the civil liberties of a protesting and insecure people." Murphy made it clear, however, that his ideas were not aimed at the FBI and did not apply to war-related concerns. "In times like these there should be central control and not a confused direction," he announced at a press conference in March 1939. "It should be in the Department of Justice and under Mr. Hoover."[3]

Roosevelt agreed. In June 1939, he had issued yet another secret directive, this time authorizing the FBI to take charge of all federal home-front investigations involving "espionage, counter-espionage, and sabotage in anticipation of the coming war." Since that moment, Hoover had been planning for hostilities in earnest. In the summer of 1939, he became chair of an intelligence committee charged with consolidating the work of other government agencies. He also began to train more agents in the tools of the intelligence trade: "document identification, electrical equipment and sound recording; methods of concealing messages; secret codes and secret writings; detection of secret inks; photographic aspects of espionage work; technical equipment usages in espionage work." By September, the main task left was simply to make the FBI's wartime jurisdiction public. While Hoover squeezed out a last few days at the beach, Murphy contacted the president to encourage a public statement clarifying the FBI's wartime jurisdiction. Roosevelt was happy to oblige.[4]

On September 6, the White House issued a press release announcing that "the Attorney General has been requested by me to instruct the Federal Bureau of Investigation of the Department of Justice to take charge of investigative work in matters relating to espionage, sabotage and violations of the neutrality regulations." The statement did not document what had come before: the 1936 directive, the 1938 expansion, the June 1939 authorization of FBI authority. It did put the rest of the law enforcement profession on notice, however, exhorting "police officers, sheriffs, and all other law enforcement officers" to share information with the Bureau and to respect federal authority. To assist Hoover in coping with this new workload, an executive order added 150 new employees to the FBI payroll.[5]

With those announcements, Roosevelt completed what he had begun in 1936, publicly rescinding Harlan Stone's order and licensing the FBI to reenter the world of political intelligence. But things did not proceed as smoothly as either Hoover or Roosevelt might have hoped. After years of distancing himself from the Palmer Raids and of attempting to rehabilitate his reputation, Hoover found himself forced to confront the controversies of his past, and to contend with same criticisms that had brought down his predecessors.

IT IS OFTEN SAID THAT GENERALS FIGHT THE PREVIOUS WAR, USING STORIES of past battles to craft strategies for the future. In the autumn of 1939, this was true of nearly everyone in Washington. Most officials had played some sort of role in the Great War. What they had concluded—indeed, what almost all Americans believed by 1939 was that the war had been a tragic mistake that led not to eternal peace and stable democracy but to the corruption and double-dealing of Versailles, and now to another disastrous war. Roosevelt acknowledged as much in his fireside chat after the invasion, vowing to maintain American neutrality. At home, he said, this generation of Americans would stick to hard-nosed facts rather than foment "rumor," having learned their lessons from false talk of German atrocities and conspiracies. Roosevelt himself would be no Woodrow Wilson, throwing into prison everyone who disagreed with him. "I cannot ask that every American remain neutral in thought," he declared, a pointed rejection of Wilson's effort to get Americans not only to act but to think as the government desired. Yet Roosevelt believed that Americans now faced a grim task of mobilization, whether they liked it or not. The challenge was to find a way to prepare for conflict while avoiding the missteps and abuses of the Wilson administration.[6]

Within the Justice Department, the previous war evoked especially painful memories, with its overlay of vigilante violence and government repression. These legacies created a conundrum for Hoover and Murphy, now charged to protect the nation without repeating the mistakes of the past. Murphy tried to articulate a path forward in his announcement on September 6. "There will be no repetition of the confusion and laxity of 20 years ago which caused havoc," he promised. "At the same time, we do not want to turn our activity into a witch hunt." Hoover, too, went out of his way to reassure the country that civil liberties abuses lay firmly in the past. In October 1939, after a brief sojourn back in Washington, he and Tolson flew to San Francisco, where Hoover was scheduled to speak before the International Association of Chiefs of Police, his first major public address since the start of the war. There, he asked the police for their help in investigating espionage, sabotage, and subversion, but warned against "over-zealous" action either by law enforcement officials or by the public at large. "We need no vigilantes in this situation," Hoover said, vowing that his model government men would be so efficient and effective as to make "hysteria" unnecessary.[7]

Coming from a veteran of German internment and the Palmer Raids, Hoover's speech appeared to acknowledge some responsibility for that era's terrible violence and excess. But Hoover was getting at something slightly different. He affirmed the essential spirit of the World War I home front. "America has room for only one ism— Americanism," he declared, echoing Wilson's slogan of "100 percent Americanism." What went wrong previously, he argued, was that the government failed to contain these high national passions and channel them toward constructive ends. If law enforcement officials wanted to be effective, but did not want the same abuses to occur, they would simply have to do a better job, administratively speaking. "Every effort must be directed in an orderly manner by thoroughly responsible, well trained, professional law enforcement officers, totally devoid of hysteria. The evil spirits which would destroy America must be met and conquered. In this, there can be no middle ground." Properly conceived, patriotic vigilance would play a key role in rooting out subversives but enforcement of national loyalty would be left to the professionals.[8]

HOOVER'S ACTIONS DURING THE FIRST MONTHS OF WAR REFLECTED BOTH ASpects of this outlook. He rejected calls for a new American Protective League, and moved quickly to discredit local groups that sought to claim its mantle. At the same time, he held on to most of the structures he had been building since 1936, which were themselves based upon what had happened during and after the Great War. In September, he officially reestablished the General Intelligence Division after three years of conducting "general intelligence" work in ad hoc fashion. He also created a custodial detention index, a card file of likely candidates for internment modeled on the system he had helped to administer two decades earlier.[9]

Hoover apparently saw no contradiction between these initiatives and his promise to protect "constitutional guarantees." To the contrary, he viewed the efficient, "unhysterical" exercise of federal power—up to and including a carefully devised detention index—as the nation's best hope for avoiding home-front chaos. He assumed that everyone would recognize the difference between an out-of-control crackdown and a properly administered intelligence operation. So with the European war finally under-way he made little effort to hide what he was up to.[10]

"In September of 1939 we found it necessary to organize a General Intelligence Division in Washington," Hoover told Congress in November. "This division now has compiled extensive indices of individuals, groups, and organizations engaged in these subversive activities, in espionage activities, or any activities that are possibly detrimental to the internal security of the United States." By that point the GID was running twenty-four hours a day, with separate sections for translation and cryptography along with an extensive library of radical and foreign-language publications. Another new unit focused on industrial espionage and factory protection, with the goal of making inroads at more than twelve thousand factories nationwide. The detection index itself had been arranged "alphabetically but also geographically" to allow for the greatest ease of access. "These indexes will be extremely important and valuable in grave emergency," Hoover explained. In the event of U.S. entry into the war, the cards would be used to identify noncitizens eligible for detention and internment under policies yet to be determined. The committee offered no objection.[11]

With this momentum behind him, in January Hoover decided to take preemptive action. On January 14, the New York field office arrested eighteen members of the pro-Nazi Christian Front, snatching up membership lists and "large quantities of arms and ammunition" in a sweep of the premises. A few weeks later, the Detroit office descended on the local Abraham Lincoln Brigade, communist sympathizers who had recruited and fought for the anti-fascist movement in Spain. Neither group had done anything especially different from what they had been doing in recent years. What changed was the drumbeat of war, and the alarmist politics that came with it.

The ensuing headlines might have come straight from Hoover's years at the Radical Division. "FBI Smashes U.S. Revolution Forces in New York Drives," one paper declared after the Christian Front arrests. But Hoover insisted that these arrests were different from what had happened under Palmer, a more restrained response to a genuine internal threat. To the press, he conjured up dreadful images of what might have happened if the Bureau had failed to act. "The government was to be sabotaged and a dictatorship was to be established," he explained of the Christian Front's supposedly grandiose plans. Under such provocation, he argued, his agents had acted as models of restraint and circumspection—just the sort of careful professionals they had promised to be.[12]

NOT EVERYONE AGREED. ON JANUARY 11, 1940, SPEAKING FROM THE FLOOR OF Congress, Representative Vito Marcantonio attacked Hoover's description of the GID and its "extensive" index of dangerous subversives. "This language is very wide and most dangerous and to me indicates preparations for a drive that will be very similar to the activities of the Palmer days," Marcantonio warned. As a representative of the communist-friendly American Labor Party, Marcantonio had special reason to be concerned, but he made the case that Hoover's latest actions imperiled everyone. Once again, he warned, the country faced a regime of "terror by index cards." Far from calming the nation's fears, Hoover was promoting "the very kind of hysteria that leads a country into war" and into another nightmare of political repression.[13]

Over the next few weeks, other progressives and liberals, many of them veterans of the "Palmer days," began to sound the alarm, urging the country to step back from such policies before it was too late. The ACLU, founded in response to the previous war's home-front abuses, called for an end to Hoover's "high handed" tactics. *The New Republic* magazine followed up with a searing article comparing Hoover's FBI to the Russian secret police and German gestapo. The magazine singled out Hoover for personal attack, arguing that his popularity made him a unique danger during wartime. "The glamor that surrounds him also conceals the growth of a power inconsistent with our conception of democratic institutions," the magazine said. The only solution was to do what Harlan Stone had done decades earlier, when he "reduced the Bureau to its normal size, after it had become swollen under William J. Burns, as it is now swollen under J. Edgar Hoover." The problem during the previous war, according to *The New Republic*, was not simply poor administration; it was the very idea of granting a man like Hoover power to determine who was and who was not a danger to the nation.[14]

If the criticism had stopped there, with grumblings from the left and its assorted factions, Hoover might have dismissed the whole matter and moved on. But these first hints of wartime controversy unleashed a range of other critics, people who had been holding their tongues when Hoover seemed so popular and well-nigh invincible. Perhaps it should have come as no surprise when those who had once spoken out against the Espionage Act and Palmer Raids began to raise the alarm about Hoover's return to raids and mass political surveillance. Hoover seemed to be caught off guard, however, bewildered that his explanations were not accepted at face value.

These critics shared some basic concerns: that Hoover had grown too powerful, that he used his power to enforce his political preferences, and that with the coming of war this situation would only get worse. Still troubled by Hoover's control over the hiring and firing of agents, in early 1940 the Civil Service Commission released a seven-page report decrying the trend toward "placing all power in the hands of a single individual in the name of efficiency." Around the same time, Montana senator Burton Wheeler helped to initiate a congressional investigation into federal, police, and private wiretapping. Like many in Washington, the senator remembered the abuses of the 1920s all too well. As Bureau director, William J. Burns had allegedly sent agents to rifle through the senator's offices, one of the events that led to Burns's expulsion.[15]

The most significant critique of Hoover that winter came from yet another veteran of the Palmer years, Nebraska senator George Norris. A progressive Republican turned Independent, Norris had been elected to the House in 1902, when Hoover was just starting elementary school, and to the Senate a decade later. In the years since, he had come to be known as one of the great independent spirits of Congress and, some argued, the nation's greatest living senator. In 1917, he had voted against U.S. entry into a war fought for Wall Street, then opposed both the Red Scare and the Treaty of Versailles. Now he argued that the nation was on the verge of committing the same mistakes once again, sacrificing liberty at home in response to a distant European conflict. He tied his worries directly to Hoover's wartime actions: the resurrection of the General Intelligence Division, the internment index, and the launching of political raids. In late February, "with considerable hesitancy," Norris sent a letter to the attorney general outlining his objections to Hoover's conduct. A few days later, he went public with his accusations on the floor of the Senate. The letter quoted Harlan Stone's indelible 1924 warning that "a secret police system may become a menace to free government and free institutions." Norris recommended that the Justice Department explore whether Hoover had now fulfilled Stone's prediction.[16]

IN THE MIDST OF THIS MOUNTING DRAMA, HOOVER DID SOMETHING STRANGE: he went on vacation again. On February 13, he and Tolson left for Miami Beach, Florida, where they rented a quaint two-story stucco villa on an island in Biscayne Bay. Officially, they were supposed to be reviving a vice investigation begun months earlier. Mostly, though, they seemed to be in strategic retreat, seizing a chance to pause and assess the situation in Washington. Hoover had spent fifteen years trying to avoid this moment, remaking himself step by painful step as a neutral, nonpartisan administrator. By the time he departed for Florida, the capital was buzzing with rumors that he would be fired anyway. Developments at the White House did not help. In January, just as Hoover's critics were whetting their knives, Roosevelt appointed Frank Murphy to the Supreme Court, leaving the attorney general's post vacant for the second time in a year. To replace Murphy, the president selected Solicitor General Robert Jackson, a devout New Dealer and another self-proclaimed champion of civil liberties.[17]

Like Murphy, Jackson remembered the previous war as a travesty of justice. He also came to office "very dubious of Mr. Hoover's policies," according to an FBI report. On February 16, three days after Hoover's departure to Florida, Jackson dismissed all charges against the Abraham Lincoln Brigade. "I can see no good to come from reviving in America at this late date the animosities of the Spanish conflict," he announced to reporters, who quickly jumped to their own conclusions about what the dismissal might mean for Hoover. "The case of J. Edgar Hoover suggests that our No. 1 G-Man may become the first American political casualty of World War No. 2," the *New York Post* declared, predicting that the combination of a new attorney general and Hoover's fierce but patient enemies would force him out of the Bureau.[18]

Hoover's unstated task in Florida was to figure out how to prevent this outcome. Winchell was on hand in Miami, huddling with Hoover and Tolson to consult about affairs in Washington. Hoover had plenty of other friends in the news business as well, especially at the Hearst and Copley chains. "Concerted Effort to Oust Head of G-Men Is Doomed to Fail under Popular Protests," one headline asserted. He also had the support of groups such as the Daughters of the American Revolution, which engaged him to speak that spring despite his troubles. But Hoover believed that Jackson was the key player, and that without a word of support from the attorney general, all the talk of firing might become a self-fulfilling prophecy. From Florida, he barked telephone instructions to his assistant Ed Tamm, charged with the unwelcome task of running interference back in Washington.[19]

At the age of thirty-three, Tamm had already worked under Hoover for almost a decade, weathering the uncertainties of the early Roosevelt transition and the pressures of the crime war. This crisis seemed different. "There have been times in years past when the practices of the FBI have been attacked," *The New York Times* noted. "But all attacks on the bureau up to now have bounced off without much damage." On February 27, the day after Norris's public criticism, Tamm informed the Justice Department that Hoover expected a public letter of support, lest the attorney general's silence give credence to unpleasant rumors. Jackson agreed but made little effort to see it through. In the meantime, perhaps encouraged by this silence, Congressman Marcantonio mounted a second attack on Hoover, scoffing at the director's apparent fondness for nightclubs and luxury vacations, and labeling Hoover the nation's top "Stork Club Detective."[20]

Tamm's updates reflect a rising panic on Hoover's part as he sat in Florida, waiting for the situation in Washington to change while negotiations with the attorney general stretched on day after day. Sometime in the midst of it all, Hoover made what must have been one of the most difficult decisions of his career. Twenty years earlier, he had helped to create the first General Intelligence Division only to see it founder and then succumb to its critics. Now, at the age of forty-five, he faced the prospect of reliving that dark period from his youth. Perhaps he simply did not want to endure the humiliation that Palmer had encountered: the congressional grilling, the questioning of motives, the mocking cartoons in the press. Or perhaps he was bluffing, hoping through dramatic action to force a response from the attorney general. On the afternoon of February 29, in conference with the attorney general, Tamm presented the ultimatum that he and Hoover had agreed upon by phone. "I informed Mr. Jackson that you would submit your resignation at once to him if he had any doubt or question as to your policies or program," Tamm reported back to Hoover. Just six months into the wartime duties he had embraced with such confidence, Hoover was prepared to resign rather than suffer through what his predecessors had experienced a generation earlier.[21]

IT IS WORTH PAUSING TO CONSIDER WHAT MIGHT HAVE HAPPENED IF JACKSON had accepted Hoover's offer. Coming at a moment when the U.S. had not yet committed to any particular wartime course, the decision might have sounded a note of homefront caution, affirming the importance of civil liberties and careful deliberation in the struggle that lay ahead. Those priorities, in turn, might have inspired a subtly different vision for what would come to be known as the "national security state," that sprawling agglomeration of military, defense, and intelligence agencies that would soon be a permanent feature of U.S. governance. As a mere individual, Hoover never came close to controlling this vast apparatus. Many of his ideas about its purpose and structure were widely shared in Washington—by liberals and conservatives, Republicans and Democrats, alike. And yet he helped to shape the emerging security state in crucial ways, both as an architect of an expanding federal surveillance system and as a cultural visionary, determined to use that system to enforce his own vision of the right and the good. The "smear campaign" of 1940, as Hoover later described it, might have set his career on a different course, with Roosevelt and Jackson giving him a handshake and a round of thanks, then dismissing him from the stage of history.

Hoover believed this scenario was possible. "No one outside the FBI and the Department of Justice ever knew how close they came to wrecking us," he later recalled of early 1940. If the wrecking ball had come through, he might be remembered as a quirky vestige of the 1930s, lumped in with Dillinger, breadlines, and Roosevelt's Blue Eagle as a Depression-era artifact. As it was, under the threat of Hoover's resignation, Jackson gave in. On the afternoon of March 1, 1940, he issued a public statement declaring that there was "nothing to justify any charge of misconduct against the Federal Bureau of Investigation." Hoover returned to Washington that night.[22]

Over the next few months, Jackson took some modest measures to constrain the FBI and to ensure Hoover would be acting under Justice Department control. On March 14, he ordered the civil liberties unit of the Justice Department to conduct a comprehensive investigation of the FBI's arrests in Detroit. A few days later, he announced a ban on wiretapping, citing a recent Supreme Court decision declaring the practice abhorrent and illegal. The Detroit inquiry, released in May, absolved the FBI of wrongdoing, declaring that "the conduct of the agents is not subject to justifiable criticism." Still, Jackson attempted to limit what a wartime FBI might do in similar situations in the future, demanding that Hoover submit to the authority of the attorney general's office in all matters of controversy.[23]

Hoover went along with Jackson's policies, supporting the attorney general's wiretapping ban and assuring the public, in a carefully worded statement, that the FBI would never tap wires "indiscriminately and in violation of fundamental civil rights." And yet the attacks of that winter continued to rankle. In late April, still mulling over the significance of what had taken place, Hoover wrote a letter to Harlan Stone, whose legacy had so often been invoked during those months, and whose vote of confidence back in 1924 had made Hoover's career and success possible.[24]

The letter began with a burst of confusion and pain. "I have, very frankly, been terribly heartsick over the vilifying 'smear' that has been directed at the FBI during the last several months," Hoover wrote to Stone. Far from taking his critics to heart, he insisted that they fundamentally misunderstood the FBI, which even now, with the war underway in Europe, remained fiercely committed to Stone's early directives. "There hasn't been the slightest deviation from any of those principles of law enforcement administration which you initiated in 1924 in this Bureau," Hoover wrote, insisting that it had been his life's struggle to enact Stone's ideas of "decency and fairness and tolerance" in bureaucratic form. The letter contained an element of deception: Contrary to Stone's instructions, Hoover's men had wiretapped and used the "third degree" and spied on Americans for political reasons.

Hoover continued in this manner for several pages, listing a succession of noble deeds that had gone underappreciated by the public. The letter also cast blame. In his struggle to figure out what went wrong that winter, he identified two chief adversaries, both of them holdovers from the Palmer days. The first were the communists, who allegedly gathered at "a secret meeting" to plan "this 'smear' campaign." The second were the weak-minded liberal dupes, "very well-meaning but misinformed persons," who succumbed to communist manipulation.

Hoover concluded his letter to Stone by affirming the public's right to criticize "any Governmental Bureau or official"—the very essence of democracy. But he also suggested that such open dialogue could be dangerous, and might need to be contained. "When it gets into the realm of imagination and suppositions, then I think it does a real harm, not only to the agency against which it is directed, but to the welfare and security of the nation." Especially in a time of war, he concluded, what was good for the FBI was good for America.[25]

CHAPTER 22

Henry E. Jones

(1940–1941)

It Won't Happen Here

Hoover's FBI expanded dramatically in 1940, building on widespread concern about a "fifth column" of spies and Nazi sympathizers within the United States. Cartoon from *Omaha World-Herald,* May 29, 1940.

© 1940 *OMAHA WORLD-HERALD*

If the invasion of Poland in September 1939 produced a shiver of fear in the United States, the invasion of France in the spring of 1940 instilled a lasting sense of dread. While Hoover was absorbed with his domestic ordeal, the world had been stuck in the so-called phony war, a period of technical hostilities but little action. Then, during a few days in early May, the Nazi army blitzed into Belgium, Luxembourg, Holland, and finally France, where the fabled French army crumpled at the Maginot Line. On June 14, 1940, Hitler's troops marched triumphantly into Paris, unfurling the swastika over the Arc de Triomphe. "As the forty-first week of the war came to a close," an American reporter wrote back to Washington, "the mighty German army appeared to be writing... an obituary for the France of 'liberte, egalite, et Fraternite.' ... France's only hope was the United States," he added, reciting pleas from Parisians for the U.S. to save them from Nazi terror. But according to pollster George Gallup, a full 93 percent of Americans still felt that the war was a European problem, and that rushing to the aid of France would involve American boys in another pointless debacle.[1]

Roosevelt did not try to convince them otherwise, at least not directly. Instead, he urged the nation to improve its defenses and reinitiated a national draft in case war should arrive on American shores. In an address to Congress on May 16, 1940, he urged Americans to ramp up war production, especially of airplanes, tanks, and other heavy equipment. Finally, he called for renewed effort against a "fifth column" of spies and saboteurs allegedly hidden throughout the western hemisphere, ready to rise up at Hitler's signal. "We have seen the treacherous use of the 'fifth column' by which persons supposed to be peaceful visitors were actually a part of an enemy unit of occupation," Roosevelt warned Congress, requesting almost a billion dollars in defense funding. In a fireside chat ten days later, he spoke again of "the Trojan Horse" and "the Fifth Column that betrays a nation unprepared for treachery": enemy saboteurs, spies, and sympathizers lying in wait. As in 1939, he counseled Americans to avoid vigilante action, but there was no mistaking the overall message: the Trojan horse was real, it had already passed through America's gates, and it was up to the FBI, above all other agencies, to stop it.[2]

This rush of concern over homegrown conspiracies and Nazi plots brought an end to Hoover's lingering ordeal. During the "phony war," Roosevelt had been willing to allow the liberals in his party—even his Republican critics—to wring their hands about civil liberties. With the invasion of France, the president lost patience, and once again committed himself firmly on Hoover's side. "The President had a tendency to think in terms of right and wrong, instead of terms of legal and illegal," Robert Jackson recalled. "Because he thought that his motives were always good for the things that he wanted to do, he found difficulty in thinking there could be legal limitations on them."[3]

The result was the single swiftest accumulation of power in Hoover's career, a grant of autonomy and discretion that surpassed anything the president had done before. In late May 1940, Roosevelt secretly rejected the Supreme Court's ban on wiretapping. "I am convinced that the Supreme Court never intended any dictum . . . to apply to grave matters involving the defense of the nation," he wrote in a confidential memo authorizing Hoover to wiretap in matters of national security, a vague and open-ended category. In mid-June, Roosevelt exempted Bureau agents from civil service regulation, formally bringing an end to the battle with the hostile commission. A few weeks later, he authorized the FBI to launch intelligence operations in Latin America, where it was feared that the Germans were building an espionage network to prepare for invasion and occupation. And in late June, he signed the Smith Act (formally known as the Alien Registration Act), which required all foreign-born residents to register with the government and outlawed violent revolutionary language. The Smith Act was virtually identical to the peacetime sedition law that Hoover and Palmer had asked for in 1920, which Congress had adamantly refused. Now, in the panicked summer of 1940, it became law without much debate.[4]

If Roosevelt's ideas were familiar to Hoover by 1940, what they authorized that year was not. Before 1940, the FBI's intelligence initiatives had been small-scale, experimental efforts, undertaken with a concern not to do too much too fast. After 1940, they became the basis for the greatest hiring boom in Bureau history, a wartime buildup that yet again changed the character of Hoover's tight-knit G-Man shop. With the invasion of France, intelligence work was no longer a sideshow to the main dramas of crime, delinquency, and vice. Beginning in 1940, it *was* the show, the most urgent and challenging aspect of Bureau duties, and the arena in which Hoover's success or failure would be measured. He had spent the winter and spring fearing for his job, convinced that the "smear campaign" would do him in. Now he suddenly had jurisdiction over the western hemisphere and carte blanche from the president to do what needed to be done. By executive authority, he could wiretap and conduct intelligence investigations anywhere in the Americas. And by congressional mandate, he could investigate anyone within the United States deemed to be a threat to the government.

Hoover did not forget the criticism that had nearly felled him in the spring of 1940. Indeed, he spent much of the war trying to win over those critics and prove them wrong. But whatever possibility there had been for a broader national discussion of free speech and civil liberties, of Hoover's failings and the desirable limits on federal power, disappeared with the invasion of France. While the rest of the country still held back, agonizing over whether to declare formal hostilities, Hoover began to mobilize an army.

HIS TOP PRIORITY, AS THE REALITY OF THE NAZI BLITZKRIEG SANK IN, WAS TO contain the supposed "fifth column" threat, the possibility that enemy agents were already operating in the United States. The issue entailed a blend of fact and fiction, an exaggerated threat accompanied on occasion by a few honest-to-goodness in-the-flesh foreign spies. He recognized that the issue would produce another round of upheaval at the Bureau, demanding "the utmost from the facilities and personnel of this organization." There was something familiar about the situation, though, with its sudden demands to scale up Bureau personnel against a backdrop of national unease. In his annual report to the attorney general, Hoover likened this "period of transition" to the first years of the crime war, when he had transformed his corps of gentleman lawyers into gun-toting G-Men. Only now the Bureau would have to remake itself as a large-scale intelligence agency, capable of forging judgments that went well beyond matters of legal evidence and criminal law.[5]

Most of the men upon whom Hoover relied to help with this project had been at his side for more than a decade. Many had been around longer than that, recruits from the first Kappa-Alpha-and-GW generation. There was Tolson, of course, whose role as Hoover's personnel and internal operations man now took on added significance. Next in line was Ed Tamm, the somber Georgetown graduate who had done so much to run interference for Hoover during the "smear campaign," along with the veteran Harold Nathan. Kappa Alpha brother Hugh Clegg ran agent training while Frank Baughman, Hoover's onetime best friend, took charge of the firearms program. Managing them all was Helen Gandy, who'd marked her twentieth anniversary at the Justice Department just months before the outbreak of war.

The relative consistency of the Bureau's leadership gave it an advantage over other federal agencies, many of them recent creations with an ever-changing roster of men at the top. So did the FBI's years of secret experimentation in domestic intelligence gathering and counterespionage. Many of the duties that fell to the Bureau were still relatively new, however, requiring each division to adapt its criminal enforcement background to the exigencies of the country's pseudo-war. The FBI lab underwent an abrupt shift, transforming itself from a criminal forensics facility into a wartime intelligence lab, focused on secret inks and microfilm technology and high-resolution cameras. At the Identification Division, what had once been a clearinghouse for criminal fingerprints evolved into a large-scale domestic surveillance program, compiling the prints of draftees, war-production workers, and foreign-born residents. The Bureau's accountants turned their attention from securities fraud to the monitoring of foreign funds. Building on the work of the General Intelligence Division, Hoover organized a new National Defense Division and continued to expand surveillance of "German groups and sympathizers, Communist groups and sympathizers, Fascist groups and sympathizers, Japanese and others." Field offices opened in Hawaii, Alaska, and Puerto Rico. A small number of agents also shipped out to foreign posts on "undercover assignments for intelligence purposes."[6]

Hoover vowed that wartime pressures would not weaken his hiring standards, or significantly alter the culture of the FBI. In search of continuity, he encouraged National Academy graduates to join the federal ranks. He also looked to local universities—GW especially—for the sort of man he had always favored. Despite his efforts to preserve the Bureau's established culture, he soon ran up against an incontrovertible fact: there were simply not enough fine-looking, well-mannered, twenty-five-to-thirty-five-year-old, white, fraternity-bred lawyers to go around. In the 1920s, when Hoover established these preferences, the Bureau had hired a handful of agents each year, carefully culling each application. By the middle of 1941, the Bureau was hiring fifty-two agents every two weeks, plus more than 160 clerks and stenographers. The sheer scale of the effort necessitated a quiet easing of the rules. Though Hoover never admitted to any change of policy, only a few of the old standards remained inviolate: there would be no women and few Black men as special agents, and anyone who "embarrassed" the Bureau would meet with swift discipline.[7]

Once hired, all of these new employees had to be trained, equipped, and paid, no easy feat at a time when federal agencies were scrambling for office space and wartime

appropriations. During the late 1930s, Hoover had launched construction of a dedicated training building at Quantico, a Marine base in northern Virginia. The three-
story brick schoolhouse opened in early 1940, just in time to become obsolete. The
Quantico dining room, designed for sixty-four students and three instructors, was
split into two shifts, serving upwards of seventy men each. At the barracks, eight trainees packed into bunk rooms meant for four, and the firing range began operating seven
days a week.[8]

Hoover's routine was changing as well, his work bleeding into the evening hours he
had once reserved for Harvey's and the Stork Club. "I am there from 9 in the morning
until 7:30 in the evening," he said of his office life in early 1941. "Then I go out to dinner, come back about 9 o'clock and usually work until 11:30 at night." He was slightly
exaggerating; office logs show that he often left for good after dinner. It was nonetheless true that *everyone* at the seat of government was working more than usual. By early
1941, the average agent was clocking four and a half hours of unpaid overtime, a point
of pride in Hoover's appropriations appearances. The Identification Division went on
an emergency 24-hour schedule. On a typical day in 1940, clerks received 12,000 new
fingerprint cards; by late 1941, an average day could mean 25,000 new prints. At the
end of 1940, the identification division held 14 million fingerprints, "the largest reserve of information based on fingerprints in the world," as Hoover noted. By the end
of 1941, that number had almost doubled, to 24 million, and the pace showed no signs
of slowing.[9]

The influx of personnel made short work of Hoover's spick-and-span office culture,
where galoshes under the desk and snacks in the drawer had once been censurable offenses. In the wartime space crunch, clerks ended up in hallways, reception areas, and
classrooms, anywhere the Bureau could squeeze out a few feet. Six years earlier, when
it opened, the Justice complex had seemed unimaginably grand and cavernous, one of
the largest government buildings ever constructed. By 1941, it was wholly inadequate,
a source of frustration, disease, and interdivisional strife. Justice planners tried to ease
the congestion by spreading out to nearby buildings: a bus station, a skating rink, a
former apartment house. The extra facilities barely made a dent in the problem, however, with dozens of new agents, clerks, and stenographers arriving each Monday morning. In January 1940, the FBI employed 2,432 men and women. By February 1941, it
had 4,477 employees, with plans to reach 5,588 by June.[10]

In the midst of this crush, a congressman suggested that the FBI might need its own
building someday. "Your Bureau is performing a service of the greatest importance to
the Nation," he declared during Hoover's congressional testimony. "I am in favor of
appropriating every dollar you need to combat alien influences and subversive activities and I would be in favor of providing you with a new building if you need one for
efficient operation." In the meantime, Congress provided money, more of it than Hoover

had ever seen. In fiscal year 1941, his budget was more than $14 million, almost seven times what he had started out with under Harlan Stone. The following year, it leaped to $25 million, and the U.S. war effort was just getting started.[11]

HOOVER'S RESPONSE TO THIS SUDDEN RUSH OF MONEY, POWER, AND PERSONNEL partially fulfilled the dark warnings proffered by civil libertarians just a few months earlier. Roosevelt's wiretapping directive allowed the FBI to launch surveillance of foreign diplomats; by early fall, taps were up and running at the German, French, Italian, Russian, and Japanese embassies. The directive also gave Hoover wide latitude to decide who else needed to be watched. Under wartime authority, he expanded such surveillance activity far beyond anything he had undertaken in 1936, with his first tentative forays into exploring "Fascism and Communism." By 1940, the category of "subversive" included virtually anyone who expressed sympathy toward a foreign power or hostility to the war effort, including striking workers and critics of White House policy. "None of these persons today has violated the specific Federal law now in force and effect," Hoover acknowledged, "but many of them will come within the category for internment or prosecution as a result of regulations or laws which may be enacted in the event of a declaration of war." Unlike criminal law enforcement, in which policemen gathered evidence after a crime had been committed, wartime surveillance was supposed to be a preventive endeavor. "To wait until [a declaration of war] to gather such information or to conduct such investigations would be suicidal," Hoover wrote.[12]

In the middle of May, at the president's suggestion, the White House press secretary dispatched several stacks of letters to Hoover with the suggestion that "you might like to go over these, noting the names and addresses of the senders." The letters came from critics of Roosevelt's war policy, including isolationists outraged at his apparent desire to entangle the United States in a European conflict. Many of the letter writers had rallied behind aviator Charles Lindbergh, who had moved to Europe after his son's kidnapping and murder only to return to the U.S. in 1939 with a medal from Hitler and an awestruck description of German air power. In a radio broadcast three days after Roosevelt's address to Congress, Lindbergh denounced the "hysterical chatter of calamity and invasion" behind the president's preparedness drive. That broadcast, combined with Lindbergh's refusal to hand back his medal from the Third Reich, led Roosevelt to conclude, "Lindbergh is a Nazi." The White House wanted the FBI to deliver updates not only on Lindbergh himself, but on his most ardent followers.[13]

This was at heart a shameless political request: the president wanted the FBI to investigate his detractors. Under the logic of war, however, the distinction between political disagreement and "disloyalty" or "subversion" was less clear than ever. In early June, Hoover opened files on Roosevelt's war critics, reporting to the White House any notable discoveries. Roosevelt made it clear that Hoover would be rewarded for the effort. "Thank you for the many interesting and valuable reports that you have made for me regarding the fast-moving situations of the last few months," he wrote to Hoover on June 14. "You have done and are doing a wonderful job, and I want you to know of my gratification and appreciation."[14]

Over the next several months, Hoover passed along dozens of other reports and updates, not only about Lindbergh and the isolationists but also about union officials, civil rights activists, communists, socialists, and members of the Bund. To assist in the gathering of information, the Bureau recruited thousands of informants, men and women willing to attend meetings, copy membership lists, and spy on their friends and family. The total number of Bureau informants recruited during the war will likely never be known, but an October memo to Roosevelt hinted at a vast recruitment effort, on a scale never before attempted by any federal agency. In a single Ohio factory, Hoover boasted, the FBI had already signed up 133 "confidential informants," each of whom "believes that he is the bureau's sole source of information within that organization." Agents were performing similar feats at 1,200 other "key industrial facilities." Even allowing for some exaggeration, it seems likely that more than 100,000 informants were spying for the FBI by the fall of 1940, and that was just within the nation's defense plants. It did not begin to include the "subversive" organizations in the FBI's files: the Bund, the Communist Party, and their lesser rivals.[15]

Hoover jealously guarded the Bureau's right to recruit informants and conduct surveillance within any group that might conceivably disrupt the war effort, including labor unions. The year 1941 produced a wave of unrest in key defense industries—aviation, electronics, automobile, coal—where Communist Party members had helped to establish powerful unions in recent years. Hoover knew enough about New Deal alliances to insist that "I, of course, have no controversy with bona fide organized labor." He maintained that the Communist Party—guided by the spirit of the Nazi-Soviet Non-aggression Pact—was fomenting industrial conflict to disrupt the American war effort, thus providing the logic for an ongoing program of labor surveillance. "I fully realize that the Bureau in initiating and carrying on investigations in this field must follow a very careful course between 'Scylla and Charybdis' and that undoubtedly some sources will accuse the Bureau of illegal activities," he wrote to Jackson in the spring of 1941, positioning himself as a martyr to the cause of national security. "I believe, however, that we must have the courage to face the yelping of these alleged Liberals."[16]

When outrage over the Bureau's activities did surface, Roosevelt was quick to laugh it off. In the summer of 1941, Hoover showed up at the White House to discuss a humiliating tale about Harry Bridges, the Australian-born union leader and alleged communist whom Hoover and Roosevelt had been worrying about since at least 1936. On a recent visit to New York, Bridges had noticed strange goings-on in the hotel room next door, and quickly concluded that he was under Bureau surveillance. Rather than confront the agents directly, he rented a room in a hotel across the street, then invited reporters and friends to join him with a pair of binoculars, allowing them to see that agents were, indeed, at the ready with wiretapping equipment. Their observations, combined with Bridges's discovery of a microphone inside his hotel phone, set off a national press cycle. "Harry Bridges Charges F.B.I. Men Spied on Him," read a headline in *The Baltimore Sun*. When Hoover sheepishly retold the story to Roosevelt, the president offered up "one of his great grins," then slapped Hoover on the back. "By God, Edgar, that's the first time you've been caught with your pants down!" he declared, laughing.[17]

Roosevelt also backed Hoover and the Justice Department in another controversial move that summer. In June, agents raided the Socialist Workers Party around Minneapolis, where members of the Trotskyist group had recently been elected to run the Teamsters local. Several weeks later, a federal grand jury indicted twenty-nine SWP members under the Smith Act, charging them with plotting the violent overthrow of the U.S. government. These were "the first peacetime sedition indictments in more than 140 years," in the words of one historian, and they came about largely in response to reports from FBI informants, who insisted that the SWP was hoarding weapons and preparing to commit acts of sabotage. When the case came to trial that fall, no stockpiles of guns were produced. The jury nonetheless convicted eighteen of the defendants, concluding that their talk of revolution constituted a grave criminal act. Roosevelt supported the decision to prosecute, hoping to shore up support from the Teamsters' more conservative national leadership.[18]

THE TUG-OF-WAR OVER HOMEGROWN RADICALISM WAS FAMILIAR TO HOOVER, a struggle that he had first engaged more than twenty years before. Other aspects of his work took him into more distant terrain, where he was less sure of his direction. The Bureau's move into wartime intelligence did not require simply scaling up. It also necessitated a change of mentality and another shift in the Bureau's culture. From 1924 through 1940, Hoover had focused on turning the Bureau into a model of professional law enforcement. Now he was supposed to transform it into a major international intelligence and counterespionage agency, capable of gathering secret information about enemy spies and, where possible, thwarting their activities.

As early experiences like the Rumrich case had shown, this proposition did not easily lend itself to Hoover's emphasis on statistics and publicity. Spies rarely take credit for their achievements; the best operations remain, by definition, secret. They let investigations run for months, even years, without knowing whether anything is really being accomplished. Successful espionage requires cunning and deceit, sometimes involving relationships with unsavory characters. None of this came naturally to Hoover. And there was almost nobody within the government from whom he could learn. As an FBI report later noted, the Bureau plunged into counterespionage work that summer "under extreme difficulties and without any precedent whatsoever to follow with regard to this type of work."[19]

The experience would no doubt have been far more difficult if not for the help of the one group on American soil that knew a great deal about such matters: the British intelligence service. The British had reached out to Hoover as the war ramped up. Though the Battle of Britain lay months in the future, by the spring of 1940 they were growing anxious about American foot-dragging, and about the bitter isolationist sentiments of men such as Lindbergh. Prime Minister Winston Churchill made no secret of his determination to bring the U.S. into the war, and he hoped to promote this aim by setting up a British intelligence outpost in New York. From there, his proxies could agitate on behalf of Britain and help the Americans build the clandestine infrastructure that would be needed for full-scale war. Churchill's vision was extralegal; no nation in the world openly allowed a foreign power to run an intelligence service on domestic soil. To make it happen, the British decided that they needed Hoover's assistance and permission.[20]

Hoover did not usually entertain this sort of offer: the arrangement was untested and controversial, and it required giving up control of his men and territory. It was also top secret, a fact that meant the FBI could not take credit for any success. Hoover agreed to meet anyway with William Stephenson, the debonaire Canadian millionaire tasked with carrying out Churchill's orders. Upon moving to New York, Stephenson made a name for himself by throwing swank cocktail parties at his Dorset Hotel penthouse. At the same time, he possessed the uncanny quality of seeming to be nowhere and nobody. The future novelist Ian Fleming, a devotee of both cocktails and spy craft, later modeled his character James Bond in part on Stephenson.[21]

Hoover was eager to work with Stephenson, though justifiably wary of the British tolerance for bending the rules. He agreed to cooperate with the British service on one key condition: he wanted the approval of the president. Roosevelt was once again happy to go along. "The President has laid down the secret ruling for the closest possible marriage between the FBI and British Intelligence," Stephenson reported in late May 1940. A few weeks later, Roosevelt directed the FBI to establish its own outposts throughout Latin America, and secretly passed along $400,000 with which to get started.

These two efforts—the establishment of a British intelligence service in the United States and an American intelligence service in Latin America—proved to be intimately linked, a process of negotiation, exchange, deception, and mutual learning on the fly. In June, with Hoover's full knowledge and cooperation, Stephenson began operating in the U.S., eventually moving into a suite of offices in New York's sparkling new Rockefeller Center. The FBI moved in on the forty-third floor of the nearby RCA building, hanging a sign advertising an "Importers and Exporters Service Company." From the outside, they appeared to be two entirely separate entities, a minor British contractor and an American small business. In truth, they were working with each other.[22]

Hoover had much to gain from Stephenson, including access to intercepted letters and British information on German agents. What Stephenson needed from Hoover was permission to operate, along with technical and communications support that would allow him to coordinate with London. Hoover obliged by setting up a dedicated transatlantic telegraph line, by establishing the FBI as the go-between for British intelligence messaging, and by turning a blind eye to British activities on U.S. soil. The FBI also helped Stephenson sneak back and forth across the Canadian border as needed.[23]

The British in turn taught the FBI how to be a spy agency. Despite his preternatural confidence, Hoover had little idea how to set up foreign outposts or run double agents or assess the cryptic messages of foreign espionage networks. As a matter of regular practice, he did not travel outside the United States. The British had been everywhere for what seemed like forever, keepers of an empire that had once spanned half the globe. Hoover dispatched Hugh Clegg to London for a round of training in espionage and counterespionage techniques. Several months later, he sent Percy Foxworth, the special agent in charge at the FBI's New York office and now the head of operations in Latin America. Agents themselves were periodically dispatched to Camp X, a secret British-run guerrilla and spy training ground just outside Toronto. There, Stephenson's men drilled hundreds, then thousands of Canadian, British, and American citizens in the arts of sabotage, self-defense, and secret codes. According to one report, Hoover himself snuck across the border to visit Camp X, and nearly fainted at the sight of German warships amassing on Lake Ontario, though it turned out to be a mirage created through specially positioned mirrors and stage sets, a bravura performance by Britain's experts in duplicity.[24]

In a postwar assessment, British analysts expressed admiration for Hoover's dogged approach to learning the entire spy trade in a few months' time. "J. Edgar Hoover is a man of great singleness of purpose," the report noted, "and his purpose is the welfare of the Federal Bureau of Investigation." Despite his sometimes prickly nature, the British trusted Hoover's discretion, deciding early on to share some of their closely held wartime secrets. They even used a code name for him, Henry E. Jones (his initials reversed). Still, the British found Hoover hopelessly ill suited for international intrigue, a man whose literal mind and by-the-book policies jarred with the quick feints and dark alliances of global spy craft. "The FBI were devoted to traditional police methods, brought up to date by lavish expenditure on laboratory and other technical equipment," a British report explained. "These methods, though admirably suited to crime detection, were sometimes found to be quite inappropriate to the efficient conduct of counter-espionage." FBI agents had been trained to gather evidence for courtroom convictions, notches in the year-end statistical tally. Spy work, by contrast, required patience and deception, and often meant acting on instinct with no hope of prosecution in sight. If and when an espionage case did reach the courtroom, often the best evidence could not be revealed, for fear of exposing illegal methods or of letting the enemy in on key secrets. The task of running double agents, foreign operatives persuaded to work for one side while ostensibly working for another, seemed impossibly vexing to the loyalty-minded Bureau.[25]

The first months of the Latin American operation—dubbed the FBI's "Special Intelligence Service"—bore out some of these concerns. Under Hoover's initial plan, Bureau men were to be dropped one by one into various countries throughout the region. Upon arrival, they would operate undercover, posing as American importers and exporters per the sign at Rockefeller Center. The agents did not receive the training that would have made such a strategy viable: no instruction in the import-export business, only limited lessons in undercover operations or Latin American history or the Spanish and Portuguese languages. Once on the ground, they discovered that they had no good way to let Hoover know what was happening. Many Latin American countries banned the transmission of coded messages over commercial wire, leaving agents with only the slow, insecure option of international mail. Even recruitment was a problem. By the end of 1940, six months after Roosevelt's directive, the Bureau had just fourteen men "either stationed or traveling in Latin America." A year later, the SIS remained "still in a strict pioneering and experimental stage," a Bureau assessment concluded, offering intelligence information "of little real value."[26]

Perhaps for this reason, by the spring of 1941 the FBI and the British authorities had begun to go their separate ways. In early June, the junior officer Ian Fleming showed up in Washington on a special assignment for naval intelligence and recorded a few of his impressions. He found Hoover loathsome: "a chunky enigmatic man with slope eyes and a trap of a mouth," utterly sexless and unimaginative. He preferred the charm of William "Wild Bill" Donovan, the decorated World War I hero and Republican former assistant attorney general who served as Roosevelt's personal intelligence adviser. Stephenson preferred Donovan as well. In the spring of 1941, his team recommended that any future wartime intelligence agency established in the U.S. "should not be controlled by the FBI, which has no conception of offensive intelligence and is incapable of a strategic mentality." On June 10, Donovan brought his own version of that claim to Roosevelt. A week later, the president invited him to lunch and offered him a job as "Coordinator of Intelligence."[27]

After more than a year in which Hoover had received one vote of confidence after another, Roosevelt's decision to promote Donovan came as a shock. The choice laid the foundation for an interagency struggle that would persist throughout the war, coming to a head in its final months. That summer, though, Hoover responded by simply pulling away from intensive cooperation with the British, and getting on with the difficult business of preparing for war.

THE FBI DID HAVE AT LEAST ONE IMPORTANT COUNTERESPIONAGE VICTORY, and that case showed how quickly the Bureau—and Hoover himself—could sometimes adapt under pressure. In late 1939, a mysterious figure named William Sebold appeared at an American consulate in Germany with the startling announcement that he was a Nazi spy, about to be shipped off to the United States. As a naturalized U.S. citizen, Sebold professed to have no interest in his assignment, and begged the consulate official to send someone from the U.S. government to meet him upon his arrival. And so on February 8, 1940, an FBI agent showed up at the quarantine post just outside New York Harbor with instructions to talk with him.[28]

Over two days of questioning, Sebold explained that he had been sent to America not only to uncover military and industrial secrets but also to set up a communications station between the Nazi government and its allegedly extensive network of U.S.-based spies. Upon learning of his plans, Hoover did not do what he had done in the 1938 Rumrich case: order immediate questioning of everyone named in the confession. Instead, he proposed that Sebold proceed with his work under the direction—and on the payroll—of the FBI. Holding back from arrest was standard double-agent procedure, something that the British had taken great pride in teaching to the naive Americans. Before Sebold, though, the FBI had barely tested its skills, and certainly not with a counterspy of such potential importance.

Their work together began with the FBI mastering the complicated German code system. Once Sebold's initial communications assured the Germans of his trustworthiness, the Bureau helped him set up a radio outpost in a ramshackle two-room cabin on Long Island, with machinery powerful enough to send and receive messages from overseas. To make the ruse work, technical agents learned to imitate Sebold's Morse code signature. The Bureau also rented an office in the heart of Times Square, providing Sebold with a location where he could meet Nazi operatives and disburse the Germans' money. Throughout, the FBI not only watched and recorded the proceedings but also controlled the flow of information. Hoover fed the German authorities enough to gain their confidence while passing along false reports and holding back what he did not want Sebold's spymasters to know.

The operation played to the FBI's strengths in forensic wizardry and technical innovation. It entailed the use of what were then fantastical new technologies: two-way mirrors, long-distance film cameras, microphones small enough to be hidden in door buzzers. It also required an enormous amount of human labor, with as many as 250 agents assigned to the case at its peak. Eager to track Sebold's contacts, agents went undercover as defense workers or as dining staff on transatlantic ships. They spent countless hours loitering outside apartment buildings, nightclubs, factories, and beer halls. Hoover relayed the gist of what was happening in a series of updates for the White House, writing with some astonishment that the FBI "has undercover Agents actually participating in a German espionage group in such a manner as to enable the director of the Federal Bureau of Investigation to know the entire activities of this ring."

In late June 1941, just days after the German invasion of the Soviet Union, Hoover got a chance to show the rest of the country what his men had been doing. On the evening of June 28, working off more than a year's information from Sebold, FBI agents arrested thirty men and three women, with plans to charge them under the Espionage Act of 1917. Hoover leaked the news first to Winchell, then relayed a "skeletonized" version of events to less favored members of the press. Returning to his old themes of science and expertise, he declared the Sebold case a model of "extensive counter-espionage," proof of what could be done through proper training, attention, and funding.[29]

The Sebold case was the best answer Hoover could have delivered to wartime skeptics. "Criticisms of Chief G-Man J. Edgar Hoover, growing out of his ability to curtail activities of anti-American groups and societies, have boomeranged on the critics," one paper declared. The trial that followed brought more favorable press coverage, with its sensational revelations of hidden cameras, secret meetings, and doctored messages to Hitler. In September, Sebold took the stand to relate his incredible tale of subterfuge, crediting the Bureau with most of the hard work. Prosecutors followed up with dramatic film footage culled from hundreds of hours of FBI surveillance.[30]

When the court adjourned for the weekend on December 5, 1941, a guilty verdict seemed certain, the crossing of the finish line in Hoover's long, uncertain race to turn the FBI into a domestic intelligence service. By the time that verdict finally came a week later, however, even Hoover was hardly paying attention. After more than two years of watching and waiting, the U.S. finally went to war in December 1941, and Hoover had to prove himself all over again.

CHAPTER 23

Enemy Aliens

(1941–1942)

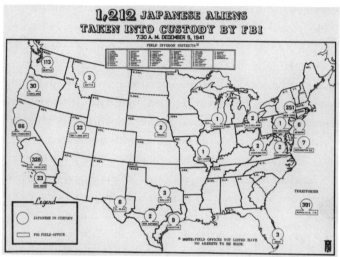

The FBI's count of Japanese nationals arrested in the wake of Pearl Harbor. The FBI ran its own arrest and internment system during the war. Hoover opposed the better-known system of mass Japanese incarceration.

FRANKLIN D. ROOSEVELT PRESIDENTIAL LIBRARY AND MUSEUM

T he call rang through to Hoover's suite at the Waldorf-Astoria around two thirty on the afternoon of Sunday, December 7. At the other end was Robert Shivers, special agent in charge of the Honolulu field office. Bypassing formalities, Shivers informed Hoover that the U.S. naval base near Honolulu was under attack; Japanese airplanes were bearing down on American battleships bunched together in the harbor. He held the telephone receiver in the air, allowing Hoover to hear the distant thud of falling bombs. Within a few minutes, the White House confirmed to the press that something momentous was underway. "The Japanese have attacked Pearl Harbor from the air and all naval and military activities on the island of Oahu," its statement declared. The United States was finally at war—not with Germany but with the Empire of Japan.[1]

Hoover had been preparing for this possibility, aware like everyone else in Washington that relations with Japan had soured months ago, and that American outposts in the Pacific would be obvious targets for Japanese attack. As early as July 1940, he had delivered a detailed report to the White House on the problem of Hawaii, where the FBI had just opened a field office. The report described the islands' communications, shipping, and food supply challenges. It also surveyed the 155,042 people of Japanese ancestry living there—mostly American citizens, but including 35,681 "aliens" whose noncitizen status attracted special Bureau scrutiny. "The loyalty of the entire group is speculative and highly questionable," Hoover wrote. He instructed the local office to "start developing intelligence information" in order to prove it. "More extended activity of this type" was likely to occur "in the event of the declaration of war," he anticipated. Two months later, the Japanese government signed the Tripartite Pact, officially allying itself with Germany and Italy.[2]

None of this preparation deterred the bombing at Pearl Harbor, but it left Hoover with a plan for what do on the afternoon of December 7, when so many others in Washington were reeling. According to that plan, the bulk of the FBI's work was to be devoted to "custodial detention," the internment scheme he had been developing since 1939. Despite many warnings about a regime of "terror by index cards," Hoover had never stopped expanding and refining the FBI's catalog of names, which now included hundreds of Japanese aliens in Hawaii and along the West Coast. By 1941, those names had been sorted into categories A, B, and C, with "A" designating the most urgent and serious threats. Those categories, in turn, had been broken down according to the reliability of the Bureau's information: A-2 indicated a highly dangerous suspect, though based on a somewhat dubious source; B-1 designated a less significant threat but a higher degree of faith in the incriminating information. Hoover was proud of the system. "If the Bureau had not compiled such a list and maintained it in an up-to-date fashion, we would be in a pitiful position today in view of the forthcoming crisis in our international relations," he had written to Robert Jackson back in the spring. Until December 7, however, such discussion had been merely hypothetical.[3]

Hoover called in to Bureau headquarters from New York three times that afternoon: at 2:50, 2:59, and 3:40. Then he raced for the airport, where a chartered plane whisked him back to Washington. Tolson was with him, and no doubt the two men spoke of what they might find when they landed: Would Congress have declared war? Would their men know what to do? Would troops be patrolling the streets? Would Washington itself be under attack? The afternoon ticked by in an agony of disconnection as they flew south over the Atlantic coast, cut off from the news and events below.[4]

With both the director and his number two man temporarily inaccessible, Hoover's assistant Ed Tamm took charge of things in Washington. What he found did not entirely accord with Hoover's well-laid plans. A power outage at Quantico had cut off communication; trainees had to gather around car radios to learn the latest news. At the Justice Department, officials had already written up a presidential order authorizing the FBI's detention program, but the man with the latest drafts in his briefcase happened to be in Philadelphia that afternoon. Even the new attorney general had gone missing. In September, Roosevelt had appointed a liberal stalwart named Francis Biddle to replace Robert Jackson, who (like Frank Murphy before him) had been bumped up to the Supreme Court. On December 7, Biddle was in Detroit delivering a speech about war bonds.[5]

Under the circumstances, Tamm sat down with Solicitor General Charles Fahy to hammer out a new draft of the executive order needed to authorize the Bureau's detention program. He also alerted field offices throughout the country to prepare for arrests of selected Japanese aliens once the president signed off. Tamm estimated it would be two hours before arrests could begin. By the time Hoover and Tolson arrived in Washington that evening, however, everyone was still waiting for the signal to get started. At 7:03, five hours after Shivers's initial call, Hoover called Fahy, hoping to hear that the president had signed the order. To his dismay, the solicitor general was just entering Roosevelt's bedroom, after a long wait for an audience. "It's pretty grim," Roosevelt declared, leaning back against a pile of pillows. Then he signed the order authorizing the FBI to begin its wartime arrests of enemy aliens.[6]

Within minutes of Roosevelt's signature, Hoover put out word to start the roundup. At 7:33, he called Shivers in Honolulu to make sure that the operation was indeed underway. Hoover expressed confidence in the FBI's index; he instructed Shivers to follow the A, B, and C classifications, then to wire lists of arrests directly to Washington to be filed in both alphabetical and numerical order. But he also allowed for end runs around the policy where needed. "If there are any of these fellows who are bad boys and who haven't been cleared A, B, or C, don't stand on any ceremony but bring them in too," Hoover said. "We're at war, now, and there's no use of a lot of fooling around as to who to arrest." His words reflected a certain amount of the vigilante spirit that he so often purported to despise. "You take those who should be taken in and we'll ask questions afterwards," he instructed.[7]

Over the next several hours, Hoover carried on similar conversations with officials scattered throughout the intelligence bureaucracy. Between eight and nine p.m., he held four emergency meetings with various Bureau and Justice officials, and took another call from Honolulu. By nine thirty, he had canceled all Bureau leaves, and ordered field offices and radio operations converted to a twenty-four-hour basis. Following White House instructions, he put an immediate halt on overseas phone communication, and requested that commercial airlines initiate a ban on Japanese freight and passengers. Most important, he issued instructions "to take into custody all Japanese who have been recommended by the FBI to the Departmental attorneys for custodial detention." Hoover estimated that at least 770 Japanese aliens would be in custody by morning, bound for internment hearings and then, most likely, detention camps.[8]

At the White House, the president's cabinet assembled to lay out its larger war plan and move toward an official declaration of hostilities. Attorney General Biddle returned to the Justice Department offices that evening "stunned and troubled" about what he had heard at the cabinet meeting, but confident that Hoover at least seemed to know what he was doing. Some of that confidence proved justified; in coming days, the FBI rounded up thousands of Japanese, German, and Italian noncitizen residents. Within a few weeks, however, Hoover's commitment to his own plan put him at odds with the Roosevelt administration, which came to embrace a Japanese internment policy far more sweeping and punitive than anything Hoover had in mind. If the war provided a test of Hoover's planning abilities, it also offered a measure of whether he meant what he said about limits, constitutional liberties, and the need to avoid vigilante hysteria.[9]

CONGRESS DECLARED WAR AGAINST JAPAN ON DECEMBER 8. OUTSIDE, THE CAPitol's wartime transformation was already underway, with marine sentries guarding all doorways. Inside, Roosevelt gathered with Congress in an emergency session. He had agonized over a speech that would convey the urgency of the hour, first declaring December 7 "a date which will live in world history," then editing the phrase to a punchier "date which will live in infamy." The cautionary example of the previous war remained on everyone's mind. Roosevelt was joined at the Capitol by Edith Wilson, widow of the late president, who had delivered his own stem-winder rousing the nation to war more than two decades earlier. Roosevelt's speech was shorter than Wilson's, just six minutes with applause included. And the vote was almost unanimous—388 to 1. The lone holdout was Jeannette Rankin, the only woman in Congress and a committed pacifist, who had also voted against war in 1917.[10]

Back at the Justice Department, Hoover was engaged in his own reckoning with the legacies of 1917. He had spent more than two years preparing for the moment when the U.S. would finally enter the war. Along the way, he made countless promises to different constituencies: that his internment program would be efficient; that it would target the right people; that his men would follow due process and respect civil liberties while containing any domestic security threat. Most of all, he had vowed to avoid the mess he had seen two decades earlier. That effort had been slow, sloppy, and insufficient, months of confusion and inaction that had allowed a vigilante mindset to take hold. This time, Hoover promised "vigil but no vigilantes."[11]

By the time he arrived back at the office on Monday morning, the first arrest reports were coming in, documenting 733 "Category A" noncitizens of Japanese ancestry taken into custody on Hawaii and the mainland, not far off from Hoover's initial prediction of 770 arrests. Shivers later boasted that the most important suspects had been rounded up within three hours, and that the FBI's index had been an impeccable guide. "The apprehension plan had previously been worked out in detail to such an extent that there were only 16 persons whom we failed to apprehend." The same held true, he claimed, once Roosevelt extended the detention program to include Germans and

Italians. Hitler would not declare war on the United States for another three days, and only then would the U.S. officially enter a state of war with Germany and Italy. At home, though, hostilities began sooner. Over the course of two hours on the afternoon of December 8, agents in Hawaii arrested more than three dozen Germans and Italians identified by the detention index as actually or potentially "dangerous," holding them along with hundreds of Japanese aliens.[12]

Over the next few days, similar roundups took place across the U.S., with special attention paid to cities like San Francisco and New York, with their large Japanese and German populations, respectively. Nationwide, approximately 1,200 Japanese aliens entered government custody within the first 48 hours after Pearl Harbor, most of them in Hawaii or along the West Coast. In New York, Ellis Island alone held 126 aliens of Japanese, German, and Italian descent. At Hoover's January 1942 appropriations testimony, he announced that the FBI had arrested a total of 1,314 Germans, 252 Italians, and 1,601 Japanese "enemy aliens" during the first month of war. By June, he reported that "apprehensions have been effected of 2,860 Germans, 1,356 Italians and 4,611 Japanese," for 8,827 arrests in total.[13]

The swiftness of these initial arrests fulfilled at least one of Hoover's stated goals: efficiency. At the same time, he knew that the arrests were only the beginning of a perilous multistep process. Now that thousands had been arrested, they would have to be processed for detention, involving hearings, evidence, lawyers, and visitors. They would have to be held somewhere, fed, housed, and treated for medical conditions. There would have to be an appeals process, some way for the prisoners to object to their internment and have their cases reexamined. For those released from custody, the FBI would have to figure out a way to track them and pick them up again if needed. The goal, as the Justice Department had agreed back in July, was to avoid "over-internment," including the detention of noncitizens "solely for careless statements made prior to the outbreak of war." But the Bureau also had to ensure that potential spies or saboteurs did not walk free. At any point, a miscalculation could result in public outcry, and perhaps even in the discrediting of the entire program.[14]

On the ground, events did not quite conform to Hoover's vision of a perfectly co-ordinated bureaucracy, bloodlessly distinguishing between the "dangerous" alien and the loyal resident. The arrests themselves were often terrifying; homes were ransacked, children plucked from their parents' arms. Agents sometimes arrested American citizens. "I was worried about my wife and sore as hell about what I considered an infringement on my constitutional rights," one of those citizens recalled. Noncitizens were often similarly bewildered and frightened, unsure of why they were being arrested. A German-born teenage girl later described FBI agents dragging her father from his bed, then taking the whole family into custody, with the exception of their German shepherd dog. "They did not say, 'We arrest you for being pro-German,' or anything like that," she recalled. "They just took us."[15]

Some of the confusion stemmed from the FBI's nebulous criteria for inclusion on the detention index. Despite its appearance of clinical accuracy, Hoover's system could be highly subjective, a matter of assessing for loyalty and potential danger in the absence of any overt act. Among Germans, mere membership in the Bund or a similar organization could be grounds for arrest. Among the Japanese, special attention was paid to community leaders such as newspaper publishers and religious leaders, on Hoover's theory that someone like "the Shinto priest who preaches in America that one's body and soul belong to the Emperor of Japan should be incarcerated as a dangerous alien enemy." In some cases, what gave the Bureau grounds for arrest was simply an inconsistency on a government registration form, or the failure to register altogether. One CIO organizer and Communist Party member made the mistake of lying on his wartime registration form, claiming to be an American citizen though he had been born in Germany and had never naturalized. The FBI arrested him as a disloyal alien, despite the fact that he had spent most of the late 1930s speaking out against the fascist threat.

Once arrested, detainees were taken to processing stations scattered throughout the country, from well-established sites such as Ellis Island to makeshift local centers. One German woman spent several months with her toddler son at a Catholic cloister near Milwaukee, under the care of nuns, while she awaited a final determination of loyalty. When FBI agents interviewed her, they asked why she had a photo of Hitler hanging in her house, why she spent so much time in and around a Bund camp, and why she had named her son Horst (supposedly after the Nazi martyr Horst Wessel). In the end, they determined that she was not a danger and sent her home to her husband, who in the meantime had burned the Hitler portrait.

Those who did end up at internment camps found wide variations in conditions, from the former Civilian Conservation Corps facility at Fort Lincoln, outside of Bismarck, North Dakota, to the chaotic family camp in Seagoville, Texas. Detainees registered a range of complaints: overcrowding, lack of communication with families, roaches and bedbugs, shortages of blankets and butter. Among the daily challenges was boredom. "Father said Sand Island was just a barbed wire fence around some barracks," the son of a German internee in Hawaii recalled. "To keep busy, most of the men sat around and talked or raked the sand. They weren't mistreated, but they couldn't imagine what was going on."[16]

Outside the fences, though, the FBI's internment program met with just the response that Hoover had anticipated. "The fact that most of the enemy aliens, most of the crackpot dupes, most of the saboteurs seem to be arrested or in hiding, is a very real tribute to Edgar Hoover and his men at the FBI," *Atlanta Constitution* editor Ralph McGill wrote in early January 1942. From that point on, Hoover's program received little attention, eclipsed by another internment plan that proved far more controversial.[17]

FIRST, THOUGH, THERE WAS AN URGENT QUESTION TO BE SETTLED: "HOW DID
they catch us with our pants down?" Texas senator Tom Connally demanded to know
during an emergency gathering at the White House on the evening of December 7.
One obvious answer was that the army and navy had failed in their jobs, anticipating
action in the Philippines or Guam but not Hawaii. But there was a case to be made that
the FBI did something wrong, too, that for all Hoover's attention to "fifth column"
activities, agents might have missed something that would have provided advance
notice of the Pearl Harbor attack. "Maybe if it spent less time tapping wires in an effort
to get Harry Bridges," scoffed the left-wing columnist I. F. Stone, "it would have more
time left for the kind of detective operations we needed on Oahu."[18]

Hoover objected to the second-guessing. "Japan held out the olive branch of peace
to official Washington while her bombers and navy slunk into Pearl Harbor on December 7, 1941, and committed one of the most outrageous stabs-in-the-back of contemporary times," he wrote in his January message to law enforcement officers, insisting
that nobody could have seen the attack coming. At the same time, he recognized the
need to explain what the FBI had been doing in Hawaii during the months before the
attack, and to take credit for the information it had in fact managed to gather. With
the emergency meeting underway, Hoover wrote to the White House to describe an
alarming phone conversation that the FBI had intercepted two days earlier. During
that call, a Japanese-born professor—"Dr. Mori"—had spent several minutes describing
to a "close relative" (probably a Japanese admiral) the naval fleet positions and weather
conditions around the Hawaiian Islands. The professor had ticked off the types of flowers
blooming in December (poinsettia and hibiscus), polite chitchat that the Bureau now
believed might have some coded significance. According to Hoover, the Hawaii FBI
office had notified military intelligence of the odd conversation, but the army and navy
had dismissed it as insignificant.[19]

Hoover may have been concerned about another strange incident as well. In late
August, the New York office had started working with an erratic German operative
turned British double agent named Dusko Popov, who had arrived in the U.S. equipped
with instructions from the Nazi government but (like Sebold before him) with no
intention of following through. Among the secret documents Popov shared with the
FBI was a German questionnaire about conditions in Hawaii. Hoover had passed that
information along to naval intelligence, but there had been little apparent follow-up.
Over the next few months, the Bureau had grown less and less enchanted with Popov,
who seemed more interested in spending FBI money and enjoying the New York nightlife than in delivering serious intelligence. In November, he left for Brazil to hook up
with German intelligence there.[20]

Roosevelt himself seemed to care more about keeping a lid on rumors and calming public fears than learning every detail of who had done what. On December 8, he appointed Hoover as temporary head of wartime censorship, assigned to supervise the publication of war-related information until the president figured out a long-term plan. In that post, Hoover was in a position to curry Roosevelt's favor—and protect the FBI's reputation—by controlling press coverage of the attack. On December 12, he agreed to run interference between the White House and the influential Washington columnists Robert Allen and Drew Pearson, authors of a series on alleged intelligence failures. "The President says you may say to Pearson and Allen that if they continue to print such inaccurate and unpatriotic statements that the Government will be compelled to appeal directly to their subscribers and to bar them from all privileges that go with the relationships between the Press and Government," the White House instructed. Hoover delivered the message, thus earning Roosevelt's gratitude as well as the advantage of muting a critical column.[21]

It was impossible to shut down all dissenting voices, though, especially once the immediate shock of the attack began to wear off. "Hoover's performance will bear watching," warned *The New Republic*, "and is one of the things which censorship must not be permitted to hide from public scrutiny as we adjust ourselves to war." The potentially dire consequences of such scrutiny became clear on December 17, when Roosevelt removed two high-ranking military officers from their commands at Pearl Harbor. At the same time, the White House announced the creation of a commission chaired by Supreme Court Justice Owen Roberts to apportion further blame. Washington columnist John O'Donnell predicted bad times ahead for Hoover. "The nation's super Dick Tracy, FBI director J. Edgar Hoover, is directly under the guns as the result of Japanese attack on Pearl Harbor and as much on the spot as the already ousted Army and Navy commanders in Hawaii," he wrote in late December. "Long-time Capitol Hill foes of FBI Chief Hoover have been whetting up their snickersnees, itching to take a crack at the detective hero." Of the three institutions arguably responsible for intelligence at Pearl Harbor, by the end of December only the Bureau had escaped punishment.[22]

Hoover rushed to his own defense, issuing a rare public rejoinder identifying a member of the press by name. "The statement of the columnist, John O'Donnell, is without a scintilla of foundation," he announced. "Jurisdiction over Japanese matters in Hawaii was vested principally in the naval authorities and not in the FBI." From the White House, Roosevelt's press secretary Stephen Early called to reassure Hoover, who composed a note back in thanks. "You do not know how much I appreciate your call today and the message you gave me," he wrote. "So far as O'Donnell's article is concerned it did make me burn because of its utter falseness." To Hoover's relief, other Democrats on the Hill hurried to follow the White House lead, speaking out in support of the FBI's "duly diligent" ways in the weeks leading up to Pearl Harbor.[23]

This position was affirmed on January 24 when the Roberts Commission released its report. The conclusions were critical of military leaders, accusing them of ignorance,

lack of preparation, and "dereliction of duty." Toward Hoover the report was far gentler, noting that "efforts were made by the Bureau to uncover espionage activities in
Hawaii," even if the Bureau failed to comprehend the full scope of "enemy activities."
To soften even that blow, Roosevelt invited Hoover to the White House on January
29 to discuss how best to use—and perhaps expand—the FBI's surveillance powers.
"The President's feeling is that the handcuffs ought to be taken off the FBI and put
somewhere else," Early explained, brushing off any further worries about Hoover's role
at Pearl Harbor.[24]

Roosevelt's stance should have been a balm to Hoover, exoneration for what could
easily have been construed as the greatest failure in Bureau history. But Hoover found
it hard to let the criticism go. "The effort to burden me with the Pearl Harbor attack
would have been ridiculous had it not been that it emanates from the same sinister
sources that are always willing to take up a smear of the F.B.I.," he fumed to New York
columnist Louis Sobol in late January. The energy he devoted to his Washington critics, along with his other war duties, may help to explain why he initially missed another
important development. Rather than calming public fears, the Roberts report inspired
a new wave of enthusiasm for an idea Hoover had dismissed back in December: mass
Japanese internment.[25]

THE WAR DEPARTMENT HAD FIRST FLOATED THE IDEA OF INTERNING ALL PEO-
ple of Japanese descent—citizens and noncitizens alike—on December 10, just three
days after Pearl Harbor. At the time, Hoover had dismissed the proposal as a symptom
of post-attack hysteria, reactionary and unnecessary by any reasonable interpretation
of the facts. His own detention program focused on noncitizens. And despite his warnings about a Japanese "fifth column," and the FBI's rush to arrest "Class A" offenders,
internal reports suggested that the number of "dangerous" people was actually quite
small.[26]

By mid-January, few politicians were acknowledging these sorts of subtleties. "Internment of All Japs Asked," read a headline in the *San Francisco Examiner* on January
21, documenting a call for all people of Japanese descent to be placed in "concentration
camps," regardless of their individual backgrounds, points of view, or personal loyalty.
General John DeWitt, the commander in charge of West Coast security, captured the
conventional view, drawing upon a long history of anti-Asian racism to declare people
of Japanese descent disloyal as a group. "The Japanese race is an enemy race," DeWitt
argued in a memo to the secretary of war. "While many second and third generation
Japanese born on United States soil, possessed of American citizenship, have become
'Americanized,' the racial strains are undiluted." This racial distinction was already en-
shrined in federal law. Under U.S. immigration law, people born in Japan were banned
from becoming U.S. citizens, while immigrants from Europe—including Germans

and Italians—could choose to become naturalized. Even in 1942, as the U.S. went to war on two fronts, there was little talk of launching mass internment for Germans and Italians.

That was partly a matter of numbers. Discriminatory naturalization and immigration laws had produced a situation in which fewer than two hundred thousand people of Japanese descent lived on the U.S. mainland. By contrast, there were millions of citizens with German and Italian ancestry, rendering mass internment administratively impossible. But the distinction was a matter of racism more than anything else. Like many Americans, General DeWitt rejected Hoover's view that it was possible to assess Japanese-Americans as individuals. "A Jap is a Jap!" he argued. Under this logic, the only way to achieve security would be to round up all people of Japanese extraction: citizens and noncitizens, loyal and disloyal, violent and nonviolent, men, women, and children alike.[27]

Perhaps War Department officials assumed that Hoover would come around to this view. If so, they underestimated his commitment to his own, very different vision of wartime internment, in which individualized investigation and professional fact-finding were supposed to prevent the sort of sweeping, indiscriminate restrictions that the government was now contemplating. Hoover spoke out against thinking of the war in racial terms. "No man should be suspected simply because he is foreign-born or has a foreign name or accent," he wrote in the summer of 1941. "Americans, unlike other nationals, are not a race. Americanism is an idea." He also had a legal argument: while noncitizens could be detained, the federal government had no constitutional right to detain U.S. citizens without due process, even in a time of war. More than that, he saw internment as bad politics, convinced that any attempt at dragnet raids or mass relocation would backfire, produce criticism, and create new dangers, including vigilantism. "Nothing could contribute more to recruiting fifth columnists than unfounded accusations or unjust oppression measures against them," he declared in a public statement. Hoover had designed his own internment program to avoid just such an outcome.[28]

His chief ally within the Roosevelt administration was Francis Biddle, the liberal attorney general who had come to office in late 1941. Hailing from the Main Line of Philadelphia, Biddle was just the kind of elite do-gooder that Hoover often assailed in his speeches. Yet the two men saw eye to eye on a surprising number of wartime issues, including Japanese internment. Their shared opposition to the policy put them in an odd political position that winter, allied against the Roosevelt White House. They nonetheless set out to convince Roosevelt to reject mass internment and take another course of action.

What Hoover and Biddle had going for them was the FBI's bureaucratic and investigative machinery—an asset that no other institution in Washington possessed to the same degree. In January, FBI agents conducted "spot" raids on Japanese households, checking for contraband and then advertising their failure to find anything. Bureau reports also helped to discredit rumors that Japanese residents were dodging the draft in unusual numbers, disclosing secret military information, or contaminating the food supply. Hoover's intelligence surveys noted that things were rapidly returning to normal and "quiet" within the Japanese business community, while farmers were hoping "that if they continue with their work as they have always done they will not be bothered." He even went so far as to argue that mass internment might cut the FBI off from key informants. "It is believed if any mass evacuation of Japanese aliens is undertaken it is probable that the few sources of information among the Japanese available at this time would be closed," he wrote. Biddle presented Hoover's position at a January 30 cabinet meeting, arguing that mass internment was both ill advised and difficult to administer, and that the FBI at any rate had the Japanese situation under control.[29]

Just how far off this was from the War Department's thinking—and from the Roosevelt administration's position—became clear in early February, when Hoover and Biddle sat down with key defense officials in an emergency meeting to iron out their differences. They all hoped to walk away with a joint press release, public evidence that ruffled feathers had been smoothed. But when Hoover and Biddle proposed that the release include an affirmation of Japanese-American loyalty and a statement rejecting mass internment of citizens, the military men refused to sign and walked out.

Two weeks later, the president signed Executive Order 9066, designating the West Coast as a military district "from which any or all persons may be excluded." Rather than the FBI or the Justice Department, it was the army that took control of moving approximately 120,000 people into ten barbed-wired "relocation" camps over the next few months. More than 70 percent of the detainees were American citizens, born and raised in the country that now accused them of disloyalty.[30]

HOOVER CONTINUED TO OBJECT TO THE MASS INTERNMENT POLICY AS THE war went on, even as he accommodated the FBI to a fait accompli. Meanwhile, his own detention program continued on a separate track, with its process of individual assessment, arrests, surveillance, and detention. By the end of the war, the FBI had arrested and detained approximately thirty-one thousand men and women, most of them of German, Italian, or Japanese descent. Of those, approximately two-thirds were released without being interned, while the final third ended up in Justice Department camps.[31]

Under the circumstances, Hoover may have taken some satisfaction in a request that arrived in 1943 asking the FBI to investigate deteriorating conditions at the Japanese mass internment facilities. Outraged at their treatment by the U.S. government, small groups of prisoners had begun to rebel against their guards, leading to riots and violent clashes. The request asked Bureau agents to assess the situation, with a focus on improving security and suppressing the riots. In a small act of bureaucratic rebellion, the

Bureau rejected those limits. Instead, Hoover handed back a meticulous indictment of the entire mass internment network, where mismanagement of "food, housing, clothing, available medical facilities, working conditions, privileges and above all the attitude and policies of the administrative staff" had led to widespread discontent.

The report reminded federal officials of what Hoover had said from the start: that the entire mass internment endeavor was doomed to fail. "It is, therefore, extremely unfortunate that the Government, the War Relocation Authority, and the public did, in the past, seize upon what they first believed to be a simple determining factor of loyalty," the report concluded. "There actually can be only one efficient method of processing the Japanese for loyalty, which consists of individual, not mass, consideration." It was a subtle protest against a policy that Hoover deemed illegal and unprofessional, a view rejected by much of wartime Washington but borne out by the judgment of history.[32]

CHAPTER 24

The Most Exciting Achievement Yet

(1942)

Hoover (seated, in pin-striped suit) at secret military commission
proceedings for eight Nazi saboteurs captured by the FBI in 1942.
Attorney General Francis Biddle is to his left, in white suit.

LIBRARY OF CONGRESS

W hen Hoover finally did come across enemy saboteurs, they turned out to be
German, not Japanese.

Well before dawn on June 13, 1942, an unarmed Coast Guard officer patrolling
the beach along Amagansett, Long Island, noticed a man standing near the shore. The
man was assisting two companions knee-deep in the water, wrestling with a rubber boat.
It was a foggy night and visibility was low, so he called out to ask what they were doing.
The man on shore replied that they were lost fishermen, coming ashore to wait for first
light. He spoke perfect English, though with a slight accent, and seemed amiable enough,
so the guardsman invited the men to sit out the night at the nearby Coast Guard station. Before they could settle on a plan, however, one of the man's companions began
to speak in German, and the man clapped a hand over his companion's mouth.

Once the German words had been spoken, the man's attitude changed. He said he
did not have a fishing license and therefore wanted to stay away from the authorities.

Then he pulled out a wad of bills and thrust $260 into the guardsman's hands. The man "told him to take it and keep quiet otherwise he and his companions would be compelled to kill him at once," a military intelligence report later noted. The shocked guardsman mumbled his assent and began to back away from the group, "afraid of being shot in the back." When he was a few hundred yards away he turned around and ran back to the Coast Guard station, where he reported that a team of German agents was attempting to invade the United States of America.[1]

Even at the Coast Guard, tasked with patrolling the nation's shores for signs of invasion and sabotage, this breathless report occasioned some skepticism. But when the guardsman showed off his crumpled bills, insisting that he had been forced to grab them and run, the rest of the station jumped into action. They raced back to the beach, where the fog still hung thick, obscuring any hope of an up-close sighting. At first light, the guardsmen noticed some sand that had been disturbed near the dunes. When they began to dig down, they found "three cases of TNT with holes bored in the TNT blocks for fuses, fuses, detonators, incendiary pens and pencils," plus "a duffle bag which contained German seamen's dungarees, shoes, and bathing trunks, all of which were soaking wet with sea water and covered with sand," according to the FBI. They transported it all back to the Amagansett station, then on to the barge office in lower Manhattan.[2]

At that point, eleven hours after the initial encounter on the beach, the Coast Guard called the FBI to report a potential case of German sabotage. The call went not to Hoover in Washington but to the New York field office, located downtown near the barge office in the federal building at Foley Square. Citing Roosevelt's 1939 order granting the FBI jurisdiction over sabotage and espionage, FBI officials seized the Coast Guard's evidence and transported it up to Foley Square, where it was laid out in the FBI shooting range to be sorted and tagged.

Hoover sent headquarters officials to supervise the investigation, but he did not go to New York himself. Instead, he stayed in Washington to manage the political side of events, reaching out to the attorney general about what appeared to be a bona fide German sabotage plot. "All of Edgar Hoover's imaginative and restless energy was stirred into prompt and effective action," Biddle later wrote of consulting with Hoover that afternoon. "His eyes were bright, his jaw set, excitement flickering around the edges of his nostrils when he reported the incident to me." The case would test nearly every part of the bureaucracy Hoover had built in recent years, from the lab's technical expertise to the investigators' manhunting prowess to the press-management strategies of Crime Records. Coming two years after the "smear campaign," it also gave Hoover a chance to complete his wartime rehabilitation.[3]

THOUGH HOOVER EXPRESSED CONFIDENCE THAT THE BUREAU WOULD "CATCH them all before any sabotage took place," the federal track record on German sabotage was dismal at best. During World War I, German agents had acted with impunity in and around New York, blowing up arms shipments leaving the harbor and targeting regional munitions plants. Everyone had expected similar sabotage attempts this time around. In May, the Atlantic shoreline had been declared a military zone, on grounds that it might be "subject to espionage and acts of sabotage, thereby requiring the adoption of military measures necessary to establish safeguards against such hostile operations." A few weeks later, Hoover met with Roosevelt to discuss the potential sabotage problem. But none of these conversations prepared Hoover for what to do about the fact that saboteurs had now landed in the Hamptons, or about the possibility that there might be other teams coming ashore elsewhere throughout the country.[4]

The best chance of capturing the Amagansett saboteurs, Hoover determined, was to lie in wait and hope that they came back for their clothing and weapons. Beginning on the afternoon of June 13, several rotating shifts of agents hid out in foxholes along the beach, while others accompanied the Coast Guard on patrol and still others took up surveillance from beachfront homes and cottages. The saboteurs failed to return, and local residents had little to offer beyond vague memories of hearing an engine grinding along the shore late at night, accompanied by the smell of diesel. Investigators would later determine that a German U-boat sent to deposit the saboteurs had run aground on a sandbar that night, stranded for several hours at low tide. The captain had gone so far as to order his men to prepare for blowing up the ship and turning themselves in as prisoners of war when, just before dawn, the tide came back in and allowed them to slip back beneath the ocean's surface.

At first, Hoover did not believe certain details of the story: How was it possible that a German U-boat had been sitting in the Hamptons, hour after hour, and nobody— even in the supposedly vigilant Coast Guard—had managed to notice? He also expressed skepticism about the guardsman's initial description of the bribe and the threats, speculating that he might have been out to meet whiskey smugglers that night and reversed course only after realizing he was talking with the wrong men. Hoover nonetheless believed that the sabotage plot was real. And he feared that the possibility of locating the men in question diminished with each passing moment.

A PHONE CALL CHANGED EVERYTHING. ON THE MORNING OF FRIDAY, JUNE 19, nearly a week after the initial encounter on the beach, an unidentified man called Hoover's office asking for the director, claiming that he had just arrived from Germany and had critical information to impart. The connection was routed to Duane Traynor, the head of counter-sabotage operations, who had heard about the landings at Amagansett. Traynor sent a car for the mysterious caller, who was staying at the Mayflower Hotel. By eleven o'clock they were seated together at Bureau headquarters.

The man introduced himself as George Dasch (also known as George John Davis), a German citizen who had lived in the United States for much of his adult life. Upon returning to Germany in 1941, he had been recruited for a special mission: the Nazis wanted him to go back to America in order to blow up aluminum factories, war plants, dams, bridges, and, where possible, department stores owned by Jews. Dasch later claimed that he'd never intended to follow through on the sabotage plan, but that he feared defying the Nazi authorities. So in late May he had boarded a U-boat headed for Long Island. It was he who had run into the Coast Guard patrolman on the early morning of June 13, just minutes after the U-boat had deposited him on the shore. With him were three other would-be saboteurs, while a second team of four was traveling in another U-boat, bound for Florida. All eight of them had lived in the United States and knew English well; two were U.S. citizens. In a wink and nod to this circumstance, the Nazi government named their mission after Francis Daniel Pastorius, an early German migrant to the United States. In another deliberate act of symbolism, they scheduled a rendezvous for the eight saboteurs on July 4, 1942, at which point both teams were supposed to begin carrying out their campaigns of destruction.

Dasch had hoped to convey his story directly to Hoover, the one man he believed might be capable of thwarting Hitler's aims. Indeed, he expressed surprise that the director was not sitting around in Washington awaiting his call. Earlier in the week, Dasch had phoned the New York office to say that he was a German citizen heading for Washington, with plans to "talk to Mr. HOOVER or his secretary" upon arrival—a call that had been taken, logged, and then dismissed by the local "nutters' desk." Now it was Traynor who met with Dasch instead, but the agent wasted little time in conveying the gist of the story to Hoover's office. With the interview underway, Hoover dispatched several agents to Dasch's hotel room, where they came across a suitcase stuffed with cash. Around the same time, New York agents reached out to the Amagansett patrolman, who tentatively selected Dasch from a photo array. By evening, Hoover was convinced that "by working on him . . . we could get the others."

Though he declined to meet with Dasch, Hoover encouraged Traynor to make the would-be saboteur feel as if the FBI was on his side. Dasch seemed to be a volatile character, and by catering to his more grandiose aspirations, Hoover hoped to turn him into a "decoy"—or perhaps even a double agent—to lure in other members of the sabotage team. Rather than keep Dasch in custody, the FBI allowed him to return to his hotel room overnight, with Traynor sleeping on the extra bed. Over the next several days, they gave Dasch whatever he wanted: restaurant meals, ham salad, scotch and soda. They provided a sympathetic ear for his claims that he was and had always been a loyal American, the buried explosives notwithstanding. In return, Dasch gave up the details of the sabotage plot, naming all his coconspirators and even turning over a handkerchief inscribed with invisible-ink instructions from the German government.[5]

Dasch's confession allowed the FBI to make quick work of his fellow Amagansett conspirators, snatching them up one after another as they made their way around New

York on June 20. The Florida team took longer to find, since Dasch knew less about their plans and whereabouts. A fellow Long Island saboteur, Peter Burger, provided a few essential clues, but the search ultimately came down to Dasch's strange handkerchief. Initially he could not remember what chemical was needed to make the secret ink reveal itself. Once he came up with ammonia, the FBI lab was able to treat the cloth and discover a list of Chicago contacts for the saboteurs. By staking out those contacts, the FBI grabbed a member of the Florida team, who initially denied knowing anything but soon led agents to Ponte Vedra, Florida, where a second cache of explosives was buried. After that, it was a matter of watching and waiting as one saboteur reached out to another.

Hoover kept a tight lid on the operation, fearing press coverage would inadvertently warn the saboteurs to run. The game of brinksmanship finally tipped his way on June 27, two weeks after the landing on Long Island, when a Florida saboteur led FBI agents to the last member of the team. At six forty-five that night, Chicago agents grabbed the eighth man and called the arrest in to headquarters. Hoover prepared to tell the story to the world.

ABOUT AN HOUR LATER, HE ALERTED NEW YORK REPORTERS TO MEET AT THE FBI field office for an important announcement.

Hoover had come to the city earlier in the day, bringing along Tolson and members of his public relations staff. Before any public announcement could be made, though, he faced the task of notifying other federal officials about what he planned to do. Eager to be the one to break the story, he decided to wait until the last minute to let anyone else know. Then he carried out the task with unsentimental efficiency. Tolson orchestrated some of the most difficult conversations, assigning handpicked FBI officials to notify their military counterparts, who were likely to resent the FBI's publicity blitz. Hoover called Biddle, who was thrilled at the news, and Biddle called Roosevelt, who was busy squiring mid-level European royals around his estate in Hyde Park. Roosevelt cheered the FBI on, joking with Biddle that the government should charge money for such a good story: "Sell the rights to Barnum and Bailey for a million and a half—the rights to take them around the country in lion cages at so much a head."[6]

At eight thirty, as planned, an "unsmiling" Hoover welcomed eight reporters into a drab conference room. Once inside, they were not allowed to leave until Hoover had completed his statement. "I want you to listen carefully," he explained. "This is serious business." Then he launched into the whole incredible tale, describing the landings at Amagansett and Ponte Vedra, the discovery of the buried weapons caches, the FBI's high-stakes manhunt, and, just hours earlier, the final arrests. He did not mention the Coast Guard's role in uncovering the initial plot. Nor did he explain how Dasch had

Hoover's parents, Dickerson Hoover and Annie Scheitlin, met and married young, in the midst of family crises. This is their wedding photo, 1879.

Hoover as the pampered baby of the family, around 1895.

Hoover's childhood home at Seward Square, just a few blocks from the Capitol.

Hoover (seated in front at center) with friends from Central High School, Washington's premier white public high school, where he was valedictorian, cadet captain, and debate champion.

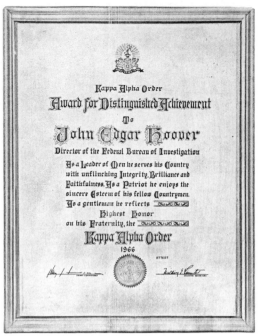

As a student at George Washington University, Hoover joined Kappa Alpha, a conservative Southern fraternity committed to racial segregation and the valorization of Confederate culture. He later selected many early Bureau officials from within Kappa Alpha. Thomas Dixon, author of *The Clansman*, was a prominent Kappa Alpha; his book became the basis for the 1915 film *Birth of a Nation*.   HERITAGE AUCTIONS

Hoover maintained a lifelong commitment to the fraternity; in 1966, he received its highest national honor.

NATIONAL ARCHIVES AND RECORDS ADMINISTRATION

As the civil rights movement gained prominence in the 1950s, Kappa Alpha embraced the Confederate battle flag as its fraternity symbol. This photo, printed in the March 1954 issue of *The Kappa Alpha Journal,* shows a portrait of Robert E. Lee hanging at a chapter house.

THE KAPPA ALPHA JOURNAL

During his first decade as Bureau director, Hoover promoted science, professionalization, and administrative efficiency. Above, Hoover (in white suit) with map showing the locations of his agents and field offices.

A publicity shot of the FBI's scientific lab equipment.

Bureau employees at work on Hoover's famous filing system.

The FBI image changed dramatically in the 1930s, as violent crime became a federal issue. This 1936 illustration shows Hoover as a leading national figure in police training and the New Deal's War on Crime.

NEW YORK DAILY MIRROR/NATIONAL ARCHIVES AND RECORDS ADMINISTRATION

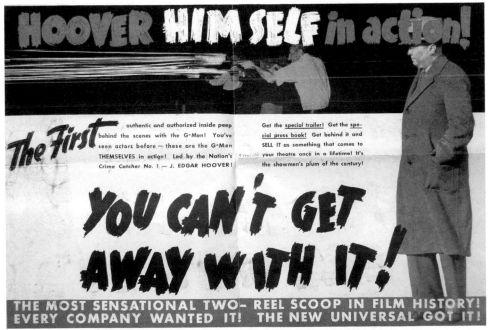

A poster for the 1936 film short *You Can't Get Away With It,* filmed at the FBI and featuring Hoover.

NATIONAL ARCHIVES AND RECORDS ADMINISTRATION

Hoover relied on public relations to make the FBI a major cultural force in the 1930s. Above, a poster for the 1935 Hollywood film *G-Men,* which presented FBI agents as gun-toting national heroes.

PICTORIAL PRESS LTD/
ALAMY STOCK PHOTO

A pamphlet offering stern advice about parenting and juvenile delinquency.

COLLECTION OF THE NATIONAL
LAW ENFORCEMENT MUSEUM

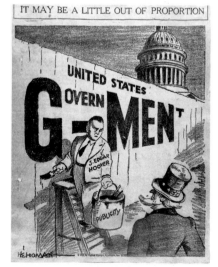

A 1936 cartoon poking fun at Hoover's fondness for publicity.

STOCKTON RECORD/ NATIONAL ARCHIVES
AND RECORDS ADMINISTRATION

Persons in Hiding, the first book published under Hoover's byline, recounted the "gangster wars" of the 1930s.

NATIONAL ARCHIVES AND
RECORDS ADMINISTRATION

During World War II, the FBI's image and purpose changed yet again. This time, Hoover acquired duties in political surveillance and domestic intelligence. At left, a 1944 magazine cover highlights Hoover's growing celebrity in Latin America.

NATIONAL ARCHIVES AND RECORDS ADMINISTRATION

A 1940 cartoon from *American Magazine* shows the FBI "stamping out" home-front espionage, a key aspect of Hoover's wartime image.

HAROLD TALBURT, *AMERICAN MAGAZINE*/ NATIONAL ARCHIVES AND RECORDS ADMINISTRATION

The Washington Armory became home to Hoover's fast-growing Identification Division, which processed millions of new fingerprints acquired from soldiers and federal employees.

FEDERAL BUREAU OF INVESTIGATION

Clyde Tolson joined the FBI in 1928 and worked by Hoover's side for the next forty-four years. Above, Tolson and Hoover in their favorite professional pose, with Hoover seated and Tolson standing to his right side.

Hoover (second from left) and Tolson (far left) at a baseball game between the FBI and the Baltimore police department, 1935. Behind Tolson, with moustache, is Frank Baughman, Hoover's college fraternity brother, now an FBI official.

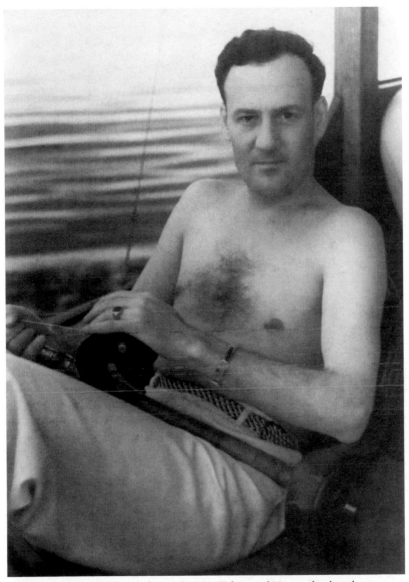

In addition to their work together at the FBI, Tolson and Hoover developed an intimate personal relationship, the most important of Hoover's life. This image, from Hoover's personal collection, shows Tolson on a fishing boat during one of their many vacations together in Florida.   COLLECTION OF THE NATIONAL LAW ENFORCEMENT MUSEUM

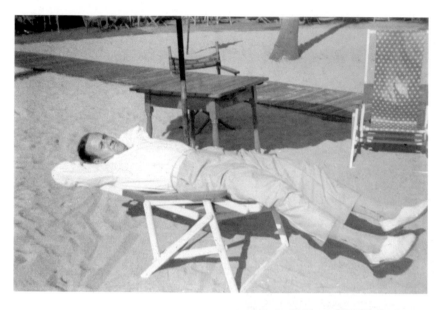

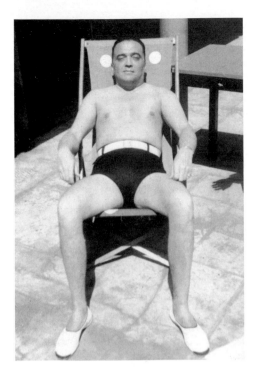

Hoover's private photo collection includes many intimate photos of Tolson (page at left) and Hoover (above) at play and at rest during their vacations together.

Hoover and Tolson found acceptance as a social couple during the 1930s, when they forged a glamorous late-night social life in cities such as New York, Washington, Miami, and Los Angeles. Above, New Year's Eve 1935/1936 at the famed Stork Club in New York.

Out on the town for the Broadway show *Hellzapoppin*, 1939.

Placing bets in 1937 at the horseracing track in Laurel, Maryland, a favorite Hoover pastime.

Hoover and Tolson fulfilled spousal roles for each other at key life moments, including professional ceremonies and family gatherings. Above, Hoover and Tolson pose in matching white suits and a sea of flowers to celebrate Hoover's twentieth anniversary at the Justice Department in 1937.

Tolson accompanies Hoover to the 1938 funeral of George Ruch, a college acquaintance and early Bureau official.

Hoover and Tolson with Tolson's family during a 1939 visit to Iowa. Hoover is center, standing; Tolson is center, kneeling.

Ellicott Hills

A Village With Walled Gardens—Between the City and Chevy Chase

4936 30th Place N.W.

To Reach: Conn. Ave. to Ellicott St., right to 30th Pl. left to 4936

A DIGNIFIED Georgian Colonial of charming simplicity and fine proportions. Quiet tones dominate the decorative scheme, creating a most restful environment that will please persons of discriminating tastes.

M ODERATE in size as to number of rooms but built on a generous scale. Spacious rooms, halls, baths, closets, porch, recreation room. Construction and workmanship of a superior character.

L OCATED in the finest residential section of the entire Chevy Chase area.

Shaded Garden — Enclosed by High Wall

IN planning the lovely garden, special thought was given to creating privacy. If one sits for a moment in the comfortable chairs on the flagstone terrace to watch the fish in the unusual pond, the pleasant shade of the trees and the comforting seclusion of the high garden walls brings the realization that the whole effect is to make outdoor living possible to an exceptional extent. The picture shows but half the extent of the garden and cannot convey the delightful effect of the green lawn dotted with shade and flowering shrubs as seen from picture windows from all of the rooms in the house.

Safely restricted to assure a permanently desirable environment

Open Daily From 10 to 9

Southern Building   # James E. Schwab   DIstrict 8157

Owner and Builder

In 1938, after his mother's death, Hoover bought a house in the newly developed neighborhood of Forest Hills, near Chevy Chase. The flyer advertises that the property is "safely restricted to assure a permanently desirable environment," a euphemism for the racial covenants that prevented Black homeowners from purchasing homes in the neighborhood.

Inside Hoover's new home. He collected antiques, including classical statutes as well as Western Americana. He also adored his terriers (posing obediently in the chair).   NATIONAL ARCHIVES AND RECORDS ADMINISTRATION

The fountain in Hoover's backyard. The brick wall around the property provided much-needed privacy.

NATIONAL ARCHIVES AND RECORDS ADMINISTRATION

Tolson, a frequent visitor, smoking in Hoover's backyard.

COLLECTION OF THE NATIONAL
LAW ENFORCEMENT MUSEUM

A Song of Men

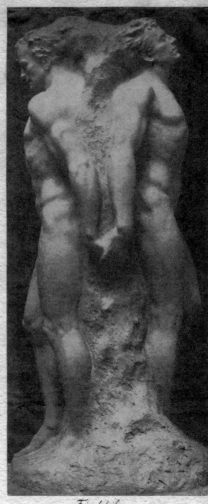

By Elsie Robinson

MEN. That rare, quiet friendship of men.

Something strange there. Beautiful, but a little terrible too.

Haig Patigian did a statue of two men who were friends. Two men who shared work and joy and adventure. Then on the turn of the tide, on the heel of a boat, shared death.

There they are in that statue, back to back, with clasped hands.

Hand to hand in good luck.

Back to back against adversity.

Sharing the weal of it— bucking the woe of it— linked.

Linked.

And yet——

There between those two sculptured backs is a mass. A rough bronze barrier that still isn't a barrier, for it does not rise between the two men. Each man is a part of it.

Each man comes out of it—comes out and reaches to clasp the hand of his friend.

Yet each man stays in it and never sees the face of his friend.

Each man, coming out of—Something.

Out of the darkness. Out of the dumbness. Out of the hunger and loneliness. Out of the wonder and urgency that is God.

Each man coming out of it and becoming himself.

Coming out in the lust and vigor of manhood— thigh and torso, proud neck and curious head. Coming out with a laugh

and a taunt and a challenge—leaping out with the zest of the awakening—reaching out with the longing for place and power—and a friend.

Then, after a thousand vain and foolish fumblings, finding that friend.

Finding that friend, like two hands meeting in darkness.

Two hands that *knew* when at last a friend was found.

Oh, the joy and the peace and the thrill of it!

Pulse talking to pulse in a language the tongue cannot speak.

Everything shared, wine, women, risk and adventure.

Everything shared, without need of a word or a look.

Everything shared.

And yet always something withheld.

Each man coming out and finding the hand of his friend yet never quite coming out.

Always there in the background, the mystery and wonder—there like a deep, dark soil in which both men are rooted. In which all men are rooted.

Always there in the background, the loneliness and the hunger—binding them both, yet holding them ever apart.

Always there in the background the Going and Coming—the vast veiled plan that neither will ever see.

There in the background between them, part of them, freeing them, binding them—*there in the background,* GOD!

Friendship —
Bronze by Haig Patigian.

This essay and photograph from Hoover's personal collection offer reflections on friendship and intimacy between men: "Everything shared. And yet always something withheld."

come to the FBI with a full confession. As Hoover told it, FBI ingenuity, efficiency, and scientific prowess alone accounted for the saboteurs' capture.

The press behaved just as he had hoped, listening with respectful silence before making a mad dash for the doors. That night, "the newspaper offices were busier than they had been since the Lindbergh kidnaping," one reporter wrote, eager not only to repeat Hoover's jaw-dropping tale but also to offer up some of the first good news of the war. Reporters competed to describe the saboteurs and their "huge terror plot" in the most satanic of terms. Hoover, by contrast, came in for levels of praise exceeding even the most awestruck accounts of the G-Man craze, with the saboteurs' arrests identified as "the domestic news sensation of the year." At least one account reminded the public of the doubts Hoover had faced in 1940, when he "was pictured sunning himself on Miami's sands" while the nation agonized over wartime civil liberties. Now, as Winchell pointed out, Hoover had come through with "the most exciting achievement yet," surpassing even the Dillinger and Sebold cases.[7]

Not everyone was quite so thrilled. Military and Coast Guard officials were furious at being shut out from Hoover's press conference, which they viewed as grandstanding and little more. Privately, they expressed concerns that Hoover had revealed far too much—that Hitler now knew exactly which of his men had been arrested and how, and would no doubt make good use of the information. Hoover had thought through these prospects, but had concluded that it was hopeless to try to keep the information secret. He also believed that the best counter-sabotage strategy would be to convince Hitler—like the American public—that the FBI had unimaginable and unassailable powers of detection.

IN MOST CASES, HOOVER'S ROLE WOULD HAVE DIMINISHED AT THIS POINT, with the arrests and the press announcement made, and with prosecution the major obstacle ahead. In this incident, his personal role became if anything more significant. On June 28, the day after Hoover's press conference, Biddle announced that "the question of prosecution has not yet been settled," admitting that "there are a number of complicated legal factors involved." The next morning, he summoned Hoover to Washington to consult about the great question facing the president and the Justice Department: Now that the FBI had nabbed the saboteurs, what should be done with them?[8]

From an investigative perspective, the fact that the saboteurs had been thwarted in their efforts was a major boon. From a legal perspective, it posed several problems—among them, whether the saboteurs had actually committed any significant crime. As an internal memo noted on June 25, "there has been no substantive violation of the sabotage, espionage, or other statutes," despite the potential for a devastating attack. And even if such charges could be brought, the outcome of a civilian trial, with its constraints of due process and high standards of evidence, was far from certain. Washington opinion demanded "Death for Saboteurs," in the words of one headline, but it was not at all clear—thanks in part to the FBI's swift preventive work—that such a verdict was possible.[9]

Given the difficulties of criminal prosecution, another idea began making the rounds in Washington: instead of working through the civilian courts, could the government mount some sort of military tribunal, treating the prisoners not as criminal conspirators but as unlawful combatants? Hoover worried that such a move might be deemed unconstitutional, especially given that two of the would-be saboteurs were U.S. citizens. "A citizen could not, of course, be tried before a tribunal of this nature as a citizen could obtain a writ of habeas corpus," he argued. Emphasizing the emergency context of war, Biddle evinced little sympathy for Hoover's position. Over the next few days, at Biddle's recommendation, Roosevelt settled on a military commission as the preferred method.[10]

Though Hoover lost that argument, the preparations for the military commission, once launched, bore his stamp. As Roosevelt envisioned it, the tribunal was supposed to operate in secret, with seven handpicked generals sitting in judgment. The task of finding a place for them to carry out their deliberations fell to Hoover, who initially leaned in favor of New York before the attorney general decided that the tribunal would have to take place in Washington, D.C. After scouting the armory and a few other possibilities, Hoover settled on just the right spot: commission proceedings should be held at the Justice Department.[11]

There were many reasons for that recommendation. The building was already air-conditioned (this would be a summer tribunal, after all) and highly secure. "There is no place where there are cells and the proper protective features except here in the Department of Justice building," Hoover explained. The location also gave Hoover at least some measure of control over the proceedings. Though the military was ostensibly in charge, Hoover would be able to approve anyone coming in and out of the building. Given the high political stakes, he wanted to prevent outsiders from gaining access to the prisoners and thus undermining the FBI's investigation.[12]

After they transferred all eight prisoners from New York to Washington, things were supposed to move quickly. "The authorities want to have this trial over with and the prisoners executed by the end of next week," Hoover explained on July 1. That estimate proved to be ambitious, however, with many complications of the proceedings yet to be worked out. Foremost among them was what to do about Dasch, whose cooperation with the FBI remained a closely held secret. During tearful negotiations in New York, he had agreed to plead guilty in order to keep up the facade of FBI impregnability and to protect his family in Germany. In return, Hoover promised to support a presidential pardon once the intense scrutiny of the trial phase had died down. But upon finding out that the case was to be heard before a a military tribunal rather than a civilian court, Dasch pulled back from his guilty plea, certain that the whole thing was a plot to execute him, too. According to Dasch, Hoover and Biddle met with him in person once the prisoners arrived in Washington, hoping to reassure him of their good intentions. "It all stands," Hoover promised of the secret agreement for clemency. "That is all I can tell you."

Hoover allegedly returned for a second visit just before the opening day of the proceedings, sitting awkwardly on a bed inside a cell as he promised to vouch for the prisoner in the days and weeks ahead. "George, I feel very sorry for your predicament and this is not what I would have chosen to do," Hoover allegedly said. Without exactly apologizing, he supposedly admitted that he would have preferred a civilian court, but that the FBI now planned to help the military commission run as smoothly as possible.[13]

THE COMMISSION HEARINGS BEGAN WITH A PARADE—OR SO IT MIGHT HAVE looked to an unknowing out-of-town visitor. On the morning of July 8, the prisoners changed out of their striped jailhouse pajamas and into civilian suits. Then they were escorted, handcuffed, through the jailhouse corridors and out to a fleet of vehicles parked outside. Once they were secure, the procession set off for the Justice Department building: a car of FBI agents in the lead, followed by an army jeep mounted with machine guns, then the armored transports carrying the prisoners. Spectators lined the sidewalks as if it was Inauguration Day. The largest crowd amassed outside the Justice building, where the vehicles rolled into the interior courtyard past the grand aluminum doors. Once the last car entered, the doors were slammed shut. Fifty armed soldiers guarded the building's entrance, while hot dog and ice cream vendors catered to those willing to wait out the day's secret proceedings.

Inside, the center of attention was room 5235, an FBI classroom that Hoover had ordered converted into an ersatz courtroom. Blackout curtains over the windows added a layer of secrecy, as did Hoover's strict procedures for who could and could not enter. In order to gain admission, every participant had to show an identification pass signed by Hoover and by General Albert Cox, the army's designated man in charge. The tight quarters and restricted access gave the hearing room a clubby atmosphere, with defense and prosecution and court recorders and commissioners all sealed in together. Hoover sat at the prosecution table with Biddle, who showed up each day in a spick-and-span white suit, a dash of summer elegance amid the grays and blues of FBI agents and military men.

Notably absent from the room were any members of the press, at the army's insistence. Hoover initially objected to the policy, then recognized that it afforded the FBI a precious opportunity to establish its own version of events as the official story. "We should get in touch with the Censor at once so as to see that no story concerning any angles of the Dasch case is cleared without first clearing with the FBI," he instructed his staff on July 7, the day before the commission hearings began. A few days later, with proceedings underway and the press hungry for details, Hoover went on the popular *March of Time* radio show to describe how his men had gone head-to-head with "Nazi scoundrels." "In foiling this diabolical scheme the agents of the FBI have again proven more than a match for Hitler's trained hirelings in the field of counterespionage," he declared, even as he warned that "more destructionists" might yet be on their way to American shores.[14]

Crucial to this story was the exclusion of the Coast Guard, whose patrolman had, after all, encountered the men on the beach. From the first, Hoover had labeled the Coast Guard both incompetent and deceitful, out to steal credit for the FBI's investigative success. Within the FBI, he complained that the Coast Guard "did nothing in this case except to obstruct and interfere with its proper development," citing a string of relatively minor errors. When asked to issue a joint press release, he refused unless the statement acknowledged the Coast Guard's "gross nonfeasance and malfeasance," a wild exaggeration of the agency's mistakes. As far as Hoover was concerned, the FBI and the FBI alone had made the case from start to finish.[15]

The commission heard a more balanced version of events, but one in which the FBI still played the defining role. The prosecution case rested largely on the testimony of FBI agents, supplemented by the physical evidence and confessions gathered at great cost and effort from June into July. Nearly every agent who came in contact with the saboteurs took the stand over the course of the commission's proceedings, describing the collection of detonators, fuses, explosives, and ingenious German devices found buried in the sand, along with summarizing the saboteurs' confessions. The touchiest areas concerned Dasch, whose help had been so invaluable. Dasch had been granted separate counsel, but that consideration did not stop him from protesting the government's alleged betrayal at great length and volume throughout the commission proceedings.

There were other annoyances, too, including allegations that FBI agents had hit and slapped the prisoners and deprived them of sleep in order to extract damning details. Even by Hoover's standards, though, it was hard to classify the proceedings as anything other than a success, a showcase of his Bureau's skills in their many varied dimensions. Outside the commission's doors, Washington was abuzz with talk of a medal for Hoover, while the media rushed ahead to declare him a "great hero" on par with General Douglas MacArthur, commander of Allied forces in the South Pacific. "Hats off enthusiastically to the FBI," one writer declared. "What a splendid job J. Edgar Hoover's excellent counter-espionage organization is doing." Another instructed his fellow citizens to "thank God" for the miraculous capacities of "John Edgar Hoover and his F.B.I. army."[16]

———

THERE WAS AT LEAST ONE PUZZLE THAT HOOVER COULD NOT SOLVE, HOWEVER:
Did a military commission of this sort even have a right to exist? The saboteurs' lawyers
insisted that it did not—that under the Civil War precedent of *Ex Parte Milligan*, the
government was duty bound to use the civilian courts if those courts were open and
functioning. Hoover had initially agreed, worrying behind the scenes that it would be
unconstitutional to try the men—especially the two American citizens—in front of
a military tribunal. Neither Roosevelt nor Biddle saw things that way, however, and
Hoover quickly gave up. Now the saboteurs' lawyers sought to put the matter before
the Supreme Court, despite the fact that the Court happened to be in summer recess.
In late July, defense counsel tracked down Justice Owen Roberts, briefly in Washington for a friend's funeral, pleading with him to take up the constitutional question
before it was too late. Aware that the commission intended to move fast, Roberts convened a small meeting of interested parties to hash out the problem at his farm in
Pennsylvania.[17]

After several rounds of phone calls and consultation, the court announced that it
would reconvene for a rare summer hearing in the matter of *Ex Parte Quirin* (named
for Richard Quirin, a member of Dasch's Long Island team). And so on July 29, the
humming commission machinery came to an abrupt halt, as everyone decamped from
the FBI classroom to the grand new Supreme Court building a few blocks away. News
photographers captured Hoover and Tolson striding up the famous outdoor stairs side
by side, Hoover in a light gray striped summer suit, Tolson a more traditional dark
color, walking in his designated position just to Hoover's right and one step behind.
Though Hoover rarely interacted with the court as a whole, he was already an insider,
well acquainted with most of the justices on the bench. In just the past few years, he
had worked closely with Justices Frank Murphy and Robert Jackson during their ten-
ures as attorney general. Felix Frankfurter was an old foe from Palmer Raids days, but
they, too, had reached a tentative accord in recent years. Presiding over them all was
Hoover's mentor and champion Harlan Fiske Stone, the man who had reached down
to save Hoover's career back in 1924, now chief justice of the Supreme Court.[18]

Hoover expressed little worry that the court would disrupt commission proceedings. "I could not visualize the Supreme Court ruling that the President's order was
unconstitutional," he told a White House aide, though he himself had argued that point
only weeks earlier. In the interim, he had gathered numerous editorials supporting
Roosevelt's position, including those arguing in favor of a swift death sentence under
headlines such as "Let Them Be Shot" and "Let's Shoot the Gang!" The court listened
patiently as defense attorneys argued in favor of civilian due process, while Biddle maintained that the president had the right to do as he saw fit with invading enemy combatants in a time of war. At noon on July 31, after two days of back-and-forth, the court

issued a unanimous ruling allowing the military commission to proceed. Loath to delay matters any further, the justices did not bother to write a full opinion, promising more attention to the matter once they convened again in the fall.[19]

And so it was back to room 5235, and to the final stretch of commission proceedings. As they mounted their closing arguments and began to address the issue of a possible death penalty, both sides turned to Hoover and the FBI to justify their positions. The defense maintained that "the very excellent preventive work which has been done by the Federal Bureau of Investigation" made the death penalty unnecessary, since the saboteurs had failed and no future schemers could outwit Hoover's G-Men. The prosecution argued that the saboteurs should hardly get credit for failing to carry out their mission, since "the only reason they did not do it was because they were caught by the FBI before they could get to the place of the crime." And when the verdict and sentences came down, it was the FBI's relationship with each man that determined whether he would live or die. On August 3, the commission closed its proceedings and sent along sentencing recommendations to be reviewed by the president.[20]

Dasch later said that he viewed Hoover's actions during those final moments as an unconscionable form of betrayal. In the closing days of the commission hearings, he allegedly ran into Hoover in the corridor outside room 5235 and demanded an audience: "Please Mr. Hoover, just one more question!" According to Dasch, his plea was met with a slap from a nearby FBI agent, at which point he crumpled to the ground in pain and despair. FBI files tell a more subdued (and more plausible) version of the encounter, in which Dasch asked to meet with Hoover but was turned away. All agreed that Hoover refused to speak with Dasch, turning his back on the man who had helped to make the FBI's greatest wartime case. "I saw the Chief disappear down the hall seemingly surrounded by an impregnable wall of justice and strength," Dasch later wrote.[21]

DASCH'S IMAGE OF HOOVER—THE COLD, HEARTLESS MAN WHO BETRAYED THE FBI's best source—would influence later histories of the case. But records suggest that Hoover tried, at least half-heartedly, to come through for both Dasch and Burger. On the afternoon of August 4, the day after the commission's conclusion, Roosevelt met with Hoover and several Justice officials to discuss how to move forward with a presidential review. Hoover recommended that the president go easy on Dasch and Burger, since "neither of these two men intended to carry out the purposes of the sabotage mission." Though they would have to be sentenced to long prison terms, given the heightened emotions of the moment, Hoover urged the president to consider "further commutation" once the war was over.

Roosevelt accepted Hoover's recommendations, ordering a thirty-year sentence for Dasch and life in prison for Burger. All the other prisoners were to be executed as quickly as possible. Then he presented Hoover with one last grim query: Would the Washington, D.C., jail be equipped to carry out the executions? Hoover answered in the affirmative, having already surveyed alternative sites before concluding that the jail where the men were already being held presented the most efficient scenario. Roosevelt provisionally approved the choice, and Hoover spent the next several days helping to refine the execution plan, deploying his administrative skills to orchestrate the deaths of six men with utmost efficiency. With most of the logistics complete, on Friday night, August 7, Roosevelt finally issued the order condemning the six men to "suffer death by electrocution," along with a life sentence for Burger and thirty years for Dasch. Still fearful of public outcry or even vigilante action, he notified the relevant government officials but not the press.[22]

The task of delivering the news to the prisoners fell to General Cox, under the logic that the executions, like the commission itself, would occur under military authority. On the morning of August 8, he made the rounds of the prisoners' cells, informing each man of his sentence along with the startling news that the executions would be carried out immediately. Most of the men "showed no sign of emotion" upon learning of their fates, according to a guard who accompanied Cox, though one "seemed to freeze" while another "dropped his head and closed his eyes." Their last meals consisted of bacon, eggs, and toast, plus wine for those who needed it. After breakfast, the guards bathed them, shaved their heads, and escorted them to the death-row cells.[23]

The execution chamber itself was a study in institutional banality, its walls painted a sickly off-yellow, chairs for the witnesses lined up in front of one-way glass. At least one historical account has placed Hoover in the witness section, but FBI documents suggest that when the moment finally came, he did not have the stomach to attend. Instead, he learned what had happened from a military guard on site, secretly tasked with observing and reporting back to the FBI. "It took approximately ten minutes to strap a man in the chair, electrocute him, take him out of the chair, place him on an Army cot, at which time a sheet was placed over his body, and then strap another man into the chair," the guard recounted. The prisoners were electrocuted in alphabetical order, just as they had been organized in Hoover's files.[24]

IT WAS NOT UNTIL THE END OF OCTOBER, EIGHTY-TWO DAYS AFTER THE EXECUTIONS, that the Supreme Court finally delivered its full decision affirming the legitimacy of Roosevelt's military commission. As several observers noted, there was something perverse about ruling on the justice of the saboteurs' deaths long after they were dead. But nobody was especially surprised about what the court had to say. As unlawful enemy combatants, the court ruled, the German saboteurs were subject to the laws of war, not to the due process of the United States courts, and could claim no right to a trial by jury.

For the two living defendants, the decision made little difference. Both Dasch and

Burger had been shocked by the swiftness of the executions, permitted to leave their cells for a fifteen-minute walk only to return and find all their friends gone missing. With the executions completed, they were transferred to Danbury federal penitentiary and then to Atlanta.[25]

The sabotage case would ultimately be remembered for its legal significance, establishing a precedent for the use of military tribunals in ambiguous theaters of war. For Hoover, though, its meaning had less to do with any constitutional implications than with what he had been able to accomplish through the mechanisms of the administrative state: the ways that he had managed the case from start to finish, through its early investigative challenges, on into the tricky arena of press revelation and secrecy, and finally into the commission, the executions, and the disposal of the bodies. Over the course of two months, the saboteurs case had tested nearly every aspect of Hoover's bureaucracy. His system had not only held up, but delivered one of the most widely hailed federal triumphs of the home front.

With the cooperation of the White House and the military, Hoover packaged and sold a story of the FBI as a ruthless and hyper-competent counterespionage force—a tale exaggerated and massaged for public consumption, but with enough truth behind it to make it stick. In the process, he completed the FBI's transformation into a hybrid institution—one part law enforcement agency, one part intelligence bureau. He also secured his place in the first ranks of Roosevelt's affections and won over some surprising wartime allies.

CHAPTER 25

American Dilemmas

(1942–1945)

During World War II, the FBI more than quadrupled in size and took on a vast range of new duties, including investigations of home-front espionage and sabotage. Hoover's celebrity increased accordingly.

NATIONAL ARCHIVES AND RECORDS ADMINISTRATION

In late July 1942, with the commission proceedings winding down, Hoover celebrated his twenty-fifth anniversary at the Justice Department. Roosevelt sent a note of congratulations. "Your leadership, foresight and direction brought the Federal Bureau of Investigation to the forefront among all law enforcement agencies of the world," he wrote, singling out Hoover's work against saboteurs and enemy aliens as a special source of pride. The president had no intention of letting Hoover rest on his laurels, however. With Hoover now a hero of the wartime administration, Roosevelt allowed the FBI to expand into still more areas of investigation, relying on Hoover to police forms of personal conduct and social conflict only loosely related to either law enforcement or national security.[1]

"Not infrequently he would call Edgar Hoover about something that he wanted done quietly, usually in a hurry," Biddle recalled, "and Hoover would promptly report it to me, knowing the President's habit of sometimes saying afterward, 'By the way,

Francis, not wishing to disturb you, I called Edgar Hoover the other day.'" In 1943, Roosevelt asked the Bureau to produce a comprehensive report on "racial conditions" in response to an alarming uptick in home-front violence. He also asked the FBI to look into the sexual practices of government officials, reflecting a budding concern that certain forms of sexual behavior—especially homosexuality—made government employees vulnerable to blackmail and intimidation. Like the counterintelligence apparatus reborn in the anxieties of conflict, the mandate to weigh in on such matters became an ongoing feature of Hoover's FBI, the final piece of its wartime legacy.[2]

No clear pattern defined Hoover's approach to his new portfolio. In some areas, he welcomed the opportunity to rethink how the Bureau worked, reaching out to former critics with offers to collaborate and establish agreed-upon protocols. In other cases, he turned back to the very methods that had led so many civil libertarians to warn about the perils of wartime surveillance. In some cases, he did both at once. Having recovered from the "smear campaign," Hoover began to forge unlikely alliances with both the ACLU and the National Association for the Advancement of Colored People (NAACP). At the same time, he continued to approve surveillance operations against both organizations. After years of locking horns with liberals and progressives, during the final years of the war Hoover acquired a short-lived reputation as something of a "liberal" himself, devoted to civil liberties and some measure of racial progress. But he also held fast to his older loyalties, working closely with groups such as the American Legion to resist the rapid social changes that home-front mobilization seemed to produce.

For Hoover as for many Americans, the waning years of the war turned out to be a time of improvisation, when old ways of doing things could be tested and discarded if necessary. That Hoover handled it as well as he did can be attributed not only to adaptability and experience, but to the support of longtime employees like Tolson and Helen Gandy, who celebrated her own twenty-fifth Bureau anniversary in 1944. Despite his ad hoc approach, Hoover left the war with more friends than he'd had going in, and with considerably more power.

EVEN BEFORE THE WAR, THE NEW DEAL HAD PRODUCED A POPULATION BOOM in Washington, with the number of city residents rising by almost 100,000 during each of Roosevelt's first two terms. After Pearl Harbor, the pace accelerated, yielding more than 100,000 new residents in 1942 alone. As during World War I, the government pushed its new army of workers into "tempos," hastily (and often shoddily) constructed office buildings intended to last only as long as the emergency itself. But there were exceptions to that rule. In Arlington, Virginia, just across the Potomac from Capitol Hill, the War Department authorized construction on a building meant to last for the ages: a squat five-sided structure known as the Pentagon, the largest office building in the world.[3]

At the FBI, wartime expansion had begun back in 1940, but the early start did little to insulate Hoover from Washington's growing office-space crisis. The number of Bureau employees continued to explode: from 4,370 in January 1941 to 7,910 in January 1942 to 12,600 by the spring of 1943. To house his growing number of employees, Hoover won appropriations for a quick-construction wing to the training barracks at Quantico. With the National Guard retreating for the Pentagon, he also laid claim to the Washington armory as a home for the Identification Division, transferring its hundreds of filing cabinets into the vast domed space. Hoover took pride in the sight of his human war machine. "It cannot be visualized," he told a reporter from *The Atlanta Constitution*. "To appreciate it you'll have to visit." In 1943, when the Duke and Duchess of Windsor came to town, FBI guides escorted them to the armory, showing off its eighty thousand square feet of floor space and ninety-foot ceilings. Defense factories displayed one side of home-front work, with their shining parades of bullets and tanks and planes. The identification division revealed another: the paperwork army required to track and process the millions of people now drawn into the federal orbit.[4]

One striking feature of the armory scene was the presence of women—more than half of all Bureau employees by the middle of 1943. Before the war, the Bureau had employed just 600 women, mostly clerks and typists. By 1943, it employed a whopping 7,800, an increase of more than 1,000 percent in just four years. There were still no female agents, but women occupied nearly every other available position, from stenographers and fingerprint clerks to statisticians, cryptographers, chemists, and accountants. "Today a new chapter in the history of women is being written behind the scenes of the Federal Bureau of Investigation," Hoover wrote in mid-1943, lauding the "tireless spirit" of his new employees. At the Identification Division, the filing staff—once 90 percent male—became 90 percent female. The code room, where skilled analysts translated top-secret messages, had no men at all. Where once G-Men had dominated the headlines, reporters now paid homage to the hardworking wartime staff of "G-Girls" and "G-Women."[5]

Other wartime changes at the Bureau were less visible but no less significant. Since its initial missteps, the Special Intelligence Service had settled onto firmer ground in Latin America, with 350 agents and other specialists plus an equal number of support staff—a division of some 700 employees by 1943. Those agents now received a bit of training before they shipped out, crash courses in Spanish or Portuguese, and in communicating with secret inks and codes. Once on the ground, they had figured out how to do other things: running informants and double agents, maintaining cover as golfers and lawyers and businessmen. The work mostly entailed listening, one agent recalled— just "pick up whatever you hear and let us know"—but SIS assignments could be dangerous, too. In January 1943, a military plane carrying SIS chief Percy Foxworth and another agent went down over Dutch Guiana, where they had been dispatched on "secret missions" related to the FBI's growing international scope.[6]

Hoover used the war to expand his reach at home as well, moving beyond the FBI to enhance his influence over especially useful and powerful domestic constituents. Foremost among them were local law enforcement agencies, long Hoover's greatest supporters, now a massive auxiliary pool of manpower available to be adapted and shaped to federal priorities. By 1942, all fifty-six FBI field offices were holding quarterly conferences with local police, instructing them in how to coordinate espionage and sabotage investigations, how to process alien enemies and keep an eye on social conditions. Added to this was the Bureau's ever-expanding force of industrial and political informants, recruited not as employees but as volunteers or contract workers, paid for specific services or (in some cases) not paid at all. By July 1942, Hoover counted 20,718 informants affiliated with the FBI in the area of defense plant protection alone.[7]

That number did not include the estimated thirty-three thousand members of the American Legion Contact Program, created in 1940 to give the FBI eyes and ears on the ground—and to give members of the Legion something productive to do. Despite the Legion's cooperation with his anti-crime and anti-delinquency drives in the late 1930s, Hoover had worried that the organization might devolve into a vigilante force, as it had after World War I. To prevent this, he decided to build upon those existing institutional ties to bring the Legion's members under direct FBI influence. Through the contact program, Legion members agreed to report allegations of potential disloyalty among friends and neighbors. Once they sent information to the FBI, however, members were supposed to hang back and let federal agents sort out what to do. "They have sensibly recognized the great difference between reporting information and acting upon information," Hoover noted in early 1941. "They are reporting it and leaving it to us to act." The arrangement both expanded and consolidated Hoover's reach, placing an energetic new grassroots army under his personal command.[8]

IN 1943, A YEAR AFTER MARKING HIS TWENTY-FIFTH ANNIVERSARY AT JUSTICE, Hoover celebrated another milestone: Tolson's fifteenth anniversary as his employee at the Bureau. Despite the distractions of war work, Hoover attempted to put in writing what the occasion meant to him, using the same elliptical but heartfelt prose that once characterized his letters to Purvis. "Words are mere man-given symbols for thoughts and feelings," he began, "and they are grossly insufficient to express the thoughts in my mind and feelings in my heart that I have for you." He tried anyway, reflecting upon Tolson's "decided influence" at the Bureau, and the ways in which the "invaluable assistance you have been to the Bureau and to me personally" had made so many triumphs possible over the years. Hoover recognized Tolson's loyalty to the institution they had built together: "just as its life has been your life, so is its success your success." He also expressed the dream that they might continue this work together long into the future. "I hope I will always have you beside me," he wrote, offering "every thought of deepest appreciation, gratitude, and thanks" to the man who had stood beside him through so much: the War on Crime, the G-Man craze, the Purvis conflict, the counterintelligence buildup, the smear campaign, Pearl Harbor, the saboteurs case—and now the challenges of evolving wartime duties.[9]

One of those duties threatened his relationship with Tolson, however, if not in ways that Hoover openly acknowledged. In 1941, as part of its draft policy, the army announced its intent to eliminate men with "homosexual proclivities" from serving in military ranks. Though the new policy applied only to military service, its effects rippled out into other areas of federal employment and into Washington society itself. After more than two decades in government, Hoover faced a world in which remaining unmarried or socializing primarily with other men—both distinctive features of his public persona—could be grounds for official scrutiny. The new policy also meant that accused homosexuals, summarily dismissed from the army, often ended up in other government jobs, nonmilitary work that came to be stigmatized as bookish, unmanly, and vaguely suspect.[10]

It did not take long for Hoover to witness how the emerging culture of suspicion could damage—or even end—a previously untroubled government career. In early 1941, he was summoned to the White House for a private meeting about Under Secretary of State Sumner Welles, one of the most respected men in the diplomatic service. According to rumor, Welles had recently made drunken sexual proposals to several Pullman porters and waiters—all of them Black men—while en route between Washington and Alabama. It was not thought to be an isolated incident. The president wanted Hoover to conduct a discreet inquiry, in hopes of finding a way to contain any political damage. A few weeks later, Hoover reported to Roosevelt that Welles had indeed propositioned several men while under the influence of alcohol, and that all too many people in Washington knew about it. "It is a common thing, unfortunately, for persons to charge men in public life with indulging in immoral acts and acts of degeneracy," Hoover lamented. In Welles's case, Hoover acknowledged the truth of the rumors, but attributed the troubling behavior to "more of a mental condition than anything else," an impulse over which the under secretary had limited control. To avoid a reoccurrence, Hoover recommended that the president appoint a "mature" companion to travel with Welles and prevent "the circulation of any story that would reflect upon his character."[11]

Hoover's suggestion failed to contain the Welles scandal. In the fall of 1942, Secretary of State Cordell Hull caught wind of the rumors and demanded a meeting with Hoover to discuss what the FBI knew. A few months later, the Republicans figured out what was happening and demanded a meeting with Hoover as well. By August 1943,

Roosevelt no longer believed he could keep his enemies quiet—and so he fired Welles, despite high regard for his diplomatic abilities.[12]

In the weeks that followed, Hoover tried to keep the true reasons for the dismissal (and the FBI's role in it) out of the newspapers. But he could not entirely control Washington gossip. One Washington resident, being interviewed by FBI agents for an unrelated case, made the mistake of mentioning a rumor that the director, too, was a "queer" who liked to hang out at New York clubs. The agents reported the remarks to Hoover, who commented, "I never heard of this obvious degenerate. Only one with a depraved mind could have such thoughts." Increasingly, though, it did not take a "depraved mind" to see that certain parts of Hoover's life did not mesh well with the war's changing cultural reality.[13]

EVEN AS HE FELT HIS WAY THROUGH THE CHALLENGES OF WARTIME SEXUAL policing, Hoover was forced to engage another issue that he might well have preferred to avoid. This was the so-called race problem, an area in which he had long held firm views, even if he rarely had expressed those views in public. Hoover still believed what Kappa Alpha had taught him long ago: that a stable social order required racial hierarchy, that Black protest threatened to disrupt that order, and that the white Southern "gentleman" offered the highest form of American citizenship. And he had built the Bureau in that vision, hiring and promoting Kappa Alpha men who already shared his ideas. Their work together often reflected what they believed. When Roosevelt ordered the Bureau to begin investigating fascism and communism in 1936, Hoover included "Negroes" and their activism—from sharecropper organizing to voter registration— under the label of subversive activity.

And yet, even here, on a subject about which he had such deep prejudices, Hoover found himself pushed to adapt to changing sensibilities during the war—and to experiment with new areas of investigation. As the Swedish economist Gunnar Myrdal observed in his wartime bestseller, *An American Dilemma*, military conflict highlighted the essential paradox of American life: How could a nation that prided itself on freedom also deny that freedom to its Black citizens? Though Hoover stopped short of fundamental changes to Bureau policy, he began to echo Roosevelt's warning that racial discrimination could undermine the war effort and disrupt home-front peace, providing the country's enemies with a powerful tool of propaganda. In one of the stranger twists of his wartime experience, he also began working with some of the very groups the Bureau was watching as potential subversives, including the NAACP.

As early as June 1941, Hoover had warned the White House "that approximately twenty-five thousand Negro delegates will participate in a 'March' on Washington" to protest discrimination within the booming defense industry. For months, A. Philip Randolph, the legendary head of the Brotherhood of Sleeping Car Porters, had been telling the White House about plans for civil rights march straight down Pennsylvania Avenue to the gates of the White House, the first of its kind. Hoover's warning reinforced Roosevelt's worry that the march would humiliate his administration, alienating the Democrats' crucial Southern wing at just the moment national unity was needed. At the last minute, Roosevelt cut a deal to save face, issuing an executive order banning discrimination in the defense industry in return for a promise to call off the march.[14]

Despite this temporary truce, rumblings of mass protest did not go away. With the United States striding forth as the last best hope for global democracy, Black men and women began to demand that democracy be realized on the home front as well. The *Pittsburgh Courier* labeled this the Double V campaign: justice and equality both at home and abroad. The U.S. military remained segregated, a redoubt of Jim Crow. Elsewhere, though, the forms of segregation erected during Hoover's childhood and early adult years were starting to crumble. In Washington, Howard University students devised the idea of holding sit-ins at local restaurants, demanding to know "Are you for 'HITLER'S way' (Race Supremacy) or the 'AMERICAN way' (Equality)?" Though they failed to desegregate the capital's lunch counters, their methods—like the canceled march on Washington—hinted at an emboldened civil rights energy.[15]

Hoover watched it all unfold, delivering reports to the White House about matters ranging from anti-poll-tax protests to plans for a "racial pilgrimage" at the Lincoln Memorial. The General Intelligence Survey, a revival of Hoover's 1919 General Intelligence Bulletin, devoted entire sections to "The Negro Situation," emphasizing the communists' "exceedingly widespread" efforts against lynching, voting restrictions, and "white supremacy" more generally. But Hoover also took an interest in groups with no communist connections at all. A 1941 report from the Oklahoma City field office noted that "there is a strong tendency for the NAACP to steer clear of Communistic activities." Hoover nonetheless conducted surveillance of the organization and amassed substantial evidence from informants within NAACP ranks.[16]

Walter White, executive secretary of the NAACP, was among the men who appeared in FBI files during these years, though his relationship with Hoover proved to be more fluid and complicated than this fact alone might suggest. Many people were surprised when they met White: Though he identified himself as a "Negro," his mixed-race heritage gave him blond hair and blue eyes, living testament to the fact that racial separation had always been an American fiction. White knew the violence of Jim Crow; he had spent years investigating race riots that killed hundreds of Americans, most of them Black men and women. He also knew the Roosevelt White House reasonably well, having positioned himself as a broker between the Democratic Party and its small but growing Black constituency. During the showdown over the March on Washington, White had sided with Randolph, helping to prod the Roosevelt administration into action.[17]

His connection with Roosevelt soon brought him to Hoover. In June 1941, as the president wrestled with the idea of an executive order banning discrimination in defense industries, White noted in a letter to Hoover that the FBI did not seem to be setting much of an example: "The general impression seems to be that the F.B.I. does not employ Negroes whatever their ability." Hoover responded with obfuscation and denial. "Please be advised that this bureau has no ban on the employment of Negroes, and, as a matter of fact, there are a number of Negroes in the employ of this Bureau at the present time," he insisted. While it was technically true that the Bureau employed a few Black men and women, Hoover's response hardly addressed the NAACP's main point. Black workers mostly occupied low-level service positions, more like servants than professional federal employees. The most visible Black employee, Sam Noisette, served as Hoover's official greeter and visitor escort—essentially, the director's personal butler. James Crawford, perhaps the second most visible Black man at the Bureau, worked as Hoover's chauffeur.[18]

The Black press found Hoover's explanations unpersuasive. "This policy of Mr. Hoover's is so analogous to the one employed by Mr. Hitler in denying membership to Jews in his notorious Gestapo and Storm Troop organization," wrote one columnist, "it is almost frightening." Over the next several years, Hoover felt compelled to take at least some sort of action. He settled on a strategy intended to produce results on paper while doing as little as possible to alter Bureau culture or practice. James Crawford had just finished driving Hoover to the Mayflower one day when he opened a surprise letter from the director's office: go directly to Quantico, the missive instructed, to be trained as a Bureau agent. Once there, Crawford turned out to be the only Black trainee in his cohort, forced to sleep alone and segregated from the other recruits. When he returned to the Bureau several weeks later, he went back to being Hoover's chauffeur, now classified as a "special agent," but under no illusions about what had inspired his on-paper promotion. "I think it was during the time when the NAACP was pressuring the Bureau because they didn't have any Negro agents," he recalled years later.[19]

This policy showcased the most cynical and entrenched aspects of Hoover's racism, his determination to preserve the Bureau's agent corps as the insular white men's club it had long been. In other areas of civil rights work, though, he showed more willingness to engage with his critics, and sometimes even to find common ground. Toward the end of 1941, White arranged a meeting with Hoover, hoping to discuss "the violation of civil liberties of Negroes" on the home front. To White's surprise, he came away intrigued by what Hoover had to say. "Mr. Hoover expressed himself as being unequivocally in favor of vigorous and prompt action by the FBI and pledged me that this would be done in every case," White reported back to the Washington branch of the NAACP, convinced that Hoover seemed to "be open to suggestions right now to a greater extent than would normally be the case." What followed was not a friendship but for a time it was a working relationship, in which the FBI learned to cooperate with the NAACP and vice versa.[20]

Hoover's willingness to engage the NAACP does not suggest that he fundamentally reexamined his own racial views, or accepted responsibility for delivering racial justice at the federal level. But it does show his ability to adapt and make pragmatic, politically astute judgments, especially in times of crisis. Another such moment arrived in the summer of 1943, when more than two hundred violent racial conflicts erupted around the country, most of them in cities overwhelmed by an influx of soldiers and defense workers, both Black and white. The worst occurred in Detroit, where scuffles between Black and white teenagers set off a three-day conflagration, ending only after the deaths of nearly three dozen people (most of them Black) and the arrival of federal troops. Hoover's response showed the ways that the war altered his official position on racial issues, even as he remained a Kappa Alpha man. On August 3, he warned the president that a riot might be stirring in Washington, laying blame on the "less desirable colored element." At the same time, he acknowledged that in order to win the war, all Americans bore responsibility for fighting racism. "Every victory for intolerance in America is a menace to democracy for all of us," he told the International Association of Chiefs of Police in a mid-August speech, calling for "vigorous, prompt and firm measures" to suppress racial violence.[21]

Hoover's speech was not merely a gesture of public liberalism intended to divert his critics. Even confidential documents, produced for internal consumption, show him grappling in new ways with the security implications of home-front racial violence. In the wake of the summer's race riots, he compiled a "Survey of Racial Conditions in the U.S.," a project not entirely unlike the one Myrdal himself had started years earlier. The FBI's version, completed in the fall of 1943, yielded a 714-page, multivolume discussion of Black life in America. Like Hoover's IACP speech, the survey did not fit easily into established political categories. It expressed grave fears about communist and Japanese manipulation of Black citizens. At the same time, it noted the "myriad factors" behind home-front conflicts, including "increased housing shortages, crowded transportation facilities and an overcrowding of amusement and recreational facilities." The report concluded that the war had changed not only the material conditions but also the attitudes of "the Negro race," now engaged in new forms of resistance to Jim Crow. "A new militancy or aggressiveness has been reported to be existent among the Negro population," the survey observed, that could soon sweep across the country and permanently alter its landscape. Though Hoover kept close watch on these developments, he had not yet decided what to do about them.[22]

AT LEAST AS SURPRISING AS HOOVER'S COOPERATION WITH THE NAACP WAS HIS wartime outreach to another group of FBI skeptics: the American Civil Liberties Union. Hoover had attempted to make peace with the ACLU during his uncertain first days as director, when Harlan Stone insisted that ACLU founder Roger Baldwin should vet Hoover's bona fides as a civil libertarian. Since then, the FBI and the ACLU had slipped back into a relationship of mutual suspicion. During the union showdown of 1936, the ACLU's Washington branch had supported the fired FBI employees, organizing pickets and letter-writing campaigns. Two years later, the group issued a pamphlet titled "Thumbs Down!" in opposition to the call for "voluntary" fingerprinting of all U.S. citizens. As the war began to spread across Europe, however, the ACLU and Hoover increasingly found common ground. In 1940, with the Nazi-Soviet Nonaggression Pact still in effect, the ACLU voted to expel any board member deemed overly sympathetic to "totalitarian" ideas, beginning with Communist Party leader (and longtime Hoover foe) Elizabeth Gurley Flynn.[23]

Hoping to build upon this momentum, in October 1941 Hoover agreed to meet with Baldwin in Washington—their first face-to-face encounter in almost two decades. Baldwin was planning to leave on a tour to examine home-front conditions along the West Coast, with an eye toward figuring out how local police might prevent the hysteria that had characterized the last war. Hoover knew what Baldwin wanted to hear. "I saw J Edgar Hoover himself, spending a most pleasant hour, in which he professed his liberalism and devotion to civil rights," Baldwin reported. After visiting several FBI field offices during his West Coast tour, Baldwin concluded that Hoover meant what he said, and that FBI agents were far more attentive to civil liberties questions than their local police counterparts. When Baldwin did raise questions, Hoover was quick to affirm a shared hope to avoid the "flagrant" civil liberties abuses and "spirit of the vigilante" that characterized the previous war. "It is my earnest desire to have the FBI stand for those principles that are so close to the hearts of all interested in maintaining our liberal form of Democracy, particularly in these very trying times," he wrote to Baldwin.[24]

Hoover's investment in Baldwin during those final months of 1941 paid off handsomely once the U.S. entered the war. In early 1942, Baldwin withdrew a critical article commissioned by *The New Republic*, tentatively titled "Civil Rights and the F.B.I." The unpublished manuscript had noted the "widespread uneasiness which has long existed among liberals and in the trade unions over the F.B.I.'s relation to civil liberties." It had attributed much of this to Hoover's red-hunting "mentality." In the end, though, Baldwin concluded that the FBI director was now a man to be given the benefit of the doubt. "An interview with Mr. Hoover convinced me that he has largely changed his views on the dangers from labor and the left," Baldwin noted in a memo for his files, the first time since the 1920s that the FBI and the ACLU saw eye to eye on critical matters.[25]

Baldwin's colleague Morris Ernst took things even further, proclaiming before all the world that Hoover was indeed a changed man. Ernst had gotten to know Hoover during the late 1930s in and around the Stork Club. Once the war began, what started as a social acquaintance evolved into a useful political alliance. Ernst saw no contradiction between serving as general counsel for the ACLU and speaking out on Hoover's behalf. To the contrary, he viewed himself as an emissary between worlds, someone who had "started with suspicions" about Hoover but who had arrived at "an increasing admiration for him" and the Bureau staff. "I listened to the blank, indiscriminate attacks on him by my Civil Liberties friends," Ernst wrote in a 1945 memoir, which included a chapter on his friendship with Hoover. "But after listening to repeated assaults on the FBI at meetings of liberals, I took the time to look into the facts." Those "facts," according to Ernst, included Hoover's deep engagement with the "philosophic interpretations" of Justices Oliver Wendell Holmes and Louis Brandeis, heroes in the civil liberties pantheon. They also included the discovery that "liberals" often attacked the FBI unjustly, and that "the assaults on Hoover ... do not stand up in the eyes of anyone desirous of looking at the complete record." If these sounded suspiciously like Hoover's own narratives, it was for good reason. Before publishing his memoir, Ernst sent the chapter to Hoover for suggestions and edits, a willing aide in the director's wartime rehabilitation.[26]

THERE WERE MANY THINGS THAT HOOVER DID NOT MENTION TO HIS FRIENDS at the ACLU. He did not tell them, for instance, that Baldwin remained on the custodial detention index, identified as a dangerous person to be snatched up in case of invasion. Nor did he let them in on the full scale of the FBI's continuing efforts to infiltrate and spy on the Communist Party, a matter that would have grave consequences after the war. A few Washington observers intuited at least some of what was what going on, however. In January 1944, *The Saturday Evening Post* published an exposé titled "Snooping on the Potomac," noting a fear among federal employees that wartime investigations would lead to the purge of "anybody who has ever been faintly liberal." The *Daily Worker* sounded the alarm as well, noting that Hoover seemed to be suffering from "hopeless political confusion," claiming the mantle of liberal and civil libertarian even as he continued to fume about "muddled emotionalists, parlor pinks, fellow-travelers, and avowed Communists."[27]

For the most part, though, Hoover surged into the final months of the war as a darling of the New Deal establishment, known as a protector of civil liberties and a vanquisher of Nazis, saboteurs, and race-baiters. With the support of the Roosevelt White House, FBI investigations formed the basis for a "Great Sedition Trial" targeting more than two dozen leaders of fascist and other far-right organizations. (The trial collapsed after the judge died unexpectedly in 1944.) Roosevelt also brought Hoover in on the war's most closely guarded scientific experiment: "a highly secret project for the development of an atomic explosive," as Hoover described it in one confidential note. By late 1944, Hoover was warning of efforts by the Soviets as well as the Germans to infiltrate the project and learn what the Americans knew, an issue that would only grow in significance during the months and years ahead.[28]

Most of those reports went through Harry Hopkins, one of the president's closest advisers and, by the end of the war, one of Hoover's own confidants and political friends. Through Hoover's updates, Hopkins learned of marches and demonstrations, informants and industrial protection, communist and civil rights activity, the ups and downs of the sabotage case. Apparently impressed by what he saw, in late 1944 Hopkins asked for an extraordinary personal favor, requesting that the FBI begin following and wiretapping his wife. The effort uncovered little of note about her activities, but it suggested something important about Hoover's wartime status: after years of tension and sniping, he was finally an insider among the New Dealers who mattered most.[29]

Hoover came through for the White House in one more matter of extraordinary personal sensitivity. In 1943, army intelligence operatives shadowed an Air Force recruit named Joseph Lash to a Chicago hotel room, where he met with Eleanor Roosevelt, a longtime friend and political ally. Ostensibly, the investigators were seeking evidence about Lash's political views and national loyalties. But they came away with recordings, captured on hotel-room bugs, purporting to show that the First Lady and her young friend were engaged in a sexual affair. When she discovered the intrusion, Eleanor Roosevelt complained vociferously to her husband, who proceeded to shut down the army's Counterintelligence Corps in response. Hoover then became the recipient of the Lash file, complete with its speculation about the First Lady's love life and its renderings of intimate letters between her and Lash.

Hoover had no great fondness for Eleanor Roosevelt, whom he viewed as a communist sympathizer with all-too-liberal racial views. Indeed, the FBI had itself copied some of her correspondence with the radical American Youth Congress during a wartime surveillance break-in in 1942. For the moment, though, Hoover kept the Lash story quiet, just as he had helped Roosevelt to hush up the Sumner Welles affair. Hoover's loyalties lay with the White House, and with the president who had made so many things possible in recent years.[30]

All told, his cooperation with White House—and his growing legitimacy among the nation's liberals—put him in a formidable position as Washington began to shift away from an urgent focus on the war to the contemplation of what might come next. In June 1944, American troops finally smashed their way onto the European mainland. With Allied victory a near certainty, Hoover—like many Washington officials— turned to considerations of the postwar order. "We have already started getting ready for some of the problems that now seem inevitable after hostilities cease," he explained. Returning to the themes that had preoccupied him before the war, Hoover predicted a rise in crime and an epidemic of juvenile delinquency, crises now exacerbated by rootless soldiers and working mothers. He also worried about a revival of revolutionary activity, and about Americans' ongoing susceptibility to "the Fascist-minded tyrant" and "the Communist-minded corruptionist." To handle it all, he envisioned a still bigger and better FBI, empowered not just to handle crime and subversion at home, but to take on global intelligence, where so much of the future battle over communism and fascism would be fought. In November 1944, with Roosevelt winning reelection to an astounding fourth term, Hoover had every reason to believe that the FBI would continue to receive the same White House support as it had for more than a decade.[31]

Instead, as the war drew to a close, he found himself forced to adapt once again to circumstances beyond his control. On April 12, 1945, Hoover was leaving the office for dinner with Tolson when an official stopped them at the elevator to say that Roosevelt had collapsed and died in Warm Springs, Georgia, and an effort was underway to locate the vice president, an obscure former senator from Missouri named Harry Truman. Just after seven o'clock that evening, Truman was sworn into office by Chief Justice Harlan Stone, the man who had done so much to alter Hoover's own fate a generation earlier.[32]

Part III

POWER AND POLITICS

(1945–1959)

Preface

T he last time the presidency changed hands, in 1933, Hoover had been a nobody, a middle-aged mid-level Republican appointee sweating over how to keep his job. Twelve years later, at the dawn of Harry Truman's tenure, he was a household name and global celebrity, better recognized and more celebrated than the new president himself. Over the course of Roosevelt's three-plus terms in office, Hoover had acquired powers unimaginable during his early days under Harlan Stone—the rights not only to arm his agents in pursuit of kidnappers and gangsters, but to conduct political surveillance and intelligence investigations throughout half of the world. In 1933, there had been no such thing as a G-Man. By 1945, the G-Man was a universally recognized type, born, bred, and popularized in Hoover's image.

Hoover himself had changed during those years. When Roosevelt came to office, Hoover had been living at home with his mother, a dutiful if parochial son of small-city Washington. By 1945 he could walk into the finest nightclubs in New York or Los Angeles or Chicago and be guaranteed a table. He had traveled the country, taking in its vistas, its hodgepodge of people, the salty pleasures of beach and ocean. And he had entertained senators and movie stars and impresarios, the crème de la crème. He had seen pain and sorrow, too: the anguish of a kidnap victim's family, the quieter loss of a sick and elderly parent. More than a dozen agents had died in his employ, ten from gunshot wounds, two in a plane crash, at least one from suicide. He shared all these experiences with a man who had first caught his attention as a charming young fraternity sort, but who had since matured into a steadfast life partner.

Throughout it all, Hoover held on to some of the strictures he had learned as a youth. He lectured about the failings of absentee parents and the virtues of Sunday school, about the need for self-discipline and fine habits and following the law. He maintained his faith in professionalism and apolitical expertise, and still believed that the right kind of man, carefully chosen, would do the right thing. For most of his early career, this good-governance administrative vision had held sway, the essence of

Hoover's self-conception as well as his public image. After 1945, his career turned in a different direction.

With the end of the war, Hoover began to use the state power he had acquired over the previous two decades to promote and enforce his other animating ideas: conservative beliefs in order and hierarchy, in religiosity and racial segregation, and above all in anticommunism as the bedrock of an American way of life. Beginning in the 1940s, Hoover emerged as the single most important architect of the so-called Red Scare, leading the federal effort to dismantle the Communist Party and sever its members from the vibrant and fluid Popular Front left. Much of what he did was aimed at the party itself, from searching out Soviet spies and investigating secret cells within the government to discrediting and prosecuting its national leadership. He engaged in a broader cultural initiative as well, linking the fight against communism with a sweeping conservative vision of what America was supposed to look like and how Americans were supposed to relate to one another.

Hoover's ability to use the FBI in support of this vision depended in part upon the by-the-book credibility he had built during his first two decades as director, among liberals and conservatives alike. It also depended upon his ability to control his bureaucracy and, where needed, to act in secret—a skill that eluded anticommunist rivals such as Senator Joseph McCarthy. For a brief moment after the war, Hoover attempted to continue with the project of expanding the Bureau, experimenting with new duties in the realms of global intelligence and lynching and civil rights. But with Roosevelt no longer in office, he ran into roadblocks, and came to accept certain constraints and limits.

If the period from 1924 to 1945 had been one of institution building—and of constructing Hoover's national reputation—the period from 1945 to 1959 was when he learned to wield power as an independent political force, no longer subordinate to other men's agendas. Aiding him in those efforts were new allies in Congress as well as state and local governments, in the media and Hollywood and the business world, even among his own former agents. Though the late 1940s brought more uncertainty and conflict, the 1950s turned out to be years of real influence in Washington, with Hoover fully accepted as a member of the city's elite. Though many people would later look back on the Red Scare as one of the darkest and most dangerous periods of American history, at the time Hoover's anticommunist politics made him more popular—and more powerful—than ever.

CHAPTER 26

Central Intelligence

(1945–1946)

Hoover (far right) after receiving the Presidential Medal of Merit
from President Harry Truman (second from right), March 8, 1946.
Despite such gestures, Truman was suspicious of Hoover's power
and tried to rein in the FBI. Also pictured are medal recipients Col.
John M. Johnson, director of defense transportation, and John
Pelley, president of the Association of American Railroads.

INTERNATIONAL NEWS PHOTOS/NATIONAL ARCHIVES
AND RECORDS ADMINISTRATION

Harry Truman planned to spend April 14, 1945, delivering the graduation speech at the FBI National Academy. His draft remarks included praise of Hoover as "my good friend," the key "moving spirit behind the Federal Bureau of Investigation." The bulk of the talk was to be devoted to social challenges as the nation transitioned from war to peace. "The dislocation of families by war work in distant plants, the growing threat of juvenile delinquency, and the psychological reactions of individuals exposed to the emotional hardships of war, all present problems of the first magnitude," Truman would have said, echoing Hoover's own forebodings.[1]

Instead of delivering that speech, Truman found himself attending Franklin Roosevelt's funeral in the East Room of the White House. The former president's body had left Warm Springs by train the day before, rolling overnight through the "black silence" of the southern countryside as thousands gathered along the tracks to weep and pay respects. At Union Station, a military guard transferred the coffin onto a caisson led by a team of white horses for a journey down Pennsylvania Avenue, past the Department of Justice. Half a million mourners lined the sidewalks and hung out of windows, observing the procession in a collective hush. At 11:14 a.m., Roosevelt's body arrived at the East Room, where the grand piano had been pushed into a corner to make room for sprays of lilies and roses around the coffin.[2]

Truman looked nervous and somewhat bewildered throughout the afternoon's service. He was not an imposing man to begin with, short and jaunty, with a preference for bow ties and straw hats. On an ordinary day, it often seemed as if he had stumbled away from a barbershop quartet into the inner sanctum of Washington politics and remained puzzled about how it had happened. For this occasion, he wore a somber formal suit, while his wife, Bess, and twenty-one-year-old daughter, Margaret, appeared at his side in dark blue dresses, a quiet and composed First Family. The service itself was mercifully brief: two simple hymns, a few words by a Washington pastor, less than twenty-five minutes all told.[3]

Hoover spent the day consulting with confidants and Justice officials, trying to figure out what the unexpected turn of events would mean for him and the Bureau in the months ahead. Roosevelt's death entailed the loss of a great patron and ally, the man who had empowered the modern Bureau and allowed it to flourish. Now in his place was an unknown and untested executive, added to the Democratic presidential ticket in 1944 largely because it was hard to define or object to Truman's muddy political views. To the degree that Truman did have a track record, it was not especially promising for Hoover. Despite the kindly speech planned for the academy graduation, as a Missouri populist Truman tended to be suspicious of professional Washington. More than once, he had aimed his objections at Hoover and the Bureau.[4]

That circumstance—the first new presidential administration in more than twelve years, and one that might well be more hostile than the previous—would have been disconcerting to any appointed official. In the spring of 1945, Hoover especially worried that it imperiled the next logical step in the FBI's evolution. During the final months of Roosevelt's presidency, Hoover had begun to discuss the possibility of expanding the FBI yet again—this time, by placing it in charge of international espionage and intelligence gathering once the war drew to a close. Roosevelt had seemed amenable to Hoover's plan, or at least willing to listen. Now the president's death and Truman's ascension meant that Hoover would be starting that conversation anew, in a political world that nobody yet understood.

BY ROOSEVELTIAN STANDARDS, TRUMAN WAS A POLITICAL NOBODY: "THE LEAST of men—or at any rate the least likely of men" to take the helm of a great nation in the midst of a cataclysmic war, in the words of one biographer. Truman had arrived in Washington from Missouri in early 1935, less than two years after the Kansas City Massacre had focused national attention on his home state. He hailed from Independence, not from Kansas City itself, a country boy and small-town haberdasher who had worked his way up from county judge to U.S. senator. Prone to romanticize his Missouri roots, he resented Hoover's portrait of 1930s Kansas City as a hotbed of lawlessness, corruption, and bloodshed. He was also sensitive to allegations against Thomas Pendergast, the infamous, potbellied boss of the local Democratic machine, who had plucked Truman out of obscurity and installed him in political office. During his earliest years in Washington, Truman had been widely mocked as "the gentleman from Pendergast," allegedly under the thumb of Missouri's most corrupt politician.[5]

Those ties first brought Truman into conflict with the FBI. Less than two years into his first term in the Senate, U.S. Marshals had seized ballots from the Kansas City municipal elections and turned them over to the Bureau to investigate allegations of fraud. The lab's testing showed widespread vote tampering and helped to produce criminal convictions against nearly 250 Pendergast operatives. A few years later, federal tax authorities went after Pendergast himself, based on evidence that he failed to report income from a massive bribe. Hoover flew to Kansas City to claim personal credit for helping to bust the ring and singled out the 1936 election fraud as "one of the most corrupt situations that has developed in that or any city for years." By the time Truman began to prepare a second run for Senate in 1940, Pendergast was behind bars at Leavenworth federal penitentiary.[6]

Truman never explicitly objected to the FBI's role in the Pendergast investigation. But his voting record over the next few years suggested a certain low-level grudge. In 1936, during Hoover's showdown with McKellar, Truman had voted against increasing the Bureau's appropriation. A few years later, he chaired a commerce subcommittee assigned to explore wiretapping legislation, with an eye toward the excesses of law enforcement. Unlike Roosevelt, he tried to take civil liberties seriously and did not suffer those who made self-serving excuses. After Pearl Harbor, he scoffed at Hoover's claim that ignorance of the attack could be blamed on the government's lack of wiretapping authority. He exhibited a similar sense of outrage in his work on the much-heralded Truman Committee, charged with investigating inefficiency, bribery, and profiteering in wartime contracts. By March 1943, Washington rumor suggested that Truman might be gearing up for "some investigation of the FBI," based on the idea that "the Bureau had been running wild" in its wartime work, though Truman insisted that "he absolutely did not" have any such intention. The following year, after Truman's election as vice president, Hoover sought to smooth things over by issuing the invitation to speak at the academy.[7]

With Roosevelt's death, Hoover hastened to postpone the speech. "Of course, I deeply regret the circumstances which made it obviously necessary to cancel the plans for the formal Graduation Exercise of the FBI National Academy," he wrote to Truman on April 13. He held out hope that Truman might yet speak at a future occasion. In the meantime, Hoover had another proposal in mind. While the rest of Washington mourned, he began to strategize about how to extend the FBI's reach throughout the world.[8]

IT HAD BEEN "WILD BILL" DONOVAN, NOT HOOVER, WHO FIRST PRODDED ROOSevelt to consider the question of peacetime intelligence. In 1942, while Hoover was busy contending with Nazi saboteurs and enemy aliens, Roosevelt had appointed Donovan to lead the Office of Strategic Services, the wartime agency charged with running intelligence, espionage, and sabotage operations throughout Europe, Asia, and Africa. From that position, Donovan had spent the past few years orchestrating high-stakes gambles: dropping paratroopers into France behind enemy lines, running operatives in intrigue-filled cities like Casablanca and Istanbul, sending undercover "businessmen" and "librarians" traipsing around the world as spies. To carry out these missions, he had recruited an elite corps of Ivy League and Wall Street standouts. On the whole, they had little experience in law enforcement or intelligence. In Donovan's view, though, such men possessed the right sort of quick wit and easy manner. In November 1944, he wrote to Roosevelt to suggest that they continue their work beyond the war as part of a new global intelligence agency. To lead it, Donovan recommended the best man in the business—not Hoover, but himself.[9]

Hoover agreed that the postwar order demanded innovation and restructuring. But he found Donovan's proposal outrageous—not least because it came from a man whose personnel and methods of management Hoover held in deep contempt. He judged the OSS chief a terrible administrator, incapable of setting up the most basic systems to track money and personnel. Hoover also distrusted Donovan's approach to screening and hiring, convinced that Ivy League bonhomie was no substitute for clear rules and manuals of procedure. He saw Donovan as a moneyed dilettante, more confident than competent. He worried as well that Donovan was seeking to encroach on FBI territory, especially in Latin America, the one international arena where the Bureau claimed wartime jurisdiction. Finally, he thought Donovan was soft on communists, all too willing to accept them into OSS ranks if they showed the right kind of insouciance and antifascist credentials. Despite the U.S.-Soviet alliance, Hoover managed to block Donovan's plan to begin open intelligence sharing with the Soviet Union, convincing Roosevelt that the Soviets could not be trusted.[10]

Hoover hoped to do the same with Donovan's 1944 proposal on postwar intelligence. As Washington debated the issue, Hoover came up with his own idea for a postwar intelligence system—led, of course, by the FBI. Where Donovan proposed building upon the OSS, Hoover recommended scaling up the cooperative arrangements that the FBI and military intelligence had developed during the war, thus cutting out or even dismantling the OSS altogether. Under Hoover's plan, the FBI would take charge of peacetime intelligence throughout the world, while military and naval intelligence would supplement those efforts in theaters of war. They would coordinate just as they had been doing since 1939, without needing to reinvent what already worked. "This plan would not call for any super-structure, but would operate with the same committee as originally set up by the President," an internal summary of the FBI proposal explained. Thus Roosevelt had been faced with two options: Hoover or Donovan, FBI or OSS, the status quo or something new. Though he did not live to make the choice, the ensuing struggle created enough bitterness to last for generations.

Hoover's chief claim to global intelligence leadership rested on the Bureau's work in Latin America, where the Special Intelligence Service, created with such urgency in 1940, had grown into a substantial network of 360 special agents and employees at its peak. The operation remained largely hidden from the public. For the men and women involved, though, SIS had become a serious venture, with agents working undercover as corporate representatives or U.S. embassy employees, among other identities. From such posts, they gathered intelligence on activities similar to those being investigated within the United States—not only Nazi smuggling and espionage but also leftist movements and potentially significant rumblings of discontent. They relayed all of it back to Washington through an elaborate communications apparatus, including several FBI-run radio channels. Under Hoover's plan, these would become the nucleus of a clandestine global communications network.

Other agencies sometimes scoffed at what came in through FBI channels: "confidential" information gleaned from top-secret sources such as the daily newspaper, in a theater of operations far from the actual war. But Hoover expressed pride in what the SIS had accomplished in a short period of time. An internal report cheered the "brilliant results" attained in Latin America as early as 1943. Hoover was particularly heartened that the FBI managed to do it all without exposing the Bureau to public scrutiny. With the end of the war looming, he proposed to Roosevelt that "the time-proven program in operation in the Western Hemisphere be extended on a world-wide basis," as an FBI assessment later described it. In Hoover's view, the FBI already knew how to function under peacetime conditions and had a corps of professional men in place to perform any necessary tasks, unlike the ill-trained and erratic OSS.[11]

He somewhat exaggerated their record. Though SIS had managed to get itself up and functioning, its quantifiable victories—in lives saved, plots thwarted, decisions influenced—were limited. If anything, FBI operatives turned out to be far more adept at gathering political intelligence than at steering wartime decision-making. Some countries where SIS operated, including Brazil, Mexico, and Argentina, harbored bona fide German or Japanese espionage networks, worth the trouble of watching. Others, such as Ecuador, lacked much of significance to the war effort. There, FBI agents spent much of their time tracking left-leaning movements, in hopes of anticipating (or even thwarting) attempts at revolution. Compared to Donovan's spectacular exploits at OSS, Hoover did not have much to offer in the way of adventure tales. But he could say with some accuracy that SIS carried out its mission on budget and without embarrassment, which was more than one could say about Donovan.[12]

Roosevelt had taken Hoover's view seriously—about the outsize strengths of the FBI as well as the weaknesses of OSS. Toward the end of the war, a presidential military aide conducted a quiet investigation of Donovan's organization, with an eye toward establishing which postwar strategy seemed most deserving. The report from that investigation turned out to reflect nearly all of Hoover's criticisms of OSS, including the idea that Donovan tolerated "poor organization, lack of training and selection of many incompetent personnel." The report accused OSS of being "hopelessly compromised to foreign governments," especially the Soviet Union, and speculated that "it may easily prove to have been relatively the most expensive and wasteful agency of the government." Investigators then offered two important conclusions, both of them beneficial to Hoover. First, they cautioned that "if the O.S.S. is permitted to continue with its present organization, it may do further serious harm to citizens." Second, they projected that any attempt to extend OSS operations beyond the war would result in a "Gestapo system" dangerous to American liberties. In the final equation, the report recommended that Donovan's proposal "be vetoed in favor of an organization" on Hoover's model.[13]

HOOVER WANTED TO MAKE SURE THAT TRUMAN UNDERSTOOD THAT PERSPECtive. On April 13, as Roosevelt's body was arriving in Washington, he summoned a young Baltimore agent named Morton Chiles to his office for a special assignment. Chiles had grown up in Independence, Missouri, and he knew the Truman family. Hoover hoped those facts might provide a point of entry for a conversation with the new president. At the director's prompting, Chiles called his father in Independence, who went to see Vivian Truman, the president's brother, who put in a long-distance call to the president. At that point Truman himself invited Chiles over for a chat.

Chiles had known Truman since the president was just "a dirt farmer," wearing "overalls with a straw hat." That day, he could see that Truman was not quite himself, "obviously still shaken up because of the awesome responsibility that he had been given." Truman seemed all too aware that he had never really fit in at the Roosevelt White House. "He told me that Roosevelt never told him anything," Chiles remembered. So the agent set about filling him in. Over the course of their hour-long meeting, Chiles explained to the president how Donovan was trying to seize hold of the postwar intelligence system, and how Hoover was trying to stop him. Chiles came away with the impression that Truman was "very grateful" for the information and "knew nothing" about all the backroom machinations.[14]

Chiles was probably right. As Truman would later admit, Roosevelt had not told him much about the war, up to and including details of the country's top-secret nuclear weapons development program. (The army briefed him on those facts on April 24, more than a week after his meeting with Chiles.) By contrast, Hoover already knew all about the Manhattan Project, along with many other wartime secrets. He also knew how valuable his own intelligence gathering could be to an untested and uncertain new head of state. By sending Chiles off to greet the president, Hoover hoped not only to get in the first word on the global intelligence controversy, but to demonstrate his usefulness to the White House.

On April 16, in his maiden speech to Congress, Truman announced his intent to carry on with Roosevelt's policies and appointees. "I want the entire world to know that this direction must and will remain—unchanged and unhampered," he declared, pleased with the roaring applause from the floor. Columnists interpreted these remarks to mean that Hoover, among others, would stay on the job. "No matter the shifts in the Dept. of Justice," columnist Leonard Lyons assured his audience, "J. Edgar Hoover will remain as head of the FBI." Things did not, however, continue quite as usual. During the Roosevelt years, Hoover had spoken directly with the president in moments of crisis. Truman preferred to communicate through the attorney general. And when Hoover needed to contact the White House, he would now do so through a set of newly appointed assistants, beginning with Harry Vaughan, a gregarious, poker-playing friend now designated as a military aide to the president.[15]

Whether purposely or not, the decision put Hoover and Truman on a collision course, as Truman surrounded himself with like-minded Missouri men and Hoover seethed at the slight to his authority. But little about Hoover's actions during the early weeks of the Truman presidency suggests any fixed enmity, or any sense that the president could not yet be won over to the FBI. To the contrary, Hoover went out of his way to ingratiate himself with Truman and to provide the same sort of political intelligence that Roosevelt had so valued. Truman faced a daunting leadership challenge: not just bringing the war to a successful close, but doing so in an atmosphere where even his own party doubted his abilities. Far from taking umbrage at what Hoover had to offer, Truman welcomed the FBI's assistance, just as he had welcomed Chiles's briefing on Donovan. "The President directs me to thank you for your special communication . . . , as he read it with much interest," Vaughan wrote to Hoover a few weeks after Roosevelt's death. "He feels that future communications along that line would be of considerable interest to him whenever, in your opinion, they are necessary."[16]

And so Hoover proceeded much as he had with Roosevelt, providing the White House with a steady stream of political intelligence. In the summer of 1945 Truman requested through an aide that the FBI "secure all information possible on White House employees," noting that "intercepts of the phone conversations of those employees would be of extreme value." The president worried over leaks coming both from Roosevelt holdovers and from members of the household staff. Hoover initiated a wiretap on Edward Prichard, a young and well-connected White House aide rumored to be close with some of the president's critics. When an aide shared logs of those conversations with Truman during a boat ride along the Potomac, the president declared them "the damnedest thing I have ever read," and encouraged the FBI to place a wiretap not just on Prichard, but on newspaper columnist (and Truman critic) Drew Pearson.[17]

Hoover declined that request. He feared that the wiretap could earn him a permanent and vocal critic in the press should it ever come out. But he remained amenable to working with Truman on a range of other politically sensitive matters. Six weeks into his term, Truman abruptly fired Attorney General Francis Biddle, replacing him with a Justice Department lawyer and Texas power broker named Tom Clark who was closer in both spirit and geography to the president's Missouri style. Around the same time, the FBI initiated a wiretap on New Deal insider turned lobbyist Tommy Corcoran, alleged to be at the center of a Georgetown-based anti-Truman cabal. That tap alone lasted almost three years, off and on. Along the way, it captured laments that Truman surrounded himself second-rate appointees and "mediocre Missourians," in Corcoran's words, and had no idea how to run the government.[18]

Privately, Truman harbored doubts about the FBI's role as collector and purveyor of political intelligence. "We want no Gestapo or Secret Police," he wrote in his journal on May 12, a month after Roosevelt's death. "F.B.I. is tending in that direction." Historians have interpreted those private musings as his genuine views: the straight-shooting, small-town man appalled at the corruption and machinations of Washington. If so, Truman did not hasten to act upon his principles. Based on the president's initial signals, Hoover had every reason to believe the techniques that had won over so many other powerful men, from Harlan Stone to Franklin Roosevelt, were now working their magic on Truman, too.[19]

MOSTLY, TRUMAN HAD MORE IMPORTANT THINGS TO DO DURING THE SPRING and summer of 1945 than to worry about Hoover and his agenda for postwar intelligence. In late April, the president ventured to San Francisco to preside over the opening of the United Nations. Over the next few weeks, Hitler committed suicide, American and Soviet troops met up at the Elbe River, and the German high command surrendered unconditionally. Truman read "a little statement" marking that "solemn but glorious hour," as he described it during a press conference on May 8. Then he announced his intent to "turn the greatest war machine in the history of the world loose on the Japanese." In July, he steamed off to Potsdam, Germany, for a meeting with Stalin and Churchill to discuss the fate of Poland and the postwar division of Germany. While there, he received word about a successful test of the country's extraordinary new weapon in the desert of New Mexico and approved its use against the people of

Japan. On August 6, while Truman journeyed back across the Atlantic, a U.S. bomber dropped the first atomic weapon ever deployed in warfare on the city of Hiroshima. Three days later, a second bomb obliterated Nagasaki, a few hundred miles to the south. Less than a week after that, Truman announced the Japanese surrender, bringing to a close the bloodiest and most destructive war in human history.[20]

Upon hearing of the Japanese surrender, Washington let loose with "four-plus years of pent-up emotion," in the words of one reporter. Confetti rained down along F Street: torn-up telephone books, ripped newspapers, shredded paper no longer needed for war procurement. Drivers laid on their horns in solidarity and then abandoned their vehicles to join impromptu jitterbug contests or to take in the "seething, shouting mass of hilarious humanity." At Lafayette Park, so many people pressed against the iron fence around the White House that military police feared it might collapse. The crowd chanted "we want Harry, we want Harry, we want Harry," and they got what they wanted: waves and smiles from their ecstatic president as he ventured out onto the White House lawn. District old-timers declared it the greatest of Washington's spontaneous celebrations, surpassing even the bonfires and parades of 1918's Armistice Day.[21]

Hoover, too, greeted the end of the war in a celebratory mood. Despite all the difficulties of the past five years, he felt the FBI had accomplished what it set out to do when the war began. "In no civilized land in time of war were civil rights and personal liberties abridged less than here in the United States," he declared in one of his first major postwar speeches. "The dragnets of World War I were unheard of in this war. The slacker raids did not recur. The lynchings and character assassins of World War I were checked. On the other hand, the sabotage which everyone said would occur did not take place." Once again, he was somewhat exaggerating his war record. It is true that the home front of the 1940s produced less of the vigilante violence that had plagued the previous war. Instead, it produced a larger, more effective, and far more fearsome security state, with the FBI at its core. In that sense, Hoover achieved what he had envisioned years earlier; the hunting of spies and saboteurs and dissenters remained mostly in the hands of professionals, and the government found less need or desire to throw dissenters in jail. What his calculus did not acknowledge was the rise in secrecy and surveillance that occurred as an analogue to these more visible developments. Hoover saw only an upside in the fact that the FBI emerged from the war some four times larger than when it began. For the nation as a whole, the downsides would soon be evident.[22]

During the war, imperatives of discretion and censorship had often constrained Hoover's effort to publicize the Bureau's exploits. As the end of the war approached, he began laying plans to craft a triumphal public narrative—and thus to persuade Truman to allow the FBI to take up where the OSS left off. In the spring of 1945, Hollywood producer Louis de Rochemont had come to Hoover's office to discuss making a movie based on the 1940 Sebold case, in which the FBI had turned Hitler's agent to the American side.[23]

Recognizing a grand opportunity, Hoover opened the Bureau to Rochemont's crews and actors, just as he had once opened it to a Hollywood seeking glamorous tales of the War on Crime. He also gave the filmmakers invaluable raw material from the FBI's files, including surveillance footage of the German embassy. Agents and clerks served as extras on the film. Hoover himself appeared on screen in a brief opening shot, seated at his desk consulting stacks of papers with Tolson standing by his right side.[24]

The debut of the film, titled *The House on 92nd Street*, came just a few weeks after V-J Day, as Hoover was beginning to ramp up his narrative push. He invited Truman's aide Harry Vaughan to attend the film's New York premiere. He also invited New York governor Thomas Dewey and former president Herbert Hoover, both of them Republicans, to round out the partisan edge. The group met for a buffet dinner at 20th Century Fox's New York offices—"a hundred or so top-names in society moviedom and politics," in the words of one news account—before sitting down to watch the incredible tale of how the FBI ran a double agent who exposed a Nazi spy ring. The film reflected Hoover's old emphasis on administration and scientific policing, with glamour shots of filing cabinets, microscopes, and a spick-and-span office set. At the same time, it showcased the Bureau's developing prowess in the areas of espionage, sabotage, and counterintelligence, just the things that Hoover wanted the Truman White House to keep in view. "I was gripped every minute," Hoover declared after the screening. "I'd forgotten how exciting it was." He hoped that the president would be impressed, too.[25]

Despite his official mantra that "the FBI is a WE organization," over the next few months Hoover personally accepted much of the credit for the Bureau's success. From 1945 into 1946, awards dinners and medal ceremonies made up a substantial part of his social schedule. As early as April 1945, the country of Panama welcomed Hoover into its Order of Vasco Nuñez de Balboa, one of several awards from Latin American nations thanking the FBI for its wartime efforts. A few months later, New York's chipper mayor, Fiorello La Guardia, granted Hoover the city's certificate of distinguished service. Even Truman found time to pin a medal on Hoover, bestowing the presidential Medal for Merit—the country's highest award for civilian service—in a small but well-publicized ceremony.[26]

Hoover wrote to Truman with "deep appreciation of the honor." But the vote of confidence that Hoover prized most came in a different form. In late September, around the time *The House on 92nd Street* made its debut, Truman issued an executive order declaring Donovan's OSS officially null and void. The spy service went out of business for good on October 1, leaving Hoover and the FBI in an ever more promising position to take over.[27]

TRUMAN SHUT DOWN OSS FOR BOTH POLITICAL AND PRINCIPLED REASONS: HE distrusted Donovan as a showman and New Deal insider, and he feared giving *any-*

one too much power in the shadowy realms of intelligence and espionage. Perhaps inadvertently, though, his attempt to limit the scope of the postwar security state only strengthened Hoover's confidence that the Bureau was now the heir apparent. By dismantling OSS, Truman effectively made the FBI the only intelligence service with an active international network and a group of experienced men ready to carry out operations—a fact that Hoover lost no time in pointing out to the White House. On September 20, just hours after issuing his executive order disbanding OSS, Truman received a new version of Hoover's proposal that the FBI lead the postwar intelligence system.[28]

The basic idea remained the same as what Hoover had proposed to Roosevelt: the FBI would do for the world what it had done for Latin America. Contained within that idea were arguments about civil liberties, concentrated power, and potential "Gestapo" tactics—in short, some of Truman's major concerns. What made the FBI the best choice to lead global intelligence, Hoover claimed, was not its ambition and daring but its acknowledgment of constitutional limits, its willingness to abide by laws and rules. He pointed to the Bureau's war record—the way it had avoided the worst abuses of World War I even while capturing Nazi spies and saboteurs. He noted the Bureau's budding relationship with the ACLU, naming both Morris Ernst and Roger Baldwin as men of impeccable integrity willing to vouch for the FBI. Perhaps most of all, he emphasized his distaste for anything resembling a gestapo, and pointed to his decades-long record of arguing against the creation of a national police.[29]

Hoover's presentation was at best a partial story. Like his public narrative, it failed to acknowledge the many ways that a more effective and professional administrative body could also be a more dangerous one. And it ignored the rise in wartime secrecy and surveillance, the millions upon millions of new files produced. But it constructed a plausible view of the known facts as Hoover saw them, in which he had managed to expand the Bureau's size and reach while avoiding the abuses of the Wilson era.

TRUMAN SOON DASHED HIS HOPES. HOOVER SPENT THE HOLIDAYS IN FLORIDA, presumably with Tolson, relaxing in a hotel with a view of the sea. Not long after they returned to Washington, he received a draft proposal from the White House. Far from embracing Hoover's narrative and his plan for postwar intelligence, Truman proposed an entirely different vision. In Truman's scheme, global intelligence would be supervised by a coordinating committee of representatives from the State, War, and Navy Departments—with the FBI excluded. Hoover fired off a confused and indignant memo pronouncing the idea "completely unworkable" and thoroughly ill informed. Not only did the directive suggest that Hoover would never lead a global intelligence agency; it also raised the prospect that the FBI's existing operations—in the domestic United States as well as in Latin America—might be subject to the committee's jurisdiction. He urged the attorney general not to approve it.[30]

To Hoover's relief, Truman's next directive, issued on January 22, clarified that the plan did not apply to "police, law enforcement or internal security functions" or to investigations conducted within the United States. Other than that, the president ignored everything that Hoover had been seeking over the past year, establishing a Central Intelligence Group (CIG), in which the FBI played no role whatsoever. No doubt many factors drove Truman's decision: civil libertarian principle, personal suspicion of Hoover, even a failure to take seriously the expertise involved in intelligence and counterespionage work. But Truman does not seem to have put much time or energy into reaching the decision, aside from listening to the interested parties and going with his gut. Hoover took the situation more seriously. As he recognized, Truman's directives had far-reaching consequences for the agencies involved—and for the future of American intelligence. With the stroke of a pen, the president split peacetime intelligence into two separate spheres: with the FBI on the domestic side and the CIG on the global. He also added fuel to the animosity already simmering between the FBI and its rivals. Most immediately, he signaled that the FBI did not have his confidence, and that the cozy relationship that Hoover had maintained with the Roosevelt White House no longer existed.[31]

Hoover got the message; he just did not care to listen. He still wanted the plan that he had wanted all along, and he believed that he could get Truman's decision reversed. In working with Hoover during the war, a British official had noted that "Hoover is the kind of man who does not bow easily to the inevitable—that is at once his strength and his weakness." In the days after Truman's directive, he stayed true to form. On January 23, he had lunch with General Dwight D. Eisenhower, the operational hero of D-Day, now the army's chief of staff. After discussing some of the travails of the European situation, Hoover turned the conversation to foreign intelligence and Truman's creation of CIG. According to Hoover's account of the meeting, Eisenhower "expressed amazement and real concern at the possibility of the FBI withdrawing from [international] operations." The general agreed that "the elimination of the FBI from foreign intelligence was most undesirable and should be corrected" as soon as possible.

Truman felt otherwise. The next day, he officially inaugurated his new era of global intelligence with a lunchtime gathering at the White House: just the president, a few staffers, a military adviser, and Admiral Sidney Souers, the naval intelligence officer appointed to lead CIG. In a mock-solemn ceremony, the president presented his guests with wooden daggers, black cloaks, and hats, anointing Souers head of the "Cloak and Dagger Group of Snoopers," under the title "Director of Centralized Snooping." Hoover was one step ahead of him, however. That morning, he had already met with Souers, extracting a promise from the CIG director that "the FBI was not to be excluded from the foreign field, but would very likely be called upon to expand its operations therein." In the meantime, Hoover could still angle to see the CIG brought under FBI influence.[32]

Hoover remained convinced that he would come out on top for several more months, as Souers tried and largely failed to get the CIG off the ground. "Complete confusion" was how one observer described a visit to CIG's offices in the War Department, where understaffing and a lack of clear hierarchy, the observer assured Hoover, meant that almost nothing was getting done. He attributed the chaos to Souers, who seemed "very sincere and wanted to do a good job," but "lacked experience" in running an office and standing up to political pressure. Hoover, by contrast, continued to oversee operations in Latin America and to keep his intelligence machine humming along. As late as April, his aides were assuring him that officials would soon "be contacting you for the purpose of obtaining an answer on how this Bureau feels about taking over the clandestine operations of worldwide intelligence." Hoover still imagined that he would be asked to step in and take over.[33]

It was not until the summer of 1946, more than a year into Truman's presidency, that Hoover fully realized that something very different was taking shape. In June, Truman began an overhaul of CIG, replacing Souers not with Hoover but with a general from military intelligence. The following month, in a definitive blow to Hoover's plans, Truman instructed the CIG to assume control over "all organized Federal espionage and counterespionage abroad," including in Latin America. Lest anyone mistake his intent, Truman ordered Hoover to do what he had instructed Donovan to do nine months earlier: disband all international operations. After two decades of constructing and expanding the FBI, Hoover was forced to dismantle something he had built.[34]

HOOVER RESPONDED TO TRUMAN'S INSULT AS ONLY A SKILLED BUREAUCRAT could, using rules, lists, and literal-minded policies to make the process of taking apart the SIS as unpleasant as possible. The new CIG team anticipated that the FBI would work slowly and carefully to execute a transfer of its Latin American facilities. Instead, on July 15, Hoover informed them that all FBI employees would be back in the United States within thirty days. Though they did not quite make that deadline, over the next few months agents throughout Latin America set about destroying what had taken a full four years to create, thus leaving their successors to start from scratch. On Hoover's instructions, they burned investigative files—"both pending and closed"—along with all lists of undercover contacts, years of work now up in smoke. Agent Samuel Papich, the last FBI man to leave Latin America, found the experience painful and demoralizing. "To turn over everything we had built," he recalled, "it broke my heart." He recognized a similar wound in Hoover—and "if you wound him," Papich noted, "he never forgets."[35]

The new head of CIG, War Department intelligence chief Hoyt Vandenberg, suspected Hoover of hostile intent. "There is grave danger in this situation that the excellent FBI organization in Latin America may disintegrate before it can be taken over by new personnel of the CIG," he complained to fellow intelligence officials. "This would be a major blow to the effectiveness of our security intelligence work in the Latin American field, from which it might take us many years to recover." When confronted with this allegation of bad faith, Hoover maintained his innocence, then explained why only a swift pullout made sense.[36]

Among confidants at the Bureau, he showed more bitterness, mulling over the injustice of being asked to assist the CIG while also being told that his men were not sophisticated enough for international intelligence work. In the margins of official memos, Hoover grumbled about CIG's "double talk" and "sadistic" methods. He also celebrated articles "debunking" CIG and describing its fly-by-night operations. His top men shared this resentment. "I pointed out . . . that it was rather inconsistent that Bureau agents were not good enough to carry on the SIS operations in the Latin Americas but at the same time their services are so indispensable that they cannot now be withdrawn or replaced," one official reported, describing a recent conversation with the attorney general.[37]

In the years to come, Hoover would downplay the idea that he had been interested in foreign intelligence, as if the pleading and wrangling with Roosevelt and Truman had been merely a concession to duty. This became the official line at the Bureau, an institutional strategy designed in part to preserve Hoover's dignity and reputation. As one official explained to a puzzled U.S. ambassador, "the Director had not sought this work for the Bureau in the beginning nor was the Bureau seeking it now." That revision of the historical record was not unlike what Hoover had accomplished in the wake of the Palmer Raids twenty-five years earlier, a cover-up of a major professional defeat.[38]

Agent Papich believed that Hoover might indeed have experienced "loser's relief" at being forced to return to the domestic sphere, the site of his greatest passion and experience. Even so, the resentment born of the battle to control foreign intelligence lingered well beyond 1946. The following year, when the Central Intelligence Group evolved into the Central Intelligence Agency, Hoover approached his counterparts with suspicion, convinced that the incompetence and recklessness he had observed at OSS had now found its home at CIA. After 1946, he approached the Truman White House with similar hostility, increasingly certain that the president was an enemy of the Bureau.[39]

CHAPTER 27

Under Color of Law

(1941–1948)

The funeral of George W. Dorsey, one of four victims of a 1946 mass lynching in Monroe, Georgia. During the 1940s, the FBI expanded into anti-lynching work, to mixed success.

AP PHOTO/*THE ATLANTA JOURNAL-CONSTITUTION*

As much as Hoover resented Truman's actions, he could not simply pack up and go home. At the very least, he did not want to. The FBI still had plenty of work to do in its established areas of authority, from domestic surveillance to statistics and crime research to basic law enforcement. And even without the global intelligence realm, Hoover saw room for postwar expansion. One of the most promising areas was also one of the most unlikely for Hoover: the investigation of the brutal, racially motivated lynchings sweeping through the American South.

Hoover never chased lynching work with the same enthusiasm that drove his bid for global intelligence. Nor, however, did he run the other way. During the 1940s, first at the prodding of Francis Biddle and then of the Truman administration, he began to experiment with drafting a more robust role for the FBI in Southern lynching investigations—and, by implication, in the domain of civil rights enforcement. He was never driven by a vision of racial equality; there was too much Kappa Alpha in his past and in his soul to allow for that. Instead, he saw lynching as a challenge to federal law enforcement authority, yet another instance in which lawless vigilantes sought to take the law into their own hands. Hoover believed that his G-Men could shore up faith in federal power by bringing lynch mobs to justice. They could also showcase their investigative and moral prowess, extending the FBI's jurisdiction into another potential growth area.

That things did not work out as planned had less to do with Hoover's initial aspirations than with the obstacles placed in his way—foremost among them the opposition of white Southerners. Though they were Hoover's allies in many other spheres, when it came to civil rights and lynching work, they attacked Hoover and the FBI as part of a federal power grab. Sometimes, they even lumped him in with the Truman administration. Faced with their opposition, Hoover soon retreated from his initial ambitions. But for a few heady years after the war, he aspired to bring lynching more fully into the repertoire of Bureau duties. Like his effort to seize control of global intelligence, it became a path not taken.

HOOVER DEFINED LYNCHING NARROWLY: AS AN ACT OF MOB VIOLENCE IN which a prisoner charged with a crime was snatched from police custody and subjected to violent retribution. By his count, between 1900 and 1944 the country had witnessed 1,963 lynchings. Broader conceptions yielded higher numbers. The Tuskegee Institute counted as many as 3,417 lynchings of Black men and women between 1882 and 1944, along with 1,291 lynchings of whites. By any definition, the salient features of lynching were its extreme cruelty—in which victims were often castrated, set on fire, or dismembered before being hanged, shot, or beaten to death—and its highly public nature, with the violence often carried out in full view of hundreds, if not thousands, of spectators. Despite this abundance of witnesses, lynchings were difficult to prosecute. Local white juries sanctioned the violence with not-guilty verdicts in those rare cases where local authorities—themselves often involved in the mob conspiracy—even saw fit to bring charges. Congress, too, refused to act. When Senator Robert Wagner (D-NY) co-sponsored a federal anti-lynching bill in 1938—only the most recent attempt to increase federal authority over lynching—it met with a weeks-long filibuster from Southern Democrats and never passed.[1]

With Congress all but hopeless and local prosecutions well-nigh impossible, Roosevelt and his Justice Department had started to brainstorm ways around the impasse—to explore if and how the scourge of lynching might be curtailed through executive or administrative action. One Democratic congressman proposed the creation of a federal commission led by Hoover, with the goal of outlining a "governmental campaign against lynching similar to the one which proved so effective against kidnapping." The Justice Department opted instead to launch a series of legal test cases in hopes of establishing federal authority to intervene when local police were either complicit or failed to act. Biddle found Hoover surprisingly amenable to the idea. "When I discussed these cases with him, suggesting that he might add to his reputation by thus espousing the liberal cause, he raised no objection to making test cases, although we both knew that his success might be at the price of intense resentment of such 'Yankee interference,'" Biddle recalled. "Without his cooperation the test cases would have never been put together."[2]

At least some of Hoover's goodwill may have stemmed from his desire to please Roosevelt, who was under serious pressure to act. But Hoover also had other reasons to sympathize with the anti-lynching cause. As an outspoken foe of vigilantism, he had little patience for violent crowds who acted on their own authority, whether they came in the form of lynch mobs or anti-German "vigilance committees." He viewed many Southern police departments with similar disdain. Though charged with upholding the law, local officials too often capitulated to—or even participated in—mob action. Finally, he may have seen a chance for a goodwill gesture toward groups such as the NAACP and ACLU, with whom he was trying to build more congenial relations.

When it came to the law itself, however, the FBI's jurisdiction rested on shaky ground. Murder was a state-law crime, not a federal offense. Roosevelt could not simply expand Hoover's purview with a handshake or the stroke of the executive pen, as he had done with sabotage, espionage, and home-front intelligence. The best authority that the Justice Department could find, after scouring the federal criminal code, was a pair of weak civil rights statutes dating back to Reconstruction. Section 51 of Title 18 authorized federal action in cases where two or more people interfered with the exercise or enjoyment of a federal right. Section 52 applied to circumstances in which public servants—usually police officials "acting under color of law"—did the same. Neither section mentioned murder, torture, or lynching. Nor did either law necessarily prohibit violence by a private individual. But unlike a federal anti-lynching law, defeated again and again in Congress, these statutes were on the books and available for creative legal interpretation.[3]

The first opportunity to test this theory emerged not long after the German invasion of France, when a local NAACP official was murdered in Brownsville, Tennessee. Hoover sent an agent to investigate. The mere presence of federal lawmen made the Brownsville inquiry an "unprecedented move," in the words of one historian. But as Hoover quickly learned, it was one thing to be willing to take on a lynching investigation; it was quite another to know how to do it effectively. The case fit the parameters of the Reconstruction statutes: the victim had been brought to a police station ("under color of law") to be interrogated about his voting-rights work (federally protected activity), only to be released into the hands of a mob, then found dead three days later in a nearby river. When it came time to establish the details of what had happened, however, Hoover's men found that few of their tried-and-true investigative techniques seemed to work. Local law enforcement refused to cooperate. Witnesses would not come forward. The Bureau agent assigned to the case seemed to have little sense of how power relations around town really worked. At one low point, he unwittingly brought a member of the lynch mob itself to help conduct interviews with the town's Black residents. With little to go on, the Justice Department chose not to convene a federal grand jury. And a Tennessee grand jury declined to hand down indictments.[4]

Despite that early failure, Roosevelt and Biddle pressed ahead—and, therefore, so did Hoover. In February 1942, the FBI sent agents into Sikeston, Missouri, to inquire into the death of a Black man who had been seized from jail, shot, tied to the back of a car, dragged through town, covered with gasoline, and then set on fire. The cruelty of the crime was staggering. With mobilization underway, it also seemed to pose a threat to American war aims. All too quickly, the lynching became "a matter of international importance and a subject of Axis propaganda," the Justice Department noted. Showing that the American system could bring justice thus became a critical part of the war effort.[5]

Eight months later, FBI agents were in Mississippi to investigate the deaths of two teenage boys, just fourteen and fifteen years old, who had been taken from jail near the town of Shubuta and hanged from opposite ends of a bridge, plunging fourteen feet before rough rope nooses finally broke their necks. Five days after that, another Mississippi lynching, this one in the town of Laurel, demanded yet another FBI investigation. In that case, the Black victim had been tried and convicted in court for murdering his white boss. When the jury deadlocked on whether to impose the death penalty, a local crowd abducted him from jail and carried out the penalty themselves.[6]

Hoover put pressure on his agents to deliver results in such cases "without fail." While their investigative performance improved somewhat, they ended up with little to show for it. Upon approaching white residents, Hoover's men ran into a "wall of silence," as he described it, far more extreme than in any other area of Bureau activity. Black residents, too, shied away from revealing anything of significance, for fear of violent retaliation from their white bosses and neighbors. And when the time came for prosecution, the Justice Department failed to make any charges stick. The federal process relied on local citizens; the U.S. Constitution required that trials take place in the district where the alleged crime was committed. The results in lynching cases were all too predictable. In Sikeston, a federal grand jury reviewed the FBI's evidence only to declare that no federal crime had been committed. In Shubuta, where the "extreme youth" of the victims called for "special attention," the Bureau managed to identify several culprits but the federal grand jury issued no indictments. In Laurel, the Justice Department secured five indictments and took the case to trial, only to have a jury declare all the defendants not guilty.

The collapse of case after case inspired a certain amount of defeatism in Washington. The most the Justice Department could hope for in convening a grand jury, one official noted, was that "at least the record will then disclose we have done our utmost." At the White House, though, Roosevelt would not give up. During the 1930s, he had expressed great ambivalence about federal civil rights measures. Under wartime pressures, he instructed Hoover and Biddle to investigate any murder in the South that met the parameters of a lynching, to publicize the results widely, and to make sure that the crimes were "vigorously prosecuted." And so they tried again in 1943—now in Baker County, Georgia, where a sheriff named Claude Screws was accused of beating a Black prisoner named Robert Hall to death with an iron blackjack. They made some progress, not only securing federal indictments against three police officials but also winning highly unusual convictions. Then the Supreme Court intervened and ruined it all. In 1945, the court ruled that because Sheriff Screws had not specifically intended to deprive his victim of a federal right, such as voting, there was no federal violation in his case. Once again, Hoover's efforts were for naught.[7]

Screws himself went on to be elected to the Georgia state senate, in a gesture of collective defiance. Still, there were glimmers of hope in what the Bureau and the Justice Department had accomplished during the war. At least one jury had delivered a set of convictions—no small feat. And the number of lynchings seemed to be in decline: from 28 in 1933 to 5 in 1940 and 2 in 1944. As with his global intelligence efforts, Hoover initially had every reason to assume that the work begun during the war would carry on into the postwar years.[8]

MANY BLACK LEADERS LOOKED TO THE END OF THE WAR WITH A SENSE OF OP-timism, hopeful that the fight against fascism, with its policies of racial genocide, might make Americans think twice about their own history of segregation, violence, and white supremacy. But far from launching an era of peaceful coexistence in American race relations, the first months of 1946 produced what the NACCP's Walter White characterized in a letter to Hoover as a "well-organized campaign of terrorism." Some of the worst attacks were aimed at Black veterans, who returned home to a heightened atmosphere of racism, hostility, and violence. On February 12, police in Batesburg, South Carolina, pulled Sergeant Isaac Woodard off an interstate bus and beat him senseless; when Woodard regained consciousness, he discovered that he was blind. Less than two weeks later, a white mob in Columbia, Tennessee, descended on the Black section of town, pillaging homes and attacking residents in a reprise of the wartime conflicts in cities such as Detroit and Chicago.[9]

The NAACP publicized both of these cases, demanding federal action to hold the perpetrators to account. The organization focused special attention on Woodard, who was still in his army uniform at the moment of the attack. Prodded along by public pressure as well as Justice Department instructions, Hoover sent agents to investigate, only to run into the same obstacles he had encountered during the war. In Batesburg, the FBI easily identified the local police chief as one of Woodard's assailants; an all-white jury acquitted him in federal court just as easily. In Columbia, agents conducted 390 interviews. Then a federal grand jury declined to indict any of the participants on grounds that the white mob's actions were "not unreasonable."[10]

The cases kept coming, each one a challenge not just to Hoover's vaunted G-Man record, but to the entire notion of federal authority on Southern soil. The most shocking attack occurred in Monroe, Georgia, a small town about an hour east of Atlanta. There, on July 25, a mob of white men forced two Black couples out of a car and shot them at point-blank range near the Moore's Ford Bridge. One of the victims, a farm laborer named Roger Malcom, had recently stabbed a white neighbor. When the lynching occurred, Malcom was being driven home from jail by his white landlord, accompanied by his wife, sister-in-law, and brother-in-law, who was an army veteran. The astonishing body count—four victims in a single afternoon—made it the "Nation's Worst Lynching," in the words of the *Atlanta Daily World*. Even as the NAACP reached out to the White House and the Justice Department, demanding to know what the federal government planned to do about the massacre, Hoover was preparing to dispatch agents to the scene.[11]

More than any previous test case, the Moore's Ford lynchings posed a simple but powerful challenge: Could a group of white men murder four Black people—two of them women, one of them a U.S. Army veteran—and get away with it? Citizens from across the country wrote to Hoover, insisting that the answer had to be no. "We don't want this crime whitewashed as other lynchings have been in the South," a group of Pennsylvania veterans declared, pleading for a serious investigation. Another letter-writer pointed out that the FBI's reputation was on the line. "You gotta prove to the whole round world right now that the FBI means business," read the anonymous note. "If it can get Capone and Dillinger, then it can get those mobsters down in Georgia if it wants to."[12]

By 1946, though, Hoover was starting to believe that it would not be quite so simple. There were the problems of jurisdiction and expertise, of the local authorities' lack of cooperation and the roadblocks in the courts. Though Hoover was loath to acknowledge it, there also were serious problems within the FBI. His all-white agent corps found it difficult to earn the trust of Black residents. Sometimes they did not even care to do so. Hoover had built the FBI in part on the model of Kappa Alpha, with all the racism—both personal and institutional—that such an approach entailed. Though he now might want to deliver in lynching cases, he had constructed an investigative force with a powerful set of internal obstacles.

He forged ahead anyway, approving a squad of twenty agents, plus stenographers and clerks, dedicated exclusively to the Georgia case. In instructions issued six days after the murders, Truman asked only that the FBI "ascertain if any federal statute can be applied to the apprehension and prosecution of the criminals." Hoover pushed his agents to go further than that, to seek not only evidence of a federal violation but also a solution to the crime itself. Over the next four months, FBI agents interviewed a whopping 2,790 people in and around Monroe, and wrote up more than ten thousand pages of reports. "Never have FBI Agents worked harder in the interests of justice," Hoover later maintained. He cited "the disgraceful killing in cold blood of four Negroes in Monroe, Georgia" as one the largest and most challenging investigations he had ever undertaken.[13]

But hard work was not enough. In interview after interview, white townspeople lied to FBI agents, purporting to know nothing about the events at Moore's Ford. They also expressed contempt for the Bureau as an invading federal force with no right to interfere in Southern affairs. "We were the most unpopular people who ever invaded Walton County," one agent recalled. That unpopularity sometimes rose to the level of physical danger. Bureau employees took to traveling in pairs, especially in "backwoods sections," in the words of one Bureau report, where "irresponsible and excitable people" threatened them with further violence.

Black residents, too, hesitated to work with the Bureau, less out of hostility to the federal presence than out of fear that what had happened to Roger Malcom and his three companions might be visited upon them as well. "The negro residents of that territory are frightened and even terrified when approached for information," a local agent informed Hoover. In an attempt to accommodate their concerns—and induce them to talk—agents tested out new techniques: interviewing everyone in a given neighborhood to avoid singling out any individual; meeting with potential witnesses in secret; actively countermanding rumors that white employers would know everything Black witnesses told the FBI. Worried that it was pointless to continue under such conditions, Hoover tried belatedly to pull back from the case. The attorney general ordered him to finish what he had started.[14]

After months of this dance, the FBI settled on ten suspects, including the white landlord who had bailed Malcom out of jail and driven his group to Moore's Ford. But they failed to come up with the murder weapon or much else in the way of physical evidence, since the lynching site had been well trampled and picked over by the time the first agents appeared. Hoover anticipated that a federal grand jury would reject their efforts—not just on evidentiary grounds, but as a matter of jurisdiction. "The most sound finding which the current grand jury could make would be that the thorough and complete investigation by the FBI, as presented to the grand jury, fails to disclose any evidence of a violation of a federal statute," Hoover warned the attorney general.[15]

Over the course of sixteen days, the grand jury heard from 106 witnesses, an extended display of the Bureau's diligence. In late December, five months after the lynchings first made headlines, the grand jury returned only a single indictment. It was for lying to an FBI agent.[16]

———

HOOVER CAME AWAY FROM THE GEORGIA CASE SIMMERING WITH FRUSTRA-
tion. He recognized that the FBI had made certain mistakes, such as arriving too late
to the crime scene and assigning an initial supervisory agent who was "both stupid and
has a bad character." Mostly, though, he blamed circumstances beyond his control. He
insisted that "lack of law and not the lack of interest" hobbled the FBI's efforts—that
he wanted nothing more than to hold lynch mobs and violent police officials to account. But after six years of "test cases," he concluded that there was little point in
continuing. In a rare confession of weakness, he admitted that "the work of the Department and the Bureau is completely ineffective, both as a deterrent and as a punitive
force." Without a federal anti-lynching law, he concluded, the FBI and the Justice Department would run up against the same obstacles again and again. "Regardless of
whether we like it," he wrote to the attorney general, "it is a fact that the Federal Statutes penalizing violations of civil liberties are inadequate weapons for efficient enforcement." Under the circumstances, he argued, it would be better to abandon lynching
work than to risk further humiliation.[17]

For now, at any rate, there was plenty of humiliation to go around. The Georgia case
had been a national sensation. So the news of its failure was a national story, too. "The
FBI knows its prestige will suffer if it fails to produce results," a syndicated article had
warned in October, around the time Hoover tried to back out of the case. Even as
Hoover earned plaudits for his success at vanquishing the Nazis, headlines complained
that "FBI Lagging in Monroe, Ga. Lynch Probe." His most radical critics seized upon
the issue to call for "the removal of J. Edgar Hoover," in the words of *The Milwaukee
Journal*, "for failing to bring the lynchers to justice." Hoover worried that worse was
yet to come. "I fear it is just the beginning of a series of editorials which will appear in
various papers of the country unless we do two things," he wrote. "It is imperative that
the civil rights cases be very promptly and vigorously handled and most carefully supervised, both in the field and at Washington." Otherwise, he thought, the federal
authorities should back out altogether.[18]

He quickly found that it was too late to get away, however. Hoover's investment
of time and resources in Monroe did little to stop outbreaks of violence elsewhere in
the South—or to keep the FBI from being pulled into still more "test" cases. Throughout the Monroe investigation, the FBI was conducting inquiries into several other
high-profile incidents of racial violence in the Deep South. Only one resulted in a
federal conviction, and even that verdict hardly produced a fitting punishment. In
Florida, a constable had whipped a Black farmhand and then forced him to drown in
the river. For those actions, the policeman earned a one-year sentence and a thousand-
dollar fine.[19]

———

WITH THE CASE-BY-CASE APPROACH INCREASINGLY STYMIED, TRUMAN DE-cided that something more needed to be done. On September 19, 1946, during the run-up to the midterm elections, he met at the White House with the National Emergency Committee Against Mob Violence, a hastily assembled conglomeration of civil rights groups who were calling for more aggressive federal action. Truman had just dealt the final blow to Hoover's Special Intelligence Service, pushing the FBI out of global intelligence. When it came to lynching, though, he wanted Hoover to expand rather than contract, to move deeper into the South and assert federal authority. At the White House meeting, Walter White read off the dismal tally of 1946: the blinding of Isaac Woodard, the riot in Columbia, Tennessee, the lynchings in Georgia. Truman found the stories wrenching. "My God!" he exclaimed. "I had no idea it was as terrible as that! We've got to do something!" [20]

Given everything the FBI had been trying to do—and everything Truman had just done to the FBI—Hoover was hardly inclined to sympathize with the president's pose of aggrieved innocence. On lynching, though, they found at least some area of common ground. Like Hoover, the president was no great believer in the social equality of the races; he used the n-word and found interracial marriage unacceptable. After the meeting with White, though, Truman concluded that the time had come to address the lynching question at the highest levels of government, and thus to move beyond the test-case approach. "I know you have been looking into the Tennessee and Georgia lynchings," he wrote to Attorney General Clark, "but I think it is going to take something more than the handling of each individual case after it happens—it's going to require the inauguration of some sort of policy to prevent such happenings." At the end of 1946, he announced the creation of the President's Committee on Civil Rights, to study "individuals who take the law into their own hands and inflict summary punishment," among other subjects, and to decide what the federal government should do with them. [21]

Despite his growing suspicion of Truman, Hoover backed the attempt to make lynching a national priority. "I hate lynchings," he wrote in 1947, "and hold in contempt anyone who would take the law in his own hands or tolerate another's playing the role of a barbaric executioner." He found it especially "deplorable" that so many white Southerners seemed willing to hide behind an "impenetrable veil of silence," choosing white supremacy over law and order. By contrast, he lauded Walter White and the NAACP for their courageous efforts in drawing attention to the issue. In the spring of 1947, not long after meeting with Truman, White asked Hoover for a brief statement endorsing the NAACP's work, to be used in the group's publicity and fundraising materials. Hoover wrote back immediately, praising the NAACP's fight for "equality, freedom and tolerance," all "essential in a democratic government." [22]

Hoover's endorsement of civil rights ended at the Bureau's front door; he continued to resist calls to reform the FBI's hiring policies. On lynching, though, he began to experiment with ways to make his agents more effective. In February 1947, two months after the collapse of the Georgia grand jury, a Black man named Willie Earle was lynched in South Carolina: cut, stabbed, and beaten before being shot in the face. In launching the investigation, Hoover tried to correct for the Bureau's mistakes at Moore's Ford. This time, the Bureau went in fast and tried to wrap up the case in days rather than months, before any "veil of silence" could settle over the town. Hoover tried to model a different relationship with the local authorities as well. The state's newly elected Democratic governor, Strom Thurmond, formally invited the FBI into South Carolina, declaring, "I do not favor lynching, and I shall exert every resource at my command to apprehend the persons who may be involved."

And the results, at first, seemed to suggest that the changes might stick. In less than a week, working in cooperation with the local authorities, Bureau agents helped to arrest thirty-one members of the lynch mob—a "record period of time," in the words of the supervising agent. No fewer than twenty-six of them confessed. The state authorities assured Hoover that they planned to prosecute the case, and to the surprise of federal officials, they came through. In early March, a South Carolina grand jury indicted all thirty-one men on charges of murder, accessory to murder, and conspiring to murder.[23]

WITH THIS MOMENTUM BEHIND HIM, HOOVER AGREED TO TESTIFY BEFORE Truman's committee, the first and only time that he would ever devote a major committee appearance primarily to the problem of lynching and civil rights. He took an active role in crafting his testimony, not content to let Crime Records handle such a sensitive subject. In a series of handwritten notes, he emphasized a desire to frame the Bureau's civil rights work not merely as a matter of legal obligation, but as part of an agenda to combat "man's intolerance of man—of denial of freedom; of tyranny; mob violence + murder." His opening statement hewed closely to these themes. "The great American crime is toleration of conditions which permit and promote prejudice, bigotry, injustice, terror and hate," he declared, before launching into descriptions of the Bureau's anti-lynching and civil rights work.[24]

He spoke of the FBI's investigations into Southern peonage, in which laborers (usually Black) were exploited, trapped, and forced by their employers (usually white) to work without wages. He talked of inquiries into Black voting rights, still limited in number but picking up over time. Both of these areas clearly fell under federal jurisdiction. But then there was lynching, the chief subject of Hoover's remarks. "No law of the jungle can approach the severity of lynch law and frenzied mob violence," he told the committee. But no federal law, he insisted, gave the FBI what it needed to investigate such violence effectively. His own statistics were bleak. Since the early 1920s, the FBI had amassed evidence in approximately 1,570 civil rights–related cases. Those investigations resulted in just twenty-seven convictions, twenty-five of them in the last five years.

In laying out the scope of the challenge, Hoover did not shy away from describing the "extreme brutality" visited upon lynching victims. On one occasion, he recalled, "an angry mob" rushed a jail and "seized the prisoner, tied his feet to a car and dragged him over the streets through the Negro section of town where his body was saturated with an inflammable liquid and burned." In another case, fifteen to twenty white men participated as a Black prisoner was "vigorously cursed, tied to the bars [of his cell], gagged and crudely emasculated," all while a friend and cellmate was forced to watch. Hoover expressed special contempt for the "terroristic slave master" who held Black citizens in fear as well as for the Southern police officials "who besmirch the good name of their chosen professions." Too often, Hoover insisted, it was sheriffs and constables—men sworn to uphold the law—who made the crime of lynching possible, either by looking the other way or by aiding and abetting the mob when it came calling. The complicity of local officials helped to explain why federal action was so vitally needed, he concluded, but also why it was so difficult at the moment.[25]

Then he took up the obvious question: Should Congress pass a federal anti-lynching law, and if so, what should that law entail? Hoover often maintained that his position as a nonpartisan law enforcement appointee precluded him from telling elected officials what to do. But he outlined what such a law might look like should Congress at last see fit to act. Even at this moment of opportunity, he argued for a limited definition of lynching. The category should apply not to all racially motivated crimes, he explained, but only to incidents in which a prisoner recently charged with a crime was seized from jail by a mob. Within those parameters, though, he called for expanding both the range of federal action and the scope of penalties available. He recommended that the law apply to private individuals, not just to law enforcement officers. He also recommended up to ten years in prison, plus a five-thousand-dollar fine, for anyone convicted under federal statutes. It was far less than a defendant might encounter if convicted of murder but more than the slap on the wrist currently available.[26]

THE COMMITTEE MEMBERS LIKED WHAT THEY HEARD. ON THE DAY AFTER Hoover's testimony, the executive secretary wrote with praise for his "magnificent job" at the witness table, and with a request for more detail about how Hoover's vision for stronger anti-lynching legislation might work. Still hoping to find common cause with the White House, Hoover responded by laying out the full range of federal rights that he believed ought to be protected from violent interference and intimidation, including the right to vote, to testify in court, to own property, to organize, assemble, strike, and picket, and to participate in federal governance—all in addition to the basic right to safety while in police custody. He argued that the FBI should not have to wait for Justice Department authorization in order to begin investigating such matters—implying that it was Justice, not the Bureau, that often dragged its feet during the first few critical days. Finally, he admitted that he, too, had more work to do, both in training his own agents and in helping to guide local police.[27]

Many of these ideas made it into the committee's report, *To Secure These Rights*, released in October 1947 to both plaudits and controversy. The report addressed a far wider range of issues than Hoover managed to cover in his testimony, including racial discrimination in housing, education, public accommodations, industrial employment, and military service. Still, some of its most powerful words addressed lynching and the role of the FBI. That situation had gone from bad to worse during the committee's deliberation, with hopes for case-by-case progress receding by the minute. Anyone who doubted this needed only look to South Carolina, where the Willie Earle trial—once so promising, with its swift investigation and thirty-one arrests—fell apart almost immediately. In May 1947, all thirty-one defendants were marched down to the courthouse under guard, their every move documented by a fleet of reporters and photographers from the national press. Less than two weeks later, after hearing the FBI's best evidence, the local jury returned a full slate of acquittals.[28]

The Black press held out hope that "Willie Earle may not have died in vain," that national outrage following his killers' acquittal would surely make him "the 'father' of a federal anti-lynching bill." The civil rights committee endorsed this idea, recommending the passage of an anti-lynching bill carrying penalties of up to twenty years in prison, plus a ten-thousand-dollar fine—twice as severe as what Hoover had proposed. About the "invaluable work" of the FBI and Justice Department the report had some kind things to say. "They deserve the highest praise for the imagination and courage they have shown," the report declared, singling out Hoover for his powerful testimony. At the same time, it highlighted many of the challenges he had identified, from the frustration of working with the "vaguely worded" federal statutes to the "hostility of local officers and local communities." The report also underscored just how new this sort of work still was for Hoover's men, who were "not always prepared to cope with the elusive and difficult aspects of a civil rights case." The committee stopped short of insisting that Hoover hire more Black agents, but it did recommend "more highly specialized training" for those already employed at the Bureau.[29]

Hoover was "keenly disappointed" by the criticism. He nonetheless acceded to the committee's instructions by incorporating civil rights work into the Bureau's biennial in-service training and brainstorming how to bring Southern departments better into line. Truman himself embraced nearly every aspect of the committee's report, delivering a landmark address on February 2, 1948, in which he urged Congress to pass civil rights legislation including a new federal law "to deal with the crime of lynching." Over the next several months, Truman did what he could from the White House, issuing an executive order to desegregate the military and committing himself to a civil rights platform, even at the risk of costing him the next election. South Carolina governor Strom Thurmond, the man who had invited Hoover to investigate the Willie Earle case, attempted to ensure that defeat by running for president on the new Dixiecrat ticket, hoping to pull white Southerners away from the Democratic Party in retaliation for Truman's civil rights stance.[30]

Though Thurmond failed to make much of a dent in Truman's campaign, Southern Democrats showed their political might by blocking anti-lynching legislation, dashing hopes for clear and unequivocal federal authority. Defeated once again, the NAACP and its allies began to give up hope for a federal anti-lynching law, applying their energies to more promising areas such as education and voting rights. Hoover, too, backed away from the issue, convinced that the possibility of greater authority in lynching investigations, like FBI control of global intelligence, was now a dead letter. He never again made a civil rights statement as powerful as his testimony before Truman's committee. Instead, he directed his energies toward the issue that would come to dominate his work and reputation in the postwar years: the problem of communism.

CHAPTER 28

The One Bulwark

(1941–1946)

Smells a Rat—By Jerry Costello

FBI

AMERICAN
COMMUNISTS

With the end of World War II, Hoover set his sights on the Communist Party, helping to spark the Second Red Scare. Cartoon by Jerry Costello, *Knickerbocker News* (Albany, New York), December 1945.

KNICKERBOCKER NEWS/
NATIONAL ARCHIVES AND
RECORDS ADMINISTRATION

W hen the press asked Hoover his priorities at the end of the war, he named communism as just one issue among many. His wartime speeches had assailed "foreign 'isms,'" including communism. But other matters, from the enemy alien problem to the potential for a postwar crime wave, received at least as much of his attention. In a major address to the police chiefs' annual convention in Miami Beach in December 1945, Hoover spoke of the FBI's triumphal war record, the need to raise police salaries, and an epidemic of postwar "lawlessness" allegedly starting to overtake American cities. The communists received just a few paragraphs, sandwiched between a critique of the nation's parole system and a disturbing portrait of its juvenile delinquents.[1]

That Hoover was not yet saying much about communism did not mean it was far from his mind, or that he was doing nothing about it. Even as Hoover wrangled with Truman about the future of lynching investigations and global intelligence, he was beginning to imagine—and to initiate—what would eventually become known as the second Red Scare. Like the first Red Scare, from 1919 to 1920, this one was rooted in war, with its vast expansions of FBI surveillance capacity. Hoover had continued to keep tabs on the Communist Party throughout the early 1940s: planting bugs and wiretaps in party offices, poring over membership lists and meeting plans, and above all cultivating human informants. He had kept much of this work quiet, however—in part to avoid another "smear campaign" from civil liberties advocates, in part because the Soviet Union was a critical U.S. ally.

He nonetheless came across some disturbing information—and it was this information, in addition to his long-standing hostility toward communism, that drove him to move the communist problem up on his list of priorities. According to Hoover's intelligence, the Soviet Union had been attempting to infiltrate the U.S. government for more than a decade, sending operatives to take up jobs and organize espionage rings throughout key federal agencies and industries. Working with them in this endeavor was the organization that Hoover had first learned to despise back in 1919: the Communist Party. The details and scope of their arrangement were still fuzzy in 1945, as Hoover sifted through the many possibilities for the FBI's postwar work. Over the next few years, as other options faded away, addressing that problem—and the broader challenges posed by domestic communism—became his chief purpose.

Many of the names brought to Hoover's attention during the war's final months would eventually become well known to the public: accused spies such as Alger Hiss and Harry Dexter White, along with accusers such as Whittaker Chambers and Elizabeth Bentley. First, though, they were part of a secret drama playing out within the federal government, as both the FBI and the Truman administration tried to make sense of the Soviet espionage problem and its implications. Though Hoover was not yet discussing the details in public, it is impossible to understand what came later without looking at what happened in 1944, 1945, and 1946, when Hoover secretly accelerated his surveillance efforts against the Communist Party, and when he first came to believe that he had a serious espionage problem on his hands.

Nearly every major feature of the postwar Red Scare—the investigations of government workers and Hollywood communists, the Hiss case and atomic spy trials, the congressional hearings, the prosecutions of the communist leaders—can be traced back to decisions and discoveries made during and immediately after the war, as the FBI struggled to choose between competing postwar visions. By the time the rest of the country understood that it was in a domestic Cold War, Hoover had already investigated many of the key players, and could boast of a well-developed supply of informants, files, and surveillance techniques at his disposal. Having turned away from other paths, whether by choice or by circumstance, he found his central postwar mission.

FOR MOST OF THE COUNTRY, THE NAZI INVASION OF RUSSIA IN JUNE 1941 PRO-duced a rapid change of sentiment: the Soviets, deemed traitors and enemies after the signing of the Nazi-Soviet Pact in 1939, were again suddenly allies in the anti-fascist fight, a crucial factor in the war against Hitler. Roosevelt had recognized their importance early on, praising Stalin for his renewed determination in facing down the Nazi threat and urging Americans to appreciate the staggering sacrifice of the Soviet people. In May 1942, as a goodwill gesture, Roosevelt commuted the sentence of Communist Party leader Earl Browder, condemned to a harsh four years in prison for passport fraud. Later that month, the president welcomed to Washington the very man who had negotiated the Nazi-Soviet pact, USSR foreign minister Vyacheslav Molotov. Roosevelt entertained Molotov at the White House, assuring him that the American people were behind the Russians 100 percent. Hollywood films such as *Mission to Moscow* picked up on that theme, depicting a benign Stalin ruling over the good-hearted and peace-seeking Russian masses. In newsreels, Americans learned of the Russians' valiant resistance to Nazi siege in the cities of Stalingrad and Leningrad. They responded with charity drives and solidarity actions.

The Communist Party had been part of this renaissance, embracing what one historian has described as "Russia's unprecedented popularity with the American public." During the harrowing twenty-two months between the signing of the pact and Hitler's invasion of Russia, party members had been pushed out of their Popular Front coalitions and into a liminal underground existence, reviled by former allies in the antifascist fight. After the invasion, the CP emerged from hiding, once again calling upon Americans to enact "National Unity for Victory over Nazi Enslavement," in the words of the *Daily Worker* newspaper. In the spring of 1943, Stalin abolished the Comintern, established in 1919 to unite the world's communist movements in global revolution. The following year, the Communist Party dissolved and reconstituted itself as the Communist Political Association, seeking mainstream acceptance as just another civic group. Fresh from the Atlanta penitentiary, Browder vowed to do away with the "old formulas and practices," and to refashion American communism for a new era of U.S-Soviet cooperation.[2]

Hoover never accepted this about-face. Despite the Soviets' importance to the war effort, he refused to believe that the CPUSA—his bête noire two decades earlier—had simply abandoned its old ideological commitments. And so he changed almost nothing about his own formulas and practices after 1941. Once the Soviets became American allies, Hoover continued to authorize surveillance of CP offices, where agents conducted regular break-ins in order to plant microphones and photograph membership lists. With that information in hand, they frequently approached employers—especially plant managers or others engaged in defense work—to warn of communists on the payroll. Hoover kept leading party members on the custodial detention index, subject to arrest and possible internment in the event of war with the Soviet Union. As the communist writer Sender Garlin noted in 1943, this was a strange way to treat an ally. "Hoover's action in placing Communists in the same category as the sworn foes of America and the United Nations coalition is certainly at variance with current developments," he wrote.[3]

Though the FBI tracked communist activity throughout the country, Hoover devoted special attention to what the party was doing in Hollywood, especially once films praising the Soviet war effort and the Russian people began to appear on American screens. In 1942, he authorized an investigation known as COMPIC (Communist Infiltration–Motion Picture Industry), intended to assess communist influence on American films. An early report estimated that "about half of the unions" in Hollywood "appear to be controlled by the Communists or follow the Communist Party line." But Hoover's real concern lay with the "intellectuals, particularly the writers, directors, actors and artists"—"the so-called cultural field"—who were allegedly propagating pro-Soviet ideas. The investigation produced long lists of communist sympathizers and party members in and around Hollywood. Among them were many of the screenwriters, actors, and directors whose names would later emerge as subjects of postwar controversy.[4]

Hoover took a similarly aggressive approach in Washington itself. Under a provision of the Hatch Act of 1939, no federal employee was henceforth permitted to belong to any organization advocating the overthrow of the government. In June 1941, Congress had apportioned $100,000 for the FBI to investigate any employees who seemed to fall into that category. Many (though not all) were alleged to be members of the Communist Party. By the start of the following year, 656 federal employees had been subjected to such "loyalty" investigations, with 125 FBI agents assigned to this new realm of work alone. The Bureau's efforts produced only a small number of firings and reprimands; of the 5,068 cases completed by the middle of 1943, 53 federal workers lost their jobs, while 44 others were subject to "administrative action other than dismissal." But like the Hollywood investigation, the loyalty queries yielded background information on thousands of men and women, stored away for later use. They also provided early practice for what would become one of the FBI's most controversial postwar duties.[5]

Hoover passed along reports of communist activity to the Roosevelt White House, making no secret of what he was up to. Though Roosevelt expressed little objection to Hoover's methods, the president questioned devoting so many resources to communism when other wartime priorities seemed more pressing. In the spring of 1942, he instructed Hoover, via the attorney general, to direct his energies elsewhere. Hoover wrote back an apologetic but indignant memo, suggesting that "the president has reached this conclusion" only because "he must have been misinformed as to the facts and record." Then the FBI continued what it was doing.[6]

As the war went on, communist activities occupied more and more of the FBI's resources, even as the CP attempted to rebrand itself as an ordinary political group. Hoover recognized "the controversial character" of singling out a domestic political organization, as he admitted to the House Appropriations Committee, especially given the backlash and criticism he had encountered so many times in the past. By the end of the war, however, he felt vindicated in his decision to carry on. In April 1945, as the Red Army closed in on Berlin, a French communist journal published a letter by a prominent party leader accusing Browder's Communist Political Association of betraying essential revolutionary and ideological commitments. Back in the U.S., party members understood the letter as a signal from Moscow to change course away from their accommodationist wartime stance. In a July 1945 meeting, they voted to resume a more militant position, ousting Browder in favor of the hard-liner William Z. Foster. Looking back on that turn of events, Browder reflected that the letter from France had been "the first *public* declaration of the Cold War," a sign that the postwar order would not yield peace and comity either abroad or at home. At Hoover's FBI, the struggle had already been underway for years.[7]

MANY OF HOOVER'S BELIEFS AND SUSPICIONS ABOUT COMMUNISM CAN BE traced back to his early years at the Radical Division, those crucial months of discovery and alarm as he watched the first American communist parties come into being. As in 1919, he viewed the party of the 1940s as an avowedly revolutionary organization, one that meant what it said when it spoke of taking over the government. Though there were no more reports of bomb plots and assassination attempts as there had been a generation earlier, Hoover remained convinced that the party supported violence and therefore operated, in effect, as a criminal conspiracy. He took no comfort from its small membership—less than a hundred thousand at its peak. What mattered to Hoover was the supposedly fanatical commitment of those members: to the party, to the Soviet Union, and to a social vision fundamentally at odds with an American way of life. On this subject Hoover remained the reactionary he had always been, inclined to see communism as a challenge to the racial, religious, and social principles he held most dear. To him, it did not matter that American communists had never come close to mounting an actual revolution, or even becoming a truly mass movement. The crucial fact, in his view, was that they would if they could. Hoover believed it was his mission to stop them.

If Hoover relied upon certain ideas forged during his early years at the Radical Division, the war also brought several important discoveries that would make the so-called second Red Scare substantially different from the first. Among them were a series of revelations about the existence of a "communist underground," a network of secret party members and Soviet operatives spread throughout the government and key national industries. During the war, Hoover learned of allegations that dozens of federal employees—including several high-ranking government officials—maintained clandestine relationships with the Communist Party. He also confronted the first credible evidence of Soviet espionage operations on U.S. soil. Though he could not yet prove his allegations, Hoover came away from the war convinced that both the Communist Party and the Soviet Union were actively seeking to undermine the U.S. government from within.

One of the earliest sketches of the party's covert activities came from a *Time* magazine editor and former communist named Whittaker Chambers, who approached the government in August 1939 with an incredible tale. Within a decade, Chambers would be one of the most famous men in America, his allegations the stuff of fierce national debate. First, though, he was part of Hoover's wartime education, one of several ex-communists who alerted the FBI to the existence of a clandestine world. Chambers had a reputation as an odd character around *Time*, where he often showed up at the office looking as if he had slept in his rumpled suit. What he conveyed to the government was even stranger. During the 1920s and 1930s, Chambers claimed, he had been a courier and contact for a secret network of communists within the federal government. While he had broken with the party in 1938, he had never told anyone in government about his former life. On September 2, 1939, the day after the German army marched into Poland, he flew from New York to Washington to meet with Assistant Secretary of State Adolf Berle, who offered to convey his story to the president. Seated under a thick canopy of trees at Berle's estate, drinking scotch and soda, Chambers poured out what would eventually become one of the most famous and contested stories in the history of American communism.

Several of the contacts Chambers identified that day were New Deal officials of Hoover's least favorite sort—perfect specimens of reformist technocracy, groomed at Harvard and Yale, vetted through Supreme Court clerkships and Ivy League social clubs. They bore unusual aristocratic names: Lauchlin Currie at the White House, Laurence Duggan and Alger Hiss at the State Department. Eventually, it would be Hiss who attracted the greatest attention and controversy, his name forever linked to Chambers. In 1939, though, when Chambers first told his story, Hiss was just one of the names on offer.[8]

Several months passed before Hoover learned of the interview with Berle, and another several years before the FBI did much with the information. In the meantime, Hoover's files on Soviet espionage grew in fits and starts. No single incident produced much in the way of prosecution or public notice. In the aggregate, though, they provided a growing body of evidence documenting "a vast illegal and conspirative Russian-controlled and dominated" espionage apparatus operating within the United States. The summary report offering those conclusions was prepared in December 1944 and ran more than six hundred pages, an early attempt to codify what the FBI knew and what it had yet to learn. Like Hoover's landmark 1919 briefs on the Communist and Communist Labor Parties, the report traveled back into Russian history, analyzing the Bolshevik Revolution before moving on to Lenin's death, Stalin's rise, and the gradual establishment of an international Soviet espionage network. According to the report, the Russians had begun to target the U.S. for espionage and infiltration as early as the Coolidge years. They stepped up their efforts considerably under Roosevelt, when the U.S. formally recognized the Soviet Union and the New Deal opened opportunities for communist sympathizers to seek out government employment. By late 1944, the FBI concluded, the Soviets appeared to have a thriving "political parallel" within American government and civic organizations, especially in groups devoted to labor, anti-fascist, and civil rights work. More ominously, they also seemed to have a robust network of men and women working inside war plants and scientific labs to steal and pass along technical secrets. The FBI's report warned that the Soviets had likely penetrated the greatest of all U.S. war projects: the "scientific experimental program to perfect an explosive of phenomenal destructiveness utilizing atomic energy," still underway in December 1944.

The report argued that the wartime authorities needed to take these incursions seriously, despite their vast menu of competing wartime claims and interests, and despite the fact that the Soviets remained an indispensable wartime ally. At the same time, it could offer only the barest outline of the full "conspiracy," or of the many sites where it might be underway. The report gave a handful of names, as well as a vast array of party officials and leaders of front groups. What stood out in the moment, however, was everything the FBI did not yet know. "The number of possible Soviet espionage agents in this country is very large," the report noted. Hoover was just beginning to sort out the details.[9]

TRUMAN SHOWED LITTLE OF ROOSEVELT'S FLEXIBILITY AND GOODWILL TO-ward the Soviet government. In late April 1945, when Molotov returned to Washington, the president lashed out with what he proudly described as a "one-two to the jaw," accusing the Soviets of acting in bad faith and failing to keep their promise to support a democratic Poland. During those early days, Hoover held out hope that the FBI and the White House might work together against the common Soviet foe, just as he had hoped they might work together on global intelligence. But things quickly fell apart here, too—and for many of the same reasons.[10]

In May 1945, as Hitler's regime collapsed throughout Europe, Hoover sent agents back to interview Chambers at *Time*, reviewing the names and scenarios the ex-communist had first described some six years earlier. One conversation continued for eight hours straight and yielded twenty-two new pages of documentation, including elaboration of the charge that the State Department's Alger Hiss had been one of Chambers's underground contacts. The following month, Hoover approved an unrelated raid on the Washington office of *Amerasia*, a left-leaning journal focused on Pacific affairs. There, agents uncovered hundreds of government documents, many of them classified, all of them presumably leaked or stolen from federal offices such as the

State Department and OSS. Though attempts to prosecute the magazine's editors mostly stalled out, Hoover came away from the arrests more convinced than ever that the swirl of allegations about spies in high places—including at the State Department—was worth pursuing.[11]

With the end of the Pacific war, what had been a trickle of information became a flood. On September 12, as OSS was winding down, Hoover wrote to the White House with news that a code clerk (subsequently identified as Igor Gouzenko) had defected from the Soviet embassy in Ottawa, Canada, with a cache of files showing "that the Soviets have an extensive espionage network in Canada." Once the Canadians permitted the FBI to interview Gouzenko, Hoover sent a follow-up report outlining what the confession seemed to indicate about conditions in the United States. In contrast to his 1944 report to Roosevelt, which had described a set of amorphous fears, this one offered a detailed account of the Soviet espionage structure. Though Gouzenko mostly knew about spies within the Canadian network, the report made it clear that "there were, of course, more agents in the United States."[12]

Further confirmation of this idea came when Louis Budenz, managing editor of the *Daily Worker*, announced in October 1945 that he was abandoning communism for Catholicism—and that he was ready to talk. In a savvy publicity stunt, Budenz let the press know the date and time of his baptism at New York's St. Patrick's Cathedral; radio commentators read his declaration of conversion on the air, relishing its description of communism as a form of "tyranny over the human spirit." Budenz spoke with the FBI over the course of five days in November, offering up personal contacts and inside knowledge gleaned from a decade in the communist orbit. As an editor rather than a member of the underground, Budenz possessed little firsthand knowledge about espionage or other clandestine activities. But he gave Hoover something arguably as valuable: testimony that the Communist Party actively engaged in recruiting and coordinating spies. Even Chambers had not yet gone quite so far, mostly describing his government contacts as communist sympathizers eager to help the American party, not necessarily the Soviet government. Budenz went on to declare that "the Communist Party in the United States is a direct arm of the Soviet Foreign Department." Any party member, he suggested, should be considered "a potential spy against the United States."[13]

Then came a confession so detailed, from such a compelling source, that it raised Hoover's alarm to another level entirely. On November 7, 1945, after several missteps and false starts, a thirty-seven-year-old Vassar graduate named Elizabeth Bentley began to talk with the Bureau about her own experience as a Soviet contact and courier. What Bentley told the Bureau she would eventually reveal to the world—in controversial appearances before congressional committees and trial juries, in news serials and a sensational autobiography. For more than two years, though, Hoover had a quiet monopoly on her information, and the chance to act upon it outside public view. Over the course of eight hours on November 7, and then for many days thereafter, Bentley laid out her life story for the FBI, starting with her New England childhood, her foreign-language studies, and her politically formative trip to fascist Italy. In the mid-1930s, back at home but worried about the state of the world, she joined the Communist Party. There she met Jacob Golos, a short and plump, intensely charismatic older man who invited her to join him in the communist underground. By the early 1940s, they were in love and spending most of their time together. Along the way Golos revealed the full scope of his work as a courier for secret Soviet contacts in the U.S. government. When he died in 1943, Bentley took over his routes and sources.

The agents who interviewed her that first day were struck not only by the astounding nature of her story but also by her skill at recall: the fact she could identify, often by name, though sometimes just by description, the many sources who provided her with information, as their officially designated courier. Some of them were shockingly high up in government, with access to important documents and real influence over federal decisions. According to Bentley, no less a personage than Harry Dexter White, the Columbia-, Stanford-, and Harvard-groomed assistant secretary of the Treasury, regularly passed information and documents to Nathan Gregory Silvermaster, a mid-ranking Treasury economist and committed Soviet operative. From there, Silvermaster took the documents home and photographed them in a secret basement lab.

And that was just one department. At the White House, Bentley named Lauchlin Currie, a former administrative assistant to Roosevelt, privy to many of the former president's secrets, as a friend of the party. At OSS, she identified no fewer than five Soviet sources, including Duncan Lee, a young confidential assistant to Donovan. Outside of government, she claimed, the columnist Walter Lippmann was unknowingly harboring a Soviet operative as his personal secretary, with access to everything that came across his desk. Bentley's bosses had even tried to plant someone at the FBI as a clerk or stenographer, she informed the interviewing agents, "some suitable American fellow who could qualify" for work on Soviet-related activities. To Hoover's relief, and perhaps to his credit, Bentley maintained that the FBI was "the only government agency that they could not crack."[14]

HOOVER HAD RECEIVED THE FIRST REPORTS ON BENTLEY'S CONFESSION ON THE morning of Thursday, November 8. He immediately prepared a "top secret" summary for the White House. Hoover acknowledged that much of Bentley's information was still "preliminary," but he was inclined to believe her. "A number of persons employed by the Government of the United States have been furnishing data and information to persons outside the Federal Government, who are in turn transmitting this information to espionage agents of the Soviet Government," he wrote. Hoover also passed along several names and promised a "vigorous investigation for the purpose of establishing the degree and nature of the complicity of these people in this espionage ring."[15]

Over the next few weeks his men conducted an investigation on a scale not seen since the saboteurs case, when Hoover had thrown hundreds of agents into tracking down the suspects, all while keeping the case out of public view. On November 9, the Washington field office dispatched two agents to New York for an urgent planning meeting to determine which "technical, physical and other investigative procedures" would be of greatest use in proving Bentley's claims. Discussion stressed the unprecedented nature of the opportunity before them. Though Bentley was no longer an active courier, she believed that her ring was still functioning, with coordination run through the Soviet embassy. And there was no reason, as yet, to think that her former contacts knew of her defection. Between them, these factors raised the possibility that the Bureau would be able to watch Soviet espionage in action, and to gather hard evidence about what had heretofore been mostly conjecture and rumor. "We shall bear down + expedite all angles of this," Hoover instructed.[16]

An effort of this scale would have been far more difficult without the FBI's wartime experience—not only the learning that had occurred in the realm of counterintelligence but also the technological and administrative infrastructure that had made such a large-scale surveillance effort possible. The war left the Bureau with thousands of files on real and alleged communists, individual portraits that could now be checked against Bentley's descriptions. As far as Hoover was concerned, Roosevelt's 1940 directive authorizing wiretapping in the name of national security was still in effect. Recalling the lessons imparted by British intelligence, Hoover approved a plan to reactivate Bentley as a double agent, back inside her old Soviet ring. In the meantime, she was to be squeezed for every bit of the "tremendous amount of information that this woman has in her possession." To ensure that her identity remained secret, Hoover approved the male code name Gregory.[17]

By early December, more than two hundred agents were at work on the Gregory plot, "the most important case confronting the Bureau at the present time," in the words of one official. Their activities included the delicate task of investigating the government employees named by Bentley (and, earlier, by Chambers), at least two of whom—Harry Dexter White and Alger Hiss—maintained prominent roles in the Truman administration. As assistant secretary of the Treasury in charge of monetary research, Harry Dexter White had helped to negotiate the 1944 Bretton Woods agreements establishing the World Bank and International Monetary Fund. Under Truman, a report noted, he "not only has access to much vital financial information, but actually makes international financial policy." From his post at State, Alger Hiss had attended the February 1945 Yalta talks and presided at the opening of the United Nations in San Francisco as its secretary general. As of late 1945, he was still employed at the State

Department as director of special political affairs. By November 10, Hoover had issued instructions for Bureau agents to locate both men, along with "various individuals" mentioned by Bentley, in order "to survey the possibility of technical or microphone surveillances." The following week, he wrote to the attorney general to request wiretaps on White, Hiss, and several other federal employees "for the purpose of determining the extent" of their involvement in "the field of espionage."[18]

To supplement the wiretaps, Hoover authorized an expansive program of physical surveillance, beginning with the labor-intensive work of tracking and following everyone involved. For weeks, agents watched as suspects traveled between home and work, ran their errands, and attended holiday parties. Bentley herself was not exempt from suspicion. Throughout November, she continued to be questioned intensively "in order that a more detailed and chronological account of the facts in her possession can be obtained." Along the way, the Bureau devised periodic tests for her, measures of her veracity and commitment. In mid-November, at the Bureau's behest, she set up a meeting with the first secretary of the Soviet embassy, alleged to be her chief contact with the Soviet government. Though he rebuffed her plea to reenter espionage work (thus quashing Hoover's plan to run her as a double agent), the fact that he showed up in the first place seemed to affirm her credibility to the FBI. And when agents cross-referenced her confession with the Bureau's wartime files and other sources, they "generally substantiated" much of what she said.[19]

According to Hoover's original plan, this spadework should have led to a quick triumph: catching somebody—any one of Bentley's names—in the act of passing along pilfered materials. By early December, though, he was starting to notice something amiss. Despite instructions to "become bolder and more ingenious" in their tactics, agents were repeatedly coming up empty-handed, unable to document even a single illegal act. On December 6, a month into the investigation, Bureau official Mickey Ladd affirmed to Hoover that serious obstacles seemed to be thwarting the investigation. The problem, as Ladd described it, was that Bentley had no tangible evidence to back up her story: no secret document or stray bit of microfilm squirreled away to show that she was who she said she was, or that she had done what she said she had. As a result, a month into one of the largest investigations in its history, the Bureau had nothing but a web of circumstantial evidence to support her story.[20]

HISTORY WOULD EVENTUALLY BEAR OUT MUCH OF BENTLEY'S TESTIMONY. AT the time, though, it looked to many insiders as if Hoover simply did not know what he was talking about. Certainly Truman thought as much, dismissing the string of urgent FBI memos as just so much hogwash, the impugning of well-respected government servants based on conjecture rather than evidence. In January 1946, just as he was launching the Central Intelligence Group, he showed Hoover what he thought of the accusations by nominating Harry Dexter White, the assistant secretary supposedly at the heart of Bentley's Treasury Department ring, to serve as the first American executive director of the new International Monetary Fund.

Hoover responded to this news in much the same way he had responded to reports of the CIG's creation—not by backing away, but by refusing to concede an inch. On January 30, he instructed Ladd "at once" to prepare a summary memo for the White House laying out the "seriousness of the charges against White" and the need for urgent action. He assured the White House that what was known was already sufficient cause for alarm, and that "in no instance" would the FBI pass along information of unknown value or reliability. What the memo actually described, however, was far more ambiguous. While Hoover acknowledged that it had become "practically impossible" to prove Bentley's charges, he insisted that a wealth of circumstantial evidence pointed in White's direction. For instance, the Bureau had found a photo lab and enlarger in the basement of White's Treasury employee and friend Silvermaster, just where Bentley had said they would be.[21]

Those allegations set off a brief flurry of activity at the White House. In the end, however, Truman found a stray camera insufficient evidence on which to impugn a career government servant. So he ignored Hoover's warnings, just as he had ignored Hoover's appeals on global intelligence. In late April, the Washington papers announced a grand farewell party at the Statler Hotel for several top Treasury officials—including White, off to assume his new job as executive director of the IMF. In announcing the departure, Truman offered a personal tribute to White. "I am confident that in your new position, you will add distinction to your already-distinguished career with the Treasury." There is no evidence the president even tried to contact Hoover.[22]

HOOVER WOULD EVENTUALLY HAVE THE FINAL SAY IN THE WHITE CASE. BUT that was years away, on the other side of a political saga that would turn White as well as Hiss, Bentley, and Chambers into national celebrities. In 1946, Hoover concluded mainly that the Truman administration could not be relied upon, in communist investigations or any other form of intelligence. He passed this attitude along to the rest of the Bureau, where a powerful sense of purpose—but also of grievance—began to take hold over the course of 1946. "With most of the intelligence and counterespionage organizations of the United States Government virtually in the process of disintegration and losing their best men," Ladd wrote to Hoover that spring, the FBI would have to chart its own course. Because even the president could not be counted upon to take the threat of subterfuge seriously, he added, "the Bureau stands as the one bulwark against the peril of Communism."[23]

That idea—that the FBI would have to take to the lead, the "one bulwark" against the growing communist challenge—lasted well beyond the temporary disappointments of the immediate postwar months. On lynching and global intelligence, Hoover largely gave up, abandoning areas where he believed the obstacles to success had become too great. When it came to communism, he doubled down. Hoover emerged from his early inquiries into Soviet espionage convinced that "a vast illegal conspiracy," as he had described it to Roosevelt, still threatened the country. So that spring, as the Bentley case collapsed around him, he went looking for new allies—not at the White House but in Congress, where he found no shortage of sympathy.

CHAPTER 29

Un-American Activities

(1946–1947)

Hoover on the cover of *Newsweek,* June 9, 1947. He emerged as the nation's best-known anticommunist years before Senator Joseph McCarthy burst on the national scene.

NEWSWEEK

Hoover and Tolson arrived in Oakland, California, aboard a Southern Pacific train on September 28, 1946. They had spent the month of August together in California, attending the horse races and soaking up the sun. Now—"smiling, but determined," as one news account described Hoover—they were returning to the West Coast for a more official occasion. Along with comedian Bob Hope and a few others, Hoover was slated to receive the highest patriotic honor bestowed by the American Legion—its Distinguished Service Medal—at the group's annual conference in San Francisco. Hoover arrived wearing his presidential Medal of Merit, pinned to his lapel by Truman back in March. At least in theory, both that medal and the one to be granted by the Legion reflected the same values: honor, patriotism, and national sacrifice. For Hoover, though, they had very different meanings by the fall of 1946. Frustrated with the Truman White House, increasingly convinced of the FBI's mission as the "one bulwark" against a mounting Red threat, he chose the American Legion convention to deliver a major public address on communism—and, implicitly, to signal a break with the president.

Hoover's remarks at the Oakland station hinted at some of what he had in mind. "There is room only for Americanism in the United States," he told reporters, posing with Tolson for photos as they stepped off the streamliner. A year earlier, such a statement might have been innocuous enough, a bland affirmation of fealty to the nation and its veterans. In the fall of 1946, midterm elections were underway across the country, with the Republican Party hoping to reclaim the House and Senate for the first time in a decade and a half. Taking aim at the very aspects of the Truman presidency that most rankled Hoover, the Republicans had declared 1946 a contest between "Republicanism" and "communism," between those willing to defend the nation against Soviet influence and those willing to look the other way. To deliver a high-profile speech on the subject of communism was to take sides in this struggle—to choose the Republicans over the Democrats and, should the Republicans win, Congress over the president.[1]

The Legion convention attracted almost four thousand attendees, most of them recent servicemen. Some had worked with the FBI as part of its wartime "contact program," designed to serve the dual purpose of containing Legion vigilantism and giving Hoover more eyes and ears on the ground. Hoover did not speak directly about the controversies over global intelligence that had put him at loggerheads with Truman. But he gestured toward some of them, describing how the Communist Party operated through a system of "diabolical plots" that the FBI was just beginning to understand. He also went on the attack toward those who refused to recognize the threat for what it was. "In our vaunted tolerance for all people the Communist has found our 'Achilles' heel,'" Hoover warned, a jab aimed in part at the Truman White House. He urged the American people—and, by implication, the White House—to "no longer be misled by their sly propaganda and false preachments on civil liberty."

The Legionnaires loved the speech, delivering ovation after ovation as Hoover marched through his grim reckoning with the conditions of 1946. The press, too, recognized something significant in the offing. The thing that "most forcibly called public attention to what Communists in America are doing was an address by J. Edgar Hoover to the American Legion," wrote the journalist Mark Sullivan, looking back on the "stern" treatment communists had received during the Palmer era. Nobody was more thrilled, however, than the Republican candidates punching their way through the midterm campaign, who recognized in Hoover's speech a valuable political gift. "The Republican Speakers' Bureau now regards J. Edgar as its best unpaid spellbinder," noted columnist Ray Tucker. From that point on, Tucker suggested, Truman's opponents would be claiming Hoover and promoting his message.[2]

When the Republicans achieved a whopping victory on November 5, winning both the House and Senate for the first time since 1930, they indeed credited Hoover. "Historians who record transitions of American opinion will probably designate September

30, 1946, as the turning point in American thinking toward this thing called Communism," Congressman Karl Mundt, Republican of South Dakota, reflected. "On that day, J. Edgar Hoover, Director of the Federal Bureau of investigation, addressed the national convention of the American Legion assembled in California in one of the most courageous and completely candid speeches in the history of the American public platform."[3]

For Hoover himself, the Republican victory marked a slightly different pivot. After the election, he stopped worrying quite so much about the man in the White House. Instead, he turned to his friends in Congress, who were eager to talk more about communism.

THE MIDTERM ELECTION SIGNALED MORE THAN A SHIFT OF PARTY RULE. IT ALSO provided an opportunity for Congress to reassert its power at a moment when many on Capitol Hill feared it was in swift decline. Under the New Deal, power and influence had shifted dramatically toward the executive branch, with its proliferating agencies and strong, unifying president. The war accelerated this trend, as new boards, administrators, and advisers gained control over previously unthinkable outlays of military and civilian resources. Hoover had benefited from the surge in executive institution building; the FBI was nothing if not the product of a booming administrative state. By contrast, Congress remained the same sluggish and partisan body, filled with men who liked to argue the fine points of procedure and seniority.

As a committee of the American Political Science Association noted in 1945, the relative decline in congressional power had been accompanied by rising public anxiety about the institution, with Americans wondering whether their creaky eighteenth-century legislature was really suited for the problems of the modern age. While the executive branch had embraced white-collar professionalism, recruiting thousands of lawyers, economists, and policy experts, Congress stuck with old patronage systems, doling out jobs to the sons of local party favorites. Compared to the thriving New Deal bureaucracies, there were not even many jobs to go around. As of 1945, many congressmen employed few or no professional staff. At the same time, they were expected to master an increasingly complex set of policy and appropriations issues. To many political observers, this status quo seemed not only undesirable, but unsustainable.

The APSA laid out some solutions: reduce the number of congressional committees, increase the powers accorded those committees, and provide appropriations to hire professional committee staff. Congress debated these ideas throughout the final months of the war, the urgency of the situation heightened by Roosevelt's death and the ascendance of a man considered by many of his Senate peers to be a deeply unworthy successor. Hearings on the matter concluded in June 1945, with the final congressional report recommending many of the same ideas promulgated by the APSA:

Congress could regain power and respect by streamlining and strengthening its structures—in other words, by becoming more like the executive branch.

In the late summer of 1946, just before the midterm elections, the House and Senate passed a Legislative Reorganization Act intended to put these ideas into effect. The reforms laid out in the bill had several important implications for an agency like the FBI. Reducing the number of committees meant concentrating congressional power in fewer hands. At the House, the number of committees shrank from forty-eight to nineteen—and thus so did the number of committee chairmen. Because of seniority rules (especially in the Senate), this change meant that power would flow upward toward the longest-serving members, who would take charge of the newly empowered committees. During the New Deal, the most senior members had often been conservative Democrats from the South, where the system of racially exclusive voting and one-party rule tended to send the same white men back to Congress year after year. Among Republicans, the most senior members tended to be more varied, ideologically and regionally speaking, but shared the distinction of being longtime Washington power brokers. Under the new system, these men would now have the power of subpoena, able to compel witnesses to appear before their committees without receiving the approval of either the executive branch or the full Congress.[4]

These were precisely the sort of politicians who tended to like Hoover, and whom he had long ago set out to charm. Though he relied on Roosevelt's patronage and flirted with wartime liberalism, Hoover had never quite fit in with the New Deal's most progressive wing. He felt more comfortable among the conservative Democrats and partisan Republicans now empowered by the reorganization law. Despite their opposition to the FBI's civil rights and lynching work, Southern Democrats continued to support Hoover on other matters. Georgia senators Richard Russell and Walter George prodded Truman to recognize Hoover with the Medal of Merit. As Truman debated what to do about the global intelligence system, Mississippi congressman John E. Rankin, a twenty-five-year veteran of Congress and a famous reactionary, had called upon Congress to make the FBI "an independent federal agency" under Hoover's sole discretion. House majority leader John McCormack, a staunch anticommunist Democrat from Massachusetts, sponsored a bill to raise Hoover's salary from $10,000 to $12,500, a measure quickly taken up by the House Judiciary Committee, which advocated for $15,000. In a nod to economy, the House finally settled on a compromise measure of $14,000, a 40 percent raise for Hoover, approved in May 1946 by unanimous voice vote.[5]

The Republicans, too, signaled their eagerness to work with Hoover as Congress prepared to switch hands. Indeed, many analysts predicted that Hoover would now be better supported than ever on Capitol Hill. "Hoover will have no trouble in getting all the money he wants from Congress," predicted Washington columnist Marquis Childs. "The FBI chief has always been more popular with Republicans than with the Democrats." To his friends in Congress, Hoover had the one thing they could never acquire: the public trust that came from being a nonpartisan, unelected government man. He also had forms of power and expertise that they could only hope to emulate.[6]

OF ALL THE CONGRESSIONAL COMMITTEES, NONE MATTERED MORE TO THE FBI than House Appropriations. So it was there that Hoover started to figure out how to build closer relationships with Congress. The judiciary committees dealt with matters closest to Hoover's heart: crime, federal law, domestic security. But appropriations held the purse strings and therefore much of the power. Congress exercised no formal oversight of FBI activities. There was no intelligence committee empowered to demand disclosures. Its leaders knew only what Hoover told them, and those disclosures came out in greatest detail during his annual appearances before the Appropriations Committees. By 1946, Hoover's testimony had acquired a ritual quality: he arrived, usually with Tolson, offered up charts and statistics displaying the FBI's efficiency and ever-growing workload, answered a few questions, and left with the praise of everyone involved. The proceedings took place in executive session, sealed off from public view, with Hoover's words transcribed, cleaned up, and released a few months later. Each year, the Bureau's budget grew, sometimes more than Hoover demanded.

Based on this history, in 1942 House Appropriations chairman Clarence Cannon approached Hoover for help in setting up a professional investigative staff. Cannon initially proposed that Hoover assign FBI agents to do the work themselves, performing whatever investigative tasks the committee might need. Hoover offered instead to loan out a few of his "best men" to get an independent investigative staff up and running. The proposal was more than a favor to a friendly politician. From the beginning, Hoover saw real advantages for himself, too. Staffing the Appropriations Committee would allow him to keep tabs on information going into the committee, thus providing access to nearly everything being weighed and measured for congressional funding. And with an investigative staff composed of FBI agents, as one internal report noted, the committee might be "somewhat influenced" to conduct those inquiries that would best serve the Bureau. Perhaps most obviously, there was little to be lost and much to be gained by staying on the good side of the men who controlled the purse strings, and by knowing what they were up to.[7]

That Hoover took the task seriously can been seen in his selection of personnel. In January 1943, he dispatched Assistant Director Hugh Clegg—one of his first and most dependable Kappa Alpha recruits, now the head of Bureau inspection and training—to supervise the creation of the new appropriations staff. He also sent R. H. Laughlin, the Bureau's chief clerk and one of its most prized office men, as the staff's ongoing supervisor. In a phone call with the committee's clerk, Hoover emphasized, "These were two of our best men and they would be able to do full justice to the important task of organizing such a unit for the House Appropriations Committee." During his months on loan to the committee, Clegg worked closely not just with Cannon, but with the committee's leading Republicans, including Illinois congressman (and future Senate minority leader) Everett Dirksen.[8]

Hoover and Cannon soon concluded that their little adventure was working out marvelously well. "As you know, this was an experiment and there was considerable doubt in some quarters as to its success," Cannon wrote to Hoover in July 1943. "But with our cooperation and especially with the excellent work of Mr. Clegg [it] has succeeded beyond all expectation." And so the "experiment" continued, with Hoover dispatching agents at regular intervals to staff the committee. In July 1946, with the reorganization bill under debate, he sent an agent named Robert E. Lee to take over the committee's investigative staff.[9]

Hoover's approach did not change when the Republicans came to power in 1947, with New York's John Taber as the new committee chair. Lee assured Hoover that "Mr. Taber has repeatedly indicated that he prefers the FBI type of personnel on our Staff work." So Hoover continued to cater to the chair's preferences—and he got most of what he wanted in return. As one headline noted, by May 1947 he was the "Envy of Colleagues" for his ability to sail through Appropriations despite the Republicans' desire to rein in wartime spending. In a year when other agencies seemed to be "running into the sharp edge of the Republican double-bladed economy sword," Hoover walked away as the one federal administrator immune to postwar budget cuts, granted every penny of the record $35 million he asked for.[10]

HOOVER HAD INTENDED FOR THE APPROPRIATIONS EXPERIMENT TO STAND alone, a quiet arrangement with an unusually powerful committee. With the passage of the Legislative Reorganization Act, however, more congressmen came calling. Hoover knew that the FBI could not provide staff for all of them. And yet he also did not want to sidestep this momentous change in governance; the stakes were too high, and the potential advantages too significant. Even before 1946, congressional committees had begun to wade into areas of critical importance to the Bureau—most notably, communism, espionage, and internal security. Now those committees were empowered to conduct more widespread investigations. Under the circumstances, Hoover decided to expand his committee relationships to focus on those closest to the FBI's purview. He began with the House Committee on Un-American Activities (HUAC).

HUAC had gotten its start back in 1938, during the surge of prewar anxieties over fascist and communist activity. These were the years when Roosevelt's secret directive had first pushed the FBI back into political surveillance, aimed at groups ranging from the Bund to the Communist Party to the CIO. HUAC targeted many of the same organizations and individuals, but far more publicly and to much greater controversy.

Chaired by Texas congressman Martin Dies, the committee of the late 1930s had sought to create headline-grabbing spectacles. It hauled in major Communist and Nazi leaders to be interrogated. The committee even conducted its own raids on suspect organizations. Hoover viewed their tactics with skepticism, concerned that such showboating would disrupt—or, worse yet, compete with—the FBI's revived surveillance activities. "The menace of the situation" was "a lot of loose talk and charges and allegations creating a hysterical public viewpoint which breaks down confidence in the constituted law enforcement agencies," he complained of HUAC in 1940. Even so, he and Dies managed to forge a working relationship, especially on the communist issue. Like his counterpart at Appropriations, Dies also took advantage of FBI expertise, hiring the former head of the Bureau's New York office as committee counsel.[11]

When Dies announced he was leaving Congress in 1944, everyone assumed that his committee would fade with him. Instead, Congressman John Rankin of Mississippi stepped in to save it, engineering a close vote to turn what had been an ad hoc venture into a permanent standing committee. HUAC also managed to survive the consolidations of 1946. After the midterm elections, New Jersey's J. Parnell Thomas, the senior Republican, took over as chairman. To Hoover, the great appeal of a reconstituted HUAC lay in the committee's ability to draw public attention to issues he deemed important—and to do so with tools off-limits to the FBI. As law enforcement officers, FBI agents were bound by a host of restrictions. They could ask questions of espionage suspects, for instance, but they could not compel them to talk. The committee, by contrast, had the power of subpoena. HUAC also had the ability to hold public hearings, where alleged communists and spies could be exposed and humiliated without the need to meet any burden of legal proof. "With such staffs they can go out and seek and obtain information," Hoover explained to the attorney general in early 1947, "and they have powers broader than those of this Bureau in that they can compel witnesses to appear and testify and can also compel the production of records and documents which this Bureau cannot do." Recognizing this serendipity, HUAC had already hired an ex-Bureau man named Louis Russell to help run its investigative staff. As their work intensified, several more ex-agents joined him.[12]

TRUMAN'S ACTIONS PUSHED HOOVER FURTHER INTO HUAC'S EMBRACE. BY CERtain measures, 1947 was the year that Truman came to take the threat of communism and Soviet power seriously, just as Hoover had been urging him to do. In other ways, their antagonism only deepened. In March 1947, alarmed at Soviet expansionism and growing crises in Greece and Turkey, the president announced the Truman Doctrine, his signature foreign-policy vision. The doctrine committed the United States to "support free peoples who are resisting attempted subjugation by armed minorities or by outside pressures"—code words for resistance to communist revolution and Soviet rule. That same month, he initiated a loyalty program mandating background checks on all two million federal employees, plus anyone hired thereafter. Under Truman's order, the government committed itself to investigating citizens' political activities and ideological leanings on a staggering new scale.

In doing so, he seemed to go out of his way to antagonize Hoover. When Truman introduced the loyalty program, he proposed far more funding for the Civil Service Commission, which would run the loyalty hearings, than for the FBI, which would have to conduct the investigations. Worse still, from Hoover's perspective, was the president's proposed bill outlining a new military and intelligence structure within the executive branch. Truman's National Security Act had many moving parts, including the creation of a National Security Council and a permanent Department of Defense. Of greatest consequence for the FBI was section 102, which proposed transforming the Central Intelligence Group, whose creation had been such an affront to Hoover, into a greatly strengthened Central Intelligence Agency. That action made permanent the divide that Truman had established early on: the FBI controlled domestic intelligence; the CIA worked everywhere else. It also reinforced Hoover's impression that the president did not appreciate or respect him.[13]

The Republicans in Congress, by contrast, went out of their way to praise and support Hoover during the first months of 1947, as they settled in for a long battle of wills with the White House. Though Truman had hoped to avoid FBI control of the loyalty program, the Republican Congress redirected most of the money to Hoover, authorizing him to launch investigations of every current and prospective government employee. In the debate over Truman's National Security Act, Republican Congressman Walter Judd (among others) stepped in to protect Hoover's prerogatives and autonomy. The so-called Judd amendment proposed to prevent the CIA "from being allowed to go in and inspect J. Edgar Hoover's activities and work." The final language of the bill ensured that the FBI would not be forced to share information with the CIA unless "essential to national security." Even then, the CIA director would have to make the request in writing. The amendment put the FBI in a class of its own, the only wing of the intelligence establishment afforded such privileges.

Like other Republicans in Congress, HUAC chairman Thomas staged a grand show of respect for Hoover to contrast with Truman's dismissiveness, repeatedly invoking the director's wisdom on questions of communism, espionage, and the national soul. HUAC supported Hoover in his battle with CIA, arguing that the Judd amendment, which proposed to protect the FBI's files and methods, did not go nearly far enough. And in March 1947, six months after Hoover's speech before the American Legion, the committee announced hearings on an issue that mattered deeply to Hoover: the legal status of the Communist Party. Thomas begged Hoover to testify before the committee, promising to "watch the questioning very carefully" and put a stop to any line of inquiry that Hoover didn't like. As he envisioned it, the hearings would present "a full-dressed public denunciation of Communism," with Hoover as the star witness. Though Hoover usually declined such requests, for HUAC—now staffed by his own men and highly responsive to his priorities—he made an exception. "I want to go on this week," Hoover concluded in late March. With that decision, he cemented an alliance that would shape the Bureau's relationship to Congress—and the nation's debate over communism—for the next two decades.[14]

HOOVER APPEARED AT A HEARING ROOM IN THE OLD HOUSE OFFICE BUILDING on the afternoon of March 26, his suit neatly pressed, Tolson by his side, testimony typed and ready. His Appropriations appearances had usually occurred in executive session, a private conversation later transcribed and edited for public release. This time, in what the press billed as "a rare public appearance," he agreed to testify under the full glare of newsreel lights, his words captured on radio and film for immediate broadcast.[15]

His testimony began with an affirmation of common purpose with HUAC. "The aims and responsibilities of the House Committee on Un-American Activities and the Federal Bureau of Investigation are the same," he declared. While "the methods whereby this goal may be accomplished differ," he went on, the two institutions worked well together, with HUAC deploying the tools of exposure and publicity while the FBI maintained its obligation "to obtain information and to protect confidence." As in his Legion speech, Hoover sidestepped most explicit discussions of espionage. Though he referred obliquely to Gouzenko's defection, there was no mention of Bentley, Chambers, White, or Hiss—all still largely unknown to the public in 1947. His vision of communism nonetheless reflected what he had learned from those investigations. "This Committee renders a distinct service when it publicly reveals the diabolical machinations of sinister figures engaged in un-American activities," he explained, hinting at dark and secret activities that could now see the light thanks to HUAC.

The committee, however, was not his only audience. Unlike his Legion speech, which had been aimed at a convention hall full of sympathizers, from the HUAC witness table Hoover chose to direct his message toward "the liberal and progressive"—those who had rallied to his side during the war but who, like Truman, seemed to doubt the urgency of the threat he was describing. Hoover had worked hard during the Roosevelt years to prove his liberal bona fides. Now, under a weaker president, with Republicans in control of Congress, he revived a narrative that he had begun to develop years before that, in the wake of the Palmer Raids. As Hoover framed it, the Communist Party of 1947 was doing just what it had done a generation earlier: manipulating well-meaning liberal "pawns" into thinking that they all wanted the same thing. Rather than seeking genuine reform, according to Hoover, the communists cynically used struggles for civil liberties, racial justice, and social welfare as "window dressing" designed "to conceal their true aims and entrap gullible followers."

Hoover held out hope that his liberal friends might yet forge a different path. "I believe the Communists' most effective foes can be the real liberals and progressives who understand their devious machinations," he insisted. But he worried about the way things were heading—especially, his remarks implied, with a man like Truman in the White House.[16]

HOOVER'S APPEARANCE ON MARCH 26 MARKED THE FIRST AND THE LAST TIME that he testified before HUAC. Out of the public eye, though, the FBI's quiet "era of cooperation" continued. Having affirmed his support of the committee, Hoover set out to combine the different methods he had described—HUAC's power of subpoena and spectacle, the FBI's skill at investigation—into a secret but robust information-sharing agreement. Within a few years, that collaboration would seem so natural that it would be hard to imagine it could have gone another way. But Hoover's decision to work with HUAC grew out of the highly specific circumstances of 1947, including his rift with Truman, the changing structure of Congress, the FBI's frustrations in the Bentley and Chambers investigations, and the outcome of the midterm elections. In those circumstances, HUAC offered what the president would not: a willingness to act, now, on Hoover's vague but suggestive information.

The testing ground for this arrangement was not Washington but Hollywood, where the FBI had spent so much time and energy during the war investigating communist influence on the film industry. Like the espionage investigations, the Hollywood query had yielded information that troubled Hoover—but without providing anything concrete, much less illegal. There were plenty of left-wingers around Hollywood; that went without saying. What Hoover had tried to determine was whether there was also a concerted and coordinated effort, by the Communist Party or the Soviet government or both, to influence American popular culture in a pro-Russian direction. Hoover came away convinced that "the American Communists launched a furtive attack on Hollywood in 1935," as he informed HUAC, but that proving it at such a late date might not be possible. So when HUAC proposed to simply haul the figures in question up before the committee and ask them point-blank about their activities, Hoover instructed the Los Angeles office to "extend every assistance."

Without the FBI's help, the famous Hollywood hearings that followed might never have happened. At the very least, they would not have played out in quite the same way. Hoover provided HUAC with nearly five years' worth of its sprawling communists-in-Hollywood investigation, the product of hundreds if not thousands of man-hours that the committee would not need to replicate. In return, he asked that HUAC keep the arrangement secret and avoid all "disclosure" that might "in any way embarrass the Bureau."[17]

Hoover would later make similar arrangements with other committees interested in communism: first, staff the committee with sympathetic men, preferably current or former FBI agents; next, provide information, on a condition of nondisclosure and total confidentiality. When it worked, the model allowed Hoover to take advantage of the committee's subpoena privileges and ability to drive national discussion without requiring the FBI to absorb much of the political risk. When it didn't, he simply stopped sharing staff and information, with the public none the wiser. The chief losers in this arrangement were the men and women who found themselves hauled before Congress and forced to answer questions about their political affiliations and activities. Thanks to Hoover's secret agreements, they often found themselves faced with vague evidence—much of it rumor and innuendo—that they could not review and, in some cases, did not even recognize.

After a series of closed hearings in Los Angeles during the spring of 1947, HUAC moved its Hollywood investigation to Washington, where it planned to use FBI evidence as the basis for a spectacular series of fall hearings. Hoover helped them along, instructing his staff to compile individual reports for the committee on some of the most prominent communists in Hollywood. For additional assistance, HUAC hired two more ex–FBI agents to conduct investigations and come up with an ideal roster of witnesses.[18]

By October, both Hoover and Thomas felt sufficiently confident to move forward with public hearings, led by a four-man subcommittee consisting exclusively of Republican members. The action took place in the same House caucus room where Hoover had testified seven months earlier, its soaring ceilings and marble walls providing an incongruously dignified setting for "what Washington expects to be the biggest show of the fall investigating season," in the words of the Associated Press. As in March, the media showed up in force, with an estimated 120 to 150 print reporters crammed around long tables toward the front of the room. Seated near the press, witnesses spoke into the same clusters of metal microphones and klieg lights that had brought Hoover's views before the nation. Some three hundred spectators squeezed into the remaining seats, hoping for a brush with celebrity or a taste of "a good old purge in the Kremlin style," as *The Boston Globe* put it.

While the committee members kept their promise to avoid any mention of direct cooperation with the FBI, Hoover's influence saturated the proceedings, from the selection of witnesses to the methods of investigation to the dramatic "facts" revealed by committee counsel. The first three witnesses were all ex-FBI men, key members of the committee's investigative staff. Following their testimony came a parade of so-called friendly witnesses—studio chiefs and celebrated actors and directors sympathetic to the committee's view, each of them vetted and approved in advance by the FBI. Many were Hoover's friends and acquaintances, including entertainment impresario Walt Disney, studio heads Louis B. Mayer and Jack Warner, and actor Adolphe Menjou. Others, such as Screen Actors Guild president Ronald Reagan, were not yet close with

Hoover but worked with local field offices as contacts and informants. Of all the friendly witnesses, none was closer to Hoover—or more publicly associated with him—than Lela Rogers, his much-hyped romance from the months after Annie's death.[19]

If the "friendly" witnesses stoked their share of debate, however, it was the "unfriendly" witnesses, called to appear during the second week of hearings, who gave the events their lasting political and legal significance. The FBI had vetted them, too, selecting a small group of writers and directors whose membership in the Communist Party could be easily proven. With the FBI's information in reserve, Thomas asked what would soon become one of the most infamous questions in American history: "Are you now or have you ever been a member of the Communist Party?" The witnesses refused to answer. Instead, they argued that HUAC's charged inquiries—indeed, its very existence—violated constitutional protections of political assembly and free speech.

The press thrilled to their combative exchanges. "Voices rose," wrote an AP reporter. "Tempers soared like skyrockets. A gavel beat a steady tattoo." After much heated back-and-forth, the "unfriendly" appearances often concluded more or less the same way, with the witnesses escorted out of the hearing room by Capitol police, while the audience jeered ("Throw out the bum!") and Thomas banged away on his gavel. Once things calmed down, the FBI usually got the last word. After the departure of each witness, the committee often revealed a thick file on his communist affiliations, much of it based on FBI material. Then Hoover's former employee Russell would present a Communist Party card proving membership.[20]

As a model for how to work with congressional committees, the hearings must have been heartening to Hoover. Alone, he had been unable to make the communists-in-Hollywood investigation into anything beyond a series of dire reports, most of them ignored by the White House. With HUAC's cooperation, he had turned that raw material into a national spectacle. In late October, Thomas abruptly declared victory, arguing that "it might be a good psychological move to discontinue while they were being well received by the public," in the Bureau's words. The following month, the House affirmed that ten of the unfriendly witnesses (popularly dubbed the "Hollywood Ten") should be held in contempt of Congress, setting off a years-long legal battle. A group of leading studio executives announced that the men would be fired from their jobs and that the industry would henceforth keep track of its communist employees— the beginning of what would become known as the Hollywood blacklist.[21]

Former FBI agents would go on to play a significant role in creating and managing the blacklist, another extension of Hoover's influence beyond the confines of the Bureau. In the meantime, Hoover seized upon the momentum provided by HUAC, the Hollywood hearings, and the Republican Congress to launch the next phase of the Red Scare.

CHAPTER 30

Three-Ring Circus

(1948–1950)

Throwing the Book at Him—By Jerry Costello

Beginning in 1948, Hoover and the FBI built major court cases against communist leaders and accused Soviet spies, including State Department official Alger Hiss. The cartoon depicts the FBI's arrest of the Communist Party's second-tier leadership.

BUFFALO COURIER-EXPRESS/ NATIONAL ARCHIVES AND RECORDS ADMINISTRATION

In the fall of 1947, while the public was focused on the Hollywood hearings, Hoover launched another secret program of cooperation—not with a congressional committee, but with the Army Security Agency (a precursor to the National Security Agency). During the war, the army had intercepted thousands of encoded cables bound for Moscow from Soviet trade and diplomatic officials stationed in the United States. Decryption experts had recently begun to decipher those cables, at which point they discovered that many of them had little to do with trade or diplomacy. Those messages, hundreds upon hundreds of them, appeared instead to document what Hoover had suspected since the war: the Soviets were running a substantial espionage network on U.S. soil. The army asked for his assistance in figuring out who the spies identified in the cables might be.[1]

Hoover jumped at the chance. After years of frustration with the Bentley and Chambers investigations, here was an opportunity to determine whether his secret turncoat sources were, after all, telling the truth. The cables promised to identify as-yet-unknown Soviet operatives, and to give the FBI the start it needed to follow them undetected. That form of identification would be far more dependable than the testimony of ex-communists, always so rife with conflicting loyalties, faulty memories, and compromised personal histories. The cables offered potentially unimpeachable evidence of Soviet officials communicating with their own representatives about the identity and recruitment of American spies—all at just the moment when the country was starting to take a real interest in the issue.

Despite their obvious benefits, however, the cables came with certain limits and risks. As the army readily acknowledged, the early evidence was "very fragmentary and full of gaps," little more than a few suggestive words decrypted at great time and cost. The Soviets used code names to identify their contacts; even if a cable could be decrypted, the task of figuring out which name fit which actual person required countless additional hours of painstaking work. If and when that information was acquired, it could not be used in court or revealed to anyone beyond a handful of government officials. From an intelligence perspective, the value of the decryptions lay in their secrecy—in the fact that the Soviets did not know what U.S. officials were able to read and see. Protecting that advantage would have to be one of the program's highest goals. It would also limit Hoover's ability to use the information publicly, or to take credit for finding it.[2]

In the end, the FBI and the army protected their evidence so well that the decryption program—ultimately code-named "Venona"—would not be fully revealed to the world until the 1990s, long after Hoover's death and after the fall of the Soviet Union. Since then, Venona has been hailed as one of the great triumphs of Cold War counterintelligence, the final proof of guilt or innocence, truth or lies, in many long-contested espionage cases. Over decades, the Venona team managed to match code names to descriptions provided by Bentley and Chambers, affirmation that these ex-communist informants were, indeed, who they claimed to be, and that Hoover had been right to believe them. The cables also identified dozens of individuals whose Soviet connections had been previously unknown to the Bureau, setting off some of the most significant espionage prosecutions of the 1940s and 1950s. In many cases the information from the cables remained partial and frustrating. Some messages merely hinted that the Soviets had taken an interest in an individual, without proof of just what the relationship entailed. Others were more definitive, offering a wealth of documentation about the theft of classified information and the arrangement of secret rendezvous. In all, Venona identified 349 people in the United States connected in one way or another to Soviet espionage, whether as information contacts or as fully committed underground agents.[3]

Taken as a whole, the Venona decryptions lend substance to Hoover's claims that Soviet espionage was a genuine problem in the 1940s, not just a figment of the anticommunist imagination. As Hoover experienced it, though, Venona also entailed frustration and uncertainty. When he encountered the project in late 1947, the scope of what he did not know—about the scale of Soviet espionage, the connections between the Communist Party and the Soviet authorities, the names and identities of participants—loomed large. And when the cables began to yield fruit the following year, the revelations created as many problems as they solved.

The project nonetheless had an energizing effect on Hoover. Even without the details in place, it seemed to confirm that his overall assessment about communist collusion with Soviet espionage was correct. It also inspired him to take more aggressive action. While Venona proceeded in secret, Hoover accelerated his efforts to expose and dismantle the party, releasing several key informants to break their silence and put their cases before the public. Together, those informants emerged as key players in three court-room dramas that took place between 1948 and 1949, sagas of personal betrayal and subterfuge far more riveting than any speech Hoover could hope to make.

WHEN THE BENTLEY INVESTIGATION HAD FIRST STALLED IN 1946, HOOVER ARgued for abandoning it and seeking out more productive areas of inquiry. He still believed what the ex-spy had revealed: that beginning in the 1930s, the Soviets had cultivated secret contacts within the American government, aided and abetted by the Communist Party. But belief was different than proof. "What we know to be true in this case is a far cry from what we are in a position to prove beyond a reasonable doubt," one Bureau official acknowledged in early 1947, citing the many frustrations—especially the lack of corroborating evidence—that had plagued the "Gregory" case from the start.[4]

Hoover saw far more potential in approaching the communist problem from other angles. If prosecutions were not yet possible, the FBI could still pursue the party through secret surveillance and infiltration measures, which might yield new evidence. Hoover could also use the bully pulpit made available by Congress and the press. As public anxiety over communism grew, still other tools became available. In mid-1947, under Truman's loyalty order, the FBI gained the right to investigate every federal employee, almost two million men and women. To guide those investigations, Hoover relied in part on the "Attorney General's List," a roster of "subversive" groups maintained and updated regularly by the FBI and Justice Department. The list included dozens of so-called communist front groups, in which the party allegedly concealed its controlling interest in order to dupe unsuspecting allies into doing its political work.

These duties gave Hoover growing influence over the political composition of the federal workforce. "Washington today should be renamed J. Edgar Hooverville," one longtime communist grumbled, citing the "panic" among federal employees at the prospect of being investigated. From Hoover's perspective, though, additional tools and methods were still needed. Among his greatest concerns was what would happen in the event of hostilities with the Soviet Union, when the FBI would no doubt be tasked with managing another loyalty detention program. During the previous war, Hoover's version of internment had targeted noncitizens, a policy that seemed to accord with the nature of the German and Japanese conflict. Should war with the Soviet Union erupt, he envisioned a radically different scenario, in which the mostly American-born members of the Communist Party would make up the true "fifth column" threat. Hoover pushed the attorney general to propose legislation that would allow the FBI to detain and intern U.S. citizens in the event of war. He also instructed the field offices to update their running detention index, with an eye toward "continuous, active and vigorous investigations" of the Communist Party's "top functionaries."[5]

With such large-scale initiatives in the offing, Hoover lost interest in pursuing the Gregory case. Beginning in 1947, he ordered agents to detain and interview the alleged members of Bentley's espionage ring—not with an eye toward prosecution, but just to let them know "that they haven't fooled us." Other than that, he planned to turn any incriminating material over to the relevant government departments and wash his hands of it. It was the attorney general who kept the inquiry going. In the spring of 1947, against Hoover's wishes, the Justice Department began to present witnesses before a grand jury in New York. Bentley testified at length, repeating her story of life inside a Soviet espionage network. So did some of the key men and women accused in her confession.[6]

The testimony in New York went on for an agonizing ten months before the grand jury concluded that it could find no grounds for indictment, despite a wealth of circumstantial evidence. Upon hearing the news, Hoover told a Justice Department attorney he had seen it coming. "I was not at all surprised at the outcome of this matter," he insisted. "I had originally, both in writing and orally, strongly urged the AG not to present the Gregory Case to the Grand Jury." At this point, hoping to save face, he offered an alternative strategy for destabilizing the communist underground. In early 1948, not long after learning of the Venona decrypts, he signed on to a proposal that the Justice Department pursue the party's leadership under the Smith Act, the little-used sedition law passed hurriedly by Congress after the Nazi invasion of France. That law made it illegal for anyone—citizen or noncitizen—"to advocate, abet, advise, or teach the duty, necessity, desirability, or propriety of overthrowing or destroying any Government in the United States by force or violence." Though he could not prove his suspicions about espionage, Hoover believed the FBI *could* demonstrate that the Communist Party violated the act's provisions about the advocacy of "force and violence." In February, he sent the attorney general eight black cardboard binders containing a 1,350-page "brief," plus 546 exhibits, designed to support that argument.[7]

The documents repeated much of what Hoover had claimed in 1919, when he wrote his first briefs on the Communist and Communist Labor Parties, arguing that their advocacy of violent revolution made noncitizen members deportable under immigration law. This time, the key date was 1945, when the party had abandoned Browder's Communist Political Association and supposedly recommitted itself to revolutionary action under the leadership of William Z. Foster, whose role as an architect of the 1919 steel strike established another point of continuity between the two historical moments. As with the 1919 briefs, Hoover's goal was less to target individuals such as Foster than to show that the party itself "advocates the overthrow of the government by force and violence," in the words of one Bureau memo. Hoover did not call for legislation that would make the Communist Party technically illegal, for fear that such a law would invite controversy and drive the party further underground, thus making it harder to track. The Smith Act seemed like an appealing alternative, because the law was already on the books and could be used flexibly.[8]

Attorney General Clark quickly came around to Hoover's point of view. "It is apparently the thought of the Department that if they can get favorable action on the case against the Communist Party as such as outlined in the Communist Party Brief," a Bureau memo explained, "they will overcome any bad publicity which might result from the Grand Jury returning in effect a no bill report on the Gregory Case." And so in late June, a full year after being empaneled to consider the problem of Soviet espionage, the New York grand jury began to learn instead about the Smith Act, the Communist Party, and the "force and violence" issue. In the Gregory case, the presentation of evidence had dragged on for ten months. For the Smith Act, it was over in less than a week, with indictments returned against twelve members of the party's national council. On July 20, FBI agents began executing the warrants. It was the first mass arrest of communist leaders in a generation.[9]

THE NEXT DAY, AS PARTY OFFICIAL ELIZABETH GURLEY FLYNN LATER OBSERVED, the second act of Hoover's "three-ringed circus" began. On the afternoon of July 21, the *New York World-Telegram* published a story it had been holding for months about a ravishing "blonde spy queen" who had been telling all to the grand jury downtown. Though the article did not name names, everyone at the FBI recognized the "spy queen" as Bentley. She had reached out to the press of her own accord, hoping to cash in on her story. In deference to the Justice Department and FBI, the reporters had held off on publication until after the grand-jury proceedings. Now that the story was out, Hoover's congressional allies saw promising fodder for a new round of hearings. The FBI almost certainly provided HUAC with Bentley's true identity and address, a continuation of the information-sharing agreement born of the Hollywood campaign. With the ink barely dry on the "spy queen" story, the committee issued a subpoena for Bentley to appear in Washington.

She testified before the committee on July 31. Speaking without notes, she described her underground life as a Soviet courier, charged with gathering information from secret communists employed by the U.S. government. She also named the key figures she had identified to the FBI, including former Treasury official Harry Dexter White, whose appointment to the International Monetary Fund had so angered Hoover. Primed to expect a blond bombshell, news outlets expressed disappointment with her brown hair and simple black dress. At the committee, however, the greatest concern was that her story was too incredible to be believed. Having opened what were supposed to be damning hearings about communist subterfuge, HUAC cast about for another witness to support her claims.[10]

Three days later, Whittaker Chambers shuffled into the committee room, his clothing unkempt and his gut spilling out over the top of his belt. He relayed a story much like Bentley's: he, too, knew of communists in government because he, too, had spent years underground. Chambers named some of the same people identified by Bentley, characterizing them as part of a "secret, sinister, and enormously powerful force" dedicated to the "enslavement" of the American people. Among them was Alger Hiss, the esteemed former State Department official, now head of the Carnegie Endowment for International Peace. Chambers claimed that Hiss had been a secret communist in the 1930s, part of a clandestine ring deep within the government. Hiss wrote to the committee immediately, demanding a chance to defend his reputation—and thus unintentionally fueling the drama that HUAC wanted.[11]

What followed over the next month was a spectacle of accusation and counteraccusation that turned Soviet espionage into a national obsession, with each side equally convinced of its righteousness. Hiss showed up to testify on August 5 crisply dressed, self-assured, and smiling at the committee as only a Washington insider could. "I am not and never have been a member of the Communist Party," he assured the nation. "I do not and never have adhered to the tenets of the Communist Party." Soon other witnesses descended on Washington to deliver similar outraged denials. On August 13, Harry Dexter White appeared before the committee to denounce Bentley's "unqualifiedly false" story. Three days later, he died of a heart attack at his New Hampshire farm, a tragedy that many attributed to the stress and harsh treatment he had faced before HUAC.

If not for his untimely death, it seems possible that White—not Hiss—would have become the focus of the summer's attention, and that Bentley—not Chambers—would have become the more famous accuser. Instead, in the weeks that followed, their messy sprawl of accusations quickly came to focus on a contest of wits between Chambers and Hiss. On August 25, HUAC brought the two men together for a hearing broadcast live on the new medium of television. Testifying first, Hiss maintained that he had last seen Chambers in 1935 and barely knew him. Chambers insisted that they had been coconspirators in the underground and, for several years in the mid-1930s, something like friends.[12]

From the vantage point of the twenty-first century, it can be hard to understand just why so many Americans seemed to care who was right or to comprehend every-thing that seemed to be at stake. There was, first, the sheer appeal of the spy story. A talented writer, Chambers made the most of his personal saga, from his early commit-ment to communist ideology to his break with the party and transformation into a conservative *Time* magazine polemicist. The tale Hiss offered was less dramatic but still compelling: as a New Deal liberal, a man who fought for global peace and social justice, he now claimed to be a victim of anticommunist hysteria, Republican backlash, and paranoid overreach. The facts themselves were few and far between. Like Bentley, Chambers seemed to have little to offer in the way of proof. So their struggle became a matter of competing worldviews. Everyone took the side that best fit their own as-sumptions.[13]

Hoover missed most of the fireworks, off in California for his annual vacation with Tolson. Upon returning to Washington in August, he found the city abuzz with talk of Hiss and Chambers. To his dismay, some of that talk cast aspersions on the FBI, which had, after all, failed to deliver on the information it had long ago acquired. "Until these lurid so-called hearings began, the FBI had a very high standing in the country," wrote the influential columnist Marquis Childs. "One of the incidental ef-fects of the 'investigation' is to make people wonder whether the FBI has been on the job." Presidential campaign season added a partisan edge to the conversation. Through-out Washington, Democrats and Republicans locked into fixed positions about whom they did or did not believe, with Democrats insisting that Hiss embodied all that was good and just about New Deal aspirations, while Republicans backed Chambers as a man willing to voice difficult truths.[14]

Hoover had already thrown in his lot with the Republicans, though he would never have admitted as much in public. A former district attorney and the current governor of New York, Republican presidential candidate Thomas Dewey had occasionally locked horns with Hoover during the crime wars of the 1930s. Ever since, though, he had been a stalwart ally. In the spring of 1948, running to win the Republican nomination for a second time, he had even made a campaign issue out of Truman's rebuff of Hoover on the global intelligence issue. "During the last war, for the first time in our history, we had many brave men planted in dangerous places all over the world," he declared in a Wisconsin primary speech. "But the President by a stroke of his pen on January 22, 1946, created a new, untried and inexperienced group." Dewey attacked Truman for destroying "the fine services J. Edgar Hoover and the F.B.I. had established." Thus he earned Hoover's gratitude and loyalty.[15]

Hoover tried to keep his support for Dewey quiet, passing along advice and inside information on the condition of confidentiality, much as he did with HUAC. But it was lost on no one that Hoover preferred Dewey to Truman. That fact put him in an awkward position as the Chambers-Hiss controversy caught fire in the summer of 1948. Everyone wanted to know what Hoover, the ultimate authority, thought about

Hiss and Chambers: Who was lying and who was telling the truth? HUAC member Karl Mundt assured Hoover that the coming Republican victory would allow him to take sides openly. "I suspect that after next January it will be made easier for us to team-up carrying forward our tasks," Mundt wrote in a private note. [16]

In the meantime, Washington was rife with speculation about how Hoover would handle the mounting political tension, in which supporting Dewey meant supporting Chambers, while Truman partisans tended to side with Hiss. "J. Edgar Hoover Caught in Middle of Spy Wrangle," one headline declared, wondering how he would get himself out. Another newspaper identified him as "the keeper of the keys and the Cerberus of the Capitol Dome," speculating that Hoover's decisions over the next few months might sway the election one way or another. That article depicted him as a fighter about to enter the political ring, torn between his executive-branch ties, which suggested he should remain silent on Hiss, and his Republican friendships, which pressured him to speak out. "The big question troubling him is this: 'When I swing, who will I try to knock out—Truman or Dewey?'"[17]

Hoover never quite had to answer that question. In mid-September, he came down with bronchial pneumonia. While he recovered in bed, the Hiss case continued to evolve, agonizingly intertwined with the election. As Dewey and Truman traded blows on the campaign trail, Chambers went on *Meet the Press* to call Hiss a liar and a communist. Hiss then sued Chambers for slander, accusing his accuser of "untrue, false, and defamatory" statements. From bed, Hoover grumbled to friends and colleagues about all the "inaccuracies, exaggerations, falsehoods, and figments of the imagination" accompanying these events. He also worried that the FBI's enmeshment in the election would undermine its reputation for nonpartisan, apolitical professionalism.[18]

On November 2, after nearly two months of illness, he finally felt strong enough to board a plane to Miami, perhaps hoping that sun, sand, and time with Tolson would help him recuperate. That night, he learned the election results: Truman scored an upset victory over Dewey and the Democrats retook both houses of Congress. The changing of the guard in Congress meant that HUAC, like other committees, would now revert into Democratic hands. And Hoover would have four more years with an adversary in the White House.[19]

Under the circumstances, Hoover refrained from going after Hiss in public, a move that would only have increased Truman's hostility. But he worked quietly with HUAC's Republican leadership behind the scenes. Among the FBI's new contacts there was a young congressman named Richard Nixon, who would soon become one of Hoover's closest and most important friends in Washington. Just after midnight on December 1, Nixon called the FBI to report that Chambers—after years of insisting that he possessed no corroborating evidence—was about to reveal a secret cache of documents in support of the Hiss allegations. HUAC investigators soon traipsed out to Chambers's Maryland farm, where he led them to his pumpkin patch and handed over several rolls of microfilm hidden in a hollowed-out pumpkin. On them were photographs of government documents Chambers had acquired during his years as a spy. Several were in Hiss's own handwriting. Together, they became known as the Pumpkin Papers.[20]

In December, based in part on this new evidence, the New York grand jury indicted Hiss on charges of perjury. Hoover was glad to see it, but he worried that the whole affair had damaged the FBI. After years of effort, after thousands of agent hours dedicated to the case, it was not the FBI, but HUAC, that had come through with the key evidence. "Something is defective in our Communist coverage," he complained to his aides. More would have to be done to fix it.[21]

THEN, WITH IMPECCABLE TIMING, CAME THE OPPORTUNITY HOOVER HAD been seeking since the army first approached him about Venona: the chance to expose an entirely new espionage ring.

The discovery occurred not at Bureau headquarters, but out at Arlington Hall, a former girls' school in Virginia where the army housed its signals intelligence service and where the painstaking decryption of the Venona cables had been taking place for more than a year. When FBI agent Robert Lamphere arrived there in late 1947, assigned as liaison to the project, he found a handful of run-down wood-frame buildings staffed by dozens of women, most of them cryptographers and scientists hired during the war, when men of similar skills and talents had been in short supply. Prospects looked bleak at first. "In its present state," an early report noted, the captured cable traffic "tends to arouse curiosity more than it does to satisfy it." Then, in the middle of 1948, while the rest of the country was focused on Chambers and Hiss and the Smith Act arrests, the Venona team "hit the jackpot," Lamphere recalled. Cross-referencing the cables with background details in FBI files, they started to decipher bits and pieces of the Soviet communications, and then to match up cover names with living, breathing individuals. One of those discoveries "struck me quite forcefully," Lamphere later wrote, since it pertained directly to the work of the FBI. In late December 1948, as Hoover fumed over the discovery of the Pumpkin Papers, the Venona team identified a Soviet operative code-named "Sima" as a political analyst in the Foreign Agents Registration Section of the Department of Justice. In that position, she had access to the FBI's loyalty and espionage investigations.[22]

Hoover relayed the news to the Washington field office on December 31, the eve of his fifty-fourth birthday. "Sima is without doubt identical with Judith Coplon, who is presently an employee in the Foreign Agents Registration Section of the Department of Justice," he wrote. The nature of Coplon's job complicated the situation: if she really was working for the Soviets, Lamphere explained, "the agency most compromised by her was the FBI"—hardly a fact that Hoover wanted to share with the Truman administration. Within hours of learning about the Coplon identification, he wrote to the attorney general recommending that she stay on the job for now, so that she could be watched and her contacts discovered. By way of explaining how the FBI had managed to identify her, he said merely that the Bureau had received information about her activities from "a highly confidential source."

Over the next several days, Hoover's agents installed wiretaps at Coplon's home and office. They also began conducting round-the-clock physical surveillance, hoping to find evidence that would corroborate the Venona identification. From these sources they learned that Coplon planned to go to New York on January 14, allegedly to visit her parents. When they followed her to the city, she turned out to be meeting with Valentin Gubitchev, a Soviet official attached to the United Nations and apparently her Russian contact. At that point, Lamphere recalled, "we had one hell of an espionage case in the making."[23]

Over the next two months, Hoover authorized the same sort of urgent and intensive investigation he had approved back in 1945, when Bentley's confession had seemed so promising. The effort involved wiretaps and surveillance not only of Coplon but of nearly everyone in her circle, from her parents to her boyfriend, a married employee at the Justice Department. It also entailed the preparation of fake reports ostensibly identifying an FBI informant within Amtorg, the Soviet government's trading arm in the U.S. They hoped that Coplon would see the documents and try to pass them along to her Soviet handlers, preferably while FBI agents were watching. Throughout it all, Hoover proceeded with two important (but sometimes contradictory) goals in mind. The first was "to get legal evidence so as to effect prosecution," as he wrote in January 1949. The other was to protect Venona—to build a case against Coplon without disclosing how she had first been identified.[24]

Coplon took the bait. In early March, the FBI sent a decoy memo her way. She immediately read it and took notes. On March 4, she traveled back to New York, "carrying the red imitation alligator make-up kit she has previously carried," as surveillance reports noted, tucked inside a "black pocketbook with gold trim." Agents followed her from Penn Station through Upper Manhattan and back to Midtown, where she met up with her Soviet contact Gubitchev and then dashed onto a bus headed south. At 9:36 p.m., agents arrested both of them around Fifteenth Street, more than two hours into the cat-and-mouse game. When they searched Coplon's purse, they found more than two dozen FBI data slips, short documents describing the location and content of various FBI files. They also found the notes Coplon had taken on behalf of her Soviet handler. This time, Hoover felt sure, it would be the FBI—not HUAC, not the Justice Department—that received the bulk of the credit.[25]

COPLON AND GUBITCHEV WERE TAKEN DOWNTOWN TO BE QUESTIONED AT
the Foley Square courthouse and federal building, where the FBI maintained a suite
of offices. Over the next year, that building would host all three rings of Hoover's anticommunist "circus": the Smith Act trial of Communist Party leadership, two perjury
trials for Alger Hiss, and the prosecutions of Coplon and Gubitchev for espionage. The
coincidence of timing and location gave off the impression that all three cases were
more or less the same, resulting from the same general anticommunist impulse. From
Hoover's perspective, though, each had a different logic, and each tested a different
aspect of the FBI's work. The Smith Act prosecution depended on years of ideological
sifting and sorting, supplemented by testimony from Hoover's army of informants.
The Hiss trials turned on the credibility of two men with conflicting stories, and thus
relied in part upon the FBI's evidentiary and forensic analysis to determine who was
telling the truth. The Coplon case came straight out of Venona, but that evidence, as
thrilling and decisive as it might have been, would remain the FBI's great secret. All
three courtroom dramas, as *Time* magazine noted in putting Hoover on its cover in
August 1949, "hinged directly on the searching investigation of thousands of U.S.
citizens made by the FBI under its director, J. Edgar Hoover." In that sense, Hoover,
too, was on trial.[26]

The first one to open, in room 110, was the Smith Act prosecution, the least sensational of the year's big cases but the one perhaps dearest to Hoover's heart. Eleven men
were on trial together, including Communist Party executive secretary Eugene Dennis
and New York City councilman Ben Davis, the party's most prominent Black member.
Recognizing an existential danger to their organization, party members staged pickets
on a traffic island outside. In the courtroom itself, the defendants engaged in tactics of
delay and disruption similar to what HUAC had witnessed during the Hollywood
hearings.

The prosecution had its own attention-grabbing strategy, however. In preparation
for the trial, Hoover allowed several undercover informants to surface and testify openly
about what they had witnessed as Communist Party members. In early April, an unassuming dark-haired man took the stand as the first of those witnesses, introducing
himself as Herbert Philbrick, a Boston advertising executive and a member in good
standing of the local CP branch. For nine years, while posing as a good communist, he
revealed, "I had been in constant communication with the Federal Bureau of Investigation." Along the way, he had delivered reams of information about fellow party
members, their ideas, and their "violent" proclivities. Philbrick's confession "drew
an audible gasp from the left side of the spectators' benches," where the defendants'
supporters tended to congregate, a reporter noted. The defendants themselves stared

"incredulously" at Philbrick for several moments before beginning to whisper, shake their heads, and consult their attorneys.

Their dismay increased over the next several weeks, as the prosecution called several additional FBI informants to the stand. After years of pretending to be true believers, they came forth to testify about nearly every aspect of party activities, including the doctrine of "violent revolution," which was supposedly to be "carried out by bands of armed workers against the existing state government," according to Philbrick. As evidence, they dissected the works of Stalin, Lenin, and Marx, along with more recent publications and teachings. But their greatest impact came from their mere presence on the stand. After years of speculation, their appearance offered the first tangible evidence of how thoroughly Hoover and the FBI had infiltrated the Communist Party.[27]

A different aspect of the Bureau's work came under scrutiny in the year's second great courtroom drama, which began on May 31, one floor up from the Smith Act case. The Hiss trials—one in the summer, another in the fall—yielded fewer surprises from the witness stand, since most of what was said had been declared months earlier before HUAC. The trials did reveal new evidence, however, much of it gathered by the FBI this time. As the first trial approached, Hoover assigned some three hundred agents to interview witnesses and hunt for key clues such as the Hiss family typewriter, on which many of the Pumpkin Papers had allegedly been reproduced. During the trial, FBI laboratory officials performed a tour de force of scientific policing, using photographic enlargements and patient explanation to show that the documents could only have been created on the Hiss machine.[28]

If things had ended there, Hoover might well have come away satisfied, convinced that whatever uncertainty had existed about the FBI's competence and determination had now been put to rest. By then, though, the Coplon trials were also underway—first in Washington, with Coplon as the sole defendant, and then back at Foley Square, where she and Gubitchev went on trial together. Compared to the Hiss case, with its tangle of accusation and counteraccusation, the Coplon prosecution should have been easy: the FBI had caught her red-handed, her purse chock-full of classified documents, a Soviet representative at her side. But Coplon's lawyer was determined to prove that this supposedly open-and-shut espionage case was actually "one of the greatest frame-ups" in American history. To make his case, he demanded to review the full contents of the FBI files associated with the data slips found in Coplon's possession. And to nearly everyone's surprise, the judge agreed to the request.[29]

It is hard to exaggerate Hoover's outrage at this decision, the first time that he was forced to turn over confidential FBI documents in open court—and this at a moment when he had thought the FBI had finally won. "I took a strong stand against making public other reports that would reveal the identities of confidential informants or embarrass innocent persons by the publication of unevaluated complaints," he explained in an irate memo to Bureau officials in late June. "I have at no time agreed or conceded that the Bureau would permit its reports containing what we considered restricted information to be introduced in evidence." By then, though, it was too late. With the permission of the court, the defense began to read Hoover's files aloud in the courtroom, each word entered into the official record. Most of the documents contained hearsay rather than bona fide evidence of espionage, but Hoover had still never intended for them to see the light of day. Coplon's second trial, at Foley Square, was even worse, with the judge demanding that Hoover disclose any and all wiretaps deployed in her case. Under duress, he admitted that the Bureau had wiretapped Coplon's parents' home, as well as her home and office phones. They had also captured at least fourteen conversations between Coplon and her attorney.[30]

DESPITE THESE COMPLICATIONS, THE JURIES ULTIMATELY SIDED WITH HOOVER in a grand slam of convictions. In October, the Smith Act case crashed to a close with a full slate of guilty verdicts, accompanied by a five-year prison sentence and a ten-thousand-dollar fine for most defendants. Three months later, Alger Hiss was convicted of perjury at his second trial and sentenced to five years in prison as well. Even Coplon was convicted not once but twice, both in Washington and in New York.

For another man, those verdicts might have been cause for celebration, a resounding vote of confidence after a difficult few months. Certainly this is how things looked to many Americans, according to Gallup polls conducted in late 1949 and early 1950. Asked their opinions of Hoover's FBI, 73 percent ranked it either "good" or "excellent." About Hoover himself, just 2 percent expressed strong disapproval, a result that Gallup characterized as "virtually without parallel in surveys that have dealt with men in public life." The company attributed this astounding result to his work on the "investigation of communist or subversive groups." After such a smashing string of victories, Gallup predicted, Hoover would now have carte blanche to proceed as he wanted.[31]

Hoover had a hard time believing it. Always inclined to view himself as a victim, he braced for a backlash from the communists and their liberal sympathizers. "I am frank to say the past few months have been among the most difficult ones that we have faced over an extended period of time," he wrote to Dewey. "There is no question in my mind but that the battle lines have now been formed and the FBI can expect to be the target of bitter attack on the part of Communists, stooges and fellow travelers as a result of body blows which have been landed against them during the past year." In preparation for the coming struggle, he devised a new filing system for investigative reports, in which any information that might "cause embarrassment to the Bureau" would be written on separate "administrative pages," easily detached from the main files in case of courtroom discovery. Requests for wiretaps and other controversial procedures would henceforth be routed separately as well, written up as "personal and confidential" letters to Hoover, labeled "June mail" to indicate their sensitive nature, and

kept under lock and key. He continued to keep Venona secret, not only from the public but apparently from the CIA and Truman as well. And when Coplon's convictions
were overturned on appeal, Hoover argued against retrying her case, for fear of endangering Venona and reopening earlier controversies. [32]

That strategy arguably paid off, as Venona soon produced the evidence that would
fuel an even more important set of espionage trials. But the emphasis on secrecy would
also increasingly isolate Hoover. He ended the year 1949 much as he had started, still
certain that the communists had the momentum and that the FBI was just catching
up. No amount of success—or of evidence to the contrary—would ever truly dislodge
that idea.

CHAPTER 31

J. Edgar Hoover, Churchman

(1948–1950)

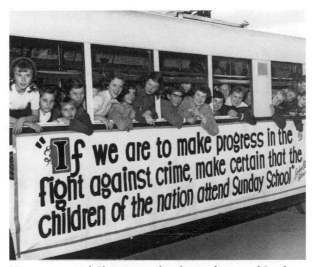

Hoover promoted Christianity, church attendance, and Sunday
school as essential tools in the struggle against crime and
communism. The quote on the side of the bus is Hoover's.
Denver Post, November 1953.

DEAN CONGER/GETTY IMAGES

Hoover was not entirely wrong that the great communist trials of 1948 and 1949
would engender criticism. As the left-wing journalist I. F. Stone noted, the materials disclosed at the Coplon trial alone revealed an "incredible vomit of slander, gossip and suspicion" within the FBI's files, much of it of little relevance to either criminal
or loyalty proceedings. Even the conservative *U.S. News & World Report* had wondered in the summer of 1949 if "much of the mystery" and "public illusion" that had
built up Hoover's stellar reputation was on the verge of being "shattered." In the weeks
that followed, the ACLU, the historic foe that Hoover had tried so hard to win over
during the war, pressed this theme home. Leading the effort was ACLU leader Roger
Baldwin, the man who had vouched for Hoover in front of Harlan Stone in 1924, and
who had come back around to Hoover's side after their conflicts in 1940. In a newspaper column, Baldwin acknowledged his "long experience with the FBI," and expressed
admiration for Hoover's "considerable restraint" and "respect for civil rights" at crucial

moments in the past. "Having said all of this," he continued, "the outstanding fact of recent years is the intrusion of the FBI into the field of political opinion."[1]

Hoover wrote to Baldwin in outrage, attacking the "flimsy" evidence deployed by the FBI's critics and insisting that "by no stretch of the imagination could the FBI be termed a secret police system." But the criticism continued, much of it coming from so-called anti-anti-communist liberals, who opposed communism but also opposed the draconian ways that men like Hoover were trying to stamp it out. In early 1950, Americans for Democratic Action, the nation's most esteemed assemblage of anti-anti-communists, joined with the ACLU in calling for investigations into Hoover's wire-tapping and loyalty policies. As individuals, ADA members, including the famed historian Arthur Schlesinger Jr., spoke out against Hoover, recalling his long history of red-hunting and mocking his well-fluffed ego. Another prominent historian, Bernard De-Voto, announced that he would no longer cooperate with the FBI if asked for the names and political associations of fellow Americans. "This feeling that the interrogation of private citizens about other citizens is natural and justified is something new to American life," he wrote in *Harper's Magazine*. "A single decade has come close to making us a nation of common informers."[2]

Hoover found it hard to contain himself. "I do not care to dignify Mr. DeVoto's compilation of half-truths, inaccuracies, distortions, and misstatements with a denial or an explanation," he wrote in a letter to *Harper's*, before proceeding to explain all the ways in which DeVoto was wrong. To his ACLU confidant Morris Ernst he offered an even longer litany of complaints. Ernst felt that Hoover was perhaps "getting a little too thin-skinned," but he promised to help out by defending Hoover in print and among his ACLU colleagues. When a Truman confidant named Max Lowenthal published a 559-page book titled *The Federal Bureau of Investigation*, Hoover's pique exploded into full-blown rage. The first book-length critique ever published about the FBI, Lowenthal's work dredged up nearly every moment of controversy and embarrassment in Hoover's career, devoting more than three hundred pages to World War I and the Palmer years. In response, Hoover mobilized friends in the press to plant critical reviews and encouraged HUAC staff to interrogate and humiliate the author.[3]

Given Hoover's well-documented popularity and string of recent victories, the ferocity of his reaction requires some explaining. Part of it can no doubt be traced to temperament: Hoover had always been anxious, always on the lookout for dangers and slights. Then there was the great, looming example of Palmer, who had been destroyed by similar critiques—indeed, by many of the selfsame critics. Added to all this was his powerful sense of righteousness, only increased by the "one bulwark" mindset of his anticommunist campaign. Hoover was sure that he was on the right side of history, and that anyone who stood against him could only be blind, treacherous, or worse. He justified intimidation and overreach against his left-leaning critics as a matter of national and institutional defense, not personal pique.

In truth, though, he probably need not have devoted quite so much time and energy to them. Baldwin, Lowenthal, DeVoto, and Schlesinger were all acting in a venerable tradition, repeating criticisms—many of them all too accurate—that had been made against Hoover since 1919 and that would come back around in later years. In the heated anticommunist atmosphere of the late 1940s, though, their small circle of liberal-left activists, intellectuals, and civil liberties advocates was not much of a match for Hoover. Since the war, he had acquired not only a wealth of new investigative and surveillance tools but also immense cultural power, much of it derived from institutions that had previously taken little interest in the FBI. Among his new allies were the nation's Christian churches, fast on the rise as a cultural and political force. For them, the fight against "atheistic communism" was never primarily a matter of facts and evidence, or even civil liberties and rights, as Hoover's left-wing critics so often claimed. It was a struggle for the nation's soul.

TOWARD THE END OF 1948, WITH THE NATION IN THE GRIP OF THE HISS-Chambers controversy, the Rev. Edward Elson published an essay promising to reveal one of Hoover's best-kept secrets. According to Elson, Hoover's image, so carefully crafted over the years, amounted to a false front. The essay noted the paradox of Hoover's celebrity. while his name might be "as familiar as those of movie stars and Presidents," nobody quite understood what made him tick—"so little is known of his private life." To understand his inner self, Elson argued, admirers would have to reckon with a singular fact. Deep down, the FBI director was not just a bureaucrat or anticommunist or law enforcement professional, but a passionate and devout Christian.

Elson named his essay "J. Edgar Hoover, Churchman." He could speak with authority because Hoover was his parishioner, a member of the National Presbyterian Church, where Elson held forth each Sunday. National Presbyterian had been created in 1947 to serve as a central church for American Presbyterians, born from a merger of Hoover's childhood church, First Presbyterian, and another congregation. From the pulpit, Elson spoke often about the perils of crime and communism, Hoover's two favorite subjects. He also performed services for the city's elite, marrying off debutantes and journalists and federal dignitaries. Truman himself attended the church's dedication in October 1947, applauding its national transformation despite his own lack of interest in formal religion and his distaste for Elson's most famous parishioner.[4]

Hoover liked Elson. Beginning in the late 1940s, he reportedly invited the minister over for a ritual of sanctification and renewal each New Year's Day (which also happened to be Hoover's birthday). Hoover had been a Presbyterian since childhood, when his brother, Dick, brought him into the church. Prior to the Red Scare, however, he rarely spoke about his religious views in public. With the end of the war and the rise of communism as his chief priority, his speeches and writing took on an increasingly

religious tone. Even as he counted Communist Party membership numbers and decrypted secret cables, he began to speak about a broader struggle between God and
godlessness. "I have been studying [communism] since 1919," he explained to a reporter in 1948. "It is really not so much a political creed as an insane kind of fanaticism,
a fanaticism that is basically atheistic—anti-God, if you like—and against the concept
of any supreme being."[5]

His essays and interviews tended to sidestep the matter of how often he actually
attended National Presbyterian. Evidence suggests that he was at best an occasional
rather than regular churchgoer, rarely up early on Sunday. But church attendance offers only one measure of his Christian faith. Though he shied away from personal
revelation in most areas, Hoover could be surprisingly open about his search for spiritual meaning. "Without belief in God, man becomes exactly what one pessimistic
philosopher has called him; an animated speck on a revolving ball, hurtling aimlessly
through endless space," he wrote in 1948. "I cannot accept such a notion." This fear of
the abyss resonated with his critique of communism as essentially materialistic, dead-
ening, and inhuman. He spoke often of a personal relationship with God. Indeed, he
described that relationship in terms not terribly different from those he used to describe his political allies in Washington. "In short," Hoover explained, "I believe in
God because God believes in me."[6]

HOOVER'S TURN TO RELIGIOSITY REFLECTED A POSTWAR TREND IN WHICH
Americans embraced church membership and religious identity in fast-growing numbers.
Though he hardly caused this surge, Hoover lent his support to it, encouraging Americans to embrace the Christian faith as a means of fighting both crime and communism. "It has been a long time since a high official in the national government has been
as outspoken as J Edgar Hoover in favor of the principles of religion," noted one admirer at the Church Street United Methodist Church of Knoxville, Tennessee. From
the authority of his federal position, Hoover linked the call to God with both fervent
anticommunism and aggressive law-and-order policy. He parceled out advice on the
subjects not only to presidents and attorneys general, but to ordinary citizens seeking
guidance about morality, crime, communism, and the dilemmas of the modern world.
In the process, he expanded his own cultural reach and helped to grow the FBI's popular constituency.[7]

As Hoover framed it, one of the chief benefits of religious faith was its prescriptive
nature: the Bible could tell Americans how to live. As a boy, he had loved to make lists
of rules for good behavior and then drive them home during Sunday school. Decades
later, he still viewed the Bible as a source of behavioral instruction, which if followed
would yield personal and professional success. He admired books like *The Greatest Story
Ever Told*, a blockbuster bestseller published by his friend Fulton Oursler in 1949,

which narrated the life of Jesus as a tale of persistence over great odds. The book's subtitle—*A Tale of the Greatest Life Ever Lived*—conveyed the sort of edifying parable that Hoover appreciated. "The Greatest Story Ever Told might well serve as a design for human life and a guide to eternity," he declared in an endorsement blurb. In his own writings, he stressed the idea of "Christian Citizenship," in which all Americans would be guided first and foremost by the Ten Commandments and the Golden Rule.[8]

Hoover focused much of his rhetoric on the country's children, whom he believed to be in danger from sin and communism alike. In his view, they had been under threat well before the war, victims of neglectful and selfish parents who refused to guide them on a righteous path. But the war itself turned the "juvenile delinquency" scare of the 1930s into a full-blown national crisis. The war had sent fathers off to the front and mothers off to the factory, all without considering what would happen to their unsupervised children. According to Hoover, many of those children had drifted into a world of petty crime and vandalism. From there, it was only a few steps "into the dreaded maze of delinquency and disease, of reformatory and prison, or, if they are not apprehended, of maiming and plundering." Even worse, these "Wild Children" were sometimes drawn to the communists' revolutionary swagger, fearless enough to believe that man's law and God's judgment did not apply to them.[9]

He relied on statistics, with all their scientific authority and exactitude, to back up his claim of an ever-growing delinquency crisis. Whether those statistics bore out a genuine crime surge or were simply a wartime fluke, Hoover took it upon himself to correct the situation. In January 1946, he lent his name to National Youth Week, a series of services and rallies organized by Protestant congregations throughout Washington to draw young people back into church. "I sincerely believe that if America is to remain devoted to the fundamentals of Christian living, more adults must assume their responsibility in bringing our young people closer to church," he declared in his official message of endorsement. On occasion, he advocated for a return to old-fashioned physical discipline. More often, he prescribed gentler methods such as following the Ten Commandments and attending Bible classes. "The Sunday School is a citadel of real spiritual influences," he explained in a press interview. "It teaches the power of prayer and the need to make God an intrinsic part of our daily lives." It also fortified young people against the temptations of crime and communism.[10]

Hoover's government position gave him influence not only with religious organizations but also with youth-oriented civic groups, to whom he regularly imparted his Christian message. Just as he lent his name to Christian groups, he worked closely with the Boy Scouts and the Boys Clubs of America, whose board he joined in 1943. He also worked with sportswriters and professional athletes, publishers and veterans groups, women's clubs and entertainers and committees for the edification of newspaper delivery boys. In 1949, a group of admirers including Washington columnist Drew Pearson and NBC executive David Sarnoff briefly floated the idea of creating an entire model school for delinquent boys in honor of Hoover's twenty-fifth anniversary as Bureau director. They got as far as acquiring a 530-acre farm in Gaithersburg, Maryland, before abandoning the idea.[11]

Hoover spoke about the declining state of American youth before government committees as well. Throughout the early 1950s, Tennessee senator Estes Kefauver conducted televised hearings addressing various aspects of the nation's alleged crime problem, from organized vice to the nefarious influence of comic books on juvenile delinquency. In that setting, Hoover revived some of his old administrative style, lauding "principles of efficiency" and cursing the "technicalities of the law" that allowed criminals to walk free. Now, however, he spoke of religious faith as well, and of the need to drag the country out of its "moral depression" lest the current system end up "supplanted by either a Socialist, Fascist or Communist form of government." Americans needed nothing less than "a return to the fundamentals upon which this Nation was founded," he told the Kefauver Committee. He prescribed "a moral reawakening" as the next great law enforcement strategy.[12]

IN ADDITION TO ITS CULTURAL POWER, HOOVER'S RELIGIOUS MESSAGE YIELDED at least one immediate benefit: it brought a rising generation of Christian leaders into his orbit as friends and allies. Among the most prominent was Norman Vincent Peale, a New York minister known nationwide as "God's Salesman." Rather than preaching salvation through born-again conversion, Peale promised inner peace and outer prosperity through *The Power of Positive Thinking*, his most famous book, published in 1952. Though he fed public anxieties about moral decline and godless communism, Peale embraced many aspects of modernity. He liked popular psychology, which gave "positive thinking" its scientific gloss. He also applauded the gospel of consumerism, which he considered less a matter of sin than of just reward. Peale welcomed the advent of modern media, particularly television and radio, which amplified his influence well beyond the thousands who thronged to hear him preach at New York's Marble Collegiate Church. Hoover admired his approach. "It is a shame all preachers do not have the ability to hold their audiences" as Peale did, he told one newspaper, comparing their "hum-drum Sunday sermons" with the vibrancy and electricity of Peale's radio voice. Hoover also claimed to be a fan of Peale's books, whose instructions in the assertion of personal will and godly action resonated with the lessons of his childhood.[13]

Peale regularly praised Hoover in his sermons and newspaper columns, declaring the director both "a great advocate of Christianity" and "our great protector against communism"—a cultural as well as a political force. He recognized Hoover as a man whose conflicted relationship with modernity reflected Peale's message; while Hoover embraced laboratory science, administrative efficiency, and public relations, he also professed to long for the stern moralism of the nineteenth century in matters of sin and religion. In the spring of 1950, Peale asked Hoover to express some of these ideas in a guest interview for his syndicated newspaper column. Hoover's message echoed Peale's positive-thinking ethos. "Religion, the bond that binds man to God, is the golden arch that leads to happiness," the essay declared. Peale returned the favor as a featured speaker at the National Academy graduation the following year. The fact that Hoover could attract someone like Peale to the academy graduation testified to Hoover's stature in American Christianity. So did a fundraising letter from the American Bible Society, which featured three great religious leaders on the value of Biblical study. The first was the influential young evangelical minister Billy Graham (also a Hoover admirer). The other two were Rev. Norman Vincent Peale and FBI director J. Edgar Hoover.[14]

Similar tributes poured forth from other Christian groups, many of them at the forefront of the postwar revival. The national organization Youth for Christ, which had given Graham his start, solicited Hoover's advice for America's young people. Hoover recommended that they all read Micah 6:8, enjoining America's youth "to love mercy, and to walk humbly with thy God." Though himself a Presbyterian, Hoover gained a particularly devoted following among Baptists, who warmed to his ideas about "what being a citizen of Christian America means," as Hoover wrote in a special column for *The Baptist Training Union Magazine*. In Houston, local Baptist congregations took out a full-page newspaper ad presenting a head-and-shoulders image of Hoover gazing upon a throng of smiling, well-dressed citizens departing from church. It also reprinted a message from Hoover urging Baptists to deploy "prayer" as a "weapon" against domestic subversion. "Men Imbued with Spiritual Values . . . Do Not Betray their Country," read a banner across the top of the ad, a direct quote from Hoover.[15]

Hoover drove this message home at the Bureau itself, where the public display of positive-thinking Christianity was fast being incorporated into what had previously been a far more secular institutional culture. Christian magazines presented FBI men as model religious citizens, devoted to God, country, family, and Hoover. According to a fanciful if sincere report in the *Central Christian Advocate* magazine, agents were among the most churchgoing Americans to be found, in the pews every Sunday unless called away on some important official duty. Even on stakeouts, the report marveled, FBI men whistled hymns to pass the time. When they were transferred to new cities, the first thing they did was to find a church to attend. After all, as another newspaper noted, "J. Edgar Hoover Says 'Go to Church.'" Agents were expected to obey his orders.[16]

They performed their righteousness not simply by attending church but by signing on with Christian fraternal organizations. In 1948, the Bureau created another Masonic chapter—the Fidelity Club—with membership encouraged for FBI employees. The mission of the Scottish Rite, Hoover's favored sect, aligned with positive-thinking Christianity: "to aid mankind's search in God's Universe for identity, for development, and for destiny," in the service of making "happier men in a happier world." Though Hoover himself no longer had much time for Masonic activities, the Masons did not view his lack of participation as a hindrance to his value as a leader. In May 1950, in a black-tie dinner at the Hotel Astor, the New York Grand Lodge awarded Hoover its medal of distinguished achievement. He accepted the honor in person, paying tribute to the founding fathers (many of them Masons) who "under the Divine Genius of the Supreme Architect of the Universe, did their work well." A few years later, without any uptick in his weekly lodge activities, the Scottish Rite promoted him to the status of thirty-third-degree Mason, its top rank and highest honor.[17]

As for Hoover's own church attendance, even the Rev. Elson acknowledged that it could be spotty. In a 1950 follow-up to his original profile of Hoover, he admitted that his favorite parishioner appeared at National Presbyterian only "on the rare weekends when the F.B.I. Director is in Washington," though he insisted that Hoover tried to attend church when out of town (a claim for which there is little evidence). But to Elson, as to the Masons, the patterns of Hoover's weekly activities mattered little in the grand spiritual scheme. Hoover was an important symbol for evangelical Christians everywhere, bound in common cause if not in the actual churchgoing experience.

ELSON'S 1950 FOLLOW-UP ARTICLE SOUGHT TO DISPEL ONE MORE RUMOR ABOUT his most famous parishioner. "J. Edgar Hoover is not a Roman Catholic and never has been," the minister wrote. In truth, Hoover was partly responsible for the confusion. Even as he joined forces with positive thinkers like Peale, he began to associate regularly with the nation's Roman Catholic leaders, who rivaled their evangelical counterparts not just in their commitments to anticommunism and Christian religiosity, but in their growing fame and celebrity.[18]

In Washington, Hoover stood out as one of the few influential Protestant officials willing to ally himself with the Catholic Church. "I am a Protestant," he told a group of laymen. "As a Protestant, I say sincerely and from experience that the Catholic Church is the greatest protective influence in our nation today." Many Catholic leaders shared Hoover's worries that the nation was succumbing to moral decline, thus making itself vulnerable to communist incursions. And they recognized Hoover as a leading voice on such matters, showering him with speaking invitations and public praise. During the 1940s and early 1950s, Hoover received an honorary degree or delivered a graduation speech at nearly every major Catholic university: Notre Dame, Marquette, Seton Hall, Catholic, Holy Cross. Under the circumstances, it made sense that some Americans were unsure about his true religious affiliation, one Catholic writer acknowledged, because "so often has J. Edgar Hoover been quoted by the Catholic Press, so often has he spoken to Catholic gatherings, so many times has he been eulogized and honored by Catholic institutions."

Hoover's top supporter in the Catholic celebrity pantheon was Bishop Fulton Sheen, a "radio priest" and leading voice of the anticommunist right. Beginning in the late

1930s, Sheen drew up to four million listeners to his NBC radio show, *The Catholic Hour*. In 1952, he added a weekly television show, *Life Is Worth Living*, which he conducted in full priestly regalia. A university-trained philosopher as well as a priest, Sheen struck a pose of reasoned contemplation, broadcasting from his book-lined office with monologues on the problem of sin and the mysteries of the afterlife, as well as those topics most dear to Hoover's heart: crime, juvenile delinquency, and communism. He shared his thoughts directly with Hoover in letters musing about Soviet tyranny and about historian Arnold Toynbee's views on the collapse of civilizations.

Sheen's flair for the dramatic produced several high-profile conversions among men and women within Hoover's orbit. In 1945, it had been Sheen who persuaded the *Daily Worker*'s Louis Budenz to renounce communism in favor of Catholicism, at which point Budenz began to speak with the FBI. In November 1948, a few months after her HUAC testimony, Sheen also baptized Elizabeth Bentley in Washington, making her conversion away from communism official. Hoover found Sheen not only politically inspiring but also "the metaphysician at his best," able to connect high-minded first principles to daunting political realities.[19]

Sheen's chief rival in Hoover's affections was Cardinal Francis Spellman, the famed head of the archdiocese of New York. In 1942, Hoover joined Spellman for a radio broadcast titled "America Fights for God-Given Rights," sponsored by the Knights of Columbus, the Catholic equivalent of the Masons. Four years later, in a gala evening at New York's University Club, Spellman presented Hoover with the highest award of the Catholic Youth Organization. Hoover warned his faithful audience to be "on guard against the strategy of the high command of American Communists," who were seeking to hide "evils" and "corruption" behind lovely phrases. Spellman pronounced the situation "terrifying." A few months later, he brought that message to the FBI itself as a keynote speaker at the National Academy graduation.[20]

What drew these celebrity priests to Hoover was the same thing that attracted their evangelical counterparts: his strong views on communism and crime, and his willingness to speak out about them. For those further down the Catholic hierarchy, there were other affinities as well. Like Hoover's FBI, the Catholic Church emphasized authority and tradition, the need to follow policy and ritual and the rules as prescribed. Catholic priests, like FBI agents, operated in a world of male sociability, set off from society at large as an especially worthy and disciplined elite. Rumors of homosexuality (some of them quite plausible) followed figures like Spellman, just as they followed Hoover. Within their respective organizations, though, such talk was denounced as itself a form of immorality and corruption, an effort to destroy otherwise heroic leaders. "I frankly believe that most of us are following in the footsteps of one who is much greater than any of us," Assistant Director Ed Tamm wrote in a private letter to a former Bureau colleague. Though a loyal Catholic, Tamm was referring not to Christ or God or the Pope, but to Hoover.

Tamm was hardly alone in seeing these connections. Just as the FBI's wartime expansion provided new opportunities for women in the clerical and scientific ranks, it opened space for would-be agents who did not fit Hoover's favored Protestant mold. Catholics rushed in to fill the void. If GW remained Hoover's prime recruiting ground, Georgetown emerged as its Catholic corollary, a local institution where well-trained boys could be plucked for government service. By 1940, there were already fifty-four Georgetown graduates employed at the FBI including Tamm, the Bureau's highest-ranking Catholic. As time went on, the Bureau also began to recruit heavily from Fordham University in New York, along with other Catholic universities throughout the East Coast and Midwest. Catholic-educated men arrived already trained for the FBI's culture of deference and conservatism. "I like to think the FBI and Fordham have the same ideas," the university's president wrote to Hoover in 1945.[21]

Hoover expressed appreciation for the way Catholic schools, especially in the lower grades, guaranteed insulation from secular and subversive influences. The Catholic church "has more than 12,000 schools without a single atheistic teacher among them," he told one parochial magazine in 1949, "not a single non-Christian or non-American principle is taught." Just as Hoover sought Protestant agents whose institutional affiliations—church, school, fraternity—indicated likely sympathy with Bureau culture, he accepted a Catholic education as a likely marker of a good fit.[22]

Once at the FBI, Catholic agents were afforded regular opportunities to reflect upon their faith, and to engage in religious expression. Beginning in the late 1940s, the FBI held an annual communion breakfast, starting with a dedicated morning mass at a local cathedral, followed by a group repast at a nearby hotel. On occasion, Hoover also sent a select group of agents—mostly but not exclusively Catholic—on weekend retreat at Manresa-on-Severn, a Jesuit center in Annapolis, Maryland. Hoover described the retreat as a chance for agents to fortify themselves against the temptations and confusions of modern life. "In a world which seems to be teetering on the brink of self-destruction, when many of our pseudo-theories are becoming loose in the seams, would it not be wise to hold the headlong plunge and seek again the simple truths which were preached by the Man of Galilee?" he asked. "During a retreat, men have an opportunity to ponder the truths of Christianity and to gain understanding of the evils which torment their everyday world."

Though Hoover did not attend the retreats, he forged a close friendship with Father Robert Lloyd, the guiding light of the Manresa retreat. Hoover referred to Lloyd—not Elson—as "our chaplain of the FBI," the one man who had done more than any other to shepherd Bureau agents into spiritual contemplation. As one Catholic magazine recognized, theirs was a common crusade, built on shared politics and a shared vision of the nation's existential plight. "The Catholic Church in America today is engaged in gigantic efforts to protect the things which Hoover knows we must preserve lest we perish," the magazine concluded. It declared Hoover, spiritually if not literally, one of theirs.[23]

MANY OF WASHINGTON'S LEADING FIGURES WOULD SOON COME TO EMBRACE Hoover's overt religiosity, with its blend of familial, spiritual, and political themes. By the mid-1950s, the city—indeed, much of the entire nation—would be in the throes of a "religious awakening," in Elson's words, in which church attendance and public displays of devotion served as signs of virtuous citizenship. No less than the celebrity ministers and radio priests of his era, Hoover helped to make this shift possible. As head of the FBI, though, he exercised forms of institutional and political power that such men could only imagine. Both his critics and admirers understood that what made Hoover's example so influential was not his depth of fervor or Biblical insight. It was the fact that he commanded a government institution capable of translating his ideas from words into action.[24]

CHAPTER 32

Atomic Drama

(1949–1951)

Ethel and Julius Rosenberg, leaving court after their conviction for atomic espionage in March 1951. Through the top-secret Venona project, Hoover had evidence of Julius's guilt, though he argued to spare Ethel's life.

LIBRARY OF CONGRESS, *WORLD-TELEGRAM* PHOTO BY ROGER HIGGINS

I n the fall of 1949, as the Hiss, Coplon, and Smith Act trials were winding down, Hoover sent an agent out to greet a ship arriving in New York Harbor. On board was a man named Harold "Kim" Philby, the latest in a string of liaisons from MI6 in London. The son of a famed scholar and diplomat, Philby had spent a lifetime being groomed for high government service: elite boarding school, then Cambridge, then knockabout experiments in journalism before recruitment into British intelligence. Toward the end of the war, he had served as head of counterespionage in Britain, working closely with the Americans on their mutual ally turned foe, the Soviet Union. Now, he was being sent to Washington to continue that work as the British point man for FBI and CIA counterintelligence.

According to Philby's supervisor, Hoover had opposed the appointment, worried that the British were trying to run intelligence operations on U.S. soil, just as they had during the war. So Philby was surprised at the warm reception he received. Aboard the ship, he offered the welcoming agent a glass of Tio Pepe sherry. Hoover's man sipped the drink dutifully but "unhappily," in Philby's description, a sour note that Philby attributed less to the FBI's ban on work-time drinking and more to the agent's lack of sophistication. "The men of the FBI, with hardly an exception, were proud of their insularity, of having sprung from the grass roots," Philby later wrote. Though he admired their solidity, he thought Hoover's agents lacked the "cosmopolitan postures" and lively curiosity necessary for truly effective intelligence work. That assumption may have made it easier to contemplate what he was really planning to do, unbeknownst to either the British or American authorities.[1]

From New York, Philby left for Washington, where the ins and outs of intelligence—and its failures—were increasingly the talk of the town. The Hiss, Coplon, and Smith Act cases were heading toward resolution but still mired in back-and-forth about Hoover's methods and the disclosure of files. Into this mix came the blockbuster news, delivered by Truman on September 23, that sensors near the Soviet Union had picked up on radioactive particles—"evidence that within recent weeks an atomic explosion occurred in the USSR." That same month, the Chinese Civil War hurtled to an end with an outcome that had once seemed unthinkable: communist victory in the world's most populous country. Taken together, the developments sent shock waves through the city, where most federal officials had assumed—or at least hoped—that the U.S. was returning to peace rather than spinning back toward global war.[2]

Many politicians, especially Republicans, blamed Truman's alleged softness on espionage for this dramatic turnaround in communist fortunes. "The Russians undoubtedly gained 3 to 5 years in producing the atomic bomb because our government from the White House down has been sympathetic toward the views of Communists and fellow travelers, with the result that it has been infiltrated by a network of spies," alleged Representative Harold Velde, a former FBI agent recently elected to Congress as a Republican from Illinois. The suspicions grew darker still in June 1950, when the communist army of North Korea crossed into South Korea, sparking a ground war that many feared would devolve into a nuclear-armed World War III.[3]

Philby knew something about how atomic politics worked in Washington. His college chum from Cambridge, Donald Maclean, had worked in the U.S. from 1944 to 1948, where he was privy to the inner workings of the Manhattan Project and Atomic Energy Commission. Philby had a different assignment, though one that would still put him in the thick of debate over how the Soviets had acquired the bomb so quickly. Specifically, he was supposed to "tighten links with CIA and loosen those with the FBI," all "without the FBI noticing" that the British now considered the CIA the go-to agency on all things Soviet. Philby knew about Hoover's resentment over the creation of the OSS and ultimately the CIA, "the only serious defeat suffered by Hoover in his political career," in Philby's view. He also heard that Hoover could be a "prima donna" who was "childishly sensitive" when it came to professional rivals. Philby himself preferred the

company of CIA men such as James Angleton, the pale, sunken-eyed mystic who had
spent time in London during the war and who was now back in Washington.

Philby met with Hoover anyway, and Hoover seems to have liked him well enough.
At the very least, he deferred to Philby's official position. The Venona team had been
sharing regular updates with British intelligence, on the logic that they might have
something in their files that would help with identification. Now Philby began visiting
Arlington Hall, home base of the Venona project, where the FBI stood ready to share
everything it had learned. Robert Lamphere, Hoover's liaison to Venona, recalled being
unable to detect Philby's much-talked-about charm. "I could hardly believe that this
unimpressive man was being spoken of as a future chief of MI-6, in line for a knighthood," Lamphere would write decades later, though his impressions may have been
clouded by all that happened in between. Philby was no more thrilled with Lamphere,
whom he later dismissed as "a nice puddingy native of Ohio," diligent and decent like
so many of Hoover's men but lacking the spark that made for greatness.[4]

One of the matters they discussed over the next several weeks involved a Soviet
source named "Homer," an as yet unidentified employee who had worked at the British
Embassy in 1945 and 1946. They also discussed "Enormoz," the Soviet code word for
the Manhattan Project and a major focus of clandestine Russian ambitions. Hoover
had realized well before the bomb became a reality that the Soviets had infiltrated the
Manhattan Project. "The most striking example of Comintern operations in this country has been uncovered in connection with the Soviet-directed espionage attempts
against military research projects dealing with atomic explosives," the San Francisco
field office noted as early as 1944. But not until Venona came along was the FBI able
to start making real progress in identifying likely culprits in this area. One apparently
worked under the name "Liberal," according to cables deciphered during 1948, handling contacts with "persons working on ENORMOZ and other spheres of technical
science." Then, in September 1949, just as Philby arrived in Washington, the Venona
team deciphered a cable identifying a high-level scientist who had provided information to the Soviets "directly from inside the Manhattan Project." That decryption in
turn set off a series of cascading revelations that would lead Hoover and the FBI to the
most famous atomic spies in American history: Julius and Ethel Rosenberg.[5]

Like the Hiss case, the Rosenberg trial would divide the country into warring camps.
Some condemned the couple as traitors. Others insisted they were innocent, citing the
suspicious coincidence between the Soviets' detonation of the atomic bomb and the
FBI's discovery of someone to blame. In truth, it was sheer happenstance that the Venona team broke those particular cables at the moment they did. The broader geopolitical stakes nonetheless shaped how Americans made sense of the charges, with some
accusing Hoover of conducting a witch hunt against innocent left-wing activists and
others insisting that under the circumstances, the charges made perfect sense. At no
point did Hoover attempt to clear up the confusion by revealing the Venona cables,

opting to let the debate spin on without disclosing what he knew. Nor did he initially come clean about the other great secret discovered by the FBI in the midst of the Rosenberg affair. Despite Hoover's positive first impressions, Kim Philby was not the man he appeared to be.[6]

THE "STARTLING BIT OF INFORMATION" REVEALED BY VENONA THAT FALL— the vital clue "directly from inside the Manhattan Project"—pointed to a Soviet agent nestled within the British scientific mission. According to the deciphered cable, he appeared to be an expert on the gaseous diffusion process involved in refining uranium, sent to the U.S. to lend his technical expertise. Within a few months, the Venona team narrowed the description down to a German-born British scientist named Klaus Fuchs, the one man whose assignments, relationships, and scientific background best fit what the cables described. By that point Fuchs was back in Britain, but still working on nuclear projects. Hoover passed along word of the FBI's suspicions to his British counterparts, who brought Fuchs in for questioning. Fuchs held out for more than a month before confessing that he had indeed spied for the Soviets both during and after the war, much of it as a high-level nuclear scientist assigned to the Manhattan Project. When the news came back around to Hoover, Lamphere recalled, "all hell broke loose at Bureau headquarters."[7]

Hoover took an intense interest in the "Foocase," ordering agents to seek out "any leads in this country" who might have aided their British scientific comrade. When it came to questioning Fuchs, though, the British wanted him all to themselves. Hoover sent an FBI representative to London on standby, with instructions that "it is vitally important that this be pressed + we get from British all they have." But all he had to go on for weeks was the hint that a Soviet operative named "Raymond" had been Fuchs's handler in the United States. Hoover denounced the British for their "outrageous attitude" in denying the FBI access to Fuchs, especially "after all of the cooperation we have extended to the British over the years." When Philby met with Hoover that winter to try to make amends, he allegedly found the FBI director "in a state of high excitement," convinced that the British were conspiring to humiliate the FBI.[8]

The British government formally arrested Fuchs on February 2, 1950. They charged him with violations of the Official Secrets Act, thus making news of his treachery public for the first time. The next day, Hoover rushed to the Senate Appropriations Committee to present what he knew, which was not all that much. With Tolson at his side, he confirmed in a closed session that Fuchs was part of "an international super-espionage ring which has fed Russia a terrifying wealth of atomic secrets," in the words of one news report. A few days later, accompanied by both Tolson and Nichols, he went into executive session again before the Joint Committee on Atomic Energy. There, he was forced to admit that the U.S. government had trusted the British to vet its own personnel—that nobody imagined that they would miss a spy so high in their ranks. After Hoover's testimony, the committee's chairman informed the press that "there can be no doubt" about Fuchs's culpability and "knowledge both as to atomic weapons and so-called hydrogen bombs." Hoover remained cagey, however, about how Fuchs had first been identified. Determined not to disclose Venona but eager to take credit, he maintained that FBI wiretaps and general surveillance had provided the essential clues.[9]

British resistance to more direct FBI involvement continued for two more months: through Fuchs's trial, conviction, and sentencing (he received fourteen years, the maximum), and then for several weeks after that. Hoover cajoled and threatened, warning London "that there would be a very bad public reaction in this country against the British Government when it became known that the FBI, who had worked upon the Fuchs Case and was instrumental in developing the early leads in the same, had been denied access to Fuchs." Finally, in late April, the British gave in. Philby delivered the good news to FBI official Mickey Ladd, who relayed it to Hoover: the FBI was at last permitted to interview the atomic spy it had helped to identify.[10]

The interview with Fuchs turned out to be highly productive. Hoover sent Lamphere and Clegg to London to do the questioning—the former, for his knowledge of Venona; the latter, for his hard-and-fast loyalty to Hoover's methods and priorities. They started off by discussing Raymond, Fuchs's American handler, about whom Fuchs apparently remembered far more than he had previously let on. Within a few weeks, the FBI had identified Raymond as Harry Gold, a Russian-born chemist who already had a thick Bureau file. On May 22, agents in Philadelphia interviewed Gold and searched his apartment, where they came across a damning local map left over from a 1945 visit to Fuchs at Los Alamos National Laboratory, in New Mexico. Back in London, Fuchs identified his old contact based on photos found in the apartment. The FBI promptly arrested Gold.[11]

That arrest produced adoring headlines in which the FBI, not the British, finally received credit for capturing an atomic spy. Over the next few weeks, there were more arrests and more headlines, as Gold confessed and provided details—many highly ambiguous—about his American and Soviet contacts. In June, the FBI arrested a former army sergeant and Los Alamos machinist named David Greenglass as part of Gold's extended network. Like Fuchs, Greenglass confessed and named his own handler: his brother-in-law, Julius Rosenberg.[12]

IN HER 1945 CONFESSION, ELIZABETH BENTLEY HAD DESCRIBED AN ENCOUNTER with a "tall, thin bespectacled" engineer named "Julius" at New York's Knickerbocker Village apartment complex. The FBI had never managed to identify Julius—indeed, had barely tried—but now the connection was obvious, since Rosenberg, an engineer, lived at the Knickerbocker. His profile also conformed with what the Venona team had discovered about the Soviet operative named "Liberal" (also known as "Antenna"), who had recruited and managed a tight group of fellow engineers, chemists, and machinists engaged in both atomic and industrial espionage during the war. One of the Liberal cables mentioned a wife named Ethel: twenty-nine years old, married for about five years—another fit with Rosenberg's profile. Other decryptions filled in background details: Liberal was a twenty-five-year-old Communist Party member living in New York, who had spent much of the war with the U.S. Army Signal Corps at Fort Monmouth, New Jersey. "So much can now be known about LIBERAL and his wife and friends that it would seem possible to identify him," the Venona team had determined in 1948. But it was not until two years later, after Greenglass's confession, that they homed in on Rosenberg as the spy the cables had described.[13]

When agents brought Rosenberg in for questioning in July 1950, Hoover was hoping that what had happened with Fuchs, Gold, and Greenglass would now occur again—that Rosenberg would confess, name names, and keep the whole investigation going. The Venona decrypts assured Hoover that they had the right man: "the operating head of a large espionage group" who "personally handled the recruiting of agents and the collection of scientific data," in the words of one FBI document. But Venona alone could only do so much. By the time Rosenberg went to trial, Venona had helped the FBI to identify 108 people who had worked with the Soviets in one manner or another—of whom a whopping sixty-four "were not previously known to us as involved in espionage." Despite this mother lode of information, vanishingly few had been arrested, and even fewer had been prosecuted in court. Without other evidence to corroborate what they knew from Venona, Hoover and the federal authorities were unable to act against even the most obviously guilty parties. As a result, many of them got off scot-free. Some, like Rosenberg's friends Joel Barr and Alfred Sarant, fled the United States, eventually ending up in the Soviet Union. Others, such as the young nuclear physicist Theodore Hall, who supplied technical information from Los Alamos, stonewalled the Bureau and then simply went on with their lives.[14]

The Rosenberg case had more going for it. Rosenberg appeared to be "possibly the most important espionage agent which we have arrested to date," in the words of one FBI assessment. The FBI also already had a highly voluble and cooperative witness. In his confession, Greenglass had ticked off the secret technical information he had provided to Rosenberg. He had second thoughts about his participation in espionage only after Rosenberg warned him to flee the country as the FBI began to close in on Gold and Fuchs. Greenglass had ignored the advice, since the family had a new baby and his wife, Ruth, had recently suffered an accident that left her with severe burns over much of her body. Instead, he chose to stay and tell the FBI what he knew, in hopes of winning leniency. Ruth agreed to talk as well. Under FBI questioning, she identified both Julius and Ethel as active participants in what amounted to an atomic espionage plot.[15]

The Greenglass statements had problems; both David and Ruth changed their stories frequently, conjuring up provocative new details at just the moments they seemed to be needed. But what they said aligned well enough with what Hoover was learning through other sources—the Venona cables, the Gold and Fuchs confessions—to give him the confidence to press ahead. In an ideal scenario, FBI agents would use the Greenglass statements to pressure Rosenberg into confessing and cooperating. But he surprised them. "ROSENBERG will not talk," one agent noted ominously in the wake of his initial interview. Rosenberg stuck with that position under interrogation and then, as of July 17, under arrest.[16]

Rosenberg's reticence inspired Hoover to consider another point of leverage. "If Julius Rosenberg would furnish details of his extensive espionage activities it would be possible to proceed against other individuals," he wrote two days after Rosenberg's arrest. "Proceeding against his wife might serve as a lever in this matter." Ethel had appeared in Venona as the twenty-nine-year-old wife of Liberal. About her involvement in espionage, though, the cables were more ambiguous. One crucial message noted that she "knows about her husband's work" but that "in view of (her) delicate health does not work" herself. Venona analysts speculated that the reference to "work" might not mean "the earning of her bread and butter, but conspiratorial work." In other words, they suspected that she knew about but did not necessarily participate in her husband's espionage activities.[17]

From this analysis the Justice Department had originally concluded that "they do not believe there is sufficient evidence developed to charge ETHEL ROSENBERG." After weeks of stonewalling by her husband, however, they changed their minds. In August, department lawyers questioned Ethel before a grand jury in New York. Like her husband, she refused to talk, aside from admitting to a general history of communist sympathies. On August 11, FBI agents arrested her as she left the Foley Square courthouse, primly dressed in white gloves and a light blue dress with white polka dots. Both she and Julius spent the next several months in prison, cut off from their two sons, ages three and seven. Hoover hoped that seeing his wife and children suffer—combined with the threat of conviction—would induce Rosenberg to talk. But as the Venona analysts noted in late February, neither Julius nor Ethel "have been in any way cooperative." Under the circumstances, Hoover agreed, the next logical step was prosecution.[18]

IF THE GOVERNMENT HAD CHOSEN AT THIS MOMENT TO REVEAL VENONA, with its frank descriptions of Julius's espionage activities (and more ambiguous words about Ethel), the Rosenberg name would have meant something very different to a generation of Americans, especially to the liberals and leftists who took up the Rosenbergs' cause as their own. It might also have spared the Rosenbergs from their fate, since what was revealed in Venona about the actual information handed over to the Soviets was somewhat less dramatic and consequential than the Rosenbergs' popular image as master atomic spies would suggest. At the very least, it would have given the Rosenbergs less reason to insist upon their innocence. But nobody, including Hoover, truly entertained the idea. As during the Coplon trial, Hoover was convinced that protecting Venona would be worth almost any amount of difficulty, since it was the government's one reliable way to trace the Soviets' connections and networks. The trial and its aftermath nonetheless swirled with rumors of "secret evidence" that explained the government's confidence in the Rosenbergs' guilt. To Hoover, the couple's refusal to admit the truth—when Hoover *knew* what Julius had done—only reinforced the idea that they were indeed heartless communist agents of the first order. Their limited success as spies mattered less than the single great fact that they had cast their lot with the Soviets.[19]

The Rosenberg trial began on March 6, 1951, in room 107 of the same Foley Square courthouse where the three-ring circus of the Hiss, Smith Act, and Coplon trials had played itself out. Hoover liked the judge, Irving Kaufman, who had served as a special assistant to the attorney general after the war and was known, in one FBI official's words, to be "historically pro-Hoover" and anticommunist. Hoover was less fond of U.S. Attorney Irving Saypol, who in prosecuting both the Hiss and Smith Act cases had revealed himself, in the view of top FBI officials, as a showboater. Both Saypol and Kaufman were Jewish—proof, according to their supporters, that the Rosenberg prosecution was not being driven by anti-Semitism. So was the Rosenbergs' codefendant Morton Sobell, a fellow Communist Party member and City College graduate. Sobell had fled to Mexico with his family, hoping to make his way to the Soviet Union. Hoover had arranged for them to be snatched up by local authorities and driven eight hundred miles back to the U.S. border.[20]

The prosecution's opening statement drew upon Hoover's black-and-white view of the communist threat. "The evidence will show their loyalty to and worship of the Soviet Union, and by their rank disloyalty to our country these defendants joined with their co-conspirators in a deliberate, carefully planned conspiracy to deliver to the Soviet Union the information and the weapons which the Soviet Union could use to destroy us," Saypol declared. The defense countered that the whole idea was a wild fantasy, that Julius was merely an innocent leftist and Ethel "basically a housewife." The jury's chief task, according to the defense, was to guard against the "bias or prejudice or hysteria" raging through American society. Hanging over both sides was the possibility of the death penalty, the first time since the execution of the Nazi saboteurs that accused traitors might be put to death on the basis of FBI evidence. Hoover viewed a death sentence not only as a potentially just outcome but also as another point of leverage toward what was still his top priority: neither convicting nor killing the Rosenbergs, but persuading them to talk.

Both Elizabeth Bentley and Harry Gold testified at the trial. But it was David Greenglass who emerged as the star witness, describing how his brother-in-law, Julius, with the quiet assistance of his sister, Ethel, had convinced him to become a Soviet spy. The family connections gave the trial a soap-opera quality—betrayal on a grand and highly personal scale. Ruth testified as well, recounting a critical scene in which Ethel, acting as her husband's assistant, had typed up some notes from Los Alamos. The Rosenbergs offered little in the way of rebuttal, taking the stand only to say that their relatives had made up the whole story. Sobell never took the stand at all. "This is a case of the Greenglasses against the Rosenbergs," defense counsel maintained—and on this point, at least, both sides could agree. On March 29, after less than a month of testimony, the jury sided with the Greenglasses, delivering guilty verdicts for all three defendants.[21]

Kaufman gave Hoover credit for the outcome. "I say a great tribute is due to the Federal Bureau of Investigation and to J. Edgar Hoover for the splendid job they have done in this case," he declared in court. When it came to sentencing, though, Hoover and Kaufman did not quite see eye to eye. Queried via back channels about his preferred scenario, Hoover recommended death for Julius as well as for Sobell, who had "not cooperated with the government and had undoubtedly furnished high classified information to the Russians." For Ethel he proposed a more lenient sentence of thirty years, in deference to her secondary role in her husband's espionage and her status as the mother of two children. He based these judgments less on what had happened at trial than on two external factors: his assessment of likely public opinion and his understanding of what the Venona cables had revealed. He expressed particular concern about the "psychological reaction" that might ensue if Ethel were sentenced to death, a young left-wing mother martyred by the American government. For David Greenglass, who had pleaded guilty, Hoover recommended fifteen years. Ruth Greenglass would not be prosecuted at all, in thanks for her cooperation.[22]

Kaufman took most of Hoover's suggestions, with one great exception. Rather than sparing Ethel and condemning Sobell, he sentenced both Julius and Ethel to death and gave Sobell thirty years. In explaining his decision, he blamed the Rosenbergs not just for facilitating the transfer of some moderately useful technical drawings, but for revealing the secret technology behind "the A-bomb" years before the Soviets would otherwise have discovered it. In the process, according to Kaufman, the Rosenbergs had subjected Americans to the threat of nuclear annihilation and enabled the start of the Korean War, with its fifty thousand U.S. casualties and counting. "I consider your crime worse than murder," he told them. "By your betrayal you undoubtedly have altered the course of history to the disadvantage of our country."

History was not yet done with the Rosenbergs, however. As Hoover had predicted, the dual death sentence, at first seen as an unequivocal FBI victory, soon began to inspire outrage throughout the world. In late 1951, American supporters organized the National Committee to Secure Justice in the Rosenberg Case, mobilizing prominent left-leaning political, intellectual, and artistic figures to push for a reversal of the verdict. Saving the Rosenbergs soon became an international cause célèbre, embraced by Pablo Picasso and Jean-Paul Sartre and even the Pope, along with millions of other sympathizers. The Rosenbergs continued to maintain their innocence, publishing sentimental jailhouse letters insisting, "We are an ordinary man and wife," persecuted only for left-wing idealism. Hoover thought the pressure campaign would—and should—backfire. "If the sentence is reduced," he wrote in May 1953, "we may well be charged with knuckling under to Communist pressure, not only abroad but in this country."[23]

Hoover held out hope to the end that the Rosenbergs, after exhausting all their appeals, would at last break down and talk. On the date of their execution, he stationed a team at Sing Sing prison to be on standby in case of any last-minute change of heart. He even made arrangements for leaping into action "if the Rosenbergs desire to talk after they go into the execution chamber and even after they are strapped into the chair." They did not. On June 19, 1953, the Rosenbergs were electrocuted just before sundown—first Julius, then Ethel—without ever naming names or disclosing to the FBI what they knew.[24]

PUBLICLY, HOOVER PROMOTED THE ROSENBERG CASE AS AN UNMITIGATED FBI victory. Among confidants, though, he acknowledged that things had not worked out entirely as planned. By refusing to talk, the Rosenbergs disrupted the thrilling chain of discovery that had begun with Fuchs. And when the next round of identifications came through, Hoover's spirits sank further. In the spring of 1951, Venona decryptions helped to identify two more men as Soviet operatives. Both were high up in British intelligence. And both were friends with FBI liaison Kim Philby. Based on this evidence, Hoover began to suspect that Philby, too, was an active Soviet spy—and that he had been sharing everything he learned about Venona with his bosses in the Soviet Union.

Hoover's path to this devastating conclusion was long, winding and painful. Not long after the Rosenberg arrests, Hoover received an honorary knighthood from the British government, bestowed by MI5 chief Percy Sillitoe—Hoover's British counterpart—in a cocktails-and-hors-d'oeuvres ceremony at the British Embassy in Washington. Throughout those months, Philby continued to entertain all manner of FBI and CIA officials at his home, often accompanied by Guy Burgess, a Foreign Service official and newcomer to Washington, assigned to the Embassy. Burgess had some of Philby's charm but none of his polish, maintaining a "poor personal appearance" as well as questionable personal behavior, according to the FBI, including drunken brawls, well-delivered insults, and the sexual company of men. But Philby liked, or at least tolerated Burgess, another old friend from Cambridge days. So the rest of the Washington intelligence establishment largely accepted the newcomer.[25]

Then, in April 1951, just days after the end of the Rosenberg trial, a new Venona decryption began to unravel the whole cozy arrangement. According to the latest break-through, the spy "Homer"—long known to be an employee at the wartime British Embassy—had taken a trip from Washington to New York in June 1944 to visit his pregnant wife. The details left no doubt that Homer was Donald Maclean, Philby's long-ago Cambridge friend who had also served in Washington. In 1948, Maclean had returned to Britain and ultimately become head of the American Department in the British Foreign Office, a post that now seemed to have alarming significance. A few days after the Homer discovery, Burgess went back to Britain to confer about the mat-ter. A few weeks after that, both men went missing, presumed to have defected to the Soviet Union.[26]

In Washington, it fell to Philby to notify the FBI about his two AWOL friends, and about the suspicion, already bubbling within British intelligence, that both had been longtime Soviet spies. During his "short interview" with Hoover, Philby assured him that the FBI could in no way be at fault—that it was the British who failed to identify the traitors in their midst. Hoover "jumped at" the absolution, according to Philby, never a "man to look a gift-horse in the mouth." Even then, though, Hoover did not see what would soon become obvious: Philby himself had been working with Ma-clean and Burgess.[27]

He finally came to that conclusion a few weeks later, after Philby had been called back to Britain amid questions about his own loyalty. High-ranking emissaries from British intelligence made a special trip to Washington to let FBI officials know of their "gravest suspicions" concerning Philby. At the CIA, a former FBI agent named Bill Harvey prepared a report on the available evidence. Like many CIA men, Harvey had joined Philby more than once for drinks, dinner, and gossip. Upon Philby's departure, Harvey undertook a study of the man, looking to fact patterns and circumstantial evidence to determine whether Philby, like Maclean and Burgess, might have been working for the Soviets. He concluded that the answer was obviously yes. Hoover was convinced, though not everyone yet agreed. Back in Britain, many of Philby's col-leagues initially rejected the notion as impossible, simply not the sort of thing that a man like Philby would do. At Hoover's FBI, faith in Philby's guilt quickly became conventional wisdom.[28]

The suspicion of Philby's betrayal "shook the Western intelligence and counterin-telligence services to their cores," Lamphere recalled. It was particularly devastating for the Venona team, which had proudly shared each new discovery with Philby. "The worst thing was that I believed he had compromised a lot of the intelligence advantage the FBI had as a result of deciphering the 1944-45 KGB messages," Lamphere later wrote. "For years I had had the optimistic feeling that, based on the breakthrough that the messages provided, we would go on and on uncovering and rolling up KGB networks in the United States. Now I understood that the KGB had to have known of our decipherment of the messages, and that our advantage was gone."[29]

Indeed, it was not just Philby who had taken a wrecking ball to the FBI's work. In 1950, amid the swirl of the Fuchs and Rosenberg cases, the Venona team learned that there was another spy with them inside Arlington Hall. A naturalized U.S. citizen born to Russian parents, William Weisband had none of Philby's aristocratic finesse or high-level access. But his job as a translator and language expert meant that he could wander the facilities, consult on top-secret decryptions, and peruse documents. Hoover's agents interviewed Weisband, hoping to elicit a confession that would lead to a prison sentence. Like the Rosenbergs, he refused to talk—and this time, there was no David Greenglass to point the finger. Weisband received a one-year sentence for contempt of court after refusing to testify before a grand jury. Then he went on with his life, albeit no longer in the employ of the U.S. government. At the FBI, he left behind a trail of shock, embarrassment, and dismay. But as the NSA later acknowledged, the Weisband disaster "was so successfully hushed" that the public and most of official Washington knew nothing about it.[30]

Philby himself maintained his innocence for another decade and then some, existing in a netherworld of suspicion and accusation. Finally, in 1962, an old acquaintance came forth with a story that he had tried to recruit her to spy for the Soviets in the 1930s. At that point, Philby's former friends in British intelligence brought him in for yet another interview. This time, he cracked. Amazingly, though, he was still not under arrest, so he defected to the Soviet Union.[31]

Venona researchers ultimately linked Philby to the Soviet code name "Stanley," putting together some of the pieces that had been sitting there all along. In the meantime, the near certainty of Philby's guilt helped to explain certain oddities and frustrations that had long plagued the FBI's counterespionage operations, starting with Elizabeth Bentley. In 1945 and 1946, Hoover had wondered why it was so hard to catch any of the people named in Bentley's confession. It turned out that Philby had passed along news of her defection almost as soon as it happened, and the Soviets had sent out warnings for the members of her network to lie low. Philby's deception also explained some of the anomalies in the Rosenberg case, including the fact that Sobell had known to flee to Mexico, and that so many other members of the Rosenberg network had evaded capture in other ways. "It is believed possible that members of the Rosenberg espionage network [redacted] may have been warned by the Soviets of their possible exposure by the FBI, and they may have fled the United States," an FBI report concluded. "While this is pure speculation, it is believed logical."[32]

In this new context, Hoover judged the Soviets harshly for allowing the Rosenbergs to be executed, rather than extracting them and providing them with refuge in the Soviet Union. For this, too, he blamed Philby. According to an FBI memo, "Philby and his Russian spy chiefs in Moscow even knew that the FBI planned to arrest the Rosenbergs and Morton Sobell, yet they chose to sacrifice them, most probably to keep Philby's identity a secret." If the U.S. had placed a high priority on Venona, in short, so had the Soviets. They went to great lengths to shield Philby and maintain his place in Washington, where he had access to everything the Americans discovered.[33]

"What it comes to," one CIA official concluded, "is that when you look at the whole period from 1944 to 1951, the entire Western intelligence effort, which was pretty big, was at what you might call minus advantage. We would have been better off doing nothing." After 1951, in any case, the revelations from Venona slowed dramatically, no longer driven by the high confidence that the Americans had gotten one over on the Soviets.[34]

Even then, though, the government did not reveal the project to the public or stop working on it altogether. In 1956, an FBI assessment took up the question of whether Venona should at last be exposed so that its information could be used in court. The memo cited the many prosecutions already guided "directly or indirectly" by Venona: Coplon and Gubitchev, Fuchs and Gold, Sobell and the Rosenbergs. But there were many other known espionage agents, including those identified long ago by Elizabeth Bentley, who were still walking free, thanks to a lack of corroborating evidence. Revealing Venona might at last bring them to justice, the memo suggested—before concluding once again, based on "a careful study of all factors," that disclosure "would not be in the best interests of the U.S. or the Bureau." Among the reasons cited was the fact that the Soviets did not, even now, know precisely how much the Americans had uncovered—which cables had been deciphered and which had not. The memo also noted that the decryptions were hard to explain and understand. Any attempt to do so might "place the Bureau right in the middle of a violent political war" about who was to blame for the Cold War, the Red Scare, and the Western world's intelligence failures.[35]

And so Hoover let things stand as they were. The debate over the Rosenbergs' guilt—and over the truth or falsity of ex-communist witnesses such as Bentley and Chambers—would remain for decades one of the major cleavage points in American society. In all that time, Hoover never questioned which side he was on. If anything, the Philby episode told him that he had not been nearly suspicious, or even paranoid, enough in the 1940s, when he first encountered the Soviet espionage question. The impossible had turned out to be true: the top British intelligence official in the United States was in fact a Soviet operative. So were dozens of other men and women, their activities described in the Venona cables but their identities as yet unknown. Hoover believed those things with great certainty, even if he could not share the full details beyond a small inside group. That disconnect only made him more impatient with critics inclined to question his methods and evidence: Hoover knew what he knew and believed what he believed, and it was up to everyone else to trust him.

From the Soviet Union, Philby looked back with contempt at all of Hoover's posturing and missteps as an intelligence chief. But he gave Hoover credit for savvy political judgment—for knowing when to fight and when to fold, when to keep secrets and when to reveal them. "Hoover is a great politician," Philby concluded. "His blanket methods and ruthless authoritarianism are the wrong weapons for the subtle world of intelligence. But they have other uses."[36]

CHAPTER 33

Hooverism

(1950–1952)

OVERSHADOWED

Despite their friendship and shared anticommunist outlook, Hoover often found himself at odds with Senator Joseph McCarthy. The cartoon depicts McCarthy's demand in 1950 for the disclosure of FBI files. Hoover fiercely resisted it. *Commercial Appeal* (Memphis), March 29, 1950.

COMMERCIAL APPEAL/
NATIONAL ARCHIVES AND
RECORDS ADMINISTRATION

Hoover met Joseph McCarthy in 1947, a full three years before anyone associated the senator's name with the issue of communism. Born to a hardscrabble farm family, McCarthy was thirty-eight years old when he arrived in Washington, tall and lean and country-boy energetic (if starting to go bald up front). He talked often of having spent his childhood engaged in shooting the skunks that endangered his family's chickens, a skill that he implied had certain uses in political life. While earning his law degree at Marquette University, he joined the boxing team and played high-stakes poker. A few years later, McCarthy was elected to the state bench, becoming the youngest circuit judge in living memory. After Pearl Harbor, he left that post to join the Marines, recognizing early on that military service would enhance his political résumé. Assigned to debrief pilots in the South Pacific, McCarthy persuaded them to take him up on safe flights and let him play with the big guns. Along the way, he acquired the photos that he would later inflate into the legend of himself as "Tail-Gunner Joe."

McCarthy had returned from the war with an eye on the Senate seat of famed Wisconsin progressive Robert La Follette Jr., son of former senator and presidential candidate Robert La Follette Sr. The aspiration reflected McCarthy's outsize confidence. Few nameless and penniless thirtysomethings would have taken on the state's kingmaker. McCarthy mostly stuck to personal attacks, excoriating La Follette as a Washington insider who had lost touch with the people. McCarthy won the Republican primary by just over 1 percent of the vote, the first defeat for the La Follette dynasty in decades. When La Follette killed himself several years later, his friends and family blamed it on McCarthy's nastiness during the campaign, and on La Follette's dismay at the culture of lies and demagoguery that their primary contest helped to unleash.[1]

In 1947, when Hoover met him, McCarthy was still a nobody by Senate standards. His first encounters with Hoover were social rather than professional, inasmuch as such distinctions were possible in Washington. Upon arriving in the city, McCarthy began to frequent Harvey's, the restaurant where Hoover and Tolson retreated every night. He also started attending the horse races at Pimlico and Bowie, among the few weekend sites where Hoover and Tolson could be found with some regularity. By April, three months into his first Senate term, McCarthy had become enough of an insider to wrangle an invitation to a postrace celebration at the home of Julius Lulley, the owner of Harvey's and one of Hoover's closest friends outside the FBI.[2]

When it came to political style, Hoover and McCarthy did not always see eye to eye. McCarthy was a populist, inclined to lampoon career federal employees as second raters drunk on their own power. "Do you like to have some government bureaucrat tell you how to manage your life?" one of his campaign ads had demanded. In other ways, though, he appealed to Hoover's sensibilities: he was a Midwestern Catholic, a self-described conservative and patriot, a man of ambition who resented the clubbiness of the East Coast elite. When McCarthy telephoned the director's office a few weeks after the gathering at Lulley's home, Hoover took the call, the first recorded instance of a professional exchange between the two men. Over the next three years, they built a relationship based on general affinity but not bound by any particular issue.[3]

McCarthy was not especially concerned with communism in the late 1940s—at least, no more than many other senators appeared to be. Instead, he focused on building a fairly conventional Washington career. Hoover helped him along toward that goal. In 1948, Hoover invited McCarthy to give the keynote address at the National Academy graduation, a reliable sign of political favor and insider status. The following year, he appeared as a guest on McCarthy's radio show, where they discussed "waste and inefficiency," the FBI's triumphs in scientific policing, and the ongoing scourge of juvenile delinquency. Not until the end did they broach the subject of communism. Even then McCarthy merely asked what the FBI was up to and Hoover responded with expressions of general concern. In May 1949, when McCarthy spoke on the Senate floor in honor of Hoover's twenty-fifth anniversary as FBI director, the senator again barely mentioned communism, praising Hoover as "the great nonpartisan figure in Washington" and leader of the nation's most efficient and outstanding government bureau.[4]

All of which made it a shock when, on February 9, 1950, McCarthy declared in a speech before the Ohio County Women's Republican Club in Wheeling, West Virginia, that "I have here in my hand" a list of 205 card-carrying communists supposedly working for the State Department. Coming less than a month after Hiss's conviction for perjury, and mere days after Klaus Fuchs's arrest, McCarthy's remarks appeared to be a signal that he was joining Hoover in the battle against communism. In truth, it was the beginning of a yearslong struggle between the two men, as personal friendship and common cause pulled in one direction, while institutional politics and professional ambition pulled in another.

McCarthy turned out to be noisy and reckless, a talented showman and propagandist. But he never had Hoover's political skills, or his interest in the slow, difficult work of institution building. By the time McCarthy burst on the national scene, Hoover had already spent years battling domestic communism and attempting to root out Soviet spies. McCarthy had played no role in any of it—Venona, the Smith Act trial, the Hiss drama, the Coplon affair, and now the Fuchs and Rosenberg cases—much less in the mundane daily work of surveillance, infiltration, and publicity. "McCarthyism," the word that came to capture the sordid side of anticommunist politics, would turn out to be mostly a surface phenomenon, a wild media drama of accusation and counteraccusation, of truth and lies. "Hooverism," the less popular term, came first, lasted longer, and mattered more.[5]

As Philby observed, Hoover was not just an investigator but a political actor, with a mind toward institutional stability and affairs of state. McCarthy knew how to attract headlines, to lob accusations that set and then reset the national conversation. Hoover knew how to create policies and alliances, and how to make them hold over the long term. McCarthy welcomed scandal and criticism and bare-knuckle partisanship. Hoover did what he could to avoid them. McCarthy showed little regard for the facts. Hoover made facts and evidence his stock-in-trade. Though he appreciated McCarthy's fervor, Hoover soon came to view the senator as a threat to the FBI. Far from making himself more valuable to Hoover by plunging into anticommunist politics, McCarthy turned himself into a problem that Hoover would spend four years attempting to solve.

MCCARTHY'S WHEELING SPEECH COULD EASILY HAVE BEEN CONSIGNED TO OBscurity, another small-time senator ranting about the Red threat and the "traitorous actions" of a coddled elite. But McCarthy kept making the speech in other settings, varying the details and tone as he moved from town to town. In Salt Lake City, he lowered the number of "card-carrying" communists in the State Department to fifty-seven. On February 20, when he spoke for nearly eight hours on the floor of the Senate, he described "81 loyalty risks," each of them "twisted mentally or physically in some way." The press ate it up. But his fellow congressmen worried that McCarthy was going too far too fast, without considering the consequences. Hoover shared those concerns. He had spent the past several years trying to make the FBI the final authority on all things communist. Now it was McCarthy in the headlines.[6]

In late February, hoping to stop McCarthy's accusations before they gathered too much momentum, the Democrat-controlled Senate voted to create a subcommittee to investigate the truth or falsity of the senator's charges. A few weeks later, committee chair Millard Tydings (D-Maryland) wrote to the White House to demand the disclosure of investigative documents that might shed light on the accusations. That included the files of the FBI. Still reeling from the Coplon trial, Hoover interpreted the request as a hostile act. And when McCarthy backed Tydings, urging the Truman administration to release the FBI's loyalty files to Congress, Hoover began to view the Wisconsin senator, too, as less friend than adversary.

Hoover did not cut off McCarthy—that would come later. Instead, he started to reassess the senator's utility to the Bureau, and to revise his own actions accordingly. When convenient, he continued to share FBI information with McCarthy, just as he did with so many other senators and congressmen. But he never entirely trusted McCarthy, and took pains to distance the Bureau from the senator. By March, he refused to be seen with McCarthy, lest the public think he was endorsing the senator's wild claims. Privately, he began to disparage McCarthy as a demagogue and a fool.[7]

But Hoover was already tied to McCarthy—indeed, to both sides of the McCarthy drama—whether he liked it or not. Like many other congressional committees, the new Tydings Committee relied on the expertise of former FBI agents, including lead counsel Edward Morgan, a retired headquarters employee. McCarthy did the same, hiring a former agent named Donald Surine, who had been fired from the FBI for consorting with a prostitute, as his chief investigator. Hoover often favored this sort of inside arrangement, with its potential for back-channeling and mutual benefit. This time, though, he worried that the presence of FBI men would imply that one side or the other was able "to get access to the files." The Tydings Committee would be looking into matters of "an extreme controversial character," Hoover wrote to the attorney general, arguing that the political circumstances "make it undesirable for the FBI to be injected into such matters." McCarthy did not seem to care about Hoover's desire to remain above the fray, however. And neither did Tydings.[8]

The next moment of confrontation came quickly. On March 21, just over a month after the Wheeling speech, McCarthy suddenly announced that he was prepared to identify "the top Russian agent" in the United States. At the time Hoover was still puzzling out leads from the Fuchs arrest, trying to link Harry Gold with the as yet unknown

Kalibr (Greenglass) and Liberal (Rosenberg). Unaware that such sensitive investigations were underway, McCarthy soon offered up the name Owen Lattimore, a political scientist and East Asia expert who had been investigated by the FBI five years earlier during the Amerasia case. McCarthy assured the public that the FBI's old investigation—once fully revealed—would show the Soviets' terrifying reach and power. "Senator McCarthy's friends said he feels so sure that the FBI files will reveal what he has called 'jarring' information about the alleged American espionage chief that he is willing to make that a test case," the Associated Press reported. Within twenty-four hours, the Tydings Committee came banging on the door of the Justice Department to insist that the FBI hand over those files—though the Democrats in charge hoped not to support but to undermine McCarthy's charges.

After "a two-hour stormy session" with the committee's leadership, the Justice Department refused the request, much to Hoover's relief. But the issue refused to go away. On March 23, Senator Brien McMahon, the second-most influential Democrat on the Tydings Committee, informed Hoover that there was still "some talk up on the Hill as to how Senator Joseph McCarthy was getting into our files." Hoover denied sharing information with McCarthy, insisting that "it did not necessarily follow that if the files were produced they would sustain [McCarthy's] allegations." In any case, Hoover thought it was McCarthy's job—not the Bureau's, and certainly not the Tydings Committee's—to prove whether the allegations were true. "I stated that I felt in this case as they did in the Coplon Case that any material in our files should be kept confidential," Hoover wrote. "That if one committee were permitted access to our files that there was no reason why another committee should not have access to them, and of course therewith the possibility that they might be used as a political football." McMahon listened patiently but made it clear that both the Tydings Committee and McCarthy would continue to seek out the Lattimore files.[9]

The attorney general ultimately presented Hoover with three possibilities for resolving the situation: (1) make the files available to the committee; (2) bring committee members in for a summary briefing "on a confidential basis"; or (3) answer specific questions submitted in writing. Hoover chose the second option, the only one that did not commit the FBI to putting anything on paper. On March 24, he met confidentially with four members of the Tydings Committee. As requested, Hoover presented a detailed summary of the Lattimore file, which showed that Lattimore was a communist sympathizer whose organization had been found in possession of classified government documents, but that he was hardly the nation's top espionage agent. Pressed for his reasoning about not disclosing the file itself, Hoover reluctantly agreed to explain himself before the full committee.[10]

When McCarthy heard what had happened, he came to Hoover in a fighting mood, demanding to know whether Hoover really planned to testify, and if so, whether he planned to reveal the full truth about Lattimore. Hoover repeated what he had told the committee: that he would speak on principle but would not address specific cases. He hinted that McCarthy should be grateful for the FBI's silence. "I remarked to McCarthy that I was just wondering if he was getting straight information or if someone was planting some funny material on him," Hoover recounted. McCarthy spat back that "he was going to keep on asking for files," to which Hoover replied testily that "that was his prerogative."[11]

Hoover arrived at the committee room on March 27 accompanied by the attorney general, along with Tolson and Nichols, who took up seats in the front row, just behind the witness table. Speaking in the "deep, confident voice" of a man "who may sometimes be wrong but is never in doubt," in one reporter's characterization, Hoover declared the confidentiality of FBI files "a grave matter of principle," the difference between an efficient, effective intelligence system and a lawless free-for-all. To release the files to Congress would be to betray men like Herbert Philbrick, the hero witness of the Smith Act trial, who had trusted the FBI to keep his identity secret for nine long years. It would also risk exposing "information of a highly restricted nature, having a direct bearing upon national security," Hoover maintained, an indirect reference to Venona and to the Rosenberg ring investigation. He likened FBI reports to "the notes of a newspaper reporter before he has culled the printable material from the unprintable," filled with undifferentiated "complaints, allegations, facts, and statements," all of which might or might not turn out to be true. It was crucial that law enforcement professionals have the chance to withhold such material, he insisted, rather than release it to those who might use it for self-interested purposes—an obvious jab at McCarthy. Appealing to "common decency," Hoover positioned himself as the responsible elder among feckless newcomers, whose methods tended to "smear innocent individuals" and foment a witch-hunt atmosphere.[12]

As a matter of "principle," Hoover's position was not appreciably different from what he had been saying since the 1920s: that the business of law enforcement, spy hunting, and countersubversion was best left to the professionals. Nor was it much of a departure from what he had said in 1949, when he had urged the attorney general to drop the Coplon case rather than permit the disclosure of FBI files. But McCarthy's sudden rise to fame and controversy gave Hoover's stance a new political meaning, especially among liberals and progressives, with whom Hoover again found himself oddly aligned. After the Coplon disclosures, *The New Republic* had huffily decried "hysteria in the Justice Department." After Hoover's Tydings testimony, the magazine lauded the FBI as a professional bellwether, and Hoover himself as a model of reason and restraint. "We confess that we were impressed," the magazine declared after Hoover's testimony, praising the "warmth and conviction" in his voice as he spoke on behalf of FBI professionalism and autonomy. "In effect, Hoover damned the whole McCarthy probe."[13]

Nearly everyone seemed to agree. "J. Edgar Hoover has won the confidence of the American people," wrote the *Philadelphia Daily News*. Eleanor Roosevelt declared herself "impressed" with Hoover and agreed that "real investigations" should be carried out at the FBI, "not in congressional investigating committees." Even Truman temporarily sided with Hoover, deeming the troublesome FBI director the lesser of two evils. On March 28, the president confirmed that his administration would not release any FBI files to Congress, citing many of the points Hoover had enumerated in testimony.[14]

Far from luring Hoover into his own camp, in his first weeks as a national sensation McCarthy managed to do what had recently seemed impossible: he pushed Hoover back into the good graces of the Truman administration and even of the American left. Though suspicious of Hoover's motives, the inveterate left-wing critic I. F. Stone conceded that Hoover had come down on the right side in this instance, "the last champion of civil liberties" with the power and influence to face down Joe McCarthy.[15]

THE TYDINGS COMMITTEE RELEASED ITS CONCLUSIONS IN MID-JULY, JUST AS the FBI was arresting Julius Rosenberg. Signed by Democratic members of the committee, the Tydings report exonerated Lattimore and condemned McCarthy's performance as "a fraud and a hoax." Republican members stuck loyally by the senator's side, writing off the conclusion as a trumped-up attack on an American patriot by a nervous and guilty Democratic Party. The debate reflected the partisan split that would characterize McCarthyism for the next several years, with Democrats opposed and Republicans in support. Hoover used those years differently. In the House, he was still working with HUAC on the communist issue. In the Senate, though, there was no committee similarly responsive to FBI influence and priorities. So in early 1951 he set about finding one, eager for a better option than Joe McCarthy.[16]

The linchpin of Hoover's strategy was another senator whose Irish name and fierce anticommunist politics often inspired comparisons to his Wisconsin colleague: Senator Patrick McCarran, Democrat of Nevada. A sheepherder turned Reno civic booster, McCarran had been elected to the Senate during the Democratic sweep of 1932. Though he owed his electoral fortunes to Roosevelt, within a few years McCarran had turned on the New Deal, a defiant Westerner opposed to concentrated federal power and Eastern pretensions of all sorts. During the next election cycle, Roosevelt had urged Nevada voters to reject McCarran as part of a nationwide bid to purge the Senate of its most conservative Democrats. But McCarran had survived with his right-wing sentiments intact. By 1951, he was one of the most powerful men in the Senate, a member of the Appropriations Committee and chair of the Judiciary Committee—the two committees, not incidentally, of greatest interest to Hoover.[17]

In the late summer of 1950, once the Tydings Committee had declared McCarthy "a fraud and a hoax," McCarran proposed the single most sweeping piece of anticommunist legislation in U.S. history. The Internal Security Act borrowed heavily from a bill introduced in 1948 by HUAC stalwarts Richard Nixon and Karl Mundt, who had tried and failed to get the Senate to sign on. Now known as the McCarran Act, the law required "subversive" organizations to register with the federal government, under the supervision of a new Subversive Activities Control Board. It also authorized the creation of domestic internment camps in the event of war, the long-awaited authorization for Hoover's planned detention program. To oversee the implementation of the law, McCarran proposed a Judiciary subcommittee with "very broad authority" to conduct "continuous study" of espionage, subversion, and internal security—in short, to give the Senate, like the House, a permanent foothold in Hoover's territory.[18]

Hoover initially refused to weigh in on the bill. "It is not the function of the director of the Federal Bureau of Investigation to make any statement regarding pending legislation," he insisted. That left everyone talking about and around him. McCarran championed the bill as a tool that Hoover surely could use, especially after all that the FBI had endured at the hands of Truman liberals. Those liberals in turn argued that McCarran's ideas would overwhelm the Bureau and potentially drive the Communist Party underground, making Hoover's work that much more difficult. Once Congress passed the bill, Truman vetoed it on similar grounds, arguing that its draconian provisions would "seriously hamper the Federal Bureau of Investigation" and force disclosure of its files. And when Congress overrode the veto, it was on the logic that the FBI—and the nation—needed to act against the menace that Hoover had spent years describing so effectively.[19]

Hoover waited until debate had died down—and the bill had passed—to make his move. In March 1951, as the Rosenberg trial was getting underway, he asked to go off the record during routine testimony before McCarran's appropriations committee. He then proposed a formal liaison relationship between the FBI and the new Senate Internal Security Subcommittee (SISS), which had been created to oversee the administration of the McCarran Act. The idea built upon Hoover's years of experience with HUAC but took it a step further. This arrangement would be not just an informal quid pro quo but an official agreement, with duties and obligations on both sides. And it would do what both sides needed: not only enhance each other's power and influence but also sideline McCarthy. On March 15, in the presence of the attorney general and several members of the Judiciary Committee, Hoover and McCarran hammered out the details. The FBI promised to respond efficiently to the subcommittee's requests for information. The subcommittee vowed, in the words of an FBI report, to "play ball with the Bureau."[20]

By design, most of the structural advantages of the agreement lay with Hoover. Though the FBI was bound to respond to requests from McCarran's subcommittee, it was up to Bureau personnel to decide which information was passed along. And Hoover did not intend to disclose "raw" files—the subject of so much recent conflict. Instead, the committee would mostly receive public information or summaries prepared by Bureau agents as "blind memoranda," without official FBI stamps or attribution and, at least in theory, untraceable to the Bureau. Like the leaders of HUAC, McCarran agreed that SISS had no right to access FBI files directly, and no right to view personnel records or loyalty files on government employees. What SISS could do was submit names and questions and wait patiently for whatever Hoover saw fit to deliver.

The agreement gave Hoover near-total discretion over what the committee saw, and over which names might be named as possible subversives and witnesses. At the same time, as with HUAC, it gave him powers and privileges normally off-limits to the FBI. Those privileges included the ability to recommend subpoenas for communist witnesses who refused to talk with the FBI. Working together, Hoover predicted, the FBI and SISS would make each other more powerful. Even better, the cooperation would happen without any public acknowledgment of Hoover's role. The subcommittee's staff included several former FBI agents. According to their lead investigator, McCarran expressed every desire to "do just about anything the director asked him to do." McCarran also agreed that SISS would present itself as the responsible alternative to Mc-Carthy, with "no muck-raking and no attempts to embarrass anybody," as Nichols put it. By working with one senator, in short, Hoover hoped to contain, influence, and counterbalance the other.[21]

McCarran's initial choice of target was intended to highlight the contrast with McCarthy. In July 1951 he began to hold public hearings on the Institute of Pacific Relations, the same think tank that had employed Owen Lattimore, McCarthy's "top Russian agent." McCarran allowed McCarthy to attend the hearings but insisted that the Wisconsin senator write down any questions and pass them along to his Democratic superiors. That left McCarran as the star of the show. His questioning of Lattimore was "one of the most acrimonious exchanges Capitol Hill has ever heard," according to *The Washington Post*. Unlike McCarthy, though, McCarran had the advantage of the FBI's assistance. With the Bureau's help, McCarran interviewed nearly everyone associated with the IPR, amassing almost six thousand pages of testimony. When it was all over, Hoover declared himself thoroughly pleased with the committee's report (which condemned Lattimore as a "conscious articulate instrument of the Soviet conspiracy"). At a meticulous 226 pages, it offered "a perfect illustration of what can be accomplished through cooperation and proper timing," in Hoover's view. It also showed what could be accomplished with McCarran rather than McCarthy.[22]

The arrangement persisted over the next several years, with Hoover and McCarran coordinating investigations into alleged communists employed in education and entertainment, labor unions and universities, the press and the United Nations. In many of those cases, Hoover helped to orchestrate the proceedings from start to finish, not only identifying who should be targeted as a dangerous subversive but also recommending the witnesses who could testify against them. SISS was, in effect, a front group for the FBI: acting in secret, the FBI helped to set the subcommittee's agenda and provided it with the information needed to see that agenda through. In return, as Hoover acknowledged, the FBI received "information I did not believe could have been gotten" another way. "As far as the FBI was concerned," he informed a senator in late 1952, "their relationship with us [has] been very satisfactory."[23]

THE SISS RELATIONSHIP MIGHT HAVE BEEN "SATISFACTORY," BUT IT WAS NOT sufficient, at least not for what Hoover hoped to achieve. Though SISS gave him a degree of control over what happened in the Senate, as HUAC had done in the House, there were still many other areas of government where the FBI exercised little if any influence. At a meeting in early 1951, while Hoover was secretly negotiating his agreement with SISS, a coalition of state governors began to complain that they had been denied access to crucial information about communist sympathizers in local defense plants or state-government jobs. They proposed creating their own committees and investigative bodies to replicate the FBI's work at the state level. Hoover viewed this prospect, like McCarthy's speeches, as a potential challenge to FBI authority. "If these people got any idea they could go out on their own in forty-eight states looking for reds there would be chaos in this country and violation of civil rights," he complained upon hearing of the governors' conversation. Hoping to placate the governors and show them the error of their ways, Hoover offered to do for them what he was already secretly doing for SISS and what he refused to do for McCarthy: set up a formal liaison relationship.[24]

Thus began the Responsibilities Program, originally conceived as a way to distinguish between federal and state responsibilities, but ultimately serving to bring the FBI into secret collaboration with the governors as with SISS. Just days after the governors' meeting, Hoover suggested that agents become more proactive in their contacts with local and state officials. Rather than wait for requests from the governors, he ordered the field offices to check the Security Index for anyone employed in "public or semi-public organizations," such as civil defense workers, government clerks, or utility employees. As with HUAC and SISS, the one major stipulation was "that any information furnished to state or local authorities along any of the above lines should not be attributed by the receiving agencies to the FBI." Hoover emphasized the need for "discreet, careful handling" by the field offices to ensure "that the Bureau's interests are protected while at the same time our responsibilities are met."[25]

He justified those expanded responsibilities on the same grounds that he had justified so much else: by providing local officials with information, the FBI would prevent them from taking the situation into their own hands, thus avoiding the proliferation of bargain-basement McCarthyism. Hoover would also enhance his own authority. By his logic, it was better to see professors, librarians, and defense workers quietly eased out of their jobs on the FBI's say-so than to endure risky episodes of public accusation and spectacle. Once the program was underway, though, it took on a life of its own, rapidly expanding beyond its initial limits. By April 1951, the Bureau was regularly notifying governors and university presidents about left-leaning faculty, administrators, and staff employed in state university systems. By May, elementary and secondary schoolteachers were included as well, on the logic, as Tolson put it, that they were in a position to "insidiously instill into the minds of children the Communist Party line." In effect, Hoover created a shadow network in which his word alone was enough to get any of them fired.

As the FBI's executive conference acknowledged, what began as a way to placate the governors ultimately emerged as "an effective weapon of harassment of the Communist Party." And like the arrangement with SISS, it worked remarkably well, at least by Hoover's standards. By the time the program closed in 1955, the FBI had disseminated information on more than nine hundred people, most of them teachers, librarians, professors, and university administrators. Of those, more than half either lost or left their jobs. Like the collaboration with SISS, it happened largely without public notice—in stark contrast to the antics of Joe McCarthy.[26]

WITH SISS AND THE RESPONSIBILITIES PROGRAM, HOOVER GAINED NEW IN-roads among the political class, back channels through which to manage the government's approach to communism out of public view. For his broader campaign to achieve success, though, he needed something else: a grassroots base of ordinary men and women ready to speak out in support of the Bureau. Hoover had already found a popular constituency on issues such as religion, crime, and juvenile delinquency. The anticommunist domain was more complicated, already overpopulated with charlatans and demagogues, and with citizen groups whose fervor, as Hoover frequently pointed out, verged on vigilante action. As with SISS, Hoover sought a disciplined group that could be relied upon both to back the Bureau's programs and to observe his preferred limits. He turned once again to the American Legion.

Hoover had chosen the Legion's convention as the launching pad for his big anti-communist speech, the one that Senator Karl Mundt had labeled "the turning point in American thinking" on the subject. Around the same time, he began to experiment with other ways to bring the Legion into closer cooperation with the Bureau. Hoover had been pleased with earlier Legion collaborations, such as the initiatives placing Bureau speakers in public schools during the 1930s and the wartime "contact program" that turned Legion members into informers. With the end of the war, he turned his attention to the men who ran the Legion's headquarters in Indianapolis and organized its massive annual conventions.[27]

Orchestrating this alliance was an FBI official named Lee Pennington, assigned by Hoover during the Roosevelt years to serve as liaison to the Legion. In 1948, Pennington began attending meetings of the Legion's National Americanism Commission, an executive committee charged with promoting patriotism over communism. Five years later, with Hoover's assent, he retired from the Bureau to take over the leadership of the commission full-time. From within the Legion, he worked to mobilize the nation's veterans in support of Hoover and the FBI. Much of that support came in the form of resolutions composed by the Americanism Commission and passed at the Legion's annual conventions, which quickly became known as "FBI Productions." A typical resolution praised the FBI's "outstanding and brilliant performance" and sought to "commend and thank the Federal Bureau of Investigation, its able director, J. Edgar Hoover and his co-workers for their fine work."[28]

The Legion also engaged in more overtly ideological work: the shock troops of Hoover-style anticommunism. In early 1950, just before McCarthy's Wheeling speech, the Legion helped to create the All-American Conference, a national coordinating body for anticommunist organizations, in hopes of developing "ways and means of strengthening government agencies in the restraint and abolition of communist activities." A few months later, when the FBI proposed reviving the contact program as a result of the Korean War, the Legion jumped at the chance to develop sources of information within its local posts. One official recalled being shocked at the "extraordinarily close cooperation between the FBI and the Legion's subversive activities program," all of it aided by "J. Edgar Hoover's 'liaison man.'" This fusion was precisely what Hoover wanted, however. Even as he derided McCarthy's attempts to whip up a popular following, Hoover continued to develop his own grassroots constituency.[29]

IF ANYONE HAD PAUSED AT THIS POINT TO MEASURE THE RELATIVE EFFICACY of Hoover and McCarthy in the anticommunist arena, they might have been surprised by what they found. McCarthy had a loud voice, a genius for drumming up controversy, and the support of much of the Republican Party. Hoover could claim an institutional and personal network that included several congressional committees, dozens of governors and state officials, a dependable popular organization, and allies on both sides of the aisle—not to mention his press contacts and publicity apparatus, plus the thousands of agents and clerks under his direct control. Certain elements of this network had been in place well before McCarthy. But McCarthy's rise pushed Hoover in new directions, underscoring the need for allies who could be relied upon "to see that the Bureau's interests are protected," as Hoover had put it.[30]

To his existing networks Hoover added still more liaison programs, including a Special Service Contact Program for prominent figures in "the business, labor, educational, religious, scientific and cultural life of this nation." He also built up informal relationships outside official structures: in the press and in private business, among civic groups and former employees. From Chicago, a group of ex-agents began to publish the magazine *Counterattack*, which named suspected communists and helped to enforce the Hollywood blacklist. In New York, Hoover got to know a new generation of anticommunist writers and editors, including Richard Berlin, the top man at the Hearst newspaper chain, and Ogden Rogers Reid, editor of the *New York Herald Tribune*. Leading businessmen sought him out for his advice on communism. So did Hollywood power brokers such as Walt Disney, who offered to incorporate a Bureau-themed display in the new theme park he was hoping to build.[31]

Faced with Hoover's formidable institutional power, McCarthy soon realized that he could not go it alone. Throughout 1951 and into 1952, Hoover continued to speak about the need for "impartiality, fairness and regard for nothing but the truth" when dealing with communists, a position that many interpreted as a sideswipe at McCarthy. The senator chose to ignore the jabs, eager to set aside their dispute over the files and to restore himself in Hoover's good graces. He seems to have recognized the depth of Hoover's institutional power, so different from his own quick-hit strategies. "No one need ever erect a monument to you," he wrote to Hoover in 1952. "You have built your own monument in the form of the FBI—for the FBI is J. Edgar Hoover." And he saw new potential for working together—not just on the issue of communism, but on another matter of mutual interest.[32]

CHAPTER 34

Inner Conflicts

(1947–1952)

Hoover and Tolson posing in honor of Tolson's twenty-fifth
anniversary at the FBI. During the 1950s, the anti-gay Lavender
Scare in Washington made them increasingly careful about how
they presented their relationship. April 2, 1953.

NATIONAL ARCHIVES AND RECORDS ADMINISTRATION

When McCarthy delivered his first full-day oration to the Senate in February
1950, he offered up profiles of eighty-one State Department employees alleged to present a danger to the nation. Most were supposedly communists or communist sympathizers, as McCarthy's Wheeling speech had promised. Two also had an
additional strike against them. According to McCarthy, No. 14 had exhibited "fla-
grantly homosexual" behavior during his time as a State Department translator.
No. 62 referenced a circle of left-leaning homosexuals whose "mental twists" allegedly
made them unfit for office. They had long ago been fired from the State Department,
but their examples highlighted what McCarthy described as a second great threat to
national security: the presence of homosexuals within the federal government. In early
March, his staff began to conduct "an inquiry for Sen. McCarthy regarding the sexual
perversion habits" of government workers, to run in parallel with his investigations of
communists.[1]

McCarthy soon dropped that plan, but other senators took it up, initiating a set of closed-door hearings in the spring of 1950 on the "Employment of Homosexuals and Other Sex Perverts in Government." Operating alongside the public spectacle of the Tydings Committee, the hearings helped to produce what came to be known as the Lavender Scare, a cultural and political parallel to the Red Scare, with "homosexuals" rather than communists as its central anxiety. McCarthy often referred to them as a single entity: "communists and queers" lurking side by side in the government. Hoover treated the two issues differently. While he had warned early and often about communism, he rarely spoke in public about homosexuality. It is not hard to imagine why. Nobody had ever accused Hoover of being a communist. By contrast, this new turn threatened to revive uncomfortable rumors about his own lifestyle and sexual identity.[2]

This is not to say that Hoover refused to participate in the Lavender Scare. Between 1950 and 1952, as he was hunting the Rosenbergs, sparring with McCarthy, and building up relations with SISS, he established a systematic program for monitoring "sex deviates" and for communicating that information to other agencies. Those policies helped to make possible the firings of thousands of government workers accused of homosexuality, a toll far higher than that of the Red Scare. They also contributed to Hoover's reputation as a purveyor of gossip and sexual secrets, as he gained access to personal information on government employees. His targets ranged from the lowliest of federal clerks up to senators, diplomats, and presidential candidates.[3]

And yet Hoover never invested in homosexual investigations with anything like the zeal or commitment that he devoted to the problem of communism. As with lynching inquiries, he was willing to do his duty but eager to back away when he could, his obligations as a lawman often in conflict with his personal agenda. Despite opportunities, he chose not to testify before Congress on the subject. And when he was forced to address the issue, he said comparatively little. Since the war, Hoover had devoted the better part of his energies to the "cause" of anticommunism, building new institutions, alliances, and methods at considerable professional risk and expense. During those same years, he often tried to avoid the homosexual issue. The Red Scare was a central feature of his life's work. The Lavender Scare he might have preferred to ignore, for both personal and professional reasons.[4]

THROUGHOUT MOST OF HIS CAREER, HOOVER HAD DEALT QUIETLY WITH INDIvidual cases of alleged homosexuality among government employees, addressing matters that came his way but rarely seeking them out. He had taken this approach during the war, when Roosevelt asked him to investigate Sumner Welles and the Pullman porters. And he assumed that the status quo would persist once the war came to an end. As of 1946, the Bureau's standing policy was to handle all such matters through oral communication, conveying allegations to the appropriate agency chief or supervisor but not going so far as to "confirm in writing."[5]

Other agencies took further steps to codify in rules and formal procedures exactly how they planned to address the issue. As early as December 1945, the Civil Service Commission instituted a policy that homosexuals should not be considered "suitable" for government jobs. Two years later, the State Department conducted an internal review and purge on the grounds that homosexuals might be subject to blackmail and thereby pressured into revealing national-security secrets. Though McCarthy never quite became its standard-bearer, the Lavender Scare owed much to the methods and style of McCarthyism, and to the images of communist treachery that it evoked. Like communists, homosexuals were depicted as members of a secret subculture with its own codes, rituals, and symbols, legible only to those on the inside. They allegedly made a point of blending in with "normal" Americans. And they rejected what Hoover had so often touted as the last best hope for civic virtue: participation in a God-fearing, well-disciplined, heterosexual nuclear family.[6]

By the time Chambers and Hiss appeared before HUAC in 1948, the homosexual issue had already gained political traction. Hiss worried that the trial and hearings would reveal his stepson's homosexuality. Chambers was concerned enough about his own past to alert the FBI that he had sought out same-sex trysts while traveling as a Soviet courier. Such examples of bona fide Soviet spies known to engage in homosexual activity were rare, however. Far more common were cases of ordinary government workers, stuck in such unglamorous jobs as postal clerk or patent processor, whose sexuality ended up being called into question. The process of deciding what to do in such cases forced federal agencies to confront a bedeviling issue: Who should count as a homosexual? By 1950, when McCarthy made his speech in the Senate, gay people were officially excluded from serving in the military, working for the government, and immigrating to the United States. But the question of who belonged in that category, and why, was far from settled.[7]

Many Americans assumed that a homosexual man could be easily recognized. "Commonly we think of the effeminate man who walks with a peculiar swing and has many mannerisms which are effeminate as being, as we say, a queer person," the head of the National Institute of Mental Health explained to Congress in 1950. That understanding was rapidly breaking down, however. In 1948, the zoologist Alfred Kinsey published *Sexual Behavior in the Human Male* (better known as "the Kinsey Report"), an eight-hundred-page scientific study purporting to reveal the truth about how America's fathers and sons behaved behind closed doors. Kinsey claimed that fully 37 percent of the nation's men had participated in at least one homosexual encounter to the point of orgasm, raising the possibility that homosexuality was not an anomaly but a widespread social practice. Thanks to Kinsey, 1948 became not just the year of the Hiss case and the Bentley revelations, but "the year everybody in the United States was worried about homosexuality," in the words of novelist John Cheever—even if nobody could quite decide what it was.[8]

Hoover knew about Kinsey's findings and rejected them. "Whenever the American people, young or old, come to believe that there is no such thing as right or wrong, normal or abnormal, those who would destroy our civilization will applaud a major victory over our way of life," he wrote in June 1948 for a *Reader's Digest* symposium on Kinsey's work. A few years later, when Kinsey criticized the director's moribund views on "crime, homosexuality, and other matters," Hoover instructed Nichols to meet with the scientist to make him "put up or shut up." But there was no containing the broader conversation about sexuality—and about homosexuality in particular—that Kinsey's work had helped to unleash.[9]

Much of that discussion drew upon psychological literature that framed homosexuality as a mental disease or personality disorder, caused in part by adverse childhood experiences. One bestseller blamed excessive mothering—or "Momism"—for causing homosexuality, encouraging suspicion of men who seemed unduly close to their mothers. Another theory suggested that it was not effeminacy but too-showy masculinity to watch out for, one of the ways that the secret homosexual might overcompensate for his hidden desires. The emphasis on individual psychology and repressed longing departed from traditional law enforcement approaches, which emphasized the commission of specific acts—sodomy, solicitation, cross-dressing—as the chief point of concern. According to the new psychological literature, homosexuality was less about external action than about internal struggle. Thus it was possible to be a "latent homosexual" even if "feelings or desires toward one of his own sex have not taken the form of actual physical acts," as the head of the National Institute of Mental Health explained to Congress.[10]

Even a casual observer could see the ways in which Hoover's life and history conformed to certain categories that were fast becoming suspect: his bachelor status, his devotion to his mother, his preference for spending time around other men. In addition, much of what might once have served as a defense against suspicion—his bromides about God and family, his emphasis on a certain swaggering masculinity—was no longer universally accepted at face value. Hoover had long emphasized self-control and inner discipline, the need to resist temptation at all costs. In the new psychological framework, that, too, could be a sign of hidden desires and inner struggles of which he himself might be only dimly aware.

HOOVER NEVER ACKNOWLEDGED PUBLICLY THAT CONCERNS OVER SECRECY and homosexuality, bachelors and security risks, had much to do with his own life. There is intriguing evidence that he worried about these issues, however. In the summer of 1947, an enterprising reporter at the *Los Angeles Times* secretly trailed Hoover and Tolson while they strolled the city on vacation. Undetected, the reporter watched them purchase ice cream at the farmers market, then wander into a nearby bookstore. Tolson bought a few lurid mass-market westerns. Hoover picked up two serious works of psychology, *Our Inner Conflicts* and *Self-Analysis*, both by the eminent German-born psychoanalyst Karen Horney.[11]

It is impossible to say how closely Hoover read these books. But if he did spend time on them, he no doubt found many themes of interest. *Our Inner Conflicts*, first published in 1945, considered the dilemma of a man whose inner self and outer persona had become incompatible, his true identity and desires concealed from the world. One possible result of that conflict, Horney suggested, would be a series of "neurotic" behaviors not unlike those Hoover exhibited on a regular basis: "perfectionist drives," "rigid self-control," the "need for admiration," "a compulsive craving for power and prestige." Such patterns attempted to compensate for—or to avoid—an essential truth that might be shattering if faced head-on. Rather than recognize an authentic self, men caught in such conflicts often projected an "idealized image" instead, preferring the formalities of rules and artifice to the difficult work of human intimacy and self-knowledge. In extreme cases, Horney argued, this conflict produced an insistence on "arbitrary rightness" as well as a knee-jerk hostility to "any questioning or criticism from outside," attributes that anyone who worked with Hoover would have recognized. Though such behavior sometimes led to acclaim and success, it often produced a "deep hopelessness" and secret anxiety. "Roughly speaking, a person builds up an idealized image of himself because he cannot tolerate himself as he actually is," she wrote. Even when this strategy yielded certain benefits, Horney concluded, it made for an exquisitely painful life.[12]

Self-Analysis, the second book Hoover purchased, offered a guide to escaping this conundrum without the aid of a psychoanalyst—and without the risk of stigma that visiting one might entail. Horney was not terribly optimistic about the prospects for self-cure. But she held out hope that committed patients might achieve clarity by mimicking the methods of formal analysis in the privacy of their own homes. To be successful, she explained, patients would need to question themselves rigorously. They would also need to break with the insistence on "arbitrary rightness" that was the greatest barrier to true insight and progress.[13]

It is hard to imagine that Hoover got very far with this process, if he engaged in it at all. As far back as Central High, "rigid self-control" had served as a point of pride, his "perfectionist drives" a key to his success. For Hoover, rejecting these qualities would have meant abandoning both his personal and professional identities. Still, the apparent flirtation with self-analysis does accord with one other fragment of evidence from this period, uncovered by the journalist Anthony Summers in his 1993 biography of Hoover. According to Summers, around 1946 Hoover briefly visited a young Washington psychiatrist named Marshall de G. Ruffin, who later went on to serve as mental health commissioner for the district superior court. Summers never interviewed Ruffin, who was dead by the 1990s, but Ruffin's wife claimed that Hoover had been "troubled by homosexuality," as her husband had indiscreetly hinted more than once. "My understanding was that Hoover got very paranoid about anyone finding out he was a homosexual," she explained to Summers, "and got scared of the psychiatry angle." While decades-old hearsay is hardly definitive evidence, especially since Ruffin allegedly burned his patient records, it does offer a possible context for Hoover's turn toward self-analysis.[14]

In any event, Hoover's curiosity about psychoanalysis seems to have produced no great transformation of the mind or soul, no new spaciousness within the tightly bound world he had created for himself. If anything, he renewed his determination to maintain the idealized image he had long projected, eliminating those traces of open affection and feminine grace that had occasionally surfaced at the FBI. A decade earlier, Hoover had celebrated his twentieth anniversary at the Justice Department by posing with Tolson in a room bursting with flowers. By the late 1940s, flowers had mostly disappeared from official ceremonies, as had any sense of playfulness, intimacy, or humor. In 1948 and again in 1953, Hoover marked Tolson's Bureau anniversary with a formal handshake in the director's office. Though the photos capture a certain affection in their smiles, Hoover and Tolson stand far apart, a well-polished desk, an American flag, and the FBI seal providing a sterile backdrop.[15]

A similar shift took place outside the Bureau. Hoover and Tolson continued to travel together: Miami in winter, California in summer, plus frequent trips to New York, Chicago, and Baltimore. But there were far fewer reports of late nights at the Stork Club or whirlwind tours of café society. Even in Washington, Hoover took a step back from the social scene. As an up-and-comer, he had angled for invitations to the embassies and the White House and had taken umbrage when Tolson was left out. After the war, he gained a reputation for avoiding such events. There were undoubtedly many reasons for Hoover's retreat from Washington society, including the more settled energies of middle age. Horney's work suggested yet another possibility. Holding on to an "idealized image" often required increasing levels of social isolation, she theorized, to avoid facing up to critical comments and challenges.

WHEN HOOVER DID VENTURE OUT, HE FOUND WASHINGTON A CHANGED CITY. It was no longer the boom-time free-for-all of the New Deal and the war, but instead a community seized by suspicion and fear. Hoover's Red Scare politics drove some of the conversation. "This city of Government employees is in a panic before the great purge," one longtime communist declared in 1947. "It is a city where everybody thinks he will be purged." The Lavender Scare added another element of anxiety, as federal offices and public establishments accused of being friendly to homosexuals came under scrutiny. *Washington Confidential*, a bestselling exposé by tabloid reporters Lee Mortimer and Jack Lait, purported to reveal a hidden "cesspool" where homosexuality, along with other forms of sinful deviance, lurked behind closed doors. The authors paid particular attention to the "garden of pansies" said to be growing in federal soil, a tight-knit community of homosexual government employees with its own "grapevine of inter-communication" and codes of behavior.[16]

Given the public interest in this sort of lurid exposé, it was perhaps inevitable that some enterprising senator or congressman would take up the issue of homosexuals in government, much as HUAC, SISS, and McCarthy had seized upon communism. The first to act was Senator Kenneth Wherry, Republican of Nebraska, one of McCarthy's few rivals for the title of "noisiest and most persistent spokesman for the extreme right within the Grand Old Party," in one journalist's description. In March 1950, while the Tydings Committee was gearing up for its showdown with McCarthy, Wherry summoned the leadership of the local vice squad to discuss homosexuality in the nation's capital. According to their estimates, some 5,000 homosexuals lived in Washington, including 3,750 federal employees. At the State Department alone, they figured that 300 to 400 homosexuals were helping to orchestrate the nation's foreign policy.

Pressed for the source of their numbers, the police officials readily admitted that these were mere guesses. Wherry's report, issued in May, nonetheless expressed deep alarm over their implications. He framed his concerns in the language of national security: any one of these thousands of homosexuals might have access to confidential information and might therefore be coerced into revealing government secrets. He raised the possibility that at least a few of them occupied positions of real power. "It was adduced that their abnormality is no respecter of persons high or low, and that there is intermingling of the afflicted in all categories of Government employment," he wrote. Wherry made no mention of the FBI or of Hoover. His argument implied that no part of the government was sacred, however, no official too highly placed to be called into question.[17]

Spurred by Wherry's report, another subcommittee came into being, headed by Senator Clyde Hoey, a Democrat. Predictably, the subcommittee employed a former FBI man to conduct its investigations. A graduate of Georgetown and an outspoken Catholic, committee counsel Francis Flanagan had made his career as a supervisor in Hoover's office. His committee work reflected FBI methods. All interviews were done quietly, in executive session, with the goal of creating "a central card index" of alleged homosexuals. Flanagan also made a point of opening the hearings not with local police testimony, but with the views of federal intelligence officials.[18]

Roscoe Hillenkoetter, head of the Central Intelligence Agency, appeared as the first witness, rattling off a thirteen-point list of dangers posed by homosexuals "from the standpoint of security." Like Wherry's report, his testimony described a scenario that could easily have applied to Hoover, emphasizing how certain forms of male professional sociability could be hard to distinguish from homosexuality. According to

Hillenkoetter, homosexual attraction often began in "the lodge" or "the fraternity," where it was easy to build bonds with other young men. From there, an enterprising homosexual might move into government work, rising within the ranks and bringing his favored men along with him. "One pervert brings other perverts into an agency, they move from position to position and advance them usually in the interest of furthering the romance of the moment," he testified. Given their tight bonds and shared secrets, Hillenkoetter warned, homosexuals had the potential to function as "a government within a government," sealed off from scrutiny by outside parties, talking mostly with each other.

When it came time for the FBI to testify, Hoover declined to appear. Instead, he sent Mickey Ladd, the number three man at the Bureau. Ladd explained the FBI's personnel practices, insisting that the Bureau would never hire "even a suspect sex deviate." He also affirmed the committee's suspicion that the Soviet Union used homosexuals as bait for unsuspecting government employees, entrapping them in compromising situations. While much of Ladd's testimony reinforced the idea of homosexuals as security risks, he also expressed a certain sympathy for their plight, pointing out that society, far more than homosexuals themselves, ought to be blamed for their hiding and lying. Ladd described homosexuality as an "affliction" rather than a choice, something innate and not easily changed. If homosexuals were vulnerable to blackmail, in other words, it was mainly because society had forced them into an untenable position.[19]

This view—that it was society, rather than the homosexual, that needed to change—found support in some of the medical testimony that followed, delivered by such august federal authorities as the surgeon general. The medical experts further complicated the question of detection, however, rejecting the stereotype of the feminized man and suggesting that even someone who "looks as masculine, acts as masculine as any of us around the table" might secretly be attracted to other men. When pressed by the committee to imagine what might happen if one of these men ended up running a federal agency, one doctor predicted that such a figure would be "extra careful about the persons that were associated with him, especially in an official capacity, in order to protect himself." It was for this reason—favoritism, not blackmail—that homosexuals should be considered "undesirable" in federal jobs, the doctor concluded.[20]

The committee's final report dismissed at least some of this testimony as interesting but extraneous, outside the central mission of identifying and ridding the government of homosexual security risks. "The subcommittee is not concerned with so-called latent sex perverts," the report declared, as long as they did not act upon their repressed desires. Instead, the report ended where it had started, with the conviction that there was a major security risk involving homosexuals in government, and that it could be eliminated through proper detection procedures. The committee called for what amounted to a zero-tolerance policy, concluding that even "one homosexual can pollute a Government office."[21]

IF HOOVER RECOGNIZED ANY DIRECT THREAT—TO HIMSELF, OR TO THE CULture of the FBI—he said little about it. Even as Crime Records churned out thousands of pages on issues such as communism and juvenile delinquency, he barely acknowledged the existence of the congressional inquiries into homosexuality. Instead, as the Hoey Committee dithered over its final report, he did what he did best, setting out to craft a policy that would meet the politicians' expectations while also maximizing his own discretion within the Bureau. He sought to avoid formal requirements that would enmesh the FBI in controversial and extended inquiries that it did not seek. He also wanted to retain control of whatever information the Bureau did acquire. Above all, he aimed to protect the Bureau from the kind of scrutiny increasingly being applied to other federal agencies.

For all the talk about "latent" and "hidden" homosexuals, Hoover's new system relied primarily on the same criteria that had always been central to the law enforcement approach: arrests for the commission of sexual acts. In the spring of 1950, within weeks of McCarthy's Senate appearance, the FBI reached out to the Washington police with a request for the names and fingerprints of everyone arrested in the city "who had been charged with perverted sex offenses." But even this tally of arrests was not so simple. Police often made arrests for disorderly conduct without noting the precise nature of the offense. In addition, they did not always indicate whether or not the person arrested was a government employee. The FBI sought to tidy up this process by asking the Washington police to flag all government employees arrested on morals charges, and by requesting similar records from around the country. In doing so, Hoover helped to reinforce the idea of homosexuality as a discrete and legible category.[22]

In his testimony, Ladd emphasized that the FBI came to such work in response to all the publicity around the issue. Once the process was underway, however, the Bureau's usual methods—list making, name naming, interviews and confidential informants—kicked in. In April, the FBI received its first roster from the Washington police: 393 people arrested "on charges of sexual irregularities" since 1947, all of whom claimed employment with the federal government, the military, or other "public organizations and institutions." The list included employees from the CIA and the Atomic Energy Commission, the Departments of Commerce and the Interior, a supervisor at the Civil Service Commission, and an auditor at the Department of Justice—even a secretary to Senator McCarthy. Hoover passed along to the White House more than sixty names of "persons arrested who claimed, at the time of their arrest, to hold highly rated positions." It included no FBI employees.[23]

Over the next few years, Hoover refined this method into a durable bureaucratic process: His agents received the information from the local police and passed it on to the relevant federal agency, investigating where necessary. Then the officials of such agencies made the hard judgments and carried out the dismissals. The process gave the FBI the benefit of detailed intelligence information without subjecting it to most of the political risk. In early 1951, Hoover reported that the FBI had uncovered 406 government employees arrested as "sex deviates" in Washington over the past ten months. A few months later, he issued a memo outlining a "uniform policy" for dealing with "reports and allegations concerning present and past employees of the United States government who assertedly are sex deviants." Hoover instructed that the appropriate executive-branch body for handling such problems was the Civil Service Commission, not the FBI. He ordered his own agents to pass along the best information they had, while retaining their own lists for future reference.

Hoover's "uniform policy" aimed to create a seamless channel from the police to the Civil Service Commission, all via the FBI. If all worked as planned, civil servants arrested for homosexual activity would not only be expelled from their jobs, but would be prevented from returning to government employment, through a centralized black-list. Hoover wanted to control that list, however, and to prevent others from accessing it. He went out of his way to insist that "no dissemination should be made" of questionable information from anonymous sources, or of "nonspecific" rumors. Even as he gathered sexual secrets on thousands of government employees, he professed to disdain the proliferation of Washington gossip.[24]

He also rejected the use of lie detectors to uncover homosexuals who had never been subject to arrest. Despite their popularity in the public imagination, Hoover had always doubted the efficacy of the machines and refused to allow agents to use lie detector results in court. When it came to homosexuality, he found the idea of scientific truth detection especially absurd. "In many cases, psychologically, the man might confess because of a guilty conscience," he told the House Appropriations Committee, in a rare public comment on the issue. "There are other sex perverts who are rather calloused [sic] and might not show such reaction." Without an overt act, in Hoover's view, there was simply no way to know whether a man might be lying about his sexual preference. Though framed as a matter of science, his testimony may also have served a more personal agenda: if one did not commit an overt act in a public place, nobody had the right to ask too many questions.[25]

BUT HE COULD NOT STOP THE QUESTIONS FROM COMING. TRUMAN HIMSELF heard some of the rumors. "One time they brought me a lot of stuff about [Hoover's] personal life," he later told a biographer, "and I told them I didn't give a damn about that. That wasn't my business." While the president never specified the nature of that "stuff," others in and around Washington were not nearly as guarded in their remarks, openly describing Hoover as a "queer" and a homosexual. Only a handful of such episodes made their way into Hoover's personnel file—no doubt just a tiny proportion of what he encountered—but his response is instructive. Upon hearing even the most idle gossip, he dispatched Bureau agents to interrogate the offending parties and trace the allegations to their origins.[26]

One rumor came to the Bureau courtesy of a Washington bakery employee. At a weekend dance in the spring of 1952, the man happened to mention that FBI agents frequented his shop. A fellow guest at the party then asked a dangerous question: "Have you heard that the Director is a queer?" The bakery worker reported this incident to his friends at the Bureau, who reported it to Hoover, who ordered them to "run this down promptly." A harrowing experience ensued. The agents assigned to the case soon identified the offending wordsmith as an employee of the National Labor Relations Board. Rather than interview him at work, they showed up at his home unannounced. Reports of the encounter use a variety of euphemisms to describe what happened next, but evidence suggests they set out to threaten and intimidate him into silence. At one moment, they "forcefully" outlined "his criminal and civil liability for the making of such statements." At another, they assailed him for his "outrageous lack of consideration and common decency" in attempting to malign a man like Hoover, "far his superior."

Unsurprisingly, the man expressed immediate regret for his remarks, begging the agents for mercy. "He stated he now realizes that he had been completely wrong in engaging in this type of gossip, agreed that his comments were completely without basis and gave his positive and definite assurance that there would be no recurrence," the agents reported back to Hoover. To make sure he had "been vigorously set straight," they left with a parting reminder that "immediate and positive action would be taken" if the FBI found he "was engaging in this type of gossip" in the future. At Hoover's instruction, they followed up by notifying the man's boss at the NLRB, who expressed regret for his "stupid employee's gossip" and only the "highest respect" for Hoover. [27]

That was just one incident. Throughout the late 1940s and early 1950s, the rumors persisted, sometimes coming from reliable sources, other times from conspiracy-minded letter writers dismissed as "crackpot" or "psychopathic." One woman wrote to the Los Angeles office to criticize "the personal character of the Director." She soon found herself face-to-face with Bureau agents, who informed her "in no uncertain terms that her repetition of such completely unfounded allegations were not appreciated." A man affiliated with the New York Medical College received a visit from agents over "vile and obscene statements regarding the Director," for which he immediately apologized, explaining that "he was just stupidly drunk" and his remarks "were absolutely without foundation." The agents warned him that a second offense "would be dealt with very severely." They came away from the interview convinced that he would not again make the same mistake.[28]

———

MOST PEOPLE IN GOVERNMENT JOBS—EVEN HIGH-LEVEL ONES—DID NOT, OF course, have Hoover's powerful lines of defense. Between April and November 1950, the height of the congressional investigations, 382 people were dismissed from federal employment due to allegations of homosexuality. At earlier moments, they might have found employment elsewhere in the government, but Hoover's lists—along with the new civil service policies—helped to foreclose that option. For some, the shame of exposure, combined with the actual or potential loss of livelihood, proved too much to take. As the Lavender Scare accelerated, reports of suicide became another part of the Washington whisper chain, desperate acts undertaken by those who felt they had nowhere else to turn.[29]

At least one FBI agent committed suicide under questionable circumstances in 1950, shooting himself in Wilkes-Barre, Pennsylvania, at the YMCA, known in many cities as a gathering place for homosexual men. And it was not just mid-rank government employees who found their careers stunted or their lives snuffed out. Throughout the 1950s, figures of real stature around Washington—men who knew Hoover personally—began to crack under the pressure of the Lavender Scare. In one tragic incident, Washington police arrested Lester C. Hunt Jr., son of Wyoming senator Lester Hunt, for soliciting sex from a man in Lafayette Park. After his son's humiliating trial, Senator Hunt withdrew his reelection bid, then shot himself in the head in his Senate office.[30]

When it came to the powerful and well connected, though, things often happened far more quietly. Over the course of the 1950s, Hoover learned of homosexual allegations against a host of influential men, including Democratic presidential contender Adlai Stevenson, columnist Joseph Alsop, presidential appointee Arthur Vandenberg Jr., and Charles Bohlen, nominated as U.S. ambassador to Russia. He handled these in much the same way he had approached the Sumner Welles situation during the war: discreetly, and with due attention to political consequences.[31]

Even McCarthy ran into problems, a victim of the churning rumor mill that he himself had helped to set in motion. In 1952, the Bureau received a letter that seemed to come from an army lieutenant alleging that "Senator McCarthy had picked him up at the Wardman Park hotel, had taken him to his home and gotten him drunk, and had committed an act of sodomy on him," according to Hoover's summary. The letter alleged that this was standard practice for McCarthy: "He is a pervert—that is the real reason why he is still a bachelor." Drawing on the latest psychological theories, the letter described McCarthy's anti-homosexual posturing as a form of overcompensation, because as everyone knew, "the best way to avoid suspicion is to accuse somebody else."[32]

McCarthy turned to Hoover in a panic, begging the FBI to investigate but to "be very circumspect" and "to be sure there is no possible leak." Despite their past differences, Hoover promised to handle it all "very, very tightly at this end," and to do what he could to track down the rumor. He kept his promise, restricting knowledge of the inquiry to a handful of top Bureau and Justice officials. "In view of the seriousness of the charges and the delicacy of the matter," Hoover "thought it was imperative that no steps be taken that might lend the possibility of this becoming known to the press before the investigation was completed," as he explained to the attorney general.[33]

The investigation itself proved to be a painful and awkward affair, requiring FBI agents to interview not only the lieutenant but also several of his friends about the details of their sexual activities. The lieutenant readily admitted to being "a queer" but denied ever sending any sort of letter about McCarthy, pleading with the agents not to bring his sexual history "into the light." In the end, he agreed to sign a statement declaring that "at no time has Senator Joseph McCarthy . . . approached me at a Bar, or any place, struck up a conversation, invited me to a home, or any place, for purposes of committing an immoral act." Hoover reported back that the original letter was "entirely a fake," conjured up by a handful of the lieutenant's friends as retribution against McCarthy.[34]

But the rumor mill was not yet done spinning. In October 1952, more than two and a half years after McCarthy first raised the issue of homosexuals in the State Department, a Las Vegas columnist alleged that the senator and a Milwaukee County Young Republican had engaged in "illicit acts with each other," concluding that McCarthy was "the most immoral, indecent and unprincipled scoundrel to ever sit in the United States Senate." Hoover once again did what he could to keep things quiet, deciding not to disseminate the information.[35]

Hoover's willingness to act on McCarthy's behalf indicates he may have sympathized with the senator's plight. He also may have been thinking about the 1952 elections, and what they were likely to mean for his future in Washington. Less than two weeks after the Las Vegas exposé, Wisconsin voters reelected McCarthy to a second term in the Senate, part of a landslide election that put the Republican Party in control of Congress and the White House for the first time in two decades.

CHAPTER 35

A Glorious Year

(1953)

Hoover (center, seated at table) testifying before allies at the Senate
Internal Security Subcommittee, November 1953. He is accompanied
by Tolson (left) and Louis Nichols (right), the architect of FBI public
relations.

Truth be told, Dwight "Ike" Eisenhower was not much of a Republican. Like
Hoover, he made his name as a nonpartisan public servant—the chief architect
of D-Day and supreme commander of Allied forces in Europe. Raised in Abilene,
Kansas, Eisenhower had spent nearly his entire adult life in the army, the embodiment
of a generation that encountered combat during the Great War and lived to see the
peace fall apart. Before World War II catapulted him to fame, he worked in procurement and other glorified administrative positions. He had no experience in electoral
politics. Indeed, he had often refused to say whether he was a Republican or a Democrat. That was part of what people liked about him. He had a big smile, a trim frame,
and the open but weathered face of a genial Midwestern farmer. At the 1952 Republican convention, he bested the arch-conservative insider, Senator Robert Taft, as the
candidate of competence and moderation. In the general election, he trounced the

brainy Democrat Adlai Stevenson, taking nearly every state outside the South. After his victory, he assured party elders that he really was their man by vowing to cast out Truman's old guard and bring a new slate of Republican appointees into power.

Presidential transitions had always been tricky for Hoover. Though appointed under a Republican president, he had now spent two decades working in Democratic administrations. Despite his bipartisan popularity, anyone who wanted to get rid of him would have been able to cite a host of errors, failings, and uncomfortable rumors. Eisenhower was not worried. If anything, he viewed the election as a chance to give Hoover the sort of support the FBI had lacked under the Truman administration. During the immediate postwar months, Eisenhower had sympathized with Hoover in his struggle to gain control of global intelligence. Since then, they had rarely interacted, but they continued to share roughly the same friends and enemies. "There had come to my ears a story to the effect that J. Edgar Hoover . . . had been out of favor in Washington," Eisenhower later wrote of his mindset in 1952. "Such was my respect for him that I invited him to a meeting, my only purpose being to assure him that I wanted him in government as long as I might be there and that in the performance of his duties he would have the complete support of my office." In a year when Republicans were determined to clean house, Hoover proved to be the great exception. "Midst inaugural comings and goings, power changes and talk of economy axes poised for a swing," a Detroit writer observed, "one Washington official—FBI Director J. Edgar Hoover—walked unconcernedly."[1]

Thus began one of the most rewarding and successful periods of Hoover's life. If 1919 had been the year that set his career in motion, 1953 became the year it all came together, with Hoover's social, political, and institutional interests unusually well aligned. For a brief moment, the persistent tensions between his professional, good-government, and nonpartisan leanings on the one hand, and his worldview as a conservative on the other, seemed to resolve without much difficulty. In 1953, Hoover's people came to power. He relished the experience.

Take what happened in Congress. Though the election displaced his ally Pat McCarran from the chairmanship of the Senate Internal Security Subcommittee, it reempowered many of the influential Republicans Hoover had courted back in 1946 and 1947, when he first ran into problems with Truman. At HUAC, former FBI agent Harold Velde became the new chair. And the committee itself, once a congressional pariah, now possessed real cachet. All but a few dozen of the Republican House members requested to be assigned to its ranks. Even Eisenhower seemed to have been drawn in. He chose his vice president, Richard Nixon, out of the committee's early leadership ranks.[2]

From Hoover's perspective, these developments showed Washington at its best, run by men who admired his methods and ideas. Eisenhower had campaigned on a promise not just to get rid of the Democrats, but to take action on the communist issue— indeed, to claim it for the Republicans. In order to do that, he needed Hoover. From his first months in office, Eisenhower championed Hoover as a symbol of the new

Republican administration: responsible but aggressive, restrained but action-oriented, especially where communism was concerned. He also helped Hoover get a taste of revenge against Truman, who had so often resisted the FBI's claims and methods. In Republican Washington, Hoover was the quintessential insider, trusted in the highest offices and empowered to do what he wanted to do.

IF EISENHOWER HAD NEVER BEEN MUCH OF A REPUBLICAN, HE ALSO HAD NEVER been much of a Christian, preferring quiet prayer and personal introspection to anything as showy as going to church. That changed once he entered the realm of electoral politics. When he arrived in Washington in January, seeking a church that would reflect this sensibility, Eisenhower turned to Edward Elson, Hoover's longtime confidant and personal minister. In order to provide a model of piety for a troubled nation, Eisenhower planned to join Elson's congregation, thus making it "the church of the Eisenhower administration," in the words of one Washington paper. On Inauguration Day, Eisenhower gathered his cabinet and innermost confidants, along with their families, for a morning ceremony of prayer and blessing at National Presbyterian. Newspapers estimated the full entourage at 180 men, women, and children, including Nixon, his wife, Patricia, and their two little girls. Elson presided over the service, welcoming the city's Republican elite to his parish. He asked the Lord to bless Eisenhower with "health of body, serenity of soul, clarity of insight, soundness of judgment."

The rest of the day attempted to preserve this mood of reverence, the most overtly pious inaugural in the city's memory. After taking the oath of office on the Capitol steps, Eisenhower began his presidency by offering a plea to "Almighty God," hastily scribbled out that morning after his return from National Presbyterian. His "little prayer," as it came to be known, implicitly acknowledged the moment's partisan shift, calling upon "all the people, regardless of station, race, or calling" to join in common purpose despite "differing political faiths." Hoover had long shared Eisenhower's belief that the law of God and the law of man should be made one. Now he thrilled to the idea of a Republican president willing to promote these values to the public at large. "This humble prayer touched Americans from coast to coast," he later wrote. "A President with such a deep religious sense and with such a sincere spiritual motivation, seeking to be guided by the right, sets an example for all the people."[3]

Eisenhower's religious example continued as the pomp and pageantry of the inauguration gave way to the routine work of governance. He quickly announced plans to join National Presbyterian as a full-time congregant, the first time that anyone could remember a president actually becoming a member of a local church. In Eisenhower's case, joining the church required special effort, since he had never been baptized. On February 1, Elson performed the baptismal rites in a private ceremony. He concluded from this experience that Eisenhower "is a man of simple faith, who is sincere in his religious doctrine."[4]

But the president's membership at National Presbyterian was also inescapably political, intended to signal the values of the new Republican order. On the evening of his baptism, he appeared on *Back to God*, a half-hour television spectacle sponsored by the American Legion. A few days later, he participated in a National Prayer Breakfast, the first of its kind, to discuss the challenges of "Government under God." From that point on, Eisenhower insisted that all cabinet meetings open with prayer. Hoover had already been engaging in similar rituals for years, from his partnership with the Legion to the communion breakfasts for FBI agents, who now saw in the Eisenhower administration a reflection of the religious ideals he had long promoted.

From National Presbyterian, the Rev. Elson affirmed the importance of these rituals for *America's Spiritual Recovery*, the title of a book he published in 1954. In contrast to the dens of homosexuality, prostitution, and gambling publicized in *Washington Confidential*, Elson described the nation's capital as "one of the most religious cities in all the world," home to the Billy Graham Evangelistic Crusade, the Daughters of the American Revolution, and the FBI National Academy. "This is the real Washington," he insisted. "This is my Washington—the symbol of America's great spiritual renaissance." During his first summer in office, as if to demonstrate Elson's claims, Eisenhower convened his cabinet to sign a document declaring that the United States drew its strength and vitality from the Bible. The following year, Congress added the words "under God" to the Pledge of Allegiance and put "In God We Trust" on the nation's postal stamps (and, later, its paper currency).

Lest anyone fail to give credit where credit was due, Elson dedicated his book to Eisenhower, "who by personal example and public utterance is giving testimony to the reality of America's spiritual foundations." Elson also included an introduction by Hoover, sealing their public partnership as minister and parishioner, both loyal to the new president. Like Elson, Hoover mourned the "devastating effects" of "Secularism" but took heart in the country's "spiritual recovery," as more and more Americans began to attend church. "There are hopeful signs for a better day," Hoover wrote, thanks in no small part to a president with "a deep religious sense" and a desire to serve as a living "example for all the people."[5]

HOOVER SAW ANOTHER HOPEFUL SIGN IN EISENHOWER'S CHOICE OF VICE PRESIdent. When Eisenhower accepted the nomination in 1952, it was as the candidate of mild centrism. Supporters urged him to balance the ticket with someone who appealed to the party's conservatives. Hence the choice of Richard Nixon, who had the added benefit of hailing from the populous state of California. An awkward physical specimen, his motions jerky and his suits too large, Nixon was not nearly as likable as Ike. But he had other useful qualities, including a willingness to get down in the political trenches while Eisenhower stood apart. Hoover found Nixon useful, too—not only as a fellow anticommunist but as a political loyalist willing to do battle on behalf of the Bureau.

Nixon had once wanted to be an FBI agent. Back in 1937, at the peak of the G-Man craze, he sent in an application listing his qualifications for the job. And as Hoover admitted, he *was* qualified. Nixon had played football in college (always a bonus at the Bureau). He'd also known how to please his law professors and deans. The FBI agents who interviewed him had come away impressed, declaring Nixon a "tactful," "self-confident," and "well-poised" fellow, "manly appearing" and "possessing [the] good physique" expected of all FBI recruits. Hoover submitted a recommendation to hire him. A few weeks later, however, a note in Nixon's file declared him "not qualified," and Tolson canceled the appointment. Hoover later hinted that Nixon had short-circuited the process in order to get started on his law career, but Nixon said he had simply never heard back.[6]

In any case, "the FBI's loss ultimately became the country's gain," as Hoover joked to a group of academy graduates. It eventually became the FBI's gain as well. Elected to Congress in the Republican sweep of 1946, Nixon had landed on HUAC just as it was starting its liaison relationship with the Bureau. His first speech in Congress, delivered in February 1947, denounced the Communist Party as a "foreign-directed conspiracy" and included long quotes from "a report by J. Edgar Hoover." For one of his first legislative initiatives, Nixon proposed a law that would require Communist Party members and front groups to register with the federal government.[7]

Far more than any other HUAC member, it was Nixon who had pushed the Hiss/Chambers confrontation forward, often (though not always) with the cooperation of the FBI. Hoover had been chagrined when Nixon, not the FBI, revealed the Pumpkin Papers. But the two men agreed all along that Chambers was the truth teller and Hiss the liar. As the case moved from Congress into the courts, Nixon attempted to mollify Hoover through acts of public tribute. During the Coplon affair, he took up Hoover's cause as his own, expressing outrage at the attorney general's decision to move forward with the trial over the FBI's wishes. As the controversy continued, he authored a resolution in recognition of Hoover's twenty-fifth anniversary as director, urging the Judiciary Committee to declare "its complete confidence" in Hoover as well as its "appreciation" for the "unselfish public service" performed over the course of two and a half decades. When Hiss's perjury conviction came down in early 1950, Nixon took to the House floor for a stem-winder outlining the hidden "lesson for the American people." He accused the Truman administration of ignoring early warnings from the FBI, brandishing a 1945 memo from Hoover to Truman that outlined a growing suspicion about Hiss. Future administrations, Nixon argued, "must give complete and unqualified support to the FBI, and to J. Edgar Hoover, its chief," lest they fall prey to the same blind spots and weaknesses.[8]

Hoover had thanked Nixon for the effusive words, especially the "very gracious references to my administration of the FBI's activities in the face of unwarranted attacks." Over the next few years, he came to see more of himself in the young congressman, as Nixon attracted "the lasting hate of the smear artists," in Hoover's words, including "the vituperation of all subversives." Hoover's enemies were Nixon's enemies. And his constituency was Nixon's constituency: the "decent people of the country," in Hoover's words, who attended church, joined the American Legion, and sponsored book groups to educate their neighbors about the dangers of communism. Such people thanked Nixon for defending Hoover. "The apparently well planned and carefully executed campaign to discredit Mr. Hoover is of great concern to me," a railroad engineer wrote to Nixon in 1949, urging him to stick with Hoover in battling "the Menace of Communism."[9]

When Nixon won the vice presidency in 1952, Hoover sent a note offering to be "of service" if and when the need should arise. "I have followed very closely the manner in which General Eisenhower and you presented your case to the country during the past several weeks," he wrote, praising the vice president for his "tireless efforts" on the nation's behalf. Hoover imagined that the election must be "a real source of satisfaction" for Nixon. The outcome satisfied Hoover as well, the start of an era in which he would be not only tolerated but championed in a Republican White House.[10]

IT WAS NOT JUST IN WASHINGTON THAT HOOVER FOUND A NEW ATMOSPHERE of welcome and belonging during the Eisenhower years. In Southern California, where he and Tolson had been vacationing for more than a decade, Hoover settled into a similar circle of like-minded men. Hoover had always loved his August month on the West Coast, where craggy beaches and overbright sun offered a welcome contrast to Washington's humidity. "Years ago, I found in Southern California a moment of peace when I felt that God was very near," he recalled to a reporter in the 1950s, describing how effortlessly the Pacific Ocean at dusk seemed to calm his nerves and strengthen his soul. He especially adored La Jolla, the touristy little beach community in San Diego where he and Tolson had been staying since the late 1930s. "If I had my way, I'd pick up the whole FBI and move it to La Jolla," Hoover claimed.[11]

Into that scene, in 1952, came a pair of Texas multimillionaires who shared Hoover's affection for La Jolla, and who sought to convert the neighborhood into a social hub for their friends, business partners, and political allies. Sid Richardson and Clint Murchison were boyhood pals who made their money fast, riding the Texas oil boom to vast riches while the rest of the country struggled through the Depression. By the time Hoover met them in the 1950s, they were in competition for the title of richest man in America. They were also ready to see what that money could do in national politics. As sons of "Solid South" Texas, they had little choice but to engage the Democratic Party. At the presidential level, however, they were keen Eisenhower supporters. Richardson alone gave an estimated $1 million to the campaign in 1952, plus $200,000 to pay for Eisenhower's various hotel expenses.[12]

Like many of their Texas counterparts, they shared a ferocious commitment to anticommunism. "We all made money fast," one oil tycoon explained. "We were interested in nothing else. Then this Communist business suddenly burst upon us." They also shared Eisenhower's enthusiasm for back-to-God politics, and for the men who could promote it on a national scale. In addition to bankrolling Eisenhower, Richardson threw his weight behind Billy Graham, helping to support the minister's Washington crusade. To Hoover, who needed neither money nor access, Richardson and Murchison offered something just as valuable. In 1952, they invited him to spend his August vacation at their new hotel in La Jolla, designed as a luxurious getaway for the most favored members of their social, business, and political community. The Hotel Del Charro soon became a second home to both Hoover and Tolson.

Murchison and Richardson designed the Del Charro to be small and unassuming, at least from the outside, with just fifty rooms in a low-slung complex near a pristine crescent pool. Hoover and Tolson usually stayed at one of the freestanding bungalows set off from the main rooms, the most private of the available accommodations. From there, they indulged in the array of delights proffered to the Del Charro's guests: poolside lunches, luaus, fashion shows, and dinners at the elegant indoor restaurant, with a blue-flowered jacaranda tree bursting out of the roof. "Its atmosphere combines the flavor of the world's most distinguished resort hotels with the charm and social attributes of a small private club," the hotel's manager boasted. For Hoover and Tolson, the Del Charro made California not only soothing but also thrilling, a taste of the old Stork Club glamour transposed to a more private setting.

The Del Charro's ultimate attraction was not the pool, tennis court, or dining room, but the people, an assemblage of concentrated wealth and political power with few rivals on either coast. Alongside Murchison and Richardson came an entourage of new-money Texas characters. Hollywood types showed up as well, including film stars John Wayne, Betty Grable, and Elizabeth Taylor. The real mystique of the Del Charro came from its political insiders, though, many of them drawn from the upper reaches of the Eisenhower administration.[13]

Among the prominent visitors to Del Charro during those early years was Richard Nixon, who arrived poolside in suit and tie with his wife, Pat, one night in the summer of 1955. The Nixons came not at the behest of Murchison and Richardson, but at the invitation of Hoover and Tolson, who had offered to throw a dinner party in the vice president's honor. The exchange suggested just how comfortable the FBI men came to feel at Del Charro: they acted not only as guests, but as hosts. Hoover wore a shiny shirt with no tie for the occasion, the sort of getup he never would have contemplated in Washington. Tolson acted as bartender. The occasion cemented social ties between the two couples. In addition, it provided Nixon with a valuable point of entrée to the Texas oilmen who had done so much to help Eisenhower's campaign. "I particularly want to thank you, too, for giving me a chance to get acquainted with your good friends from Texas," Nixon wrote to Hoover after the dinner.[14]

Hoover and Tolson proved to be among the most famous and pampered of the hotel's guests, if also among the most inclined toward seclusion and privacy. Murchison and Richardson picked up the hotel tab for them, beginning with the prohibitive room rate of a hundred dollars per day. They also granted Hoover and Tolson sure-thing opportunities in the Texas oil fields, in which the investments would pay out in boom times but would not lose money if the fields dried up. According to legend, Richardson delighted in treating Hoover just like anyone else, barking at him to "get your ass out of that chair and get me another bowl of chili!" At the same time, the Texas hosts went out of their way to please their powerful guest. On one occasion, upon hearing Hoover muse over the gorgeous citrus trees in Florida, Murchison allegedly flew in several fruit trees—peach, plum, and orange—and had them planted overnight outside the director's cabana.

An even greater tribute was the purchase of the nearby Del Mar horse-racing track, which Hoover loved to frequent. One Texas politician described some awkward encounters when Hoover found himself elbow-to-elbow with the "mobsters" who also enjoyed the track (though apparently "a few of them he got along with quite well"). Richardson and Murchison addressed this shadier side of the business by promising to donate the track's proceeds to fight juvenile delinquency and support underprivileged boys, citing Hoover's example as inspiration. They even expressed hopes that Hoover would run their charitable organization, Boys Inc., once he retired from the Bureau.[15]

Critics soon attacked the Del Mar as a giant tax dodge, a way for Murchison and Richardson to fund high times for their inner circle while depriving the public coffers of much-needed revenue. Eventually Hoover's financial relationship with his Texas patrons, including the no-lose oil investments, would come under scrutiny as well. During the early Eisenhower years, however, life and work hummed along smoothly: signs to Hoover that he had stuck by the right principles during the Truman years, and had earned friends and admirers in high places.[16]

EISENHOWER'S VICTORY EVEN BROUGHT A CERTAIN GRUDGING ACCOMMODA-tion between Hoover and the federal institution he distrusted above all others: the Central Intelligence Agency. Since its formation in 1947, the CIA had grown into the most significant, if also the most mysterious, of the intelligence services—"even more important than the FBI," in the judgment of columnist Drew Pearson. While Hoover focused on domestic anticommunism, the CIA had taken on the world, encouraged by the National Security Council not simply to gather information but to "counter Soviet and Soviet-inspired activities" through a variety of covert means. By the end of 1948, the agency had manipulated its first foreign election, throwing millions of dollars around Italy in an effort to stave off communist victory. Over the next few years, it tried (and usually failed) to build up forces of anticommunist spies, guerrilla fighters, and Western-minded intellectuals behind the Iron Curtain.[17]

Nobody outside of the CIA knew precisely what the agency was up to. But Hoover had picked up enough information to know that he didn't like it. He found the CIA's broad secrecy privileges unfair, given how often the FBI had been forced into fights to keep its policies and files under wraps. "A lot of this stuff about confidential operations is horsefeathers," he said, contradicting his own oft-held stance. "A few things must be kept secret, but the taxpayers have a right to know how an agency is spending their money." He also worried about the CIA's personnel practices. The agency had scaled up in just a few years, without using what Hoover viewed as proper methods, training, and screening. He accused the agency of harboring communists, homosexuals, and spies—and in at least a few of those cases, his suspicions turned out to be true. One Venona cable even hinted that Walter Bedell Smith, director of the CIA beginning in 1950, might have been turned by the Soviets during his time in Moscow as American ambassador.

Such, at least, were the reasons Hoover offered when asked about his obvious hostility toward the agency. As any insider could see, though, there was also a more personal side to the rivalry. Hoover still resented Truman's rebuff and the loss of the FBI's South American operations. Beginning in 1947, he simply extended those resentments to the CIA. He viewed the agency as a group of arrogant freelancers out to violate the very norms and laws that the FBI was supposed to protect. FBI officials referred to the CIA's covert operations group as a "gang of weirdos" and Bedell Smith himself as "a 'stinker' & not a little one either," in Hoover's words. When his own officials attempted to cooperate nonetheless, Hoover dismissed their entreaties as "slobbering palaver." "We know they have no use for us," he declared. And he, in turn, had no use for an agency that he believed never should have been created.[18]

As the first new president in the agency's history, Eisenhower faced a host of urgent questions: What should he do with Truman's creation? Who should lead it? Were there limits to what the CIA could or should be doing in the midst of the Cold War? Hoover had strong opinions on the matters. On December 30, 1952, weeks before the inauguration, he met with Eisenhower to discuss them. Hoover's first priority was to prevent the agency from being handed over to former OSS chief Bill Donovan, who was once again making a bid to be put in charge. Eisenhower acceded to that request. But the man he chose instead had his own history of run-ins with the FBI. Less than three weeks after his meeting with Hoover, Eisenhower announced the nomination of longtime CIA official Allen Dulles as head of the agency.[19]

Like Donovan, Dulles came out of the OSS, a son of privilege recruited to war-time adventurism from a white-shoe law firm. Hoover therefore viewed him with suspicion—"a 'Charley McCarthy' for Donovan," as one FBI report put it in 1947, with Donovan as the master ventriloquist and Dulles as his dummy. There were few ties of culture or common sympathy to help mend the rift. Dulles had come of age as the consummate Republican insider, his path to power all but assured from birth. His grandfather and uncle had both served as secretary of state—an honor that Eisenhower now bestowed upon his brother, John Foster Dulles.

Of the two, Allen was the more gregarious and sociable. He was also deadly serious about the need for a centralized intelligence apparatus. In 1947, Dulles had met be-hind closed doors with congressmen writing the National Security Act, the law that brought the CIA into being. Many observers assumed that he would be appointed to direct the agency the following year, after Thomas Dewey won election as president. With that in mind, in 1948 he helped to author a report recommending that the CIA take a greater role in domestic counterintelligence, thus consolidating the nation's anti-communist and anti-Soviet activities under one roof. The idea did not go over well with Hoover. "Irrespective of the merits or demerits of that it seems to me they ought to get CIA in shape first," he wrote icily. The agency "already has more than it properly handles or digests." He retaliated by recommending the formation of an intelligence-coordinating committee with no CIA involvement—a move that one agent later char-acterized as the "low point" in FBI-CIA relations.[20]

All of which meant that Dulles had his work cut out for him in 1953. On March 4, he called upon Hoover at Bureau headquarters, expressing his "highest regard and respect for the FBI" as well as his "intention to maintain good cooperative relations." Hoover met the gesture with less tact, warning Dulles that he wanted "cooperation from the heart" and not just "lip service." The two men sat down in person only a hand-ful of other times over the course of the Eisenhower years. Slowly, though, Hoover began to accept the inevitable: that the CIA was here to stay. Although he never liked that fact, he found that having a supportive president in the White House at least made it easier to work side by side.[21]

THE EISENHOWER YEARS WOULD LATER BE HELD UP AS AN EXAMPLE OF COVERT intelligence run amok: CIA-backed coups in Guatemala and Iran, a spy tunnel carved out beneath the city of Berlin, secret testing of LSD on unwitting subjects. Less often noticed are the ways that those years also empowered the FBI, providing Hoover not merely with cultural ballast and genial social outings, but with the institutional and political support to carry out many of his long-term aims. From his first days in office, Eisenhower stressed the centrality of the FBI to his vision of anticommunism and domestic security. Hoover embraced the license that Eisenhower afforded him.

The idea of promoting the FBI as a signature feature of the Republican White House came largely from one man—not Hoover but Herbert Brownell, Eisenhower's pick for attorney general. A corporate lawyer by trade, Brownell boasted a long and determined history within Republican politics. As Dewey's campaign manager, he had borne much of the blame for the surprise loss in 1948. By 1952, he had set out to find a winning candidate and settled on Eisenhower far earlier than most. Brownell had helped convince Eisenhower to run, and then stayed by his side as a "wise counsellor and trusted confidant," in the words of one profile. As *Time* pointed out, he had two things that Eisenhower desperately needed: a "legal mind" and a "political brain." When Eisenhower appointed him attorney general, everyone understood that the president would be relying on Brownell for strategic advice. "The shortest half-mile in Washington after Jan. 20 will be the one running from the Justice Department to the White House," the *Washington News* predicted.[22]

The close association between the president and the attorney general might have gone badly for Hoover, becoming a means of excluding the FBI from decision-making power. But Brownell arrived in office with two goals in mind. First, he wanted to reorganize the Justice Department, which he deemed to be in "pretty bad shape," unable to keep all its employees properly paid and working together. Second, Brownell sought to ensure that whatever happened at Justice—including at the FBI—provided political benefits to the president. Brownell saw Hoover as an underutilized resource with enormous institutional power and popular acclaim that could be captured for Republican ends. He also recognized that Hoover felt battered and underappreciated after almost eight years under Truman. "I think his experiences during the Truman administration had been frustrating to him," Brownell later reflected.[23]

What followed was a pageant of symbolic and practical support that could hardly have been imagined during the Truman years. Under Brownell's leadership, the Department of Justice relaxed its oversight of "bugs" (or microphone plants), giving Hoover carte blanche to run the FBI as he saw fit. Brownell also pushed Congress to enact legislation allowing wiretap evidence to be used in espionage cases, a change Hoover had sought ever since the Coplon trials. Eisenhower supported that initiative and added to it with Executive Order 10450, which would become one of the most infamous measures of his presidency. The policy expanded Truman's government employee loyalty program to include offenses related to the "habitual use of intoxicants to excess," "drug addiction," and "sexual perversion," as well as to "sympathetic association with a saboteur, spy, traitor, seditionist, anarchist, or revolutionist." Eisenhower made the FBI a key authority on such matters, ordering Hoover to conduct investigations into any government employee deemed suspicious. If and when the FBI found cause for concern, such employees could be fired and banished forever from federal employment. Under Eisenhower's policy, in short, Hoover could make or break the career of almost any federal employee in Washington.[24]

The program resulted in a swift escalation of both investigations and dismissals of government employees, especially at the State Department, where former FBI agent R. W. Scott McLeod took the lead. Following the model set by the congressional committees, McLeod hired several former agents to assist with his investigations and met repeatedly with Hoover for advice and encouragement. According to one estimate, in just seven months McLeod succeeded in ousting nearly two hundred State Department employees for offenses ranging from homosexuality to alcoholism to political subversion. Such a record would have been impossible, he wrote to Hoover, "if it were not for the fact that you have offered your cooperation." By the fall of 1953, Eisenhower reported a total of 1,456 employees dismissed across the federal agencies. In a graduation speech before the National Academy, Brownell contrasted this record with that of the Truman years, when so much of the FBI's work had been ignored or disparaged. "We are now making certain that this fine work is not wasted," he told the graduating police officers, assuring them that the FBI finally had the "backing" and "follow-through" that it needed.[25]

JUST WHAT BROWNELL MEANT BY THIS BECAME CLEAR ON NOVEMBER 6, 1953, when he took the opportunity of an afternoon talk before the Executives' Club of Chicago to revisit a case that had long rankled Hoover. Brownell's remarks that afternoon set off "one of the greatest controversies of our controversial times," in the words of Washington columnist Doris Fleeson. The subject was the late Harry Dexter White, the Treasury official whose promotion to the IMF had first convinced Hoover that he could not rely on Truman. Parts of the story had been aired before, most notably in White's 1948 appearance before HUAC, which had been followed by his heart attack and death. Brownell brought it up again in 1953 to showcase Hoover's version of events, in which White was no mere victim of committee pressure and rumor mongering, but a longtime Soviet source whose disloyalty had been ignored by Truman. "I can now announce officially, for the first time in public, that the records in my department show that White's spying activities for the Soviet government were reported in detail by the F.B.I. to the White House by means of a report delivered to President Truman," Brownell informed the surprised Chicago executives.[26]

Hoover himself was feeling far more confident about White than he had been in 1946, when even he admitted that the evidence had been circumstantial rather than definitive. Among the documents revealed by Chambers during the Hiss affair had been a memo in White's handwriting, apparent substantiation that the assistant treasury secretary had passed along government information. Two years later, the Venona team had linked White "conclusively" to the cover name "Jurist," who appeared in at least one Soviet cable as an "active" source. Hoover's ongoing bitterness toward Truman showed up in his comments about the Venona discovery. "Wouldn't it be swell to

send substance to [Truman's aide] Ad. Souers for information of the President," he
wrote. But Truman did not know the details of Venona, and Hoover was determined
to keep it that way.[27]

Truman denied that he had ever been informed of White's alleged Soviet connections. "I don't know what they're talking about. No such thing happened," he maintained. Almost immediately, Hoover's ex-employee Harold Velde, now head of HUAC,
sent Truman a subpoena, the first time that anyone could remember a former president
being called before Congress as a hostile witness. Truman refused to respond, ratchet-
ing up the situation into what one paper described as "a political brawl of almost unprecedented rancor." On November 11, five days after the Chicago speech, Eisenhower
held a press conference in which he expressed support for Brownell and Hoover, confirming that he had encouraged Brownell to go public with the White story. Five days
later, having endured more than a week of such talk, Truman took to the airwaves to
deliver a "volcanic outburst" in rebuttal, pointing out that the New York grand jury
had itself rejected the FBI's supposedly stellar evidence of Soviet espionage by government officials. In an eleven p.m. broadcast carried live on both television and radio,
Truman insisted that the matter was wildly overblown, and that Brownell had "lied to
the American people" by suggesting that Truman would knowingly appoint a Soviet
source to high international office. He said that the FBI had admitted that its information about White was inconclusive. According to Truman's version of events, everyone
agreed that White should move on to the IMF without any public disclosure in order
to allow the FBI investigation to continue.[28]

At this point Hoover's Republican friends at the Senate Internal Security Subcommittee stepped in with an offer: Did Hoover want to testify before the committee and
give his own account of what had happened? The negotiations occurred quickly. Truman's broadcast ended around midnight on November 16. The next afternoon, the
hundreds of spectators and reporters in the Senate caucus room gasped with surprise—
and then burst into applause—as Hoover pushed open the main doors and strode to
the witness table, an unannounced guest at the day's proceedings. During previous
committee appearances, reporters had been struck by Hoover's poised and methodical
affect. This time, they described him as "red-faced," "annoyed," and "tight-lipped," his
wrath barely contained. Beyond the caucus room, far more people were watching than
even just a few years earlier, thanks to the rapid spread of television. "We'd never seen
Hoover on TV before," one viewer reflected. "It was quite an experience."[29]

Hoover repeated much of what he had said before, explaining that the FBI did not
make policy but only followed the lead of Congress and the White House. In this case,
however, he felt duty bound to correct the record, even if it meant contradicting a
former president. With clipped precision, he retold the events of 1945 and 1946, insisting that "at no time was the F.B.I. a party to an agreement to promote Harry Dexter
White." According to the media, "it wasn't what he said but the way that he said it"

that made his testimony effective, "forceful, fairly and with a vibrant, competent ring to his voice." By the time he was finished, he had shown himself to be the "decisive witness" in the White controversy, according to *The New York Times*, as well as "probably the most powerful figure on Capitol Hill."[30]

In the days that followed, the praise for Hoover reflected his status as the toast of Eisenhower's Washington, a man of gravitas and long experience, now backed by both Congress and the White House. "I don't think I ever saw a more impressive witness," gushed a Dallas radio host. "I thrilled at the sight of Hoover—a great patriot, a great administrator, a great official dedicated to keeping your country free." In Washington, columnist John O'Donnell noted that the streets of the capital seemed "strangely empty" during Hoover's testimony, with everyone inside glued to the television or the radio, "looking and listening to the greatest story of foreign spying and internal treason ever told in the history of the Republic." O'Donnell declared November 17, 1953, one of the most exciting days the city had ever seen. "A century hence, if our Republic still survives in its tradition of freedom, our children's children will be reading in their history books how FBI Chief J. Edgar Hoover told the U.S. Senate of his efforts to block the Communist conspiracy of the Roosevelt-Truman era," he predicted.[31]

Public opinion polls bore out the perception of Hoover's testimony as an unmitigated triumph—not only the final word in the White case but also a sign that Hoover deserved the trust and free rein that Eisenhower and Brownell had been offering. According to a Gallup survey, 78 percent of Americans came away with a favorable opinion of Hoover, while just 2 percent expressed any doubts. (The other 20 percent registered no opinion at all.) Gallup once again declared the numbers all but unparalleled in the annals of American politics. "On other occasions the public has tossed bouquets to Government officials," the pollster explained, "but rarely is the attitude as favorable as that expressed in today's vote." By Gallup's calculations, thirty-nine out of forty Americans either liked or accepted what Hoover had done, whether they happened to be Democrats, Independents, or Republicans.[32]

Among the dissident few were longtime critics whose concerns about Hoover's concentrated power and increasingly conservative politics would eventually find a wider audience. But for at least a moment in 1953, with friends in the White House and the American public firmly behind him, even Hoover found it difficult to worry. On the night after his testimony, he attended a formal dinner at the White House, joining Eisenhower, Brownell, and Rev. Elson to honor the justices of the Supreme Court. The next day, he ventured out to the Bowie racetrack to enjoy opening-day festivities. When reporters approached him for further reflections on the White case, Hoover said he would prefer to enjoy lunch with friends on that warm and golden afternoon, offering only a "contented smile" in the way of comment.[33]

CHAPTER 36

No Sense of Decency

(1953–1954)

After years of controversy, Joseph McCarthy met his downfall in 1954. Cartoon depicts the Army-McCarthy hearings, where McCarthy claimed to have a letter from Hoover about communist infiltration of the army. Hoover denied the letter's authenticity.

READING TIMES/NATIONAL ARCHIVES AND RECORDS ADMINISTRATION

On November 23, a week after his appearance at the Senate, Hoover dined with Eisenhower once again. Crammed into a banquet room at the Mayflower Hotel, they were joined by hundreds of other people, including Brownell and Secretary of State John Foster Dulles, to celebrate the fortieth anniversary of the Anti-Defamation League. To mark the occasion, the League staged an hourlong televised variety show, with acts from comedians Lucille Ball and Desi Arnaz, newsman Walter Cronkite, and Broadway belter Ethel Merman, Hoover's old friend from his Stork Club days. Even in such august company, Hoover stood out as a man of consequence. "A significant development at the banquet was the spontaneous applause which greeted each mention of the name of FBI Director J. Edgar Hoover," one paper reported. When it came time for the speech that would close out the show, Eisenhower chose to focus his attention on another figure who had been making a stir in Washington. He never mentioned the subject's name, speaking in parable about Wild Bill Hickok, the Wild West gunslinger who supposedly made it a point to "meet anyone face to face with whom you disagree" and to act with integrity when he did. But everyone understood that the message was directed at a particular man: Senator Joseph McCarthy, the one Republican who did not much like what had happened in the Harry Dexter White matter, and who seemed determined to turn the spotlight back in his own direction.[1]

In theory, McCarthy should have been thrilled that Eisenhower was focusing on "communists in government," the issue on which the senator had made his name. Instead, McCarthy saw a threat to his own prominence. As a Republican, he had benefited from the Eisenhower sweep, assuming control of the Senate's Committee on Government Operations (now known as the McCarthy Committee). But he never quite managed to fit in with the Eisenhower crowd, which viewed the senator as an uncouth and irresponsible caricature of anticommunism. The White affair brought these conflicts into the open. In his midnight broadcast, Truman had accused the Eisenhower administration of embracing "McCarthyism," which he defined as the "use of the big lie and the unfounded accusation." McCarthy worried that the opposite was happening, that "the old battler, Joe McCarthy" was being "pushed off the front pages" in favor of Hoover, Eisenhower, and Brownell, as one radio show put it. So he set out to reclaim the limelight.[2]

In a live television broadcast on the night after Eisenhower's ADL address, McCarthy delivered what would become one of the most notorious speeches of his career—on par with the Wheeling episode, at least among Republicans. He initially framed the address as a response to Truman. Toward the end of the speech, however, he turned to the Republican Party, confessing fears that Eisenhower, like Truman, might not have what it takes to root out communist treachery. "Let me make it clear that I think the new Administration is doing a job so infinitely better than the Truman Acheson regime that there is absolutely no comparison," he declared. But better, he suggested, was not good enough.[3]

As the conservative columnist and FBI ally George Sokolsky reflected a few days later, McCarthy's "blockbuster" of a speech "shook and split the Republican party," at just the moment when the White episode had seemed to deliver such a clear and unifying punch. The story of McCarthy's fall from grace over the year that followed has become one of the great legends of American political history, a combination of morality tale and hard-boiled combat, the symbolic end of the Red Scare. As the Republican Party split apart on the McCarthy question, Hoover found himself once again forced to choose sides against a friend. But the showdown of 1954 also turned out to be a period of pride and satisfaction, in which Hoover solidified his status as one of the Eisenhower administration's favored sons. When it was all over, one paper asserted, there were "no clearcut winners—only losers." But this was not quite true. By the end of 1954, Hoover was the nation's unchallenged anticommunist authority, his combination of good-government bromides and conservative political zeal more popular than ever.[4]

WHEN HE RAN FOR PRESIDENT, EISENHOWER HAD HOPED TO GET THROUGH the campaign without coming into much contact with McCarthy, whose methods he loathed. In an election year with so much at stake for Republicans, though, he was reluctant to alienate a senator who had powerfully captured the public imagination. Hoover's office recognized Eisenhower's tolerance of McCarthy as political expediency and nothing more. "Despite fact that Eisenhower and McCarthy have reached some form of working agreement," a Bureau assessment noted, "the relationship between the two men is far from being friendly." At a campaign stop in Wisconsin, Eisenhower ordered an aide to stand between him and McCarthy, lest the senator attempt to sneak up and embrace him for the cameras.[5]

The Republican sweep in November 1952 offered McCarthy a chance to start anew—not only with Eisenhower but also with Hoover. The spat over FBI files that had divided them after Wheeling was more than two years in the past. McCarthy seemed eager to put the whole thing behind them. In the wake of the election, the Republican leadership awarded him the chairmanship of the Senate's Committee on Government Operations, an obscure and relatively powerless committee, but one in which he saw great potential to revive his anticommunist work. Created to root out corruption and inefficiency in federal expenditures, the committee maintained a Permanent Subcommittee on Investigations. McCarthy saw no reason that the subcommittee couldn't investigate other matters as well. He immediately reached out to Hoover to express hopes for "closer cooperation with and more extended use of the FBI and its facilities" as he set out to make his committee famous.[6]

He had good reason to think Hoover might go along. Despite their methodological differences, the two men still shared an outsize commitment to anticommunism. By 1953, McCarthy also shared more and more of Hoover's social world. Like Hoover, the senator had become a darling of the Texas oil set, pampered and celebrated by the country's richest men. During the 1950 election, Clint Murchison had given McCarthy ten thousand dollars to defeat Millard Tydings, the senator who had sounded the alarm against McCarthy's tactics. (Tydings lost after McCarthy's staff distributed a fake, composite photograph showing Tydings with Communist Party leader Earl Browder.) Murchison gave the Wisconsin senator a similar gift in 1952, this time targeting Connecticut senator William Benton, who had tried to get McCarthy expelled from the Senate. The oilman claimed to have "spoken to J. Edgar Hoover about McCarthy," and to have gotten Hoover's sign-off before taking action. According to Murchison, Hoover's only complaint was that McCarthy was "not general enough" in his accusations—that the senator claimed to have facts and details that only the FBI could or should know.[7]

With his committee assignment secured after the 1952 election, McCarthy took pains to create additional ties to Hoover, starting with his choice of investigative staff. Donald Surine, the former FBI agent personally recommended by Hoover, was still working as the senator's chief investigator. Several other staffers departed after McCarthy's reelection, but he quickly replaced them with men close to the FBI, in hopes of establishing the same sort of relationship that Hoover maintained with other committees. For general counsel, McCarthy chose Francis Flanagan, the former FBI agent who had run the Senate inquiry into homosexuals in government. As research director, he hired ex-communist Howard Rushmore, now a prolific journalist for the Hearst chain, who prided himself on publicizing the "quiet but grim struggle between the FBI and the Communist Party." And when Flanagan and Rushmore departed after just a few months on the job, McCarthy recruited still more FBI men, including Frank Carr, the head of communist investigations at Hoover's New York office, and Jim Juliana, who had worked as Carr's assistant. "With these newcomers on board," one McCarthy biographer has noted, "every major staff position . . . was filled by a former FBI agent or a man with superb contacts inside the Bureau."[8]

The most important of these new staffers was Roy Cohn, an awkward but energetic young lawyer out of New York, personally recommended by several members of Hoover's old Stork Club crowd. The son of a well-off New York judge, Cohn was pudgy, brainy, and never quite at ease. He had rushed through childhood, enrolling in Columbia University at sixteen and emerging three and a half years later with both an undergraduate degree and a law degree. Like Hoover, he went straight into government work, performing clerical tasks at the district attorney's office while he waited to turn twenty-one. At that point, he was finally able to take the bar exam and become an assistant U.S. attorney. During his first months on the job, Cohn had worked on the Smith Act prosecutions at Foley Square. From there, he moved on to the position of confidential assistant to U.S. Attorney Irving Saypol, the prosecutor in the Rosenberg case. Cohn had questioned David Greenglass during the Rosenberg trial, earning a reputation as a relentless but well-informed interrogator. Hoover may have seen something of himself in Cohn's precocious rise: here was another young man brimming with legal talent, personal ambition, and a passion for anticommunism.[9]

Cohn frequented the Stork Club and 21, where he eased his way into the confidence of Hoover's friends Leonard Lyons and Walter Winchell. Like Hoover, Cohn made a practice of passing along gossip and insider tips, experimenting with the reputation-shredding methods that would come to define his career. As a young gay man struggling to conceal his desires, he also may have found some of the same relief and acceptance that Hoover did in the Stork Club's live-and-let-live atmosphere. Among the men Cohn got to know during these years was G. David Schine, the handsome blond son of hotel magnate Junius Myer Schine. Hoover knew the elder Schine from winter vacations in Miami, where the Schine family owned several luxury hotels. In New York, David Schine and Cohn became "very, very close friends," in the words of Cohn's aunt, as well as regular nightclub companions. Just how close they were became a matter of speculation once Cohn joined McCarthy's staff and plunged into a Washington scene still in the throes of the Lavender Scare. In 1952, not long after meeting Cohn, Schine composed an eight-page pamphlet describing the nefarious history of global communism, subsequently distributed in Schine hotels "as a public service" and cited as justification for Cohn to hire Schine as a consultant to the McCarthy Committee. Despite the pamphlet's many inaccuracies, Hoover claimed to "have read it and enjoyed it tremendously." His praise was a testament less to the pamphlet's quality than to Schine's status as a member of his social network.[10]

Hoover met Cohn himself in 1952, in the midst of wrangling over communist-related grand jury matters. According to Cohn, he had been trying to contact Hoover for weeks when suddenly the director called out of the blue and invited him over for a private chat. "Within ten minutes I was seated across the desk from him," Cohn recalled. It turned out to be a meeting of the minds, with Cohn complaining about the blindness and foot-dragging of the Truman administration and Hoover promising to back him up if he ran into trouble. At the time, Cohn was working in Washington as special assistant to Attorney General James McGranery, who assigned him to coordinate with the FBI on communist investigations and to serve as an all-around fixer if things went wrong. When Elizabeth Bentley started drinking heavily and got mixed up with an abusive boyfriend, it was Cohn who stepped in to set the man straight. Cohn also played a role in the attempted perjury prosecution of Owen Lattimore, the last gasp in the legal saga of McCarthy's "top" Soviet agent. All of which made Cohn an obvious candidate when McCarthy started asking around for another lawyer to help run his Senate committee. Cohn was thrilled when both Hoover and Nixon showed up for a party celebrating his appointment—"heady wine," as he later wrote, for a twenty-five-year-old just beginning to test the promise of life in Washington.[11]

AS COMMITTEE CHAIRMAN, MCCARTHY ADOPTED THE HIT-AND-RUN STYLE HE had introduced back in 1950: a bold (if vague) accusation, followed by a quick turn to another target if and when objections were raised. Now, though, he had subpoena power, a substantial budget, and an expanded professional staff to help him. For his committee's first target he selected Voice of America, the State Department's worldwide radio operation, established during the war to promote American interests and spread American values around the world. On February 16, less than a month into the Eisenhower administration, the McCarthy Committee opened hearings in New York (predictably, at the Foley Square courthouse) and began calling up witnesses. To prove his claim that Voice of America was in cahoots with the communists, he focused on the fact that two of its transmitters were located on sites with considerable atmospheric interference. "Would not the best way to sabotage that [pro-American] voice be to place your transmitters within that magnetic storm area, so that you would have this tremendous interference?" he demanded of a Voice of America engineer as the klieg lights glared and the cameras rolled. And so it went, week after week, from February into March, a parade of witnesses pummeled and then dismissed by the indignant senator.

Throughout it all, McCarthy continued to praise Hoover, and to hint at cooperation between his committee and the FBI. During the Voice of America hearings, he grilled *New York Post* editor James Wechsler, a former Young Communist League member, about the newspaper's frequent criticisms of Hoover: "Have you ever, in your editorial columns, over the last 2 years, praised the FBI?" At hearings on alleged subversion in the Government Printing Office, McCarthy attacked the organization's leadership for failing to heed Hoover's warnings: "Man, you had the FBI report! What more did you need?" In September 1953, he published an article in *The Evening Star* extolling the virtues of coordination between congressional committees and the FBI. He cited Hoover's 1947 HUAC testimony, in which the director had outlined the committees' unique powers. He also pronounced Hoover "one of the most competent and outstanding men in Washington."[12]

Hoover was not so enthusiastic about McCarthy, but he remained open to working with the senator during the early months of the Eisenhower administration. If anything, Hoover seems to have wanted to save McCarthy from himself. In May, he met with McCarthy to discuss J. Robert Oppenheimer, the esteemed scientist and father of the atom bomb, whose left leaning affiliations had frequently been noted. McCarthy wanted to hold hearings on Oppenheimer but Hoover warned him that "there were several other committees in Congress which probably might resent his taking on this investigation." When the conversation veered into a discussion of Hank Greenspun, the Las Vegas editor who had exposed the rumors of McCarthy's homosexuality, Hoover offered similar advice. Rather than sue Greenspun, a situation that might attract undue attention to the issue, Hoover suggested that the senator hand the matter off for confidential inquiry by the Senate Internal Security Subcommittee, now safely in Republican hands. McCarthy professed to find the idea "well worth while exploring," more in deference to Hoover than in admiration for the rival Senate body.[13]

The one jarring note that summer came from a situation that should have drawn them further together: McCarthy's decision to staff his committee with former FBI men. The committee's new staff director, Frank Carr, had been working for the FBI when McCarthy lured him away, always a black mark in Hoover's book. Worse still, the growing number of FBI employees on McCarthy's staff began to inspire questions about whether the fix was in—whether Hoover was indeed allowing McCarthy access to FBI files, as critics had long suggested. Hoover worried about both perception and reality. "Ex-agents trying to make good on the committee job are not going to drop an iron curtain on their past knowledge of Bureau cases, informants, etc.," he admitted.

In July, he sent Nichols to meet with McCarthy and explain why hiring Carr was a bad idea. When McCarthy's secretary (soon to be his wife), Jean Kerr, came to plead the case back to Hoover, he reiterated that the presence of FBI men "would, no doubt, be seized upon by critics of the Senator and of the FBI as a deliberate effort to effect a direct 'pipe line' into the FBI." Hoover warned that the Bureau would have to be "far more circumspect in all of its dealings with the McCarthy Committee" if the appointment went through. When McCarthy went ahead and hired Carr anyway, Hoover cut them off altogether.[14]

Hoover's decision that summer to stop sharing information with McCarthy put the FBI ahead of most Republican politicians, including Eisenhower, who expressed their private displeasure with McCarthy but feared to take any action. And even Hoover did not go so far as to critique the senator in public. That August, he found himself with McCarthy at the Del Charro, playing shuffleboard and sipping drinks by the pool. When cornered by a local reporter about his opinion of his fellow hotel guest, Hoover delivered a qualified but not unsympathetic statement. "Certainly, he is a controversial man," he said, citing the senator's background as an ex-Marine, "amateur boxer," and Irishman to explain his combative style. He nonetheless declared McCarthy "earnest" and "honest" in all endeavors, unfairly criticized by the forces that tended to surface "whenever you attack subversives of any kind."[15]

EVEN AFTER MCCARTHY'S DENUNCIATION OF HIS "REPUBLICAN FRIENDS" THAT November, Eisenhower held out hope that the party would find a way to bring McCarthy back into the fold. McCarthy made the task impossible. During the fall of 1953, after his return from the Del Charro, he initiated hearings into alleged security lapses at Fort Monmouth, the New Jersey army base where Julius Rosenberg and members of his ring had been stationed during the war. In early 1954, he homed in on the case of Irving Peress, an army dentist who had gone to college with Rosenberg and moved in communist circles. Though army higher-ups had ordered Peress dismissed, he had been accidentally promoted to the position of major, a bureaucratic lapse that McCarthy framed as evidence of lax procedures toward communists. "Who promoted Peress?" he demanded, calling up General Ralph Zwicker, the highly decorated commander of New Jersey's Camp Kilmer, where Peress had once been stationed. When Zwicker refused to say who was responsible for the decision, McCarthy berated him as no better than a Fifth Amendment communist, "not fit to wear that uniform"— accusations all but designed to alienate Eisenhower, a career army man.[16]

It was only at this point, with the army under attack and McCarthy doubling down on his critique of fellow Republicans, that Eisenhower determined the White House could no longer stay above the fray. In early March 1954, he learned that Edward R. Murrow, the revered CBS broadcaster, planned a full half-hour program dedicated to unmasking McCarthy's methods. In conjunction with that, the president initiated his own full-court press against the senator. On March 8, Eisenhower authorized Nixon to begin preparing an anti-McCarthy speech. On March 9, Republican senator Ralph Flanders denounced McCarthy from the Senate floor as a traitor to "the Republican family." And on March 11, Eisenhower quietly approved the army's release of a report accusing McCarthy and Cohn of trying to strong-arm military officers in order to obtain favorable treatment for the now-drafted David Schine—accusations that would soon result in the "Army-McCarthy hearings" and produce the final agonizing episodes of McCarthy's career.

The fallout from these events has since become a well-worn morality tale of how the Eisenhower administration brought a dangerous rogue senator to heel. Less often noted is how critical the FBI was to the administration's anti-McCarthy strategy. In going after McCarthy, Eisenhower worried that the Republicans would lose control of the anticommunist issue, and that the White House itself would be tainted with the "soft on communism" charge. To "take [the] Red play away from McCarthy," as Eisenhower put it, the White House set out to promote Hoover as the nation's model anticommunist: the serious, responsible, professional alternative to McCarthy. In a televised speech in April, Eisenhower warned that certain unnamed figures had "greatly exaggerated" the threat of communism. To the degree that such fears were justified, however, the nation could rest assured that Hoover was already on the job. "Our great defense against those people is the FBI," Eisenhower declared, labeling Bureau agents "a great bulwark" against communism. A few days later, at the president's urging, Brownell delivered a follow-up address "bragging on [the] FBI," in Eisenhower's words. In that speech, Brownell renewed his call for "powerful constitutional weapons" to aid the FBI in its work—and thus to sideline Joe McCarthy.[17]

With such enthusiastic backing from the administration, there was little question about which side Hoover would choose. On April 9, he wrote to Eisenhower to express a humble desire to live up to the "support and confidence" outlined in the president's broadcast. "I think it will go down in history as one of the greatest speeches made by any President of the United States," he wrote.[18]

ON THE MORNING OF APRIL 22, 1954, BACK IN THE SENATE CAUCUS ROOM, GENeral Miles Reber took the stand as the first witness in the Army-McCarthy hearings, a political pageant of such intensity and animosity that it made the Tydings Committee (the Senate's original anti-McCarthy effort) look like a garden party. According to Reber, even as McCarthy had been railing about Fort Monmouth and suspicious pink dentists, Cohn had been quietly pressuring the army on behalf of his friend David Schine, who had been drafted into service. At first, Cohn had sought a reserve officer's commission, in hopes of saving Schine from overseas combat. When that failed and

Schine entered the army as a private, Cohn demanded outrageous privileges for his friend, including regular weekend passes and freedom from kitchen duty. The hearings were supposed to determine whether there was any connection between Cohn's desire to get what he wanted and McCarthy's decision to target the army for investigation.[19]

Hoover knew all about Cohn and Schine and the army, a situation that had been the subject of Washington gossip for months. Back in 1950, as a favor to Schine's father, Hoover himself had made inquiries about the young man's draft status, offering the services of the New York field office in a failed bid to help Schine secure a naval officer's commission. Three years later, once Schine joined McCarthy's staff, Hoover had continued to approach the situation with sympathy. The first reports about Cohn's behavior began to trickle in toward the end of 1953, as Bureau contacts passed along concerns "that Senator McCarthy could be placed in such an embarrassing spot if news ever leaked out that the senator and Cohn were endeavoring to obtain special privileges for Schine." By early 1954, as the news indeed started to leak, agents were reporting that Cohn seemed to be calling army representatives "at all hours of the night," threatening that "we'll make it tough for you" unless the army did what he wanted. Hoover remained loyal to Schine as long as he could. As late as February, well after the FBI knew what Cohn was doing, Hoover agreed to serve as a character reference for Schine, who was then making a bid for assignment to the military police. Once the hearings began, he quickly changed positions.[20]

As the chief subject of controversy, McCarthy himself could not chair the Army-McCarthy hearings, though they were being conducted under the auspices of his own subcommittee. Leadership fell instead to Karl Mundt, the pipe-smoking senator from South Dakota and the committee's second-ranking Republican. Like Nixon, Mundt had gotten to know Hoover as a member of HUAC, entering into the anticommunist fray long before being elected to the Senate. By 1954, the two men were on a first-name basis, but their relationship was not without tension. In March, just before the start of the hearings, the FBI received news that Mundt had told a newspaper of the FBI's quiet arrangements with congressional committees. Hoover dispatched Lou Nichols to have a "heart to heart talk" with the senator about the need to keep all Bureau cooperation confidential. Mundt pledged his fidelity while acknowledging, according to Nichols, that "with a friendly administration and with a friendly Attorney General, perhaps [the FBI] did not need Congress as much as we might on other occasions." That insight—that the FBI was once again working with the White House as well as Congress—helped to shape what happened next.[21]

The Army-McCarthy hearings were televised in full. On their screens, Americans saw a belligerent, intoxicated Senator McCarthy, temporarily relieved of his committee chairmanship, acting more in the role of defendant than prosecutor. At his side was

Roy Cohn, whose grimaces, eye rolls, and occasional bouts of laughter let viewers know what he thought of the proceedings. From start to finish, the hearings were suffused with innuendo about Cohn's outsize affection for Schine: "You and David Schine have been what we might call warm, personal friends, have you not?" army counsel Joseph Welch asked during one round of questioning, suggesting that they "have perhaps double dated together?" Brought in from Boston to represent the army, the bow-tied, patrician Welch turned out to be surprisingly effective on television, his sly humor a sharp contrast with Cohn's petulance and McCarthy's bombast.

For the first few weeks of the hearings, nobody paid much attention to the FBI— just as Hoover preferred. Then, on May 4, without any advance warning to Hoover, McCarthy pulled from his ever-growing pile of papers a 1951 letter in which the FBI director warned the leadership of Fort Monmouth about a serious communist infiltration problem in their ranks. McCarthy had made no mention of such a letter during his weeks of hearings on the Fort Monmouth situation during the fall. Now, with Secretary of the Army Robert Stevens in the witness chair, McCarthy sought to prove that the army had known about the danger lurking at Fort Monmouth and failed to act. The dramatic revelation threatened to turn the hearings back against the army. McCarthy's transparent suggestion, moreover, was that the secretary was going after Cohn and McCarthy for exposing the army's missteps.

By introducing the letter, McCarthy had hoped to claim Hoover's authority as his own. Instead, he opened up an opportunity for the army's team to present themselves as the true protectors of the FBI's reputation and legacy. Still on the witness stand, Secretary Stevens refused to look at the letter without Hoover's explicit permission, citing its "personal and confidential" nature. Welch went a step further, insisting that the committee would now have to hear directly from Hoover to validate or invalidate the letter's authenticity. At that point, the subcommittee decided it had no choice but to send a staff member—one of the many former FBI agents serving in its ranks—to confer in private session with the director.

Hoover had it within his power to turn the proceedings in McCarthy's favor, to grant credibility to a fellow anticommunist warrior in an hour of need. But as Mundt had recognized, Hoover now valued the White House far more than he needed McCarthy. Hoover spent two hours with the committee's liaison. During that time, they examined the letter that McCarthy had submitted: two and a quarter pages long, dated January 26, 1951, addressed to General Alexander Bolling, a top army intelligence officer, and signed in type by "J. Edgar Hoover, Director." They also reviewed a fifteen-page FBI memo of the same date, covering much of the same material, with Bolling as the recipient and Hoover as the sender. Under those circumstances, it would have been easy enough for Hoover to affirm that McCarthy's letter was based on genuine FBI information. Instead, as the *Star* reported, he "disowned the McCarthy document" as an unauthorized item of unknown provenance. Hoover did not appear in the caucus room, leaving it to his former employee to explain, "Mr. Hoover advised me that this is not a carbon . . . copy of any communication prepared or sent by the FBI to General Bolling," though "the language is, in some instances, identical."

"As I understand your testimony," Welch translated, the letter "is a carbon copy of precisely nothing."

"The testimony created a new uproar," the *Star* reported, casting McCarthy once again as a liar and dissembler. McCarthy seemed stunned by Hoover's rejection, insisting (correctly) that the letter reflected FBI research and that the FBI should be able to confirm that. His outrage increased when Brownell notified the committee that he would not release the fifteen-page FBI report, citing the "confidential" nature of Bureau files—and thus making it impossible for McCarthy to prove or disprove his claims.[22]

As the hearings moved on to other subjects, McCarthy continued to demand that the attorney general release the FBI report, just as material had been divulged about that "very important dead spy" Harry Dexter White. He also attempted to go around the attorney general, appealing to employees of the executive branch to break with official policy and send along supporting materials. With those words—what amounted to solicitation by a sitting senator of unlawful leaks—McCarthy drew a response direct from the president. In private conversation with an aide, Eisenhower compared McCarthy to Hitler, calling the senator's appeal "the most disloyal act we have ever had by anyone in the government." The president was somewhat more restrained in a public statement issued the next day. Asserting the primacy of the executive branch in "the enforcement of our laws and presidential orders," he issued a warning to "any individual who may seek to set himself above the laws of the land."

The final weeks of the hearings went from bad to worse for McCarthy, with the senator consuming alcohol in ever-greater quantities, often stumbling into the afternoon sessions half-drunk. When Cohn took the stand on June 9, he faced more innuendo about his relationship with Schine and his claims about the Monmouth situation. Angered by Welch's persistent questioning, McCarthy tried to change the subject by announcing that a young lawyer in Welch's office had once belonged to the National Lawyers Guild, classified by the attorney general as a communist front. In private negotiations, Cohn had agreed with Welch that McCarthy would avoid the subject in return for Welch avoiding inquiry into Cohn's draft status. When the attack came anyway, Welch met it with an eloquent parry. "Let us not assassinate this lad further, Senator," he told McCarthy. "You have done enough. Have you no sense of decency, sir, at long last? Have you left no sense of decency?" Of the thousands of words spoken over the course of thirty-six days—some 2,986 pages of testimony—these were the ones that came to define the Army-McCarthy hearings, and thus to seal McCarthy's fate.[23]

———

BY THE TIME MCCARTHY TOOK THE STAND LATER THAT AFTERNOON, THERE was little chance of turning things around. He tried anyway over the course of the next day and a half, propping up a large map of the United States and proceeding to lecture the exhausted committee about Marx, the Bolshevik Revolution, and the imminent nature of a "brutalitarian" communist threat. His presentation sounded much like what Hoover himself had said on countless occasions, but it was too late to earn back the director's—or the nation's—favor.[24]

As the hearings wound down, observers struggled to find the proper words to convey their disgust, labeling the affair "one of the most disgraceful episodes in the history of our government." And yet Hoover himself seemed to emerge unscathed. In May, at the height of the controversy over the letter, he had celebrated his thirtieth anniversary as Bureau director, an occasion that inspired dozens of ritual tributes to the one "irreplaceable man in Government," in Pat McCarran's words. Mundt had taken time away from the hearings to support a resolution in honor of Hoover's anniversary.[25]

In the weeks that followed, participants on all sides competed to outdo each other in their admiration for Hoover. On the stand, Cohn "made an impassioned speech in praise of Mr. Hoover and congressional investigations," one news report observed. Cohn's adversary, Joseph Welch, was no less solicitous, repeatedly declaring that "he loves, cherishes and reveres J. Edgar Hoover," in the words of liberal commentator Murray Kempton. McCarthy himself insisted throughout the hearings, "I don't know of any wrongdoings in the Federal Bureau," absolving Hoover of all blame for the army's mistakes and treachery. "Usually the mention of the name of the FBI chief— a virtual deity in the caucus room—was enough to start a stampede for the microphones among the Senators, none of whom will yield to one another in their admiration of Mr. Hoover," wrote *Star* reporter Mary McGrory. In one of the most contentious political spectacles in American history, Hoover's supposed greatness emerged as the one point of consensus. "The entire inquiry," a London writer observed, "seems to have benefited no one except J. Edgar Hoover." The senator himself noticed the strange phenomenon in which even his avowed enemies rushed to agree about the FBI's unimpeachable authority. "J. Edgar Hoover's shoulders must be getting awfully lame from so many people here hanging upon his coattails," McCarthy grumbled, even as he attempted to cling to them himself.[26]

In popular memory, the Army-McCarthy hearings mark the dismal climax of the Red Scare, the moment the country definitively rejected anticommunist hysteria in favor of more restrained methods and attitudes. In truth, the months following the hearings produced some of the most draconian anticommunist legislation in American history, much of it justified as a way to support the FBI and push back against

McCarthy. As early as May, Brownell had laid out a plan "to expand and intensify" the Justice Department's anticommunist initiatives, in the words of one reporter. Over the next few months, Congress passed several bills in support of this effort, including the Communist Control Act, which stripped the Communist Party of its legal status. To accommodate Hoover's long-standing concern that such a law would simply drive the communists underground, Eisenhower and his Republican allies in Congress eliminated criminal penalties for individual party members. But the act was still the single most significant piece of anticommunist legislation in years—and it came after, not before, the Army-McCarthy hearings. The final bill passed all but unanimously in both the House and Senate.[27]

Hoover and Brownell flew out to Denver in September to meet Eisenhower and discuss what to do with the newfound power at their disposal. They emerged from their meeting with a triumphant message. "It is the aim of this Administration to utterly destroy the Communist Party, U.S.A. and its activities in the U.S.," Brownell announced in a local press conference. Seated by his boss's side, Hoover followed up with praise for a new law granting immunity to ex-communists willing to talk with the FBI. His mere presence made news—"one of his rare appearances before newsmen," in the words of the Associated Press.[28]

Given this "rare" opportunity, the press were eager to hear from Hoover about another great question of the moment: What did he think of Joe McCarthy? On this subject, however, Hoover had little to say. As a newspaper had noted back in June, with the hearings winding down, Hoover had exercised real "circumspection" when it came to "dealing with the malignant Senator." That had not changed by the end of summer, even as criticism of McCarthy mounted nearly everywhere else. The senator had once again stopped by the Del Charro during Hoover's August visit. This time, though, Hoover had refused to see him, or to answer press queries about the matter. In Denver, Hoover said simply that the FBI welcomed the "constructive support" of any congressional committee, without specifying which committees—and which senators—fit that description. It was a far cry from the previous summer, when Hoover had glowingly described McCarthy as "a vigorous individual who is not going to be pushed around" even in the fiercest of political battles.[29]

REPUBLICANS SUFFERED SERIOUS LOSSES IN THE 1954 MIDTERM ELECTIONS, bringing an end to their brief, heady period of one-party control in Washington. Hoover's favored congressional committees flipped back into Democratic hands, necessitating yet another reshuffling of staff and priorities. McCarthy was forced out of his committee chairmanship as well, his reign brought to a close not by any righteous backlash but through the ordinary mechanisms of electoral politics. His fellow senators nonetheless claimed the final word. Back in July, the Republican moderate Ralph

Flanders had introduced a resolution of censure against McCarthy, listing off dozens of violations of decency and respectable behavior. Yet another Senate committee whittled them down to just two major charges, both involving McCarthy's behavior toward fellow senators rather than his more egregious attacks on committee witnesses. On December 2, with the elections safely out of the way, the Senate voted, 67 to 22, to censure McCarthy—a rare rebuke to one of their own. The vote carried no official consequences; McCarthy was not stripped of his seniority or tossed out of the Senate. But it made him persona non grata around Washington.[30]

Hoover let others do the talking, acceding to a narrative in which the FBI, with its supposed professionalism, restraint, and commitment to confidentiality, became the preferred alternative to McCarthy's public browbeating and wild exaggeration. In the spring of 1955, with McCarthy's censure still fresh in political memory, Eisenhower put another seal of approval on that narrative by awarding Hoover the National Security Medal, a newly invented honor for outstanding employees within the intelligence field. The Rose Garden ceremony on the morning of May 27 drew a who's who of Hoover's administration friends: Nixon was there, along with much of Eisenhower's cabinet. McCarthy, it went without saying, was not invited. Eisenhower took advantage of the occasion to emphasize those qualities that implicitly distinguished Hoover from the senator, issuing a citation that noted the director's "exceptional tact," "recognized integrity," and "high personal prestige." After the ceremony, Nixon hosted a celebratory lunch for Hoover and Tolson.

Later that day, Hoover wrote to the deputy attorney general that he was "deeply moved" by the ceremony—indeed, that he considered it "a high light in my life." Perhaps the greatest affirmation, though, was the fact that he was still standing there at all. As one writer observed during the Harry Dexter White affair, Hoover displayed a remarkable ability to outlast nearly everyone else who touched the fractious issue of communism, especially those hapless politicians who tried to claim the issue for themselves. "McCarthys may come and go, but Hoover remains—the link between all administrations, countenanced even in the New Deal's heyday, and now the most powerful political-police chief the world has known."[31]

CHAPTER 37

Massive Resistance

(1954–1957)

Officials of the NAACP, including Thurgood Marshall (far right)
and executive secretary Roy Wilkins (second from left),
campaigning in 1956 against racial violence and segregation in
Mississippi. Despite Hoover's racism, the FBI and the NAACP
developed a working relationship during the 1940s and 1950s.

DONALDSON COLLECTION/MICHAEL OCHS ARCHIVES/GETTY IMAGES

No sooner had the McCarthy controversy been put to rest than another crisis demanded Hoover's attention. On May 17, 1954, while much of the public was glued to the Army-McCarthy hearings, the Supreme Court issued a long-awaited decision in the case of *Brown v. Board of Education of Topeka*, better known around Washington as the "schools case." Writing for a unanimous court, Chief Justice Earl Warren ruled that racial segregation in public schools violated the constitution's guarantee of equal protection, a sweeping reversal of the "separate but equal" doctrine that had upheld the Jim Crow system for more than half a century. In doing so, he forced the FBI back into civil rights work.

Hoover knew Warren reasonably well and, for the most part, trusted his judgment. As state attorney general and then governor of California, Warren had forged an amicable relationship with the FBI, soliciting Hoover's aid in state law enforcement and accepting tips through the Responsibilities Program. Since moving to Washington as chief justice in the fall of 1953, Warren had dined with Hoover at the White House and appeared as the guest speaker at an academy graduation. Their only significant moment of disagreement had occurred during the war, when Warren had championed Japanese internment while Hoover played the role of cautious civil libertarian.[1]

With *Brown*, they switched positions. The decision launched Warren's reputation as one of the century's great liberals, the towering giant of rights-based jurisprudence. For Hoover, it meant a growing conflict between his duties as a federal lawman and his conservatism on matters of race and social protest.

FOR WASHINGTON RESIDENTS SUCH AS HOOVER, DESEGREGATION WAS NO DIS-tant matter. It was local and intensely personal. In 1948, after years of activism, a self-appointed National Committee on Segregation in the Nation's Capital had published a report declaring the city "the capital of white supremacy" and urging Americans to "break the chains that bar a quarter of a million Negroes in Washington from their equal rights as Americans." During the 1952 presidential campaign, in a nod to such efforts, Eisenhower had vowed to eliminate "every vestige of segregation in the District of Columbia." The following year, even before Warren arrived in town, the Supreme Court affirmed Reconstruction-era laws declaring the city's restaurants open to all patrons, regardless of race.

Those rulings and speeches changed only so much. In 1954, the city mostly remained separated into Black and white. As a governing logic, though, the support for desegregation reversed much of what Hoover had seen and experienced in his early life, when the edifice of segregation had been imagined and built. Hoover's birth occurred just sixteen months before *Plessy v. Ferguson*, the Supreme Court decision that affirmed the legitimacy of "separate but equal." He had come of age in largely segregated institutions, from his elementary school to his high school and university, and on up to the FBI itself. The Stork Club, Harvey's, the Mayflower, the Del Charro—all were restricted to primarily white clientele, though Black waiters, dishwashers, and maids often kept the businesses afloat. When Hoover went home, it was to a neighborhood constructed to attract white residents and to exclude everyone else.

The push for desegregation altered his world. The Supreme Court's restaurant ruling applied to Hoover's regular haunts, even if no mad rush to accommodate Black patrons ensued. A separate decision banning the enforcement of racial covenants in housing made obsolete the "safely restricted" terms under which Hoover had purchased his home. Over the course of the 1940s, federal employers such as the Library of Congress began to roll back the segregationist policies put in place during Hoover's youth, though as the 1948 report on segregation noted, exclusion remained the default policy within the federal government. Under Truman, the military began to desegregate as well, making the war in Korea the first major Cold War conflict fought with integrated troops.[2]

The Washington public schools, where Hoover had discovered his talents as a star student, followed suit. In 1950, with the city's Black population on the rise and its white population in decline, the school board proposed to convert Hoover's alma mater, Central High, into a "Negro school." The idea sparked outcry from Central alumni, who pointed to the school's record in producing distinguished white public servants such as Hoover. But the school board pushed ahead. By the end of 1950, Hoover's beloved alma mater ceased to exist under the Central High name, after some seventy years as the city's premier white high school.[3]

The Supreme Court's 1954 rulings brought another round of upheaval. On the same day as *Brown*, the court issued a separate decision about public education in Washington, where the school system was governed by federal rather than state authority and therefore required different legal reasoning. As with *Brown*, the court found segregation unconstitutional, deciding in favor of Black students who had attempted to enroll in a whites-only junior high school. Eisenhower promptly ordered the city's schools to desegregate in time for the start of the 1954–1955 school year, expressing the hope that Washington would serve as a "pilot model" for the nation.[4]

The public-school ruling did not apply to Hoover's other alma mater, George Washington University, the site of such intense FBI recruitment over the years. But the desegregation campaign had an impact there, too. Of all the city's historically white universities, GW had been the last holdout in favor of segregation. "There are no colored students in The George Washington University," its president, Cloyd Marvin, had declared as late as 1938, insisting that Negro students could be better served at Howard or other Black institutions. Over the next several years, GW clung to its segregationist practices even as other local universities began to accept Black students. With *Brown*, GW, too, finally gave in. Reflecting the evolution in elite white opinion, Marvin conceded that "in light of the principles enumerated by the Supreme Court, in light of our holding a Federal Charter, and in light of our relationship to government departments through contracts, it was felt we could not lag behind the new social front that is establishing itself."[5]

That left Hoover's fraternity, Kappa Alpha, as the last segregationist holdout among the key educational institutions of his youth. If anything, the fraternity's emphasis on racialized "Old South" rituals only increased as Jim Crow began to crumble. The GW chapter still held the parties and football-related festivities that had been so important to Hoover. Now they also staged Confederate dress balls (part of "Old South Week End") and put on blackface minstrel shows (in 1950, the theme was a "Cotton Pickin' Party"). Some fraternity chapters went beyond that, staging "secession ceremonies" and mock assassinations of Union leaders. At all such events, the Confederate battle flag occupied a place of honor as the fraternity's unifying emblem, displayed over the front door to chapter houses as well as at dances and parades. The fraternity's journal took credit for inspiring a new "fad of displaying the Battle Flag" as a symbol of support for Jim Crow.[6]

Hoover had little to say in public about the controversies at Central, GW, and Kappa Alpha. But what he did say suggests that his fundamental loyalties had changed little over the years. In late 1954, a few months after *Brown*, he gave permission for *The Kappa Alpha Journal* to reprint one of his articles on communism. He composed a personal note to go with it, praising "faithful adherence to the principles of Kappa Alpha" as a high virtue.[7]

HOOVER'S ONGOING SYMPATHY FOR KAPPA ALPHA SUGGESTS A POWERFUL CONtinuity in his racial views. Taught as a young man to regard segregation as a bedrock of the social order, he did not simply abandon those ideas when the Supreme Court declared otherwise. But his personal views on race were not the only—or even the chief—consideration on his mind as he began to contemplate what the FBI should do in the wake of *Brown*. He remembered what had happened in the 1940s, when the FBI had tried but failed to bring federal power to bear against Southern lynch mobs. Now he worried that the FBI was heading into a similar morass. Though it gave federal backing to desegregation, *Brown* did not explain how to enforce the law, or how to strike a reasonable balance between federal, state, and local jurisdictions. Figuring that out would be up to Hoover.

He worried as well about what desegregation would mean for his signature issue of anticommunism—whether it would help to solidify the consensus he had built or break it apart. Hoover had long disdained Black activists as dupes of the Communist Party, fellow travelers in effect if not always in fact. At the same time, he recognized that American racial violence and exclusion provided easy fodder for communist propaganda. The Soviet government loved nothing more than to point out American hypocrisy on such cherished values as equality, opportunity, democracy, and the rule of law. So did the domestic Communist Party, as FBI files documented at great length. If anticommunism fed Hoover's suspicion of civil rights organizations, it also pushed him to act against the most egregious forms of racial injustice as a way of defending America from its ideological enemies.

The Justice Department had filed amicus briefs before the Supreme Court advocating desegregation on Cold War grounds. "Racial discrimination furnishes grist for the Communist propaganda mills," it warned, with segregation in the nation's capital the greatest embarrassment of all. Once the *Brown* decision came down, the Republican National Committee quickly declared that it "falls appropriately within the Eisenhower Administration's many-frontal attack on global Communism"—an attack in which Hoover was supposed to be at the vanguard. Hoover approached *Brown* acutely aware of these pressures, and of the need to deliver a law enforcement response that would shore up American credibility. Whatever else it might be, desegregation was now a practical problem that he would have to solve in order to maintain the FBI's broader standing and legitimacy.[8]

One sign of Hoover's pragmatism on the question could be seen in his ongoing relationship with the NAACP. It was the NAACP that had engineered *Brown* and the other school desegregation suits, part of a long-term strategy to dismantle the legal edifice of Jim Crow. Leading that effort was a brilliant young attorney named Thurgood Marshall, a graduate of Howard University School of Law and one of the most effective civil rights lawyers in the nation. In 1940, at the age of thirty-two, he helped to create the NAACP's Legal Defense and Education Fund as the launching pad for many of the high-profile cases now reshaping the racial landscape. A savvy political thinker, he also recognized the value of government relationships developed outside the courtroom, even if that meant getting along with an unreformed Kappa Alpha like Hoover.[9]

Marshall came to this discovery the hard way: by making Hoover angry. Throughout the 1940s, Marshall had regularly lent his voice to complaints about racism in the FBI's hiring practices, as well as in its methods of investigating civil rights–related crimes. In late 1946, in the wake of the Georgia lynchings, he had taken those complaints to Hoover and to the attorney general, composing unsparing letters in which he described the FBI's "one-sided" record on crimes "where Negroes are the victims." Hoover had responded with his usual defensiveness, insisting to the attorney general that Marshall was "most careless," that the charges were far too vague to be actionable, and that the NAACP was out to get the FBI. He also contacted Walter White, who had shown at least some sympathy for the FBI during the war and the subsequent anti-lynching campaign. "The repeated efforts on the part of Thurgood Marshall to embarrass the FBI" were unacceptable, Hoover complained, urging White to intervene on the FBI's behalf. Apparently recognizing the peril of alienating the country's chief law enforcement official, White seems to have encouraged Marshall to meet with Hoover and smooth things over. "I . . . have no faith in either Mr. Hoover or his investigators and there is no use in my saying I do," Marshall wrote back, refusing to concede that "anything in my letter" could be labeled "untrue."[10]

The meeting came off anyway. On the morning of October 22, 1947, Marshall arrived at Hoover's office to discuss the FBI's civil rights record. Just what was said is not recorded in Marshall's file. But a later report noted that after 1947, "Marshall refrained from further unfounded criticism." Hoover made his own friendly gestures in return, promising that any communications from Marshall would receive the director's prompt and personal attention.[11]

In the years thereafter, they worked together (if only grudgingly), especially on the issue of communism. Like nearly everyone in Washington, Marshall described himself as a devout anticommunist. Under the pressures of the moment, he and other NAACP leaders went out of their way to show that they, too, could be relied upon to do their part. As Bureau documents noted with some frequency, the Communist Party often encouraged its members to join the NAACP and other civil rights organizations in hopes of influencing or even controlling their agenda. In response, the NAACP's national board vowed in 1950 to expel any local chapter dominated by communists. The NAACP also forbade members of "Communist and Communist front organizations" to participate in its activities. White personally assured the FBI's New York office "that the NAACP will in no fashion whatever work with the Civil Rights Congress" or other alleged communist front groups. Within its own ranks, the NAACP publicly identified a handful of local chapters where Communist Party members had come to exercise at least a modest degree of influence. Assessing these efforts, a 1953 FBI report on "The Communist Party and the Negro" praised the NAACP as a "pragmatic and expedient" organization, securely on the right side of the communist question.[12]

The report's conclusions did not stop Hoover from approving a "COMINFIL" ("communist infiltration") investigation of the NAACP beginning in February 1954. Under its auspices, agents were authorized to use "discreet" inquiries through "reliable sources" to track what was happening within the organization. Marshall received in-person updates from the FBI on the infiltration inquiry, even soliciting details to be incorporated into his speeches. He also publicly cited Hoover as proof that the NAACP was on the right side of the line when it came to communism. "Edgar Hoover, boss of the FBI, says we are not subversive," he affirmed at one NAACP gathering.[13]

When *Brown* came along, it only made sense for the FBI and NAACP to talk about working together. In late 1952, White reached out to Hoover to discuss preparations for possible outbreaks of violence should the court decide in the NAACP's favor. "There may be several outfits which capitalize on racial and religious bigotry which may attempt to stir up trouble," he warned. He hoped that Hoover and the NAACP might join forces "in preventing others from creating disorder." Even White underestimated the ferocity of the response to come, however, and the way it would strain the fragile truce between the two organizations.[14]

HOOVER'S RELATIONSHIP WITH MARSHALL AND THE NAACP REFLECTED ONE side of his professional outlook: that of the pragmatic lawman, willing to make alliances of necessity. His friendship with Mississippi senator James Eastland reflected another. One of the most committed segregationists in Congress, Eastland espoused ideas familiar to Hoover, from his passionate denunciations of "Oriental Communism" to his glorification of the Old South. When Eastland became head of SISS (Hoover's favorite Senate subcommittee) in late 1954, Hoover viewed it as a positive thing for the

Bureau. At the same time, he soon found himself at odds with Eastland over *Brown*—and over the use and power of federal law enforcement to support the Supreme Court's decision. The same imperatives that drove Hoover into uneasy cooperation with the NAACP brought him into conflict with men such as Eastland, who were otherwise his great champions and allies.[15]

Eastland had been born in 1904 into a crucible of Mississippi racial violence. Just months before his birth, his father had led a lynch mob seeking vengeance for the murder of Eastland's uncle. The mob killed at least three people before finally capturing the alleged murderers, a Black couple. Eastland's relatives beat the suspects, cut off their fingers and ears, and tortured them with corkscrews before burning the couple alive in front of a crowd a thousand strong. Named for his murdered uncle, Eastland had been groomed to take over his family's plantation holdings, and to maintain the social and political order on which it rested. Upon arriving in Washington in 1941, he had carved out a place for himself as an outspoken champion of white supremacy. He opposed any federal policy that might disrupt it.[16]

On the day of the *Brown* ruling, Eastland announced that Southern states "will not abide by nor obey this legislative decision by a political court." In the weeks that followed, those words became the rallying cry of a formidable movement dedicated to undermining and resisting any attempt to dismantle Jim Crow. Virginia senator Harry Byrd, another longtime fixture of the Southern congressional stable, eventually labeled this movement "massive resistance," an explicit plan by states from Virginia to Mississippi and Texas to defy the Supreme Court order. In the midst of the brewing conflict, Hoover ended his formal liaison arrangement with Eastland's subcommittee. He still continued to work with the senator and to feed him information, however, convinced that Eastland was doing "a grand job and had made a great contribution to the American people." Hoover sympathized with Eastland's dismay over *Brown*. As a federal lawman, though, he refused to sanction open defiance of the law and the courts. The rise of massive resistance put these commitments into conflict.[17]

Eastland's Mississippi quickly emerged as a spiritual and practical center of massive resistance, the first state to declare its rebellion and to spawn groups dedicated to seeing the cause through. In the summer of 1954, a rally in Indianola marked the launch of the Citizens' Councils of Mississippi, intended to provide the self-anointed "best" white citizens of the state with an outlet for organizing against *Brown*. The group ostensibly emphasized legal means, contrasting itself with the lynchers and vigilantes of the Ku Klux Klan. But its rhetoric often obscured any real distinction between legal and illegal, nonviolent and violent. In retaliation for registering to vote or attempting to attend white schools, the Citizens' Councils recommended boycotts of Black-owned stores, the firing of Black employees, and the calling in of debts.[18]

The councils' rhetoric, combined with their growing membership, brought them to Hoover's attention just as the McCarthy crisis was starting to dissipate. In December 1954, the Justice Department wrote to Hoover recommending "that an investigation be made," with the aim of determining whether the Citizens' Councils should be included on the attorney general's list of subversive organizations. Despite his general sympathy with Eastland and other Southern leaders, Hoover complied immediately, ordering agents in the New Orleans and Memphis offices to prepare a comprehensive evaluation. When the first reports arrived in February, they described a booming organization—thirty thousand members in twenty-five branches throughout Mississippi—with an ambitious political agenda. "Objectives include act to oppose voters seeking Negro vote, discourage Negro registration, educate citizens to advantages of segregation and dangers of integration, mobilize public opinion and devise legal means to cope with problems," one FBI report said. Echoing the councils' own claims, local agents maintained that the group anticipated "no violence to maintain segregation" and that the councils' members called for "a war of nerves" rather than a war in the more literal sense.[19]

This purported commitment to nonviolence did not halt the FBI's investigation. As the councils continued to grow and spread beyond Mississippi, Hoover decided to "intensify" the Bureau's efforts, ordering field offices "to be alert for the formation of Citizens' Councils" in their territory and to furnish the Bureau "immediately" any information received. Like most of Hoover's efforts related to civil rights, this required some tricky work where jurisdiction was concerned. As a May 1955 memo noted, "current Bureau policy is that we do not investigate groups that advocate and employ legal means." Hoover made an exception, however, for groups created specifically to target "racial minorities," on the theory that "such groups' activities may result in civil rights violations."[20]

Of all his civil rights initiatives during these years, Hoover's decision to investigate the Citizens' Councils is perhaps the most surprising. The councils advertised themselves as the law-abiding, respectable wing of massive resistance. Given his well-known sympathies with white Southerners, Hoover could well have accepted this at face value and looked the other way, as many Southern leaders chose to do. That he took a different path says less about his personal sympathies than about his fury at those who would defy federal law, and about his expanding definition of justifiable domestic intelligence. Even as he moved forward, Hoover remained aware of the political costs should its investigation be discovered. "Bureau's position in connection with conducting inquiries re these groups is extremely delicate," a deputy warned. "We could be charged with investigating citizens organizations which have committed no violations over which we have jurisdiction." In recognition of this fact, headquarters urged field agents to conduct their inquiries "most discreetly."[21]

HOOVER'S CONCERNS OVER THE NEW WHITE SUPREMACIST GROUPS BECAME even more urgent once massive resistance turned deadly. While the FBI poked around the Citizens' Councils, another wave of racial violence swept across the South. As in 1946, it provoked passionate calls for the federal authorities to step in and prevent the atrocities—or, where prevention was not possible, to bring the perpetrators to justice.

The worst of the violence took place in Mississippi, Eastland's home turf and the birthplace of the Citizens' Councils. Upon visiting the state for the first time in April 1955, *Jet* reporter Simeon Booker recalled being shocked by the open antagonism and threats aimed at civil rights proponents, most of them middle-class Black men and women seeking nothing more than the right to cast a vote and participate in American life as full citizens. On one of his first days in the state, Booker attended a rally where a Black store owner and minister named Reverend George Lee spoke about the voting-rights struggle. Less than a month later, a convertible pulled up alongside Lee as he drove through his hometown of Belzoni. The occupants shot him twice in the face. He crashed his car into a nearby house, then stumbled out pleading for help. By the time a taxi transported him to the hospital, he was dead, a casualty of massive resistance.

Booker's distress at encountering such violence would soon lead him to reach out to the FBI, and then to start sharing information about what he saw and experienced through his reporting work. When that fact was revealed decades later, after a storied career at *Jet* magazine, friends and colleagues expressed shock at his decision to cooperate with the Bureau. Booker defended it as the obvious thing, no different from what White, Marshall, and other NAACP leaders were doing in Washington. "Any young reporter . . . who thinks it was inappropriate to maintain contacts in Hoover's FBI is simply clueless as to what it took to watch your back in the South of the 1950s and '60s," he later wrote. In a situation with few good options, Hoover's grudging offers of cooperation often seemed better than nothing, according to Booker: they provided a chance not only to be "used" by Hoover's agents, but to use them in turn for tips that could save lives and produce important stories.[22]

The Lee murder itself occasioned little notice outside the Black press. As the weeks went on, though, the "Reign of Terror" in Mississippi, as the NAACP put it, became impossible to ignore. In Brookhaven, a veteran and farmer named Lamar Smith spearheaded a local voter registration effort only to be gunned down by white men in front of the town courthouse. A few months after that, sixty-five-year-old Gus Courts, a store owner who had worked with Lee on the Belzoni campaign, was shot through his shop's plate-glass window. He managed to escape with serious but not fatal injuries. And in late August, a fourteen-year-old boy named Emmett Till, down from Chicago to visit his mother's relatives, bought some bubble gum from a general store in the town of Money. During the transaction, he may have whistled at the young white woman running the cash register. A few nights later, a group of white men descended upon his uncle's house, dragged Till out of bed, and drove him to a shack in the woods, where they proceeded to torture and then shoot him before throwing his body in the Tallahatchie River.

The Till murder made the summer's violence in Mississippi into a national and even international story, the case that finally prodded many white observers to grapple with the brutality and senselessness of the state's racial regime. Unlike Lee, Smith, and Courts, Till was just a kid—a kid from the North, no less, unfamiliar with how the South set up its social rules and enforced them. Till's mother, Mamie, determined to ensure that "the world can see what they did to my boy," brought his body back to Chicago for an open viewing. Thousands of mourners filed past his coffin over Labor Day weekend, aghast at his bloated body and distended features, all for the crime of allegedly flirting with a white girl.[23]

If the Till case captured the headlines, from Hoover's perspective it was the least of the summer's crimes—or at any rate, the one least deserving of Bureau attention. During the first frantic hours after Till's disappearance, a local agent dispatched overnight teletype updates to Washington, concerned that there would be grounds for federal involvement. But both Hoover and Brownell quickly agreed that the Bureau lacked jurisdiction. They came to a different conclusion about the other crimes, where the connection to voting rights seemed to leave more room for federal action. On May 9, Hoover launched an investigation into the Lee murder, dispatching agents to interview witnesses and gather ballistics evidence. The Bureau ultimately identified two chief suspects, both members of the local Citizens' Council. Upon reviewing the evidence, however, the Justice Department determined that the link between Lee's murder and his voting rights work was too weak to move forward with a federal indictment.[24]

As in the lynching investigations of the 1940s, Hoover found the Lee case to be an exercise in frustration: Bureau agents went in and solved the crime, only to be told that their efforts were for naught. The same held true with the Courts and Smith shootings, which proceeded—and ultimately failed—along similar lines. The outcome of the Till case was perhaps worst of all, a miscarriage of justice in which the federal government stood by as a local white jury acquitted Till's assailants of murder. Hoover blamed everyone else for what went wrong, casting fault on Southern politicians and policemen, on the Justice Department and the weakness of federal law, on the NAACP for pushing too hard, and on the Citizens' Councils for pushing back. He never seems to have entertained the idea that he himself might have done something different.

Those who endured the violence firsthand were not so ready to absolve him. In the face of such naked miscarriages of justice, legalistic explanations about federal jurisdiction satisfied few interested parties—least of all Hoover's uneasy allies at the NAACP. On September 7, the NAACP's national leadership assembled for a meeting with Justice Department officials, hoping to persuade the attorney general—and thus the Eisenhower administration—to use the full power at their disposal to combat white Southern violence. From Mississippi itself, the call was taken up by Dr. T. R. M. Howard, founder of the Regional Council on Negro Leadership and one of the state's most prominent Black voices. On September 25, in a speech before some twenty-five hundred participants at an NAACP membership meeting in Baltimore, Howard lambasted the FBI, wondering why an organization that managed to uncover so many spies and saboteurs "can never seem to work out who is responsible for killing Negroes in the South." He laid the blame not on jurisdictional problems or the intransigence of the white South, but at the feet of "J. Edgar Hoover, himself."[25]

Hoover turned to Thurgood Marshall to defend the FBI, arguing in a letter that the Bureau had tried hard in Mississippi but failed for lack of jurisdiction. Writing back, Marshall affirmed that the FBI had done "a full complete job in so far as the Mississippi situations are concerned." He lamented along with Hoover that federal law is "not adequate in such situations and should be strengthened." Howard was not nearly so conciliatory, insisting once again that Hoover should be brought to account. In January, Hoover lashed back and released a public letter denouncing Howard's "false charges." In the letter, Hoover professed to be on the same side as Howard, appalled at Mississippi's wave of violence. At the same time, he pleaded a lack of power and jurisdiction, begging for the sort of understanding that Marshall had extended earlier. "This bureau is doing everything within the scope of existing legislation in civil rights matters," Hoover insisted, "and our fair and prompt investigations have done much to increase public respect for and consciousness of civil rights." To Howard, though, the moment for worrying about jurisdictional fine print had passed long ago.[26]

THE CONFLICT WITH HOWARD REFLECTED ONE OF THE PAINFUL FACTS OF THE Southern situation as Hoover saw it by the end of 1955: despite all the energy devoted by the FBI to its "limited inquiries," things were getting more volatile rather than less. In November 1955, a new county grand jury refused to indict on kidnapping charges in the Till case, sparking another round of outrage and recrimination over federal impotence. The following month, the Black community of Montgomery, Alabama, launched a much-heralded bus boycott in protest of segregation only to be met with bombings, threats, and assaults. Two months after that, acting on orders from the Supreme Court, the University of Alabama opened its doors to its first Black student, an aspiring librarian named Autherine Lucy. After several days of violence in protest, the university suspended her.

Along with this deteriorating situation came heightened resistance to Bureau action—not only from Howard or the NAACP, but from Hoover's onetime fans and sympathizers within the white South. In the fall of 1955, Hoover received a letter from Robert Patterson, founder of the Mississippi Citizens' Councils, who accused the FBI of working in cahoots with the NAACP "to intimidate Southerners who will not submit to its radical integration aims." In Georgia, where FBI agents were investigating Cobb County's all-white jury selection process, the state legislature passed a resolution "severely" censuring both Hoover and Brownell for "flagrant violation of the Constitution" and undue interference in state affairs. Not to be outdone, Mississippi's legislature passed its own bill restricting FBI investigative activities (though the governor vetoed it on grounds that the state had nothing to hide).[27]

Hoover responded to this criticism with disdain, as the grumblings of lawless, small-minded vigilantes. In the end, though, he was far more lenient toward the South's segregationists than toward civil rights groups on the other side. In January 1956, South Carolina senator Strom Thurmond went public with his suspicion that the FBI was secretly investigating the Citizens' Councils. From SISS, Eastland followed up with a personal query, insisting to FBI officials that the councils had been a "very stabilizing" force against "the 'hotheads' and 'rednecks.'" Under such pressure, Hoover backtracked from his commitment to investigate all groups targeting racial minorities. Agreeing (implausibly) that the Citizens' Councils showed no signs of violence or "extralegal measures," in late 1956 he canceled the investigation into council activities, even as he continued to investigate the NAACP and other civil rights groups for their supposed allegiances to communism.[28]

To Hoover, the white South's intransigence only underscored what he had long believed: that civil rights was a lose-lose situation for the Bureau, and one best avoided. Brownell adopted a different interpretation—and it was his opinion, not Hoover's, that would win the day. In his view, the South's willingness to thumb its nose at federal law meant that a better and stronger federal civil rights law was now necessary. On January 5, 1956, Brownell called Hoover to his office for a consultation about a civil rights bill he planned to introduce at an upcoming cabinet meeting. As Brownell envisioned it, the bill would expand and strengthen the Justice Department's ability to act in civil rights cases, including the creation of a new Civil Rights Division. He wanted Hoover to help present the idea to Eisenhower's cabinet. Brownell understood that Hoover might harbor personal doubts about desegregation. "Considering the atmosphere in which he was raised, he had a point of view (that he didn't carry into his law enforcement activities) which did not favor school integration," Brownell later explained. But he saw another side of Hoover, too: the professional public servant and federal lawman.[29]

And so, on March 9, 1956, Hoover accompanied Brownell to the White House for a meeting of Eisenhower's Cabinet. Hoover's presentation that day showed less of the outrage and certainty that had characterized his testimony before Truman's committee a decade earlier, when he had still hoped that the FBI might make a true success of the anti-lynching campaign. Then, he had described Southern violence as a scourge that could be—indeed, had to be—stopped by a determined federal government. Now, he described it as an understandable, if problematic, reaction to *Brown*'s attack on racial traditions that had been "handed down from generation to generation." White

Southerners were terrified by "the specter of racial intermarriages" and the prospect of social equality, Hoover explained. "The current tensions represent a clash of culture when the protection of racial purity is a rule of life ingrained deeply as the basic truth." At the same time, he conceded that the federal government had a duty to enforce the law, whether the white South liked it or not. The question was how.[30]

Brownell's bill was supposed to solve this problem. Actually getting it passed, though, was another story, as Truman had learned years before. Three days after Hoover's cabinet presentation, the Southern Democrats of Congress released a "Southern Manifesto," declaring the *Brown* decision "a clear abuse of judicial power" and vowing to resist the intrusion of "outside meddlers"—including federal authorities—who attempted to enforce the ruling. Eastland signed the document, as did nearly every other Southern member of Congress, a declaration of political war against the Eisenhower administration.[31]

That Brownell's bill eventually passed anyway is testament to the political skills of Senate majority leader Lyndon Johnson, a man with whom Hoover would soon build perhaps the greatest political alliance of his career. What happened along the way, however, only heightened Hoover's frustration with civil rights work, and accentuated the jurisdictional confusion that had existed for years. In an effort to make the bill palatable to Southern lawmakers, the Senate stripped away several provisions of Brownell's proposal, narrowing it from a broad civil rights bill into a much more limited defense of voting rights. Senators also added a clause reaffirming the right to local jury trials in all substantial voting rights cases, a measure intended to ensure the failure of any federal prosecution under the new law.

In Hoover's view the FBI acquired a controversial new set of duties without any increased likelihood of success. Deputy attorney general William Rogers said it was like "giving a policeman a gun without bullets."[32]

IN THE WAKE OF THE BILL'S PASSAGE, HOOVER ONCE AGAIN TRIED TO EASE HIM-self out of civil rights work, to convince Brownell to set the Bureau free to do what it did best: hunt criminals and communists. In October 1957, he met with Brownell to discuss the recent crisis in Little Rock, Arkansas, where Eisenhower had sent federal troops to enforce the desegregation of Central High School. The FBI had been dispatched to Little Rock to assess the situation weeks before the troops came in. Like the National Guard, the Bureau's agents met with fierce resistance from local politicians. Given the deteriorating situation, Hoover suggested to Brownell that future civil rights inquiries might best be conducted not by the FBI but by the Justice Department's new Civil Rights Division. "I made this observation because of the intolerable situations [which] have developed during the last years and months in trying to handle the investigative work in this field," he explained.[33]

Brownell rejected the idea, and Hoover apparently never brought it up again. A few months later, when a Southern legislative aide suggested the same thing, Hoover dismissed it as a fantasy of someone acting out of emotion rather than logic and devotion to duty. "It is amazing how utterly unobjective some individuals get," he wrote to fellow Bureau officials in early 1958. "We have a job to do and we will do it."[34]

CHAPTER 38

Master of Deceit

(1956–1959)

An advertisement for Hoover's bestselling book, *Masters of Deceit*, published in 1958. Hoover tried to keep anticommunism front and center in the late 1950s, when many Americans were losing interest.

Despite his misgivings about the new civil rights law, by 1957 Hoover could say that history mostly seemed to be going his way. Eisenhower's reelection in 1956 had affirmed the influence and popularity of a Republican circle that revered the FBI. And the one man who had for so long disrupted party unity, who had almost torn the Republicans apart in 1953 and 1954, was no longer in a position to wreak havoc. Shunned by his fellow Washingtonians, Joe McCarthy had spent the past few years drinking away his shame, occasionally emerging to warn of a resurgent Red menace or to champion Hoover as a presidential nominee. On May 2, less than four months into Eisenhower's second term, he died of acute hepatitis at Bethesda Naval Hospital. Accompanied by Tolson, Hoover attended a brief memorial service in Senate chambers, expressing "sorrow over the passing of a friend." With that, McCarthyism reached its dismal end. Hooverism, by contrast, was stronger than ever.[1]

Hoover's staying power did not go unnoticed in the national press, where the

months after McCarthy's death brought a rush of tributes to Hoover's status as the
city's great "indestructible" survivor, an object of "universal respect," "almost a legend
in his own lifetime." First among his admirers was Pulitzer Prize winner Don Whitehead, one of the deans of the Washington press corps. Two years earlier, he had approached Hoover with the idea of writing a book that would recount "the FBI's birth,
development and struggles," in Hoover's words. Just after the inauguration, he published *The FBI Story*, supposedly an objective "report to the people" but actually, as one
reviewer noted, an "authorized biography" in all but name. The book occupied the
number one slot on the *New York Times* bestseller list from February through May
1957, securing Hoover's place in the literary pantheon even as the nation bade a less-
than-fond farewell to McCarthy.[2]

Whitehead's book warned that the grand struggle that had joined Hoover and
McCarthy together—the world-historical "fight against communism"—was not yet
complete. But here, too, things seemed to be going Hoover's way. In early 1956, Soviet
premier Nikita Khrushchev acknowledged some of the worst crimes of the Stalin regime in a speech before his party's twentieth Congress, setting off anguished debates
and recriminations among communists throughout the world. At home, the American party was fast descending into chaos, its members frustrated, disillusioned, and
fleeing the party ranks. An FBI assessment declared Khrushchev's speech "one of the
greatest psychological blows" in the movement's history. After a decade of Red Scare
politics, it was widely assumed that the American communist party would soon collapse altogether.[3]

Certainly the Supreme Court seemed to think so. In June 1957, a month after Mc-
Carthy's death, the court issued a series of decisions restricting the methods available
to the FBI and other government agencies in their pursuit of communist activists. One
decision drastically narrowed interpretation of the Smith Act, which Hoover had used
to such good effect against party leadership. Another ruled that defendants had the
right to review FBI informant files if and when the government planned to call the
informant to appear as a witness during trial. The Court offered mostly technical reasons. But its decisions also reflected a new confidence that communism had, at last,
been crushed in the United States. To the court, as to many Americans in 1957, the
Communist Party now looked less like an existential threat than like a pitiable group
of diehards clinging to a discredited ideology. Under the circumstances, the court suggested, there was no need for expansive measures to contain them.[4]

Hoover could see that certain aspects of the anticommunist fight were indeed
going well, that the old worries over spies in high places or communist domination of
the labor movement could be safely consigned to the past. And yet he found it hard to
rest easy in 1957—much less to think that the FBI had truly, at last, achieved victory.
He remained haunted by the example of his youth, when the Radical Division had
helped to destroy the early parties only to see the communists rise again, stronger and

better organized, a decade later. To much of the country, the collapse of the Communist Party seemed to present an opportunity to move on from the Red Scare, with Hoover duly recognized as its conquering hero. To Hoover, that desire was itself now a problem. As he conceived it, the great enemy of 1957 was not so much the party itself. It was the public apathy that might allow the communists time to rest and regroup.

And so Hoover set out to find new ways to counter that apathy, convinced once again that the FBI would have to be the "one bulwark" within an indifferent nation. No doubt he feared what would happen to the FBI if the nation's attention turned to other issues: Would it still occupy a place of prestige? Would his power and influence wane? But he was also a victim of his own paranoid logic, which allowed no room for victory—or even for progress—on the subject of communism. Hoover's understanding began with the premise that the Communist Party was a fanatical, secret conspiracy, deceitful down to its very core. As such, its defeat could never be shown by the available evidence. There would always be something hidden, always an additional chapter to the story. Another man might have accepted the Supreme Court's judgment that the domestic Red Scare was over, that its excesses and abuses could now be curtailed from a place of both safety and chagrin. Hoover saw nothing but unending struggle—not just against the Communist Party, but against the naysayers who claimed it was safe to relax and worry about other issues.

That included the Supreme Court itself. In the summer of 1957, just after McCarthy's death, Hoover set out to deploy his "unique skill in manipulating Congress, the press, the public, and his nominal superiors in the White House and the Justice Dept." in order to amend the court's recent decisions. The result was a House bill that allowed judges to review and redact FBI informant files before turning them over to defendants— a crucial check on the process of disclosure demanded by the Court. In August, after weeks of back-channeling and a "dazzling display of [Hoover's] finesse as a legislative operator," in the words of a *New York Post* columnist, the House voted in favor of the bill 315–0. The Senate passed the same bill with just two dissenting votes. And on September 3, six days before approving the Civil Rights Act, Eisenhower signed the bill into law, the first of Hoover's triumphs in his attempt to extend Red Scare politics into the new era.[5]

Over the next several months, Eisenhower continued to show his support for Hoover as the reigning authority on all matters anticommunist. In November, the president put in a special appearance at the National Academy graduation, smiling alongside Norman Vincent Peale as Hoover presented the president with an honorary gold FBI badge. Two months later, Eisenhower awarded Hoover one of the inaugural presidential medals for "distinguished federal civilian service," an attempt to recognize the model employees of the administrative state. "Hoover is politically untouchable," *Newsweek* concluded in a cover story about him, "as bipartisan as the Washington Monument, as much an institution as the Smithsonian." James Wechsler, the left-liberal editor of the

New York Post reluctantly agreed. He classified Hoover fourth behind Eisenhower, John Foster Dulles, and Senate majority leader Lyndon Johnson as one of the most powerful men in Washington—and as the only one who could count on support from both Democrats and Republicans. "Here then indeed is the sacred cow, elephant, and donkey united in a single being," Wechsler wrote, describing Hoover as that rare creature capable of being political and apolitical all at once. To Wechsler's dismay, Hoover appeared to be "above and beyond criticism" for "more than 90 per cent of the U.S. press."[6]

And yet Hoover, always looking out for the next great danger, remained convinced that much work still lay ahead. At a moment when other men might have taken a bow and retired, Hoover put his power and popularity to work to ensure that the American people would remain on guard against communism.

HOOVER HAD INFORMED THE WHITE HOUSE OF HIS INTENTIONS AS EARLY AS March 8, 1956, when he put in a rare appearance before the National Security Council to discuss "The Present Menace of Communist Espionage and Subversion," as he titled the day's "top-secret" presentation. Eisenhower was there, along with Nixon, Brownell, Allen Dulles, and more than a dozen executive-branch officials, all eager to hear how Khrushchev's speech, delivered just weeks earlier, seemed to be reshaping Cold War possibilities. Hoover assured the president that the FBI would continue using the techniques at its disposal to track what was left of the party, including mail opening, informant networks, and microphone surveillance. Even so, he saw a need for innovation to counterbalance the nation's growing apathy about communism. By the end of the meeting, Hoover had secured Eisenhower's implicit approval to use "every available means" to carry on the fight. With that sanction in hand, he set out to establish a targeted "counterintelligence" experiment that would take advantage of the turmoil then racking the party.[7]

COINTELPRO (short for "counterintelligence program"), as that initiative came to be known, would eventually expand well beyond the Communist Party, becoming by far the most notorious program of Hoover's career. But it started small, tested first on the country's few remaining communists and only later adapted to other groups. Like so many of Hoover's innovations, COINTELPRO was not a fact but a process: of learning and dodging, of adjusting to new pressures and new capacities. In 1956, his chief aim was to disrupt and discredit the Communist Party at a time of high vulnerability. The way to do this, as Hoover conceived it, was no longer to prosecute party members or to haul witnesses up in front of a congressional committee, techniques now viewed with increasing skepticism in both the courts and the press. The FBI would instead bring its strategy in-house, using its resources to manipulate, misinform, and disrupt the party in secret. Under COINTELPRO, there would be no more grand trials or dramatic committee-room confrontations. Instead, Hoover envisioned a slow accretion of slights and miseries—"along the line of 'keeping the pot boiling,'" as one FBI memo explained, until the lid blew off.[8]

For the background knowledge necessary to plan such an operation, Hoover turned to William Sullivan, a rising young official in the Domestic Intelligence Division. Born in Massachusetts, Sullivan had taken a roundabout way into the FBI, earning a degree in history and then teaching high school English for several years before entering government service. The war brought him to the Bureau, one of the thousands of new employees whose backgrounds did not quite conform to Hoover's traditional expectations. Sullivan was a Democrat and a self-styled intellectual, more at home with words than with people. He stood several inches shorter than Hoover. "Brash, brilliant, brimming over with self-esteem," in the words of one colleague, Sullivan was no traditional G-Man, either in looks or in temperament. But he had found his calling in the anticommunist struggle, where his keen analytical mind and literary bent gave him an edge at articulating the ideological stakes.[9]

In August 1956, as Hoover began to think through the contours of COINTELPRO, Sullivan proposed that a secret monograph on the "present-day weaknesses, needs, and reasoning of the Communist Party" be "rushed" into production. As Sullivan envisioned it, the report would "serve as a type of text or guide or source book" for the forthcoming "program of disruption"—the bible of COINTELPRO. Six weeks later, he delivered a nearly hundred-page document tailored to questions that agents and informants in the new program might have about the party's internal disputes. The report highlighted Khrushchev's speech, which inspired "widespread disappointment, dissatisfaction, disillusionment, confusion, and defeatism among Party leaders and rank-and-file members alike." According to Sullivan, many communists seemed to be wrestling with the moral status of the party, unsure whether to quit or carry on. "Questions never before asked are being raised," he wrote. "Complaints never before made are being aired." Those questions and complaints left the party in "the most critical, perilous, and weakened condition in the 37 years of its existence." With the Communist Party "on the brink of bankruptcy," Sullivan concluded, the FBI had an unprecedented opportunity to push it over the edge.[10]

Hoover agreed that the situation appeared "made to order for an all-out, disruptive attack against the Party on a broader scale than heretofore attempted by the Bureau." In a letter of authorization distributed in early September, he encouraged agents to toss out their old ideas and think anew about ways to destabilize the party—"not by harassment from the outside which might only serve to bring the various factions together but by feeding and fostering from within the internal fight currently raging." He acknowledged that the Bureau needed to tread carefully, taking into account the fact that party members would be on the alert for more traditional forms of FBI interference.

He also demanded that any proposed action be routed through his office for central approval, identifying COINTELPRO as a personal project of the highest priority.[11]

For its initial phases, Hoover's office recommended two techniques. The first was the anonymous letter, which could be sent to a party member or friendly press contact to highlight some unflattering aspect of communist policy or experience. The second, more versatile method involved the use of informants to spread rumors and stoke division within party circles. Simply wasting the party's time—diverting meetings into "non-productive, time-consuming channels"—was a virtue, in Hoover's view. So was preventing resolution on contentious party issues. Hoover instructed the FBI's informants to spend as much time as possible stirring up anger between white and Black activists; the right-wing, left-wing, and ultra-left factions; rank-and-file members and party leaders; the Stalinists and their Trotskyist rivals. If all went well, he surmised, the sheer misery of the fights might induce members to quit or to offer themselves to the FBI as collaborators.[12]

Thanks to the party's already weakened state, most of these goals proved shockingly easy to accomplish. By November 1956, when assistant director Alan Belmont offered an assessment of COINTELPRO's first sixty days, the Bureau already had four "basic programs" underway, with several more in the works. The most ambitious was Hoover's national initiative for "keeping the Party divided" by using informants to "raise controversial issues and criticisms of Party programs"—the core strategy of COINTELPRO. Beyond that, the field offices seized upon opportunities to target specific aspects of party life. Observing the communists' internal chaos, the rival Socialist Workers Party, a tiny Trotskyist sect, launched a recruitment drive aimed at "bringing about defections of CP members." The FBI did its best to help out, smuggling membership lists and meeting locations to the SWP. Hoover's agents also passed the lists to the Internal Revenue Service, identifying 336 "underground leaders" who allegedly failed to pay their taxes while fleeing from the law.[13]

Hoover tracked such efforts closely over the next several months, alternately congratulating and cajoling the field offices as they felt their way through the delicate assignments. By February 1957, FBI headquarters was "convinced that this program has contributed materially to the disruption and confusion inside the CP." Hoover nonetheless demanded greater accomplishments in the months that followed. "The Bureau will not accept any plans for standing idly by in the hope that the Party will destroy itself through internal dissension," read a message to the field in April 1957. "You will be expected to plan activities that will trigger latent controversies and accentuate the active areas of conflict." The FBI was no longer in the business of watching and waiting. Under COINTELPRO, agents were supposed to make things happen.[14]

The Supreme Court decisions that so angered Hoover a few months later only enhanced his commitment to COINTELPRO. Despite the last-minute scramble in

Congress, the court had severely restricted many of the techniques that Hoover had relied upon in the past: Smith Act prosecutions, informant testimony, congressional committees, and registration requirements. COINTELPRO, by contrast, remained entirely within his control, a secret effort that required neither courts nor prosecutors nor public support.

That secrecy, in turn, gave Hoover time to learn on the job and to refine the program's contours as needed. In June 1957, he discovered that local communists in Cleveland seemed to be catching on to COINTELPRO, whispering among themselves that "the FBI has evidently launched a campaign of ideological harassment through anonymous mailings." In response, Hoover temporarily called off the use of such letters throughout the country. Over time, his office compiled a list of refinements that would make the mailings less easily identifiable as FBI forgeries: limiting their number of recipients, including spelling errors and typos, using commercial-size paper (eight and a half by eleven inches) rather than government-issue paper (eight and a half by ten inches) for any printing jobs.[15]

Other fine-tuning followed, along with a cascade of ideas for making the program more effective. In April 1957, a top-ranking FBI official recommended that the Bureau start writing fake pamphlets to be distributed to party members, rather than wait around for a disgruntled ex-communist or investigative journalist to write useful essays spontaneously. By the end of the year, the practice had become a standard part of COINTELPRO, with Bureau researchers either producing or distributing investigations of topics such as the Soviets' anti-Semitic atrocities and the various failures of domestic party leaders. One field office went so far as to propose a pamphlet framing longtime party chief William Z. Foster as a government informant and agent provocateur. Hoover encouraged agents to use satire as well as exposés to upset party members, on the logic that a "campaign of ridicule" aimed at communist stereotypes and clichés "might well prove to be deadly."[16]

By 1958, this effort seemed to be yielding the "desired type of disruptive tangible results," according to an internal FBI assessment. In January, the communists' *Worker* newspaper suspended daily operations for the first time in thirty-four years, pleading a lack of funds. Within local chapters, "factionalism, paralysis and demoralization" were fast reaching "an advanced stage," according to the Chicago office. In smaller cities such as New Haven, Connecticut, the local chapter was barely hanging on, its "breakdown" all but complete.[17]

Many of the developments had little to do with FBI activity one way or another. As Hoover's own files noted, the party was on the ropes well before COINTELPRO. But Hoover hailed the signs of collapse as proof of COINTELPRO's effectiveness, even as he harbored concerns that things were not always as they seemed. When the *Worker* scaled back its publication schedule, FBI documents warned that it was a ruse designed to keep party squabbles out of public view rather than "a forerunner of the death of the Communist Party." The party's emergency fundraising drive was dismissed as nothing more than "a clever plan designed to hoodwink Party members" into turning over their wages. Despite clear signs of the party's weakness, Hoover managed to view 1958 as even more perilous than 1956 and 1957. Though he could take pride in the occasional FBI success, on the whole he still felt that not nearly enough was being done.[18]

Given his single-minded zeal on such matters, it is impossible to separate the growth of COINTELPRO from Hoover's personal psychology on the communist issue, in which the nation's enemies were always making headway, while the Bureau stood helpless and shackled on the sidelines. The program's clandestine nature and centralized structure only enhanced his personal influence, providing Hoover with almost total control over the scope of operations. And yet contrary to later myth, he did not keep COINTELPRO entirely secret. In closed testimony before congressional committees during these years, he described the Bureau's "intensive program designed to infiltrate, penetrate, disorganize and disrupt the Communist Party-USA." He also wrote to the attorney general about a "program designed to promote disruption within the ranks of the Communist Party." His reasons for these disclosures were no doubt self-protective: if and when COINTELPRO came to light, he could say that he had permission from his ostensible superiors. But the disclosures also reveal something important about the depth of Hoover's support in Washington during the era. Though many people would later profess to be outraged about what the FBI was doing, in the late 1950s nobody in Congress or the Justice Department seemed inclined to interfere or to ask too many questions.

The same held true for the president. In May 1958, Hoover notified the White House in writing about the FBI's success in encouraging "disillusionment and defection among Party members" through the use of disruptive techniques. In November 1958, he expanded upon those claims in person before a meeting of Eisenhower's cabinet. With Tolson's assistance, Hoover distributed copies of a "top-secret" booklet outlining Russian intentions and intelligence techniques. The presentation stressed recent FBI victories, including the 1957 arrest of Colonel Rudolf Abel, an undercover Soviet espionage agent who had been posing for years as a New York photographer. Hoover also provided a remarkably frank description of the FBI's own counterintelligence activities, including its new program "designed to intensify any confusion and dissatisfaction among [party] members." He spoke openly of informant machinations and "simulated Party documents," of anonymous mailings and manipulated votes and IRS investigations. He also repeated his view that the "loss of CP membership makes no difference," that despite their manifold weaknesses and existential struggles, the communists were as strong as ever. Nobody seems to have registered any objection, either to Hoover's interpretation of world events or to his account of COINTELPRO.[19]

———

AMONG THE EVIDENCE THAT HOOVER SHARED WITH THE CABINET THAT DAY, hoping to persuade them of the party's continuing strength, was the incredible tale of a "CPUSA representative" who had recently returned from a secret odyssey to Moscow. According to Hoover's account, which was enhanced by "top secret" drawings illustrating each stage of the journey, the man flew from New York to Moscow and then on to Beijing in a daring attempt to restore relations between the American party and its powerful counterparts abroad. In Moscow the American met with "top-ranking" members of the presidium, as well as with the head of the Soviet party's international department. From there, he flew to China, where he spent two weeks in conversation with the "highest-ranking Chinese officials," including no less a personage than the revolutionary turned dictator Mao Tse-tung.[20]

The dramatic story drove home one of Hoover's central points: though the American party might look weak, it was busy preparing for a resurgence, aided and abetted by global communism's two Great Powers. But Hoover never mentioned an aspect of events that might have cast serious doubt on that thesis. The "CPUSA Representative," recently designated as international liaison between the American party and its friends in Moscow, was actually a Bureau informant, the central figure in a high-stakes espionage effort known as Operation SOLO.

The opportunity for SOLO, like the impetus for COINTELPRO, emerged from the confusion sparked by Khrushchev's speech. In late 1956, with the American party in free fall and desperate for funds, party leadership decided that the time had come to revisit its methods of communicating with the Soviet Union. During the 1930s and early 1940s, communication had been relatively easy, with party members regularly traveling back and forth between the U.S. and Russia. With the dawn of the Cold War, however, travel had become far more restricted, especially for open party members. By 1956, the American party had resorted to communicating with the Soviets through a former acolyte who accepted deportation to Scotland after his Smith Act conviction, an arrangement that neither side found satisfactory. Into this void came talk of designating a new go-between, someone who could be trusted with Soviet money as well as Soviet instructions, thus shoring up the American party in its time of need. In early 1957, Hoover put out a call for the field offices to "capitalize on this situation" by identifying informants "who could be developed as a courier between the Communist Party, USA, (CP, USA) and the Communist Party of the Soviet Union (CPSU)." He deemed the project "of extreme importance," the best chance since Venona "not only to determine the degree and type of control the Soviet Union exercises over the CP, USA, but to develop admissible evidence proving such control."[21]

The man chosen for the mission was Morris Childs, an ailing but resilient fifty-six-year-old Chicago informant. Born near Kiev and brought to the U.S. as a child, he had converted early to communism, a charter member of the party during the wilderness years of the 1920s. In 1929, he left the United States to attend the Lenin School in Moscow, mastering a curriculum that ranged from guerrilla warfare and sabotage to the intricacies of Marxist theory. Upon his return, Childs worked for the party in Chicago, even running for Senate as the communist candidate from Illinois. In 1945, during the great shake-up following the war, he became editor of the *Daily Worker*, among the most influential posts in the communist pantheon. Two years later, he fell ill with heart problems and found himself pushed out of his editorial post. This accident of timing insulated him from the worst of McCarthyism but soured him on his comrades.

His younger brother, Jack, first agreed to inform for the FBI, upset at how the party had treated Morris. In 1952, under a program known as TOPLEV (short for "top-level" officials), the FBI encouraged Jack to recruit Morris, too. After a few exploratory meetings, Jack reported back that Morris was indeed "in a suitable frame of mind which would make him receptive to a contact by Bureau agents." Hoover wasted no time in exploiting the opportunity. During his initial interviews with Bureau agents, Morris hinted that "he had information of a broader scope and of better quality" than even the redoubtable Whittaker Chambers. Based on this promise, Hoover authorized a starting salary of a hundred dollars per week. He also approved plans to send Morris to the Mayo Clinic at the FBI's expense. The FBI hoped that proper treatment for Morris's heart disease would allow him to reactivate as a party member—now on the FBI payroll.[22]

One of Hoover's main interests at the time was the COMFUGs, Bureau shorthand for the "communist fugitives" who had fled underground in the face of Smith Act prosecutions. As CG-5824-S, his informant designation, Childs provided clues about no fewer than 350 "key individuals," making him "the personification of the Bureau's long-range informant development program." Along with his brother, Morris also proved invaluable in helping the Bureau to understand the secret financial networks supporting the party, with their confounding array of front businesses and clandestine arrangements. By the time the opening for a Soviet courier came along, Morris was one of the most prolific and dependable of Hoover's high-ranking informants. It made sense to try to maneuver him into the position.[23]

The plan worked spectacularly well. In early 1958, the Soviets invited Morris to Moscow as the newly recognized international representative of the American party. Anxious to see the trip come off smoothly, FBI agents intervened with the State Department to acquire a passport. FBI officials also agreed to pay their informant's Chicago bills while he was abroad. In April, he set off for Moscow with instructions from Hoover to be on the alert for any evidence that the USSR "directs and controls" the American Communist Party. He returned three months later with the incredible tales that Hoover would ultimately convey to the cabinet, including descriptions of audiences with the Soviet party elite in Moscow and the detour to China to meet with Mao Tse-tung.[24]

Hoover received the accounts of Childs's adventures in seventeen separate debriefing documents, compiled after interviews that ran up to eleven hours per day. Much of it he shared through "prompt dissemination" to Eisenhower, Nixon, John Foster Dulles, and a select group of other high-ranking administration figures. As with Venona, he did not disclose the nature or identity of his source. Hoover himself was less interested in diplomatic intelligence than in what Childs revealed about the domestic party. At the November cabinet meeting, he revealed that Moscow would be sending two hundred thousand dollars to the American party in an attempt to stabilize its finances and hold on to remaining members. As a down payment, Childs received a shipment of seventeen thousand dollars in cash not long after his return. He passed it along to the FBI to be photographed and documented before handing it over to party leaders.[25]

Over the next decade and a half, Childs would undertake fifty-one more missions through SOLO, traveling not only to the Soviet Union and China but also throughout Latin America and Asia, where he met with a panoply of famous revolutionaries. His brother, Jack, would take over the financial side of the courier operation, helping to smuggle some $28 million from Moscow into the United States, incontrovertible evidence of Russian influence on the American party. Jack's reports, like those of his brother, told amazing but true tales: of a personal meeting with Fidel Castro in Cuba, of clandestine rendezvous with Soviet contacts in the New York subway system, of a "secret service school" operated from private apartments in Moscow, where he was trained in the use of microfilm, invisible ink, codes, and ciphers. But none quite recaptured the excitement of that first trip, when Hoover realized what an "outstanding" coup his men had pulled off. In thanks, he sent a letter to Morris and his wife, instructing that his note be placed in an FBI safe once it had been shown to the informants. He also approved a thousand-dollar bonus, the first of many to come.[26]

OF EVERYTHING HOOVER HAD DONE SINCE 1919 IN THE NAME OF FIGHTING communism, COINTELPRO and SOLO ranked among the most significant. Their impact would extend into the 1960s, when they would influence—and distort—politics at a variety of levels, from the manipulation of grassroots activists to the provision of intelligence for high-stakes geopolitical decision-making. But those programs were secret, their existence known to only a handful of men and women. They could not, therefore, do what Hoover had long argued would be crucial to the success of his anticommunist fight: mobilize public opinion to reject communism as an evil, illegitimate, and godless force. For that, Hoover developed the FBI's third major anticommunist initiative of the post-McCarthy era.

In March 1958, he published *Masters of Deceit*, a book-length distillation of everything he had learned over the past four decades about "Communism in America and How to Fight It," in the words of the book's subtitle. At Crime Records, Sullivan helped to write the book, drawing upon much of the information he had gathered for his secret background memo early in COINTELPRO. Though Hoover did not write the words on the page, there can be no question that the book, like so much of what came out of Crime Records, reflected his concerns and worldview. *Masters of Deceit* repeated many of his familiar bromides. Communists were "evil" and "anti-God," out to dupe the public through "shabby, deceitful phrases." It also emphasized Hoover's message about the perils of apathy. "The present menace of the Communist Party in the United States grows in direct ratio to the rising feeling that it is a small, dissident element and need not be feared," the book maintained, articulating the same worry that Hoover had pressed on the cabinet. Though produced in full public view, *Masters of Deceit* was itself a counterintelligence operation of sorts, aimed at discrediting the party. "We cannot afford the luxury of waiting for communism to run its course like other oppressive dictatorships," the book warned the American people. The language was almost identical to what Hoover told his own agents working on COINTELPRO.[27]

At Henry Holt publishers, *Masters of Deceit* was all but guaranteed an enthusiastic reception because Clint Murchison, Hoover's oilman patron from La Jolla, happened to own the company. As the publication date approached, Hoover made a point of sending advance copies to anyone who mattered within the Eisenhower administration, including Allen Dulles and the new attorney general, William Rogers, who replaced Brownell in late 1957. He also sent it along to friends outside Washington, many of whom were quick to offer promotional support. After testifying at the Smith Act trial, informant Herbert Philbrick had published his own anticommunist tell-all, *I Led Three Lives*, subsequently made into a dramatic television series. In 1958, he threw his celebrity behind *Masters of Deceit*, appearing on a local Boston station to recommend the book to area readers. Boston archbishop Richard Cushing went even further, declaring the book "the classic text book pertaining to Communism" and helping to distribute some two thousand copies. The ACLU's Morris Ernst came through with a cover spot in the respectably bookish *Saturday Review*, while Kappa Alpha ordered up a laudatory feature in its national fraternity journal. The American Legion, still Hoover's number-one institutional admirer, bought copies for every member of its press association.[28]

The FBI itself gave the book its greatest push, mobilizing agents to extoll its virtues and hand out copies. Each field office was expected to contact local bookstores, along with the local press, on matters of publicity and sales. Those who did the best received bonuses and raises. On one occasion, Sullivan traveled to Ohio to speak before the Citizens' Committee of Cincinnati, a grassroots group invented by the local field office to impress Hoover. Sullivan arrived to find a fleet of trucks packed with copies of *Masters of Deceit*, with a free book promised to anyone who showed up for the event.

"Needless to say," he later wrote, the reviews produced through these methods tended to be "excellent."[29]

Press coverage by those less firmly bound to Hoover proved somewhat more mixed. Newspapers across the country syndicated *Masters of Deceit* as an article series, accepting his publisher's offer of direct access to "The Book J. Edgar Hoover Had to Write." Other publications, especially those on the left, tended to view the book's arrival with more skepticism, less a matter of historic urgency than an attempt to renew public hysteria over an issue better laid to rest. Writing in the *New York Post*, one critic described *Masters of Deceit* as merely the latest twist on a "self-manufactured myth." The author dismissed Hoover as a mental lightweight, "intellectually ill-prepared" to comprehend the nuances of the communist struggle.[30]

Equally harsh criticism came from investigative journalist Fred Cook, who accused Hoover of "fanning the embers of McCarthyism" while trying to pose as a disinterested expert. Cook followed up his review with a sixty-page investigation for *The Nation* magazine. While the article critiqued nearly every phase of Hoover's career, it reserved special ire for his "grandiose magnification of the subversive menace." Cook found Hoover's demagoguery and repressive policies far more dangerous than the actions of a few thousand party members.[31]

The harsh words of his would-be judges had little effect on the book's sales. *Masters of Deceit* entered the *New York Times* bestseller list at No. 5 and quickly jumped to the No. 1 spot, where it stayed for six weeks. Over the next several years, the book sold more than two million paperback copies, in addition to 250,000 hardcover sales. Hoover allegedly distributed more than half of the profits to himself, Tolson, and Nichols, though the book was written by his taxpayer-funded staff. He also earned something else of inestimable value. At a moment when McCarthy's death might have signaled the end of anticommunism as a national preoccupation, Hoover managed to keep it front and center.[32]

THE SUCCESS OF *MASTERS OF DECEIT* ONLY ENHANCED HOOVER'S REPUTATION in Washington, especially among Republicans who had promoted him as the responsible alternative to McCarthy. Eisenhower found no more awards to dole out, but he expressed his appreciation for Hoover in other ways. There were private notes of support and camaraderie. And there were invitations to exclusive White House events. In September 1959, in one of the strangest-bedfellow occasions of his presidency, Eisenhower invited Hoover to a white-tie state dinner with none other than Khrushchev, the first Soviet premier to set foot on American soil. The official dinner speeches heralded a new era of peace and cooperation in U.S.-Russian relations, but Hoover's presence signaled something else: a fixed enmity now forty years in the making, flexible in its contours and methods but unchanging in its essential principles.[33]

In the same week as the Khrushchev dinner, the film version of *The FBI Story* premiered at Radio City Music Hall in New York. Hoover had already seen the film, breaking down in tears after the private screening in Washington, when he told film director Mervyn LeRoy it was "one of the greatest jobs I've ever seen." Former Crime Records chief Lou Nichols, now a private citizen, went to see it as an anonymous member of the New York public, contacting Hoover that same evening to say that the film looked "great," at once an "institutional picture" and a personal tribute to the FBI's "guiding genius."[34]

If Hoover had been a different man, such a moment might have inspired thoughts of retirement, of laying down the burdens that he had assumed thirty-five years earlier, when he first accepted Harlan Stone's challenge to reenvision the Bureau. But Hoover could not quite believe that the institution he had forged in his own likeness, and that he had mobilized in the service of his own ideology, could carry on without him.

Part IV

THE WAR AT HOME

(1960–1972)

Preface

The glory of the 1950s had been the way the pieces all came together. During his first two decades as director, Hoover had focused on building the FBI: acquiring and adjusting to new duties, pleasing his superiors, hiring the right men, and setting the right policies in place. With the end of World War II, he had begun to forge a new path, using the Bureau's growing power to promote and enforce his anticommunist vision. In 1945, few Americans had been focused on communism as their top concern. A decade later, they were thinking of little else—and when they thought of communists, they often thought of Hoover. Conservatives cheered his blistering language and willingness to use state power in support of the "American way of life." Liberals appreciated his restraint and words of caution, relieved to have an alternative to Joe McCarthy. Despite the occasional outcry, his effort to turn the FBI into the nation's "one bulwark" against subversion had made him popular, in Washington as throughout the country.

That balance collapsed in the 1960s, as the issue of communism began to fade and other, more divisive matters took center stage. First among them were race and civil rights, areas in which Hoover had never been able to reconcile his personal views and professional obligations. Unlike communism, civil rights divided the country, and Hoover found himself caught in the middle. He tried to offer just enough to keep each side satisfied while pursuing his own agenda, just as he had during the Red Scare. But the trick did not quite work this time. As during the 1940s and 1950s, he mounted campaigns against the most extreme elements of the segregationist South, especially the Ku Klux Klan. Those efforts were far outstripped, however, by his surveillance, harassment, and intimidation of civil rights leaders and activists. Over the course of the 1960s, he departed more and more from his vision of the FBI as a professional, apolitical institution and a bastion of upright, objective Government Men. The contradictions that he had negotiated for so long—between liberalism and conservatism, between his faith in apolitical governance and his commitment to an ideological cause—finally collapsed in on themselves. So did the American consensus that had once sustained him.

Electoral politics played a role in this shift. Hoover turned sixty-five on January 1, 1960, entering the new decade as an elder statesman, out of sync with the new generation's youthful energies. Had things gone another way, he might have been forced to step down a few years later, at the mandatory federal retirement age of seventy. He was saved from this fate by two friends who happened to end up in the White House. The first was Lyndon Johnson, Hoover's longtime neighbor on Thirtieth Place. The second was Richard Nixon, his old ally in the anticommunist cause. With their help, the FBI continued to expand into new areas—most notably, civil rights and organized crime. But some of Hoover's biggest challenges came in figuring out when to cooperate with his friends in the White House and when to resist.

Outside the White House, opinion about Hoover was more divided. He began the 1960s widely celebrated as the nation's greatest living public servant. He ended it as one of the country's most polarizing and controversial men. He bore some responsibility for this shift, as he jettisoned what had once been the signal feature of the FBI—its professional, apolitical ethos—in favor of an overt commitment to new ideological crusades. His changing fortunes also reflected broader political trends, as the country split over issues of race and civil rights, "law and order," and the war in Vietnam. When Hoover died—suddenly, and still in office—Nixon called him "one of the giants" of American history, but his presence had shrunk. Hoover had become a standard-bearer less for the unbounded promise of federal power than for its dangers. By 1972, he would be a smaller and more bitter man than he had once been, looking to preserve the past rather than make the future.

CHAPTER 39

New Frontiers

(1960–1961)

Hoover (center) with newly elected President John F. Kennedy (left) and Attorney General Robert Kennedy (right), February 1961. Kennedy was the first president younger than Hoover.

AP PHOTO/HENRY BURROUGHS

As far as Hoover was concerned, 1960 was supposed to be Richard Nixon's year. Hoover had endured eight presidential contests since becoming Bureau director. In 1960, he had a chance to help secure the presidency for a close friend who could be trusted to support the Bureau and respect Hoover's priorities. Nixon was eighteen years younger than Hoover, nearly a full generation removed. Over the course of Eisenhower's presidency, Hoover had nonetheless come to recognize qualities in the vice president that made their differences of age, background, and lifestyle insignificant. Nixon had always shared Hoover's anticommunist affinities. During the Eisenhower years, they also found a broader commonality of spirit and outlook. Neither man made friends easily: Nixon was famously awkward, Hoover famously aloof. That social unease may have helped draw them together, two middle-class nobodies making good on the world stage. They shared a tendency to view critics as enemies and to see themselves as visionaries under siege by lesser mortals. Out of this strange combination of personal and ideological sympathies emerged something resembling a friendship.

Politics always came first, of course. There, Hoover and Nixon had encountered few conflicts during the Eisenhower years. Like Hoover, Nixon had supported McCarthy until political expediency dictated otherwise. At that point, he had turned on the senator with resolve. Nixon's rejection of McCarthy had provided ample opportunity to praise Hoover as the desirable alternative, a man of lawful restraint as well as passionate anticommunist conviction, a servant of God but also a servant of the state. Throughout Eisenhower's second term, Hoover and Nixon worked together to follow the shifting tides of Soviet and communist thought, with Hoover providing regular updates from SOLO and Nixon bringing him in on global events. Nixon regularly called Hoover at home, as often as twice a day.

The high point of Nixon's engagement with the communist issue had come in the summer of 1959, when he departed the United States for Moscow. His official purpose was to preside at the opening of the American National Exhibition, a world's-fair-style showcase designed to introduce the Soviet people to American products, habits, and culture. On vacation in La Jolla, Hoover tuned in to Nixon's televised exchanges with Khrushchev, staged to take place in the exhibit's mock-up of a pristine suburban kitchen (and known forever after as the "Kitchen Debate"). Hoover came away enthralled with Nixon's composure and insight when face-to-face with the communist foe. "To say that I am impressed is a gross understatement," he wrote to Nixon in early August. "The excellent manner in which you have met and overcome every obstacle placed in your path during your tour is typical of the 'Nixon know-how' which everyone has come to expect. You again have proven yourself as one of our truly outstanding statesmen"—all just in time for campaign season.

While Hoover respected Nixon's political skills, he expressed even greater admiration for the personal qualities that allowed Nixon to persevere "under such trying conditions." In 1954, when Nixon had appeared before the FBI Academy graduation, Hoover had taken the opportunity to narrate his friend's growth of character, beginning with Nixon's hardscrabble upbringing in California, where the future vice president "acquired his education the hard way, his workday starting at 4:00 a.m. in the store of his father." Hoover told Nixon's story much as he told his own: a childhood of few privileges and stern lessons, followed by early success as a result of self-discipline, religious conviction, and superior talent.[1]

In short, Hoover liked Nixon quite a lot. The sympathies appeared to be mutual. As vice president, Nixon had gone out of his way to invite Hoover to luncheons and dinners with visiting dignitaries, including former French president Charles de Gaulle and King Mohammed V of Morocco. On other occasions, they met up purely for pleasure. One New Year's Eve, Nixon threw Hoover a surprise birthday party at Maxim's restaurant in Miami—a "perfect" event, in Hoover's view, and one "I shall long remember." In honor of Hoover's thirty-fifth anniversary as FBI director, Nixon made a show of taking his elder-statesman friend out to lunch, stopping by the Justice building to pick up Hoover in the vice-presidential car. While some of this had the air of the younger supplicant honoring the grand old czar, there were also more casual exchanges, weekend dinners and spur-of-the-moment cocktails in each other's homes. Years later, Nixon would estimate that he had been to Hoover's house at least a dozen times. "I know nobody else in public life that I have seen more on a social level than Hoover," he would say. He described Hoover as "my closest personal friend" in Washington during the 1950s—"much closer, for example, than Eisenhower or any member of the Cabinet."[2]

Within that friendship, Nixon accepted Tolson as Hoover's social partner. Invitations went to Hoover and Tolson as a pair, while acceptances and declines came back the same way. After the Nixons visited the Del Charro, Hoover wrote to say "how much Clyde and I enjoyed having Pat and you with us for at least a short while in La Jolla." When forced to decline a luncheon invitation back in Washington, he sent a personal note to let Nixon know "how sorry Clyde and I are that we were unable to join Pat and you" for the special occasion. At moments when it really mattered, such as Nixon's return from the Soviet Union, the foursome did their best to get together for a lunch or a nightcap, despite everyone's busy schedules. During less pressured periods, Hoover welcomed Pat's Washington gatherings as comfortable spaces to unwind, "always so warm and relaxing as well as fun."[3]

Over the course of the 1950s, Hoover and Tolson spent enough time with the Nixons to develop regular haunts, favorite foods, and inside jokes, the stuff of which long-term friendships are made. Hoover and Nixon spoke regularly by phone, and when Hoover missed Nixon's call marking his thirty-third anniversary as FBI director, he took the opportunity to let Nixon know in writing that "it is grand to have a friend such as you." Somewhat improbably, in a city full of utilitarian maneuvering and transient relationships, Hoover had found a friend in Nixon. Now he had a chance to see that friend occupy the White House.[4]

NIXON WAS NOT A BORN CAMPAIGNER. HE COULD BE AWKWARD AND OFF-putting, with a grating laugh and forced smile, at once too calculating and too eager to please. By contrast, his Republican primary challenger, New York governor Nelson Rockefeller, had all the ease of born privilege, a sophisticate at home in the worlds of high art, culture, and business. So did the Democrats' chosen man, John F. Kennedy, just forty-three years old, with a floppy brown haircut and toothy grin that made him look even younger. Much attention was paid to Kennedy's Catholic faith, with its implied ties to the ancient world of the Vatican. But Kennedy himself campaigned as the candidate of the future, envisioning the 1960s as a glorious "New Frontier" filled with "invention, innovation, imagination," "a turning-point in history." Hoover was not looking for any new frontiers, though. He wanted a president who would extend the politics of the 1950s, a decade when the FBI had achieved so much fame, success, and influence.[5]

And so Hoover set out to help Nixon, quietly setting aside his oft-advertised claim that the FBI stood apart from electoral politics. He had provided behind-the-scenes advice to Republican candidate Thomas Dewey in 1948, hoping to push Truman out of the White House. What he did for Nixon in 1960 was on a whole different scale. Four days before the Republicans convened in Chicago to choose their candidate, Hoover called Nixon's secretary, Rose Mary Woods, to pass along rumors about Kennedy's ill health, including the fact that the Democratic candidate had fainted recently while meeting with the governor of New Jersey. Hoover thought Nixon should include a reference to Kennedy's weakness during his Republican convention speech. "Indicate it will be a hard fight—wants everyone to join and fight," Hoover suggested. "Then say—I am fit and well and able to do it."[6]

Hoover's tips continued from vacation in California, where according to his assessment nearly everyone seemed to be a Nixon supporter. Hollywood director Mervyn LeRoy, fresh off The FBI Story, had recently signed on as a founding member of Celebrities for Nixon, an ambitious attempt to counter Kennedy's Rat Pack glamour. The Texas oil crowd stood behind Nixon, too, "notwithstanding that this whole group of Texans are died-in-the-wool Democrats," as Hoover wrote to Pat Nixon on September 8. The Murchisons were keen to hold a fundraising luncheon with "some of the friends you met at La Jolla," Hoover reported to the Nixons, while Effie Cain, wife of oilman Wofford Cain, was busy pinning Nixon buttons "on all persons that she met." Hoover gathered a few of the buttons and sent them along to Pat as a sign of the Texans' enthusiasm.[7]

Nixon's momentum sagged somewhat in late September, when he went up against Kennedy in the first televised presidential debate and came away a sweaty second-best. Hoover remained optimistic, however, passing along polls that continued to show both candidates with a fighting chance. On a more personal note, he invited Nixon to use his cottage at the Key Biscayne Hotel during the American Legion convention in Miami Beach, where both men (along with Kennedy) were scheduled to speak. Like few other public figures, Hoover understood how hard it could be to reconcile intense public scrutiny with personal awkwardness. "If he wants a few hours of relaxation, he will have it certainly," Hoover assured Nixon's secretary, promising the vice president "complete privacy if he so desires."[8]

On Election Day, office logs show Hoover refusing outside phone calls, canceling his appointments, and leaving the office just before noon. He appears to have stayed with the election drama well into the wee hours of the night, as returns in states such as Illinois, California, Minnesota, and Michigan came in too close to call. After midnight, when things seemed to be turning for Kennedy, Nixon put in a dispirited appearance in a hotel ballroom, observing that "if the present trend continues, Senator Kennedy will be the next President of the United States." The trend did continue, if just barely. Kennedy squeaked through with 49.72 percent of the popular vote to Nixon's 49.55 percent (303 to 219 in the electoral college), one of the closest elections in presidential history.[9]

Many Republicans viewed the results as a case of outright theft, accusing the Kennedy team of manipulating votes in Democratic strongholds such as Texas and Chicago. Hoover tried to remain upbeat, assuring Nixon that this was not the end of the political road. "Your courage, sincerity and rockbound patriotism were truly exhibited to the American public at 3:30 a.m. today when you, despite the emotions you must have been suffering, so eloquently thanked the people of this Nation and your backers for their help and, in addition, asked them to unite in a common cause," he wrote. And yet Hoover, like many Nixon sympathizers, could not quite reconcile himself to what had happened. "The United States and the Free World need a man of your stature desperately," he wrote, while adding, "As a personal friend, I know that a setback will not color your determination and fighting spirit in any manner whatsoever." Despite the loss, Hoover predicted great things ahead for his "close friend and advisor," urging Nixon to stay with the cause "for many years to come." Then he turned to face what just months earlier had seemed such an unlikely prospect: John F. Kennedy was about to become president.[10]

KENNEDY'S ELECTION MARKED A COMING-OF-AGE MOMENT FOR HOOVER: FOR the first time, he was older than the president. He had not survived so long in Washington by throwing his power around recklessly, or by alienating up-and-coming politicians. Even as he fulminated and gossiped with Nixon, he had remained on polite terms with the Kennedy campaign, neither praising nor criticizing their bluff young candidate. And if Hoover had little interaction with Kennedy himself, he did boast at least one important personal link. For more than a decade, Hoover had gone out of his way to cultivate the goodwill of Kennedy's father, Joe, a relationship that he now counted upon to ease the presidential transition.

Hoover and Joe Kennedy had plenty of reasons to like each other. They were creatures of the same generation, self-made but socially self-conscious, faintly scornful of men who had the world handed to them from birth. While Hoover was rocketing up through the Justice Department, Joe Kennedy had been making a name for himself as a banker, businessman, Hollywood mogul, and liquor distributor. Public legend pegged him as a bootlegger, an outlaw exaggeration that Joe himself seemed to appreciate. Like

Walter Winchell, Joe Kennedy was one of those larger-than-life figures who seemed to intrigue Hoover, a dangerous man with an enormous appetite for power and a willingness to operate both inside and outside the law.

Hoover and Joe seem to have met, predictably enough, through government work. In 1938, Franklin Roosevelt appointed Joe as ambassador to the Court of St. James's in London, a satisfyingly aristocratic post for an Irishman who felt he had something to prove. Two years later, when one of his subordinates stole hundreds of confidential cables between Churchill and Roosevelt, the government called on Hoover to help. As it turned out, Joe was not long for Britain anyway. By the end of 1940, Roosevelt had recalled him in embarrassment over comments that Hitler seemed unbeatable and the West might as well concede the fact. Joe spent the war years moping around his estates in Hyannis Port, Massachusetts, and Palm Beach, Florida, in exile from Washington. During this difficult period, Hoover had reached out with the news that young John, then a naval lieutenant, seemed to be embroiled in a sexual affair with Inga Arvad, a married Danish journalist and suspected Nazi spy. The Bureau never proved the espionage charges, but they did overhear the couple making love in a South Carolina hotel room. Acting on Hoover's tip, Joe pressured his son to end the relationship.

Hoover's critics have since pointed to the Arvad episode to show how Hoover got his hooks into the Kennedys, how he used the son's indiscretions to strong-arm the father into cooperation. But this image of a reluctant Joe Kennedy trembling before a vengeful Hoover hardly captures the relationship that developed over the next several years. Whatever secrets first brought them together, Hoover and Joe apparently came to enjoy each other's company. In 1943, Joe bought a part interest in Hialeah, the legendary Florida racetrack where Hoover liked to relax over Christmas break. He and Hoover crossed paths there many times, swapping horse tips and sharing intrigue from Washington. Like Nixon, Joe treated Hoover and Tolson as a social couple, inviting them to his home in Palm Beach, sending cases of scotch their way at Christmastime. At a time when Joe had few allies in Washington, Hoover made him feel useful and still accorded him an insider's respect. Joe, in turn, welcomed Hoover into the Kennedy family's strange, closed society of Harvard reserve and Irish-Catholic bonhomie.[11]

Toward John Kennedy himself Hoover seems to have devoted little time or attention. As a congressman, Kennedy developed a reputation as a playboy but also an intellectual, known to dabble in book-writing and other highbrow pursuits. It seemed inconceivable to Hoover, as to most Washington players, that this skinny, boyish Ivy Leaguer would ever become much of a national force. It was not until the summer of 1960, with Kennedy poised to capture the Democratic nomination, that Hoover formally paused to take stock. On July 13, in the midst of the Democratic convention, his aides prepared a summary memo on Kennedy "in view of strong possibility he will be Democratic candidate for President." The memo provided the basic who's who: Kennedy's time as a naval lieutenant and decorated PT boat hero, author of two books and winner of the Pulitzer Prize. Politically, the memo pegged Kennedy as an unexceptional realist, a man who "tempers his political liberalism" with "realistic conservatism," in the words of one columnist. The report also alluded to the fact that Senator Kennedy, citing health issues, had failed to show up and vote against Joe McCarthy in 1954.

Beyond his doctrinal plasticity, Kennedy's outstanding characteristic seemed to be an attraction to the wrong kind of supporters and the wrong kind of women. "As you are aware," the memo explained, "allegations of immoral activities on Senator Kennedy's part have been reported to the FBI over the years." Arvad was just the beginning. According to the report, Kennedy frequented establishments owned by "notorious hoodlums," often accompanied by pop crooner and organized-crime favorite son Frank Sinatra. Kennedy also appeared to be engaged in almost constant sexual intrigue, despite his 1953 marriage to socialite Jacqueline Bouvier. Just three months before the Democratic convention, the Bureau received reports that Kennedy and Sinatra spent the night with "show girls from all over town" at the Sands Hotel in Las Vegas, a known hotbed of organized crime. Closer to home, a Georgetown woman accused Kennedy of conducting an affair with her young tenant, a staffer in his Senate office.[12]

Popular legend suggests that Hoover used this information to pressure Kennedy into keeping him on as FBI director. But there is little evidence that Kennedy, coming off of a close election, eager to placate the conservatives in his own party, seriously considered any other course. On the morning of November 10, Kennedy called to speak with Hoover by phone, one of his first acts as president-elect. Later that day, in a statement from his family's Hyannis Port compound, Kennedy announced that Hoover would remain in office. Queried by the press, Hoover sounded a note of restrained enthusiasm about working with the new president. Others seemed less pleased. "We are off to the new frontiers," grumbled columnist and Kennedy associate Fletcher Knebel, "via the same old trading post."[13]

IF KENNEDY'S ELECTION CAME AS A DISAPPOINTMENT TO HOOVER, THERE WAS at least one silver lining: Lyndon Johnson, Kennedy's choice for vice president. In the early 1940s, as a lanky young congressman from East Texas, Johnson had purchased a home on Hoover's block of Thirtieth Place. Since then, the two men had developed a neighborly rapport—not exactly the tight bond that Hoover shared with Nixon, but something far more personal than one might expect of the FBI director and the Senate majority leader. The vice presidency arguably entailed a demotion for Johnson, who had amassed unparalleled power and influence in the Senate. For Hoover, though, Johnson's election to the number-two spot could hardly have been more fortuitous. At a moment of transitional uncertainty, Hoover's relationship with Johnson, like his friendship with Joe Kennedy, offered up the promise of insider sympathy.

By the time Johnson moved onto Hoover's block in 1943, he was already considered a rising star on the Hill, a young man with "energy, initiative and the ability to strike hard in the right places," in the words of one appreciative journalist. His house resembled Hoover's: a sturdy brick colonial in front of a spacious backyard bursting with hollyhocks, roses, hydrangeas, and lilies. From the beginning, Johnson and his wife, Lady Bird, opened their home to all manner of transient Texans, inviting naval officers, aides, and politicians to crash on the third floor. They also made a practice of inviting their neighbors over for brunch and afternoon drinks to talk politics and neighborhood affairs. Hoover accepted when he could—a familiar presence, if not quite a regular.[14]

If Hoover liked Nixon for certain commonalities of temperament and spirit, he may have liked Johnson for his differences. At six feet four, Johnson was an outsize presence in almost everything he did: loud and profane and unafraid to take up space. When he got what he wanted, he gushed with enthusiasm, pledging allegiance unto his dying hours. When things did not go his way, he could turn fearsome, subjecting his targets to the in-your-face technique—finger wagging, massive body planted far too close for comfort—known around Washington as the Treatment. Hoover's tirades with his staff, usually carried out by memo rather than tantrum, looked like the epitome of politesse compared to Johnson's. The Texan had none of Hoover's concern for propriety (he forced aides to take instruction while he sat on the toilet), and he reveled in his lack of discipline. He cared little for God, at least for Hoover's moralizing, avenging version. Instead, he cared about Texas, the Democratic Party, the legacy of the New Deal, and the political success of Lyndon Johnson, not necessarily in that order.

Still, Hoover and Johnson had enough in common to make a go of it. Johnson was a Southern Democrat, a proud member of one of Hoover's favorite constituencies, though he had refused to sign the pro-segregation Southern Manifesto or to endorse massive resistance. More important, he was a man who took power seriously—he liked to wield it, but he also liked to talk and gossip about it, one of the capital's most skilled and dedicated backroom dealmakers. Though Hoover spent most of his spare time with Republicans, he and Johnson shared some key acquaintances, including Hoover's Del Charro patrons Sid Richardson and Clint Murchison, who had supported Johnson in his swift rise through Texas politics. Hoover and Johnson also shared a distaste for idealists and Harvard types, preferring to see themselves as self-made men of action.

Mostly, theirs was a friendship of proximity, the sort of casual familiarity and affection known to develop among neighbors of long standing. At one end of Thirtieth Place was Hoover's peaceful well-dusted home, a place where adults congregated only in the most civilized manner. A few doors down and across the street, the Johnson house featured an entirely different sort of energy—"general bedlam," in Lady Bird's description. The Johnson girls spent much of their childhood outside, playing with the neighborhood kids in the backyard, racing their little red car up and down the sidewalk, and occasionally helping themselves to Hoover's roses. Johnson himself could often be seen walking their pet beagle, just as Hoover regularly walked his own little cairn terriers along Thirtieth Place.[15]

Johnson's signal achievement as Senate majority leader had been the passage of the Civil Rights Act of 1957, in which he attempted to placate his Southern friends while showing that he was not, himself, like all the rest. Hoover was no fan of the bill in its final form, but he appreciated that Johnson was willing to use his Senate power for the FBI at other moments. As majority leader, Johnson helped to usher through the legislation undoing the Supreme Court's demand that the FBI open up informant records to defense attorneys. In the fall of 1960, with the election underway, he went so far as to support a bill guaranteeing Hoover a lifetime sinecure: the full payment of the FBI director's salary until the day he died, whether or not he remained on the job. The bill had to be rushed through in the ten days before Congress recessed. Johnson pulled out all the stops to make it happen.[16]

Like Nixon, Johnson saw political benefit in identifying with Hoover, especially as the Texas legislator sought to become a more national figure—to shed his reputation as "a Southern reactionary who would not be supported by a united Democratic Party," in the words of a SOLO report describing Soviet conventional wisdom. While eyeing the Democratic nomination in 1959, he had invited Hoover and Tolson to join him in Austin for a charity event followed by an afternoon trip to the nearby LBJ Ranch. At the luncheon, Johnson introduced Hoover as his old friend from Thirtieth Place. "There are advantages and disadvantages to having J. Edgar Hoover as a neighbor," he added, to guffaws from the audience. When it came to politics, though, being close to Hoover had been mostly upside for the new vice president.[17]

KENNEDY'S DECISION TO REAPPOINT HOOVER PROVIDED A GESTURE OF CONTI-nuity, assurance that he did not plan to upend the old order at a moment of Cold War uncertainty. So did his reappointment of Allen Dulles, still head of the CIA. Most of his other national security appointments were bolder, more in line with the vague New Frontier themes of "youth" and "progress." Defense Secretary Robert McNamara was just forty-four, famed as the Harvard "Whiz Kid" who engineered a financial turn-around at Ford. National security adviser McGeorge Bundy was younger still. At thirty-four, he had become dean of Harvard's Faculty of Arts and Sciences and now at forty-one he was to be Kennedy's inside man on foreign policy. And then there was the president's pick for attorney general, the youngest and most controversial of them all. After announcing Hoover's reappointment, Kennedy floated the idea of tapping his younger brother Robert (or "Bobby"), just thirty-five years old, for the position of Hoover's boss.

All of Kennedy's appointees shared traits that put Hoover on edge: Ivy Leaguers confident of their own brilliance but, by Hoover's standards, ignorant about how Washington really worked. By reputation, Bobby was potentially the worst of the lot. First, he was the president's brother, an act of nepotism that smacked of royal-family arrogance. Second, he was widely known in Washington as the least likable and most pugnacious of the Kennedys: the "Black Prince," in Adlai Stevenson's words. *The New York Times* howled in outrage at the prospect of a brother-to-brother appointment, pleading with Kennedy to base his cabinet appointments on expertise rather than political loyalty.

Hoover tried to keep an open mind. He knew Bobby somewhat better than he knew the president, and he liked at least some of what he saw. Bobby had gotten his start in Washington on McCarthy's committee, where as Roy Cohn's assistant and then as Democratic counsel he had shown himself to be a formidable anticommunist brawler. Even after the committee fell apart, Bobby refused to abandon McCarthy. Like Hoover, he attended the senator's Washington funeral, and he even flew out to Wisconsin for the private family services. In 1955, after a trip to Russia, he made a point of meeting with Hoover to reassert his anticommunist bona fides. By 1957, he was staff counsel for the McClellan Committee, a reconfigured version of McCarthy's investigative subcommittee, now led by Democratic senator John McClellan and focused on labor racketeering and organized crime.

Those topics had brought Bobby into contact with the FBI, which provided the committee with advice and background information. So Hoover had reason to think that he and Bobby might be able to work together once again. Yet he also knew that Bobby deserved his reputation as "a son of a bitch," in Truman's words, because he had seen that side, too. Despite serving on the McCarthy Committee, Bobby had puffed himself up in righteous anger about the senator's abuse of witnesses and demanded that the FBI disclose its files—a noble sentiment but not one that Hoover appreciated. Toward Cohn, Bobby had remained belligerent; once they allegedly came close to a fistfight outside the committee room. As counsel for the McClellan Committee, Bobby had pushed to ride along with FBI agents when they arrested Teamsters leader Jimmy Hoffa, an idea that appalled Hoover even after Bobby pulled back and admitted the inappropriate "rashness of such a request."

By the 1960 presidential election, the memos accumulated in Bobby's Bureau file were nothing if not inconsistent, veering wildly from high praise ("most cordial") to general condemnation ("completely uncooperative"). So when Bobby himself visited the director's office on December 14, 1960, to ask whether or not he should accept appointment as attorney general, he must have wondered what was about to ensue. Hoover apparently felt that he had to say yes to the president's brother. "I didn't like to tell him that," he later explained, "but what could I say?"[18]

JOHN KENNEDY ANNOUNCED HIS BROTHER'S APPOINTMENT ON DECEMBER 16, two days after Bobby's meeting with Hoover. Almost immediately, the press began to speculate about how the director might respond to his thirty-five-year-old boss, gently reminding the younger man that "the indestructible Mr. Hoover is thus far undefeated in the wars of Washington." Within the Justice Department, though, there was little indication at first that anything radically new was afoot. Since 1917, Hoover had served under no fewer than fifteen attorneys general. Making room for a sixteenth— even a controversial one, the brother of the president—did not seem to require any great innovation. When the Senate came asking for any "derogatory information" about the attorney general designate, Hoover assured them he had none and that they should feel free to approve the appointment. A few weeks later, he personally delivered a mounted FBI badge to Bobby's office, "making him an honorary Special Agent." He also appointed Bureau official Courtney Evans, the former liaison to the McClellan Committee, well liked by both Kennedy brothers, to serve as the FBI's emissary to the new administration.[19]

The Kennedy brothers sent back their own signals of respect and welcome. On January 29, Hoover attended the president's first major reception at the White House, a gathering for some three hundred top executive-branch officials. Rather than welcome in the new men with a dull ceremony, Kennedy flung open the state dining room for a gala, complete with martinis and highballs. "It's wonderful," Hoover told the wire services. "I can't ever remember attending a similar party in the White House." Despite his disappointment at Nixon's loss, despite his own resistance to change, Hoover recognized something exciting in the Kennedy presidency, a style that Washington had never seen. For a few splendid weeks, he thought he might be part of it.[20]

CHAPTER 40

Top Hoodlums

(1957–1961)

Bobby Kennedy in his Justice Department office, May 1961. Hoover disliked his casual style as attorney general.

AP PHOTO/BYRON ROLLINS

For those first few weeks, Bobby tried to play by Hoover's rules. "I really deferred to him," Bobby later insisted. "I mean, I made a real effort because I recognized the fact that I was young and coming in there and all the rest of the business." But he never forgot the fundamental fact of their relationship: whether Hoover liked it or not, the attorney general was the boss and the Bureau director his subordinate. Bobby came to his new position with a rich boy's insouciance: confident about giving orders, certain of his ability to master the details. Some of the younger Bureau agents found this charming, a crack of light in the wall of Bureau discipline. Hoover and his inner circle did not. Within a few weeks, they were at odds with their young boss over issues ranging from organized crime to the dress and conduct policies at Justice. The relationship never recovered.

There was, first, the matter of shirtsleeves. Though Bobby usually showed up to work in a suit and tie, as the day wore on he often shed these encumbrances, first removing the jacket, then the neckwear, then loosening his collar and rolling up his cuffs. To

Hoover, this was tantamount to reporting for work in pajamas. Bureau regulations still required agents to wear dark suits, white shirts, and ties at all times, along with hats whenever they ventured outside. Hoover viewed this not merely as a convenient uniform but as a symbol of professionalism, a sign that they took their jobs seriously. "It is ridiculous to have the Attorney General walking around the building in his shirt-sleeves," he complained to Bureau aides. "Suppose I had had a visitor waiting in my entrance room. How could I have introduced him?"

Bobby had other bad habits, too. For his permanent office at Justice, he rejected the attorney general's traditional quarters in favor of a cavernous, wood-paneled reception room—"enormous," one reporter recalled, "as long as a football field." And in fact he did play touch football in the office, a Kennedy-family diversion now brought indoors. Bobby also liked to play darts, flinging sharp-tipped metal projectiles at a target on the wall, pocking up the fine walnut paneling when he missed. Hoover saw both games as "pure desecration—desecration of government property." On one occasion, he and Tolson ventured to Bobby's office for a meeting only to find the attorney general distracted by his dart game, half-listening to their reports. According to Kennedy confidant Arthur Schlesinger, Hoover and Tolson concluded that it was "the most deplorably undignified conduct they had ever witnessed on the part of a Cabinet member." They left the meeting early, appalled at the attorney general's lack of propriety.[1]

Even on his own turf, Hoover was not entirely safe. Bobby liked to wander the halls at Justice, including the FBI's offices, popping into various meetings, introducing himself personally to even the lowest-level clerks. Hoover found the practice outrageous, a violation of accepted hierarchy and an implicit warning that his men would have to be on their toes at all times. On February 1, a group of clerks happened to be on break when Bobby stopped by the photostat room. "It is unfortunate that the 'break' came at just this time," Hoover wrote, embarrassed that his employees were not hard at work. On another occasion, Bobby provoked a major internal incident by attempting to use the Bureau gym after hours. According to a flurry of memos, he appeared at the gym's basement door around 7:40 p.m., during a routine tour of the facilities, only to find it locked. After a few phone calls attempting to get the gym opened, he gave up and said he'd try again tomorrow. Hoover was furious—not only with the agents who had failed to open the gym but also with the attorney general. "This certainly proves the point we have been stressing—our employees should always be busy; engage in no horseplay + be properly attired," he insisted. "No one knows when + where A.G. may appear." To a man who craved order, Bobby's spontaneity was disorienting.[2]

Sometimes the attorney general even appeared unannounced in Hoover's personal office, the one man aside from the president with the implied right to barge past Helen Gandy. Not once but twice on February 17 he stopped by with "an unidentified male friend"; Gandy noted dryly in the office log that he was "just passing by." On another occasion, he brought several of his children to visit while Hoover was out and allowed them to rummage through the director's papers. For official exchanges, Bobby made Hoover come to him by means of a loud, insistent buzzer placed on Hoover's desk. According to one agent, Hoover had been perplexed when he first saw the contraption, "a strange object . . . with wires trailing off under the carpet." Once a technician explained what it was, Hoover supposedly ordered it ripped out and placed on Gandy's desk. The attorney general insisted that he wanted direct access to Hoover, though, and the device was reinstalled.[3]

Hoover found the buzzer humiliating, a reminder of his subordinate status. Bobby could not resist rubbing it in. Justice Department lawyers recalled his glee at being able to summon the FBI director. "He hit a goddamn buzzer and within sixty seconds, the old man came in with a red face, and he and Bobby jawed at each other for about ten minutes," one marveled years later. "Nobody had ever buzzed for Hoover!" another recalled. Bobby had every right to reassert some measure of control over the Bureau, including his demand that communication between the FBI and the White House go through the attorney general. But the way he did it made the whole thing seem both insulting and personal.[4]

As a child of wealth, Bobby knew instinctively that power could be exercised not just by imposing rules, but by flouting them. This, at least, was the message delivered by Brumus, a lumbering, slobbering Newfoundland dog who had been a gift from the famed satirist James Thurber. Bobby made a habit of bringing the dog into the office, where Brumus proceeded to mark territory by urinating on the carpets. According to legend, Brumus once deposited a steaming pile near the entrance to Hoover's reception room. Hoover assembled an executive conference to determine what to do about the unnerving situation in which the attorney general was arrogantly flouting the law that forbade animals in federal offices. In the end, though, Brumus remained a fixture of the Kennedy Justice Department, a symbol of all that separated it from Hoover's Bureau.[5]

By early February, the tensions between the two sides had become obvious enough to attract the attention of reporters. At *The New York Times*, thirty-three-year-old Anthony Lewis composed a celebratory feature about the new youth-oriented culture at Justice, describing how even the "most experienced and hard-boiled" government lawyers now grudgingly conceded that Bobby had managed to shake things up. In Lewis's telling, everything that enraged Hoover—the casual dress, the erratic hours, the disregard for hierarchy—became evidence of a transformative and positive change. Where Hoover saw chaos and impudence, Lewis saw a much-needed infusion of energy. More than a change of policy, he noted a "sharp change in the mood of the Justice Department," with staid federal attorneys suddenly swept up in the urgency of the new political decade. "As much as one can judge so vague a thing," Lewis concluded, "morale has risen."[6]

And that may well have been true at Justice, where Bobby was free to appoint his own deputies and make his own decisions. At the Bureau, Hoover still dominated the institutional culture, and his agents quickly came to regard the attorney general with contempt. They privately referred to Bobby's office as "the playpen" or "rumpus room." Letters to Hoover derided the man himself as a "boy wonder." By late February, the situation was dire enough that one FBI official felt compelled to intervene with Bobby's press secretary in an effort to get the attorney general to tone things down. "I . . . suggested that the Attorney General's predecessors who were somewhat older than the present Attorney General functioned in a very dignified and sedate manner," the official wrote. He assured Hoover that even Bobby's own staff recognized "that the Attorney General has a very unorthodox and direct approach to everything—including the Bureau."

The memo suggested that these were perhaps just growing pains, that the whole matter might "'simmer down' as the newness of the situation was overcome." Hoover was not convinced. By the end of February, his early gestures toward cooperation began to give way to a growing intransigence. "If we are asked a question then we may answer it," he wrote in response to the official's memo. Other than that, Bobby should expect no further favors from the Bureau.[7]

IF IT HAD JUST BEEN A CLASH OF CULTURES, HOOVER AND HIS THIRTY-FIVE-year-old boss might eventually have reached some sort of accord. But the conflict also concerned real power and institutional prerogatives, matters on which Hoover saw little room for compromise. On January 23, just three days into his term as attorney general, *The Wall Street Journal* reported that Bobby was planning a "multi-agency drive" against organized crime, an area where it was implied that federal authorities—including the FBI—had fallen behind in recent years. To coordinate the effort, he proposed the creation of a federal Crime Commission, independent of any existing agency. Hoover viewed both ideas as threats to FBI prerogatives: the former an insult to what the Bureau was already doing, the latter a restriction on what it might yet do. He set out to teach his boss something about how the politics of crime and law enforcement worked in Washington.[8]

Looking back on this conflict, Kennedy partisans would claim that the attorney general was simply trying to fill a void created by the FBI, that Hoover had ignored organized crime until a young, farsighted superior showed up one day to set him straight. That explanation is only partly true. As Hoover liked to point out, the FBI made its name fighting organized crime in the 1930s: What were the Dillinger and Barker and Karpis gangs, if not "organized" criminal enterprises? Since then, his men had helped to investigate high-profile gangsters ranging from Irish mob boss Roger Touhy to Las Vegas mastermind Bugsy Siegel. His Ten Most Wanted list, established in 1950, often featured fugitives connected to organized crime. But Hoover had argued throughout that organized crime, like most other forms of illegal activity, was best addressed at the local level—and in any case, did not yet fall under the jurisdiction of the FBI. His approach served the purpose of insulating FBI agents from the temptations of graft, vice, and corruption that Hoover feared might undermine their squeaky-clean image. It was also in keeping with Hoover's long-standing visions of the FBI as a professional model for local police, but not necessarily as a substitute for their manpower.[9]

His greater misjudgment, repeated well into the mid-1950s, was that organized crime itself existed only on a local rather than national level—that there was no Mafia, or national crime-boss syndicate, coordinating activities from the top down. But that idea, too, had collapsed long before Bobby came to office. In November 1957, state police in Apalachin, New York, raided a party at which several dozen crime bosses had gathered for a national confab. At that point, Hoover had conceded the need for federal action and secretly launched his own organized-crime initiative. That effort had been underway for more than three years when Bobby announced that the federal government would finally do something—indeed, anything—about the national problem of the Mafia. Hoover was not inclined to forgive the insult.

Despite his self-righteousness, Hoover was partly to blame for the fact that nobody, including the attorney general, recognized what the FBI was up to. In the wake of Apalachin, one agent recalled, "the press came knocking at Mr. Hoover's door" with excited questions: "Who are these guys? How are they affiliated with each other? What is the nature of their business? Why were they meeting? Does this prove there is in fact such a thing as the Mafia?" But Hoover, uncertain about his jurisdiction, unclear about the nature of the problem, refused to answer.

Unbeknownst to the public, he did take action, however. As early as 1953, Hoover had authorized the creation of a small "Top Hoodlum Program" designed to target the most powerful mob bosses in major American cities. In the wake of Apalachin, that investigation expanded quickly. Agents soon determined that "the Mafia does exist in the U.S.," in the words of one summary memo. "It exists as a special criminal clique or caste engaged in organized crime activity," with members drawn primarily from those of "Sicilian Italian origin and descent." When it came to fleshing out the details, however, progress had been fitful and often unsatisfying, with agents circling around their well-protected targets, unable to discover anything meaningful or to persuade anyone on the inside to talk. In response, Hoover had stepped up the pressure, vowing to give the initiative his "utmost personal attention." But he still hesitated to discuss the issue in public.

Of all the field offices, Chicago came in for the greatest pressure from Hoover. He still recalled how Al Capone had once ruled the city, and how Purvis and the Chicago office had been forced to take up arms during the 1930s. In the late 1950s, as agents began to chip away at Mafia networks, they found direct ties back to Capone and to the criminal machine he had helped to build three decades earlier. Among the "top hoodlums" identified by the Chicago field office was Murray Humphreys, a tall and genial Welsh-born fixer who traced his professional roots all the way back to the Capone gang. Two decades younger but no less formidable was Sam "Momo" Giancana, whose squat frame, Sicilian background, and snarling demeanor better fit popular ideas of who and what a Mafia boss was supposed to be. By the time Kennedy came to office, Hoover's office had labeled both men "armed and dangerous." They reserved even choicer epithets for Giancana. According to the Bureau, he possessed a "vicious temperament" and "psychopathic personality" that made him especially fearsome.

Figuring out how to approach such a man—how to investigate him without endangering agents' lives or showing the Bureau's hand—had proved to be no simple matter. Hoover had rejected the use of undercover agents for fear that their activities might "embarrass" the Bureau. That had left three options: physical surveillance, informant recruiting, and the use of bugs or wiretaps. The first two came with outsize challenges, given their targets' sophisticated methods for evading law enforcement and their brutally enforced code of silence. So Hoover had turned to microphones and wiretaps. Bugging technology was still awkward at best, with all-too-large microphones that had to be hidden behind walls and then connected directly to a Bureau outpost through a tangle of physical wires. Under the circumstances, though, Hoover "figured they had no choice but to go into bugging whole hog," in the words of a Justice Department official.

The strategy "worked beautifully," in the official's assessment, providing Hoover with first a trickle and then a flood of information about the nation's most elusive and influential crime bosses. In July 1959, the Chicago office succeeded in planting a bug at a would-be tailor shop frequented by Humphreys. In truth, the building was a secret meeting place where he met with fellow "hoodlums" and spoke freely about their plans. FBI agents nicknamed their microphone "Little Al," in honor of the late great Al Capone.

Hoover listened in via daily transcripts shipped to Washington. His demands required grueling work from agents and clerks; each day, they not only transcribed the conversations but also provided interpretive notes explaining to Hoover who was talking and what they might be talking about. Through the bugs, Hoover learned of the extensive gambling and prostitution networks maintained by Humphreys, along with his plans for retaliation against rivals and hand-in-glove relations with Giancana. The mobsters even spoke of something called the Commission, a group of major crime bosses who met regularly to divide up territory and negotiate disputes. The Chicago office worried about sending that news on to Hoover. "Hadn't Mr. Hoover been saying for years that there was no national body of organized crime?" Chicago agent William Roemer asked. "Our evidence amounted to heresy!" But after demanding that the recording be sent to Washington for review, Hoover accepted the new reality.

The bugs were far from perfect instruments of law enforcement. Because they often entailed illegal trespass, their evidence could not be used in court. Those dubious origins also meant that—as with SOLO, Venona, and so many of his most cherished secret operations—Hoover continued to stay quiet about what the Bureau was doing. He did not share everything he knew with the Justice Department, for fear that leaks and sloppy handling of information might expose and destroy the entire operation. Even so, he did not take kindly to Bobby's suggestions that the country suddenly needed an organized-crime initiative and a new federal Crime Commission to run it.[10]

GIVEN THE KENNEDY FAMILY'S HISTORY, ORGANIZED CRIME WAS A STRANGE choice of priorities in any case. Joe Kennedy's investment portfolio was rumored to brush up against organized crime "at a hundred points," in the words of writer Burton Hersh. So were his social habits, which included countless hours gambling and womanizing in Las Vegas, the country's improbable new playground for organized crime. John Kennedy inherited some of his father's preferences and questionable contacts, despite his family-man image. Bobby had carved out a more distinctive profile, less the bon vivant than the flashing, hot-tempered enforcer of his own political vision. As counsel for the McClellan Committee, he had made his name as the great Washington scourge of "labor racketeering," the ill-defined realm where union corruption met with organized-crime activity. To the befuddlement of many Democratic allies, his investigations took him deep into the bowels of industrial unions and urban political machines, two key party constituencies. Now they also put him up against Hoover, whose help had been "absolutely invaluable," as he acknowledged in *The Enemy Within*, his fast-paced 1960 book on the committee's activities.[11]

Hoover responded not by openly defying his boss's orders (he rarely did that) but by setting out his own priorities and following them through. If an organized-crime push was coming, he wanted to be out in front, prepared to show that the FBI could and would do what was needed. In Chicago, the epicenter of the Bureau's organized-crime effort, he increased the main squad from five men to seventy. He also encouraged agents to show off just how much the Bureau had already done. In February, the Justice Department asked for a "full-scale investigation" of Humphreys, the very man the FBI had been bugging for well over a year. At that point, Hoover ordered the Chicago office to share its intelligence, hoping to show that the FBI had not, in fact, been lying down on the job. The one exception involved direct knowledge of the FBI's bugs, most of them top secret and installed illegally. There, he encouraged agents to use "suitable phraseology" to obscure what was happening, at least until they could sort out whom to trust within the Kennedy Justice Department.

In that sense Hoover sought to produce what Bobby most wanted: evidence that could be used in federal prosecution. During the late 1950s, the Top Hoodlums program had operated mainly as a counterintelligence effort, in which the Bureau gathered information without regard for any potential of courtroom prosecution. "Our goal was to learn the innermost secrets of the mob and then use that information in an attempt to thwart its operations," Roemer explained, not to face down "the mob" before a judge or jury. Now Hoover ordered the field offices to shift directions and to focus on investigations likely to bring "top hoodlums you currently have under investigation to trial in the immediate future." He attached "extreme importance" to achieving "a successful prosecutive conclusion"—and thus to pleasing the new attorney general.[12]

If this looked like cooperation, though, it was cooperation with limits. And it was Hoover, not Bobby, who defined what the limits would be. From Bobby's first days in office, Hoover concluded that he could live with a stepped-up organized-crime effort, essentially more of what the Bureau was already doing. What he could not abide was the other half of Bobby's proposal: the formation of a Crime Commission with the power to override FBI authority and to set the federal law enforcement agenda. Just days after Kennedy's inauguration, the United Press wire service ran an article outlining Hoover's view that "the daily exchange of information" between FBI agents and local law enforcement still offered the country's most effective crime-fighting model. The article pointed out that "FBI Director J. Edgar Hoover has cited this type of cooperation as an argument against establishment of a federal crime commission, favored by some officials."[13]

Within a few weeks, the dispute was serious enough to inspire speculation about whether the president and his brother would tolerate such open defiance, even from a legend such as Hoover. On February 23, Hoover made his way to the White House for a briefing, his first of the new presidential administration. Aware of growing tensions, the media speculated that the president had summoned Hoover in order to fire him. Hoover put out a different version of events. "He is not going to resign and he is not going to be asked to resign," the sympathetic columnist Paul Harvey announced on March 8, relying on FBI tips. The real purpose of the meeting, Harvey explained, was to discuss how to reconcile Bobby's desire for a Crime Commission with Hoover's opposition to it.[14]

Whatever was said at the meeting, in the following weeks Bobby's enthusiasm for the commission dropped markedly, while his public praise of Hoover notably increased. His final acquiescence came on April 6, during his inaugural press conference as attorney general. His status as the president's dashing younger brother drew a crowd, with 174 reporters, along with two radio teams, crammed into his football field of an office. Bobby took the opportunity to outline a sweeping vision for fighting organized crime, just as he had suggested from the moment of his appointment. This time, however, there was no mention of a Crime Commission. Instead, he called for eight new laws that would give the FBI greater power and discretion to combat organized crime.[15]

For anyone paying close attention, the reversal was astonishing. Bobby had come into office calling for an independent commission, outside Bureau control, to take the reins of federal law enforcement. Now he was championing legislation that would serve to enhance Hoover's power. "It is my firm belief that new laws are needed to give the FBI increased jurisdiction to assist local authorities in the common battle against the rackets," Bobby announced, without acknowledging any change of heart whatsoever.[16]

Reporters felt Bobby did surprisingly well for a greenhorn, combining an ambitious agenda with a touch of the Kennedy charm. Behind the scenes, though, it was Hoover who carried the day. Less than three months into the new administration, he proved that he was still a man to be reckoned with, and sent the new attorney general down to his first public defeat.[17]

A SECOND DEFEAT CAME JUST DAYS LATER—AND IT, TOO, INVOLVED ORGA-nized crime, though not in a way that either Hoover or Bobby quite anticipated. On April 17, after months of planning, the CIA dispatched fourteen hundred half-trained Cuban exiles onto the beaches of the Bay of Pigs in Cuba, where the socialist turned communist Fidel Castro had led a successful revolution two years earlier. Castro's troops made quick work of the invading force. As things fell apart, President Kennedy balked at sending air cover because the entire operation was supposed to come off without any hint of American involvement. The attempt at secrecy failed. On April 20, three days after the invasion, he tacitly acknowledged American backing, a dispiriting and embarrassing loss in "the eternal struggle of liberty against tyranny."[18]

The Bay of Pigs debacle fit well with Hoover's evolving assessment of the Kennedy brothers as young and arrogant and ill-prepared for the hard work of running the country. According to one aide, Hoover received a last-minute briefing in advance of the invasion but played no role in its conception—or in its collapse. "Mr. Hoover listened to Bobby, but we were just strictly sidelined by him on the entire matter," the aide explained. "I think the director was relieved that he did not have a role." Even so, Hoover saw the chance to strike a blow on the FBI's behalf. A few days after the invasion, he delivered a report to the attorney general documenting the many missteps of his old adversaries at the CIA, beginning with the sheer organizational chaos of its early years.[19]

Hoover's grumbling might have brought an end to the Cuba story if not for an incident that had taken place months earlier in Las Vegas. In late October 1960, just days before the election, a housekeeper at the Riviera hotel had entered the room of comedian Dan Rowan and found it littered with wiretapping and bugging equipment, apparently left behind midway through a surveillance setup. She called the police, who in turn called the FBI on the premise that the situation might involve a violation of federal wiretapping laws. The local field office quickly deduced that Rowan was dating girl-group singer Phyllis McGuire, who also happened to be dating none other than Chicago Mafia boss Sam Giancana, one of Hoover's "top hoodlums." Tracking the surveillance equipment led to a former FBI agent named Robert Maheu, who admitted that he had been hired to orchestrate the bugging.

Confronted by his former colleagues, Maheu at first maintained that an anonymous Los Angeles attorney had paid him to contract out the surveillance work, for reasons he refused to specify. Then on April 18, the day after the Bay of Pigs invasion, he suddenly changed his story. In a shocking admission that quickly made its way up to Hoover's office, Maheu confessed that the CIA had hired him as a liaison to the Chicago underworld, in hopes that the CIA and the Mafia might join forces against Castro in Cuba. According to CIA thinking, the mob was already furious about Castro's seizure of casinos and crackdown on illicit business in Havana—and would therefore make excellent partners for the U.S. government in its campaign to undermine Castro's fledgling regime. In this revised version of the story, Maheu said he had orchestrated the Las Vegas surveillance to check up on whether Giancana had been leaking information about the scheme to Phyllis McGuire, the girlfriend he shared with Rowan.[20]

It was an incredible story: the Mafia and the CIA working together, at the very moment that Hoover and Bobby were loudly proclaiming a war on organized crime. It was so incredible, in fact, that Hoover might not have believed it—except that a CIA official soon confirmed that it was true. In early May, confronted with Maheu's story, CIA director of security Sheffield Edwards admitted that "Maheu was used as an intermediary with Sam Giancana, relative to CIA's anti-Castro activities." Gobsmacked by this turn of events, Hoover decided that he wanted to know everything: about the Mafia, about the CIA, about the possible involvement of the attorney general and the White House. "Here was CIA, coddling characters the Bureau was supposed to be investigating," CIA liaison Samuel Papich recalled. "That irritated the hell out of Hoover—and when J. Edgar got mad, boy, he got mad!"[21]

Over the next several months, Hoover sent agents out to interview (and reinterview) the major players. In one especially fraught incident, a team of FBI men intercepted Giancana at Chicago's O'Hare airport, in hopes that a surprise confrontation might induce him to talk about his CIA cooperation. Enraged at being trapped near the plane's gate, Giancana indeed railed about Cuba, warning that "the United States Government is not as smart as it would like to think it is," according to an FBI report. He also encouraged agents to take his threats "to their 'boss', who in turn would report the results to their 'super boss,' who would thereupon report to his 'super super boss'"—by whom he apparently meant Hoover, Robert Kennedy, and John Kennedy. "I know all about the KENNEDYs," he warned, "and one of these days we are going to tell all."

When asked to clarify his comments, Giancana "uttered an obscenity" and refused to say another word. But Hoover took it all as confirmation of what he already believed: that the Kennedys were reckless and arrogant and up to no good, and that they were keeping things from the Bureau.[22]

ULTIMATELY, IT WAS BOBBY KENNEDY WHO CAME TO HOOVER ON A "HIGHLY confidential basis" to reveal what had really happened between the CIA and Giancana. According to the attorney general, the CIA actually employed Maheu—and thus Giancana—not to gather intelligence in Cuba or to assist with the Bay of Pigs invasion, but "to hire some gunmen to go into Cuba and kill Castro" for a fee of $150,000. It was another bout of stunning information: the Mafia and the CIA in cahoots to assassinate a foreign leader. Hoover saw it as all too typical of CIA practices. "I only wish we would eventually realize CIA can never be depended upon to deal forthrightly with us," he wrote around that time. "Certainly my skepticism isn't based on prejudice nor suspicion but on specific instances all too many in number."[23]

Skepticism continued to dominate his relationship with Bobby Kennedy as well. But, as both sides grudgingly acknowledged, they had little choice other than to move forward together. In May 1961, once the Crime Commission question had been settled, Hoover brought the attorney general's office in on the fact that the FBI had been using "microphone surveillances" in organized crime cases "even though trespass is necessary." According to FBI liaison Courtney Evans, the attorney general was "pleased" by the news and offered no objection. In August, they conferred on the use of wiretaps in organized crime cases. Once again, the attorney general failed to shrink back in horror. Instead, he threw his support behind the legislative package wending its way through Congress, which granted the FBI new authority to investigate interstate gambling and racketeering—"powerful new weapons to crack down on underworld rackets," in one newspaper's description, as well as "the most sweeping legislation of its kind in nearly 30 years."[24]

Over the next few years, with these new laws at their disposal, the FBI and the Justice Department carried out at least some of the crusade that Kennedy had envisioned during his first heady weeks in office. But Hoover never quite reconciled himself to Bobby's leadership, and rarely managed to offer his full cooperation. In 1962, the FBI helped to persuade gangster Joseph Valachi to inform on his fellow mob bosses, making him "the greatest song bird ever to flee the cage of La Cosa Nostra," in one official's description. At the Justice Department, a "Get Hoffa Squad" did just what its name entailed, pursuing the Teamsters leader relentlessly before winning a conviction for jury tampering in 1964. Humphreys, too, was eventually arrested—though he died that same night, finally brought down by heart problems.[25]

Giancana proved to be more complicated. In August 1961, a few weeks after the confrontation at the airport, Hoover authorized the Chicago field office to plant a microphone at the Armory Lounge in Forest Park, Illinois, Giancana's favorite hangout and place of business. What he heard there led him into not just the Mafia and the CIA, but also back to the White House.

CHAPTER 41

The Federal Bureau of Integration

(1957–1961)

Hoover, Attorney General Bobby Kennedy, and others hung in effigy at a rally of the National States' Rights Party in Anniston, Alabama, September 5, 1961. Though Hoover investigated civil rights activists and resisted calls to protect them, many segregationists viewed him as an invasive pro-civil-rights force.

JIM LOWRY/NATIONAL ARCHIVES AND RECORDS ADMINISTRATION

Less than a month after the Bay of Pigs, another crisis erupted. This one was not of John Kennedy's own making but it would become the moral issue that defined much of his presidency. The story began on May 4, 1961, when a group of thirteen men and women calling themselves Freedom Riders boarded two commercial buses out of Washington, determined to test whether Black and white citizens could ride through the Deep South side by side. Their journey became major news ten days later, when white mobs in Alabama met them with all the fury of massive resistance, setting their first bus on fire and beating the Freedom Riders with pipes, clubs, and fists.[1]

Before this moment, Hoover had approached civil rights as a fraught but still second-rank political issue, with a tendency to flare up and burn out. Beginning with the Freedom Riders, it moved to the center of national politics—and of Hoover's concerns—and did not leave that position for more than a decade. As one of the opening salvos of this new era, the Freedom Riders episode adopted an increasingly popular method of civil rights agitation: nonviolent direct action. That method, in turn, changed how Hoover understood the FBI's duties and its relations with Southern law enforcement.

Hoover had long been suspicious of anyone, especially Black activists, who spoke out against racism and Jim Crow. But during the 1940s, he had viewed civil rights work at least in part as a matter of enforcing "law and order." Lynchings, especially, tapped into his long-standing hostility toward vigilantes and local police officials who claimed the right to take the law into their own hands. With the rise of nonviolent direct action, he began to turn more and more of that hostility on civil rights activists themselves, framing them as provocateurs and agitators stirring up trouble where none was needed. The NAACP of the 1940s and 1950s had pushed for the law to be changed—and then for those changes to be enforced through federal power. The new generation of activists, frustrated at the slow pace of racial transformation, tried to speed things along through more confrontational methods. Hoover viewed these forms of civil disobedience and direct action as tantamount to lawbreaking—even when federal law happened to be on the protesters' side. In the 1960s, he came to view "law and order" not as a directive that might protect Black Southerners and civil rights organizers, but as something that would have to be imposed upon them.

In this shifting terrain Hoover began to rethink how the FBI would relate to its growing roster of civil rights duties—and to the Southern police departments who were, inevitably, involved in the enforcement process. The 1957 Civil Rights Act had raised expectations about what the FBI could and should do on civil rights. But it had provided little clear guidance about how to do it. So Hoover crafted his own limits, based in part on his ideological animus toward the civil rights movement and in part on his long-standing institutional interests. As during the lynching investigations, he made it known that the FBI would investigate in cases where federal jurisdiction appeared to apply, engaging freely in surveillance and counterintelligence work. But he drew strict lines elsewhere: he would not allow FBI agents to be used as guards or soldiers on behalf of civil rights demonstrators, even in the face of near-certain violence directed their way. Those tasks were better left to local law enforcement, he argued, which had both the manpower and the jurisdiction to carry them out. The problem, of course, was that Southern police departments usually had even less interest in protecting demonstrators and their rights than he did.

The Freedom Riders presented the first major test of these limits, and of Hoover's attempt to persuade Southern police departments to do the guarding and protecting in the FBI's stead. By the time it was all over, his refusal to intervene in the face of serious violence would make him a target of criticism from civil rights supporters, who argued that the FBI had a duty to provide protection and keep the peace. At the FBI,

Hoover would narrate the Freedom Rides differently, as a saga of trust and betrayal, in which local police deserved most of the blame.

The White House often backed Hoover in these exchanges. Despite their growing tensions in other realms, Hoover and the Kennedy administration initially agreed when it came to federal intervention in civil rights matters, choosing caution over any bold new moves. Each hoped to preserve his ties to the white South: Kennedy because he wanted to hold the Democratic coalition together; Hoover because he relied upon the cooperation of local law enforcement as well as the sympathy of Southern Democrats. Though Kennedy and Hoover would later be depicted as polar opposites on the civil rights question, in 1961 they faced the emerging Southern crisis with common concerns. Neither one expressed much enthusiasm for making civil rights a federal issue.

HOOVER ONCE BELIEVED THAT HE HAD SOLVED THE PROBLEM OF SOUTHERN law enforcement. "In the late twenties and early thirties there was great reluctance upon the part of the local authorities to cooperate with the FBI," he explained to Bobby Kennedy, "and it took us several years before we could break down this reluctance, but we finally did so." His ace in the hole had been the FBI National Academy, where local officers came to train and then carry the FBI's methods back to their hometowns. Through the academy, Hoover had built up a network of sympathetic policemen throughout the South, widely known as the least modernized and least professional of the nation's law enforcement regions. Some of their sympathy came from a shared racial outlook: Hoover had built the FBI on the model of Kappa Alpha, where white Southern men were prized. But academy men also learned new things from Hoover during their time in Washington. Many left as true believers in his style of law enforcement professionalism, with its emphasis on statistics and index cards and forensic science. More often than not, they remained willing to work with the FBI once they returned home.[2]

Civil rights cases were the great exception. During the lynching investigations of the 1940s, Hoover had often found himself at odds with local police; indeed, the police were often in cahoots with the lynch mobs under investigation. *Brown* and the desegregation challenges of the 1950s heightened those tensions, casting the FBI as an unwelcome interloper in a states-rights region. Then came the 1957 Civil Rights Act, which thrust the Bureau definitively into civil rights and voting rights issues but only added to its jurisdictional confusion. According to the logic of massive resistance, to be a segregationist increasingly meant to oppose all forms of federal power, including the presence of FBI men on Southern soil. For the legions of academy graduates working in the South—as for Hoover himself—that created a set of unwelcome contradictions. None of them wanted segregation dismantled. But their professional duties regularly found them locked in conflict. By the late 1950s, it seemed impossible, or at least extremely difficult, to express loyalty both to the Southern racial order and to the FBI.

Plenty of men tried. Pick almost any major city or state in the South and somewhere in the law enforcement picture, most likely near the top, there was probably an academy graduate or former Bureau agent. In North Carolina, where lunch-counter sit-ins captured the nation's attention, the commissioner of motor vehicles and public safety was Edward Scheidt, former head of the Bureau's powerful New York office. In New Orleans, Guy Banister, formerly in charge of the FBI's Chicago office, worked as the assistant superintendent of police before founding his own private investigative agency. In Mississippi, ostensibly so hostile to federal authority, FBI men could be found in a variety of key positions. Hugh Clegg, one of Hoover's earliest Kappa Alpha recruits and his right-hand man in building the academy, was now on the chancellor's staff at the University of Mississippi, in the thick of a desegregation struggle. Zack Van Landingham, a twenty-seven-year Bureau veteran, worked as chief investigator for the Mississippi State Sovereignty Commission, a statewide agency founded in 1956 to track and disrupt civil rights activity.

In theory, the Sovereignty Commission was supposed to embody the distinction between federal and local authority, with a founding mission "to protect the sovereignty of the state of Mississippi and her sister states from encroachment thereon by the Federal government or any branch, department, or agency thereof." In reality, it showed just how complicated that relationship could be. Among its first members was a state senator and former FBI agent named Earl Evans. Two years after its founding, the commission hired Van Landingham to modernize its files and keep it up to speed on the latest investigative techniques. He modeled the commission's internal structures on what he had seen at the FBI, setting up a Bureau-style index card file to track civil rights activists and touring the state to deliver Hooveresque lectures on juvenile delinquency. The commission also established a lending library to promote approved conservative ideas and made *Masters of Deceit* one of the first books available.[3]

In his original vision, Hoover counted upon his former employees, like the academy graduates, to smooth the FBI's relationship with Southern law enforcement. He often came away disappointed. Take what had happened in Poplarville, Mississippi, in April 1959, when a Black man named Mack Charles Parker had been snatched from jail and murdered by a mob of white citizens. With the encouragement of both Eisenhower and the state's reform-minded governor, Hoover had sent some sixty agents into town to question residents and track the available evidence. Within weeks, they produced a 370-page report describing the lynching in detail and naming the men involved in the conspiracy.

The episode was nonetheless a disaster for Hoover—and a warning about the tenuous state of his relations with Southern law enforcement. From the moment agents arrived in town, the residents of Poplarville had complained about federal interference, accusing Hoover's men of "harassment" and "gestapo tactics." Local police were no friendlier. "We encountered open hostility from some officials in the Poplarville area," Hoover later acknowledged. In response, his former agents had tried to defend the Bureau. In a speech before a local civic group, Van Landingham insisted that the FBI's investigation helped to preserve rather than undermine the "total and complete segregation of the races in Mississippi" by showing that the system could right itself. Hugh Clegg backed him up by attempting to organize local ex-agents into a chapter of the Society of Former Special Agents, from which they could sing Hoover's praises. But the rest of Hoover's former employees around the state, men he had trained and indoctrinated, rejected that idea, and refused to speak out on the Bureau's behalf. Clegg felt their decision "showed weakness" and "a very wishy-washy attitude." He apologized to Hoover on their behalf.

Under the circumstances, Hoover was not surprised when the local prosecutor refused to consider the FBI's report or to allow FBI agents to testify in front of the grand jury. A federal grand jury, convened by the Justice Department but populated by local residents, rejected the attempt to find a federal statute that would make prosecution viable. Hoover was livid about the pointless effort and expense—$87,150 of taxpayer funds, all down the drain. He was furious, too, that federal power looked so impotent in the face of local resistance. "We were able to establish the identity of a number of members of the mob who participated in the abduction of Parker and obtained admissions from some of the participants," he noted in his appropriations testimony. Then "the Pearl River County grand jury met at Poplarville . . . and ignored the case."[4]

WHEN KENNEDY ARRIVED IN OFFICE, HOOVER INITIALLY ASSUMED THAT LITtle would change. Despite rumblings of party secession over the years, in 1960 the Solid South remained a bedrock of the Democratic coalition. Georgia and Louisiana had given Kennedy greater margins of victory than his home state of Massachusetts. Hoping for just this outcome, Kennedy had hedged on civil rights during the campaign. His boldest proclamation was the vow to eliminate discrimination in federally subsidized housing with "a stroke of the Presidential pen." Once in office, however, he moved slowly, failing to sign much of anything.[5]

The Freedom Ride was an attempt to force his hand. As civil rights leaders pointed out, major pillars of the Jim Crow system had long ago been declared unconstitutional. Little was being done, however, to translate those fine words into deeds. The *Brown* decision, now seven years old, had little to show for itself beyond partial school desegregation in willing cities such as Washington, D.C. Another troubling example could be found in interstate transportation, where the Supreme Court had ruled as early as 1946 that segregation violated the Constitution. In December 1960, during the interregnum between Kennedy's election and his assumption of office, it extended that ruling to bus stations and other transit facilities, declaring separate water fountains, lunch counters, restrooms, and seating areas unconstitutional as well. By the spring of 1961, however, the "Colored" and "White" signs were still hanging, and drivers were still forcing Black interstate passengers to the back of the bus. The Congress of Racial Equality (CORE), a small civil rights group based in New York and Washington, sought to challenge that situation, and to call attention to the Kennedy administration's lack of action.

Their Freedom Ride plan was brilliantly simple: leaving from Washington on May 4, an interracial group of men and women would ride south, with the goal of arriving in New Orleans on May 17 to mark the seventh anniversary of *Brown*. Along the way, they would test compliance with the Supreme Court decisions by sending "colored" passengers to use "white" restrooms and eat at "white" counters (and vice versa), and by seating themselves aboard the buses in violation of segregation ordinances. On paper, this was no more than an exercise of constitutional rights. But everyone understood that federal court decisions and Southern practices were two different things. The friction between them could be explosive.

The chief goal of the Freedom Ride was to insist that the federal government enforce its own laws, to make it impossible for John and Robert Kennedy—and, by extension, Hoover—to sit on the sidelines. A full two weeks before departing, CORE sent letters to the FBI, the Justice Department, and the White House outlining the Freedom Riders' itinerary and asking for federal protection. Receiving no reply, the group reached out again through journalist Simeon Booker, the FBI's longtime contact at *Jet* magazine, who planned to ride along with the activists and document their journey. On May 3, Booker met briefly with Bobby Kennedy, who said that CORE should let him know if they ran into any problems. Booker also spoke with at least one FBI official. On the night before their departure, he called FBI headquarters to say that the Freedom Ride was preparing to head out and that they were concerned about the prospect of violence.[6]

Had he been a different sort of man, Hoover might have decided to make a grand gesture: to offer FBI protection to the Freedom Riders, or at least to assure them that federal authorities would be working to keep them safe. Instead, he took the opportunity to articulate the limits of FBI involvement. FBI agents would gather intelligence, observe any conflicts, and conduct the needed investigations, he informed the attorney general, but they would not act as bodyguards, intervene to prevent violence, or interfere with the jurisdiction of local police. According to CORE director James Farmer, Hoover's approach included recruiting an informant among the riders—perhaps Booker, perhaps someone else. Other than that, the FBI mostly ignored the start of the Freedom Ride. So did the national press, the Justice Department, and the White House.[7]

The only hint of official acknowledgment came from Bobby Kennedy, who ventured south in early May to deliver a speech at the University of Georgia. The occasion for the speech was Law Day, recently established as a federal holiday to counterbalance the May Day long celebrated by communists and leftists. In that appearance, he affirmed the supremacy of Supreme Court decisions, "however much we might disagree with them." He also begged white Southerners to avoid acts of violence and lawbreaking, assuring them that the federal authorities meant business. "I say to you today that if the orders of the court are circumvented, the Department of Justice will act," he proclaimed. A week later, as their bus headed into Birmingham, Alabama, the Freedom Riders put that claim to the test.[8]

TO MOST AMERICANS, BIRMINGHAM WAS WELL KNOWN AS A HOTBED OF RACIAL violence—a city "fragmented by the emotional dynamite of racism, reinforced by the whip, the razor, the gun, the bomb, the torch, the club, the knife, the mob, the police and many branches of the state's apparatus," as one *New York Times* writer described it in 1960. To Hoover, it was infamous for a slightly different reason. Long before most other Southern law enforcement officials rose against the Bureau, Birmingham's public safety commissioner, Eugene "Bull" Connor, had rejected Hoover's leadership. A die-hard Southern segregationist unwilling to compromise with federal power, Connor was more than a policeman. He was one of Birmingham's chief power brokers and helped to call the shots around town. He was also widely known for his sympathy with the Ku Klux Klan, which often acted as an auxiliary arm of the Birmingham police.[9]

Connor had come to office in the 1930s as a Hoover-style reformer, promising to bring the latest science to a police culture dominated by handshakes and cronyism. As a young man, he had supported civil service rules and appealed to the FBI for help in establishing the city's first crime lab. Beginning in the 1940s, however, Connor had turned on Hoover, concerned with the rise in lynching investigations and the enforcement of civil rights. From that point on, he had refused to enroll Birmingham police officers at the FBI Academy, shipping them off instead to a Louisville, Kentucky, training school that specialized in "Southern" police techniques. By the late 1950s, with civil rights conflicts in full bloom, he had taken to openly denouncing the FBI as a tool of Northern liberals.

Connor was forced nonetheless to deal with Hoover's men, because in Birmingham, as elsewhere, former agents and academy graduates were an indelible part of the law enforcement landscape. When Connor took an unexpected four-year hiatus from office beginning in 1953, his replacement as public safety commissioner quietly started sending local officers back to the academy. One of those men was Jamie Moore, a "large, heavy-set, pleasant amiable southern gentleman," in the words of one Bureau report, appointed as Birmingham's chief of police by the new commissioner. FBI instructors had seen in Moore a way to crack the culture of resistance that Connor had introduced. "Moore can be expected to be a loyal supporter of the Bureau," they noted, the highest praise that could be afforded an academy graduate. When Connor returned to the commissioner's office in 1957, he was appalled to find a Hoover loyalist running the police department. "You don't fit into the picture as my chief of police," he informed Moore, and promptly launched a campaign to remove him from office. But Moore faced him down, holding on to the post while also winning election as the president of the Alabama chapter of the FBI National Academy Associates. As the Freedom Riders approached the city in the spring of 1961, he still held both positions.[10]

HOOVER KNEW THAT THERE MIGHT BE VIOLENCE IN BIRMINGHAM ONCE THE Freedom Riders arrived—not just because of the city's reputation, but because a key source had told him so. As early as April, before the activists left on their trip, the local FBI field office sent along rumblings of a plot being hatched between the local police and the Klan's outlaw vigilantes. The information came from a man named Gary Rowe, a former Marine turned Ku Klux Klan member and, as of 1960, a paid informant for the Bureau. Hoover put his hopes for the police in academy graduates like Moore, but he counted on men like Rowe to keep the FBI in the know about Klan activities.[11]

Hoover had set his sights on infiltrating the Klan as early as the 1940s. As with the lynching investigations, his initial efforts came to little in terms of prosecution or jail time. But they did produce some rudimentary lists and files, the start of a long-term inquiry. Hoover carried that inquiry into the massive resistance era, relying on the FBI's growing roster of secret intelligence-gathering techniques to enhance the Bureau's knowledge. Among his initiatives was a small-scale but ongoing effort to cultivate Klan informants. Some were "plants," recruited by agents to join the Klan on the FBI's behalf. Others were existing Klan members who proved willing, for one reason or another, to go on the Bureau payroll.[12]

Rowe fell somewhere in between. In 1960, the Klan's Eastview 13 Klavern in Birmingham had set its sights on recruiting him. As part of their due diligence, a local Klansmen had called the FBI to ask, oh so casually, if Rowe had any connection to the Bureau. Intrigued by the strange question, local agents had gone to Rowe themselves to ask if he might indeed be willing join the Klan—but on behalf of J. Edgar Hoover. To both sides, he seemed like a ready-made Klansman: "young, twenty-six, and strong," in one historian's description, "with a hair-trigger temper and a habit of solving problems with his fists." He also happened to be a "cop buff" with a history of idolizing law enforcement, an attitude that primed him to say yes to the Bureau's offer.

Hoover's instructions in recruiting informants like Rowe called for "a thorough, intensive background investigation and careful personal scrutiny" of all candidates. Rowe passed the Bureau's test, but his behavior since then showed just how fine the line between acceptable and unacceptable behavior could be. In the summer of 1960, he became his klavern's "Night-Hawk-in-Chief," charged with recruiting members and personally hoisting the burning cross. By fall, he had moved up to an "Action Squad" that carried out the group's most secretive and violent operations. Under those auspices, in April 1961 he had participated in an attack on an elderly white couple temporarily caring for a Black child. He also helped to plan the much more ambitious scheme aimed at the Freedom Riders, all while keeping the FBI in the loop.

As Rowe and his fellow Klansmen envisioned it, the attack on the Freedom Riders was supposed to play out in several distinct stages. On Sunday, May 14, when the Freedom Riders would be departing Atlanta and heading west into Alabama, a few Klansmen would buy tickets aboard the buses, posing as ordinary passengers. Once the vehicle or vehicles crossed the Alabama state border, those men would begin intimidating and attacking the activists. Then, when they reached the town of Anniston, about sixty-five miles east of Birmingham, a large crowd of supporters would be waiting to lend a hand. If either bus made it beyond Anniston, thirty more Klansmen would be on call at the Birmingham bus terminals to deliver the final blows.

Ordinarily, on learning of such a violent plot in the making, the FBI would contact the city police, expecting the local authorities to inform and protect everyone involved. But according to Rowe, the Birmingham police knew all about the scheme, and had agreed to play their part by delaying any intervention once the beatings began. Sergeant Thomas Cook, a Connor loyalist and the Klan's main point of contact with the police department, promised that the Klansmen could "beat 'em, bomb 'em, maim 'em, kill 'em" for a full fifteen minutes before worrying that the police would come in. Under the circumstances, Hoover tried to finesse the situation by turning to police chief Jamie Moore—"confident that Chief Moore, a graduate of the FBI Academy, would safeguard the Freedom Riders," in the words of Bull Connor's biographer.

Moore quickly betrayed Hoover's trust. On the night of Saturday, May 13, he called the local field office to say that he was leaving town, ostensibly to visit his mother for Mother's Day, when the Freedom Riders were due to arrive in Birmingham. He suggested that they communicate any future updates about the buses to Sergeant Cook, the very man (as both Moore and the FBI knew) who was helping to plan the attacks. Hoover still might have done something at this point: instructed his agents to protect the buses, warned the attorney general, even alerted the Freedom Riders themselves. But it was the weekend, he was not in the office, and there is no evidence that anyone thought he would want to take such action. Instead, with Moore out of the picture, local agents kept Cook up-to-date about the Freedom Riders' schedule, calling in when the buses left Atlanta for Birmingham. In effect, they helped to make sure that the Klan was ready once the Freedom Riders arrived.[13]

The attacks came off more or less as Rowe had predicted in his advance reports, a well-coordinated, multistage assault masquerading as spontaneous mob violence. The Greyhound bus ran into trouble first, just as it pulled into Anniston. Having caught wind of rumors describing a bloodbath in the offing, hundreds of townspeople lined the route, many still dressed in their Sunday best, to "welcome" the Freedom Riders into town. The bus station itself appeared to be locked and deserted until a whooping gang of Klansmen, armed with bats, pipes, and pistols, came rushing toward it. While they slashed the tires and pounded on the metal frame, the police were nowhere to be seen. Eventually a desultory band of officers showed up to escort the bus away, only to abandon it once again at the town line. A few miles outside Anniston, the bus rolled to a stop, disabled by its slashed tires, and became a sitting target for the carloads of Klansmen trailing behind. After several more minutes of jeering and taunting, someone threw a burning pile of rags into the bus through a broken window, sending black smoke swirling through the interior. A few minutes later, just after the passengers had fled the burning bus, the gas tank exploded. The confrontation finally ground to a halt when highway patrolmen showed up and fired warning shots into the air. They looked the other way as the Klansmen dispersed, failing to note any license plates or physical descriptions.

The second bus, from Trailways, showed up in Anniston an hour later to find a deserted station and no mention of what had taken place. Fatefully, the driver proceeded on to Birmingham, where the next phase of the plan was already underway. Several Klansmen had boarded this second bus back in Atlanta, posing as passengers. Before the bus pulled out of Anniston, they began to terrorize riders, pummeling their targets into unconsciousness and then hauling their bodies to the back of the bus. The greatest violence came in Birmingham itself, where several dozen Klansmen lay in wait. They allowed the passengers to exit the bus and enter the terminal before the assault began, a full fifteen minutes during which the unarmed passengers—including several innocent bystanders—were beaten, kicked, and punched, sometimes by half a dozen men at a time. When the fifteen minutes were up, the Birmingham police finally appeared to clear the station and enforce the law.

IF THE KLANSMEN HAD BEEN ABLE TO KEEP THEIR MOUTHS SHUT, THE WHOLE saga might have ended then and there, just another of the gruesome flare-ups that seemed to characterize the Southern struggle over segregation. But the plotters had boasted around town about what was going to happen, and so photographers and reporters were on site when the Trailways bus rolled in. Their ranks included Howard K. Smith, a national correspondent for CBS. That afternoon, Smith began to broadcast a string of national radio reports, describing how what appeared to be "spontaneous outbursts of anger" were actually "carefully planned and susceptible to having been easily prevented or stopped had there been a wish to do so." By the next morning, when Hoover returned to the office, the violence visited upon the Freedom Riders was front-page news. Even in Birmingham, the local paper ran a page-one photograph of the melee at the bus terminal: a circle of angry white men punching, kicking, and beating a hunched-over victim.[14]

One of those men was Gary Rowe, the Bureau's prize informant. "The Old Man's going to shit," Rowe's handler supposedly declared upon seeing the photograph, terrified at the prospect that Hoover would learn about Rowe's participation in the beating. The field office decided not to send that particular piece of news on to Washington. In the process, they preserved Rowe's reputation as "the most alert, intelligent, productive, and reliable informant on Klan and racial matters currently being operated by the Birmingham office," leaving Hoover none the wiser.[15]

Elsewhere, though, Hoover found plenty to worry about. On May 12, he had sent a message to the Justice Department "to the effect that 30 Klansmen were to be stationed at the Birmingham bus terminal on 5/14/61," with another thirty waiting in the wings if needed. Despite the detailed advance warning, neither the FBI nor the Justice Department made any effort to step in directly as the mobs assembled and the buses rolled along. Instead, when the appointed day came, FBI agents observed Hoover's carefully prescribed limits: they let the violence play out at the Birmingham bus station, insisting that it was up to the local police—whether Jamie Moore or Bull Connor or Thomas Cook—to contain the conflict. Only after the attacks were over did they mobilize to investigate, beginning with interrogations of the Anniston victims at the hospital. At that point the Justice Department jumped into action as well. Unlike Hoover, Bobby Kennedy would claim he "never knew [the Freedom Riders] were traveling down there . . . before the bus was burned in Anniston," implying that if he had only known, he surely would have done something. In truth, he just wasn't paying attention.[16]

But the crisis was not over yet—and the question of who, if anyone, would protect the riders soon became a major point of tension between Hoover and the attorney general. On Monday, May 15, after being treated at the hospital, the Freedom Riders returned to the Birmingham bus terminal, determined to move on to their next stop. They soon discovered that no bus driver would take them to Montgomery—indeed, that it was too dangerous even to wait out negotiations at the terminal, as a new crowd amassed outside. When they finally conceded the inevitable and headed for the airport, the situation was no better, with a restive mob assembling and bomb threats coming in.

At this point, the strategies of the FBI and the Justice Department began to diverge. They never quite came back together. Hoover wanted to stay out of it all, aside from conducting investigations after the fact. Bobby Kennedy saw a major problem looming for the White House and tried to head it off through cajoling and political pressure. From Washington, the Justice Department's John Seigenthaler made his way to Birmingham, huddling with the Freedom Riders at the airport as he tried to arrange an escort out. Hoover's men on the ground watched but did little. Despite the obvious issues, Hoover remained adamant about working through the local police department:

FBI agents would not serve as guards or soldiers for anyone, he insisted. He finally extracted a half-hearted promise from Jamie Moore that the police would protect the Freedom Riders from further assault, if they could. When Bobby asked how many agents the FBI had on the ground, Hoover refused to say—just enough, he maintained, to carry out the FBI's properly delimited duties. That night, with negotiations still underway, Hoover left the office at 6:09 p.m., more or less the usual time. Bobby stayed behind to help secure the Freedom Riders' safety.[17]

The airport standoff continued until 10:38 p.m., when the plane carrying the Freedom Riders finally took off from Birmingham. But even that did not bring the crisis to a close. Two days later, a group of students out of Nashville decided to carry on where their injured comrades had left off, arriving in Birmingham in hopes of continuing the previously scheduled journey. This next round of Freedom Riders made it only as far as Montgomery before another organized mob set upon them at the bus station. Following Birmingham's lead, the Montgomery police held back for several minutes before even attempting to intervene. It was enough time to inflict severe injuries on several Freedom Riders and bystanders. To celebrate their victory, the Montgomery rioters built a bonfire outside the bus station and burned the clothing, suitcases, and other personal items they had snatched from their victims. Hoover's agents watched and took notes as it happened.[18]

The next night things got still worse. Determined not to cower in the face of assault, more than a thousand Black residents gathered at Montgomery's First Baptist Church, one of the sites where the famed Montgomery bus boycott had been dreamed up and carried out five years earlier. The roster of speakers featured several of the injured Freedom Riders as well as leading figures from the local and national movements, who spoke not only about the power of nonviolence but also about the need for federal intervention. Even as they made their case, yet another mob was gathering outside, some two thousand white residents bearing torches, rocks, and chains, threatening to set the church ablaze and to attack anyone who tried to escape.

Hoover offered them little help. Desperate to stave off a full-blown riot, the Justice Department attempted to mobilize a makeshift band of federal "marshals"—mainly tax collectors and border agents—to contain the violence in Montgomery. But when Bobby asked the FBI for extra cars to help shuttle the marshals, Hoover said no, insisting that the FBI needed all its men and equipment. As the crisis accelerated, he avoided Bobby's calls and provided only half of the hundred agents requested to fill out the marshals' ranks. Only after receiving a message forwarded by the president himself did Hoover grudgingly throw in his lot with the rescue effort. That evening, after hours of delay, an agent arrived at Maxwell Air Force Base, where the marshals were amassing, to volunteer the FBI's services.[19]

Even the president's intervention induced no long-term change of heart, however. When the Freedom Rides picked up once again, Hoover refused to entertain the idea of an FBI escort for the buses as they moved through Alabama and into Mississippi. "As long as I am Director of this Bureau I do not intend to allow it to be misused by pressure groups," he informed Bobby, casting the bus riders not as innocent victims but as the people who had instigated the whole conflict.[20]

Coming on top of their personal differences and the tension over organized crime, the Freedom Rides episode confirmed what was already becoming clear in the Hoover-Kennedy relationship: Hoover would do what he wanted and no more. And yet in those areas where Hoover *was* willing to act—gathering intelligence and conducting investigations—he moved quickly and professionally. On May 20, he sent assistant director Al Rosen to Alabama to oversee an expanded investigation of the violence. He also transferred at least sixty-five agents into Montgomery to start working the case. The following day, the FBI renamed the investigation FREEBUS, a catchall title that swept up the attacks in Anniston, Birmingham, and Montgomery, plus the ongoing Freedom Rides still cruising into the South, into a single file. Less than twenty-four hours after that, Hoover was able to inform an exhausted Bobby that the FBI had arrested four Klansmen in the Anniston bus burning, with more soon to come.

For the Freedom Riders themselves, all the pain and risk ultimately yielded some measure of progress. Under pressure from the attorney general's office, the Interstate Commerce Commission banned segregation in interstate transit facilities, an overdue affirmation of the Supreme Court's decisions. By Hoover's standard, though, the entire Freedom Rides episode looked like just one more pointless loss. Throughout May, FBI agents continued to sweep through Alabama's big cities and small towns, gathering information and thoroughly spooking the Klan, which began to talk of the need to "go underground and meet in small groups in private homes," according to Rowe, just as the communists had once done. Agents also began looking for "any action by the police which might be indicative of a failure to afford protection to members of the freedom ride," in hopes that local law enforcement officials, including Jamie Moore, would be held responsible for their betrayal at the bus depots. By early June, the Bureau had expended some forty-eight hundred agent hours on the Anniston bus burning alone. Hoover later boasted that six men were convicted in that episode. But in Birmingham itself—just as in Georgia in 1946 and Poplarville in 1959—local juries refused to convict anyone for the bus station attacks.[21]

When it was all over, many observers—including the attorney general—viewed Hoover's efforts as too little too late, a cleanup inquiry undertaken only after he had failed to prevent repeated acts of violence. From Hoover's perspective, though, even this limited involvement came with real costs for the FBI's reputation. In early September, white supremacist leader J. B. Stoner held a rally in Anniston and hanged in effigy his five most hated people: Robert Kennedy, CORE leader James Farmer, two Alabama FBI agents, and Hoover himself. Stoner referred to the FBI as the Federal Bureau of Integration, a derisive but popular nickname in the white South.[22]

The name reflected a partial truth: compared to most local law enforcement, the FBI *was* the more progressive force, at least willing to investigate and hold Klansmen to account. But Hoover never wanted that particular badge of honor and did not deserve it. In response to the great moral challenge of the new decade, he fought to maintain limits rather than to push boundaries, to indulge his own prejudices rather than challenge them.

CHAPTER 42

Patron Saint of the Far Right

(1961–1962)

Hoover (center) with Senator Thomas Dodd (left), a former FBI agent, at the Freedoms Foundation at Valley Forge, February 1962. The Foundation was one of many conservative groups that revered Hoover in the 1960s.

NATIONAL ARCHIVES AND RECORDS ADMINISTRATION

In the spring of 1961, as the Freedom Riders were just beginning to flirt with the idea of a bus trip, *Time* magazine noted another form of activism taking hold across the land. This one came from the right—part of a "wave of conservatism," in the words of its standard-bearer, the iron-jawed Arizona senator Barry Goldwater, "that could easily become the phenomenon of our time." As *Time* described it, by 1961 the wave had spread from the secretive anticommunist cells of the John Birch Society to the mass meetings of Young Americans for Freedom, where thousands of white boys and girls gathered to demonstrate their opposition to liberalism, atheism, civil rights, and communism— and their support of the conservative values Hoover had long espoused. "Nobody knows for sure its present strength or its future potential," Goldwater declared during YAF's first rally in New York's Manhattan Center. "But every politician, newspaperman, analyst and civic leader knows that something is afoot that could drastically alter our course as a nation."[1]

Hoover was among those who realized that something was indeed afoot. Even as he struggled to address the challenges of civil rights, organized crime, and an all-too-casual attorney general, he was also watching the rise of the "New Right," a movement with ideas close to his heart but methods not always to his liking. The new conservatives revered Hoover as a "patron saint," in the words of one journalist, the most prominent federal appointee willing to speak out in favor of their values. Hoover did not view them with equal admiration. He never investigated the burgeoning New Right with the same fervor he applied to the left or the civil rights movement. Nor, however, did he let his conservative admirers off scot-free. Instead, he tried to have it both ways: to encourage the movement while warning against its conspiracies and excess.[2]

That approach had worked well during the McCarthy years, when Hoover positioned himself as the responsible anticommunist alternative to far-right demagogues and vigilantes. It had held during massive resistance as well, when he managed to both investigate and sympathize with the white South. But this was the 1960s, not the 1950s. He found it harder than ever to strike the right balance between his conservative outlook and his professional identity as a federal bureaucrat.[3]

HOOVER HAD A SOFT SPOT FOR THE CONSERVATIVE MOVEMENT'S ENFANT TERRIBLE, a Yale man and oil-fortune heir named William F. Buckley Jr. Despite a life of privilege, Buckley had grown up thinking of himself as a Hoover-style outsider: a Catholic within WASP society, a member of a proud conservative "remnant" surrounded by preening liberals. In 1951, fresh out of college, he published *God and Man at Yale*, a passionate indictment of the socialist ideas and collectivist mindset that supposedly infected his alma mater. Three years later, he followed up with a rousing book-length defense of McCarthy and McCarthyism. Like Hoover, Buckley saved his greatest ire not for communists, but for the eggheads, pinks, fellow travelers, and dupes who aided and abetted their cause. In 1955, expanding on these ideas, he founded *National Review*, a weekly magazine intended to give members of the emerging conservative movement a place to hash out their differences.

National Review was to Buckley what *Masters of Deceit* had been to Hoover: an effort to sound the alarm about the communist threat, and especially about the need to maintain vigilance in the wake of McCarthy's downfall. Buckley also adopted some of Hoover's have-it-both-ways attitude toward his fellow anticommunists and conservatives. A self-admitted elitist, Buckley aimed to make the right more modern and therefore more respectable, to jettison some of the embarrassing anti-Semitism and isolationism that had been so prominent before the war. He also aimed to separate his style of conservatism from the likes of the Ku Klux Klan, though there the line could be harder to draw. Buckley argued that the federal government had no right to mandate

school integration and that "the white community in the South" was justified in excluding Black voters "because, for the time being, it is the advanced race."[4]

Hoover admired Buckley's ability to promote conservative ideas while separating
himself from the most extreme elements within the growing right-wing surge. Buckley
in turn promoted Hoover as one of the few federal officials who seemed to understand
the urgency of what the conservative movement was doing. While a student at Yale in
1949, Buckley had invited Lou Nichols, Hoover's PR chief, to visit campus and defend
the FBI's record on civil liberties. The following year, in recognition of that assistance,
Nichols invited Buckley and his wife on a "special tour" of Bureau facilities in Washington. The FBI pulled out all the stops: an hour-and-forty-five-minute private escort
through the exhibit rooms, lab, communications center, and traffic diorama, culminating in the chance to shoot a tommy gun at the firing range. Along the way, Buckley
spoke of his admiration for Hoover's "ability to withstand political, subversive and
academic attacks." The highlight, of course, was meeting Hoover himself.[5]

In the years since, Buckley had maintained a loose but friendly relationship with
Hoover and the Bureau, meeting occasionally with Nichols and offering to send along
relevant writing for prepublication review. Conservative intellectuals could be a difficult audience for Hoover; they tended to dismiss his disquisitions on Sunday school and
juvenile delinquency as unsophisticated pandering. Through *National Review*, Buckley gave Hoover's ideas unstinting praise as well as a patina of intellectual respectability. The only notes of discord came from Hoover's position as a member of the vast
administrative state, seemingly at odds with the magazine's libertarian sensibility. Even
there, however, *National Review* tended to allow him the benefit of the doubt. "That
an organization with such inherently dangerous powers has functioned at all times
strictly within the limits of the Constitution is a triumph of the men who make up that
organization," editor Frank Meyer wrote of the FBI in 1957. With Buckley at the helm,
National Review depicted Hoover as Hoover liked to depict himself: as a federal bureaucrat who respected states' rights and the limits of his own power even while going
toe-to-toe with his ideological enemies.[6]

NATIONAL REVIEW REPRESENTED ONE SIDE OF THE NEW CONSERVATIVE ACTIV-
ism: intellectual, self-regarding, ambitious to be respectable and respected within elite
conversation. But there was another side to the movement, a sprawling set of grassroots
organizations that embraced Hoover's anticommunist message as their first principle.
Beginning in the late 1950s, hundreds of thousands of Americans had taken the anticommunist battle into their own hands, founding a network of civic groups, media
outlets, bookstores, philanthropic efforts, propaganda outlets, and publishers dedicated
to "educating" the American public about the ongoing threat. By all appearances, this
was just what Hoover had asked for in *Masters of Deceit*—a bona fide "conservative

revival," in the words of one historian, with the communist question front and center. But Hoover viewed their arrival as at best a mixed blessing.[7]

The grassroots right treated *Masters of Deceit* as a foundational text, one of the few books that every movement member was expected to read and digest. As early as 1958, the budding Midwestern activist Phyllis Schlafly put *Masters of Deceit* at the top of her Reading List for Americans, a compilation of favored anticommunist and free-market treatises. The John Birch Society similarly included *Masters of Deceit* on its list of "approved books," alongside founder Robert Welch's *The Life of John Birch* and Buckley's *McCarthy and His Enemies*. Other Hoover acolytes took more direct action, not just recommending his book, but purchasing it in bulk to be distributed as an essential guide for fellow citizens. In Miami, a local exterminator spent his own money to paint ads for the book on benches at city bus stops. "Learn How to fight Communism! Read: Masters of Deceit," the copy instructed, accompanied by a cartoon of Fidel Castro on his knees. In 1961, the American Legion helped to sponsor Operation Alert, an effort to put the book into the hands of high school students with the goal of "disseminating maximum authentic information on the nature and methods of the communist threat."[8]

What they all appreciated about *Masters of Deceit* was not simply its anticommunist message. Hoover's book also brought the movement a certain gravitas, the reassurance that even the most paranoid anticommunist need not be relegated, as liberals often suggested, to the "lunatic fringe." When Hoover spoke about communism, his admirers assumed that he was drawing upon his store of expert knowledge, acquired over almost four decades at the helm of the Bureau. He exercised a public authority almost unheard of among far-right heroes. "You, I feel, are the only one that can tell me what I would like to know," one self-proclaimed "housewife" from Tyler, Texas, wrote to Hoover in 1961, pleading for information about how to be "a patriotic American and inform myself as a good citizen should." Hoover received similar letters from many other conservative admirers, wondering what they should do to fight communism and which organizations they should join.[9]

There was a certain irony in their lionizing of Hoover, because—like the writers of *National Review*—most of the new conservatives purported to oppose concentrations of federal power, especially in areas such as civil rights and social welfare. But Hoover managed to be the exception to the rule, the great far-right hero within the federal bureaucracy. "Give us presidents like Barry Goldwater, vice presidents like J. Edgar Hoover," one enthusiast wrote to a Shreveport paper in 1960, nursing the dream that Hoover might run for electoral office as a conservative. In Texas, the state chapter of the Constitution Party (soon renamed the Conservative Party) went so far as to nominate Hoover as its presidential candidate, an honor he politely but firmly declined.[10]

When Hoover came under attack, the movement's columnists, publishers, and activists proved to be stalwart defenders, willing to hurl invective and accusation that might have been unbecoming from a federal servant himself. According to an essay in the John Birch Society's *American Opinion* magazine, everyone understood that Hoover's position within the government prevented him from saying what he truly felt and thought. "He has to consider the continuing effectiveness of his Federal Bureau of Investigation," the magazine explained, "one of the few remaining strong bulwarks against the Communist advance in this country." In this view, it was up to the movement to defend the FBI against its attackers and to say what Hoover could not—even when Hoover himself hinted that they might be better off keeping quiet.[11]

OF ALL THE GROUPS INVOLVED IN THE NEW RIGHT SURGE, ONE HELD SPECIAL significance for Hoover. It was composed of his own former agents, men who had once worked at the Bureau and then left to carry his cause into the private marketplace. The trend had started during the McCarthy years, when dozens of entrepreneurial agents departed for jobs as investigators and lecturers on communism. Since then, it had accelerated in dramatic fashion. At almost any gathering sponsored by one of the new right-wing groups, former Bureau men were sure to be on the roster, warning darkly about subversion. Most of them no longer worked in law enforcement, opting for roles as radio and television hosts, columnists and writers, fixtures on the right-wing lecture circuit. They still made use of what Hoover had taught them—not just in anticommunist intelligence, but in the arts of public speaking and propaganda. Through his former agents, Hoover not only witnessed the new conservative movement; he helped to produce it.

The most important of these ex-agents was Dan Smoot, a Crime Records veteran who parlayed his Bureau training into a pioneering role in right-wing media. Born to an impoverished Missouri family, Smoot had joined the FBI during the war. In 1947, he transferred to Crime Records, where he spent several years learning to anticipate "what Mr. Hoover would probably say" in the form of press releases and proxy speeches. In the early 1950s, Smoot took those skills to H. L. Hunt, a Texas oilman who was seeking to create a new network of right-leaning press, radio, and television ventures, many of them staffed by former FBI men. Hunt offered Smoot a job hosting *Facts Forum*, a radio and television show that purported to present both the left and right sides of major political issues. Smoot soon departed in order to give "only one side—the side that uses fundamental American principles." By the early 1960s, he had built his own small radio, television, and print empire and turned himself into one of the New Right's first media darlings.[12]

If Smoot emerged as the most prominent member of his cohort, it was not for lack of competition. From Utah, former agent W. Cleon Skousen published *The Naked Communist*, a 1958 treatise often paired with Hoover's *Masters of Deceit* on conservative reading lists. Herbert Philbrick, Hoover's star witness at the Smith Act trials, followed up the success of his television show, *I Led Three Lives*, with a prolific writing and speaking schedule. Married FBI "counterspies" Paul and Marion Miller made their own bid for fame with the 1960 publication of Marion's memoir, *I Was a Spy: The Story of a Brave Housewife*. Even in Congress, former agents stood out as some of the most outspoken apostles of the new conservatism. In 1957, ex-agent H. Allen Smith won election to Congress as a Republican from southern California. Two years later, Samuel Devine, a wartime agent and former head of the Ohio Un-American Activities Committee, followed suit as a congressman from "conservative Columbus," in the words of one local observer. Together with former agent turned senator Thomas J. Dodd, they staked out positions far to the right of the congressional mainstream, echoing what they had learned from Hoover.[13]

All these former employees—whether in Congress or on the far-right lecture circuit—made use of the public speaking and research skills acquired at the Bureau. They also took advantage of what was perhaps Hoover's single greatest gift to his former agents: the credibility that came with the FBI name. "For three and a half years while an FBI agent, I worked exclusively on communist investigations," Smoot boasted in one of his early newsletters. "I followed commie leaders around, night and day, studied their speeches, kibitzed on their secret meetings, read their stupid literature." Skousen openly identified himself as one of Hoover's "special administrative assistants," a claim that somewhat exaggerated his work at the Bureau but was proudly repeated in articles promoting his books and lectures. Congressman Devine reminisced about his years of working under Hoover and encouraged fellow Ohioans to celebrate May 10, 1961, as J. Edgar Hoover Day, officially designated by the governor. Congressman Smith sang Hoover's praises from the floor of Congress.[14]

Hoover initially appreciated the flattery. When Skousen sent along a signed copy of *The Naked Communist*, Hoover approved a letter of thanks. With Philbrick his office kept up a regular, friendly correspondence, trading tips and gossip. About Smoot he was less enthusiastic but willing to tolerate a certain amount of agitation. "Smoot's remarks in his lectures and the tenor of many of the articles in his publication smack of right-wing arch-conservatism," a 1958 FBI memo noted, recommending that the Bureau be careful in its dealings with him but not cut off ties altogether.[15]

HOOVER'S ATTITUDE BEGAN TO CHANGE IN THE SPRING OF 1961, WHEN THE White House and the media started to notice what was happening—and did not like what they saw. The *Time* issue released in March 1961 marked one moment of public discovery, the dawning realization that the far right was gaining ground fast. *Time* focused on the John Birch Society as a paranoid, conspiratorial club, tracing how secret Bircher "cells" operated under the "hard-boiled, dictatorial direction" of founder Robert Welch. The magazine also laid out the more outlandish aspects of Welch's worldview, including his desire to impeach Supreme Court justice Earl Warren and his suggestion that Dwight Eisenhower's brother Milton had been running the country for years as Ike's "superior and boss within the Communist Party." A few days later, two senators rose on the floor of Congress to denounce the Birch Society as a dangerous force, a symptom of all that was going wrong in an overwrought, overheated nation. One was a conservative Republican, the other a liberal Democrat, moved to speak by a shared conviction that Eisenhower was *not*, in fact, a secret communist. Their comments marked the beginning of a national controversy over the "ultra-conservative, semi-secret" Birch Society and the New Right movement of which it was a part.[16]

On another issue with such bipartisan consensus, Hoover might have sided with the senators. But this was no ordinary issue. The John Birch Society was already linked to the FBI—through the activities of former agents and informants, through their admiration for *Masters of Deceit*, and especially through their faith that Hoover would serve as their guiding light. In the days after the Senate speeches, Welch wrote to Hoover several times, asking that the FBI stand up for the Birch Society as a respectable patriotic force. "The whole question, as to whether America survives against the distraction and enslavement planned for it by the Communists," Welch explained, "depends on how well and how firmly the anti-Communists stand together."[17]

Far from plunging into the debate on the Birchers' behalf, Hoover initially hoped to ignore the matter, gambling that whatever might be required of the Bureau could be accomplished discreetly, behind the scenes. On March 14, a few days after the Senate speeches, he instructed all field offices to steer clear of the Birch Society and withhold Bureau publications from its members "in view of this irresponsible organization's attempt to capitalize on the FBI's prestige," in the words of an FBI memo. He extended a similar dictum to the Christian Anti-Communism Crusade, which sponsored daylong and sometimes weeklong mass meetings featuring lectures on "The Communist Program of Conquest" and "Communist Fronts and Captive Organizations," among other topics. Reacting to the growing concern in Washington and the national media, Hoover concluded that the dangers of association with such groups would outweigh any benefits. "We must stick to no comment to all inquiries," he wrote to Bureau officials, and "not be drawn into this brawl."[18]

His one public statement on the matter that spring came in the form of a tepid message in the April 1961 *Law Enforcement Bulletin*, still his favorite platform from which to issue a controlled political communication. The "Director's Note" opened with a statement that any Bircher might have embraced: "America, historically an impregnable fortress against tyranny, is engaged in a mortal struggle with world communism." But the rest of the essay revived Hoover's old warnings about the dangers of "vigilante" behavior, now updated to engage in the debate over the ultraright. "Attributing every adversity to communism is not only irrational, but contributes to hysteria and fosters groundless fears," he declared, calling for citizens to embrace "thoughtful, reliable, and authoritative sources of information" rather than conspiracy theories. He hoped that, among other benefits, the statement might please the Kennedy administration. "I specifically pointed out the need for an objective and dispassionate approach in fighting the communist menace," he pointed out to Bobby. "I felt this step was necessary because of the rash of vigilante-type individuals and organizations springing up throughout the country."[19]

And for a while, it seemed as if that might settle the matter, as if Hoover might get his wish for the whole issue simply to die away. At the end of April, national attention shifted to the Bay of Pigs, then on to the Freedom Rides. During the summer, though, the uproar about the New Right returned—and with it Hoover's dilemma. In June, President Kennedy traveled to Vienna to meet with Khrushchev, fueling a surge of apocalyptic worries in Birch Society circles. Later that month, the Supreme Court upheld a law requiring the Communist Party to register with the federal government, an unexpected coup seized upon by Birchers and others to call for a new Red Scare. Kennedy raised his own alarm in a speech on July 25, assailing Khrushchev for Soviet aggression in Berlin, "the great testing place of Western courage." A few weeks after that, the East German government raised the stakes even higher by starting construction on the Berlin Wall.[20]

Hoover and Tolson left for La Jolla just after Kennedy's speech. But California was hardly the place to get away from the New Right debate. When they had begun their annual pilgrimage a decade earlier, La Jolla had seemed like a true retreat, comfortably distant from Red Hollywood. Since then, the defense industry had filled in the gaps, planting look-alike suburbs all along the southern coast to house a boom generation of Cold War workers. With this new landscape had come a right-wing movement far more energetic and committed than could be found in the rest of the nation. Southern California, especially, was its epicenter.[21]

Arguably the most controversial player there was not Welch but Fred Schwarz, the odd little Australian doctor who founded the Christian Anti-Communism Crusade. When Schwarz launched his first "anticommunism school" in Orange County in March 1961, the local government excused seven thousand children from class so that they could attend the event. Since then, he had expanded into a series of mass gatherings throughout the state, each one seemingly bigger than the last. As Hoover and Tolson arrived for their vacation in late July, local papers featured glowing accounts of ex-agent Cleon Skousen's recent speech before an "overflow crowd" in Santa Monica, calling for a "rising ground swell in America against communism" and possible withdrawal from the United Nations. Up in Sacramento, the alarmed attorney general of California was preparing to release a long-awaited report on the secret agendas and activities of the Birch Society.[22]

Hoover paid close attention. "I am very much concerned about some of these people like Schwartz [sic], the Birch Society etc.," he confided to Nixon's secretary, warning that his old friend should not get mixed up "with these wild-eyed people of the right" if he decided to run for governor of California. As Hoover discovered, how-ever, it was not so easy to draw a hard and fast line between the "wild-eyed people" and those whose support one might solicit. Even as Hoover spent his days lounging by the pool and taking in the races at Del Mar, his former agents continued to burn up the Southern California countryside with lectures on "How the West Can Win" and why "all American government foreign aid is immoral." Their efforts peaked just after Hoover and Tolson returned to Washington, when Schwarz staged a four-day rally at the Los Angeles Memorial Sports Arena, broadcast live on television throughout Southern California. "See and hear for yourself the true nature of the Communist menace to our country," said the ads. Some forty-five hundred people responded, returning to the stadium night after night. On three of those four evenings, the headline speakers were former agents or FBI informants—Dodd, Skousen, and Philbrick.[23]

Hoover returned from California determined to create some distance from these onetime protégés, lest the controversy over their activities redound to the FBI's disad-vantage. In early September, Tolson ordered Smoot, Skousen, and Schwarz removed from the Bureau's mailing lists and banned them from receiving Bureau publications. Crime Records also appears to have reached out to syndicated columnist George So-kolsky, always ready to aid the Bureau in print. A few days after Hoover's return from California, Sokolsky published a column scoffing at the pretensions of the former FBI agents who claimed to know so much about communism and its attendant ills. "I have learned that a former FBI agent is generally just former," he wrote. "Employment by the FBI is not a permanent badge of efficiency, knowledge or responsibility." Though he did not name names, there was no mistaking *which* agents he viewed as cause for concern. "The reason I emphasize this point is that there is an upsurge of conservatism in this country and there are many opportunists who jump on the conservative bandwagon and who claim special knowledge and special advantages," Sokolsky wrote. He pre-dicted a hard road ahead for those who failed to distinguish between the charlatans who claimed the mantle of the FBI and the true anticommunist experts at the FBI itself.[24]

THROUGHOUT MOST OF 1961, PRESIDENT KENNEDY REMAINED SILENT ON THE Birch Society question. In October, he changed his mind. The precipitating event was a five-night Schwarz-sponsored "Town Meeting on Americanism" in Glendale, Cali-fornia, featuring lectures by Skousen and the Miller informant duo along with a roster of other Hoover-friendly celebrities. On November 18, the day after the meeting con-cluded, Kennedy showed up in Los Angeles, scheduled to speak before a hundred-dollar-a-plate dinner at the Hollywood Palladium. From the stage where Lawrence Welk usually performed his soft-shoe anthems, Kennedy delivered an explicit warning that "discordant voices of extremism"—"those on the fringes of our society"—now posed a serious threat to the nation's internal cohesion. "At times these fanatics have achieved a temporary success among those who lack the will or the wisdom to face unpleasant facts or unsolved problems," he declared. Sometimes, they even appeared to be patriotic, men and women acutely sensitive to the "strains and frustration" of the Cold War. Luckily, Kennedy explained, there was an easy way to identify those who had crossed over from concern into fanaticism: they were the ones who primarily worried about domestic communism, "convinced that the real danger is from within. . . . You and I and most Americans, soldiers and civilians, take a different view of our peril," he assured his audience. "We know that it comes from without, not within."[25]

Kennedy did not mention Hoover by name. But the ties between the FBI and the New Right did not go unnoticed within the administration and its liberal allies. Not long after Kennedy's speech, United Auto Workers president Walter Reuther composed a lengthy memo on "The Radical Right in America Today," citing the John Birch Society, Schwarz's crusade, and Hunt's Life Line as dangers to American unity. The memo noted how Hoover's anticommunist language seemed to encourage their followers. He "exaggerates the domestic Communist menace at every turn and thus contributes to the public's frame of mind upon which the radical right feeds," Reuther complained. What was needed now was an effort "to rein in" men like Hoover, "who have created the unreasoned fear of the domestic Communist movement in the minds of the American people."[26]

Hoover did not find out about Reuther's memo until 1963, when journalists Donald Janson and Bernard Eismann published *The Far Right*, a wide-ranging exposé that identified Smoot, Skousen, and Philbrick "among those promoting extremism," in the words of an FBI summary. Hoover did not have to be privy to the strategies of the Kennedy White House, however, to see that he could not sit on the sidelines forever. Just weeks after Kennedy's speech he decided to offer a rejoinder, his first substantive public statement about the controversy that had been roiling the country for months. Like Kennedy, he chose a venue that would demonstrate his political influence and provide a room full of supporters to applaud his message. In Hoover's case, this meant a gala dinner sponsored by the Mutual of Omaha insurance company, which had selected him to receive its 1961 Criss Award for outstanding public service. The award came with ten thousand dollars, a gold medal, and a lavish dinner for some two hundred handpicked guests at the Mayflower Hotel. To join him for the occasion, Hoover selected a roster of men who reflected his deepest and oldest relationships, beginning with Tolson. He also invited several allies within the right-wing media pantheon, including Sokolsky, Hearst publisher Richard Berlin, and columnist Fulton Lewis Jr.[27]

With this friendly audience as a backdrop, Hoover delivered one of the most remarkable speeches of his career, a blistering polemic at once achingly self-righteous and carefully calculated, an act of official defiance and mollification all at once. Rather than capitulate to Kennedy's assessment of domestic communism, Hoover doubled down on the message that had so endeared him to the likes of the Birch Society and the Anti-

Communism Crusade. "We are at war with the communists and the sooner every red-blooded American realizes this the safer we will be," he declared. "Fear, apologies, defeatism and cowardice are alien to the thinking of true Americans! As for me, I would rather be DEAD than RED!" At the same time, he gave liberals—and the president himself—something to hold on to. After whipping up the crowd's sense of embattlement, he concluded by urging that Americans "not be taken in by those who promote hysteria . . . , whether they be the proponents of chauvinism of the extreme right or the pseudo liberalism of the extreme left."[28]

The speech made a sensation in the press, where reporters could choose whichever side of that equation they happened to prefer. His old *New York Post* critic James Wechsler shook his head at the sheer audacity of Hoover's attempt to have it both ways. "The ceremonies again dramatized Mr. Hoover's ability to remain a 'non-controversial' figure, perennially advanced as the Presidential nominee of the extreme right wing even as he retains the plaudits of some sections of the liberal community," Wechsler wrote. Noting that the remarks would "assure the rabid rightists that his heart belongs to them," the columnist observed that Hoover had also managed to placate liberals, signaling to them that his heart was with the government and its traditions of responsible expertise. All in all, Wechsler concluded, it was a bravura performance by a master of the political arts: "Let it never be said that he doesn't know what he's doing." But even Hoover could not sustain the balance forever.[29]

AFTER THE CRISS AWARD, HOOVER CONTINUED TO CRITICIZE THE BIRCH SOCIety and other so-called extremists, if often in an oblique manner. That February, in a speech before the conservative Freedoms Foundation at Valley Forge, in Pennsylvania, he stepped up his attack on not only the "pseudo-liberals of the extreme left" but also the "pseudo-patriots of the extreme right." Kennedy accepted such words as the best he was likely to get from Hoover. "As a vigilant, experienced American, who has real credentials as a Communist fighter—J. Edgar Hoover—has said, such actions play into communist hands and hinder, rather than aid, the fight against communism," the president explained. Amazingly, Hoover's approach also earned him plaudits on the other side of the political spectrum. As the Birch Society controversy reached its peak in early 1962, Barry Goldwater himself reached out to Hoover for "guidance" on how to manage the ocean of inquiries flooding his office. Beyond Washington, self-styled "respectable" conservatives such as Buckley soon began to echo Hoover's stance. In February, in one of the most debated episodes of Buckley's career, *National Review* reluctantly distanced itself from Welch in terms similar to Hoover's Criss speech, warning that the Birch Society founder would hinder rather than help the conservative cause. Later that month, William Randolph Hearst Jr. weighed in. "For America's sake I hope all sincere anti-Communists get out of such outfits as the Birchers," he wrote. Instead, he urged Americans to follow Hoover, "who as head of the FBI really knows what he is talking about."[30]

Hoover's domestic intelligence chief, William Sullivan, later marveled at his boss's balancing act. "If a liberal came in, the liberal would leave thinking that, 'My God, Hoover is a real liberal!' If a John Bircher came in an hour later, he'd go out saying, 'I'm convinced that Hoover is a member of the John Birch Society at heart.'" To say that Hoover could manage both constituencies, however, is not to say that he escaped the Birch Society controversy entirely unscathed. Sokolsky noted how painful the split was within the conservative movement. "Many of my old friends feel that I have deserted them," he wrote in a February column. Hoover, too, experienced a backlash from the Birchers and other far-right admirers, the loss of their previously unshakable faith in his righteousness. He received many bewildered letters, signed by one or another "disillusioned FBI admirer," pointing out that "even an implied repudiation from a man of your stature carries with it tremendous weight." Hoover's former employees took the repudiation particularly hard. "For God's sake, George, why are you attacking your friends?" Philbrick demanded of Sokolsky in early March.[31]

By that point, though, the split was done. One historian has defined the moment as a division between "responsible" and "extremist" conservatives—two different but related political cultures existing side by side. With his tepid criticism of the Birchers, Hoover put himself in the first camp, a passionate but "responsible" conservative within a liberal Democratic administration, at once the great national figurehead of anticommunism and a man who could be counted upon to draw a line between the experts and the masses.[32]

Even as the Kennedys grudgingly took what they could get from Hoover, it was increasingly the "responsible right" that would embrace him, providing him with social and ideological ballast that would define his political community for the next decade. And yet in critical ways Hoover remained distinct from men like Buckley and Sokolsky and Goldwater, icons of so-called responsible conservatism. They were provocateurs and politicians, interested in shifting public debate. Hoover exercised real state power, a fact that made him both valuable and potentially dangerous to the conservative cause. In all the discussion of "pseudo-liberals" and "pseudo-conservatives," of "extremists" and "responsible" moderates, there was little mention of what the FBI was actually doing with its accumulated power. If Hoover had been serious about constraining the New Right, he would have targeted groups such as the John Birch Society in the ways he had once gone after the Communist Party. Instead, his focus remained more or less where it had always been. Like the Birchers, Hoover remained focused on battling communism above all other priorities.

CHAPTER 43

In Friendship

(1961–1962)

Since He's Been Wearing Those Rose-colored Glasses Everything Looks Red To Edgar!

Hoover accused many civil rights organizations and activists, including the Rev. Dr. Martin Luther King Jr., of harboring communist ties. He used that claim to justify widespread surveillance and disruption. Cartoon is from the *Baltimore Afro-American*.

COURTESY OF THE AFRO AMERICAN NEWSPAPERS ARCHIVES

On the morning after the siege of Freedom Ride supporters inside the Montgomery church, Hoover asked for a background memo on one of the Black ministers trapped inside. The man was a "prominent integrationist," agents reported back, a leader of the Montgomery bus boycott in the mid-1950s and a pioneer in the techniques of nonviolent direct action that had become increasingly popular ever since. He maintained a few vaguely communist connections; he once thanked the Socialist Workers Party for supporting the bus boycott and had been known to attend meetings with communist-friendly progressives. But as far as the reporting agent could tell, the Rev. Dr. Martin Luther King Jr. had "not been investigated by the FBI" in any serious way. "Why not?" Hoover asked, two hastily scrawled syllables that would soon set off one of the most expansive and controversial investigations in FBI history.[1]

There is something absurd about the idea that Hoover had barely heard of King in 1961. It had been more than five years since King came to national attention during the Montgomery bus boycott, when at the age of twenty-six he stepped forward as the campaign's public face and chief strategist. The son of a prominent Atlanta minister, King had been as surprised as anyone to find himself cast in that position. His early ambitions had been far more conventional: college, divinity school, then a Ph.D. at Boston University, all in hopes of carrying on his father's ministerial legacy. But when history intervened, King rose to meet the moment. Timing and circumstance happened to intersect particularly well with his talents, as they did for Hoover a generation earlier.

Since the boycott, King's name had appeared several times in Bureau files. When he helped to organize a prayer pilgrimage at the Lincoln Memorial in 1957, Bureau reports noted his presence and apparent interest in school desegregation. After he was stabbed the following year during a book tour in Harlem, agents noted that the communist leader Ben Davis volunteered to donate blood. As recently as February 1961, Crime Records had analyzed an essay that King wrote for *The Nation* magazine, concluding that King was "in error" when he referred to the FBI as a segregated institution but that "he obviously would only welcome any controversy or resulting publicity." Hoover felt the FBI should not play into King's hands by delivering a public response.[2]

If his "Why not?" notation a few months later did not reflect a total absence of information about King, it did say something important about Hoover's priorities: before the summer of 1961, King as an individual did not much matter at the Bureau. Until the Freedom Rides, Hoover had shown little appetite for learning the fine points of King's history or knowing much about the movement's emerging generation of leaders. The Kennedys initially gave him little reason to change. In the weeks after the Freedom Rides, the Justice Department held a few inconclusive meetings with civil rights leaders, promising support for voter registration in exchange for a deescalation of sit-ins and bus rides. Mostly, though, they simply moved on to Cold War crises like the Vienna summit and the construction of the Berlin Wall.

Hoover's lack of interest largely held over the next several months. Rather than learn much about King himself, Hoover quickly came to focus on two advisers close to King, both of whom maintained ties with the Communist Party. Many historians have depicted Hoover's approach as Cold War opportunism, in which he imposed a tried-and-true anticommunist framework onto an exciting young movement. With little to go on besides his own biases and paranoia, this story suggests, Hoover seized upon the defunct communist affiliations of a few mid-level advisers to justify an extended campaign of vilification and harassment. FBI documents suggest that the story is not quite so simple. Hoover approached the King investigation with his prejudices intact, including the racism that often made him see calls for justice as a threat to national security. But he did not need to go out of his way, or dig deep into the recesses of a paranoid psychology, to come up with a link between King and communism. As FBI files show, King was indeed working closely with two men, Stanley Levison and Jack O'Dell, who were connected, both present and past, to the Communist Party's clandestine apparatus. In Cold War Washington, Hoover was not the only one who found that news alarming.[3]

———

IT TOOK NO GREAT LEAP OF THE IMAGINATION TO THINK THE COMMUNIST
Party and the new generation of civil rights activists might somehow be linked. Since
the 1930s, communists had been denouncing Jim Crow as a system of class oppression
and white America as an agent of racist imperialism. So it made sense that some of the
men and women now involved in the civil rights surge might have a touch of red in
their pasts. Certainly this was true of several men in King's inner circle, who had been
youthful converts to communism before concluding that the party's rigidity (along
with the threat of government suppression) made the communists a moribund vehicle
for transforming Black life. Wyatt Tee Walker, executive director of King's Southern
Christian Leadership Conference, had cut his teeth in the Young Communist League
during the 1940s. So had Bayard Rustin, the penetrating organizer who had counseled
King through the Montgomery bus boycott and emerged as one of the movement's
most influential nonviolent strategists. (Rustin also happened to be gay, a matter that
attracted the FBI's attention and created tensions within King's group of Christian
ministers.)[4]

Hoover built files on all these men, convinced that their youthful communism made
their loyalty forever suspect. But the figure who truly alarmed him in 1961, as the
Bureau began to investigate King, presented a different issue altogether. A white New
York businessman and liberal activist, Stanley Levison did not openly acknowledge
party membership, in the past or in the present, or even admit a serious interest in
communism. But according to Morris and Jack Childs, the trusted and well-protected
informants of SOLO, Levison had long been one of the party's most important secret
fundraisers and financiers, as well as an active participant in its underground apparatus. In the early 1960s, when the Bureau realized that Levison was one of King's
advisers, Hoover was surprised to learn that Levison was still working with the party.
Hoover did not pause to consider that the situation might be relatively benign: that
Levison might feel torn between old loyalties and new opportunities to support the
cause of racial justice. Instead, he worried about a possible Soviet connection. He had
seen stranger things turn out to be true: Julius Rosenberg really *was* an atomic spy, and
Kim Philby, one of the highest officials in British intelligence, really *had* colluded with
the Soviets for decades. The implications of the Levison story seemed almost as explosive: at a moment of peak Cold War tension, the Soviet Union might be whispering in
the ear of one of the civil rights movement's emerging leaders.[5]

Jack Childs had alerted the Bureau to Levison's communist ties as early as 1952,
when the party leadership was facing stiff jail sentences under the Smith Act. According to Jack's initial debriefing, that year Levison was serving secretly as a Communist
Party fundraiser, courier, and underground facilitator, a vital link in the party's clan-

destine financial network. The Bureau had barely heard of Levison in 1952 despite its intensive investigation of the party, but there appeared to be an easy explanation for that fact. According to Jack, Levison's work was so covert that only a handful of high-ranking party insiders knew any of the details. Based on this tip, Hoover began to seek out more information.[6]

What he found was not especially alarming, at least on the surface. To the outside world, Levison appeared to be a supremely ordinary figure: a middle-aged Jewish businessman with a slight paunch and a pair of horn-rimmed glasses—"nothing outstanding," in the words of an early Bureau report. Born and raised in New York, he appeared to have flirted with radical causes in his youth before settling into a conventional bourgeois life. By the 1950s, he lived on the Upper West Side with his wife and son. He spent most of his time tending to various small businesses, including a Ford dealership in New Jersey and a laundry in Ecuador. He had a twin brother named Roy, who co-owned several of the businesses. He held a law degree from St. John's University that he rarely used. When he was not tending to work and family, Levison devoted his time to liberal politics as New York treasurer for the American Jewish Congress, planning rallies on behalf of the Rosenbergs and against the likes of Joe McCarthy.[7]

According to Jack's account, however, there was another side to Levison—one that was rarely shown to anyone outside the innermost circle of the Communist Party. While supposedly living a bourgeois existence, Levison began participating in the Communist Party's secret apparatus, using his outward respectability to provide cover for clandestine financial transactions. Beginning in the late 1940s he solicited money from wealthy contacts, ran side businesses on the CP's behalf, and donated tens of thousands of dollars to CP coffers. Jack knew all this because he worked directly with Levison as a point man for the party's "reserve fund," a secret stash of money designated for bail and other emergency expenses. Levison ran the so-called Wall Street Group, an assemblage of heiresses, bankers, and other bourgeois types willing to contribute money and expertise. By Jack's estimate, during the mid-1940s Levison and his brother, Roy, donated at least ten thousand dollars per year to the party and helped to solicit thousands more from anonymous party "angels."[8]

Jack's own brother, Morris, bore out these claims. When Morris decided to rejoin the party at the FBI's behest in 1952, it was Levison who showed up in Chicago as an emissary from the CP leadership, assigned to vet Morris's reliability and motivations. And when Morris made his first trip to New York in order to recontact old party friends, it was Levison who escorted him to a safe-house apartment and then to the private homes of party leaders. Levison schooled Morris in clandestine technique, instructing him to rely exclusively on public transportation and to take roundabout routes to any party engagement. He also built elaborate ownership structures for CP businesses, often serving as the front man and owner in name. FBI files emphasized that Levison's activities were "intended as a fund raising enterprise for the party and not, to Informant's knowledge, for espionage purposes" or for the "smuggling of atomic bombs." This did not do much to reassure Hoover. In 1953, a year after Jack's initial revelations, the New York field office added Levison's name to the Security Index, convinced of his importance "in both open Communist Party activity and the Communist Party underground apparatus."[9]

In the meantime, Hoover sought confirmation of Levison's CP activities from other sources. In March 1954, a full seven years before the Freedom Rides piqued his interest in King, Hoover approved a wiretap on Levison's home phone, a labor-intensive operation that lasted for nine months. When Levison left home, he was often followed by Bureau agents, who noted the details of his travels. When he departed New York altogether, they worked ahead of time to plant microphones and wiretaps in his hotel rooms. On at least one occasion, when Levison left his hotel for another appointment, agents appear to have broken into his room and photographed key financial documents and correspondence.[10]

These operations produced enough corroborating evidence about Levison's party activities to support the general outlines of the Childs brothers' claims. In May 1954 Hoover confirmed to the New York office that "the subject has become increasingly active in Communist party affairs and has assumed some degree of control over Communist Party financial transactions." The New York office agreed with this assessment and recommended that Levison be identified henceforth as a "Key Figure" within communist circles. With this justification in hand, the FBI pressed for still more information about his background, going so far as to interview his ex-wife and her new husband, a former business partner of Levison's, about the possibility that Levison might be a Soviet spy. His ex-wife dismissed the possibility out of hand, but her husband (himself a former communist, now living under an assumed name) was not so sure. He described Levison as "cold, calculating and constantly looking for weaknesses in individuals upon which he could play."[11]

That vague comment—hardly from an unbiased source—appears to be the closest the Bureau ever came to tying Levison to any sort of espionage. Even without any direct Soviet connection, the material uncovered by the Bureau during those years was enough to prove that Levison played a secret and important role in the Communist Party's domestic finances. That alone made him a subject of enduring suspicion. By 1955, when Hoover approved a second wiretap on Levison's phone, the Bureau believed it had established the following facts: First, Levison handled tens of thousands of dollars per year in CP money and business transactions. Second, he knew details about the CP's leadership and underground activities, including the locations and identities of federal fugitives. Finally, he had managed to do all this in secret, while maintaining his position as a well-regarded businessman and pillar of the Jewish community.[12]

LEVISON MET KING IN 1956, JUST AS THE MONTGOMERY BUS BOYCOTT BEGAN TO attract national attention. By that point, he was starting to perform many of the same tasks for civil rights groups that he had for the Communist Party: fundraising, strategizing, outreach to wealthy New Yorkers. That year, to provide a vehicle for channeling Northern money into the Southern movement, he helped to found an organization called In Friendship. The socialist labor leader A. Philip Randolph played a key early role in the group, cosponsoring a benefit rally at Madison Square Garden. Levison worked behind the scenes, along with two of his closest allies: Ella Baker, the pioneering NAACP organizer and nonviolent strategist, and Bayard Rustin, who met with King in Montgomery. Together, they laid a plan for In Friendship "to connect the Negro struggle with the labor movement," in Levison's words, and thus build a cross-regional, race-and-class coalition.[13]

The first historians to write about Levison's activities suggested that he broke with the Communist Party around this time, as he transitioned into working with King. Now, with better access to the FBI's files, it seems clear that this was not true. In April 1956, according to SOLO, Levison handed $4,500 in cash to the party's head of finances, who in turn handed some of the money to Jack Childs for safekeeping. In the months that followed, the FBI spotted Levison with his party contacts all over the city: descending into subway tunnels, meeting on the steps of the public library, sipping coffee at Chock full o' Nuts. For the year 1956, according to Bureau files, Levison and his brother channeled up to $41,000 to the Communist Party (the equivalent of about $425,000 in today's money). Party officials gave the two brothers a joint pseudonym—"Lee"—to help cover their tracks.[14]

The Madison Square Garden benefit for In Friendship proved to be a solid if not quite so spectacular success, raising $27,000 for the Southern civil rights effort. In reporting on the spectacle, *The New York Times* identified King as one of "three Southern Negroes who had been involved in recent incidents in the South," not yet a nationally recognized figure. Like many other observers, though, Levison had seen the potential for something more in King's powerful rhetorical abilities and skill at elevating civil rights from a regional struggle to a moral imperative. Later that year, Levison sat down with Baker and Rustin at his Upper West Side apartment to hash out a plan for a national organization under King's leadership, a vehicle to channel the nascent energies of the Montgomery boycott into a larger Southern movement. It would ultimately be known as the Southern Christian Leadership Conference, the organization that would be linked with King until the end of his life.

Over the next several months, Levison showed his commitment to King by devoting hundreds of hours to getting the SCLC off the ground. By the end of the year, he was also doing King's taxes and helping to ghostwrite his first book, *Stride Toward*

Freedom. He helped to shore up King's personal finances, passing along two gifts of five thousand dollars each in 1957 and 1958, courtesy of a wealthy New York family with ties to the Communist Party. Levison proved particularly valuable as an emissary to Northern white society, helping King to craft messages and speeches that would strike the right political notes. Out of these efforts emerged a close personal bond. "Levison became King's closest white friend and the most reliable colleague of his life," King biographer Taylor Branch wrote of their first years together.[15]

Initially, neither Hoover nor anyone else at the FBI understood the depth of connection between the two men. But Bureau officials did begin to develop a theory about Levison's work within the broader civil rights movement. According to Jack Childs, in 1957 the brothers Levison contributed twenty-five thousand dollars to the Communist Party, one of its largest single contributions. Within months, though, Levison's connection to the party was reported to be "deteriorating." Hoover suspected, based on this fragmentary information, that Levison might be distancing himself from the party in order to move even deeper underground as the communists' inside man within the civil rights movement.[16]

Once that assumption was in place, it became almost impossible to dislodge, with each new rumor seeming to build upon the last. In the summer of 1958, party leader Eugene Dennis told Morris Childs that Levison was now secretly "at the head" of a party group devoted to working with "mass organizations" such as the American Jewish Congress and the NAACP. In October, the coordinator of the CP's financial network complained that "he was unable to contact STANLEY LEVISON because STANLEY was 'busy and involved' with the Youth March on Washington," a civil rights initiative in which King was also taking part. A few days after that, Childs reported that Dennis and party activist James Jackson had met with communist contacts high up in the civil rights hierarchy—"the most secret and guarded people, who are in touch with, consult with, and guide LUTHER KING [*sic*] and A. PHILLIP RANDOLPH." Though neither Dennis nor Jackson would disclose the names of these contacts, they did reveal that they were "Party guys, far removed from the top level of the Party" but "playing an important role in guiding these fellows (KING and RANDOLPH)." At least one of the "guys," Childs reported, seemed to be connected to the American Jewish Congress. The description fit Levison.[17]

At no point did Hoover seem to entertain the idea that communist leaders might be exaggerating their own influence and power over Levison, or over the broader civil rights movement. Nor did he consider that Levison might be trying to avoid his old CP friends and shift his energies over to King's far more promising efforts. Hoover's vision largely converged with the communists': the Party was secretly exercising influence over the civil rights movement.

By this circular logic, even the most innocuous behavior became reason for suspicion. And yet Hoover was also sitting on some genuinely combustible facts. According to Jack Childs, the Levison brothers pledged $12,000 to the CP in 1959, a full two years after Levison helped to found King's SCLC. In 1960, they pledged another $12,000. And in the spring of 1961, when Hoover began investigating King in earnest, CP leaders estimated that they could expect another $8,000 from the Levison brothers over the coming year.[18]

THERE WAS AT LEAST ONE OTHER ASPECT OF LEVISON'S ACTIVITIES THAT HOOVER found suspicious. That was his support for a man named Hunter Pitts O'Dell, better known to friends as Jack. Born in Detroit in 1923, O'Dell spent much of his adult life in the Deep South. During that time, he had served as an organizer for the Communist Party, doggedly working against Jim Crow and in favor of labor rights at a moment when neither effort had much regional traction. In 1958, he moved to New York after a belligerent appearance before HUAC in Atlanta. He met Levison around that time, and the two men grew into steadfast allies. Levison soon recommended O'Dell for a job at the New York office of the SCLC. King accepted the recommendation. As with Levison, however, newly released Bureau files suggest that there was no definitive abandoning of one organization in favor of the other. Based on information from the Childs brothers, among other sources, Hoover had reason to think that O'Dell, too, kept up a relationship with the Communist Party after he started working with King. The FBI acted on this assumption.

Unlike Levison, O'Dell had spent much of his adult life as an open party member. Raised in Detroit, he grew up working-class, witness to the local triumphs of the autoworkers' unions but also to the sufferings of his grandfather, a janitor at the Detroit Public Library. He came to the Communist Party through the militant politics of the National Maritime Union, one of Hoover's least favorite labor organizations. By the middle of the 1950s, he had emerged as "one of the Party's top southern policy makers," in the words of one historian, a position for which there was admittedly little competition.[19]

One of O'Dell's chief adversaries during these years was Guy Banister, Hoover's former special agent in charge in Chicago, who had left the FBI to run a citywide Bureau of Investigation as deputy chief of police in New Orleans. In March 1956, Banister ordered a raid on O'Dell's home, seizing what was described to the newspapers as "the finest collection of Communist literature" ever captured in the Deep South. The police shared the collection with Hoover's friends at the Senate Internal Security Subcommittee, which was scheduled to hold local hearings in New Orleans. The papers included dozens of books and articles by the likes of W. E. B. Du Bois, Stalin, and William Z. Foster. The seized documents also showed a familiarity with underground life; police found two Social Security cards made out with false names. When SISS questioned

O'Dell about what the police had found, he declared his contempt for the proceedings and refused to answer any questions about his political affiliations or party membership, citing the Fifth Amendment against self-incrimination.[20]

The Bureau kept a close eye on O'Dell in the years that followed, as he encountered a series of legal obstacles that drove him out of the South and into New York's communist circles. In early January 1959, Jack Childs reported that O'Dell planned to fill in for CP official James Jackson as head of the party's "Negro and Southern work" while Jackson went off to Moscow. The following month, the New York office reported that O'Dell had entered CP headquarters for a meeting of the National Executive Committee, an exclusive gathering of some two dozen top party leaders. Bugs inside captured O'Dell advocating a "united front approach" that would put the party's organizing energies behind the civil rights cause. He was especially excited to gather signatures for another March on Washington, where King, Randolph, and others would call once again for Eisenhower to take action. According to Morris Childs, O'Dell finished out the year by joining the party's National Executive Committee under the cover name "Cornelius James," one of three committee members operating under pseudonyms. Morris himself was elected to the committee as "C. Martin."[21]

At this point came an episode that would loom large in Hoover's theory about King, O'Dell, and Levison, and about how the CP had schemed to put the three men together. In February 1960, Hoover learned that O'Dell was allegedly "on the payroll of the National Office of the CPUSA but efforts were being made to get him something away from the Party." As if in accordance with this plan, Levison soon met with several leaders of the SCLC to discuss staffing. During that meeting, the men determined that the New York office needed someone to manage fundraising and direct mail. Levison recommended O'Dell. Just a few years after allegedly joining the Communist Party's National Executive Committee under a pseudonym, O'Dell began to work for the SCLC.[22]

That is where the Bureau found him a year later, when Jack Childs delivered one more sensational piece of evidence. In the summer of 1961, Jack embarked on a trip to Moscow, where he was supposed to be trained on how to handle the transfer of Soviet money. While there, he attended "secret service" schools held in unmarked apartments throughout the city, learning how to manage code names, microfilm, invisible ciphers, and other tools of the trade. One day, a Soviet official handed over a list of code names identifying the most important communists in the U.S. The list included approximately fifty names, mostly top-ranking party officials. Among them was the name "O'Dell Pitts," to be identified in future correspondence as "Tread." An FBI memo later corrected the roster: "O'DELL PITTS, mentioned in this list as 'TREAD,' is HUNTER PITTS O'DELL." In other words, the man now running King's SCLC New York office mattered enough to Soviet intelligence to earn a code name. So he mattered more than ever to Hoover.[23]

———

THE INFORMATION ABOUT LEVISON AND O'DELL, ABOUT CODE NAMES AND SE-
cret funds, came with one major drawback. As with Venona, Hoover could not disclose
how he knew what he knew. His instructions to Bureau officials warned in the strictest
of terms not to reveal anything that might jeopardize SOLO. Those directives applied
to all communications with the Justice Department and the White House. In 1962,
as the FBI proceeded with its investigation of King, Hoover decided to bring the Kennedy brothers in on the tale of Levison and O'Dell and the secret machinations of the
Communist Party. At the same time, he refused to say how the FBI got its information,
or offer any real proof for his claims. He shared enough to cause consternation at the
White House, given Kennedy's overtures to King as an emissary to the civil rights
movement. But both the president and the attorney general also doubted Hoover's
judgment. Their decision to broach the subject with King came out of this nexus of
concern and mistrust.

The back-and-forth over disclosure—What would Hoover tell the White House,
and what would the White House tell King?—soon became a major source of tension.
Hoover found himself in much the same position he had occupied at the height of the
Venona revelations: convinced that his sources provided unimpeachable insight into a
secret communist network, but unwilling to explain how he'd gained such knowledge.
Even as the White House expressed unease about Hoover's allegations, he grew ever
more convinced that he was onto something big: that Levison and O'Dell provided a
missing link between the Communist Party and the civil rights movement. On January 4, 1962, Hoover learned that Levison had written King's recent speech before the
AFL-CIO calling for solidarity between the civil rights and labor movements. Four
days later, he wrote a pointed memo informing the attorney general that Levison was
"a secret member of the Communist Party" and appealing for a strategy to deal with
what was fast becoming an untenable situation.[24]

The AFL-CIO speech seems to have marked a turning point for the FBI, evidence
not only of Levison's behind-the-scenes support for King's activism but also of willful
attempts to shape its message. Over the next several days, Hoover transitioned from
the passive delivery of information into a more active role in pushing the Kennedy
administration to figure out what to do. On January 9, and then again on January 10
and 12, he spoke with Bobby Kennedy by phone. On January 13, Courtney Evans reported that the president himself wanted to speak with Hoover—not because "there
was any problem," but just to review "conditions generally." In all likelihood, Hoover
and Kennedy discussed the Levison-O'Dell situation, because a few days later, a presidential aide was dispatched to warn King away from his "communist" associates.[25]

John Seigenthaler drew the unpleasant duty. At the end of King's visit to the White
House in January, Seigenthaler walked him out to his car, a seemingly friendly gesture

that soon turned serious. "I was somewhat indirect in explaining the problem," Seigen-thaler later explained. "I mean, this was sensitive, delicate. Obviously I didn't have to mention the Bureau, or Hoover, for him to understand about whom I was talking." The gist of Hoover's message came across anyway. On the president's instruction, Sei-genthaler informed King that both Levison and O'Dell were active, if secret, Com-munist Party collaborators. King acknowledged the information but said he wanted proof, unwilling to condemn apparently loyal friends and movement allies on mere say-so.[26]

With Hoover now fully committed to action on the matter, the allegations proved difficult for King to escape. On January 24, 1962, Hoover delivered his annual House appropriations testimony, reminding the country that the Communist Party had long sought "to infiltrate the legitimate Negro organizations." Around the same time, he quietly began to share the allegations about King's communist friends with select con-gressmen and senators. His actions provoked a round of inquiries from the Justice Department, where Bobby Kennedy was pushing for additional information. After scrutinizing the files, however, Hoover determined that he had shared enough. "King is no good any way," he wrote on February 3. "Under no circumstances should our informant be endangered."[27]

And so the information simply continued to pile up: some of it exculpatory, some of it alarming, much of it purely speculative. "Hoover's memos were very, very persua-sive," Seigenthaler recalled, even with many of the details withheld. "You would think Levison was evil incarnate, guiding the movement on a direct line from the Kremlin." One new discovery involved a secret meeting between Levison and Viktor Lesiovsky, a Soviet official at the United Nations secretariat, suspected by the FBI of being the head of Soviet intelligence in the U.S. Hoover's level of alarm rose in tandem with each revelation.[28]

Under the circumstances, Bobby Kennedy finally decided he had little choice but to follow the FBI's lead and increase the level of federal surveillance. On February 27, in preparation for this new phase, Hoover instructed material related to King's communist affiliations reclassified as a "Security Matter—C," in which "C" stood for "communist." A few days later, he began making plans to have new bugs and wiretaps installed in Levison's home and office. On March 16, FBI agents broke into Levison's office to plant a hidden microphone. A few days later, acting on an order signed by Rob-ert Kennedy, they installed a wiretap as well.[29]

Hoover's goal was to confirm what the Childs brothers had been telling him for years: that both Levison and O'Dell were "secret communists" who had never actually split from the party. What he found instead pointed the FBI in a new direction.

CHAPTER 44

Decadent Thinking

(1957–1962)

Hoover consulting with President John F. Kennedy, 1963. Hoover was aware of Kennedy's extramarital affairs and the president knew it.

NATIONAL ARCHIVES AND RECORDS ADMINISTRATION

On February 27, 1962, the same day that he designated King a "communist" security matter, Hoover alerted the White House about another troubling set of associations—one that, like the Levison-King connection, posed serious political risks for the president. According to Hoover, on November 7 and again on November 15, a Los Angeles freelance artist named Judith Campbell had placed telephone calls to Evelyn Lincoln, the president's secretary, through the White House switchboard. The memo claimed "the relationship between Campbell and Mrs. Lincoln or the purpose of these calls is not known." But the FBI knew enough about Campbell herself to cause concern. According to the memo, Campbell was also in touch with Sam Giancana, the Chicago Mafia boss who had contracted with the CIA to carry out the Castro plots—and who was still the subject of a major federal investigation.[1]

In truth, Hoover knew more than that. The phone calls hinted that the president was engaged in a sexual relationship with Campbell, even as Kennedy promoted himself as a family man, his gracious wife and two small children the very picture of American domesticity. In itself, that did not make Campbell especially unique. Since becoming president, Kennedy had indulged in an "astounding *immensity*" of extramarital sexual activity, in the words of one historian. What made Campbell different was her connection to the country's "top hoodlums"—not only Giancana but also John Roselli, who had played a key role in the Castro plots. FBI files identified Campbell as both Roselli's "paramour" and Giancana's "friend." In other words, she appeared to be carrying on intimate relations with one or even two leading Chicago mobsters at the same time that she was "shacking up with John Kennedy in the east," as one source bluntly described it. Though Hoover did not yet know the full scope of the situation, he envisioned a political crisis in the making.[2]

On March 22, nearly a month after his initial note to the White House, he sat down with Kennedy to hash things out in person. The luncheon took place at the White House, the first time since their wrangling over the Crime Commission that Hoover had met with the president in such an intimate setting. There is no written record of the meeting, designated in advance as an off-the-record exchange. If they discussed Campbell, as seems likely, Hoover must have found the conversation awkward at best. Two days earlier, his aides had prepared a memo outlining the known facts about Campbell, on the assumption that "the Director may desire to bear this information in mind in connection with his forthcoming appointment with the President." Under the circumstances, Kennedy had little choice but to disavow Campbell, or at least to appear to do so. That afternoon, a few hours after Hoover's departure, he called Campbell for the last time through the White House switchboard, ostensibly to break off their relationship. Like King, Kennedy appears to have recognized Hoover's power and to have resisted it. "Get rid of that bastard. He's the biggest bore," Kennedy supposedly told a White House aide as Hoover left the meeting.[3]

But there was no getting rid of Hoover. He kept Kennedy's secret, aside from some gossip among friends. But the episode did not improve his opinion of the president any more than it enhanced Kennedy's opinion of Hoover. Coming on top of the Castro plots, the tensions over King and civil rights, and the growing difference in personal style, the Campbell affair left Hoover more convinced than ever that the country's charming young president lacked the self-discipline necessary for real leadership. Under Kennedy's leadership, Hoover concluded, the 1960s seemed to be awash in "decadent thinking" and "self-indulgence," with Americans choosing personal pleasure over devotion to duty.[4]

HOOVER'S WAS IN PART A GENERATIONAL LAMENT, THE COMMENTARY OF A MAN born in the late nineteenth century, increasingly baffled by modern ways and manners. Now nearly seventy years old, he was no longer the vigorous reformer known for his rapid speech and crackling personal energy. He tried to cover up his aging just as he hid so much else, puzzling with reporters over the great mystery of how he, alone among his peers, managed to avoid the ravages of time. "This is a flattering question," he said. "If the years have not 'kept pace' with me, perhaps it is because I have been too busy to stop long enough for them to 'catch up.'"[5]

Had reporters been able to peer behind the facade, however, they would have found an entire team of doctors attending to Hoover, in some cases through biweekly and even weekly calls at his Bureau office, an aging man's attempt to keep up with his younger staff. In 1961, he consulted up to a dozen medical specialists. As time went on, the doctors' visits increased, with Hoover sometimes consulting multiple physicians in a single day. That came on top of his annual August checkups in La Jolla, where the Scripps Clinic regularly certified his ongoing health. Just as he cultivated reporters and politicians, Hoover made a point of befriending his doctors. At the Criss Award dinner in December, where he had delivered his speech about "pseudo-patriots" of the left and right, at least a dozen physicians were in attendance, each invited by Hoover as a gesture of personal honor.[6]

Some of this medical hoopla resulted from pure hypochondria. Hoover attempted to fend off disease and age just as he repelled other enemies: through self-discipline, pattern recognition, and heightened vigilance. By 1960, he was also on a diet, instructing Annie Fields to eliminate all starchy food. According to Bureau officials, as he grew older his insistence on cleanliness and order began to mutate into a full-blown abhorrence of germs, bacteria, and other invisible, microbial threats. At least some of his health problems were real, though, and required serious medical intervention. In late 1962, he was admitted to the George Washington University Hospital for what Tolson described as "minor corrective surgery"—in reality, a prostate operation, one of the least dignified bodily insults visited upon aging men. He remained on sick leave for six weeks.[7]

Tolson, too, was beginning to show his age, the movie-star good looks now fading into the merely pleasant, though still trim, profile of a sixtysomething man. Not long after Hoover's health scare, Tolson was hospitalized for a duodenal ulcer and then for heart surgery, just two of many serious ailments that would beset him over the next several years. Tolson's declining health may have come as a shock to both men: he was five years Hoover's junior, and he had always been in better shape, thinner and more athletic. He smoked constantly, however, and now, in his early sixties, he had been smoking for decades.[8]

Perhaps hoping to lift both of their spirits, Hoover reached out to the White House with a plea to honor Tolson with the President's Award for Distinguished Federal Civilian Service, the same award Hoover had received under Eisenhower. The application— "Proposed nomination of Clyde A. Tolson, Associate Director, Federal Bureau of Investigation"—was hardly a work of flowery sentiment. But it can be read as a love poem of sorts, delivered in bureaucratese, the language Hoover knew best. The document narrated Tolson's life as a parable of bootstraps discipline. It also extolled his virtues as a model Bureau man, beginning with his hiring in 1928, when he naively thought his Bureau job would be a short-term endeavor. "Instead, this initial association with the FBI and Director J. Edgar Hoover developed into a career which has spanned three decades," the report noted, "and has witnessed the notorious gangster era of the 1930s, World War II, the Korean military conflict and the present-day national menaces of crime and subversion in America." What got him through, according to the report, were the outstanding personal qualities that so many Americans now seemed to lack, including "innate intelligence," "imaginative genius," "dogged determination," "astute judgment," "boundless energy," "patriotic zeal," and "unerring ability to produce extraordinary results in a minimum of time."

These were among the highest compliments that Hoover could bestow. But perhaps the greatest testament to their life together came from Tolson. "I like my work," he explained in a quote included as part of the report. "The satisfaction that comes with doing my job is enough for me. I have no other ambition in life."[9]

BOBBY KENNEDY WAS SITTING ON THE BOARD OF ADVISERS THAT REJECTED Tolson's application, instead granting the award to candidates from the Agriculture, Defense, and State Departments. No doubt this was a personal jab at Hoover, one of the many slights that made up their increasingly testy back-and-forth. Out of earshot, Bobby could be cruel about the relationship between Hoover and Tolson—or, as he preferred to describe them, "J. Edna" and Clyde. According to aides, he liked to crack jokes about Hoover's masculinity, scoffing at the director as a "fucking cocksucker" who preferred to "squat to pee." When Tolson was admitted to the hospital, Bobby wanted to know why: "What was it, a hysterectomy?" The gossip about this sort of comment sometimes made its way back to Hoover. In February 1962, a wiretap captured one Philadelphia mobster guffawing to a friend that Bobby "wants EDGAR HOOVER out of the FBI because he is a fairy." "Listen to this," the voice said, "EDGAR HOOVER is not married and neither is his assistant, read back in his history."

According to William Hundley, head of the Justice Department's organized crime section, Bobby went beyond this idle chatter and briefly initiated an investigation into Hoover's private life, hoping to prove, once and for all, that the director preferred sex with men. Hundley came away convinced that the gossip "was all bullshit," and that Hoover was the restrained, self-disciplined workaholic he had always seemed to be.[10]

One now-infamous story from these years has received outsize attention for casting doubt on this conclusion. According to the journalist Anthony Summers, sometime in 1958 Hoover attended an intimate gathering in a suite at the Plaza hotel: just Hoover, Roy Cohn, and Lewis Rosenstiel, a liquor magnate who had recently hired Hoover's PR chieftain, Lou Nichols, away from the Bureau. Rosenstiel allegedly brought his wife, Susan, along for the occasion. She later professed her astonishment at what she witnessed that day, from the moment that a woman named Mary, "wearing a fluffy black dress, very fluffy, with flounces, and lace stocking and high heels, and a black curly wig" bid her good evening. Mary was actually Hoover, she claimed. He supposedly went on to engage in sex play with two teenage boys hired for the occasion. Then he did it again the following year, this time in a red dress and black feather boa, once more with Susan Rosenstiel watching.[11]

Certain aspects of her story fit with the circumstances of Hoover's life. In the late 1950s, he still traveled regularly to New York, where he was known to socialize with Cohn, who was friendly with Rosenstiel. By then, Cohn was engaged in what would become a famously prodigious gay sex life, even as he continued to insist to the outside world that he was a conservative heterosexual man. If the broad outlines of the Plaza encounters conform with a few of Hoover's known patterns, however, the details do not. As historians have noted, the incidents read like nothing so much as a standard pulp fantasy of cross-dressing excess: the boa, the flounces, "Mary" and the teenage boys. Susan Rosenstiel herself is the weakest part of the story. She was paid for her disclosures, a practice rejected by many journalists as incentive to lie and exaggerate. And she showed elsewhere that she was indeed willing to lie when the circumstances demanded it. In the 1970s, she was convicted of perjury in the wake of her divorce from Lewis, earning her the rare distinction of serving time in prison for lying.[12]

In any case it is difficult to imagine Hoover taking that sort of risk, whatever his personal desires may have been. Throughout the late 1950s, when the Plaza encounters were alleged to have taken place, Hoover remained acutely aware of just how dangerous allegations of homosexuality could be, even as the worst pressures of the Lavender Scare were starting to ebb. One of his major concerns involved the Soviets, who made a practice of investigating the sexual transgressions of well-placed Americans. In 1960, Hoover noted at least three recent cases in which Americans visiting Russia "indulged in homosexual activities and pictures were taken and they were confronted with these pictures and threatened with exposure unless they agreed to carry out espionage in this country."[13]

Recent evidence suggests that the Soviets were also targeting Hoover himself during these years. In 1992, a retired high-ranking KGB archivist named Vasili Mitrokhin fled the collapsing Soviet Union with thousands of pages of handwritten notes documenting the agency's foreign intelligence operations. Contained in those notes was a passage showing how the KGB had used "active measures"—forgeries, anonymous letters, paid informants, leaks to newspapers—to spread gossip about Hoover's sexual orientation. "To compromise E. Hoover as a homosexual, letters were sent to the main newspapers on behalf of an anonymous organization," Mitrokhin recorded. According to Mitrokhin's notes, those letters attacked Hoover for acting like "a moralist and a pillar of the American society" even as he "turned the FBI into a faggots' den."[14]

The Soviets apparently did not get very far with their campaign against Hoover. During his lifetime, no "main newspapers" ever published such bald or explicit accusations. But he continued to exercise vigilance when it came to press depictions of his private life, which did occasionally include a wink and a nod. When the left-leaning *New York Post* launched a major investigative series on the Bureau in 1959, publisher Dorothy Schiff noted the unusually hostile nature of Hoover's countercampaign; he refused to talk to her reporters, threatened his agents with punishment, and asked any congressmen who did talk to retract their statements. "I wondered why Hoover had lost his head," she wrote. "Why was he so scared? Drawing upon my knowledge of psychology, I decided he must be afraid that something damaging about his private life would be revealed." Schiff assured everyone that "the *Post*'s primary concern was Mr. Hoover as a public man," that "we have no scandalous facts to present about his private affairs." This was not especially comforting, however, since even to raise the question was to insinuate the possibility of a "scandalous" answer.[15]

Hoover's worry about his reputation may help to explain his behavior in one of the saddest and cruelest personal encounters of his later years. In 1959 Melvin Purvis, the man who had once been the object of so much affection and attention, returned to Washington as majority counsel for a Senate judiciary subcommittee. Press reports emphasized the strange nature of his new post: here was Purvis, once the great hero of the Dillinger case, "now 55 with hair graying at the temples," back in Washington but apparently cut off from the Bureau. Over the years, Hoover had maintained an extensive file on his old friend's doings but refused all personal contact. As the file noted, Purvis had run into serious health issues during that time, including "arthritis in his neck and shoulders, apparently accompanied by extreme pain." In late 1959, not long after returning to Washington, he experienced a major personal loss when an old friend committed suicide. "Life is preposterous," the friend apparently told his family before shooting himself. "You go through the motions and then you wake up and realize something is missing—something big is missing."

Purvis seemed to recognize a void as well. In February 1960, after returning home to South Carolina, he shot himself in the face with a .45 Colt automatic pistol. Within hours, according to Crime Records, the Bureau was "deluged" with press inquiries about Purvis. But Hoover refused all comment, either to the media or to Purvis's family.[16]

Purvis's wife and sons, taken aback by the cruelty of this final rejection, sent a telegram to Hoover mourning the damage he had inflicted over the years. "We are honored that you ignored Melvin's death," they wrote. "Your jealousy hurt him very much but until the end I think he loved you." Far from reconsidering his actions, Hoover took the message as affirmation that he had been right to distance himself from Purvis, that there was still something dangerous and volatile about what had happened between them in the 1930s. "It was well we didn't write," he remarked in a handwritten note on the telegram, "as [they] would no doubt have distorted it."[17]

GIVEN SUCH CONCERNS, PERHAPS HOOVER SHOULD HAVE WELCOMED THE NEWS about Frank Kameny. A former government astronomer, in the late 1950s Kameny sued the federal government over his dismissal for homosexuality, adopting the language of discrimination, civil rights, and equal protection. He lost his case, but the effort appealed to other Washington men living "with a Sword of Damocles hanging over them," as one ally later put it, never sure from one day to the next whether they would be rooted out and fired from government positions. In the summer of 1961, they founded the Mattachine Society of Washington, a local chapter of the nation's first dedicated gay-rights organization. The group hoped to bring the Lavender Scare to an end once and for all, and to open up new possibilities for the men and women who had once been its targets. Hoover saw nothing liberatory in the effort. Upon learning of the chapter's existence, he ordered the Washington field office to start tracking its activities.[18]

According to agents' reports, the initial meeting was modest but spirited—"16 well-dressed men" convened for discussion and snacks at the Hay-Adams hotel. As a rule, Bureau agents resisted frequenting venues where gay men gathered, for fear that observers might conclude that they were there for the wrong reasons. Only after the Mattachine meeting dispersed did they descend on the hotel to grill the manager and waitstaff. According to Kameny, after that first meeting Bureau agents also began to show up in unexpected places, asking people close to the group to disclose membership lists and become informants. Kameny interpreted the FBI's actions as a deliberate attempt at intimidation. Properly assembled and presented to the Civil Service Commission, the information gathered in such exchanges could get a man permanently blackballed from federal employment.

To Hoover's shock, the Mattachine men responded in a way that would have been unthinkable during the Lavender Scare: they complained to the attorney general. In June 1962, Kameny fired off an angry letter to Bobby Kennedy, alleging illegal harassment by the FBI and demanding an end to federal investigation of the society. Hoover could hardly believe the gall and suggested that they all ignore the communication. But the Mattachine men were determined not to be ignored, and over the next several months, they mounted a campaign to irritate and provoke Hoover at one of his most vulnerable spots. They knew the rumors about his homosexuality. "I was gay, the people I was hearing it from were gay and the boxes Hoover and Tolson were in were boxes owned by gay men," West Coast activist and Mattachine founder Harry Hay later recalled of the gossip about Hoover and Tolson together at Del Mar. "They wouldn't be in that crowd otherwise." As a 1961 memo noted, Hay's own short-lived magazine had once gone so far as to print the "allegation that there were homosexuals in 'key positions' in the FBI," thus earning the lasting scrutiny and hostility of the Los Angeles office. Kameny took a less direct approach, appealing to Hoover's sense of justice while also hinting that he knew a thing or two about homosexuals at the FBI. A year after founding the Washington chapter, he wrote to Hoover suggesting that the FBI rethink its "policies of repression, persecution, and exclusion" toward homosexuals. "We realize that this area presents you with many potential problems, some of them quite subtle and touchy ones of politics and public relations," he wrote—not least because among the "roughly a quarter-million" homosexual federal employees, there were "a number in your own bureau."[19]

Hoover refused to write back, but the jabs kept coming, delivered mostly outside public view. Affecting a pose of informational awareness, the society began to invite Hoover to special events and lectures around Washington, including a talk by Donald Webster Cory, author of *The Homosexual in America*. "The lecture, entitled 'The Homosexual—Minority Rights, Civil Rights, Human Rights,' is one which we feel may be of interest to you," the invitation explained, enclosing a complimentary ticket for Hoover. When Hoover failed to attend, they added him to the mailing list for their newsletter, the *Gazette,* providing the Bureau with regular updates on their "attempts to legalize the activities of homosexuals," in the words of one Bureau summary.

Finally, this provoked a response. "This material is disgusting and offensive and it is believed a vigorous objection to the addition of the Director to its mailing list should be made," an FBI memo noted. At that point Hoover decided that the Mattachine leadership should be brought into headquarters for a face-to-face chat with Bureau agents. The public relations office took the lead on the arrangements, tracking down Kameny as well as the editor of the offending newsletter. To Bureau agents' astonishment, when the two men arrived at the Crime Records office a few weeks later they seemed perfectly at ease, explaining that they sent the newsletter to every official in Washington and hardly understood why Hoover would object. They also—"somewhat facetiously"—invited Hoover to attend their upcoming national convention and participate more fully in their activities.[20]

The interviewing agents followed a preplanned script: the FBI did not make policy, but it was in fact federal policy that homosexuals be expelled from their jobs. The meeting lasted just eight minutes, but the agents left with an uneasy feeling. "Whether or not these mailings to the Bureau are discontinued," they wrote, making the best of a bad situation, "it has been clearly made a matter of record that the receipt of such items is considered offensive and are not desired."[21]

Their concerns proved to be well placed. A few weeks after the meeting, the Mattachine men wrote to the Bureau with a final offer: they would take Hoover off their mailing lists if he would remove all their names and organizational information from Bureau files. At this point, Hoover more or less gave up and decided to stop responding.[22]

Elsewhere in Washington, though, they were starting to attract more favorable attention. In 1975, the federal government would rescind its ban on the employment of homosexuals in the civil service, due largely to the work of activists such as Kameny. The change came too late for Hoover.[23]

DESPITE HOOVER'S WARNINGS ABOUT JUDITH CAMPBELL, JOHN KENNEDY CONtinued to produce an array of sexual scandals and annoyances throughout his time at the White House. In May 1962, actress Marilyn Monroe appeared onstage at Madison Square Garden for the president's forty-fifth birthday gala, dressed in a white ermine coat and sequined evening gown, to puff out a seductive, breathy "Happy Birthday, Mr. President" song before thousands of well-wishers. Kennedy declared her sultry performance an entirely "sweet" and "wholesome" event, a winking reference to the rumor that he and Monroe were having an affair. There were stories that Bobby was seeing Monroe as well, gossip that the attorney general dismissed as having moved well "beyond any semblance of the truth" but that Courtney Evans, forced to mediate between the White House and the FBI, suspected might be true. That gossip in turn produced a raft of conspiracy theories, at least some of which Hoover attempted to investigate.[24]

One involved a dustup over Mariella Novotny, a call girl who had worked the New York society scene in 1960 and supposedly ended up in the arms of then-senator John Kennedy. She came to Hoover's attention via Scotland Yard, which was busy investigating the Brits' own high-powered sex scandal, known as the Profumo affair. In an interview with British authorities, Novotny denied having a sexual relationship with Kennedy, though she recalled "a rumor that was going around New York that the president had many girlfriends." With Hoover's permission, Evans passed the news along to Bobby, who declared the allegations "preposterous" but admitted that everyone should be prepared for "more similar stories" as time went on. "He would like for us to continue to advise him of any such matters coming to our attention on a personal basis," Evans reported back to Hoover, "as he could better defend the family if he knew what was being said." In truth, inviting Hoover further into the family's business was probably the last thing Bobby wanted.[25]

Then there was Ellen Rometsch, potentially the most scandalous of them all: a German émigré, five feet seven, with black hair, green eyes, and a penchant for "heavy makeup," in the FBI's description. Rometsch had made her name as a "party girl" at Washington's Quorum Club, an exclusive if dumpy Capitol Hill pleasure palace frequented by congressmen and senators. When Hoover caught wind of her activities and her alleged relationship with the president, he initiated a national-security investigation based on her place of birth in East Germany. Agents ultimately concluded she posed no serious Cold War threat. Hoover nonetheless took pains to ensure that she would not "get a visa" to return to the United States and tell tales about the president. Her story did not disappear, however. Once the newspapers began to rumble about the "high executive branch officials" known to be "friends and associates of the part-time model and party girl," the attorney general and the president saw little choice but to ask for Hoover's help.[26]

After years of tension and sniping and second-guessing, their entreaty must have been satisfying for Hoover, an acknowledgment that his political skills and connections could, on occasion, be of use even to the Kennedys. In particular, they wanted him to speak on the president's behalf with Senators Mike Mansfield and Everett Dirksen, the Democratic and Republican leaders of the Senate, respectively, who were threatening hearings into the national-security angle of the Rometsch story. Hoover initially toyed with Bobby, suggesting that the attorney general simply share the FBI's report on the available evidence. In the end, though, he agreed to serve as middleman on the logic that "they would give more credence to what I had to say than any statement" from a nepotism-addled attorney general. In a private meeting at Mansfield's house, Hoover explained that while "there were of course a number of Senators and a number of Congressmen who were clients of these so-called 'call girls,'" the senators should have no cause for concern about espionage or leaks. He also implied that the senators should perhaps be careful when it came to throwing stones in glass houses. While assuring them that "there had been no breach of security," he noted that "the matter of immorality . . . has been rather common in the Senate and the House," not just the White House. Under the circumstances, everyone would be well-advised to "keep quiet."[27]

In thanks for the meeting, John Kennedy invited Hoover to lunch at the White House. Like Hoover's earlier visits, this one has often been portrayed as an exercise in arm-twisting, with Kennedy as the aggrieved innocent and Hoover as the scheming villain, gloating over his knowledge of the president's foibles. But it is also possible that Hoover sympathized in some small way with the president, a powerful man made vulnerable by unruly and unconventional desires. Bobby hinted at such a possibility in the midst of the Rometsch investigation, reminding Hoover that "there are always allegations about prominent people that they are either homosexuals or promiscuous." Those words might be construed as a nod to Hoover's own supposed secrets. Either way, the FBI and the Kennedys were now in it together.[28]

CHAPTER 45

The Most Dangerous Negro

(1963)

The Rev. Dr. Martin Luther King Jr., speaking at the March on Washington in August 1963. After the march, an FBI memo declared King "the most dangerous Negro" in America.

BOB ADELMAN/LIBRARY OF CONGRESS

When he began to piece together the connections between Levison, King, and O'Dell back in 1961, Hoover had assumed that it would be easy to handle the situation: he would tell the White House, the White House would tell King, and the alleged communists in question would quietly be ousted from positions of influence. The wiretaps and bug installed at Levison's home and office were the next step in that process. Through surveillance, Hoover planned to gather evidence that would support his allegations of ongoing communist connections and put further pressure on King. He did not find what he was seeking. As agents began to transcribe dozens and then hundreds of hours of private conversation, they came across few contacts between Levison and Communist Party leaders, much less with the Soviet Union. What they found instead was a wealth of detail about the civil rights movement's strategies.

Somewhat to Hoover's surprise, the political intelligence gleaned from the wiretaps added to his political influence at the White House over the course of 1963, a crucial year of civil rights negotiation. It did not, however, help him to resolve the growing conflict between his racial views and his duties as a federal lawman, or between the FBI, the Justice Department, and the White House. As the movement reached a crisis point in 1963, Hoover displayed a new openness to mobilizing his men on behalf of the Kennedys' agenda—even to working with Black activists on occasion. At the same time, he grew more hostile toward King, who was fast becoming one of his top public enemies.

HAD HE CARED TO DO SO, HOOVER MIGHT HAVE USED THE EARLY LEVISON WIRE-taps to develop a nuanced sense of King as a rising movement leader, driven by high ambition and acute caution. But he was still interested in a narrower project: getting Levison and O'Dell out of King's orbit. In late April 1962, presumably at Hoover's behest, the Senate Internal Security Subcommittee subpoenaed Levison to appear for questioning. Under oath, he barely tolerated their inquiries. "I am a loyal American and I am not now and never have been a member of the Communist Party," Levison declared before refusing to answer any further questions. Hoover scoffed at the denial, especially because the Childs brothers continued to report from party sources "that Stanley Levison, because of his association with the King movement, is doing the most important work in the CP today." Stymied in his effort to use SISS to force a confession, Hoover settled for identifying Levison once again as a "key figure" in the Communist Party.[1]

Toward O'Dell, Hoover adopted a somewhat different strategy, relying not on the subpoena power of SISS but on the secret pressures and manipulations of counterintelligence. In July, Hoover received word that O'Dell was still "considered by the CPUSA, as being a member of its National Committee." With that revelation in hand, he authorized the writing of an anonymous note about O'Dell's communist past, to be distributed without attribution to friendly Southern newspapers. The goal, according to the New York office, was not only to ensure that O'Dell would be fired from the SCLC, but to "cause other Negro organizations . . . to clean out anyone who possibly could cause embarrassment because of Communist affiliation or background." Several major newspapers took the bait, publishing identical articles that described O'Dell as "a concealed member" of the party's national council.[2]

At this point King made his first significant miscalculation in dealing with Hoover, one that would cost him dearly in the months ahead. Under pressure to respond to the O'Dell allegations, King issued a carefully worded public statement denying any knowledge of his employee's communist leanings, either past or present, and vowing to get to the bottom of the matter. The statement described O'Dell as a mere "technician" at the SCLC, brought in to help with "the mechanization of our mailing procedures." Hoover believed both claims were false: that King had been briefed by the White House about O'Dell's communist associations, and that O'Dell was in fact a key insider at SCLC. King's statement also maintained that O'Dell had resigned pending an "exacting and fair inquiry." But this, too, turned out to be untrue. As Hoover soon learned, O'Dell was temporarily being paid through a side channel on the assumption that SCLC would "probably rehire him," in Levison's words, once the furor blew over.[3]

A sympathetic interpretation of King's actions would attribute them to personal and political loyalty, the desire to protect valued colleagues from red-baiting. Hoover merely saw an example of King's willingness to harbor communists despite being warned against it. His anger increased the next month, when King complained in a press interview that Hoover often assigned white Southern-born agents to Southern field offices, leaving the FBI too "friendly with the local police" and overly "influenced by the mores of the community." King cited the case of Albany, Georgia, where the SCLC, working with other civil rights organizations, had recently launched a campaign of marches, boycotts, and nonviolent civil disobedience. In Albany, according to King, the FBI's Southern-born agents inevitably "sided with segregationists," preferring to fraternize with the police rather than protect the rights of demonstrators.[4]

Of everything Hoover had learned about King in the past few years, it was this minor criticism that seems to have caused the greatest personal animus. Indignant at the suggestion of bias, Hoover instructed his aides to tally up the records from the Albany office, counting which agents had been born where. Upon discovering that four out of five hailed from Northern states, he told them to contact King and correct the record—at which point King made another small but fateful mistake. Though an FBI official left two messages at the SCLC, King did not call back. FBI memos concluded that he "obviously does not desire to be given the truth" and labeled him a "vicious liar."[5]

This conviction—that King was a man of lies and deceit, hopelessly compromised by his association with communists—guided Hoover's interpretation of events over the next several months, as the SCLC began to lay plans for what would become its moment of greatest national impact: an anti-segregation campaign in Birmingham, Alabama. Racism explains much of Hoover's animus: as King became more prominent and influential, Hoover increasingly viewed him as a disrupter and a threat, in violation of the natural order. If asked, though, Hoover would have denied any ulterior motivation; according to him, King was simply lying and deserved what he got. In January, King rehired O'Dell based on the idea that O'Dell had left the Communist Party "quite awhile before" going to work at the SCLC—a claim that Hoover found preposterous. That same month, both O'Dell and Levison traveled to Dorchester, Georgia, for a top-secret, small-group strategy session in advance of the Birmingham campaign. To Hoover, their inclusion at that meeting proved that they were still powerful insiders at the SCLC, helping to determine the future direction of the civil rights movement despite their connections to the Communist Party.[6]

And yet when an opportunity came to act against Levison, to bring the whole tale out into the open, Hoover hesitated and backed away. In February 1963, the Justice Department floated the idea of prosecuting Levison for failing to register under the McCarran Act. In order to make the case, they needed a witness who could testify with credibility about Levison's secret party activities. Unwilling to expose SOLO, Hoover dispatched agents to consult with more than a dozen other ex-communists and informants, hoping that they might make the identification. When they all failed to recognize Levison, Hoover chose to protect SOLO rather than move forward, citing the fact that "a highly sensitive source who is not available for interview or testimony" remained the only provider of information.[7]

The aborted prosecution left Hoover stuck where he had been for more than two years: convinced that Levison and O'Dell were part of the communists' clandestine apparatus, but unable to force a separation from King or to get anyone else to make a move. The one hint of action came from Levison himself, who in March 1963 arranged to meet with Lem Harris, the communists' point man on finances and fundraising. According to Jack Childs, Levison explained over lunch that he had recently become disillusioned with the party, convinced that "the CP is 'irrelevant' and ineffective." Though he and other supporters continued to contribute money to the party "out of habit and sentiment," he explained, the time had come for a permanent break. "I was . . . tough . . . and I think I established my firm view, firm position," Levison told his brother a few days later, in a conversation captured on the FBI's wiretaps.

Harris came away with a different impression. "The LEVISONS and O'DELL are still Party members, but do not desire to be openly 'linked up' with the Party," Childs reported to the FBI, citing Harris's interpretation of events. "Although they are 'disenchanted' with the Party, they are not quitting." Jack received a similar report from Isadore Wofsy, another top party-finance official. "The LEVISONS wish to 'run' MARTIN LUTHER KING independently, without any interference from the Party," he told the FBI, "however, the LEVISONS wish to 'remain Party people.'"[8]

How should one interpret these conflicting claims? It seems most likely that Levison was, indeed, splitting from the party. After years of increasing distance, of trying to treat his former comrades fairly, he may simply have decided to throw in his lot with the cause that mattered more. But Hoover believed just the opposite—that the meeting confirmed rather than repudiated his own long-standing theory about Levison's true loyalties: If Levison had really been distancing himself from the party for years, why on earth did he need to meet with Harris as late as March 1963—some six years after he started working with King—in order to renounce the whole operation? And why, if he had nothing to hide, had he apparently never told King anything about it?

IN THE END, THE IMPULSE BEHIND LEVISON'S MEETING MAY HAVE HAD LESS TO do with any concerns internal to the Communist Party than with the SCLC's upcoming plans for Birmingham. During the conclave at Dorchester, the SCLC leadership had laid the groundwork for a campaign of nonviolent civil disobedience there, hoping to capitalize upon the city's reputation as "the most segregated city in America," in King's words. At that gathering, Levison reminded everyone about what Birmingham had been like during Bull Connor's early years, when the labor movement had gone up against the police only to be driven back through "forced brutality" and intimidation, just like the Freedom Riders. The plan now was to make Connor's methods work in the movement's favor, to produce a spectacle of such moral clarity that it would move both the city and the nation to turn against segregation.[9]

Hoover had his own strategy to work out for Birmingham, where his ability to influence the local authorities remained tenuous at best. After the Freedom Rides, he had made half-hearted gestures toward limiting contact with many Southern police departments, hoping to protect the Bureau from "unwarranted criticism." Once King accused the FBI of assigning too many Southern-born agents to Southern offices, Hoover had adjusted that policy, too, transferring additional Northern agents into the region "in order that the criticism which has arisen against the Bureau in its work in the civil rights field might to some degree be minimized." Hoover resented having to make the changes. "I personally do not approve of this policy because I think law enforcement should work as a team," he explained to Bobby Kennedy. He especially objected to the idea that the FBI had been pressured into action by Black leaders like King. "I think the limit of palliation and appeasement has been reached," he declared.[10]

Birmingham presented its own special problems. In 1963, National Academy graduate Jamie Moore was still there as police chief, bouncing between his role as Connor's subordinate and his desire to maintain decent FBI relations. And now there was another ex-FBI man in the mix, a former agent, arch-segregationist, and Connor devotee named Arthur Hanes, elected as Birmingham's mayor in 1961. Between them, Moore and Hanes represented two sides of Hoover's legacy: Moore the professional lawman, ostensibly devoted to expertise, local-federal cooperation, and scientific methods; Hanes the passionate conservative and standard-bearer for segregation, willing to stretch and evade the law in order to promote his cause.

One man who was certain the FBI should stay as far away as possible was Alabama governor George Wallace, who had been elected on a commitment to preserve "segregation now, segregation tomorrow, segregation forever," as he promised in his 1963 inaugural address. Wallace had never liked the FBI. As a circuit-court judge in the 1950s, he vowed to arrest any FBI agent who set foot in his territory. Since then, he had often swept the FBI into his denunciations of federal power, demanding resistance from all self-respecting white Southerners. Hoover took notice. When Wallace complained in 1962 that Alabama citizens were being harassed by FBI agents investigating voting rights, Hoover did not afford the governor even the courtesy of a phone call. "To contact him would only take cognizance of his tirades, [and] encourage further unwarranted politically-inspired assaults against the Bureau," an aide explained. Privately, Hoover labeled Wallace "a rat."[11]

He found it more difficult to separate from Hanes (the Birmingham mayor), who shared many of Wallace's views but often bragged about his past under Hoover's tutelage. During his three years at the Bureau, Hanes had been a standard G-Man: Southern-born, a college athlete turned law student, even "a handsome version of J. Edgar Hoover," in one historian's assessment. As an agent in the late 1940s, he had worked briefly in the field offices before taking up administrative work at headquarters. In 1951, he left to become head of security at Hayes Aircraft, a major Birmingham employer, and soon joined the Citizens' Council. His ability to move between worlds caught Bull Connor's attention. "He's the son of a Methodist minister, a football player, and an FBI man," Connor had said, promoting Hanes as an ideal mayoral candidate.[12]

Once elected, Hanes shut down the city's parks, pools, golf courses, and recreational facilities rather than desegregate them. In Washington, Hoover took flak for those actions. "Mayor Hanes expressed attitudes with respect to negroes which were extremely insulting to the convictions of most American citizens and which may justly earn the appellation, un-American," one concerned citizen wrote to Hoover, wondering if the FBI supported the racist views of its progeny. Hoover disavowed Hanes's attitudes. "His opinions, of course, are his own," he wrote back. But the questions persisted: How could the FBI have produced such a man? And what did it mean that one of the South's most virulent segregationist mayors described himself as a great Hoover admirer?[13]

With neither the mayor nor the governor as an appealing ally, Hoover was left with police chief Jamie Moore, the same man who had abandoned the Freedom Riders. While Hoover was now more cautious about working directly with him, Moore's academy background proved crucial in the early stages of planning how to handle the upcoming protests in Birmingham. Partly through academy circles, Moore had recently made common cause with Laurie Pritchett, the police chief of Albany, Georgia, where the SCLC had staged its last major round of demonstrations. Pritchett, too, was an academy graduate, a true believer in Hoover-style professionalism. Drawing upon those lessons, he had fashioned his own approach to policing civil rights demonstrations.

According to Pritchett, the Birmingham police had made a colossal mistake by allowing the Klansmen to beat the Freedom Riders—not because such violence was wrong, but because it played into the hands of the protesters. Without that spectacular violence, he argued, nobody would have noticed a bus trip by a handful of civil rights agitators. With it, they became martyrs and media darlings. In Albany, he set out to deprive the demonstrators of any such satisfaction. When they protested lawfully, the police stood by and watched. When they broke the law, officers calmly arrested them and took them to jail. Pritchett even helped to orchestrate King's release from jail, rather than allow him to stay inside and become an object of sympathy. Borrowing Gandhian language, Pritchett described his strategy as nonviolent passive resistance—

only in this case, it was a strategy for the police. His approach earned plaudits through-out the Northern press, where he was depicted as a new type of enlightened Southern lawman.

The imperative to get around Pritchett's tactics helped to bring King and the SCLC back to Birmingham, where Connor seemed likely to authorize an old-fashioned beat-down and thus attract sympathetic attention for the movement. Eager to head this off, Moore invited Pritchett down to Birmingham for a consultation. Pritchett showed up partly out of curiosity about Connor, "expectin' some big robust man" but instead finding a paunchy senior citizen with a receding hairline and too-thick glasses. Con-nor described plans to use police dogs and fire hoses to control the protesters. Pritchett advised Moore to "deactivate" the hoses "immediately" but expressed pessimism about whether the Albany approach could succeed with a hothead like Connor in charge.[14]

At first, though, it seemed as if the containment plan might really work. On April 6, when several dozen protesters gathered to pray and march, Moore followed Pritch-ett's lead and warned them calmly through his bullhorn that they were parading with-out a permit. Connor himself instructed the Klan to stay far away from the marchers, for fear of replicating the Freedom Riders debacle. After several days of restraint, how-ever, the Birmingham police departed from Pritchett's example by arresting King and then holding him in jail. King seized the opportunity afforded by eight days of solitude to compose what would become his famous "letter from a Birmingham jail," its initial draft scribbled along the margins of daily newspapers.

The differences between Birmingham and Albany grew still more significant over the next several weeks. On May 2, movement organizers launched a "children's march," drawing hundreds of students—some as young as six—out of school to walk, sing, and dance in the streets before submitting to arrest. The following day, facing hundreds more young marchers, Connor decided that he'd had enough and issued the order that both sides had long expected. For several minutes on May 3, in full view of photogra-phers and news reporters, the Birmingham police turned their dogs and fire hoses on the children. The resulting images—a high school sophomore fending off a German shepherd lunging toward his chest, children crouching in pain and terror as streams of water hit their fragile bodies—did just what the academy men had feared: they at-tracted national attention to King and the protesters, and thus made the Birmingham police into symbols of everything wrong with Southern law enforcement.

For all their lasting power and significance, the most dramatic forms of police vio-lence lasted only a short time. On May 4, when the children went out again, the fire hoses and dogs were still there but used with more discretion, less a full assault than an implied menace. On May 5, the firefighters refused to turn on their hoses at all. By that point, Kennedy aide Burke Marshall had arrived in town as an emissary from the Justice Department, hoping to broker a deal between the protesters and the white busi-ness owners downtown. Within days, the city announced a historic (if limited) accord, setting in motion the desegregation of its department stores, restaurants, and public facilities.

Less noticed were the changes taking place in law enforcement at the same time. In 1963, Birmingham policeman Mel Bailey, yet another of Hoover's academy graduates, began a thirty-three-year stint as sheriff of Jefferson County, the start of an uneven move away from Connor's methods. Both Connor and Hanes were soon out of office for good, having lost a special election. While critics drew a straight line between Hoover's racism and Hanes's "rabidly segregationist" mayoralty, it was Hoover's other disciples, the academy graduates and police professionalizers, who emerged with greater power in their hands. Though it would be remembered as a fearsome example of Connor-style brutality, Birmingham also showcased Hoover's preferred approach to policing, in which conservative race politics and modern police methods went hand in hand.[15]

IN THE EARLY STAGES OF THE BIRMINGHAM DEMONSTRATIONS, BOTH HOOVER and the White House had maintained that there was no federal role to be played. That began to change in mid-May after the children's marches, when a series of bombings aimed at the city's civil rights leadership shattered any illusion that nonviolence was destined to carry the day. On May 11, explosions went off in two locations: one at the home of King's brother, A. D., a local preacher, and a second beneath one of the SCLC's rooms at a local hotel. King had left Birmingham earlier that day, but a crowd gathered to register its outrage on his behalf, pelting the police with bottles and rocks—in one case even tackling and stabbing an officer. Hoover accepted responsibility for the bombing investigations under the Civil Rights Act of 1960, which allowed the FBI to investigate cases in which either the suspects or explosives were thought to have crossed state lines. Kennedy went well beyond that, into bolder and more decisive action. After months of contemplation, he concluded that a federal civil rights law banning discrimination in public accommodations would be needed to settle the Southern question.

Kennedy delivered on that idea a month later, in an impromptu television address that would come to be seen as the high point of his presidency. On the morning of June 11, in a show of defiance against a federal court decision ordering the desegregation of the University of Alabama, Governor Wallace made a self-described "stand in the schoolhouse door," a staged confrontation in which he bodily attempted to block the first Black students from entering the university before stepping aside for federal troops. That night, disgusted at Wallace's insurrectionary posturing, Kennedy appealed to Congress in a somber thirteen-minute television address backing a new law that would guarantee equal access to public accommodations, including restaurants, stores, schools, transit hubs, and universities. "The events in Birmingham and elsewhere have so increased the cries for equality that no city or state or legislative body can prudently choose to ignore them," he declared. It was a profound shift from where his own presidency had begun, and it presaged greater enforcement activity by the federal authorities.[16]

Hoover had been part of the process by which the president arrived at his new position, if only in indirect ways. In early June, the Levison wiretaps revealed plans afoot for a March on Washington to pressure the White House into supporting a federal civil rights law. "The threat itself may so frighten the President that he would have to do something," King told Levison, by way of explanation. Hoover sent those words along to the White House. So when Kennedy surprised everyone with his televised address less than a week later, it was in part an effort to outflank King, and to shift the pressure of the march away from the White House and onto Congress.[17]

But new pressures kept emerging. And more and more, they drew Hoover in. Just after midnight on the evening of Kennedy's speech, Medgar Evers, field secretary of the Mississippi NAACP, collapsed in the driveway of his Jackson home, the victim of a gunshot to the back. He died almost immediately, presumed to be a victim of Klan retaliation against Kennedy's civil rights stance. Hoover sent agents in to investigate, since Evers's voting-rights work, combined with the timing of the shooting, made his murder a possible federal violation.

In the meantime, the FBI continued to pursue information about King's plans as the civil rights movement surged into a new phase, its ambition for a federal civil rights law now backed by the president. By throwing his support behind the law, Kennedy had tied himself to King—and made himself more vulnerable to accusations that might besmirch the civil rights leader. On June 17, less than a week after the president's speech, Bobby called Hoover to say that he was ready to confront the Levison-O'Dell issue again, and to warn King not to be in touch with either man "directly or indirectly." In that conversation, Hoover repositioned himself as an ally concerned about the ways that Levison and O'Dell might taint King's righteous efforts. "If King continues this association, he is going to hurt his own cause," he declared, adding that "nothing could be worse" for the movement's future.[18]

Kennedy proceeded with sending his civil rights bill to Congress, a leap of faith by a Democrat still dependent upon the South for reelection. Meanwhile, the Justice Department worked closely with Courtney Evans to figure out how much they could say to King without jeopardizing SOLO. O'Dell was the easier case, given his open history of Communist Party membership—though officials still worried about disclosing any current evidence of "Communist influence or control." Levison remained more of a challenge, since his role in party finances had always been known to so few individuals. Based on Evans's advice, Burke Marshall decided that "it was not in the best interest of the United States to inform Dr. King that we had any firm information that Levison was under communist control." Instead they would once again ask King to trust them, and hope that this time he would do as they asked.

The plan went into effect on Saturday, June 22, 1963, in the midst of a civil rights summit at the White House. Before the meeting began, Marshall pulled King aside to discuss Levison and O'Dell, following the limits laid out by the FBI. Lest the warning be dismissed again, Bobby personally followed up with King, letting him know how important it was to the White House. Then, just when King might have thought the worst was over, the president himself asked for a few moments of private discussion. Strolling through the Rose Garden with King, Kennedy laid out an extreme version of what Hoover had described over the past two years, identifying Levison as a fixture of the Soviets' secret U.S. apparatus, O'Dell as a member of the national board ("the number five Communist in the United States"), and Levison as O'Dell's clandestine party guide and mentor. The bottom line was clear: "They're Communists. You've got to get rid of them," Kennedy said, especially if King wanted the White House to continue moving forward with a civil rights agenda. He insisted throughout that the warnings were in King's interest, that they were both lucky to be getting another chance to fix the situation before it ended up on the front pages.

King conceded that O'Dell was probably a lost cause, an open communist with a well-established history that could be used as a political weapon. On Levison, though, he dug in again, refusing to believe what the president said about his friend's communist background. "I know Stanley, and I can't believe this," he told the president. "You will have to prove it." That day, the White House put in two calls to Hoover, one at 11:53 a.m. and another at 12:30 p.m. But Hoover never gave permission to disclose the details that King was seeking.

What would have happened if Hoover had actually done as King had asked, if he had finally shared the wealth of detail amassed by the Childs brothers over the previous decade? Possibly King would have continued to defend his colleague, arguing that communists had fought for noble causes including labor rights, anti-fascism, and racial equality. Or perhaps he would have felt betrayed by Levison's apparent secrecy and subterfuge. In either case, it seems unlikely that the loss of Levison would have made a dramatic difference for the broader movement, given its momentum and growing mass appeal. But King did not see things that way. When Marshall came back to him with only "vague allegations of Levison's unspecified Soviet contacts," in the words of one historian, King once again sided with his friend and dismissed the whole matter as a figment of Hoover's imagination.[19]

ON JUNE 23, THE DAY AFTER THE WHITE HOUSE MEETING, HOOVER ANNOUNCED that the FBI had arrested Medgar Evers's murderer, a Mississippi Citizens' Council member named Byron De La Beckwith. Around the same time, King gathered a group of SCLC officials to speak with O'Dell, just as he had promised the president he would do. O'Dell resented facing down the FBI's accusations. "Hoover can kiss my ass! I am not the issue!" he insisted. But Hoover was one step ahead, having leaked reports of O'Dell's ongoing employment at the SCLC to *The Birmingham News*, among other papers. Conceding the inevitable, King wrote a letter of dismissal to O'Dell, but not without taking a jab at Hoover. Though he never mentioned Hoover's name, King noted that in Cold War America "any allusion to the left brings forth an emotional response," painting Hoover-style anticommunism as fundamentally irrational and outdated. In asking for O'Dell's resignation, he also pointed out that nobody had yet supplied firm evidence that O'Dell maintained "any present connections with the Communist party."[20]

When it came to Levison, though, King held true to what he'd told the president in the Rose Garden: he would not sever ties without proof. And since proof was not forthcoming, he tried instead to perform an end run around the president's request. His latest idea was to rely on friendly go-betweens—New York lawyer Clarence Jones and the rising young singer Harry Belafonte—when he needed to get in touch with Levison. Under the new arrangement, Belafonte recalled, "I would go to a friend's house and call a third party, who would relay the message that Stan should call their mutual friend. Stan would then go out to a pay phone and call me at the friend's house. Both parties were then on 'safe phones,' as we called them, and the FBI was, we hoped, left out of the loop." Belafonte occasionally experienced his own twinges of doubt about Levison. "Was Hoover right?" he sometimes wondered. "Maybe Stan *was* an active communist, taking his orders from Moscow." But he set that "paranoia" aside in order to help King get out from under the FBI's pressure and scrutiny.

King appears to have believed that the new setup would satisfy the White House—that he and the Kennedys were tacitly in cahoots against Hoover, seeking to save face rather than address a bona fide national security threat. He was mistaken. On King's behalf, Jones disclosed the new plan to the Justice Department. Rather than offering a wink and a nod, Bobby was quietly horrified. In July, he proposed something that even Hoover had not fully entertained: wiretaps not merely on Levison, but on King himself. Courtney Evans claimed to have discouraged the idea, pressing the attorney general to think about "the repercussions if it should ever become known that such a surveillance had been put on King." But Bobby insisted that he was not worried and that he wanted "as complete coverage as possible," according to Evans.[21]

The attorney general backed off from his ambitions a few days later, approving a wiretap on Jones but not one on King. By that point, though, Hoover was already thinking about his own next move, with or without the attorney general. On August 28, from the steps of the Lincoln Memorial, King delivered seventeen of the most stirring minutes of oratory in all of American history while Hoover sat at Bureau headquarters, keeping his schedule clear in case of emergency. Belafonte later speculated about what the day must have been like for Hoover, as "not just 100,000, but more than 250,000—more people than we imagined in our wildest dreams" amassed along the National Mall in support of racial equality. "What, I wondered, must J Edgar Hoover be thinking at that moment, holed up in his dark little den at the FBI?"[22]

One thing Hoover was thinking was that perhaps the time had come to make nice with civil rights protesters, given their growing power and influence. With the march underway, the radical journalist William Worthy, head of the tiny but outspoken Freedom Now Party, vowed to bring the struggle to Hoover's doorstep with a sit-in at FBI headquarters. To head off that confrontation, Hoover made a surprise decision to invite Worthy and his fellow Freedom Now leaders to the Bureau for a sit-down conference. Worthy had long excoriated Hoover as the worst of the worst, a pillar of white supremacy. He nonetheless accepted Hoover's invitation, arriving at the director's reception room the next morning for what was surely one of the strangest confabs in civil rights history. Hoover remained silent as Worthy and his companions described the "lack of law enforcement" in civil rights cases and the fact that "the FBI had not measured up to its responsibilities." Once they finished speaking, he launched into his own monologue, rattling off the FBI's investigative successes and blaming any frustrations on its lack of jurisdiction. Hoover felt that Worthy left the meeting less "sarcastic" than when he went in, and decided that such personal exchanges might be a way of managing the future. He instructed that Freedom Now representatives "be promptly and courteously received" if and when they showed up at FBI offices. "It is felt that by such an approach, not only can the Bureau forestall any 'sit-ins' and unfavorable publicity," he wrote, "but do much to enable Negro leaders to understand the true role of the FBI in these investigations."[23]

If Hoover had, in fact, adopted that model, the next several years might have looked radically different: a dialogue in good faith between the FBI and the civil rights movement, as the country attempted to make progress on racial justice. But Hoover was also thinking about other things, and those ideas would have far greater consequences than his one-off meeting with a minor player. On August 23, five days before the March on Washington, the Domestic Intelligence Division had submitted a "detailed memorandum concerning the efforts of the Communist Party, USA, to exploit the American Negro." The memo argued that while the communists were taking a renewed interest in the civil rights movement, the movement did not seem much interested in them—an argument that Hoover had made frequently in the 1950s. He no longer believed that the communists were quite so ineffective, however, and pushed back hard against any suggestion that the Bureau could rest easy. "This memo reminds me vividly of those I received when Castro took over Cuba," he wrote, accusing his aides of overlooking obvious evidence of communist influence. "I for one can't ignore the memos re King, O'Dell, Levison, Rustin, Hall et al as having only an infinitesimal impact on the efforts to exploit the American Negro by the Communists."[24]

His note set off a new round of activity at the Bureau, as officials rushed to reassess their strategies and to ensure that they followed Hoover's dicta. It also ultimately changed the Bureau's approach to King, who was no longer to be considered merely a target of communist influence, but a growing problem in his own right. In the wake of the march, Sullivan composed an obsequious memo backtracking on his office's previous claims and acknowledging that "the Director is correct," as always. Intuiting what Hoover seemed to want, Sullivan argued that the moment had come to face the King issue head-on, without relying on advisers or friends as points of entrée, and without waiting for the White House to force King into action. "Personally, I believe in the light of King's powerful demagogic speech yesterday he stands head and shoulders above all other Negro leaders put together when it comes to influencing great masses of Negroes," Sullivan wrote, in what would become one of the most influential memos in Bureau history. "We must mark him now, if we have not done so before, as the most dangerous Negro of the future in this Nation from the standpoint of communism, the Negro and national security." Over the next few months, with the approval of both Hoover and Bobby Kennedy, the FBI installed wiretaps at King's home and offices.[25]

CHAPTER 46

The President Is Dead

(1963)

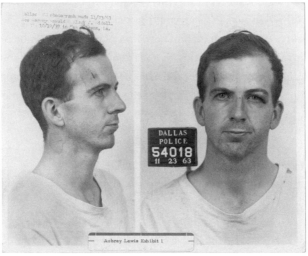

Mug shots of Lee Harvey Oswald, arrested for the assassination of
President John F. Kennedy, November 22, 1963.

NATIONAL ARCHIVES AND RECORDS ADMINISTRATION

When a bomb tore through Birmingham's 16th Street Baptist Church on
September 15, 1963, less than a month after the March on Washington, many
people assumed that it would be the FBI's biggest case of the year. The congregation
had been at the epicenter of the summer's protests: "a large Negro church in which
many pro-integration demonstrations" had been held, in the words of an "urgent" telegram to Hoover from Birmingham that afternoon. The bomb struck just as the church
was filling up for Sunday services. Four girls—eleven-year-old Denise McNair, along
with fourteen-year-olds Carole Robertson, Cynthia Wesley, and Addie Mae Collins—
had been looking into a mirror in the basement restroom when the explosion burst in
on them, ripping off their Sunday-best dresses and burying them beneath a pile of steel,
stone, and brick.[1]

The writer James Baldwin, at the peak of acclaim for the essays in his collection,
The Fire Next Time, declared Hoover responsible for their deaths. "I blame J. Edgar
Hoover in part for the events in Alabama," he told *The New York Times*, citing the

FBI's dismal record on racial violence. "Negroes have no cause to have faith in the FBI." James Wechsler, Hoover's inveterate critic at the *New York Post*, wondered if this brutal crime, coming after years of federal hesitation, might finally do Hoover in. "The bomb that destroyed four children in Birmingham should have finally shattered the Hoover myth," he wrote, while conceding that "such legends die hard." The statistics from Birmingham spoke for themselves: at least forty racially motivated bombings since 1947, with not one successful arrest or conviction.[2]

Hoover still blamed those numbers on forces outside the FBI, describing civil rights as thankless work in which "both sides in the racial issue" attacked the FBI from "their respective points of view." Even to Hoover, though, the church bombing had been so terrible—and so heavily publicized—that sitting back seemed impossible. When a Justice attorney telephoned the FBI that night, the official on duty assured them that Hoover and the rest of the Bureau "considered this a most heinous offense and that we had entered the investigation with no holds barred." They did so under the 1960 Civil Rights Act, which had expanded the FBI's jurisdiction in bombing cases. Based on this authority, Hoover ordered an investigation undertaken that afternoon with "all possible speed."[3]

For the moment, Hoover refrained from making any public statement about the bombing, fearing that he would seem to be "coming in the back door to capitalize on a tragic incident," in the words of one Bureau official. The best way to send a message, they decided, was to get to the heart of the matter as fast as possible and to speak out "only when we have accomplishments." But before Hoover could announce any accomplishments or do much to redeem his record on Southern bombings, an even more spectacular crime intervened. It turned the nation's attention away from Birmingham and toward Dallas.[4]

HOOVER HAD JUST RETURNED FROM LUNCH WHEN THE REPORT FLASHED OVER the ticker on November 22. Three minutes later, at 1:43 p.m., he reached Bobby Kennedy at Hickory Hill, in Virginia, where the attorney general was enjoying a poolside tuna sandwich. "I have news for you," Hoover said, as a nearby workman began to run toward Kennedy's pool, transistor radio in hand. "The president's been shot." The wounds were serious, even critical, Hoover reported. The gunman remained at large. He promised to find out more, then hung up and took a call from the field office in Dallas, where the president had been rushed to Parkland Hospital, the right side of his skull and brain shattered by at least one bullet.

Bobby later expressed astonishment at Hoover's flat, unapologetic tone, his near-total lack of concern or sympathy. This would soon become a standard portrait of those first awful minutes: Hoover stoic and uncaring; Bobby racked by grief, panic, and fear. Under the circumstances, though, Hoover's emotional distance had certain advantages.

Bobby's secretary, Angie Novello, had refused to make the phone call, unwilling to be the first one to relay the terrible news. Hoover did what he felt his position demanded. The attorney general might be the president's brother, but he was also Hoover's boss. Hoover concluded that his boss ought to be informed about a major crime in the making.[5]

There were two more phone calls out to Bobby in Virginia that afternoon, as the Bureau went into mass alert. The first came at 2:10 p.m., when Hoover called to report that "the president is dead" nearly half an hour before the public announcement from Dallas. Deputy attorney general Nicholas Katzenbach remembered that even then Bobby was furious at Hoover. "Hoover just called me," he told Katzenbach, in the latter's account. "The president is dead. I think Hoover enjoyed giving me the news." In Hoover's own version, the exchange was not nearly so stark. "I asked the attorney general whether or not he wanted to go to Dallas, and told him that we would facilitate the trip," Hoover recalled. "He said no; his plans were nebulous."

Hoover's final call that afternoon reported that the president's body was heading east on Air Force One, and that Lyndon Johnson had been sworn in as president. He also noted that the FBI "had moved in even though this was not a federal crime." The instinct to discuss jurisdiction at such a moment did not further endear him to Bobby. As a Bureau official later pointed out, however, this was simply what Hoover did in times of crisis. "I think Mr. Hoover's reaction was like it would have been in any other incident: 'What is the FBI's responsibility insofar as this matter is concerned? What is the principal thing the FBI should do at this time?'" The answers were not so obvious. As Hoover would explain many times over the next twenty-four hours, the murder of the president was just that: an act of murder, falling under the jurisdiction of the local authorities.[6]

Throughout the country, news of the president's death brought routines to a halt. At the Bureau, by contrast, Hoover's great bureaucratic machine shifted into high gear. Whatever the fine points of jurisdiction, it was clear that the country would be looking to the FBI to do *something*; as with Birmingham, hanging back was not an option. In Dallas, agent James Hosty ascribed a surreal quality to the afternoon, as if the rules and regulations designed for other cases could not possibly apply in a crime of this magnitude. "The president of the United States was gunned down less than six blocks from where I was eating lunch," he later wrote. "And then FBI headquarters was asking me to help find the president's assassin." Hoover's first assumption, widely shared by other law enforcement officials, was that a right-wing zealot had carried out the assassination. His initial instructions prodded his agents in this direction. "All offices immediately establish whereabouts of bombings suspects, all known Klan and hate group members, known racial extremists," he ordered in an "urgent" message to the field offices.[7]

In Washington, oddly, there was less to do. Just as at earlier moments of high crisis,

Hoover spent the afternoon by the phone, awaiting news. Assistant director Alan Belmont took operational charge of the afternoon's events, staying on the line with Dallas, spitting out instructions, and demanding impossible answers. Hoover remained one step removed, sealed off in the director's quarters, less the master of events than the final repository of other men's information. He accepted just one more direct call from Dallas that afternoon: special agent in charge Gordon Shanklin phoned at 2:17, presumably to report that police officer J. D. Tippit had just been shot along a tree-lined residential street. About half an hour later, Dallas police apprehended the chief suspect in that shooting, a young man named Lee Harvey Oswald, who was also wanted for questioning in the president's murder.[8]

The Oswald arrest sent the FBI's energies veering in another direction, away from roundups of "hate group" contacts and into drill-down scrutiny of a single man. In Dallas, Hosty recalled a jolt of dread upon hearing Oswald's name: he had been keeping tabs on Oswald for almost a year, not because of any assassination plot but due to Oswald's bizarre past. In 1959, after a stint in the Marines, Oswald had defected to the Soviet Union and attempted to renounce his American citizenship. Three years after that, he had returned to the United States with a Russian wife and baby daughter, bouncing between Texas and his hometown of New Orleans before settling in Dallas. Since then, it had fallen to Hosty, among others, to try to figure out what was going on.

The chief suspicion was that Oswald or his wife, Marina—or both—had been sent to the U.S. as Soviet sleeper agents, to be activated at a propitious moment. "To me Lee and Marina were just routine espionage cases," Hosty later explained. "All I was trying to find out was whether either one of them was a spy for the Soviets." Despite the high stakes, he had never interviewed Oswald, for fear of revealing too much about the FBI's counterespionage methods. He had tried to speak with Marina, but to no avail. Just weeks before the assassination, Oswald had delivered an outraged note to the field office telling Hosty to lay off or "appropriate action" would be taken. That note, along with Oswald's file, was sitting in Hosty's file drawer at the Dallas field office.

Upon realizing these connections, Hosty thought of "Old Man" Hoover, hoping against hope that Hoover would understand that Oswald had not appeared to pose any violent threat. In the meantime, he located the office file on Oswald and brought it to his boss, Shanklin, who put him on the phone with Belmont at headquarters, who ordered Hosty down to the Dallas police department to participate in Oswald's interrogation.[9]

Around the time of Oswald's arrest, Hoover was on the phone with oilman Billy Byars, apparently the one Texas friend he sought out that afternoon, presumably to gain a firsthand report from the ground. By the time Richard Nixon called in an hour and a half later, Hoover had been fully briefed on the latest developments in Dallas and sounded confident of Oswald's guilt. "I said, 'What happened?'" Nixon recalled. "'Who was it? One of those right-wing nuts?' Hoover responded, 'No, it was a Commonest.'"

He never said Communist, incidentally, always Commonest." For at least a few hours that afternoon, Oswald's story seemed to align neatly with Hoover's worldview.

Even under these conditions, in conversation with trusted allies and close friends, there was something notably aloof about Hoover's demeanor that day. Nixon himself later described the afternoon as an "agonizing" ordeal, recalling how a doorman rushed toward his cab in New York with "tears . . . streaming down his cheeks" to report that the president had been killed. Nobody ascribed any such emotion to Hoover. Nor did Hoover himself ever describe the afternoon that way. In his few personal accounts of the assassination, he proceeded methodically through events: first the news ticker, then the call to Bobby, then the business of finding a murderer. At no point did he pause to express any great personal grief or official regrets, or any sense that the FBI could have or should have saved the president.[10]

Hoover also seemed ready to accept the simplest solution to the crime, to wrap up the whole matter right then and there. Even as his agent snuck into the Dallas police station to participate in Oswald's interrogation, Hoover was assuring confidants in Washington that "very probably we had in custody the man who had killed the President in Dallas" though "this had not definitively been established." When assistant attorney general Norbert Schlei called just after five o'clock, seeking to gather background information for a public announcement, Hoover calmly ticked off the available facts. "I stated [Oswald] was born an American but tried unsuccessfully to lose his American citizenship; came back to this country in 1962." He also passed along at least one mistake, suggesting that Oswald had visited Cuba "several" times in recent years. Hoover made no attempt to hide the FBI's past interactions with Oswald. Nor did he show much concern that Oswald might not have acted alone. Instead, he seemed to take the facts at face value. Most likely, he informed Schlei, the president had been killed by a man who was at once "a nut" and "an extreme radical of the left."

Hoover's confidence would later fuel speculation: Why was he so certain about Oswald? What could account for his calm in the midst of so much emotion and chaos? In conversation with Schlei that afternoon, Hoover hinted at one explanation: almost alone among men in government, he had seen this sort of thing before. At the age of sixty-eight, Hoover was one of the few federal officials who could claim a living memory of another presidential assassination, the shooting of William McKinley by the anarchist Leon Czolgosz in 1901, when Hoover was six. As Hoover described it, Czolgosz was not so different from Oswald, both a radical and a fantasist who believed that shooting the president would inspire a revolution. During Hoover's childhood, the nation had been racked with debates over whether Czolgosz was a madman or a true anarchist. As Hoover now recounted to Schlei, he himself had been one of the people who helped to put the debate to rest. "I advised Mr. Schlei that Czolgosz, who killed President McKinley, was a student of Emma Goldman and that I later prosecuted her for deportation from the United States."

If Schlei found it strange to be discussing Hoover's early glories at a moment of national panic, he did not register any objection. Instead, after more discussion of Oswald, he expressed his thanks—"Mr. Schlei stated I had been very helpful"—and then hung up, prepared for a long night at Justice headquarters.[11]

HOOVER MADE NO PLANS TO STAY LATE, AS HE MIGHT HAVE DONE IN HIS younger years. He left the office at 6:01, content to leave matters in the hands of sub-ordinates. Lyndon Johnson found him at home later that evening, in the first of many phone calls that would pass between the two men in the days to come. Johnson had been in Dallas that morning, riding with his wife, Lady Bird, in his own open-top car, a respectful seventy-five feet behind the president. The Secret Service had raced him to Parkland Hospital, then out to Love Air Field, where they smuggled him onto Air Force One. Jackie Kennedy had arrived at the plane half an hour later. She stood at Johnson's side while he recited the presidential oath, her cheerful pink suit stained brown by her husband's blood. They arrived back in Washington at 5:58, just as Hoover was preparing to leave the office. At 6:10, Johnson spoke briefly from the tarmac at Andrews Air Force Base, his first public words as president. "I will do my best," he said plaintively into a bank of microphones, "that is all I can do." Then he departed for his old suite in the Executive Office Building, not yet ready to lay claim to the Oval Office. At 7:26, after speaking with Dwight Eisenhower and Harry Truman, the last two occupants of the White House, he placed a call to Hoover.[12]

Johnson no longer lived down the street on Thirtieth Place, but he and Hoover had remained fast friends, exchanging a steady run of birthday gifts and holiday greetings. Johnson had been bitterly unhappy as vice president, a hulking, twangy Texan among lithe brain trusters, "treated more or less as an orphan by the Kennedy administration," in the words of one FBI official. This was part of what sustained his friendship with Hoover: both men viewed the Kennedy presidency as something to be endured rather than engaged, and both reserved a special dark place in their hearts for the president's brother. Bobby had been merciless toward Johnson, closing him out of key administrative meetings and mocking him privately as "Rufus Cornpone," a rube in a world of sophisticates.[13]

Johnson's phone call to Hoover that evening lasted just three or four minutes, hardly enough time to mark the momentous occasion. By all accounts, Johnson appeared as calm as Hoover by that point, all business and leadership. It was too soon to speak of politics, or to acknowledge that the assassination, for all its present horror, might be a good thing for both Hoover and Johnson. This first call was transactional, with one important piece of business to be accomplished. Despite the vagaries of federal jurisdiction, that night Johnson "asked me to take over completely the investigation of the assassination," Hoover later wrote.[14]

Only then did Hoover accept that the Kennedy assassination, like the escalating violence in the South, would require a sweeping, long-term commitment from the FBI. Around ten p.m., authorized from his home on Thirtieth Place, Hoover shared Johnson's instructions with the field offices. "The Bureau is conducting an investigation to determine who is responsible for the assassination," his message read. "This matter is of utmost urgency and should be handled accordingly."[15]

WHILE HOOVER SLEPT, OTHER MEN IN WASHINGTON AND DALLAS SPENT THE night wired and awake, trying to move the nation through a tragedy of as yet unknown dimensions. At Bethesda Naval Hospital, doctors performed an autopsy on the late president's body, removing what was left of his brain before concluding that he had been killed by bullet wounds to the head and upper back. At four thirty a.m., they released the body back to Jackie Kennedy, and a naval ambulance sped through the empty Washington streets with both Jackie and Bobby aboard, heading for the White House. Staff had decorated the East Room as a site of mourning, with a raised black catafalque toward the center. A Marine guard carried the casket into the room, now lit by candles in homage to those critical hours when Abraham Lincoln's body, similarly pocked by an assassin's bullet, had lain there a century earlier.[16]

Half a continent away in Dallas, the night belonged to Oswald, the peculiar young man whose alleged actions had set the whole tragedy in motion. At midnight local time, Dallas police gave the press its first glimpse of him: short and disheveled, in a wrinkled white T-shirt torn at the neck, his left eye bruised and just beginning to swell. An hour and a half later, Oswald was arraigned for the crime of murder in the death of John F. Kennedy.[17]

At the FBI field office, SAC Shanklin held court at his desk throughout the night, chain-smoking cigarettes, calling the Dallas police and then Bureau headquarters and then the police again, the chief point of contact between two distraught bureaucracies. His agent Hosty later described Shanklin as a "nervous" man, "afraid of his own shadow" more often than not. "To survive with J. Edgar Hoover as his boss," Hosty wrote, "he always had to be looking over his shoulder." But that night everyone at the Dallas office was nervous—not just about what had happened the previous day, but about what might happen once the director awoke the next morning. Updates flowed in to Hoover's office throughout the early morning hours: Dallas police found a rifle on the sixth floor of the Texas School Book Depository; the rifle belonged to A. Hidell; A. Hidell was one of Oswald's pseudonyms; the rifle was heading east on an Air Force jet to be examined at the FBI lab. At four a.m., Shanklin wrote up a lengthy overview, the first master summary of investigation, to be ready for the director first thing in the morning.[18]

Hoover was in no rush to reengage the matter. November 23 was a Saturday, and

Hoover no longer went into the office on Saturdays, usually spending the morning at Thirtieth Place and the afternoon at the track. Even on this Saturday, he started out following the usual routine. He received a briefing from headquarters summarizing Shanklin's memo. At ten a.m., as if he had spent the whole night deep in the details, Hoover called Johnson from home with an update on the investigation.

Hoover's decision not to go into the office that morning did not significantly alter the developing investigation. But it may have introduced elements of uncertainty and misinformation into the call with Johnson that could otherwise have been avoided. Hoover began by speaking as if the police and FBI investigations had seamlessly melded into a single investigative effort. "This man in Dallas," he explained, "we, of course, charged him with the murder of the president." As on the previous day, Hoover expressed confidence in Oswald's guilt but warned that "the case as it stands now isn't strong enough to be able to get a conviction" despite the discovery of Oswald's rifle. According to the latest reports, Oswald had acquired the rifle through a mail-order catalog, a detail that Hoover found particularly upsetting. "It seems almost impossible to think that for $21 you could kill the president of the United States," he told Johnson. Hoover reminded the new president that "no one knows this"—that the information he was conveying would be kept from the press as long as possible to allow the investigation to develop.

Unlike their brief exchange the previous night, this conversation went on for some time—at least ten minutes, possibly as many as fifteen. Hoover did most of the talking, clipping along at his martial pace, while Johnson listened, occasionally interjecting a question or two. Some of what Hoover conveyed that morning was truly bizarre, a concoction of newly discovered facts and eager leaps of imagination. The Bureau knew, for instance, that Oswald had made a visit to the Soviet embassy in Mexico City (and soon it would be realized that he had visited the Cuban consulate there as well). Though nearly every aspect of that trip remained a mystery, Hoover informed Johnson that it was not Oswald but a doppelgänger who had gone to Mexico, using Oswald's name. This was a minor detail, just one of many conveyed during the phone call. But it was strange enough to raise Johnson's level of alarm about a possible conspiracy behind the assassination. Perhaps this was Hoover's intent—to impress Johnson and show that only the FBI could uncover the greatest of secrets. More likely, he simply did not yet understand the details of the developing investigation, and he had nobody by his side to correct him.[19]

At this point, perhaps sensing that he was on uncertain footing, Hoover came to the obvious conclusion: his presence was required at headquarters, even though it was a Saturday. Once there, he assumed the same pose he had adopted in the hours after the shooting: he was calm, dispassionate, and faintly impatient, seeking not to mourn the president but to move the investigation toward a swift conclusion. Around twelve thirty, some twenty minutes after arriving at headquarters, he issued a message informing all special agents in charge that "Lee Harvey Oswald has been developed as the principal suspect in the assassination of Pres. Kennedy." He ordered them to resume normal contact with the right-wing informants and suspects they had rushed to locate the previous day.[20]

Those instructions marked another shift in the Bureau's direction. Even as they continued to run down new leads, they increasingly focused on gathering evidence of Oswald's complicity. As Hoover had suggested to Johnson, the problem was not only one of guilt or innocence, but of securing enough evidence to convict Oswald in court. Looking back, some of his men would wonder if he had moved too soon. "Hoover's obsession with speed made impossible demands on the field," Courtney Evans recalled. "I can't help but feel that had he let the agents out there do their work, let things take their normal investigative course, something other than the simple Oswald theory might have developed." But Hoover was under enormous pressure, Oswald was by far the most credible suspect, and not pursuing that investigation aggressively enough would have yielded its own complaints and problems.[21]

Indeed, if Hoover had limited interest in pursuing other paths that afternoon, it was partly because he was seeking to do what he often did best: protect the Bureau. To inquire more expansively into the previous day's events was, in his mind, to court disaster—not only for the FBI but also for the nation and possibly the world. Oswald was a newly returned Soviet defector; one wrong comment—one off-the-cuff hint that the Bureau suspected the Soviets had killed the president—and the world might find itself embroiled in a major international incident, perhaps even on the brink of nuclear war. Then there were the more immediate concerns about Bureau operations, and about what might be revealed if the investigation wandered down too many twisting paths. Given free rein to pursue all avenues, what would agents inadvertently reveal about SOLO, or about the Bureau's investigations of organized crime? How many of those efforts would be disrupted or exposed to public view? Hoover may have ordered the resumption of standard informant proceedings that afternoon not just because he believed in Oswald's guilt, but because other options seemed so perilous.

Finally, there was the great, consuming question of blame—of whether the Bureau would be held responsible for failing to prevent the assassination. Already that morning, the Dallas police chief had revealed in a press conference that "the FBI knew [Oswald] was in Dallas." The Secret Service, too, would undoubtedly try to shift responsibility onto the FBI. Hoover would have to make judgments about what his own agents had done or not done in the days and hours leading up to the assassination. He would have to decide, too, whether those judgments should be made public, or whether they would be contained within the Bureau.

Such institutional priorities helped to guide Hoover's actions that afternoon. He did not venture out into the field or pay his respects at the White House, where John Kennedy's body lay in state for viewing by congressmen and other government officials. Instead, he sat at his desk, the grand arbiter and filter of other men's information, fielding calls up the chain of command. According to his office log, Hoover did not speak with anyone outside the Bureau that afternoon. He made only a single call to the White House, in a failed attempt to contact Bobby Kennedy.

He did reach out in writing to Johnson, sending a five-page report to the White House that outlined what the Bureau knew. Unlike Hoover's phone call with Johnson that morning, this report was largely accurate, describing Oswald's background, family and known associates, the forensic details of the bullets and rifle. Then, apparently satisfied that things were under control, Hoover left the office. It was 5:51 p.m. on Saturday evening, almost thirty hours since Kennedy's murder. With a suspect in jail and new evidence emerging by the moment, it seemed safe to assume that the worst was behind them.[22]

HOOVER WAS STILL AT HOME THE NEXT DAY, WHEN THE DALLAS POLICE ES-corted Oswald into a windowless corridor below the main city jail. The police planned to move Oswald to a more secure county facility, where he would be locked up and interrogated until his trial several months hence. It was, by any reckoning, a delicate operation. The night before, someone had called the local Bureau field office to warn that a "syndicate" planned to kill Oswald in retaliation for the president's murder. The Bureau had in turn warned the police. Hoover was not in on that exchange—he was at Thirtieth Place—but it did not take special knowledge to see that the transportation of the man who was now the world's most famous prisoner might require some extra discretion and planning.

As Hoover later complained, however, the Dallas police were suffering from "tele-visionitis" that day. When Oswald emerged into the corridor, cameramen and report-ers swarmed his police entourage, with Oswald, handcuffed but unshackled, in the middle. They walked together a few steps before a man stepped from the crowd to Oswald's left, extended his arm, and shot Oswald in the gut. Many Americans wit-nessed the murder live on television, in what was supposed to be NBC's brief cutaway from Kennedy memorial coverage. The morning's pageantry had been spectacular: the slain president's casket mounted on a simple black carriage, drawn from the White House to the Capitol by six gray horses, one rider missing from each pair. But it was Oswald's shooting—the first murder ever broadcast live on television—that riveted the nation.[23]

Like Kennedy two days earlier, Oswald was rushed to Parkland Hospital, where he died in surgery just after two p.m., without a word to the Bureau agents stationed outside the operating room. His death meant that the assassination investigation would have to take a radically new path, one that would lead not to criminal conviction but to some other, more nebulous conclusion. Now there would never be a confession, or even a chance to ask basic questions. And there would be no trial, no public sifting of evidence, no impartial jury to weigh the facts and come to a court-sanctioned decision. When Hoover awoke that morning, it had all seemed surprisingly simple: a suspect was in custody, his rifle and bullets at the lab, the background evidence building nicely. Now the Kennedy assassination was no longer a criminal matter but a fast-evolving source of speculation, uncertainty, and finger-pointing.

Hoover did not go downtown that afternoon, but he was paying close attention, developing his own narrative of what had happened and what would need to come next. At four p.m., he laid out his understanding in a phone call to Johnson's aide Walter Jenkins. "There is nothing further on the Oswald case except that he is dead," Hoover noted in a masterful act of understatement. There was, however, now the issue of Oswald's murderer, a small-time Dallas strip-club owner named Jacob Rubenstein, better known as Jack Ruby. Hoover had already concluded that Ruby was a lowlife. "He runs two night clubs in Dallas and has the reputation of being a homosexual," Hoover noted, an assessment that he would later revise but never entirely reject. And Ruby was now the FBI's problem.

All of that could wait, however; Ruby was in police custody in Dallas and any trial would be months away. "The thing I am most concerned about, and so is Mr. Katzenbach," Hoover explained in his four p.m. phone call, "is having something issued so we can convince the public that Oswald is the real assassin." Already, Oswald's murder was sparking rounds of speculation: How could he be murdered in a building swarming with police? How did Ruby get into the station? Did Ruby murder Oswald in order to silence him? The few words that Oswald uttered in public before his murder helped to fuel the rumors. "I'm just a patsy," he had insisted during a fleeting encounter with the press. Hoover showed little patience for what he viewed as mere victim posturing, the sort of claims offered up by even the most ordinary criminals trying to save their own skins. He professed to be far more concerned about containing the rumor and speculation, and preventing it from undermining confidence in the police, the Bureau, and the federal government.[24]

Late Sunday afternoon he dispatched two Bureau supervisors to Dallas to prepare an official report for the White House—and to be back in Washington with the report by Tuesday. "This was, of course, an impossible assignment," recalled Fletcher Thompson, one of the men sent off to Dallas. "But we had to do our best." The actions of the Dallas office did not help, in at least one crucial area. According to agent Hosty, on the night of Oswald's murder he was ordered by his boss, Shanklin, to destroy the threatening note that Oswald had delivered just weeks earlier. Hosty later speculated that Shanklin's instructions must have come from higher up, perhaps from an FBI official channeling Hoover. But it was Hosty himself who committed the act. Assured that there would now be no trial—and thus no need to preserve the evidence—he walked down the hall, tore the note into pieces, and flushed it down the toilet.[25]

———

OSWALD'S DEATH DID LITTLE TO CHANGE HOOVER'S MIND ABOUT THE PRESI-
dent's assassination. In a statement issued on the night after Oswald's murder, Hoover
affirmed that Oswald and Oswald alone had most likely killed Kennedy. Now, though,
there was yet another problem: much of the country did not seem to believe that the
situation was so simple—and there was talk that even an official FBI report might not
convince them otherwise. With Oswald dead and speculation running rampant, official Washington was starting to mull over the idea that the president, Congress, or
even the State of Texas ought to appoint a committee to look into the evidence. From
Hoover's perspective, this meant that the assassination was no longer merely a tragedy,
a criminal case, or an investigative challenge. With competing investigations in the
offing, the FBI's credibility might come under threat.

Johnson had declared Monday a national day of mourning, a time to pause from
routine business and absorb the magnitude of the nation's loss. Most federal offices
were closed and dark, their flags lowered to half-mast. The FBI, with its roster of urgent
tasks to complete, was open for business. Hoover treated Monday as another routine
workday, arriving at 9:30 to an office already buzzing and clacking. He spoke with the
Bureau officials he had assigned to conduct an internal review of pre-assassination
contacts with Oswald. Then, at 10:25, he took another call from the president.[26]

After a few opening pleasantries, Johnson got to the point: according to White
House sources, *The Washington Post* planned to run an editorial calling for the creation of a presidential commission to oversee the assassination investigation and sift
through the work of the Dallas police, Secret Service, CIA, and FBI. Johnson wanted
to stop it, and he wanted Hoover's help. He still hoped the FBI would prepare a single
definitive report. "If you get too many cooks messing with the broth, it'd mess it up,"
Johnson thought. He urged Hoover to use "any influence you got with the Post" to
squash the editorial.

Hoover did not need to be persuaded. It had been almost twenty years since the
Pearl Harbor commission, more than forty years since the hearings on the Palmer
Raids, but the memories still burned: the humiliation and nitpicking scrutiny, the
second-guessing by political men with their own agendas. Already, citizens were writing in to question whether the FBI could have prevented the president's shooting,
whether agents should have been paying more attention to Oswald and his Russian
wife. Hoover responded with indignation. "At this time in the Nation's bereavement,
I am disturbed by your implied accusation of negligence," read a letter dispatched over
his signature to critical correspondents. The last thing he wanted was to have the Bureau's files scrutinized by competing commissions, each wrangling to outdo the other
for headlines. "It's a regular circus then," he complained to Johnson. In any case, neither one of them wanted it hashed out in the *Post*. "I view it like the *Daily Worker*,"

Hoover joked, agreeing to do what he could to shut down the *Post*'s editorial and to take care of things while Johnson headed off to St. Matthew's Cathedral, then Arlington Cemetery, to attend Kennedy's funeral.[27]

An FBI official called his contacts at the *Post*, but won only a temporary reprieve. Rumors of a commission persisted and gave agents on the ground a new reason to panic. "As this talk in Washington grew stronger with each passing day," Hosty recalled, "the intensity level in the Dallas FBI office grew proportionately. Each day the agents were pushing themselves harder and harder." On Tuesday, November 26, Hoover's emissaries returned from Dallas as promised, a tentative report on both the Ruby and Oswald cases in hand. Now, though, Hoover insisted that "the Presidential report on both matters should not be prepared until *all* allegations and angles have been completed."[28]

In truth, it was already too late to contain the sprawling public crisis to a single FBI investigation. Despite Johnson's agreement on Monday morning that a federal commission would be "a regular circus," as the week went on he began to conclude that it might be the best of the available options and that anything else might produce an ongoing parade of multiple and opposite truths. Johnson would have preferred for the FBI to issue its report and for the public to accept whatever Hoover said as the single honest answer. "Then the American public will have assurance from an agency with all the impressive credentials of the FBI that Oswald, acting alone and not as part of a conspiracy, fired the fatal bullets last Friday," explained a dispatch from the Associated Press. Already, though, critics were pointing to a vast range of remaining questions. The State of Texas was flirting with conducting its own court of inquiry. So were several committees of Congress, including Hoover's friends at Judiciary. By Thursday, papers were reporting that Senators Mike Mansfield and Everett Dirksen—the two men Hoover had met with just weeks earlier to head off inquiries into Kennedy's dalliances—were now entertaining the idea of hearings to sift through the FBI's evidence.[29]

On Friday afternoon, Johnson broke the bad news to Hoover in a phone call. "Me and you gonna talk like brothers," he said, before describing his decision to appoint a presidential commission to investigate the assassination. Johnson framed it as the only possible choice: a presidential commission would reduce public speculation and give a focal point of authority to quiet the country down. But he was nervous about how Hoover might react. "You're more than the head of the Federal Bureau as far as I'm concerned," he told Hoover, fumbling for praise and promises of access. "You're my brother and personal friend."

Hoover seemed flattered by the words, so different from what he had experienced during the Kennedy years. Perhaps as a result, he responded to this latest development with the same stoicism with which he had greeted the news of Kennedy's death. It had been a full week since Hoover made that first call to Bobby, poolside at Hickory Hill. Now he assured his old friend Lyndon Johnson that this—Johnson's first major decision as president—would be just fine. "I certainly appreciate your confidence," he told Johnson as they said goodbye that afternoon. Then he set out to manage, influence—and, sometimes, to mislead—the commission that Johnson created.[30]

CHAPTER 47

The Commission

(1963–1964)

Hoover (center) in a White House ceremony exempting him from
mandatory federal retirement at age seventy. President Lyndon
Johnson, a longtime friend and supporter, is shaking Hoover's hand.
Deputy attorney general Nicholas Katzenbach is at right. Future
vice president Hubert Humphrey is on stairs, far left. May 1964.

Once Johnson settled on the idea of a presidential commission, a fraught question
arose: Who should be asked to serve on it? Johnson wanted "absolutely top-
flight folks," men whose gravitas and credibility would legitimize the commission's
proceedings. He also needed representation from a variety of constituencies, including
both Democrats and Republicans. Johnson promised Hoover that the commission's
true purpose was not to cast doubt on the FBI's findings about Oswald. Rather, it was
to lend credibility to the FBI's inquiry and to tamp down the many rumors already
bubbling up. Outside the FBI, the list of possible coconspirators in the assassination
seemed to be expanding by the hour: Fidel Castro, the Soviets, the Mafia. Left unchecked, such rumors might metastasize into major political and foreign-policy crises.
At his darkest moments, Johnson worried that they could even spark World War III.

So choosing the right people was important. By the time he spoke with Hoover about the commission, Johnson already had a few names in mind. Before he approached them, though, he wanted Hoover's advice. Though Johnson did not say it outright, he understood that the commission would have a hard time completing its work without the FBI's cooperation. Hoover readily approved a few of the names offered by Johnson, including former CIA director Allen Dulles ("a good man") and Georgia senator Richard Russell ("an excellent man"). Others, such as former World Bank president John McCloy, he viewed less favorably but without rancor. He flat-out rejected only the liberal Republican senator Jacob Javits, floated by Johnson as just the kind of man whose ego could ruin the whole effort. "Javits plays to the front page a lot," Hoover agreed.

The president's final roster reflected Hoover's preferences—with one exception. During their phone call, Johnson neglected to mention the single most important figure on the list: Chief Justice Earl Warren, Johnson's chosen man for the position of chair. The silence was no oversight. Since the court's "Red Monday" decisions in the communist cases of 1957, Hoover's friendship with Warren had devolved into a sullen standoff. But Johnson thought he needed the cooperation of both Hoover *and* Warren to make the commission work—Hoover to conduct a credible investigation, Warren to lend his imprimatur to the FBI's report. So he moved ahead with Warren's appointment while assuring Hoover that the White House was really on the FBI's side. "You just put down some of the things you think oughta happen," Johnson instructed Hoover, "and I won't involve you, or quote you, or get you in jurisdictional disputes or anything, but I'd like to at least advocate 'em as my opinion." When Johnson announced the commission's roster just hours later, Hoover registered no objection to the final list. "The President discussed this with me," he affirmed to FBI officials, only slightly stretching the truth. "I am in accord."[1]

IF JOHNSON WAS CAREFUL ABOUT MANAGING HIS FBI DIRECTOR, HOOVER HAD his own strategy for managing the president. At the center of that plan was Cartha "Deke" DeLoach, Johnson's favorite contact at the Bureau. Born in Claxton, Georgia, DeLoach came to the Bureau during the war, just another tall, lean Southern boy in Hoover's ranks. He soon found his place as the FBI's star liaison man, assigned to act as its ambassador to key institutions in and around Washington. DeLoach had served as an early liaison to the CIA, where he managed to please Hoover by infuriating the agency's leadership. From there, he moved on to more congenial positions, including liaison to the American Legion and, later, to select members of Congress. DeLoach showed a special talent for getting along with Southern good old boys, plying them with brandy and inside tips. He also worked smoothly with the press, deploying just the right blend of defensiveness and generosity. In 1959, Hoover rewarded him with a promotion to head of Crime Records, in charge of all external relations, from media outreach to politics to crime statistics. Accepting the job, DeLoach promised "no 'cry-ing' on my part'" if and when the Bureau found itself in choppy waters.[2]

Johnson had been one of the Southern politicians whom DeLoach courted during those years, first during Johnson's time as Senate majority leader and then as vice president. Along the way, DeLoach also developed a close relationship with Walter Jenkins, Johnson's chief aide and right-hand man out of Texas. DeLoach and Jenkins were both Catholic fathers, each with a brood of children, a soft spot for golf, and a fierce loyalty to their respective bosses. Almost without trying, they came to like each other and to work together. In 1962, at Hoover's behest, DeLoach helped Jenkins coordinate a response to the Billie Sol Estes scandal, in which a Texas businessman accused Johnson of corruption and double-dealing. From such experiences, Johnson concluded that he could trust and work well with DeLoach. In late November, after the assassination, Hoover nudged DeLoach to make the most of that history as liaison to the Johnson White House. Johnson thought the idea "mighty gracious" of Hoover. "I sure appreciate that," he said during the November 29 phone call. "We salute you for knowin' how to pick good men!"[3]

Here, too, though, there was one aspect of the situation that Johnson chose not to mention. In little more than a year, Hoover would be turning seventy, the mandatory retirement age for federal workers. At that point, the unthinkable might happen: Hoover would step down and be replaced by a younger man such as DeLoach. If Hoover played his cards right, though, there was another option on the table. As president, Johnson had the right to exempt Hoover from retirement.

THE WARREN COMMISSION MET FOR THE FIRST TIME ON THE MORNING OF December 5 in a secluded wood-paneled room at the National Archives. All seven members were present: Warren, Russell, McCloy, and Dulles, plus Senator John Sherman Cooper (R-Kentucky), Congressman Hale Boggs (D-Louisiana), and Congressman Gerald Ford (R-Michigan). Warren opened the meeting by acknowledging "the very sad and solemn duty" before them. From there, it was down to business. Warren expressed the fond hope that their work would not take long. Toward that end, he proposed that the commission forgo hiring its own investigators or conducting its own investigation. Instead, Warren proposed that they focus on reviewing—and hopefully rubber-stamping—the work already done by the FBI. "Our job here is essentially one for the evaluation of evidence as distinguished from being one of gathering evidence," he told the members. Warren proposed that they hold all proceedings in secret to avoid fueling day-to-day speculation in the press. Their work would begin in earnest once the FBI submitted a summary report on the case against Oswald.[4]

Warren's proposal should have been just what Hoover wanted: a quick and efficient exchange, presumably ending in affirmation of the FBI. But Hoover approached that

first meeting with suspicion, on high alert for any sign that the commission in general—
and Warren in particular—was trying to upstage and discredit the Bureau. Hoover
declined to send a representative to the proceedings, arguing that it made more sense
to engage once the FBI submitted its final report. In the meantime, a sudden rush of
press coverage offered detailed previews about what the report was likely to contain.
Hoover denied any role in planting the articles. "I thought no one knew this outside
the FBI," he wrote with indignation in one internal memo. But the commission's members thought it was Hoover himself behind the stories. Boggs labeled it all "the most
outrageous leak I have ever seen," insisting that "it almost has to come from the FBI."
According to that theory, Hoover was divulging the contents ahead of time in order
to claim credit and limit the commission's range of action.[5]

If it could be hard to find Hoover's fingerprints on the press disclosures, it was
considerably easier when it came to the issue of commission staff. Even under Warren's
quick-and-dirty proposal, the commission would need to hire at least a few professional lawyers to sift through the required reading and prepare the commission's own
report. To direct this work, Warren selected an Eisenhower-era Justice official named
Warren Olney. The choice should have pleased Hoover, who had worked closely with
Olney during the Eisenhower years. But he found the prospect "horrible," and deemed
Olney himself a model of misguided liberalism. So DeLoach went off to deliver confi-
dential briefings to the commission's members about Olney's "miserable personality."
Fortunately for Hoover, the commissioners were already inclined to resist appointing
Olney, on grounds that he was too close to Warren. By the time the commission met
on December 6, the Olney appointment was all but dead. Instead, Warren hired J. Lee
Rankin, an Eisenhower Justice official more to everyone's liking.[6]

That hire occurred just in time for Hoover to deliver what all agreed would be the
FBI's signal contribution to the commission's work: its much anticipated investigative
summary. At four hundred pages, the report was a substantial piece of work, assembled
under great duress and delivered on December 9, less than three weeks after the assassination. The report laid out the case against "Oswald, avowed Marxist," from his defection to the Soviet Union through his hiring at the Texas School Book Depository,
from where he fired the fatal shots. It also admitted that the FBI had been in contact
with Oswald on several occasions before the fateful day, but had failed to understand
the threat he posed. Most recently, the Dallas and New Orleans offices had been tracking his involvement in the Fair Play for Cuba Committee, a pro-Castro organization.
Not long before the assassination, he had ventured to Mexico City, where he made
contact with the Soviet embassy and Cuban consulate.[7]

If the report included certain details about Oswald and his interactions with the
FBI, what Hoover left out proved to be at least as important as what he put in. The
purpose of the report, as Hoover had explained to the White House, was not to assess
the range of possible explanations for the president's murder but to "convince the pub-

lic that Oswald is the real assassin." In keeping with this mission, the report excluded aspects of the investigation unrelated to Oswald. It also excluded material that called into question the FBI's methods, judgment, and actions. The result was a report that delivered important information but did not fully address many of the country's—and the commission's—lingering questions.[8]

Warren recognized a problem right away. "Well, gentlemen, to be very frank about it, I have read that report two or three times," he declared at the commission's meeting on December 16, "and I have not seen anything in that yet that has not been in the press." Other members ticked off obvious questions that seemed to have gone unanswered: How did Oswald become an "expert marksman"? What did the State Department have to say about Oswald's Mexico visit? In some areas, such as Oswald's previous attempt to assassinate the far-right zealot General Edwin Walker, they wanted more detail. "It just doesn't seem like they're looking for things that this commission has to look for in order to get the answers that it wants and it's entitled to," Rankin complained. The commissioners had hoped that the FBI's report would settle the big questions. Instead, it left many of them wide open.[9]

The situation was arguably worse than even the commissioners understood. The thrust of their initial complaints emphasized oversight and "shoddy" work rather than any deliberate obfuscation. But Hoover was, indeed, withholding information, some of which would not be revealed for years to come. He did not, for instance, disclose what he had learned about the CIA's collaboration with the Mafia against Castro— possible motive for Castro now to retaliate against Kennedy. Nor did he discuss the FBI's recent raids on a Cuban exile training camp near Oswald's then-residence in New Orleans, where agents uncovered vast supplies of dynamite, bomb casings, napalm, and guns. Hoover's reasons for protecting such evidence were not necessarily objectionable: these were independent operations, and he did not think they were relevant to the question of Oswald's guilt or innocence. But the effect, over the long run, was to fuel rather than tamp down talk of conspiracies and deep-state machinations.[10]

Hoover was especially sensitive about information that might reveal the FBI's own clandestine methods—especially in high-value operations such as SOLO and COINTELPRO. By a quirk of timing, SOLO informant Morris Childs had been in Moscow when the assassination occurred. He returned with a reassuring account of what the day had been like inside the Kremlin. According to Childs, the Soviets, too, were worried about conspiracy-mongering; they thought "some irresponsible general" might believe rumors of Soviet involvement and fire off a few missiles in revenge. Hoover shared the concern that all of the assassination rumor-mongering might spin out of control—yet another reason he sought to contain the range of evidence presented to the Warren Commission.[11]

Finally, Hoover did not disclose what would have been among the most shocking secrets of all: the fact that he believed his own agents had acted with "gross incompetency" in the weeks leading up to the assassination. Beginning on December 10, the day after he submitted his report to the commission, Hoover meted out discipline to seventeen FBI employees for "shortcomings in connection with the investigation of Oswald." The complaints varied, from the Bureau's failure to include Oswald on the Security Index to Agent Hosty's decision not to interview him. DeLoach urged Hoover to delay the punishments, lest they lend credence to the notion that the FBI had been derelict in its treatment of Oswald. Hoover refused to wait, but he did concede one important point. Rather than let the world know his opinion of his agents, he decided to turn the disciplinary actions into yet another Bureau secret.[12]

HOOVER'S REPORT HAD BEEN A GAMBLE: HE BET THAT THE FBI COULD ASSEMBLE the evidence, present it to the commission, and have it accepted at face value. When that failed to happen, relations with the commission began to break down. For the first few weeks after the assassination, everyone had assumed that they would all end up in the same place—that the commission would affirm the FBI, foreclose any remaining rumors, and allow the country to move on. After the FBI's report, the road to that destination got much longer.

Warren identified this new state of affairs at the commission's next meeting, held at the National Archives on December 16. A week earlier, he had anticipated an efficient review of the FBI's summary report, followed by a quick wrap-up of extraneous questions. Now he concluded that the commission would have to review the FBI's entire investigation page by page, including all interviews, forensic evidence, and surveillance reports. Members would also have to change their mindset. The commission had started out granting Hoover the benefit of the doubt. Now, as commission member Richard Russell pointed out, they would have to shift to a "Devil's Advocate" stance, double-checking the FBI's work and probing every corner to determine if anything seemed to be missing. Russell recommended that the commission treat the FBI's words as if they were "going to use them to prosecute J. Edgar Hoover" rather than Lee Harvey Oswald.[13]

Warren made this shift of attitude known in a press conference immediately after the meeting. Speaking from outside the commission's meeting room, Warren said that the FBI's much-hyped report had arrived in "skeleton form," raising more questions than it answered. "In order to evaluate it," he explained, "we have to see the material on which the report was based." Without contacting Hoover, he announced that the commission would be demanding the "raw" materials from the FBI investigation. And they wanted such materials immediately.[14]

Hoover reacted as if he had been punched in the face. "This statement by the Chief Justice I felt was entirely unwarranted and could certainly have been phrased better so as not to leave the impression, at least by innuendo, that the FBI had not done a thorough job," he complained to colleagues. He recognized, though, that he, too, would now have to make a shift—if not of mindset, then at least of strategy. He ordered the FBI to send the commission "all reports, whether of substantial nature or so-called 'nut reports.'" By December 20, they had delivered 2,960 pages of material, with more on the way. It was the same method he had used during his fit of pique over Truman's shutdown of the Special Intelligence Service in 1946: when it was impossible to change the rules, follow them with a vengeance.[15]

Hoover carried on with his kill-them-with-kindness approach throughout December and into January, as the commission scrambled to get its staff up and running. To Bureau officials, he emphasized the importance of sending along everything and anything. "I wouldn't care if it filled a whole building," he wrote after the commission requested to see all the physical evidence (bullets, clothing, rifles, etc.) related to the assassination. The process became a source of rueful joking around the Bureau. "Better have some extra wood + nails as Warren may want to see the 'raw' material!" Hoover wrote in response to a demand for all diagrams, scale models, and physical reconstructions used in the Bureau investigation. But behind the humor was a powerful sense of indignation at the commission's refusal to trust the FBI and to take Hoover at his word.[16]

That feeling reached new heights after January 22, when Warren summoned the commission for an emergency early-evening meeting. Gerald Ford, then a junior congressman from Michigan and the youngest member of the commission, recalled an "atmosphere of tension" as he was pulled from House duties and hustled off to the commission's headquarters. With the members assembled around a large wooden table, chief counsel J. Lee Rankin disclosed a bombshell. According to what Rankin described as credible sources, Oswald had been working as an FBI informant at the time of the assassination. Rankin even had details: Oswald had been hired in September 1962 at a rate of two hundred dollars a month, operating as informant number 179.

The members expressed astonishment at the news. The "implications of this are fantastic, don't you think so?" Hale Boggs exclaimed. Even more fantastic was the realization that the commission had no way to prove or disprove the allegations. The obvious thing was just to ask Hoover. By now, though, there were serious doubts about whether Hoover would tell the truth. "I am confident that the FBI would never admit it," Rankin said, "and I presume their records will never show it." Allen Dulles defended Hoover at another meeting a few days later, but only so far. "I would believe Mr. Hoover," he said, while conceding that "some people might not." In any case, Dulles agreed that "you can't prove what the facts are." The commission could do nothing but question the accusers, give Hoover a chance to respond, and live with the answers.

Warren affected bravado. "I am not going to be thin-skinned about what Mr. Hoover might think," he announced to the commission. But he left the task of actually confronting Hoover to the unlucky Rankin. In late January, well after the informant story broke in the press, Rankin screwed up his courage to face Hoover and ask the question. Hoover issued the expected denial. "I told Mr. Rankin that Lee Harvey Oswald was never at any time a confidential informant, an undercover agent, or even a source of information for the FBI," he noted in a memo for the record, "and I would like to see that clearly stated on the record of the commission and I would be willing to state so under oath." Then he lit into Rankin about the commission's "carping criticism" of the FBI and its willingness to entertain such ridiculous ideas.[17]

Some of Hoover's rage was personal; he did not appreciate being challenged and prodded and second-guessed, especially by a mid-ranking former Justice official. But there was genuine confusion in his response, too—a sense that the commission was betraying its presidential mission for reasons that he did not entirely understand. As Johnson had first presented it, the commission existed in order to contain rumors, to shore up faith in the intelligence community, and to prevent the outbreak of World War III. Instead, it seemed to be chasing gossip and casting doubt on the official story of the assassination, with no apparent endgame in sight.

But Hoover, too, was caught in the dilemma that Rankin had articulated: even if the commission trusted him, he had no way to prove absolutely that he was telling the truth. In early February, he submitted an affidavit stating that Oswald was never an FBI informant, laying out in painstaking detail how the FBI informant system worked and why, therefore, it would be impossible for Oswald to have been an informant without Hoover knowing it. He supplemented his statements with affidavits from nine other Bureau employees, each of whom attested to the same basic set of facts. The informant story was indeed false, conjured up as a joke then passed along as fact by a too-eager reporter in Dallas. But to Hoover's dismay, the rumor never entirely subsided.[18]

HOOVER DID NOT INTEND TO LET HIS AUTHORITY SLIP AWAY SO EASILY. IF WARren and Rankin no longer trusted him, there were plenty of men around Washington who did—or who were at least willing to go along to get along. Chief among them was Gerald Ford, identified early on by columnist Doris Fleeson as the commission's one "certain FBI defender." On December 17, the day after Warren's press conference, Ford had sought out DeLoach, implicitly offering to serve as Hoover's eyes and ears inside the commission. After checking in with Hoover, DeLoach accepted the suggestion and sent Ford on his way with a locked briefcase for safekeeping FBI documents.[19]

As their conflict with the Warren Commission deepened, Hoover and DeLoach turned more and more to such political arrangements, calling in favors from congressmen and senators, from editors and reporters and even their few friends at the CIA. In Hoover's view, the commission was no longer primarily a bureaucratic challenge, to be managed through document dumps and the manipulation of staff. After mid-January it was a political problem, requiring the action of political men.

One of DeLoach's first stops was Mississippi senator James Eastland, still the head of the Senate Internal Security Subcommittee and a Bureau ally in matters other than civil rights. On February 7, in the wake of the informant controversy, DeLoach intercepted Eastland just off of the Senate floor. The two men retreated to Eastland's office, locked the door, and began to assess the damage. Eastland had just heard the informant rumor, but DeLoach brushed it off as old news—and "absolutely false" to boot. The imperative of the moment, he explained, was to prevent the rumor from taking on a life of its own around Washington. Eastland offered to circulate Hoover's affidavit around Capitol Hill as the authoritative document on the matter. DeLoach suggested to a member of Eastland's SISS staff that it would helpful to know the source of the rumor that had reached the senator. That way, the rumormonger could be "tied down and made to put up or shut up" before spreading any more gossip about the Bureau.

From there, DeLoach made his way through the Senate, seeking out sympathetic audiences with key figures. He spoke with commission member Richard Russell, who had urged Warren to act as if they were going to "prosecute J. Edgar Hoover" but now worried that "extreme liberals" were taking over the commission. DeLoach also met with Senator Roman Hruska, who suggested that he reach out to Senate minority leader Everett Dirksen, who was purportedly worried that "this matter could completely discredit the FBI." Together, at Hoover's instruction, DeLoach and Hruska made their way to a local hospital, where Dirksen was laid up. DeLoach showed him Hoover's affidavit, after which Dirksen reportedly "felt much better." Then it was on to the House, beginning with Ford and Boggs, the two commission members.[20]

While DeLoach focused on Congress, William Sullivan, the architect of COINTELPRO and now head of the Domestic Intelligence Division, took on the national security agencies. On February 7, Sullivan just happened to sit with Allen Dulles at a Boy Scout–sponsored breakfast. Dulles assured him that the commission was after the truth, not after the FBI. But other CIA men were not so sure. That same day, another FBI official spoke with James Angleton, the agency's counterintelligence chief and now one of the most pro-FBI men in its ranks. He came away convinced that the only way to dispel public doubts about the informant question was for the Warren Commission to issue a statement of support for the Bureau.

Hoover scoffed at this possibility. "I want nothing from the Warren Commission," he told Sullivan. He concentrated instead on charming and convincing the press firsthand. Throughout the winter and into the spring, he consulted frequently with his favored press contacts, including William Randolph Hearst and Richard Berlin at the Hearst chain. After years of retreat from Washington socializing, he also forced himself to attend luncheons and soirees where members of the press were likely to gather. On April 2, he attended a banquet in Johnson's honor as a guest of the White House News Photographers Association and *The Saturday Evening Post*. Three weeks later, he dragged himself up to New York for the annual luncheon of the Banshees, an assemblage of some two thousand editors and publishers. Less than a week after that came the Gridiron dinner in Washington, always among the poshest press rituals of the season. "I wish the entire personnel of the FBI could know the strain you have been under for the past several days, particularly in connection with the many editors that you have briefed, met and talked to," DeLoach wrote to Hoover in the midst of their press blitz. But DeLoach had only added to the strain by hosting a cocktail party at his home for the members of the American Society of Newspaper Editors. Hoover spent much of that evening talking with Gerald Ford, who seemed eager to show the assembled editors that the FBI and the commission were still on speaking terms.[21]

Absent from much of this activity was the one man Hoover had so often counted upon in the past—not only to manage his press relations, but to soothe his soul. Tolson went out on sick leave just after the assassination with a stomach "flare-up" and "a very bad back condition," as Hoover described it to a friend. Over the next several weeks, while Hoover was absorbed in negotiations with the Warren Commission, Tolson's condition went into swift decline. His illness made "my burdens heavier in the office," Hoover admitted. It also disrupted the routines that kept Hoover in decent spirits, including their usual vacation to Miami. In all, Tolson was out of the office for three months: through the early negotiations over commission staff, Hoover's delivery of the FBI report, and the informant controversy. For the first time in decades, he even missed Hoover's annual appearance before the House Appropriations Committee, a circumstance so unusual that the committee chairmen noted it for the record.[22]

Hoover's worry about Tolson, combined with the stress of the Warren Commission, made him even more volatile than usual—quick to demand results, even quicker to dismiss those who did not deliver. From February into March and April, Hoover continued to do the commission's bidding with an uneven mix of resentment and efficiency, going so far as to plant a wiretap and bug in Marina Oswald's home at the commission's request. Within the FBI, though, his contempt for Warren and the rest of the commission's staff knew no bounds. "It is getting to be more + more intolerable to deal with this Warren Commission," he complained, whether because its staff lawyers were "not too bright" or its requests mostly "impractical + absurd." Hoover was no more generous toward his own employees, accusing them of unforgivable "shortcomings" and "grossly" mishandling the commission's requests.[23]

Hoover's one great comfort came from the White House, where Johnson continued to act as if the FBI could no wrong. He showered Hoover with Christmas gifts and phone calls, lunch invitations and pleas for elder-statesman wisdom. Many of these exchanges involved matters far afield from the Warren Commission, including the Billie Sol Estes scandal, which was slowly winding its way toward the Supreme Court. DeLoach later recalled meeting with Johnson at least two or three times a week during the period following the assassination. They also spoke regularly over the White House hotline that Johnson had installed in DeLoach's home bedroom. And DeLoach talked with Johnson's aide Walter Jenkins even more frequently than with the president himself. On occasion Hoover, Johnson, DeLoach, and Jenkins all got together, partly to talk politics, but also just for fun. On March 9, a full month after the informant controversy broke in the press, Johnson invited them all to the White House for an afternoon of lunch and swimming in the pool. While there, they discussed Johnson's new poverty program and some pending appointments. The point of the afternoon, though, seems to have been to let Hoover know that he was still on the inside. Later that day, Johnson called Tolson at home just "to see how you're doing" and to affirm that Hoover "is about the best thing I've got left around this town."[24]

Johnson soon came up with a far more significant way to show his appreciation. On May 6, Hoover went to the White House to assist with the presentation of a youth medal for "bravery and service." While he was there, Johnson let him in on a secret plan to be executed a few days hence. Hoover returned to FBI headquarters "bursting with good news," in the description of Dallas agent James Hosty, who happened to be in town to testify before the Warren Commission. Hosty had expected the worst of his meeting with Hoover, more browbeating about shoddy work and investigative oversights. Instead, "like a child who had just discovered one more nickel in his pocket to spend at the carnival," Hoover decided to let him in on what Johnson had said.

"The president told me that the country just couldn't get along without me," Hoover explained. Johnson planned to exempt Hoover from mandatory retirement, several months in advance of the director's seventieth birthday.[25]

THE OFFICIAL HONORS TOOK PLACE TWO DAYS LATER IN THE WHITE HOUSE flower garden, with Johnson presiding and Hoover as the guest of honor. Tolson managed to be there, just a few steps away from the center of action. With them was a who's who of Washington, including many of the senators and congressmen Hoover had sought out for help over the past few months. Hoover called them "some of my very best friends"—as always, blending the personal and the professional.

Johnson himself fit that mold, at once a down-home neighbor and a hardheaded student of power. The formal remarks written for the occasion emphasized Hoover's formidable status as a "household word" and "hero to millions of decent citizens." Johnson's smile, though, showed real affection. Hoover was beaming, too, his mouth agape as Johnson presented him with an official plaque. After the ceremony, they all retreated for lunch in the president's private living quarters, yet another personal touch. Reporters found the whole event surprisingly "sentimental," given the two legendarily ruthless men involved. All the same, nobody expressed much surprise at Johnson's decision. "It was about as likely that Mr. Johnson would advocate free beer in the high schools as it was that he would not recommend Mr. Hoover's term be continued," one columnist wrote. Indeed, it was not clear who was exercising power over whom: whether Hoover had wrangled the concession of all concessions from Johnson, or whether Johnson now had Hoover at his beck and call.[26]

If any questions remained about Hoover's status around Washington, they were put to rest over the next several days. In Congress, now dominated by an overwhelming Democratic majority, the House celebrated Hoover's fortieth anniversary as FBI director with a unanimous resolution honoring "one of the most remarkable records of service to God and country in our nation's history." At the Senate, individual speakers delivered tributes to "the number one crime and Communist buster in this country" (Strom Thurmond) and to the "glow of inspiration, of competence, of zeal for public service which Mr. Hoover generates" (former agent Thomas Dodd). American Legion chapters sent commendations. So did the Society of Former Special Agents and the FBI National Academy Associates, two groups that owed their existence to Hoover. Even Bobby Kennedy sent along a note of congratulations. "In the past few months, I have not had the pleasure of associating with you as closely as formerly," he wrote, with tactful understatement. "I regret this but would not want this occasion to pass without congratulating you on this milestone."[27]

From Hoover's perspective, the timing could hardly have been better. On May 8, he was with the president in the flower garden. On May 10, the tributes poured forth. And on May 12, in a subtle but unmistakable gesture of capitulation, Earl Warren broke down and called Hoover directly. They met in Warren's private office at the Supreme Court for lunch the next day. Then, on May 14, after months of sniping and scheming and second-guessing, Hoover finally testified in front of the Warren Commission.

His remarks that day affirmed what he had been saying for months: that Oswald had acted and acted alone. In the end the commission affirmed that conclusion as well. To Hoover's chagrin, the Warren Commission's final report contained some mild criticism of the FBI for an "unduly restrictive" policy that kept it from sharing information about Oswald with the Secret Service. Mostly, though, the document read quite a lot like the FBI's original report, delivered back in December. In that sense, Hoover won the day: the commission affirmed his basic conclusions about the assassination. It also fulfilled the instructions that Johnson had laid out in November: to commit to a single narrative and to prevent the assassination from spiraling into an even greater crisis.[28]

If the immediate moment left Hoover with at least some taste of victory, though, the years ahead bore out some of his initial fears. Though Johnson had charged both the commission and the FBI with tamping down rumors and conspiracies, the blind spots and elisions in their work would become fodder for public suspicion, including several rounds of congressional inquiry, over the next several decades. Hoover anticipated the backlash. "This will be a matter of controversy for years to come, just like the Lincoln assassination," he acknowledged during his testimony. "There will be questions raised by individuals, either for publicity purposes or otherwise, that will raise some new angle or new aspect of it." For the moment, he suggested, there was nothing to be done except to move on and hope that "the facts" would someday win out.[29]

CHAPTER 48

Freedom Summer

(1964)

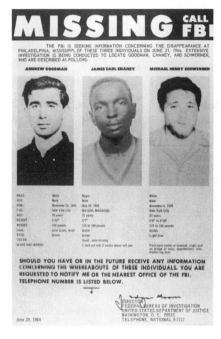

FBI flyers seeking information in the June 1964 disappearance of three civil rights workers at Philadelphia, Mississippi.

FEDERAL BUREAU OF INVESTIGATION

With the question of retirement settled and the Warren Commission's testimony behind him, Hoover may have longed for a few weeks of peace and quiet. But 1964 was an election year, and Lyndon Johnson wanted his help. Hoover could hardly say no, given the lease on life he had just been granted by the White House. Still, he was not entirely thrilled about the president's requests. In order to win the Democratic nomination and then the election, Johnson believed he would have to show the country that he was not just another good-old-boy Southern Democrat. And in order to do that, he hoped to pass the civil rights bill that Kennedy had once championed. That was why he wanted Hoover's assistance.

Hoover did not share Johnson's fondness for civil rights legislation or ambitious social policy; both men understood that. What Johnson envisioned was an alliance of interests, in which Hoover would approach civil rights with the same dexterity he had demonstrated in managing the Warren Commission. Since entering the Oval Office,

Johnson had made it clear that he planned to run for the presidency as a new sort of a liberal—still a Texan, but one now draped with the Kennedy cloth. In his State of the Union speech, he committed to Kennedy's dream of a civil rights law that would "abolish not some, but all racial discrimination." He also vowed to lead an "unconditional war on poverty" and erase the blights of malnutrition, overcrowding, unemployment, and ignorance from the world's most affluent land. Johnson justified both efforts as Cold War measures: America would show the world that capitalism could deliver equality and justice better than Soviet communism. But what he proposed was a far cry from how Hoover conceived of that struggle.[1]

Hoover had far more in common with the man who was shaping up to be Johnson's likely Republican opponent: Arizona senator Barry Goldwater, "the apostle of conservatism and the favorite candidate of right-wing Republicans," in the words of *The New York Times*. Though heir to a Phoenix department-store fortune, Goldwater presented himself as a cowboy, partial to the hats, boots, and sunset-backed poses that identified him as a man of the West. Goldwater's supporters viewed him as the ultimate outsider candidate, an unlikely successor (and intended rebuke) to the moderate Eisenhower-Nixon administration. He found his base in the groups who had caused such a fuss in the early Kennedy years: members of the John Birch Society and proud ticket holders for anticommunism crusades. Hoover continued to criticize them. "I think the extreme right is just as much a danger to the freedom of this country as the extreme left," he told the Warren Commission. But his hesitation had little effect on his reputation among Goldwater supporters, who continued to embrace Hoover as one of their own. "A wonderfully well accepted American patriot who would make a great running mate for you is J. Edgar Hoover," one admirer wrote to the senator in early 1964. While Johnson's civil rights allies tended to look upon Hoover with suspicion, Goldwater supporters recognized a kindred spirit.[2]

Nevertheless it was Johnson who had saved Hoover's job, and it was Johnson who now demanded Hoover's loyalty. So, beginning in the summer of 1964, Hoover mobilized the FBI in support of Johnson's civil rights agenda. He never abandoned his own goal of containing the civil rights movement and undermining leaders such as King. Indeed, Johnson never asked him to. The president welcomed Hoover's ability to provide intelligence on the movement and its leaders. At the same time, he looked to Hoover for help in achieving one of the great moral triumphs of his presidency.

HOOVER'S FIRST FAVOR TO JOHNSON INVOLVED THE "DANGEROUS," "UNPRINCIpled," "opportunistic" man at the helm of the civil rights movement, whose support Johnson needed in order to see the Civil Rights Act through Congress. Martin Luther King's stature had grown exponentially since the March on Washington; *Time* had named him 1963's Man of the Year. Within the Bureau, though, King's reputation continued to decline, thanks in no small part to the wiretaps that Bobby Kennedy had approved just weeks before his brother's assassination. By December 1963, Hoover had four taps running at SCLC's Atlanta headquarters and a crucial fifth one at King's home. He was also wiretapping King's lawyer and adviser Clarence Jones, along with the much-maligned Stanley Levison. From those taps Hoover learned that King was still consulting Levison. He also learned something more startling: despite being married with four children, King regularly engaged in trysts with "girlfriends" scattered throughout the country.

Like Hoover, domestic intelligence chief William Sullivan recognized the potential inherent in these discoveries. The connections between Levison, O'Dell, and the Communist Party had often been murky and difficult to prove, a matter of secret party memberships and even more secret sources of information. The sexual affairs told a story anyone could comprehend: here was a man of the cloth, a self-proclaimed moral arbiter, who apparently did not practice what he preached. A few days before Christmas, while Hoover was entering into negotiations with the Warren Commission, Sullivan's office asked for permission to explore a counterintelligence campaign against King, using both the long-standing allegations of "King's unholy alliance with the Communist Party" and the newer discoveries about his personal life. As they envisioned it, the FBI would use the same COINTELPRO techniques that it had deployed so effectively against the Communist Party. Hoover signed off immediately.[3]

Over the next several months, that signature would license one of the most expansive disruption and harassment operations in Bureau history—all of it aimed at King, who was, even by the FBI's own account, engaged in no illegal activity. If the King campaign attracted outsize Bureau attention, though, it was different mostly in scale and scope from how Hoover treated the rest of the movement. As the civil rights movement morphed and expanded in the mid-1960s, so, too, did FBI surveillance. By 1963, the Bureau had recruited informants within several major civil rights organizations, including the NAACP, still mired in its love-hate relationship with the Bureau. At King's SCLC alone, agents identified "twelve key employees" to be targeted for surveillance, including the director of public relations, who was rumored to be a heavy drinker and therefore ripe for Bureau recruitment. Bayard Rustin, the organizational genius behind the March on Washington, also remained high on Hoover's list of suspicious figures. "While there may not be any direct evidence that Rustin is a communist neither is there any substantial evidence that he is anticommunist," an FBI report noted in 1964, in a model example of damned-if-you-do, damned-if-you-don't reasoning. Hoover instructed that there should be "no de-emphasis in the investigation concerning Rustin" and "no stone being left unturned."[4]

So it went for nearly every individual and organization that touched the civil rights cause, whether from the far left or the near middle. Among the most intense targets of Bureau surveillance was the Nation of Islam, characterized in FBI reports as an "all-Negro, fanatically anti-white" and "violent" organization, in contrast to King's non-violent, integrationist sensibility. The Bureau had been watching the NOI since at least the early 1950s, alarmed by its emphasis on Black self-empowerment and its embrace of Islam over Christianity. But it was not until the end of the decade that Hoover began to see the organization as a potential national force, rather than merely an extremist "Cult." A combination of informants and technical surveillance provided reams of information about Elijah Muhammad, the NOI's patriarch and guiding light. Years before initiating surveillance on King, Hoover used that information to try to discredit Muhammad and disrupt the NOI, authorizing anonymous letters about Muhammad's extramarital affairs and surveillance of his "hideaway" apartments.

In recent years, Hoover's attention had shifted somewhat to Muhammad's most famous disciple, Malcolm X (often identified in Bureau files by his given name, Malcolm Little). Malcolm X broke with the Nation of Islam but the FBI kept its surveillance going, documenting his rising influence as well as his internal disputes with his former allies. In December, he described the Kennedy assassination as "chickens coming home to roost" and said he was "glad" to see it, an inflammatory statement that raised Bureau alarm. By 1964, he was talking about "the ballot or the bullet" as the choices available to Black Americans—and unlike King, he did not necessarily recommend the former. In response, Hoover authorized a wiretap at his residence, sought to exacerbate his divide with Muhammad, and tracked his movements abroad. The media often portrayed Malcolm X as King's chief rival, with a distinct vision of how best to attack and defeat American racism. At the FBI, Hoover cared little for such distinctions and treated them more or less the same.[5]

ON DECEMBER 23, A MONTH AND A DAY AFTER KENNEDY'S ASSASSINATION, SUL-livan convened a meeting about King. A planning memo laid out some of the possible questions to be addressed: "What do we know about the background of King's girl-friends and their husbands?" "Could we convert any of their weak points to strong points for us?" "What are the possibilities of using Mrs. King?" "What are the possibilities of placing a good looking female plant in King's office?" Five men from Hoover's seat of government attended the meeting, along with two agents brought in from Atlanta. Over the course of nine hours, they discussed how to use wiretaps, bugs, press leaks, photographs, gossip-spreading, physical surveillance, tax inquiries, anonymous letters, and other counterintelligence techniques against King—all while avoiding "embarrassment to the Bureau." By early evening, they had settled on a multipronged program, designed to unfold in stages over several weeks and months. The first order of business was to expand surveillance of anyone connected with SCLC: all employees, financial institutions, and donors. Next, agents would gather anything they could find "concerning weaknesses in his character which are of such a nature as to make him unfit to serve as minister of the gospel," as Sullivan put it in a summary memo. Finally, "at an opportune time," they would "expose King as an immoral opportunist," presumably through media or congressional contacts. Sullivan recommended a ninety-day period in which the Bureau would expand its surveillance and gather additional information about "the clerical fraud and Marxist" before taking more ambitious action.

Hoover granted his "OK," a standard scrawl at the bottom of the two-and-a-half-page memo. After a pause for the Christmas holidays, the King team began to put their plan into effect. The linchpin of Sullivan's strategy involved expanding from wiretaps into hidden microphones that would record King not merely talking about his assignations, but actually carrying them out. King spent most of his time on the road, journeying wearily between speaking engagements, collapsing for the night in hotel rooms. From the wiretaps agents hoped to learn in advance about his travel plans. Once they knew where he would be staying, they would arrive early at the hotel, place microphones in his room, then sit back and listen.[6]

A chance to test the plan presented itself within days. In early January, the FBI learned that King was due in Washington to observe Supreme Court oral arguments in an Alabama libel case. He planned to stay at the posh Willard Hotel just down the street from the White House, the same place Kappa Alpha had once hosted its annual tea dances. In preparation for King's arrival, Sullivan assembled a small group from the Washington field office, including its best "sound man" (skilled in bugs and wiretaps) and "hotel contact man" (who maintained the Bureau's local network of sympathetic hotel staff), to determine the most efficient way "to effect technical coverage on King." With the help of a friendly source at the Willard, the "sound man" settled on the lamps in a typical Willard room as the most promising site for surveillance. From there, he acquired two identical lamps, wired them with transmitters, and handed them off to a housekeeper, who innocently placed them in King's room. Before King arrived on January 6, Sullivan's team took up residence in two nearby rooms equipped with radio receivers and tape recorders. At least once each day, they removed the logs and tapes from the hotel room and walked them over to the Washington field office. The rest of the time, they remained isolated in the monitoring rooms, one floor above King.[7]

Only Hoover and a handful of other federal officials, agents, and confidants have ever heard the recordings. (After Hoover's death, a court order placed the tapes under embargo for fifty years, set to expire in 2027.) But they spoke a good deal to each other and to allies outside the Bureau about what they thought they heard. According to Hoover, the evening was filled with sexual activities of an "immoral + degenerate" nature, involving not only King and more than one woman but also several of his fellow ministers. One agent recalled hearing King proclaim, "I'm fucking for God!" and "I'm not a Negro tonight," amid the many other sounds—sighs, laughter, the clink of glasses—coming from the room. A written summary of the recordings, apparently prepared by Bureau officials in early 1968, added detail to those recollections. According to the document, written in a tone of bristling outrage, the dozen or so people gathered in the room that night engaged in a fantastical "sex orgy," complete with "excessive consumption of alcohol and the use of the vilest language imaginable." King allegedly participated in and even joked about the full range of activity, declaring himself a proud founding member of the "International Association for the Advancement of Pussy Eaters."

As the historian David Garrow first noted in a 2019 article for the British magazine *Standpoint*, the summary contained a far more serious allegation as well. "When one of the women protested that she did not approve" of the group's sexual practices, the report alleged, a Baptist minister from Baltimore "immediately and forcibly raped her." A handwritten note, presumably added by Sullivan or another Bureau official, claimed that "King looked on, laughed and offered advice" while the rape took place. These allegations remain just that: allegations. Without the release of the tapes, the summary account tells us only what Bureau officials—and Hoover himself—believed to have occurred, as interpreted through their own racial biases and through surveillance that allowed them to hear but not see what was happening. In any case, it does not absolve either Hoover or his agents of their own misconduct.[8]

If a rape did take place at the Willard that evening, at the time Hoover made little distinction between that criminal violation and the other "natural or unnatural sex acts" alleged to have occurred, in the summary report's charged language. His interpretation of the recordings drew upon racial stereotypes about Black men's rapacious, unbounded sexuality. It also built upon Hoover's outrage at Kennedy's secret philandering: here was yet another public figure who acted the part of the saintly family man while indulging private appetites. Hoover would ultimately treat the white man and the Black man very differently, however. Even before the Willard incident, he had begun to rely on language of filth and degradation to describe King. "This is disgusting," he wrote in the margins of a wire-service report announcing King's award from a Catholic lay group for "Christ-like behavior." After the night at the Willard, Hoover's comments grew more vicious. "King is a tom cat with obsessive degenerate sexual urges," he wrote on one of Sullivan's reports. In conversation with Bureau officials, Hoover cheered that the Willard tapes "will destroy the burrhead," deploying a racial epithet that said far more about Hoover's own moral failings than about King's.[9]

JOHNSON DELIVERED HIS STATE OF THE UNION ADDRESS ON JANUARY 8, 1964, two nights after the Bureau's discoveries at the Willard. In that speech, he declared racial justice to be "a moral issue" that "must be met" by swift passage of the civil rights bill. To another president and another FBI director, the timing of those two events— the Willard surveillance and the call for civil rights legislation—might have created an inexorable conflict. Neither Johnson nor Hoover saw the situation that way. On January 14, Hoover dispatched DeLoach to brief the White House on what the FBI

This 1968 cartoon captures Hoover's astonishing longevity in office. He served as Bureau director under eight presidents—four Republicans and four Democrats.

WASHINGTON DAILY NEWS/NATIONAL ARCHIVES AND RECORDS ADMINISTRATION

In the 1950s, Hoover was forced to choose between two key anticommunist allies: President Dwight D. Eisenhower and Senator Joseph McCarthy. Above, McCarthy (far left) and Hoover (far right) pose with Clyde Tolson (second from left) and Royal Miller (second from right) at Hoover's favorite vacation spot, the Del Charro Hotel in La Jolla, California.   NATIONAL ARCHIVES AND RECORDS ADMINISTRATION

Hoover ultimately chose Eisenhower over McCarthy. Pictured here pinning a medal on Hoover in 1955. Vice President Richard Nixon, one of Hoover's closest Washington friends, is on the steps to Eisenhower's right.

Elected in 1960, John Kennedy (below, at center) was the first president younger than Hoover—and the one who liked him least. Hoover preferred Vice President Lyndon Johnson, who lived on his street and cultivated his friendship. At left, Hoover and Johnson in Austin, Texas, in 1959, when Johnson was senate majority leader. Johnson hosted Hoover's speech to a local charity, then whisked Hoover and Tolson off for a visit to the LBJ Ranch.

Hoover (far right) with President Kennedy (center) and Attorney General Robert Kennedy (second from right) in 1962, looking glum on the occasion of the president's appearance at the FBI National Academy graduation.

As president, Lyndon Johnson relied on Hoover to support his political and legislative agenda. Hoover came through, though he did not always agree with Johnson's priorities, especially on civil rights. Above, Johnson signs the 1964 Civil Rights Act and hands a pen to Hoover.

Johnson's late-night televised press conference during the 1967 Detroit "riot." He saw Hoover (far left) as a useful symbol of law and order.

In 1966, Hoover gave Johnson a new beagle puppy—a gesture back to their days as neighbors on 30th Place. Johnson named the dog Edgar (pictured on hind legs; the other dog is Freckles).

Hoover's friendship with Nixon—the closest he had with any president—began in the late 1940s, when Nixon was a Congressman. Here, Hoover greets Vice President Nixon and wife Patricia at the Del Charro Hotel, where Hoover and Tolson hosted a 1955 dinner in the Nixons' honor.

As president, Nixon publicly honored Hoover while secretly hoping to ease him out of office. Above, Nixon and Hoover at the 1969 graduation ceremonies of the FBI National Academy, staged in the East Room of the White House. Hoover is presenting Nixon with an honorary gold FBI badge.

At Nixon's invitation, Hoover celebrated his seventy-seventh birthday aboard Air Force One. Neither man knew that it would be Hoover's last. With them are Secretary of State William Rogers and his wife, Adele.

A prolific landscape artist, Samuel Noisette worked at the FBI for more than forty years, most notably as Hoover's official greeter. He was one of the few Black men classified as an FBI agent within what the NAACP described as Hoover's "lily white" corps.   LIBRARY OF CONGRESS

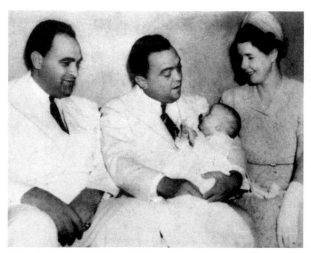

FBI official Louis Nichols (left) was Hoover's public relations chief and liaison to Capitol Hill. He named his first-born son John Edgar, after Hoover.

NATIONAL ARCHIVES AND RECORDS ADMINISTRATION

Hoover's secretary, Helen Gandy, worked for him for more than half a century.

LIBRARY OF CONGRESS

The three FBI officials on this page played key roles in Hoover's relationship with the Johnson and Nixon administrations. Above, Cartha "Deke" DeLoach (left) served as liaison to the Johnson White House (pictured here with Hoover, right, and son, Deke Jr., in 1962). NATIONAL ARCHIVES AND RECORDS ADMINISTRATION

As head of the Domestic Intelligence Division, William Sullivan (left) ran COINTELPRO, the FBI's now-infamous program of disruption and harassment aimed at groups such as the Communist Party, the Black Panthers, and the Ku Klux Klan.

NATIONAL ARCHIVES AND RECORDS ADMINISTRATION

W. Mark Felt (right) was the number-three FBI official when Hoover died. He went on to become Watergate's "Deep Throat." Pictured here in 1967 with his wife, Audrey, and Hoover.

DP PICTURE ALLIANCE/ALAMY STOCK PHOTO

Hoover's outspoken conservative views, especially on communism and civil rights, attracted support on the 1960s New Right. Above, Hoover speaks at the 1962 annual convention of the American Legion, an important popular constituency for the FBI. AP PHOTO/ED WIDDIS

A 1960 advertisement on a bus bench in Miami, sponsored by a local exterminator, urges Americans to read Hoover's anticommunist tract, *Masters of Deceit*. GRAPHIC HOUSE/ARCHIVE PHOTOS/GETTY IMAGES

Hoover spoke often about the importance of Christian faith for combating crime and communism, his two signature issues. This 1951 advertisement in the *Houston Press* shows the popular resonance of his message among evangelicals. HOUSTON PRESS/NATIONAL ARCHIVES AND RECORDS ADMINISTRATION

During the 1960s, Hoover's popular image fractured around issues such as civil rights, Vietnam, and the New Left. Above, civil rights activists stage a protest at the FBI's Denver field office in March 1965, calling for more robust federal action in support of civil and voting rights. DENVER POST/GETTY IMAGES

Cartoons of the era mocked Hoover for his thin skin in response to valid criticism. On the left, the cartoonist Herblock notes that the Warren Commission's 1964 criticism of the FBI does not fit with Hoover's preferred image of infallibility. On the right, a 1967 cartoon shows Hoover hopping mad over congressional inquiries. A 1964 HERBLOCK CARTOON, © THE HERB BLOCK FOUNDATION

Doonesbury
by GB Trudeau

In 1971, antiwar activists in Media, Pennsylvania, broke into an FBI office and stole its files, including those documenting the FBI's surveillance of New Left groups. This Doonesbury cartoon satirizes the FBI's emphasis on policing student radicals and civil rights activists rather than organized crime.

Hoover and Tolson maintained their partnership—both professional and personal—until the end of Hoover's life. Above, Tolson (far left) doles out advice during Hoover's historic 1964 press conference in Jackson, Mississippi. DeLoach is to Hoover's right.   NATIONAL ARCHIVES AND RECORDS ADMINISTRATION

Hoover and Tolson continued to dine out together well into the 1960s.

NATIONAL ARCHIVES AND RECORDS ADMINISTRATION

Hoover and Tolson tried to project an image of vigor as they aged. Pictured striding past the Washington monument in a staged photo, around 1964.

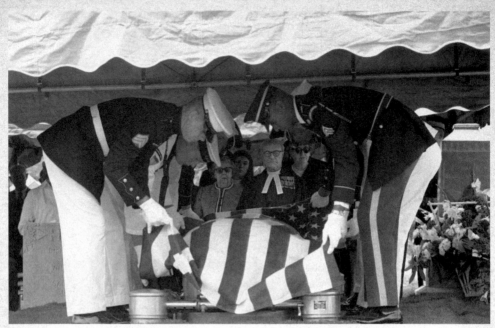

Hoover's funeral in May 1972 was a national event: broadcast live on all three major television networks, with a eulogy delivered by President Nixon. The burial ceremony at Congressional cemetery was a smaller affair. Above, soldiers fold the flag atop Hoover's casket, to be handed to Tolson.

AP PHOTO/CHARLES HARRITY

A distressed and frail Tolson being guided into a car after Hoover's funeral. Tolson resigned from the FBI upon Hoover's death.   BETTMANN/GETTY IMAGES

had found at the Willard, eager to keep the president in the loop. As Johnson's emissary, Walter Jenkins read the FBI's report "word for word" and declared King's behavior "repulsive." Then he recommended that the FBI move forward with what it was already planning to do. According to DeLoach, Jenkins believed that "the FBI could perform a good service to the country if this matter could somehow be confidentially given to members of the press." DeLoach assured Jenkins that "the Director had this in mind" for the future.[10]

Johnson apparently made no mention of the Willard incident or any of the FBI's plans when he met with King and other civil rights leaders on January 18. But even as Johnson assured King that the civil rights bill would be forced through the House "without a word or a comma changed," Hoover was beginning to test whether Congress might also be a useful vehicle for exposing King. On January 29, Hoover appeared before a House appropriations subcommittee to deliver his annual testimony. When it came time to discuss civil rights, he warned vaguely about the potential for "infiltration, exploitation, and control of the Negro population" by the Communist Party. Then he moved off the record to discuss King's communist ties and sexual activities. Everyone understood what happened to "off the record" comments in Washington: they entered the Capitol Hill whisper chain, passed from congressman to staffer to reporter in backroom chats. Coming in the midst of a congressional showdown over Johnson's civil rights bill, Hoover's comments spread rapidly.

Still, on February 10, less than two weeks after Hoover's testimony, the House passed the civil rights bill, exactly as Johnson had hoped. A week later, Jenkins summoned DeLoach to the White House and asked for the full King file—not just the revelations from the Willard and the wiretaps, but the years of background material on Levison and O'Dell. The impetus for the meeting supposedly came from Johnson's civil rights aides, who worried that Hoover's rumormongering about King might endanger the civil rights bill as it made the treacherous passage from House to Senate. Bobby Kennedy, too, was rumored to be sorting out how to make a move, either for or against King. DeLoach assured Jenkins that Hoover had everything under control. The FBI would take no action that might imperil Johnson's political agenda.

Hoover mostly lived up to that promise. In mid-March, hoping to disrupt the civil rights bill's passage through the Senate, Louisiana congressman and HUAC chair Ed Willis called on DeLoach with a proposition: the committee wanted to subpoena Hoover to testify on the record about King's many foibles. DeLoach also received a query from Virginia congressman Howard W. Smith, a passionate anticommunist who was now head of the House Rules Committee. Smith's effort to derail the civil rights bill by adding a clause outlawing sex discrimination was backfiring spectacularly, resulting in legislative language that now included women as a protected class. Now he saw a chance to strike another blow through the FBI. Both legislators were "seriously disturbed about the fact that there appeared to be considerable derogatory information about King and apparently no one in the Congress was taking steps to advise the general public," DeLoach reported to Hoover. The tricky calculation, all agreed, was "the timing of exposing King."[11]

If Hoover had embraced Willis's idea—going before HUAC to testify about Levison and O'Dell and the Willard—he would have seriously damaged King's reputation. But he would also have disrupted Johnson's plans and risked exposing the Bureau's operation. So he decided to remain silent, at least until after the presidential election.

THE FBI CONTINUED TO GATHER INFORMATION ON KING THROUGHOUT THE spring of 1964, as the Senate took up the civil rights bill and then settled in for another filibuster. Their hotel-room bugging captured King making a tasteless joke during a televised rerun of John Kennedy's funeral. "Look at her!" King supposedly crowed as Jackie Kennedy bent down over her husband's casket, "sucking him off one last time"— a comment that Hoover promptly shared with Bobby Kennedy. In Los Angeles and Atlanta, agents overheard King in conversation with a "girl friend" and "another girl friend," their identities and backgrounds immediately subject to FBI inquiry. In Detroit, a team of the Bureau's "very best men" bugged his hotel room and considered ginning up a police raid to catch him in the act. The most sensational new developments came from Las Vegas, where an investigator for the gaming commission interviewed a white showgirl and sometime prostitute who said she'd spent a night with King, gospel singer Clara Ward, and another male friend of King's. Together, they supposedly engaged in "unnatural" acts. Like Hoover, the investigator recognized the implications of this blockbuster claim. "The good doctor doesn't exactly practice what he preaches, or does he?" he asked in a gleeful memo.[12]

In June came the last phase of debate over the civil rights bill. West Virginia senator Robert Byrd filibustered the bill for more than fourteen hours. But the final word went to Goldwater, who delivered a mournful eight-minute speech on the evening of June 18 decrying the imminent destruction of Americans' "God-given liberties." The next day, supposedly beaten down by what Goldwater described as Johnson's "sledgehammer political tactics," the Senate voted to pass the bill. The victory cost Johnson dearly among Southern Democrats, who now regarded him as a cross between a fool and a race traitor. On June 19, though, the most difficult phase seemed to be over, with the Senate votes tallied and definitive.[13]

Then a crime out of Mississippi threw the whole calculus out of balance.

THE FBI'S RESIDENT AGENT IN JACKSON, MISSISSIPPI, RECEIVED THE PHONE call just after ten p.m. on Sunday, June 21. According to the worried voice on the line, three young civil rights workers—Andrew Goodman, Michael Schwerner, and James

Chaney—had gone missing that afternoon somewhere in Neshoba County, Mississippi. Goodman and Schwerner were white left-leaning activists from New York.
They had come to Mississippi as an advance guard for Freedom Summer, a bold new
voter-registration project that placed Northern volunteers, including white college
students, in local Black homes. Chaney, a twenty-one-year-old Black man, lived in
Mississippi, observing, absorbing, and objecting to its indignities. The three men had
gone to Neshoba to investigate a recent church burning but failed to call in for their
four p.m. safety check. The chain of alarm that followed extended first to the Freedom
Summer regional office, then to the jails, and finally, six hours later, to the local Bureau
office.

The FBI agent at Jackson took no action that first night, other than telling the
worried civil rights workers to "keep me informed." Nor did he do much the following
morning, perhaps hoping that the young men would still show up. By Monday evening, however, it was clear that they would not be returning anytime soon and that
they had likely suffered a torturous fate. Just before six p.m., Bobby Kennedy ordered
the FBI into the case and notified the president about the unfolding crisis. Half an
hour later, Walter Cronkite announced to the country that "three young civil rights
workers disappeared . . . on Sunday night near the central Mississippi town of Philadelphia, about fifty miles northeast of Jackson." The case would be treated, for now, as
an interstate kidnapping, even though everyone feared that the boys were already dead
somewhere in the swamps of Mississippi.[14]

Hoover ordered a fleet of agents into Neshoba County, where they quickly found
that they were not popular men. At the Freedom Summer offices, both volunteers and
locals felt that help had come too little, too late, while local whites showed the same
hostility and contempt they had displayed for years in lynching investigations. By four
p.m. Hoover nonetheless had some real news for the president. "I wanted to let you
know we found the car," he told Johnson by phone. "Nobody knows this at all, but the
car was burned, and we do not know yet whether any bodies are inside of the car." A
few hours later, he called back to report that the bodies were not in the car, and that
the investigation would be continuing.[15]

Hoover had little more news to offer over the next several weeks, as the investigation began to slow and then stall, hampered by the silence that always seemed to descend over white residents in such cases. He nonetheless proved useful to Johnson,
helping the president to manage the final push toward civil rights legislation even as
heightened emotions and deep uncertainty about the missing young men kept Mississippi on the verge of an "explosion." For all his political experience, Johnson had never
before dealt with this sort of ongoing unsolved crime, or with the blend of public
scrutiny and high contingency it entailed. Hoover had decades of accumulated wisdom. Unlike Kennedy, Johnson was willing to listen.

Between June 23 and 25, Hoover and Johnson spoke on the phone no fewer than eight times. In those conversations, Hoover advised the president to keep press comments about Mississippi to a minimum. He also agreed to run interference with the state's law enforcement, unrelievedly hostile to Johnson but still occasionally willing to work with Hoover. Johnson recognized the value of Hoover's Southern network; now, at a moment of crisis, the director was one of the few executive-branch officials able to command respect and cooperation where it was needed most. From Washington, Hoover was designated to serve as an emissary to Mississippi governor Paul Johnson (no relation to the president), who was refusing to accept calls from either the White House or the attorney general's office. When Hoover called, the governor evaded him, too, but Hoover managed to get a message passed along through local contacts. As he proudly reported back to the White House, Hoover suggested that the governor supply state patrolmen to search for the bodies and deliver a public statement in support of bringing "the perpetrators of this crime to justice." Hoover admitted that the situation was touch-and-go. "Now whether he'll say that or not, I don't know," he acknowledged.

The president's chief goal was to keep the situation contained until he could wrap up the civil rights bill, so agonizingly close to becoming the law of the land. At two p.m. on July 2, the House voted to accept the Senate's revised version of the legislation. Three hours later, Hoover called Johnson with an update about the Mississippi situation before the president took the final step of signing the bill into law. "If this thing blows up, I want to be in a position of saying I took precautions," Johnson explained, "and I put all the people that Edgar Hoover could spare down there to try to track down these violators and perpetrators of these crimes." Hoover assured him that a crack team was now in place and that the Bureau was working around the clock to find the missing men.[16]

With that assurance in hand, Johnson made his way to the East Room of the White House to perform one of the most significant deeds of his presidential life. At Johnson's invitation, Hoover ventured over to observe the ceremony, a florid old figure seated amid some one hundred other handpicked witnesses, including Bobby Kennedy and Martin Luther King. Just after seven p.m., with the television cameras rolling live for the nightly broadcast, Johnson sat down at a small table and looked directly into the television camera. "We believe that all men are entitled to the blessings of liberty," he read, his Texas drawl making the words seem all the more significant. "Yet millions are being deprived of those blessings—not because of their own failures, but because of the color of their skin." As applause swept through the room, he signed the Civil Rights Act of 1964, outlawing racial discrimination in public accommodations. He used seventy-two pens to sign the bill, a ceremonial gesture intended to recognize the many different hands that had gone into making the moment possible. He handed one pen each to Kennedy and King, in tribute to the fierce labor they had devoted to the civil rights cause. Another pen went to Hoover.[17]

———

IN THEIR CONVERSATIONS BEFORE THE SIGNING CEREMONY, HOOVER AND Johnson had agreed that the Bureau would need to make a big splash in order to demonstrate that the civil rights bill meant what it said: the federal government was now taking charge of desegregation. The great cautionary example was what had happened after *Brown*, when delays in enforcement had allowed white Southerners to rally together in the massive-resistance campaign. This time, Hoover proposed swift action. Though the FBI had always stationed agents in small offices throughout Mississippi, the Bureau had never maintained a full field office in the state. Now, he suggested, the FBI should open a field office in the state capital of Jackson, where tensions over the missing civil rights workers and the Freedom Summer "invasion" posed an immediate threat to the law's peaceful enactment.

Johnson loved the idea. When he arrived at the East Room on the evening of July 2 to sign the bill, he had already approved a basic outline of Hoover's plan. Earlier that afternoon, local Bureau agents had rented an entire floor "in an air-conditioned building" in downtown Jackson, as Hoover informed the president, and efforts to bring in the necessary filing cabinets, phones, safes, and desks were already underway. Johnson took this as a promise that Hoover would support a more robust exercise of federal enforcement power in Mississippi, especially now that the civil rights bill made segregation in public accommodations illegal. Their only point of disagreement concerned the degree to which Hoover was willing to put his own reputation—and his political relationships in the South—on the line for this particular cause. Johnson wanted Hoover to go to Jackson and open the office himself, to use the same leverage that had induced the governor to cooperate in the kidnapping case in order to get Mississippi officials on record in support of enforcing the new law. "I'm perfectly willing to do so," Hoover said before offering a list of reasons why it might not be a good idea.[18]

Johnson won in the end. In a statement released on July 9, Hoover announced that he planned to go to Mississippi the next day, implicitly inaugurating a new era of federal law enforcement in the South. Early on July 10, he and Tolson boarded an air force jet out of Washington and set off on their first-ever trip to Mississippi. DeLoach flew ahead to coordinate local arrangements, and to ensure that the day's pageant conveyed a seamless message of local, state, and federal cooperation. From the airport, all three were driven to the governor's house in downtown Jackson, a white-pillared, antebellum mansion and a monument to Old South nostalgia. Their escort consisted of both highway patrolmen and FBI agents, all supposedly dedicated—for the day, at least—to ensuring the legitimacy of federal power. Even Governor Johnson participated in the pageantry, welcoming Hoover, Tolson, and DeLoach into his home to discuss how they might all work together.

Hoover was unusually blunt in that conversation, handing over the names of known Mississippi Klansmen, including those employed by the state highway patrol, and urging the governor to purge official ranks. Once they stepped back into public view, however, both men exuded nothing but optimism and agreement. During a stop inside the state capitol's senate chamber, the governor pointed out a subtle connection to Hoover's past. Engraved on the ceiling was the phrase "Dieu et les Dames"—"God and the Ladies"—the motto of Kappa Alpha.

That moment was more than a mere tourist coincidence, one man honoring another's college years. It also reflected a shared history and outlook: you, the governor hinted, understand why the men and women of the white South fought so hard against this day. And Hoover did understand. Though his professional duties required him to act, he, too, had succumbed with reluctance to the politics of the moment. Nobody else in American government could strike quite the same balance: at once an emissary of federal power and an icon of Old South culture and values.

Hoover adopted a similar position at the afternoon's press conference, staged from the FBI's new headquarters in downtown Jackson. The office was as yet a Potemkin affair, all temporary walls and hastily thrown-together displays of books. Despite soaring temperatures, Hoover wore the usual dark suit and crisp white shirt, the official costume of a G-Man. With sweat trickling down his forehead and onto his bifocals, he read a prepared statement for the fifty-plus reporters who had assembled for the event, many of them dispatched from the major papers and networks in Washington, Los Angeles, and New York. When he was finished, a full supporting cast of Mississippi officials stepped to the podium to offer words of praise and agreement. "We're delighted to have the FBI here in Jackson," the governor enthused. "Mr. Hoover and his party is welcome to this state." Not to be outdone, Mayor Allen Thompson urged the people of Jackson to embrace the "wonderful" FBI presence. To visiting newsmen, accustomed to the usual Southern diatribes against federal power, it was an extraordinary—even baffling—moment. "In Mississippi," wrote Chicago reporter Nicholas von Hoffman, "Hoover is one of the most popular—perhaps at this juncture the only one popular— of all federal officials."

In all the praise and excitement, reporters tended to miss a sobering aspect of Hoover's visit: though he had traveled to Mississippi to promote the observance of the new federal law, he had barely spoken with civil rights supporters. Nor had he invited any Black men or women to participate in his press conference. As Hoover was leaving the press conference, Mississippi NAACP field director Charles Evers, brother of the slain civil rights leader Medgar Evers, intercepted him and asked to meet. Hoover sat down with him for about half an hour but showed little of the goodwill and understanding he had expressed toward white officials. "Mr. Evers stated he sometimes becomes discouraged, particularly because of the constant threats of his life," Hoover wrote in a summary memo for the White House. "I told him that while I could understand his feelings, he must expect some degree of personal danger."

Later that evening, when Evers contacted Hoover again, the director was even less sympathetic. Evers had hoped that Hoover might want to meet personally with local civil rights workers and perhaps gain a firsthand impression of conditions on the ground. Instead, Hoover flew off to New York with Tolson the next morning, avoiding a scheduled trip to Neshoba County. He left Evers with a reminder that the FBI's willingness to engage came with certain conditions. "I specifically made the point that the FBI had solved the murder of his brother at great cost and sacrifice, yet we had never hesitated in our quest for solution," Hoover reported to the White House. "I added that despite this hard-earned success, a number of Mr. Evers' followers, both before and after the solution of the murder, had unjustifiably criticized the FBI." He warned Evers that "such tactics are divisive and do nothing to resolve the troublesome issues confronting the American people." He said nothing about the divisiveness coming from within the FBI.[19]

CHAPTER 49

All the Way with LBJ

(1964)

Hoover and President Lyndon Johnson, friends and allies. Johnson described Hoover as the only trustworthy man in Washington.

Less than a week after Hoover's visit to Mississippi, the city of New York exploded. The incident that "triggered the seething unrest," as Hoover would later describe it, involved a fifteen-year-old Black boy named James Powell, who lived in the Bronx but happened to be attending summer school on the wealthy Upper East Side. On the morning of July 16, Powell was walking to school with friends when a white building superintendent sprayed them with a hose. The man vowed, according to Powell's friend, to "wash the black off" them. They chased their tormenter into his building; some witnesses said they threw bottles and garbage-can lids, too. When they reemerged, laughing, Powell caught the attention of Thomas Gilligan, an off-duty white police officer shopping nearby. Gilligan later maintained that Powell rushed him with a knife, a claim widely questioned by other witnesses. Seizing his service weapon, Gilligan fired off three quick shots at the children. Two of them hit Powell. The boy died on the sidewalk in front of a group of school-age children from his nearby summer program.

As *Time* later noted, this was the sort of incident—the killing of a Black teenager by a white police officer—"that in other, quieter times would have passed almost unnoticed." In the summer of 1964, with Birmingham and Mississippi seared into the national consciousness, with the president's ink barely dry on the new civil rights law, it sparked a rebellion. For the next week, Harlem residents took to the streets, sometimes chanting in organized protest, sometimes throwing bottles, bricks, and Molotov cocktails at the police. The images of the crackdown were as dramatic as anything out of Birmingham. *Time* printed a photograph of an armed-and-helmeted white police officer chasing a group of skinny Black boys, his baton poised to smash down on their unprotected heads. What most worried Johnson, though, was the opposite impression: that not enough was being done to contain the riots, that his civil rights act was now encouraging rebellion, looting, and disorder. Throughout the country, columnists were starting to joke about "Goldwater riots," shorthand for the idea that Black vandalism or urban disorder automatically meant more votes for the Republican.[1]

Hoover was eager to assist Johnson—to show that he could handle New York the same way he had handled Mississippi. On July 21, five days into the disaster, Johnson had drafted a press release announcing that the FBI would be taking on the Harlem investigation. Then he called Hoover, who agreed to put in a personal appearance in New York, just as he had done in Mississippi, in support of Johnson's plan. Johnson was thrilled at first, but soon grew worried that Hoover would be setting a pattern, boxing himself in to appear anywhere and everywhere a racial disturbance might occur. They settled on a more contained approach: Hoover would consult with the city and state officials, and would keep the president abreast of what he learned.

On Johnson's behalf, Hoover spoke with New York mayor Robert Wagner and governor Nelson Rockefeller, urging them to handle the crowd-control situation without relying on federal intervention or troops. At the same time, he assured Johnson that the FBI was firmly in control on the investigative side. He promised to produce a report describing what had happened in Harlem. Preferably, the report would show that Johnson's civil rights law was not responsible for the violence—and it would make that point well before the election.[2]

THOUGH JOHNSON WAS EAGER FOR HOOVER'S COOPERATION IN NEW YORK AND Jackson, a nagging problem remained: the FBI had still not found the three missing civil rights workers in Neshoba County. Lest the nation lose sight of this fact, on July 21, while Hoover and Johnson were busy sorting out plans for Harlem, King announced that he would be visiting the site of their abduction, along with other Mississippi areas where voter registration work was in progress. Local Klansmen promptly vowed not to let King leave the state alive. Their announcement, in turn, set off a minor panic at the White House. As Bobby Kennedy put it to the president, "If he gets killed, it creates all kinds of problems."[3]

Hoover knew about the rumored plots against King. "There are threats that they're going to kill him," he told Johnson when the president called just after noon on July 21. But Hoover had no intention of doing much about it. He had refused to notify King about previous death threats. He also still resisted attempts to induce his men to perform guard duty. "Once we start protecting them, we are going to have to do it for all of them," he had complained to Bobby Kennedy just minutes before speaking with Johnson. In that conversation, he vowed that they were not going to act as bodyguards for King or anyone else. When Johnson called, though, Hoover softened. "Talk to your man in Jackson and tell him that we think it would be the better part of wisdom, in the national interest, that they work out some arrangement" for protecting King, the president begged. Under pressure from Johnson, Hoover did what no other president, ally, or critic had been able to make him do: he sent a detail of FBI agents to perform guard duty for a civil rights leader.[4]

The bugs and taps were still in place, as was the scheme to "neutralize" King when the time seemed right. But for a few crucial days that July, the FBI placed itself between him and the Klan. Agents were there when King landed at the Jackson airport, acting not just as a party of observers but as a personal security detail. From there, they followed him wherever he went: to a pool hall and mass meeting in Greenwood, back to Jackson, then another mass meeting, and finally out to Neshoba County. Along the way, King offered occasional criticism of the Bureau. In an interview with Walter Cronkite, he noted that "if the FBI was so talented," it "should be able to solve the crime involving the three missing civil rights workers from Mississippi," in the words of an FBI summary. Though the words no doubt rankled Hoover, he did not react or respond in kind. Instead, on July 22, he let Johnson know, "We got Martin Luther King through the evening safe and sound." He promised to keep doing so as long as the president wanted.[5]

Secretly, the FBI was also making progress on the very case that King had accused them of neglecting. In late July, at the same time King was accusing the FBI of dragging its feet, a member of the Mississippi Highway Patrol decided to start talking. Like many of the Southern lawmen who had quietly aided the Bureau over the years, he did so at considerable risk. To gain his information, Hoover authorized payments of up to thirty thousand dollars, perhaps even more if necessary (though it remains unclear if and how much money changed hands). Everyone understood that the strategy of buying information reflected desperation rather than skill. "Under no circumstances should there be any indication in subsequent press, that would disclose our modus operandi," Al Rosen wrote on July 31, hoping to protect "the Bureau's prestige."[6]

On August 4, acting on their hard-won tip, agents hauled construction equipment out to a twenty-foot-high earthen dam on a farm outside Philadelphia, Mississippi.

From there, they began scraping away layer after layer of dirt. After two hours, they could smell "faint traces of the odor of decaying organic material." At three p.m., they saw the heels of a man's boots poking up through the soil. By the end of the day, they had uncovered the corpses of three young men, stacked atop each other and buried deep in the dam. Without the tip-off, nobody would have been able to find them.[7]

Johnson was ecstatic at the discovery, not just because it signified progress in a horrific crime, but because it showed what federal authority could accomplish in Mississippi. On August 5, he called Hoover to make sure that the director understood how grateful he was. "I didn't know how long it'd take, but I knew . . . you'd bring in results," Johnson told Hoover, an affirmation of the implied promise between the White House and the Bureau. Hoover warned Johnson that the next steps in Mississippi might be difficult, because both the local sheriff and his deputy appeared to be involved in the murders. Johnson expressed confidence that Hoover would stick with the case no matter the obstacles. "If you just think that you are going to get off the payroll because you're getting a little older, you're crazy as hell," the president said, in what might be construed as both a compliment and a warning. "I don't retire the FBI."[8]

UNTIL THIS MOMENT, JOHNSON'S PRESSURE HAD ARGUABLY BROUGHT OUT THE best in Hoover, inspiring the director to look beyond his rigid self-interest, to transform his Government Men once again into avenging angels of federal power. By forcing the FBI into the civil rights battle, and by constraining the exposure of King, Johnson pushed Hoover into the role of statesman and peacemaker, the one man capable of easing the white South into its new legal regime. He had given FBI agents a chance to showcase their investigative prowess, then championed them when they came through. Johnson viewed Hoover mostly as a political asset, but his attitude had broadened rather than narrowed Hoover's range of action. With Johnson's prodding, Hoover showed that the FBI was still capable of producing solid and professional work. Then, in August, Johnson asked Hoover for a favor that would have shattered any illusion of Hoover's apolitical professionalism or support for civil rights, if it had become widely known.

Their scheme involved the Democratic National Convention in Atlantic City, scheduled for August 24–27, where Johnson would, if all went well, be affirmed as his party's nominee. Johnson saw threats to that prospect coming from two directions. First were the men he perceived as party rivals, ambitious fellow Democrats who might set out to steal the convention and thus deny him the nomination. Second was a Freedom Summer delegation planning to truck into Atlantic City under the banner of the new Mississippi Freedom Democratic Party, where they would stage a convention-floor fight against the lily-white Mississippi delegation. Johnson viewed both insurgencies as personal affronts, displays of ingratitude and hostility from the very people he had worked so hard to appease. He was also bitter about the possibility of a convention-floor challenge from Bobby Kennedy, his own attorney general, who might attempt to capitalize on public sympathy over the assassination. But it was the MFDP that threatened to crack the Democratic coalition so essential to Johnson's political success. Seating the Black delegates, Johnson feared, would lead to a walkout from the white South. Not seating them would undermine his hard-won moral authority on civil rights. Hoover was once again supposed to help hold it all together.

This time, there would be no statesmanlike ceremony, no special appearance by Hoover. Instead, Johnson wanted bugs, taps, and confidential informants. According to DeLoach, Hoover privately complained that "Lyndon is way out of line" in asking the FBI to conduct surveillance at a political convention. But Hoover knew "when he was trapped." On July 25, he left for La Jolla with Tolson. While he was gone, DeLoach took charge of planning for the convention.[9]

What Johnson wanted above all was a "showcase convention," as DeLoach later described it, with "no 'incidents,' no angry demonstrators on TV, no pictures of police cracking the heads of civil rights protestors." In early August, Hoover instructed De-Loach to assemble a "special squad" of agents who could be counted upon to act with discretion on the president's behalf. To supplement the agents, he ordered the FBI's best, most experienced civil rights informants to amass in Atlantic City. One of those informants, Julius Hobson, ran the Washington office of CORE; he knew all the major figures who would be coming to town for the convention, including King. Several of the agents themselves would pose as reporters for NBC News, with the company's approval and cooperation. Aiding them all would be an extensive array of taps and bugs planted at meeting halls and local hotels where civil rights "agitators," including King, were likely to be staying.[10]

Hoover returned to Washington in late August, just in time to watch the operation play out. The convention opened to immediate controversy, with Alabama governor George Wallace denouncing the entire proceeding as a desecration of white supremacy, while the Freedom Summer activists prepared to deliver their own televised version of events. They had traveled north with a full-scale model of the torched and blackened station wagon where Goodman, Chaney, and Schwerner endured their final moments. They also brought a secret weapon in the form of Mississippi sharecropper Fannie Lou Hamer, whose eloquent testimony about the passion and pain she experienced in attempting to register to vote in Mississippi proved to be the convention's greatest televised sensation. Bureau informants kept track of it all, transmitting verbatim reports from the MFDP strategy sessions held in the basement of a local church, while agents posing as reporters followed up with "interviews" and off-the-record conversations with civil rights activists. Based in part on such information, Johnson scheduled a surprise press briefing from Washington in an attempt to distract from Hamer's speech.[11]

Johnson refused to come to Atlantic City until the nomination had been secured.

So it was up to DeLoach's team to keep the president apprised of what was happening along the boardwalk and inside the convention hall. They worked through the two Johnson aides assigned to manage events on the ground in Atlantic City: the always loyal Walter Jenkins and the younger Bill Moyers. DeLoach delivered twice-daily reports to them, one in the morning and one in the evening, documenting various plans for demonstrations, ongoing political calculations, and unseemly late-night goings-on. One noted that King would likely back Johnson no matter what happened with the MFDP, for fear that Goldwater's "coalition of racists and the extreme reactionary conservatives of the North" might actually capture the White House. Another documented King's plans to meet up with a woman from Philadelphia at a motel room near the turnpike as soon as he could get away. According to Senator Richard Russell, the president stayed up late poring over the Bureau's intelligence and strategizing about the next day's sessions. "He loves this," Russell noted in his private diary. "Hoover has apparently been turned loose and is tapping everything."

In truth, neither Bobby Kennedy nor the MFDP stood much chance of unseating a popular incumbent president. But this is not what Johnson believed at the time, and he credited "the presence of [Bureau] men, although completely unobserved by all except my immediate assistants" with helping him to keep the convention on his side. In total, DeLoach provided forty-four pages of on-site intelligence to the White House, much of it relating the private conversations and strategy sessions of civil rights leaders. That information, DeLoach concluded, "enabled [the Johnson team] to make spot decisions and to adjust Convention plans to meet potential problems before serious trouble developed."[12]

One of those decisions involved offering two at-large delegate slots to the MFDP, whose members promptly rejected it. Members of the official all-white delegations from Mississippi and Alabama walked out as well, though without upending the entire convention as Johnson had feared. Johnson finally arrived in the city on the evening of August 26, once the controversy had been more or less settled, prepared to accept the party's nomination as its presidential candidate the following day. Hoover never left Washington, but he paid close attention to DeLoach's reports. On September 1, he awarded DeLoach a three-hundred-dollar bonus for achieving "successful results" in one of the strangest and most politically sensitive operations ever undertaken by the Bureau.[13]

DeLoach later admitted that the FBI should never have been in Atlantic City, that Hoover should have held the line at such blatant political use of his men. "At best," he wrote, "it was demeaning; at worst, it was a serious breach of the law." That fall, though, he knew better than to express any reservations about the director's blossoming alliance with Johnson. "While this was rather a unique experience for us," he wrote to Hoover on September 8, "I do hope that our work, in some small manner, further contributed to the President's great confidence in you and the FBI."[14]

———

AT LEAST ONE EVENT MADE HOOVER'S JOB EASIER DURING THE FINAL MONTHS
of 1964. In early September, just after the Atlantic City convention, Bobby Kennedy
resigned as attorney general in order to run for the Senate from New York. He tried to
make peace as he left, sending personal notes to both Hoover and Tolson thanking
them for "having made an important contribution to the country in a time of maximum need." After almost four years of rancor, Hoover saw no need to placate his now-
former boss. On September 3, Bobby threw a farewell party in the Justice Department
courtyard for some two thousand employees. Hoover and Tolson declined to attend,
though they may have heard strains of "When Irish Eyes Are Smiling" wafting up
through the Justice corridors.[15]

Nobody thought Bobby was gone from Washington forever. "RFK Goodby Sounds
like 'I'll Be Back,'" *The Boston Globe* noted. Meanwhile, Hoover had other problems to
handle. On September 24, the Warren Commission delivered its report to the president
in a somber ceremony in the White House Cabinet Room. Less than forty-eight hours
later, Hoover released his own report—not on the assassination but on the summer's
riots in Harlem. Throughout September, at Johnson's request, he had been collaborating with former New York governor Thomas Dewey about the report's scope, which
had ballooned to include recent racial uprisings in Brooklyn and Philadelphia, as well
as in smaller cities like Paterson, New Jersey, and Dixmoor, Illinois. As DeLoach noted,
the president hoped to "convince the American public that the Johnson Administration is actually attempting to do something about the many riots going on." Hoover
delivered more or less what the president wanted. The final report reflected some of
Hoover's usual preoccupations. According to the FBI, "hoodlums" and "irresponsible
Negroes," many of them inspired by Malcolm X, helped to fuel the disorder in Harlem.
Mostly, though, the report was a marvel of careful messaging, in which Hoover catered
to Johnson's preferred view. After decades of scoffing at the "sentimentalists" and
"bleeding hearts" who emphasized poverty as a cause of crime, Hoover concluded that
"underlying economic and social conditions" had precipitated the summer's episodes
of unrest. He even ruled out speculation that the Communist Party had played a role
in planning the violence.[16]

To Hoover's conservative allies, the FBI's stance was thoroughly perplexing. "We
must hope that future attempts to conscript the FBI as a propaganda agent for the
administration's policies will fail," grumbled *National Review*, warning that Hoover
was putting his "hero" status among conservatives in jeopardy. At the White House,
though, it was yet another example of the president's genius in establishing his alliance with Hoover. Against all odds, Johnson "maneuvered his anticommunist FBI
director into issuing a report that endorsed the war on poverty [and] helped blunt the
Goldwater Republican challenge," one historian has noted. Though Hoover had spent

forty years insisting that the FBI could not be swayed by political concerns, he turned out to be as susceptible as anyone to Johnson's masterful blend of praise, coercion, and power.[17]

HOOVER PERFORMED ONE MORE FAVOR FOR JOHNSON BEFORE THE ELECTION. This one was as much personal as it was political. On October 7, after a party at the *Newsweek* office, Walter Jenkins—the FBI's chief contact at the White House—walked to the local YMCA and entered the men's bathroom. There, he met a homeless army veteran and proceeded to have sex with him. Neither man realized that the vice squad was watching as part of a sting operation. The police arrested Jenkins and took him down to the station for booking. A week later, when *Evening Star* reporters learned of the arrest and threatened to write about it, Jenkins reached out to Johnson adviser Abe Fortas, confessing that he was devastated by the impending scandal and wanted to die. Fortas checked Jenkins into the George Washington University Hospital. Then he called DeLoach, who volunteered to see if anything could be done to hush up the police report. When it turned out that the news was already on its way into print, they brought Hoover into the loop to assist the Johnson campaign one more time.[18]

The Republicans came out punching hard. On behalf of the Goldwater campaign, they demanded to know whether Jenkins had revealed national security information during these assignations, and whether he had ever been subject to a thorough security check. Within twenty-four hours, hoping to insulate his own campaign, Johnson formally ordered the FBI to investigate and report back, just as it had done in Harlem. Behind closed doors, Hoover professed once again to be outraged by Johnson's presumption, including not only the pressure to issue an immediate press release absolving Jenkins of any taint but also to find out who had tipped off the press in the first place. "I told Fortas this is not in accord with what I think should be done," Hoover complained. As during the convention, however, he also concluded "that I will have to carry out these instructions." Over the next few days, Hoover dispatched agents to interview everyone involved, including Jenkins's friends, family, and coworkers.[19]

What they found was not a grand national security conspiracy, but a sad tale: Jenkins, father of six, had been arrested in the same bathroom, for the same purpose, five years earlier. His security clearance had been completed a year before that encounter— hence the ostensible ignorance of the White House about his sexual activities. Both DeLoach and Johnson professed to be baffled that they had been working side by side with a man who kept such secrets and who seemed to exhibit all the signs of vigorous heterosexual manhood. "There has never been the slightest inclination of homosexuality," DeLoach said, recalling how he and Jenkins had attended church, gone on walks, and cracked jokes together—even "played golf at least fifty times." Johnson, too, seemed perplexed that his own aide could have succeeded in hiding such a significant fact. DeLoach assured him that "these things in Washington have come up quite often before" and that the FBI would figure out how to handle it.[20]

Hoover did not find the incident nearly as confusing. He speculated that Jenkins—like Sumner Welles and so many others over the years—had simply lost control of himself, succumbing to the sort of temptation that might befall any man. As Hoover explained to Johnson on October 19, four days into the investigation, Jenkins had been under enormous stress, with the election and his White House duties to manage. As a result, he had a breakdown, leading to his homosexual activity. "I stated I thought in regard to Mr. Jenkins that they will find it was something mental," Hoover recalled to Tolson, "and if so, it would be well if a medical report can be prepared in due time that this man's condition requires institutionalizing." Nobody seems to have questioned how, exactly, a few drinks and a loss of self-control would inexorably lead a man to the basement of the YMCA.[21]

Johnson's political opponents saw no reason to give anyone—Jenkins, Johnson, or even Hoover—the benefit of the doubt. On October 15, in a routine gesture of sympathy, Hoover had sent flowers to Jenkins in the hospital, along with a card wishing for a speedy recovery. Six days later, with the investigation in full swing, someone mentioned this fact to the press. The subsequent coverage emphasized Hoover's conflict of interest: Why was he investigating a man to whom he had sent flowers? More difficult was the innuendo that Hoover might have more in common with Jenkins than he wished to acknowledge.[22]

Hoover acted tough. "I've got a pretty powerful hide on that," he told Johnson. "I've listened to it so long." What he did not do, to Johnson's relief, was renounce Jenkins. On October 22, with less than two weeks to go before the election, Hoover issued a report absolving Jenkins of any national security violations. To the Goldwater camp, this seemed like yet another example of Johnson-Hoover collusion: "misuse" of the FBI "for blatantly political purposes," in the words of one Republican senator. While Hoover was doing Johnson a political favor, however, the report also seems to have reflected what he actually believed. "My feeling of Jenkins, and I know him officially and personally, is that I like him and feel sorry for him," he wrote in a memo to Tolson and other Bureau officials. "It is a pitiful case and I think it is time for people to follow the admonition of the Bible about persons throwing the first stone and that none are without sin."

Johnson expressed gratitude for Hoover's approach. "You handled it with thoroughness and with diligence and with compassion," he told Hoover by phone. Such words were not often spoken about the FBI director, especially when it came to sensitivity about other men's vulnerabilities. But the Jenkins story brought out something human in both Hoover and Johnson, a point of private connection between two quintessentially political men.[23]

It did not hurt that the politics worked out as well. On November 3, less than two weeks after the Jenkins report, Johnson won the presidential election in one of the great landslides of American history, trouncing Goldwater with more than 90 percent of the electoral college and 61 percent of the popular vote. The next day, Hoover wrote to Johnson offering "congratulations on your overwhelming victory." He promised, during the four years ahead as during the campaign itself, "to assist you in the many problems that lie ahead."[24]

CHAPTER 50

The Most Notorious Liar

(1964–1965)

Rev. Dr. Martin Luther King Jr. leaving Hoover's office after their first and only sit-down meeting, December 1, 1964. Newly released documents help to show the full extent of the FBI's surveillance and harassment campaign against King. LIBRARY OF CONGRESS, NYWT&S COLLECTION

For almost a year, with the civil rights bill and then Johnson's election hanging in the balance, Hoover had postponed his plan to "expose" Martin Luther King. In November 1964, with those hurdles behind him, he took up where he had left off. For his initial audience, he chose the small but dogged Washington women's press briefing group, an offshoot of the more powerful National Press Club, which did not deign to admit women as members. As a regular practice, the women's club had scheduled private meetings with high-profile Washington officials to explore "their responsibilities, current problems of interest, etc.," as they explained to DeLoach. After some initial skepticism, Hoover and DeLoach concluded that the meeting offered an opportunity for Hoover to promote his agenda for the new presidential term. It also provided a chance to test the waters about King and other hot-button issues. "I explained . . . that the ladies must fully understand that some of the Director's comments may have to be 'off the record,'" DeLoach noted in a memo.[1]

On the morning of Wednesday, November 18, more than two dozen women filed into Hoover's office. Hoover was always "shy on such occasions," DeLoach recalled, "and tried to avoid them." When avoidance was not possible, he covered up his nervousness by speaking so fast and breathlessly that nobody else could get a word in edgewise. His monologue on November 18 proved especially dizzying, as if the pent-up frustration of the previous four years needed to be released all at once. Hoover took aim at the Warren Commission: "unfair and unjust," he declared, "a classic example of Monday morning quarterbacking." He attacked the Birchers ("I have no respect for the head of the society"), gun owners ("There are licenses for automobiles and dogs; why not guns?"), even Congress itself ("Naturally I get more and more irritated when I see Congress passing along to us matters that should be handled by the states"). DeLoach had set aside an hour for the briefing, but Hoover continued on into a second hour, then a third. He spoke on crime and states' rights, on lie detectors and juvenile delinquents, on the Neshoba County crime and the corruption of Southern law enforcement.

Of everything Hoover said that morning, however, one set of comments stood out. Without any special notice, he turned to the subject of King, who was then having a banner few weeks as the recently announced recipient of the Nobel Peace Prize. Hoover seized the occasion not to comment on the prize, but to "correct" the record on King's two-year-old criticism of the Bureau for staffing its Southern offices with Southern-born agents. "In view of King's attitude and his continued criticism of the FBI on this," Hoover told the reporters, "I consider King to be the most notorious liar in the country." Then he went off the record for "further comments," just as he had done before the appropriations committee. There is no reliable account of what he said, but it is not hard to imagine the range of possibilities: Levison and O'Dell, the girlfriends and assignations, King's claim that he obeyed a higher law than that imposed by mere courts and policemen.

DeLoach later claimed that he tried to get Hoover to retract the "notorious liar" comment. "I grabbed pencil and paper, scrawled a note, and passed it over to Hoover. It read, 'Don't you think you should insist that the remark about King was off the record?'" Hoover refused—not just once, but three times—in response to DeLoach's increasingly insistent notes. "DeLoach advises me to tell you ladies that my calling Dr. King a notorious liar should be off the record," he informed the room. "I won't do this. Feel free to print my remarks as given."[2]

And so they did. Measured by the firestorm that followed, Hoover made a terrible decision that day, committing to a remark that would ultimately become one of the most "notorious" episodes of his career. And yet DeLoach's version of events also suggests that Hoover was no rambling old man—that Hoover knew, or thought he knew, what he was doing. This was Walter Winchell's opinion, presumably culled from conversations with Hoover. The FBI director's performance, Winchell wrote, "was not, as assumed by editorial page critics, a sudden tantrum" about King. Hoover had simply "delayed his blast until after Election Day so that the White House would not be involved."[3]

THE NEXT MORNING, NICHOLAS KATZENBACH RELUCTANTLY ENTERED THE director's office to discuss what to do. A former law professor, festooned with degrees from Yale, Princeton, and Oxford, Katzenbach had been recruited into government during the Kennedy years as an assistant attorney general, a member of the brash young team that had so alienated Hoover. In 1963, he had faced off against George Wallace at the schoolhouse door, his bald pate and slump-shouldered tall-man's posture a famous contrast to Wallace's defiant snarl and squat frame. After the assassination, he had pushed for the Warren Commission, and then for full transparency in the FBI's posthumous investigation into Oswald. Now he had become acting attorney general, appointed to keep things running while Bobby Kennedy moved on to his new job as the junior senator from New York.[4]

With Katzenbach, Hoover tried to backtrack about the King comment, no doubt aware that it was not going over well among administration liberals. "I'm very sorry," he said. "It was a mistake to see all those women reporters." Hoover blamed DeLoach for orchestrating the event and for convincing everyone that it was a good idea. Grudgingly, Katzenbach decided to close ranks and declare his support for Hoover. Later that day, when the reporters asked him if he agreed with Hoover's comments about King, the acting attorney general replied, with studied neutrality, "I'm pleased with the FBI's job in the South." He then added, "Civil rights leaders often feel that more should be done. Generally, it's impatience on their part."[5]

Those same civil rights leaders were already at the White House, however, complaining to Johnson that his FBI director was out of control and ought to be disciplined. The meeting had been scheduled days earlier, with Johnson hoping to discuss his civil rights agenda for the new term. The participants—including NAACP executive director Roy Wilkins, long a friendly Bureau contact—now found the meeting hijacked by a discussion of Hoover. "We stand with Dr. King in his conviction that the FBI has not provided adequate protection to Negroes in the South," Wilkins told the press. Nearly every faction of the movement seemed to agree, united in their indignation about Hoover's comments if not on questions of strategy and tactics. That same day, a spokesman from CORE called to tell DeLoach that his group would be issuing a statement in solidarity with King, even though "CORE leaders considered the FBI as a friend of theirs," as DeLoach reported to Hoover. Hoover might have welcomed the advance warning as a tribute to his years of engagement, some of it mutually beneficial, with the nation's civil rights groups. Instead, he declared them all a bunch of "hypocrites."[6]

The press mostly responded with shock at Hoover's attempt to malign a soon-to-be Nobel laureate. Even his admirers seemed to think he had gone too far. "Please sir, shut up," one fan suggested. "You are, we'll all acknowledge, a top-flight administrator, an excellent cop, and a highly accomplished empire builder and bureaucrat. But that doesn't give you any right to call some of our most distinguished citizens liars and bleeding hearts while you are still on the public payroll." *Newsweek* editor Ben Bradlee (soon to become editor of *The Washington Post*) commissioned a story about rumors that Johnson planned to fire Hoover. Bradlee also let it be known around town "that the FBI had told him that Martin Luther King was a sexual degenerate," but that he disapproved of the FBI's underhanded tactics far more than he disapproved of King.[7]

King himself happened to be off in the Bahamas, attempting to relax and work on his Nobel speech. By the middle of Friday afternoon, reporters began to helicopter onto the sandy expanse near King's hotel in order to find out what the man himself had to say. Put on the spot, King conjured up a surprisingly generous, if patronizing, response. "I cannot conceive of Mr. Hoover making a statement like this without being under extreme pressure," he told reporters. "He has apparently faltered under the awesome burdens, complexities and responsibilities of his office." The FBI later captured a less sympathetic perspective via wiretap. King's father urged his son, via Coretta, "to be moderate in his approach to this problem," but King—like Hoover—was in no mood for compromise. "Hoover is old and getting senile," he told a friend, "and should be hit from all sides."[8]

DeLoach persuaded Hoover not to hit back that first weekend. For the most part, Hoover listened. On Friday, he appeared at a reception hosted by the widow of a prominent Washington developer, taking up a roost by the door and chatting with senators as if nothing were amiss. The criticism and mockery rankled, however, especially because Hoover felt he had done nothing wrong—that he was, once again, the victim of a hostile press. After all, King *had* lied, sometimes directly to the president. Plus, the Bureau was now devoting hundreds if not thousands of agents to civil rights cases—even, back in July, to protecting King himself. Hoover seemed genuinely baffled by the uproar over his comments, and by the media's refusal to pursue his off-the-record hints. "I cannot understand why we are unable to get the true facts before the public," he wrote to DeLoach. "We can't even get our accomplishments published."[9]

Many of Hoover's closest friends—men who had been with him for decades—shared this sense of grievance, calling in to assure Hoover that he would survive and even prosper once things settled down. "History has a way of putting such incidents in perspective and in the end you will come through with your reputation untarnished," Nixon wrote. Indeed, the one man whose opinion really mattered, Lyndon Johnson, seemed to find the whole episode highly amusing, one of the few times he'd caught Hoover in a major public misstep. In conversations with DeLoach, the president treated Hoover like a dotty old uncle, sometimes prickly and theatrical but still worthy of family love. "We all get to feeling sorry for ourselves once in a while, and feeling like somebody's picking on us," he told DeLoach two days after Hoover's press conference.[10]

When questioned by reporters, Johnson announced gravely that he would not consider dismissing Hoover, despite the very serious outcry over the director's remarks. To his aides, he offered what would become one of the most famous phrases of his presidency. Asked why he would not, at last, get rid of the sixty-nine-year-old FBI director, Johnson allegedly explained in his most down-home, East Texas patois, "It's probably better to have him inside the tent pissing out, than outside pissing in."[11]

JOHNSON MIGHT HAVE BEEN LESS AMUSED IF HE HAD UNDERSTOOD THE FULL scope of what Hoover and the FBI were planning. Though DeLoach apparently believed that a full retreat was in order, Sullivan insisted that the time was ripe to push ahead in their long-delayed counterintelligence campaign against King. Hoover agreed with Sullivan.

They waited until Saturday to begin carrying out the plan. "Sometime during the morning," recalled Seymor Fred Phillips, an agent in the Domestic Intelligence Division, "Sullivan came into my office and asked me for some unwatermarked stationery. I secured some from my secretary's desk and after checking it through the light, I offered it to Sullivan." A bit later, Sullivan called over to ask for the SCLC's address in Atlanta. When Phillips stopped by to deliver the information, his boss "seemed to be busily at work at a typewriter on a stand next to his desk." Sullivan inquired once again if the paper on which he was typing was truly, definitively untraceable.

What he was typing during those Saturday hours, on that unwatermarked paper, was a single-page letter addressed to King, allegedly written by a Black man disillusioned by his hero's moral failings. "King, In view of your low grade, abnormal personal behavior I will not dignify your name with either a Mr. or a Reverend or a Dr.," the letter began. "And, your last name calls to mind only the type of King such as King Henry the VIII and his countless acts of adultery and immoral conduct lower than that of a beast." The letter went on to describe the varieties of "sexually psychotic" crimes allegedly committed by King: "all your adulterous acts, your sexual orgies extending far into the past." Its language conjured up the degraded images often attributed to Black men in American culture, labeling King an "evil, abnormal beast," a "dissolute, abnormal moral imbecile," and a "filthy, abnormal animal." At the same time, it showed a frightening level of specificity, describing sexual escapades with other "ministers of the Gospel," and going so far as to identify one of King's West Coast "playmates" by name. The message concluded with a vague threat and a deadline: "King, there is only one thing left for you to do. You know what it is. You have just 34 days." Once he completed the letter, Sullivan placed it in a sealed envelope along with an audio "highlights" reel gleaned from the FBI's hotel-room recordings.

Few people know precisely what ended up on that tape; it is under court embargo until 2027, along with the rest of the King recordings. And there are other lingering mysteries: What did Sullivan believe was the "one thing" that King knew to do? And why did it have to happen on Christmas, thirty-four days from November 21? King and his confidants saw a dire possibility. "There was no question that there was a strong suggestion that Martin commit suicide in this sick letter," recalled Andrew Young, one of King's closest advisers.

Whatever they were seeking, Hoover and Sullivan wanted above all to make sure that the operation could not be traced directly to the Bureau. Around noon, Sullivan summoned Phillips again—this time, with instructions to take the mysterious package over to Bureau headquarters. The next phase of the operation fell to agent Lish Whitson, who received a phone call from Sullivan at home that afternoon with instructions to drop everything and proceed immediately to the north terminal of Washington's National Airport. Once there, Whitson was approached by a young man who identified him as "Mr. Whitson" and then thrust a brown-paper package, approximately eight inches square and one inch thick, into his hands. Whitson had been told to fly to Miami. Once there, he called Sullivan for further instructions. As Whitson would inform congressional investigators more than a decade later, he "did as directed and upon calling Sullivan was instructed to address the package to Mr. Martin Luther King." From there, he had the package weighed, added the proper postage, and dropped it into the U.S. mail, addressed to King, with no return address. On Sunday, he flew to Washington. On Monday, back in the office, he informed Sullivan that the whole journey had gone well. Sullivan promised "someday" to "tell you all about" what had been inside the package.[12]

WHILE SULLIVAN ORCHESTRATED THE MAILING TO KING, HOOVER AND DELOACH launched another, related project: containing the damage to Hoover's reputation as a result of the "notorious liar" comment. For days after the briefing, Hoover hesitated to reengage the press, grumbling away in private memos and phone conversations but refusing public comment. Then, on Tuesday night, once Whitson was safely back from Florida, Hoover broke his silence. The forum was a black-tie dinner for 1,114 patrons in the grand ballroom of Chicago's Hilton Hotel, a benefit for Loyola University's medical school. Hoover was the guest of honor, recipient of the newly inaugurated Sword of Loyola prize, in "tribute to a national or international figure who exhibits a high degree of courage, dedication, and service." And perhaps, after the previous week's uproar, it did take a certain misguided courage for Hoover to continue to speak his mind.

He came with a script and mostly followed it, decrying the "bleeding hearts" who coddled juvenile delinquents and the criminals who took advantage of the system. At some point, however, he apparently departed from his Crime Records text to deliver a rebuttal to King—indeed, to all the critics and civil rights sympathizers who'd had so much to say over the past five days. "It is a great misfortune that the zealots or pressure groups always think with their emotions and seldom with reason," he declared. "They have no compunction carping, lying and exaggerating with the fiercest passion, spearheaded at times by Communists and moral degenerates." He did not name any specific "degenerates," but he did not need to. The speech was aimed not at the genteel Catholics in the room but at King and his allies, who would surely read his remarks in the press and realize that he had no intention of backing down.[13]

They got the message. On November 27, three days after Hoover's talk, NAACP executive director Roy Wilkins contacted DeLoach to request an emergency face-to-face meeting. He apologized for the disruption—it was Thanksgiving weekend—but he felt that the matter could not wait. "Wilkins stated he personally knew about whom the Director was talking," DeLoach reported, "although many other Negroes did not know." According to Wilkins, movement leaders recognized that the FBI might be planning to expose King's infidelities, with dire consequences to follow. Wilkins stipulated the "truthfulness of the sexual degenerate allegations and communist allegations against King," according to DeLoach, and maintained "that he personally did not mind seeing King ruined." But Wilkins also knew that "if King was ruined the entire civil rights movement would be ruined," an outcome he was keen to avoid. The timing for a scandal could hardly have been worse: King was just days away from receiving the Nobel Prize. And he had already announced plans for a voting-rights campaign in Selma, Alabama. Wilkins pleaded with DeLoach for time in which his fellow civil rights leaders could put a little pressure on King—perhaps even persuade him (in a painful twist of logic) to stop attacking Hoover. In the meantime, Wilkins expressed a desperate hope that "the FBI would not expose King before something could be done," such as convincing King to leave public life and take up the presidency of "a small college." DeLoach replied disingenuously that the FBI would never engage in gossip-mongering and gutter talk. That said, "if King wanted war we were prepared to give it to him."[14]

That war was, of course, already well underway, with DeLoach as one of its chief instigators. While Sullivan's package made its way from Miami to Atlanta, DeLoach was busy strategizing about what to do with *Communism and the Negro Movement*, a misleadingly titled thirteen-page summary report on King that the FBI periodically updated and circulated around Washington. In its latest iteration, the report contained two pages on "King: His Personal Conduct." It also contained the old allegations about Levison, O'Dell, and "the continued dependence of King upon former Communist Party, USA members." In October 1963, Hoover had sent the report around to allies in the military and the executive branch, but Bobby Kennedy had insisted on recalling them, for fear that they would be leaked and backfire on the president. The new version was even more salacious. Hoover hoped that this time somebody other than the FBI would take up the work of exposure.[15]

He started with the White House. On December 4, DeLoach spoke with Johnson aide Bill Moyers, who had been given a copy of the report to review. Moyers informed DeLoach that "it was both his and the President's opinion" that the FBI should go ahead with distributing the report around Washington. To make sure there was no mistake about what he was hearing, DeLoach confirmed with Moyers that "he appeared to be telling me that we should go ahead and disseminate" the information to key government officials, including the compromising material about King's sex life. According to DeLoach, Moyers "answered in the affirmative." Over the next few days, Hoover's office sent the report to at least a dozen Johnson administration officials, including Katzenbach, Defense Secretary Robert McNamara, and Secretary of State Dean Rusk.[16]

At that point, King finally broke down and contacted Hoover directly. He had not yet received Sullivan's package. Nor did he know in any great detail about Hoover's dissemination campaign. But it did not take inside knowledge to see that a rift with Hoover could be dangerous, hardly the position from which to launch a new voting-rights campaign. Just after noon on December 1, King's colleague Andrew Young reached out to the Bureau to discuss the possibility of a sit-down meeting between King and Hoover. DeLoach played the offer as an insult, informing Young—apparently with a straight face—that "it was useless of them to request a 'peace meeting' with us as long as the crusade of defamation against Mr. Hoover and the FBI was to be carried on by Rev. King." After a bit of negotiation, however, all parties agreed to stage a summit. As they envisioned it, King would come to Hoover's office and they would discuss matters privately, away from the prying eyes of the press.[17]

King arrived at Hoover's office that afternoon at three thirty, accompanied by Young and two other advisers. DeLoach tried to hurry the group straight through Hoover's reception room, but noted disapprovingly that King "slowly posed for the cameras and newsmen" who had rushed over on short notice. DeLoach stayed on hand to take notes throughout the meeting, and to run interference if the situation demanded it. His staff prepared a background memo to remind Hoover of King's past as "a hypocrite, a fraud and a cheat who, under the guise of religion and patriotism, is deceiving millions of Americans." Hoover apparently had no interest in discussing such matters in King's presence. Instead, after listening to King for a few minutes, he "took the ball away" from his guest, as he later boasted to Katzenbach, and never quite gave it back.

Hoover enjoyed a home-court advantage. It was his office, his vast mahogany desk perched high on its platform. Some of his remarks to King bordered on the absurd, including the idea that "the FBI shares the same despair which the Negroes suffer" when the Bureau ran into criticism or a lack of cooperation. In other areas, though, his ideas were not so far off from what King—in another, less fraught and less threatening context—might have wanted to hear. Hoover lamented the all-white juries empaneled throughout the South, along with the "outrageous miscarriage of justice" that often resulted from the actions of "redneck sheriffs" and other "trashy type of characters." He boasted of his trip to Mississippi and his agreement with Governor Johnson "to put an end to violence and brutality" against Black citizens. He talked of the Neshoba County investigations, of the FBI's passionate hope for a guilty verdict, and of his own "full sympathy with the sincere aspects of the civil rights movement." In most ways, though, the content hardly mattered. As Hoover explained to Katzenbach, the only truly important thing was that the conversation happened at all—"that I had gone through with it."[18]

King seems to have found the whole episode thoroughly bizarre, like a lecture from an ancient professor grown too fond of hearing his own voice. After the meeting, King thanked his hosts, then stepped out into Hoover's anteroom to make a statement to the press. News photographers captured him looking dazed and downcast, clutching his hat in one hand as he moved past a glass door etched with Hoover's name. King had written his statement before the meeting and now read it aloud. "I am pleased that I have had the opportunity to meet with Mr. Hoover this afternoon and I might say that the discussion was quite amicable," he declared. "I sincerely hope that we can forget the confusions of the past and get on with the job . . . of giving and providing freedom and justice for all the citizens of the nation."[19]

IN THEORY, THE SUMMIT BETWEEN KING AND HOOVER DEMONSTRATED THAT their breach had healed, that everyone decided to consign the "notorious liar" episode to the past. Three days later, FBI agents swept through Neshoba County and snapped up twenty-one white men—including the local sheriff and deputy sheriff—for their roles in the summer's triple murder. Six days after that, King delivered his Nobel acceptance speech in Oslo, Norway. "I accept the Nobel Prize for Peace at a moment when 22 million Negroes of the United States of America are engaged in a creative battle to end the long night of racial injustice," he declared in the opening intonations of an anguished but ultimately hopeful address. For the first time since Hoover's press conference, it seemed as if the FBI might be on the same side in that long and bloody struggle.[20]

But Hoover was not ready to let go of his campaign against King. Indeed, he had never intended to do so. On December 2, the day after their meeting, he ordered full transcripts of the recordings made in King's hotel rooms, overruling DeLoach's argument that this "tremendous amount of work" might be put off for a while, now that "the controversy has quieted down considerably." The Bureau also continued to interfere in King's private affairs. In advance of the Nobel ceremony, Hoover approved plans to brief American diplomats in Stockholm, Copenhagen, and other Scandinavian capitals on "both the communist influences on King and King's degenerate nature," in hopes that they would refuse to meet with the civil rights leader. Once King returned from Oslo, the Bureau took note of scurrilous rumors that his entourage had been "running naked, drunk white prostitutes up and down the halls of the hotel" and that local police had been called after one of the prostitutes allegedly robbed King's brother.[21]

In Washington, Sullivan sneaked off to National Airport to brief Dr. R. H. Edwin Espy, general secretary of the National Council of Churches of Christ, about the latest King gossip. Widely known as a white liberal and champion of civil rights, Espy assured Sullivan that the council would never again provide money or support to King's work, and that his fellow Protestant clergy were united in their disgust for "King's moral depravity." Cardinal Francis Spellman apparently felt the same way. After receiving a similar briefing, he agreed to intervene with the Pope himself in hopes of denying King an audience at the Vatican. Hoover met personally with the Black radio and television preacher Elder Lightfoot Solomon Michaux, a self-proclaimed "Hooverite." With DeLoach's assistance, Michaux released a four-page open letter lambasting King and suggesting that the civil rights leader apologize to Hoover.[22]

FBI officials found more hesitation among their press contacts, the most trusted of whom received oral briefings as well as a copy of the King report. Despite cluckings of sympathy, no reputable editor or reporter wanted to be responsible for exposing King, especially at the moment of his Nobel triumph. Still, the prospect of an imminent press report worried Katzenbach, who flew out to the Johnson ranch just before Christmas to register his concern with the president. He found that Johnson was not especially concerned, however, and certainly had no intention of chastising Hoover or of reining him in. When Hoover's seventieth birthday rolled around on January 1—the day that he should have been required to retire from federal service—Johnson made no move to nudge Hoover in that direction. Correctly observing the situation, pop astrologer Jeane Dixon predicted that "President Johnson, to a greater extent than his predecessors, will work closely with FBI director J. Edgar Hoover" in the year ahead.[23]

She was right. In the final calculus, far from alienating the president, the King debacle allowed Hoover to demonstrate his enduring popularity—to remind Johnson, among others, that many more Americans shared Hoover's worldview than shared King's. In February 1965, three months after Hoover's press conference, the Harris organization conducted a poll measuring his reputation among the American people. The results showed that "despite recent criticism, FBI director J. Edgar Hoover still has the solid backing of nearly 8 of 10 Americans for the job he is doing as the nation's number one law man." When asked to stack up Hoover against King in their recent confrontation, a full 50 percent of the public took Hoover's side, while just 16 percent expressed greater sympathy with King. (The other 34 percent chose "not sure" or "neither.")

The poll did not identify the respondents' race. Nor did it consider the possibility that opinion about Hoover might be sharply divided by racial background. To the Harris pollsters, the results were unequivocal. "It is evident that recent civil rights controversies have not led to widespread disenchantment with J. Edgar Hoover," they wrote. "In the estimate of most people, [he] remains what he has been for at least a generation: a powerful symbol of law and order, a pillar of security in an uncertain nation and world." In early March Hoover returned in triumph for a luncheon at the Women's National Press Club, where he occupied the head table along with the attorney general. That same month, he attended the annual Gridiron dinner, where he put on an even more defiant show by sitting next to the NAACP's Roy Wilkins. Though there had been no single grand exposé of King, both Washington and the media world were thoroughly saturated with gossip and rumor on the subject. Hoover's cues were not hard to interpret.[24]

And there was one more moment—this one entirely outside public view—that must have fueled Hoover's confidence for 1965. On January 5, King's wife, Coretta, opened a bulky but unassuming brown-paper package with a Florida postmark. Between the Oslo trip and other business, she had allowed the package to languish for weeks, assuming it was just another of her husband's recorded speeches. Instead, she found an alarming letter inside—"King, there is only one thing left for you to do. You know what it is. You have just 34 days"—along with a muffled tape reel of her husband's hotel-room activities. Alerted by his stunned wife about the package's contents, King rushed home to listen to the tape and to figure out how bad the situation was. Though they could not prove it, everyone suspected that the tape and letter had come from the FBI, an immediate threat and a long-term warning wrapped up in one. "They are out to break me," King noted wearily in a phone conversation, all of it overheard on FBI wiretaps and duly transcribed for Hoover.[25]

CHAPTER 51

White Hate

(1964–1965)

'Are You One of Us Working for Them, or One of Them Working for Us?'

In 1964, Hoover launched a COINTELPRO campaign against the Ku Klux Klan and other white supremacist groups. As the cartoon suggests, many people thought FBI agents had more in common with Klansmen than with civil rights activists.

WASHINGTON DAILY NEWS/ NATIONAL ARCHIVES AND RECORDS ADMINISTRATION

Even after the battle with King subsided, Hoover continued to complain about one aspect of the resulting public debate. Whatever else they might have concluded about Hoover and King as individuals, civil rights advocates had agreed without hesitation that the FBI was not doing nearly enough to protect Black lives in the South. Hoover had insisted all along that there was more to the story. But he felt constrained from talking about it, for many of the same reasons that he would not discuss the true depths of his anti-King efforts. Unbeknownst to all but a few government officials, during the same fall that he had escalated his campaign against King, Hoover also launched a counterintelligence program targeting the Ku Klux Klan and other white supremacist groups. He called it COINTELPRO–White Hate.

Hoover had hinted at what was going on during the "notorious liar" press conference, when he blamed the Klan for "all the lynchings and bombings of homes in the South" before assuring the women's press club that the FBI had penetrated the organization and knew "pretty well who they are." He brought it up again during his private meeting with King, boasting that his men were putting the "fear of God" into the Klan by imitating "the manner in which we infiltrated the communists and the Soviet espionage services." Nobody quite seemed to catch his meaning, however—perhaps because they could not imagine Hoover's FBI actually engaged in clandestine warfare against gun-toting, white Southern men. This is precisely what was happening, however. At the very moment that he was seeking to destroy King's career and reputation, Hoover was mounting "a four-year underground fight against Klansmen the like of which the South had never seen," in the later words of his favorite journalist, Don Whitehead.[1]

To Hoover, the dual approach made perfect sense. After almost twenty years of being immersed in Southern racial conflicts, he had come to view civil rights activists and Klansmen as part of the same debilitating turn toward lawbreaking and disorder. The fact that one group used torture, intimidation, and murder as its methods while the other practiced nonviolence was almost incidental to him. Both groups, in his view, broke the law and assaulted the status quo. And both created unwelcome problems for federal officials—from the FBI on up to the president—by promoting conflict and instability.

Where anyone stood on questions of segregation and racial hierarchy, freedom and citizenship, was to some degree beside the point. Hoover never escaped the racism of his Kappa Alpha years; nor did he try to. With the passage of the Civil Rights Act, he also doubled down on the idea that segregationist violence—indeed, the very existence of a group like the Ku Klux Klan—constituted an unacceptable challenge to federal authority. In the fall of 1964, just weeks after the law's passage, he concluded that the time had come to go after the Klan with the same methods he had used to good effect against the communists and, now, against King. "If an enthusiastic approach is made to this new endeavor," he wrote in September, "there is no reason why the results achieved under this program will not equal or surpass our achievements in similar-type programs directed against subversives."[2]

IT WAS DURING A PHONE CALL ABOUT SETTING UP THE NEW FBI OFFICE IN MISsissippi that Johnson had broached the idea of really doing something about the Klan. He had been up late reading the Bureau's reports on the Communist Party, with their jaw-dropping inside details. What if the Bureau, seizing on the momentum provided by the Civil Rights Act, could do the same thing to the Klan? he wondered aloud to Hoover. After all, both groups tried to keep their membership secret. And both, according to Johnson, posed serious dangers to the country's peace and stability. "On Communists, they can't open their mouth without your knowing what they're saying," Johnson said. "Now I don't want these Klansmen to open their mouth without your knowing what they're saying." He did not state the obvious: that this level of infiltration could take place only through extensive use of wiretaps, informants, bugs, and counterintelligence methods. He did acknowledge, however, that the whole conversation was best kept quiet. "Nobody needs to know it but you," he told Hoover.[3]

Some level of Klan infiltration was already underway, a fact of which Johnson may have been only dimly aware. In Birmingham, Gary Rowe was coming up on his fifth year as "the best informant we had in the Ku Klux Klan," in one agent's description, alternately participating in and trying to restrain the actions of his fellow members. And he was only one among many. Taken together, the Bureau's growing ranks of Klan informants revealed a "deep, widespread revival" of white resistance in the South that summer, as Hoover put it in a report to Johnson, with the various Klan groupings at the center of the storm. Far from seeing the Civil Rights Act as the resolution of a civil rights struggle, Klansmen viewed the law as an abomination—and they did not wait long to convey that message back to Washington. On July 11, the day after Hoover's press conference in Mississippi, several Klansmen noticed a car with Washington, D.C., plates driving along the Broad River Bridge in Georgia. Assuming that they were face-to-face with "one of President Johnson's boys," they shot into the car and killed Lemuel Penn, a veteran, Howard University graduate, and D.C. school administrator.[4]

Thanks in part to its informant network, the FBI made arrests in the Penn case within a month. But Hoover knew better than to rely on individual prosecutions, with their dismal track record before all-white juries, to stem the Klan's growth. He recognized that "many of the sheriffs" and "a number of the chiefs of police" in Deep South cities were Klansmen, as he told Johnson. After more than two decades immersed in controversies over lynching, voting rights, and the civil rights struggle, he also understood that an overt federal presence could be a tricky proposition. The near guarantee of local white resistance made the prospect of secret operations especially appealing, a chance to do what Johnson wanted done without further alienating the white South. The downside, of course, was that the Bureau could not claim credit for its actions, even in the face of accusations that it was sitting by and doing nothing.[5]

Sullivan proposed bringing the Klan formally into COINTELPRO in late July 1964, when the FBI had temporarily paused its campaign of vilification against King and sent agents to protect him in Mississippi. In a "personal and confidential" letter to Hoover, written after "giving this racial problem constant thought," he recommended a plan not unlike what Johnson had suggested over the phone. "My idea is: This Division can bring to bear all the techniques, skills, and procedures which it has used to successfully penetrate the Communist Party and espionage organizations to now penetrate these hate organizations causing us so much trouble," he wrote. To which Hoover delivered a one-word response: "Expedite."[6]

Hoover formally announced the program to the field offices in early September, using language almost identical to what Sullivan had declared just a few months earlier about King. "The purpose of this program is to expose, disrupt and otherwise neutralize the activities of the various Klans and hate organizations, their leadership and adherents," he wrote, outlining twenty-six groups—including several Klan offshoots, the Nazi Party, and the National States Rights Party—to be targeted in the new initiative. Like the original COINTELPRO, the White Hate campaign would be tightly run out of the Bureau's Washington offices, with all ideas submitted to Hoover's office for approval. Its goal, too, was not merely to gather information, but to sow confusion and encourage the groups to destroy themselves from within. The techniques deployed in earlier operations were now fair game: writing anonymous letters, spreading rumors, using informants as provocateurs, planting false stories in the press. The governing rule, as always, would be preventing embarrassment to the Bureau.[7]

If the White Hate program owed its basic structure to earlier efforts, there were also a few key differences. As one assistant director noted in a July 30 memo, the new program made no pretense of a Klan connection with espionage or international subversion "inasmuch as they are not controlled by a foreign power." For the first time, the Bureau would be undertaking a purely domestic counterintelligence operation, aimed at native-born Americans with no known ties to another country. Even with King, there had been at least the veneer of foreign subterfuge: King was connected to Levison, who was secretly connected to the Communist Party, which was secretly allied with the Soviet Union. The White Hate program broke from this logic to identify white supremacist groups as "subversive" by virtue of their violent reputations rather than their international ties or revolutionary vision.[8]

In Mississippi, most of the action came out of the new Jackson office, where Special Agent in Charge Roy Moore organized roving squads to track and intimidate known Klan members. At the national level, the program emphasized psychological rather than physical techniques, with the goal of fueling paranoia, factionalism, and despair. With Hoover's approval, the lab drew up a cartoon series mocking the Klan for its infiltration by the FBI. "Who, me? Worried about FBI informers?" a terrified Klansman blurted out in one cartoon, looking in terror at a headline announcing "Klan Infiltrated by FBI." A second drawing, titled "Ku-Kluxers Koloring Komics," showed a Klansman in full masked-and-robed regalia declaring to readers, "I am an informant. Color me Fed!" Slated for a "disruptive, anonymous mailing," the cartoons reflected a Bureau assumption that the macho, posturing Klan would be especially "sensitive to ridicule." The Bureau also assumed that Klansmen would not—indeed, could not—read anything more complicated than a simple letter or cartoon. When one agent proposed writing a harsh critical history of the Klan for distribution to members, Hoover vetoed the idea. Unlike the intellectually nimble communists, FBI correspondence noted, Klansmen were "emotionally unprepared to completely absorb and fully comprehend the significance" of such material. When the Bureau faked letters written by Klansmen, they made sure to include spelling and grammatical errors, and to keep the messages short.

In addition to poking fun and building paranoia, COINTELPRO–White Hate did its best to make life difficult for Klansmen, especially for local leaders charged with holding meetings and collecting dues. In one Florida town, an anonymous Bureau mailing persuaded county supervisors to withhold funds for a paved road near Klan headquarters. In another incident, agents reached out to friendly media contacts and convinced them not to provide press coverage for a seemingly benign Klan-sponsored turkey shoot. Bureau agents printed flyers showing the wrong time and place for Klan meetings, and made a point of interviewing Klan members in public locations, where other men could see them and wonder if they were working with the authorities. They dug up information on tax and fire code violations, then anonymously passed on the evidence to the relevant authorities. In Georgia, agents targeted James Venable, leader of the National Knights of the Ku Klux Klan and, according to Bureau sources, a thoroughgoing "psychotic." They sought to feed his psychosis, conjuring up plans to spread rumors that other white supremacists were "using him" and to leak "material concerning VENABLE" to local newspapers. They also made plans to track down Venable's landlord and convince him to cancel the lease on local Klan headquarters.[9]

Agents relied on informants not only to provide the information that made such actions possible but also to sow confusion and conflict from within. In Alabama, Gary Rowe recalled being encouraged to "screw as many wives as you can; plant as much hate and dissent in the goddamn families as you can; do anything you can to discredit the Klan, period. No holds barred." Other informants served in more limited but no less critical roles. During the fall of 1964, the FBI recruited two men who would go on to testify in the Neshoba County murders, stunning their fellow Klansmen much as Herbert Philbrick had stunned his friends in the Communist Party during the Smith Act trials a decade and a half earlier. If anything, the Klan was turning out to be far easier pickings than the Communist Party had been. A shocking number of Klansmen, many of them poor, seemed only too happy to trade information and wreak havoc in exchange for money. Between 1964 and 1965, the Bureau nearly doubled its number of informants.[10]

On occasion, those informants actually succeeded in preventing acts of violence, either by persuading their fellow Klansmen to back away or by warning the FBI in advance, at which point agents sometimes had a chance to intervene. In situations where they had to choose between preventing violence and keeping their cover, though, they were often instructed to opt for the latter. Hoover's priority was to keep the pressure on and to maintain a steady flow of information, not to stop any given crime from occurring. Over the long term, it was hoped, the disruptive techniques would make the organizations utterly ineffective, all without the trouble of a courtroom trial.

Hoover seemed to be thrilled with the program's early progress. "The important thing to remember is never to let up," he wrote to the Atlanta field office, already immersed in similar operations against King. From the Domestic Intelligence Division, officials promised that the accomplishments of 1965 would dwarf anything Hoover had yet seen. "We anticipate our counterintelligence action against Klan and hate organizations, now in its formative steps, will be effectively increased during the coming year," Sullivan wrote on January 6. "We will take advantage of any situation which presents itself."[11]

ON THE DAY HE WROTE THOSE WORDS, A "SITUATION" WAS ALREADY STARTING to present itself in Selma, Alabama, a small, dusty town about an hour and a half outside Birmingham. King had visited Selma on January 2, three days before he discovered the existence of the FBI's "suicide letter" and tape, and four days before Sullivan wrote his promise to Hoover about the Klan COINTELPRO. The visit marked King's first extended stay in Alabama since 1963, when he had faced off with Bull Connor in Birmingham. King's goal in returning to hostile territory was not merely to influence local politics, but to push for voting rights legislation at the federal level, just as the Birmingham campaign had helped to build momentum for the 1964 Civil Rights Act. At the FBI, though, many things had changed since Birmingham. Two years earlier, there had been no Civil Rights Act, no Lyndon Johnson in the Oval Office, and no COINTELPRO–White Hate. There had also been no bugs or wiretaps on King himself, and no obvious personal enmity between the civil rights leader and the FBI director.

Like Bull Connor, Selma's county sheriff, Jim Clark, was a dedicated massive resister; he wore a pin with the word "Never" in his lapel. And like Connor, Clark failed to see how unleashing police violence might backfire on his cause. On February 1, King led a march to the Selma courthouse, where he was arrested and submitted to imprisonment. From there, the situation escalated quickly. While King festered in jail, Malcolm X arrived in Selma to offer his own words of wisdom. Little more than two weeks later, he was dead, shot during a speech at the Audubon Ballroom in New York City by gunmen from the Nation of Islam. FBI informants witnessed the assassination, just as they had witnessed so much else in his short life. When it came time to investigate the murder, Hoover allowed them to speak with New York police but insisted that they not disclose their informant status.[12]

Back in Selma, Bureau agents played a similarly passive role. Twenty agents were present for what became known as the Bloody Sunday march, in which police attacked protesters as they attempted to cross the Edmund Pettus Bridge. The agents took photographs and film footage, and counted up the ensuing injuries. But they arrested only three white men, all of them accused of assaulting an FBI agent. Katzenbach objected to Johnson: "That didn't look right, Mr. President, from the public viewpoint, you know—all the Negroes that were beat up and the people we arrested were the people who beat up the FBI agent." As if to confirm Katzenbach's assessment, on March 8, the day after Bloody Sunday, protests arrived at the Justice Department, where student activists staged a sit-in at the attorney general's office, singing and chanting for several hours before being dragged out by police. Another group—up to 170 demonstrators at its peak—managed to sneak back in two days later, much to the department's embarrassment. News photographers captured Katzenbach kneeling down and trying to persuade the activists to let him use his own office. While the students wisely avoided Hoover's suite, they brought the protest to the Bureau in New York, where more than a thousand people assembled outside the local office to demand federal action in Alabama.[13]

As with the King controversy, Hoover resented what he saw as a lack of gratitude, though the protesters could not possibly know everything the Bureau was doing to combat the Klan and other white supremacist groups. He remained adamant that the FBI would not perform guard duty. But he also remained eager to deploy his arsenal of secret methods against many of the groups the protesters most reviled. By early January the FBI had "over 100 separate counterintelligence operations" underway against "White Hate" organizations. In late January, even as conflict was rising in Selma, the Jackson office laid out a comprehensive plan for targeting Sam Bowers, the Imperial Wizard of the White Knights of the KKK and arguably the most significant Klansman in all of Mississippi. Because Bowers seemed to prize anonymity, agents proposed printing up Klan literature and mailing it out to key state officials with Bowers's name and return address attached. They also envisioned writing Klan meeting cards signed by Bowers, and addressing them (allegedly by mistake) to Klan members' next-door neighbors, thus revealing the identity of both Bowers and his followers.

In Alabama, too, Gary Rowe was busy keeping the Bureau informed about local Klan activities, and about what his friends had in store for the protesters in Selma. At the Bureau's request, he compiled an updated list denoting every member of the state's two most significant Klan groups, along with what weapons they claimed to own. He managed to survey eighteen members, who boasted a total of eighteen pistols and thirty-five rifles plus an alarming supply of hand grenades, dynamite, and blasting caps. As if to drive the point home, bombs began showing up again in Birmingham in March, while the rest of the world was watching Selma. Over the course of twenty-four hours, Hoover's men managed to defuse no fewer than six time bombs scattered throughout the city. Rowe warned that the violence was not over yet, that the Klan was planning something bigger and better for King's next march.[14]

HOOVER KEPT JOHNSON APPRISED OF THESE ACTIVITIES, PRODUCING REGULAR updates for the White House advertising "our accomplishments" against the Klan. Perhaps sympathetic to Hoover's frustration at not being able to spread the word more widely, Johnson honored him with one of the least likely invitations of either man's career. Hoping to build upon public outrage over the beatings at Selma, Johnson called

Congress back into special session in mid-March to take up the issue of voting rights. At 10:22 on the morning of March 15, Hoover received a phone call from Lady Bird Johnson, inviting him to join her in the president's box that night for an important address to Congress on the subject.[15]

When Hoover appeared as instructed in the House chamber several hours later, he found himself in odd company, just one of several guests handpicked to symbolize Johnson's coalition in favor of voting rights. In the front row, Hoover was seated next to Lady Bird and her twenty-one-year-old daughter, Lynda Bird, recently invited on a private FBI tour. Seated in the box as well was U.S. Information Agency director Carl Rowan, the highest-ranking Black official in the federal government. Johnson also invited former Florida governor LeRoy Collins, head of the Johnson administration's Community Relations Service, who had long acknowledged the inevitability—if not the desirability—of desegregation, and who served as a useful stand-in for the moderate wing of the white Democratic South. Four clergy members from the Selma protests were there, too. They offered a reminder not only of King's ministerial authority but also of the Reverend James Reeb, a white Unitarian minister murdered by white supremacists in Selma during the week between Bloody Sunday and Johnson's address.

Johnson entered the chamber through the center aisle of the main floor, attempting to ignore the empty seats of Southern representatives who refused to attend, including the entire Virginia and Mississippi delegations. Arriving at the podium, he looked more solemn than usual, nodding slightly but not smiling as he waited out the gallery's standing ovations. As the journalist Tom Wicker noted, Johnson's "slow Southern accent" gave special weight to the words he spoke over the next forty minutes, one of the most moving and inspired addresses in all of presidential history. After more than a century of foot-dragging, he urged Congress to act on voting rights—not in another century, not in a few years or months, but immediately. And he urged the entire nation to speak with one voice. "It is not just Negroes, but really it is all of us, who must overcome the crippling legacy of bigotry and injustice," he said before uttering the hallmark words of the civil rights movement: "And we shall overcome."

Lynda Bird, seated just a few feet down from Hoover, reflected afterward, "It was just like that hymn, 'Once to every man and nation comes a moment to decide.'" And for the moment, at least, Hoover decided to throw in his lot with Johnson's version of the civil rights cause. According to press reports, he "listened intently to the President's address and applauded constantly," whether because he, too, was swept up in the moment or because he knew how to put on a good show.[16]

SIX DAYS LATER, ON MARCH 21, THE SELMA MARCHERS SET OUT ONCE AGAIN to cross the Edmund Pettus Bridge, with the goal of making it all the way to Montgomery over the course of the next several days. This time, they moved with federal protection, thanks to the court order of an Alabama federal judge as well as Johnson's decision to make the marchers' cause his own in Washington. Johnson had been nervous about sending federal troops and reached out to Hoover for advice, phoning from Air Force One "in a highly agitated condition" on the night of March 18. Johnson made it clear "that he didn't want anything to go wrong," and Hoover responded accordingly, ordering "20 more Agts sent in at once" ("we can't dilly-dally about it") along with "additional cars if necessary." The president found Hoover's actions partly but not entirely reassuring. Given Hoover's well-known resistance to performing "guard duty," Johnson finally did what he had been reluctant to do on other occasions: federalize the National Guard to protect the marchers. As the march set off, its several hundred participants—teenagers and rabbis, ministers and housewives and seasoned activists—were dwarfed by vast columns of soldiers, jeeps, and policemen.[17]

Hoover's agents made up only a small part of that contingent, and their duties, per design, did not include furnishing protection to any protesters. In their own way, however, agents tried to keep the march safe and chugging along smoothly. When marchers worried that their trucked-in water supply had been poisoned, agents discovered that the funny taste came from an excess of the cleaning agent creosote, an attempt to make up for the truck's past as a sewage unit. Agents also followed up on rumors of bombs planted at tents along the route and kept watch on cars bearing "anti-integration signs" and Confederate flags. Despite the potential for violence, "no serious incidents" occurred, as Hoover reported to Johnson. So the marchers trudged on, enduring sunburn and exhaustion but nothing too much worse.[18]

On March 25, the whole show arrived at the Alabama state capitol for an afternoon's worth of jubilant speech-making and song. The high point, as expected, was King's oration, a part-scripted, part-improvised journey through the terror and inspiration of the civil rights struggle. King promised, with an eye to Johnson's voting rights bill, that it would be "not long" before the glories of freedom and true citizenship were available to all. "The arc of the moral universe is long, but it bends toward justice," he assured the tearful crowd, as his message was broadcast live to millions of Americans.[19]

FBI agents assigned to the march believed they had played at least some role in making that moment happen, even if the marchers, still resentful of Hoover's watch-and-film stance, did not necessarily see things that way. "There had been visible proof that a peaceful march could be held in any part of the United States," a supervising official later reflected. "And there was a lot of pride on the part of law enforcement." But there was shame and disappointment, too, because the story of Selma did not end with an inspiring speech on the Montgomery capitol steps. That night, as the marchers were being ferried by car back to Selma, four Klansmen night-riding along Highway 80 pulled up beside an Oldsmobile station wagon and fired into the driver's side window. One of those blasts struck a march volunteer named Viola Liuzzo near her left ear and severed her spinal cord, "causing almost instantaneous death," in the Bureau's description. Liuzzo was a mother of five from Detroit. She said she had felt called to answer King's plea for racial solidarity. She was also a white woman driving a Black male passenger in a car with a bumper sticker declaring "All the Way with LBJ," a social crime for which she had been executed.[20]

THE LIUZZO MURDER SHOWED THE LIMITS OF HOOVER'S KLAN INITIATIVES. Despite months of counterintelligence work, despite its hundreds of informants, the FBI failed to prevent a White Hate murder from marring the year's most important civil rights demonstration. Within twenty-four hours, though, Hoover had turned the episode around. Johnson called in to FBI headquarters three times on the night of the murder—first at 12:55, then at 1:07 and again at 1:11—hoping for an update or at least a bit of solace. At 8:10 the next morning, Hoover called back with the news Johnson most wanted to hear: the FBI had solved the Liuzzo case and was getting ready to arrest the perpetrators.

Hoover's reports to Johnson that morning betrayed many of his long-standing prejudices. Rather than sympathize with Liuzzo, he defamed her as a drug addict and sex seeker, allegedly out for a "necking party" with her teenage Black passenger (claims for which there was little evidence). He warned Johnson against speaking directly with her husband, a Teamsters employee who Hoover "wouldn't say [was] a bad character" but who was definitely one of their "strong-arm men." Still, there was no getting around the fact that the FBI had pulled off something spectacular—proof that its new anti-Klan initiative, if not yet perfected, was at least starting to work. One of the four Klansmen in the car that targeted Liuzzo was none other than informant Gary Rowe, who had called in to his contact just after midnight. Rowe claimed that he had not fired his own gun, an assertion that the FBI accepted without too much initial probing. He also delivered the names of the three men who had murdered Liuzzo, along with a detailed story about what they had been doing earlier in the evening, how they had carried out the shooting, and where they had gone once the deed was done.

Johnson was gobsmacked at the FBI's quick work. "Anybody that could have a man in that car—that's the most unthinkable thing I ever heard of!" he spluttered to Hoover a few weeks later. "It makes me scared, by God, to even talk back to my wife! Afraid you'll have somebody there arresting *me*!" Neither Hoover nor Johnson spent much time contemplating why Rowe had not tried to stop the murder. What mattered that morning was getting the news out and grabbing the "chance to show what good work the FBI has done," as Johnson put it to Hoover. The president already had a press conference planned for late morning to honor several "notables of the space age." In a conversation just after nine thirty, he proposed that Hoover and Katzenbach rush into the room during that conference to deliver the startling news about the Liuzzo case. "I think it might make it a little dramatic," Johnson suggested.

As it turned out, Hoover's men did not make the arrests in time to meet Johnson's press-conference deadline. But around 12:40, Johnson broke into the nation's regularly scheduled daytime programming with the Liuzzo announcement. Standing at his side were Hoover and Katzenbach, who had decided to enter calmly alongside the president rather than dash in with breaking news. The news itself was "dramatic" enough: the arrests of four Klansmen for Liuzzo's murder, less than twenty-four hours after the fatal shot. Johnson identified all four by name (including Rowe, who had been arrested to conceal his role as an informant). He also identified "Mr. Hoover and the men of the FBI" as the ones who had made it happen through "their prompt and expeditious and very excellent performance." Far more than the Birmingham bombing or the Mississippi murders, the Liuzzo case allowed Johnson to present the FBI as what he wanted it to be: an all-knowing, ever-watchful check on the excesses of Klan violence in the South. "If Klansmen hear my voice today," Johnson said, "let it be both an appeal and a warning to get out of the Ku Klux Klan now and return to a decent society before it is too late."[21]

ROWE SPENT THE NEXT SEVERAL WEEKS UNDER FBI PROTECTION, MOVING FROM house to house and hotel to hotel under the code name "Thomas Dixon," after the famous Kappa Alpha author of *The Clansman*, the novel on which the KKK's favorite film, *The Birth of a Nation*, was based. On April 21, 1965, after nearly a month of trying to avoid raising suspicions, he testified against his fellow Klansmen before an Alabama grand jury, bringing an end to his career as an FBI informant. His sacrifice did not add up to much initially, as the first two state trials in the case ended in a hung jury and an acquittal. Despite the setback, Hoover argued that it was "important that the case be pressed with vigor because it is a 'symbol' in the minds of the civil rights people." And when Rowe finally testified in federal court, something incredible happened: a jury of white men convicted three fellow white men of violating the civil rights of a protester.[22]

Years later skeptics would raise questions about whether Rowe was quite the hero the FBI made him out to be, and about whether his claim that he never fired his gun ought to be considered believable. In 1965, though, the conviction looked like a pure victory, with Hoover and his men now sure "that they finally, after years of dire frustration, had the Klan 'by the balls,'" in the words of one journalist. In conversation with the attorney general, Hoover declared the trial "the turning point"—the beginning of the end for the Klan. And by some measures he turned out to be correct. Between 1965 and 1968, the Klan began to fall apart much as the Communist Party had done a decade earlier, unable to withstand the juggernaut of prosecution, in addition to the FBI's ongoing campaign of exposure, surveillance, and disruptive measures. Over the course of the White Hate program, Hoover received a total of 444 proposals from the field, of which he approved 285. According to the Bureau's estimates, 139 of those produced results, ranging from the discrediting of particular Klan leaders to the sowing of paranoia and discord.[23]

Throughout those years, Hoover never lost sight of his original intentions with COINTELPRO: not to go after White Hate extremists, but to contain and control the communists and their left-wing allies. After 1967, he increasingly returned to that vision, sidelining the Klan effort in favor of what would ultimately become a far more infamous series of programs targeting the sprawling, energetic movements of the emerging New Left. For many agents on the ground, though, it was the Klan operation that would eventually become the greatest point of pride. "The best thing we did during all those years was knock down the Klan," one agent later reflected, describing how men like Bowers and Venable went from "invincible" to marginal in a matter of months. Even liberals normally skeptical of Hoover's methods and intentions were inclined to make an exception where the Klan program was concerned. "It is unfortunate that the value of these activities would in most cases be lost if too extensive publicity were given to them," Katzenbach wrote to Hoover in the fall of 1965, after reviewing a report on the FBI's Klan penetration techniques. "However, perhaps at some point it may be possible to place these achievements on the public record, so that the Bureau can receive its due credit."[24]

CHAPTER 52

Hoover Knows Best

(1965–1966)

In 1965, Hoover
authorized a dramatic
television series based
on FBI case files.
The FBI starred Efrem
Zimbalist Jr. (left) as
Inspector Lewis Erskine.
Cover is from July 1967.

TV GUIDE/© 1967 TVGM
HOLDINGS

On March 3, 1965, four days before the Selma marchers first set out to cross the Edmund Pettus Bridge, Hoover had ventured to the White House to discuss another matter of urgent concern. According to him, the country was in the throes of a crime wave as serious as what Franklin Roosevelt had confronted in the 1930s, when the likes of John Dillinger and Machine Gun Kelly had roamed the countryside. Hoover argued that the rising crime rate foretold a broader social collapse, with growing numbers of Americans holding the entire concept of "law and order" in contempt. He lumped all manner of problems under that rubric, from the 1964 uprising in Harlem to the Klan murders in Neshoba County. At the same time, he singled out ordinary, seemingly apolitical, street-level crime as a growing problem in its own right. He warned Johnson that the crime issue threatened much of what the White House hoped to accomplish on poverty and civil rights. And on this subject, as on so many others, Hoover thought he could be an asset to the president.[1]

The 1964 campaign had already pushed crime to the front of the national agenda as something that all Americans, not just a handful of police officials, were told to fret about. Goldwater had made it a centerpiece of his candidacy. George Wallace, running as a third-party candidate, had complained that "if you are knocked in the head on a street in a city today, the man who knocked you in the head is out of jail before you get to the hospital." Though Johnson won the election, the concerns laid out during the campaign did not disappear. In December 1964, according to a Harris poll, fully 73 percent of Americans believed that crime was on the rise. They thought the federal government should do something about it.[2]

Hoover believed that he knew what should be done—not just because crime was one of his areas of expertise, but because he had been through it all before. Though the crime debate of the 1960s was increasingly framed in terms of race, civil rights, and a growing "urban crisis," to Hoover it also looked like what had happened in the 1930s, when the FBI had made its reputation as a crime-fighting force. It was then that Hoover had begun to keep the nation's crime statistics, a bureaucratic triumph that allowed him to exercise influence over the issue's framing and reception. As those statistics now began to presage another crisis, he turned to methods and ideas from that era, including the calls to arm local police with advanced weaponry, to step up professional training, and to use the federal government as a coordinating mechanism for local police. He also launched his own cultural initiatives, adapting the public relations experiments of the 1930s—the era that created the vaunted "G-Man"—for the modern television viewer.

To younger audiences, these methods could make him seem dated, an old man out of touch with changing times. Even inside the FBI, some junior agents scoffed at Hoover's gangster-fighting language and throwback style. By other measures, though, Hoover was ahead of the curve, one of the key officials who had helped to establish the terms and policies through which the country—and now the president—understood what was happening on American streets. From his decades of fulminations on criminal "rats," delinquents, and the "sob sisters" who aided them, Hoover had developed a ready-made tough-on-crime language—what one columnist described as good old-fashioned "lawnorder" talk. From his technocratic side came a menu of policy options about how to solve the problem, beginning with political and monetary support for the nation's police. In 1965, he brought all these ideas to Johnson, certain that the president did not need to reinvent Roosevelt's War on Crime but merely to recycle it.[3]

HOOVER'S STORY OF WHAT WAS HAPPENING WITH CRIME AND POLICING BEGAN with the numbers—and the numbers looked grim. According to the FBI's statistics, crime increased 12 percent between 1960 and 1961, and then kept up more or less that same pace in every year that followed. In 1964, it rose 13 percent compared to 1963, including an alarming 9 percent growth in murders. That made for an increase of more than a quarter of a million episodes of "serious crime," in Hoover's words, each one adding to the nation's growing ranks of victims. And things only appeared to be getting worse. Between 1963 and 1968, the nation's murder rate nearly doubled, by far the greatest increase in Hoover's three-plus decades as the collector of national crime data.[4]

From these numbers Hoover constructed a portrait of a nation under siege. "Today, thousands of Americans live in fear," he wrote. "They fear for their lives, the safety of their families, their homes, and their businesses. The cause of their fear is CRIME." To explain how the crime spike had occurred, he turned not to structural causes such as poverty or racism but to the factors he had been lamenting for decades: moral decline, parental neglect, and lenient probation and parole policies. He also added another element drawn from the 1930s: in the throes of social crisis, Americans were losing respect for established authority, especially for the police on the front lines of struggle. That phenomenon, too, could be documented in numbers. In 1964, killings of police officers reached an all-time high, with a total of fifty-seven murders.[5]

To Hoover, both the politics and the statistics brought back the awful years of 1933 and 1934, when his green agents had been gunned down with impunity. Back then, he had solved the problem by arming his men. He had also argued for a radical alteration in law enforcement methods, beginning with "scientific" police reform and extending to the film codes, with their mandate to turn the police into heroes. Now the rising crime rate seemed to be mixed up with countless additional factors: race riots and the Beatles, civil disobedience and the Ku Klux Klan and the cultural power of the American teenager. Those were hard to quantify, but they were all connected, in Hoover's view, to a crisis of historical proportions—part of the "unceasing conflict between the forces of law and order and a criminal element which is bold, arrogant and constantly increasing in numbers."[6]

Unless, as many experts suggested, Hoover's numbers were exaggerated. Even as he delivered what appeared to be hard facts, criminologists and social scientists pushed back with the same analysis that they had offered in the 1930s: Hoover's great crime wave was partly a fiction, a matter of manipulation and distortion on the part of the FBI. In March 1965, *The New York Times* published a story quoting several experts who felt "the FBI figures are terribly in need of adjustment" but who "don't dare say so publicly," for fear of incurring Hoover's wrath. Speaking under cover of anonymity, they pointed to innocuous explanations for the alleged surge in crime: perhaps it was due to economic prosperity (when more people owned cars, there was more car theft) or to the simple fact that millions of babies born in the postwar boom were now teenagers and young adults, the age groups most likely to engage in criminal activity.[7]

Or perhaps, as many experts have argued both then and since, all the talk of crime and juvenile delinquency was mostly a coded conversation about race. Modern crime statistics often reclassified the by-products of poverty and youthful exuberance as serious infractions, thus creating an impression that urban Black teenagers posed a special danger to the social order. The statistics were also based on the number of arrests, a calculation that tended to show where the most policing was happening, not necessarily the most crime. Those logical leaps distorted the crime picture, making it ripe for misinterpretation. In crime, as in so many other issues, law enforcement officials like Hoover could often see what they wanted to see.[8]

Still, there were certain classifications, such as murder, in which the numbers were hard to fudge. And it was here that Hoover made his best case. "These are not statistical abstractions conjured up by the FBI," *The Washington Daily News* wrote, responding to Hoover's critics. "No amount of FBI-baiting can soften the shocking impact of these figures." Indeed, what mattered, politically speaking, was not whether the statistics were true but whether the public believed them—whether the numbers that Hoover was describing, and the narrative he assigned to explain them, seemed to accord with Americans' lived experience.[9]

AMONG THE CITIES WHERE THE CRIME ISSUE LOOMED LARGEST WAS WASHING-ton, D.C., for seven decades the site of so many of Hoover's personal and political struggles. "The District has not been spared in the general increase in crime now being experienced throughout the United States," Johnson declared in a message to Congress in February 1965, proposing a commission to explore "crime and law enforcement in the District." According to FBI statistics, crime in the district went up 34 percent in the first six months of 1964 alone, with rape, robbery, assault, and burglary up 47 percent. Then, in the first three months of 1965, homicide and "non-negligent manslaughter" more than doubled compared to the same period in 1964. Those numbers meant that crime in Washington was actually growing faster than in the nation at large.[10]

Much of the ensuing debate concentrated on a single fact: in the 1960 census, the capital crossed a threshold, becoming the first major city in the U.S. with a majority-Black population. As many scholars have argued, the relationship between that development and the rising crime rate was far from straightforward. But many contemporary observers found it impossible to separate the two. "What shocks the visitors is that in the very shadow of the greatest power instrumentalities on earth, there is this bewildering paradox—inability to guarantee safety for the individual on the street," a visitor from Michigan noted. "A race problem? Yes, it is in large part." Even where race went unmentioned, there was no mistaking the rising tide of anxiety expressed by the political class about the capital's changing population. "No matter how its cause is justified or how sugarcoated the sociologists try to make it, Washington is a crime-ridden city," an Alabama congressman declared in the spring of 1965. "The streets are not safe at night. In fact, daylight muggings, robberies, assaults, and rape are commonplace."[11]

Hoover lent his professional imprimatur to this narrative, not only by citing alarming statistics, but by publicizing gruesome stories of street crime committed by Black men. When Washington police shot and killed a Black man for snatching a white woman's purse in 1963, Hoover blamed the parole system for setting the man free in the first place, calling for "an aroused public, determined no longer to tolerate consideration for the hardened criminal in preference to the rights of the law abiding citizen." On other occasions, he cast aspersions on the "young hoodlums" who preyed upon middle-class residents. Though he rarely spoke directly of race, he often deployed racialized stereotypes in his depiction of juvenile offenders, describing them as hardened "gang" members wielding guns and switchblades, with a "callous contempt" for all "acceptable standards of behavior." "Marauding teen-age thugs are degrading many American communities with brutal sidewalk muggings and assaults on defenseless and elderly citizens," he wrote in 1962, blasting the juvenile courts for going easy on the "beastly punks" who preyed on the rest of society.[12]

He included himself among the ranks of the vulnerable, a lifelong district native who no longer felt free to stroll around his own city. "You can't safely walk the streets of Washington, D.C., even in the daylight," he lamented in late 1964, during the same press conference where he denounced King. The wooded expanse of Rock Creek Park, just a few blocks from Hoover's home, offered little reprieve. "I used to walk there," Hoover complained. "I can't do it now because of conditions in the city." By his own description, Hoover was just another elderly white district resident, worried about the changes taking place in their midst.[13]

BUT OF COURSE HOOVER WAS NOT JUST ANOTHER WASHINGTON RESIDENT. HE had the ear of the White House, and on this issue, as on so many others, Johnson was inclined to listen. On March 8, five days after meeting with Hoover and just twenty-four hours after Selma's Bloody Sunday, Johnson took up the crime problem in a special message to Congress. His chief concern was slightly different from Hoover's: Johnson worried that the crime issue might disrupt the momentum behind his Great Society programs. His statement nonetheless bore Hoover's imprint. Though Johnson emphasized the elimination of poverty as a "long-run solution" to crime, most of his speech focused on policing and on the need to revive a culture of respect for law enforcement. He picked up on Hoover's language to describe the immediate crisis. "Crime has become a malignant enemy in America's midst," Johnson declared, asserting that Americans no longer felt safe in their homes or places of business, much less out along city streets. He cited FBI statistics to justify their sense of unease. "Since 1940 the crime rate in this country has doubled," he said. "It has increased five times as fast as our population since 1958." In order to reverse the trend, he called on Congress "to give new recognition to the fact that crime is a national problem"—and that the federal government would have to play a greater role in supplying and supporting local police. He also singled out Hoover as a visionary who long ago recognized the "need" for the federal government to assume leadership on the issue.[14]

Johnson labeled his initiative the War on Crime, borrowing from the 1930s formulation and from his own recent declaration of a War on Poverty. In July, he expressed a renewed "hope that 1965 will be regarded as the year this country began in earnest a thorough, intelligent, and effective war against crime." Over the next several months, his proposed Law Enforcement Assistance Act (LEAA) sailed through Congress. On August 2, the House approved the law 326–0. In early September, the Senate passed it along without dissent. On September 22, Johnson signed it into law with a characteristically ambitious promise: "I will not be satisfied until every woman and child in this Nation can walk any street, enjoy any park, drive on any highway, and live in any community at any time of the day or night without fear of being harmed."

The chief purpose of the LEAA was to offer federal money to law enforcement agencies seeking to modernize their operations, whether through professional training or through the acquisition of the latest police technology. In the first War on Crime, such advances had helped to produce the FBI National Academy, as well as the Bureau's early experiments with tommy guns, bulletproof vests, and armored cars. Now the technology differed but the impulse both to militarize and to professionalize the world of law enforcement remained the same. In addition to paying for training in areas such as forensic detection, the LEAA set aside money for heavy equipment such as tanks and military-grade rifles and (as in the 1930s) bulletproof vests. The Washington police received $1.2 million to hire 350 additional officers and detectives, to build up its fleets of station wagons, scout cars, patrol wagons, and motor scooters, and to provide the force with walkie-talkies and more advanced communications systems.[15]

Hoover recognized the political power inherent in the disbursal of funds under the LEAA and sought to exercise what influence he could. Johnson made that task easier with his selection of former FBI official Courtney Evans, Hoover's liaison to the Kennedy White House, as the man in charge of doling out the federal money. "Evans is in a position where he is giving out a lot of money to groups and individuals around the country in this Law Enforcement Assistance Act and it could be a powerful instrument in the political field," Hoover noted. Evans was smart enough to offer Hoover some of the money. "He indicated that if the FBI were to need funds around the first part of 1966, he would be most receptive to a request from us in the amount of several hundred thousand dollars," a friendly inside source reported.[16]

Hoover soon launched the National Crime Information Center (NCIC), his latest experiment in "scientific policing" and file-management innovation. The NCIC adapted these concepts for the age of computers, setting up the first nationwide system for recording and retrieving local crime records. The idea, as Hoover described it, was to establish a "vast communications network" that would allow every police depart-ment in the country to retrieve information in "a matter of seconds" rather than hours or days. In Hoover's view, this system would help to counterbalance what was still the criminal's greatest advantage: the ability to move from jurisdiction to jurisdiction while the police were forced to stop at the borders. This same logic had helped to drive the changes of the 1930s, when the FBI acquired faster cars and more powerful guns. With the NCIC, Hoover explained, a few keystrokes allowed for an "uninterrupted flow of up-to-the-minute crime data" in out and of the FBI's Washington headquarters, "a big advancement in scientific crime detection."[17]

Hoover's other ambition was to expand and improve the National Academy, among his proudest achievements from the Roosevelt era. The school still operated out at Quantico, the Virginia military base where Hoover had set up shop in the 1930s, with two hundred local and international police officers in each twelve-week class. He now envisioned an academy equipped to house and teach twelve hundred students at a time, with bigger and grander dormitories, offices, classrooms, and shooting ranges. After extensive back-and-forth with the White House, Congress, and the new bureaucracy created by the LEAA, the money he wanted came through.[18]

Johnson also borrowed one more critical idea from Hoover's past. In July 1965, he announced the members of a federal Crime Commission intended to mimic the famed Wickersham Commission of the early 1930s. Hoover had been outraged when Bobby Kennedy proposed something similar as attorney general. He offered little resistance to Johnson. In early September, Johnson invited the body's nineteen members to the White House for a luncheon and brainstorming session. After a few introductory re-marks, he turned the floor over to Hoover, one of the few men working in government who had participated in the Wickersham Commission. Hoover took the opportunity to lay out a vision strikingly similar to the one he had developed in the 1930s, describ-ing the crime rate as a symbol of social decline and "a shocking indictment of the American way of life."[19]

THE LEAA REFLECTED THE PROFESSIONALIZING, "SCIENTIFIC" APPROACH THAT had been central to Hoover's early G-Man image. But that image could not have come into being without another great innovation of the Roosevelt years: the buildup of the FBI's skills in public relations. In 1965, as Johnson's War on Crime gained momentum, that same impulse inspired Hoover to branch out into color television with a one-hour dramatic series: *The FBI*.

Hoover initially resisted moving into television, just as he had once resisted entreaties from the film industry. He feared its sensationalizing qualities, along with the possibility that the FBI would lose control of its own story. But after months of strategizing and wheedling, DeLoach came back with a persuasive offer: a seventy-five-thousand-dollar onetime payment, plus five hundred per week to the FBI Recreation Association in exchange for access to selected FBI files and expertise. It helped that the offer came from men Hoover knew and trusted. At Warner Bros., the show's originating studio, Jack Warner had helped to oversee nearly every successful FBI-themed film of the past three decades, from *G-Men* in 1935 to *The FBI Story* in 1959. One of Hoover's main contacts at ABC, the show's network home, was James Hagerty, Eisenhower's former press secretary and a great Bureau supporter. The show's chief sponsor would be the Ford Motor Company, where John Bugas, one of Hoover's original G-Men and head of the FBI's Detroit office throughout the Roosevelt years, had long been second-in-command. The final member of the team, producer Quinn Martin, was fresh off the hit series *The Untouchables*, which portrayed the heroics of Roosevelt-era federal law enforcement with voice-over narration by Walter Winchell.[20]

ABC wanted less nostalgia in Hoover's show. "It would be suicide to go back to the days of John Dillinger and stuff like that which the public has seen six times," the vice president of programming explained. "We're interested in the silent, behind-the-scenes work that seldom makes headlines." Not everyone believed that the network could pull it off. Even before the first episode, skeptics registered concern that the show would distort the Bureau's work, providing a glossy portrait with all the warts and blemishes brushed away. "No one could question Hoover's determination to do what he feels is best for the bureau," wrote one reporter, "but a sustained commercial television series extolling his men and his policies week after week will look strange to a world for whom the civil rights battle in the United States and the Warren Commission's criticism of the FBI are vividly in mind." San Francisco columnist Arthur Hoppe envisioned a hopelessly didactic pageant centered on "the story of your selfless government agents who selflessly serve you night and day. Selflessly." He proposed to call it *Hoover Knows Best*, a play on the small-town comedy *Father Knows Best*, famous for its treacly plots and relentless moralizing.[21]

As the embodiment of the modern G-Man, Warner's producers chose a square-jawed actor named Efrem Zimbalist Jr., best known for his recent star turn in the detective show *77 Sunset Strip*. During the 1964 presidential election, Zimbalist had campaigned for Goldwater. While this might have hurt him in certain Hollywood circles, when it came to launching *The FBI* his involvement in law-and-order politics only enhanced his qualifications. Zimbalist played the character of FBI inspector Lewis Erskine, a jack-of-all-trades investigator ready to be dispatched across the country solving crimes. As part of his training, Zimbalist spent several weeks at the National Academy, absorbing the peculiarities and traditions of Bureau culture.

The show premiered on Sunday, September 19, 1965, the same week that Johnson signed the LEAA into law. Certain elements of the episode would have been familiar to any devotee of the 1930s G-Man genre: the agents in their dark suits and white shirts, the stolid reminders that "the FBI investigates" but does not prosecute or decide the law. Despite these gestures to the past, producer Quinn Martin sought a more nuanced, human view of the modern agent's life. "The movies made them look like robots," Martin complained of the G-Man oeuvre. "They came out of a file cabinet in the morning, walked around like machines, went back in a drawer at night. And I don't want that." To soften the FBI's image, the first episode showed Erskine lounging in bed, bleary-eyed and annoyed when his supervisor called him in to work. It also featured a drawn-out flirtation between Erskine and a voluptuous blond businesswoman who fell for him the moment he interviewed her.[22]

Hoover worried about these sexualized touches, just as he worried about the episode's sensational plot, in which the fugitive turned out to be a mass murderer who liked to choke women with their own hair. From retirement, Lou Nichols rushed to assure Hoover that the show was a public relations success. "I think that some of the viewers may have expected more of an institutional program presented from the documentary approach, and in this respect I think the program could have been improved upon," Nichols told Hoover. "However, we have got to remember that prime television time is directed to the man on the street and a presentation to survive must have high entertainment value." The first week's numbers showed moderate success. Nielsen rated *The FBI* the twenty-sixth most popular show of the week—tied with *The Lawrence Welk Show*, and just one spot behind *The Ed Sullivan Show*, which ran in the same Sunday-night slot. A *Star* poll ranked *The FBI* the most popular of ABC's eleven new shows, with more than 73 percent of viewers giving it the thumbs-up.[23]

Critical opinion proved less charitable. "One has to be surprised, after viewing this program, that the FBI would lend its proud name to this piece of melodramatic swill," read a review in *The Washington Post*. "Producer Martin may have access to FBI files on closed cases, but the script was the most banal kind of shoot-em-up trash and romantic nonsense." If Hoover agreed with certain aspects of this critique, he made no move to stop the show. Instead, he began to take a more active role in its production, dictating terms and conditions that would deliver a message more in line with his own priorities. At Hoover's direction, the show largely dispensed with women and romance by the end of the first season. It also began to emphasize punishment, concluding episodes with an account of jail time meted out to the suspect, along with a "Wanted" poster of a real-life criminal fugitive. Over time, Hoover and Tolson added other demands, including the elimination of any portrayal of police brutality, wiretapping, "extreme acts of violence," and civil rights cases. As these changes took hold, the same publications that once complained about the show's "melodramatic" qualities began to lament its portrayal of the FBI agent as "a kind of one-dimensional automaton who solves crimes and rounds up criminals." Hoover viewed the shift as a success, though, convinced that what had worked for the 1930s would now work for the War on Crime of the 1960s.[24]

TRY AS HE MIGHT, THOUGH, HOOVER COULD NOT STOP TIME. AND THERE WAS at least one realm in which his old solutions and priorities no longer seemed to work. Since the height of the Red Scare in the 1950s, liberals had been quietly raising questions about the FBI's methods, arguing that Hoover's insistence on secrecy and FBI autonomy did not adequately protect civil liberties—a return of the critique that had felled Palmer so long ago. In 1965, those questions acquired new urgency. To Hoover's chagrin, the Supreme Court agreed to hear the case of Fred Black, a Washington lobbyist recently convicted of tax fraud whose hotel room had been secretly bugged by the FBI. In Congress, Representative Edward Long launched hearings into wiretapping by federal agencies. From Justice, Katzenbach announced that all wiretaps would henceforth be approved by his office. Even Johnson felt pressured to weigh in, issuing a directive that forbid federal wiretapping except in cases of "internal security." Hoover professed not to care about any of it. "I don't see what all the excitement is about," he wrote in a memo to FBI officials in February 1965. But his actions suggested otherwise.[25]

His greatest concerns focused on the Supreme Court, which had dealt such powerful blows to the FBI in recent years. The justices praised Hoover in their 1966 *Miranda* decision, holding up the FBI as a model for its longtime practice of informing arrested suspects about their constitutional rights. The *Black* case was more of a problem. Though Black himself did not know his hotel room had been bugged, higher-ups at the Justice Department—including Katzenbach and now-Solicitor General Thurgood Marshall—felt duty-bound to disclose the fact before the Supreme Court. Hoover took their decision as a personal betrayal—"the greatest crisis" in FBI history, he declared. He worried that it would not only expose the Bureau's bugging practices, but reveal far too much about Black's ties to former Johnson aide Bobby Baker, whose backroom dealmaking and financial shenanigans had long threatened to tarnish the Johnson presidency. He was also outraged that Bobby Kennedy, now a senator, denied knowing anything about the FBI's bugging practices during his time as attorney general. Convinced that Katzenbach was in cahoots with Kennedy, Hoover tried to use his White House contacts— including Supreme Court Justice Abe Fortas, a die-hard Johnson loyalist—to make an end run around the Justice Department. DeLoach acknowledged that speaking with Fortas "bordered on a violation of judicial ethics," but went ahead with it anyway. On June 14, 1966, they met for a secret breakfast session to discuss the political machinations and implications of the *Black* case. When they were done, Fortas agreed "to slip in the back door and see the President" in the hopes that Johnson would put pressure on Katzenbach.[26]

Their efforts failed. In the end, the Supreme Court ruled in Black's favor and blamed Hoover for the illegal bugging, though the fallout to the FBI's reputation was less serious than Hoover had feared. He had similarly mixed success with Congress, where Long's Judiciary subcommittee was investigating federal wiretapping. Hoover wanted the FBI excluded from the committee's purview, so he turned to James Eastland, his old ally from SISS, still the chair at Judiciary. Eastland assured Hoover that Long would not ask about the FBI. But as with the Supreme Court, things did not work out quite as Hoover planned. Despite Eastland's promise, Long made a gesture toward probing the FBI's surveillance practices. Preparing for testimony, Katzenbach requested that the FBI temporarily suspend all of its bugs "so that he would be in a position to state that there was no coverage of microphones by the FBI." Once the testimony was over, he implied, they could go back to business as usual.[27]

Except that there was no going back—not in the atmosphere of "Congressional and public alarm and opposition to any activity which could in any way be termed an invasion of privacy," as Hoover summarized the situation. Hoping to get out in front of the politics, he proceeded to do something shocking: he voluntarily banned all such activity. "I was, frankly, astounded to hear this," Katzenbach recalled of the moment when Hoover agreed that the FBI's use of bugs should be more heavily supervised. The development was especially astounding given Hoover's law-and-order language. But from 1965 into 1966, Hoover continued to impose additional restrictions: no more "black bag jobs" (which entailed breaking and entering and were, by the FBI's admission, "clearly illegal"), no more mail covers, no more polygraphs, no more sifting through suspects' trash. When the Bureau's "sound-trained Agents" (experts in bugging and wiretapping) were due for a refresher course, Hoover canceled it, for fear of implying that the FBI actively encouraged such practices. And when they sought to use other techniques that might brush up against a now-forbidden category of clandestine surveillance, they were required to gain the approval of headquarters.[28]

As one FBI official later commented, these developments should have "gladdened the hearts of civil libertarians," a stark contrast with Hoover's approach to the War on Crime. But few people outside of the FBI knew what was happening. And there were plenty of exceptions to the rules. FBI records show a dramatic drop in the use of black bag jobs: from 80 in 1964 down to 0 in 1967. In other areas, though, the restrictions seem to have been more apparent than real. After a temporary pause, the FBI continued to break into foreign embassies. The Bureau also continued to wiretap in national security cases—albeit with a new limit of twenty domestic wiretaps and sixty related to foreign intelligence at any given moment. Perhaps most importantly, Hoover held on to the one program that would eventually make all of the others seem relatively benign. Cut off from other methods of surveillance and harassment, he quietly doubled down on COINTELPRO.[29]

AT THE FBI, EMPLOYEES GREETED THE NEW RESTRICTIONS WITH BEFUDDLE-ment. After decades of being trained and encouraged in the use of bugs and wiretaps, suddenly they were supposed to stop, with no regard for the investigative consequences? The organized crime section took it especially hard. "It was a heinous slaughter, devastating our coverage of the mob," agent William Roemer later wrote of being told to dismantle bugs he had spent years trying to plant. Even headquarters officials were aggrieved, ascribing Hoover's change of heart not to political savvy but to a loss of nerve born of old age.[30]

There was some truth to that view. FBI promotional materials depicted the director as the same live wire he had been at the height of the G-Man era. The reality was different. Hoover still arrived at the office—suit pressed, a fresh flower in his lapel—around nine a.m. each day. From that point on, though, his office life bore little resemblance to the bustling world of *The FBI*. Hoover's office greeter, Sam Noisette, was now sixty-five years old, still graciously welcoming visitors, but with the air of a man who learned his trade and manners some four decades earlier. Helen Gandy was almost seventy. Like her boss, she needed a special exemption to avoid mandatory retirement.[31]

The stability of his office staff reflected Hoover's loyalty to those who served him capably—and the loyalty he was often able to inspire in others. By 1965, however, this seemingly virtuous quality was turning the FBI into a gerontocracy. "We have employees in the Bureau who are in their 80s," Hoover proudly informed *Time* magazine. "I've always been against retiring a man by age." But even Hoover himself was slowing down, and everyone inside the Bureau could see it. Unlike Inspector Erskine, ready to hit the road at a moment's notice, he spent most of his day in the office, presiding over ceremonial handshakes and talking on the phone. He rarely met with his younger executives in person. "It had to be something real bad to have him want you to come down and talk to him," recalled Tom Bishop, a supervisor at Crime Records.[32]

Often, just after lunch, Hoover took a nap—sometimes for several hours. Everyone pretended he was doing paperwork, but the truth seems to have been an open secret. Employees also looked the other way when he received his "vitamin shots," intended to boost his energy levels. Descriptions of what the shots contained have ranged widely, from the innocuous vitamin B_{12} to high-powered amphetamines. Whatever they contained, the shots revealed Hoover struggling to keep up appearances as his famously youthful energy began to flicker and fade.

Part of that struggle involved Tolson's health. Despite Hoover's optimism, Tolson never truly recovered from his hospitalization in 1963. He managed to return to work and to keep up the regular vacation schedule: California in August, Miami in December. Then, just as Hoover and Johnson were launching the new War on Crime, he ended up back in the hospital. In 1966, with Tolson "critically ill," Hoover abandoned their summer plans in La Jolla. "Of course, I have had to cancel all of these arrangements in view of Clyde's condition," he wrote to a friend. "He has lost considerable weight and is quite weak from being in bed and will have to go through, I think, a substantial period of recuperation." Acquaintances who visited Tolson expressed shock at his physical transformation: the way he dragged his legs and slurred his speech, how his right eye spontaneously bled as the result of a blood clot. At one point he weighed just 135 pounds with a six-foot frame, a frail old man dependent on those around him. Hoover took on the role of caretaker, moving Tolson into the house at Thirtieth Place to be watched over during the daytime by Annie Fields. "Clyde has now left the hospital and is convalescing at my home since he does not have a full-time maid over at his apartment and I have a cook and housekeeper who lives in and can see that he gets the proper nourishment and attention he must have in order to regain his strength," Hoover explained to a friend. At the Bureau itself, a more jagged worry sometimes burst through. "My God, Deke. I almost lost him last night," he gasped to DeLoach after one especially harrowing episode.[33]

His caretaking duties left him with both less time and less desire for social outings, though he did make periodic efforts to show up for the awards that still came his way. Now an elder statesman, Hoover found himself collecting lifetime achievement awards from groups he had initially joined as a young man. In October 1965, the regional Supreme Council of the Scottish Rite Masons granted him its highest honor, the Grand Cross. The following year, Kappa Alpha followed suit with a national award. At the ceremony, according to the fraternity's in-house magazine, Hoover spoke "movingly" of how "the principles of our Order have remained with him and have been a profound influence in his life."[34]

One other honor that year also forced Hoover to reflect upon his past. In the early 1960s, the Methodist denomination had announced a plan to raze his childhood home at 413 Seward Square in order to make room for the Capitol Hill United Methodist Church, a modernist brick structure. Hoover did not object, pooh-poohing the efforts of preservationists who proposed that his home be saved as a historic site. The congregation decided to recognize his life and career nonetheless. In June 1966, the church dedicated its new "J. Edgar Hoover Window," a thirty-two-by-twenty-two-foot, seven-panel, stained-glass extravaganza spectacularly lit for passersby on Pennsylvania Avenue. "It is the largest memorial window in the city of Washington," Hoover reflected, "and seeing it for the first time yesterday, I must say it is the most beautiful one that I have ever seen."[35]

Of all the sentiment-laden awards and citations parceled out during these years, though, the one that may have meant the most to Hoover went to someone else. On May 23, 1965, two months after introducing the LEAA and the War on Crime, Johnson announced that Clyde Anderson Tolson would receive the Distinguished Federal Civilian Service award, the honor that Hoover had tried so hard—and failed so miserably—to win for Tolson during the Kennedy years. When the day of the ceremony arrived, Tolson was too sick to attend. Hoover appeared at the White House in his stead, accepting the medal and then rushing to the hospital to place it in his hands.[36]

FOR THE YOUNGER MEN WHO WORKED WITH HOOVER, THE GREAT FACT OF HIS age posed a problem at once omnipresent and unmentionable. "Clearly Hoover was showing his age of almost seventy," Katzenbach later wrote, "and it was not clear to me to what extent he was in fact guiding his subordinates." Thirty-eight-year-old Ramsey Clark, who succeeded Katzenbach as attorney general in late 1966, expressed similar concerns. The son of former attorney general Tom Clark, who had worked closely with Hoover during the Truman administration, Ramsey tended to view Hoover's ideas about how to fight crime—even how to count it—as the outdated products of an earlier generation. He also found Hoover hopelessly "self-centered," so in love with the FBI's image and approach that he would "sacrifice even effective crime control" rather than entertain any new ideas.[37]

Some of Hoover's top aides shared these views, worried that an aging Hoover was relying too heavily on old approaches and methods. In late 1965, not long after the launch of *The FBI*, Hoover promoted forty-five-year-old DeLoach to the Bureau's number three position. Despite his status as a Hoover protégé, DeLoach feared that the director's age was starting to affect operations, denying the Bureau the "fresh air" it needed to grow and thrive. He tried to suggest ways to bring in other perspectives, such as inviting outside experts to debate law enforcement issues in the Bureau's newsletter. Hoover rejected that advice, insisting that "our Agents know well enough" and that "we don't have to bring any outsider in." The younger agents were just being lazy, Hoover maintained, while supervisors who should have known better were indulging them. "This Bureau today has no time to 'wet nurse' anyone, whether it be an executive or whether it be a subordinate," he declared.[38]

Despite such frustrations, DeLoach promised to "be here as long as you want me or need me," and to help pass Hoover's values along to the next generation. The old FBI culture proved to be a hard sell, however. During the 1930s, the G-Man craze had injected the Bureau into the consciousness of little boys, who saw in Hoover's corps a glamorous, gunslinging opportunity to fight for truth and justice. By the 1960s, the members of the younger generation—those millions of baby boomers reaching peak employment age—had started to look askance at the Bureau and its operations. In

1964, investigative reporter Fred Cook added to this "negative reputation" with the publication of *The FBI Nobody Knows*, the first book-length exposé of FBI operations since Max Lowenthal's *Federal Bureau of Investigation* a decade and a half earlier. The book began by describing a hopeful young agent signing up for the FBI, lured by the "lofty ideal it projected of honest, dedicated law enforcement and unselfish public service." By the end of the second paragraph, the young agent found himself "revolted by the reality" of life at the FBI. Without anyone noticing, according to Cook, Hoover had created a "ruthless autocracy" that "ruled and dictated the private lives of agents," forcing them into a strange, paranoid subculture out of sync with the culture, politics, and values of the 1960s. Hoover reacted just as he had for decades when faced with criticism: he ordered an investigation of the author.[39]

Bureau officials attempted to get around the generational problem by emphasizing neutral factors such as job security and educational opportunity in their recruiting appeals. In many areas, though, they found little room to maneuver. In the fall of 1962, Hoover appointed forty-nine-year-old W. Mark Felt to lead the FBI's training division, where new agents received their introduction to Bureau culture. Felt bore Hoover's cultural stamp with pride, as tall, square-jawed, and deep-voiced as Lewis Erskine himself. But rather than solicit Felt's ideas about how to adapt this style for a new generation, Hoover instructed him to double down on the old policies, including the Bureau's restrictions on weight, hairstyle, and dress. "I stressed the necessity for the Training Division to promptly screen out any undesirable new employees, clerks or agents," Hoover wrote in a memo describing his instructions to Felt. Among the undesirables were not only men who failed to adhere to the Bureau's clean-cut style but also those who resisted its internal political culture and "the importance of the indoctrination of Bureau personnel."[40]

Like most employees, Felt knew all too well that Hoover meant what he said. At the Kansas City field office, Felt had received a letter of censure for hiring a man whose lips were judged too "large" and "prominent" to meet Bureau specifications. More recently, Hoover had fired a single twentysomething identification clerk after discovering that the man allowed a young woman to sleep in his apartment for two nights. The clerk sued for reinstatement and back pay, arguing that any reasonable person understood that "a little premarital necking" was now an acceptable social practice. Hoover's decision to fire him, the clerk argued, had been "arbitrary and capricious." The "Sex and the Single FBI Man" lawsuit set off a round of mockery. "You mean you sleep in that suit, white shirt and conservative tie?" one columnist wrote, imagining a hot-and-heavy temptress doing her best to seduce an FBI agent. The jokes had little impact at the Bureau. As Fred Cook noted, the director's "old-maidish prejudices about whether a man smokes or reads *Playboy* or how he parts his hair" remained part of what defined life at the FBI.[41]

When pressed, Hoover could admit that the FBI now represented a bygone way of life, that his cultural preferences—like his law-and-order policies—owed as much to the past as to the present. "Perhaps we are inclined toward Puritanism in an increasingly permissive world," he reflected. He had established his fundamental ideas long ago, however, and he had no intention of changing.[42]

CHAPTER 53

Commies in Colleges

(1965–1967)

Hoover initially viewed the student New Left as a form of communism in disguise. Cartoon is from the *Nashville Banner*, 1966.

NASHVILLE BANNER

There was one more area in which Hoover refused to let go of ideas that others deemed outdated. That was the subject of communism, the issue that had lit up his political consciousness four and a half decades earlier and that remained central to his understanding of how politics worked. In the Soviet Union, the mantle of leadership was passing from Khrushchev to Leonid Brezhnev. The center of the Cold War was shifting as well, away from the Kennedy-era hot spots of Cuba and Berlin. In 1962 Hoover expanded COINTELPRO to include Puerto Rican radical and nationalist groups, which he feared might be seeking to follow Cuba's revolutionary path. A few years later, Johnson ordered Hoover's men into the Dominican Republic alongside the Marines, instructing them to ferret out communist plots and help vet U.S.-friendly leaders. Even more pressing U.S. military action was taking place in the former French colony of Indochina, known to most Americans as Cambodia and Vietnam. Kennedy had sent thousands of "advisers" to Vietnam to orchestrate a pushback against the communist forces in the north. Johnson turned the simmering conflict into a full-scale, if undeclared, war. In 1964, the first full year of Johnson's presidency, the U.S. sent more than 20,000 troops to Vietnam. By the end of 1965, it was almost 185,000. That number would double and then almost double again as Johnson insisted that "an Asia so threatened by Communist domination would certainly imperil the security of the United States itself."[1]

  At home, by contrast, the infrastructure put in place to contain the Communist Party seemed to be crumbling, as the concerns of the 1940s and 1950s gave way to a low-level contempt for the party's few thousand remaining members. In late 1964, the Supreme Court ruled that party members could once again obtain U.S. passports, just one of several decisions further relaxing the strictures of the Red Scare. Hoover disagreed with the decision, arguing once again that capitulation would allow the party to rebuild. The passport ruling "afforded the Party a golden opportunity to reward its 'more deserving' members by providing them with an expense-free trip to the Soviet Union," he complained to the White House, "where they will be feted, indoctrinated and imbued with an enthusiasm to return to the United States and work with renewed vigor in their nefarious aims of infecting our Nation with communism."[2]

  For information about the party's internal workings, Hoover continued to rely on SOLO, the informant operation that gave him direct access not only to key allegations about Levison, O'Dell, and King but also to the party's international activities. Many of their reports came to focus on Vietnam, where the Soviets found Johnson's actions "very serious and very dangerous," all but devoid of "long-range" thinking. Hoover shared those reports with the White House. He also tracked the Soviet funds flowing into Communist Party coffers: some $2.9 million between September 1958 and June 1965. As usual, Hoover did not publicize the details of these findings, for fear of exposing a "highly valuable" operation. But the information fueled his conviction that the Communist Party was still far more sinister and foreign-influenced than most Americans understood, and that it was up to the Bureau to stick with the anticommunist cause when nobody else cared to do so.[3]

  Indeed, Hoover felt so strongly about the communist issue that he almost missed what was actually happening on the American left in the 1960s. Far from embracing communism, a new generation of activists was starting to rethink its views on war and peace, civil rights and civil liberties, the Soviet Union and China and Vietnam. They called themselves the New Left. At first, Hoover did not know what to make of them.

IF THE NEW LEFT HAD A SINGLE MOMENT OF ORIGIN, IT MAY HAVE BEEN JUNE 1962, when a group of white college students met in Port Huron, Michigan, to write a manifesto. Many were the children of socialist or communist parents, "red-diaper babies" raised on stories of Hoover and McCarthy and the terrors of the Red Scare. Their project, undertaken with no shortage of generational self-regard, was to devise a plan to preserve the left's nobler traditions—struggles for racial justice, labor, and international peace—while jettisoning some of the Communist Party's baggage. They called themselves Students for a Democratic Society, and they adopted the identity of "anti-anti-communists," critical of the party but far more worried about men like Hoover. Rejecting the binaries of the Red Scare, they envisioned a free-flowing and welcoming New Left, dedicated to civil rights, antinuclear activism, and "participatory democracy"—and, over time, opposition to the Vietnam War.[4]

Hoover did not initially take any special interest in their activities. Far from perceiving the dawn of a "new" left, he saw just a variation on his old communist enemy. When free-speech demonstrations erupted at the University of California, Berkeley, in 1964, Hoover assumed they were a communist-inspired effort to influence the minds of college students. He received a fifty-five-page report on Berkeley in late October, on the cusp of the presidential election. From that report he learned that thirty-eight of the hundreds of students involved in the demonstrations had communist backgrounds or connections—enough, as he misinterpreted it, to show that the Communist Party was attempting to manipulate the students. In response, he launched a preliminary inquiry into SDS, seeking evidence of communist infiltration.[5]

The question of how to characterize SDS might have remained a parochial dispute if not for what happened on April 17, 1965, less than a month after the end of the Selma march and six weeks after Johnson's declaration of a War on Crime. On that day, SDS staged its first major protest against the Vietnam War, attracting some fifteen thousand supporters to Washington. A second group of protesters caught up with Johnson at his ranch in Texas, where they staged an "Easter Vigil" outside the gates. When he returned to Washington, Johnson summoned Hoover to discuss just who this SDS seemed to be. Hoover explained that they were dupes of the Communist Party.[6]

Johnson adopted Hoover's interpretation of SDS, eager to dismiss the war's critics as stupid, disloyal, or worse. "The kids are running up and down parading, and most of them are led by Communist groups," he told a reporter the day after meeting with Hoover. To counteract the threat, Johnson and Hoover mounted a joint publicity campaign, reaching out to key media figures and members of Congress who might be willing to spread the word about the communist/SDS connection. In conversations throughout late April, Johnson informed his circle that Hoover was getting ready to dole out the same treatment to the college kids that he had afforded the communists. Like Hoover, he singled out the children of communist parents as the hidden link between the party and SDS.[7]

Having secured the president's support, Hoover took the next logical step: he began to apply some of the same pressure techniques against the New Left that he had used against the old. In late 1964, he approved an information exchange with California governor Pat Brown, sending along the names of more than a dozen students and five faculty members deemed too close to the communist orbit. The following month, he met with CIA director John McCone, a Berkeley graduate who agreed that the "young punks" on campus would have to be reined in.[8]

These methods of contact came straight from the Responsibilities Program of the 1950s, with its network of governors, college presidents, and local officials. Hoover also relied on the congressional-committee networks he had formed during those years. In 1965, he used his Appropriations testimony to name the forty-three individuals with "subversive backgrounds" who were behind the turmoil at Berkeley—his "Commies in Colleges" theory of the New Left, as one headline described it. Crime Records also contacted HUAC and SISS, the latter now chaired by former FBI agent Thomas Dodd. When Hoover proposed that Dodd look into communist influence on the anti-war movement, the senator jumped at the chance, eventually producing a 235-page report demonstrating that the movement was, as Hoover liked to claim, "under Communist control."[9]

At the FBI itself, the field offices scaled up their observation of anti-war protests and their recruitment of informants. From these sources Hoover gained a detailed rendering of SDS activities, ranging from its Economic Research and Action Project, which placed college students as organizers in poor communities, to its more visible run of teach-ins, sit-ins, and rallies. He also came face-to-face with what the students thought of him. Interviewed for a local television show in Chicago, SDS leaders scoffed at Hoover's description of their group as a communist front, ascribing it to his "strange paranoia" on the subject.[10]

And Hoover did, indeed, seem paranoid, unable to recognize SDS members as anything other than closet communists or Soviet dupes. In October, the New York office tried to explain that "the Communist Party has not 'infiltrated' the Students for a Democratic Society," though party members did what they could to "exploit" anti-war feeling. Hoover lashed back, declaring their analysis "merely an exercise in semantics between 'infiltrated' + 'exploit.'" Rather than listen to his own agents, he took to delivering sarcastic comments about their incompetence and willful blindness. "And yet you can find no Communist influence in this outfit!" he wrote in the margin of a news clipping describing SDS's growing influence.[11]

Whatever their personal opinions, agents had little choice but to follow Hoover's directives. They added SDS leaders to the Security Index, still the FBI's go-to list of "subversives" to be detained in the event of a national emergency. To the attorney general, Hoover suggested that prominent student leaders be prosecuted under sedition statutes, just like the top figures of the Communist Party. With Hoover's encouragement, Crime Records prepared blind memoranda for dissemination to "cooperative anticommunist news sources," describing the "subversive elements" behind SDS, as well as the "widespread moral laxity" at their retreats, protests, and conventions.[12]

SDS nonetheless surged ahead, the passionate core of a fast-growing anti-war and student movement. In April 1965, the presence of fifteen thousand demonstrators in Washington had been enough to alarm Johnson and prod Hoover into action. The following spring, thousands more turned out for the International Days of Protest staged in cities across the globe. In April 1967, that number increased dramatically for a demonstration in Central Park, the staging ground for a mass march to the United Nations. As Hoover watched these events unfold, he pushed for "maximum coverage" of SDS. He did not, however, question his premise that the New Left was just the Old Left, now dressed in peace-and-rainbow stylings.[13]

BY 1967 HOOVER WAS ALSO WATCHING ANOTHER GROUP OF "SUBVERSIVE" STUdents, if for slightly different reasons. These were the brash young activists of the Student Nonviolent Coordinating Committee (known as SNCC, or "Snick"). Founded in 1960 after the lunch-counter sit-ins at Greensboro, North Carolina, SNCC had evolved in creative tension with King's SCLC: the fabled "shock troops" of the civil rights movement, in contrast to King's role as peacemaker and public ambassador. SNCC members had staged many of the sit-ins at the Justice Department, including the protests in Katzenbach's office after Bloody Sunday in Selma. But most of their work took place in the Deep South, where staffers and volunteers routinely risked their lives to carry out the drudge work of voter registration and grassroots organizing. SNCC activists had played crucial roles in Freedom Summer, the Mississippi Freedom Democratic Party, and the Selma march, where they could often be identified by their working-class garb of denim overalls and white shirts, sometimes with a tie thrown on for good measure. Another distinctive feature was their "freedom of association" policy, in which SNCC welcomed cooperation with communist-affiliated groups at a time when other mainstream civil rights organizations refused to do so. In 1966, SNCC added to its distinctiveness by expelling most of its white staffers on the grounds that an influx of white, college-educated activists threatened to deny Black members, especially local people in the South, the ability to set the group's political direction. At that point, "SNCC began a radical change from a civil rights organization to a hate group preaching violence and black supremacy," in the FBI's alarmist interpretation. Hoover stepped up his level of scrutiny.[14]

The "dominant figure" shaping SNCC's political outlook was Stokely Carmichael, a tall and eloquent Howard University graduate and, as of 1966, the organization's national chair. Born in Trinidad and raised in New York, Carmichael knew something of the Old Left; during high school, he had struck up a friendship with Eugene Dennis Jr., son of the former Communist Party leader Eugene Dennis, one of Hoover's targets in the 1948 Smith Act arrests. Carmichael began exploring civil rights activism while studying philosophy at Howard, volunteering to swap in as a bus passenger after the Klan assault at Birmingham halted the first Freedom Ride. After graduation, he returned to Mississippi as a project director for Freedom Summer. From there, he moved on to Lowndes County, Alabama, known as "Bloody Lowndes" for the relentless violence visited upon local Black residents. Over the course of his work, Carmichael became convinced that the FBI and the federal government could not be relied upon to do "a damn thing" to stop such violence.[15]

Carmichael had been at Selma, but the march that made him famous—and that piqued Hoover's interest in his activities—occurred the following year. On June 5, 1966, James Meredith, the aspiring political science major who had integrated the University of Mississippi, began a solo March Against Fear from Memphis to Jackson. Meredith hoped to demonstrate that it was safe for a Black citizen to walk alone through the Deep South. The next day, a white man shot him several times near the Mississippi border, wounding him seriously but not fatally. In Washington, a dozen SNCC members descended on the FBI in protest, picketing outside the main doors of the Justice Department and demanding federal action. Disinclined to wait around for Hoover, Carmichael joined forces with King and other civil rights leaders to pick up the march where Meredith left off. Several days into their odyssey, after being jailed and released on a charge of trespassing, Carmichael delivered one of the most influential speeches in the history of the civil rights movement, second only to King's 1963 address at the National Mall. "We've begged the federal government," he told a crowd of some six hundred supporters. "That's all we've been doing, begging and begging." From that day on, he announced, they would beg no more. "The only way we gonna stop them white men from whuppin' us is to take over," Carmichael declared. "What we gonna start sayin' now is Black Power!"[16]

In the weeks that followed, his "Black Power" speech would often be depicted as a break with King, the rejection of an integrationist vision and the forms of compromise that integration entailed. At the FBI, though, it had the opposite effect, catapulting Carmichael into the same category as King: he was now a dangerous and subversive force who would have to be carefully watched and curtailed. Support came from the White House, where "the President was very concerned about the activities of Stokely Carmichael and the Student Nonviolent Coordinating Committee (SNCC)," as a Johnson aide informed DeLoach. Well-tutored by Hoover, Johnson brought to the subject the same suspicions he applied to SDS, convinced that SNCC, too, was "tied in" with the Communist Party. He asked that the FBI deliver "at least several times a week, a memorandum on the activities of Carmichael and his group."[17]

Hoover requested a wiretap on Carmichael, but Attorney General Clark, himself imbued with a touch of New Left spirit, refused to approve it. In lieu of a wiretap, FBI agents focused their attention on compiling Carmichael's "wild and inflammatory statements." Though still technically chairman of SNCC, Carmichael spent most of 1966 and 1967 traveling the country as an independent speaker, laying out his philosophy of Black Power and its implications. He claimed to be building upon Malcolm

X's calls for self-defense and Black political power in the face of white violence and indifference. What Hoover heard, though, was what he had heard decades earlier from the Communist Party: advocacy of violence. "The term 'black power,' first popularized nearly a year ago by Stokely Carmichael, has given rise to serious apprehension among the American people because of the threat of violence and reverse racism that seems implied in Carmichael's use of these two words," Hoover wrote to the White House in March 1967, as he pondered whether Carmichael, like the communists, could be prosecuted for sedition.

Even more alarming, from Hoover's perspective, was Carmichael's attempt to forge an alliance with SDS and the broader anti-war movement—thus bringing together several of the most "subversive" strains in American political life. "He has coupled his espousal of 'Black Power' with a condemnation of the war in Vietnam and the draft," Hoover wrote to the White House just weeks before SDS staged its rollicking 1967 protest at the United Nations. Carmichael spoke at the rally, denouncing Johnson as a warmongering "buffoon." He spoke again the following month in Washington, pleading with Johnson to end the war in Vietnam in the name of universal humanity. In that speech, he claimed that he would rather be "Red than dead," a New Left twist on the Cold War "better dead than Red" slogan.[18]

For all of his revolutionary posturing, Carmichael had few formal ties to the Communist Party, much less to the Soviet Union. Like the members of SDS, he considered himself a polyglot revolutionary, borrowing from movements around the world. Hoover saw that stance, too, as an insidious form of disloyalty—if not an espionage concern, then potentially a serious revolutionary challenge. On May 16, 1967, the same day as Carmichael's Washington speech, the House Appropriations Committee released Hoover's annual testimony to the press. He singled out Carmichael for condemnation. Hoover depicted the SNCC leader not only as the "chief architect of 'black power,'" but as a clandestine ally of the Revolutionary Action Movement (RAM), a tiny, obscure left-wing sect that Hoover characterized with outsize alarm as "a highly secret, all-Negro, Marxist-Leninist, Chinese-communist-oriented group."[19]

Questioned by reporters about his connections to communism, Carmichael labeled the allegations "infantile," the sort of simplistic claptrap that had long been Hoover's stock-in-trade. Hoover himself he derided as a mere "note-taker," standing by while civil rights workers "were getting our heads beat in the South." Like his counterparts in SDS, Carmichael accused Hoover of deliberately misrepresenting New Left politics, trying to make them fit into pernicious and outdated frameworks. In truth, Carmichael said, "I don't know what Communist-oriented means."[20]

CARMICHAEL RESIGNED AS CHAIR OF SNCC IN THE SPRING OF 1967, HEADING off for a tour of revolutionary Cuba and North Vietnam. That did not stop Hoover from blaming him—along with his supposed allies in SNCC, SDS, RAM, and the Communist Party—for what happened in the weeks that followed. Over the course of three months during the summer of 1967, the nation's cities witnessed well over one hundred racial uprisings, an escalation of the violence that had begun three years earlier in Harlem and erupted again at Watts, in Los Angeles, during the summer of 1965. In Newark, New Jersey, twenty-six people died in just four days, most of them Black residents killed by police and National Guard troops. In Detroit, the worst-hit city, the number of deaths rose even higher, with guardsmen and police firing live ammunition into crowded neighborhoods in an effort to suppress what Michigan governor George Romney described as "uncontrollable arson, looting, and the threat to human life by snipers." Called upon to explain what was happening, Hoover blamed the conflicts this time not on poverty or despair or racism—the obvious social causes—but on left-wing radicals like Carmichael, who sought to fan the flames of discontent. If they did not necessarily set the initial spark, he insisted, they "more or less light the kerosene . . . that will make it into a fire."[21]

Johnson hesitated to get involved in Newark, waiting days to speak out for fear that an association with the violence would tarnish his remaining civil rights initiatives. When Detroit erupted just days later, he saw no choice but to act. On the night of July 24, 1967, Johnson summoned Hoover and a handful of other advisers to the White House for an emergency conference, convinced that he would need a coordinated federal strategy to contain the violence. Just before nine, the small group—including Attorney General Clark, Secretary of Defense Robert McNamara, and Supreme Court Justice Abe Fortas—gathered for dinner and discussion. As the hours ticked by, Hoover recalled, "the situation grew progressively worse," with grim reports from Detroit of "fires, shooting, looting, and general disorder." When the meeting began, Johnson still hoped to avoid sending federal troops into the melee, for fear they might shoot civilians and leave him accused of having blood on his hands. Within a few hours, everyone could see that some sort of federal intervention was inevitable.

Hoover was there less to advise on police tactics than to provide "intelligence coverage," as he described it—to tell Johnson who was behind the whole mess. Johnson had his own suspicions. "The President stated that he had been of the opinion that there was a concerted action and a pattern about all of these riots," Hoover recorded in a memo the following day, describing Johnson's conviction that self-conscious agitators, rather than spontaneous mobs, were responsible for the violence. Hoover may have taken a certain pleasure in noting the president's mindset, so obviously a reflection of what Johnson had absorbed from his FBI tutelage. He discouraged Johnson from seeking a single individual or group to blame. Still, he reinforced the president's assumption that communists, anti-war activists, and Black Power advocates were helping to foment unrest. If he had not actually planned the riots, Carmichael certainly helped to inspire them with his "violent and militant" speeches, Hoover informed

Johnson. The communists then jumped into the fray once the chaos began. In Hoover's view, "militant" elements did more to shape the riots' meaning than to initiate events, but their actions still posed a worrisome challenge.

Johnson said little about these conversations in the televised statement he cobbled together that evening. Instead, he emphasized another of Hoover's favorite themes: the need for "law and order." At midnight, Johnson went live from the White House to announce that federal troops were entering the city of Detroit, where "law and order have broken down." Hoover stood with him, just as he had after the Mississippi murders and the Liuzzo shooting, the eldest of the five men flanking the president. Johnson spoke for less than eight minutes. He emphasized that "law enforcement is a local matter" but that the "extraordinary circumstances" in Detroit demanded federal action.

The following morning, Hoover plunged into the task that Johnson had assigned him during the emergency conference: finding out whether an organized conspiracy to foment urban rebellions in fact existed. "The most important and pressing request of the President is for an over-all memorandum in depth as to any pattern that is being followed in these riots which we are having," Hoover wrote to his top officials. Just after ten thirty, he talked by phone with Johnson, who seemed vastly relieved that "no federal troops had shot anybody" overnight but who still believed that some sort of "central connection" held all the riots together. Hoover did not identify a single communist-backed conspiracy but offered up a few candidates who might be blamed nonetheless. Among them was H. Rap Brown, the new chairman of SNCC and "one of the worst in the country."[22]

In his written report, delivered to Johnson on July 26, Hoover expanded upon the "agitator" theme. A brief investigative summary attributed the riots to "spontaneous outbursts of mob violence," usually sparked by a "minor incident involving police action." From the first page, however, the report qualified this claim, arguing that "volatile situations were triggered into violent outbreaks by the exhortations of 'Black Power' advocates," while other "violent, criminal, subversive extremist elements" seized the day "as the disorder grew and spread." Hoover devoted entire sections to topics under discussion well before Newark or Detroit: "Black Power," "The Role of Demagogues," "Antiwar and Civil Rights Movements Linked." It reserved special scorn for Carmichael, Brown, and King, all "false prophets in the civil rights field." Hoover downplayed what should have been obvious: that Carmichael, Brown, and King found receptive audiences not because of communist manipulation, but because they described some of the real despair, racism, and struggle in American society and politics.[23]

AFTER THE HARLEM RIOT IN 1964, HOOVER'S REPORT HAD BEEN THE FINAL SAY, the last moment anyone in the federal government tried to make sense of what had taken place. After Detroit, Johnson opted for a different strategy, appointing a presidential commission—like the Warren Commission and the Crime Commission before it—to sift through the evidence. To chair the commission, he selected Illinois governor Otto Kerner, an administration loyalist who had once served as a general in the Illinois National Guard.[24]

Kerner in turn selected Hoover as the commission's first major witness. On the morning of August 1, in closed session before a handful of commission members, Hoover described how some routine arrests at a "so-called illegal liquor joint" in Detroit had escalated into an armed confrontation with police. But he devoted the bulk of his testimony to his favorite subjects: communism, Black Power, the New Left, and the threats they posed to national stability. According to Hoover's analysis, the summer's riots never would have taken place without "the demagogic exhortations" of agitators intent on "fomenting violence by open advocacy of disrespect for law and order." Indeed, what was distinctive about 1967, in Hoover's view, was the intersection of older revolutionary sentiment with the new language of Black Power. "The Summer of 1967 has brought a new development," he told the commission. "Volatile situations have been triggered into violent outbreaks by the exhortations of 'Black Power' advocates."

He did not hesitate to name names—first among them, Stokely Carmichael and H. Rap Brown. In preparing for his testimony, Hoover had pushed Crime Records to find outrageous quotes from both men. He personally added a few that were "more vicious than what we had." Hoover insisted on including King among the figures to be blamed for the riots. "Much harm is being done by those who hypocritically prate of 'nonviolence', yet incite to violence the ignorant or the misinformed," he told the Kerner Commission. He blamed all three for stirring up "young Negro hoodlums," already "a constant and ever-increasing source of trouble and concern to law enforcement." Though ostensibly invited before the commission to provide real evidence, he spent much of his testimony reiterating stereotypes and myths.

His recommendations for what to do were relatively modest: more training and better pay for the police and National Guard, a renewed push to "make law-enforcement a profession and not merely a dumping ground for political hacks." He also supported the new "anti-riot" laws being proposed at the federal level, strategically crafted to target activists like Carmichael and Brown, who often crossed state lines between speeches. He called upon the commissioners to look to "the better type Negro" to exercise a "restraining influence" within urban communities, singling out the NAACP as the most dependable civil rights organization. After appointing DeLoach as liaison to the committee, he turned over three volumes of FBI research documenting what had happened in Detroit, Newark, and other cities that summer. Much of it had less to do with the violence itself than with the threat allegedly posed by the Black Power movement.[25]

———

THE COMMISSION REJECTED HOOVER'S CONSPIRATORIAL THINKING. INSTEAD, they saw America for what it was: "two societies, one black, one white—separate and unequal." Rather than blaming communists, student radicals, or Black Power demagogues for creating discontent in the inner cities, the commission blamed white racism, with all the soul-crushing indignities and denials of ambition that it entailed. "White society is deeply implicated in the ghetto," the commission wrote in one of the bluntest statements on the subject ever to emerge from the federal government. "White institutions created it, white institutions maintain it, and white society condones it."[26]

Hoover pushed back. "There is racism but not as predominantly as the Kerner Commission found it to be," he told Ramsey Clark. In any case, he had already decided not to wait around for the commission's conclusions. In mid-August, while he was in California, Hoover finally conceded that whatever was happening in America, the FBI could no longer exclusively blame the communists. In August, he authorized another major counterintelligence program, this one aimed at "black nationalist, hate-type organizations" such as SNCC and at key Black Power leaders including Carmichael and Brown. The following year, he launched COINTELPRO–New Left, seeking to "expose, disrupt and otherwise neutralize" both the anti-war and student movements. Between them, the programs marked a shift away from the emphasis on communism that had dominated Hoover's thinking for almost three decades and made him into a formidable adversary for the New Left generation.[27]

CHAPTER 54

Messiah

(1968)

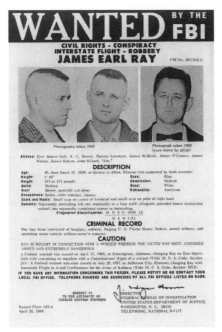

The FBI identified James Earl Ray as the man who shot and killed Martin Luther King Jr.

FEDERAL BUREAU OF INVESTIGATION

O n July 26, 1967, with Detroit still smoldering, Johnson took more than an hour out of his schedule to host a White House luncheon for Hoover. The occasion was Hoover's fiftieth anniversary at the Justice Department: half a century since he'd graduated from law school, assessed his limited options, and taken the leap into government service. At the time, the country was tearing itself apart over an unpopular foreign war and the draft necessary to fight it. In the summer of 1967, Hoover may have wondered gloomily just how much had really changed. Americans in 1917 had worried that their society was falling apart, as thousands of homegrown radicals called for revolution and thousands more resisted the war. Half a century later, he was dealing with the same problems.

But he was no longer a bewildered junior lawyer looking to his bosses for hints about how to behave. He was the boss himself, summoned to the White House for an afternoon of appreciation, with every chance in the world to tell the president what to do. DeLoach attended the lunch, still the steady go-between in matters involving Hoover and the White House. So did Tolson, weak and sometimes confused when things moved quickly, but loyal to the last. Joining them was a small coterie of Justice officials, including Solicitor General Thurgood Marshall, Hoover's longtime on-again, off-again correspondent at the NAACP, now on the cusp of appointment to the Supreme Court.[1]

Johnson expected little credit for promoting a Black man to such high office. In 1964 and 1965, he had assumed he would be forever hailed as a civil rights hero—a white Southerner who went to battle against his party to fulfill the dream of full Black citizenship. He had since come to view himself as a victim of his own success, assailed by the very people—college students, Black activists, white liberals—who owed him the most. This change of attitude brought him closer to Hoover, one of the few Washington power brokers who seemed to understand, in Johnson's view, what it was like to have critics coming at you from all sides. During his early years as president, Johnson had relied on Hoover but often pushed the FBI in a more liberal direction, especially on civil rights. Now he rarely bothered with the push and pull. Their list of common enemies seemed to grow with each passing day: not just Bobby Kennedy and the Communist Party, but the New Left, Black Power, and anti-war movements.

They still affirmed their friendship with compliments and gifts, many of them gestures back to happier times on Thirtieth Place. In 1966, when Johnson's daughter Lucy left for Austin with one of his favorite dogs, Hoover surprised the president with a wriggling beagle puppy as a replacement. Johnson named the dog Edgar and invited Hoover over to stroll the White House grounds while little Edgar did his business. During phone calls, they commiserated about the so-called Georgetown Set, liberal elites who wasted their time away at "high-level cocktail parties and receptions and these things with which this town is plagued," as Hoover put it in one conversation. They also bemoaned the rise of Minnesota senator Eugene McCarthy as the self-proclaimed anti-war candidate for the Democratic nomination.[2]

The months after Hoover's fiftieth-anniversary luncheon brought other unwelcome developments. Hoover had done what he could to help Johnson with the anti-war problem, authorizing DeLoach to set up a meeting between the president and the head of the American Legion, in hopes of rallying Legion members behind the war. Such machinations were supposed to turn around Johnson's sagging poll numbers. "It shows quite definitely that the President's popularity downtrend is halted," Hoover wrote optimistically in the spring of 1966, passing along a Gallup poll. But the downtrend continued. In October 1967, thousands of anti-war protesters staged a march from the Lincoln Memorial to the Pentagon, where they were photographed slipping flowers into soldiers' rifles in the name of peace. In early 1968, the war itself took a turn for the worse, as troops from North Vietnam flooded into the south in a surprise attack known as the Tet Offensive. FBI intelligence showed Johnson's enemies ready to take advantage of events. "Possibility of delivering decisive blow to LBJ's war policy is very great," read an excited message from communist leader Gus Hall to Soviet officials, intercepted by way of SOLO.[3]

The rising hostility took a toll on Johnson. In mid-February, he phoned Hoover in a panic over leaks of war policy. "I don't want anybody to know I called you but I want you personally to [do] one big job," he said. The job he envisioned was a standard-issue national security task: keep an eye on key foreign embassies and see who might be leaking to whom. He also wanted Hoover to tighten up security among congressional committee staff. Johnson's tone reflected a growing pessimism, as well as a sense that Hoover was now one of the last trustworthy men in Washington. "You're the only guy in the government that's watching it," he told Hoover. "And I think we'd have already lost the government if you hadn't. So I just want to order you now to be more diligent than you've ever been in your life." Hoover agreed to "give it my personal attention" and discretion.[4]

Events over the next few weeks did little to improve Johnson's mood. On March 12, McCarthy nearly beat Johnson in the New Hampshire primary. Four days later, sensing Johnson's vulnerability, Bobby Kennedy announced his own bid for the Democratic nomination. Johnson took it personally. "I was being forced over the edge by rioting blacks, demonstrating students, marching welfare mothers, squawking professors, and hysterical reporters," he later recalled. Then "the thing I feared from the first day of my Presidency was actually coming true. Robert Kennedy had openly announced his intention to reclaim the throne in the memory of his brother."[5]

And so two weeks after Kennedy's announcement, to the shock of many supporters, Johnson offered his own surprise. At the end of a televised speech about his plans to achieve peace in Vietnam, he tacked on the news that "I shall not seek, and I will not accept, the nomination of my party for another term as your President." In the way of explanation, he cited the "divisive partisanship" plaguing the nation and expressed hope that his decision would help to heal that divide.

Certain friends had known ahead of time about Johnson's plans. Hoover had not. The following morning, DeLoach checked in with Johnson's secretary and with Walter Jenkins in Texas, to try to get a read on the president's motives. He reported back to Hoover that Johnson "made the decision because he is extremely tired, very sick of all the criticism being heaped upon him, and because of the deteriorating Vietnam situation." In short, he was giving up and letting other men take over.[6]

With this information in hand, Hoover dispatched a farewell note to his old friend. He expressed a "deep feeling of sorrow" at Johnson's announcement, recalling the "long years of association and personal friendship" they had shared. He acknowledged Johnson's right "to enjoy some of the pleasures which have been denied during a brilliant career of dedicated public service." He did not, however, express any desire to follow the president's lead. Despite age and illness, despite the "giant stampedes" heading his way, too, Hoover made it clear that he planned to stay in office and fight his way through the next crisis.[7]

THAT CRISIS CAME FOUR DAYS LATER IN MEMPHIS.

Martin Luther King was standing on the balcony of his room at the Lorraine Motel, looking out over the parking lot below. As witnesses later described it, there was a loud popping sound, then King stumbled and collapsed onto his back, his arms spread out at his sides as if nailed to the cross. A bullet had pierced the right side of King's face, then sliced down through his jaw and neck. An hour later, at 7:05 pm, doctors at nearby Saint Joseph's Hospital declared him dead, the victim of an unknown assassin.

Hoover and DeLoach were both gone for the evening when news of the shooting came in from Memphis. Faced with deciding whom to alert first, headquarters put the call through to DeLoach, who was at home preparing hamburgers for dinner. He took a moment to absorb the news. Then he hung up the phone and called Hoover.[8]

To anyone who had been around the FBI on November 22, 1963, the day of Kennedy's assassination, the events looked disturbingly familiar. There was the quotidian setting, the single bullet from an unknown shooter, the tragedy so immense in its implications that at first it seemed hard to absorb. This time, there was also another budding crisis with which to contend. Since 1964, Hoover had been on record as one of King's fiercest critics, an enmity so deep and severe that it was the first thing most Americans thought of when they heard the words *King* and *FBI* together. Around Washington, his even more vicious whisper campaign against King was an open secret. It did not take much to imagine that Hoover would now come under attack—at the very least, for fomenting the hatred and suspicion that led to King's death; at the extreme, for possibly aiding and abetting the assassination itself.

Indeed, recent months had seen a reescalation of his campaign against King—some of it public, much of it highly secret. From 1965 into 1966, Hoover had canceled many (though not all) of the wiretaps and bugs on King's home, office, hotel rooms, and associates. Then, in April 1967, King began to speak out against the Vietnam War. Hoover had seized upon King's anti-war sentiments as evidence that the minister was still being manipulated by communists. King "is an instrument in the hands of subversive forces seeking to undermine our nation," he wrote to Johnson on April 19. Hoover felt that renewed attention would now be necessary.

Ramsey Clark recalled being shocked at the "very uninhibited way" Hoover talked about King. "It had to me qualities of racism," Clark said, in an all-too-kind understatement. Other Washington figures objected less, either because they shared Hoover's views or because they perceived some measure of benefit in remaining quiet. Southern politicians such as Strom Thurmond and Robert Byrd relished their FBI briefings about

King. In private conversation, Johnson allegedly referred to King as "that goddamned n—— preacher" even as the White House pushed ahead on fair housing legislation, one of Johnson's last civil rights achievements.[9]

By early 1968, much of the FBI's attention had become focused on the Poor People's Campaign, an ambitious attempt by King to combine economic and racial justice agendas in a massive weeks-long demonstration in Washington. As King had envisioned it, tens of thousands of supporters would descend on the city and set up camp near the National Mall, where they would live until Congress and the president acceded to their demands. King had framed the campaign as a chance to execute nonviolent strategy on a new and ambitious scale, in the heart of the capital itself. To Hoover, the idea looked like nothing so much as a summons to violence, lawlessness, and revolution. Internal FBI correspondence predicted "great violence and bloodshed" along with "irreparable propaganda damage around the world." To forestall this eventuality, Sullivan recommended that they "leave no stone unturned."[10]

On March 4, 1968, a month before King's assassination, Hoover had sent a message to forty-one field offices outlining what this new phase of FBI action would entail. As he described it, the chief threat was not merely the Washington protest. It was the possibility that King would succeed in uniting the dueling factions within the civil rights and Black Power movements. Hoover saw three men in the country who could become that sort of "messiah" figure: Carmichael, the Nation of Islam's Elijah Muhammad, and King himself. He ordered his men to prevent any such leader from rising to power.[11]

The month between that memo and King's assassination had brought a surge of energy at the Bureau, with Sullivan coordinating a national effort to attack the "messiah" problem. King seemed to understand that the situation was closing in on him. In late March, he traveled to Memphis to join a protest in support of striking sanitation workers. Though he had called for a peaceful demonstration, the parade broke down in what the press described as another major "riot." FBI officials interpreted the melee as evidence "that acts of so-called nonviolence advocated by King cannot be controlled." Immediately following the march, the FBI distributed anonymous articles to friendly press contacts about King's supposedly violent tendencies. They also circulated a blind memo about his escape to a white-owned hotel in the midst of the conflict. In Washington, Senator Byrd delivered a speech, almost certainly written by Crime Records, that emphasized King's cowardice and adopted the FBI's mocking "messiah" language.[12]

King returned to Memphis in early April determined to rewrite the script being imposed upon him. He called for another march, this one militantly and unequivocally nonviolent. He stayed at the Lorraine, the city's most prominent Black-owned motel. But even King had a hard time mustering faith in the movement's forward progress, or in his own ability to continue to carry its burdens. On the evening of April 3, he spoke at the local Masonic Temple about the need "to bring the colored peoples of the world out of their long years of poverty, their long years of hurt and neglect." He wondered, though, whether he would survive long enough to see that dream fulfilled. "Longevity has its place," he declared. "But I'm not concerned about that now. I just want to do God's will." Twenty-four hours later, he was dead, murdered on his hotel balcony.[13]

DELOACH RECOGNIZED THAT THERE WOULD BE NO SEPARATING THE SHOOT-ing from Hoover's campaign against King. "I hung up the phone with a sinking heart," he later wrote. "The repercussions would be enormous." Hoover did not initially grasp the full implications. When DeLoach called after conveying to his wife that "some idiot shot Martin Luther King," Hoover's main interest seemed to be avoiding what had happened after the Kennedy assassination, when the FBI had been forced, based on tenuous jurisdiction, to take responsibility for a bitterly difficult and controversial case. "Do not accept responsibility for the investigation," he told DeLoach. "This is a local matter."

Those instructions held for about ten minutes. Disregarding Hoover's preferences, Attorney General Clark told DeLoach to assume federal control of the investigation. He justified the move in the way that the Justice Department had explained so many of its Southern interventions: the shooting deprived King of his federally protected civil rights. And so Hoover reversed course, just as he had in 1963. Under pressure from above, he instructed DeLoach to take charge of the investigation, but to make sure it did not turn into a "political circus."[14]

Clark thought he understood why Hoover adapted so quickly to the change of plans. "The FBI's reputation was at stake, and there was nothing more important to Hoover than the bureau's reputation," he later explained to author Hampton Sides. "Hoover was afraid people were going to say *he* did it. So he was all out for finding the killer." Once Hoover made that decision, Clark noted, the commitment was total. On the evening of April 4, Hoover's massive bureaucratic machine cranked into motion, from the ballistics, forensics, and fingerprint experts at headquarters down to the low-liest field office recruits. In Memphis, agents commandeered the "big box" of evidence collected by the local police and raced it to the airport, where an agent personally escorted the box to Washington. Among the items already uncovered was what appeared to be the murder weapon, a Remington Gamemaster .30-06 slide-action rifle found wrapped in a bedspread and abandoned just down the block from the motel. In Washington, headquarters was "bustling" by the time DeLoach arrived a few hours after the shooting, "with agents manning telephones and staff members shuttling files from one office to another." FBI officials streamed back into the office overnight, with one notable exception: Hoover stayed home.

Even Hoover did not get much sleep that night, however. Just before nine p.m.,

Lyndon Johnson broadcast a statement from the White House confirming "the brutal slaying tonight of Dr. Martin Luther King" and pleading with Americans to reject "lawlessness" as a response. Unlike the previous year, when he had insisted that Hoover stand at his side after the Detroit riots, he did not invite Hoover to participate. As Johnson pleaded for calm, though, major cities were already erupting in paroxysms of grief and violence. In Washington, entire blocks were on fire, with swift-moving bands of looters and protesters—it was hard for police to tell the difference—venturing perilously close to the White House itself.[15]

Around two a.m., in the midst of the uproar, Clark called Hoover to say that he planned to leave soon for Memphis, where the National Guard had been called in to preserve order. Clark wanted to establish a strong federal presence on the ground, and he thought an FBI official should come along to help signal that. They agreed on DeLoach. It went without saying that Hoover himself was better off staying in Washington and trying to keep a low profile.[16]

EARLY ON APRIL 5, DELOACH AND CLARK BOARDED A PRESIDENTIAL PLANE AND set off for Memphis to launch what would become the most labor-intensive, time-consuming, and expensive investigation to that point in FBI history. They stopped by the local field office, where most of the staff had been awake all night. From there, it was on to a series of meetings with local politicians and law enforcement. Already, the city was buzzing with talk of a conspiracy by King's enemies, including the FBI and the local police. Clark held a morning press conference in which he dismissed the rumors and proclaimed himself "very hopeful" about a quick resolution to the case. Then, in the late afternoon, he and DeLoach headed back to the airport. They arrived just as King's body was being loaded onto a plane bound for Atlanta. King's wife, Coretta, had flown in to be with him on this final journey, and Clark boarded her plane to express his deep sorrow and regret. DeLoach stayed behind out of concern that "she might resent my coming," given "Mr. Hoover's longtime feud with her husband."[17]

Despite the complications of his position—and despite his ongoing resentment of King—Hoover had good reason to be optimistic about DeLoach's report from Memphis. The FBI had the murder weapon. They also had an abandoned suitcase filled with cosmetics, socks, and other odds and ends, any one of which might yield a critical clue or fingerprint. Several witnesses had seen a man running down the street after the shooting, then jumping into a white Mustang and racing away. Investigators did not yet know who he was, but they had traced him to a boardinghouse across the street from the Lorraine, where he had registered under the name John Willard. They quickly established that he had fired the fatal shot out of a window in the bathroom. It seemed like only a matter of time before this surfeit of evidence—human, physical, and circumstantial—would lead the FBI to a clear suspect.[18]

Hoover may also have been relieved that the shooting happened in Memphis, rather than in a city like Birmingham or Montgomery, where the FBI presence might have met with scorn and resistance from local police. The Memphis chief of police, Frank Holloman, was a former Bureau agent—and one who had managed to remain more or less in Hoover's good graces. Before moving to Memphis, he had been a supervisor in Hoover's office. As part of that job, he had also tended to Hoover's house, making sure the lawn was mowed and the roses trimmed. In short, he knew Hoover's preferences and methods as well as almost anybody. And he still seemed willing, by and large, to bow to Hoover's wishes.

The Bureau maintained important contacts in other Memphis communities as well, including those closest to King and his movement. Among them was a local photographer named Ernest Withers, known throughout the movement for his searing portraits of the Freedom Rides and other famous moments of protest. Withers had been secretly providing information to the Bureau since 1961, sending along photographs of local activists, Nation of Islam members, and other persons of interest who happened to come through town. Like the NAACP officials who worked with the Bureau, Withers was a committed anticommunist. He was also suspicious of the younger generation of radicals, with their calls to revolution, armed struggle, and Black Power, giving him common cause both with Hoover and with King's inner circle.[19]

BACK IN WASHINGTON, THE SECOND NIGHT WAS WORSE THAN THE FIRST. AS DeLoach and Clark flew into the city on April 5, they could see a "smoky haze" hanging low over the downtown area, with flames bursting through in patches. Theirs was one of the only flights in the air, because local airports had been closed to commercial traffic. Johnson ordered the White House and Capitol protected at all costs, and young soldiers stood wrapped around the buildings, rifles and bayonets at the ready. Around the country, thousands of soldiers were pressed into similar duty. By the time it was all over, forty people were dead nationwide, with twenty-one thousand arrested. In Washington alone, the uprising resulted in more than $50 million worth of damage.[20]

Johnson recalled a "sick feeling" as his great political city descended into something approaching a race war. He thought of the stories he had heard about federal troops patrolling the capital during the Civil War and "wondered, as every American must have wondered, what we were coming to." Hoover had a more personal cache of memories on which to draw. To him, the events of 1968 may have evoked the riot of July 1919, during his first month as head of the Radical Division. Back then, it had been white mobs inflicting much of the violence, seeking to install and enforce Jim Crow through racial terror. Now the country was witnessing a form of Black rebellion against the vestiges of that racial system.[21]

Hoover still blamed King for encouraging lawbreaking and civil disobedience.

And he still believed that nonviolent protest actually produced violence by luring antagonistic parties into direct conflict. But none of that, at least in theory, was supposed to matter in the search for King's killer. "Our sole objective is to apprehend the assassin," he declared. On April 11, as if heeding Hoover's call, the Atlanta police located the suspect's white Mustang, abandoned in the parking lot of an apartment complex. Around the same time, FBI agents attached a new name to their wanted man: not the pseudonym John Willard, but Eric Starvo Galt.[22]

Then they came up with another name, one they felt certain would stick. Galt's pattern of movement seemed to be characterized by short stays in rented rooms, frequent changes of alias, and a lot of keeping to himself. FBI agents concluded from this pattern that he might already have been a fugitive, on the run from a previous conviction. On April 18, they began comparing the fingerprints lifted from the discarded gun and other evidence with the fifty-three thousand fingerprint cards of known federal fugitives. One day into the process, they came up with a match.

DeLoach was sitting with Tolson at an FBI executives' meeting when the fingerprint supervisor called him with the news: the man they wanted was not named Eric Starvo Galt but was in fact federal fugitive 405942G, a Missouri prison escapee named James Earl Ray.

THE IDENTIFICATION OF RAY WAS A TOUR DE FORCE OF HOOVER'S EXPERT BUreaucracy, from the first mad dash from Memphis with the evidence to the tension-filled but tedious hours of sifting through thousands of fingerprint cards. Now, after two weeks of silence, he unleashed his publicity system with full force. On April 19, Hoover issued a public statement naming Ray and crediting the FBI's "systematic and exhaustive search of latent fingerprints" with the final identification. He followed the statement with the distribution of 230,000 "Wanted by the FBI" posters throughout North America. The flyers featured Ray's mug shots from his 1960 arrest, along with a recent photo of him in a tuxedo, acquired from a bartending school he had attended in Los Angeles. Hoover designated Ray as the fugitive of the week on *The FBI* television show, where details of a real-life federal crime now wrapped up every episode.[23]

Then the investigation suddenly stalled out. Hoover spent late April into May pressuring his thousands of agents to take the next step—to move from an identification of Ray into locating the man himself. To aid in that process, he contemplated placing wiretaps on Ray's siblings, a proposal quickly scotched by the attorney general. In the meantime, other events sprang up to provide distraction—most notably, a mass protest at Columbia University, where New Left activists occupied several campus buildings, rifled through professors' offices, and posed for photos at the university president's desk before being dragged out and beaten by police. In the aftermath, Hoover pushed "for increased coverage on college campuses," even as he continued to push even harder for agents to find King's assassin.[24]

Critics noted Hoover's suspicious lack of momentum. Indeed, as far as they could tell, he had all but given up. In late April, the ACLU's Southern regional director called for Hoover to be removed from the investigation and replaced with someone "in whom Negroes and all other Americans have faith and confidence." The Black press delivered a similar no-confidence vote. "Let me make it plain, very plain: America's blacks never have and do not now trust either J. Edgar Hoover or the FBI," the journalist Louis Lomax declared. Democratic primary candidate Eugene McCarthy promised that if elected president, he would replace Hoover with a new FBI director.[25]

Added to these indignities was the great inescapable fact of Bobby Kennedy's presidential campaign. Kennedy had been delivering a campaign speech in Indianapolis when he received word of King's death. Jettisoning his prepared remarks, he told the mostly Black crowd about the evening's tragedy, then spoke off the cuff, but with deep passion, about the rage and agony that his family had endured in the wake of his brother's murder, five years ago. He pleaded for calm—and Indianapolis, almost alone among major American cities, responded. As a result, to Hoover's astonishment, Kennedy was suddenly being hailed as a civil rights hero. A month later, he won the Indiana primary in a surprise upset, attracting not only Black votes but also the votes of the city's white, largely Catholic working class. After that, many liberals declared him a shoo-in for the nomination, the one man who could hold together a fracturing Democratic Party.

Hoover could hardly believe what he was seeing: the arrogant playboy now hailed as a statesman and peacemaker. He was particularly outraged about Kennedy's attendance at King's funeral, as if the former attorney general and the civil rights leader had been such great allies all along. In mid-April, Hoover's aides began gathering a list of the King-related wiretaps that Kennedy had approved as attorney general. With those details in hand, DeLoach reached out to the powerful Washington columnist Drew Pearson, an on-again, off-again friend of the Bureau. DeLoach "showed me some amazing documents involving Bobby Kennedy and wiretaps," Pearson noted in his diary. Later that month, Pearson published a column describing how Kennedy had not only approved but even recommended installing a wiretap in 1963. The column included the old accusations about King's contact with "various Communists" and originally included some of the FBI's sexual gossip, though many newspapers edited out the latter.

To Hoover's fury, Kennedy denied the whole thing, as if the FBI did not in fact have the man's signature right there on the wiretap orders. But Hoover was hemmed in by his own denials, too. When confronted by Clark about leaking the Kennedy information, both Hoover and DeLoach took umbrage at the suggestion, pointing out that they were also being criticized for placing the King wiretaps. In at least one way,

though, the Pearson column did its work. As Pearson's colleague Jack Anderson acknowledged to DeLoach, the column was meant to deliver "a death blow prior to the
Oregon primary." On May 28, four days after its publication, Kennedy lost the Oregon
election to McCarthy.[26]

Kennedy mounted a comeback in California the next week. On the night of his
June 4 primary victory, he was celebrating with supporters at the Ambassador Hotel
when a gunman walked right up, in full view of dozens of witnesses, and shot him in
the head. Kennedy died at the hospital in the early morning hours of June 6, the latest
of Hoover's enemies to be brought down by an act of violence that seemed to symbolize everything wrong with America.

THIS TIME, THERE WERE NO RIOTS, JUST A DEEPENING SENSE OF DESPAIR. THERE
was also little mystery about who had committed the murder. After the shots rang out,
bystanders tackled Sirhan Sirhan, a twenty-four-year-old Palestinian who was just
standing there, gun in hand. At four a.m., Johnson called Hoover to confirm that the
White House would be kept abreast of all developments. Hoover instructed DeLoach
"to help in any way we could" but insisted that "the King matter" remain top priority.[27]

Kennedy's funeral took place on June 8 at St. Patrick's Cathedral in New York, his
adopted home state as senator. Hoover happened to be in the city, staying at the nearby
Waldorf-Astoria, but he made no attempt to attend the funeral. The day turned out to
be momentous anyway. That morning, British authorities arrested a man named Ramon
George Sneyd as he attempted to depart London for Brussels. Sneyd was actually James
Earl Ray. The Canadian authorities had matched the name with Ray's photo during a
painstaking review of more than a hundred thousand passport applications. It was just
the extraordinary breakthrough Hoover had been waiting for.[28]

Given Kennedy's funeral, Hoover could have waited to announce Ray's arrest, allowing the British to hold their prisoner in secret, at least for a few hours, just as they
had once held Klaus Fuchs. He does not appear to have entertained the idea. Because
it was a Saturday, DeLoach received the news first. After confirming Ray's identification, he called Hoover in New York. "Fine, have the usual press release prepared,"
Hoover instructed by phone. In Washington, DeLoach called in his favorite *Star* reporter, Jerry O'Leary, for a "lead start." Then, with Kennedy's funeral still underway,
he announced the big news and "the heavens came down" around them.[29]

In his story the next day, O'Leary marveled at the sheer scale of the effort that had
been required to pull off Ray's arrest: three thousand full-time agents, $1.4 million,
more than half a million miles logged on the Bureau's fleet of cars. He attributed the
FBI's success not only to Hoover's emphasis on technical expertise and effective coordination, but to the extra pressure and worry brought on by his fractious history with
King. "Hoover and every one of his 6,700 agents was aware that failure to find King's

slayer would be attributed by some to Hoover's public dispute with King a few years ago," O'Leary wrote. That assessment barely started to capture the vast scope of Hoover's campaign against King, most of which would not be publicly known for several more years. But even O'Leary could not help but hint at the cruelty inherent in Hoover's timing of the announcement. That morning, Coretta King had been attending Kennedy's funeral in New York. She learned of Ray's arrest only once she walked out of the church and heard that Hoover had made a public announcement.[30]

Later that day, a funeral train transported Kennedy's body to Washington, where he was due to be buried in Arlington Cemetery. More than two million people lined the tracks along the way, mourning not only Kennedy, but the promise—of youth, of peace, of racial reconciliation—that so many Americans had seen in his candidacy. At the same time, another set of tributes was getting underway in Congress: statements celebrating the genius of J. Edgar Hoover and all he stood for. Some congressmen simply praised the FBI for "one of its most outstanding jobs" in effecting Ray's arrest. Others used the occasion to make a political point. "I hope these selfish critics who have accused Mr. Hoover and the FBI of giving less than their best where crimes against civil rights activities are concerned will once and for all realize that their unfounded charges, are preposterous and entirely out of order," said Senator Roman Hruska. Senator Robert Byrd, who had scorned King as a false messiah just days before the assassination, railed against the legions of naysayers who "do not know the true character of Mr. Hoover and his associates." Hoover had found his needle in a haystack, and its point was sharp and unyielding.[31]

Attorney Melvin Belli suggested that Hoover take advantage of whatever goodwill the Ray arrest had produced to hang up his hat once and for all. "He should resign on this note of high triumph and depart," Belli wrote. "Such a chance may not come his way again." Hoover chose not to listen. Instead, he turned to the last remaining task of the King assassination case: getting Ray out of London and safely into an American prison.[32]

OSWALD'S SHOOTING HAD SHOWN THE WORLD WHAT COULD HAPPEN WHEN police mismanaged a high-profile prisoner. Both then and since, Hoover had criticized the Dallas police for negligence. Now his top priority was to make good on those claims by ensuring that Ray survived the journey from London to Memphis and from federal to local custody. Within hours of announcing Ray's arrest, Hoover ordered two FBI agents overseas to begin the extradition process. They flew the first leg of their trip in Lyndon Johnson's private plane, a favor from a grateful president.

Hoover hoped that the whole thing could be wrapped up swiftly, that the FBI would soon be done with the assassination investigation and on to other business. Instead, he found himself "more or less stymied in legal technicalities in Great Britain," as he complained to Ramsey Clark on June 20. Among those creating the obstacles was Arthur Hanes, the former FBI agent who had served as mayor of Birmingham during King's demonstrations, then went on to defend the Klansmen who had killed Viola Liuzzo in Selma. To Hoover's disgust, Hanes showed up in the assassination case as Ray's lawyer, still with "a strong smell of the Klan about him." Hanes tried to prevent the FBI from interviewing Ray while in transit and requested to fly back across the Atlantic with his client. Hoover "was absolutely opposed to that," as he informed the attorney general. He was also opposed to meeting with Hanes or acknowledging any connection between the lawyer's current activities and his time as an FBI agent.[33]

It was not until mid-July that all the "technicalities" were worked out. On July 16, FBI officials met with the agents selected for the trip and reviewed "how to handle themselves upon delivery of the prisoner, during flight, and at touchdown in Memphis." Two days later, the agents left for London. By seven p.m. East Coast time on July 18, they were heading back across the Atlantic with Ray, accompanied by a doctor who could testify that they had not abused their prisoner while in flight.[34]

DeLoach recalled the hours that the flight was in the air as among the longest of his life. Hoover and Tolson had left for California midday, landing in Los Angeles just before Ray took off from London. DeLoach stayed behind at headquarters, awaiting news of the touchdown. As the hours ticked by, he replayed the Oswald shooting in his mind: Jack Ruby stepping forward, the gun in Oswald's belly, the "muffled explosion" followed by Oswald's "anguished look" as he slumped forward and collapsed. "This could not, would not happen to James Earl Ray," he repeated—until he learned that, in fact, it hadn't. Just before five a.m., he received word that the plane had touched down at a naval air base near Memphis, where an armored personnel carrier was waiting to whisk Ray off into the early morning.

Once the convoy departed for jail, DeLoach "breathed a sigh of relief," called Hoover, and began to orchestrate the FBI's retreat from the assassination inquiry, now in the hands of local law enforcement. But Hoover soon discovered that it was not quite so easy to put the case to rest. In March, Ray pleaded guilty to King's murder, accepting a ninety-nine-year sentence and thus seeming to close the case. As he registered his plea in court, though, he insisted to the judge that there was more for the FBI to learn. "I don't exactly accept the theories" put forth by the attorney general and "Mr. J. Edgar Hoover," he explained. When asked which "theories" he meant, he specified "the conspiracy thing" and hinted that he had not, in fact, acted alone.[35]

That "conspiracy thing" has since come to taint what once appeared to be an unblemished—indeed, unassailable—FBI triumph. Inspired by Ray's claims, generations of lawyers, investigators, and writers have floated a variety of alternative theories, including the suggestion that Hoover himself, enraged at King, frustrated by the FBI's counterintelligence failures, helped to orchestrate the assassination. In the 1970s, after Hoover's death, a House committee concluded that the FBI did, indeed, fail to adequately explore clues suggesting a possible conspiracy. But they found no credible evidence that Hoover or the FBI played any role in the assassination itself—because, indeed, no credible evidence exists.[36]

If anything, they argued that Hoover's history of animosity toward King "had the effect of inspiring an intensified investigation," lest the FBI be accused of slacking on the job. While Hoover may have pushed his agents to deliver on a culprit, though, he bears responsibility for the assassination itself in at least one important sense. At the committee hearings, one member asked "whether the FBI created a moral climate" that encouraged white Americans to view King as an urgent and existential threat. On that question, at least, the record is clear. The answer is yes.[37]

CHAPTER 55

Nixon's the One

(1968–1969)

By the time Richard Nixon became president, he and Hoover had been friends for twenty years. Pictured in 1971 at the FBI National Academy graduation.

Since his 1960 loss to Kennedy, many former allies had written off Nixon as a political has-been, a man whose chance to seize the presidency had been stymied by a few thousand votes, then demolished by the charm of Camelot. Nixon wrote himself off in 1962, when he lost the California governor's race and assembled a "last press conference" to inform his adversaries that "you won't have Nixon to kick around anymore." Hoover had encouraged his friend to enter the governor's race as a strong anticommunist candidate. After the loss, he ignored all professions of retirement, assuring Nixon that "many chapters are yet to be written about your past and future service" to the nation. "The greatest fighters in the history of our country have, without exception, suffered numerous reverses," he wrote to Nixon on the day after the election. Even in defeat, Hoover thought of himself as someone who shared most of Nixon's goals and almost all of his enemies.

Out of this sense of common mission—and common grievance—their friendship had continued not just unscathed but strengthened by the trials of the Kennedy and Johnson years. Their correspondence throughout the 1960s displayed affection and openness, qualities rare for either man. "It is such a real pleasure to be able to relax and not have to guard every word and to know that one is with real, understanding friends," Hoover wrote to Nixon's wife, Pat, after an especially meaningful gathering. During the darkest days of the Kennedy administration, Hoover had spent hours complaining of his predicament. "I remember sitting with Hoover in his house during a visit to Washington in 1961," Nixon recalled, "listening to him go on about 'that sneaky little son of a bitch,' who happened to be the President's brother and Hoover's boss." Nixon provided what Hoover needed most during those years. He was knowledgeable and discreet, happy to strategize, and eager to listen.[1]

Hoover did the same for Nixon. Though they no longer lived in the same city or shared the same church, Nixon continued to consult Hoover about major life decisions. After the loss in California, he asked Hoover whether he should stay out west or venture east and start a new life. "It was just like old times to enjoy superb food, good hospitality and stimulating conversation with friends with whom you feel you can safely let down your hair," he wrote after a dinner at Hoover's house, as he wrestled with the choice. Once he decided to settle in New York, joining a well-connected corporate law firm, they visited regularly, keeping up with holiday greetings and gift exchanges and treating each other more or less as family. When Nixon's thirteen-year-old daughter, Julie, performed a water ballet for Hoover and Tolson during one of their California vacations, Hoover took the time to write a note of thanks. "It was a most beautiful exhibition and I could understand that you girls had worked hard on both the decorations and the ballet in order to make it so perfect."[2]

When crisis struck during those years, Hoover and Nixon came back together almost instinctively, rushing to provide the same mutual support that had gotten them through earlier times of trial. In November 1963, it was Hoover who provided Nixon with the first solid details about Kennedy's death, taking the time to brief Nixon by phone even in the midst of the post-assassination chaos. During the King controversy of late 1964, Nixon expressed his private outrage at the news coverage, identifying with Hoover as a victim of the pseudo-liberal press. "As I look at the cartoons and read of the vitriolic comments in the columns and editorials," he wrote in a personal letter, "I am reminded of some of the things I went through during the years I was in Washington. I just wanted you to know that you can number me among the legion of friends who are standing with you during these attacks." Now that shared sense of embattlement was bringing them together once again.[3]

THE TRUTH WAS THAT NIXON AND HOOVER DIDN'T JUST LIKE EACH OTHER. In 1968, they needed each other more than ever. At the age of seventy-three, Hoover could no longer survive in office without a sympathetic man in the White House. For Nixon, matters were more complicated but no less urgent. Everyone agreed that his greatest challenge for the Republican nomination would come from the party's conservative wing, where true believers and inside operatives had nominated Goldwater in 1964. Despite the landslide loss to Johnson, most of them still felt it was the best thing they had ever done. While liberals painted Nixon as a far-right reactionary, conservatives viewed him as an Eisenhower moderate, all too ready to compromise. Nixon needed to convince conservatives that he was on their side. So Hoover's status as a "patron saint" of the far right was valuable.[4]

Despite his collaborations with Johnson, most conservatives still expressed admiration for Hoover, viewing him as one of the last holdouts in a federal government lurching toward the left. Almost alone among members of the Johnson administration, he seemed to be willing to speak out in favor of conservative verities on crime, religious faith, anticommunism, and, in more coded terms, race and segregation. His open hostility toward King, the New Left, civil disobedience, Stokely Carmichael, anti-war protesters, and the muddle-headed liberals who supported them only added to his luster. After all, Hoover controlled an institution that could inflict real damage on those groups. For any conservative seeking a role model within the Johnson administration, Hoover was as good as it got. "I'd a lot rather have my own kids grow up hero-worshipping J. Edgar Hoover than Mario Savio or Stokeley [sic] Carmichael," explained California superintendent of public instruction Max Rafferty, famous for his own diatribes against out-of-control teens and the national turn toward lawlessness.[5]

Conservatives throughout the country agreed. Between 1964 and 1968, Hoover received national awards from right-wing groups including the American Educational League, a self-proclaimed promoter of "Southland" values; the American Security Council, an anticommunist research agency staffed by former FBI employees; Young Life, an umbrella organization for teenage evangelicals; and We the People!, a political group affiliated with the far-right Christian Crusade. At the same time, he retained overwhelming popularity among mainstream Republicans. In a 1965 Gallup poll, 84 percent of Republicans gave the FBI a "highly favorable" rating, making Hoover's Bureau by far the most popular institution in the survey. By comparison, 50 percent of Republicans expressed "highly favorable" views of the American Medical Association, making it a distant second. Just 3 percent admired the John Birch Society and 1 percent supported the Ku Klux Klan.[6]

Nixon's popularity—among Republicans but especially among conservatives—was not nearly as secure as Hoover's. "I know my positions on civil rights and foreign aid and reciprocal trade haven't changed," he told a *New York Times* reporter during an exploratory interview in 1966, "and the conservatives—the real conservatives—don't like that." To drive the problem home, he rummaged around his desk and produced a recent poll of subscribers to right-leaning magazines. Asked to name the nation's "most trusted" conservatives, readers came up with a list that included Barry Goldwater, Ronald Reagan, William F. Buckley, and J. Edgar Hoover—but excluded Nixon. Upon declaring his candidacy, Nixon had set out to woo these other men, meeting with Goldwater and his fellow conservative Republicans, hosting elaborate gatherings for the *National Review* crowd and their acolytes at Young Americans for Freedom. Their support turned out to be grudging and uneven, though, especially once Reagan declared his own primary campaign. Only Hoover was an unequivocal Nixon man.[7]

And of them all, Hoover was arguably the most valuable. Despite his growing disconnect with the younger generation, many of his views—especially on crime and policing—seemed ready-made for the 1968 campaign. According to a Gallup poll released in February, crime now ranked as the number one domestic concern for most Americans. Hoover remained the nation's most prominent exponent of the "law-and-order" approach. Under the pressures of the campaign, Nixon now chose to adopt it as his own signature issue.[8]

Nixon published his first major statement on the subject in an October 1967 article in *Reader's Digest*, the dependable old warhorse of American conservatism. The title—"What Has Happened to America?"—echoed Hoover's jeremiads, with their laments over the nation's moral and political decline. The language that followed was pure Hoover as well: race riots as harbingers of "urban anarchy"; "permissiveness," "indulgence," and misplaced "sympathy" for criminals as the liberal rot at the heart of the system. Following a script Hoover had helped to write, Nixon argued that racial discrimination and poverty could never fully explain the alarming rise in urban violence. Instead, Americans should look to something far more "virulent," such as the "decline in respect for public authority and the rule of law in America." Nixon shared Hoover's militancy on the question. "We should make no mistake," he wrote. "This country cannot temporize or equivocate in this showdown with anarchy; to do so is to risk our freedoms first and then our society and nation as we know it." On the campaign trail, Nixon presented himself as the last hope of a society headed toward chaos and moral breakdown. By early 1968, the campaign had distilled these proclamations down to a handily vague slogan: "Nixon's the One."[9]

The intended audience was that subset of citizens Hoover had long courted as his base: the Sons and Daughters of the American Revolution, American Legion members, small-town editors and policemen, white citizens wary of civil rights. Nixon would experiment with catchy new names for this group—"the silent center," "the silent majority," "the forgotten Americans"—but there was nothing new in thinking about them as a coherent network of support. Hoover had been doing it for decades. Now the Republican Party was beginning to strategize about how to combine them into its political base, with Nixon as their standard-bearer. In 1968, it seemed as if the white

South might go Republican for the first time. Nixon's task was to find positions that would resonate across the regional divide—a plan that would come to be known as the Southern Strategy. "Law and order" was at the top of the list.

Nixon's chief competition on the issue came not from Vice President Hubert Humphrey, the front runner for the Democratic nomination, but from former Alabama governor George Wallace, Hoover's longtime critic from Birmingham days, now the renegade far-right candidate of the American Independent Party. Wallace had once taken pleasure in denouncing the FBI's Southern incursions. Now, in a reversal of his former stance, he sought to one-up Nixon in his support for Hoover. As Wallace's stand-in at the Alabama governor's office, his wife, Lurleen, declared May 11, 1968, as "J. Edgar Hoover Day." Without consulting Hoover, Wallace's campaign also flirted with the idea of the FBI director as a vice-presidential running mate. Fortunately for Nixon, Hoover never entertained the possibility; like many Americans, he privately thought Wallace harbored "psychoneurotic tendencies." But Wallace insisted that they shared the same values, and that his running mate should have "the qualities possessed by a man like J. Edgar Hoover."[10]

Nixon took a more understated approach to the law-and-order issue. Where Wallace complained in openly racist invective that "*swaydo*-intellectuals explain [crime] away by saying the killer didn't get any watermelons to eat when he was ten years old," Nixon spoke of "permissiveness toward violation of the law." Where Wallace warned that "the Supreme Court is fixing it so you can't do anything about people who set cities on fire," Nixon called for "better training and higher standards for police." A week after the Kerner Commission released its report lamenting "two societies," "separate and unequal," Nixon went on the radio to affirm that "our first commitment as a nation in this time of crisis and questioning must be a commitment to order." When Democratic primary candidate Eugene McCarthy called for Hoover to step down, Nixon jumped into the fray, affirming that Hoover "is the kind of man I want to head the FBI, if I should have the opportunity to make that decision." Nixon also began to go after Ramsey Clark, holding up the attorney general as a symbol of liberal softness toward Black Power agitators, street-level criminals, and the New Left—in other words, the antithesis of Hoover.

And so it went for several months, through the Columbia conflict, the assassinations and riots, Johnson's signing of another crime bill, and threats of further conflict in the streets. None of these events required much adjustment of rhetoric. They fit nicely into Nixon's warning that "far from being a great society, ours is becoming a lawless society." Hoover affirmed Nixon's populist message. "America is NOT a sick society," he declared in the August 1968 *Law Enforcement Bulletin*, released on the eve of the Republican convention in Miami. "It is time for Americans to shed their apologetic demeanor and stop belittling themselves. The hard-working, tax-paying, law-abiding people of this country are responsible for its growth and development."[11]

Their joint efforts paid off on August 8, when Nixon strode onto the blue-carpeted stage in Miami to accept the Republican nomination for president. He won on the first ballot, swatting off challenges from Reagan and Nelson Rockefeller, but naysayers in the audience still doubted that a two-time loser like Nixon could bring home the victory. Nixon mustered what bravado he could, declaring that in addition to getting out of Vietnam, his top priority was law and order, the domestic issue that mattered most to "the great majority of Americans, the forgotten Americans." He promised to restore order to the streets by curtailing anti-poverty programs and firing Ramsey Clark. He also repeated his promise to redefine "civil rights" for the law-and-order age. "The first civil right of every American is to be free from domestic violence," he declared.[12]

It went without saying that he would rely on the man the protesters hated most to make it all happen. "There's a lot of Hoover's approach to law enforcement that happens to be the approach of the Republican Party," a Nixon strategist noted after the convention. "We'll quote him. We'll say what he has been saying for years." *The Wall Street Journal* summed up the conventional wisdom even more succinctly. "The Hoover approach is about to get a new, nationally televised testimonial," it predicted, with Nixon as chief witness and spokesman.[13]

NIXON'S STANCE THRILLED HOOVER. HERE WAS A MAJOR-PARTY PRESIDENTIAL candidate, a sincere friend and trusted ally, organizing an entire campaign around themes Hoover had been promoting for decades. But no matter how much he might yearn for Nixon's victory, Hoover still retained some of his old wariness toward electoral politics. Too much of his public image and goodwill in Congress still rested on the idea that he was, in fact, beholden to no political faction. Even Nixon championed Hoover's supposed independence. "He has kept the FBI out of politics," the candidate declared. "That's the kind of man we need and that's the kind of a man I will have as head of the FBI." If Hoover could not cooperate directly with Nixon's campaign, though, someone else loyal to his interests and sensitive to the FBI's priorities—someone who knew the law-and-order platform inside out—might be called upon to do some of that work. In late July 1968, Nixon announced the creation of a six-member "senior advisory committee on campaign policy and strategy" that happened to include Hoover's old deputy and public relations whiz, Lou Nichols. [14]

Since leaving the Bureau, Nichols had devoted most of his time to Schenley Industries, the liquor distributor run by Hoover's friend (and alleged Plaza playmate) Lewis Rosenstiel. But he had remained in close touch with Hoover, regularly phoning, visiting, performing favors, and offering praise and advice. In 1965, Nichols helped to create the J. Edgar Hoover Foundation, a charitable organization devoted to perpetuating "the ideas and purposes to which the Honorable J. Edgar Hoover has dedicated his life." To do so, he worked closely with the Freedoms Foundation in Valley Forge, Pennsylvania, where a newly created J. Edgar Hoover Library on Communism aspired to become "the outstanding library on communism in the United States." By 1968, the library featured anticommunist classics such as Herbert Philbrick's *I Led Three Lives* as well as a growing collection of radical paraphernalia, including peace buttons snatched from the "Communist W. E. B. Du Bois's club during a riot," according to one display caption. Above it all hung a "huge color photograph" of Hoover himself, made possible by Nichols's labors.[15]

Hoover was flattered by the attention, but it was something else that made Nichols useful in 1968. In addition to his work for Hoover, Nichols had a long history with Nixon and deep roots within the Nixon camp. He had worked on the 1960 campaign, earning a gushing letter from Nixon about "how deeply grateful I am for all that you did for our cause." Two years later, when Nichols proffered advice on the California governor's campaign, Nixon had assured him, "I think our chances are excellent but it is going to be a hard, tough battle." Like Hoover, Nichols had stuck by Nixon "when everyone else was treating him like a has-been," in the words of one acquaintance. On one occasion, he met Nixon at the airport in a chauffeured limousine to give his "has-been" friend an illusion of influence and power.[16]

That connection made Nichols a potentially useful link between Nixon and Hoover. In January 1968, Nichols set up a meeting with Hoover and Strom Thurmond (another fierce Nixon supporter), officially to pass along a ten-thousand-dollar check from a Thurmond-related charity to Hoover's foundation. Nichols also requested a few extra minutes to discuss an unspecified "three or four other matters" with the director. Hoover's calendar hints at what at least one of those matters may have been: around the same time, Hoover was scheduled to meet with Ronald Reagan, Nixon's chief conservative rival and at that point still a presidential contender. Hoover's executive team worried about the propriety of talking too openly with Nichols. They recommended "that when Mr. Nichols calls Miss Gandy on Wednesday morning, he be advised that the Director's heavy schedule precludes him from discussing these additional matters."[17]

The meetings themselves continued, though, once every few months throughout election season. In 1968, Nichols persuaded Rosenstiel to donate $1 million to the Hoover Foundation. On May 8, the three men gathered in Hoover's office, presumably to discuss the gift. On August 19, eleven days after Nixon accepted the nomination, Nichols met with Hoover once again. As Nixon aide John Ehrlichman later recalled, everyone understood that Nichols formed a key part of the chain linking Nixon to Hoover, someone who "fed Nixon information" from the FBI and presumably brought it back. "But Hoover was more than a source of information," Ehrlichman added. "He was a political adviser to whom Nixon listened."[18]

UNDER THE CIRCUMSTANCES, VICE PRESIDENT HUMPHREY DID NOT EXPECT much from Hoover. But he, too, asked for favors on occasion. A civil rights liberal and champion of the War on Poverty, Humphrey preferred to talk about equality and justice rather than law and order. But like Johnson, he appreciated Hoover's political instincts and willingness to do battle with the New Left, which had long targeted him as a supporter of the Vietnam War. Asked in early August if he planned to get rid of Hoover, Humphrey hedged his answer—apparently calculating, in the words of *Parade* magazine, that "Hoover is a political asset" even within a divided Democratic Party. A few days later, he gave Hoover an opportunity to prove him correct. Worried over rumors of protest and disruption at the upcoming Democratic National Convention in Chicago, Humphrey asked Hoover to create a "special squad" like the one the FBI had made for Johnson in 1964. Hoover agreed to go along, assuring Humphrey that the FBI "had already initiated" widespread surveillance throughout the city. To the Chicago office he was more restrained. "We are not going to get into anything political," Hoover insisted, while instructing them to conduct thorough infiltration and surveillance of the incoming "kooks" and "troublemakers."[19]

The Chicago police had their own plan. On the convention's opening night, a phalanx of blue-shirted, helmet-clad police officers marched into Grant Park to clear out the thousand or so protesters amassed in opposition to the war and the Democratic establishment. They brought tear gas and billy clubs and proceeded to use them not just once, but night after night. The protesters dug in, armed mostly with outrage, which proved to be not quite enough. As one witness later reflected, for the young Americans trapped behind makeshift barricades, the "convention became a lacerating event, a distillation of a year of heartbreak, assassinations, riots." For Nixon, it turned out to be a great propaganda victory: here was the breakdown of law and order that he had been describing. And the Democrats appeared to be the ones responsible.[20]

By the time the gas and smoke cleared, the delegates inside the convention hall had chosen Humphrey as the Democratic nominee. In the aftermath, Humphrey encouraged the FBI to investigate what had happened outside, and Hoover once again agreed to do as asked. By September 6, a week after the convention, the FBI had conducted 416 interviews, with plans to conduct another two hundred or so before reaching any final conclusion. When it came time for Hoover to offer a preliminary interpretation of events, though, he sounded like a Nixon man. On September 18, testifying before a presidential commission, he blamed the protesters, not the police, for instigating the violence. "If it is true that some innocent people were the victims of unnecessary roughness on the part of the police," he said, "it is also true that the Chicago police and the national guard were faced with vicious attacking mobs who gave them no alternative but to use force." As he had for half a century, Hoover positioned himself as the great Washington avenger of the nation's beleaguered police, the one federal official who truly understood their needs and challenges. In 1968, that position had obvious political connotations.[21]

Many observers found his interpretation hard to stomach, given the shocking levels of police violence seen live on television. "For a man with experience in police work, he took an extraordinarily simplistic line about the Chicago cops' performance during the Democratic National Convention," *Time* magazine complained. Senator Albert Gore of Tennessee questioned whether Hoover's FBI could objectively investigate the conflict in Chicago. A second Democratic senator called for Hoover's resignation. But these men were never Hoover's intended audience. Far more important were the 81 percent of Americans who agreed in a September Harris poll that "law and order has broken down in this country," and the 84 percent who said that "a strong President can make a big difference in directly preserving law and order." As even *Time* acknowledged, Hoover's comments about the Democratic convention resonated with this group. "Public opinion . . . continued overwhelmingly to support Hoover's view," the magazine admitted.[22]

Hoover kept a low profile in the weeks after his testimony, as the presidential contest entered its final, high-pressure stage. But he found plenty to do behind the scenes. In late October, Johnson came running with a last-minute request that the FBI surveil and wiretap the South Vietnamese embassy, for fear that Nixon was secretly negotiating to delay a peace settlement. Hoover did as the president requested, ordering agents to follow the Washington socialite Anna Chennault, suspected of serving as Nixon's go-between. As late as November 4, the day before the election, Johnson's aides hoped that the investigation might yet "blow the roof off of the political race," according to DeLoach. But the effort came and went without any definitive conclusion, the last in the great run of secret collaborations between Hoover and Johnson.[23]

Nixon would later become convinced that the FBI had bugged his campaign plane at Johnson's behest, a misunderstanding that Hoover would alternately encourage and dismiss. When it came to the campaign itself, though, everyone understood that Hoover and Nixon were a package deal. The Republican message was chock-full of "Hooverisms," one reporter noted, most of them related to "crime, disorder, and dissent." Nixon's vice-presidential running mate, Maryland governor Spiro Agnew, threatened to name sixty-two left-wing leaders mixed up with communism and praised Hoover as "a great American." The Nixon campaign recorded last-minute radio ads featuring FBI crime statistics, while the candidate highlighted the Democrats' crime-related failures. "I charged that Humphrey had exaggerated and overemphasized poverty as a cause of crime and that contrary to what the administration believed and preached, the war on poverty was not a war on crime," Nixon recalled in his memoir.[24]

And then there was Nichols, the link between the Nixon campaign and the backroom expertise of the FBI. Most of his energies went into campaign security, known euphemistically as "poll-watching." In October, he helped to recruit a hundred former FBI agents, along with an alleged hundred thousand "trained volunteers," to run surveillance at polling locations deemed particularly susceptible to anti-Nixon sentiment. Speaking with the press, Nichols insisted that some three million votes would be at stake on Election Day due to Democratic "miscounting, ballot tampering and 'ghost' voting." Some reporters saw less lofty ideals at work. Rather than attempting to protect electoral integrity, they suggested, the goal was to intimidate Democratic voters. "If you see a man in a dark suit and a trench coat at your voting precinct tomorrow, fear not," one article advised on the day before the election. "You're supposed to think he's an FBI agent, but he's really just a masquerading member of a Nixon 'Honest Ballot Squad.'" In truth, many of Nichols's recruits *were* FBI agents at heart if no longer by name, men whose training, bearing, and loyalties had endured beyond the end of their government jobs.[25]

Nixon needed the help. In the final tally, he barely edged out Humphrey in the popular vote, with 31.8 million to Humphrey's 31.3 million, and an alarming 9.9 million for Wallace. The close results meant that the new president owed the men who had helped to ensure that those key votes would end up in the Republican column. He also owed a debt to the architects of his law-and-order message, "the most important domestic issue in the presidential election and arguably the decisive factor in Richard Nixon's narrow triumph over Hubert Humphrey," in the words of one historian.[26]

Nixon's victory put Hoover in the best political position he had occupied in almost a decade. Despite Johnson's personal loyalty, the president's ideology and constituency had never fully aligned with Hoover's. Now the Nixon administration promised a true fusion of interests—personal, political, ideological. With Nixon's election, columnist Leonard Lyons predicted, "J. Edgar Hoover can now remain as head of the FBI as long as he wants to."[27]

ON NOVEMBER 12, A WEEK AFTER THE ELECTION, HOOVER MET JOHNSON AT THE White House for lunch, bidding a nostalgic goodbye to one friend while preparing to welcome another. "As a personal friend, neighbor and subordinate, I have enjoyed your company in both historic and relaxing moments," Hoover wrote to Johnson in thanks. "Today's luncheon was perhaps one of the best of these moments." When Nixon visited the White House a few weeks later, Johnson made a point of getting Hoover on the phone for an unprecedented conference call between the FBI director and both the current and future presidents. In a burst of self-pitying melodrama, Johnson confessed to Nixon that it was sometimes Hoover alone who had been there for him, "a pillar of strength in a city of weak men." "Dick, you will come to depend on Edgar," the outgoing president warned. "He's the only one you can put your complete trust in."[28]

Two days after his lunch with Johnson, Hoover zipped north by train for a meeting with Nixon at presidential transition headquarters, a lavish suite of rooms on the thirty-ninth floor of New York's Pierre Hotel. Nixon's aide John Ehrlichman thought Hoover "looked unwell" when he arrived: "florid and fat-faced, ears flat against his head, eyes protruding." But Hoover was in better shape than he appeared to be and seems to have gotten what he wanted out of the hourlong encounter. "Edgar, you are one of the few people who is to have direct access to me at all times," Nixon told him, promising insider status within the new administration and a return to the glories of the Eisenhower years.[29]

What followed over the next several months was a political romance that exceeded even Johnson's yearslong pageant of medals, invitations, and joint appearances. Over the Christmas holiday in Florida, Nixon invited Hoover to join him for a "mainly social" visit at Key Biscayne. In late January, Hoover donned a tuxedo for Nixon's first dinner party as president, an intimate gathering of ten in the White House family dining room. Among the other attendees were Secretary of State William Rogers and National Security Advisor Henry Kissinger. Like all Nixon officials, they were expected to treat Hoover with deference and respect, one of the cardinal rules of the new administration. When it came time to deliver Hoover's White House pass a few days later, Nixon aide John Ehrlichman made a point of carrying out the task in person.[30]

Looking back, DeLoach remembered how flattered Hoover was by all the attention. "The director was in his glory," DeLoach said. "Richard Nixon was 'his man.'" For a few months at least, this seems to have translated into a certain lightness of spirit, a feeling that Hoover was again at one with a Republican administration and its priorities. "Back at FBI headquarters, we began to hear him saying 'Dick said this . . . Dick did that.'" And the honors kept on coming, even as the ritual hype of the presidential transition began to pass. In February, Nixon recommended large raises for both Hoover and Tolson: from $30,000 to $42,500 for the top man, from $28,500 to $40,000 for his number two. In March, it was lunch at the White House again, this time an exclusive gathering with Nixon, Ehrlichman, and the new attorney general, Nixon campaign manager John Mitchell. In April, Hoover and Tolson journeyed to Camp David for yet another group dinner, followed by a film screening.[31]

Nixon capped it all off on May 28 with one of the most elaborate pageants of support for the FBI ever staged by an American president. That day, he opened the grand East Room of the White House for the graduation ceremonies of Hoover's National Academy. At the president's invitation, all one hundred graduating officers, along with their wives, enjoyed not only formal speeches and handshakes but also a private coffee reception with top administration officials. Nixon himself served as graduation speaker and personally handed each man his diploma. Hoover stood at his side, smiling and helping to coordinate the smooth exchange of paper.[32]

The speech Nixon gave that day touched on all the law-and-order truisms of the campaign trail: that Americans faced grave internal dangers, that only "establishing and maintaining respect for law" would protect them, that it was the police who had become America's "second-class citizens," scorned and abused. He also spoke about his first encounter with the FBI, back in 1937, when Hoover was on the rise as a national hero and young lawyers everywhere dreamed of hunting the likes of John Dillinger.

Nixon described how he had submitted his agent's application and then waited, desperately hoping to learn that he, too, would soon be a G-Man.[33]

In telling the story, Nixon repeated Hoover's claim that congressional appropriations cuts—not Nixon's own résumé—had led to his rejection. "That will never happen again," Nixon announced, vowing to fight Congress to get the FBI whatever it might need. Hoover had something for Nixon, too, a small token of respect to make up for the errors of the past: a shiny gold FBI agent's badge.[34]

As a public show of unity, the event could hardly have been more successful, proof that Hoover's values were Nixon's, too. And Nixon paid tribute to the more personal side of their relationship as well. On October 1, he ventured to Hoover's house for dinner, along with Attorney General John Mitchell and presidential aide John Ehrlichman—an inversion of the Washington hierarchy in which the FBI director would normally go to the president. Ehrlichman found Hoover's decor bizarre and slightly sad: a collection of "dingy, almost seedy" furniture, along with hundreds of photographs of celebrities from the '30s and '40s. Tolson was there but barely, wandering downstairs to say hello before heading back up to the bedroom where he was recuperating from his latest illness. Hoover flew in steaks from Clint Murchison's Texas ranch in a gesture toward his long-ago dinners with Nixon at the Del Charro and therefore a signal of his insider status. Ehrlichman was not impressed with the food, but he did express admiration for one aspect of Hoover's hospitality. Without anyone quite noticing, Hoover was able to direct conversation where he wanted it to go, and to gain Nixon's approval for whatever he wanted.[35]

Outside observers recognized the dinner's political message. "an exhilarating hope and enthusiasm for the control of crime," as a federal judge exclaimed to Nixon. Over the next few months, though, Hoover learned that his partnership with the new administration also entailed certain costs. With a Republican in the White House, the liberals and Democrats who had held their tongues throughout the Johnson years began to come for Hoover, decrying him as a dangerous reactionary, no longer the master state-builder and figure of bipartisan renown. To Hoover's surprise and dismay, Nixon was not always there to defend him. As the administration began to put "law and order" into action, Hoover and Nixon discovered that they did not, in fact, always share a set of common interests, and that friendship and politics could be a volatile mix.[36]

CHAPTER 56

The Gospel of Nihilism

(1969–1970)

SOMEBODY'S ASLEEP

(Reprinted from CHICAGO TRIBUNE)

Hoover criticized the New Left as a force of "lawlessness" and "anarchy." The cartoon is from the *Chicago Tribune*, June 1968, two months before protests and violence at the Democratic National Convention in Chicago.

After Johnson's election in 1964, Hoover had felt emboldened to unleash his long-delayed counterintelligence assault on Martin Luther King, beginning with the "notorious liar" press conference and escalating to the anonymous letter and hotel-room tapes. Four years later, after Nixon's election, he made a similar decision. Banking on his ideological and personal sympathy with the Nixon White House, he intensified the Bureau's counterintelligence efforts against the Black Power movement and the New Left.

The bulk of Hoover's efforts soon came to focus on the Black Panther Party for Self-Defense, later shortened to Black Panther Party (BPP), a group that had not even existed when Johnson came into office. Founded in Oakland in 1966, over the course of little more than two years the Black Panthers had become the most visible and controversial of the country's emerging Black radical organizations, usurping King and even Stokely Carmichael as the movement's self-proclaimed "vanguard." In the late fall of 1968, with Nixon's election secure, Hoover issued instructions to "submit imaginative and hard-hitting counterintelligence measures aimed at crippling the BPP." By the time Nixon took office in January, the Panthers were the target of a Bureau counterintelligence effort that surpassed in both its ambition and its cruelty anything done to the Communist Party, the Ku Klux Klan, or King himself.[1]

Hoover justified this escalation partly through his changed interpretation of what was happening on the New Left. During Johnson's early presidency, Hoover had emphasized the continuities between the Communist Party and groups like SNCC and SDS, depicting the New Left as a younger, more flamboyant version of the Old. Since 1967, however, he had begun to question this view, citing a sudden uptick in acts of "revolutionary terrorism" and violent clashes with police, fueled by "a pathological hatred for our way of life" among young radicals. The adjective he chose for this phenomenon was "anarchistic," a term with particular resonance for a man whose professional identity had been forged in the crucible of World War I. By 1968, most Americans—including most government officials—had no living memory of what had happened early in the twentieth century: the anti-war protests and slacker raids, the bombings and attempted assassinations, the jailing and deportation of Emma Goldman. For Hoover, though, these had been formative experiences, touchstones for the revolutionary tumult of the Nixon years.[2]

IF HOOVER HAD BEEN ASKED AT ALMOST ANY POINT IN HIS CAREER TO CONJURE up his most terrifying vision of domestic insurrection, he might have described the Black Panthers. To their admirers, the group's members offered a shining model of unapologetic Black militancy. To Hoover, they looked like "young hoodlums," even if they called themselves Marxist revolutionaries. They showcased a political philosophy and style all their own. The Panthers wore leather jackets, sunglasses, and black berets, a distinctive mod look beloved by the news media. They talked about themselves as committed Marxists—leaders in a global revolt against colonialism, racism, capitalism, and imperialism. Sometimes they even carried weapons, usually shotguns or semiautomatic rifles slung over the shoulder, one part self-defense and another part "urban guerrilla."

In 1966, members of the founding Oakland branch started bringing those guns on neighborhood patrols to police the city's police, well-known for its brutality and callousness toward Black residents. The following year, they made national news by showing up at the California state capitol, weapons in hand, to protest a gun-control bill designed to strip them of the right to bear arms. A few months after that, founder Huey Newton, a nasal-voiced, clean-cut Oakland law student, was arrested for shooting and killing a police officer during a traffic stop. After being treated for a gunshot wound to the stomach, he survived to become the first great national symbol of the Panther rebellion, with calls to "Free Huey!" a regular feature at New Left gatherings.

Hoover's attentions were mostly elsewhere during the Panthers' first few years, caught up with King, Carmichael, SDS, and the fallout from Detroit and Newark. In late 1967, he launched an initiative to recruit "ghetto-type informants" paid to keep the Bureau abreast of "racial feelings and unrest." At the same time, he expanded the FBI's scattered "racial informants" programs, a category that included not only "ghetto-type" but also "White Hate" informants, as if Klan violence and urban uprisings were simply two sides of the same coin. Even his COINTELPRO instructions barely acknowledged the Panthers for their first year or two. In his August 1967 order authorizing counterintelligence operations against "Black Nationalist, Hate-Type Organizations," Hoover singled out SNCC, SCLC, and the Nation of Islam, along with three smaller groups, as the primary targets for Bureau attention. He never mentioned the Black Panthers.[3]

From the first, "Black Nationalist" COINTELPRO took advantage of the techniques already tried and tested on other groups: anonymous letters, cartoons and media campaigns, pretext phone calls and rumor spreading, intimidation of landlords, employers, and donors. But there were several distinctive features, crafted to exploit the vulnerabilities of young Black activists. One strategy involved cooperation with local police, a method that had been complicated, if not impossible, during the anti-Klan campaign in the South. When it came to Black activists, Hoover generally found himself in accord with urban police chiefs, who shared many of his prejudices and suspicions. They proved eager to use special squads and street-level muscle to supplement FBI intelligence gathering. During a typical incident in Washington, an elementary school run by the Nation of Islam found itself slapped with health and safety violations thanks to an FBI tip-off to local authorities. In another instance, the Albany, New York, field office came up with a plan for the police to target Black activists with traffic tickets "until a backlog of 'unpaid' tickets is accumulated and the issuance of an arrest warrant is necessary," with the arrest then "held in abeyance until such time as racial violence may appear imminent." Hoover vetoed that plan for fear of "actually causing violence." But he encouraged the field office to push ahead with its "imaginative thinking" about how best to cooperate with and utilize the local police.[4]

The goal behind all this highly individualized, often petty harassment was as sweeping as anything Hoover had dreamed of vis-à-vis the Communist Party. In addition to thwarting the rise of a Black "messiah" who might inspire the masses, he sought to stop the country's fractured civil rights and Black Power organizations from uniting into a powerful racial-justice alliance. "An effective coalition of black nationalist groups might be the first step toward a real 'Mau Mau' in America, the beginning of a true black revolution," he warned the field offices, borrowing the movement's language of global anti-imperial revolt. To preclude that outcome, he argued, the Bureau would have to "prevent militant black nationalist groups and leaders from gaining respectability" and to limit the likelihood that they might achieve any sort of "long-range growth."

Hoover's initial instructions had identified three men with the charisma and public following to lead a unified movement: Martin Luther King, Stokely Carmichael, and Nation of Islam leader Elijah Muhammad. After King's assassination, Hoover increased his focus on Carmichael, whose youthful magnetism contrasted sharply with the declining physical prowess of Muhammad, who was nearly as old as Hoover. Since leaving SNCC, Carmichael had refashioned himself as a roving intellectual, working out his ideas in a new book titled *Black Power: The Politics of Liberation in America*. He unequivocally rejected the "isms" of the Old Left. "Communism is not an ideology suited for black people, period," he declared in 1968. But Hoover no longer acknowledged that communist infiltration had been the original logic behind his investigations of SNCC. By 1968 he shifted seamlessly to warning instead that Carmichael might "form a united front of civil rights and black nationalist groups" under the Black Power banner.[5]

Hoover's interest in Carmichael led inexorably to the Black Panthers. In Lowndes County, Alabama, Carmichael had worked on a voter registration and community organizing effort that adopted the black panther as its symbol. As his fame grew, he became a Black Panther in name if not necessarily in practice, briefly taking up the title of "honorary prime minister" in homage to his growing status as a global revolutionary icon. It seemed obvious what should come next: SNCC and the Panthers would unite in a common assault on the status quo. In June 1968, in one of the first mentions of the Panthers to appear in COINTELPRO files, the New York office noted that the Panthers and SNCC seemed to be sharing local office space and getting along quite nicely. "Every opportunity will be seized to disrupt their seemingly harmonious relationship," the field office assured Hoover.[6]

But Hoover was not content to let such assurances stand. Throughout the summer of 1968, as he hoped for a Nixon victory, he issued increasingly dire warnings to the field, pressuring his men "to use every possible technique to disrupt and neutralize the extremist black nationalists." Those efforts began to pay off by the end of the summer. In late August, the Los Angeles field office concluded with satisfaction that "the Counterintelligence Program has resulted in the neutralization of the growth of membership and the relative financial strength of SNCC." At that point Hoover redirected the Bureau's gaze. In the summer of 1969, he declared that the "Black Panther Party"—not SNCC or SCLC or the Nation of Islam—"without question, represents the greatest threat to the internal security of the country."[7]

Despite their revolutionary style and armed showmanship, the Panthers proved to be no match for the FBI. As anti-colonial activists and Marxist revolutionaries, they had lofty goals, including a potential alliance with the anti-war movement and the white activists of the New Left. But as young people, their aspirations often outstripped their political and organizational savvy—or their ability to withstand a carefully planned state assault. At the top, Panther leadership was swirling with turf battles and mutual recriminations that the FBI found easy to exploit. In one May 1969 operation, Hoover authorized a plan to send Carmichael a fake note, written on duplicated Panther letterhead, expelling him from the organization. But Carmichael soon resigned of his own volition, citing infighting, factionalism, and irreconcilable ideological differences that had little to do with any FBI machinations.[8]

In addition to encouraging this sort of divisiveness, Hoover pushed the field offices to find evidence of "immorality" among the Panthers. He hoped that such material would discredit them as he had once hoped it would discredit King. Hoover's racism inclined him toward the misplaced view that "a typical black supporter of the BPP is not disturbed by allegations which would upset a white community." He nonetheless encouraged agents to seek out the personal and sexual vulnerabilities of Panther leaders, including evidence of interracial relationships, which were presumed to be damning to a white audience. Over the course of 1968 into 1969, the FBI documented instances of sexual promiscuity and "jiving with the white girls" to be exploited through the use of anonymous letters to would-be supporters. Where such evidence could not be found, the FBI manufactured it. In one tragic incident, the Bureau spread the false rumor that the white Hollywood actress and Panther supporter Jean Seberg was bearing the child not of her husband but of a Panther. Humiliated by the sensational media coverage, Seberg went into premature labor, lost the baby, and years later committed suicide.[9]

Neither Hoover nor his field agents showed any great compassion when confronted with such human frailty and pain. If anything, their files show a certain glee about their ability to break down Black activists and make them suffer. When Philadelphia police arrested one "extremist" who had been moving from town to town trying to avoid police harassment, the local field office noted with pleasure that he "lay down on the floor of his residence, beat the floor with his fists and cried." When SNCC leader James Forman ended up in a psychiatric hospital, thanks in part to fear and paranoia induced by the FBI, the New York field office redoubled its counterintelligence efforts. The cruelty was all the more striking given that most of their targets were teenagers and twentysomethings experimenting with revolutionary politics and social transformation for the first time.[10]

Few aspects of Panther life received as much attention as the issue of gun violence, ready-made for both police and counterintelligence action. The Panthers' armed theatricality made them media sensations. It also made them susceptible to derogatory coverage about their alleged propensity for violence. At least some of that coverage was planted by the FBI. Often Hoover publicized existing facts: that some Panthers referred to the police as "pigs"; that they called for true revolutionaries to "off the pigs"; that Panther leaders Huey Newton and Eldridge Cleaver had both been charged with shooting police officers. On other occasions, the FBI went out of its way to prod the Panthers into situations where violence was likely to result. In the fall of 1968, Hoover noted that a rivalry between the Panthers and the US Organization, a small Black nationalist offshoot in California, was fast "taking on the aura of gang warfare with attendant threats of murder and reprisals." Rather than attempt to tamp down the situation, he encouraged local field offices to "fully capitalize" upon it. In early 1969, the rivalry erupted into a gun battle on the UCLA campus, with US members shooting and killing two Panthers. Local FBI officials admitted that they could not take credit for causing the conflict. But they were pleased to note "a definite disruption within the overall black nationalist movement," along with "a great deal of consternation within the black community."[11]

By the spring of 1969, with Nixon in office, talk of violence—both real and imaginary—began to result in mass arrests. In early April, a Panther defector accused cofounder Bobby Seale of ordering the murder of a former California chapter member. (Seale dismissed the accusation as "something FBI pig J. Edgar Hoover would say.") Across the country in New York, police arrested twenty-one local Panthers, charging them with an elaborate scheme to bomb the city's department stores, botanical gardens, educational facilities, and police stations. The following month, members of the New Haven chapter were arrested and charged with the torture-murder of a fellow Panther who had been accused of being an FBI informant. Among those arrested was Seale himself, who just weeks earlier had called upon sympathizers "to recognize the rotten FBI pig agents as their dedicated enemies and to go forth and get rid of all the pigs and enemies of the people." He had visited New Haven around the time of the murder.[12]

Even in areas of Panther activity far removed from threats and shoot-outs, Hoover was inclined to see a violent conspiracy at work. In early 1969, the Panthers created a free breakfast program for children, acting upon research suggesting that children who did not eat a nutritious breakfast were less likely to succeed in school. Hoover saw in the program an effort not to feed hungry youngsters, but to indoctrinate Black youth. "The BPP is not engaged in the 'Breakfast for Children' program for humanitarian reasons," he wrote, but "to fill adolescent children with their insidious poison." He called upon his men to disrupt it.[13]

HOOVER WAS HARDLY THE ONLY GOVERNMENT OFFICIAL TO VILIFY THE PANthers in 1969. What set him apart was his ability to move beyond words and mobilize a well-trained, ideologically disciplined, professional corps to do his bidding. Fifty years earlier, during the last wave of "anarchistic" revolt, his Radical Division had been a fledgling operation, its administrative capacity wholly out of line with the gargantuan nature of its task. Now he had the power to contain, manipulate, infiltrate, and even destroy entire organizations and movements.

Hoover was not just worried about the Panthers' advocacy of self-defense, or the possibility of "unification" with like-minded Black activist groups. Even more alarming was their budding alliance with white middle-class college kids, who were beginning to emulate Panther style and rhetoric. When Hoover had begun to pay attention to the New Left four years earlier, he had seen its members mostly as pathetic communist dupes. By 1968, he was convinced that he was looking at something much more expansive and genuinely revolutionary—less like the disciplined, hierarchical, pro-Soviet Communist Party than like the sprawling far-left movements he had confronted as a young man. The New Left "as a movement is difficult to define," Hoover wrote in "Analysis of the New Left: A Gospel of Nihilism" for *Christianity Today*. "The New Left is a *mood*, a *philosophy* of life, a *Weltanschauung*, a way of looking at *self, country*, and the *universe*." The FBI's internal statistics reflected this shift away from a narrowly defined Old Left. In 1963, when Johnson took office, more than 80 percent of the FBI's Security Index was composed of alleged communists. By 1969, when Nixon entered the White House, that number was down to 57 percent and falling fast.[14]

The New Left's "loosely-bound, free-wheeling, college-oriented" sensibility made it both harder to define and more effective than the Communist Party, according to Hoover. Its young members thrived mainly on a spirit of rebellion, without getting bogged down in disputes over membership dues and party lines. A handful also found themselves drawn to the cult of revolutionary violence. "New Left leaders have constantly exhorted their followers to abandon their traditional role of 'passive dissent' and resort to acts of violence and terrorism as a means of disrupting the defense effort and opposing established authority," Hoover wrote to the field offices during the summer of 1968. And there were acts to go along with the words. During the first ten months of 1969, the FBI documented approximately 80 bombings at draft boards and ROTC centers, along with showy protests such as burning draft cards with napalm. In 1970, there were 3,000 bombings (plus 50,000 bomb threats) throughout the country. Hoover saw in these episodes not a desperate cry against an unjust war, but a heightening of revolutionary impulses passed down from the first anarchist generation.[15]

Hoover's initial COINTELPRO–New Left message to the field offices reflected some of the emphasis on potential violence that characterized his approach to the Panthers. "The Bureau has been very closely following the activities of the New Left and the Key Activists," he wrote on May 10, 1968, "and is highly concerned that the anarchistic activities of a few can paralyze institutions of learning, induction centers, cripple traffic, and tie the arms of law enforcement officials." But these were white middle-class college kids, not Black urban militants, a situation that came with far different challenges and constraints. "Can I infiltrate a college classroom?" one agent recalled asking himself. "Can I go and listen to a professor? Can I talk to a professor in a college class-room? Can I go to his office? Can I put an informant in the college classroom? Or even on the campus?" In general, Hoover's answer was yes, but he warned repeatedly about the special conditions that applied to working in and around universities, where some students came from backgrounds that afforded them real social and political power.[16]

While the campaign against the Panthers embraced arrests, frame-ups, and police cooperation, the New Left COINTELPRO concentrated on the gentler, more psycho-logical side of the counterintelligence playbook, the blind memos and anonymous mailings designed to humiliate and harass. During the program's first month, Hoover authorized plans to drum up news coverage about the iffy academic records of Antioch College activists; to inform the DMV about a left-wing professor's expired license plates; and to consult with University of Delaware administrators about denying rec-ognition and funding for an SDS chapter on campus.[17]

Subsequent memos laid out additional options, including the publication of "ob-noxious pictures," secret communications with parents and college administrators, the manufacture of fake campus pamphlets, and even the occasional ginning up of drug-related arrests. From the Newark office came a proposal to take photos of "six of the dirtiest and most unkempt SDS demonstrators" at Princeton, to be circulated in an anonymous mailing to donors, alumni, and members of the campus Conservative Club. In Los Angeles, agents retrieved the diary of a local New Left leader (who had suppos-edly "discarded" it) and proposed to forge a handful of "cryptic" entries hinting that the young diarist was a government informant. The entries "would contain phone numbers which would, when called, be identified as Army intelligence or secret service agencies," the proposal suggested.[18]

Some of these operations produced immediate consequences; after an "intensive investigation" by the Boston office, one landlord evicted approximately twenty people living in an SDS collective. Far more often, they were slow-burn ideas, intended to transform what might otherwise have been a unified, purpose-driven movement into a sprawling mess of suspicion and logistical chaos. Wasting activists' time was a high priority. In advance of the protests at the Democratic convention, Chicago agents cop-ied 250 housing request forms to be filled out for nonexistent out-of-town protesters—petty harassment intended to "cause considerable confusion." Hoover was especially enthusiastic about proposals that made student activists look foolish, incompetent, or worse. "Ridicule is one of the most potent weapons which we can use," he wrote in July 1968, echoing the message he had once applied to the Klan.[19]

Added to all this was the grunt work of infiltration and surveillance, activities that made up the bulk of the Bureau's escalating New Left activity. By August 1968, all field offices claimed to be running informants within student and anti-war organizations, with greater concentrations in major offices such as New York, Chicago, and Los An-geles. A year later, Hoover counted more than two thousand agents at work on New

Left assignments, with approximately a thousand undercover informants distributed throughout the country. He still forbade his own men from going undercover. "As long as I am director of the FBI, I'll not have any agent wearing old clothes or long hair," he declared. When they wanted to, though, agents could blend in far better with the SDS than with the Panthers. They were young, white, college-educated men close in background if not in outlook to many of their intended targets.[20]

Like the Panthers, SDS was already shot through with rivalries over ideology, tactics, and organizational power—factors ready-made for FBI exploitation. The fiercest of them consisted of a fight between the Progressive Labor Party (PLP), an Old Left faction now dominated by Maoists, and the equally militant but more free-flowing and media-savvy Revolutionary Youth Movement (RYM, also known as the National Office faction). In his June message for the *Law Enforcement Bulletin*, Hoover predicted that these "bitterly and hotly contested" differences might burst into the open at the SDS national convention that summer. Hoping to capitalize on that prospect, he secretly ordered the convention flooded with informants instructed to vote in favor of the RYM candidates, for fear that the serious-minded PLP might turn a "shapeless and fractionalized" SDS into an actually "disciplined organization." In the end, RYM did Hoover's work for him by storming out of the convention, declaring itself "the real SDS" and seizing control of the group's headquarters, bank accounts, and printing equipment.

Hoover counted the crack-up as real progress. "The SDS as the mainstay of the New Left Movement is now seriously divided and, to this extent, weakened," the Cleveland office reported after the convention, "and the National Office faction is gradually being forced into a position of militant extremism which hopefully will isolate it from other elements." That judgment proved correct in the long term, as infighting and disillusionment led thousands of students to flee the group. In the short term, though, things got worse rather than better. To mark the transformation of SDS into a truly revolutionary organization, the new leadership adopted the singular name Weatherman, borrowed from a song of anti-war bard Bob Dylan, who had written that American youth did not "need a weatherman to know which way the wind blows." Within a year of taking over what had once been the largest student protest organization in American history, Weatherman declared that "our job is to lead white kids into armed revolution," that the age of protests and marches was over, and that "revolutionary violence is the only way."[21]

IT IS INCONCEIVABLE THAT ANY LAW ENFORCEMENT OFFICIAL WOULD SIMPLY have stood by while bands of young people, small in number but serious in intent, began building bombs, attacking military installations, and extolling the virtues of armed revolt. But Hoover's FBI went well beyond identifying individuals likely to commit criminal acts. In his view, entire movements—even dangerous ways of thinking— were responsible for the escalating violence. They all needed to be contained through government action. The FBI contributed to the growing sense of desperation by stoking fear and disorder among activists, encouraging informants to embrace radical positions, and by showing young people—both overtly and covertly—that the authorities were, indeed, not to be trusted. Hoover purported not to understand how anyone could argue for the necessity of violence in a country where free speech and the democratic process failed to deliver justice. As much as any man in government, though, he helped to create the conditions that made such arguments plausible.

Weatherman's first major salvo, in October 1969, signaled the new state of affairs. The trial of eight activists accused of conspiracy to riot outside the Democratic convention was underway in a Chicago courtroom, where Panther leader Bobby Seale would soon be gagged and bound to his chair after an attempt to serve as his own lawyer infuriated the judge. With the whole country paying attention, Weatherman leadership issued a call for the nation's young revolutionaries to descend on Chicago and wreak revenge for the previous year's police beatings and assaults. "We're not urging anybody to bring guns to Chicago, we're not urging anyone to shoot from a crowd," one activist explained, "but we're also going to make it clear that when a pig gets iced, that's a good thing, and that everyone who considers himself a revolutionary should be armed, should own a gun." To symbolize the coming clash, in early October Weatherman bombed the statue of a policeman at Haymarket Square, the site of the dramatic 1886 anarchist bombing and trial that had once galvanized Emma Goldman and her generation of revolutionaries.

The Days of Rage, as Weatherman called its own confrontation with the police, proved less inspiring. On the evening of October 8, a few hundred young people gathered early in Lincoln Park, armed not with guns but with less lethal fare: metal chains, blackjacks, lead pipes. Then, despite the nationwide call to arms, nobody else showed up. They went through with their rampage anyway, tearing through Chicago's Gold Coast neighborhood en masse, smashing windows and glass doors along the way. The police chased them through the streets, shot six of them (though none fatally), beat several dozen, and arrested even more than that.

Despite its spectacular failure, the Days of Rage confirmed Hoover's view that the New Left was becoming increasingly "anarchistic." It also produced an opportunity to move ahead with another aspect of his agenda: ensuring that, whatever else happened, the young guerrillas of the former SDS and the armed "vanguard" of the Panthers did not join forces.[22]

HOOVER HAD WARNED OF THAT POSSIBILITY AS EARLY AS MAY. "THE STUDENTS for a Democratic Society (SDS) and the BPP are cooperating in several ways to exploit their common revolutionary aims," he instructed the Chicago office. "Together these organizations pose a formidable threat." To thwart those efforts, the Bureau set out to convince the Panthers that SDS, especially its Weatherman faction, "was a core of elite white chauvinistic students" with little but their own egos in mind. The Days of Rage fed that story. Though he had once boasted that "we work very closely with the SDS," Chicago Panther leader Fred Hampton turned on Weatherman after their Lincoln Park antics. "We do not support people who are anarchistic, opportunistic, adventuristic, and Custeristic," he declared. He inadvertently echoed Hoover's own critique of Weatherman tactics amid his own call for a new anti-imperial, revolutionary coalition.[23]

Just twenty-one years old in the fall of 1969, Hampton had already made a name for himself as a powerful orator and effective local organizer, rising through the youth ranks of the NAACP and then becoming chairman of the local Panther chapter before he was old enough to vote. From the perspective of the Chicago office, that made him a "Key Agitator" and potential Black "messiah," albeit one as yet without a national following. Though Hampton spurned Weatherman theatrics, he worked diligently to create alliances with other groups, including local Chicago gangs and even so-called hillbilly rights groups, which advocated on behalf of poor white migrants from states like Kentucky and Tennessee. For Hoover, this was the prospect most to be avoided. And because Hampton was a Black radical and not a white student, the means chosen were extreme. What Hoover did to Hampton in the months following the Days of Rage ranks with the "suicide letter" to King as among the most merciless actions of his career.[24]

The Chicago police carried out the worst of it. But they were prodded along by Hoover's men. The FBI carefully documented Hampton's run-ins with the law, including an arrest for taking ice cream from an ice cream truck and handing it out to neighborhood children. In early 1969, a tip from the local field office led to Hampton's arrest on that charge in the midst of a live television interview—an episode that "proved highly embarrassing to the BPP," in the Bureau's approving words. Over the next several months, the Panthers and police engaged in several shoot-outs and violent confrontations, each one contributing to a heightened atmosphere of dread. In early October, just a few days before the Weatherman debacle in Lincoln Park, they exchanged gunfire at the local Panther office; police followed up by ransacking the place. On November 13, another gun battle, this one lasting a full half hour, resulted in the deaths of two police officers.[25]

Into this tinderbox the FBI brought a match in the form of William O'Neal, a local Panther informant recruited under Hoover's stepped-up informant initiatives. After the police murders, O'Neal's FBI handler summoned him for a meeting, asking for information about what the local Panther chapter, including chairman Fred Hampton, seemed to be doing and saying in response to the shoot-out. They met again later that month, at which point O'Neal drew a map of Hampton's apartment, presumably to aid the police in a planned raid. As Hampton's bodyguard, O'Neal knew the layout well, including where Hampton slept. He indicated everything on his diagram, which the Chicago field office promptly shared with the police. In late November and early

December, O'Neal's handler spoke five to seven times with police contacts and met in person at least once. On December 3, he reported to Hoover that Chicago police were "currently planning a positive course of action relative to this information."[26]

The following morning, at four forty-five a.m., fourteen Chicago officers burst in on the "Panther crib" where several people, including Hampton, were fast asleep. Ostensibly in search of illegal guns, they came in carrying not only their service revolvers but also heavier weapons—including at least one machine gun—from both official and personal collections. Their first barrage killed a Panther named Mark Clark. After that, the police began shooting wildly. According to later reports, Clark got off a single, reflexive shot as he died—the only shot fired by the Panthers that night. The police fired up to ninety-nine bullets, including two shots delivered point-blank into Hampton's forehead. At the end of it all, "FRED HAMPTON, Illinois Chairman of the BPP, lay dead," in the words of an FBI report, with bullet wounds near his right ear and right eye.[27]

Initial news coverage described a gun raid gone bad. In Panther circles, though, word spread quickly that Hampton had been "murdered in his bed," in the words of Panther leader Bobby Rush—and that Hoover had been at least tangentially responsible. When blood tests suggested that Hampton had been drugged, those suspicions took on new weight. "A pig agent must have given it to him because Fred never used any drugs and J. Edgar Hoover has said he has infiltrators in the Black Panther Party," Rush told the press. Hoover may or may not have known in advance about the drugging or about the precise plan for the raid; such local operational details sometimes made their way up to headquarters, sometimes not. Either way, he helped to make Hampton's death possible: by vilifying the Panthers and pressuring his men to act, by authorizing and orchestrating the larger COINTELPRO effort, and by encouraging FBI field offices to coordinate their efforts with local police.[28]

And when it was all over, he applauded it as just the sort of operation he had long been seeking. On December 8, O'Neal's handler wrote to Hoover to recommend a special payment to the informant for providing information of "tremendous value." "The raid was based on the information furnished by informant," the memo noted, claiming credit for helping to orchestrate the raid if not for firing the fatal shots. Hoover approved a three-hundred-dollar bonus for O'Neal above and beyond his regular stipend.[29]

RATHER THAN SLOWING DOWN THE CYCLE OF POLITICAL VIOLENCE THAT plagued Nixon's first year in office, Hampton's killing accelerated it. Among Chicago activists, the death "instilled a sense of militancy and resistance, that certain things would not be tolerated," one alderman recalled. For the members of Weatherman, one participant remembered, "It was the murder of Fred Hampton more than any other factor that compelled us to take up armed struggle." On December 6, two days after Hampton's death, Weatherman took credit for bombing two police cars in Chicago. A few months later, they became the Weather Underground Organization (WUO), a clandestine armed network dedicated to waging "war" against an American society "too fucked-up" to recognize its own evil. Of the three thousand bombings in the United States over the course of 1970, only a handful could be directly attributed to the WUO. But theirs took on a special significance—emblematic, in Hoover's words, of the "terroristic violence" being embraced by the "fanatics" of the American left.[30]

Meanwhile, the Panthers remained embroiled in their own violent exchanges with the authorities. Arrested in 1969 for the alleged plot to bomb major sites throughout New York, the "Panther 21" won a blanket acquittal two years later. By that point, though, the organization was in uneven decline as a national force, unable to sustain what had always been an against-the-odds struggle. In late 1969, when Hampton was killed, some 10 percent of BPP members were already police or federal informants. Added to that problem was a vicious rivalry between party leaders Huey Newton and Eldridge Cleaver, who demanded that their members choose sides between them. The FBI sought to accentuate their disagreements through rumors and fake letters—all to swift effect. In 1971 Hoover pronounced "the differences between Newton and Cleaver" entirely "irreconcilable" and moved on to identifying "future targets."[31]

In that sense, Hoover got at least some of what he had wanted back in 1968, when he pushed his men to move more aggressively against what he viewed as a "nihilistic" and "anarchistic" left. It is less clear that the rest of the country ended up better off. Despite what Hoover claimed, the young revolutionaries of the late 1960s stood for ideas shared by many Americans: that the country's progress on racial justice was too slow and insufficient, that the war in Vietnam was a painful and deadly mistake. Their turn to violence hurt rather than helped their case, but Hoover would have come for them anyway, just as he had once targeted the nonviolent civil rights movement. It was a far cry from what he had once promised Harlan Stone, after his early-life encounters with "anarchistic" movements forced a civil liberties reckoning. Now there were important people urging him to go even further and do even more to contain the left— beginning with Richard Nixon.

CHAPTER 57

The Man Who Stayed Too Long

(1970–1971)

Anti-war activists accused by Hoover (in poster) of plotting to kidnap National
Security Advisor Henry Kissinger. By the early 1970s, Hoover's once-stellar
reputation was in free fall, especially on the left.

LEE LOCKWOOD/THE CHRONICLE COLLECTION/GETTY IMAGES

On June 5, 1970, while the FBI was busy brainstorming how to "intensify" the
split between Weather Underground and the Panthers, Nixon convened a meeting of intelligence officials at the White House. He hoped to discuss the state of the
New Left, Black Power, and anti-war movements—and to pressure Hoover not to rein
in FBI activity but to be more aggressive. Nixon understood the meeting as an intervention in history, a moment to face the fact that America was coming apart and the
New Left was largely to blame. "We have moved from the 'student activism' which
characterized the civil rights movement in the early 60s through the 'protest movements' which rallied behind the anti-war banner beginning with the march on the
Pentagon in 1967 to the 'revolutionary terrorism' being perpetrated today," he read
from talking points written up in advance of the meeting. To remedy this "new and
grave crisis," he turned to the one man who had been wrestling with the left longer than
anybody else in the room, appointing Hoover as the chair of a committee to bring the
intelligence agencies together in support of the president's agenda.[1]

Nixon did not know all the details of COINTELPRO, or the fact that Hoover's agents were already deep inside some of the most abstruse debates and rivalries of the New Left. What he did know was that Hoover seemed strangely hesitant to use certain other techniques that had long been staples of the domestic intelligence system. Despite their many loopholes, the directives that Hoover had issued in 1965 and 1966—no bag jobs, no mail covers, tight controls on bugging and wiretapping—still held sway at the Bureau. Indeed, the years since had further convinced him that the public and the courts were in no mood to tolerate, much less applaud, clandestine techniques that had once been routine. To Nixon, though, his decisions looked like a puzzling unwillingness to do what needed to be done in the midst of a national crisis. After all this time—and despite many public words to the contrary—Nixon thought that Hoover was losing his nerve.

To prod the FBI into action, Nixon selected Thomas Charles Huston, a young army intelligence officer turned White House staffer, one of the most outspoken conservatives in the upper reaches of the executive branch. Huston had come to politics as a leader of Young Americans for Freedom, the conservative analogue to SDS. As an organization, YAF still loved Hoover; in 1969, it sponsored a nationwide *Masters of Deceit* contest, with a thousand-dollar prize for the best essay on the book's anticommunist principles. As a person, Huston was more skeptical—not only of Hoover, but of any unelected bureaucrat who chose to spend a lifetime in government. He believed that "the bureaucracy must be treated as the enemy," a powerful force with its own culture and interests. Huston took it as his mission to "harass, brow-beat, do whatever is necessary" to bring people like Hoover in line with the White House agenda.[2]

Given the director's long friendship with the president, Huston might have assumed that hardball tactics would not be necessary. During Nixon's first eighteen months in office, Hoover had mostly been a willing partner, happy to do favors when the president asked. There were exceptions, though, and new signs that reflected just the problems Huston feared. In the spring of 1969, concerned over Vietnam-related leaks, Nixon and National Security Advisor Henry Kissinger had approached Hoover with a request for help. Hoover went along at first, installing at least seventeen wiretaps—on White House and National Security Council staffers as well as reporters—and reporting to Kissinger on the findings. As the weeks went on, however, he began to worry that the taps would be exposed—thus subjecting the FBI to charges of political spying or, worse yet, suppression of the free press. By the middle of 1969, he was demanding that the taps be authorized in writing by someone higher up, preferably the attorney general or the president. In the end, hoping to placate Hoover, the attorney general agreed to put his name to paper, and Kissinger himself came to Hoover's office "to express his personal appreciation" for what the FBI had done. Everyone recognized that "this coverage represents a potential source of tremendous embarrassment to the Bureau and potential disaster for the Nixon administration," in the words of one FBI memo. Contained in that analysis was the idea that one side might have to be cut loose to protect the other.[3]

Even where Hoover appeared to go along willingly with Nixon's requests, there was often an edge to the exchange, a wariness about who was gathering information on whom. In 1969, Nixon asked Hoover to investigate rumors about a "coterie of homosexuals" at the White House, in which high-ranking aides supposedly met after hours in secret rendezvous. Hoover soon pronounced the whole thing ridiculous, much to the relief of White House counsel John Ehrlichman and chief of staff H. R. Haldeman, both of whom had been named as members of the ring. In retrospect, though, Ehrlichman came to view the exoneration as a form of intimidation in its own right—a reminder from Hoover that he could make or break their reputations anytime he chose to do so.[4]

Hoover convened the first meeting of his New Left intelligence committee on Monday, June 8, three days after the gathering at the White House. It did not go well. When Hoover announced that they were being asked to present a historical analysis of the left, Huston interrupted to say that this was not at all what the president wanted—that Nixon was more interested in developing a strategy for the future than in wallowing in the past. Hoover left the meeting infuriated at Huston's arrogance, dismissing the young staffer as a "hippie intellectual" with no respect for the work of government.[5]

Over the next two weeks, with Hoover's grudging permission, Huston met with top officials from the various intelligence agencies to hammer out a plan for the president. When Nixon received their draft report, he liked what he saw. Hoover did not. Huston's report called for an all-out ideological war against the New Left, including surveillance and disruption tactics far more ambitious than what the FBI was currently doing. Where the report went especially wrong, in Hoover's view, was in its call for a council of officials from various intelligence agencies to supervise the effort, and its recommendation that Hoover lift the restrictions he had put in place on wiretaps, bugs, mail covers, and other clandestine techniques. In Hoover's assessment, the plan asked the FBI to interrupt its current operations and assume a greater risk of exposure at just the moment that COINTELPRO was yielding real results. Hoover had no issue with surveillance and counterintelligence, in other words. He just wanted to be the one in charge, and he did not want to get caught.

And so he set out to stop Huston's plan, drawing upon the best of his bureaucratic skills. He began by marking up the report with footnotes, each registering a distinct objection. Where the report recommended an "intensification" of electronic surveillance, Hoover maintained that "the FBI does not wish to change its present procedure." Where the report called for "relaxing restrictions" on covert mail opening, he noted that the practice was "clearly illegal" and likely to result in "serious damage . . . to the intelligence community" if revealed to the public. In response to a suggestion that the federal agencies expand their use of campus informants, Hoover warned of "leaks to the press which would be damaging and which could result in charges that investigative agencies are interfering with academic freedom."[6]

The footnotes were in place by the time Hoover gathered the committee for its second official session on June 25—by all accounts, one of the most dreadful afternoons in intelligence history. Tasked with reviewing Huston's report, Hoover decided to go through the document page by page, asking for separate comments on each of forty-three pages, footnotes included. When the moment came for Huston to chime in, Hoover dismissed him, calling him by the wrong name (Hoffman, Hutchinson) before returning to the leisurely review process. In a follow-up memo to the White House, an infuriated Huston complained that Hoover was being "bull-headed as hell," refusing to accept "a single conclusion drawn or support a single recommendation made." "Twenty years ago he would never have raised the type of objections he has here," Huston complained, "but he's getting old and worried about his legend." He recommended that Nixon call the director in for a "stroking session," convinced that Hoover would listen only to the president.[7]

Nixon declined to take Huston's advice about meeting with Hoover. Instead he gave verbal assent to the Huston report's recommendations, authorizing Huston to ignore Hoover and put the plan into effect. When Hoover received Huston's notice announcing the new policy, he "went through the ceiling," in the words of one aide, demanding that Attorney General John Mitchell take up the matter directly with Nixon. In the meantime, Hoover did not exactly defy the president's wishes. Instead, he agreed to move forward—but only under a direct, written order from the president or the attorney general. "Despite my clear-cut and specific opposition to the lifting of the various investigative restraints referred to above and to the creation of a permanent interagency committee on domestic intelligence," he told Mitchell, "the FBI is prepared to implement the instructions of the White House at your direction." In other words, Hoover had no intention of being the fall guy for any "illegal" activities Nixon might be seeking.[8]

Nixon could read between the lines, and quickly rescinded his approval of the Huston Plan. "I knew that if Hoover had decided not to cooperate, it would matter little what I had decided or approved," he later explained. Appalled at watching Nixon give way to an unelected, seventy-five-year-old bureaucrat, Huston composed a last-ditch message appealing to the dignity of the president's office. "At some point, Hoover has to be told who is President," he wrote in late August 1970, once the battle was all but lost. "It makes me fighting mad, and what Hoover is doing here is putting himself above the President." It was a fair point, but not one that Nixon cared to acknowledge.[9]

HAD THE POLITICS ALIGNED DIFFERENTLY, HOOVER'S BUREAUCRATIC VIRTUOS-ity might have earned him a certain amount of respect within the White House—

proof that even at the age of seventy-five, he still knew how to do political battle and win. Instead, the meltdown of the Huston Plan confirmed for many Nixon staffers what they had only begun to whisper about during the campaign: that Hoover was growing too old and obstreperous, and that perhaps it was time for him to go.

The FBI itself was growing rapidly. During Nixon's first few years in office, Hoover's budget nearly doubled, to $334 million (about the same as the State Department's), while the number of agents grew by about 30 percent, up to 8,900 by the end of Nixon's first term. At the same time, Hoover seemed less and less in control. While agents still feared and respected his power, they also spent a good deal of time strategizing about how to avoid his rules and get around his personal authority. Hoover's mercurial disciplinary system, once a fearsome pillar of Bureau culture, now looked to many of them like random and unnecessary punishment. In response, they adopted a "tell the man nothing" policy as a means of collective protection. Hoover knew it was happening. "I am noting more and more that officials of the Bureau are making decisions and committing the Bureau to certain action in substantive matters without first consulting me about them," he complained to Tolson. He did little to change his methods, though. One agent later described the situation as a "degenerate dictatorship": Hoover was still at the top, with his long-standing policy of "blind loyalty" in place. But fewer and fewer agents were buying into his system.[10]

Congress had tacitly recognized this problem in its 1968 crime bill, which sought to intervene in the structure of the FBI director's position. Under the new law, the president, not the attorney general, would nominate Hoover's successor to be approved by the Senate, the routine process for cabinet-level appointments. The next FBI director would be appointed for just ten years, longer than two presidential terms but far shorter than Hoover's tenure. The changes recognized how much Hoover had done to enhance the status of the FBI director's position over the past four and a half decades but also sought to take back some of that power. The idea was to preserve the position's apolitical character while ensuring that nobody else would stay in office for quite so long.[11]

The law had nothing to say on the next obvious question: Who could possibly replace Hoover? For years the easy answer had been DeLoach, the FBI's point man on all things public and political during the Johnson years. By 1969, though, DeLoach had lost his patron in the White House and his seamless relationship with Hoover was starting to fray. Despite his frequent protestations of loyalty, DeLoach had grown frustrated by many of the same things that baffled ordinary agents: Hoover's obstinance, his resistance to criticism, his blithe disregard for others' advice. In late April 1970, Hoover reprimanded DeLoach for planning a trip to American Legion headquarters in Indianapolis at the very moment when protesters were preparing to descend upon New Haven, Connecticut, where Bobby Seale and other Panthers were heading to trial. After years of swallowing his pride in such situations, DeLoach finally cracked, firing off a testy memo insisting upon his right to be treated as more than a mere underling.

"I have never deserted my post at any time when needed," he wrote to Hoover. "To the contrary, I give up ample leave each year simply because I feel that my responsibilities demand my presence in the office. I work every Saturday and many Sundays. It is most unusual for me to get a good night's sleep because of telephone calls from the office." A month later, following several rounds of "agonizing deliberation," DeLoach decided to submit his resignation. After more than a quarter century of working together, Hoover sent DeLoach on his way with a set of gold cufflinks, a few gold buttons, a mounted gold badge, and good wishes for a new life as a Pepsi executive.[12]

DeLoach's departure left William Sullivan, architect of Hoover's campaigns against Martin Luther King, the Klan, and the New Left, as the next most obvious candidate. Hoover liked Sullivan and even called him by his first name, a rare honor within the formal Bureau. But Sullivan, too, sometimes ran afoul of Hoover's temper. After receiving his own reprimand before the New Haven trial, he apologized in a self-critical memo. "Because of the nature of our work in the Bureau, necessarily we have to be pragmatists in the main," he wrote. "When something works out well, we have done the right thing, and when it does not, obviously we have done the wrong thing which happened in my case." Hoover rewarded his diffidence with a promotion into DeLoach's job, placing Sullivan in charge of all investigative, intelligence, and public relations operations. No sooner did Sullivan take up the post than he, too, began to lose patience with Hoover. In October 1970, just three months into his new job, he made the mistake of admitting publicly that the Communist Party is "not nearly as extensive or effective as it was a number of years ago." Hoover chastised him for minimizing the situation, predicting that Sullivan's words "will no doubt result in difficulty" convincing Congress and the public to fund ongoing anticommunist work. Rather than fight Hoover, Sullivan gave in. "I would prefer not to give any more speeches as long as I remain in the Bureau," he wrote in a memo to Tolson—an early hint that he, too, might not be around to succeed Hoover as director.[13]

THE INFIGHTING TOOK ITS TOLL ON HOOVER, NOT LEAST BECAUSE TOLSON, HIS one true intimate and ally, could no longer provide the accustomed support. By 1970 Tolson was blind in one eye, tended to drag one of his legs, and could no longer use his hands with any dexterity. Hoover insisted that Tolson come into the office anyway, a daily spectacle of agony that put many younger officials on edge. Even as Hoover bid farewell to DeLoach, he refused to let Tolson retire, finagling another special deal to avoid the mandatory retirement age of seventy. "My alter ego is Clyde Tolson," he explained to a reporter. "He can read my mind. It doubles my work when he is not here." In truth, Tolson could barely keep up with his Bureau duties. Hoover tried to encourage him with tough love, walking several steps ahead rather than falling back to Tolson's pace. He also considered setting up a punching bag for Tolson to hit when it all became too much. "I can leave my problems behind when I leave the office at night," Hoover said. "Tolson can't and he needs to get rid of his tensions." In Hoover's narrative, it was Tolson who was sick, Tolson who was growing old, Tolson who was finding it difficult to cope. But Hoover's volatile treatment of his subordinates suggests that he, too, needed an outlet for his frustrations.[14]

He directed at least some of his anger toward the press, where speculation about his retirement and declining competence had started to chip away at his once-invincible image. According to Gallup, the FBI still boasted an impressive approval rating in the summer of 1970, with 71 percent of the public reporting a "highly favorable" view. All the same, approximately half of Americans felt that Hoover needed to retire. The polls reflected an important shift in Hoover's public identity. For much of his career, he had succeeded in promoting himself as a bipartisan figure, admired by Democrats and Republicans alike. By 1970, he could no longer pull it off. "Now the case of J. Edgar Hoover has been added to the list of issues—ranging from the war in Viet Nam, to race relations, welfare and the plight of the cities—which are the source of deep division across America today," wrote pollster Louis Harris. Hoover's strongest support came from Nixon's so-called Silent Majority: working- and middle-class whites, residents of the South and Midwest, with incomes under fifteen thousand dollars and a high school education or less. His favorable ratings were falling precipitously among "younger adults, Easterners and persons with a college background," according to Gallup—in other words, among college-educated liberals. The surveys did not separate out Black opinion, but there Hoover's reputation was no doubt declining even faster, as his tirades against King and the Panthers did their work. According to Harris, the chief complaint among those surveyed was "that the FBI head is beyond his prime and is no longer doing as effective a job as could be done." But that sentiment only captured part of what was taking place. After a lifetime of straddling the liberal-conservative divide, Hoover was now despised by one side and beloved by the other.[15]

One sign of his declining support among liberals came from former attorney general Ramsey Clark, who wrote of Hoover's "petty and costly" style of leadership and "self-centered concern for his reputation" in his new book, *Crime in America*, published in the fall of 1970. A similar critique was proffered by William Turner, a former agent whose writing in *Ramparts* magazine had made him the New Left's go-to authority on the FBI. The Washington press corps began to gang up as well, promising to reveal Hoover's juiciest secrets after years of adulation. The most influential attack came from Washington Merry-Go-Round columnist Jack Anderson, heir to his former boss Drew Pearson's position as king of the political muckrakers. Day after day Anderson took it upon himself to expose the seamier side of Hoover's reign: how Hoover had allegedly seen a psychiatrist; how he siphoned off money from Bureau book deals into his personal accounts; how Clint Murchison had repeatedly allowed "the durable old G-man and his faithful companion Clyde Tolson, both bachelors" to stay at the Del

Charro for free. Anderson went so far as to collect and analyze the trash Hoover left behind his house, a deliberate invasion of privacy in revenge for the FBI's "peephole practices." (He found that Hoover liked spaghetti and meatballs, crab bisque soup, and peppermint ice cream but needed heartburn medicine to help with digestion.)[16]

At the *Los Angeles Times*, reporter Jack Nelson took things still further. In his own series of articles, he attacked Hoover for matters ranging from the personal gifts he demanded from his agents to the FBI's lack of accountability on racial violence. There was even talk of pushing toward the third rail of FBI coverage: the rumors of Hoover's homosexuality. When Hoover caught wind of that possibility, he called Nelson's editor in for a vicious dressing down. "He was intense," the editor recalled in a panicked memo. "It was quite evident that he was upset, particularly on the question of the homosexual charge." Hoover threatened to sue for criminal slander and succeeded in getting that particular article shut down.[17]

He fumed over the press coverage as "hokum," "an absolute lie," and "just a lot of hog-wash," while individual reporters and critics earned even more unsparing labels: "sick columnist," "skunk," "whore-monger," "bleeding-heart," "jerk" with "mental halitosis." Like Nixon, he reserved much of his bitterness for *The New York Times* and *The Washington Post*, Eastern liberal papers supposedly conspiring to destroy his reputation. Under duress, he often extended that view to other publications. "I put the *Sun* in the same category as the *Washington Post* and the *New York Times*," he informed the Baltimore SAC in May 1970, responding to the coverage of a local Panthers case. Such papers were "left-wing and trying to downgrade law enforcement and not support it."[18]

DeLoach had once made it his job to prevent Hoover from engaging in direct spats with the press. Sullivan either lacked the independent judgment to save Hoover from himself or cared less about doing so. The results were disastrous. In November 1970, furious about Ramsey Clark's attacks, Hoover called the former attorney general a spineless "jellyfish" during a newspaper interview. The following month, *Time* quoted him musing aloud about the violent tendencies of Mexicans and Puerto Ricans ("They don't shoot very straight. But if they come at you with a knife, beware") and King's moral vicissitudes ("I held him in complete contempt because of the things he said and because of his conduct").

Even on occasions when Hoover's words were carefully scripted, he showed increasing levels of vitriol and instability. In an appearance before the appropriations committee, he outlined a fantastical "conspiracy" by anti-war activists "to kidnap a highly placed government official" (later revealed to be Kissinger) and hold him hostage until Nixon called off the bombing campaign in Southeast Asia. In a hectoring "Open Letter to College Students," he urged young people to resist the entreaties of campus "extremists" who "ridicule the flag, poke fun at American institutions, seek to destroy our society." From college administrators, he demanded the "courage and guts" to expel such students and to control their own faculty, who were "worse than the hippies." When the former governor of Kentucky went so far as to punch a "long-haired student" in the midst of a demonstration, according to the local paper, Hoover sent a note cheering the bold action. He even found it hard to sympathize with the four students shot and killed by National Guardsmen during an anti-war demonstration at Ohio's Kent State University, informing the White House that "the students invited and got what they deserved."[19]

To liberals and leftists, Hoover's diatribes made him seem more out of touch than ever, a relic from the benighted and preachy past. But even Nixon and his aides worried that Hoover's political value was fast eroding. "Several new controversies have changed the minds of some of Hoover's most ardent defenders in the White House," former Nixon counsel Clark Mollenhoff noted in early March 1971. "Some moderates and conservatives are now expressing the view that the 76-year-old Hoover must be replaced before the 1972 campaign gets under way." In a letter to the president around the same time, speechwriter Pat Buchanan took note of Hoover's declining approval ratings and argued that it was time to cut the FBI director loose. "My strong recommendation would be to retire Hoover now in all the glory and esteem he has merited and deserved," Buchanan wrote, "and not let him—for his own sake and ours—wind up his career a dead lion being chewed over by the jackals of the Left."[20]

BUT THE "JACKALS" WERE JUST GETTING STARTED, AND WHEN THE NEXT BITE came, it did more damage to Hoover's reputation than any single event in his lifetime. On the night of March 8, 1971, burglars broke into the tiny FBI resident office in Media, Pennsylvania, a drowsy suburban town southwest of Philadelphia. They left behind the office valuables—cameras, radios, typewriters, Dictaphones, guns—but took something immeasurably more precious to Hoover. After picking the locks on the office filing cabinets, they cleared out the documents, making off with stacks of paper showing what the FBI did day-to-day. It was the first time since the Coplon case, twenty-two years earlier, that raw files had slipped out of Hoover's control. Even worse, these files were floating around in public, and he had no idea who took them, what the burglars planned to do with them, or how to get them back.

Local agents discovered the break-in around seven forty-five a.m. on March 9, realizing within minutes that "all serials and notes in these cabinets are missing," as they explained in a horrified cable to Washington. When Hoover arrived at the office and heard the news, he "went into a towering rage," in the words of one witness. Within hours, he opened the MEDBURG ("Media Burglary") investigation and dispatched almost two hundred agents on "urgent" and "top priority" status to Philadelphia, where it was assumed that the burglars would be found within local anti-war and New Left circles. That assumption was confirmed when a group calling itself the Citizens'

Commission to Investigate the FBI contacted a Reuters reporter to announce that it had "removed files from the Media, PA, office of the FBI" and planned to study the files to determine "the nature and extent of surveillance and intimidation carried on by this office." Apparently not realizing the significance of the tip, Reuters declined to make much of the story, and the local papers reported only that a burglary had taken place at the Media office without specifying what had been stolen. For almost two weeks, Hoover held out hope that the secret would hold until the FBI could locate the burglars and retrieve the files, thus preventing a "serious" blow to the Bureau's operations and reputation. "Final damage will hinge primarily on extent of disclosure of various documents and whether they are revealed to unfriendly, subversive or hostile elements," a Bureau assessment predicted.

Democratic senator George McGovern dashed Hoover's hopes on March 22, when an aide called the FBI to report the arrival of a mysterious envelope at McGovern's Senate office. Inside were photocopies of more than a dozen FBI files, plus a note from the Citizens' Commission urging him to "disseminate it (or not) according to your own judgment." One of the enclosed FBI documents spoke about interviewing anti-war protesters as a way to "enhance the paranoia endemic in these circles." Another revealed Hoover's orders to investigate every Black student union in the country on grounds that "the violence, destruction, confrontation and disruptions on campuses" made widespread surveillance necessary. Left-wing activists had long speculated about the FBI's practices, certain they were being watched and manipulated. Now they had the documents to prove it.

In addition to sending the documents to McGovern, the burglars delivered copies to Congressman Parren Mitchell of Maryland and to three newspapers despised by Hoover: the *Los Angeles Times*, *The Washington Post*, and *The New York Times*. Though Mitchell, McGovern, and the *Los Angeles Times* turned the documents over to the FBI, the *Post* and *The New York Times* decided to move ahead with publication. The *Post* justified its decision on the basis that "the records afford a glimpse, not often granted to the general public or even to committees of Congress, of some of the ways in which the FBI works." Other glimpses emerged periodically over the next several weeks, as the burglars mailed out their haul in strategic increments.

The worst of the documents exposed previously confidential surveillance programs, including Hoover's instructions to recruit "ghetto informants" to report on urban conditions and civil rights protests. Others revealed some of the quirks and petty indignities of life under Hoover, including his insistence that the FBI reject all "long hairs, beards, mustaches, pear-shaped heads, [and] truck drivers" seeking Bureau employment. But the most important revelation of all went unnoticed, at least at first. Among the dozens of documents released by the commission was an article from *Barron's* magazine recommending that college administrators crack down on student dissenters. Attached was a cover sheet ordering the dissemination of the article under the auspices of New Left "COINTELPRO," the first time that the word "COINTELPRO" had appeared outside of government circles. Reporters covering the story missed that detail—which did not, in any case, signify much to those not in the know. Hoover took this as a hopeful sign, urging the field offices to "continue aggressive and imaginative participation in the program" even as he instructed them to cut back on what they were committing to paper. By the end of the month, though, his sense of caution took over. On April 28, after fourteen years of "neutralizing" and "disrupting" social movements that ran afoul of FBI priorities, Hoover reluctantly ordered a halt to COINTELPRO.[21]

AMONG LIBERALS AND LEFTISTS, THE RELEASE OF THE MEDIA DOCUMENTS marked the end of whatever was still left of Hoover's reputation as the limited-state, good-government figure that they had once embraced and admired. House Democratic leader Hale Boggs came out swinging with a series of House-floor speeches detailing Hoover's failures, weaknesses, and abuses of power. Boggs claimed to be a disappointed Hoover admirer. "What I am going to say I say in sorrow, because it is always tragic when a great man who has given his life to his country comes to the twilight of his life and fails to understand it is time to leave the service and enjoy retirement," he explained. In addition to the subterfuge exposed in the Media documents, Boggs accused Hoover of wiretapping members of Congress, then using what he knew to buy their silence. He called on fellow politicians to stand up to the director for once rather than cowering in fear.[22]

Several members of Congress took him up on the challenge, mustering the courage to deliver their own speeches about Hoover as an example of state-based professionalism fallen into disgrace. Most were liberal Democrats and (not coincidentally) likely candidates for a 1972 run against Nixon. Maine's Edmund Muskie assailed Hoover for sending agents to observe the first Earth Day, as innocuous and peaceful as protests in 1971 could get. Massachusetts senator Ted Kennedy, endeavoring to carry on his slain brothers' legacy, called for Hoover to step down and open the FBI to congressional investigation. McGovern gave an even more frank assessment of Hoover's reign, delivered at some length to *Playboy* magazine. "Hoover should have resigned 25 years ago," McGovern said. "He has become paranoid." As proof, he cited "the FBI's own documents, from the files in Media, Pennsylvania," which showed how little Hoover cared about observing constitutional limits and how willing the FBI director was to lie to the nation.[23]

The press made the most of the drama. During April and May, several major national newsmagazines put Hoover on the cover—and not, this time, to pay homage to his professionalism and integrity. *Newsweek* purported simply to be raising questions: "Hoover's FBI: Time for a Change?" *Life* was more forthright, depicting Hoover as a Roman patriarch, his bust carved in marble as the "Emperor of the FBI." *Time* got cute by noting that the current controversies seemed to be "Bugging J. Edgar Hoover," while *The New York Times* gave him a new moniker: "The Man Who Stayed Too Long." Worried that any reaction by Hoover would only make things worse, friends and allies begged him not to respond directly to the press but "to let my friends on the Hill take care of it," as Hoover grumbled to Deputy Attorney General Richard Kleindienst.[24]

Those friends did at least some of what they promised, though their response arguably exacerbated the partisan divide building around the director and the methods he employed. From April into May, as the left jeered at Hoover's "paranoid" tendencies and old-man prejudices, a loyal array of congressmen put themselves on record as his staunch supporters. Among them were several former FBI agents now serving in the House. "I am shocked, I am disgusted, and I am upset by the stench of red herring in this Chamber," one declared. In the Senate, longtime allies such as Barry Goldwater, James Eastland, and Strom Thurmond stepped up to praise Hoover yet again as "one of our greatest living Americans," in Goldwater's words, now being subject to "slander unworthy of the halls of Congress." On May 10, Hoover's forty-seventh anniversary as Bureau director, more than seventy members of Congress, a large percentage of them Republicans, put themselves on record with statements extolling Hoover's virtues.[25]

Among conservatives, the Media documents only increased enthusiasm for Hoover's FBI, with its willingness to tackle "those tough and distasteful things" necessary to keep Americans safe, in the words of columnist James Kilpatrick. "The case against the F.B.I. is very weak," William F. Buckley agreed in his newspaper column, dismissing the criticism of Hoover as "mostly ideological" carping, designed to allow leftists and criminals to run amok. Few commentators made much distinction between Hoover and the broader institution; after more than four decades, they were one and the same. California governor Ronald Reagan, the rising star of the conservative movement, saluted Hoover in a speech before the California Peace Officers' Association as "one of America's greatest law enforcement officials," now being subjected to an unfair and deeply "bitter verbal assault." A newsletter affiliated with Phyllis Schlafly raised the possibility of a conspiracy—"Can the 'Get Hoover' campaign be traced to a common Communist source?"—while Norman Vincent Peale urged Hoover to ignore the whole thing. "Please tell him to pay no attention to all the pipsqueaks," Peale instructed his audience at a Knights Templar dinner gala. "They are nothing more than gnats on the hide of an elephant—and I certainly meant no disrespect by the term, elephant."[26]

Under the circumstances, Nixon saw little choice but to throw in his lot with Hoover, despite the tensions over the Huston Plan—and despite the growing desire among White House staffers to be rid of Hoover altogether. On April 16, the president sat down for a long and searching interview in front of the American Society of Newspaper Editors, an institution all but guaranteed to give wide publicity to whatever he said. He devoted several minutes to Hoover, portraying his old friend as a well-meaning public servant "taking a bad rap on a lot of things" in what should have been his joyful twilight years. He also showed how well he knew Hoover, predicting that the "unfair and malicious criticism" coming out of Media would lead Hoover to "dig in" rather than consider retirement. When Hoover expressed his thanks during a phone call with Nixon, the president explained, "I always stick by my friends—you know that." It was an acknowledgment of their long history together, if not necessarily an accurate account of the president's latest thoughts about his FBI director.[27]

Just as Nixon had predicted, Hoover refused to entertain the idea of stepping down. "I have a motto in my office which reads as follows: 'When the going gets tough, the tough get going,'" he wrote to a friend in California. "This is my philosophy and the way I am meeting the current attack." He apparently concluded that in order to move forward, he would have to stop letting other men speak on his behalf. For his grand reentrance he chose a dinner in honor of Martha Mitchell, the gregarious and much-gossiped-about wife of the attorney general. On the night of May 24, Hoover showed up at the Shoreham Hotel in a tuxedo for the occasion, heading directly to the bar for a stiff glass of Jack Daniel's before turning to face the crowd.

The room was full of reporters, mostly members of the American Newspaper Women's Club, which sponsored the event. They were stunned to see Hoover there. "J. Edgar Hoover, to understate it, is not a regular on the Washington party scene," one newspaper noted. They soon began peppering him with questions: not only about the latest round of criticism and his possible retirement, but about the youth counterculture and the new fashion of hot pants and the relative merits of country comedian Minnie Pearl, who was the evening's entertainment. It was a perilous situation for Hoover, in which he might at any moment burst out with the sort of comments that had been getting him into so much trouble. On the whole, though, he stuck with his mandate to appear cheerful and relaxed. Questioned by reporters about his critics, he merely smiled and shrugged. "It doesn't bother me at all," he insisted. "I've been under that kind of pressure for 40 years."[28]

When asked to introduce Martha Mitchell, Hoover delivered his lines with a rare touch of self-deprecation. "I know that those of you who subscribe to an alleged National picture magazine may have had difficulty recognizing me in the conventional clothes I am wearing this evening," he read from a prepared script, referring to the *Life* spread depicting him as a Roman ruler, "but, like ordinary people, we 'Emperors' do have our problems, and I regret to say that my toga did not get back from the cleaners on time."[29]

FOR A FEW WEEKS AFTER THE MITCHELL DINNER, IT LOOKED AS IF HOOVER AND Nixon might be back on track, their political alliance secure despite all the twists and turns. The idyll did not last. On June 13, *The New York Times* began printing a series of classified papers revealing government deception in the planning and execution of the Vietnam War (soon to be known as the Pentagon Papers). The fact that the papers had been leaked by someone in the defense establishment thrust Nixon and Hoover back into the situation that had plagued them for much of 1969 and 1970, with Nixon pushing Hoover to be more aggressive in hunting down the leaker and Hoover, in Nixon's words, "dragging his feet." Hoover worried about media sensitivities toward the presumed leaker, a RAND Corporation analyst named Daniel Ellsberg. He also had personal ties to Ellsberg's father-in-law, the toymaker Louis Marx, and hesitated to insult his friend. "We ought to be awful careful what we do in this case of this man Ellsberg," Hoover warned Nixon on July 1, arguing that the press would be only too happy "to make a martyr out of him." But Nixon "did not care about any reasons or excuses," as he later acknowledged in his memoir.[30]

Over the next several weeks Nixon made two fateful decisions in response to Hoover's reluctance to pursue Ellsberg. First, he authorized the creation of the Plumbers, a team of independent intelligence operatives—including former FBI agent G. Gordon Liddy—who would act at the behest of the White House, fixing "leaks" and doing the dirty tricks that Hoover refused to do. He also decided, reluctantly and with trepidation, that the time had come at last to ease his old friend Hoover out of office.

The confrontation took weeks of planning, as Nixon aides speculated about the right strategies and made their case about why it had to happen now. Above all, Nixon wanted to prevent Hoover from exposing the White House wiretaps and other secrets. There was also the broader political equation to consider. After building his campaign around Hoover's law-and-order politics, Nixon did not want to risk a revolt by his own silent majority on Hoover's behalf. He could also use Hoover's anticommunist bona fides as he prepared to open diplomatic relations with China. Picking up on Nixon's dilemma, columnists Rowland Evans and Robert Novak noted that Hoover was unlikely to resign voluntarily. "Any private White House suggestion that he do so likely would trigger a public blast from Hoover, stirring the director's legion of supporters and shaking Mr. Nixon's tenuous conservative constituency," they wrote. "Besides, administration officials fear any official criticism of Hoover would play into the hands of the far left's campaign to discredit law enforcement."[31]

The upshot was that Hoover would, indeed, have to retire willingly. "If he does go, he's got to go of his own volition," Nixon explained to Attorney General John Mitchell. "That's what we get down to, and that's why we're in a hell of a problem." His staff spent the late summer and early fall of 1971 brainstorming how to make that happen, entertaining ideas as far-fetched as allowing Hoover to keep his car and personal staff after retirement, or even bumping him up to the Supreme Court. Throughout it all, Nixon continued to treat Hoover as the same confidant he had always been. In mid-June, Hoover attended Tricia Nixon's wedding at the White House, an invitation reserved for the family's "oldest and closest friends." On July 1, after the Supreme Court ruled that the Pentagon Papers could continue to be published, Nixon called Hoover to complain that the justices were a bunch of "clowns" and "bastards," and that *Wash-*

ington Post publisher Katharine Graham was nothing more than an "old bag." (Hoover preferred to describe her as "an old bitch.")[32]

While Nixon dithered, the uncertainty began to create problems at the FBI, with its backlog of ambitious younger officials. Sullivan caught on early to the discontent at the Nixon White House, and sought to nudge it along with regular complaints and updates. Still hoping to position himself as the modern, with-it heir to Hoover's power, he fired off memo after memo laying out his critique of Bureau culture, from his fellow officials' "lack of objectivity, originality, and independent thinking" to the fact that ordinary agents "said what they did because they thought this was what the Director wanted them to say." The plan backfired, though, and Sullivan soon found himself, like DeLoach before him, cast out of the director's inner circle. In July 1971, Hoover sidelined him by promoting Inspector W. Mark Felt into the newly invented position of deputy associate director. The title made Felt the number-three man at the Bureau, though his actual job, as Hoover made clear in a one-on-one meeting, was mainly to "control Sullivan." Recognizing the slight for what it was, Sullivan decided to go out with a bang. In late August, he wrote a letter to Hoover scorning the "'yes men,' 'rubber stamps,' 'apple polishers,' flatterers, self-promoters and timid, cringing, frightened sycophants" who populated the Bureau's upper ranks. To no one's surprise, Hoover asked him to resign. "I don't want yes men but I want men to give me their views, and, when I make a final decision, I want them to carry them out," Hoover explained, apparently seeing little irony in the idea that Nixon might want the same thing from his own FBI director. In his final act of defiance, Sullivan handed over the transcripts of the so-called Kissinger wiretaps—the ones Hoover had placed on presidential staffers and press figures—to an assistant attorney general loyal not to the FBI but to the White House.[33]

Nixon's own confrontation with Hoover came a few weeks later. The president's staff instructed him to be forthright about setting a real retirement date while promising that Hoover would leave office with "full honors (medal, dinner, etc.)," unmistakably showered in glory. They even wrote out the best way to deliver the news. "Edgar, as you can imagine I've been giving your situation a great deal of thought," read Nixon's script. "I am absolutely delighted that you have weathered the attacks upon you and the Bureau so well." But, the script went on, the time had come for Hoover to announce that he would serve just one more year "and that then you will retire on 'senior status'" following the presidential election.[34]

When the moment arrived, though, Nixon "flinched," in Ehrlichman's words. Hoover came to the White House for breakfast at Nixon's invitation, sitting alone with the president for almost an hour. According to Nixon, Hoover expressed no great enthusiasm about retiring. Nor, however, did he refuse to do so. Instead, he adopted the same strategy he had used with the wiretaps and with the Huston Plan, agreeing to go along with Nixon's agenda as long as it came as a direct request. Faced with the prospect of firing Hoover rather than gently easing him into retirement, Nixon backed off. Instead of letting Hoover go, Nixon ended up promising approximately a 20 percent increase in personnel for the FBI's foreign offices.

Over the next several weeks, Nixon puffed himself up to nudge Hoover out of office but came away defeated again and again. "I was told five times that Hoover would be fired," one Justice official recalled. "The last time, for sure, they told me was on October 5, 1971." In his memoirs, Nixon maintained that he simply could not bring himself to "desert a great man, and an old and loyal friend, just because he was coming under attack." To his aides, though, he revealed something more acute: a fear of Hoover's skill at wielding power, and a sense that even the president was no match for the FBI director. Perhaps because of their friendship and deep affinity, he recognized in Hoover a determination to carry on no matter the cost. "We may have on our hands here a man who will pull down the temple with him, including me," Nixon warned.[35]

Hoover relished the victory, not yet aware that it would be the last great triumph of his career. Despite everything that had gone wrong in recent months—the Huston Plan tensions, the theft of the Media documents, the erosion of his reputation—he looked forward to 1972 as a year when he would once again be able to assert his own priorities. "There has to be somebody at the top to make those decisions," he explained to a subordinate. "The President and the Attorney General have left me here," he added, and "I intend to continue to make them."[36]

CHAPTER 58

One of the Giants

(1972)

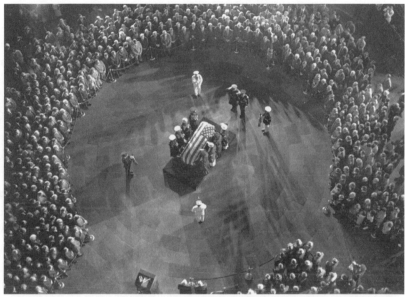

Hoover's body lying in state at the Capitol, May 3, 1972. Hoover is the only federal civil servant ever to be accorded that honor.   ASSOCIATED PRESS

In late December 1971, despite everything, Hoover joined Nixon for dinner at the little white ranch house in Key Biscayne, known affectionately among insiders as the Southern White House. The meal evoked old times together in Miami: fat stone crabs like the ones they shared in the fifties, followed by a Grand Marnier soufflé, the dessert that was "our favorite in the days when we visited Maxim's," as Hoover wrote to Nixon in a note of thanks. Though several other cabinet members and advisers attended, the occasion was deliberately informal. Nixon and Hoover sat for photographs in flowered easy chairs, one of the presidential dogs sprawled at their feet. When Nixon flew back to the capital a few days later on Air Force One, he invited Hoover to ride along as an honored guest. As the plane approached Washington, Nixon surprised Hoover with a birthday cake covered in white frosting and edged with red and orange flowers. The official photo shows Hoover grinning across at the president, a little boy delighted but self-conscious at being the center of attention. It was his seventy-seventh birthday and he appeared to be just where he wanted: surrounded by friends and well-wishers, welcomed at the innermost sanctum of presidential power.[1]

The impression did not last. The bureaucratic struggles of the past few years had been too bitter, and Hoover's interests too much at odds with those of the White House, to make for any permanent reconciliation. Though Hoover had won most of those bruising battles, the victories had damaged his relationships not just in the White House, but in Congress, the media, and the Bureau itself.

ON JANUARY 1, HOOVER'S ACTUAL BIRTHDAY, ANTI-WAR PROTESTERS KICKED off the year with a picket line outside the White House. Many wore flak jackets and blue jeans—the "usual anti-war garb," in one reporter's scornful words—but others came dressed in suits, ties, and dresses to mark the dawn of the new year. Around two p.m., as the picket line broke up, they gathered for a bonfire on the White House Ellipse. In the bright cold of the afternoon, they shared wishes for peace, then launched into a series of "anti-war Christmas carols." One was dedicated to Hoover. "Sing choirs of agents, sing in adoration," they belted to the tune of "O Come All Ye Faithful." "Sing ye, o sing ye, to J.E.H."[2]

Around the FBI, though, few people remained to sing Hoover's praises. DeLoach and Sullivan were gone. Hoover's own generation, the men and women who had been at his side since the beginning, was barely hanging on. Tolson was sicker than ever, shuffling into the office for just a few hours each day. Sam Noisette retired in 1968 and chauffeur James Crawford stepped down after hospitalization for brain surgery. Helen Gandy went on medical leave in March 1972, a rare concession to human frailty. Hoover kept up a jokey front. "If I did not know you better," he wrote to Gandy as she lay ill at home, "I might think you were just taking advantage of this beautiful spring weather we are having."[3]

But there was no avoiding the basic math, or the ongoing string of personal losses. Frank Baughman, Hoover's dashing comrade from Kappa Alpha, died in the fall of 1971 after what the papers described as a "short illness." When Hoover appeared in Daytona Beach to attend Baughman's funeral, reporters were shocked at what they saw. "He quite obviously had difficulty maintaining his balance on his arthritic-torn legs," one wrote, describing Hoover as "grim-faced" and "tired-looking" behind his dark sunglasses. Several agents swarmed Hoover as an official escort but, perhaps afraid to touch the great man, they could not prevent him from stumbling on the stairs between the funeral home and the sidewalk. When Hoover reached his white limousine, he was forced to reach down and lift his deadened legs into the seat by hand. He "now appears to be a man silently suffering great physical pain," one observer concluded.[4]

Not long after returning from Daytona, Hoover learned that Walter Winchell was in the hospital, suffering from the excruciating final stages of testicular cancer that had metastasized to his bones. Winchell's life had been one long saga of misery in recent years: the suicide of his only son in 1968, followed by the death of his long-time partner in 1970 and the loss of his beloved newspaper column. Press coverage now said that Winchell was in "serious but not critical condition," and Hoover dispatched an upbeat note bidding him "a quick and complete recovery." After four decades of friendship, this was their last correspondence. Winchell died three weeks later, a shrunken wraith at just 110 pounds.[5]

Hoover conceded nothing about his own state. "I am indeed fortunate in being blessed with excellent health," he told *The New York Times* in December 1971. But even his tried-and-true allies were no longer persuaded by the false front. In January, the *Star*'s Jeremiah O'Leary, long one of Hoover's greatest Washington acolytes, wrote an article hinting that the time had come for the director to step down. "The last year was a rough one for Hoover and the FBI," O'Leary wrote. "The brusque and thin-skinned director at times seemed cast in the role of a man besieged." The article included hurtful comments from an array of anonymous FBI officials (most likely including Sullivan and DeLoach), who attributed Hoover's decline to the fact that "he no longer has around him the kind of take-charge guys who used to save him from snap decisions and the hip-shooting that have been getting him into the headlines lately." Even they expressed a certain mournfulness about watching him falter. "Nobody wants to see him humbled after all these years," an anonymous agent told O'Leary. "But he ought to leave of his own accord and with honor instead of while wolves are tearing at him."[6]

While Hoover remained in office, though, the wolves kept coming, as fierce and fast as ever. In April, Congressman Cornelius Gallagher charged the Bureau with "corruption at its worst," and with planting "innuendo" about Hoover's political enemies—Gallagher included—in national magazines. (In private conversation, he threatened to reveal on the House floor that "the director of the FBI and the Deputy Director of the FBI have been living as man and wife for some 28 years," a charge that he never dared utter in public.) From the ranks of ex-agents, a dissenter named Robert Wall emerged to renounce the FBI as "a repressive organization, seeking to suppress organizations which it thinks deviates from the orthodoxy." From the world of publishing, not one but two biographical exposés promised to reveal his innermost secrets. "Unlike God, John Edgar Hoover admits to no mistakes," one of them began, followed by more than two hundred pages dissecting and dismissing the most treasured myths of Hoover's half century in office.[7]

By all accounts Hoover appeared to be annoyed but unbowed by the attacks, unwilling even now to give in and step down. In late April, he traveled to New York for the annual lunch of the Banshees, an ingathering of the most powerful publishers in the news industry, where his host William Randolph Hearst Jr. found him cheerful and "in the pink of health." Upon his return to Washington, he plunged back into business as usual. On the night of May 1, he went to dinner at Tolson's apartment, then returned home to Thirtieth Place and ventured upstairs to bed. Sometime over the next few hours, his heart stopped. He died alone, but with the world still watching.[8]

THE OFFICIAL STORY, RECORDED IN A MEDICAL EXAMINER'S "DEATH REPORT," is that Annie Fields ("female, Negro, 59 years") found Hoover's body. She had prepared Hoover's breakfast, but grew concerned around eight thirty when he didn't appear on time. She waited a few minutes, then went up to his bedroom, where she found him in "an unconscious condition in bed." Another version (and perhaps the more likely one) suggests that it was actually James Crawford who found Hoover. Though he had retired from the Bureau in January, Crawford had come to Thirtieth Place to supervise the installation of some rose plants, one of the few people Hoover trusted to do work around the house. When Fields noticed that Hoover hadn't come down for breakfast, she asked Crawford to go upstairs, since Hoover was known to sleep in the nude. In that version of the story, Hoover was found not peacefully in bed, but sprawled on the floor, as if he had fallen while returning from the bathroom.[9]

In any case, it was either Fields or Crawford who called Tolson, who called Gandy, who called Assistant to the Director John Mohr, the highest-ranking official on the Bureau's administrative side. Mohr later estimated that Gandy phoned "a few minutes after 9 o'clock," at which point Hoover's death became a political event. Mohr notified Acting Attorney General Richard Kleindienst, who instructed him to make sure that Hoover's office was "secure" before the news leaked out too widely. Back at Thirtieth Place, Hoover's personal physician arrived to examine the body and proclaimed the cause of death to be "hypertensive cardiovascular disease." At the Bureau, word spread quickly among Felt and other top officials.[10]

Nixon, too, soon learned of the morning's events. Upon hearing from Haldeman that Hoover had died overnight, after forty-eight years as FBI director, Nixon burst out with an expression that was one part surprise, one part grudging admiration. "That old cocksucker!" he supposedly exclaimed, before turning to the question of what, exactly, was supposed to happen next.[11]

NIXON SEEMS TO HAVE EXPERIENCED HOOVER'S DEATH AS AN AUTHENTIC blow, the loss of a man who had been part of his inner circle since his first rough-and-tumble years in Washington. "He was my best personal friend in government," Nixon told his special counsel, a claim that he would repeat countless times in the subsequent days. In conversations with aides, speechwriters, and cabinet members, Nixon described Hoover over and over again as a friend "in a very close and intimate sense," with "about ten times as much" history together as Nixon's next closest relationship in Washington.[12]

Nixon did not forget that he had been trying—and failing—to push Hoover out for at least the past year. Instead, he expressed gratitude that the end had come the way it did: Hoover dying with his boots on, never giving the "bastards" in the "goddamn press" the satisfaction of actually forcing him out. Nixon could now freely rewrite Hoover's final year, casting the White House as the director's great defender "through thick and thin." "Oh, he died at the right time, didn't he?" Nixon asked Haldeman. "Goddamn it'd have killed him . . . to lose that office. It would have killed him."[13]

As Nixon described things, Hoover was no longer the intransigent old man of the past few years, but a tough and brilliant friend of a quarter century's standing. Hoover's death was also, inescapably, a political occasion—"the biggest death story since Eisenhower" in 1969, according to Nixon, and one that could yield substantial benefits for the White House. "While we're all sad about it," he told one aide, Hoover's demise was sure to revive talk of the "law-and-order issue," a subject on which "there is no better way for me to identify than to identify with my friend Hoover." It also raised the question of who would possibly attempt to fill Hoover's shoes. In that sense Hoover's death was far *more* significant than Eisenhower's, since Eisenhower had long been out of power, whiling away the time at his farm in Gettysburg, Pennsylvania, when he succumbed to heart disease. Hoover died before loosening his grip on the director's position. He left behind an institution suddenly leaderless for the first time in forty-eight years.[14]

The most urgent order of business for Nixon should also have been the simplest: somebody had to let the public and the press know that Hoover was dead. Within minutes of receiving the news, Nixon began discussing how best to break the story and frame it to White House advantage. Kleindienst believed that the attorney general should deliver the briefing, since Hoover had been, after all, a Justice employee. Nixon felt it should come from the president. "I just have the feeling that I ought to make the announcement of his death," he explained around ten thirty. Nixon insisted that Hoover was a "national" figure, not just someone who happens to "work for the Attorney General."[15]

While the White House argued over logistics, the FBI was banned from revealing Hoover's death to anyone beyond a handful of top officials. The mandate created several awkward situations. When Helen Gandy called Crime Records to ask them to clear Hoover's schedule for the day, she had no explanation to offer for the sudden change of plans. A reporter showed up anyway for a prearranged morning interview, so officials at Hoover's office hemmed and hawed and left her sitting in the reception area. The intrepid journalist happened to be Lynda Bird Robb, Lyndon Johnson's eldest daughter, who was planning a fluff piece on Hoover's cairn terriers for *Ladies'*

Home Journal. Given her connections, Mohr finally broke down and authorized an agent to tell her the "bad news." From a pay phone outside the Justice Department, she relayed the message to her father in Texas.[16]

Nixon himself called Johnson a few minutes later, a matter of courtesy from one Hoover friend to another. "I know how much you thought of him," Nixon told Johnson, offering the comfort that "at least he outlived his detractors." Johnson said only, "I'm very sorry he's gone," calling Hoover a "good man" who would be missed by many. That afternoon, he sent Tolson a one-sentence telegram at home. "Lady Bird and I grieve with you," he wrote, a familial gesture of respect toward the relationship that Hoover and Tolson had built together.[17]

For the public announcement, Nixon and Kleindienst settled on a compromise: Kleindienst would reveal the death, then Nixon would enter the room, unannounced, to add a few personal words. Around 11:10, almost three hours after the discovery of Hoover's body, Kleindienst issued a statement from the White House briefing room announcing, "J. Edgar Hoover passed away during the night at his residence. His personal physician informed me that his death was due to natural causes." At that point Nixon walked in, looking as shaken as if he had just heard the news himself. In a ragged voice, he spoke of a "profound sense of personal loss," identifying Hoover as "one of my closest personal friends and advisors" for more than two decades. To honor Hoover's legacy, he ordered flags on federal buildings to be lowered to half-mast.[18]

Nixon fulfilled another set of personal obligations that evening, phone calls to the two people he felt might be grieving Hoover's death most acutely. One was Gandy, whom he praised as the "great secretary" who had made Hoover "a great man." The other was Tolson, who had stayed away from the FBI all day and was said to be in bad shape. "Clyde, on this day, I know you were Edgar's closest friend," Nixon began before starting to falter. In the way of condolence, he offered not only his "sympathies" but also a vow to push back one last time against the naysayers and the doubters who had plagued Hoover in his final months. "All of his damned detractors are going to look damned small," Nixon promised.[19]

THE HOUSE OF REPRESENTATIVES CONVENED AT NOON, FORTY-FIVE MINUTES after Nixon's briefing-room elegy. Over the next several hours, its members did little but talk about Hoover. For the first time since at least 1969, most of what they said was complimentary, the trials and tribulations of recent years washed away in a flood of nostalgia. House majority leader Hale Boggs, whose attacks had eviscerated Hoover just the previous year, set the rapturous tone. "There is no man who has served this country with greater dedication, with greater love, and with greater productivity," he now declared. Boggs compared Hoover's death to Roosevelt's sudden collapse in the spring of 1945, at a moment when the country could hardly imagine life continuing under another president. "It is equally difficult to comprehend the passing of Mr. Hoover," Boggs maintained.

Thus began a grand spectacle of bipartisan tribute. A few minutes after noon, Congressman Williamson Stuckey of Georgia introduced a resolution to place Hoover's body in state at the Capitol rotunda, an honor previously accorded just twenty-one times, always to elected officials or members of the military. The House passed the measure with no objections. So did the Senate, which rushed to tack on a second resolution in Hoover's honor. In the mid-1960s, construction had begun on a new building for the FBI, located just across Pennsylvania Avenue from the main Justice headquarters. With Hoover now gone, the Senate voted to name the building in his honor, with support from both the House and the president.[20]

Hoover had given his final interview to the Springfield, Missouri, *News & Leader,* one of the small-town publications that had always loved him best. In that interview, published on April 23, 1972, he repeated his preferred version of his life story, in which he grew the FBI from obscurity to greatness based on "certain basic principles"—among them, a commitment to "merit," to "non-political" professionalism, and to respecting limits of federal jurisdiction. With his death, that well-worn narrative became the foundation for countless obituaries, editorials, and feature articles, testament to the lasting power of the original Hoover myth. "He rigorously forbade FBI men from engaging in partisan politics in any way, shape or form," *The Providence Journal* wrote in a typical obituary. The *Journal* was just one of dozens of publications to fall back on a story that had been told to them for decades by one of the most effective publicity operations in government.[21]

In article after article, the highlights of Hoover's early life were laid out for the nation to weigh and measure: his family's deep roots in Washington, his God-fearing but humble childhood, his birthright of career government service. The 1930s and 1940s still came across as Hoover's glory days, with the FBI's heroic victories over Dillinger and Pretty Boy Floyd and the Nazi saboteurs. But smaller, more personal memories received their due as well. The busboy at the Mayflower described how he always buttered Hoover's toast on both sides, then trimmed off the crusts and cut it into two equal pieces—"one for Mr. Hoover, one for Mr. Tolson." To mark Hoover's death, the Mayflower left his customary front-corner table empty, crisscrossed by red, white, and blue ribbons to remind fellow guests of the director's lifelong patriotism.[22]

In many parts of the country, the public's judgment was laudatory to the point of hero worship, especially among the white middle-class constituencies who had long risen to Hoover's defense. "The FBI director has come possibly closer than any other public figure to speaking out for the average man and women [*sic*] in America—the great mass of people sometimes referred to as a 'silent majority,'" declared the *Chronicle* of Augusta, Georgia. *National Review*, still the essential text of the conservative movement, marveled at Hoover's ability to please such audiences while leading "an agency that is in many ways the very image of the modern superstate—faceless, powerful, adapted to the latest technology, almost inhumanly efficient." The magazine attributed this feat to Hoover's origins in the early twentieth century, when belief in federal power had yet to become a stand-in for what the editors sneeringly dismissed as liberal values. By implication, no future director would be able to do what Hoover had done: carry on as a devout conservative and a technocratic state builder at the same time.[23]

Whether liberal or conservative, though, nearly everyone agreed on one point: the outstanding feature of Hoover's career was how long it had lasted. "J. Edgar Hoover stood guard over America through the trials of the twenties, the turmoil of the thirties and the horrors of war in the forties, fifties, and sixties," one Democratic congressman recalled in an admiring speech on May 2. Most Americans could not remember a time without Hoover as FBI director, prodding and scolding the nation to live up to his vision. Whatever one might think of that vision, the fact that he was now gone seemed profoundly strange, "as if the Washington Monument was no more," in the words of the *Chicago Tribune*. And unlike the collapse of a physical structure, there could be no rebuilding what was lost. "There probably will never be anybody like Mr. Hoover again," a *Christian Science Monitor* writer concluded. "Nor should there be."[24]

TWENTY-SEVEN HOURS AFTER THE DISCOVERY OF HOOVER'S BODY, A BLACK hearse pulled up to the steps of the Capitol, where a military honor guard stood waiting in a funereal downpour. Hoover's official ceremony of mourning began at the base of the Capitol steps, as the honor guard hoisted his casket onto their shoulders and began a long, dignified trudge up to the rotunda. Hoping to shield Hoover's body from vandals, Gandy and Mohr had chosen a lead-lined casket weighing more than half a ton, and the honor guard nearly buckled under the weight. Once inside the Capitol, they laid the casket down atop a rough pine catafalque, draped in black velvet, that had originally been built to receive Abraham Lincoln's body. John Kennedy had been honored the same way in 1963, after the shock of his assassination. Two other presidents, Herbert Hoover and Dwight Eisenhower, had lain in state at the Capitol as well. Hoover was the first unelected civil servant ever to be accorded the honor.

Edward Elson, Hoover's minister of long standing, now the Senate chaplain, was on hand to accept the body and offer a short blessing. Just after eleven o'clock, hundreds of other federal dignitaries began to stream into the rotunda, amassing in a circle behind the velvet ropes around Hoover's casket. Nearly the entire Senate came, trickling out from chambers and offices throughout the Capitol. The House opened and then closed its official proceedings so that members could process to the rotunda together, with none other than Hale Boggs up front. All nine Supreme Court justices showed up, their black robes setting them apart from the crowd. So did most of the

Cabinet plus a few assorted governors, including California's Ronald Reagan, who happened to be in town. Nixon stayed away, preserving his star power for the church funeral scheduled for the following day. Other than that, nearly everyone who mattered in Washington seemed to be present—an unmistakable display, even in death, of Hoover's power and influence. Fifteen of the congressmen were former FBI agents, huddled together in a group. The top fifteen officials of the Bureau stood next to them, with one important exception. Said to be "taking this pretty hard," according to Mohr, Tolson appears to have stayed home.

Chief Justice Warren Burger delivered the four-minute eulogy, a posthumous seal of approval from the highest court in the land. He narrated Hoover's life as the story of a local boy made good, rising "from modest beginnings" to "the pinnacle of his profession." Burger pointed out the critical role that Harlan Stone had played in Hoover's career by giving the untested young administrator a chance to reform the struggling Bureau. From that point on, Burger said, Hoover had navigated "crisis after crisis" with impressive equanimity, balancing "efficiency in enforcement of laws" with "constitutional limitations." He attributed Hoover's success to the director's willingness to express his "patriotism" and "Christian faith" even when others seemed inclined to scorn them.

As the senators, congressmen, justices, and cabinet officers dispersed back to the nation's business, the public began to trickle in, moving in a slow, circular procession along the velvet ropes. First in line to pay their respects were Lou Nichols and his son, John Edgar, who had witnessed the ceremony from back in the crowd, with Nichols weeping quietly. FBI employees and other law enforcement officers would have the rotunda to themselves from eight to ten in the evening, after the day's work had been done. Other than that, the rotunda was open to all who wished to attend, and they came in droves, "mourners from every walk of life," in the words of one wire-service report, up to a thousand people per hour. Many were tourists: Girl Scouts, student groups, or families on a pilgrimage to Washington, happy to take in a free glimpse of history. Others were local residents, police officers and federal workers who saw something of themselves in Hoover. As *The Evening Star* pointed out, Hoover was "nothing if not a proper Washingtonian," that rare born-and-bred creature who attained the highest ranks of government work. "Today in Washington, a city that was built and populated by bureaucrats, they are mourning the man who was probably the most powerful of them all," the paper observed. All told, approximately six thousand people viewed Hoover's body during the twenty-two hours that he lay in state.[25]

Not everyone who showed up at the Capitol during those hours came with respect and good wishes. At noon, as Burger was delivering Hoover's eulogy, a small cluster of congressmen, staffers, and anti-war protesters began their own vigil outside in the pouring rain on the Capitol steps, reading out the names of the war dead, young men whose lives were cut short long before they could realize their ambitions. Overnight, it turned into a candlelight "liturgy on the air war," featuring quotations from Vietnamese peasants and U.S. bomber pilots about the damage the war was doing, read by anti-war celebrities such as folk singer Judy Collins and Daniel Ellsberg, who had leaked the Pentagon Papers. Upon hearing rumors that the protesters planned to storm the Capitol and overturn Hoover's catafalque, the White House sent operatives to the scene with instructions to mingle and try to turn the situation to Nixon's political advantage—by attacking the protesters if necessary. Though they pushed around at least one anti-war demonstrator, the most vocal counterprotest came from the thirty College Republicans who showed up with signs reading, "Support Our President," eager to heckle their left-wing rivals.

According to *The Washington Post*, Hoover's mourners largely avoided both gatherings, aside from the occasional complaint that the anti-war protesters were being "disrespectful" to the late FBI director. The protesters themselves could not help but point out the day's strange math, with "a handful" of Americans mourning the deaths of some forty-eight thousand soldiers while "thousands" showed up to pay their respects to a single federal servant.[26]

AT THE WHITE HOUSE, THE MOST PRESSING QUESTION ON THE AFTERNOON OF May 3 was who would succeed Hoover—a man who, almost by definition, could not be replaced. "The death of J. Edgar Hoover . . . poses a grave problem for President Nixon in terms of politics, administration, and national security," one columnist noted, observing that Nixon's choice could not possibly satisfy everyone. As they contemplated Hoover's legacy, the newspapers offered up lists of possible successors: FBI insiders such as Felt or Mohr, or perhaps a prominent police chief such as Philadelphia's Frank Rizzo. Nixon had his eye on someone less obvious: a lanky ex-submariner and assistant attorney general named L. Patrick Gray. A Nixon supporter, Gray possessed certain essential qualities that Hoover had lacked. He was understated, pliable, modest, and loyal to the White House.[27]

Nixon's idea was not necessarily to appoint Gray as permanent FBI director, but to use him as a placeholder, an "acting director" who could fill the position until after the November election. Strategizing about how to present this choice to the public, Nixon instructed press secretary Ron Ziegler to frame it as an act of homage to Hoover, a way of keeping the FBI insulated from "the whims of partisan politics." To other aides, he was more frank about his agenda. Under the 1968 crime bill, any permanent FBI director would have to be approved by the Senate, currently under Democratic control. Given the continuing fallout from the Media burglary, confirmation hearings were likely to "open up the whole damn FBI business," Nixon speculated, and to produce "the goddamnedest investigation" of the FBI that the country had ever seen. In Nixon's nightmare vision, the next several months would be consumed by revelations about the

FBI's secret surveillance policies and harassment of Martin Luther King. A Senate investigation might even reveal the wiretaps that Hoover had initiated on behalf of the White House, a political disaster that could cost Nixon the election.[28]

Appointing Gray as acting director was supposed to solve that problem. In addition, it would give the White House "a presence in the bureaucracy over there," as Nixon and Haldeman agreed in one conversation, an insider voice less loyal to the FBI than to the president. Ehrlichman expanded upon this strategy in a lengthy memo to Nixon, prepared in the harried hours after Hoover's death and before Nixon's meeting with Gray. As a public servant, Gray was well known for his "loyalty, ability and demonstrated competence," Ehrlichman wrote—with an emphasis on the first of the three. Nixon could thus ask Gray to defuse whatever land mines Hoover might have left behind: "to locate and sequester all surreptitious investigation of the Administration or its personnel in which Hoover may have engaged for protective purposes." The chief job of the acting director, as Ehrlichman described it, was not to preserve Hoover's mythical nonpartisan independence, but to bend the FBI, at long last, to Nixon's will. "Gray's primary assignment is to consolidate control of the FBI, making such changes as are necessary to assure its complete loyalty to the Administration," Ehrlichman wrote. The Nixon White House underestimated just how difficult that would be. The mission would ultimately put Gray on a collision course with what was, even in death, still Hoover's institution.[29]

Nixon made it clear that he expected more deference from Gray than he had gotten from Hoover. At the same time, he hoped Gray would hold on to at least some of Hoover's hard-punching style. "You've got to be a conspirator, you've got to be totally ruthless, you've got to appear to be a nice guy, but underneath you need to be steely tough," Nixon informed his new FBI director. "You know that, believe me, is the way to run that bureau."[30]

FELT LATER RECALLED THE SHOCK AND DISMAY THAT SWEPT THROUGH THE Bureau's upper ranks at the news of Gray's appointment on May 3. "It did not cross my mind that the president would appoint an outsider to replace Hoover," he later wrote, lamenting the "many trained executives" passed over in favor of Gray. As the number-three man under Hoover and Tolson, Felt had assumed that he would at least be in the running for the job. He also counted himself a Hoover man, trained to resist encroachments by outsiders and to protect the Bureau's autonomy in the face of political pressure. That afternoon, though, Felt grudgingly welcomed Gray to the FBI. "Frankly, most of us were hoping the president would select an insider," he told his new boss, "but I can assure you that all of us will do everything we can to help you."[31]

Not all Hoover's former employees were so accommodating. According to John Mohr, Gray had put in a mysterious appearance at the Bureau not long after Hoover's death, inquiring into Hoover's "secret files," the object of Washington gossip and speculation for at least a generation. Gray was acting in his capacity as assistant attorney general, not yet as FBI director. Perhaps as a result, Mohr brushed him off. Gray returned the next morning, just before nine a.m., to ask again about where the secret files were hidden. This time, Gray was more "agitated," Mohr recalled, and Mohr "got a little agitated myself," suspicious that Gray was less concerned with protecting Hoover's legacy than with locating any "secret files that would embarrass the Nixon administration." When Gray warned, "I am a hardheaded Irishman and nobody pushes me around," Mohr spat back that *he* was "a hardheaded Dutchman," ready to do what needed to be done to safeguard Hoover's Bureau.

There were, in fact, two major sets of files in Hoover's office, materials that had been sequestered from the general system under his explicit instructions. The first was the Official & Confidential File, 164 folders containing information of such exquisite sensitivity that it was kept under lock and key in Hoover's filing cabinets. Their title suggested a systematic designation, but the collection was mostly a hodgepodge of reports and rumors, some dating as far back as the investigation into the 1920 Wall Street bombing. If there was no hard-and-fast rule for what made it into the O&C File, though, certain investigations were obvious: the inquiries into John Kennedy's sexual assignations, the "special" performed for Johnson at the 1964 Democratic convention, the wiretaps, bugs, and dirty tricks against King. In one of his few moments of official engagement following Hoover's death, Tolson ordered the O&C File transferred to Mark Felt, who was, implicitly, supposed to shield them from any outside query. That included inquiries from the Nixon White House, which was assumed to be looking out for its own interests, and not necessarily those of Hoover's Bureau.

The other collection consisted of what was known as the Personal File, papers of special significance for Hoover's private life rather than necessarily for the Bureau's business. Hoover had begun sorting through those folders in the months before his death, fearful that he would soon be forced to retire and lose control of their contents. He gave up quickly. Gandy later insisted that the files consisted overwhelmingly of personal correspondence—"letters from and to, and the original letters from, and the carbon of letters to personal friends." Congressional investigators would conclude, with good evidence, that official Bureau documents were in there as well. In either case, what Gandy did next constitutes a painful loss for the historical record. Before his death, Hoover asked her to destroy the entire Personal File. She began carrying out his wishes on the day he died and continued on for at least two months, tearing up each piece of paper before sending it along for shredding or incineration.[32]

AROUND THE SAME TIME THAT HOOVER HAD ORDERED THE PERSONAL FILE destroyed, he also set about revising his will, the last best evidence of who and what really mattered to him. The final version was the document of a patriarch, albeit one without a wife or children, aimed at rewarding the handful of intimates whose relationships with him had involved submission and dependency. A lump sum of $5,000 went to Gandy, who had spent more than half a century keeping his schedule and executing his wishes. To James Crawford and Annie Fields, whose domestic labors had been so critical to his life at Thirtieth Place, he gave $3,000 and $2,000, respectively. Crawford also received Hoover's clothing, which he was supposed to split with Hoover's longtime receptionist Sam Noisette. Hoover gave nothing to his nieces and nephews, or to any blood relative, the final indignity in a lifetime of unraveling family relations. But he did recognize his two namesakes—John Edgar Ruch, son of his college friend and Palmer Raids coconspirator George Ruch, and John Edgar Nichols, Lou Nichols's son—with gifts of jewelry and cufflinks. Everything else—the house and dogs, the photographs and autographs, the oil investments and jade collection and nude statuary—went to Tolson, now recognized as the equivalent of Hoover's spouse and next of kin.[33]

Hoover's funeral operated according to a different logic, less a mapping of personal sentiment and obligation than a final grand political show. Nixon attended to many of the details, consulting with speechwriters and aides about the proper venue and setting, and about the political message he hoped to send. "We're gonna have a hell of a ceremony for him," Nixon had vowed within hours of Hoover's death, picturing something "big"—a "national memorial" befitting Hoover's status and popularity. Nixon had hoped to stage the funeral out at Arlington National Cemetery, with its magnificent outdoor amphitheater, but Hoover had requested to be buried in the family plot at Congressional Cemetery, making the stalwart National Presbyterian Church a more logical choice. Nixon accommodated that request—apparently Hoover's only one—as long as the funeral included one key element. "It might be that I have to give the eulogy myself," he told Haldeman, convinced that his personal history with Hoover made him the "one who can do it right."[34]

Over the next day and a half, Nixon met several times with the young speechwriter assigned to draft the eulogy. He spent the morning of May 4 rehearsing their words in the Oval Office, as aides popped in and out to discuss Vietnam, talks with the Soviets, and the delicate question of funeral seating arrangements. At the Capitol, police stood at attention while the military honor guard carried Hoover's thousand-pound casket back down the steps and into a waiting hearse. From there, a motorcade—one patrol car, plus eleven officers on motorcycles—escorted the hearse across town to National Presbyterian in time for the eleven o'clock funeral. Toward the end of the journey, as the motorcade approached the church along Nebraska Avenue, officers from the Metropolitan and Park police joined in the pageantry, lining the road in one last law-and-order salute.[35]

Edward Elson opened the service with a prayer spoken from a low wooden table positioned just behind Hoover's flag-draped casket. Many of the readings that followed might have been spoken at any Presbyterian funeral, well-worn passages intended to wrest meaning out of death. Elson also spoke more personally of Hoover's religious journey—how the young man had supposedly longed to become a minister, how he came to believe that enforcing the law could be a way of serving God—and expanded the morning's readings to include passages that Hoover might have liked. From Corinthians, Elson spoke of putting away "childish things" and taking up the burdens of manhood. From Ephesians came the admonition to "stand against the wiles of the devil" and to maintain discipline in the face of temptation. From Timothy came a passage declaring, "I have fought a good fight, I have finished my course, I have kept the faith," sentiments Hoover surely would have appreciated.

The only other speaker that day was Nixon himself, somber if not tearful as he spoke from a raised white pulpit at the front of the room. The eulogy contained little that had not been said in the papers: Hoover as law-and-order icon, as nonpartisan patriot, as professional administrator, respected if not always loved by much of the country. Certain comments had an edge to them, as Nixon decried the "disorder, disruption and disrespect for law" sweeping the land and recalled Hoover's scorn for the "permissiveness" that allowed it to happen. He declared Hoover "one of the giants" of American history, a public servant who "stayed at his post" from the difficult days after World War I up through the present, as "eight Presidents came and went, while other leaders of morals and manners and opinion rose and fell." When the eulogy was complete, Elson joined Nixon for a moment of silence, their backs to the pews and their heads bowed in respect. After a prayer of amen sung by the Army Chorus, the honor guard hoisted Hoover's casket onto their shoulders and led the way out of the church, followed by a procession of dark-suited, mostly gray-haired G-Men according to rank.

Only then did the more personal side of Hoover's life once again take precedence, as a motorcade—eleven vehicles this time, plus the motorcycle escort—rolled off for Congressional Cemetery. Of the two thousand people at the funeral, just a few dozen made their way to the cemetery, where Hoover was to be buried alongside his mother, his father, and the sister he had never met. Like the political pageant at National Presbyterian, this smaller, more intimate service reflected something important about how Hoover had lived his life: after seventy-seven years, despite all his fame and influence, his parents and siblings were still his only close family members. But the ceremony also recognized that there were other relationships that had mattered—one above all. Before Hoover's coffin was lowered into the ground, the honor guard removed the American flag draped across the top and folded it into a crisp-cornered triangle. Then they handed it to Tolson, in quiet acknowledgment of his forty-four years at Hoover's side. The crowd drifted off before the casket could be lowered into the ground, laying Hoover to rest in the federal city of his birth, where he had made such an indelible imprint as a Government Man.[36]

Epilogue

On the night of June 17, 1972, just over a month after Hoover's funeral, five men broke into the headquarters of the Democratic National Committee at the Watergate complex in Washington. They had pulled off a similar operation three weeks earlier, planting listening devices on selected phones before slinking back into the night. Now they were returning to adjust the wiretaps. To ensure that they could get out the way they got in, they placed a piece of duct tape over the lock on the door to the underground parking garage. When a security guard noticed the tape during inspection rounds, he called the police, who arrested all five men, thus setting in motion the improbable political saga known as Watergate.

Over the next two and a half years, as Watergate slowly but inexorably consumed his presidency, Nixon found himself thinking back upon his friendship with Hoover, longing for the sort of protection that he imagined Hoover might have been able to provide. Despite their differences over the past few difficult years, Nixon clung to the idea of Hoover as a true loyalist and ally, the one dependable soul in a city of feckless men. "There were times—and Lyndon Johnson told me this same thing—when I felt that the only person in this goddamned government who was standing with me was Edgar Hoover," Nixon mused in the winter of 1973, as everything was starting to unravel. White House counsel John Dean took the idea even further, arguing that Hoover might have been the one person able to contain the Watergate scandal before it reached the White House. "I think we would have been a lot better off during this whole Watergate thing if he'd been alive," Dean told Nixon, "'cause he knew how to handle that Bureau."[1]

As it was, Watergate proved impossible for Nixon to contain—and the same forces that brought him down ultimately came for Hoover's FBI. After years of anguish and disillusionment over Vietnam, Watergate unleashed a new age of cynicism about government conduct and about the men and women who chose to make politics their profession. By 1975, that sense of outrage extended to the FBI, as Congress delivered for the first time on its long-standing promise to investigate Hoover's secretive and insular institution. When it was all over, decades of FBI secrets—from COINTEL-PRO to wiretapping to what Hoover had done to Martin Luther King—were laid bare to public scrutiny. Just before his death, Hoover had spoken with a senator about his wish to have been born twenty years earlier, so that he might have passed on before seeing what became of the modern world. As it turned out, he died just in time to avoid witnessing the public repudiation of his life's work and the destruction of his reputation.[2]

GRAY BEGAN HIS TERM AT THE FBI BY TRYING TO DO WHAT HOOVER HAD DONE in 1924: crack open the windows to let in some fresh air. In the weeks after Hoover's death, Gray announced in quick succession that he planned to hire women as agents, expand minority recruitment, and allow existing employees to grow out their hair. He cut down on Hoover's "awesome and formidable" flow of paperwork, reasoning that "there had to be a better way to manage and control this organization of superb human beings." He also tried to shift the FBI's internal culture, in which Hoover "had these guys so brainwashed they even talked like him." He abolished Crime Records, banned the use of the phrase "seat of government," and set up an office of planning and evaluation to explore what other changes might be necessary. Despite his status as *acting* director, Gray hoped to make the FBI "more open to legislative scrutiny, more responsive to public needs, and much less defensive and self-promotional," as his son later recounted.[3]

Gray did not understand what he was up against. Before he suggested a single reform, his appointment had already sparked "a wave of bitterness and suspicion between senior FBI officials and the White House," as the *Washington Daily News* noted in early May. Once the reforms began to take hold, that "bitterness and suspicion" began to coalesce into a bureaucratic rebellion, carried out by men who had trained under Hoover. Lou Nichols tried to warn Nixon of the peril ahead, drawing upon the goodwill he had earned through his service in the 1968 campaign. "I fear that a tragic mistake has been made, altho I hope not," he wrote in a May 19 letter, warning of the smoldering discontent among top FBI officials over the appointment of an outsider.[4]

Mark Felt stayed on as Gray's acting associate director, now the Bureau's number-two man. On the surface, he treated Gray as he had treated Hoover, soliciting favor by hanging Gray's "beautiful autographed picture" on the office wall and sending flowers to the hospital when his boss got sick. Beneath that surface, though, Felt was roiling with a career man's resentment. More than any other official, Felt interpreted Gray's appointment as a personal insult. He also worried about Gray's ability—or even desire—to withstand pressure from the White House, and to preserve the hard-won autonomy, privileges, and secrets of Hoover's Bureau. Like other executives, he mocked his new boss as "Three Day Gray," a reference to Gray's penchant for spending time away from Washington giving speeches or meeting field agents. He also set out to undermine Gray through a method that Hoover had once used with exquisite skill: manipulating the press. Felt was at once an opportunist and an avid student of Hoover's methods, especially when it came to protecting the Bureau's freedom of action.[5]

Into this stew of ambition, uncertainty, and competing agendas came the Watergate burglary—at first, nothing more than a bungled dirty trick by a few mid-level operatives. As the highest-ranking official with investigative experience, Felt was appointed to take charge of the federal inquiry. On the side, he plunged into what would become the most famous episode of leaking in the history of journalism. Within days of the burglary, he began sharing investigative details with a young *Washington Post* reporter named Bob Woodward, already an acquaintance and the occasional recipient of tips. Around the *Post* office, Felt became known by the pseudonym "Deep Throat."

Felt denied his role as Deep Throat until 2005, when, in ill health, he finally confessed to *Vanity Fair* and then published an updated memoir. Today, some close observers still doubt that Felt's revelation is the whole story, suggesting that Deep Throat must have been a composite or that Woodward and his partner, Carl Bernstein, must have had other sources. Whether Deep Throat was a hero, protecting the nation from malfeasance on high, or a self-interested actor, seeking professional advancement, remains a contested question. Whatever his motivation, Felt helped to keep the Watergate story alive at a moment when even Washington insiders showed little interest. But he did not, as the heroic legend might suggest, entirely get away with it. By October, Nixon suspected that Felt himself was the leaker, thanks to a tip from a press source. The White House decided not to act on the information, for fear that Felt would "go out and unload everything," in Haldeman's words, just as they had once worried that Hoover might "bring down the temple."[6]

That gamble paid off, at least in the short run. Nixon won the 1972 election in a landslide, taking every state except Massachusetts. The victory only accelerated his problems at the FBI. Having delayed the appointment of a permanent FBI director until after the election, in early 1973 Nixon faced the same dilemma he had encountered after Hoover's death: Should he appoint an outsider or one of Hoover's men? He chose to continue on with Gray, a misstep that one historian later described as Nixon's "most fateful and disastrous decision in this crucial period." Nixon acknowledged that Gray would have to be "careful" during the nomination hearings, given his reputation as a Nixon loyalist. Once it was all over, though, Nixon had hoped that Gray would be more like his predecessor as FBI director. Hoover "knew that he could trust me, I knew that I could trust him and as a result, he told me things," Nixon explained to his nominee, conveniently forgetting the struggles and mutual animosity that had characterized Hoover's final years. "The moment you're confirmed then I think we've got to have the kind of relationship we had with Hoover."[7]

Gray never got the chance to try. Far from being "careful" at the hearings, he was gloriously, ineptly honest, far more open than Hoover ever would have been. Where

Hoover had always refused to supply "raw" FBI files to Congress, Gray volunteered to let the committee review the entire Watergate investigation (an offer that left the Nixon White House apoplectic). He also revealed an agreement, made just days after the burglary, to allow White House counsel John Dean to sit in on all Watergate-related interviews. White House aides found the scene excruciating. "Let him twist slowly, slowly in the wind," Ehrlichman mused as the hearings wore on. In April, Nixon mercifully withdrew his nomination, but the revelations continued. Soon the press revealed that Dean had given Gray a stack of papers retrieved from the safe of Watergate burglar Howard Hunt and asked him—not in so many words—to dispose of the contents. "Had I been a Hoover," Gray later reflected, he would have held on to the files and used them "against Dean, Ehrlichman and the President." Instead, he burned them in the fireplace of his Connecticut home. Once the details came out, he took the whole disaster to heart. Gray contemplated suicide in the months after the hearings, but worried that "if I took my own life," there might be "no one to defend me."[8]

After Gray's withdrawal, Hoover's former deputy Lou Nichols wrote in to express "heartfelt sympathies," but also to note that the whole disaster could have been avoided simply by giving Hoover-era veterans the respect they deserved. "I cannot help but believe that had you summoned a few of the old timers at the very outset, you could have been spared a lot of grief, and I feel the results could have been entirely different," Nichols wrote. But Nixon showed less interest than ever in listening to the old guard. To replace Gray as acting director, he appointed William Ruckelshaus, a moderate lawyer and top administrator from the Environmental Protection Agency. Looking ahead, Nixon made no secret of the fact that he wanted the FBI "cleaned out"—starting with Felt, who resigned under pressure in June 1973.[9]

It would be another fourteen months before Nixon himself resigned, the first president ever to give up and leave office midterm. As the noose tightened, he continued to long for Hoover. "He'd have scared them to death," Nixon mused to Dean during the Gray hearings. "He's got files on everybody, God damn it." Nixon was exaggerating Hoover's power—but in any case, Hoover was not there to save him. To the contrary, the conflicts and tensions of Hoover's final years continued to play out as Nixon battled his way through the last painful months in office. As the Senate took up its own Watergate investigation, committee chairman Sam Ervin pushed well beyond the burglary and into the operations that had once caused Hoover so much worry: the Kissinger wiretaps, the Huston Plan, the creation of the Plumbers.[10]

When the final moments came, it was the attempt to interfere with the work of the FBI that helped to bring Nixon down. In late July, after months of court battles and political grandstanding, the White House was forced to turn over what would soon be known as the "smoking gun" tape, a conversation between Nixon and Haldeman recorded just a week after the Watergate burglary. In that conversation, they complained that Gray could not "control" the FBI, and that the burglary investigation was moving "in some directions we don't want it go." To head it off, they agreed to ask CIA leaders to call up the FBI and explain, untruthfully, that the "directions" they were following involved CIA operations and should be left alone. Upon its release, the conversation showed that Nixon had taken an active role in the cover-up after the burglary. It also fulfilled Nichols's warning that going to battle with Hoover's FBI—trying to bend the institution to another man's political will—might well prove to be "a tragic mistake." On August 8, 1974, three days after the tape's release, Nixon resigned the presidency.[11]

THE FBI TELEVISION SHOW WAS NOT RENEWED FOR ABC'S FALL BROADCAST schedule that year, its noble-agents theme increasingly at odds with the national temper. By that point, the Bureau had yet another director, former Kansas City police chief Clarence Kelley, who managed to be nominated by Nixon and approved by the Senate before Watergate engulfed everything. Kelley was more like what the old guard had wanted: he had served under Hoover for twenty-one years, from 1940 through 1961, though mainly in the field offices rather than under Hoover's thumb in Washington. As the first permanent director since Hoover, Kelley continued and extended many of the reforms initiated by Gray, slowly easing the FBI away from its insular Kappa Alpha culture and toward a more diverse, less hierarchical vision. At the same time, he sought to differentiate himself from Gray by launching an internal review of the FBI's Watergate investigation. Completed in July 1974, a month before Nixon's resignation, the report acknowledged certain missteps but mostly blamed "senior associates at the White House" who "conspired with great success for nine months to obstruct our investigation." Included among them was Gray, whose "naivete (or his villainy, depending on your point of view)" had forever tarnished the FBI's reputation for independence.[12]

Even as Kelley attempted to put Watergate to rest, other controversies began to crop up, most of them with roots in the bitter struggles of Hoover's final years. In July 1973, just days after Kelley assumed office, the Socialist Workers Party filed suit against the FBI for harassment and civil rights violations, based in part on the files stolen in Media, Pennsylvania. In December, after winning a judgment under the Freedom of Information Act, NBC reporter Carl Stern went public with an exposé of COINTELPRO—again based on initial clues from the Media burglary. The FBI never managed to find the burglars, an embarrassing failure in a high-profile case. When the conspirators finally revealed themselves in 2014, they were more or less the people Hoover had suspected all along: local anti-war activists committed to calling their government to account, including a professor from Haverford College and another from Temple University.[13]

Congress began its own investigations of the FBI in early 1975, taking advantage of Hoover's death and the momentum of Watergate to carry out what it had so often threatened but failed to do during his lifetime. In the House, a committee chaired by New York Democrat Otis Pike demanded documentation of the FBI's domestic surveillance programs and wiretapping policies, subjects that Hoover had long hoped to hide from congressional scrutiny. Toward the end of 1975, another House committee began asking questions about the disposition of Hoover's files in the hours and days following his death. The next year, the Justice Department itself started looking into corruption within the FBI's supposedly incorruptible ranks.

But it was the Senate that stole the limelight, just as it had during Watergate. In early 1975, Senator Frank Church of Idaho, one of the body's most liberal Democrats, announced that a newly designated select committee would be looking into the operations of not only the FBI but also the CIA, the NSA, and the rest of the intelligence establishment. Throughout 1975 and into 1976, the Church Committee kept the public riveted with hearings on CIA assassination plots, Mafia collusion, and secret LSD experiments. The Committee also revealed much of what Hoover had sought to keep hidden at the FBI. After a single day of hearings on Hoover's domestic intelligence policies, Senator Walter Mondale declared the witnesses' matter-of-fact descriptions "some of the most disturbing testimony that can be imagined in a free society."[14]

The committee's final report on the FBI hearkened back to the Palmer era, when "repressive activity" by federal authorities had first shocked the nation. "History Repeats Itself," the committee concluded, leaving Americans back where they had started half a century before. Throughout Hoover's career, the committee determined, the FBI had broken the reasonable rules and restraints set in place by Harlan Stone. As a result, "too many people have been spied upon" and "to [sic] much information has been collected," the committee concluded, resulting in a stifling of free speech far more hidden and subtle but no less dangerous than what had occurred during the Palmer era.

The committee supplemented its main narrative on the FBI with a series of reports on particularly egregious episodes supervised by Hoover. One examined the investigation into the Kennedy assassination, concluding that the FBI's actions were woefully "deficient" and that Hoover (among others) deliberately withheld information from the Warren Commission. Other reports looked into "COINTELPRO: The FBI's Covert Action Programs Against American Citizens," "The FBI's Covert Action Program to Destroy the Black Panther Party," and the neutral-sounding but jaw-dropping "Dr. Martin Luther King, Jr., Case Study." Beyond simply describing what had happened, the reports included copies of internal FBI correspondence, complete with Hoover's handwritten notes and signature. Through those documents, Americans learned for the first time of the anonymous letter sent to King, with its degrading sexual language and its call for King to undertake the "one thing"—suicide, in his friends' interpretation—that would set the situation right. They learned about the FBI's determination to "neutralize" the Black Power movement and prevent a Black "messiah," about its cartoons and fake rivalries and press campaigns. Certain aspects had been whispered about and reported on before, but it was different to see the documents firsthand, to read of Hoover openly plotting and discussing how to destroy entire social movements. "Unsavory and vicious tactics have been employed," the committee wrote, listing "anonymous attempts to break up marriages, disrupt meetings, ostracize persons from their professions, and provoke target groups into rivalries that might result in deaths," among other outrages.

The Church Committee hearings remain the single most significant inquiry ever undertaken by Congress into the conduct of the nation's intelligence agencies. And unlike so many of the controversies over civil liberties during Hoover's lifetime, they resulted in real reform. At the heart of the committee's analysis was the idea that Hoover's power, like the power of the CIA and other intelligence agencies, stemmed from a "failure to apply the wisdom of the constitutional system of checks and balances"— in other words, the failure of Congress to watch and contain the executive branch. To remedy the problem, Congress established the House and Senate intelligence committees, permanent bodies with the right to demand facts and documents from the intelligence agencies. It also broadened and strengthened the Freedom of Information Act, allowing ordinary citizens to do the same. At the Justice Department, Attorney General Edward Levi created new guidelines on domestic surveillance, with the goal of disrupting the secret bureaucracy that Hoover had established.[15]

The courts took action, too. In 1977, a federal district judge ruled that the recordings and transcripts from King's hotel rooms should be sealed for fifty years. In 1978, Felt, Gray, and domestic intelligence specialist Ed Miller were charged with conspiracy to violate the civil rights of Weather Underground members and their families during investigations into the New Left. According to the charges, the three men had conspired after Hoover's death to revive the wiretapping and bag-job techniques that had been curtailed in the mid-1960s. Though the charges against Gray were eventually dropped, a jury convicted Felt and Miller, the first intelligence officers ever convicted in criminal court for abusing Americans' civil liberties.[16]

All of this would have been anathema to Hoover—constraints that he would never have agreed to, or at least would have fought tooth and nail. And yet there were certain ways in which his example, even in death, also prevented more widespread reforms from taking place. The most popular interpretation of the Church Committee's report was that Hoover himself was mainly to blame—and that his death had taken care of most of the problems. The committee tried to push back against this view, insisting that a "long line of Attorneys General, Presidents, and Congresses" had "given power and responsibility to the FBI, but . . . failed to give it adequate guidance, direction, and control." But the story line that stuck ascribed responsibility mostly to Hoover, to his unique bureaucratic prowess and manipulation. Even on the committee, many members cast themselves—and, by extension, the rest of the public—as innocents, duped and deceived by a uniquely villainous man. "Virtually every family in the country would have screamed in protest no matter how much they disliked Dr. King or the Panthers or the Communists," one senator declared during the Church hearings, if only they had known and understood the full extent of what was happening.[17]

Lost in the wave of condemnation was one of the central facts of Hoover's life: whether or not they knew every detail of what he was up to, millions of people, from presidents down to the smallest of small-town editors, had always aided and supported him—not despite but because of his willingness to target those who challenged the status quo. At the highest ranks, certain government officials had in fact known a good deal about what Hoover was doing. They were routine recipients of briefings on "the application of disruptive techniques and psychological warfare," as Hoover put it in notes for one off-the-record appearance before Congress. "I want to assure you," Kelley added in a statement after Hoover's death, "that Director Hoover did not conceal from superior authorities the fact that the FBI was engaging in neutralizing and disruptive tactics against revolutionary and violence-prone groups." The statement exaggerated Hoover's openness, but it contained a grain of truth. Presidents, congressmen, and attorneys general understood the basic outlines of what Hoover was up to—and often chose not to know more.[18]

Even in 1975, there were those who tried to make the case that Hoover's FBI had been a response to the collective will, channeling a sense of national fragility and vindictiveness toward internal dissenters that was widely shared by many Americans. "We had cities being burned; we had educational institutions being bombed," one FBI official reminded the Church Committee of the COINTELPRO years. "So I don't find any basis in my mind to argue with their good-faith belief they were faced with a danger." A. Mitchell Palmer had made a similar case before Congress during the early 1920s, insisting that the raids, the Radical Division, and the anti-Red crusade had all been a matter of giving the public what it wanted. As in the 1920s, though, the argument failed to stick. In death Hoover ended up as the nation's greatest political villain, his name forever linked to the worst and most sordid aspects of the FBI's history, and to the idea that the government could not be trusted to protect the rights of Americans. What had begun during Hoover's life—the decline of his once-storied reputation as a Government Man—continued for years after his death, until almost nobody was willing to defend him.[19]

A HANDFUL OF POLITICIANS DID CONTINUE TO CHAMPION HOOVER AND THE FBI even after the Church revelations, if in ever-smaller numbers. Barry Goldwater, who served on the committee, accused his fellow members of adopting a "freewheeling, self-righteous, and frequently moralizing" tone in their zeal to destroy the intelligence agencies, whose abuses were, in any case, "thoroughly ventilated, if not overdrawn." After the conviction of Felt and Miller, Ronald Reagan came to the rescue, issuing a pardon and proclaiming them men of "high principle." Both statements confirmed what was increasingly the case—that defense of the FBI, like the defense of law and order, would increasingly be seen as a conservative issue.[20]

At the FBI itself, director Kelley initially shied away from criticizing Hoover, hoping to placate the Bureau's old-guard loyalists even as he eased the institution into a more temperate and uncertain future. After the Church Committee's reports, he felt compelled to respond, and to go on record with his own assessment of Hoover's virtues and vices. He chose Westminster College in Fulton, Missouri, as the setting for the historic occasion, the same place where Winston Churchill had famously warned of an "Iron Curtain" descending on Europe a generation earlier. Kelley began by lamenting how much of his time as FBI director had been spent "attempting to reconstruct and then to explain FBI activities that occurred years ago," under Hoover's leadership. Then he did something that Hoover never would have considered: he offered an apology. "Some of these activities were clearly wrong and quite indefensible," said Kelley. "We most certainly must never allow them to be repeated." The worst abuses he ascribed to "the twilight of Mr. Hoover's administration," when (it was implied but not said) the famous G-Man had somehow lost his way. At the same time, he asked that the American people try to take a balanced view of the men and women who had built the FBI under Hoover. They were neither the "superhuman" G-Men of long-standing popular myth, he insisted, nor "demons obsessed with grinding up American rights and sweeping them into the gutter."[21]

Hoover would get no such benefit of the doubt. In the decades since his death, the abuses exposed by the Church Committee have continued to define his legacy; his name conjures up images of backroom scheming and abuse of power, of secrets and lies and the politics of fear. He has been depicted as a racist and a demagogue, a single-minded seeker of power, a small-minded and twisted man intolerant of even his own desires— all rightly so. During his lifetime, Hoover did as much as any individual in government to contain and cripple movements seeking racial and social justice, and thus to limit the forms of democracy and governance that might have been possible. His actions damaged the lives of thousands of people—liberals and journalists, civil rights workers and congressmen, Black Panthers and communists. It is only fitting that his targets should have their say, and that their experiences should help to define his legacy.

And yet there is a certain loss in this image of Hoover as a one-dimensional villain, the embodiment of all that is worst in the American political tradition. For one thing, it makes him a too-easy scapegoat; his guilt restores everyone else's innocence. It also obscures what once seemed to be an ennobling vision of government service as a realm where professionalism, self-sacrifice, expertise, and efficiency would reach their highest form. One tragedy of Hoover's life is that he became what he swore he would never be, and thus undermined the very ideals that he had found so captivating as a young man.

But there, too, his story is not so singular, either as a human experience or as a political parable. Hoover built his image—however false and distorted it might have been—at least in part on the idea that public service was something to be admired, and that the federal government might act as a force for good. And he did this while holding firm to conservative principles; indeed, he saw no conflict between the two. Today, that kind of balancing act seems far more difficult. In his zeal to protect the "American way of life," Hoover helped to accelerate a turn against the federal government—indeed, against the very idea of government service—that is still a major feature of the modern right. At the same time, his reactionary politics and the abuses they inspired have made him—and the forms of government power for which he came to stand—anathema among leftists and liberals. The man who once garnered a 98 percent approval rating now has few admirers and almost nobody willing to claim his legacy, even within the FBI.

In 1975, in the midst of the Church Committee's investigations, President Gerald Ford dedicated the J. Edgar Hoover FBI Building, a hulking brutalist monolith built as the FBI's stand-alone headquarters on Pennsylvania Avenue. Today the building is slated for likely demolition, with a new headquarters to be constructed somewhere less conspicuous, perhaps in Maryland or Virginia. That building will no doubt bear a different name—and it should, for Hoover does not deserve the honor. But ceasing to honor him should not mean forgetting the complexities of his life and legacy. Whatever else he may have been, Hoover exerted unparalleled influence over American politics and society for more than half a century, as a committed conservative and as a government servant, as a single-minded bureaucrat and as a confused, sometimes lonely man. We cannot know our own story without understanding his, in all its high aspiration and terrible cruelty, and in its many human contradictions.[22]

ACKNOWLEDGMENTS

My mother rarely spoke of her childhood in Washington, D.C. I knew that her father worked at the Bureau of Engraving and Printing. I knew that her mother divorced her father and married the lead political cartoonist at the Scripps-Howard chain. To my surprise, researching J. Edgar Hoover's life helped me to fill in some of the gaps in her family history. It turns out that my grandfather attended George Washington University alongside Clyde Tolson; one went into the Bureau of Engraving and Printing, the other into the Bureau of Investigation. My step-grandfather also knew Hoover (and presumably Tolson) from the Washington press scene.

There are fewer traces of my mother herself, a young woman in a mid-century man's world. She died in 2008, before I began writing this book and before I knew what to ask about her childhood. I lost my father a few years later. Their steady and loving influence are here nonetheless.

I owe a major debt to my sister Karen, who offered housing, encouragement, and nephew fun in Boston and especially Washington, where she conveniently lived for several years within a few blocks of the FBI's J. Edgar Hoover Building. She always said "yes" rather than "again?" when I proposed a research trip. Plus, she managed to raise a spectacular fifth-grader during the time it took me to write this book.

In Washington, David Plotz, Hanna Rosin, Judith Plotz, and Paul Plotz provided two crucial summers' worth of housing, allowing me to explore Hoover's hometown in depth. At the FBI, John Fox was an indefatigable guide to Hoover-related research materials and an excellent lunch companion. Archivists at the National Records and Archives Administration—especially Richard Peuser—offered crucial support in accessing and understanding FBI records, while the research staff at the National Law Enforcement Museum—especially Lauren Sydney—provided invaluable access to Hoover's personal papers and photo collection. The staff at the FBI's Freedom of Information division responded to research queries with diligence (despite my status as a member of their "prolific requesters" list). At Yale, James Kessenides and Bill Landis guided me to Hoover-related sources within the library system and ordered new materials when needed. At the Associated Press, Matthew Lutts was especially helpful with photos and permissions, as was Amy Cary at Marquette University and Kirsten Carter at the FDR Library.

Many scholars and historians shared their research tips and Hoover-related materials, including Ray Arsenault, Mark Bradley, Arthur Eckstein, Mark Feldstein, Irwin Gellman, Steve Gillon, Brian Hochman, Ernie Lazar, Jennifer Luff, Daniel Mendelsohn, Luke Nichter, Jessica Pliley, Susan Rosenfeld, Joel Silverman, Timothy Stewart-Winter, Aaron Stockham, Athan Theoharis, and Jason Ward. Tony Summers and Robbyn Swann invited me into their home for a week and allowed me to poke around in their vast Hoover archive. Ed Gray granted early access to his father's papers and facilitated my first close-up view of bear cubs climbing trees.

A remarkable cohort of research assistants contributed time and talent to this book, including Kate Birkbeck, Jeff Friedrich, Anastasiia Posnova, Noah Remnick, Joshua Tait, Gabriel Winant, and Emily Yankowitz. In the project's fledgling stages, Nick Handler traveled far and wide to presidential libraries and D.C.-area archives; now, a decade later, he is a professor in his own right and we are lucky for it. Jacob Wasserman spent a summer at the National Archives and Records Administration, where he came across the first unredacted version of the "suicide letter" sent to Martin Luther King and did a deep dive into German internment records. Jay Driskell performed superb work in Washington and elsewhere; his professionalism and good humor kept the project moving along at crucial junctures. Andrina Tran is a historian, editor, and researcher of many talents. I relied on her insight and skill, especially in the final stages of the book. Readers can thank Andrina for strategic cuts to what could have been an even longer manuscript. Adam Waters and Joe Landman were top-notch fact checkers as the book went to press.

Several scholarly workshops, conferences, and lecture series gave me the chance to discuss my research with willing and thoughtful audiences, including the Cambridge American History Seminar, the 20th-Century American Politics and Society Workshop at Columbia, Princeton's American Political History Seminar, the Johns Hopkins Seminar in History, the Carl Becker lecture series at Cornell, and the Elmer Louis Kayser Memorial Lectures at George Washington University (Hoover's alma mater). Conferences sponsored by Harvard, the University of Michigan, the American Historical Association, and the Organization of American Historians, among others, provided inspiring interlocutors. At Yale, it was a thrill to discuss the FBI present and past with former director James Comey and my colleague Asha Rangappa (herself a former FBI agent), among many other campus events. I appreciate that students in my American Century lecture course, as well as my undergraduate and graduate seminars, allowed me to go on and on about Hoover. They reinforced my sense that he is a fascinating character but reminded me that humans born in the twenty-first century don't necessarily know him as a household name.

The New York Times, The Washington Post, Slate, The Nation, and the *Journal of Policy History* offered especially useful opportunities to write about Hoover over the years. *The New York Times Magazine* published the unredacted King "suicide letter" after I came across it in the archives (with Jacob Wasserman's help). In documentary film, I am especially grateful to directors Sam Pollard (*MLK/FBI*), Stanley Nelson (*The Black Panthers*), Alex Gibney *(Enemies)*, Susan Bellows (*The Bombing of Wall Street*), and Sharon Grimberg (*McCarthy*) for allowing me to talk about Hoover on camera.

The Yale History Department believed in me when this project was still in early stages. As individuals, many Yale faculty have taken time to offer advice, mentorship, collaboration, and insight along the way, including David Blight, Laura Engelstein, David Engerman, Joanne Freeman, Paul Freedman, Tamar Gendler, John Gaddis, Bryan Garsten, Glenda Gilmore, Emily Greenwood, Valerie Hansen, Elizabeth Hinton, Jonathan Holloway, Matt Jacobson, Paul Kennedy, Jennifer Klein, Naomi Lamoreaux, Katie Lofton, Mary Lui, Joanne Meyerowitz, Alan Mikhail, Sam Moyn, Bill Nordhaus, Steve Pitti, Paul Sabin, Emma Sky, Arne Westad, and Jay Winter. At the Grand Strategy program, Mike Brenes, Dan Kurtz-Phelan, Heather McGhee, Victoria Nuland, Rory Stewart, Jake Sullivan, and Evan Wolfson inspired me with ideas great and small. Caryn Carson, Liza Joyner, Liz Vastakis, and Kaitlyn Wetzel offered critical administrative assistance. Support from the Grand Strategy program and Yale's Keroden Fund helped to make such a large-scale research and writing project possible.

I am especially grateful to the many scholars, historians, and friends who took time to read and offer their expert views on sections of the manuscript. This book is much better thanks to their generosity, though whatever mistakes remain are all my own. Their ranks include John Fox, Glenda Gilmore, Anthony Gregory, Elizabeth Hinton, David Huyssen, Katie Lofton, Fred Logevall, Lerone Martin, Shari Motro, Donna Murch, Tim Naftali, Phil Shenon, Ellen Schrecker, and Timothy Stewart-Winter. Max Holland gave a thorough vetting to the chapters on the 1960s and 1970s, as did David Garrow, who knows almost everything there is to know about King and the FBI. My writing group—Edward Ball, Claire Potter, and Paul Sabin—patiently read vast swaths of the manuscript out of order and in draft form. We became fast friends along the way (though I was last to deliver a full book manuscript).

I did not subject most of my friends, in New Haven and elsewhere, to forced bouts of manuscript reading. I am nonetheless grateful for the many hours that they spent listening to my triumphs, anxieties, and frustrations (especially Myra Jones-Taylor, Tony Leiserowitz, Jenn Marlon, Matt Taylor, and Molly Worthen). My medical-care providers at Yale, NIH, and elsewhere kept me functional and pain-free enough to make my continued work on the project possible. Dan Perkins believed in this book and witnessed its evolution from idea to research to words on the page, though we did not see it through to the end together.

At Viking, Wendy Wolf embraced the book early on, waited patiently for a draft, and then gave it the enthusiastic but disciplined edit it needed. I appreciate her willingness to say yes more often than no. Andrew Wylie never wavered in his support for the book, or for me. He was the first to read (and like) the whole manuscript, a vote of confidence that came just when I needed it. At the Wylie Agency, Scott Moyers placed the book with Viking before deciding to return to the publishing side of the business. Fred Courtright did impressively efficient work in tracking down textual permissions. The great editorial and production crew at Viking, especially Terezia Cicel and Paloma Ruiz, made sure that all the working parts fit together.

I am fortunate that several of my closest friends also happen to be sensationally good writers and historians—and that they were willing to read this manuscript in full. Emily Bazelon is an extraordinary person—a true and steady walking companion, a great journalist, and one of the most generous souls I know. Kim Phillips-Fein has been my coconspirator in writing history, thinking about politics, and figuring out how to live a decent life since we met in graduate school. I fell in love with John Witt while I was struggling to finish this project. He makes all things seem possible. I am grateful to be sharing my life with him—and with Gus and Teddy, who have already taught me more about baseball, life, and family than they may know.

My son Nick has lived with our friend Edgar as long as I have—longer, if we measure by percentage of years on earth. When he was in third grade, I made a presentation for his class in which I talked a bit about Hoover and then fingerprinted the whole lot of them. I assured them that the book would be done by the time they finished middle school. Nick is now in college. From our bedtime "history facts" to our summers in Washington to our presidential-history road trips, he tolerated having a historian for a mom with good cheer, great curiosity, and the spirit of an enthusiast. This book is dedicated to him.

NOTES

Introduction

1. *The FBI Story*, directed by Mervyn Leroy (Warner Brothers, 1959); Demaris, *Director*, 69–71; interview of Cartha DeLoach by Susan Rosenfeld, November 12, 2005, FBI OH; McHugh, "Hoover Was Able," *San Diego Union*, May 4, 1972, B159, JEHS; LeRoy, *Mervyn LeRoy*, 200–1. On "bulldog," see, for example: Mitchell, "Unknown Side," *Prison Evangel*, May–June 1960, B129, JEHS; Talburt, "Nixon, Hoover," *WDN*, November 15, 1968, B144, JEHS; Anderson, "Millionaire Picked Up," *WP*, December 30, 1970, B150, JEHS.

2. For a review of the literature on Hoover and the FBI, including major biographies, see the Note on Sources.

3. For a review of relevant historiography in U.S. political history, see the Note on Sources.

4. "FBI Director Hoover Backed," *CR*, February 17, 1965, B138, JEHS.

5. For a discussion of this book's primary research, see the Note on Sources.

Chapter 1: The Oldest Inhabitants (1800–1895)

1. "Weekly Review," 1:2, F14, B2, NLEM; Nichols to Allen, August 17, 1953, F1, S-JEHC.

2. "Suicide by Drowning," *WS*, April 10, 1880; Certificate of Death, District of Columbia: 264595, F4, S-JEHC.

3. Hoover, "If I Had a Son," *Woman's Day*, June 1938, B57, JEHS.

4. Census (1820); Green, *Washington*, 1:23.

5. Census (1860, 1870, 1880); *CD* (1862–1884); https://www.ancestry.com/family-tree/person/tree/115676412/person/240142486827/facts.

6. Census (1820); "Border State Representatives," *BS*, May 9, 1862. The census entry is for Michl Hoover, almost certainly Hoover's great-great-grandfather.

7. Reynolds, "Was J. Edgar Hoover Black?" *WP*, November 22, 2011; Posner, "Is It True Hoover 'Passed' for White?" *Globe and Mail*, August 14, 2000; Spannaus, "The Mysterious Origins of J. Edgar Hoover," *American Almanac*, August 2000; Summers, *Official & Confidential*, 349–51; Maxwell, *F.B. Eyes*, 35–42; McGhee, *Secrets Uncovered*.

8. Quoted in Green, *Washington*, 1:172–3; "Oldest Inhabitants," *WP*, July 5, 1888; "Discussed Early Days," *WP*, April 3, 1902; *CD* (1853); Coast Survey (1853), 81.

9. "The Last of Earth," *WP*, May 29, 1878; "Local News," *WS*, May 27, 1878; Coast Survey (1853), 81; *Washington, D.C., U.S., Marriage Records, 1810–1953* (Lehi, UT: Ancestry.com Operations, 2016); "Border State Representatives," *BS*, May 9, 1862; Census (1860).

10. Green, *Washington*, 1:168–9; *Centennial Celebration of the United States Coast and Geodetic Survey*; Odgers, *Alexander Dallas Bache*; Slotten, *Patronage, Practice, and the Culture of American Science*; Jansen, *Alexander Dallas Bache*; Kevles, "Not a Hundred Millionaires."

11. Coast Survey (1853), 81; Coast Survey (1854), 88; Coast Survey (1855), 101; Coast Survey (1856), 88; Coast Survey (1857), 117; Coast Survey (1858), 159; Coast Survey (1859), 176, 179; Coast Survey (1860), 102, 184–5; Coast Survey (1861), 75; Coast Survey (1863), 60; "Local News," *WS*, May 27, 1878.

12. Coast Survey (1867), x, 42–3; Coast Survey (1876), 64; Coast Survey (1877), 66; F9, B3, NLEM.

13. Coast Survey (1876), 64; Coast Survey (1877), 66; "Local News," *WS*, May 27, 1878; Coast Survey (1878), 10.

14. Coast Survey (1878), 10.

15. "Hitz Family," F5, B373, HHB; "Copy of the Translation," F5, B373, HHB; "In Memoriam," F12, B1, NLEM; Meier, *United States and Switzerland*, 126–9.

16. Green, *Washington*, 1:183; "Hitz Family"; Meier, *United States and Switzerland*, 126–9.

17. "Appointment," *BS*, May 31, 1864; Meier, *United States and Switzerland*, 126–9; "The Swiss National Festival," *BS*, July 23, 1872; "A Council for the Poor," *WP*, January 22, 1878; "Swiss Colony in Tennessee," *BS*, September 21, 1869; "Ways That Are Dark," *WP*, November 11, 1878; "Copy of the Translation."

18. Photos: "Annie Scheitlin, Dated 1867," "Portrait of Annie Hoover," PB1, NLEM; interview, Dorothy Davy, S-JEHC; Summers, *Official & Confidential*, 16; *CD* (1863–1880).

19. "Is Hitz a Citizen?" *WP*, December 3, 1882; "Mr. Hits Not a Diplomat," *WP*, December 7, 1882; "Suicide by Drowning"; "City Talk and Chatter," *WP*, April 12, 1880; Meier, *United States and Switzerland*, 130.

20. "Suicide by Drowning."

21. "Change in the Swiss Consulate," *WP*, July 19, 1881; "Guilty as Indicted," *WP*, May 14, 1886; "Five Years Each,"

WP, June 6, 1886; "Messrs. Hitz and Prentiss Released," *WP*, December 14, 1886; "A New Trial Denied," *WP*, May 30, 1886; "Journal—Private," NLEM; *CD* (1883–1895); "The Amateur Authors," *WP*, May 23, 1889.

22. "Journal–Private," NLEM.

Chapter 2: Little Edgar (1895–1905)

1. "Journal—Private," NLEM.

2. F111, B2, NARA-P.

3. "White House Reception," *BS*, January 2, 1895; Diary, January 1, 1910, F9, B1, NLEM.

4. *Washington, DC: A Guide to the Nation's Capital*, 42; Gilmore, "District of Columbia Population History 1800–2020," https://matthewbgilmore.files.wordpress.com/2021/04/population2020.jpg; Green, *Washington*, 2:84.

5. Asch and Musgrove, *Chocolate City*, 119–84.

6. Theodore Roosevelt Birthplace, "Roosevelt Pets," https://www.nps.gov/thrb/learn/historyculture/the-roosevelt-pets.htm; "The Family of Theodore Roosevelt," Theodore Roosevelt Association, https://www.theodoreroosevelt.org/content.aspx?page_id=22&club_id=991271&module_id=339183. On Roosevelt's personality, see esp. Goodwin, *Bully Pulpit*.

7. "Weekly Review," 1:2, 1:6, 1:4, 1:5, F14, B2, NLEM.

8. Photo, F: "Hoover Family Home," PB1, NLEM; *CD* (1891, 1892); "To Be Named Seward Place," *WP*, December 10, 1902.

9. Photo, F: "Hoover Family Home"; Powers, *Secrecy and Power*, 9.

10. Census (1900).

11. Asch and Musgrove, *Chocolate City*, 185–216; Theoharis and Cox, *Boss*, 21; "Ebenezer United Methodist Church, AKA 'Little Ebenezer,' turns 180," Streets of Washington, http://www.streetsofwashington.com/2018/05/ebenezer-united-methodist-church-aka.html.

12. *Washington, DC: A Guide*, 158–60, 180–1; "Jefferson's Legacy," Library of Congress, http://www.loc.gov/loc/legacy/bldgs.html; Theoharis and Cox, *Boss*, 25.

13. Nichols to Allen, August 17, 1953, F1, S-JEHC; Diary, 1909, "Cash Accounts," F9, B1, NLEM.

14. Gentry, *J. Edgar Hoover*, 63; Annie to Hoover, October 6 [ca. 1906], F17, B2, NLEM; Annie to Hoover, September 4, 1912, B19, NLEM; Dickerson to Hoover, undated [ca. 1904], F: "Undated Letter to JEH from father," B19, NLEM.

15. *Coast Survey* (1895), 101; *Coast Survey* (1897), 90.

16. "Cadet Officers Appointed," *WP*, October 14, 1898; "Won by the Easterns," *WS*, November 24, 1897; "Class Day at Eastern," *WP*, June 16, 1899; "Class Day at E.H.S.," *WP*, June 21, 1899; *Coast Survey* (1899–1900), 128–9; Talley, "Capital's Famous Hoover Brothers," *WP*, October 7, 1934; *CD* (1906), 624; Theoharis and Cox, *Boss*, 26.

17. Talley, "Capital's Famous Hoover Brothers"; Trohan, "Chief of the G-Men," *CT*, June 21, 1936, B27, JEHS; "High School Days End," *WP*, June 3, 1901; "Teachers Go To fair," *WP*, June 26, 1904; "Teachers Plan Trips," *WP*, July 6, 1904.

18. *Official Guide to the Louisiana Purchase Exposition* (Saint Louis: Official Guide Co., 1904), 94–8, https://archive.org/details/cu31924015340114; Kramer, *Blood of Government*, 264–5; Dickerson to Hoover, F: "undated letter to JEH from his father," B19, NLEM.

19. Annie to Hoover, October 6 [year undated], F17, B2, NLEM; Dickerson to Hoover, October [illegible], F "undated letter to JEH from father in Boston," B19, NLEM.

20. "Journal—Private," NLEM; Diary, April 10, 1908, F9, B1, NLEM; "Miss Elizabeth Snowden," *WS*, May [illegible], 1956, F1, S-JEHC.

21. Diary, March 21, 26-28, April 9, 1908; February 27, July 28–30, August 16-25, September 2-8, 1909; August 8–22, 1910, F9, B1, NLEM; Green, *Washington*, 2: 202.

Chapter 3: The Boy Problem (1905–1909)

1. "Slayer a Suicide," *WP*, October 24, 1905; *U.S., Naval Enlistment Rendezvous, 1855–1891* (Provo, UT: Ancestry.com Operations, 2014); *Washington, D.C., U.S., Compiled Marriage Index, 1830–1921* (Provo, UT: Ancestry.com Operations, 2014); *Virginia, U.S., Select Marriages, 1785–1940* (Provo, UT: Ancestry.com Operations, 2014).

2. "Slayer a Suicide"; "Dead Man's Head," *WT*, October 24, 1905; "Murder and Suicide," *WS*, October 24, 1905; "Found Wife Murdered," *BS*, October 24, 1905; "Found Wife and Man Dead," *BG*, October 24, 1905.

3. Report card, fifth grade, F16, B2, NLEM.

4. For the masculinity crisis, see especially Lears, *Rebirth of a Nation*; Bederman, *Manliness and Civilization*; Hilkey, *Character Is Capital*; Murphy, *Political Manhood*; Pettegrew, *Brutes in Suits*; Putney, *Muscular Christianity*; Rotundo, *American Manhood*.

5. Roosevelt, "Strenuous Life." For more on the "strenuous life" theme, see Dalton, *Theodore Roosevelt*.

6. Forbush, *Boy Problem*, 47; Putney, *Muscular Christianity*, 100.

7. "Weekly Review," 1:5, 1:16, F14, B2, NLEM.

8. "Weekly Review," 1:6, 1:4, 1:7, F14, B2, NLEM; Hoover to Walker, 1949, F1, S-JEHC.

9. Diary, 1909, "Things Easily Forgotten," F9, B1, NLEM; Diary, August 2, 1909, January 10, 1910, September 3, 1909, F9, B1, NLEM; "Weekly Review," 1:4.

10. Demaris, *Director*, 7; Nichols to Allen, August 17, 1953, F1, S-JEHC.

11. Interview of Anna Hoover Kienast, S-JEHC; Demaris, *Director*, 8.

12. Hirshbein, *American Melancholy*, 1, 13.

13. National Research Council, *Depression in Parents*, 15–8, 119–82.

14. *Washington, D.C., U.S., Compiled Marriage Index, 1830–1921*; Census (1900, 1910, 1920); *CD* (1886, 1887, 1889, 1907, 1909, 1914, 1919); Theoharis and Cox, *Boss*, 24.

15. Diary, March 25–30, 1908, F9, B1, NLEM; Diary, 1909, Memoranda, F9, B1, NLEM; "Last Honors to John Hitz," *WP*, March 30, 1908; Elson, "The J. Edgar Hoover You Ought to Know," *Chaplain*, September/October 1950, B105, JEHS.

16. Putney, *Muscular Christianity*, 73-74, 116, 94; Bederman, "'The Women Have Had Charge,'" 438.

17. Powers, *Secrecy and Power*, 14; "Installs Dr. Weidley," *WP*, April 4, 1906.

18. Mitchell, "Unknown Side," *Prison Evangel*, May/June 1960, B129, JEHS; Agee, "FBI Chief Says," *Columbus Enquirer*, May 11, 1963, B135, JEHS; Diary, January 5, 12, 19, 1908, F9, B1, NLEM.

19. Mitchell, "Unknown Side"; "Life Is a Roseate Thing," *WP*, January 8, 1906; Diary, 1908, F9, B1, NLEM; "Memoranda," Diary, 1909, F9, B1, NLEM.

20. "Journal—Private"; Theoharis and Cox, *Boss*, 30; "Social and Personal," *WP*, July 1, 1908; wedding announcement, June 30, 1908, F12, B1, NLEM; interview of Dorothy Davy, S-JEHC; *CD* (1909), 1073.

21. *CD* (1908), 670; Census (1910); Theoharis and Cox,

Boss, 27; Demaris, *Director*, 9; "Journal—Private," NLEM; Interview log, F: "Robinette, Fred II," S-JEHC.

Chapter 4: Jump High and Leap Quick (1909–1913)

1. O'Neill, "J. Edgar Hoover's School Days," *American Boy & Open Road*, September 1954, B116, JEHS; Powers, *Secrecy and Power*, 25–6; *CHR* (December 1909), 29; *Centennial History*, 81; *Brecky* (1912), 91–4.

2. Hoover, "FBI Chief Remembers Experiences," *High Point Enterprise*, January 4, 1961, B131, JEHS.

3. *Centennial History*, 8, 83; *Brecky* (1909), page unmarked/dedication.

4. *Brecky* (1913), 8–9, 30; *Centennial History*, 81; *CHR* (November 1909), 12.

5. Diary, September 22–26, 1909, F9, B1, NLEM; *Centennial History*, 90; Report card, 1911–1912, F16, B2, NLEM; Theoharis and Cox, *Boss*, 32; *Centennial History*, 91.

6. "Grins and Chagrins," *CHR* (November 1909), unpaginated; *CHR* (February 1909), 10; *CHR* (December 1908), 12; *CHR* (April 1909), 10; Putney, *Muscular Christianity*, 39.

7. Census (1870); *CHR* (November 1909), 18; *CD* (1914); *Centennial History*, preface.

8. Talley, "Capital's Famous Hoover Brothers," *WP*, October 7, 1934; *CHR* (May 1909), 19.

9. *CHR* (October 1911), unpaginated; *Brecky* (1912), 80.

10. Diary, January 3, 1910, NLEM; Photo, F9, B3, NLEM.

11. *Brecky* (1912), 80; *Centennial History*, 90.

12. Diary, January 7, 1910; *CHR* (November 1912), 16.

13. Dance card, March 25, 1913, F12, B1, NLEM.

14. *Brecky* (1913), 77, 122; Harter, "G-Man Success," *WH*, January 29, 1937, B38, JEHS; "Lawrence (Biff) Jones," *WP*, February 13, 1980.

15. *CHR* (April 1911), 18; *CHR* (April 1910), unpaginated.

16. *CHR* (March 1913), 25; O'Neill, "J. Edgar Hoover's School Days"; *Centennial History*, 90; *CHR* (March 1912), 17; *CHR* (January 1913), 20; *CHR* (February 1913), 20; *CHR* (December 1909), unpaginated.

17. "Older Than the City," *WP*, November 2, 1901; "Dr. Talmage to Preach," *WP*, December 16, 1899; "Must Have a Purpose," *WP*, November 27, 1899.

18. "The Director-II," *New Yorker*, October 2, 1937, B46, JEHS; *Organized Sunday School Work*, 450–3.

19. "Big Day for Children," *WP*, September 25, 1905; Hoover, "FBI Chief Remembers," *High Point Enterprise*, January 4, 1961, B131, JEHS.

20. Hoover to Cummiskey, January 30, 1947, F28, S-JEHC; "Tells Joy of Living," *WP*, January 25, 1909; "Assembly's Church Services," *WP*, March 17, 1905.

21. "Christianity and Strikes," *WP*, September 29, 1902.

22. "Union Is Improbable," *WP*, September 4, 1905; "The Nation's Capital," *WP*, November 9, 1903; "Plan Fight on Liquor Evil," *WP*, July 1, 1907; "White Girl Weds a Negro," *WP*, March 20, 1903; "Question of Race in S.S. Congress," *WP*, May 20, 1910.

23. Hoover to Cummiskey, January 30, 1947, F28, S-JEHC.

24. Hoover to Cummiskey; Hurd, *Institutional Care*, 579. The precise date of Dickerson's stay at Laurel is difficult to determine. Theoharis suggests it was sometime around the fall of 1912. Theoharis and Cox, *Boss*, 34. Summers dates it slightly later. Summers, *Official and Confidential*, 23.

25. Braslow, *Mental Ills*, 38–40; Harmon, "Hydrotherapy," 492; Hurd, *Institutional Care*, 579.

26. Dickerson to Hoover, September 8, 1912, F9/8/12, B19, NLEM; Annie to Hoover, September 4, 1912, F9/4/12, B19, NLEM. A photo album in Hoover's personal papers suggests that Annie and Dickerson did visit Wytheville, perhaps to pick him up or drop him off. F: "Hoover Family Album-1912," PB1, NLEM.

27. Theoharis and Cox, *Boss*, 41; Summers, *Official and Confidential*, 24; interview log, Dorothy Davy, F4, S-JEHC.

28. *Brecky* (1913), 76, 132, 120-3, 127; *CHR* (March 1913), 21–5; "Cadets Are Reviewed," *WP*, May 7, 1913; "Company K's Flag," *WP*, May 21, 1913.

29. *CHR* (December 1912), 17; *CHR* (March 1913), 24.

30. *Brecky* (1913), 78, 86, 76.

31. *CHR* (ca. May 1912), 17.

Chapter 5: Dieu et les Dames (1913–1917)

1. "Lawrence (Biff) Jones," *WP*, February 13, 1980; Gray, "Alumni Notes," *CHR* (November 1912), 25; "David Hazen Blakelock," *Brecky* (1913), 69.

2. Theoharis and Cox, *Boss*, 39, 41; *CD* (1914); interview of Dorothy Davy, S-JEHC; Davy, interview log, F4E, S-JEHC; Robinette, interview log, F351, S-JEHC; *CD* (1918); "Dr. MacLeod to Visit Springfield," *WP*, May 11, 1913; "Ask Pastor to Remain," *WP*, June 18, 1913; "Lent Rules Churches," *WP*, March 22, 1914.

3. Weyl, *New Democracy*, 1.

4. On Wilson, see especially Cooper, *Woodrow Wilson* and *The Warrior and the Priest*; Cook, *Democracy and Administration*; Schaffer, "New South Nation"; Yellin, *Racism in the Nation's Service*; Greenidge, *Black Radical*.

5. "J. Edgar Hoover's School Days," *American Boy & Open Road*, September 1954, B116, JEHS; Conaway, *America's Library*, 89.

6. "Alumni Notes," *CHR* (November 1912); Powers, *Secrecy and Power*, 42; "Cosmos Club," *CD* (1909); Rosenberg, *Nation's Great Library*, 23–41.

7. Library of Congress, "Abstract of Official Record of Employee," November 4, 1925, FBI JF; Library of Congress, Order Division, annual reports: July 1, 1913–June 30, 1914, July 1, 1914–June 30, 1915.

8. Cooper, *Ten Thousand Public Enemies*, 58; Library of Congress, "Abstract of Official Record of Employee."

9. Rosenberg, *Nation's Great Library*, 26–7, 83–4, 25.

10. *CT* (1914), 18; "Prof. Jones Opposes 'Varsity Athletics," *Hatchet*, March 13, 1914; "Ninety-Sixth Annual Commencement," June 6, 1917, B19, NLEM.

11. "Big Increase," *Hatchet*, October 6, 1913; "Ninety-Sixth Annual Commencement"; Novak, "Desegregation of George Washington University."

12. Hoover, law school notebooks, NLEM; *CT* (1914), 102; *CT* (1916), 76; "Law School Opens," *Hatchet*, October 6, 1913.

13. "Clark to Speak," *Hatchet*, March 27, 1914; "Start Movement," *Hatchet*, April 10, 1914; "Bennett Champ Clark," *CR*, July 16, 1954; "Law School Dinner," *Hatchet*, April 17, 1916; "Lawyers Dine," *Hatchet*, May 12, 1916.

14. *KAJ* (February 1914), 183.

15. *KAJ* (March 1916), 171; *KAJ* (November 1921), 156; Trelease, *White Terror*, 4; *KAJ* (January 1922), 145.

16. *KAJ* (March 1916), 171; "Brief History of the Mississippi State Capitol," Mississippi Legislature, http://www.legislature.ms.gov/about-the-capitol/history-of-the-capitol/; von Hoffman, *Mississippi Notebook*, 38.

17. *KAJ* (November 1925), 9–11; *Race Problems*, 49–50, 57, 54; Godshalk, *Veiled Visions*, 35–56; Miller, *Appeal to*

Reason, 3; "Kappa Alphas Honor Graves," *AC*, November 12, 1907.

18. Keene, "Dixon, Thomas," *American National Biography*; "Dixon's Play Stirs Wrath," *AC*, October 16, 1905; Slide, *American Racist*, 19–65; "Kappa Alphas Plan Banquet," *AC*, April 28, 1907; "Banquet Tonight," *AC*, November 18, 1910; "Kappa Alpha Frats," *AC*, November 13, 1910.

19. "Kappa Alpha Alumni Meet," *WP*, October 16, 1913; "Kappa Alpha Dinner Gay," *WP*, January 26, 1914; John Temple Graves, "World's Grandest Monument Waiting in Sight of Us for the Confederate Dead," *Hearst Sunday American*, July 19, 1914, Library of Congress, https://www.loc.gov/item/rbpe.01403900/; *KAJ* (November 1925), 46–7.

20. "History of Stone Mountain Memorial Association," Stone Mountain Memorial Association, https://stonemountainpark.org/about-us/history-of-smma/; Benbow, "Birth of a Quotation"; Gordon, *Second Coming of the KKK*, 12–23.

21. "Kappa Alphas to Banquet," *WP*, April 16, 1916.

22. "Kappa Alphas to Banquet"; "Important Bills Are Introduced," *WP*, December 12, 1915; *KAJ* (January 1915), 63.

23. *KAJ* (July 1914), 545; *KAJ* (March 1919), 250; *KAJ* (February 1914), 254.

24. *CT* (1916), 262; "Kappa Alpha," *Hatchet*, October 16, 1916; "Alpha Nu Xmas Smoker," *WP*, December 17, 1916; "Kappa Alphas to Banquet."

25. *KAJ* (February 1914), 181; *KAJ* (March 1919), 5.

26. *CD* (1915–1918); Tucker, "In Re: Thomas Fr Baughman," September 20, 1919, FBI FOIA 67–691 (Baughman); *KAJ* (March 1916), 149, 171–4; "Frat Men at Smoker," *WP*, May 17, 1915.

27. Johnson, *Lavender Scare*, 41–2; Syrett, *Company He Keeps*, 206; *KAJ* (January 1915), 21; *KAJ* (February 1914), 181.

28. *KAJ* (January 1915), 93; *KAJ* (April 1915), 82.

29. *CT* (1916), 86.

30. "Ninety-Fifth Annual Commencement," June 7, 1916, F16, B2, NLEM; "Ninety-Sixth Annual Commencement," June 6, 1917, B19, NLEM.

Chapter 6: The Great Adventure (1917–1918)

1. Hastings to D. N. Hoover, April 6, 1917, F: "Dickerson Hoover Resignation Letter," B19, NLEM.

2. On World War I and civil liberties, see especially Cottrell, *Roger Nash Baldwin*; Walker, *In Defense of American Liberties*; Murphy, *World War I and the Origins of Civil Liberties*; Scheiber, *Wilson Administration and Civil Liberties*; Kornweibel, *"Investigate Everything"*; Capozzola, *Uncle Sam Wants You*; Ellis, *Race, War, and Surveillance*.

3. "Speaks on 'Socialism,'" *Hatchet*, February 13, 1914; "Law School Notes," *Hatchet*, October 24, 1913.

4. Green, *Washington*, 2:205; "Student Military Camps for This Summer," *Hatchet*, February 4, 1916; Kennedy, *Over Here*, 185; "Pacifists in Riots," *WP*, April 3, 1917. On war opposition, see Kazin, *War Against War*.

5. "Favors Nation in Khaki," *WP*, April 20, 1917; Kennedy, *Over Here*, 149–50; "Ninety-Sixth Annual Commencement," June 6, 1917, B19, NLEM.

6. "Kappa Alpha," *Hatchet*, October 5, 1917; "J. Edgar Hoover," F: "AG Personal File—J. Edgar Hoover 1933–1947," B114, HSC; Powers, *Secrecy and Power*, 41.

7. Green, *Washington*, 2: 237-250.

8. For the home front and voluntarist politics, see esp. Hawley, *Great War*; Wiebe, *Search for Order*; Kennedy, *Over*

Here; Whalan, *World War One*; Neiberg, *Path to War*; Capozzola, *Uncle Sam Wants You*.

9. Green, *Washington*, 2:237, 249–50; Census (1920); Summers, *Official and Confidential*, 31–2.

10. "Washington Takes Its Last Nightcap," *NYT*, November 1, 1917; Nicolay, *Our Capital*, 512.

11. Oath, July 26, 1917, FBI JF; "History of the Department's Four Main Buildings," United States Department of Justice, https://www.justice.gov/opa/video/history-department-s-four-main-buildings-1870-present.

12. McCormick, "Thomas Watt Gregory," *American National Biography*; "Southern Society Reelects Calhoun," *WP*, June 1, 1917; *AR/AG* (1918), 16–7, 47.

13. "All Disloyal Men Warned by Gregory," *NYT*, November 21, 1917; Jensen, *Price of Vigilance*, 90, 41.

14. Oath, July 26, 1917; *AR/AG* (1918), 15.

15. Wilson, "Address to a Joint Session of Congress Requesting a Declaration of War Against Germany," April 2, 1917, American Presidency Project, https://www.presidency.ucsb.edu/documents/address-joint-session-congress-requesting-declaration-war-against-germany.

16. Witcover, *Sabotage at Black Tom*; Kennedy, *Over Here*, 68–73; Capozzola, *Uncle Sam Wants You*, 10.

17. On the APL, see especially Mills, *League*; Jensen, *Price of Vigilance*. For badge, see Jensen cover image.

18. *AR/AG* (1918), 681–3, 724, 25–34; Capozzola, *Uncle Sam Wants You*, 177.

19. Hoover, "Memorandum for Mr. O'Brian," December 28, 1917, DOJ 9-16-12-1726-5; Powers, *Secrecy and Power*, 51–3; Hoover, "Memorandum for Mr. O'Brian," December 17, 1917, DOJ 9-16-12-1384-6; Hoover, "Memorandum for Mr. O'Brian," December 29, 1917, DOJ 9-16-12-1954-8.

20. Hoover, "Memorandum for Mr. O'Brian," December 28, 1917; Hoover, "Memorandum for Mr. O'Brian," December 17, 1917.

21. *AR/AG* (1918), 27, 36; Wasserman, "Internal Affairs," 11.

22. Debs, "On the Proposed National Platform," *St. Louis Labor*, August 12, 1916, Marxists Internet Archive, https://www.marxists.org/archive/debs/works/1916/0804-debs-proposednationalplatform.pdf.

23. Avrich and Avrich, *Sasha and Emma*, 269–78.

24. *AR/AG* (1918), 53–4. On the IWW during World War I, see especially Strang, *Keep the Wretches in Order*; Preston, *Aliens and Dissenters*, 88-207.

25. Lumpkins, *American Pogrom*, 1–2; Kornweibel, *"Investigate Everything,"* 181–4, 170–4.

26. *AR/AG* (1918), 29; NARA, "World War I Enemy Alien Records," https://www.archives.gov/research/immigration/enemy-aliens/ww1.

27. O'Brian to McCarthy, May 22, 1918, DOJ 9-16-19-51-161; O'Brian to Cahill, May 24, 1918, DOJ 9-16-19-51-169; O'Brian to McDermott, May 29, 1918, DOJ 9-16-19-51-180; Special Assistant to McCarthy, May 3, 1918, DOJ 9-16-19-51-214; Kane to Attorney General, May 6, 1918, DOJ 9-16-19-51; *AR/AG* (1918), 28–31.

28. Geisler, "Memorandum for Mr. O'Brian," November 7, 1918, FBI JF; Powers, *Secrecy and Power*, 41–2.

29. Green, *Washington*, 2:247-9.

30. Chief clerk to Abercrombie, November 2, 1918, FBI JF; Geisler, "Memorandum for Mr. O'Brian," November 7, 1918.

31. "City Wild with Joy," *WP*, November 12, 1918; Oath, November 13, 1918, FBI JF.

Chapter 7: The Radical Division (1919)

1. *KAJ* (March 1919), 283–5; *KAJ* (November 1921), 156; *KAJ* (March 1950), 5.

2. Lenin, "Letter to American Workers."

3. Coben, *A. Mitchell Palmer*, 197. For a biographical overview, also see Coben, "A. Mitchell Palmer," *American National Biography*.

4. *An Act to Exclude and Expel from the United States Aliens Who Are Members of the Anarchistic and Similar Classes*, Public Law 65-221, *U.S. Statutes at Large* 40 (1918): 1012. For Galleani and his followers, see Avrich, *Sacco and Vanzetti*, 3–164; Simon, *America's Forgotten Terrorists*.

5. Ackerman, *Young J. Edgar*, 45.

6. Avrich, *Sacco and Vanzetti*, 140–1.

7. "'Bolshevik Work,' Says Hardwick," *AC*, May 1, 1919.

8. "Sixteen Bombs Held Up," *BG*, May 1, 1919; "Government Gives Warning," *WP*, May 1, 1919; Avrich, *Sacco and Vanzetti*, 141–4.

9. "Ole Hanson Would Hang," *NYTr*, May 2, 1919; "Dies in May Day Riot," *WP*, May 2, 1919; "A National Danger," *WP*, May 3, 1919.

10. Avrich, *Sacco and Vanzetti*, 81, 149–56.

11. "U.S. and D.C. Officials Confer," *WS*, June 3, 1919; *Illegal Practices*, 580; "'Attempt to Terrorize Has Failed,'" *WP*, June 4, 1919.

12. "2,000 'Reds' on Lists," *WP*, June 19, 1919.

13. Ackerman, *Young J. Edgar*, 40, 50–2, 45.

14. Theoharis and Cox, *Boss*, 57.

15. Flynn to agents, August 12, 1919, in Poindexter, 30–4.

16. Schmidt, *Red Scare*, 159.

17. "Memorandum upon Work of Radical Division, August 1, 1919 to October 16, 1919," October 18, 1919, R63, EGP; Ackerman, *Young J. Edgar*, 66.

18. "Report of Radical Section for Week Ending September 12, 1919," September 12, 1919, R63, EGP; "Radicalism and Sedition Among the Negroes," *NYT*, Nov. 23, 1919; Denney, "'To Wage a War,'" 36; Maxwell, *F.B. Eyes*, 52-58.

19. Hoover, "Memorandum for Mr. Creighton," August 23, 1919, R63, EGP; Palmer to Warden, September 8, 1919, R63, EGP; Hoover, "Memorandum for Mr. McGlasson," September 15, 1919, R63, EGP.

20. Hoover, "Memorandum of Conference with Commissioner-General of Immigration," September 8, 1919, R63, EGP; Hoover, "Immigration Hearing in Deportation Case of Alexander Berkman," September 25, 1919, R63, EGP; "Report on Radical Section for the week ending October 10, 1919," October 10, 1919, R63, EGP.

21. Hoover, "Report upon New York Trip," October 10, 1919, R63, EGP.

22. "Text of Senator Poindexter's Resolution," *NYT*, October 15, 1919; Ackerman, *Young J. Edgar*, 106–10; Goldman, *Living my Life*, 704.

23. Schmidt, *Red Scare*, 267–8, 273; Activities of DOJ.

24. "Law to Crush 'Reds,'" *WP*, November 16, 1919; Wilson, Seventh Annual Message to Congress, December 2, 1919, American Presidency Project, https://www.presidency.ucsb.edu/documents/7th-annual-message.

25. "Court Fight Lost by Berkman and Goldman Woman," December 9, 1919, B1, JEHS; "For Immediate Publication," December 10, 1919, R63, EGP; Hoover to Ernst, September 13, 1944, FBI FOIA 94-4-5366-14 (Ernst); "Berkman Must Go," *NYT*, December 12, 1919.

26. Ackerman, *Young J. Edgar*, 157; "Emma Goldman and 250 'Reds' to Be Deported Today," *SLPD*, December 21, 1919.

27. "Extension of Remarks of Hon. William N Vaile," *CR*, January 5, 1920, B1, JEHS; "249 Reds Sail," *NYH*, ca. December 21, 1919, B1, JEHS.

Chapter 8: New Elements (1920)

1. "Memorandum upon Work of Radical Division, August 1, 1919 to October 16, 1919," October 18, 1919, R63, EGP.

2. "Platform and Program of the Communist Labor Party of America," in *Palmer on Charges*, 392–297. For the Socialist split, see Shannon, *Socialist Party*, 126–49.

3. Draper, *Roots of American Communism*, 188–90.

4. "Brief on the Communist Party," in *Palmer on Charges*, 321–31; "Status of the Communist Labor Party," in *Palmer on Charges*, 375–77; Hoover to Caminetti, December 24, 1919, F4, DOJ 205492.

5. Hoover to Durham, January 7, 1920, F3, DOJ 205492; George, *Red Dawn*, 25.

6. "Brief on the Communist Party," in *Palmer on Charges*, P2, 321.

7. Hoover to Caminetti, December 22, 1919, F4, DOJ 205492; *Illegal Practices*, 21.

8. Hoover to Caminetti, November 25, December 17, December 18, 1919, DOJ 203557.

9. Powers, *Secrecy and Power*, 103; *Illegal Practices*, 21.

10. For an example of Hoover's revisionist claims, see Knebel, "J. Edgar Hoover," *Look*, May 31, 1955, B118, JEHS; Burke to Kelleher, December 27, 1919, in *Illegal Practices*, 12–4.

11. Post, *Deportations Delirium*, title.

12. Hoover, "Memorandum for the Chief Clerk," January 2, 1920, F4, DOJ 205492; Burke to Kelleher, December 27, 1919.

13. Knebel, "J. Edgar Hoover"; Smith to Immigration, January 3, 1930, IB 54809; Dunn to Immigration, January 3, 5, 1920, IB 54809; Hoover to Caminetti, January 3, 1920, IB 54809; Hoover to Caminetti, January 3, 1919 [sic], F4, DOJ 205492.

14. "More than 1500 Alleged Radicals Arrested," *BS*, January 3, 1920; Schmidt, *Red Scare*, 290–1.

15. "Reds by the Thousands," *NYT*, January 5, 1920; "Let Radicals Out Under $1,000 Bail," *NYW*, January 4, 1920, B1, JEHS.

16. "Washington Opens Hearing on 'Reds'," *NYT*, January 22, 1920, B1, JEHS; "Minutes of Meeting in the Office of the Secretary," January 21, 1919 [sic], IB 54844-77; Ackerman, *Young J. Edgar*, 207–12, 259.

17. Kane to Wilson, January 12, 1920, in *Illegal Practices*, 346; Boynton to Attorney General, January 13, 1920, F3, DOJ 205492; Ackerman, *Young J. Edgar*, 191–4.

18. Hoover to Caminetti, January 6, 1920, F3, DOJ 205492.

19. Post, *Deportations Delirium*, 12-18, 70; Ackerman, *Young J. Edgar*, 164-169.

20. Hoover to Caminetti, March 16, 1920, F10, DOJ 205492; "Expert on Reds Coming Here," April 7, 1920, *Boston American*, B1, JEHS; untitled, *Boston Post*, April 14, 1920, B1, JEHS; Ackerman, *Young J. Edgar*, 241–9. On *Post's* bureaucratic politics, also see Guariglia, "Wrench in the Deportation Machine."

21. "Will Deport Only Real Communists," *NYT*, April 10, 1920.

22. Caminetti to Peters, April 12, 1920, IB 54809.

23. Link, *Papers of Woodrow Wilson*, V 65, 187.

24. "Palmer Says Men Behind Walk-Out Aim at Soviet Rule," *NYTr*, April 15, 1920; Caminetti to Hoover, April 19, 1920, IB 54809.

25. "Over Status of Members of Communist Party," *SLPD*, April 25, 1920; "Makes Hot Reply," *BG*, April 25, 1920, B1,

JEHS; "U.S. Agents Said to Be Active in Communist Party," *NYTr*, April 25, 1920.

26. "Attorney-General Palmer Has Four Extra Guards," *SLPD*, May 2, 1920; "Palmer's Riot Predictions Fail," *NYTr*, May 2, 1920.

27. Ackerman, *Young J. Edgar*, 290; *Investigation of Post*, 262.

28. Hoover, "Memorandum for the Attorney General," May 25, 1920, DOJ 209264-3.

29. "Note," ca. May, 1920, FBI Fold3 341761.

30. Ackerman, *Young J. Edgar*, 284, 299; King to "Our Members and Friends," May 5, 1920, FBI Fold3 379228 (National Popular Government League/NPGL); "Memorandum for Mr. Ahern," May 8, 1920, FBI Fold3 379228 (NPGL); Kemon, "National Popular Government League," May 19, 1920, FBI Fold3 379228 (NPGL).

31. Hoover, "Memorandum for the Attorney General," May 25, 1920, DOJ 209264-3.

32. *Palmer on Charges*, 46, 53, 34.

33. "Take Up Frisco Trips," *WS*, ca. August 1920, B1, JEHS.

34. "Bomb Plot, Says Palmer," *NYT*, September 18, 1920; *Illegal Practices*, 19–20, 649. Also see Gage, *Day Wall Street Exploded*.

Chapter 9: No. 2 (1921–1924)

1. Certificate of Death, District of Columbia: 264595, F4, S-JEHC.

2. Russell, *Shadow of Blooming Grove*, 512.

3. McCartney, *Teapot Dome Scandal*, 62. For background on Harding, Daugherty, and the Harding presidency, see especially McCartney, *Teapot Dome Scandal*; Russell, *Shadow of Blooming Grove*; Sinclair, *Available Man*; Murray, *Harding Era*; Adams, *Incredible Era*. For McLean as Bureau agent, see Adams, *Incredible Era*, 315.

4. Russell, *Shadow of Blooming Grove*, 508, 335; McCartney, *Teapot Dome Scandal*, 233, 10; "Daugherty's 'Pal' Suicide," *LAT*, May 31, 1923; "Smith, Suicide," *BS*, May 31, 1923.

5. For Burns, see especially Gage, *Day Wall Street Exploded*, 136–41, 261–76; Caesar, *Incredible Detective*. For other details, see "Burns Talked of to Succeed Flynn," *NYT*, April 1, 1921; Hoover, "Report upon New York Trip," October 10, 1919, R63, EGP.

6. Hoover and Cooper, "The Amazing Mr. Means," *RD*, March 1937, B39, JEHS.

7. Redacted to redacted, ca. December 1917, S1, FBI 67-3654 (Gandy), S-JEHC; Summers, *Official and Confidential*, 32; Hoover to Gandy, August 22, 1921, S1, FBI 67-3654 (Gandy), S-JEHC.

8. Lowenthal, *Federal Bureau of Investigation*, 4–5.

9. Pliley, *Policing Sexuality*, 67; Theoharis et al., *FBI: Comprehensive Reference Guide*, 4.

10. "For National Bureau of Identification," *NYT*, September 25, 1921.

11. *AR/AG* (1922), 67; Burns to SACs, November 15, 1923, FBI 66-04, F5, B1, Sr73: "SAC letters," AT; Burns to SACs, August 21, 1923, FBI 66-04, F5, B1, Sr73: "SAC letters," AT.

12. Pliley, *Policing Sexuality*, 106–58.

13. Ackerman, *Young J. Edgar*, 86; Grant, *Negro with a Hat*, 155, 338, 363. For Garvey and the Bureau, see also Ewing, *Age of Garvey*.

14. Theoharis et al., *FBI: Comprehensive Reference Guide*, 10, 47; "A Byte out of FBI History: Imperial Kleagle of the Ku Klux Klan in Kustody," March 11, 2004, FBI, https://www.fbi.gov/news/stories/2004/march/kkk031104.

15. Gage, *Day Wall Street Exploded*, 284, 297–306; Spolansky, *Communist Trail*, 23–30.

16. Gage, *Day Wall Street Exploded*, 299; Davis, *Power at Odds*, 130–5; Russell, *Shadow of Blooming Grove*, 547–8, 567–70.

17. Wheeler, *Yankee from the West*, 213–4.

18. *Daugherty*, 2–33, 73–89; Russell, *Shadow of Blooming Grove*, 621.

19. Murray, *Harding Era*, 432.

20. McCartney, *Teapot Dome Scandal*, 238.

21. Russell, *Shadow of Blooming Grove*, 620; Wheeler, *Yankee from the West*, 215.

Chapter 10: The New Sleuth (1924–1925)

1. Whitehead, *FBI Story*, 65–7; Nichols to Mason, October 19, 1950, FBI 62-8782 (Stone), F3, B1, Sr52, AT. For Stone's background, see Mason, *Harlan Fiske Stone*, 11–165.

2. Hoover to Stone, July 13, 1939, F: "General Correspondence, Hoover, John Hoover, 1935–1943," B17, HFS.

3. Stone, "Memorandum for Mr. Hoover," May 13, 1924, FBI 62-8782 (Stone), F3, B1, Sr52, AT.

4. *CC2*, 3.

5. *AR/AG* (1924), 60–72.

6. "J. H. Hoover Gets," *DW*, December 22, 1924, B1, JEHS; Frankfurter to Stone, April 3, 1924, F001757-003-0433, FF; Stone to Frankfurter, April 7, 1924, F001757-003-0433, FF; Ackerman, *Young J. Edgar*, 374–5.

7. Baldwin to Stone, August 6, 1924, S1, B1, FBI NARA 57-561 (Hoover); Cottrell, *Roger Nash Baldwin*, 140–4; Stone, "Memorandum for Mr. Hoover," August 7, 1924, S1, B1, FBI NARA 67-561-9 (Hoover).

8. Hoover to Ryan, June 7, 1924, FBI 62-8782, F3, B1, Sr52, AT; Updegrove, "In Re: Guarding Attorney General," June 3, 1924, FBI 62-8782, F3, B1, Sr52, AT; Hoover, "Memorandum for Mr. Martin," July 29, 1924, FBI 62-8782, F3, B1, Sr52, AT; Hancock to Hoover, October 23, 1924, FBI 62-8782, F3, B1, Sr52, AT; Hoover to Nathan, September 18, 1924, S1, FBI FOIA 61-883-2 (Nathan).

9. Demaris, *Director*, 4–7; Theoharis and Cox, *Boss*, 108.

10. "Stone and Mellon," *WP*, December 23, 1924, B1, JEHS; "History," University Club, https://www.universityclubdc.com/history. On Masonic culture, see especially Dumenil, *Freemasonry and American Culture*; Carnes, *Secret Ritual and Manhood*.

11. Frankfurter to Stone, January 22, 1925, F001757-003-0465, FF; Stone to Frankfurter, January 24, 1925, F001757-003-0465, FF; Schlesinger, *Crisis of the Old Order*, 57.

12. For Herbert Hoover's philosophy, see especially Hoover, *American Individualism*. For his law enforcement vision, see especially Calder, *Origins and Development of Federal Crime Control Policy*; McGirr, *War on Alcohol*.

13. "Outline of the Instructions," ca. August 1929, S1, FBI FOIA 62-21747 (Wickersham); Small, "Days of 'Old Sleuth,'" untitled newspaper, December 29, 1924, B2, JEHS.

14. "Head of the Secret Service," *National Magazine*, March 1925, B2, JEHS.

15. "New Boss," *Birmingham Post*, January 6, 1925, B2, JEHS; Stokes, "Hoover Banishes," *AC*, December 27, 1924, B1, JEHS; Billings, "Real Gentleman Successor," *Eagle*, April 16, 1925, B2, JEHS. For a typical photo, see "SH-H-H," *Register* (Springfield, Missouri), December 27, 1924, B1, JEHS.

16. "Mason Made Chief," *Fellowship Forum*, December 27, 1924, B1, JEHS; "New Boss"; Small, "Days of 'Old Sleuth.'"

17. McGirr, *War on Alcohol*.

18. Hoover to Nathan, May 9, 1925, S1, FBI FOIA 67-83 (Nathan); *AR/AG* (1924), 63; *AR/AG* (1925), 109; JEH APP (1927), 102.

19. Hoover to Nathan, May 9, 1925.

20. *AR/AG* (1925), 122–3.

21. Ring, "New Police Strategy," *WS*, May 10, 1925, B2, JEHS.

Chapter 11: Kappa Alpha Bureau (1925–1928)

1. JEH APP (1926), 57; JEH APP (1929), 60, 62; JEH APP (1927), 101; JEH APP (1928), 47; Theoharis et al., *FBI: Comprehensive Reference Guide,* 4; JEH APP (1930), 74.

2. Stokes, "Hoover Banishes Gumshoe Sleuths," *AC*, December 27, 1924, B1, JEHS.

3. "Application for Appointment," April 19, 1921, S1, FBI FOIA 67-883 (Nathan); Nathan to Neale, September 19, 1920, S1, FBI FOIA 67-883 (Nathan); Purvis and Tresniowski, *Vendetta*, 18–9; Nathan, "A Modern Helen," F2, B1, MHP; Wile, "Washington Observations," *WS*, June 30, 1930, B2, JEHS; Nathan, "Memorandum for the Director," June 24, 1932, S1, FBI FOIA 67-822-148 (Purvis).

4. Burns, "Memorandum for Mr. Holland," May 6, 1924, S1, FBI FOIA 67-883 (Nathan); Nathan to Hoover, January 2, 1925, S1, FBI FOIA 67-883 (Nathan); Hoover to Nathan, January 9, 1925, S1, FBI FOIA 67-883 (Nathan); Hoover, "Memorandum for [redacted]," March 20, 1925, S1, FBI FOIA 67-883 (Nathan); "Appeal from Classification Allocation," undated (ca. October 1928), S2, FBI FOIA 67-883 (Nathan).

5. "Registration Climbing," *Hatchet*, October 24, 1913; *Hatchet*, February 17, 1925.

6. *CT* (1928), 107; Clegg OH.

7. *CT* (1926), 255; Theoharis et al., *FBI: Comprehensive Reference Guide*, 315, 323, 338; *CT* (1924), 145; "Little Opposition," *Hatchet*, October 21, 1924; *CT* (1920), 253; *CT* (1922), 21; "Application for Appointment," October 7, 1931, FBI FOIA 67-21916-2 (Edwards).

8. Hoover to Tolson, March 14, 1928, S1, FBI NARA 67-9524-28 (Tolson); Tolson to Hoover, June 23, 1928, S1, FBI NARA 67-9524-46 (Tolson).

9. Tracy to Hoover, February 11, 1928, S1, FBI NARA 67-9524-14 (Tolson); Kemp, "Clyde A. Tolson," February 2, 1928, S1, FBI NARA 67-9524-11 (Tolson).

10. Tracy to Hoover, February 11, 1928, S1, FBI NARA 67-9524-14 (Tolson); White, "Clyde A. Tolson," February 7, 1928, S1, FBI NARA 67-9524-15 (Tolson); Hoover to Keith, January 26, 1928, S1, FBI NARA 67-9524-3 (Tolson).

11. Baker to AG, January 27, 1928, S1, FBI NARA 67-9524-8 (Tolson).

12. *CT* (1924), 44; *CT* (1926), 177; "Law School Dance," *Hatchet*, February 3, 1925; "Speakers to Address," *Hatchet*, November 18, 1924; "Gate and Key," *Hatchet*, April 21, 1925; Tracy to Hoover, February 11, 1928, S1, FBI NARA 67-9524; *CT* (1921), 271; "Hottel Re-Elected," *Hatchet*, December 23, 1924; "Special Agent Guy Hottel," September 24, 1934, FBI FOIA 67-46399-16 (Hottel); *CT* (1925), 58; *CT* (1926), 166.

13. Hoover, "Memorandum for Assistant Director Nathan," September 28, 1931, S2, FBI FOIA 67-883-164 (Nathan).

14. Sargent to Nathan, April 28, 1925, S1, FBI FOIA 67-883-22 (Nathan); Hoover, "Memorandum for Division Seven," June 1, 1931, S2, FBI FOIA 67-883-157 (Nathan); Hoover to Clegg, November 14, 1931, S1, FBI FOIA 67-6524-136 (Clegg); Sisson to Tolson, January 9, 1931, S1, FBI NARA 67-9524-128 (Tolson); Chesnut, "True Stories of Uncle Sam's Own," *WS*, April 19, 1931, B2, JEHS.

15. Bureau of Investigation, *Manual of Instruction* (1927). On the history of "obscene" matters, see Charles, *FBI's Obscene File.*

16. Watson, "Revamp Department of Justice," *Pittsburgh Press*, March 18, 1925, B2, JEHS; Lee, *In the Public Interest*, 39–40.

17. JEH APP (1928), 55–6; "How a Federal Detective Works," *National Spectator*, January 9, 1926, B2, JEHS; "Efficiency Rating Sheet," September 30, 1928, S1, FBI NARA 67-9524 (Tolson); Egan, "Memorandum for the Director" with report, December 6, 1934, S3, FBI FOIA 67-7489 (Purvis).

18. Clegg OH.

19. Hoover, "Memorandum for Mr. Nathan," August 6, 1931, S1, FBI NARA 67-9524 (Tolson); "Memorandum for Mr. Nathan," November 26, 1928, S1, FBI NARA 67-9524 (Tolson).

20. "Memorandum for Mr. Tolson," March 5, 1931, S1, FBI NARA 67-9524-130 (Tolson).

21. "How a Federal Detective Works"; JEH APP (1928), 54; Whitehead, *FBI Story*, 86–8; Theoharis et al., *FBI: Comprehensive Reference Guide*, 353.

22. JEH APP (1929), 65.

23. JEH APP (1928), 52–3. On the Osage case, see Grann, *Killers of the Flower Moon.*

24. Clegg OH; "Hoover Termed," *Washington Brevities*, October 8, 1932, B2, JEHS.

25. Bayliss to Mapes, March 26, 1929, F: "DOJ: Bureau of Investigation," B25, Cabinet Offices, HHoo; Bayliss, "Re: JE Hoover," March 1929, F: "DOJ: Bureau of Investigation," B25, Cabinet Offices, HHoo.

Chapter 12: Depression Days (1929–1932)

1. For bureaucratic autonomy, see especially Carpenter, *Forging of Bureaucratic Autonomy* and *Reputation and Power.* Also see Doig and Hargrove, *Leadership and Innovation*; Cook, *Bureaucracy and Self-Government*; Lewis, *Public Entrepreneurship.*

2. Justice Research and Statistics Association, "Historical Data," https://www.jrsa.org/projects/Historical.pdf; McGirr, *War on Alcohol*, 193.

3. Calder, *Origins and Development of Federal Crime Control Policy*, 5, 78. For the politics of crime during the Herbert Hoover years, also see McGirr, *War on Alcohol*, 188–229; "Symposium: Wickersham Commission," *Marquette Law Review.*

4. Clegg OH; Eig, *Get Capone*, 151, 209.

5. JEH APP (1932), 59.

6. National Commission on Law Observance and Enforcement, "Report on Criminal Statistics," April 1, 1931, S1, FBI FOIA 62-21747-121x (Wickersham), 5–6.

7. "Police Heads," untitled newspaper (Altoona, PA), July 8, 1925, B2, JEHS; IACP, resolution, June 6, 1929, S1, FBI NARA 67-561 (Hoover); JEH APP (1931-second deficiency), 503–4.

8. JEH APP (1931-second deficiency), 503–4.

9. National Commission on Law Observance and Enforcement, "Report on Criminal Statistics," April 1, 1931.

10. "Business Leaders Face 1930 Confidently," *WP*, January 1, 1930; "Business Leaders Face 1931 with Courage," *WP*, January 1, 1931; "2 Cabinet Officials Optimistic," *WP*, January 1, 1932.

11. Cahill, "Vast Construction," *WP*, January 1, 1931; Cahill, "New Business Year," *WP*, January 1, 1931; Cahill, "Capital Trade," *WP*, January 1, 1932.

12. "Kindly Neighbors Care," *WP*, January 1, 1930; Cottrell, "Capital Families Incomes," *WP*, January 1, 1931.

13. On Bonus Army, see Ellis, *Nation in Torment*, 158–85.

14. "Chief of Justice Department," *Livingston Enterprise*, August 16, 1925, B2, JEHS; "U.S. Justice Bureau Chief Visits," *Seattle Post-Intelligencer*, August 20, 1925, B2, JEHS; "Alibi Framers," *Jacksonville Journal*, October 13, 1931, B2, JEHS; "Highlights from Addresses," *National Police Officer*, October 1930, B2, JEHS; "Still Hunting a Jury!" *Chicago Herald and Examiner*, June 17, 1926, B2, JEHS; Hoover, "Memorandum for Mr. Nathan," March 30, 1931, S1, FBI NARA 67-9524 (Tolson); Hoover to Stone, August 19, 1939, F: "General Correspondence, Hoover, John Edgar, 1935-1943," B17, HSF.

15. Wile, "Washington Observations," *WS*, September 27, 1929, B2, JEHS; "Each One a Hoover!" *Cincinnati Enquirer*, December 6, 1928, B2, JEHS; Ellis, *Nation in Torment*, 150, 167; Fish, 1:2, 29; Hoover to Lowenthal, March 6, 1930, S2, FBI FOIA 62-21747-75 (Wickersham).

16. "Peter Carter Says," *WH*, August 3, 1933, B3, JEHS.

17. Temporary Secretary, March 3, 1926, F: "Memo Dated 3/3/26," NLEM; Theoharis et al., *FBI: Comprehensive Reference Guide*, 243, 230; Moser, "Investigators Boost Sports Association," *WT*, April 17, 1935, B9, JEHS; *CT* (1926), 253.

18. JEH APP (1934), 83.

19. JEH APP (1931), 56; Thode, "Memorandum for Mr. Hoover," June 6, 1928, B1, S1, FBI NARA 57-561-15 (Hoover).

20. JEH APP (1931-second deficiency), 499; Hoover, "Memorandum for Mr. Tolson," March 25, 1931, S1, FBI NARA 66-2396-228 (Tolson).

21. Clegg OH; Riley, "Federal Diary," *WH*, September 2, 1933, B3, JEHS.

22. "FBI Law Enforcement Bulletin," December 1, 2012, FBI.gov, https://leb.fbi.gov/2012/december/fbi-law-enforcement-bulletin-a-history; Theoharis et al., *FBI: Comprehensive Reference Guide*, 234.

23. "The Establishment of a Technical Laboratory," March 20, 1934, F: "Justice Department, FBI, 1933–1934," B10, OF10B, FDR; Appel, "Application for Appointment," July 17, 1934, FBI FOIA 67-966-174 (Appel).

24. JEH APP (1931), 63–4; Hoover, "Memorandum," September 1, 1932, S1, FBI V [illegible] (Bonus March); Mitchell to Hoover, September 9, 1932, S1, FBI V [illegible] (Bonus March); Fish 1:2, 37, 46; Luff, *Commonsense Anticommunism*, 121–41.

25. Sisk, "Unknown Persons," February 16, 1934, P1, FBI V NY-62-3057 (Lindbergh kidnapping).

26. Collier, "Condon Says He Knows," *WS*, May 15, 1932, B2, JEHS. On the early politics of kidnapping, see Frydl, "Kidnapping and State Development"; Cox, *Snatch Racket*, 1–118. On Lindbergh kidnapping, see especially Gardner, *Case That Never Dies*; Fisher, *Ghosts of Hopewell*.

Chapter 13: Chairman of the Moral Uplift Squad (1927–1932)

1. "Society: Cabinet Women," *WP*, March 22, 1932.

2. For bachelor culture, see especially Chudacoff, *Age of the Bachelor*; Gustav-Wrathall, *Take the Young Stranger*.

3. "John Edgar Hoover," *Richmond News Leader*, May 3, 1972, B229, JEHS; Demaris, *Director*, 8–9; Purvis and Tresniowski, *Vendetta*, 49.

4. Purvis and Tresniowki, *Vendetta*, 57; Hoover to Purvis, April 10, 1934, F3, B1, MHP.

5. Hoover to Purvis, April 3, 1934, F3, B1, MHP. This letter refers to the "Uplight Squad" but "uplift" squad is his more common, and more obvious, formulation.

6. Purvis and Tresniowski, *Vendetta*, 16–7, 25–36; Purvis, *American Agent*, 22-28; Barber, "Melvin H. Purvis," January 18, 1927, S1, FBI FOIA 67-7489-8 (Purvis).

7. Purvis, *American Agent*, 24; Barber, "Melvin H. Purvis," January 18, 1927, S1, FBI FOIA 67-7489-8 (Purvis).

8. Purvis and Tresniowski, *Vendetta*, 37–8, 46–8.

9. "Chicago Efficiency Ratings," July 1, 1930, S1, FBI FOIA 67-7489 (Purvis); Connelley to Hoover, April 17, 1930, S1, FBI FOIA 67-7489-99 (Purvis).

10. Schilder, "Efficiency Rating Sheet," March 31, 1930, S1, FBI FOIA 67-7489 (Purvis); Hoover, "Memorandum for Mr. Purvis," March 12, 1929, FBI FOIA 67-7489-65 (Purvis); Hoover, handwritten note, March 15, 1929, S1, FBI FOIA 67-7489 (Purvis).

11. Purvis, "Memorandum for the director," April 2, 1929, S1, FBI FOIA 67-7489-67 (Purvis); Purvis to Hoover, November 7, 1929, F1, B1, MHP; Hoover to Purvis, November 9, 1929, F1, B1, MHP; Purvis to Hoover, January 20, 1930, F1, B1, MHP.

12. Sisson to Purvis, February 27, 1930, S1, FBI FOIA 67-7489-93 (Purvis); Schilder to Connelley, March 17, 1930, FBI FOIA 67-7489-96 (Purvis); Sisson to Purvis, July 10, 1930, F1, B1, MHP; Purvis to Hoover, July 24, 1930, FBI FOIA 67-7489-106 (Purvis); Sisson to Purvis, August 16, 1930, S1, FBI FOIA 67-7489-108 (Purvis); Sisson to Purvis, August 29, 1930, S1, FBI FOIA 67-7489-110 (Purvis); "Memorandum of Telephone Call," October 9, 1930, S1, FBI FOIA 67-7489-117 (Purvis); Sisson to Purvis, November 4, 1930, S1, FBI FOIA 67-7489-124 (Purvis); Purvis to Hoover, November 7, 1930, S1, FBI FOIA 67-7489-122 (Purvis); Purvis and Tresniowski, *Vendetta*, 42.

13. Purvis and Tresniowski, *Vendetta*, 42–3; "Lawyers Club Hears Sleuth," *Cincinnati Post*, February 12, 1931, B2, JEHS.

14. Hoover to Purvis, March 10, 1931, F2, B1, MHP.

15. Purvis to Hoover, March 12, 1931, F2, B1, MHP.

16. Hoover to Purvis, March 16, 1931, F2, B1, MHP; Purvis to Hoover, March 20, 1931, F2, B1, MHP; Hoover to Purvis, March 23, 1931, F2, B1, MHP.

17. Hoover to Purvis, August 16, 1932, F2, B1, MHP; Hoover to Purvis, October 15, 1931, F2, B1, MHP.

18. Purvis to Hoover, February 16, 1934, F3, B1, MHP; Hoover to Purvis, June 2, 1931, F2, B1, MHP; Hoover to Purvis, August 3, 1932, F2, B1, MHP; Hoover to Purvis, June 2, 1931, F2, B1, MHP; Hoover to Purvis, September 26, 1932, F2, B1, MHP.

19. Hoover to Purvis, October 15, 1931, F2, B1, MHP.

20. Purvis to Hoover, December 6, 1931, F2, B1, MHP; Hoover to Purvis, May 10, 1933, F2, B1, MHP.

21. Hoover to Purvis, September 24, 1932, F2, B1, MHP; Purvis to Hoover, February 16, 1934, F3, B1, MHP; Hoover to Purvis, September 25, 1933, F3, B1, MHP.

22. Hoover to Purvis, February 13, 1932, F2, B1, MHP; Hoover to Purvis, October 21, 1932, F2, B1, MHP; Hoover to Purvis, July 28, 1934, F3, B1, MHP.

23. Hoover to Purvis, October 21, 1932, F2, B1, MHP; Hoover to Purvis, September 16, 1932, F2, B1, MHP; Hoover to Purvis, September 17, 1932, F2, B1, MHP; Nathan, "A Modern Helen," F2, B1, MHP; Nathan to Purvis, October 14, 1932, F2, B1, MHP.

24. Purvis to Hoover, July 1, 1933, F2, B1, MHP; Hoover to Purvis, July 15, 1933, F2, B1, MHP; Purvis to Hoover, July 19, 1933, F3, B1, MHP.

25. Hoover to Purvis, July 22, 1933, F3, B1, MHP.

26. Hoover, "Memorandum for Mr. Purvis," September 10, 1931, F2, B1, MHP; Hoover to Purvis, August 26, 1931, F2, B1, MHP; Hoover, "Memorandum for Division Six," September 8, 1931, F2, B1, MHP; Hoover to Purvis, March 10, 1931; "How a Federal Detective Works," *National Spectator*, January 9, 1926, B2, JEHS.

27. Hoover to Purvis, September 26, 1932 F2, B1, MHP; Purvis and Tresniowski, *Vendetta*, 43; Hoover to Purvis, July 26, 1932, F2, B1, MHP.

28. Purvis to Hoover, August 11, 1932, F2, B1, MHP; Clegg, "Report of Inspector H.H. Clegg," February 27–March 11, 1932, S1, FBI FOIA 67-7489 (Purvis); Hoover to Purvis, October 25, 1932, F2, B1, MHP.

29. Purvis, *American Agent*, 71.

Chapter 14: Government Men (1933)

1. On state development and the 1930s War on Crime, see especially Potter, *War on Crime*; Burrough, *Public Enemies*; O'Reilly, "New Deal for the FBI"; Denney, "'To Wage a War'"; Frydl, "Kidnapping and State Development"; Gregory, *Building Law and Order*. On the Kansas City Massacre, see especially Unger, *Union Station Massacre*. For examples of the FBI's triumphal histories, see especially Hoover, *Ten Thousand Public Enemies*; Whitehead, *FBI Story*.

2. Roosevelt, Inaugural Address, March 4, 1933, American Presidency Project, https://www.presidency.ucsb.edu/documents/inaugural-address-8.

3. Theoharis and Cox, *Boss*, 111–5; "Walsh Plans Changes," *Philadelphia Inquirer*, March 1, 1933, FBI 62-28331, F2, B1, Sr51, AT; "Memorandum for Mr. Hoover," March 2, 1933, FBI 62-28331, F2, B1, Sr51, AT; Hoover, "Memorandum for Mr. Nathan," March 2, 1933, FBI 62-28331, F2, B1, Sr51, AT; "Senator Walsh Dies on Train," *Philadelphia Inquirer*, March 3, 1933, FBI 62-28331-4x, F2, B1, Sr51, AT.

4. Gentry, *J. Edgar Hoover*, 155; Kennedy, *Freedom from Fear*, 129–30.

5. Mason, *Harlan Fiske Stone*, 152; McSwain to Roosevelt, July 25, 1933, F: "F.B.I. 1933–1934," B10, OF10B, FDR; Seymour to Roosevelt, July 20, 1933, F: "F.B.I. 1933–1934."

6. Hoover to Purvis, April 25, 1933, F2, B1, MHP; "Memorandum re. Article," April 7, 1933, F: "F.B.I. 1933–1934," B10, OF10B, FDR; McCormack to McIntyre, July 7, 1933, F: "F.B.I. 1933–1934," B10, OF10B, FDR; Roosevelt and Brough, *Rendezvous with Destiny*, 236.

7. Tucker, "Hist! Who's That?," *Collier's*, August 19, 1933, B3, JEHS.

8. Theoharis et al., *FBI: Comprehensive Reference Guide*, 318. The most thorough account of the case is Unger, *Union Station Massacre*. Where not otherwise cited, details of the massacre and investigation can be found there and in Burrough, *Public Enemies*.

9. Burrough, *Public Enemies*, 51–2; *CT* (1925).

10. Hoover, "Memorandum for Mr. Nathan," June 17, 1933, S1, FBI V 62-28915-16 (Kansas City Massacre/KCM); Jones to Hoover, June 17, 1933, S1, FBI V 62-28915-6 (KCM); Burrough, *Public Enemies*, 53–4; Hoover, "Memorandum for the Attorney General," June 19, 1933, S1, FBI V 62-28915-12 (KCM); Hoover to Vetterli, June 17, 1933, S1, FBI V 62-28915-7 (KCM); Tolson, "Memorandum for the Director," June 20, 1933, S1, FBI V 62-28915 (KCM); Hoover, "Memorandum for Mr. Tolson," June 22, 1933, S3, FB VI 62-28915 (KCM).

11. "Cummings Picked to Succeed Walsh," *NYT*, March

3, 1933; Parrish, "Homer Stille Cummings," *American National Biography*. For Cummings's legal and administrative views, see especially Cummings, *Liberty under Law and Administration*; Cummings and McFarland, *Federal Justice*.

12. *AR/AG* (1933), 98; Powers, *Secrecy and Power*, 183.

13. "Underworld Weapons," *Cincinnati Enquirer*, July 5, 1933; "U.S. Pushes War," *CT*, July 30, 1933; "J.E. Hoover Heads," *NYT*, July 30, 1933.

14. Denney, "'To Wage a War,'" 17.

15. Burrough, *Public Enemies*, 130–3; Chaplin, "Federal 'G' Men," *WH*, October 15, 1933, B3, JEHS.

16. JEH APP (1935), 66–77.

17. "Lone Island Picked," *NYT*, October 13, 1933; "Roosevelt Orders War," *NYT*, July 27, 1933.

18. Unger, *Union Station Massacre*, 57; Bureau of Investigation, *Manual* (1927), 16; Purvis, *American Agent*, 55–6, 66.

19. Potter, *War on Crime*, 140; "Memorandum for Mr. Tolson," April 23, 1934, S1, FBI FOIA 67-11938 (Pennington); Burrough, *Public Enemies*, 59, 166, 169, 247.

Chapter 15: The Black Chamber (1934)

1. The best recent accounts of the FBI's role in the Dillinger case are Burrough, *Public Enemies*, and Purvis and Tresniowski, *Vendetta*. Where not otherwise cited, details of the Dillinger case can be found in these sources. For broader context, see especially Gorn, *Dillinger's Wild Ride*; Ruth, *Inventing the Public Enemy*; Girardin and Helmer, *Dillinger*; Toland, *Dillinger Days*. For federal policy, see Potter, *War on Crime*; Gregory, *Building Law and Order*. On Hoover's reluctance, see Burrough, *Public Enemies*, 154.

2. For "Black Chamber" references, see Hill, "Human Side of the News," *WT*, July 26, 1934, B4, JEHS; "Criminals' Nemesis," *WP*, May 26, 1935, B10, JEHS.

3. Purvis, *American Agent*, 99.

4. Purvis and Tresniowski, *Vendetta*, 46; Purvis to Hoover, November 29, 1933, S1, FBI FOIA 67-7489 (Purvis); Purvis, *American Agent*, 49.

5. Purvis and Tresniowski, *Vendetta*, 86–8; "Sankey Link in Lindbergh Case Fails," *WP*, February 2, 1934.

6. Hoover to Purvis, February 6, 1934, F3, B1, MHP.

7. Hoover to Purvis, April 3, 1934, F3, B1, MHP.

8. For Purvis's description, see Purvis, *American Agent*, 1–9.

9. Burrough, *Public Enemies*, 313; *CT* (1925), 47.

10. Burrough, *Public Enemies*, 314–9; Purvis and Tresniowski, *Vendetta*, 116.

11. Purvis and Tresniowski, *Vendetta*, 131, 136.

12. "Colleagues Carry Slain Agent," *WN*, April 27, 1934, B4, JEHS; Hoover, "Memorandum for the Assistant to the Attorney General," April 25, 1934, S1, FBI FOIA 67-7489-249 (Purvis).

13. Purvis and Tresniowski, *Vendetta*, 132; Burrough, *Public Enemies*, 367–8; Hoover to SAC, June 22, 1934, S1, FBI FOIA 67-6524 (Clegg).

14. Purvis and Tresniowski, *Vendetta*, 139.

15. F206, B4, NARA-P.

16. *AR/AG* (1934), 124.

17. "Cummings Puts $10,000 Price," *BS*, June 24, 1934; Hoover to Purvis, May 29, 1934, S2, FBI FOIA 67-7489-260 (Purvis).

18. Hazelrigg, "Twilight of Gangster Era," *NYHT*, July 29, 1934, B4, JEHS; "Government Bent on Wiping Out," *NYT*, July 24, 1934, B4, JEHS.

19. "U.S. Bases Its Gangster Drive," *Tulsa Tribune*, July 31, 1934, B4, JEHS; Tamm, "Memorandum for the Director," September 24, 1934, S64, FBI V 62-28915-2657 (KCM).

20. Lockerman, "'A Girl among Man-Hunters,'" *ChiT*, October 7, 1935, B14, JEHS; Burrough, *Public Enemies*, 414–5.

21. Purvis and Tresniowski, *Vendetta*, 171; Burrough, *Public Enemies*, 414; Unger, *Union Station Massacre*, 151; Tamm, "Memorandum for the Director," October 1, 1934, S63, FBI V 62-28915 (KCM).

22. Tamm, "Memorandum for the Director," September 24, 1934; Tamm, "Memorandum for the Director," September 25, 1934, S64, FBI V 62-28915-2617 (KCM); Tamm, "Memorandum for the Director," October 1, 1934, S63, FBI V 62-28915-2628 (KCM); Burrough, *Public Enemies*, 450; Unger, *Union Station Massacre*, 153–4.

23. Burrough, *Public Enemies*, 427.

24. "Purvis Puts New Notch," *BS*, October 23, 1934.

25. Burrough, *Public Enemies*, 477; Purvis and Tresniowski, *Vendetta*, 259.

26. "Slain Agents Fired 60 Shots," *NYT*, November 29, 1934; "Nelson Slain," *Indianapolis Star*, November 29, 1934; Macaulay, "Speeding the Downfall," *BS*, December 9, 1934.

Chapter 16: It's FBI Now (1934–1935)

1. CrimeConf, 19, 7; Powers, *Secrecy and Power*, 195.

2. CrimeConf, 17, 19.

3. Wicker, "Washington," *NYT*, July 25, 1965, B139, JEHS. On Hoover's turn to public relations, see especially Powers, *G-Men*; Cecil, *Branding Hoover's FBI*; Cecil, *Hoover's FBI and the Fourth Estate*.

4. Roosevelt, "Fireside Chat on Banking," March 12, 1933, American Presidency Project, https://www.presidency.ucsb.edu/documents/fireside-chat-banking.

5. "Author Cooper Kills Self," *WTH*, September 30, 1940, S17, FBI FOIA 94-3-4-20-677x1 (Cooper); Cooper, *The Eagle's Eye*.

6. Cooper to Hoover, April 22-23, 1933, S1, FBI FOIA 62-21526-9 (Cooper); Hoover to Cooper, April 27, 1933, S1, FBI FOIA 62-21526-9 (Cooper); Hoover, "Brains Against Bullets," *American Magazine*, February 1934, S2, FBI FOIA 62-21526 (Cooper).

7. Lester, "Memorandum for Mr. Tolson," August 26, 1934, FBI 62-43811, F1, B1, Sr35, AT; Hoover to Purvis, November 14, 1934, F3, B1, MHP.

8. *The Public Enemy*, directed by William Wellman (Burbank, CA: Warner Bros. Pictures, 1931).

9. "Detection and Apprehension," F: "General Correspondence, Hoover, John Edgar, 1928-1934," B17, HFS; Moley, *Hays Office*, 32–88, 240–1. On the early politics of the film code, also see Doherty, *Hollywood's Censor*; Doherty, *Pre-Code Hollywood*; Powers, *G-Men, 51-73*.

10. Doherty, *Hollywood's Censor*, 60–2.

11. Moley, *Hays Office*, 241–3; Doherty, *Hollywood's Censor*, 69–71.

12. Hoover to Purvis, January 2, 1935, F3, B1, MHP; "Hoover, Nemesis of Crime," *WH*, January 2, 1935, B8, JEHS; "War on Crime," *WT*, January 1, 1935, B8, JEHS.

13. "J.E. Hoover Remains Head," *CT*, July 30, 1933; Houser, "Uncle Sam's Sherlocks," *NYWT*, December 14, 1933, B3, JEHS; "Moley's Crime Sleuth," *NYWT*, August 5, 1933, B3, JEHS; F98, B2, NARA-P.

14. "Washington Wayside," *WS*, July 22, 1935, B12, JEHS; Milne, "Boss of G-Men Tells How They Do It," *Boston Sunday Post*, June 9, 1935, B11, JEHS; U.S. General Services Administration, s.v. "U.S. Department of Justice Building," http://www.gsa.gov/portal/ext/html/site/hb/category/25431/actionParameter/exploreByBuilding/buildingId/321.

15. "National Broadcasting Company," July 17, 1935, S7, FBI FOIA 62-21526-200 (Cooper); Fox, "The Birth of the FBI's Technical Laboratory," https://www.fbi.gov/history/history-publications-reports/the-birth-of-the-fbis-technical-laboratory1924-to-1935; Theoharis et al., *FBI: Comprehensive Reference Guide*, 250–1.

16. "Hoover Battles Crime," *WT*, June 13, 1935, B11, JEHS; Milne, "Boss of G-Men," *Boston Sunday Post*, June 9, 1935, B11, JEHS; Alexander, "The Director," *New Yorker*, September 25, 1937, B45, JEHS; Kipling, "If," F22, B2, NLEM.

17. F65, B1, NARA-P; "Where Is Thy Sting?" *Indianapolis Times*, January 17, 1935, B8, JEHS; Milne, "Boss of G-Men"; "Federal Crime Museum," *Pittsburgh Press*, June 4, 1935, B10, JEHS; "Hoover Battles Crime."

18. Potter, *War on Crime*, 170; Theoharis et al., *FBI: Comprehensive Reference Guide*, 14.

19. "Seal & Motto," FBI, https://www.fbi.gov/about-us/history/seal-motto.

20. Collier, "It's F.B.I. Now," *WS*, June 28, 1935, B11, JEHS; Tolson, "Memorandum for the Director," November 5, 1934, S3, FBI FOIA 62-21526 (Cooper); Cooper to Hoover, December 24, 1934, S4, FBI FOIA 62-21526 (Cooper).

21. Tolson, "Memorandum for the Director," December 11, 1934, S3, FBI FOIA 62-21526 (Cooper); Hoover, "Memorandum for Mr. Tolson," November 2, 1934, S3, FBI FOIA 62-21526 (Cooper).

22. Cooper to Tolson, January 8, 1935, S4, FBI FOIA 62-21526 (Cooper); Lester, "Memorandum for Mr. Tolson," January 10, 1935, S4, FBI FOIA 62-21526 (Cooper); Tolson, "Memorandum for the Director," January 11, 1935, S4, FBI FOIA 62-21526 (Cooper).

23. G. G. G., "10,000 Public Enemies," *WP*, March 10, 1935, B9, JEHS; Driscoll, "Cream of the United States, *NYHT Books*, March 3, 1935, B9, JEHS; Duffus, "Government's War on Crime," *NYT Book Review*, March 3, 1935, S6, FBI FOIA 62-21526 (Cooper).

24. Cooper, *Ten Thousand Public Enemies*, 5, 27.

25. Byrnes, "Long Shots and Close-Ups," *Bulletin*, April 5, 1935, B9, JEHS; Powers, *G-Men*, 66.

26. Powers, *G-Men*, 53; "Entertainment for Impending Week," *WP*, May 9, 1935, B10, JEHS.

27. *G-Men*, directed by William Keighley (Burbank, CA: Warner Bros. Pictures, 1935); Powers, *G-Men*, 51–64.

28. Martin, *Hollywood's Movie Commandments*, 134; Powers, *G-Men*, 53.

29. Clegg OH; Powers, *Secrecy and Power*, 200–1; Broun, "It Seems to Me," *WDN*, May 22, 1935, B10, JEHS.

30. "National Broadcasting Company," July 17, 1935, S7, FBI FOIA 62-21526-200 (Cooper). On Hoover's early public relations initiatives, see especially Powers, *Secrecy and Power*, 202–7; Cecil, *Branding Hoover's FBI*, 27-72; Powers, *G-Men*, 3-187.

31. JEH APP (1937), 78; Hoover to Ford, October 30, 1936, film poster: "You can't get away with it," F65-HM-2, B5, NARA-P.

32. Theoharis et al., *FBI: Comprehensive Reference Guide*, 229.

Chapter 17: Right-Hand Man (1935–1936)

1. Purvis and Tresniowski, *Vendetta*, 260; Hoover to Purvis, November 14, 1934, F3, B1, MHP. For correspondence about the film, see October 26–30, 1934, FBI FOIA 80-84 (Purvis).

2. Hoover to Purvis, January 2, 1935, F3, B1, MHP; Hoover, "Memorandum," November 23, 1934, S3, FBI FOIA 67-7489 (Purvis); Egan, "Memorandum for the Director," December 6, 1934, S3, FBI FOIA 67-7489 (Purvis);

Tolson, "Memorandum for the Director," March 8, 1935, S3, FBI FOIA 67-7489 (Purvis); Hoover to Purvis, March 9, 1935, S3, FBI FOIA 67-7489 (Purvis)

3. Hoover, "Memorandum for Mr. Tolson," April 4, 1935, S3, FBI FOIA 67-7489 (Purvis); Purvis and Tresniowski, *Vendetta*, 273; Hoover, "Memorandum," July 10, 1935, S3, FBI FOIA 67-7489-375 (Purvis); "Purvis Quits Post," *NYS*, July 12, 1935, B12, JEHS.

4. Hoover, "Memorandum for Mr. Sornborger," December 13, 1929, S1, FBI NARA 67-9524-90 (Tolson); Hoover, "Memorandum for Mr. Gardner," October 2, 1930, S1, FBI NARA 67-9524-120 (Tolson); "Distinguished Men Play on Summit," untitled (Uniontown, PA), July 26, 1930, B2, JEHS; PB85, NLEM.

5. Winchell, "Double G-Men," *NYM*, September 26, 1935, B14, JEHS; Winchell, "On Broadway," *WH*, December 7, 1935, B16, JEHS; interview, Anita Colby, S-JEHC; Summers, *Official and Confidential*, 84; Gabler, *Winchell*, 265.

6. Theoharis et al., *FBI: Comprehensive Reference Guide*, 357; Burrough, *Public Enemies*, 54; Unger, *Union Station Massacre*, 79.

7. Clegg OH; Purvis and Tresniowski, *Vendetta*, 134; Tolson, "Memorandum for the Director," March 8, 1935, S3, FBI FOIA 67-10595-165 (Purvis).

8. Hoover, "Memorandum for Mr. Tolson," November 8, 1934, S2, FBI NARA 67-9524 (Tolson).

9. Hoover to Tolson, November 10, 1932, S2, FBI NARA 67-9524-157 (Tolson). For early examples, see Tolson to Cooper, May 22, 1933, S1, FBI FOIA 62-21526-14 (Cooper); Tolson, "Memorandum for the Director," May 29, 1933, S1, FBI FOIA 62-21526-17 (Cooper); Cooper to Tolson, ca. July 20, 1935, FBI FOIA 62-21526-207 (Cooper); Hoover to Cooper, July 20, 1935, S7, FBI FOIA 62-21526 (Cooper); Cooper to Hoover, ca. September 1934, S3, FBI FOIA 62-21526-84 (Cooper).

10. "Certificate of Medication Examination," September 1934, FBI FOIA 67-46399-15 (Hottel); PB2, NLEM.

11. *CT* (1923), 98; *CT* (1924), 135, 145; *CT* (1925), 133, 227; *CT* (1926), 177; "Great 'Pep' Rally Planned," *Hatchet*, November 25, 1924; "GWU Takes First Game," *Hatchet*, September 30, 1924; "Annual Hop," *Hatchet*, December 2, 1924; "Hottel Re-Elected," *Hatchet*, December 23, 1924; "Gate and Key," *Hatchet*, April 21, 1925; *CT* (1925), 227; Roberts, "Guy Lewellyn Hottel," September 20, 1934, FBI 67-46399-7 (Hottel); interview, Guy Hottel, S-JEHC.

12. Roberts, "Guy Lewellyn Hottel"; Tolson to Glavin, September 16, 1934, FBI FOIA 67-46399 (Hottel).

13. Quinn, "Memorandum for Mr. Tolson," March 9, 1935, FBI FOIA 67-46399-30 (Hottel); Hoover to Hottel, March 16, 1935, FBI FOIA 67-46399-28 (Hottel); Hoover, "Memorandum for Mr. Sornborger," May 16, 1935, FBI FOIA 67-46399-34 (Hottel); Tolson, "Guy L. Hottel," April 24, 1935, FBI FOIA 67-46399-35 (Hottel); Tolson, "Memorandum for the Director," July 26, 1935, FBI FOIA 67-46399-41 (Hottel); Tolson, "Memorandum for the Director," August 24, 1935, FBI FOIA 67-46399-41 (Hottel); Tolson, "Guy Hottel," October 26, 1935, FBI FOIA 67-46399-47 (Hottel); Keith to Hoover, September 3, 1935, FBI FOIA 67-46399-43 (Hottel).

14. Interview, Guy Hottel, S-JEHC; Summers, *Official and Confidential*, 81–3; Hoover, "Memorandum for Mr. Tolson," April 19, 1936, FBI FOIA 67-46399-87 (Hottel); Clegg, "Memorandum for the Director," July 22, 1936, FBI FOIA 67-46399-98 (Hottel); Tolson, "Memorandum for the Director," July 28, 1936, FBI FOIA 67-46399-99 (Hottel);

Tolson, "Memorandum for the Director," August 11, 1936, FBI FOIA 67-46399-101 (Hottel); Hottel to Hoover, May 20, 1937, FBI FOIA 67-46399-128 (Hottel).

15. Powers, *Secrecy and Power*, 205.

16. Untitled, *WH*, January 28, 1935, B8, JEHS. For examples, see F125, B2, NARA-P; F162, B3, NARA-P.

17. "The Cochrane Eye," *Detroit Free Press*, September 12, 1935, B14, JEHS; F125, B2, NARA-P; F162, B3, NARA-P; Hoover, "Memorandum for Mr. Tolson," June 8, 1935, S2, FBI NARA 61-9524-192 (Tolson); "First Lady Tours," *Indianapolis Star*, April 19, 1936, B21, JEHS.

18. Interview of Charles E. Kleinkauf, FBI OH; "'Public Enemies'; See Hoover," *WS*, December 4, 1935, B16, JEHS; F227-228, B4, NARA-P; "Capital's Star Parade," *WP*, October 28, 1939, B71, JEHS; F43, B1, NARA-P; "Furr Confident of Winning," *WP*, July 22, 1936, B29, JEHS; "Head 'G' Man Greets Shrine Head," *Cleveland Plain Dealer*, June 11, 1935, B11, JEHS; F38, B1, NARA-P.

19. "Hoover Assails Crime Aides," *WT*, January 18, 1935, B8, JEHS; "Meet 'Doctor' Hoover," June 11, 1935, S2, FBI NARA 67-561-58 (Hoover); "The Cover," *KAJ*, May 1935, B10, JEHS; "Bullet Proof Limousine," *Buffalo Courier-Express*, May 23, 1935, B10, JEHS.

20. "Edgar Hoover and Harry Hopkins," *Hartford Times*, April 24, 1936, B21, JEHS; Essary, "Now," *WT*, July 24, 1935, B12, JEHS; "Capital Stuff," *NYDN*, May 7, 1935, B10, JEHS; "John Edgar Hoover," *Time*, August 5, 1935, B13, JEHS.

21. F5, B1, NARA-P; "Men Watch a Fight," *BG*, August 19, 1936, B30, JEHS; "Relaxing after Kidnap Victory," *Post Gazette*, June 14, 1935, B11, JEHS; Lyons, "Corpses Derelicti," *Broadway Gazette*, September 28, 1935, B14, JEHS; F99, B2, NARA-P; "Washington Wayside," *WS*, June 6, 1935, B10, JEHS.

22. F98, B2, NARA-P; F240, B4, NARA-P.

23. Gabler, *Winchell*, 199; Frank to Hoover, September 7, 1934, S2, FBI V 62-31615-12 (Winchell). Also see Stuart, *Secret Life of Walter Winchell*; Weiner, *Let's Go to Press*; Stowe, "The Politics of Café Society."

24. Winchell, "On Broadway," *WH*, March 22, 1935, B9, JEHS; Hoover to Dunn, May 28, 1934, S2, FBI V 62-31615-3 (Winchell); Sackett to Hoover, June 5, 1934, S2, FBI V 62-31615-4 (Winchell); Tracy to Hoover, September 17, 1935, S2, FBI V 62-31615-28 (Winchell).

25. Gabler, *Winchell*, 186–90, 262–7; Blumenthal, *Stork Club*.

26. Gabler, *Winchell*, 188; "Champ and Head G-Man Greet New Year," *WS*, January 1, 1936, B17, JEHS; F182, B3, NARA-P.

27. Winchell, "On Broadway," *NYM*, September 26, 1935, B14, JEHS; Lyons, "The Lyons Den," *NYP*, January 8, 1936, B14, JEHS; Beebe, *Stork Club Bar Book*, 110.

28. Winchell, "On Broadway," *NYM*, September 26, 1935; Winchell, "On Broadway," *WH*, August 7, 1935, B13, JEHS.

29. Winchell to Hoover, August 1935, S3, FBI FOIA 67-7489 (Purvis); Summers, *Official and Confidential*, 85–6.

30. Chauncey, *Gay New York*, 313–42; Blumenthal, *Stork Club*, 137–8, 146; Summers, *Official and Confidential*, 84.

31. Winchell to Hoover, February 9, 1936, S2, FBI V 62-31615 (Winchell); "Chief G-Man in Florida," *Birmingham News*, February 18, 1936, B18, JEHS; "J. Edgar Hoover Views Races," *MH*, February 18, 1936, B18, JEHS; Roman, "Angler's Notes," *Miami Tribune*, February 22, 1936, B18, JEHS; PB62, 63, NLEM; interview, Guy Hottel, S-JEHC.

32. PB51, PB61, PB62, PB2, PB57, NLEM.

33. Theoharis et al., *FBI: Comprehensive Reference Guide*, 357.

Chapter 18: Sob Sisters and Convict Lovers (1935–1938)

1. Hoover, "The Influence of Crime on the American Home," *American Railway Journal*, 1936, B17, JEHS.

2. "Ripley Leads as Boys' Idol," *WH*, April 5, 1936, B20, JEHS.

3. Friedman, *Crime and Punishment*, 161–2.

4. Hoover to Cooper, December 21, 1934, S3, FBI FOIA 62-21526 (Cooper); Milne, "Boss of G-Men Tells How They Do It," *Boston Sunday Post*, June 9, 1935, B11, JEHS.

5. "Washington Wayside," *WS*, July 17, 1935, B12, JEHS; "Hoover Enlarges 'Enemy' List," *NYS*, July 9, 1935, B11, JEHS.

6. Hill, "Human Side of the News," *Pittsburgh Sun-Telegraph*, July 23, 1935, B12, JEHS; Cribbins, "J. Edgar Hoover," *New World Sun*, August 3, 1935, B13, JEHS.

7. "Lawes Assails Hoover Views," *NYWT*, July 10, 1935, B11, JEHS; "Lawes Finds Views of Hoover Cruel," *NYT*, July 11, 1935, B12, JEHS.

8. "Hoover, Chief G-Man," *Detroit News*, July 10, 1935, B11, JEHS.

9. JEH APP (1937), 87; "President Favors 'Crime School,'" *WT*, February 11, 1935, B8, JEHS.

10. JEH APP (1937), 86–8; Haakinson, "'G-Men's University' Opened," *Lincoln Star*, June 23, 1935, B11, JEHS; Theoharis and Cox, *Boss*, 130.

11. "America's Youth Problem," *Ohio American Legion News*, October 14, 1937, B46, JEHS.

12. "J. E. Hoover Strikes Back," *Detroit News*, November 9, 1937, B48, JEHS; "Print Law Need Seen," *LAT*, June 28, 1936, B27, JEHS; Myers, "Crime and Relaxed Home," Central Press Association, June 25, 1936, B27, JEHS; Hoover, "Crime and Your Home," *This Week*, February 6, 1938, B52, JEHS.

13. Routh, "G-Man J. Edgar Hoover," *Baptist Student*, October 1938, B63, JEHS; "Religion in a Troubled World," *Religious Digest*, June 1938, B57, JEHS.

14. "FBI Pledge," January 12, 1938, S2, FBI FOIA 67-883-244 (Nathan); "FBI Pledge," February 2, 1938, S2, FBI FOIA 67-39021-230 (Nichols); "FBI Pledge," February 8, 1938, S1, FBI FOIA 67-61295-75 (Smith).

15. "Chief of America's Heroic G-Men," *Shelby Sentinel*, June 12, 1936, B27, JEHS.

16. Myers, "Crime and Relaxed Home," Central Press Association, June 25, 1936, B27, JEHS; "Asks Kiwanis to Join Crime War," *Newark Evening News*, June 24, 1936, B27, JEHS; "Federal Agent Paints Dark Picture," *Greensboro Daily News*, April 24, 1936, B21, JEHS; "Boss of G-Men Guest," *Detroit Times*, June 19, 1936, B27, JEHS; "J. Edgar Hoover Hits Politicians," *NYWT*, September 19, 1936, B32, JEHS; "J. Edgar Hoover Expounded," *Kansas City Journal-Post*, September 22, 1936, B32, JEHS; "Head G-Man Lays Youthful Crimes," *Philadelphia Record*, May 31, 1936, B25, JEHS; "Hoover Tells Folly," *CT*, June 23, 1936, B27, JEHS; "Text of Address," *Megaphone*, May 28, 1936, B25, JEHS; Connor, "G-Men Taking Up Oratory," *Chicago Daily News*, January 29, 1936, B17, JEHS; Hoover, "Memorandum for Mr. William Stanley," June 6, 1934, S1, FBI FOIA 67-39021-9 (Nichols); Tolson, "Memorandum for the Director," October 25, 1935, S1, FBI FOIA 67-39021

(Nichols); "Certificate of Medical Examination" (Nichols), S1, FBI FOIA 67-39012 (Nichols); Hall, "Louis B. Nichols," June 13, 1934, S1, FBI FOIA 67-39021 (Nichols); Clegg, "Memorandum for the Director," November 5, 1935, S1, FBI FOIA 67-39012-56 (Nichols); Untitled, July 7, 1936, S1, FBI FOIA 67-30921-82 (Nichols); Hoover, "Memorandum for Mr. Tolson," July 15, 1396, S1, FBI FOIA 67-39021-84 (Nichols).

17. "Asks Kiwanis to Join," *Evening News*, June 24, 1936, B27, JEHS; Hoover, "Law Enforcement and the Citizen," *Police and Peace Officers' Journal*, February 1935, B8, JEHS; "G-Man Hoover Urges Revival," *Memphis Press-Scimitar*, May 29, 1936, B25, JEHS.

18. "Text of Address."

19. "Federal Agent Paints Dark Picture"; "Abuse of Parole," *Arkansas Gazette*, June 13, 1937, B42, JEHS; "Clubwomen Called into Crime War," *Cleveland News*, October 14, 1937, B46, JEHS; Christianson, "Character Education," *Clubwoman*, January 1938, B49, JEHS.

20. Holleran to Hoover, May 6, 1938, S1, FBI FOIA 94-1-3197 (American Legion); Hoover to Holleran, May 10, 1938, S1, FBI 94-1-3197 (American Legion); Hoover to Mason, August 16, 1938, S1, FBI FOIA 94-1-3197 (American Legion).

21. JEH APP (1937), 60; "Congressional Tribute," *Pittsburgh Post-Gazette*, April 7, 1936, S1, FBI FOIA 67-9287 (McKellar); S. 4169, 74th Cong, 2nd session, February 24, 1936, S2, FBI V 67-561 (Hoover); "Hoover Pay Raise Approved," *NYHT*, June 2, 1936, B26, JEHS.

22. "Senators Quiz J.E. Hoover," *ChiT*, April 17, 1936, B21, JEHS; Hoover to Griffin, April 20, 1936, S2, FBI FOIA 67-9287 (McKellar).

23. Hoover to Biddle, April 17, 1936, S1, FBI FOIA 67-9287-A-19 (McKellar).

24. Foxworth, "Memorandum for the Director," April 13, 1936, S1, FBI FOIA 67-9287-A-28 (McKellar); Lester, "Memorandum for the Director," April 20, 1936, S1, FBI FOIA 67-9287-A-58 (McKellar); Hoover to Stapleton, April 19, 1936, S1, FBI FOIA 67-9287-A-34 (McKellar).

25. "Record of Telephone Call" (Connor), April 16, 1936, S1, FBI FOIA 67-9287-A-22 (McKellar); Vetterli to Tolson, April 17, 1936, S1, FBI FOIA 67-9287-A-84 (McKellar); "New Deal Idea of 'Economy,'" *Philadelphia Daily News*, April 20, 1936, S2, FBI FOIA 67-9287 (McKellar); "Don't Curb the G-Men," *Trenton Evening Times*, April 17, 1936, S2, FBI FOIA 67-9287 (McKellar); untitled, *Evening Union*, April 17, 1936, S2, FBI FOIA 67-9287-A-164 (McKellar).

26. *CR*, April 22, 1936, S3, FBI FOIA 67-9287 (McKellar).

27. "Senate Roars 'Nay,'" April 22, 1936, S1, FBI FOIA 67-9287 (McKellar); "Record of Telephone Call," April 22, 1936, S1, FBI FOIA 67-9287-A-12, A-21 (McKellar); Hoover to Marsh, April 26, 1936, S1, FBI FOIA 67-9287-A72 (McKellar). Also see "Record of Telephone Call," April 22, 1936, S1, FBI FOIA 67-9287-A-12, A-13, A-21, A-63, A-65 (McKellar); Hoover to Glass, April 23, 1936, S1, FBI FOIA 67-9287 (McKellar); Hoover to Robinson, April 23, 1936, S1, FBI FOIA 67-9287 (McKellar); Hoover to Nye, April 23, 1936, S1, FBI FOIA 67-9287 (McKellar).

28. "G-Men Quiz Karpis," *WN*, May 2, 1936, B22, JEHS; Powers, *Secrecy and Power*, 207–8; Karpis, *My Story*, 232–42; "G-Men Transfer Karpis," *Evening Gazette*, May 2, 1936, B22, JEHS; Whitehead, *FBI Story*, 109.

29. "Karpis Arrest Hoover's First," *Sentinel*, May 2, 1936, B22, JEHS.

30. Clegg OH.

31. Turrou, *Where My Shadow Falls*, 132. For overviews of Hoover's 1936–1937 anti-prostitution campaign, see Pliley, "Vice Queens and White Slaves" and *Policing Sexuality*, 183–206.

32. "Woman Seized in Park Ave.", *NYWT*, February 5, 1936, B18, JEHS; "G-Men Smash N.Y.-Connecticut White Slave Ring," *NYJ*, August 22, 1936, B31, JEHS; Turrou, *Where My Shadow Falls*, 139–40; "White-Slave Hunt," *NYT*, August 23, 1936, B31, JEHS; "G-Men Probe," *Honolulu Advertiser*, January 1, 1937, B37, JEHS.

33. Tamm, "Memorandum for the Director," July 8, 1937, S1, FBI NARA 31-44269 (AC raids); Hoover to SAC New York, March 16, 1937, FBI NARA 31-46384-68 (Baltimore raids); Turrou, *Where My Shadow Falls*, 136; "Memorandum for the Director," August 25, 1937, S10, B101, FBI NARA 31-44269 (AC raids); "G-Men Arrest 125," *NYM*, August 30, 1937, B44, JEHS; Whitley, "Memorandum for the Director," August 30, 1937, S10, FBI NARA 31-44269-248 (AC raids); "Federal Agents Arrest 125," *NYHT*, August 30, 1937, B44, JEHS.

34. "Mencken Gives Vice Lecture," *WH*, July 31, 1937, B43, JEHS; Hoover, "War on the Sex Criminal!" *This Week*, September 26, 1937, B45, JEHS.

35. Alexander, "The Director," *New Yorker*, September 25, 1937, B45, JEHS.

Chapter 19: The Gathering Storm (1936–1938)

1. Hoover, "Confidential Memorandum," August 24, 1936, B22, F136, HO&C.

2. On the formation of the CIO, see especially Zieger, *CIO*, 22–65.

3. On populist challenges to Roosevelt, see Brinkley, *Voices of Protest*.

4. Hoover, "Confidential Memorandum," August 24, 1936; Hoover, "Memorandum for Mr. Tamm," September 10, 1936, B22, F136, HO&C. Hoover, "Confidential Memorandum," August 25, 1936, B22, F136, HO&C.

5. Cummings to Roosevelt, October 20, 1938, F: "AG Personal File: Espionage Committee: Oct 1938," B100, HSC.

6. CCH6, 556–7; CC2, 25.

7. For American fascism in the 1930s, see Fronczak, "Fascist Game." For the South, see Gilmore, *Defying Dixie*, 106–294.

8. Canedy, *America's Nazis*, 49–70, 73–4, 113, 133–4.

9. "Cummings Weighs 1,000-Page Study," *WP*, January 6, 1938, B50, JEHS; "FBI Report Said to Clear Nazi Bund," *Arkansas Gazette*, January 13, 1938, B50, JEHS; Canedy, *America's Nazis*, 142.

10. Canedy, *America's Nazis*, 73–4.

11. For an overview of American communism in the 1930s, see Klehr, *Heyday of American Communism*; Fried, *Communism in America*, 227–46. For communists and civil rights, see especially Gilmore, *Defying Dixie*; Kelley, *Hammer and Hoe*.

12. Cummings to Roosevelt, October 20, 1938; Manly, "Seize Records," *CT*, September 29, 1939, B71, JEHS; "G-Men Clear Landlords," *WN*, March 13, 1939, B66, JEHS; "FBI Sees Relief Used," *WP*, March 13, 1939, B66, JEHS.

13. Klehr, *Heyday of American Communism*, 224, 238.

14. Cummings to Roosevelt, October 20, 1938; Hoover, "Confidential Memorandum," August 24, 1936.

15. Cummings to Roosevelt, October 20, 1938; Klehr, *Heyday of American Communism*, 230.

16. Hoover, "Confidential Memorandum," August 24,

1936, B22, B136, HO&C; Klehr, *Heyday of American Communism*, 232–3, 239–40.

17. Ward, "Say J.E. Hoover Fired," *BS*, July 17, 1936, B29, JEHS.

18. "Pickets Fight 'Injustices,'" *NYA*, July 23, 1936, B29, JEHS; "Hearing Denied," *NYHT*, July 21, 1936, B29, JEHS.

19. Thompson to Hottel, "John Edwards," November 25, 1944, FBI FOIA 67-21916-180 (Edwards).

20. "Hearing Denied"; "To All Trade Unionists," F: "Hoover, J. Edgar," B35, GJ; Ward, "Washington Weekly," *Nation*, July 25, 1936, B29, JEHS.

21. Moser, "Lodge Ouster," *WT*, July 27, 1936, B29, JEHS.

22. "D.J. Lodge Scores Hoover," *WS*, August 18, 1936, B30, JEHS; "Hoover 'Ghost' Speaks," *WP*, September 1, 1936, B31, JEHS; "Justice Unit Suspended," *WT*, July 25, 1936, B29, JEHS; Collins to Mead, December 7, 1936, F: "Hoover, J. Edgar," B35, GJ.

23. Edwards to Hoover, August 15, 1936, FBI FOIA 67-21916-169 (Edwards); Thompson to Hottel, "John Edwards," November 25, 1944; Hart, "Federal Diary," *WP*, February 12, 1937, B39, JEHS.

24. On the Rumrich case, see Jeffreys-Jones, *Nazi Spy Ring*. For a firsthand account, see Turrou, *Nazi Spies*.

25. Hoover to Donovan, August 1, 1941, P2B, FBI V 77-58706 (Donovan); Turrou, *Nazi Spies*, 297; Beall, "Counter-Spy Bureau Urged," *NYT*, October 8, 1938; Batvinis, *Origins of FBI Counterintelligence*, 53.

26. Allen, "President's Concern Spurs Legislation," *NYP*, October 8, 1938, B63, JEHS; Cummings, "Memorandum," October 14, 1938, F: "AG Personal File: Espionage Committee: Oct 1938," B100, HSC.

27. Cummings to Roosevelt, October 20, 1938.

28. Hoover, "Memorandum," November 7, 1938, F136, B22, HO&C.

Chapter 20: Mothers and Sons (1938–1939)

1. "Cancer Drive Draws Praise," *Illinois State Register*, February 13, 1937, B39, JEHS; Demaris, *Director*, 8.

2. "Notes of IV with Fred Garfield Robinette," April 30, 1989, F351, S-JEHC; Hoover, "The 700,000 Unhappiest Mothers," *Lookout*, August 7, 1938, B61, JEHS; "Animal Lovers Pay Tribute," *WP*, October 4, 1936, B32, JEHS; "A Christmas Gift," December 15, 1953, B112, JEHS.

3. "Notes of IV with Fred Garfield Robinette."

4. Hoover to Tolson, February 14, 1938, S2, FBI NARA 67-9524-263 (Tolson); "Mrs. Hoover Dies," *WN*, February 23, 1938, B53, JEHS; Turrou, *Nazi Spies*, 65; "Mrs. Anna Hoover Dies," *WS*, February 23, 1938, B53, JEHS.

5. Hoover to McLean, March 11, 1938, B6, EWM; interview, Guy Hottel, S-JEHC.

6. Muir, "Madding Crowd," *MDN*, March 17, 20, 1938, B54, JEHS.

7. Gabler, *Winchell*, 262–3; Untitled, *NYDN*, May 2, 1938, B55, JEHS; Considine, "On the Line," *NYM*, June 23, 1938, B60, JEHS; "City Welcomes 1939," *NYM*, January 1, 1939, B65, JEHS.

8. "Sh! G-Man No. 1 Is Here!" *Kansas City Star*, May 17, 1938, B56, JEHS; Winchell, "On Broadway," *NYM*, June 1, 1938, B57, JEHS.

9. Gordon, "J. Edgar Hoover and Girl," *WN*, April 1, 1938, B54, JEHS; "G-Man's Chief Stepping Out," *LAT*, April 10, 1938, B55, JEHS.

10. Gwin, "Hoover Seeks Wife," *BG*, August 1, 1939;

Winchell, "On Broadway," *NYM*, April 25, 1938, B55, JEHS; Winchell, "On Broadway," *NYM*, April 27, 1938, B55, JEHS; S1, FBI FOIA 9-2139 (Rogers); "Lela Rogers," *NYT*, May 29, 1977; Wright, "Ginger Rogers' Mother May Wed," *Los Angeles Daily News*, June 10, 1938, B58, JEHS. For early threats against Rogers, see FBI FOIA 9-2696-A (Rogers) and FBI FOIA 9-3139 (Rogers).

11. "Ginger Rogers' Mother on Spot," *Boston Herald*, June 10, 1938, B58, JEHS; "Hoover Mum on Romance," *MDN*, June 10, 1938, B58, JEHS.

12. Gordon, "J. Edgar Hoover and Girl"; "G-Man's Chief Stepping Out."

13. Interview notes, Katherine Huff Miller, F30, S-JEHC; Gentry, *J. Edgar Hoover*, 219; PB36, NLEM; F487, B8, NARA-P.

14. Winchell, "On Broadway," *NYM*, April 27, 1938; Winchell, "Man about Town," *NYM*, February 27, 1939, B66, JEHS; interview, Guy Hottel, S-JEHC.

15. Tolson, untitled, July 1, 1938, S2, FBI NARA 67-9524 (Tolson); F340, B6, NARA-P.

16. "Ellicott Hills," F616, B10, NARA-P; Gentry, *J. Edgar Hoover*, 217.

17. "Ellicott Hills"; PB52, NLEF; Brown, "Our Times," *Detroit Times*, August 27, 1946, B95, JEHS; "J. Edgar Hoover Speaks Out," *Time*, December 14, 1970, B150, JEHS.

18. PB17, NLEM; Shelton, "Neighbors Reminisce," *WS*, May 7, 1972, B159, JEHS. For house interior, see especially F300, B6; F608, B10; F1895, B35, NARA-P.

19. F300, B6; F608, B10, NARA-P.

20. Robinson, "A Song of Men," B119, NLEM; Gustav-Wrathall, *Take the Young Stranger*, 67.

21. PB2, 36, 52, NLEM; interview notes, Roberta Johnson, F9, S-JEHC.

22. Demaris, *Director*, 33–4.

23. Hoover, *Persons in Hiding*, 308, dedication page.

24. Cooper, *Designs in Scarlet*, 355; Hoover to Patterson, September 30, 1940, S17, FBI FOIA 94-3-4-20-677X1 (Cooper).

25. "Kidnap Aid Reported Seized," *Chicago Herald and Examiner*, January 21, 1938, B51, JEHS; "G-Men Score Again," *Spooner Advocate*, ca. January 20, 1936, B50, JEHS; "Hoover Believed," *Milwaukee News*, January 20, 1938, B50, JEHS; "Ross Kidnapper Tries to Escape," *Minneapolis Star*, January 21, 1938, B51, JEHS; "Hoover in 'Break' Try!" *Chicago Times*, January 21, 1938, B51, JEHS.

26. Denlinger, "Training G-Men," *NYWT*, B54, JEHS; "Hoover's Story of Ross Murder," *WT*, January 21, 1938, B51, JEHS.

27. "G-Man Hoover Leads Kidnap Hunt," *Atlanta Georgian*, June 2, 1938, B57, JEHS; Miller, "Family Tragedy," 842–78; F308, B6, NARA-P; "Cash Boy Dead," *MH*, June 9, 1938, B58, JEHS; "Hoover's Statement," *MH*, June 9, 1938, B58, JEHS. On the Cash kidnapping, see Miller, "Family Tragedy and FBI Triumph in the South"; Waters and Waters, *The Kidnapping and Murder of Little Skeegie Cash*.

28. "Hoover to Lead Levine Hunt," *NYM*, June 14, 1938, B65, JEHS; "Chief G-Man Talks," *Cleveland Plain Dealer*, June 22, 1938, B60, JEHS; "Levine Boy's Bound Body," *NYT*, May 30, 1938; "Dramatic Surprise Sprung," *NYJA*, November 2, 1938, B63, JEHS; Winchell, "On Broadway," *NYM*, November 2, 1938, B63, JEHS; "Sherlock Winchell," *Newsweek*, September 4, 1939, B71, JEHS; Gabler, *Winchell*, 274–80; Gentry, *J. Edgar Hoover*, 219.

29. Clerf to Breeding, January 27, 1939, F: "1/27/39 Letter . . . ," B1, NLEM.

30. "Yet He Went On," F12, B1, NLEM.

Chapter 21: Terror by Index Card (1939–1940)

1. Gardner, "Stocks Close Week with Rally," *WP*, August 27, 1939; Folliard, "Capital Tense," *WP*, September 4, 1939.

2. "Guy Hottel of F.B.I. Weds," *WS*, September 26, 1939, B71, JEHS; Friedheim, "Murphy Orders G-Men," *Pittsburgh Sun-Telegraph*, January 6, 1939, B65, JEHS.

3. Zipes, *Justice and Faith*, 139-199; "Murphy Drafts Plan," *NYHT*, January 26, 1939, B65, JEHS; "Growing Espionage Met," *NYT*, March 24, 1939.

4. Roosevelt, "Memorandum for the Secretary of State [et al]," June 26, 1939, F: "FBI, 1939," B10, OF10B, FDR; Batvinis, *Hoover's Secret War*, 11; Duffy, *Double Agent*, 112; Murphy to Roosevelt, September 6, 1939, F1939, B10, OF10B, FDR.

5. "Nation-wide Aid to F.B.I. Asked," *LAT*, September 6, 1939, B71, JEHS; Roosevelt to Murphy, September 13, 1939, F1939, B10, OF10B, FDR.

6. Roosevelt, "Fireside Chat," September 3, 1939, American Presidency Project, https://www.presidency.ucsb.edu /documents/fireside-chat-13.

7. "Nation-wide Aid to F.B.I. Asked," *LAT*, September 6, 1939, B71, JEHS.

8. Hoover, "Law Enforcement Faces Problems," *Iowa Sheriff*, October 1939, B71, JEHS.

9. "F.B.I. Chief Opposes Spy Vigilantes," *WS*, November 1, 1939, B72, JEHS; JEH APP (1940-emergency), 302–7.

10. Hoover, "Law Enforcement Faces Problems."

11. JEH APP (1940-emergency), 304–5.

12. "FBI Smashes U.S. Revolution Forces," *Florence Evening Star*, January 15, 1940, B73, JEHS; "F.B.I. Arrests 18,'" *NYHT*, January 15, 1940, B73, JEHS.

13. "The President's Message," *Equal Justice*, February 1940, B74, JEHS.

14. Untitled, *NR*, February 19, 1940, B74, JEHS.

15. "Criticism Aimed at G-Men Head," *Pittsburgh Press*, February 9, 1940, B74, JEHS; Lamke, "Memorandum for the Attorney General," February 1, 1940, F10, B94, RJ; U.S. Senate, Committee on Interstate Commerce, "Investigating Wire Tapping," 76th Congress, 3d session, March 12, 1940, F8, B94, RJ.

16. Lowitt, *George W. Norris*, 2:293–9; Cole, "Norris, George W.," *American National Biography*; Norris to Jackson, February 22, 1940, R11, NO&C; "Norris Is 'Worried,'" *NYT*, February 27, 1940, B74, JEHS.

17. "Hoover Returns to Miami Beach," *MDN*, February 14, 1940, B74, JEHS; "Hoover Like Feudal Baron," *MH*, February 28, 1940, B74, JEHS.

18. Biddle, *In Brief Authority*, 108; Tamm, "Memorandum for the Director," March 1, 1940, R11, NO&C; Department of Justice, "For Release," February 16, 1940, R11, NO&C; Franklin, "FBI's Difficulties Traced to Spy Scare," *NYP*, March 18, 1940, B75, JEHS.

19. "Hoover like Feudal Baron," *MH*, February 28, 1940, B74, JEHS; Prevost, "Concerted Effort to Oust Head of G-Men," *Detroit Free Press*, March 3, 1940, B74, JEHS; *CR*, April 18, 1940, B76, JEHS; Tamm, "Memorandum for the File," February 20, 1940, R11, NO&C; Tamm, "Memorandum for the Director," March 1, 1940, R11, NO&C.

20. Barkley, "Critics Open Fire," *NYT*, March 17, 1940, B75, JEHS; Tamm, "Memorandum for the Director," March 1,

1940, R11, NO&C; Warren, "Hoover 'Stork Club Detective,'" *New York News*, February 28, 1940, B74, JEHS.

21. Tamm, "Memorandum for the Director," March 1, 1940.

22. Whitehead, *FBI Story*, 170; "Hoover Raid on 'Reds' is Defended," *MDN*, March 1, 1940, B74, JEHS; "Hoover Returns to Washington," *MDN*, March 1, 1940, B74, JEHS.

23. Griffin, "Orders Probe into Arrests Made by F.B.I.," *BS*, March 15, 1940, B75, JEHS; *CR*, March 18, 1940, B75, JEHS; DOJ press release, March 15, 1940, F6, B94, RJ; "Jackson Clears F.B.I. in Recruiting Arrests," *Detroit Free Press*, May 5, 1940, B76, JEHS.

24. *CR*, March 18, 1940.

25. Hoover to Stone, April 23, 1940, F: "General Correspondence: Hoover, John Edgar, 1935–1943," B17, HFS.

Chapter 22: Henry E. Jones (1940–1941)

1. Folliard, "Germans Take Paris," *WP*, June 16, 1940.

2. Roosevelt, "Message to Congress on Appropriations for National Defense," May 16, 1940, American Presidency Project, https://www.presidency.ucsb.edu/documents/message-congress-appropriations-for-national-defense-1; Roosevelt, "Fireside Chat," May 26, 1940, American Presidency Project, https://www.presidency.ucsb.edu/documents/fireside-chat-10.

3. Jackson, *That Man*, 74.

4. Roosevelt, "Memorandum for the Attorney General," May 21, 1940, F6, B94, RJ; Roosevelt to Smith, June 13, 1940, F: "Justice Dept., FBI, 1940," B10, OF10B, FDR; *History of the SIS Division*, 1:1, FBI V; Haverty-Stacke, *Trotskyists on Trial*, 37–41; Belknap, *Cold War Political Justice*, 22–7.

5. AR/AG (1940), 151.

6. "Present Status of Espionage and Counter Espionage Operations," October 24, 1940, F341-432, B12, OF10B, FDR; AR/AG (1940), 154.

7. "Present Status of Espionage and Counter Espionage Operations"; JEH APP (1941), 138; JEH APP (1941-second deficiency), 273.

8. Kluttz, "F.B.I. Ready to Meet Any War Emergency," September 27, 1939, *WN*, B71, JEHS; "The FBI Academy: A Pictorial History," FBI, https://www.fbi.gov/services/training-academy/the-fbi-academy-a-pictorial-history; JEH APP (1941-second deficiency), 268.

9. JEH APP (1941-first deficiency), 181; JEH LOGS, 1941; JEH APP (1942), 188; "Present Status of Espionage and Counter Espionage Operations"; Batvinis, *Origins of FBI Counterintelligence*, 80–1.

10. JEH APP (1942), 196-197, 175; JEH APP (1941-second deficiency), 275; JEH APP (1941-first deficiency), 184.

11. JEH APP (1941, supp), 183; Theoharis et al., *FBI: Comprehensive Reference Guide*, 4.

12. Hoover, "Re: Washington Embassies," September 27, 1940, F300-340, B12, OF10B, FDR; Hoover to Jackson, April 1, 1941, B17, F91, HO&C.

13. Early to Hoover, May 18, 1940, F: "FBI 1940," B10, OF10B, FDR; Olson, *Those Angry Days*, 103.

14. Roosevelt to Hoover, June 14, 1940, F17, B2, NLEM.

15. "Present Status of Espionage and Counter Espionage Operations."

16. Hoover to Jackson, April 1, 1941, F91, B17, HO&C.

17. Affidavit of Harry Bridges, August 29, 1941, F40, B14, HO&C; "Harry Bridges Charges F.B.I. Spied on Him," *BS*, August 26, 1941; Biddle, *In Brief Authority*, 166.

18. Haverty-Stacke, *Trotskyists on Trial*, 1–137; for quote, see 73.

19. *History of the SIS Division*, 1:41, FBI V. On reorganization, see Fox, "Intelligence Analysis and the Bureau."

20. Batvinis, *Hoover's Secret War*, 25.

21. Olson, *Those Angry Days*, 117–8; Riebling, *Wedge*, 4–13.

22. Stevenson, *Man Called Intrepid*, 84; West, *British Security Coordination*, xxv–xxvii; "Memorandum Prepared by Assistant Secretary of State Berle, June 24, 1940, and Approved by the President," F: "FBI 1941–1942," B11, OF10B, FDR; Batvinis, *Hoover's Secret War*, 107, 30; *History of the SIS Division*, 1:3, FBI V.

23. West, *British Security Coordination*, 4; Stevenson, *Man Called Intrepid*, 165.

24. Clegg OH, 43–5; *History of the SIS Division*, 1:4, FBI V; Stevenson, *Man Called Intrepid*, 187–98, 190. Also see Stafford, *Camp X*.

25. West, *British Security Coordination*, 3, 351; Batvinis, *Hoover's Secret War*, 26.

26. *History of the SIS Division*, 1:2–10, FBI V.

27. Godfrey, "Intelligence in the United States," July 28, 1941, CAB 81-103, National Archives (Kew), London, UK; Riebling, *Wedge*, 4–13.

28. For the Sebold case, see Duffy, *Double Agent*. Where not otherwise cited, details of the case can be found in this source.

29. "FBI Agents Smash Huge Nazi Spy Ring," *NYM*, June 30, 1941, B80, JEHS; "Nab 29 in Spy Round-Up," *Grand Rapids Herald*, June 30, 1941, B80, JEHS.

30. "Courts, Officials, Veterans in Tribute To G-Man," *Morning Herald*, October 11, 1941, B81, JEHS.

Chapter 23: Enemy Aliens (1941–1942)

1. Whitehead, *FBI Story*, 182; White House Press Release, December 7, 1941, Franklin D. Roosevelt Presidential Library and Museum, https://www.fdrlibrary.org/documents/356632/390886/Pearl+Harbor+Documents.pdf/405ef5ca-fb07-4a76-b651-2c756814eda4.

2. Hoover to Watson, July 3, 1940, F165-209, B12, OF10B, FDR.

3. Fox, *America's Invisible Gulag*, 5; Hoover, "Memorandum for the Attorney General," April 1, 1941, F91, B17, HO&C.

4. JEH LOGS, December 7, 1941; Whitehead, *FBI Story*, 182.

5. "Interview with Judge Fahy and Francis Shea," January 24, 1978, F: "Fahy, Charles," B117, JT; "Investigator," January 16, 1942, F2, B1, S73, AT; Biddle, *In Brief Authority*, 205.

6. Batvinis, *Hoover's Secret War*, 13–5; JEH LOGS, December 7, 1941; "Interview with Judge Fahy and Francis Shea."

7. "Conversation between the Director and Special Agent in Charge," December 7, 1941, F6, B126, JT.

8. JEH LOGS, December 7, 1941; Hoover to Watson, December 7, 1941, F1000-1032, B15, OF10B, FDR; Hoover, "Memorandum," December 7, 1941, F1000-1032, B15, OF10B, FDR.

9. Biddle, *In Brief Authority*, 206.

10. "U.S. Capital Put under Army Guard," *Austin Statesman*, December 8, 1941; "FDR's 'Day of Infamy' Speech" 33: 4 (2001), National Archives, https://www.archives.gov/publications/prologue/2001/winter/crafting-day-of-infamy-speech.html.

11. Hoover, "The Citizen and the FBI," *Catholic Digest*, November 1941, B81, JEHS.

12. Hosokawa, *Nisei*, 237; Hoover, "Memorandum," December 7, 1941, F1000-1032, B15, OF10B, FDR; Shivers to Hoover, December 12, 1941, F3, B126, JT; Shivers to Hoover, "Re: Japanese Air Raid," December 12, 1941, F3, B126, JT; Fox, *America's Invisible Gulag*, 78.

13. Reeves, *Infamy*, 3–4; JEH APP (1942-deficiency), 138; Hoover, "Memorandum for the Attorney General," June 1942, F136, B22, HO&C.

14. Fox, *America's Invisible Gulag*, 9.

15. Hosokawa, *Nisei*, 237; Fox, *America's Invisible Gulag*, 63–4.

16. *CR*, May 11, 1942, B82, JEHS; Fox, *America's Invisible Gulag*, 32–139; Biddle, *In Brief Authority*, 209.

17. McGill, "One Word More," *AC*, January 1, 1942, B82, JEHS.

18. Toland, *Infamy*, 13; Stone, "The Shake-Up We Need," *Nation*, December 27, 1941, B82, JEHS.

19. Hoover, "America at War," *Peace Officer*, January 1942, B82, JEHS; Hoover, "Memorandum," December 7, 1941, F1000-1032, B15, OF10B, FDR.

20. Batvinis, *Hoover's Secret War*, 141–54.

21. Hoover, "In Re: Censorship," December 8, 1941, F1039, B15, OF10B, FDR; Hoover to Early, December 12, 1941, F: "Federal Bureau of Investigation," B29, STE; Early, "Memorandum for Honorable J. Edgar Hoover," December 12, 1941, F: "Federal Bureau of Investigation," B29, STE.

22. T. R. B., "Washington Notes," *NR*, January 5, 1942, B82, JEHS; O'Donnell, "Capitol Stuff," *WTH*, January 29, 1941, B82, JEHS.

23. "Hoover Replies to Charges on Hawaii Spies," *WTH*, December 29, 1941, B82, JEHS; Hoover to Early, December 29, 1941, F: "Federal Bureau of Investigation," B29, STE; *CR*, February 16, 1942, B82, JEHS.

24. Roberts Report, 20, 12; "F.D. to 'Take Handcuffs Off,'" *NYM*, January 29, 1942, B82, JEHS.

25. Sobol, "New York Cavalcade," *NYJA*, January 31, 1942, B82, JEHS.

26. Hosokawa, *Nisei*, 244–5; Robinson, *By Order of the President*, 78; Demaris, *Director,* 121-2.

27. "Internment of All Japs Asked," *San Francisco Examiner*, January 21, 1942, B82, JEHS; Reeves, *Infamy*, 41, xix.

28. Hoover, "Big scare," *American*, August 1941, B81, JEHS; "Aliens: Friends or Foes?" *NYM*, March 25, 1942, B82, JEHS.

29. Biddle, *In Brief Authority*, 215; General Intelligence Survey, February 1942, 23-27, F: "FBI Reports: General Intelligence Survey in the U.S. (1942)," B144, HH; Robinson, *By Order of the President*, 98–100.

30. Biddle, *In Brief Authority*, 216–7; Robinson, *By Order of the President*, 100–1, 108; Reeves, *Infamy*, xv–xvi.

31. Fox, *America's Invisible Gulag*, 39.

32. "FBI Survey of Japanese Relocation Centers," 1:1–2, 5, F: "Japanese Relocation," B150, HH.

Chapter 24: The Most Exciting Achievement Yet (1942)

1. Hinman, "Subject: Landing of Enemy Agents from Submarine," June 13, 1942, S1, B18, FBI NARA 98-10288 (Dasch); Hoover, "Memorandum for Mr. Tolson," June 15, 1942, S1, B18, FBI NARA 98-10288 (Dasch).

2. Hinman, "Subject: Landing of Enemy Agents from Submarine"; Hoover, "Memorandum for Mr. Tolson."

3. Biddle, *In Brief Authority*, 327. The most comprehensive books on the saboteurs case are Dobbs, *Saboteurs*, and O'Donnell, *In Time of War*. Where not otherwise cited, details of the investigation and tribunal can be found in these works. Also see Johnson, *Betrayal*; Rachlis, *They Came to Kill*; Fisher, *Nazi Saboteurs on Trial*.

4. Biddle, *In Brief Authority*, 327; Saboteurs, 1:80.

5. McWhorter, "Memorandum for the Fil," June 14, 1942, B27, FBI NARA 98-10288 (Dasch); Dobbs, *Saboteurs*, 125;

Hoover, "Memorandum for Mr. Tolson," June 19, 1942, S1, B8, FBI NARA 98-10288-28 (Dasch); "Log re: George John Dasch," S3-additions, B19, FBI NARA 98-10288 (Dasch)

6. Tamm, "Memorandum for Mr. Ladd," June 27, 1942, S3-additions, B19, FBI NARA 98-10288-98 (Dasch); Biddle, *In Brief Authority*, 327–8.

7. Tamm, "Memorandum for Mr. Ladd"; "Hoover Released Story," *Editor & Publisher*, July 4, 1942, B83, JEHS; "The Invaders," *Newsweek*, July 6, 1942, B83, JEHS; "Eight Nazi War Plant Saboteurs," *Memphis Commercial Appeal*, June 28, 1942, B83, JEHS; Gordon, "Mead's Effort to Honor J. Edgar," *WDN*, July 16, 1942, B83, JEHS; Dobbs, *Saboteurs*, 194.

8. "Seize More Spies," *Kansas City Times*, June 29, 1942, B83, JEHS; Hoover, "Memorandum for Mr. Tolson," June 29, 1942, S2, B19, FBI NARA 98-10288-281 (Dasch).

9. Tamm, "Memorandum for the Director," June 25, 1942, S3, B19, FBI NARA 98-10288-135 (Dasch); Vincent, "Death for Saboteurs," *Atlanta Journal*, June 29, 1942, B83, JEHS.

10. Hoover, "Memorandum for Mr. Tolson," June 29, 1942.

11. Hoover, "Memorandum for Mr. Tolson," July 1, 1942, S2, B19, FBI NARA 98-10288-288 (Dasch); Hoover, "Memorandum for Mr. Tolson," July 1, 1942, S2, B19, FBI NARA 98-10288-286 (Dasch); Hoover, "Memorandum for Mr. Tolson," July 1, 1942, S3, B19, FBI NARA 98-10288-186 (Dasch); Hoover, "Memorandum for Mr. Tolson," July 1, 1942, S2, B19, FBI NARA 98-10288-287 (Dasch).

12. Hoover, "Memorandum for Mr. Tolson," July 1, 1942, S2, B19, FBI NARA 98-10288-286 (Dasch); Hoover, "Memorandum for Mr. Tolson," July 1, 1942, S2, B19, FBI NARA 98-10288-288 (Dasch).

13. Hoover, "Memorandum for Mr. Tolson," July 1, 1942, S2, B9, FBI NARA 98-10288-288 (Dasch); Dasch, *Eight Spies*, 143–5.

14. Hoover, untitled, July 7, 1942, S10, B21, FBI NARA 98-10288-880 (Dasch); Nichols, "Memorandum for Mr. Tolson," July 9, 1942, S9, B21, FBI NARA 98-10288-681 (Dasch); Dobbs, *Saboteurs*, 229; "Hoover Warns of Nazi Plots," *WTH*, July 11, 1942, B83, JEHS.

15. Hoover, "Memorandum for Mr. Tolson," July 22, 1942, S10, B21, FBI NARA 98-10288-897 (Dasch); Hoover, "Memorandum for Mr. Tolson," July 31, 1942, S13, B23, FBI NARA 98-10288-1159 (Dasch).

16. Baldwin, "Boost for the F.B.I.," ca. July 1942, B83, JEHS; Light, "So What!" *St. Paul Pioneer Press*, July 11, 1942, B83, JEHS; Johnson, *Betrayal*, 168.

17. Hoover, "Memorandum for Mr. Tolson," June 29, 1942.

18. "Hoover Attends Hearing," *Houston Press*, July 31, 1942, S2, FBI NARA 67-9524 (Tolson).

19. Hoover, "Memorandum for Mr. Tolson," July 24, 1942, S11, B22, FBI NARA 98-10288-989 (Dasch); Hoover, "Memorandum for the Attorney General," July 11, 1942, S7, B20, FBI NARA 98-10288-570 (Dasch).

20. O'Donnell, *In Time of War*, 231, 242.

21. Dasch, *Eight Spies*, 147; Glavin, "Memorandum for the Director," August 1, 1942, S14, B32, FBI NARA 98-10288-1210 (Dasch).

22. Hoover, "Memorandum," August 5, 1942, F136, B22, HO&C.

23. McKee to Hoover, "Re: George John Dasch," August 10, 1942, S19, B35, FBI NARA 98-10288-1604 (Dasch).

24. O'Donnell, *In Time of War*, 248; Ladd, "Memorandum for the Director," August 5, 1942, S15, B34, FBI NARA 98-10288-1323 (Dasch); Ladd, "Memorandum for the Director," August 8, 1942, S16, B34, FBI NARA 98-10288-1380 (Dasch); Traynor, "Memorandum for Mr. Ladd,"

August 10, 1942, S16, B34, FBI NARA 98-10288-1362 (Dasch); McKee to Director, August 10, 1942, S19, B35, FBI NARA 98-10288 (Dasch).

25. Ladd, "Memorandum for the Director," August 12, 1942, S17, B34, FBI NARA 98-10288-1444 (Dasch).

Chapter 25: American Dilemmas (1942–1945)

1. Roosevelt to Hoover, July 25, 1942, F: "7/25/42 FDR Letter to Hoover," B1, NLEM.

2. Biddle, *In Brief Authority*, 182.

3. Lewis, *Washington*, 356–64.

4. JEH APP (1943), 101–3; Hoover, "Memorandum for the Attorney General," April 8, 1943, B36, JRJ; "Vastness of FBI's Records Annex," *AC*, October 22, 1943, B88, JEHS; "High Spots," *Script*, October 23, 1943, B88, JEHS.

5. "Women Workers Constitute Over Half of FBI Personnel," *WS*, July 11, 1943, B87, JEHS; Hoover, "Women and the FBI," *General Federation Clubwoman*, February 1943, B85, JEHS; Gordon, "FBI's Hoover Wanted Wife in 1939," *WDN*, December 7, 1943, B88, JEHS; "Women Replace Men in Many FBI Positions," *Philadelphia Inquirer*, July 11, 1943, B87, JEHS; "G-Girls of FBI Credited with Solving Many Crimes," *Richmond Times-Dispatch*, July 11, 1943, B87, JEHS; "And Now We Have G-Women—Gee!" *Chieftain*, July 12, 1943, B87, JEHS.

6. Batvinis, *Hoover's Secret War*, 110–6; FBI, *History of the S.I.S. Division*, 11–21, FBI V; Batvinis, *Origins of FBI Counterintelligence*, 215–25; Becker, *FBI in Latin America*, 22; interview of William T. Baker, FBI OH; "35 Killed in Crash of U.S. Plane," *New York World-Telegram*, January 21, 1943, B85, JEHS.

7. JEH APP (1943), 108–9; Hoover to Hopkins, July 18, 1942, F2215-2238, B16, OF10B, FDR.

8. Theoharis, "FBI and the American Legion Contact Program," 277; JEH APP (1942), 192.

9. Hoover to Tolson, October 21, 1943, S2, FBI 67-9524 (Tolson), NARA. The letter mistakenly says that Tolson is receiving his Ten Year Service Key, though it also notes more accurately that his FBI service began in April 1928.

10. Bérubé, *Coming Out under Fire*, 12. Also see Canaday, *Straight State*, 91-173.

11. Hoover, "Memorandum," January 3, 1941, B157, B24, HO&C; Hoover, "Memorandum," January 30, 1941, F157, B24, HO&C.

12. Charles, *Hoover's War on Gays*, 37–51.

13. Tucker/Shaffer, "Memorandum for SAC," July 27, 1944, F33, B13, HO&C; Conroy, "Personal & Confidential," July 5, 1944, F33, B13, HO&C.

14. Hoover to Watson, June 21, 1941, F833-854, B14, OF10B, FDR.

15. Asch and Musgrove, *Chocolate City*, 279.

16. Hoover to Hopkins, November 28, 1942, F: "Miscellaneous FBI Reports Nov.–Dec. 1942," B151, HH; Hoover to Hopkins, August 26, 1942, F: "Miscellaneous FBI Reports July–Sept 1942," B151, HH; "General Intelligence Survey in the United States," August 1942, F: "General Intelligence Survey in the United States, 1942," BB144, HH; CC3, 416.

17. On White's early life and career, see Sullivan, *Lift Every Voice*, 61–236; White, *Man Called White*, 1–205; Janken, *Walter White*, 1-260.

18. White to Hoover, June 17, 1941, F: "Federal Bureau of Investigation, 1940–42," GO File, NAACP; "Hoover Says F.B.I. Employs Negroes," July 25, 1941, F: "Federal Bureau of Investigation, 1940–42," GO File, NAACP.

19. Mackay, "A Note to Mr. Hoover," *Tri-State News*, March 28, 1942, B82, JEHS; Demaris, *Director*, 38.

20. White to Marshall, December 17, 1941, F: "Federal Bureau of Investigation, 1940–42," GO File, NAACP.

21. Sugrue, *Origins of the Urban Crisis*, 29; FBI, *Survey of Racial Conditions*, 78–81, B21, OF10B, FDR; Bradley, *Very Principled Boy*, 11–20; "FBI Head Calls Riots Disgrace to the Nation," *Journal and Guide*, August 21, 1943, B87, JEHS.

22. FBI, *Survey of Racial Conditions*, 3, 428, 14, B21, OF10B, FDR.

23. "Civil Liberties Union Aims to Picket Dept. of Justice," undated ca. 1936, F: "Hoover, J. Edgar," B35, GJ; ACLU; "Thumbs Down!" February 1938, B52, JEHS; Walker, *In Defense of American Liberties*, 130–4. Also see additional documents in B35, GJ.

24. Baldwin, "Memo re–J. Edgar Hoover," October 20, 1941, F5, B858, MC001, ACLU; Baldwin to Hoover, October 28, 1941, F5, B858, MC001, ACLU; Hoover to Baldwin, November 1, 1941, F5, B858, MC001, ACLU.

25. "Civil Rights and the F.B.I.," March 12, 1942, Sr3, RNB; "Memo by Roger Baldwin," July 1943, Sr3, RNB.

26. Salisbury, "The Strange Correspondence of Morris Ernst and J. Edgar Hoover," *Nation*, January 25, 2007; Barbas, *Rise and Fall of Morris Ernst*, 266-9, 283-6, 296, 302–5; Ernst, *The Best Is Yet*, 23–6; Ernst to Hoover, August 30, 1944, FBI FOIA 94-4-5366-14 (Ernst).

27. Walker, *In Defense of American Liberties,* 127; Pringle, "Snooping on the Potomac," *SEP*, January 15, 1944, B89, JEHS; Gordon, "FBI Chief Talks like a McCormick Editorial," *DW*, April 20, 1944, B90, JEHS; Cottrell, *Roger Nash Baldwin*, 277.

28. Biddle, *In Brief Authority*, 233–43; Hoover to Hopkins, November 16, 1944, F: "FBI Reports-Miscellaneous-1944, 1945," B151, HH; Hoover to Hopkins, February 9, 1945, F: "FBI Reports-Miscellaneous-1944, 1945," B151, HH.

29. Winchell, "On Broadway," *NYDN*, July 1, 1942, B83, JEHS; Hoover to Hopkins, July 10, 1942, S7, B20, FBI NARA 98-10288 (Dasch); Hoover to Hopkins, July 18, 1942, F2215-2238, B16, OF10B, FDR; Hoover to Hopkins, August 26, 1942, F: "Misc July–Sept. 1942," B151, HH; Hoover to Hopkins, September 4, 1942, F: "Misc July–Sept. 1942," B151, HH; Hoover to Hopkins, November 21, 1942, F: "Misc July–Sept. 1942," B151, HH; Hoover to Hopkins, March 4, 1944, F: "FBI Reports-Miscellaneous-1944, 1945," B151, HH; F87, B17, HO&C.

30. Cook, *Eleanor Roosevelt*, 466-7; Theoharis, *From the Secret Files of J. Edgar Hoover*, 59-65.

31. Cowell, "J. Edgar Hoover's 20 Years with the FBI," *St. Louis Globe-Democrat*, May 21, 1944, B90, JEHS; *CR*, April 10, 1946, B94, JEHS; Hoover, "Youth Running Wild," *Signs of the Times*, August 8, 1944, B91, JEHS; "FBI Chief Warns of Reds, Fascists," *NYJA,* April 18, 1944, B90, JEHS.

32. Gentry, *J. Edgar Hoover*, 317; Biddle, *In Brief Authority*, 360–1; McCullough, *Truman*, 347.

Chapter 26: Central Intelligence (1945–1946)

1. Hoover to Truman, April 13, 1945, F10B: "National Academy," B103, White House Central File (WHCF), HST; Hoover to Connolly, April 13, 1945, F10B: "National Academy," B103, WHCF, HST; "Extension of Remarks," *CR*, April 20, 1945, B92, JEHS.

2. Kluckhohn, "Crowds in Tears," *NYT*, April 14, 1945; Kluckhohn, "Rites at Capital," *NYT*, April 15, 1945.

3. "Roosevelt Funeral," *SLPD*, April 15, 1945.

4. JEH LOGS, April 14, 1945.

5. McCullough, *Truman*, 349; Ferrell, *Truman and Pendergast*, 18. Also see Hartmann, *Kansas City Investigation*.

6. "Byte out of History: FBI Involvement in Early Election Fraud Case in Kansas City," August 6, 2015, FBI, https://www.fbi.gov/news/stories/fbi-involvement-in-early-election-fraud-case-in-kansas-city; JEH APP (1940), 128; Ferrell, *Truman and Pendergast*, 45–61, 58.

7. Hoover, "Memorandum," April 15, 1936, S1, FBI FOIA 67-9287-A-18 (McKellar); Manly, "Truman Holds FBI," *WTH*, February 4, 1942, B82, JEHS; Tamm, "Memorandum for the Director," March 12, 1943, R11, NO&C.

8. Hoover to Truman, April 13, 1945, F10B: "National Academy Folder," B103, WHCF, HST.

9. Waller, *Wild Bill Donovan*, 106–314. On OSS and the Ivy League, see especially Winks, *Cloak & Gown*.

10. Correlations summary of William J. Donovan file, "NY Let., 6/8/43," S1C, FBI V 77-58706 (Donovan); Waller, *Wild Bill Donovan*, 224–5.

11. FBI, *History of the SIS Division*, 80, 136–40, 22, "Maximum Coverage by Special Agents and Special Employees," 1941–1947, FBI V; Becker, *FBI in Latin America*, 19.

12. For an analysis of anticommunist activity, see Becker, *FBI in Latin America*.

13. Park, "Memorandum for the President," March 12, 1945.

14. Gentry, *J. Edgar Hoover*, 321; "Memoir of Former Special Agent of the FBI Morton P. Chiles," FBI OH.

15. Truman, "Address before a Joint Session," April 16, 1945, American Presidency Project, https://www.presidency.ucsb.edu/documents/address-before-joint-session-the-congress; Lyons, "Lyons Den," *NYP*, April 18, 1945, B92, JEHS; McCullough, *Truman*, 367; Sullivan, *The Bureau*, 38.

16. Vaughan to Hoover, April 23, 1945, F: "FBI," B102, OF10B, WHCF, HST.

17. Theoharis and Cox, *Boss*, 244-5; Ladd to Director, May 23, 1945, F2, B1, HO&C; Gurnea to Director, "White House Survey," Aug. 13, 1945, F160, B24, HO&C; CC2, 37.

18. Holland, "Tapping of 'Tommy the Cork,'" *Washington Decoded*, December 1, 1999. For the Corcoran wiretaps, see B1, HO&C. For Biddle's firing, see Biddle, *In Brief Authority*, 364–6.

19. Ferrell, *Off the Record*, 22; McCullough, *Truman*, 367; Frank, *Trials of Harry Truman*, 136.

20. For quote, see Truman, "The President's News Conference on V-E Day," May 8, 1945, American Presidency Project, https://www.presidency.ucsb.edu/documents/the-presidents-news-conference-v-e-day.

21. Francis, "Washington Lets Loose," *LAT*, August 15, 1945; "Crowd Yells," *WP*, August 15, 1945; Ripley, "Screaming Salute," *CSM*, August 15, 1945.

22. Hoover, "Reconversion," *On Guard*, January 1946, B94, JEHS.

23. JEH LOGS, April 22, 1945.

24. *The House on 92nd Street*, directed by Henry Hathaway (Los Angeles: 20th Century Fox, 1945); JEH LOGS, April 22, 1945; "FBI Filmed Nazis," *NYT*, September 13, 1945, B93, JEHS.

25. "Hoover, J. Edgar," September 10, 1945, B102, OF10B: "FBI, Cross-Reference Sheets," WHCF, HST; Hoover to Hoover, September 8, 1945, F "J. Edgar Hoover Correspondence," B90, Post-Presidential File, HHoo; Cassini, "These Charming People," *WTH*, September 17, 1945, B93, JEHS.

26. McNair, "Dinner Parties," *WP*, April 6, 1945, B92, JEHS; "Hoover Paid Honor," *WDN*, January 26, 1944, B89, JEHS; "Mayor Puts," *NYHT*, December 30, 1945,

B93, JEHS; Photos, F783, B13, NARA-P; "Medal to J.E. Hoover," *NYT*, March 16, 1946.

27. Hoover to Truman, March 11, 1946, F: "Hoover letter to Truman," B20, NLEM.

28. Riebling, *Wedge*, 64–5.

29. "A Plan for U.S.," undated, S8, FBI FOIA 62-80750 (CIA). Though this document is included in preparation for possible 1947 testimony, it refers to the FBI conducting active operations in the western hemisphere, suggesting it originally dates from an earlier period.

30. Smith, "U.S. and Us," *WTH*, December 21, 1945, B93, JEHS; "Beachcombing," *Miami Beach Daily Sun*, December 11, 1945, B93, JEHS; "Executive Order," draft, January 12, 1946, S1, FBI FOIA 62-80750 (CIA); Hoover to AG, "Proposed Executive Order," January 15, 1946, S1, FBI FOIA 62-80750 (CIA).

31. Truman to Secretary of State, January 22, 1946, S1, FBI FOIA 62-80750 (CIA).

32. West, *British Security Coordination*, 48; Hoover, "Memorandum for Mr. Tolson," January 25, 1946, S1, FBI FOIA 62-80750-9 (CIA); Weiner, *Legacy of Ashes*, 13; JEH LOGS, January 24, 1946.

33. Roach to Ladd, "National Intelligence Organization," February 1, 1946, S1, FBI FOIA 62-80750 (CIA); Ladd to Hoover, "Present Activities," April 11, 1946, S1, FBI FOIA 62-80750 (CIA).

34. Riebling, *Wedge*, 73–4.

35. Hoover to Vandenberg, July 15, 1946, CIA CREST; Presley to Carson, "Closing of San Jose," August 22, 1946, S4, FBI FOIA 62-80750-181 (CIA); Riebling, *Wedge*, 75; Roethe to File, "Summary of Interviews with Sam J. Papich," March 5, 1975, MFF.

36. Vandenberg, "Memorandum for the Members," ca. August 5, 1946, CIA CREST; Hoover to Attorney General, "Special Intelligence Service," August 8, 1946, S3, FBI FOIA 62-80750 (CIA).

37. Ladd to Director, "National Intelligence Authority," April 24, 1946, S1, FBI FOIA 62-80750 (CIA); Ladd to Director, "Central Intelligence Group," July 23, 1946, S3, FBI FOIA 62-80750-134 (CIA); Brown, "Intelligence Mission," ca. February 6, 1947, S6, FBI FOIA 62-80750-297 (CIA); Tamm to Director, August 10, 1946, S3, FBI FOIA 62-80750 (CIA).

38. Untitled, October 29, 1946, S5, FBI FOIA 62-80750-235 (CIA); Carson to Director, "Interview with William D. Pawley," August 22, 1946, S4, FBI FOIA 62-80750 (CIA).

39. Riebling, *Wedge*, 76.

Chapter 27: Under Color of Law (1941–1948)

1. Hoover, "Protecting Our Freedom," F46, B14, HO&C; Dray, *At the Hands of Persons Unknown*, viii, 361.

2. "Ludlow Asks Hoover," *BS*, July 18, 1938, B61, JEHS; Biddle, *In Brief Authority*, 260.

3. "Civil Rights and Domestic Violence: A Summary," March 15, 1947, F46, B14, HO&C; Dray, *At the Hands of Persons Unknown*, 439-40; Wexler, *Fire in a Canebrake*, 108-9.

4. Ward, *Hanging Bridge*, 103–4; "Elbert Williams-Notice to Close File," United States Department of Justice, https://www.justice.gov/crt/case-document/elbert-williams-notice-close-file.

5. Ward, *Hanging Bridge*, 104; Dray, *At the Hands of Persons Unknown*, 440.

6. Ward, *Hanging Bridge*, 92-115.

7. Ward, *Hanging Bridge*, 104, 101, 119; Dray, *At the*

Hands of Persons Unknown, 440-1; Wexler, *Fire in a Canebrake,* 109, 124.

8. Dray, *At the Hands of Persons Unknown,* 440-1; "Lynchings in the United States, 1900-1945," F46, B14, HO&C.

9. White to Hoover, August 21, 1946, F: "Federal Bureau of Investigation racial issues and violence investigations, 1946–1949," GO File, NAACP; Exhibit #2, #9, "Civil Rights and Domestic Violence: A Summary," March 15, 1947, F46, B14, HO&C; Dray, *At the Hands of Personsl Unknown,* 370-4. On Woodard, see Gergel, *Unexampled Courage.*

10. Exhibit #2, "Civil Rights and Domestic Violence: A Summary," March 15, 1947, F46, B14, HO&C; Dray, *At the Hands of Persons Unknown,* 372; Gergel, *Unexampled Courage,* 4.

11. Wexler, *Fire in a Canebrake,* 76-9; 93-5.

12. Pitch, *Last Lynching,* 50.

13. Exhibit #1, "Civil Rights and Domestic Violence: A Summary," March 15, 1947, F46, B14, HO&C; Wexler, *Fire in a Canebrake,* 81, 113, 190, 235; Pitch, *Last Lynching,* 120, 128; Hoover, "Protecting Our Freedom," F46, B14, HO&C.

14. Dray, *At the Hands of Persons Unknown,* 383; Pitch, *Last Lynching,* 64, 70-2, 117-8.

15. Pitch, *Last Lynching,* 84, 127.

16. Exhibit #1, "Civil Rights and Domestic Violence: A Summary," March 15, 1947, F46, B14, HO&C; Wexler, *Fire in a Canebrake,* 189–90.

17. Pitch, *Last Lynching,* 56, 111; Wexler, *Fire in a Canebrake,* 153.

18. Brooks, "FBI Is on a Spot," *Knoxville News-Sentinel,* October 4, 1946, B95, JEHS; Wexler, *Fire in a Canebrake,* 127; "Lynchings Hit," *Milwaukee Journal,* September 7, 1946, B95, JEHS; Pitch, *Last Lynching,* 111.

19. Wexler, *Fire in a Canebrake,* 154-5. Another case was in Minden, Louisiana. See Exhibit #5, "Civil Rights and Domestic Violence: A Summary," March 15, 1947, F46, B14, HO&C.

20. Egerton, *Speak Now Against the Day,* 414; Wexler, *Fire in a Canebrake,* 151.

21. Frank, *The Trials of Harry S. Truman,* xx, 151, 375-6; Wexler, *Fire in a Canebrake,* 151–2; Truman, "Executive Order 9808," December 5, 1946, at https://www.trumanlibrary.org/library/executive-orders/9808/executive-order-9808.

22. Hoover, "Inside Labor," *NYP,* July 3, 1947, B98, JEHS; Hoover to White, April 14, 1947, F: "FBI, 1946-1949," GO File, NAACP.

23. Exhibit #7, "Civil Rights and Domestic Violence: A Summary," March 15, 1947, F46, B14, HO&C; Gravely, *They Stole Him out of Jail,* 17-20, 44-7; Bass and Thompson, *Strom,* 82–4; Fredrickson, *Dixiecrat Revolt,* 50–65. On Thurmond and lynching, see Crespino, *Strom Thurmond's America,* 51–6.

24. Hoover, "General Problem," F46, B14, HO&C.

25. Hoover, "Protecting Our Freedom," F46, B14, HO&C; "Civil Rights and Domestic Violence: A Summary," March 15, 1947, F46, B14, HO&C.

26. Hoover, "Memorandum for Mr. Tolson," March 22, 1947, F46, B14, HO&C; "Civil Rights and Domestic Violence: A Summary," March 15, 1947, F46, B14, HO&C.

27. Carr to Hoover, March 21, 1947, F46, B14, HO&C; Hoover to Carr, March 24, 1947, F46, B14, HO&C.

28. *To Secure These Rights;* Gravely, *They Stole Him out of Jail,* 115; Fredrickson, *Dixiecrat Revolt,* 61–3.

29. Gravely, *They Stole Him out of Jail,* 202; *To Secure These Rights,* 158, 114, 24, 26, 124, 118, 123–4.

30. Tamm to Director, November 10, 1947, FBI 94-45366-28 (Ernst); Truman, "Special Message to the Congress on Civil Rights," February 2, 1948, American Presidency Project, https://www.presidency.ucsb.edu/documents/special-message-the-congress-civil-rights-1. On the 1948 election, see Frederickson, *Dixiecrat Revolt,* 150–86.

Chapter 28: The One Bulwark (1941–1946)

1. "Hoover, F.B.I. Chief," *Sewanee Alumni News,* August 1941, B81, JEHS; Hoover, "Reconversion," *On Guard,* January 1946, B94, JEHS.

2. Isserman, *Which Side Were You On?,* 124–32, 191.

3. Garlin, "Does G-Man Hoover Know," *DW,* July 30, 1943, B87, JEHS; O'Reilly, *Hoover and the Un-Americans,* 48.

4. "Communist Infiltration," February 18, 1943, S1, FBI IA 100-138754 (COMPIC).

5. Schrecker, *Many Are the Crimes,* 110; Morgan, "FBI Probes," *Los Angeles Examiner,* January 17, 1942, B82, JEHS; JEH APP (1945), 228.

6. Biddle, "Memorandum for J. Edgar Hoover," May 29, 1942, F: "AAG/FBI," B36, JRJ; Hoover, "Memorandum for the Attorney General," June 1, 1942, F136, B22, HO&C.

7. JEH APP (FY 1945), December 3, 1943, 229; Isserman, *Which Side Were You On?,* 216–21, 233–8; Johanningsmeier, *Forging American Communism,* 304–13; Barrett, *William Z. Foster,* 222–5.

8. On Chambers, see especially Tanenhaus, *Whittaker Chambers;* Weinstein, *Perjury.* Where not otherwise cited, background information on Chambers/Hiss may be found in these works. For the meeting with Berle, see Tanenhaus, *Whittaker Chambers,* 159–62.

9. Tanenhaus, *Whittaker Chambers,* 169-70; "Comintern Apparatus," December 15, 1944, FBI IA 100-203581-3702 (COMRAP).

10. Gaddis, *The United States and the Origins of the Cold War, 1941-1947,* 205; Bohlen to President, "Memorandum of Conversation," April 23, 1945, *Foreign Relations of the United States: Diplomatic Papers, 1945, Volume V, Europe* (Washington, D.C.: U.S. Government Printing Office, 1967), 256, Office of the Historian, https://history.state.gov/historicaldocuments/frus1945v05/d196.

11. Tanenhaus, *Whittaker Chambers,* 203; Klehr and Radosh, *Amerasia Spy Case;* Weinstein, *Perjury,* 367.

12. Hoover to Connelly, September 12, 1945, F: "Atomic Bomb," B145, Subject File, President's Secretary File, HST; Knight, *How the Cold War Began,* 1–13; "Soviet Espionage Activities," October 19, 1945, F: "C," B145, Subject File, President's Secretary File, HST.

13. Budenz, *This Is My Story,* 349; Ybarra, *Washington Gone Crazy,* 571; Isserman, *Which Side Were You On?,* 239.

14. For background on Bentley, see Olmsted, *Red Spy Queen;* Kessler, *Clever Girl.* For quote, see Conroy to Director and SAC, November 8, 1945, S1, FBI IA 65-56402-4 (Silvermaster).

15. Hoover to Vaughan, November 8, 1945, S16, FBI IA 65-56402-403 (Silvermaster).

16. Mumford to Ladd, "Elizabeth Terrill Bentley," November 9, 1945, S1, FBI IA 65-56402-10 (Silvermaster); Ladd to Director, "Elizabeth Terrell Bentley," November [illegible], 1945, S1, FBI IA 65-56402-21 (Silvermaster); Kessler, *Clever Girl,* 138; Olmsted, *Red Spy Queen,* 103.

17. Spencer, "Elizabeth Terrill Bentley," November 16, 1945, S1, FBI IA 65-56402-25 (Silvermaster).

18. Ladd to Director, "Nathan Gregory Silvermaster," December 12, 1945, S8, FBI IA 65-56402-235 (Silvermaster);

Hendon to Tolson, "Bentley Case," November 19, 1945, S1, FBI IA 65-56402-38 (Silvermaster); Ladd to Hoover, "Elizabeth Bentley," November 10, 1945, S16, FBI IA 65-56402 (Silvermaster); Hoover, "Memorandum for the Attorney General," November 19, 1945, S24, FBI IA 65-56402-581x2 (Silvermaster); Hoover, "Memorandum for the Attorney General," November 17, 1945, S24, FBI IA 65-56402-581X (Silvermaster); Hoover, "Memorandum for the Attorney General," November 28 [illegible], 1945, FBI IA 65-56402-581x (Silvermaster).

19. Spencer, "Elizabeth Terrill Bentley," November 16, 1945; Olmsted, *Red Spy Queen*, 73-6; Kessler, 138-9; Ladd to Director, "Nathan Gregory Silvermaster," December 12, 1945.

20. Stewart to Hottel, "Special Squad Conference," November 30, 1945, S16, FBI 65-56402-409 (Silvermaster); Ladd to Director, "Nathan Gregory Silvermaster," December 6, 1945, S13, FBI IA 65-56402-28 (Silvermaster).

21. Ladd to Hoover, "U.S. Delegates," January 30, 1946, S25, FBI IA 65-56402-621 (Silvermaster); Hoover to Vaughan, February 1, 1946, S21, FBI IA 65-56402-473 (Silvermaster).

22. Hoover, "Memorandum for Mr. Tolson," February 25, 1946, S22, FBI IA 65-56402-505 (Silvermaster); Ladd to Director, "Harry Dexter White," February 20, 1946, S23, FBI IA 65-56402-571 (Silvermaster); Ladd to Hoover, "Gregory," May 8, 1946, S46, FBI IA 65-56402-103 (Silvermaster).

23. Ladd to Hoover, "Gregory," April 17, 1946, S38, FBI IA 65-56402 (Silvermaster).

Chapter 29: Un-American Activities (1946–1947)

1. Flaherty, "Dempsey Here," *Los Angeles Examiner*, August 1, 1946, B95, JEHS; JEH LOGS, July 26–August 29, 1946; "Gangsterism, Communism," *Oakland Tribune*, September 29, 1946, B95, JEHS; "Legion to Honor," *San Francisco Examiner*, September 13, 1946, B95, JEHS; Powers, *Secrecy and Power*, 284.

2. "FBI Head Terms," *Cincinnati Enquirer*, October 1, 1946, B95, JEHS; *Address by J. Edgar Hoover* (New York: Herbert-Spencer, 1946), B95, JEHS; "FBI Chief Warns," *BS*, October 1, 1946, B95, JEHS; Sullivan, "Decline," paper unknown, ca. October 1946, B95, JEHS; Tucker, "Ray Tucker's Letter," *Brooklyn Eagle*, October 22, 1946, B95, JEHS.

3. SAC Salt Lake City to Director, "Communist Matters," June 23, 1947, S1, FBI FOIA 62-75421 (Mundt).

4. American Political Science Association, *Reorganization of Congress*; Davidson, "Legislative Reorganization Act of 1946"; Postell, "The Decision of 1946."

5. Connelly to George, December 5, 1945, F: "OF10B FBI," B102, WHCF, HST; Connelly to Russell, December 5, 1945, F: "OF10B FBI," B102, WHCF, HST; "Rankin Wants," *San Antonio Light*, January 30, 1946, B94, JEHS; "Bill Would Raise," *WS*, March 27, 1946, B94, JEHS; "House Group Favors," *WTH*, April 13, 1946, B94, JEHS; "Pay Rise," *NYT*, May 3, 1946, B94, JEHS.

6. Childs, "Communism in Politics," *WP*, December 2, 1946, B95, JEHS.

7. Hoover, "Memorandum for Mr. Tolson," January 4, 1943, FBI 62-40772-62x1 (House Appropriations); Laughlin, "Memorandum for the Director," January 20, 1943, 62-40772-81 (House Appropriations).

8. Hoover, "Memorandum for Mr. Tolson," January 7, 1943, FBI 62-40772-62x2 (House Appropriations); Clegg,

"Memorandum for the Director," February 24, 1943, FBI 62-40772-63 (House Appropriations).

9. Cannon to Hoover, July 25, 1943, FBI 62-40772-68 (House Appropriations); Lee, *In the Public Interest*, 97.

10. Lee to Hoover, July 14, 1948, FBI 62-40772-117 (House Appropriations); Callahan to Tolson, "Assignment of Agents," July 13, 1948, FBI 62-40772-118 (House Appropriations); Jarrell, "FBI Head Envy," *Morning World-Herald* (Omaha), May 19, 1947, B97, JEHS.

11. Hoover to Jackson, October 21, 1940, F10, B89, RJ. On FBI and HUAC, see O'Reilly, *Hoover and the Un-Americans*.

12. Hoover, "Memorandum for the Attorney General," March 18, 1947, R3, FBI SR 61-7582 (HUAC); Nichols to Tolson, "Committee on Un-American Activities," March 25, 1947, R3, FBI SR 61-7582 (HUAC); "Un-American Acts," ca. April 1945, R3, FBI SR 61-7582 (HUAC); O'Reilly, *Hoover and the Un-Americans*, 41–44.

13. "Special Message to the Congress on Greece and Turkey: The Truman Doctrine," March 12, 1947, Harry S. Truman Library and Museum, https://www.trumanlibrary.gov/library/public-papers/56/special-message-congress-greece-and-turkey-truman-doctrine; Morgan, *Reds*, 304–5; "The National Security Act of 1947—July 26 1947," Oxford University Press, https://global.oup.com/us/companion.websites/9780195385168/resources/chapter10/nsa/nsa.pdf. On the politics of the loyalty investigations, see Storrs, *Second Red Scare*.

14. Riebling, *Wedge*, 76–8; Nichols to Tolson, March 18, 1947, R3, FBI SR 61-7582 (HUAC); Nichols to Director, "Committee Un-American Activities," March 25, 1947, R3, FBI SR 61-7582 (HUAC). On competing visions for National Security Act, see especially Hogan, *Cross of Iron*, 23–68.

15. "Today in Congress," *WTH*, March 26, 1947, B96, JEHS; "Hoover Says Reds," *Dallas Morning News*, March 27, 1947, B96, JEHS.

16. "J. Edgar Hoover and Communism," *CR*, March 27, 1947, F1, B8, "Internal Security File," Eleanor Bontecou Papers, HST.

17. "J. Edgar Hoover and Communism," *CR*, March 27, 1947, F1, B8, "Internal Security File," Eleanor Bontecou Papers, HST; Nichols to Tolson, May 13, 1947, R3, FBI SR 61-7582 (HUAC). On the Hollywood hearings, see Doherty, *Show Trial*.

18. Doherty, *Show Trial*, 62-63; Tamm, "Memorandum for the Director," July 11, 1947, Sr250, S4, FBI IA 100-138754 (COMPIC).

19. "Filmdom Red Inquiry," *WP*, October 19, 1947; Phillips, "Un-American Committee," *NYT*, October 26, 1947; Gould, "Committee Probing," *BG*, October 23, 1947; Hood to Hoover, October 13, 1947, R3, FBI SR 61-7582-478 (HUAC); Doherty, *Show Trial*, 101-105.

20. "Movie Writer," *AC*, October 28, 1947; Norton, "Anti-Communist Films," *BS*, October 22, 1947; Edwards, "Probers Expose," *CT*, October 30, 1947. On Reagan, see Rosenfeld, *Subversives*, 112–123.

21. Fletcher to Ladd, "Communist Infiltration," July 21, 1949, Serial 1003, P2, S9, FBI IA 100-138754 (COMPIC), VI-107; Doherty, *Show Trial*, 299-311.

Chapter 30: Three-Ring Circus (1948–1950)

1. On Venona, see especially Haynes and Klehr, *Venona*; West, *Venona*; Schechter and Schecter, *Sacred Secrets*; Romerstein and Breindel, *Venona Secrets*; Blum, *In the Enemy's House*; Benson, *Venona Story*; Benson and Warner, eds.,

Venona. For a critical perspective, see Schrecker and Isserman, "Papers of a Dangerous Tendency: From Major Andre's Boot to the VENONA Files," in Schrecker, *Cold War Triumphalism.* For the FBI, see Lamphere, *FBI-KGB War;* Fox, "In the Enemy's House: Venona and the Maturation of American Counterintelligence," paper presented at the 2050 Symposium on Cryptologic History, October 27, 2005.

2. Belmont to Boardman, "[Redacted] Espionage-R," February 1, 1956, FBI FOIA [unnumbered] (Venona).

3. Haynes and Klehr, *Venona,* 9.

4. Bradley, *Very Principled Boy,* 136–7.

5. "Eisler Calls Washington," *NYDN,* June 13, 1947, B97, JEHS; Steinberg, *Great "Red Menace,"* 95.

6. Bradley, *Very Principled Boy,* 137-138.

7. Hoover, "Memorandum for Mr. Tolson," April 1, 1948, P137, FBI 56402 (Silvermaster); Steinberg, *Great "Red Menace,"* 108; Bradley, *Very Principled Boy,* 149; Morgan, *Reds,* 313.

8. Steinberg, *Great "Red Menace,"* 96–7.

9. Fletcher to Ladd, "Gregory Case," March 19, 1948, P137, FBI 65-56402 (Silvermaster).

10. Flynn, "Life of the Party," *DW,* June 29, 1948, B101, JEHS; Weiner, *Enemies,* 158. On Bentley and HUAC, see Olmsted, *Red Spy Queen,* 114–139; Kessler, *Clever Girl,* 148–188.

11. On Chambers and HUAC, see Tanenhaus, *Whittaker Chambers,* 212-334.

12. Weinstein, *Perjury,* 21, 55–62. On the White case, see especially Craig, *Treasonable Doubt.*

13. On the social significance of the Hiss case, see especially Swan, *Alger Hiss, Whittaker Chambers, and the Schism in the American Soul.*

14. JEH LOGS, July 26-September 3, 1948; Childs, "Calling Washington," *WP,* September 3, 1948, B100, JEHS.

15. New York to Director, July 14, 1938, S1, FBI FOIA 62-45146 (Dewey); "Text of Dewey's," *NYHT,* April 2, 1948, B99, JEHS. On tensions from the 1930s, see for instance: Tamm, "Memorandum for the Director," October 19, 1937, FBI FOIA 62-45146-11 (Dewey).

16. Mundt to Hoover, August 31, 1948, S1, FBI FOIA 62-75421 (Mundt). For Hoover's quiet cooperation with Dewey, see F57, B14, HO&C; Sullivan, *The Bureau,* 41–5.

17. "J. Edgar Hoover Caught," *Las Vegas Evening Review Journal,* September 27, 1948, B100, JEHS; Richards, "Dewey Hunts FBI," *New York Star,* September 29, 1948, B100, JEHS.

18. "J. Edgar Hoover Confined," *WS,* September 17, 1948, B100, JEHS; "J. Edgar Hoover Seriously Ill," *Flint News Advertiser,* September 17, 1948; Tanenhaus, *Whittaker Chambers,* 283; Hoover to Ernst, October 4, 1948, FBI FOIA 94-4-5366-43 (Ernst).

19. JEH LOGS, November 2-16, 1948.

20. Gellman, *Contender,* 225–233.

21. Fletcher to Ladd, "Sam David Whittaker Chambers," December 20, 1948, R10, FBI SR 100-409206 (Hiss).

22. "I.D. Special Analysis Report #1," August 30, 1947, NSA Venona; Lamphere and Schachtman, *FBI-KGB War,* 85, 97. For Lamphere's early experiences with Venona, see Lamphere and Schachtman, *FBI-KGB War,* 78-98.

23. Director to SAC WFO, "Judith Coplon," December 31, 1948, S1, FBI V 65-58365 (Coplon); Lamphere and Schachtman, *FBI-KGB War,* 100, 104. On the Coplon case, see especially Lamphere and Schachtman, *FBI-KGB War,* 99-125; Mitchell and Mitchell, *Spy Who Seduced America.*

24. Ladd to Director, "Judith Coplon," January 17, 1949, P1, FBI V 65-58365-26 (Coplon).

25. Delavigne to Hottel, "Judith Coplon," March 4, 1949, P10, FBI V 65-5128-110 (Coplon); Ladd to Director, "Judith Coplon," March 7, 1949, S1, P2, FBI V 65-58365-186 (Coplon).

26. "The Watchful Eye," August 8, 1949, B102, JEHS.

27. On the Smith Act trial, see especially Martelle, *Fear Within;* Belknap, *Cold War Political Justice,* 77–121; Morgan, *Reds,* 312–20. For quotes, see *I Led Three Lives,* 284–289. For the account of another FBI informant, see Calomiris, *Red Masquerade.*

28. For analysis of the Hiss trial evidence, see especially Weinstein, *Perjury,* 399–526, 623–48; Tanenhaus, *Whittaker Chambers,* 339–442. For a defense of Hiss, see Hartshorn, *Alger Hiss, Whittaker Chambers and the Case that Ignited McCarthyism;* also see algerhiss.com. For historical controversies, see Jacoby, *Alger Hiss and the Battle for History.*

29. Mitchell and Mitchell, *Spy Who Seduced America,* 40.

30. Hoover, "Judith Coplon Case," June 28, 1949, P7, FBI V 65-14932-496 (Coplon); Michell and Mitchell, *Spy Who Seduced America,* 57-282.

31. Gallup, "Only 3%," *WP,* August 21, 1949, B102, JEHS; Gallup, "J. Edgar Hoover Gets," *Public Opinion News Service,* February 24, 1950, B103, JEHS.

32. Hoover to Dewey, March 2, 1950, S3, FBI FOIA 62-56146 (Dewey). On June mail, see Theoharis and Cox, *Boss,* 256–61. Whether or not Truman knew about Venona has been a subject of scholarly debate. For the negative view, see especially Moynihan, *Secrecy,* and Haynes and Klehr, *Venona.* For claims that Truman did know, see Schechter and Schecter, *Sacred Secrets.*

Chapter 31: J. Edgar Hoover, Churchman (1948–1950)

1. Stone, "Dr. Condon's Challenge," *Daily Compass,* June 13, 1949, B101, JEHS; "Spy Trials Cripple," *USNWR,* July 9, 1949, B102, JEHS; Baldwin, "Statement," October 11, 1949, F2, B613, ACLU.

2. Hoover to Baldwin, October 10, 1949, F1, B862, ACLU; ACLU, "News Release," January 9, 1950, F15, B996, ACLU; "Speech by Joseph Rauh," February 24, 1950, F15D, B285, General File, WHCF, DDE; Schlesinger, "Week in History," *Chicago Sun-Times,* March 5, 1950, B103, JEHS; DeVoto, "Due Notice," *Harper's,* September 1949, B102, JEHS.

3. "FBI Chief Charges," *WP,* December 1, 1949, B102, JEHS; Ernst to Hoover, February 13, 1948, FBI 94-5366-32 (Ernst); Lowenthal, *Federal Bureau of Investigation;* Morgan, *Reds,* 322–4.

4. Elson, "J. Edgar Hoover—Churchman," *Presbyterian Life,* November 27, 1948, B100, JEHS; "In Bridal Procession," *WP,* February 29, 1948; "Mary Lonergan," *NYT,* May 20, 1951; "Second Cousin," *Toronto Globe and Mail,* February 6, 1950; "Presbyterian Dedication," *WP,* October 18, 1947.

5. Summers, *Official and Confidential,* 158; Meik, "Red Fascism," *Deseret News,* February 5, 1948, B99, JEHS.

6. Hoover, "Why I Believe in God," *School Bank News,* June 1948, B99, JEHS.

7. "That Man Hoover," *Church Street Methodist Church,* December 5, 1947, B98, JEHS. On Hoover and religion, see especially Johnson and Weitzman, eds., *The FBI and Religion* and Martin, *Gospel of J. Edgar Hoover.*

8. Oursler, *Greatest Story Ever Told*; "Laymen Endorse," *El Paso Times*, February 26, 1949, B101, JEHS; Hoover, "To Be an American," *Baptist Training Union Magazine*, July 1945, B115, JEHS.

9. Hoover, "Wild Children," *American Magazine*, April 1943, B86, JEHS.

10. "City-Wide Rally," *WP*, January 19, 1946, B94, JEHS; Dutton, "F.B.I. Head Says," *LAT*, August 19, 1951, B107, JEHS.

11. Hoover to Hoover, October 4, 1943, B90, Post-Presidential Papers, HHoo; "J. Edgar Hoover Joins," *Boys Club Bulletin*, November 1943, B88, JEHS; Fine, "Tips on Tables," *WN*, July 29, 1949, B102, JEHS.

12. "We Must Prevent," *Illinois Policeman and Police Journal*, March–April 1951, B106, JEHS.

13. George, *God's Salesman*; Flaherty, "Hoover Hits Crime," *Los Angeles Examiner*, October 23, 1956, B122, JEHS; Knebel, "J. Edgar Hoover," *Look*, May 31, 1955, B118, JEHS. On Peale, see especially Lane, *Surge of Piety*, 81–101. On Hoover's relationships with ministers, see especially Martin, "Bureau Clergyman," 3–5.

14. Hoover, "Neglect by Parents," *Daily Times*, April 6, 1950, B104, JEHS; "Norman Vincent Peale Answers," *Look*, June 14, 1954, B115, JEHS; "FBI National Academy," *CR*, April 3, 1950, B104, JEHS; "Reverse Side of Letter," American Bible Society, 1958, B125, JEHS.

15. "Golden Texts," *Youth for Christ Magazine*, February 1953, B110, JEHS; Hoover, "To Be an American"; "Men Imbued with Spiritual Values," *Houston Press*, September 29, 1951, B107, JEHS.

16. Barton, "FBI Men Go," *Central Christian Advocate*, November 22, 1951, B107, JEHS; "J. Edgar Hoover Says," *Vineland Times Journal*, October 15, 1955, B119, JEHS.

17. Jones, "Nation's Watchdog," *Northern Light*, F7, B1, NLEM; Clausen, "What Is the Scottish Rite?" (Washington: Supreme Council, 1973), F7, S-JEHC; "Noble J. Edgar Hoover," *Meccan*, April–June 1950, B104, JEHS; "Red Menace," *NYJA*, May 3, 1950, B104, JEHS; "FBI Head," *Hickory Daily Record*, October 18, 1955, B119, JEHS.

18. Elson, "J. Edgar Hoover You Ought," *Chaplain*, September–October 1950, B105, JEHS.

19. Rosswurm, *FBI and the Catholic Church*, 56, 1, 80–6; Hoover, "Our Future," May 10, 1942, F: "Justice Dept., FBI 1941–2," B11, OF10B, FDR; "MU to Honor Chief," *Milwaukee Journal*, May 17, 1950, B104, JEHS; "FBI Head," *Sunday Call*, May 28, 1944, B90, JEHS; Clendenin, "J. Edgar Hoover Awarded," *Alumnus*, Fall 1954, B116, JEHS; "Ninety-Sixth Commencement," June 1944, *Holy Cross Alumnus*, B90, JEHS; Reeves, *America's Bishop*; Sherwood, *Rhetorical Leadership*, 9–42; Olmsted, *Red Spy Queen*, 80, 115.

20. "J. Edgar Hoover Talks," *Lincoln Journal*, March 22, 1942, B82, JEHS; "Hoover Warns," *NYJA*, January 9, 1946, B94, JEHS; "FBI Graduates," *WTH*, June 27, 1946, B94, JEHS.

21. Rosswurm, *FBI and the Catholic Church*, 9–52, 105. On homosexuality, see, for instance, Signorile, "Cardinal Spellman's Dark Legacy," *New York Press*, May 7, 2002; Gentry, *J. Edgar Hoover*, 347.

22. "FBI Director Lauds," *Pilot*, July 17, 1949, B102, JEHS.

23. DeLoach to Hoover, March 20, 1956, S4, FBI V 67-338728-230 (DeLoach); "Sixty-Nine F.B.I. Men," *Manresan*, May 1943, B86, JEHS; Rosswurm, *FBI and the Catholic Church*, 10, 50–2; "Hoover on Retreats," *Catholic*

Mirror, November 1951, B107, JEHS; Brieg, "Mr. F.B.I.," *Information*, November 1953, B111, JEHS.

24. Elson, *America's Spiritual Recovery*, 33.

Chapter 32: Atomic Drama (1949–1951)

1. Philby, *My Silent War*, 137.

2. Truman, "Statement by President Truman in Response to First Soviet Nuclear Test," September 23, 1949, Wilson Center, https://digitalarchive.wilsoncenter.org/document/134436.

3. Oshinsky, *Conspiracy So Immense*, 102.

4. Philby, *My Silent War*, 135, 78, 150; Lamphere and Schachtman, *FBI-KGB War*, 130.

5. "Comintern Apparatus," December 15, 1944, S63, FBI IA 100-203581 (COMRAP); Erskine to Chief AS-90, "Study of [Redacted] Messages," April 16, 1948, NSA Venona; Lamphere and Schachtman, *FBI-KGB War*, 133.

6. On Philby, see especially Macintyre, *Spy among Friends*; Hamrick, *Deceiving the Deceivers*; Newton, *Cambridge Spies*; Knightley, *Master Spy*.

7. Lamphere and Schachtman, *FBI-KGB War*, 133, 137. For the Fuchs case, see especially Williams, *Klaus Fuchs, Atom Spy*; Moss, *Klaus Fuchs*.

8. Hoover, "Memorandum to Mr. Tolson," February 2, 1950, P12, FBI V 65-58805-587 (Fuchs); Ladd to Director, "Emil Julius Klaus Fuchs," February 5, 1950, P33, FBI V 65-58805-1089 (Fuchs); Ladd to Director, "Foocase," March 13, 1950, P17, FBI V 65-58805-713 (Fuchs); Philby, *My Silent War*, 151.

9. "Briton Admits," *WTH*, February 4, 1950, B103, JEHS; "FBI Atom," *Chicago Daily News*, February 6, 1950, B103, JEHS; Lamphere and Schachtman, *FBI-KGB War*, 137–8; Levin, "Briton Held," *Chicago Sun Times*, February 7, 1950, B103, JEHS; "Wire Tapping Trapped," *WDN*, February 8, 1950, B103, JEHS.

10. Hoover, "Memorandum for Mr. Tolson," April 5, 1950, P27, FBI V 65-58805-9417 (Fuchs); Ladd to Director, "Emil Klaus Fuchs," April 28, 1950, S32, FBI V 65-58805-1052 (Fuchs).

11. Ladd to Director, "Emil Klaus Fuchs," April 28, 1950, S38, FBI 65-58805-1149 (Fuchs); Lamphere and Schachtman, *FBI-KGB War*, 143–60.

12. "FBI Trails," *WTH*, May 24, 1950, B104, JEHS; "Harry Gold Spy," *WS*, May 25, 1950, B104, JEHS.

13. Roberts, *Brother*, 166; Erskine to Chief AS-90, "Study of [Redacted] Messages," April 27, 1948, NSA Venona; Erskine to Chief AS-90, "Special Study," August 12, 1948, NSA Venona.

14. Roberts, *Brother*, 419–20; Ladd to Director, "[Redacted], Espionage-R," February 28, 1951, FBI V [unnumbered] (Venona); Schneir, *Final Verdict*, 37. On Hall, see Albright and Kunstel, *Bombshell*.

15. Ladd to Director, "[Redacted], Espionage-R," February 28, 1951, FBI V [unnumbered] (Venona); Roberts, *Brother*, 240-68.

16. Whelan, "Re: Julius Rosenberg," June 16, 1950, S1, FBI IA 65-15348-13 (Julius Rosenberg).

17. Radosh and Milton, *Rosenberg File*, 99; Erskine to Chief AS-90, "Special Study," August 13, 1948, NSA Venona.

18. Whelan, "Re: Julius Rosenberg," July 17, 1950, S3, FBI IA 65-15348-111 (Julius Rosenberg); Ladd to Director, "[Redacted], Espionage-R," February 28, 1951, FBI V [unnumbered] (Venona); Roberts, *Brother*, 271.

19. Schneir, *Final Verdict*, 162.

20. Radosh and Milton, *Rosenberg File*, 288, 99–100, 137–8.

21. Roberts, *Brother*, 298–376. For quote, see 368.

22. Cunningham, "Cause of Treason," *Boston Sunday Herald*, B106, JEHS; Radosh and Milton, *Rosenberg File*, 279–81; Lamphere and Schachtman, *FBI-KGB War*, 225–6.

23. Roberts, *Brother*, 381.

24. Radosh and Milton, *Rosenberg File*, 326, 351, 336, 376-7, 416; Lamphere and Schachtman, *FBI-KGB War*, 265-6. For the execution controversy, see Clune, *Executing the Rosenbergs*.

25. Gordon, "Now It's 'Sir J.,'" *WN*, October 18, 1950, B105, JEHS; Brooks, "Assistant Secretary," *WS*, October 18, 1950, B105, JEHS; SAC SFO to Director, "Donald Maclean," July 14, 1951, P1C, S1, FBI V [unnumbered] (Cambridge Five); Macintyre, *Spy among Friends*, 142-9.

26. Macintyre, *Spy among Friends*, 149-50; Haynes and Klehr, *Venona*, 52-5.

27. Philby, *My Silent War*, 162–3.

28. Riebling, *Wedge*, 87-94, 102-6; Macintyre, *Spy among Friends*, 158-9; Lamphere and Schachtman, *FBI-KGB War*, 232.

29. Lamphere and Schachtman, *FBI-KGB War*, 228–38.

30. Johnson, *American Cryptology during the Cold War, 1945-1989*, 277-8; Haynes, Klehr, and Vassiliev, *Spies*, 398-405; Haynes and Klehr, *Venona*, 48-51.

31. Macintyre, *Spy among Friends*, 244-282.

32. West, *Venona*, 138–9; "David Greenglass Case," undated, P31, S6A, FBI V [unnumbered] (Cambridge Five).

33. Martin, *Wilderness of Mirrors*, 44.

34. Macintyre, *Spy among Friends*, 276.

35. Belmont to Boardman, "[Redacted], Espionage-R," February 1, 1956, FBI V [unnumbered] (Venona).

36. Philby, *My Silent War*, 147–8.

Chapter 33: Hooverism (1950–1952)

1. For biographies of McCarthy, see especially Tye, *Demagogue*, and Oshinsky, *A Conspiracy So Immense*. Also valuable is the documentary *McCarthy*, directed by Sharon Grimberg (PBS/American Experience). Where not otherwise noted, background on McCarthy can be found in these works. For useful earlier biographical accounts, see especially Rovere, *Senator Joe McCarthy*; Cook, *Nightmare Decade*; Reeves, *Life and Times of Joe McCarthy*.

2. Oshinsky, *A Conspiracy So Immense*, 56; Cassini, "These Charming People," *WTH*, April 3, 1947, B97, JEHS; Dixon, "Washington Scene," *WTH*, April 7, 1947, B97, JEHS.

3. Oshinsky, *A Conspiracy So Immense*, 52; JEH LOGS, May 5, 1947.

4. Hoover to McCarthy, February 3, 1948, S6A, FBI 94-37780-2 (McCarthy); McCarthy to Hoover, April 13, 1949, S6A, FBI FOIA 94-37708-7 (McCarthy); Jones to Nichols, April 11, 1948, S6A, FBI FOIA 84-37708-9 (McCarthy); "Transcribed Remarks," S6A, FBI FOIA 84-37708-9 (McCarthy); "J. Edgar Hoover," *CR*, May 10, 1949, B101, JEHS.

5. For an example of contemporary use of "Hooverism," see "J. Edgar Hooverism," *DW*, October 3, 1946, B95, JEHS. For historical analysis, see Schrecker, *Many Are the Crimes*, 203.

6. Oshinsky, *A Conspiracy So Immense*, 108–14.

7. Hoover, "Memorandum for Mr. Tolson," March 23, 1950, S12B, FBI FOIA 121-23278-61 (McCarthy).

8. Hoover, "Memorandum for the Attorney General," March 10, 1950, S11B, FBI FOIA 121-23278-28 (McCarthy).

9. Oshinsky, *A Conspiracy So Immense*, 136; "4 Spy Suspects," *WS*, March 22, 1950, B103, JEHS; Ladd to Director, March 22, 1950, S12A, FBI FOIA 121-23278 (McCarthy); Hoover, "Memorandum for Mr. Tolson," March 23, 1950, S12B, FBI FOIA 121-23278-61 (McCarthy).

10. Ladd to Director, March 24, 1950, S12B, FBI FOIA 121-23278-63 (McCarthy); "George Warns," *Atlanta Journal*, March 25, 1950, B103, JEHS; Holland, "Showdown Near," *WS*, March 25, 1950, B103, JEHS. For an assessment of the evidence on Lattimore, see especially Haynes and Klehr, *Amerasia Case*, 28-55.

11. Hoover, "Memorandum for Mr. Tolson," March 24, 1950, S12A, FBI FOIA 121-23278 (McCarthy).

12. "F.B.I. Put Files," *NYHT*, March 28, 1950, B103, JEHS; Untitled, *NR*, April 10, 1950, B104, JEHS; Hoover, "The FBI Loyalty Files," *HC*, March 30, 1950, B104, JEHS.

13. Ickes, "Hysteria in the Justice Department," *NR*, July 4, 1949, B102, JEHS; Untitled, *NR*, April 10, 1950, B104, JEHS.

14. "Confidence," *Philadelphia Daily News*, March 29, 1950, B103, JEHS; Roosevelt, "Conservative Has," *WDN*, March 30, 1950, B103, JEHS; "Senate-Truman Clash," *WS*, March 29, 1950, B103, JEHS.

15. Stone, "J. Edgar Hoover as Defender," *New York Compass*, March 26, 1950, B103, JEHS.

16. Oshinsky, *A Conspiracy So Immense*, 168–72; Tye, *Demagogue*, 185–7.

17. On McCarran and the FBI, see especially Ybarra, *Washington Gone Crazy*; Gerard, "A Program of Cooperation.'"

18. Belmont to Ladd, "Senate Subcommittee," April 28, 1951, FBI 62-88217-63 (SISS), F: 60-90, B1, Sr20, AT.

19. Anderson, "Estes' Claim Hoover," *Chattanooga News-Free Press*, October 9, 1950; Ybarra, *Washington Gone Crazy*, 509–34; "Text of Truman's Message," *BS*, September 23, 1950.

20. Stockham, "Lack of Oversight," 207; Nichols to Tolson, "McCarran Committee," March 22, 1950, FBI 62-88217-29, F: X-59x1, B1, Sr20, AT.

21. Ybarra, *Washington Gone Crazy*, 538, 547–8; Nichols to Tolson, "McCarran Committee," March 30, 1951, FBI 62-88217-29, F: X-59x1, B1, Sr20, AT.

22. Marder, "Lattimore Lashes Out," *WP*, February 27, 1952; Ybarra, *Washington Gone Crazy*, 397, 569–605.

23. Gerard, "A Program of Cooperation," 126–278; Hoover, "Memorandum for Mr. Tolson," November 25, 1952, FBI 62-88217, F691-926, B3, Sr20, AT.

24. Nichols to Tolson, February 2, 1951, and Hoover to Attorney General, "Release of Subversive Information," February 3, 1951, FBI 62-93875-1, F1, B1, Sr42, AT; Hoover, "Memorandum for Mr. Tolson," February 6, 1951, FBI 62-93875-6, F1, B1, Sr42, AT.

25. Hoover to SACs, "Re: Responsibilities of the FBI," February 17, 1951, FBI 62-93875, F1, B1, Sr42, AT.

26. Thom and Jung, "Responsibilities Program," 357, 358, 361; Rosenfeld, *Subversives*, 32, 35. Thom and Jung put the number slightly lower (369).

27. SAC Salt Lake City to Director, "Communist Matters," June 23, 1947, S1, FBI FOIA 62-75421 (Mundt).

28. "Biographical Sketch," F17, B160, HAP; Pennington to Ladd, "National Convention," October 25, 1948, FBI IA 94-17998-816 (AL-National Americanism Commission); Hoover, "Memorandum for Mr. Tolson," October 27, 1953, S3, FBI FOIA 67-11938-388 (Pennington); Hoover to Pennington, November 5, 1953, S3, FBI FOIA 67-11938-388 (Pennington); Hoover to Connell, November 16, 1953, S3, FBI FOIA 67-11938-388 (Pennington); Powers, *Secrecy and Power*, 398.

29. Little "United Front," S18, FBI IA 94-1-17998 (AL-National Americanism Commission); "Trends and Developments," February 1950, S18, FBI IA 94-1-17998 (AL-National Americanism Commission); Pennington to Ladd, "American Legion Contacts," July 26, 1950, S18, FBI IA 94-1-17998-922 (AL-National Americanism Commission); Baumgardner to Fletcher, "The Inside Story," October 21, 1948, S14, FBI IA 94-1-17998-818 (AL-National Americanism Commission).

30. Hoover to SACs, "Re: Responsibilities of the FBI," February 17, 1951, FBI 62-93875, F1, B1, Sr42, AT.

31. "Action Taken," August 7, 1950, F: "I," B146, Subject File: FBI, President's Secretary File, HST; Woltman, "Ex-FBI Agents," *NYWT*, ca. June 12, 1947, FBI IA NY 62-9189 (American Business Consultants). For examples of *Counterattack*'s defense of the FBI, see *Counterattack,* June 16, 1950, December 1, 1950. For early Berlin consultation, see JEH LOGS, May 23, 1950, June 9, 1950. For Reid, see Nichols to Reid, December 10, 1953, F: "Hoover, J. Edgar," B7, Sr1, G755, ORR. For Disney, see SAC Los Angeles to Director, "Walt Disney," December 16, 1954, S1, FBI V 94-4-4667 (Disney); Mason to Tolson, "Walt Disney," March 7, 1956, S1, FBI V 94-4-4667 (Disney).

32. "Hoover Answers Ten Questions on the F.B.I.," *NYT Magazine*, April 16, 1950, F16, B996, ACLU; McCarthy to Hoover, July 30, 1952, S6B, FBI FOIA 94-37708-71 (McCarthy).

Chapter 34: Inner Conflicts (1947–1952)

1. Johnson, *Lavender Scare,* 15–6; Keay to Belmont, March 10, 1950, S11B, FBI FOIA 121-23278 (McCarthy).

2. Hoey; Oshinsky, *A Conspiracy So Immense,* 157.

3. For "thousands," see Johnson, *Lavender Scare,* 166.

4. On the FBI and the Lavender Scare, see especially Johnson, *Lavender Scare*; Charles, *Hoover's War on Gays.* Also see Canaday, *Straight State*; Lvovsky, *Vice Patrol*; *The Lavender Scare*, directed by Josh Howard (PBS/American Experience).

5. Ladd to Director, "Review of State Department," July 20, 1950, S16C, FBI FOIA 121-23278-22 (McCarthy).

6. Hoey Hearings, 2728; Charles, *Hoover's War on Gays,* 71.

7. Tanenhaus, *Whittaker Chambers,* 343-5; Weinstein, *Perjury,* 407-8; Canaday, *Straight State,* 3–4, 10–3.

8. Hoey Hearings, 2268; Johnson, *Lavender Scare*, 53–5.

9. Jones, *Alfred C. Kinsey*, 632; Nichols to Tolson, January 5, 1950, S3, FBI V 62-87653 (Kinsey); Nichols to Tolson, "Professor Kinsey," January 11, 1950, S3, FBI V 62-87563 (Kinsey).

10. Johnson, *Lavender Scare,* 9, 95; Canaday, *Straight State,* 214-21; Hoey Hearings, 2258–72.

11. Beck, "Farmers Market," *LAT*, August 6, 1947, B98, JEHS.

12. Horney, *Our Inner Conflicts*, 14–7, 96-114.

13. Horney, *Self-Analysis,* 7–36.

14. Summers, *Official and Confidential,* 94–5; F414A: "Ruffin de, Marshall," Summers-JEHC.

15. F99, B2, NARA-P; PB85, NLEF.

16. "Eisler Calls Washington," *NYDN*, June 13, 1947, B97, JEHS; Lait and Mortimer, *Washington Confidential,* ix, 90.

17. Oshinsky, *A Conspiracy So Immense*, 131; Wherry, 5, 2.

18. Johnson, *Lavender Scare,* 101–5.

19. Hoey Hearings, 2099–102, 2131–2.

20. Hoey Hearings, 2268, 2278.

21. Hoey, 2, 4.

22. Hoey, 12-3; Charles, *Hoover's War on Gays*, 88-95.

23. Hoey Hearings, 2143-4; Hoover to Souers, April 10, 1950, F: "FBI: S," B147, PSF: Subject File, HST.

24. Charles, *Hoover's War on Gays*, 95–6; Hoover, "Re: Sex Deviates," June 20, 1951, S26, FBI FOIA 66-02-1112X (Sex Deviates Program).

25. "Hoover Doubts Lie Detector," *WP*, April 10, 1950, B110, JEHS.

26. Miller, *Plain Speaking,* 393; Demaris, *Director,* 106.

27. Ladd to Director, March 24, 1952, S5B, FBI V 67-561-279 (Hoover); Ladd to Director, March 26, 1952, S5B, FBI V 67-561 (Hoover); Ladd to Director, April 1, 1952, S5B, FBI V 67-561-280 (Hoover).

28. Malone to Tolson, November 4, 1953, S5B, FBI V 67-561-295 (Hoover); [Illegible] to Director, November 8, 1953, S5A, FBI V 67-561-298 (Hoover); SAC New York to Director, "Robert A. Collins," June 11, 1954, S5A, FBI V 67-561 (Hoover).

29. Johnson, *Lavender Scare,* 117.

30. "Letters to the Day," *New London Day*, April 29, 1950, B104, JEHS; Johnson, *Lavender Scare,* 140-1; McDaniel, *Dying for Joe McCarthy's Sins.*

31. Charles, *Hoover's War on Gays,* 112-9, 148-51, 131-41.

32. Hoover, "Memorandum for Mr. Tolson," January 17, 1952, S2, FBI FOIA 62-96332-3 (McCarthy); [Redacted] to [Redacted], December 27, 1952, S2, FBI FOIA 62-96332 (McCarthy).

33. Hoover, "Memorandum for Mr. Tolson," January 16, 1952, S2, FBI FOIA 62-96332-1 (McCarthy); Hoover, "Memorandum for Mr. Tolson," January 18, 1952, S2, FBI FOIA 62-96332-8 (McCarthy).

34. Hoover, "Memorandum for Mr. Tolson," January 17, 1952, S2, FBI FOIA 62-96332-6 (McCarthy); Hoover, "Memorandum for Mr. Tolson," January 23, 1952, S2, FBI FOIA 62-96332-12 (McCarthy); "I, Lieut. [Redacted]," January 16, 1952, S2, FBI FOIA 62-96332 (McCarthy); Hoover, "Memorandum for Mr. Tolson," January 18, 1952, S2, FBI FOIA 62-96332-7 (McCarthy).

35. Belmont to Ladd, "Senator Joseph McCarthy," November 19, 1952, S2, FBI FOIA 62-96332-35 (McCarthy); Greenspun, "Where I Stand," S2, FBI FOIA 62-96332 (McCarthy).

Chapter 35: A Glorious Year (1953)

1. Powers, *Secrecy and Power*, 316; Hayden, "FBI Stays Safely," *Detroit News*, February 1, 1953, B110, JEHS. For recent interpretations of Eisenhower, see especially Hitchcock, *Age of Eisenhower*; Galambos, *Eisenhower*; Johnson, *Eisenhower*; Smith, *Eisenhower;* Newton, *Eisenhower.*

2. Oshinsky, *A Conspiracy So Immense,* 250-2.

3. "Cabinet Trio," *WTH*, December 5, 1953, B112, JEHS; "Ike's Family," *Minneapolis Star*, January 20, 1953; Elson, *America's Spiritual Recovery*, 53–6, 10.

4. "Ike and Wife Join," *ChiT*, February 2, 1953.

5. Kruse, *One Nation under God*, 73–4, xii-xiii; Elson, *America's Spiritual Recovery*, 58–9, 168, 170, 9–11.

6. "Application for Appointment," April 23, 1937, FBI FOIA 67-102459 (Nixon); Hanson to Director, "Report of Interview," July 17, 1937, FBI FOIA 67-102459 (Nixon); Hoover to Keenan, July 24, 1937, FBI FOIA 67-102459-10 (Nixon); Glavin to Director, "Richard M. Nixon," March 18, 1954, FBI FOIA 67-102459 (Nixon); Hoover, "Introduction of Vice President," June 11, 1954, FBI FOIA 67-102459 (Nixon); Adams to Callahan, "[Redacted], Former

Special Agent," June 9, 1969, FBI FOIA 67-102459 (Nixon); Gellman, *Contender*, 5–8.

7. Hoover, "Introduction of Vice President"; Untitled, *CR*, February 18, 1947, B96, JEHS.

8. Nellor, "Nixon Assails Strategy," *WTH*, June 13, 1949, B101, JEHS; "H. Res. 262," June 22, 1949, S5C, FBI V 67-561 (Hoover); Nixon, "The Hiss Case," January 26, 1950, in Perlstein, *Richard Nixon*, 19–59.

9. Hoover to Nixon, January 31, 1950, F2, B19, PPS 320.103, RN; Hoover, "Introduction of Vice President"; O'Neill to Nixon, June 23, 1949, F1, B19, PPS 320.103, RN.

10. Hoover to Nixon, November 5, 1952, F3, B19, PPS 320.103, RN.

11. "FBI Director Hoover Recalls," *WS*, January 26, 1958, B125, JEHS; McHugh, "Hoover Boost All-America," *San Diego Union*, March 31, 1963, B135, JEHS.

12. Burrough, *Big Rich*, 219. Where not otherwise cited, background details on Murchison and Richardson can be found in this source.

13. Burrough, *Big Rich*, 204, 190–1, 225–8; "Hotel Del Charro" clipping, F30, S-JEHC.

14. Ribbel, "FBI Chief, Nixon," *San Diego Tribune*, August 10, 1955, B118, JEHS; Phleger, "Director of FBI," *San Diego Union*, August 11, 1955, B118, JEHS; Photo, PB54, NLEM; Nixon to Hoover, September 1, 1955, F6, B19, PPS 320.103, RN.

15. Anderson, "Millionaire Picked Up," *WP*, December 31, 1970, B150, JEHS; Burrough, *Big Rich*, 227; "Would Buy Half-Dozen," *Detroit Free Press*, July 13, 1954, B115, JEHS; "2 Texans," *NYT*, July 13, 1954, B115, JEHS; "Bing's Baby," *San Diego*, August 1967, B142, JEHS; Connally, *In History's Shadow*, 137.

16. Burrough, *Big Rich*, 242–3.

17. Pearson, "Washington Merry-Go-Round," *Louisville Courier Journal*, July 27, 1950, B105, JEHS; Weiner, *Legacy of Ashes*, 26–8.

18. Knebel, "How Hoover Rules," *Look*, June 14, 1955, B118, JEHS; Riebling, *Wedge*, 125–6, 100; Weiner, *Enemies*, 153.

19. Waller, *Wild Bill Donovan*, 361.

20. Weiner, *Legacy of Ashes*, 23–38; Riebling, *Wedge*, 94–5, 119-21; "Director's Notation," undated (ca. 1948), S14, FBI FOIA 62-80750-866 (CIA). On Dulles, also see Talbot, *Devil's Chessboard*; Waller, *Disciples*; Kinzer, *The Brothers*.

21. Ladd to Director, "Allen W. Dulles," March 5, 1953, S1, FBI IA 62-83338-10 (Dulles); Weiner, *Enemies*, 188-9.

22. Lucey, "No One Has," *WN*, January 7, 1953, B110, JEHS; Cover, *Time*, February 16, 1953. For Brownell's recollections, see Brownell, *Advising Ike*.

23. Brownell and Flanigan, interview re: Hoover, August 24, 1988, B270, HB.

24. Theoharis, *Boss*, 371–5; Stockham, *Lack of Oversight*, 23–4; "Executive Order 10450," April 27, 1953, National Archives, https://www.archives.gov/federal-register/codification/executive-order/10450.html.

25. Charles, *Hoover's War on Gays*, 124–6; Oshinsky, *A Conspiracy So Immense*, 264; Leviero, "1,456 Ousted," *NYT*, October 24, 1953; "Brownell Denounces," *WS*, June 12, 1953, B110, JEHS.

26. Fleeson, "The Last Chapter," *WS*, November 18, 1953, B112, JEHS; "Brownell on White Case," *NYHT*, November 17, 1953, B111, JEHS.

27. Weinstein, *Perjury*, 255-8; Ladd to Director, "[Redacted]-Espionage," October 16, 1950, FBI V (Venona).

28. Jonas, "Truman Promoted 'Spy,'" *WS*, November 6,

1953, B111, JEHS; Roper, "Senate Group Probes," *WS*, November 7, 1953, B111, JEHS; "Eisenhower's Remarks," *NYHT*, November 12, 1953, B111, JEHS; Reston, "A Prophetic Omission," *NYT*, November 17, 1953, B111, JEHS; "Text of Truman's Speech," *NYHT*, November 17, 1953, B111, JEHS; Walsh, "U.S. Response," *WS*, November 17, 1953, B111, JEHS.

29. "Hoover to be Called," *WS*, November 17, 1953, B111, JEHS; Lawrence, "Hoover Says," *NYT*, Nov. 18, 1953, B112, JEHS; Knowles, "New White Serial," *NYT*, November 18, 1953, B111, JEHS; Reston, "Hoover Star," *NYT*, November 17, 1953, B111, JEHS; Fleeson, "The Last Chapter," *WS*, November 18, 1953, B112, JEHS; "Nick Kenny Speaking," *NYM*, November 19, 1953, B112, JEHS.

30. "Hoover's Statement,"*NYHT*, November 18, 1953, B112, JEHS; "Nick Kenny Speaking"; Reston, "Hoover Star.".

31. "Behind the News," WFAA, November 17, 1953, B111, JEHS; O'Donnell, "Capitol Stuff," *NYM*, November 18, 1953, B112, JEHS.

32. Gallup, "Public Gives J. Edgar Hoover," *WP*, December 26, 1953, B112, JEHS.

33. Shumaker, "White House Fetes," *WTH*, November 18, 1953, B112, JEHS; McNair, "Supposed They Talked," *WP*, November 18, 1953, B112, JEHS; Catling, "Hoover Forgets Furor," *BS*, November 19, 1953, B112, JEHS.

Chapter 36: No Sense of Decency (1953–1954)

1. Sampson, "Ike Backs Right," *WP*, November 24, 1953, B112, JEHS; "Face-to-Face Justice," *WTH*, November 24, 1953, B112, JEHS.

2. Oshinsky, *A Conspiracy So Immense*, 349; "Behind the News," WFAA, November 17, 1953, B111, JEHS.

3. "Text of Senator McCarthy's Speech," *NYT*, November 25, 1953.

4. Sokolsky, "These Days," *WTH*, December 3, 1953, B112, JEHS; Oshinsky, *A Conspiracy So Immense*, 472.

5. Morgan, *Reds*, 423; Oshinsky, *A Conspiracy So Immense*, 237.

6. SAC WFO to Director, "U.S. Senator Joseph R. McCarthy," November 2[8], 1952, S6B, FBI FOIA 94-37708-76X (McCarthy).

7. Davis, "'Joe Is Doing the Job,'" *NYP*, July 7, 1953, S3, FBI FOIA 62-96332 (McCarthy); Oshinsky, *A Conspiracy So Immense*, 303.

8. Rushmore, "FBI Battling," *NYJA*, October 7, 1951, B107, JEHS; Oshinsky, *A Conspiracy So Immense*, 250-5, 318-21.

9. On Cohn, see especially Hoffman, *Citizen Cohn*; Elias, *Gossip Men*; Zion, *Autobiography of Roy Cohn*. For a recent documentary see Tyrnauer, *Where's My Roy Cohn?* For Cohn's account of his time on the McCarthy committee, see Cohn, *McCarthy*.

10. Hoffman, *Citizen Cohn*, 142-7; Summers, *Official and Confidential*, 190; Schine, "Definition of Communism," 1952, FBI FOIA 62-98588 (Schine); Hoover to Schine, December 10, 1952, FBI FOIA 62-98588 (Schine).

11. Demaris, *Director*, 155; Olmsted, *Red Spy Queen*, 174–7; Hoffman, *Citizen Cohn*, 134-8; Cohn, *McCarthy*, 47–8.

12. Oshinsky, *A Conspiracy So Immense*, 266–9, 282, 326; McCarthy, "Can FBI Do It Alone?" *WS*, September 25, 1953, B111, JEHS.

13. Hoover, "Memorandum for Mr. Tolson," May 13 [illegible], 1953, S3, FBI FOIA 62-96332 (McCarthy).

14. Charles, *Hoover's War on Gays*, 91; Nichols to Tolson, July 23, 1953, Miscellaneous AZ Folders, NO&C; Hoover,

"Memorandum for Mr. Tolson," July 14, 1953, F105, B19, HO&C; Nichols to Tolson, July 23, 1953, S28B, FBI 62-16607-1 (McCarthy); Executives' Conference to Director, "Dissemination of Information," October 14, 1953, S17B, FBI 121-23278 (McCarthy); Theoharis, *Chasing Spies,* 208-9.

15. Dunne, "FBI Chief," *Evening Tribune,* August 22, 1953, B110, JEHS; PB78, NLEM.

16. Oshinsky, *A Conspiracy So Immense,* 365-78.

17. Nichols, *Ike and McCarthy,* 172, 221-2; "Flander's Address," *WP,* March 10, 1954; "Text of President Eisenhower's Address," *WP,* April 6, 1954, B114, JEHS; Holland, "Brownell Outlines," *WS,* April 10, 1954, B114, JEHS.

18. Hoover to Eisenhower, April 9, 1954, F: "Hoover Letter to President Eisenhower," B20, NLEM.

19. Army-McCarthy, 33-83; Oshinsky, *A Conspiracy So Immense,* 418-23.

20. Rosen to Ladd, "G. David Schine," March 30, 1953, FBI 62-98588-4 (Schine); Belmont to Ladd, "General Walter Bedell Smith," August 5, 1953, FBI 62-98588 (Schine); Keay to Belmont, "Gerald David Schine," February 19, 1954, FBI 62-98588-16 (Schine); Jones to Nichols, "Gerard David Schine," February 25, 1954, FBI 62-98588 (Schine).

21. Nichols to Tolson, August 23, 1948, S1, FBI FOIA 62-75421-19 (Mundt); Hoover to Mundt, August 24, 1948, S1, FBI FOIA 62-75421 (Mundt); Mundt to Hoover, November 13, 1948, S1, FBI FOIA 62-75421-22 (Mundt); Nichols to Tolson, April 14, 1954, S2, FBI FOIA 62-75421-68 (Mundt).

22. Army-McCarthy, 1664-1665, 703-713, 721-725, 734, 758-774; "McCarthy Is Disputed," *WS,* May 5, 1954, B114, JEHS; "Brownell Fights Release," *WS,* May 6, 1954, B114, JEHS.

23. Oshinsky, *A Conspiracy So Immense,* 434, 457-71; Army-McCarthy, 2366-81, 2429, 2986.

24. Army-McCarthy, 2438-441; "McCarthy Takes Stand," *WP,* June 10, 1954, B115, JEHS.

25. Oshinsky, *A Conspiracy So Immense,* 471; "J. Edgar Hoover," *CR,* May 5, 1954, B114, JEHS; Jones to Nichols, "Senator Karl E. Mundt," June 30, 1954, S2, FBI FOIA 62-75428-71 (Mundt); Hoover to Mundt, July 1, 1954, S2, FBI FOIA 62-75428 (Mundt).

26. Lewis and McNeil, "Ike Comes to Bat," *WN,* June 2, 1954, B115, JEHS; Kempton, "Lost," *NYP,* July 1, 1954, B110, JEHS; Marder, "McCarthy Is Blasted," *WP,* June 17, 1954, B115, JEHS; McGrory, "Hearings," *WS,* June 17, 1954, B115, JEHS; "Don Iddon's Diary," *Daily Mail,* May 26, 1954, B114, JEHS.

27. Johnson, "Better Check," *Collier's,* June 25, 1954, B115, JEHS; McAuliffe, "Liberals and the Communist Control Act of 1954"; Trussell, "Senate," *NYT,* August 13, 1954, B115, JEHS.

28. "Brownell, Hoover," *NYDN,* September 13, 1954, B116, JEHS; "Red Fight," *WP,* September 3, 1954, B116, JEHS.

29. "C.I.A. Is a Good Issue," *Louisville Courier Journal,* June 25, 1954, B115, JEHS; "Re: Senator Joseph McCarthy," ca. August 23, 1954, S7, FBI FOIA 94-37708 (McCarthy); "Red Fight," *WP,* September 3, 1954, B116, JEHS; "FBI Head Lauds," *Great Falls Tribune,* August 25, 1953, S3, FBI FOIA 94-37708 (McCarthy).

30. Tye, *Demagogue,* 448-56; Oshinsky, *A Conspiracy So Immense,* 474-91.

31. Photo, May 27, 1955, F1242, B20, NARA-P; Eisenhower, remarks, F: "FBI Corres., May 1955-Jan. 1957," B47, WR; Hoover to Rogers, May 27, 1955, F: "FBI Corres., May

1955-Jan. 1957," B47, WR; Baldwin, "Nation DOES need," *National Guardian,* December 14, 1953, B112, JEHS.

Chapter 37: Massive Resistance (1954–1957)

1. Clegg OH; JEH LOGS, October 22, 1947; "FBI Promises," *SFC,* October 29, 1947, B98, JEHS; Nichols to Tolson, "Governors Conference," February 10, 1951, S1, FBI 62-93875-68 (Responsibilities Program), Sr42, B1, AT; Executives' Conference to Director, "Dissemination of Information," October 15, 1953, S17B, FBI FOIA 121-23278 (McCarthy); Shumaker, "White House Fetes," *WTH,* November 18, 1953, B112, JEHS; "Chief Justice Assails," *WS,* November 20, 1953, B112, JEHS. On Warren and Hoover, also see Newton, *Justice for All,* 63, 197.

2. Asch and Musgrove, *Chocolate City,* 273-5, 297-9; Mayer, "Eisenhower Administration," 25, 29. Also see Quigley, *Just Another Southern Town.*

3. Carper, "Board Transfers," *WP,* March 9, 1950; Carper, "Capital Closes," *WP,* June 18, 1950.

4. Asch and Musgrove, *Chocolate City,* 312-14; Dent, "Plans for Desegregation," *Atlanta Daily World,* July 8, 1954.

5. Novak, "Desegregation of George Washington University," 23, 38.

6. "Alpha Nu," *KAJ* (January 1948), 46; "Alpha Nu," *KAJ* (November 1949), 54; "Alpha Nu," *KAJ* (May 1950), 54; photo, *KAJ* (November 1949); photo, *KAJ* (March 1950), 29; "Confederate Flag," *KAJ* (January 1952), 8.

7. Hoover, untitled letter, December 14, 1954, *KAJ* (January 1955), 39.

8. Dudziak, *Cold War Civil Rights,* 100, 109.

9. On Marshall's early years, see esp. Tushnet, *Making Civil Rights Law;* Sullivan, *Lift Every Voice;* Rawn, *Root and Branch.*

10. Marshall to Clark, December 27, 1946, S4, FBI V 62-86660-1 (Marshall); Hoover, "Memorandum for the Attorney General," January 10, 1947, S4, FBI V 62-86660 (Marshall); "Thurgood Marshall," October 18, 1947, S4, FBI V 62-86660-3 (Marshall); Cleveland to Evans, "Thurgood Marshall," September 20, 1961, S9, FBI V [illegible] (Marshall); Marshall, "Memorandum to Mr. White," January 23, 1947, F: "FBI Racial Issues and Violence Investigations, 1946–1949," Group 2: SrA, GO File, NAACP.

11. JEHS LOGS, October 22, 1947; Cleveland to Evans, "Thurgood Marshall," September 20, 1961, S9, FBI V [illegible] (Marshall); Hoover to Marshall, October 6, 1947, F: "FBI Racial Issues and Violence Investigations, 1946–1949."

12. Sullivan, *Lift Every Voice,* 374; Berg, "Black Civil Rights and Liberal Anticommunism," 89, 90-4; White to Scheidt, December 15, 1950, F: "Federal Bureau of Investigation Racial Issues and NAACP Investigations, 1950–1953," Group 2: SrA, GO File, NAACP; FBI, "The Communist Party and the Negro," February 1953, FBI IA.

13. Belmont to Boardman, "Communist Infiltration," October 21, 1955, S1D, FBI V 61-3176-1077 (NAACP); "Communist Infiltration," July 19, 1954, S1A, FBI V 61-3176-769 (NAACP); Baumgardner to Belmont, "Communist Infiltration," February 1956, S4, FBI V 62-86660 (Marshall); Nichols to Tolson, February 8, 1956, S4, FBI V 62-86660 (Marshall); Nichols to Tolson, June 15, 1956, S4, FBI V 62-0-71397 (Marshall); "Subversive Character of NAACP," *CR,* February 23, 1956, B120, JEHS.

14. White to Hoover, December 17, 1952, F: "Federal Bureau of Investigation Racial Issues and NAACP Investigations, 1950–1953."

15. On Eastland, see especially Asch, *Senator and the Sharecropper;* Zwiers, *Senator James Eastland.*

16. Asch, *Senator and Sharecropper*, 6-47.

17. "Mississippi Representative Hopes," *NYT*, May 18, 1954; Hoover, "Memorandum for Mr. Tolson," March 28, 1955, FBI 94-4-5130, F4, B8, Sr90, KO; Gerard, "A Program of Cooperation," 354–5. On massive resistance, see especially Bartley, *Rise of Massive Resistance*; Crespino, *In Search of Another Country;* Crespino, *Strom Thurmond's America*; McRae, *Mothers of Massive Resistance*; Ward, *Defending White Democracy*.

18. On the Citizens' Councils within massive resistance, see especially McMillen, *Citizens' Council*.

19. Tompkins to Hoover, "The Citizens' Councils," December 10, 1954, S1, FBI IA 105-34237 (Citizens' Councils); Hoover to Tompkins, December 17, 1954, S1, FBI IA 105-34237 (Citizens' Councils); Men, "Association of Citizens' Councils," February 16, 1955, S1, FBI IA 105-34237 (Citizens' Councils).

20. Hoover to Tompkins, "Association of Citizens' Councils," December 16, 1955, S4, FBI IA 105-34237 (Citizens' Councils); Director to SAC, "Citizens' Councils," March 22, 1955, S1, FBI IA 105-34237 (Citizens' Councils); Belmont to Boardman, "Citizens' Councils," May 16, 1955, S2, FBI IA 105-34237 (Citizens' Councils).

21. Belmont to Boardman, "Citizens' Councils," October 13, 1955, S2, FBI IA 105-34237-45 (Citizens' Councils); Belmont to Boardman, "Citizens' Councils," June 16, 1955, S2, FBI IA 105-34237 (Citizens' Councils).

22. Booker, *Shocking the Conscience*, 3–21, 103; Department of Justice, Civil Rights Division, "George Lee—Notice to Close File," July 12, 2011, United States Department of Justice, https://www.justice.gov/crt/case-document/george-lee.

23. On Till, see especially Gorn, *Let the People See*; Anderson, *Emmett Till*.

24. Interview of Lynn Smith, FBI OH; Department of Justice, Civil Rights Division, "George Lee—Notice to Close File."

25. Gorn, *Let The People See*, 228; "Probe of South's FBI," *BS*, September 26, 1955, B119, JEHS. On Howard, see Beito and Beito, *Black Maverick*; Beito and Beito, *T. R. M. Howard*.

26. "Hoover," *Philadelphia Afro-American*, October 15, 1955, B119, JEHS; "FBI Chief Accuses," *Clarion Ledger*, January 19, 1956, B120, JEHS.

27. Patterson to Hoover, September 15, 1955, S2, FBI IA 105-34237-38 (Citizens' Councils); "State House Backs," *AC*, January 18, 1956, B120, JEHS; "Statesmanlike Veto," February 23, 1956, *CR*, B120, JEHS.

28. "Thurmond Hits," *Morning News* (Florence, SC), January 6, 1956, B120, JEHS; Nichols to Tolson, "Citizens' Councils," January 18, 1956, S4, FBI IA 105-34237-189 (Citizens' Councils); Belmont to Boardman, "Citizens' Council," December 13, 1956, S7, FBI IA 105-34237-315 (Citizens' Councils).

29. Belmont to Boardman, "Association of Citizens' Councils," January 4, 1956, S4, FBI IA 103-34237 (Citizens' Councils); Brownell to Nixon, April 9, 1965, Dwight D. Eisenhower Presidential Library, Museum & Boyhood Home, https://www.eisenhowerlibrary.gov/sites/default/files/research/online-documents/civil-rights-act/1956-04-01-cabinet-paper.pdf; Flanagan, interview with Herbert Brownell, August 24, 1988, B270, HB.

30. Hoover, "Racial Tension and Civil Rights," March 1, 1956, Dwight D. Eisenhower Presidential Library, Museum & Boyhood Home, https://www.eisenhowerlibrary.gov/sites/default/files/research/online-documents/civil-rights-eisenhower-administration/1956-03-01-hoover-statement.pdf

31. "Declaration of Constitutional Principles," (1956); Crespino, *Strom Thurmond's America*, 105–7.

32. Caro, *Years of Lyndon Johnson: Master of the Senate*, 830-1003. For quote, see 997.

33. "FBI Head Defense," *Arkansas Democrat*, October 26, 1947, B124, JEHS; Lewis, "F.B.I. Head Says," *NYT*, September 28, 1957, B124, JEHS; Hoover, "Memorandum for Mr. Tolson," October 7, 1957, S8, FBI IA 105-34237 (Citizens' Council).

34. Nease to Tolson, January 22, 1958, F85, B16, HO&C.

Chapter 38: Master of Deceit (1956–1959)

1. Director to SAC New York, May 7, 1957, S5B, FBI FOIA 62-96332 (McCarthy); Montgomery, "Capital McCarthy Rites," *Daily Defender,* May 7, 1957.

2. Bell, "The Indestructible J. Edgar Hoover," *Family Weekly*, February 9, 1958, B125, JEHS; Whitehead, *FBI Story*, preface, foreword; "FBI Story Has Defects," *Pittsburgh Post-Gazette*, August 17, 1957, B124, JEHS. For best-seller lists, see http://www.hawes.com/1957/1957.htm.

3. Whitehead, *FBI Story*, 326; Belmont to Boardman, "Communist Party, USA," March 7, 1958, S13, FBI G 100-3-104 (COINTELPRO CPUSA).

4. Lichtman, *The Supreme Court and McCarthy-Era Repression,* 92-109. For a full account of the "Red Monday" decisions, see Sabin, *In Calmer Times*.

5. Shannon, "The FBI and Congress," *NYP*, August 18, 1957, B124, JEHS; "File Protection Voted," *WP*, August 28, 1957, B124, JEHS; Warner, "F.B.I. Files Bill," *NYHT*, August 31, 1957, B124, JEHS; "Bill Designed," *WS*, September 3, 1957, B124, JEHS.

6. Hoover to Eisenhower, November 8, 1957, F: "OF 5-F-1 FBI, National Academy," B107, WHCF, DDE; "Graduation Exercises," November 8, 1957, F: "OF 5-F-1 FBI, National Academy," B107, WHCF, DDE; "First Annual President's Awards for Distinguished Federal Civilian Service," June 1958, F6, B1, NLEF; "Handcuffs on the FBI?" *Newsweek*, September 2, 1957, B124, JEHS; Wechsler, "The One-Interest Press," *Progressive*, May 1957, B123, JEHS.

7. Memorandum, "Subject: Discussion at the 279th Meeting of the National Security Council," March 9, 1956, B7, NSC Series, DDE; Davis, *Assault on the Left*, 5; Weiner, *Enemies*, 191.

8. Belmont to Boardman, "CP, USA-Counterintelligence Program," August 28, 1956, FBI 62-116395-430-440.

9. For a brief biography, see Theoharis et al., *FBI: A Comprehensive Reference Guide*, 354-5. For Sullivan's personal narrative, see Sullivan, *The Bureau*. For quote, see DeLoach, *Hoover's FBI*, 270.

10. Sullivan to Belmont, "Current Weaknesses," August 22, 1956, S1, FBI G 100-3-104 (COINTELPRO CPUSA); Sullivan to Belmont, "Current Weaknesses," October 9, 1956, S2, FBI G 100-3-104 (COINTELPRO CPUSA); "Current Weaknesses," October 1956, S2, FBI G 100-3-104 (COINTELPRO CPUSA).

11. Director to SAC New York, "Communist Party-USA," September 6, 1956, FBI JFK 62-116395-430-440; Director to SAC New York, "Communist Party, USA," September 7, 1956, FBI FOIA 100-3-104 (COINTELPRO CPUSA).

12. SAC Philadelphia to Director, "Communist Party, USA," October 21, 1957, S9, FBI G 100-3-104 (COINTELPRO CPUSA).

13. Belmont to Boardman, "Communist Party, USA," November 9, 1956, S3, FBI G 100-3-104 (COINTELPRO CPUSA); Hoover to SAC New York, "Communist Party, USA," October 11, 1956, S1, FBI G 100-3-104 (COINTELPRO CPUSA); Hoover to Commissioner, IRS, "Communist Party, USA," October 23, 1956, S2, FBI G 100-3-104 (COINTELPRO CPUSA).

14. Belmont to Boardman, "Communist Party, USA," February 13, 1957, S4, FBI FOIA 100-3-104 (COINTELPRO CPUSA); Director to SAC New York, "Communist Party, USA," April 19, 1957, S5, FBI FOIA 100-3-104 (COINTELPRO CPUSA).

15. Director to SAC Cleveland, "Communist Party, USA," June 7, 1957, S7, FBI G 100-3-104 (COINTELPRO CPUSA); Belmont to Boardman, "Communist Party, USA," June 20, 1957, S7, FBI G 100-3-104 (COINTELPRO CPUSA); Director to SAC New York, "Communist Party, USA," July 18, 1957, S7, FBI G 100-3-104 (COINTELPRO CPUSA); SAC San Francisco to Director, "Communist Party, USA," July 5, 1957, S7, FBI G 100-3-104 (COINTELPRO CPUSA); Director to SAC New York, "Communist Party, USA," November 13, 1957, S9, FBI G 100-3-104 (COINTELPRO CPUSA).

16. Belmont to Boardman, "Communist Party, USA," April 16, 1957, S6, FBI G 100-3-104 (COINTELPRO CPUSA); Hoover to SAC New York, "CPUSA-Counterintelligence Program," December 14, 1956, S6, FBI G 100-3-104 (COINTELPRO CPUSA); Belmont to Boardman, "Communist Party, USA," September 3, 1957, S8, FBI G 100-3-104 (COINTELPRO CPUSA); Belmont to Boardman, "Communist Party, USA," March 7, 1958, S13, FBI G 100-3-104 (COINTELPRO CPUSA); Director to SAC Los Angeles, "Communist Party, USA," May 7, 1957, S6, FBI G 100-3-104 (COINTELPRO CPUSA); SAC New York to Director, "Communist Party, USA," September 30, 1958, S18, FBI G 100-3-104 (COINTELPRO CPUSA); Director to SAC New York, "Communist Party, USA," October 10, 1958, S18, FBI G 100-3-104 (COINTELPRO CPUSA).

17. Belmont to Boardman, "Communist Party, USA," April 25, 1958, S18, FBI G 100-3-104 (COINTELPRO CPUSA); "Discontinuance of the 'Daily Worker,'" January 8, 1958, S11, FBI G 100-3-104 (COINTELPRO CPUSA); SAC Chicago to Director, "Communist Party, USA," March 20, 1958, S13, FBI G 100-3-104 (COINTELPRO CPUSA); Director to SAC New Haven, "Communist Party, USA," October 13, 1958, S18, FBI G 100-3-104 (COINTELPRO CPUSA).

18. "Discontinuance of the 'Daily Worker'"; "Financial Manipulations," June 19, 1958, S15, FBI G 100-3-104 (COINTELPRO CPUSA).

19. "Director's Material: FY 1959," FBI JFK 62-116395-340-347; Director to Attorney General, "Communist Party, USA," May 8, 1958, FBI JFK 62-116395-340-347; Hoover to Cutler, May 8, 1958, FBI JFK 62-116395-340-347; Gray, "Minutes of Cabinet Meeting," November 6, 1958, F: "Cabinet Meeting of November 6, 1958," B12, Cabinet Series, DDE; "Excerpt from Former FBI Director Hoover's Briefing," November 6, 1958, FBI JFK 62-116395-340-347.

20. Gray, "Minutes of Cabinet Meeting," November 6, 1958, and FBI, "Travel by CPUSA Representative" in "Charts Re: Current Communist Subversion," F: "Cabinet Meeting of November 6, 1958," B12, Cabinet Series, DDE.

21. Director to SAC Albany, "Communist Party, USA," November 2, 1956, S1, FBI V 100-428091 (SOLO); Direc-

tor to SAC New York, "Communist Party, USA," January 23, 1957, S3, FBI G 100-3-104 (COINTELPRO CPUSA).

22. Barron, Operation SOLO, 17–41, 44; SAC New York to Director, "Communist Party, USA, TOPLEV," May 9, 1952, S1, FBI IA 134-46 (Morris Childs); "Urgent," ca. April 15, 1952, S1, FBI IA 134-46 (Morris Childs); SAC Chicago to Director, "Communist Party-USA," May 1, 1952, S1, FBI IA 134-46 (Morris Childs); "Urgent," ca. May 2, 1952, S1, FBI IA 134-46 (Morris Childs); SAC Chicago to FBI Minneapolis, July 9, 1952, S1, FBI IA 134-46 (Morris Childs). David Garrow was the first historian to identify and describe the SOLO operation. See Garrow, FBI and Martin Luther King; Powers, "Double Agent," New York Times Book Review, April 21, 1996; Draper, "Our Man in Moscow," New York Review of Books, May 9, 1996.

23. Untitled, ca. December 1, 1952, S2, FBI IA 134-46 (Morris Childs); SAC Chicago to Director, "CG-5824-S," April 16, 1953, S3, FBI IA 134-46-87 (Morris Childs).

24. SAC Chicago to Director, March 3, 1958, P1, FBI V 1100-428091 (SOLO); Belmont to Boardman, "SOLO," March 10, 1958, P1, FBI V 100-428091-3 (SOLO); Belmont to Boardman, "SOLO," April 7, 1958, P1, FBI V 100-428091-85 (SOLO); Belmont to Boardman, "SOLO," April 24, 1958, P1, FBI V 100-428091 (SOLO); Director to SAC Chicago, "SOLO," March 12, 1958, P1, FBI V 100-428091-4 (SOLO).

25. SAC Chicago to Director, "SOLO," August 21, 1958, P3, FBI V 100-428901-51 (SOLO); SAC Chicago to Director, July 29, 1958, P2, FBI V 100-428901-41 (SOLO); Hoover, "Memorandum for Mr. Tolson," July 25, 1958, P2, FBI V 100-428091 (SOLO); FBI, "Soviet Financial Aid" in "Charts Re: Current Communist Subversion," F: "Cabinet Meeting of November 6, 1958," B12, Cabinet Series, DDE; SAC Chicago to Director, "SOLO," September 30, 1958, P5, FBI V 100-428091-88 (SOLO).

26. Barron, Operation Solo, 4; SAC New York to Director, "SOLO," June 12, 1964, P63, FBI V 100-428091-3911 (SOLO); SAC New York to Director, "SOLO," December 20, 1961, P39, FBI V 100-428091 (SOLO); SAC New York to Director, July 15, 1961, FBI V 100-428091-1373 (SOLO); Director to SAC Chicago, "SOLO," September 3, 1958, P3, FBI V 100-428091-61 (SOLO).

27. Sullivan, The Bureau, 89; Hoover, Masters of Deceit, 331–3, 78.

28. Powers, Secrecy and Power, 344; Hoover to Dulles, February 27, 1958, S2, FBI IA 62-83338 (Dulles); Rogers to Hoover, February 11, 1958, F: "FBI Corres." April 1957–August 1958, B47, WR; Philbrick, I Led Three Lives; Grams, I Led 3 Lives; Philbrick, "New Books," NYDN, January 25, 1958, S3, FBI FOIA 100-365248 (Philbrick); SAC Boston to Director, "Herbert A. Philbrick," April 1, 1958, S1, FBI FOIA 100-365248-222 (Philbrick); Rosswurm, FBI and the Catholic Church, 68; Ernst, "Battle Against," Saturday Review, March 8, 1958, B125, JEHS; "Hoover Book Reveals," KAJ, January 1959; Starr, "J. Edgar Hoover Sees," Trumpet, 1960, B217, JEHS.

29. Sullivan, The Bureau, 88–91.

30. King Features Syndicate, 1958, B239, JEHS; Shannon, "The Celebrity," NYP, May 26, 1958, B125, JEHS.

31. Cook, "The Virus," Nation, May 24, 1958; Cook, "The FBI," Nation, October 18, 1958.

32. Schoenwald, Time for Choosing, 45–6; Demaris, Director, 88; Sullivan, The Bureau, 90–1; Ungar, FBI, 273.

33. Eisenhower to Hoover, May 6, 1959, F1172: "Hoover, J. Edgar," B970, PPF, WHCF, DDE; Hoover to Eisen-

hower, May 8, 1959, F1172: "Hoover, J. Edgar," B970, PPF, WHCF, DDE; Hoover to Eisenhower, June 17, 1959, F1172: "Hoover, J. Edgar," B970, PPF, WHCF, DDE; Furman, "Peace Is Theme," *NYT*, September 16, 1959; "President Is Host," *NYHT*, September 16, 1959.

34. "A Matter of Pride," *NYM*, September 24, 1959, B128, JEHS; Demaris, *Director*, 68; Nichols to Hoover, October 1, 1959, S7, FBI FOIA 65-39021-701 (Nichols).

Chapter 39: New Frontiers (1960–1961)

1. Hoover to Nixon, August 4, 1959, F11, B19, PPS320, RN; "Graduation Exercises," June 11, 1954, FBI FOIA 67-102458-22 (Nixon); Weiner, *Enemies*, 179.

2. Hughes to Hoover, May 3, 1960, F12, B19, PPS320, RN; Hoover to Nixon, November 27, 1957, F8, B19, PPS320, RN; Hoover to Nixon, January 2, 1958, F9, B19, PPS320, RN; UPI, May 8, 1959, S6A, FBI V 67-561 (Hoover); NT 719-12.

3. Hoover to Nixon, September 7, 1955, F6, B19, PPS320, RN; Hoover to Nixon, October 28, 1958, F9, B19, PPS320, RN; Nixon to Hoover, September 17, 1959, F11, B19, PPS320, RN; Hoover to Pat Nixon, June 28, 1960, F13, B19, PPS320, RN.

4. Hoover to Nixon, May 19, 1957, F8, B19, PPS320, RN.

5. "Address of Senator John F. Kennedy Accepting the Democratic Party Nomination," July 15, 1960, John F. Kennedy Presidential Library and Museum, https://www.jfklibrary.org/archives/other-resources/john-f-kennedy-speeches/democratic-party-nomination-19600715.

6. Hoover, "Memorandum for Mr. Tolson," April 27, 1948, F57, B14, HO&C; Woods to Nixon, "Memorandum," July 21, 1960, F13, B19, PPS320, RN.

7. "Celebrities for Nixon," *LAT*, August 17, 1960, B129, JEHS; Hoover to Pat Nixon, September 8, 1960, F13, B19, PPS320, RN.

8. Hoover to Woods, October 5, 6, 11, 14, 1960, F13, B19, Pre-Presidential Papers, Special Files, RN.

9. JEH LOGS, November 8, 1960; JEH APPT, November 8, 1960; Pietrusza, *1960*, 405.

10. Hoover to Nixon, November 9, 1960, F13, B19, Pre-Presidential Papers, Special Files, RN.

11. Nasaw, *Patriarch*, 444–7, 523-69; Theoharis, *From the Secret Files of J. Edgar Hoover*, 15-34; Hersh, *Bobby and J. Edgar*, 60-5; Hoover to Kennedy, May 5, 1953, F14, B9, FBI 94-37808-8 (Joseph Kennedy), HO&C.

12. Jones to DeLoach, "Senator John F. Kennedy," July 13, 1960, B17, F96, HO&C; SAC Los Angeles to Director, "Crimdel-CRS," April 1, 1960, B17, F96, HO&C; DeLoach to Tolson, June 10, 1959, "Senator John F. Kennedy," F13, B8, HO&C; Kater to McGill, April 29, 1959, F13, B8, HO&C; Hersh, *Dark Side of Camelot*, 107–10. On Kennedy's early life, see especially Logevall, *JFK*.

13. JEH LOGS, November 10, 1960; UPI, November 10, 1960, B130, JEHS; Knebel, "Potomac Fever," *WS*, November 12, 1960, B130, JEHS.

14. "Capital Hill Aware," *Austin American-Statesman*, November 4, 1943; LBJ-HM10; "Texas Journalist," *WP*, March 11, 1943; Caro, *Years of Lyndon Johnson: Means of Ascent*.

15. LBJ-HM13; LBJ-HM12; DeLoach, *Hoover's FBI*, 379.

16. Interview of Cartha DeLoach, FBI OH; UPI, August 31, 1960, B129, JEHS; UPI, September 9, 1960, B130, JEHS.

17. SAC New York to Director, "SOLO," March 13, 1960, P18, FBI V 100-428091-646 (SOLO); "J. Edgar Hoover in Austin (1959)," November 9, 1959, Texas Archive of the

Moving Image, https://texasarchive.org/2013_02715; LBJ -HM28.

18. Dallek, *Camelot's Court*, 85–91, 59; "Ministry of Talent," *NYT*, November 23, 1960; interview of Roy Cohn by James A. Oesterle, March 24, 1971, at jfklibrary.org/sites /default/files/archives/RFKOH/Cohn ,%20Roy%20M /RFKOH-RMC-01/RFKOH-RMC-01-TR.pdf; Pietrusza, *1960*, 63; Jones to DeLoach, "Robert Francis Kennedy," September 19, 1959, S1B, FBI V 77-31587-35 (RFK); Schlesinger, *Robert Kennedy and His Times*, 111–2, 231; Jones to Nichols, "Robert Francis Kennedy," July 20, 1955, S1A, FBI V 71-31587-27 (RFK); JEH LOGS, December 14, 1960.

19. "Dillon Appointed Secretary," *NYT*, December 16, 1960; Novak, "Brother Bobby," *WSJ*, December 19, 1960; DeLoach to Mohr, January 13, 1961, S1B, FBI V 77-51387 (RFK); Hoover, "Memorandum for Mr. Tolson," January 23, 1961, S1B, FBI V 77-51387 (RFK); RFK to Hoover, July 29, 1958, S3, FBI V 67-163462 (Evans).

20. Shannon, "Kennedy, Wife, Greet 300," *LAT*, January 30, 1961; "White House 'Comes Alive,'" *Illinois State Register* (UPI), January 30, 1961, B131, JEHS.

Chapter 40: Top Hoodlums (1957–1961)

1. Schlesinger, *Robert Kennedy and His Times*, 254, 257, 256; Hersh, *Bobby and J. Edgar*, 218.

2. Reinneberger to Callahan, "Attorney General Robert Kennedy," February 1, 1961, S1B, FBI V 77-51387 (RFK); Rosen to Parsons, "Attorney General Robert F. Kennedy," February 1, 1961, S1B, FBI V 77-51387-67 (RFK); Edwards to Mohr, "Attorney General's Efforts," February 1, 1961, S1B, FBI V 77-51387-72 (RFK).

3. JEH LOGS, February 17, 1961; Hersh, *Bobby and J. Edgar*, 219, 238–9; Liddy, *Will*, 95.

4. Schlesinger, *Robert Kennedy and his Times*, 256–7.

5. Hersh, *Bobby and J. Edgar*, 238–9.

6. Lewis, "Swifter Pace Set," *NYT*, February 5, 1961, B131, JEHS.

7. Branch, *Parting the Waters*, 403; [Redacted] to Hoover, March 13, 1961, S2, FBI V 77-51387 (RFK); Auerbach to Hoover, "Edwin O. Guthman," February 20, 1961, S1B, FBI V 77-85663 (RFK).

8. Beecher, "Crime Crackdown," *WSJ*, January 23, 1961.

9. For a critical view of Hoover, see Schlesinger, *Robert Kennedy and His Times*, 261–85. For the FBI's early organized-crime efforts, see DeLoach, *Hoover's FBI*, 302-5.

10. DeLoach, *Hoover's FBI*, 302; Roemer, *Roemer*, 23, 25, 29, 78, 87, 122–4, 200; Summers, *Official and Confidential*, 258; "Chicago 92-349," September 12, 1960, S2, FBI V NA (Giancana); Gale to DeLoach, "Telephone and Microphone Surveillance," December 13, 1966, F36, B14, HO&C. For Top Hoodlum's date of origin, see "Turning Point: Using Intel to Stop the Mob, Part 2," https://archives.fbi.gov /archives/news/stories/2007/august/mobintel2_080907.

11. Hersh, *Bobby and J. Edgar*, 285, 287; Kennedy, *Enemy Within*, 177.

12. Roemer, *Roemer*, 167, 80; Director to SAC Chicago, "Murray Humphreys," February 10, 1961, S8, FBI V 92-3088-59 (Humphreys); Director to SAC Chicago, "Murray Llewelyn Humphreys," February 7, 1961, S8, FBI V 92-3088-58 (Humphreys).

13. "Hoover Opposes," *State Times*, January 22, 1961, B131, JEHS.

14. JEH APPT, February 23, 1961; Baggs, "A View of the News," *Miami News*, February 27, 1961, B131, JEHS;

Harvey, "Hoover Isn't on the Carpet," *Port Huron Times Herald*, March 8, 1961, B131, JEHS.

15. Roevekamp, "Kennedys Swing into Line," *CSM*, March 1, 1961; Lewis, "Robert Kennedy Mocks," *NYT*, April 7, 1961.

16. "Attorney General Seeks," *CSM*, April 7, 1961.

17. Clayton, "Bobby Kennedy Meets Press," *WP*, April 7, 1961.

18. Kennedy, "Address before the American Society of Newspaper Editors," April 20, 1961, John F. Kennedy Presidential Library and Museum, https://www.jfklibrary.org /archives/other-resources/john-f-kennedy-speeches/ameri can-society-of-newspaper-editors-19610420. On Bay of Pigs, see especially Naftali and Fursenko, *One Hell of a Gamble*, 77–100; Rasenberger, *Brilliant Disaster*.

19. Strober and Strober, *"Let Us Begin Anew,"* 331; Weiner, *Enemies*, 226–7.

20. Keeney to O'Connor, "Summaries of File #84-46-5," July 1, 1975, S4, FBI V 62-116395-354 (Castro). For a full account, see Maier, *Mafia Spies*. For Maheu's story, see Maheu and Hack, *Next to Hughes*, 108-34.

21. Rosen to Belmont, "Arthur James Balletti," February 2, 1962, S1B, FBI V 139-1201-8 (Castro); Riebling, *Wedge*, 164.

22. Hill, untitled, July 18, 1961, S11, FBI V 92-3088 (Humphreys); Roemer, *Roemer*, 145–52.

23. Director to Attorney General, "Central Intelligence Agency's Intentions," March 6, 1967, S1B, FBI V 62-80570 (Castro); "The Role of the FBI," p. 52, April 29, 1966, FBI JFK 62-116395-546.

24. DeLoach to Tolson, "Knowledge of Usage," June 2, 1966, S4, FBI V 67-163462 (Evans); Evans to Belmont, "Organized Crime," July 7, 1961, S4, FBI V 66-04-3467 (Evans); DeLoach to Tolson, "Knowledge of Usage," December 24, 1965, S4, FBI V 66-5815-1255 (Evans); "Potent Rackets Bills," *WP*, September 14, 1961, B132, JEHS.

25. DeLoach, *Hoover's FBI,* 313; Roemer, *Roemer*, 180–1. For an inside account of the Justice Department's anti-Hoffa campaign, see Sheridan, *Fall and Rise of Jimmy Hoffa.*

Chapter 41: The Federal Bureau of Integration (1957–1961)

1. On the Freedom Rides, see especially Arsenault, *Freedom Riders*; May, *Informant*, 22–78. Where not otherwise cited, background information on the Freedom Rides can be found in these sources.

2. Hoover, "Memorandum for the Attorney General," September 30, 1963, S2B, FBI V 157-1025 (Bapbomb).

3. O'Reilly, *"Racial Matters,"* 95; Borne, *Troutmouth*, 144–224; Clegg, "Testimonial to J. Edgar Hoover," *Mississippi Law Enforcement Officers Association Journal*, November–December 1965, B139, JEHS; Hoover, "Memorandum for Mr. Tolson," May 26, 1961, S5, FBI FOIA 67-6524 (Clegg); Smead, *Blood Justice*, 147, 68–9; Katagiri, *Mississippi State Sovereignty Commission*, 34, 45–52, 8–9, 88.

4. Branch, *Parting the Waters*, 257–8; Smead, *Blood Justice*, 161, 151–2, 147–8, 181; JEH APP (1961), 359; DeLoach to Tolson, "Mack Charles Parker," May 19, 1959, S5, FBI FOIA 67-6524 (Clegg). For a full account of the Parker lynching and the FBI investigation, see Smead, *Blood Justice*.

5. "Remarks of Senator John F. Kennedy at National Conference on Constitutional Rights and American Freedom," October 12, 1960, John F. Kennedy Presidential Library and Museum, https://www.jfklibrary.org/archives/other

-resources/john-f-kennedy-speeches/constitutional-rights -conference-nyc-19601012.

6. Arsenault, *Freedom Riders*, 110–1; O'Reilly, *"Racial Matters,"* 83; Branch, *Parting the Waters*, 413.

7. For the informant claim, see Strober and Strober, *"Let Us Begin Anew,"* 296.

8. "Text of Attorney General," *NYT*, May 7, 1961.

9. Salisbury, "Fear and Hatred," *NYT*, April 12, 1960.

10. Nunnelley, *Bull Connor*, 24–7, 46, 82, 48, 63–5; Rogers to Tamm, "Jamie Moore," November 16, 1956, FBI FOIA 1-7828-8 (Moore); Hoover to Moore, September 15, 1960, S1, FBI FOIA 1-7828 (Moore).

11. On Rowe, see especially May, *Informant*; McWhorter, *Carry Me Home*. For Rowe's own account, see Rowe, *My Undercover Years with the Ku Klux Klan.*

12. Hoover to Allen, September 3, 1946, F: "K," B146, Subject File, President's Secretary File, HST. For informant work in the 1950s, see interview of Fletcher D. Thompson, FBI OH.

13. May, *Informant*, 2–14, 19, 21, 22–5, 29–31; McWhorter, *Carry Me Home*, 167; Arsenault, *Freedom Riders*, 136; Nunnelley, *Bull Connor*, 98; O'Reilly, *"Racial Matters,"* 88.

14. Arsenault, *Freedom Riders*, 165; May, *Informant*, 43.

15. McWhorter, *Carry Me Home*, 212; May, *Informant*, 46.

16. McGowan to Rosen, "Freebus," May 24, 1961, S1, FBI FOIA 157-373 (Freebus); Schlesinger, *Robert Kennedy and His Times*, 295.

17. Arsenault, *Freedom Riders*, 172–6; JEH LOGS, May 15, 1961; O'Reilly, *"Racial Matters,"* 89.

18. Arsenault, *Freedom Riders*, 176; McGowan to Rosen, "Freedom Ride," May 20, 1961, V1, FBI FOIA 157-373 (Freebus).

19. Arsenault, *Freedom Riders*, 220; JEH LOGS, May 20, 1961; Parsons to Tolson, "National Non-Violent Freedom Committee," May 20, 1961, V2, FBI FOIA 157-373-173 (Freebus); Branch, *Parting the Waters*, 468.

20. O'Reilly, *"Racial Matters,"* 93.

21. Parsons to Tolson, "National Non Violent Freedom Committee," May 20, 1961, S2, FBI FOIA 157-73-173 (Freebus); Rosen to Parsons, "Freedom Ride," May 21, 1961, S1, FBI FOIA 157-373-98 (Freebus); Arsenault, *Freedom Riders*, 247, 425; May, *Informant*, 53; O'Reilly, *"Racial Matters,"* 86; Hoover to Dirksen, September 24, 1963, S2A, FBI V 157-1025-235 (Bapbomb); McWhorter, *Carry Me Home*, 247.

22. Lowry, photo, *Anniston Star*, September 5, 1961, F1705, B31, NARA-P; "Five Hanged," *WS*, September 6, 1961, B123, JEHS; "FBI on Frameup Rampage," *Thunderbolt*, May 1959, B127, JEHS; Winchell, "Debunking the Bunk," *NYJA*, December 3, 1964, B137, JEHS.

Chapter 42: Patron Saint of the Far Right (1961–1962)

1. "A Wave of Conservatism," "The Americanists," *Time*, March 10, 1961.

2. Dudman, *Men of the Far Right*, 163.

3. On the conservative movement in the late 1950s and early 1960s, see especially Nash, *Conservative Intellectual Movement*; McGirr, *Suburban Warriors*; Perlstein, *Before the Storm*; Phillips-Fein, *Invisible Hands*; Nickerson, *Mothers of Conservatism*; Schoenwald, *A Time for Choosing*; Huntington, *Far-Right Vanguard*; Critchlow, *Phyllis Schlafly and Grassroots Conservatism*; Webb, *Rabble Rousers*.

4. Judis, *William F. Buckley, Jr.*, 138. For Buckley, also see

Bogus, *Buckley*; Bridges, *Strictly Right*; Nash, *Conservative Intellectual Movement*; Felzenberg, *A Man and His Presidents*.

5. Nichols to Tolson, October 20, 1950, FBI FOIA 94-42995 (Buckley); "Hats Off," *Yale News*, October 25, 1949, B102, JEHS; "William Frank Buckley," October 26, 1950, FBI FOIA 94-42995-3 (Buckley).

6. Nichols to Tolson, April 24, 1953, FBI FOIA 94-42995-6 (Buckley); Meyer, "The FBI Story," *NatR*, February 2, 1957.

7. McGirr, *Suburban Warriors*, 5.

8. Critchlow, *Phyllis Schlafly and Grassroots Conservatism*, 39; "Initial List," S3, FBI IA 62-104401 (JBS); "Truly Nolen," *Miami News*, February 29, 1961, B131, JEHS; Lotto, "Reds Fear," *NYJA*, November 4, 1961, B132, JEHS; "Columbia Alert," *Columbia Record*, November 24, 1961, B132, JEHS.

9. Hough to Hoover, September 9, 1961, FBI FOIA 67-69602-312 (Skousen).

10. "Calls for 'More of the Same,'" *Shreveport Journal*, July 25, 1960, B129, JEHS; Morehead, "Texans Propose," *Dallas Morning News*, May 31, 1960, B129, JEHS; "Nomination Rejected," *Houston Chronicle*, June 15, 1960, B129, JEHS; Hoover to Logan, June 3, 1960, S1, FBI FOIA 100-8085-55 (Constitution Party).

11. McDowell, "A Review of Reviews," *American Opinion*, May 1958, S1, FBI IA 62-104401 (JBS).

12. Smoot, *People Along the Way*, 171; Smoot, "Who is Dan Smoot?," *DSR* (3:1), January 7, 1957; Hendershot, *What's Fair on the Air?*, 65-101.

13. Skousen, *Naked Communist*; Philbrick, *I Led Three Lives*; Miller, *I Was a Spy*; McGirr, *Suburban Warriors*, 95; "Samuel Devine Dies," *WP*, undated; "Ohio Solon," *Baltimore Afro-American*, January 23, 1960.

14. Smoot, "What the Communists," *DSR* (4:5), February 3, 1958, 5–6; SAC Los Angeles to Director, "W. Cleon Skousen," February 17, 1961, FBI FOIA 94-47468 (Skousen); "J. Edgar Hoover Day," *CR*, May 18, 1961, B131, JEHS; "DiSalle Honors," *Labor Union*, May 5, 1961, B131, JEHS; "Extension of Remarks of H. Allen Smith," *CR*, May 1, 1958, B125, JEHS.

15. Skousen to Hoover, March 24, 1958, FBI FOIA 94-47468 (Skousen); Hoover to Skousen, April 2, 1958, FBI FOIA 94-47468 (Skousen); Jones to Nease, "Article, 'A Yank Named Yankus,'" August 22, 1958, S1, FBI FOIA 62-102576-13 (Smoot). For Philbrick correspondence, see S4, FBI FOIA 100-365248-253 (Philbrick).

16. "A Wave of Conservatism," "The Americanists," *Time*, March 10, 1961; "Senator Scores," *NYT*, May 9, 1961. On the John Birch Society, see especially Mulloy, *World of the John Birch Society*.

17. Welch to Hoover, March 22, 1961, S19, FBI IA 62-104401 (JBS); Welch to Hoover, March 23, 1961, S19, FBI IA 62-104401-1112 (JBS).

18. DeLoach to Mohr, "John Birch Society," March 14, 1961, S15, FBI IA 62-104401-851 (JBS); "Learn how you can combat communism!" F11, B45, HAP; Los Angeles to Director, April 2, 1961, S16, FBI IA 62-104401 (JBS).

19. "Hoover to All Law Enforcement Officials," *LEB*, April 1961; Hoover to RFK, April 5, 1961, S17, FBI IA 62-104401 (JBS).

20. For Kennedy's speech, see "Radio and Television Report to the American People on the Berlin Crisis," July 25, 1961, at https://www.jfklibrary.org/archives/other-resources/john-f-kennedy-speeches/berlin-crisis-19610725.

21. JEH LOGS, July 27, 1961. On right-wing politics in southern California, see McGirr, *Suburban Warriors*; Nickerson, *Mothers of Conservatism*.

22. "Ex-FBI Agent," *LAT*, July 27, 1961; Gillam, "Mosk Labels Birch," *LAT*, August 3, 1961.

23. Hoover to Woods, November 8, 1961, F14, B19, PPS320, RN; "Kiwanis Club," *LAT*, July 27, 1961; "Commentator Calls," *LAT*, July 23, 1961; "Tonight on TV," *LAT*, August 28, 1961; Fleming, "Break Ties," *LAT*, August 30, 1961.

24. DeLoach to Tolson, "Fred C Schwarz," September 8, 1961, FBI FOIA 94-47468 (Skousen); JEH APPT, August 25, 1961; Sokolsky, "These Days," *WP*, September 5, 1961, S2, FBI FOIA 62-102576-56 (Smoot).

25. "Americanism Town Meeting," *LAT*, November 12, 1961; Fleming, "Palladium All Dressed Up," *LAT*, November 19, 1961; "Text of Kennedy's Palladium Speech," *LAT*, November 19, 1961.

26. Mallett, *Reuther Memorandum*, 49–56.

27. Jones to DeLoach, "'The Far Right,'" June 5, 1963, S6, FBI FOIA 61-9556 (Reuther); Guest list, December 7, 1961, F: "Personal Recollections," B1, EMG; "$10,000 Prize," *NYT*, December 8, 1961. For an account of backroom shenanigans at the Criss dinner, see DeLoach, *Hoover's FBI*, 106-9.

28. "Remarks of J. Edgar Hoover," December 7, 1961, F14, B19, PPS320, RN.

29. Wechsler, "To J. Edgar," *NYP*, December 13, 1961, B132, JEHS.

30. "Fake Patriots Assailed," *Evening Bulletin*, February 22, 1962, B133, JEHS; "Red Strength," *CR*, January 18, 1962; DeLoach to Mohr, "Inquiry," January 23, 1962, S2, FBI FOIA 62-91161-43 (Goldwater); "The Question of Robert Welch," *NatR*, February 13, 1962; Hearst, "Editor's Report," *NYJA*, February 18, 1962, B133, JEHS.

31. Demaris, *Director*, 74; Sokolsky, "These Days," *WP*, February 21, 1962, B133, JEHS; Morrell to DeLoach, February 27, 1962, S27, FBI IA 62-104401 (JBS); [Redacted] to Hoover, February 26, 1962, S3, FBI FOIA 100-402036 (Schwarz); Philbrick to Sokolsky, March 1, 1962, S4, FBI FOIA 100-265248 (Philbrick).

32. Schoenwald, *Time for Choosing*, introduction.

Chapter 43: In Friendship (1961–1962)

1. Scatterday to Rosen, "Martin Luther King, Jr.," May 22, 1961, S1, FBI FOIA 100-106670 (MLK).

2. "Correlation Summary: Martin Luther King, Jr.," September 28, 1960, S1, FBI FOIA 100-106670-11 (MLK); "Reverend Martin Luther King, Jr," November 14, 1961, S1, FBI FOIA 100-106670 (MLK); Jones to DeLoach, "Article in 'The Nation,'" February 7, 1961, S1, FBI FOIA 100-106670 (MLK).

3. On the FBI's investigation of King, see especially Garrow, *The FBI and Martin Luther King, Jr.*; Garrow, *Bearing the Cross*; Branch, *Parting the Waters*; Branch, *At Canaan's Edge*; Branch, *Pillar of Fire*; O'Reilly, *"Racial Matters"*; *MLK/FBI*, directed by Sam Pollard (2020).

4. Branch, *Parting the Waters*, 285. On Rustin, see especially D'Emilio, *Lost Prophet*; Podair, *American Dreamer*; Anderson, *Bayard Rustin*.

5. Historians have long debated the nature of Levison's relationship to the Communist Party. Writing in the 1970s, Arthur Schlesinger described Levison simply as a "good-hearted and undiscriminating liberal," with only passing acquaintance with the Communist Party (Schlesinger, *Robert Kennedy and his Times*, 356). A decade later, King biogra-

pher Taylor Branch labeled Levison "a fiercely independent thinker, of eclectic political interests" that included the Communist Party, but only prior to Levison's association with King (Branch, *Parting the Waters*, 209). Historian David Garrow, who has done more than anyone to document the FBI's investigation of Levison, concluded in 2002 "beyond any possible question" that Levison "was a highly important Party operative" in the 1950s but that his involvement "declined precipitously" around 1956 or 1957, as he took up work with King (Garrow, "The FBI and Martin Luther King," *Atlantic*, July/August 2002, https://www.theatlantic.com/magazine/archive/2002/07/the-fbi-and-martin-luther-king/302537/). The only book-length study of Levison himself, Ben Kamin's *Dangerous Friendship*, similarly argues that Levison broke with the party around 1956. In recent years Garrow has revised his view of Levison's activities to include ongoing involvement with the Communist Party after 1957. See especially Garrow, "The Troubling Legacy of Martin Luther King," *Standpoint*, June 2019, https://www.davidgarrow.com/wp-content/uploads/2019/05/DJGStandpoint2019.pdf. For Garrow's earlier interpretations of Levison, also see Garrow, *Bearing the Cross*, and Garrow, *FBI and Martin Luther King, Jr.*

6. SAC New York to Director, "NY 694-S," June 9, 1952, S1, FBI IA 134-91 (Jack Childs).

7. SAC New York to Director, "Stanley Levison, Roy Levison," June 9, 1952, S1, FBI FOIA 100-392452-1 (Levison); Garrow, *FBI and Martin Luther King, Jr.*, 32; Branch, *Parting the Waters*, 208–9; New York, "Stanley David Levison," September 21, 1953, S2, FBI FOIA 100-111180-57 (Levison); "Exhibit Number 1," April 25, 1964, FBI JFK 62-116395-672.

8. SA (A) to SAC New York, "CP, USA-Funds," July 9, 1956, S7, FBI FOIA 100-111180 (Levison); SAC New York to Director, "NY 694-S," June 9, 1952, S1, FBI IA 134-91 (Jack Childs); SAC New York to Director, June 24, 1952, S1, FBI IA 134-91 (Jack Childs).

9. SAC Chicago to Director, "CG-5824-S," October 6, 1952, S2, FBI IA 134-46-4 (Morris Childs); SAC Chicago to Director, "CG-5824-S," December 8, 1952, S2, FBI IA 134-46-35 (Morris Childs); SAC Chicago to SAC New York, "Stanley Levinson or Levison," October 17, 1952, S1, FBI FOIA 100-111180 (Levison); SAC New York to Director, "NY 694-S," June 9, 1952; SAC New York to Director, "Smuggling of Atomic Bombs," S2, FBI FOIA 100-111180 (Levison); SAC New York to Director, "Stanley David Levison," June 19, 1953, S2, FBI FOIA 100-392452-3 (Levison); New York, "Stanley David Levison," September 21, 1953, S2, FBI FOIA 100-111180-57 (Levison).

10. For 1954 wiretap, see Sub1 ELSURs, FBI FOIA 100-111180 (Levison); Banister to Director, April 8, 1954, S3, FBI FOIA 100-111180 (Levison); Banister to Director, April 29, 1954, S4, FBI FOIA 100-111180-208 (Levison); SAC Chicago to SAC New York, "Stanley Levison," September 3, 1954, S5, FBI FOIA 100-111180-426 (Levison); Belmont to Hoover, "Stanley D. Levison," April 28, 1954, FBI JFK 62-116395-EBF-1008; Banister to Director, April 24, 1954, FBI JFK 62-116395-EBF-1008; Hoover, "Memorandum for the Attorney General," April 21, 1954, FBI JFK 62-116395-EBF-1008; Boardman to Director, "Stanley David Levison," April 20, 1954, FBI JFK 62-116395-EBF-1008.

11. Director to SAC New York, "Stanley David Levison," May 6, 1954, S4, FBI FOIA 100-111180-212 (Levison); SAC New York to Director, "Stanley David Levison," July

6, 1954, S5, FBI FOIA 100-392452-66 (Levison); SAC New York to Director, "Security Informant Program," July 28, 1954, S4, FBI FOIA NY 100-111180 (Levison); New York, "Jay Richard Kennedy," August 19, 1954, S4, FBI FOIA NY 100-111180 (Levison). The husband, Jay Richard Kennedy, went on to play a complicated but interesting role as a CIA informant, novelist, and civil rights insider. See Garrow, *FBI and Martin Luther King, Jr.*, 30–4.

12. For 1955 wiretap logs, see "Levison ELSURs," Sub3, FBI FOIA NY 100-111180 (Levison).

13. Kamin, *Dangerous Friendship*, 64.

14. SAC New York to Director, "CP, USA-Funds," April 11, 1956, S7, FBI FOIA 100-111180-667 (Levison); SA [Redacted] to SAC New York, "CP, USA-Funds," July 9, 1956, S7, FBI FOIA 100-111180-675 (Levison); SAC New York, "Stanley David Levison," July 25, 1956, S7, FBI FOIA 100-111180-677 (Levison); SA [Redacted] to SAC New York, "Stanley Levison," September 27, 1956, S7, FBI FOIA 100-111180-691 (Levison); SAC New York to Director, "CP, USA, Funds," October 20, 1958, S17, FBI IA 134-91-1490 (Jack Childs); SAC Chicago to Director, "Communist Party-USA, Funds," April 15, 1958, S14, FBI IA 134-91-1308 (Jack Childs). For historians, see note 5.

15. SAC New York, "Cominfil Railroad Industry," October 22, 1956, S7, FBI FOIA 100-111180-697 (Levison); "Civil Rights Lag," *NYT*, May 25, 1956; Garrow, *Bearing the Cross*, 83–90, 116–7; Branch, *Parting the Waters*, 211–2, 208, 227; Kamin, *Dangerous Friendship*, 87; Baumgardner to Sullivan, "Communist Party, USA," March 25, 1964, FBI JFK 100-3-116-1200; Garrow, "Troubling Legacy of Martin Luther King," 32.

16. SAC New York to Director, "CP, USA, Funds," October 20, 1958, S17, FBI IA 134-91-1490 (Jack Childs).

17. SAC Chicago to Director, "SOLO," August 29, 1958, S5, FBI V 100-428091-80 (SOLO); SAC New York to Director, "CP, USA, Funds," October 23, 1958, S17, FBI IA 134-91 (Jack Childs); SAC New York to Director, "CP, USA," November 4, 1958, S17, FBI IA 134-91 (Jack Childs).

18. SAC New York to Director, "CP, USA, Funds," October 20, 1958, S17, FBI IA 134-91-1490 (Jack Childs); "Atlanta Hearings," *Baltimore Afro-American*, August 9, 1958; SAC New York to Director, "CP, USA Funds," March 16, 1961, S24, FBI IA 134-91-2380 (Jack Childs). On O'Dell, also see Navasky, *O'Dell File*.

19. McWhorter, *Carry Me Home*, 106–7. For O'Dell's background, also see Navasky, *O'Dell File*; Branch, *Parting the Waters*, 573–97; Garrow, *FBI and Martin Luther King, Jr.*, 50–1.

20. Branch, *Parting the Waters*, 573–4; "Police Map," *New Orleans States*, May 8, 1956, S2, FBI FOIA 100-14516-548 (King); "O'Dell Test," ca. March 1956, S2, FBI FOIA 100-14516-548 (King); "Former Resident Charged," *Morning Advocate*, March 28, 1957, S2, FBI FOIA 100-14516-548 (King); SAC New Orleans to Director, "Hunter Pitts O'Dell," November 20, 1962, S2, FBI FOIA 100-106670 (King); United States Congress, Senate, Committee on the Judiciary, *Scope of Soviet Activity in the United States, Part 13: Hearings before the Subcommittee to Investigate the Administration of the Internal Security Act and Other Internal Security Laws of the Committee on the Judiciary, United States Senate, Eighty-Fourth Congress, Second Session, on April 10–12, 1956* (Washington, D.C.: U.S. Government Printing Office, 1956), 755–76.

21. SAC New York to Director, "James Jackson," January

12, 1959, S20, FBI IA 134-46-1835 (Morris Childs); SAC New York to Director, "CP, USA," March 4, 1959, S20, FBI IA 134-46-1853 (Morris Childs); SAC Chicago to Director, "CG 5824-S*," August 18, 1961, S24, FBI IA 134-46-2363 (Morris Childs); Bland to Sullivan, "Martin Luther King, Jr.," September 6, 1963, F24, B12, HO&C.

22. "Hunter Pitts O'Dell," undated, FBI JFK 62-116395-672.

23. SAC New York to Director, "Urgent," July 15, 1961, S31, FBI V 100-428091-1373 (SOLO); SAC New York to Director, "SOLO," July 18, 1961, S33, FBI V 100-428091-1469 (SOLO); SAC New York to Director, "SOLO," July 26, 1961, S33, FBI V 100-428091-1468 (SOLO).

24. Bland to Sullivan, "Stanley David Levison," February 3, 1962, S8B, FBI FOIA 100-392452-135 (Levison); Director to Attorney General, "Martin Luther King, Jr.," February 14, 1962, S8B, FBI FOIA 100-349542 (Levison).

25. JEH LOGS, January 9, 10, 12, 1962; Evans to Belmont, January 13, 1962, S2, F13, B8, HO&C.

26. Hersh, *Bobby and J. Edgar*, 348–9.

27. JEH APP (1963), 344; Branch, *Parting the Waters*, 564; Bland to Sullivan, "Stanley David Levison," February 3, 1962.

28. Hersh, *Bobby and J. Edgar*, 349; Weiner, *Enemies*, 231.

29. Director to SAC Atlanta, "Martin Luther King, Jr.," February 27, 1962, S1, FBI FOIA 100-106670 (King); SAC New York to Director, "Stanley David Levison," March 16, 1962, S8B, FBI FOIA 100-392452-146 (Levison); SAC New York to Director, "Stanley David Levison," March 20, 1962, S8B, FBI FOIA 100-392452-147 (Levison); wiretap log, March 20, 1962, Sub7 ELSURs, FBI FOIA 100-111180-7-1 (Levison).

Chapter 44: Decadent Thinking (1957–1962)

1. Hoover to O'Donnell, February 27, 1962, FBI PA 92-3267-125 (Campbell).

2. Pietrusza, *1960*, 155; Hersh, *Dark Side of Camelot*, 390; Evans to Belmont, "Judith E. Campbell," March 15, 1962, FBI PA 62-116929 (Campbell); "John Roselli," March 10, 1962, S1B, FBI V 92-3267 (Castro); Evans to Belmont, "Judith E. Campbell," March 20, 1962, F96, B17, HO&C.

3. JEH APPT, March 22, 1962; Evans to Belmont, "Judith E. Campbell," March 20, 1962, F96, B17, HO&C; Branch, *Parting the Waters*, 569.

4. Warner, "Patriotism," *Chicago Sun Times*, June 29, 1962, B133, JEHS; "FBI Chief Cites," *Journal*, October 10, 1962, B134, JEHS.

5. Gardner, "Keep Young Look!," circa June 14, 1960, B129, JEHS.

6. The doctors most frequently identified in Hoover's office logs include Omundson, Kennedy, Meyer, Cajigas, Choisser, Geier. See JEH APPT, JEH LOGS, 1960–1963; "Recollection 12," F: "Personal Recollections," B1, EMG.

7. Harris, "Bachelor Cop," *Seattle Post-Intelligencer*, April 3, 1960, B128, JEHS; "FBI Chief Better," *WP*, November 16, 1962; "J. Edgar Hoover," *Times Union*, May 10, 1964, B138, JEHS; JEHS LOGS, November 9–December 21, 1962.

8. Gentry, *J. Edgar Hoover*, 650; Powers, *Secrecy and Power*, 363. For Tolson smoking, see PB36, PB62, NLEM.

9. "Proposed Nomination," NLEM.

10. "List of Guests, June 12, 1963," DI: JFKPOF-094-055-p0004, F: "Distinguished Civilian Service Awards Board," Sr7, President's Office Files, JFK; Hersh, *Bobby and J. Edgar*, 301–2; Mahoney, *Sons & Brothers*, 98; Gentry, *J.*

Edgar Hoover, 479; "Continuation of Conversation," February 17, 1962, F30, S-JEHC.

11. Summers, *Official and Confidential*, 247–59.

12. For critiques of the Rosenstiel story, see especially Kessler, *The Bureau*, 106–9; Theoharis, *J. Edgar Hoover, Sex, and Crime*, 38–59; Charles, *Hoover's War on Gays*, 1–10; Potter, "Queer Hoover," 355–81. On Cohn, see von Hoffman, *Citizen Cohn*.

13. Hoover, "Memorandum for Mr. Tolson," March 23, 1960, S18, FBI V 100-428091 (SOLO).

14. "United States of America: Intelligence Games/Active Measures," Sr1, V6, P5, Ch. 12:3, 432, MITN; Andrew and Mitrokhin, *Sword and the Shield*, 1–22; 234–6. Translation of archival material courtesy of Anastasiia Posnova.

15. "Publisher Hits," *Daily Oklahoman*, October 7, 1959, B128, JEHS.

16. Kennedy, "Rambler," August 19, 1959, S7, FBI 67-7489 (Purvis); Rosen to Hoover, "Melvin Horace Purvis," October 15, 1959, S7, FBI 67-7489-578 (Purvis); Purvis and Tresniowski, *Vendetta*, 324, 327, 2; "Former FBI Man," March 1, 1960, S7, FBI 67-7489 (Purvis); "Dillinger's 'Killer,'" *Los Angeles Examiner*, March 1, 1960, S7, FBI 67-7489 (Purvis); DeLoach to Mohr, "Former SAC," February 29, 1960, S7, FBI 67-7489 (Purvis).

17. Purvis to Hoover, March 7, 1960, S7, FBI FOIA 67-7489 (Purvis).

18. Johnson, *Lavender Scare*, 179–85; Mattachine Society, "Discrimination against the Employment," February 28, 1963, S6, FBI GA 100-403320 (Mattachine). Also see Cervini, *Deviant's War*, 80–179.

19. WFO to Director, "Mattachine Society," August 8, 1961, S6, FBI GA 100-403320 (Mattachine); Jones to DeLoach, "William Dufty," June 10, 1959, S5, FBI GA 100-403320 (Mattachine); Kameny to RFK, June 28, 1963, S6, FBI GA 100-403320 (Mattachine); Hoover to RFK, July 9, 1962, S6, FBI GA 100-403320 (Mattachine); Summers, *Official and Confidential*, 84; Jones to DeLoach, "Unc," April 11, 1961, S6, FBI GA 100-403320 (Mattachine); Kameny to Hoover, August 28, 1962, S6, FBI GA 100-403320 (Mattachine).

20. Schuyler to Hoover, June 4, 1963, S6, FBI GA 100-403320 (Mattachine); Jones to DeLoach, "Mattachine Society," July 20, 1964, S6, FBI GA 100-403320 (Mattachine).

21. Jones to DeLoach, "Franklin E. Kameny," August 7, 1964, S6, FBI GA 100-403320 (Mattachine).

22. Johnson to [Redacted], October 1, 1964, S6, FBI GA 100-403320 (Mattachine); Jones to DeLoach, "Franklin E. Kameny," October 9, 1964, S6, FBI GA 100-403320 (Mattachine).

23. Johnson, *Lavender Scare*, 210–1.

24. "Robert F. Kennedy," undated, S1, FBI V 61-9454 (Monroe); Evans to Belmont, "Meyer Lansky," F12, B8, FBI 92-2831-585, HO&C; Hersh, *Bobby and J. Edgar*, 320–32; Summers, *Goddess*, 336; Jones to DeLoach, "'Photoplay' Article," July 9, 1963, S1, FBI V 105-40018-4 (Monroe); "One Year Later," ca. 1963, S1, FBI V [NA] (Monroe).

25. Bates to Director, June 29, 1963, F13, B9, HO&C; Evans to Belmont, "Christine Keeler," July 24, 1963, F13, B9, HO&C; Evans to Hoover, "Interview by the Attorney General," July 3, 1963, F96, B17, HO&C; Hersh, *Bobby and J. Edgar*, 360–4; Hersh, *Dark Side of Camelot*, 390–8.

26. SAC WFO to Director, "Elly Rometsch," July 15, 1963, FBI PA 105-122316 (Rometsch); Hoover, "Memorandum to Mr. Tolson," October 30, 1963, FBI PA 105-122316 (Rometsch); Hoover, "Memorandum to Mr. Tolson," October 26,

1963, F22, B12, HO&C; Hersh, *Bobby and J. Edgar*, 364–9; Hersh, *Dark Side of Camelot*, 387–90, 398–406.

27. Hoover, "Memorandum to Mr. Tolson," November 7, 1963, FBI PA 105-122316-94 (Rometsch); Hoover, "Memorandum to Mr. Tolson," October 28, 1963, FBI PA 105-122316-24 (Rometsch).

28. JEH APPT, October 31, 1963; Evans to Belmont, "Route in Envelope," July 3, 1963, F96, B17, HO&C.

Chapter 45: The Most Dangerous Negro (1963)

1. SAC New York to Director, "Stanley Levison," April 2, 1962, S8B, FBI FOIA 100-392452 (Levison); SAC New York to Director, "Stanley Levison," May 3, 1962, S8B, FBI FOIA 100-392452-153 (Levison); DeLoach to Sullivan, "Testimony," May 3, 1962, S8B, FBI FOIA 100-392452-156 (Levison); Garrow, *FBI and Martin Luther King, Jr.*, 47–8; SAC New York to Director, "Martin Luther King, Jr.," May 3, 1962, FBI JFK 62-116395-EBF-1073; SAC New York to Director, "Stanley Levison," June 4, 1962, S2, FBI FOIA 100-106670 (King).

2. "Martin Luther King, Jr.," March 26, 1968, S80, FBI FOIA 100-106670 (King); SAC New York to Director, "CPUSA," September 28, 1962, S2, FBI FOIA 100-106670 (King); SAC New York to Director, "Hunter Pitts O'Dell," December 4, 1962, FBI FOIA 100-106670 (King).

3. SAC New Orleans to Director, "Hunter Pitts O'Dell," November 20, 1962, S2, FBI FOIA 100-106670 (King); SAC New York to Director, "Hunter Pitts O'Dell," December 12, 1962, S9A, FBI FOIA 100-392452 (Levison).

4. Rosen to Belmont, "Racial Situation," November 20, 1962, FBI JFK 62-116395-EBF-951.

5. DeLoach to Mohr, "Racial Situation," January 15, 1963, S3, FBI FOIA 100-10670 (King).

6. Garrow, *Bearing the Cross*, 669.

7. Branch, *Parting the Waters*, 696–7; Hoover to Yeagley, "Stanley David Levison," February 12, 1963, S9B, FBI FOIA 100-392452 (Levison).

8. SAC New York to Director, "Stanley David Levison," March 21, 1963, FBI JFK 62-116395-EBF-1073; Garrow, *Bearing the Cross*, 235; SAC New York to Director, "Stanley David Levison," April 3, 1963, S9B, FBI FOIA 100-392452-196 (Levison); SAC New York to Director, "Martin Luther King," June 13, 1963, FBI JFK 62-116395-EBF-1073; SAC New York to Director, "Communist Infiltration," August 21, 1962, FBI JFK 62-116395-EBF-949; SAC New York to Director, "Martin Luther King," July 31, 1963, FBI JFK 62-116395-EBF-1073.

9. King, *Why We Can't Wait*, 49; Garrow, *Bearing the Cross*, 229. On the Birmingham campaign, see especially McWhorter, *Carry Me Home*. When not otherwise cited, background information on the campaign can be found here.

10. Hoover, "Memorandum for the Attorney General," September 30, 1963, S2B, FBI V 157-1025 (Bapbomb).

11. FBI Mobile to Director, February 6, 1956, S1, FBI FOIA 62-102939 (Wallace); "Wallace Warns," *Dothan Eagle*, February 6, 1956, B120, JEHS; Rosen to Belmont, "[Redacted] et al," January 9, 1962, S1, FBI FOIA 62-102939 (Wallace); SAC Mobile to Director, "Alabama Circuit Judge," March 6, 1956, S1, FBI FOIA 62-102939-8 (Wallace). For background on Wallace, see Carter, *Politics of Rage*.

12. Adams to Callahan, "Arthur J. Hanes," June 18, 1968, S1, FBI FOIA 67-175292 (Hanes); King to Director, "Arthur Jackson Hanes," November 20, 1947, S1, FBI FOIA

67-175292 (Hanes); "Citizens Councils," *CSM*, May 22, 1956; McWhorter, *Carry Me Home*, 180–1, 187, 196.

13. [Redacted] to Hoover, December 23, 1961, FBI FOIA 67-175292-65 (Hanes); Hoover to [Redacted], December 29, 1961, FBI FOIA 67-175292 (Hanes).

14. Eskew, *But for Birmingham*, 210; Garrow, *Bearing the Cross*, 179–88, 203–19; McWhorter, *Carry Me Home*, 308–9, 339–41; Nunnelley, *Bull Connor*, 140–1.

15. McWhorter, *Carry Me Home*, 379–80, 403; Bailey, interview, *Eyes on the Prize*, November 2, 1985, Washington University Digital Gateway, http://digital.wustl.edu/e/eop/eopweb/bai0015.0941.006sheriffmelvinbailey.html. For quote, see Wechsler, "The Lessons," *NYP*, May 14, 1963, B135, JEHS. For long-term shifts in Southern policing, see Randolph, "Civil Rights Arrested."

16. "President John F. Kennedy's Civil Rights Address," June 11, 1963, YouTube video, 13:23, courtesy of John F. Kennedy Presidential Library and Museum, posted by C-SPAN, June 6, 2013, https://www.youtube.com/watch?v=7BEhKgoA86U.

17. General Investigative Division, June 6, 1963, S4, FBI FOIA 100-106670-132x2 (King).

18. Hoover, "Memorandum for Mr. Tolson," June 17, 1963, S4, FBI FOIA 100-106670-150 (King). On Evers, see FBI V 157–901 (Evers).

19. Marshall to Hoover, "Hunter Pitts O'Dell," September 20, 1963, F24, B12, HO&C; Branch, *Parting the Waters*, 835–8; Garrow, *Bearing the Cross*, 272–3, 275; JEH LOGS, June 22, 1963.

20. McWhorter, *Carry Me Home*, 468–9; Garrow, *Bearing the Cross*, 275; King to O'Dell, July 3, 1963, S106, FBI FOIA 100-106670-3656 (King).

21. Belafonte, *My Song*, 275, 282; Evans to Belmont, "Communist Influence," July 16, 1963, F24, B12, HO&C; McWhorter, *Carry Me Home*, 471.

22. Hoover, "Memorandum for the Attorney General," July 23, 1963, F24, B12, HO&C; Evans to Belmont, "Martin Luther King, Jr.," July 25, 1963, F24, B12, HO&C; JEH LOGS, August 28, 1963; Belafonte, *My Song*, 279–80.

23. SAC Letter 63-44, "Visits by Civil Rights Groups," September 4, 1963, FBI-JFK 62-116395 477-Bulky (2); Joseph, *Waiting 'til the Midnight Hour*, 46–50, 65–7, 84–7.

24. Baumgardner to Sullivan, "Communist Party, USA," August 23, 1963, FBI JFK 62-117290-1321-Bulky.

25. Sullivan to Belmont, "Communist Party, USA," August 30, 1963, S7, FBI FOIA 100-106670 (King); Hoover, "Memorandum for the Attorney General," October 7, 1963, S106, FBI FOIA 100-106670 (King); Evans to Belmont, "Martin Luther King, Jr.," October 10, 1963, S106, FBI FOIA 100-106670 (King); Evans to Belmont, McMahon to File, "Martin Luther King, Jr.," October 17, 1963, FBI JFK 62-116395-837-1037; Bland to Sullivan, "Martin Luther King, Jr.," October 18, 1963, FBI JFK 62-116395-1153-Bulky; Evans to Belmont, "Martin Luther King, Jr.," October 21, 1963, FBI JFK 62-116395-1153-Bulky; Sizoo to Sullivan, "Martin Luther King, Jr.," October 22, 1963, FBI JFK 62-116395-837-1037; SAC New York to Director, "Martin Luther King, Jr.," October 25, 1963, FBI JFK 62-116395-1153-Bulky; New York to Director, "Martin Luther King, Jr.," November 1, 1963, FBI JFK 62-116395-1153-Bulky; McMahon to File, "Cominfil," November 4, 1963, FBI JFK 62-116395-837-1037; SAC Atlanta to Director, "Dr. Martin Luther King, Jr.," November 27, 1963, FBI JFK 62-116395-1153-Bulky; SAC New York to Director, "Mar-

tin Luther King, Jr.," December 12, 1963, FBI JFK 62-116395-1153-Bulky; SAC Brennan to Sullivan, "Martin Luther King, Jr.," April 18, 1968, S106, FBI FOIA 100-106670-3950 (King). For wiretap planning, also see F24, B12, HO&C.

Chapter 46: The President Is Dead (1963)

1. Birmingham to Director, "Unsubs," September 15, 1963, S1, FBI V 157-1025-1 (Bapbomb); McWhorter, *Carry Me Home*, 23–5, 520–3. For a general account of the bombing and investigation, see McWhorter, *Carry Me Home*. Two other Black children were also killed in Birmingham that day: 13-year-old Virgil Ware was riding his bicycle when he was shot by white-supremacist vigilantes; 16-year-old Johnny Robinson died after being shot in the back by a police officer. See McWhorter, *Carry Me Home*, 531.

2. "Rally to Mourn," *NYT*, September 19, 1963, B135, JEHS; Wechsler, "Missing G-Men," *NYP*, September 18, 1963, B135, JEHS.

3. Hoover to Dirksen, September 24, 1963, S2A, FBI V 100-1025-235 (Bapbomb); Rosen to Belmont, "Unsub," September 15, 1963, S1A, FBI V 157-1025-25 (Bapbomb); Director to Attorney General, "Unknown Subjects," September 16, 1963, S1, FBI V 157-1025 (Bapbomb).

4. Belmont to Tolson, "Birmingham Bombings," September 17, 1963, S1D, FBI V 157-1025-211 (Bapbomb).

5. Interview with J. Edgar Hoover, June 4, 1964, F91, B44, WMP; JEH LOGS, November 22, 1963; Manchester, *Death of a President*, 195–6; Thomas, *Robert Kennedy*, 276; Schlesinger, *Robert Kennedy and His Times*, 607-9. For an assessment of recent literature on the Kennedy assassination, see Gage, "Who Didn't Kill JFK?" *Nation*, December 18, 2013.

6. JEH LOGS, November 22, 1963; Thomas, *Robert Kennedy*, 277; interview with J. Edgar Hoover, June 4, 1964, F91, B44, WMP; Katzenbach, *Some of It Was Fun*, 130; Strober and Strober, *"Let Us Begin Anew,"* 448

7. Hosty, *Assignment: Oswald*, 14–5; Director to All Offices, November 22, 1963, S1, FBI MFF 62-106090 (JFK HQ).

8. JEH LOGS, November 22, 1963.

9. Hosty, *Assignment: Oswald*, 16-26, 51-2. On Oswald's time in the Soviet Union, see Savodnik, *Interloper*.

10. JEH LOGS, November 22, 1963; Aitken, *Nixon*, 316; interview with J. Edgar Hoover, June 4, 1964, F91, B44, WMP.

11. Hoover, "Memorandum for Mr. Tolson," November 22, 1963, S1, FBI MFF 62-106090 (JFK HQ File).

12. JEH LOGS, November 22, 1963. For a general account of the day, see Caro, *Years of Lyndon Johnson: Passage of Power*, 307–436.

13. Johnson to Hoover, F: Hom-Hoq, B23, "Master File" Index, VP series, LBJ; Strober and Strober, *"Let Us Begin Anew,"* 193; Caro, *Years of Lyndon Johnson: Passage of Power*, 159–306.

14. Hoover to McGaughey, December 5, 1963, F60-63, B1, EMG.

15. Hoover to SACs, November 22, 1963, S1, FBI MFF 62-109060 (JFK HQ).

16. Caro, *Years of Lyndon Johnson: Passage of Power*, 373.

17. WCR, 196-7.

18. Hosty, *Assignment: Oswald*, 16–7.

19. Holland, *Kennedy Assassination Tapes*, 68–75.

20. JEH LOGS, November 23, 1963; Director to SACs, November 23, 1963, S1, FBI MFF 62-109060 (JFK HQ).

The exact time of the communication is difficult to determine from the available copies, but several time stamps indicate 12:30 as the most likely time of delivery.

21. Summers, *Not in Your Lifetime*, 93.

22. "Dallas Police Chief Curry speaks," November 23, 1963, https://www.youtube.com/watch?v=0iNEodi-GU8; JEH LOGS, November 23, 1963; Holland, *Kennedy Assassination Tapes*, 73-4.

23. Hoover to McGaughey, December 5, 1963, F60-63, B1, EMG.

24. Untitled memo for the record, November 24, 1963, at https://www.archives.gov/files/research/jfk/releases/docid-32263509.pdf.

25. Interview of Fletcher D. Thompson, FBI OH; Hosty, *Assignment Oswald*, 58-61.

26. JEH LOGS, November 25, 1963.

27. Holland, *Kennedy Assassination Tapes*, 92–6; Hoover to Marks, November 25, 1963, S1, FBI MFF 62-109060 (JFK HQ).

28. Hosty, *Assignment: Oswald*, 97; interview of Fletcher D. Thompson, FBI OH; CC5, 34.

29. "FBI Presses," *ChiT*, November 28, 1963; Clayton, "Dozens of Questions," *WP*, November 27, 1963; Clayton, "2 Senate Leaders," *WP*, November 28, 1963.

30. Holland, *Kennedy Assassination Tapes*, 135–49.

Chapter 47: The Commission (1963–1964)

1. Holland, *Kennedy Assassination Tapes*, 153, 135–49; Shenon, *Cruel and Shocking Act*, 59, 60; Untitled, "Attached is...," November 29, 1963, S1, FBI MFF 62-109090 (Warren Commission).

2. On DeLoach's FBI career, see especially DeLoach, *Hoover's FBI*. For details, also see: interview of Cartha DeLoach, FBI OH; Hoover to DeLoach, January 28, 1959, P4, FBI V 67-338728-398 (DeLoach); January 28, 1959, P4, FBI V 67-338728-298 (DeLoach).

3. DeLoach to Mohr, "bilsul," June 28, 1963, F22, B12, HO&C; Holland, *Kennedy Assassination Tapes*, 369.

4. WCES, December 5, 1963; Shenon, *Cruel and Shocking Act*, 71.

5. Belmont to Tolson, "Assassination of the President," December 2, 1963, S1, FBI MFF 62-109090 (Warren Commission); CC5, 34; WCES, December 6, 1963; Demaris, *Director*, 276.

6. Belmont to Tolson, "Assassination of the President," December 3, 1963, S1, FBI MFF 62-109090-8 (Warren Commission); Shenon, *Cruel and Shocking Act*, 71.

7. FBI, "Investigation of Assassination of President," FBI Summary Report (WC Doc. 1), FBI MFF.

8. Shenon, *Cruel and Shocking Act*, 80.

9. WCES, December 16, 1963.

10. On Hoover's evasions, see especially Shenon, *Cruel and Shocking Act*.

11. Baumgardner to Sullivan, "SOLO," December 4, 1963, S51, FBI V 100-428091-3394 (SOLO).

12. CC5, 50-52; Shenon, *Cruel and Shocking Act*, 151–2.

13. WCES, December 16, 1963.

14. Ottenberg, "Warren Group Probing," *WS*, ca. December 20, 1963, S1, FBI MFF 62-109090-19 (Warren Commission).

15. Hoover, "Memorandum for Mr. Tolson," December 26, 1963, S1, FBI MFF 62-109090-50 (Warren Commission); Shenon, *Cruel and Shocking Act*, 86; Rosen to Belmont, "Lee Harvey Oswald," December 20, 1963, FBI MFF 62-109090 (Warren Commission).

16. Malley to Rosen, "Lee Harvey Oswald," January 21, 1964, S2, FBI MFF 62-109090 (Warren Commission); Gauthier to Callahan, "Assassination of President Kennedy," January 2, 1964, S1, FBI MFF 62-109090 (Warren Commission).

17. Ford and Stiles, *Portrait of the Assassin,* 14; WCES, January 22, 1964; Hoover, "Memorandum for Mr. Tolson," January 31, 1964, S3, FBI MFF 62-109090 (Warren Commission).

18. Sullivan to Belmont, "Lee Harvey Oswald," February 5, 1964, S3, FBI MFF 62-109090 (Warren Commission); "I, J. Edgar Hoover," February 5, 1964, S3, FBI MFF 62-109090 (Warren Commission); Hoover to Rankin, February 6, 12, 1964, S3, FBI MFF 62-109090 (Warren Commission); Shenon, *Cruel and Shocking Act,* 136-7.

19. Fleeson, "Members of Assassination Probe," *WS,* December 3, 1963, B135, JEHS; DeLoach to Mohr, "Lee Harvey Oswald," December 17, 1963, S1, FBI FOIA 94-40611 (Ford); Shenon, *Cruel and Shocking Act,* 86.

20. DeLoach to Mohr, "Assassination of the President," February 7, 1964, S2, FBI FOIA 62-52026 (Thurmond); DeLoach to Mohr, "Assassination of the President," February 7, 1964, S5, FBI MFF 62-109090 (Warren Commission).

21. Sullivan to Belmont, "Mr. Allen W. Dulles," February 7, 1964, S6, FBI MFF 62-109090-94 (Warren Commission); Brennan to Sullivan, "Lee Harvey Oswald," February 10, 1964, S3, FBI MFF 62-109090 (Warren Commission) (Hoover's handwriting is difficult to read); JEH LOGS, February 6, 10, 14, 17, 18, 20, 25, March 13, 18, 1964; JEH APPT, January 31, April 2, 1964; Hoover, "Memorandum for Mr. Tolson," February 17, 1964, S4, FBI MFF 62-109090 (Warren Commission); "Whale of a Wow," *NYJA,* April 25, 1964, B136, JEHS; "President Heads," *WS,* April 26, 1964, B136, JEHS; DeLoach to Hoover, April 17, 1964, S5, FBI V 67-338728 (DeLoach); DeLoach to Reedy, April 8, 1964, F: "DeLoach," B117, WHCF, LBJ; Hoover to Ford, April 17, 1964, S1, FBI FOIA 94-40611-20 (Ford).

22. Hoover to McGaughey, December 5, 1963, F60-63, B1, EMG; JEH APPT, January 29, 1964, 286.

23. Shenon, *Cruel and Shocking Act,* 224-5; Jevons to Conrad, "Assassination of President," March 12, 1964, S7, FBI MFF 62-109090 (Warren Commission); Branigan to Sullivan, "Lee Harvey Oswald," February 14, 1964, S5, FBI MFF 62-109090 (Warren Commission); Branigan to Sullivan, "Lee Harvey Oswald," February 26, 1964, S6, FBI MFF 62-109090 (Warren Commission); Rosen to Belmont, "President's Commission," February 26, 1964, S4, FBI MFF 62-109090-116 (Warren Commission); Downing to Conrad," March 3, 1964, S8, FBI MFF 62-109090 (Warren Commission).

24. Interview of Cartha DeLoach, FBI OH; JEH APPT, March 9, 1964; LBJD, March 9, 1964; Branch, *Pillar of Fire,* 246-7; LBJ-T 2420. For Hoover's gift and pleasantry exchanges with Johnson, see F: "J. Edgar Hoover," Name File, WHCF, LBJ.

25. JEH APPT, May 6, 1964; Hosty, *Assignment: Oswald,* 151.

26. "Remarks of the President," May 8, 1964, F: "Hoover, Mr. J. Edgar," B968, WH Social File, LBJ; Photo, F1978, B38, NARA-P; JEH APPT, May 8, 1964; UPI, untitled, May 8, 1964, B136, JEHS; Bain, "National Sacred Cow," *Globe and Mail,* May 11, 1964, B136, JEHS.

27. "House Praises," *Salt Lake Tribune,* May 8, 1964, B136, JEHS; "Tribute," *CR,* May 11, 1964, B136, JEHS; Foley to Johnson, received May 7, 1964, F: "Hoover, J. Edgar," B388, WHCF, LBJ; JEH APPT, May 8, 1964; Ken-

nedy to Hoover, May 12, 1964, F: "General Correspondence, Hoover," B25, AG Papers, JFK.

28. JEH LOGS, May 12, 1964; JEH APPT, May 13, 1964; Newton, *Justice for All,* 572; WCH5, 97-120; WCR, 24.

29. WCH5, 100-1.

Chapter 48: Freedom Summer (1964)

1. Johnson, "Annual Message to the Congress on the State of the Union," January 8, 1964, American Presidency Project, https://www.presidency.ucsb.edu/documents/annual -message-the-congress-the-state-the-union-25.

2. Bigart, "Goldwater Fills Rally," *NYT,* May 13, 1964; WCH5, 101; [Redacted] to Goldwater, January 30, 1964, S2, FBI FOIA 62-98961 (Goldwater).

3. Sullivan to Belmont, "Communist Party, USA," August 30, 1963, S7, FBI FOIA 100-106670 (MLK); Baumgardner to Sullivan, "Communist Party, USA," December 19, 1963, S7, FBI FOIA 100-106670 (MLK); "Questions to be Explored at Conference 12/23/63," FBI JFK 62-116395-EBF-650.

4. SAC Chicago to Director, "Communist Party, USA," May 14, 1959, FBI JFK 62-116395-EBF-949; SAC Atlanta to Director, "Communist Party, USA," April 14, 1964, FBI JFK 62-116395-EBF-650; Director to SAC Atlanta, "Communist Party, USA," July 23, 1964, FBI JFK 62-116395-EBF-650; Director to SAC New York, "Communist Party, USA," April 24, 1964, FBI JFK 62-116395-EBF-650.

5. Director to Yeagley, "Nation of Islam," February 5, 1963, FBI JFK 62-116395-672 (2); Director to Murray, "Elijah Mohammed," December 30, 1952, FBI JFK 62-116395-672 (2); Marable, *Malcolm X,* 182-3, 269-73, 302-4. For wiretap authorization, see Hoover, "Memorandum for the Attorney General re: Malcolm K. Little," April 1, 1964, FBI JFK 62-116395-EBF-1426.

6. "Questions to Be Explored at Conference 12/23/63," FBI JFK 62-116395-EBF-650; Sullivan to Belmont, "Communist Party, USA," December 24, 1963, S7, FBI FOIA 100-106670 (MLK).

7. "Re: Interview of Retired FBI Special Agent (SA) Wilfred L. Bergeron," July 8, 1975, FBI JFK 62-116395-349-380; "Re: Interview of FBI Special Agent (SA) William D. Campbell," July 14, 1975, FBI JFK 62-1116395-387-400.

8. Director to official, handwritten memo, ca. January 22, 1964, FBI JFK 62-116395-EBF-1125; Branch, *Pillar of Fire,* 207; Garrow, "Troubling Legacy"; Untitled report, page begins "brought to Washington . . . ," FBI JFK 62-116395-1153-Bulky; Untitled report, page begins "unnatural act, King . . . ," FBI JFK 62-116395-1153-Bulky.

9. Untitled report, page begins "brought to Washington . . ."; UPI, untitled, November 9, 1963, S6, FBI FOIA 100-106670-264 (MLK); Sullivan to Belmont, "Communist Party-USA," January 27, 1964, F24, B12, HO&C; Garrow, *FBI and Martin Luther King, Jr.,* 106.

10. "Annual Message to the Congress on the State of the Union"; DeLoach to Hoover, "Re: Reverend Martin Luther King, Jr.," January 14, 1964, FBI JFK 62-117290-1321-Bulky.

11. Branch, *Pillar of Fire,* 210, 243-4; JEH APPT, January 29, 1964; Hoover, "Memorandum for Mr. Tolson," February 5, 1964, S8, FBI FOIA 100-106670 (MLK); DeLoach to Mohr, "Martin Luther King," March 16, 1964, S10, FBI FOIA 100-106670-320 (MLK).

12. Branch, *Pillar of Fire,* 249-50; SAC Atlanta to Director, "Justification for Continuation" (w/ addendum), March 20, 1964, FBI JFK 62-116385-934-Bulky; Sullivan

to Belmont, "Communist Party-USA," March 19, 1964, FBI JFK 62-116395-934-Bulky; "For Telephonic Briefing," March 19, 1964, FBI JFK 62-116395-934-Bulky; "Communist Party, USA," June 1, 1964, FBI JFK 62-116395-1153-Bulky; "Memo: Gaming Control Board," May 18, 1964, FBI JFK 62-116395-1153-Bulky.

13. Albright, "Sen. Goldwater," *WP*, June 19, 1964.

14. Watson, *Freedom Summer*, 74–6, 86.

15. Germany and Carter, *Presidential Recordings*, 8:64–5, 117.

16. LBJ-T 3837, 3838, 3841, 3853, 3857, 3869, 3891, 3893, 3897; Germany and Carter, *Presidential Recordings*, 8:64–201, 94–5, 391–5.

17. JEH APPT, July 2, 1964; Johnson, "Radio and Television Remarks Upon Signing the Civil Rights Bill," July 2, 1964, at http://www.lbjlibrary.net/collections/selected-speeches/november-1963-1964/07-02-1964.html; "President Johnson Signs Civil Rights Act," July 2, 1964, at https://www.c-span.org/video/?300956-1/civil-rights-act-50th-anniversary; Watson, *Freedom Summer*, 121; Branch, *Pillar of Fire*, 387-9.

18. Germany and Carter, *Presidential Recordings*, 8:392–3.

19. Watson, *Freedom Summer*, 144; Hoover to Jenkins, July 13, 1964, F: "HU-2/ST24: 1/1/64-7/16/64," B26, WHCF, LBJ; Shoemaker, "Hoover Heading," *Jackson Daily News*, July 10, 1964, B137, JEHS; JEH APPT, July 10, 1964; DeLoach, *Hoover's FBI*, 181-2; von Hoffman, *Mississippi Notebook*, 38; Branch, *Pillar of Fire*, 397; interview of Ernest Cochrane, FBI OH; O'Leary, "Popular Hoover," *WS*, July 11, 1964, B137, JEHS; Hoffman, "Use of 1864 Law," *Chicago Daily News*, July 11, 1964, B137, JEHS.

Chapter 49: All the Way with LBJ (1964)

1. On Harlem, see Flamm, *In the Heat of Summer*. For quotes, see Hoover to Jenkins, September 14, 1964, F135, B22, HO&C, Watson, *Freedom Summer*, 152; Perlstein, *Before the Storm*, 336.

2. Hoover, "Memorandum for Mr. Tolson," July 21, 1964, S13, FBI FOIA 100-106670 (MLK); Hoover, "Memorandum for Mr. Tolson," July 21, 1964, S3, FBI FOIA 62-98961 (Goldwater); Hoover, "Memorandum for Mr. Tolson," July 22, 1964, S3, FBI FOIA 62-98961 (Goldwater); JEH LOGS, July 21-22, 1964. On the FBI's investigation, see F135, B21, HO&C.

3. LBJ-T, 4292; Watson, *Freedom Summer*, 180.

4. Beschloss, *Taking Charge*, 460–2; Branch, *Pillar of Fire*, 198; Hoover, "Memorandum for Mr. Tolson," July 21, 1964, S13, FBI 100-106670 (MLK).

5. Hoover, "Memorandum for Mr. Tolson," July 21, 1964, S13, FBI FOIA 100-106670-396 (MLK); Director to New Orleans, "Itinerary of Dr. Martin Luther King," FBI FOIA 100-106670-397 (MLK); Director to New Orleans, "Reported Itinerary," July 20, 1964, S13, FBI FOIA 100-106670-395 (MLK); Rosen to Belmont, "Reverend Martin Luther King, Jr.," July 21, 1964 S13, FBI FOIA 100-106670-401 (MLK); Hoover to Jenkins, July 23, 1964, S13, FBI FOIA 100-100670 (MLK); McGowan to Rosen, "Reverend Martin Luther King," July 22, 1964, S3, FBI FOIA 100-106670-405 (MLK); Hoover, "Memorandum for Mr. Tolson," July 22, 1964, S13, FBI FOIA 100-106670 (MLK).

6. Rosen to Belmont, "Unknown Subjects," July 31, 1964, S1, FBI V 44-25706 (MIBURN); Watson, *Freedom Summer*, 198–9.

7. FBI, "Prosecutive Summary," V2, December 19, 1964, S5, FBI V 44-25706 (MIBURN).

8. LBJ-T, 4760.

9. DeLoach, *Hoover's FBI*, 5; JEH LOGS, July 25, 1964; Morgan, untitled, *Evening Tribune*, July 29, 1964, B137, JEHS.

10. DeLoach, *Hoover's FBI*, 3-9; DeLoach to Mohr, "Special Squad," August 29, 1964, S5, FBI V 67-338728-450 (DeLoach).

11. JEH LOGS, July 23-August 24, 1964; JEH APPT, July 23-August 24, 1964; DeLoach to Mohr, "Special Squad," August 29, 1964, S5, FBI V 67-338728 (DeLoach). On the convention, see Watson, *Freedom Summer*, 237-61. On Hamer, see Blain, *Until I Am Free*.

12. DeLoach, *Hoover's FBI*, 7–9; DeLoach to Jenkins, "Morning Summary of Activities," August 26, 1964, FBI JFK 62-116395-1134-1145; DeLoach to Jenkins, "Afternoon Summary of Activity," August 25, 1964, FBI JFK 62-116395-1134-1145; Dallek, *Flawed Giant*, 162-3; DeLoach to Mohr, "Special Squad," August 29, 1964, S5, FBI V 67-338728 (DeLoach).

13. Hoover to DeLoach, September 1, 1964, S5, FBI V 67-338728 (DeLoach).

14. DeLoach, *Hoover's FBI*, 9; DeLoach to Hoover, September 8, 1964, S5, FBI V 67-338728 (DeLoach).

15. Kennedy to Tolson, September 2, 1964, S3, FBI V 9524-416 (Tolson); Apple, "Kennedy Quits," *NYT*, September 4, 1964.

16. Casey, "RFK Goodby," *BG*, September 4, 1964; DeLoach to Hoover, September 9, 1964, F135, B21, HO&C; Hoover to Jenkins, September 14, 1964, F135, B22, HO&C; "Summary Analysis," September 14, 1964, F135, B22, HO&C.

17. Untitled, *NatR*, October 13, 1964; O'Reilly, *"Racial Matters,"* 235.

18. Beschloss, *Reaching for Glory*, 54-84; Charles, *Hoover's War on Gays*, 269-77; Stewart-Winter, "The Fall of Walter Jenkins and the Hidden History of the Lavender Scare," in Canaday et al, *Intimate States*, 211-34.

19. Beschloss, *Reaching for Glory*, 76-7; Hoover, "Memorandum for Mr. Tolson," October 15, 1964, S1, FBI FOIA 161-2848-2 (Jenkins). Also see Goldwater to Hoover, October 19, 1964, S4, FBI FOIA 62-98961-227 (Goldwater); "Goldwater Asks," *WS*, October 20, 1964, B137, JEHS.

20. Beschloss, *Reaching for Glory*, 69-71.

21. Hoover, "Memorandum for Mr. Tolson," October 19, 1964, S1, FBI 161-2848-18 (Jenkins).

22. DeLoach to Mohr, "Walter Jenkins," October 16, 1964, S6, FBI FOIA 161-2848 (Jenkins); Untitled, Washington Capital News Service, October 21, 1964, B137, JEHS; Van Der Linden, "Did FBI Chief Really," *Jackson Daily News*, October 23, 1964, B137, JEHS; Franklin, "Hoover Assailed," *NYT*, October 28, 1964, B137, JEHS; Beale, "Barry Advises," *WS*, November 29, 1964, B137, JEHS.

23. Beschloss, *Reaching for Glory*, 90-2; "President Misused FBI," *NYDN*, October 24, 1964, B137, JEHS; Hoover, "Memorandum for Mr. Tolson," October 23, 1964, S2, FBI FOIA 161-2848-39 (Jenkins).

24. Hoover to Johnson, November 4, 1964, F: "11/23/63–11/30/64," FG135-6, B188, WHCF, LBJ.

Chapter 50: The Most Notorious Liar (1964–1965)

1. DeLoach to Mohr, "Sarah McClendon," November 5, 16, 1964, FBI JFK 62-116395-EBF-951.

2. DeLoach, *Hoover's FBI*, 203–5; "Hoover Raps Warren," *BS*, November 19, 1964, B137, JEHS; "Hoover Hits

Courts," *WS,* November 19, 1964, B137, JEHS; Branch, *Pillar of Fire,* 526.

3. Winchell, "It Takes All Kinds," *NYJA,* November 27, 1964, B137, JEHS.

4. For Katzenbach's account of his time as attorney general, see Katzenbach, *Some of It Was Fun.*

5. Katzenbach, *Some Of It Was Fun,* 186; Buchanan, "Hoover's Great," November 21, 1964, B137, JEHS.

6. Sterne, "Hoover Seen 'Faltering,'" *BS,* November 20, 1964, B137, JEHS; DeLoach to Mohr, "Val Coleman," November 19, 1964, FBI JFK 62-116395-1192-1200X.

7. "Memo to J. Edgar," *Medford Mail Tribune,* November 20, 1964, B137, JEHS; "Newsweek Says," *WP,* November 30, 1964, B137, JEHS; DeLoach to Mohr, "Ben Bradlee," December 1, 1964, FBI JFK 62-116395-EBF-1125.

8. Sterne, "Hoover Seen 'Faltering'"; Baumgardner to Sullivan, "Martin Luther King, Jr," November 20, 1964, FBI JFK 62-116395-1192-1200X; Branch, *Pillar of Fire,* 527; Sides, *Hellhound on His Trail,* 40.

9. McNair, "Society Sleuths," *WP,* November 21, 1964, B137, JEHS; Rosen to Belmont, "Telegram from Martin Luther King, Jr," November 20, 1964, S20, FBI FOIA 100-106670-581 (MLK).

10. Nixon to Hoover, November 30, 1964, F2, B20, PPS320, RN; Beschloss, *Reaching for Glory,* 149.

11. Bridge, "Talk of Replacing," *WP,* December 1, 1964; Halberstam, "Vantage Point," *NYT,* October 31, 1971. For doubts about the authenticity of the quote, see Demaris, *Director,* 232.

12. Wannall to Adams, "Senstudy 75," April 23, 1975, FBI JFK 62-116395-101-150; Garrow, "Troubling Legacy of Martin Luther King"; Young, *Easy Burden,* 327-8; "Work Paper: Recollections of SA Seymor Fred Phillips," April 29, 1975, FBI JFK 62-116395-1192-1200X; Anonymous to King, F24, B12, HO&C; Gage, "What an Uncensored Letter."

13. "Mrs. Lewis," *ChiT,* November 25, 1964, B137, JEHS; "Hoover Says," *WS,* November 25, 1964, B137, JEHS; Branch, *Pillar of Fire,* 529-30.

14. DeLoach to Mohr, "Roy Wilkins," November 27, 1964, FBI JFK 62-116395-1192-1200X; interview of Cartha DeLoach, FBI OH.

15. "Communism and the Negro Movement," November 27, 1964, FBI JFK 62-116395-EBF-951; Sullivan to Belmont, "Communism and the Negro Movement," October 18, 1963, FBI JFK 62-11639-726-810; Evans to Belmont, "Communism and the Negro Movement," October 25, 1963, FBI JFK 62-116395-340-347; Director to Attorney General, October 25, 1963, FBI JFK 62-116395-340-347; Hoover, "Memorandum to Mr. Tolson," October 25, 1963, FBI JFK 62-116395-340-347; Sizoo to Sullivan, "Communism and the Negro movement," October 25, 1963, FBI JFK 62-116395-340-347.

16. DeLoach to Mohr, "Martin Luther King," December 7, 1964, FBI JFK 62-116395-340-347; Hoover to McNamara, December 7, 1964, FBI JFK 62-116395-340-347; Hoover to Rusk, December 7, 1964, FBI JFK 62-116395-340-347; Hoover to Katzenbach, December 7, 1964, FBI JFK 62-116395-340-347. For planning, see Sullivan to Belmont, "Communism and the Negro Movement," November 27, 1964, FBI JFK 62-116395-726-810.

17. DeLoach to Mohr, "Martin Luther King," December 1, 1964, S21, FBI FOIA 100-106670-570 (MLK).

18. DeLoach to Mohr, "Martin Luther King," December 2, 1964, S21, FBI FOIA 100-106670 (MLK); Jones to DeLoach, "Martin Luther King, Jr.," December 1, 1964, S21,

FBI FOIA 100-106670-647 (MLK); Hoover, "Memorandum for Mr. Tolson," December 1, 1964, S19, FBI FOIA 100-106670-563 (MLK).

19. Branch, *Pillar of Fire,* 535; Sterne, "Early Arrests," *BS,* December 2, 1964, B137, JEHS.

20. Press release, December 4, 1964, B10, V13, P19 (FBI), DOJ Administrative History, LBJ; King, "Acceptance Speech," December 10, 1964, at https://www.nobelprize.org/prizes/peace/1964/king/lecture/.

21. Belmont, "Summary—Highly Sensitive Coverage," December 2, 1964, S105, FBI FOIA 100-106670-1024 (MLK); Baumgardner to Sullivan, "Martin Luther King, Jr.," November 30, 1964, FBI JFK 62-116395-1192-1200X; Legat London to Director, "Martin Luther King, Jr.," December 10, 1964, FBI JFK 62-116395-1192-1200X; Baumgardner to Sullivan, "Martin Luther King, Jr.," December 17, 1964, FBI JFK 62-116395-789-Bulky; untitled report, page begins "Nobel Peace Prize Junket," FBI JFK 62-116395-1153-Bulky.

22. Sullivan to Belmont, "Martin Luther King, Jr.," December 16, 1964, FBI JFK 62-117290-1321-Bulky; Baumgardner to Sullivan, "Martin Luther King, Jr., September 8, 1964, FBI JFK 62-117920-1321-Bulky; Martin, "Bureau Clergyman."

23. Katzenbach, *Some of It Was Fun,* 154-5; Montgomery, "Crystal Ball," *NYJA,* January 3, 1965, B137, JEHS.

24. "FBI Director Backed," *CR,* February 17, 1965, B138, JEHS; JEH APPT, March 9, 1965; Photo, *WS,* March 10, 1965, B138, JEHS; Jones to DeLoach, "General Wallace Martin Greene, Jr.," March 16, 1965, S3C, FBI V 62-78720 (Wilkins).

25. Garrow, *FBI and Martin Luther King, Jr.,* 133-4; Branch, *Pillar of Fire,* 556-7; Garrow, *Bearing the Cross,* 372-5.

Chapter 51: White Hate (1964–1965)

1. "Hoover Raps Warren," ca. November 19, 1964, B137, JEHS; DeLoach to Mohr, "Martin Luther King," December 2, 1964, FBI JFK 62-116395-EBF-951; Whitehead, *Attack on Terror,* 2.

2. Director to SAC Atlanta, "Counterintelligence Program," September 2, 1964, S1, FBI V 157-9-1 (COINTELPRO–White Hate).

3. Germany and Carter, *Presidential Recordings,* 8:393-4.

4. May, *Informant,* 115; Kantor, "White Racism," *WDN,* July 23, 1964, B137, JEHS; Shipp, *Murder at Broad River Bridge,* 14.

5. Germany and Carter, *Presidential Recordings,* 8:219.

6. Sullivan to Hoover, July 24, 1964, FBI JFK 62-116395-546. On COINTELPRO-White Hate, see especially Cunningham, *There's Something Happening Here*; Drabble, "To Ensure Domestic Tranquility."

7. Director to SAC Atlanta, "Counterintelligence Program," September 2, 1964, S1, FBI V 157-9-1 (COINTELPRO–White Hate).

8. Gale to Tolson, "Investigation of Ku Klux Klan," July 30, 1964, S1, FBI V 157-9 (COINTELPRO–White Hate).

9. Interview of Billy Bob Williams, FBI OH; Baumgardner to Sullivan, "Counterintelligence Program," January 19, 1965, S1, FBI V 157-9 (COINTELPRO–White Hate); Director to SAC Miami, "Counterintelligence Program," April 15, 1965, S1, FBI V 157-9 (COINTELPRO–White Hate); Baumgardner to Sullivan, "Counterintelligence Program," April 20, 1966, S1, FBI V 157-9 (COINTELPRO–White Hate); Cunningham, *There's Something Happening*

Here, 126, 124, 73–4; Baumgardner to Sullivan, "Counterintelligence Program," May 10, 1965, S1, FBI V 157-9-10 (COINTELPRO–White Hate); SAC Atlanta to Director, "Counterintelligence Program," October 14, 1964, Sub2, FBI 157-9 (COINTELPRO–White Hate); SAC Atlanta to Director, "Counterintelligence Program," October 14, 1964, Sub2, FBI V 157-9-2-9 (COINTELPRO–White Hate).

10. May, *Informant*, 310; Hoover to Katzenbach, September 2, 1965, S1, FBI V 157-9 (COINTELPRO–White Hate).

11. Director to SAC Atlanta, "Counterintelligence Program," March 15, 1965, Sub2, FBI V 157-9 (COINTELPRO–White Hate); Baumgardner to Sullivan, "Communist Party, USA," January 6, 1965, S1, FBI V 157-9 (COINTELPRO–White Hate).

12. Hoover to Moyers, February 3, 1965, S23, FBI FOIA 106700 (MLK); Branch, *Pillar of Fire*, 578–9; Closson and Bromwich, "J. Edgar Hoover Hid," *NYT*, November 18, 2021.

13. Branch, *At Canaan's Edge*, 49, 59; "Demonstrators Ejected," *Globe and Mail*, March 9, 1965; "From Rights Demonstrators," *Austin Statesman*, March 10, 1965; "Justice Dept. Routs," *Newsday*, March 9, 1965; "Thousands across Nation," *AC*, March 10, 1965.

14. Baumgardner to Sullivan, "Communist Party, USA," January 6, 1965, FBI V 157-9 (COINTELPRO–White Hate); SAC Jackson to Director, "Counterintelligence Program," January 28, 1965, FBI V 157-9-6 (COINTELPRO–White Hate); May, *Informant*, 118–24.

15. Belmont to Tolson, "Recent Shootings," August 31, 1965, S1, FBI V 157-9 (COINTELPRO–White Hate); JEH LOGS, March 15, 1965.

16. "Speed Action," *NYP*, March 16, 1965, B138, JEHS; JFH APPT, January 19, 1965; JEH LOGS, January 19, 1965; McCardle, "Mrs. LBJ," *WP*, March 16, 1965, B138, JEHS; Branch, *At Canaan's Edge*, 111–2.

17. Hoover, "Memorandum for Mr. Tolson," March 19, 1965, S3, FBI IA 44-28544 (Selma); Belmont to Tolson, "Forthcoming Civil Rights March," March 19, 1965, FBI IA 44-28544-177 (Selma).

18. Rosen to Belmont, "March from Selma," March 24, 1965, FBI IA 44-28544-275 (Selma); McGowan to Rosen, "March from Selma," March 24, 1965, FBI IA 44-28544-134 (Selma); McGowan to Rosen, "March from Selma," March 24, 1965, FBI IA 44-28544-218 (Selma); "March from Selma," March 22, 1965, FBI IA 44-28544-3 (Selma).

19. Branch, *At Canaan's Edge*, 164–70.

20. May, *Informant*, 146–7; "March from Selma," March 26, 1965, FBI IA 44-28544-287 (Selma).

21. LBJD, March 26, 1965; May, *Informant*, 166, 171; Beschloss, *Reaching for Glory*, 245–6, 248–9, 279; Branch, *At Canaan's Edge*, 177; "Transcript of Johnson's Statement on Alabama Arrests," *WP*, March 27, 1965, B138, JEHS.

22. May, *Informant*, 180–2, 253, 265.

23. May, *Informant*, 183; Hoover, "Memorandum for Mr. Tolson," December 3, 1965, FBI V [unnumbered] (Tolson); Davis, *Assault on the Left*, 7.

24. Interview of Ernest M. Cochrane, FBI OH; Katzenbach to Hoover, September 3, 1965, S1, FBI V 157-9 (COINTELPRO–White Hate).

Chapter 52: Hoover Knows Best (1965-1966)

1. JEH APPT, March 3, 1965; "Johnson and Chiefs Discuss Curb on Crime," *ChiT*, March 4, 1965, B138, JEHS.

2. Flamm, *Law and Order*, 35, 51–2.

3. Strout, "Law-and-Order Debate," *CSM*, September 14, 1968.

4. "U.S. Crime at Peak," *NYT*, March 1, 1961, B131, JEHS; "Serious Crimes Rise," *NYDN*, March 10, 1965, B138, JEHS; Flamm, *Law and Order*, 2; Justice Research and Statistics Association, "Historical Data," *Crime and Justice Atlas 2000*, https://www.jrsa.org/projects/Historical.pdf.

5. Hoover, "Message from the Director," *LEB*, November 1967; Pakenham, "13 Pct. Rise," *ChiT*, July 27, 1965, B139, JEHS.

6. Hoover, "Battlefield," *Army Digest*, October 1968, B144, JEHS.

7. Schumach, "Experts Say," *NYT*, March 22, 1965, B138, JEHS.

8. On the racial politics of crime and juvenile delinquency in the early 1960s, see Hinton, *From the War on Poverty to the War on Crime*. 27-95.

9. "Crime and Statistics," *WDN*, March 15, 1968, B225, JEHS.

10. Johnson, "Special Message to the Congress on the Needs of the Nation's Capital," February 15, 1965, American Presidency Project, https://www.presidency.ucsb.edu/documents/special-message-the-congress-the-needs-the-nations-capital; Flamm, *Law and Order*, 42; "Area Killings Double," *WS*, June 9, 1965, B138, JEHS.

11. Chipman, "Crime, Delinquency," April 28, 1963, B135, JEHS; "Extension of Remarks: Hon James Martin," *CR*, May 26, 1965, B138, JEHS. Also see Hinton, *From the War on Poverty to the War on Crime*; Flamm, *Law and Order*; Forman, *Locking Up Our Own*.

12. "Aroused Public," *DN*, March 22, 1963, B135, JEHS; "Who's to Blame?" *USNWR*, January 1, 1962, B133, JEHS; Hoover, "Message from the Director," *LEB*, November 1962.

13. "Hoover Raps Warren," ca. November 19, 1964, B137, JEHS; "J. Edgar Hoover Speaks," *Time*, December 14, 1970, B150, JEHS.

14. Johnson, "Special Message to the Congress on Law Enforcement and the Administration of Justice," March 8, 1965, American Presidency Project, https://www.presidency.ucsb.edu/documents/special-message-the-congress-law-enforcement-and-the-administration-justice.

15. Pakenham, "13 Pct. Rise," *ChiT*, July 27, 1965, B139, JEHS; Hinton, *From the War on Poverty to the War on Crime*, 80-8; Flamm, *Law and Order*, 51. On the militarization of police in the 1960s, also see Schrader, *Badges without Borders*; Camp, *Incarcerating the Crisis*.

16. Hoover, "Memorandum for Personal Files," June 14, 1966, F37, B13, HO&C; [Redacted] to Trotter, "Courtney A. Evans," October 12, 1965, P6, FBI 67-163462-305 (Evans).

17. "Department of Justice During the Administration of President Lyndon B. Johnson," B10, V13, P19 (FBI), DOJ Administrative History, LBJ; "Message from the Director," *LEB*, January 1967.

18. Casper to Mohr, "Joseph I. Woods," November 28, 1966, FBI JFK 62-116395-EBF-1125; interview of Cartha DeLoach, FBI OH; Hoover, "Memorandum for Mr. Tolson," May 26, 1965, P7, FBI V [unnumbered] (Tolson); Leary, "$10 Million Expansion," *WS*, May 27, 1965, B138, JEHS.

19. Pakenham, "13 Pct. Rise," *ChiT*, July 27, 1965, B139, JEHS; Hinton, *From the War on Poverty to the War on Crime*, 80-3; Ottenberg, "Johnson Gives Backing," *WS*, September 8, 1965, B139, JEHS.

20. Powers, *G-Men,* 229-254; interview of Cartha DeLoach, FBI OH; Warner Bros. to DeLoach, April 13, 1966, F3, B4, HO&C; O'Leary, "The FBI,' *WS,* January 2, 1972, B158, JEHS; Warner Bros. to DeLoach, December 11, 1964, F3, B4, HO&C; Roberts, "Authentic FBI Series," *Boston Traveler,* January 13, 1965, B138, JEHS; Hagerty to Hoover, January 12, 1965, F: "FBI 1965-1973," B125, JH; Memo, July 28, 1965, F: "FBI 1965-1973," B125, JH; JEH LOGS, January 11, 1965; Gould, "Is J. Edgar Hoover Using TV," *MJ,* February 21, 1965, B138, JEHS.

21. Molloy, "ABC Will Push," *Miami Herald,* February 5, 1965, B138, JEHS; Gould, "Is J. Edgar Hoover Using?" ; Hoppe, "Scram, Acidosis," *SFC,* March 5, 1965, B138, JEHS.

22. Kondracke, "Zimbalist Plugs," *WS,* June 15, 1971, B155, JEHS; Donnelly, "The FBI Gives TV," April 28, 1965, *WDN,* B138, JEHS; Rich, Untitled, *Citizen News,* July 9, 1965, B139, JEHS; Turner, "FBI Will Have Human," *Chicago Daily News,* June 29, 1965, B138, JEHS.

23. Nichols to Hoover, September 27, 1965, S7, FBI FOIA 67-39021-745 (Nichols); Adams, "'Bonanza' Leads," *NYT,* October 12, 1965, B139, JEHS; Boyle, "'The FBI' Rated," *WS,* October 25, 1965, B139, JEHS.

24. Laurrent, "Premier of 'The FBI,'" *WP,* September 20, 1965, B139, JEHS; "Zimbalist," *WP,* July 24, 1966, B140, JEHS; "Ho Hum!" *News-Dispatch,* February 17, 1972, B229, JEHS; Bishop to DeLoach, "ABC-TV Series," November 7, 1969, S6, FBI 67-338728 (DeLoach).

25. Katzenbach, *Some of It Was Fun,* 182-7; Administrative History of the Department of Justice: Wiretapping and Electronic Surveillance," November 1963-January 1969, F: "Wiretapping," B139, Personal Papers of Ramsey Clark, LBJ; Hoover to Gross, December 7, 1966, P6, FBI V 67-163462 (Evans); Belmont to Tolson, "Long Committee," February 27, 1965, FBI JFK 62-116395-1428-Bulky.

26. Charns, *Cloak and Gavel,* 36-63; Theoharis and Cox, *Boss,* 368-95; DeLoach to Tolson, June 14, 1966, F37, B13, HO&C. On Long, see Hochman, *Listeners,* 179–92.

27. Hoover, "Memorandum for Mr. Tolson," July 14, 1965, FBI JFK 62-116395-EBF-752X; Theoharis and Cox, *Boss,* 360-8; Stockham, *Lack of Oversight,* 250-4.

28. CC2, 109-10; Katzenbach, *Some of It Was Fun,* 182-3; Sullivan to Belmont, September 30, 1965, FBI JFK 62-116395-EBJ-752X; Sullivan to DeLoach, July 19, 1966, FBI JFK 62-116395-1428-Bulky; Sullivan to DeLoach, "'Black Bag' Jobs," July 19, 1966, F36, B13, HO&C; Hoover, "Memorandum for Mr. Tolson," January 6, 1967, B13, F36, HO&C; Miller to Conrade, "Senate Subcommittee on Administrative Practice," July 26, 1965, FBI JFK 62-116395-EBF-752X.

29. Felt, *FBI Pyramid,* 101; "Re: Request Pertaining to Surreptitious Entries," October 17, 1975, FBI JFK 62-116395-837-1037; Sullivan to Belmont, September 30, 1965, FBI JFK 62-116395-EBJ-752X; Director to New SAC New York, "Telephone Surveillances," November 29, 1966, FBI JFK 62-116395-EBJ-1008.

30. Roemer, *Roemer,* 227; CCH2, 97.

31. CC3, 931-2; CCH2, 97; "Service Award," *WS,* B142, JEHS; Bonner, "Sam Noisette," December 23, 1972, *WP;* Adams to Callahan, "Helen W. Gandy," February 20, 1967, S3, FBI 67-3654 (Gandy), S-JEHC; Gandy to Hoover, February 24, 1967, S3, FBI 67-3654 (Gandy), S-JEHC; Hoover to Gandy, February 24, 1967, FBI 67-3654 (Gandy), S-JEHC.

32. "J. Edgar Hoover Speaks," *Time,* December 14, 1970, B150, JEHS; interview of Thomas E. Bishop, FBI OH.

33. Powers, *Secrecy and Power,* 356; Gentry, *J. Edgar Hoover,* 692, 650; Hoover to McGaughey, July 29, 1966, F66, B1, EMG; Hoover to McGaughey, August 9, 1966, F66, B1, EMG; Hersh, *Bobby and J. Edgar,* 217.

34. "Remarks of J. Edgar Hoover," October 19, 1965, F7, B1, NLEM; "J. Edgar Hoover Presented," *KAJ,* January 1967, B141, JEHS.

35. Jones to DeLoach, "Proposal," S6, FBI NARA 67-561 (Hoover); "J. Edgar Hoover Window," PB80, NLEM; Hoover to McGaughey, June 27, 1966, F66, B1, EMG.

36. Washington Capital News Service, May 23, 1965, B138, JEHS; Hoover to Johnson, June 2, 1965, F12/1/64-1/13/67, FG135-6, B188, WHCF, LBJ.

37. Katzenbach, *Some of It Was Fun,* 183; Clark, *Crime in America,* 81–2.

38. Hoover, "Memorandum for Mr. Tolson," December 9, 1965, S6, FBI V 67-338728-471 (DeLoach); interview of Cartha DeLoach, FBI OH; Hoover, "Memorandum for Mr. Tolson," March 25, 1966, FBI V [unnumbered] (Tolson).

39. DeLoach to Hoover, April 8, 1965, S6, FBI V 67-338728-460 (DeLoach); Cook, *FBI Nobody Knows,* 1; Powers, *Secrecy and Power,* 362–3.

40. Casper to Mohr, "W. Mark Felt," October 24, 1962, S4, FBI FOIA 67-276567-330 (Felt); Hoover, "Memorandum for Mr. Tolson," October 29, 1962, S4, FBI FOIA 67-276576-331 (Felt).

41. Malone to Mohr, "[Redacted], Special Agent," September 7, 1961, S4, FBI FOIA 67-276576 (Felt); Hoover to Felt, September 12, 1961, S4, FBI FOIA 67-276576-296 (Felt); Basham, "FBI Clerk," *WS,* September 20, 1967, B142, JEHS; "Court Urged," *WP,* September 21, 1967, B142, JEHS; "Sex and the Single FBI Man," *SFC,* September 21, 1967, B142, JEHS; Hoppe, "Mr. Hoover's Unkissed Agents," *WS,* September 25, 1967, B142, JEHS; Cook, *FBI Nobody Knows,* 11.

42. Hoover, "How J. Edgar Hoover Felt," *TV Guide,* May 20, 1972, 30; Powers, *G-Men,* 244.

Chapter 53: Commies in Colleges (1965–1967)

1. "Vietnam War Allied Troop Levels 1960–73," American War Library, https://www.americanwarlibrary.com/vietnam/vwatl.htm; Johnson, "The President's News Conference: Why We Are in Viet-Nam," July 28, 1965, American Presidency Project, https://www.presidency.ucsb.edu/documents/the-presidents-news-conference-1038. For the Dominican Republic, see Weiner, *Enemies,* 253-63. For COINTELPRO, see FBI V 105-93124 (COINTELPRO Puerto Rican Groups).

2. Hoover to Watson, May 3, 1965, P86, FBI V 100-428091 (SOLO).

3. "Soviet Comments Regarding President Johnson," June 19, 1964, P64, FBI V 100-428091 (SOLO); Hoover to Moyers, January 7, 1965, P80, FBI V 100-428091 (SOLO); Baumgardner to Sullivan, "SOLO," July 9, 1965, P91, FBI V 100-428091 (SOLO); Director to SAC Chicago, "SOLO," February 8, 1961, FBI V 100-428091-1178 (SOLO).

4. SDS, *Port Huron Statement.*

5. Rosenfeld, *Subversives,* 203–4; SAC New York to Director, "Students for a Democratic Society," December 2, 1964, S1, FBI G 100-439048 (SDS).

6. "Students for a Democratic Society," April 29, 1965, S5, FBI G 100-439048 (SDS); CC3, 484–6.

7. Beschloss, *Reaching for Glory,* 292–3, 295.

8. Rosenfeld, *Subversives,* 227, 237–41; Hoover, "Memorandum for Mr. Tolson," January 28, 1965, S7, FBI V unnumbered (Tolson).

9. Rosenfeld, *Subversives*, 253; van der Heuvel, "Warns of Big Increase," *NYDN*, May 18, 1965, B138, JEHS; Baumgardner to Sullivan, "House Committee on Un-American Activities," May 25, 1965, S6, FBI G 100-439048 (SDS); Beschloss, *Reaching for Glory*, 295–6; Davis, *Assault on the Left*, 32.

10. SAC Chicago to Director, "Students for a Democratic Society (SDS)," June 7, 1965, S6, FBI G 100-439048-308 (SDS).

11. Baumgardner to Sullivan, "Communist Infiltration," October 22, 1965, S12, FBI G 100-439048 (SDS); report on "Students for a Democratic Society," ca. October 1965, S12, FBI G 100-439048 (SDS); Cromley, "Record of Protest," ca. October 22, 1965, S12, FBI G 100-439048 (SDS).

12. Baumgardner to Sullivan, "Communist Infiltration," May 18, 1965, S5, FBI G 100-439048 (SDS); Director to Attorney General, "Students for a Democratic Society," May 19, 1965, S5, FBI G 100-439048 (SDS); Jones to Wick, "Communist Infiltration," August 11, 1966, S19, FBI G 100-439048 (SDS); "Students for a Democratic Society," August 11, 1966, S19, FBI G 100-439048 (SDS).

13. "Students for a Democratic Society," May 13, 1965, S5, FBI G 100-439048 (SDS); Baumgardner to Sullivan, "Communist Infiltration," August 2, 1966, S19, FBI G 100-439048 (SDS).

14. Joseph, *Waiting 'til the MIdnight Hour*, 137; Branch, *At Canaan's Edge*, 59–65; Hoover to Johnson, July 26, 1967, SMG. On SNCC, also see especially Carson, *In Struggle*; Ransby, *Ella Baker and the Black Freedom Movement*, 252–369; Joseph, *Stokely*, 45–148.

15. On Carmichael, see especially Joseph, *Waiting 'til the Midnight Hour*, 118–73; Joseph, *Stokely,* 1–124. For "damn thing," see "Stokely Carmichael," July 13, 1966, P1, FBI V 100-446808-2X (Carmichael).

16. Baker and Albright, "Shooting Spurs Rights," *WP*, June 8, 1966, B140, JEHS; Joseph, *Stokely*, 2; Joseph, *Waiting 'til the Midnight Hour*, 142.

17. DeLoach to Tolson, "Stokely Carmichael," August 10, 1966, P1, FBI V 100-446080 (Carmichael).

18. "Telephone Surveillances Denied by the Attorney General," ca. April 1, 1968, F: "Federal Bureau of Investigation, Volume 1," B29, National Security File, LBJ; Joseph, *Waiting 'til the Midnight Hour*, 164–5; "Stokely Carmichael," September 3, 1966, P5, FBI V 100-446 (Carmichael); Hoover to Stegall, March 24, 1967, F: "Student Nonviolent Coordinating Committee (Stokely Carmichael) Jan.–Nov. 1967," B73B, Office Files of Mildred Stegall, LBJ; "Student Nonviolent Coordinating Committee," April 21 and May 17, 1967, F: "Student Nonviolent Coordinating Committee (Stokely Carmichael) Jan.–Nov. 1967."

19. Kling, "Carmichael Linked," *ChiT*, May 17, 1967.

20. "Carmichael on Hoover," *WP*, May 18, 1967, B142, JEHS.

21. Gillon, *Separate and Unequal,* 4; Hoover testimony, August 1, 1967, SMG. For police violence and urban uprisings, see Hinton, *America on Fire*.

22. LBJD, July 24, 1967; Hoover, "Memorandum for Mr. Tolson," July 25, 1967, S8, FBI V unnumbered (Tolson); "Address to the Nation Regarding Civil Disorder, 7/24/67. MP593," YouTube video, 7:51, posted by TheLBJLibrary, May 23, 2012, https://www.youtube.com/watch?v=ZTpz4ti2Gc4; LBJ-T 12005.

23. Hoover to Johnson, July 26, 1967, SMG.

24. Gillon, *Separate and Unequal*, 45, 80–1.

25. Hoover testimony, August 1, 1967, SMG; Hoover,

"Memorandum for Personal Files," July 31, 1967, S8, FBI V [unnumbered] (Tolson); JEH APPT, August 3, 1967.

26. *Report of the National Advisory Commission on Civil Disorders*, 1, vii.

27. Hoover, "Memorandum for Mr. Tolson," June 20, 1968, FBI 44-38861-4660, reprinted in MLK-HSAC, V7, 88–94; Director to SAC Albany, "Counterintelligence Program," August 25, 1967, S1, FBI V 100-448006 (COINTELPRO–Black Extremist); Brennan to Sullivan, "Counterintelligence Program," May 9, 1968, S1, FBI V 100-44968 (COINTELPRO–New Left).

Chapter 54: Messiah (1968)

1. LBJD, July 26, 1967.

2. Washington Capital News Service, untitled, September 28, 1966, B140, JEHS; LBJD, September 22, 1966; photo, F2204, B54, NARA-P; LBJ-T 10286.

3. Theoharis and Cox, *Boss*, 399; Hoover to Watson, March 3, 1966, F: "12/1/64–1/13/56," FG135-6, B188, WHCF, LBJ; SAC New York to Director, "SOLO," March 21, 1968, P122/S94, FBI V 100-428091-6837 (SOLO).

4. LBJ-T 12715.

5. Goodwin, *Lyndon Johnson and the American Dream*, 359.

6. Johnson, "President's Address," March 31, 1968, at American Presidency Project, https://www.presidency.ucsb.edu/documents/the-presidents-address-the-nation-announcing-steps-limit-the-war-vietnam-and-reporting-his; DeLoach, *Hoover's FBI*, 395.

7. Hoover to Johnson, April 1, 1968, F: "Hoover, J. Edgar," B388, WHCF, LBJ.

8. Young, *Easy Burden,* 463-5; Sides, *Hellhound on his Trail,* 168, 193; DeLoach, *Hoover's FBI*, 223. For a comprehensive account of the King assassination investigation, see Sides, *Hellhound on His Trail*. Where not otherwise cited, details of the investigation can be found in this source.

9. Garrow, *FBI and Martin Luther King, Jr.*, 182; HSCA MLK, 7:141; DeLoach to Tolson, "Martin Luther King," January 19, 1968, FBI JFK 62-117290-132-Bulky; DeLoach to Mohr, "Senator Strom Thurmond," September 15, 1965, S2, FBI FOIA 62-52026-85 (Thurmond); Young, *Easy Burden*, 434.

10. Sullivan to DeLoach, "Martin Luther King's," March 30, 1968, FBI JFK 620117290-1321-Bulky.

11. Director to SAC Albany, "Counterintelligence Program," March 4, 1968, S1, FBI V 100-448006 (COINTELPRO–Black Extremist).

12. Lane and Gregory, *Murder in Memphis*, 108; Moore to Sullivan, "Sanitation Workers Strike," March 28, 1968, S80, FBI FOIA 100-106670 (MLK); Moore to Sullivan, "Counterintelligence Program," March 29, 1968, FBI JFK 62-117290-1321-Bulky.

13. King, "I've Been to the Mountaintop," April 3, 1968, in Carson and Shepard, *A Call to Conscience*, 222.

14. DeLoach, *Hoover's FBI*, 223–5.

15. Sides, *Hellhound on His Trail*, 201, 207; interview of Robert Fitzpatrick, FBI OH; Jevons to Conrad, "Unknown Subject," April 5, 1968, S2, FBI MFF 44-38861 (MURKIN); DeLoach, *Hoover's FBI*, 226.

16. HSCA, 7:122.

17. Sides, *Hellhound on His Trail,* 231-2, 245–8; DeLoach, *Hoover's FBI*, 229.

18. Jevons to Conrad, "Unknown Subject," April 5, 1968, S2, FBI MFF 44-38861 (MURKIN).

19. HSCA-MLK, 4:236-240; Lauterbach, *Bluff City*, 201–8, 107–98.

20. Sides, *Hellhound on his Trail*, 280.

21. Johnson, *Vantage Point*, 538; Flamm, *Law and Order*, 146.

22. Washington Capital News Service, "Clark 4/11 NX," FBI JFK 62-117290-1321-Bulky; Rosen to DeLoach, "MURKIN," April 11, 1968, S7, FBI MFF 44-38861-820 (MURKIN).

23. Sides, *Hellhound on His Trail*, 320–1, 326; "For Immediate Release," April 19, 1968, F24, B12, HO&C.

24. HSCA-MLK, 7:8-13; Director to SAC Albany, "Counterintelligence Program," May 28, 1968, S1, FBI V 100-449698 (COINTELPRO–New Left).

25. "Ouster of Hoover," *Milwaukee Journal*, April 29, 1968, B143, JEHS; Lomax, "King Killer," publication unknown, ca. May 1968, B143, JEHS; "Replace Hoover," *BS*, April 22, 1968, B143, JEHS.

26. Brennan to Sullivan, "Martin Luther King," April 18, 1968, S106, FBI FOIA 100-106670 (MLK); Pearson, *Washington Merry-Go-Round*, 578, 580–1; Pearson and Anderson, "Kennedy Ordered," *WP*, May 24, 1968, B143, JEHS; DeLoach to Tolson, "Approval of Wire Taps," May 21, 1968, FBI JFK 62-116395-1153-Bulky; Ritchie, *Columnist*, 252-5.

27. Hoover, "Memorandum for Mr. Tolson," June 5, 1968, P10, FBI V unnumbered (Tolson).

28. Sides, *Hellhound on his Trail*, 351–71.

29. DeLoach, *Hoover's FBI*, 250; interview of Cartha DeLoach, FBI OH.

30. O'Leary, "Scotland Yard," *WS*, June 9, 1968, B143, JEHS.

31. Andrews, "Capture of James Earl Ray," *CR*, June 10, 1968, B143, JEHS; Hruska, "Commendation," *CR*, June 10, 1968, B143, JEHS; Byrd, "Capture of James Earl Ray," *CR*, June 10, 1968, B143, JEHS.

32. Belli, untitled, *Daily Mirror*, June 19, 1968, B143, JEHS.

33. DeLoach to Tolson, "Murkin," June 8, 1968, FBI JFK 62-117290-1321-Bulky; interview of Kenneth Bounds, FBI OH; Hoover, "Memorandum for Mr. Tolson," June 20, 1968, P10, FBI V [unnumbered[(Tolson); Vinson to Director, "James Earl Ray," July 17, 1968, S66, FBI MFF 44-38861 (Murkin); Hoover, "Memorandum for Mr. Tolson," July 16, 1968, S65, FBI MFF 44-38861-4852 (Murkin); Rosen to DeLoach, "Murkin," July 26, 1968, S1, FBI FOIA 67-175282 (Hanes).

34. DeLoach to Tolson, "Murkin," July 16, 1968, S65, FBI MFF 44-38861-4889 (Murkin); Rosen to DeLoach, "Murkin," July 18, 1968, S65, FBI MFF 44-38861-4893 (Murkin).

35. JEH APPT, July 18, 1968; JEH LOGS, July 18–19, 1968; DeLoach, *Hoover's FBI*, 253–4; Sides, *Hellhound on His Trail*, 382–3; Ray, 24.

36. HSCA Report, 5–6. For alternate theories of the assassination, see Pepper, *The Plot to Kill King;* Weisberg, *Frame-Up*; Nelson, *Who Really Killed Martin Luther King, Jr.?*; Lane and Gregory, *Murder in Memphis*.

37. HSCA-MLK, 7:4, 7:61.

Chapter 55: Nixon's the One (1968–1969)

1. "Remarks of Richard Nixon," November 7, 1962, https://cdn.nixonlibrary.org/01/wp-content/uploads/2017/07/24093803/1962-Last-Press-Conference.pdf; Nixon, *RN*, 238, 595–6; Hoover to Nixon, November 7, 1962, F1, B20, PPS320, RN; Hoover to Nixon, December 12, 1960, F13, B19, PPS320, RN.

2. Nixon to Hoover, April 6, 1963, F2, B20, PPS320, RN; Hoover to Julie Nixon, August 24, 1961, F14, B19, PPS320, RN.

3. Nixon, *RN*, 252–3; Nixon to Hoover, November 30, 1964, F2: "Hoover, J. Edgar," B20, PPS320, RN.

4. Dudman, *Men of the Far Right*, 163.

5. Rafferty, "American Civil Liberties Union," *Florida Times-Union*, August 21, 1967, B142, JEHS; Ledbetter, "Max L. Rafferty," *NYT*, June 14, 1982.

6. "J. Edgar Hoover Cited," *Herald Examiner* (Los Angeles), October 19, 1964, B137, JEHS; Jones to DeLoach, "Tenth Anniversary," April 9, 1965, S3, FBI FOIA 100-425828-99 (American Security Council); "American Security Council Honors 11," *Chicago Sun Times*, April 29, 1965, B138, JEHS; Olofson, "FBI Chief Tells," *Omaha World-Herald*, February 7, 1964, B136, JEHS; Akers, "Young life," *Gazette Telegraph* (Colorado Springs), February 16, 1964, B136, JEHS; "Right-Wing Group," *Chicago Daily News*, August 20, 1965, B139, JEHS; Gallup, "3 of 100 in GOP," *NYHT*, December 19, 1965, B139, JEHS.

7. Smith, "Nixon on Nixon," *NYT*, September 4, 1966; Perlstein, *Nixonland*, 173–4, 283.

8. Scammon and Wattenberg, *Real Majority*, 39.

9. Nixon, "What Has Happened to America?," *Reader's Digest*, October 1967; Perlstein, *Nixonland*, 202, 232, 235.

10. "Ceremonial to Honor," *Mobile Press-Register*, May 5, 1968, B143, JEHS; SAC Mobile to Director, "Alabama Circuit Judge George Wallace," March 6, 1956, S1, FBI FOIA 62-102939-8 (Wallace); Carter, *Politics of Rage*, 354; O'Reilly, *"Racial Matters,"* 172; "Wallace Strategists Happy," *WS*, September 17, 1968, B144, JEHS.

11. Perlstein, *Nixonland*, 224; Nixon, "What Has Happened to America?"; "Nixon Would Use Force," *NYT*, March 8, 1968; Semple, "Nixon Telethon Ends," *NYT*, May 27, 1968; Nixon, "Address Accepting the Presidential Nomination at the Republican National Convention in Miami Beach, Florida," August 8, 1968, American Presidency Project, https://www.presidency.ucsb.edu/documents/address-accepting-the-presidential-nomination-the-republican-national-convention-miami; Hoover, "Message from the Director," *LEB*, August 1968.

12. Nixon, "Address Accepting the Presidential Nomination."

13. Kohlmeier, "Hoover Loses," *WSJ*, October 10, 1968, B144, JEHS.

14. Hope, "Nixon Confident," *WS*, May 27, 1968, B143, JEHS; "Nixon Advisers Named," *NYT*, July 25, 1968.

15. Cheshire, "The Director and the Foundation," *WP*, June 1, 1969, B146, JEHS; DeLoach to Jones, "Freedoms Foundation," August 10, 1964, S7, FBI FOIA 67-39021 (Nichols); "Snow Job," *Philadelphia*, February 1968, B143, JEHS.

16. Nixon to Nichols, November 8, 1961 and August 31, 1962, F: "Nichols," B560, PPS320, RN; Cheshire, "The Director and the Foundation," *WP*, June 1, 1969, B146, JEHS.

17. Nichols to Hoover, January 9, 1968, S7, FBI FOIA 67-39021-756 (Nichols); JEH APPT, January 18, 1968; Jones to Bishop, "Louis B. Nichols," January 12, 1968, S7, FBI FOIA 67-39021-755 (Nichols).

18. Winchell, "$1 Million Gift," *NYDN*, May 31, 1968, B143, JEHS; Cheshire, "The Director and the Foundation," *WP*, June 1, 1969, B146, JEHS; JEH APPT, May 8, August 19, 1968; Ehrlichman, *Witness to Power*, 156–7.

19. Untitled, *Parade*, *WP*, August 11, 1968, B144, JEHS; DeLoach to Tolson, "Democratic National Convention," August 7, 1968, FBI JFK 62-11695-1428; Hoover, "Memorandum for Mr. Tolson," August 15, 1968, FBI JFK 62-11695-1428; DeLoach to Tolson, "Democratic National Convention," August 22, 1968, FBI JFK 62-11695-1428.

20. Johnson, "Bosses Strike Back," *Smithsonian*, August 2008.

21. Temple to Johnson, September 6, 1968, F7/1/68, B188, FG 135-6, WHCF, LBJ; Leach, "Hoover Backs Chicago," *Chicago American*, September 18, 1968, B144, JEHS; "FBI Chief Defends," *Herald and News*, September 18, 1968, B144, JEHS.

22. "Investigations," *Time*, September 27, 1968, B144, JEHS; Thomasson, "Hoover Asked to Quit," *WDN*, September 19, 1968, B144, JEHS; "81% in a Poll," *NYT*, September 10, 1968.

23. Hoover, "Memorandum for Mr. Tolson," October 29, 1968, FBI JFK 62-116395-551-Bulky; DeLoach to Tolson, "Call from Bromley Smith," October 29, 1968, FBI JFK 62-116395-551-Bulky; Hoover, "Memorandum for the Attorney General," October 29, 1968, FBI JFK 62-116395-551-Bulky; Hoover to White House Situation, October 30, 1968–November 8, 1968, FBI JFK 62-116395-551-Bulky; DeLoach to Tolson, "Embassy of South Vietnam," October 30, 1968, FBI JFK 62-116395-551-Bulky; DeLoach to Tolson, "Check of Phone Calls," November 19, 1968; DeLoach to [illegible], "Embassy of [Redacted]," November 4, 1968, FBI JFK 62-116395-551-Bulky. On the Chennault affair, see especially Hughes, *Chasing Shadows*, and Locker, *Nixon's Gamble*, 2–12.

24. "Everybody Bugs Everybody," at https://millercenter .org/the-presidency/secret-white-house-tapes/everybody -bugs-everybody-else; Kohlmeier, "Hoover Loses Immunity," *WSJ*, October 10, 1968, B144, JEHS; Sunderland, "Agnew Says," *BS*, September 12, 1968, B144, JEHS; Stewart, "The Happy Hatchet Man," *BG*, September 12, 1968; Perlstein, *Nixonland*, 349; Nixon, *RN*, 321.

25. Dietsch, "Poll Watching Record," *WP*, November 2, 1968, B144, JEHS; "A Nixon Aide," *NYT*, October 29, 1968, B144, JEHS; Rottenberg, "Each Party Strives," *WSJ*, November 4, 1968.

26. Perlstein, *Nixonland*, 354; Flamm, *Law and Order*, 2.

27. Lyons, "Lyons Den," *NYP*, November 11, 1968, B144, JEHS.

28. JEH APPT, November 12, 1968; Hoover to Johnson, November 12, 1968, F7/1/68, B188, FG 135-6, WHCF, LBJ; LBJD, December 12, 1968; Nixon, *RN*, 357–8.

29. JEH APPT, November 14, 1968; Ehrlichman, *Witness to Power*, 156.

30. Untitled, Washington Capital News Service, December 30, 1968, B144, JEHS; Untitled photo, *WP*, January 21, 1969, B145, JEHS; "President Richard Nixon's Daily Diary," January 29, 1969, Richard Nixon Presidential Library and Museum, https://www.nixonlibrary.gov/sites /default/files/virtuallibrary/documents/PDD/001 %20January%2021-31%201969.pdf; Untitled, Washington Capital News Service, January 30, 1969, B145, JEHS; Ehrlichman to Wong, January 25, 1969, F1, B3, FG 17-5, WHCF, RN.

31. DeLoach, *Hoover's FBI*, 407–8; Callahan to Mohr, "Salaries of FBI Director," February 14, 1969, B2, S7, FBI NARA 67-561 (Hoover); JEH APPT, March 14, 1969; Hoover to Nixon, April 28, 1969, and Tolson to Nixon, April 29, 1969, F1, B3, FG 17-5, WHCF, RN; "Nixon Calls FBI Chief," April 26, 1969, *WP*, B146, JEHS; Untitled, Washington Capital News Service, April 26, 1969, B146, JEHS; Haldeman, *Haldeman Diaries*, 53.

32. Chapin, "Memorandum for Mr. Hugh Sloan," March 27, 1969, F1, B3, FG 17-5, WHCF, RN; "Alabamian Gets Nixon," *Birmingham News*, May 29, 1969, B146, JEHS.

33. Nixon, "President Nixon urges," *LEB*, July 1969; "Respect for Laws," *Birmingham News*, May 29, 1969, B146, JEHS.

34. "Nixon Lauds Graduates," *Milwaukee Journal*, May 29, 1969, B146, JEHS.

35. Ehrlichman, *Witness to Power*, 160-2; Untitled, Washington Capital News Service, October 1, 1969, B147, JEHS.

36. Hauk to Nixon, October 3, 1969, FG 17-5, F1, B3, Subject Files, WHCF, RN.

Chapter 56: The Gospel of Nihilism (1969–1970)

1. Director to SAC Baltimore, "Counterintelligence Program," ca. November 1968, S5, FBI V 100448006-482 (COINTELPRO–Black Extremist).

2. Hoover, "Message from the Director," *LEB*, September 1, 1968. For "anarchistic," also see "U.S. Violence," *Houston Chronicle*, June 23, 1968, B143, JEHS; Hoover, "Analysis of the New Left," *Christianity Today*, August 18, 1967, B142, JEHS.

3. CC3, 492-493; FBI, "Development of Racial Informants," September 1967, FBI IA monograph, 10; Director to SAC Albany, "Counterintelligence Program," August 25, 1967, S1, FBI V 100-448006 (COINTELPRO–Black Extremist). For Panther history, see especially Murch, *Living for the City*; Williams, *From the Bullet to the Ballot*; Malloy, *Out of Oakland*; Nelson, *Black Panthers*; Bloom, *Black Against Empire*; Rhodes, *Framing the Black Panthers*; Self, *American Babylon*.

4. SAC SFO to Director, "Counterintelligence Program," October 27, 1967, S1, FBI V 100-448006 (COINTELPRO–Black Extremist); SAC Albany to Director, "Counterintelligence Program," May 29, 1968, S2, FBI V 100-448006 (COINTELPRO–Black Extremist); Director to SAC Albany, "Counterintelligence Program," June 12, 1968, S2, FBI V 100-448006 (COINTELPRO–Black Extremist). On the policing of breakfast and community programs, see especially Murch, *Living for the City*, 169-190.

5. Director to SAC Albany, "Counterintelligence Program," March 4, 1968, S1, FBI V 100-448006 (COINTELPRO–Black Extremist); Joseph, *Waiting 'til the Midnight Hour*, 225; Director to SAC Boston, "Counterintelligence Program," February 8, 1968, S1, FBI V 100-448066 (COINTELPRO–Black Extremist).

6. SAC New York to Director, "Counterintelligence Program," June 26, 1968, S2, FBI V 100-448006 (COINTELPRO–Black Extremist); Joseph, *Stokely*, 84.

7. Director to SAC New York, "Counterintelligence Program," July 10, 1968, S2, FBI V 100-448006 (COINTELPRO–Black Extremist); SAC Los Angeles to Director, "Counterintelligence Program," August 30, 1968, S3, FBI V 100-448006 (COINTELPRO–Black Extremist); "Hoover Calls Panthers," *WP*, July 16, 1969, B147, JEHS.

8. Director to SAC San Francisco, "Counterintelligence Program," May 2, 1969, S9, FBI V 448006-406 (COINTELPRO–Black Extremist); Joseph, *Waiting 'til the Midnight Hour*, 243.

9. Director to SAC Albany, "Counterintelligence Program," August 25, 1967, S1, FBI V 100-448006 (COINTELPRO–Black Extremist); Director to SAC San Francisco, "Counterintelligence Program," July 11, 1969, S11, FBI V 100-448006-1116 (COINTELPRO–Black Extremist); Director to SAC San Francisco, "Counterintelligence Program," May 27, 1969, S10, FBI V 100-448006-964 (COINTELPRO–Black Extremist); Director to SAC San Diego, "Counterintelligence Program," June 17, 1969, S11, FBI V 100-448006 (COINTELPRO–Black Extremist).

10. SAC Philadelphia to Director, "Counterintelligence Program," August 30, 1967, S1, FBI V 100-448006 (COINTELPRO–Black Extremist); SAC New York to Director, "Counterintelligence Program," August 7, 1968, S5, FBI V 100-448006-228 (COINTELPRO–Black Extremist).

11. Director to SAC Baltimore, "Counterintelligence Program," ca. November 1968, S8, FBI V 100-448006 (COINTELPRO–Black Extremist); SAC Los Angeles to Director, "Counterintelligence Program," March 17, 1969, S8, FBI V 100-448006 (COINTELPRO–Black Extremist).

12. "Panther Seal Charges Spies," SFC, April 8, 1969, B146, JEHS.

13. Director to SAC San Francisco, "Counterintelligence Program," May 28, 1969, S10, FBI V 100-448006-955 (COINTELPRO–Black Extremist); Director to SAC San Francisco, "Counterintelligence Program," May 27, 1969, S10, FBI V 100-448006-964 (COINTELPRO–Black Extremist); Director to SAC San Francisco, "Counterintelligence Program," May 13, 1969, S9, FBI V 100-448006 (COINTELPRO–Black Extremist).

14. Director to SAC Cincinnati, "Counterintelligence Program," February 29, 1968, S1, FBI V 100-448006 (COINTELPRO–Black Extremist); Hoover, "Analysis of the New Left," Christianity Today, August 18, 1967, B142, JEHS; Row to Callahan, "Security Index Card Statistics," January 17, 1963, FBI JFK 62-116395-429; Row to Callahan, "Security Index Card Statistics," January 21, 1969, FBI JFK 62-116395-429.

15. Director to SAC Albany, "New Left Movement," October 28, 1968, FBI JFK 62-116395-1428-Bulky; Davis, Assault on the Left, 77, 140; Joseph, Waiting 'Til the Midnight Hour, 249.

16. Hoover to SAC Albany, "Counterintelligence Program," May 10, 1968, S1, FBI V 100-449698 (COINTELPRO–New Left); interview of William E. Dyson, FBI OH.

17. Cunningham, There's Something Happening Here, 51.

18. Director to SAC Albany, "Counterintelligence Program," July 5, 1968, S1, FBI V 100-449698 (COINTELPRO–New Left); Davis, Assault on the Left, 47; Cotter to Brennan, "Counterintelligence Program New Left," July 21, 1970, S1, FBI V 100-449698 (COINTELPRO–New Left).

19. SAC Boston to Director, "Students for a Democratic Society (Weatherman)," February 26, 1970, S2, FBI V 100-449698 (COINTELPRO–New Left); Brennan to Sullivan, "Counterintelligence Program," August 15, 1968, S1, FBI V 100-449698 (COINTELPRO–New Left); Director to SAC Albany, "Counterintelligence Program," July 5, 1968, S1, FBI V 100-449698 (COINTELPRO–New Left).

20. Cunningham, There's Something Happening Here, 56; Davis, Assault on the Left, 141; Sullivan, The Bureau, 158.

21. Hoover, "Message from the Director," LEB, June 1969; Eckstein, Bad Moon Rising, 60–2, 86.

22. Ayers, "A Strategy to Win," New Left Notes, September 12, 1969. On Weatherman and the FBI, see especially Varon, Bringing the War Home; Eckstein, Bad Moon Rising; Chard, Nixon's War at Home; Green and Siegel, Weather Underground.

23. Director to SAC Chicago, "Counterintelligence Program," May 21, 1969, S10, FBI V 100-448006 (COINTELPRO–Black Extremist); Director to SAC Baltimore, "COINTELPRO–New Left," April 22, 1949, S9, FBI V 100-448006 (COINTELPRO–Black Extremist); Davis, Assault on the Left, 113; Varon, Bringing the War Home, 81.

24. For background on Hampton, see especially Williams, From the Bullet to the Ballot; Haas, Assassination of Fred Hampton.

25. For context and overview on Hampton's murder, see Williams, From the Bullet to the Ballot, 167-190. For details, see Haas, Assassination of Fred Hampton, 61-64; Davis, Spying on America, 120; "Shooting of Nine Chicago Police Officers," November 17, 1969, FBI JFK 62-116395-1420-Bulky.

26. Mitchell to SAC Chicago, "Black Panther Party," November 21, 1969, FBI JFK 62-116395-B670-2/2; Haas, Assassination of Fred Hampton, 198, 225-6.

27. "Black Panther Party" (BPP), November 21, 1969, FBI JFK 62-116395-B670,-2/2; "Sergeant Daniel R. Groth," December 22, 1969, S1, FBI V 44-44202 (Hampton); Hass, Assassination of Fred Hampton, 207-8, 185.

28. Haas, Assassination of Fred Hampton, 94; Kifner, "3 Panthers Snub," NYT, January, 1970.

29. Kifner, "F.B.I. Files Say," NYT, May 7, 1976. For recent details about O'Neal, see Leonard and Gallagher, "We Obtained F.B.I. Documents on How and Why Fred Hampton Was Murdered," Jacobin, March 31, 2021.

30. Haas, Assassination of Fred Hampton, 100, 113; Burrough, Days of Rage, 84–5; "A Declaration of a State of War (Communiqué #1)," Genius, https://genius.com/Weather-underground-a-declaration-of-a-state-of-war-communique-1-annotated; Powers, Secrecy and Power, 448; CCH2, 333.

31. Williams, From the Bullet to the Ballot, 176; CC3, 198–207.

Chapter 57: The Man Who Stayed Too Long (1970–1971)

1. "Presidential Talking Paper," undated, F: "HRH Security/FBI," B147, Special Files, Staff Member and Office Files: H. R. Haldeman, RN; CC3, 936–8.

2. "Masters of Deceit," Human Events, December 13, 1969, B147, JEHS; Kutler, Wars of Watergate, 97.

3. Hoover, "Memorandum for Mr. Tolson," November 16, 1970, FBI JFK 62-116395-547-551; Locker, Nixon's Gamble, 37-43, 134. Graff puts the number of wiretaps at eighteen rather than seventeen. Graff, Watergate, 13-5.

4. Haldeman, Haldeman Diaries, 66; Ehrlichman, Witness to Power, 159-60.

5. CC3, 938–9.

6. "Special Report Interagency Committee," June 1970, CCH2, 173, 175–6, 181.

7. CC3, 945; Huston to Haldeman, "Domestic Intelligence Review," July 1970, CCH2, 189–92.

8. CC3, 955–6; Hoover to Mitchell, "Interagency Committee on Intelligence," July 27, 1970, CCH2, 315.

9. Nixon, RN, 474–5; Huston to Haldeman, "Domestic Intelligence," August 5, 1970, CCH2, 249.

10. Graves, Nixon's FBI, 90; Murtagh to Chairman, November 18, 1975, FBI JFK 62-116395-1134-1145; Hoover, "Memorandum for Mr. Tolson," February 8, 1966, S7, FBI V [unnumbered] (Tolson).

11. Title VI, Omnibus Crime Control and Safe Streets Act of 1968, Govinfo, https://www.govinfo.gov/content/pkg/COMPS-1696/pdf/COMPS-1696.pdf.

12. DeLoach to Tolson, "Interdepartmental Information Unit," April 30, 1970, S6, FBI V 67-338728 (DeLoach); DeLoach to Hoover, June 4, 1970, S6, FBI V 67-338728 (DeLoach); DeLoach to Hoover, August 12, 1970, S6, FBI V 67-338728 (DeLoach).

13. Felt and O'Connor, G-Man's Life, 101; Sullivan to DeLoach, "Availability," May 20, 1970, S7, FBI FOIA 67-205182 (Sullivan); Hoover to Sullivan, June 10, 1970, S7,

FBI FOIA 67-205182 (Sullivan); "F.B.I. Aide," *NYT*, October 13, 1970, B149, JEHS; Sullivan to Tolson, October 13, 1970, S7, FBI FOIA 67-205182 (Sullivan); Sullivan to Tolson, "Public Speeches," October 14, 1970, S7, FBI FOIA 67-205182-613 (Sullivan).

14. Gentry, *J. Edgar Hoover*, 650–1; Adams to Callahan, "Clyde A. Tolson," March 17, 1970, S4, FBI NARA 67-9524-447 (Tolson); Tolson to Hoover, March 23, 1970, S4, FBI NARA 67-8524-446 (Tolson); O'Leary, "J. Edgar Still Looks," *WS*, December 31, 1967, B142, JEHS; Felt and O'Connor, *G-Man's Life*, 166.

15. "Poll Finds," *NYT*, August 9, 1970, B148, JEHS; Harris, "U.S. Is Split," *ChiT*, May 6, 1971, B154, JEHS; "Hoover's Record," *Charlotte Observer*, May 9, 1971, B154, JEHS.

16. Clark, *Crime in America*, 82; Turner, *Hoover's FBI*; Feldstein, *Poisoning the Press*, 137-40; Anderson, "$100-a-Day Suites," *WP*, May 12, 1971, B154, JEHS; Anderson, "Millionaire Picked Up," *WP*, Dec. 31, 1970, B150, JEHS.

17. Nelson, *Scoop*, 156–66.

18. Hoover, handwritten notes on: Anderson, "Hoover's Letters," *WP*, January 1, 1971, B151, JEHS; Harwood, "Snooping and Shouting," *WP*, April 8, 1970, B148, JEHS; Tully, "Will Hoover Retire In '72?" *Alexandria Gazette*, June 16, 1970, B148, JEHS; Eveslage, "Police No. 1 Target in America," *American Free Press*, September 1970, B149, JEHS; Gulliver, "Hoover Critic," *AC*, December 3, 1970, B150, JEHS; Miller, "Congressman Anderson's," *WSJ*, December 18, 1970, B150, JEHS; "Buffalo Minister," *Buffalo Evening News*, April 11, 1970, B148, JEHS; Wicker, "Calvin Coolidge's Revenge," *NYT*, November 19, 1970, B149, JEHS. Also see NT 6-84; Hoover, "Memorandum for Mr. Tolson," May 1, 1970, S10, FBI V unnumbered (Tolson).

19. Clawson, "FBI's Hoover," *WP*, November 17, 1970, B149, JEHS; "Hoover Reveals," *Boston Record American*, December 7, 1970, B150, JEHS; "Hoover Says Anti-War," *WS*, Nov. 27, 1970, B149, JEHS; Hoover, "Open Letter," September 21, 1970, F; "An Open Letter to College Students," B20, NLEM; Clawson, "FBI's Hoover Scores," *WP*, November 17, 1970, B149, JEHS; Sinclair, "Hoover Praises Chandler," *Courier-Journal*, May 28, 1970, B148, JEHS; Hoover, "Memorandum for Mr. Tolson," May 11, 1970, S10, FBI V [unnumbered] (Tolson).

20. Mollenhoff, "Nixon seen set," *Tampa Times*, March 1, 1971, B152, JEHS; Oudes, ed., *From: The President*, 217–8.

21. On the Media burglary, see Medsger, *Burglary*, especially 113-272; *1971*, directed by Johanaa Hamilton (2014). For details, see Philadelphia to Director, "Unsub; Break In," March 9, 1971, S1, FBI 52-94527-3 (Medburg); O'Leary, "The FBI," *WS*, January 2, 1971, B158, JEHS; Brennan to Sullivan, "Burglary of FBI Resident Agency," March 15, 1971, S3, FBI 52-94527 (Medburg); Hoover to SAC, Albany, "Counterintelligence Programs," April 28, 1971, S2, FBI V 157-9 (COINTELPRO White Hate).

22. *CR*, April 5, 1971, B152, JEHS; *CR*, April 22, 1971, B153, JEHS.

23. "Kennedy," *BG*, April 8, 1971, B152, JEHS; "Playboy Interview," *Playboy*, August 1971, B156, JEHS.

24. "Hoover's FBI," *Newsweek*, May 10, 1971, B154, JEHS; "Emperor of the FBI," *Life*, April 9, 1971; "He May Be the Man," *NYT*, April 18, 1971, B153, JEHS; "Bugging J. Edgar Hoover," *Time*, April 19, 1971, B153, JEHS; Hoover, "Memorandum for Mr. Tolson," April 15, 1971, S10, FBI V unnumbered (Tolson).

25. *CR*, April 22, 1971, B153, JEHS; Goldwater to Nixon, April 15, 1971, F: "EX FG 17-5 Federal Bureau of Investigation [3 of 8, January–April 1971]," B3, WHCF, RN; *CR*, April 5, 1971, B152, JEHS; "East Lauds Hoover, FBI," *Clarion Ledger*, May 6, 1971, B154, JEHS; *CR*, April 1, 1971, B152, JEHS; *CR*, May 10, 1971, B154, JEHS.

26. Kilpatrick, "Why J. Edgar Hoover," *WS*, March 16, 1971, B152, JEHS; Buckley, "Questions about the FBI," *Memphis Press-Scimitar*, April 27, 1971, B153, JEHS; "Reagan Lauds," *Sacramento Bee*, May 10, 1971, B154, JEHS; "Campaign against the FBI," *The Mindszenty Report*, May 1971, B154, JEHS; "'Gnats on the Hide,'" *Knight Templar*, April 1971, B152, JEHS.

27. "President Says Hoover," *WS*, April 17, 1971, B153, JEHS; NT 001-123.

28. Hoover to McGaughey, June 14, 1971, F71, B1, EMG; Quinn, "The Night the Director," *WP*, May 25, 1971, B154, JEHS; Crawford, "Score Two for Martha," *WDN*, May 24, 1971, B154, JEHS; Untitled, *Hamilton Journal*, June 16, 1971, B155, JEHS; "Hoover Breaks 3-Yr. Seclusion," *ChiT*, May 25, 1971, B154, JEHS.

29. "Remarks of J. Edgar Hoover," May 24, 1971, S7, B2, FBI NARA 67-561-377 (Hoover).

30. Nixon, *RN*, 512–4; NT 6-84.

31. Evans and Novak, "Nixon Dilemma," *WP*, April 5, 1971, B152, JEHS.

32. NT TR 587-3; "Who Went, Who Didn't," *WP*, June 13, 1971, B155, JEHS; NT 291-11; NT-LOG 575-7; NT 6-84.

33. Ponder to Tolson, "Disagreements," September 9, 1971, S7, FBI FOIA 67-205182 (Sullivan); Felt and O'Connor, *A G-Man's Life*, 117–8; Sullivan, *Bureau*, 243; Hoover, "Memorandum for Mr. Tolson [et al]," October 1, 1971, S8, FBI FOIA 67-205182-637 (Sullivan).

34. "Scenario for Conversation," undated, F: "[Hoover, J. Edgar] Company President," B20, Special Files, Staff Member and Office Files: John D. Ehrlichman, RN; Untitled memo attached on Ehrlichman to Nixon, "Director of the FBI," October 27, 1971, F: "[Hoover, J. Edgar] Company President," B20, Special Files, Staff Member and Office Files: John D. Ehrlichman, RN.

35. Ehrlichman, *Witness to Power*, 166–7; Nixon, *RN*, 597–9; Gray and Gray, *In Nixon's Web*, 9; NT 601-033.

36. Hoover, "Memorandum for Mr. Tolson," October 1, 1971, S8, FBI FOIA 67-205182-637 (Sullivan).

Chapter 58: One of the Giants (1972)

1. "Dinner at Key Biscayne," *WP*, December 29, 1972, B157, JEHS; Hoover to Nixon, January 3, 1972, F: "Ex FG 17-5 Federal Bureau of Investigation [5 of 8, September 1971–May 1972]," B3, WHCF, RN; "Charles G. ('Bebe') Rebozo, FBI Director J. Edgar Hoover, the President, and Secretary of State William P. Rogers before Dinner at Key Biscayne Florida, 188/28/1971," ARC Identified 194750, RN-WHPO; "His Spirit," *Chicago Sun Times*, January 1, 1972, B158, JEHS; Untitled photo, *NYT*, January 2, 1972, B158, JEHS; Untitled photo, PB34, NLEM.

2. Ross, Untitled, Washington Capital News Service, January 1, 1972, B158, JEHS.

3. Hoover to McGaughey, September 27, 1971, F71, B1, EMG; Gentry, *J. Edgar Hoover*, 20; Hoover to Gandy, March 1, 1972, S3, FBI 67-3654 (Gandy), S-JEHC.

4. "Baughman Rites," *Orlando Sentinel*, September 20, 1971, B156, JEHS; McIntosh, "Reflection on FBI Chief," ca. November 1971, B157, JEHS; JEH LOGS, September 9–10, 1971; Kelly and LaPrise, "Hoover Attends," *Daytona Beach News-Journal*, September 10, 1971, F: "Baughman Sept 71," S-JEHC.

5. Gabler, *Winchell*, 542–9; Hoover to Winchell, January 26, 1972, S58, FBI V 62-31615-1289 (Winchell).

6. "Hoover, Almost 77," *NYT*, December 6, 1971, B157, JEHS; O'Leary, "The FBI," *WS*, January 2, 1972, B158, JEHS.

7. Facter, "Gallagher Charges," *Hudson Dispatch*, April 20, 1972, B158, JEHS; Elder, "Rep. Gallagher Charges," *WS*, April 20, 1972, B158, JEHS; Gentry, *J. Edgar Hoover*, 588–9; "Ex-G-Man," *Buffalo Courier-Express*, January 14, 1972, B158, JEHS; Messick, *John Edgar Hoover*, 1; Nash, *Citizen Hoover*.

8. Hearst, "A Time for Sadness," *Baltimore News American*, May 7, 1972, B229, JEHS; Felt, *G-Man's Life*, 148-9.

9. "Death Report," CCR 21-617, May 2, 1972, F1: "Hoover: Funeral," B1, NLEM; Gentry, *J. Edgar Hoover*, 19–21. Ungar places a third person at the death scene, Hoover's new driver, Tom Moton. Ungar, *FBI*, 37-8.

10. Files, 65; District of Columbia Department of Public Health, "Certificate of Death, 72-03405," F: "Copies (10) of JEH Death Certificate," B1, NLEM.

11. Gentry, *J. Edgar Hoover*, 28.

12. NT 23-152; NT-TR 719-12.

13. NT 335-16, 334-11, 23-133; NT-TR, 717-19.

14. NT 334-36, 23-133.

15. NT 23-103.

16. DeLoach, *Hoover's FBI*, 414–7; Elsasser, "National Crimefighter," *ChiT*, May 3, 1972, B159, JEHS.

17. NT 717-8; Johnson to Tolson, May 2, 1972, F: "Hoover," B73, Post-Presidential Papers, Name File, LBJ.

18. AP, "J. Edgar Hoover Is Dead," *Detroit News*, May 2, 1972, B159, JEHS; Nixon, "Statement by the President," May 2, 1972, F: "GEN FG 17-5 Federal Bureau of Investigation," B4, WHCF, RN; Breasted, "Nixon Calls Him 'Truly Remarkable," *NYDN*, May 3, 1972, B159, JEHS.

19. NT 334-36, 23-118.

20. *Memorial Tributes to J. Edgar Hoover in the Congress of the United States* (Washington, DC: U.S. Government Printing Office, 1974), 29–30, 37, 3–13; Untitled, Washington Capital News Service, May 2, 1972, B159, JEHS; "Individuals Who Have Lain in State or in Honor," U.S. House of Representatives, https://history.house.gov/Institution /Lie-In-State/Lie-In-State-Honor/.

21. Farmer and Freeman, "J. Edgar Hoover 77," *Springfield News & Leader*, April 23, 1972, reprinted in *Memorial Tributes*, 16; "J. Edgar Hoover," *Providence Journal*, May 3, 1972, B229, JEHS.

22. Delaney, "Mourning," *WS*, May 3, 1972, B159, JEHS.

23. Untitled, *Augusta Chronicle*, May 3, 1972, B229, JEHS; "J. Edgar Hoover, RIP," *NatR*, May 26, 1972, 572–3.

24. *Memorial Tributes*, 35; "J. Edgar Hoover," *ChiT*, May 3, 1972, B229, JEHS; Canham, "Mr. Hoover's place," *CSM*, May 8, 1972, B159, JEHS.

25. Gentry, *J. Edgar Hoover*, 42; untitled, Washington Capital News Service, May 3, 1972, B159, JEHS; Robertson, "Hoover Lies," *NYT*, May 4, 1972; Seppy, "High officials," *AP*, May 3, 1972; Levey, "Throngs View," *WP*, May 4, 1972; Felt and O'Connor, *G-Man's Life*, 146; Burger, "Eulogy," May 3, 1972, reprinted in *Memorial Tributes*, xvii–xviii; Elsasser, "Hoover Eulogized," *ChiT*, May 4, 1972, B159, JEHS; "J. Edgar Hoover," *WS*, May 3, 1972, reprinted in *Memorial Tributes*, 223; Fialka, "Nation's Capital," *WS*, May 3, 1972, B159, JEHS; "6,000 file," *WDN*, May 4, 1972; "The Lincoln Catafalque," Architect of the Capitol, https://

www.aoc.gov/what-we-do/programs-ceremonies/lying-in -state-honor/lincoln-catafalque.

26. Valentine, "Mourners Pass," *WP*, May 4, 1972; "Counter Protest," *NYT*, May 4, 1972; "1,000 Quakers," *NYT*, May 4, 1972; Lukas, *Nightmare*, 194–6.

27. Greene, "Capitol Stuff," *NYDN*, May 3, 1972, B159, JEHS; Antevil, "FBI Has New Most-Wanted," *NYDN*, May 3, 1972, B159, JEHS; Stuart, "Who Will Take FBI Helm?" *CSM*, May 3, 1972, B159, JEHS.

28. NT 335-16, 334-14, 334-36.

29. NT 717-15; Ehrlichman to Nixon, "Meeting with Richard Kleindienst, Pat Gray," May 3, 1972, FG 17-5: "Federal Bureau of Investigation [5 of 8, September 1971–May 1972]," B3, Subject Files, WHCF, RN.

30. NT-TR 719-12.

31. Felt and O'Connor, *G-Man's Life*, 148, 154.

32. HO&C; Files, 88–90, 36–49.

33. "Will—John Edgar Hoover," July 19, 1971, F1, B1, NLEM.

34. NT-TR, 717-10, 717-19.

35. NT 335-14, 335-24, 23-125; NT-LOG 719-3, 719-7, 719-8; "Nixon Eulogizes Hoover at Last Rites," *WS*, May 4, 1972, B159, JEHS.

36. "Services for the Honorable J. Edgar Hoover," May 4, 1972, F1, B1, NLEM; Nixon, "Eulogy by the President for J. Edgar Hoover," May 4, 1972, F1, B1, NLEM; Van Riper, "Nixon Calls Hoover," *NYDN*, May 5, 1972, B159, JEHS; Levey, "Nixon Eulogizes Hoover," *WP*, May 5, 1972, B159, JEHS; Spencer, "'He Was a Great Patriot,'" *WS*, May 5, 1972, B159, JEHS.

Epilogue

1. NT-TR 858-003; NT-TR 865-14.

2. Hoover, "Memorandum for Mr. Tolson," April 13, 1971, S9, FBI V [unnumbered] (Tolson).

3. Gray and Gray, *In Nixon's Web*, 42–3, 183, 288; Gray, "At EEG House," August 4, 1980, B: "LPG Handwritten Ipswich Narratives, 1980," LPG. Also see Gray's handwritten notes in the margins of Felt, *FBI Pyramid*, in LPG: 153, 111, acknowledgments.

4. "In the Offing," *WDN*, May 6, 1972, B159, JEHS; Nichols to Nixon, May 19, 1972, F6, B4, FG 17-5, RN.

5. Felt to Gray, September 20, 1972, S5, FBI FOIA 67-276576-430 (Felt); Gray to Felt, December 1, 1972, S5, FBI FOIA 67-276567-432 (Felt); Weiner, *Enemies*, 309.

6. Woodward, *Secret Man*, 59; Kutler, *Abuse of Power*, 170–1; Woodward and Bernstein, *All the President's Men*. Felt's memoir went through several editions. It was first published in 1979 as *The FBI Pyramid: From the Inside*, without the Deep Throat revelations. In 2007, he published a revised edition with John O'Connor under the title *A G-Man's Life: The FBI, Being Deep Throat, and the Struggle for Honor in Washington*. Most recently, to coincide with the film *Mark Felt* (2017), it was released as *Felt: The Man Who Brought Down the White House*. For the original *Vanity Fair* story, see O'Connor, "I'm the Guy They Call Deep Throat." For a rigorous, objective take on Felt's career, see Holland, *Leak*. Also see Gage, "Deep Throat, Watergate, and the Bureaucratic Politics of the FBI." For the ongoing debate, see Holland, "Beyond Deep Throat," *Newsweek*, October 9, 2014.

7. Kutler, *Wars of Watergate*, 247; NT-TR 858-003.

8. Gray, "At EEG House," August 4, 1980, B: "LPG Handwritten Ipswich Narratives, 1980," LPG; Gray and Gray, *In Nixon's Web*, 213; Holland, *Leak*, 129–50.

9. Nichols to Gray, April 24, 1973, S7, FBI FOIA 67-30921-779 (Nichols); Kutler, *Abuse of Power*, 345.

10. NT-TR 865-14.

11. NT-TR 741-002.

12. "FBI Watergate Investigation: OPE Analysis," July 5, 1974, FBI V 139-4089 (Watergate); Kelley and Davis, *Clarence Kelley*.

13. The burglars revealed themselves in Medsger, *Burglary*; Hamilton, *1971*. For the SWP and Stern, see Medsger, *Burglary*, 366–9; 331–3.

14. CCH6, 61. On the post-Watergate investigations, see Olmsted, *Challenging the Secret Government*.

15. CC2, 21, 5, iii; CC5, 6; CC3, iii, 159, 180, 187-223.

16. "F.B.I. Ordered," *NYT*, February 1, 1977; Robinson, "FBI Tap Data," *WP*, February 1, 1977; Horrock, "Gray and 2 Ex-F.B.I. Aides," *NYT*, April 11, 1978; Kiernan, "Ex-FBI Officials," *WP*, November 7, 1980.

17. CCH6, 2, 77.

18. Untitled notes: "Top Secret-Off the Record," ca. 1962, FBI JFK 62-116395-340-347 (Church Committee); "Statement of Clarence M. Kelley," November 18, 1974, FBI JFK 62-116395-1134-1145.

19. CCH6, 71.

20. CC2, 389-391; Reagan, "Statement on Granting Pardons to W. Mark Felt and Edward S. Miller," April 15, 1981, Ronald Reagan Presidential Library and Museum, https://www.reaganlibrary.gov/archives/speech/statement-granting-pardons-w-mark-felt-and-edward-s-miller-0.

21. "Kelley Apologizes," *LAT*, May 9, 1976; "FBI Apologizes," *Newsday*, May 9, 1976; "FBI Director Kelley apologizes," *ChiT*, May 9, 1976; "Back to Basics," *Newsday*, May 19, 1976.

22. "History of FBI Headquarters," FBI, https://www.fbi.gov/history/history-of-fbi-headquarters.

NOTE ON SOURCES

To research J. Edgar Hoover is to live with paradox. There is at once too much material and too little. No historian or biographer could possibly read every page produced by Hoover's bureaucracy. But given his fondness for secrecy and obfuscation, it can still be difficult—sometimes impossible—to find out what one wants to know. In writing this biography, I have added to the research pile by acquiring and analyzing thousands of pages of never-before-used documents. I have also taken advantage of decades of painstaking and inspiring work by fellow historians, biographers, and FOIA researchers.

This Note on Sources highlights distinctive features of both the primary and secondary resources featured in this book. The Primary Sources section describes a range of archival and government documents, with emphasis on the many newly accessible sources consulted and acquired for this project. The Secondary Sources section provides a selective guide to those works by historians, scholars, and journalists that have been most useful—indeed, absolutely critical—in the writing of this book. It also offers a brief historiographical overview of the scholarly subfields that most directly influenced the book's interpretation and analysis. For a full list of works consulted, as well as complete citations to the works referenced in this Note, readers will want to consult the Bibliography at the end of this book.

PRIMARY SOURCES

It has often been said that Hoover embodied Ralph Waldo Emerson's view of an institution as "the lengthened shadow" of a single man. The primary sources available to document Hoover's life come mostly from the institution he led for almost half a century. In the quarter-century since the last crop of Hoover's biographies, hundreds of important new FBI files have become available, including the records of SOLO, Venona, and the Church Committee. While they cover a vast range of subjects, they also share certain features. Hoover was famously insistent that FBI files should never be revealed to the world. While his secrecy creates interpretive challenges, it also means that FBI files can be remarkably revealing. Hoover made a practice of writing his unfiltered thoughts in blue pen on the margins of files and newspaper articles. This running tally of his views is a great gift to biographers. At the same time, many FBI files still contain painful levels of redaction, with entire passages and even pages blacked out. All historical research requires judgment about what information we have and what we do not or cannot know. FBI files make this conundrum acutely apparent.

The greatest repository of records on Hoover is still the FBI itself. The Bureau makes available hundreds of FBI files on famous individuals and major subjects. Researchers may consult such files through the FBI's online reading room, The Vault. Among the most important are the 125 sections of the SOLO file. *G-Man* is the first Hoover biography to make use of these fascinating documents. The Vault also provides access to internal files vital to understanding Hoover's institution, including his office logs and appointment books. Over the course of my research, I supplemented the FBI's publicly available material by filing dozens of FOIA requests on subjects ranging from FBI personnel (Harold Nathan, Guy Hottel, Dan Smoot) to important political allies (Barry Goldwater, James Eastland, Hoover's stable of ex-agents in Congress) to right-wing organizations such as the John Birch Society and Christian Anti-Communism Crusade. FOIA was also crucial in instances where The Vault provides only partial or limited versions of investigative or personnel materials. FBI historian John Fox shared important material from Hoover's early career as a junior Justice Department official and other key moments.

FBI documents no longer in the Bureau's custody are housed in Record Group 65 at National Archives II in College Park, Maryland. Especially valuable for this biography was the reprocessed version of Hoover's Official and Confidential file. In 2014 (thanks my diligent research assistant Jacob Wasserman), I located the first unredacted copy of the FBI's "suicide" letter to Martin Luther King (described in chapter 50) in that collection. Readers can find more about that document in my 2014 essay for *The New York Times Magazine*.

Newly available from NARA as well are the thousands of documents released online under the John F. Kennedy Assassination Records Collection Act. Included in that release were voluminous records from the Church Committee, which have only begun to be examined by historians. Thanks to that release, this book contains many new details about Hoover's COINTELPRO program, including instances in which he quietly disclosed at least some of its contours and contents both to Congress and to the White House. The Records Act release also contains new material about Hoover's investigation of Martin Luther King, FBI surveillance policies, and other important areas of controversy.

NARA houses a wealth of early case files, including relatively untapped materials on German internment, vice and prostitution, and civil rights investigations. NARA is also home to the J. Edgar Hoover Scrapbook collection, in which Hoover compiled press clippings, cartoons, and editorials covering most of his life and career. I read well over one hundred boxes worth of press materials, which were a key source for understanding Hoover's public image and impact as well as the contours of his social life. NARA also maintains Hoover's official photograph collection, from which I have drawn many of the images reproduced in this book. Finally, NARA is home to several important collections housed in other records groups, including RG 60 (the Department of Justice).

One of the great benefits of writing in the twenty-first century is the wealth of FBI material available through sources and repositories not created by the FBI itself. *G-Man* is the first major Hoover biography published since the release of the Venona papers, available online through the National Security Agency (as well as in more limited form at the Vault). I accessed key records on the FBI's early disputes with the CIA directly through the CREST system at NARA; those are now available online as well. Supplementing these official repositories are a wealth of FBI files compiled independently by researchers and historians and generously made available online for public use. The indefatigable Ernie Lazar has spent years filing targeted FOIA requests for important political and investigative files; those are now available to the public at the Internet Archive. The Mary Ferrell Foundation has compiled nearly all records related to the assassinations of John F. Kennedy, Robert F. Kennedy, and Martin Luther King, along with records and reports of the Church Committee and other investigative bodies. The National Security Archive at George Washington University contains an ever-growing body of intelligence-related documents, as do the Government Attic, MuckRock, and Black Vault sites. At Marquette University, the FBI collections compiled by Athan Theoharis and Kenneth O'Reilly are among the nation's most valuable one-stop shopping destinations for Bureau files (though their contents require a visit to the archives and are not available yet online). Still other FBI files are available through the commercial databases and microfilm collections listed in the notes and bibliography.

Where possible, I have tried to indicate the originating repository of the FBI files I have examined—not only to give credit where credit is due, but to allow other researchers to find the files with greatest ease. Thanks to evolving FBI redaction and release procedures, it is often possible to find slightly different versions of the same FBI file in multiple locations. A similar difficulty holds true for FBI file numbers. The same document may have multiple identifying numbers (field office file versus headquarters file designations, for instance). Within reason, I have tried to provide sufficient evidence in my citations to account for these discrepancies. Where possible, each citation includes at least one consistent file number as well as the general subject matter of the file in question, along with its originating repository. In many cases, citations have been grouped together when multiple successive paragraphs relied on the same series of books or documents. The bibliography contains full citations for source abbreviations used in the endnotes.

* * *

Beyond FBI materials themselves, the most valuable source of documentation on Hoover's life is the J. Edgar Hoover Collection housed at the National Law Enforcement Museum in Washington, DC. That collection contains a wealth of personal material, including Hoover's childhood diaries and his private photograph collection, with its hundreds of striking images of his life with Clyde Tolson. The museum itself includes an exhibit of Hoover's office, which is well worth a visit.

Sophisticated new genealogical and newspaper databases made it possible to uncover other aspects of Hoover's family and early life that he never discussed and apparently did not want the world to know. This book documents his grandfather's suicide and his aunt's murder for the first time, based on news reports. This biography also contains the first extended analysis of Kappa Alpha's history and racial politics, much of it drawn from the fraternity's *Kappa Alpha Journal*. I reconstructed Hoover's days at Central High largely through materials available at the Sumner School Archives in Washington, D.C. My description of his time at George Washington University came from his college yearbooks and school newspaper as well as his private collection.

Additional material on Hoover's social and personal life can be found in the archives of friends and interlocutors, many of them included here for the first time. The Melvin Purvis Papers at Boston University offer the single most revealing repository about Hoover's inner life during his early years as director. At Stanford's Hoover Institution, the Emmett McGaughey Papers provides an intimate view of Hoover late in life. The Mitrokhin Archive at Cambridge offers glimpses of Soviet efforts to investigate Hoover's personal life. The William Manchester Papers at Wesleyan contain Hoover's reflections on the Kennedy assassination, based on an interview conducted just after the president's death. At the Library of Congress, the papers of Evelyn McLean contain an especially revealing letter written by Hoover in the wake of his mother's death, while the Harlan Fiske Stone papers document Hoover's surprisingly personal relationship with his early mentor. At the FBI, the files of Cartha DeLoach, Morris Ernst, Melvin Purvis, Clyde Tolson, and Walter Winchell are especially revealing on a personal level. In preparation for his 1993 biography of Hoover, Anthony Summers and his team of researchers conducted dozens of interviews with Hoover's friends, fans, and foes alike. I am grateful to him and to Robbyn Swan for inviting me into their home and sharing their voluminous research files, including recordings of selected interviews. I am also grateful to Ed Gray, who has undertaken the task of making the papers of his late father (and Hoover's successor) L. Patrick Gray available to researchers. Those papers are now at the Library of Congress. (For this book's many additional personal debts, see the Acknowledgments.)

On Hoover's political relationships and networks, the nation's presidential libraries are a vital resource. For this book, I consulted every presidential library from Herbert Hoover's through Richard Nixon's. The Johnson and Nixon collections, including both oral histories and textual documents, are especially useful, reflecting Hoover's longtime and close relationships with both presidents. For blow-by-blow reconstructions of key historical moments, the Johnson and Nixon audio recordings also have few rivals in presidential history. Outside of the presidential library system, researchers owe a special debt to Michael Beschloss, Douglas Brinkley, Max Holland, Stanley Kutler, Luke Nichter, and the team from the University of Virginia's Miller Center (among others) for making some of the most important recordings accessible in annotated, scholarly form. Beyond the White House, I have consulted the papers of multiple politicians, including Congressman John Rooney's at Brooklyn College and Senator James Eastland's at University of Mississippi. At least as important as the papers of Hoover's friends are those of his critics and enemies. The ACLU Papers at Princeton and the Papers of the NAACP (available through ProQuest) were especially valuable for this biography.

The published primary sources consulted for this book are too numerous to discuss, but a few bear special mention. The psychological works of Karen Horney provide an intriguing framework for understanding Hoover's "inner conflicts." I tracked them down after seeing a brief news article mentioning Hoover's purchase of Horney's books. The memoirs of Harry Belafonte, Simeon Booker, and Andrew Young offer especially useful insights into the FBI's relationship with the civil rights movement. Kim Philby's memoir, while hardly dependable in a factual sense (like Philby himself), presents a sharp character portrait of Hoover. Several attorneys general, including Francis Biddle and Nicholas Katzenbach, wrote valuable memoirs as well; they are perhaps most surprising not for their frustrations with Hoover, but for their sympathy and admiration for the man. For the FBI's institutional history, the published reports and hearings of the Church Committee remain a vital resource, though it is now almost half a century since the committee completed its work.

The many memoirs of former FBI agents offer crucial perspective from inside the Bureau. Books by Melvin Purvis and Leon Turrou, while somewhat breathless, cover Hoover's early years as director, as do the writings of Courtney Ryley Cooper. On Venona and the FBI's early experiments in counterespionage, Robert Lamphere's autobiographical book *The FBI-KGB War* is a vital resource. Dan Smoot's memoir describes connections between the FBI and the mid-century conservative movement. On the FBI and organized crime, the best memoir is William Roemer's. On the FBI and the Kennedy assassination, James Hosty's memoir is especially valuable. Three of the officials who vied to become Hoover's successor—Deke DeLoach, William Sullivan, and Mark Felt—published essential if sometimes conflicting accounts of their experiences. So did G. Gordon Liddy, whose memoir describes his transition from FBI agent to Nixon Plumber. Ed Gray compiled his father's reflections into a valuable memoir. The latest contribution is Paul Letersky's *The Director*, a lively account published in 2021 by a former agent who worked in Hoover's office.

Complementing these published works is an extraordinary collection of oral histories compiled by the Society of Former Special Agents of the FBI and the Former Agents of the FBI Foundation and now available online. Taken together, those interviews offer an unparalleled glimpse of what it was like to live and work in Hoover's shadow.

SECONDARY SOURCES

Until the final year of his life, nobody dared publish a biography of Hoover. After his death, historians and journalists rushed in to fill the gap. The four most significant biographies of Hoover date from the late 1980s and early 1990s, just long enough after his death to allow for the opening of archival materials and the epic work of researching the full sweep of his career. Richard Gid Powers came first with *Secrecy and Power* (1987), still the biography that best situates Hoover in his life and times. Athan Theoharis's *The Boss*, written with John Stuart Cox (1988), concentrates on civil liberties questions and FBI policy while contributing new details about Hoover's family life and background. Curt Gentry's *J. Edgar Hoover* (1991) offers a rollicking investigation of Hoover's career, with an emphasis on exposing FBI secrets. Anthony Summers's *Official and Confidential* (1993) contains details gleaned not only from archival sources, but from key interviews with Hoover's acquaintances and critics.

To varying degrees, all four of these biographies promise to reveal the truth behind the great Hoover façade. *G-Man* does this as well, but from a distinct point of origin. This book does not treat Hoover as a rogue actor. Rather, it aims to situate him within broad currents of American political history—to move him from the margins to the center of our understanding about what the American Century was and how it worked.

* * *

For that purpose, three areas of scholarly work have been particularly important. The first is the literature on American political development and the rise of the administrative state. As scholars such as Brian Balogh, Daniel Carpenter, Stephen Skowronek, and James Sparrow (among many others) have shown, the administrative state came of age alongside Hoover, with crucial origins in the Progressive Era. Though Hoover's FBI acquired a distinctive stamp, he deployed ideas and methods held widely throughout federal policymaking circles. Carpenter has described the vast range of tools—including the deliberate cultivation of a reputation for professionalism and accomplishment—that career officials such as Hoover used to achieve stability, longevity, and some measure of bureaucratic autonomy. Sparrow has shown the unparalleled impact of World War II on state expansion. By the 1950s, vast swaths of the federal government were operating within what Balogh has described as a "prominis-trative" state, relying on a combination of private and public methods of administration, professionalism, and expertise. Though often described within the context of "liberal" state development, these methods and developments spanned parties and ideologies. They operated in conversation with but separate from electoral politics. As Hoover's example shows, they extended beyond the social welfare and regulatory state and into the security state as well.

If Hoover shared certain ideas with self-described liberal and progressive administrators, though, he also borrowed heavily from—indeed, helped to shape and define—certain distinctively conservative ideological traditions. Since the 1990s, historians such as Kevin Kruse, Lisa McGirr, Rick Perlstein, and Kim Phillips-Fein (among many others) have developed a rich literature on the history of modern American conservatism, a second key area of historiographical engagement for this biography. Much of that literature has focused on non-state actors (businessmen, intellectuals, grassroots and party activists). To the degree that state actors have come under consideration, historians have tended to focus on conservative politicians such as Barry Goldwater, Ronald Reagan, and Strom Thurmond. One goal of this book is to bring the historiographies of American political development and U.S. conservatism into closer conversation with each other.

Hoover prompts us to think differently about the origins of modern conservatism—not only to look back to the Progressive Era, but to think about those conservatives operating within and helping to develop the modern state. If at some moments Hoover sounded like a progressive administrator, at others he sounded like a card-carrying member of the conservative movement, ferociously opposed not only to radical left movements of all sorts but also to the liberal policymakers, politicians, and intellectuals whom he accused of aiding and abetting them. His great skill was to maintain both identities at once. Historian Jonathan Schoenwald has highlighted the distinction between "responsible" and "extremist" conservatives during the 1960s—between those like Hoover who considered themselves players within the Washington establishment and those who stood outside, often hoping to tear it down. Though Hoover placed himself in the former camp, he was also seen as a hero to the latter. Indeed, he was one of the few federal bureaucrats who could claim such a feat. Critics of the state admired Hoover not despite but because of his institutional power, especially his ability to use the federal government's formidable police and investigative might to contain and discredit the American left. In his classic work on conservatism, George Nash identified anticommunism as the glue that held together an uneasy conservative coalition. As the nation's most prominent anticommunist—more famous and certainly more respected than Joe McCarthy—Hoover was a key part of that project: a conservative state-builder during the supposed age of liberal consensus.

Of course, as historians such as Michael Flamm, Elizabeth Hinton, Khalid Muhammad, Stuart Schrader, and Heather Ann Thompson (among many others) have pointed out, the nation's politics on the issues of crime and policing have never divided neatly along partisan or ideological lines. In recent years, historians have developed a wide-ranging and incisive literature on policing, incarceration, and the rise of the U.S. security state. Two themes from this literature are especially useful in thinking about the significance of Hoover's life and legacy. One is the wide degree of agreement across party lines about crime and policing, whether in the Progressive Era, the New Deal or the 1960s and beyond. The other is the centrality of race in constructing these evolving regimes of law enforcement and carceral policy. Like his friend and patron Lyndon Johnson, Hoover often enforced his racialized vision through the tools of the liberal state—including the forms of bureaucratic autonomy and professionalism so central to the literature on American political development. At the same time, his life underscores that many of these ideas, themes, and mechanisms were not new in the 1960s. Hoover's life prompts us to think about the 1960s and 1970s not as a rupture in the history of crime and incarceration, but as part of something we might describe as a Long War on Crime.

* * *

The vast literature on the FBI itself has of course been *the* crucial resource in the writing of this book—one for which I offer deep thanks to the many historians and journalists who have spent years puzzling over redactions, filing FOIA requests, and otherwise trying to bring the Bureau's history to light. All students of the subject owe an especially significant debt to two scholars, Athan Theoharis and Richard Gid Powers, who not only wrote two of the first and best biographies of Hoover, but who performed uncommon service to fellow scholars and citizens by making a range of archival and reference materials available. Together with Susan Rosenfeld and Tony Poveda, they compiled *The FBI: A Comprehensive Reference Guide* (1999), still the most reliable guide for basic questions of FBI history. They also produced scholarly editions (often on microfilm, the technology of a bygone age) of important FBI material, including Hoover's Official and Confidential File. The list of their published work available in the bibliography only begins to capture the scope and significance of their influence.

Several other historians, journalists, and scholars have taken on the daunting task of attempting to tell the FBI's institutional story from start to finish. During Hoover's lifetime, books by Max Lowenthal and Fred Cook sounded the alarm on Hoover's abuses, while Don Whitehead pushed back with Hoover's help. After Hoover's death, Sanford Ungar published the first major synthesis of Bureau history; it has held up well. For more recent but no less essential single-volume synthetic histories, see the work of Rhodri Jeffreys-Jones, Ronald Kessler, and Tim Weiner.

Many recent scholars and journalists have chosen (wisely) to focus on particular cases, themes, or historical periods rather than to engage the full Hoover era. Their works are too numerous to describe in full here, but a few warrant special mention. I relied upon the works below and many others to fill out my understanding of Hoover across vast swaths of time and subject matter. Without them, my own book could not have been written.

On Hoover's early life, the work of Kenneth Ackerman is essential. On the FBI in World War I and the Red Scare, see especially the work of Mark Ellis, Joan Jensen, Regin Schmidt, Jeffrey Simon, and Theodore Kornweibel. The FBI's institutional growth during the 1920s and 1930s has been a fruitful area of scholarly insight and analysis in recent years. See the work of James Calder, Matthew G.T. Denney, Kathleen Frydll, Anthony Gregory, Lisa McGirr, Kenneth O'Reilly, Claire Potter, and Daniel Richman & Sarah Seo. Bryan Burrough offers a riveting overview of the major gangster cases of the 1930s. For more targeted case studies from the era, see the work of Carolyn Cox, Jonathan Eig, David Grann, Elliott Gorn, Vivien Miller, Alston Purvis, and Robert Unger, among others. On FBI public relations, Richard Gid Powers wrote the pioneering work, while Matthew Cecil is now the go-to scholar. On the FBI's policing of sex and gender before World War II, see the work of Douglas Charles, Jessica Pliley, and Mary Elizabeth Strunk. For understanding Hoover in the context of debates over masculinity, homosexuality, and bachelorhood in the early twentieth century, I relied especially upon the work of George Chauncey, Howard Chudacoff, Daniel Hurewitz, and Nick Syrett. On Walter Winchell and café society, works by Neal Gabler, Ralph Blumenthal, and David Stowe were especially useful. For speculation about Hoover's sexuality, see the writings of Douglas Charles, Christopher Elias, Ronald Kessler, Claire Potter, Anthony Summers, and Athan Theoharis. For the history of Washington, D.C., I relied especially on the books of Chris Myers Asch and George Derek Musgrove, Constance McLaughlin Green, and Tom Lewis.

World War II and the invention of U.S. intelligence has inspired an extensive if uneven literature, much of it focused on the OSS and CIA rather than the FBI. Ray Batvinis and Mark Riebling offer the best overviews of the FBI's attempts to learn the intelligence trade. On World War II and the security state, the works of Douglas Charles, Matthew Dallek, and Lynn Olson offer useful context. On Nazi espionage, I relied especially on books by Ray Batvinis, Michael Dobbs, Peter Duffy, Rhodri Jeffreys-Jones, and Pierce O'Donnell. On the FBI's wartime internment and political surveillance, see the work of Mark Becker, Stephen Fox, Donna Haverty-Stacke, and Maurice Isserman. Books by Tim Weiner and Douglas Waller provide especially useful background on Hoover's early rivalry with the CIA.

The history of lynching in the U.S. has inspired a vast and grim scholarly literature, much of it concentrated in the late nineteenth and early twentieth centuries. On the major cases of the 1940s, the period of Hoover's greatest involvement, historical treatment has been somewhat more limited. To reconstruct the FBI's activity in this area, I relied primarily on case studies by Richard Gergel, William B. Gravely, Anthony Pitch, Howard Smead, Jason Ward, and Laura Wexler. Phillip Dray's work provided a useful overview. Patricia Sullivan's study of the NAACP was crucial for understanding the organization's early work.

The postwar Red Scare has received a great deal of attention as well, though not necessarily with the FBI as its central subject. On the broad phenomenon of McCarthyism, the work of Ellen Schrecker and Landon Storrs is especially insightful. Works by Michael Belknap, David Caute, Ted Morgan, David A. Nichols, Arthur Sabin, Michael Steinberg, and Michael Ybarra offer crucial political and legal context. On the FBI's relationship with Congress, the works of Christopher Gerard, Kenneth O'Reilly, and Aaron Stockham are essential. Excellent biographies of Joseph McCarthy by David Oshinsky and Larry Tye fill out the portrait of the man and his era. For a cultural analysis of Roy Cohn, McCarthy, and Hoover, see Christopher Elias's new book. On the FBI and Hollywood, see the work of Thomas Doherty and John Sbardellati. Irwin Gellman's work provides useful detail about Hoover's early relationship with Nixon.

The era's Soviet espionage dramas have inspired an extensive literature in their own right, much of it based on painstaking work in once-secret files. It would have been impossible to make sense of Hoover's role in these cases without this collective labor. On the Hiss/Chambers case, the works of Sam Tanenhaus and Allen Weinstein are essential. On the Rosenbergs, I relied on the investigative work of Sam Roberts as well as Joyce Milton and Ronald Radosh. For Elizabeth Bentley and her circle, the key works are by Mark Bradley, Bruce Craig, Lauren Kessler, and Kathryn Olmsted. Marcia Mitchell and Thomas Mitchell contributed the first book-length study of the Judith Coplon case. John Barron's work on SOLO builds upon pioneering work by David Garrow. On Venona (which has inspired its own minor sub-field), the works of Robert L. Benson, John Earl Haynes, and Harvey Klehr are foundational, while more recent books by Howard Blum and Nigel West fill out important narrative and detail. For more on Soviet defectors and recent archival discoveries, see the work of Christopher Andrew, John Earl Haynes, Harvey Klehr, Jerrold and Leona Schechter, and Allen Weinstein and Alexander Vassiliev.

Intertwined with the Red Scare was the Lavender Scare, an area in which new work has greatly deepened historical understanding in recent years. On the FBI itself, the scholarship of Douglas Charles is essential. For sexual policing elsewhere in the federal government, see the work of Michael Berube, Margot Canaday, and David Johnson. The edited collection *Intimate States* contains several essays relevant to the FBI work—mostly notably, Timothy Stewart-Winter's article on Walter Jenkins. Eric Cervini's recent book focuses on the experiences and activism of Frank Kameny.

As several historians have recognized, Hoover was not only a state-builder but a culture-maker. On the FBI and religion, see works by Lerone Martin and Steve Rosswurm, along with the recent collection edited by Sylvester A. Johnson and Steven Weitzman. For the religiosity of the 1950s, the work of Kevin Kruse provides useful context. Within the literature on conservatism, Heather Hendershot's study of right-wing media contains valuable material on former FBI agent Dan Smoot. The work of Lisa McGirr and Michelle Nickerson describes the right-wing anticommunist surge in southern California.

The literature on Hoover and the FBI in the 1960s and 1970s is by far the most extensive of any era. Almost without exception, Hoover is cast as a villain, if often one among many. On Hoover's relationship with the Kennedys, Burton Hersh offers the most detailed recent work. On civil rights, the crucial moral and political issue of the 1960s, there is a wealth of historical literature, though much of it addresses the FBI as one subject among many. For an overview of the FBI's surveillance of Black Americans, see the work of Kenneth O'Reilly. David Garrow's foundational research remains a go-to source for historians concerned with King and the FBI, along with Taylor Branch's three-volume King biography. The scholarship of William Nunnelley and Yasuhiro Katagiri contains especially valuable material on the FBI's relationship with Southern police departments. On the Klan and COINTELPRO–White Hate, the research of David Cunningham and John Drabble is useful.

Many of the flashpoint events and figures of era have received detailed attention in case studies, though they have not necessarily focused on the FBI. For the Freedom Rides, see Ray Arsenault's work. On Birmingham, Alabama, and FBI informant Gary Rowe, the books of Gary May and Diane McWhorter are especially useful. On Freedom Summer, see Bruce Watson's riveting account. On Malcolm X and the FBI, Manning Marable's biography is still the indispensable source, along with Clayborne Carson's edited edition of the relevant FBI files. The Black Panthers have seen a surge in scholarship in recent years; I relied especially on the work of Donna Murch and Jakobi Williams. Peniel Joseph's books are invaluable for understanding the FBI's relationship to SNCC, Stokely Carmichael, and the major organizations and incidents of the Black Power era. On FBI informant Ernest Withers, see the work of Marc Perrusquia and Preston Lauterbach.

The assassinations of the 1960s have produced a dizzying array of research, of uneven quality. On the FBI and the Kennedy assassination, the work of Philip Shenon and Max Holland stands out for its intelligence and integrity. On the King assassination investigation, Hampton Sides has provided the best account. On race, policing, and law-and-order politics in the 1960s and 1970s, an increasingly large and even booming literature includes the work Michael Flamm, James Forman, Elizabeth Hinton, Julilly Kohler-Hausmann Stuart Schrader especially. On the Kerner Commission, see Steve Gillon's recent book.

Some of the most exciting new scholarship on the FBI itself has focused on the 1960s and 1970s. Bryan Burrough provides a compelling overview of major cases (as he did for the 1930s), with an emphasis on FBI campaigns against New Left and Black radical groups. Seth Rosenfeld has focused on the state of California, including the first substantive account of the FBI's relationship with Ronald Reagan. On COINTELPRO, works by Aaron Leonard and Connor Gallagher, David Cunningham, and James Kirkpatrick Davis include valuable discoveries. Alexander Charns and Brian Hochman have taken up the issue of wiretaps, bugs, and civil liberties during the era. On the Weather Underground, Jeremy Varon provides a transnational perspective, while Arthur Eckstein's new study contains important material about the FBI's campaign against the group. On the Nixon era, new work by Daniel Chard and Melissa Graves develops both the personal and institutional politics. Betty Medsger has written the key work on the Media burglary. On the FBI's role in Watergate and related scandals, see the work of Mark Feldstein, Garrett Graff, Ken Hughes, Stanley Kutler, Ray Locker, and Donald Ritchie. Max Holland has written the definitive secondary work on Mark Felt. Kathryn Olmsted and Katherine Scott have examined the Church Committee and the Congressional investigations of the 1970s that marked the end of the Hoover era.

BIBLIOGRAPHY

General Abbreviations

B: Box
F: Folder
P: Part
PB: Photo Box
R: Reel
S: Section
Sr: Series
V: Volume

Records of the Federal Bureau Of Investigation

BI: Records of the Bureau of Investigation, RG 65, M1085, National Archives and Records Administration, College Park, MD

FBI: Records of the Federal Bureau of Investigation, held at FBI, Washington, DC

FBI FOIA: Records of the Federal Bureau of Investigation, obtained by the author through the Freedom of Information Act

FBI Fold3: Records of the Bureau of Investigation, available through fold3 by Ancestry

FBI G: Records of the Federal Bureau of Investigation, available through "Federal Response to Radicalism in the 1960s" (Gale/Cengage) and "Federal Surveillance of African Americans, 1920–1984" (Gale/Cengage)

FBI GA: Records of the Federal Bureau of Investigation, available through Government Attic (governmentattic.org)

FBI IA: Records of the Federal Bureau of Investigation, available through Internet Archive (archive.org)

FBI JFK: Records released by the National Archives and Records Administration under the President John F. Kennedy Assassination Records Collection Act of 1992 (https://www.archives.gov/research/jfk/release)

FBI MFF: Records of the Federal Bureau of Investigation and related agencies, available at Mary Ferrell Foundation (maryferrell.org)

FBI NARA: Records of the Federal Bureau of Investigation (RG 65), available at National Archives and Records Administration, College Park, MD

FBI OH: FBI Oral History Heritage Project of the Former Agents of the FBI Foundation and the Society of Former Special Agents of the FBI

FBI PA: Records of the Federal Bureau of Investigation, available through Paperless Archives (paperlessarchives.com)

FBI SR: Records of the Federal Bureau of Investigation (microfilm), published by Scholarly Resources

FBI V: Records of the Federal Bureau of Investigation, available at the Vault (vault.fbi.gov)

HO&C: "The J. Edgar Hoover Official and Confidential File," RG 65, National Archives and Records Administration, College Park, MD

JEH APP: Testimony of J. Edgar Hoover before the House Committee on Appropriations (1924–1972)

JEH APPT: Appointment calendars of J. Edgar Hoover, available at the Vault (vault.fbi.gov)

JEH LOGS: Daily logs of J. Edgar Hoover, available at the Vault (vault.fbi.gov)

JEHS: J. Edgar Hoover Scrapbooks, RG 65, National Archives and Records Administration, College Park, MD

LEB: FBI Law Enforcement Bulletin

NARA-P: Photographs Accumulated by FBI Director J. Edgar Hoover, ca. 1933–1972, RG 65, National Archives and Records Administration, College Park, MD

NO&C: Louis Nichols Official & Confidential File, edited by Athan Theoharis, University Publications of America (microfilm), 1990

Archival Collections

Boston University, Howard Gotlieb Archival Research Center, Boston, MA
    Ladislas Farago Papers
    Melvin H. Purvis Collection (MHP)
Brooklyn College, City University of New York, Brooklyn, NY
    Papers of John Rooney

Charles Sumner School Museum and Archives, Washington, DC
 Public school collections (Sumner)
Dwight D. Eisenhower Presidential Library, Abilene, KS
 Papers of Dwight D. Eisenhower (DDE): Pre-Presidential Papers, White House Central Files, President's Secretary's File, White House/Office of the Special Assistant for National Security, Post-Presidential Papers
 Papers of Herbert Brownell (HB)
 Papers of James Hagerty (JH)
 Papers of Maxwell Rabb
 Papers of William P. Rogers (WR)
The Emma Goldman Papers: A Microfilm Edition (EGP), edited by Candace Falk, Ronald J. Zobray et al., Alexandria, VA: Chadwyck-Healey, 1990
Franklin D. Roosevelt Presidential Library, Hyde Park, NY
 Papers of Franklin D. Roosevelt (FDR): Official File, President's Personal File, President's Secretary's File
 Papers of Eleanor Roosevelt
 Papers of Francis Biddle (FBiddle)
 Papers of Francis Corrigan
 Papers of Gardner Jackson (GJ)
 Papers of Harry Hopkins (HH)
 Papers of Henry Morgenthau
 Papers of Henry Wallace
 Papers of James H. Rowe Jr. (JRJ)
 Papers of John Toland (JT)
 Papers of Oscar Cox
 Papers of Stephen T. Early (STE)
 Papers of Sumner Welles
Harry S. Truman Presidential Library, Independence, MO
 Presidential Papers of Harry S. Truman (HST): President's Secretary's File, White House Central File
 Papers of Eleanor Bontecou
 Papers of J. Howard McGrath
 Papers of Tom Clark
Herbert Hoover Presidential Library, West Branch, Iowa
 Papers of Herbert Hoover (HHoo): Presidential Papers, Post-Presidential Papers
John F. Kennedy Presidential Library, Columbia Point, Boston, MA
 Presidential Papers of John F. Kennedy (JFK): National Security Files, White House Central Files
 JFK and RFK Oral History Collections
 Papers of Nicholas Katzenbach
 Personal Papers of Robert F. Kennedy
LBJ Presidential Library, Austin, TX
 Lady Bird Johnson's Home Movies (LBJ-HM), LBJ Presidential Library YouTube channel (https://www.youtube.com/channel/UCwRQxHVCyShQyky_HzHdZEQ)
 Lyndon B. Johnson's Daily Diary Collection (LBJD) (http://www.lbjlibrary.net/collections/daily-diary.html)
 Oral History Collection
 Papers of Drew Pearson
 Papers of Lyndon B. Johnson (LBJ): Confidential File, Department of Justice Administrative History, Famous Names, National Security File, Post-Presidential Papers, Senate Series, Social File, Vice President Series, White House Central Files
 Papers of Ramsey Clark
 Recordings and Transcripts of Telephone Conversations and Meetings (LBJ-T) (https://www.lbjlibrary.org/the-lbj-telephone-tapes)
 White House Aides Files: Bill Moyers, George Reedy, Joseph Califano, Mildred Stegall, Walter Jenkins
Library of Congress, Washington, DC
 Papers of Evalyn Walsh McLean (EWM)
 Papers of Harlan Fiske Stone (HFS)
 Papers of Harold Hitz Burton (HHB)
 Papers of Herbert A. Philbrick (HAP)
 Papers of John J. Walsh
 Papers of Robert H. Jackson (RJ)
Marquette University, Raynor Memorial Libraries, Milwaukee, WI
 Papers donated by Athan Theoharis (AT): "FBI Investigation and Surveillance Records, 1919"
 Kenneth O'Reilly Research Materials (KO), FBI Records
National Archives and Records Administration, College Park, MD/Washington, DC
 Background papers for CIA staff officer Thomas F. Troy's *Donovan and the CIA: A History of the Establishment of the Central Intelligence Agency* (TT), 1940–80
 Records of the Central Intelligence Agency (CIA CREST)
 Records of the Department of Justice (DOJ), RG 60
 Records of the Immigration and Naturalization Service (IB), RG 85
 Records of the Judge Advocate General (Army), RG 153
 also see Records of the Federal Bureau of Investigation, page 795
National Law Enforcement Museum, Washington, DC
 J. Edgar Hoover Collection (NLEM) *(some box and folder numbers may have changed due to transfer and reprocessing)*
National Security Agency
 Papers of the VENONA Project released by NSA (NSA Venona)
Princeton University, Seeley G. Mudd Manuscript Library, Princeton, NJ
 Papers of the American Civil Liberties Union (ACLU), 1912–1990
 Roger Nash Baldwin Papers (RNB)
Private collections
 Papers of L. Patrick Gray (LPG), Library of Congress (originally in possession of Ed Gray, Hanover, New Hampshire)
 Research files of Anthony Summers and Robbyn Swan (S-JEHC), in possession of the author
 Research files of Claire Bond Potter, in possession of the author
 Research files of Luke Nichter, in possession of the author
 Research files of Mark Feldstein, in possession of the author
 Research files of Steven M. Gillon (SMG), in possession of the author
ProQuest History Vault
 Papers of the NAACP (NAACP)
Richard Nixon Presidential Library and Museum, Yorba Linda, CA
 Papers of Richard Nixon (RN): Pre-Presidential Papers, White House Central File, White House Staff Member and Office Files *(some box and folder numbers may have changed due to transfer and reprocessing)*

White House Tapes (NT), including logs (NT-LOG) and transcripts (NT-TR) (https://www.nixonlibrary.gov/white-house-tapes); also see nixontapes.org

Stanford University, Hoover Institution Library and Archives, Stanford, CA
  Papers of Emmett C. McGaughey (EMG)

University of Cambridge, Churchill College, Churchill Archives Centre, Cambridge, UK
  Papers of Vasili Mitrokhin (MITN)

University of Maryland, Library of American Broadcasting, College Park, MD
  Papers of Helen Sioussat

University of Mississippi, Department of Archives & Special Collections, Oxford, MS
  James O. Eastland Collection

University of Southern Mississippi, Center for Oral History and Cultural Heritage, Hattiesburg, MS
  Oral history with Mr. Hugh H. Clegg, 1975–1976 (Clegg OH)

University of Tennessee, Betsey B. Creekmore University Special Collections and University Archives, Knoxville, TN
  Don Whitehead Journalistic Collection

University of Virginia, Albert and Shirley Small Special Collections Library, Charlottesville, VA
  Papers of Homer Stille Cummings (HSC)

Wesleyan University, Special Collections & Archives, Middletown, CT
  Papers of William Manchester (WMP)

Yale University, Sterling Memorial Library, New Haven, CT
  Papers of Frank Donner
  Papers of Ogden Rogers Reid
  Papers of William F. Buckley

Published Government Records

Activities of DOJ: *Investigation Activities of the Department of Justice: Letter from the Attorney General Transmitting in Response to a Senate Resolution of October 17, 1919, a Report on the Activities of the Bureau of Investigation of the Department of Justice Against Persons Advising Anarchy, Sedition, and the Forcible Overthrow of the Government.* Washington, D.C.: U.S. Government Printing Office, 1919.

AR/AG: Annual Reports of the Attorney General

Army/McCarthy: *Hearings before the Special Subcommittee on Investigation of the Committee on Government Operations, "Special Senate Investigation on Charges and Countercharges Involving: Secretary of the Army Robert T. Stevens, John G. Adams, H. Struve Hensel, and Senator Joe McCarthy, Roy M. Cohn, and Francis P. Carr.* Washington, D.C.: U.S. Government Printing Office, 1954.

CC2 (Church Committee, Book 2): *Intelligence Activities and the Rights of Americans: Book II, Final Report of the Select Committee to Study Governmental Operations with Respect to Intelligence Activities, United States Senate.* Washington, D.C.: U.S. Government Printing Office, 1976.

CC3 (Church Committee, Book 3): *Supplementary Detailed Staff Reports on Intelligence Activities and the Rights of Americans: Book III, Final Report of the Select Committee to Study Governmental Operations with Respect to Intelligence Activities, United States Senate.* Washington, D.C.: U.S. Government Printing Office, 1976.

CC5 (Church Committee, Book 5): *The Investigation of the Assassination of President John F. Kennedy: Performance of the Intelligence Agencies, Book V, Final Report of the Select Committee to Study Governmental Operations with Respect to Intelligence Activities, United States Senate.* Washington, D.C.: U.S. Government Printing Office, 1976.

CC6 (Church Committee, Book 6): *Supplementary Reports on Intelligence Activities: Book VI, Final Report of the Select Committee to Study Governmental Operations with Respect to Intelligence Activities, United States Senate.* Washington, D.C.: U.S. Government Printing Office, 1976.

CCH2 (Church Committee Hearings, Vol. 2): *Hearings before the Select Committee to Study Governmental Operations with Respect to Intelligence Activities of the United States Senate, Ninety-Fourth Congress, First Session: Volume 2, Huston Plan.* Washington, D.C.: U.S. Government Printing Office, 1976.

CCH6 (Church Committee Hearings, Vol. 6): *Hearings before the Select Committee to Study Governmental Operations with Respect to Intelligence Activities of the United States Senate, Ninety-Fourth Congress, First Session: Volume 6, Federal Bureau of Investigation.* Washington, D.C.: U.S. Government Printing Office, 1976.

CD (City Directory): *Washington, D.C. City Directory, 1860–1925* (online database). Provo, UT: Ancestry.com Operations, 2000.

Census: *1800–1940 United States Federal Census* (online database). Provo, UT: Ancestry.com Operations, 2010.

Coast Survey: Reports of the superintendent of the U.S. Coast and Geodetic Survey, 1858–1896. Washington, D.C.: U.S. Government Printing Office.

CrimeConf: *Proceedings of the Attorney General's Conference on Crime, December 10–13, 1934.* Washington, D.C.: U.S. Government Printing Office, 1934.

Daugherty: U.S. Congress, Senate, Select Committee on Investigation of the Attorney General. *Investigation of Hon. Harry M. Daugherty, Formerly Attorney General of the U.S. Vol. 1: Hearings before the United States Senate Select Committee on Investigation of Attorney General, Sixty-Eighth Congress, First Session, on Apr. 1–4, May 12–22, 26–29, 1924.* Washington, D.C.: U.S. Government Printing Office, 1924.

Files: U.S. House, Subcommittee of the Committee on Government Operations, *Inquiry into the Destruction of Former FBI Director J. Edgar Hoover's Files and FBI Recordkeeping*, Ninety-Fourth Congress, First Session, December 1, 1975. Washington, D.C.: U.S. Government Printing Office, 1975.

Fish: U.S. Congress, House, Special Committee on Communist Activities in the United States. *Hearings before a Special Committee to Investigate Communist Activities in the United States of the House of Representatives, Seventy-First Congress, Second Session, Pursuant to H. Res. 220, Providing for an Investigation of Communist Propaganda in the United States.* Washington, D.C.: U.S. Government Printing Office, 1930–1931.

FRUS: *Foreign Relations of the United States.* Washington, D.C.: U.S. Government Printing Office.

Hoey: Clyde Roark Hoey, U.S. Congress, Senate, Committee on Expenditures in the Executive Departments. *Employment of Homosexuals and Other Sex Perverts in Government. Interim Report Submitted to the Committee on Expenditures in the Executive Departments by Its Subcommittee on Investigations Pursuant to S. Res. 280, 81st Congress, a Resolution Authorizing the Committee on Expenditures in the Executive Departments to Carry Out Certain Duties. December 15 (Legislative day, November 27), 1950.* Washington, D.C.: Ward & Paul, 1950.

Hoey Hearings: U.S. Congress, Senate, Committee on Expenditures in the Executive Departments. *Investigations Subcommittee, Hearings Pursuant to S. Res. 280, Executive Session, Eighty-First Congress, Second Session, on July 14, 1950–September 8, 1950.* Washington, D.C.: U.S. Government Printing Office, 1950.

HSCA: *Hearings before the Select Committee on Assassinations of the U.S. House of Representatives, Ninety-Fifth Congress, Second Session.* Washington, D.C.: U.S. Government Printing Office, 1978.

HSCA Report: *Final Report of the Select Committee on Assassinations, U.S. House of Representatives, Ninety-Fifth Congress, Second Session: Summary of Findings and Recommendations.* Washington, D.C.: U.S. Government Printing Office, 1979.

Illegal Practices: U.S. Congress, Senate, Committee on the Judiciary. *Charges of Illegal Practices of the Department of Justice: Hearings before the United States Senate Committee on the Judiciary, Sixty-Sixth Congress, Third Session, on Jan. 19, 25, 27, Feb. 1, Mar. 3, 1921.* Washington, D.C.: U.S. Government Printing Office, 1921.

Investigation of Post: U.S. Congress, House, Committee on Rules. *Investigation of Administration of Louis F. Post, Assistant Secretary of Labor, in the Matter of Deportation of Aliens: Hearings before the Committee on Rules, House of Representatives, Sixty-Sixth Congress, Second Session.* Washington, D.C.: U.S. Government Printing Office, 1920.

Palmer on Charges: U.S. Congress, House, Committee on Rules. *Attorney General A. Mitchell Palmer on Charges Made against Department of Justice by Louis F. Post and Others. Hearings before the Committee on Rules, House of Representatives, Sixty-Sixth Congress, Second Session.* Washington, D.C.: U.S. Government Printing Office, 1920.

Poindexter: U.S. Attorney-General; U.S. Congress, Senate. *Investigation Activities of the Department of Justice: Letter from the Attorney General Transmitting in Response to a Senate Resolution of October 17, 1919, a Report of the Activities of the Bureau of Investigation of the Department of Justice against Persons Advising Anarchy, Sedition, and the Forcible Overthrow of the Government.* Washington, D.C.: U.S. Government Printing Office, 1919.

Ray: James Earl Ray sentencing hearing, available at http:// jfk.hood.edu/Collection/Weisberg%20Subject %20Index%20Files/R%20Disk/Ray%20James%20Earl %20Trial%20Transcript%203-10-69/Item%2003.pdf.

Roberts Report: *Attack upon Pearl Harbor by Japanese Armed Forces: Report of the Commission Appointed by the President of the United States to Investigate and Report the Facts Relating to the Attack Made by Japanese Armed Forces upon Pearl Harbor in the Territory of Hawaii on December 7, 1941.* Washington, D.C.: U.S. Government Printing Office, 1942.

Saboteurs: Trial transcript, Court Martial Case 334178 (German Saboteurs), RG 153. Accessed in National Archives Online Catalog. NA identifier: 6121078, RG 153.

WCES: Warren Commission Executive Sessions. Available at Mary Ferrell Foundation.

WCH: Hearings of the *Investigation of the Assassination of President John F. Kennedy: Hearings before the President's Commission on the Assassination of President Kennedy.* Washington, D.C.: U.S. Government Printing Office, 1964. Available at Mary Ferrell Foundation.

WCR: *The Warren Commission Report: Report of the President's Commission on the Assassination of President John F. Kennedy.* New York: St. Martin's Press, 1964.

Wherry: U.S. Congress, Senate, Committee on the District of Columbia. *Report of the Investigations of the Junior Senator of Nebraska on the Infiltration of Subversives and Moral Perverts into the Executive Branch of the U.S. Government.* [S.l]: [s.n.], 1950–1951.

Wickersham: *National Commission on Law Observance and Enforcement: Report on Criminal Statistics* (Vol. 3). Washington, D.C.: U.S. Government Printing Office, 1931.

Newspapers and Magazines (selected, with abbreviations)

AC: The Atlanta Constitution

BG: The Boston Globe

Brecky: Brecky (yearbook of Central High School, Washington, DC)

BS: The Baltimore Sun

ChiT: Chicago Tribune

CHR: The Review (student newspaper of Central High School, Washington, DC)

CR: Congressional Record

CSM: The Christian Science Monitor

CT: Cherry Tree (yearbook of George Washington University)

DSR: Dan Smoot Report

DW: Daily Worker

Hatchet: The University Hatchet (student newspaper of George Washington University)

HC: The Hartford Courant

KAJ: The Kappa Alpha Journal

LAT: Los Angeles Times

MDN: Miami Daily News

MH: Miami Herald

MJ: The Milwaukee Journal

NatR: National Review

NR: The New Republic

NYDN: New York Daily News

NYH: The New York Herald

NYHT: New York Herald Tribune

NYJA: New York Journal-American

NYJ: New York Journal

NYM: New York Mirror

NYP: New York Post/New York Evening Post

NYS: The New York Sun

NYT: The New York Times

NYTr: New-York Tribune

NYW: The World (NY)

NYWT: New York World-Telegram/New York World-Telegram and The Sun

RD: Reader's Digest

SEP: The Saturday Evening Post

SFC: San Francisco Chronicle

SLPD: St. Louis Post-Dispatch

WDN: Washington Daily News

WH: The Washington Herald

WN: Washington News

WP: The Washington Post/Washington Post and Times-Herald

WS: The Washington Star/Evening Star

WSJ: The Wall Street Journal

WT: The Washington Times

WTH: Washington Times-Herald

Published Primary Sources

Anderson, Jack. *Peace, War, and Politics: An Eyewitness Account.* New York: Tom Doherty Associates, 1999.

Barth, Alan. *The Loyalty of Free Men*. New York: Viking, 1951.

Beebe, Lucius. *The Stork Club Bar Book*. New York: Rinehart & Company, 1946.

Belafonte, Harry, with Michael Shnayerson. *My Song: A Memoir*. New York: Alfred A. Knopf, 2011.

Bentley, Elizabeth. *Out of Bondage: The Story of Elizabeth Bentley*. New York: Devin-Adair, 1951.

Bernstein, Carl, and Bob Woodward. *All the President's Men*. New York: Simon & Schuster, 1974.

Beschloss, Michael R., ed. *Reaching for Glory: Lyndon Johnson's Secret White House Tapes, 1964–1965*. New York: Simon & Schuster, 2001.

———. *Taking Charge: The Johnson White House Tapes, 1963–1964*. New York: Simon & Schuster, 1997.

Biddle, Francis. *In Brief Authority*. New York: Doubleday, 1962.

Booker, Simeon. *Shocking the Conscience: A Reporter's Account of the Civil Rights Movement*. Jackson: University Press of Mississippi, 2013.

Bowers, Scotty. *Full Service: My Adventures in Hollywood and the Secret Sex Lives of the Stars*. New York: Grove Press, 2012.

Brinkley, David. *Washington Goes to War*. New York: Ballantine, 1988.

Brinkley, Douglas, and Nichter, Luke A., eds. *The Nixon Tapes, 1971–1972*. Boston: Mariner, 2015.

Brownell, Herbert. *Advising Ike: The Memoirs of Attorney General Herbert Brownell*. Lawrence: University Press of Kansas, 1993.

Budenz, Louis Francis. *Men without Faces: The Communist Conspiracy in the USA*. New York: Harper, 1950.

———. *This Is My Story*. New York: McGraw-Hill, 1947.

Calomiris, Angela. *Red Masquerade: Undercover for the FBI*. Philadelphia: J. B. Lippincott, 1950.

Carson, Clayborn and Kris Shepard. *A Call to Conscience: The Landmark Speeches of Dr. Martin Luther King, Jr.* New York: Warner Books, 2001.

Centennial Celebration of the United States Coast and Geodetic Survey, April 5 and 6, 1916. Washington, D.C.: U.S. Government Printing Office, 1916.

Chambers, Whittaker. *Witness*. New York: Random House, 1952.

Churchill, Ward, and Vander Wall, Jim. *The COINTELPRO Papers: Documents from the FBI's Secret Wars against Dissent in the United States*. Cambridge, MA: South End Press, 2002.

Clark, Ramsey. *Crime in America: Observations on its Nature, Causes, Prevention and Control*. New York: Simon & Schuster, 1970.

Coan, Blair. *The Red Web: 1921–1924*. Boston: Western Islands, 1969.

Cohn, Roy M. *McCarthy*. New York: New American Library, 1968.

Collins, Frederick L. *The FBI in Peace and War*. New York: G. P. Putnam's Sons, 1943.

Comfort, Mildred. *J. Edgar Hoover: Modern Knight Errant*. Minneapolis: T. S. Denison, 1959.

Cooke, Alistair. *A Generation on Trial: U.S.A. v. Alger Hiss*. London: Rupert Hart-Davis, 1950.

Cook, Fred. *The FBI Nobody Knows*. New York: Macmillan Company, 1964.

Cooper, Courtney Ryley. *Designs in Scarlet*. Boston: Little, Brown and Company, 1939.

———. *The Eagle's Eye: A True Story of the Imperial German Government's Spies and Intrigues in America from Facts Furnished by William J. Flynn*. New York: McCann Company, 1919.

———. *Ten Thousand Public Enemies*. Boston: Little, Brown and Company, 1935.

Cummings, Homer, and Carl McFarland. *Federal Justice: Chapters in the History of Justice and the Federal Executive*. New York: Macmillan Company, 1937.

Cummings, Homer. *Liberty under Law and Administration*. New York: Charles Scribner's Sons, 1934.

Dasch, George John. *Eight Spies against America*. New York: Robert M. McBride & Company, 1959.

Daugherty, Harry M., and Thomas Dixon Jr. *The Inside Story of the Harding Tragedy*. New York: Churchill Company, 1932.

DeLoach, Cartha D. "Deke." *Hoover's FBI: The Inside Story by Hoover's Trusted Lieutenant*. Washington, DC: Regnery, 1995.

Dennis, Peggy. *The Autobiography of an American Communist: A Personal View of a Political Life, 1925–1975*. Berkeley, CA: Creative Arts Books, 1977.

Dilling, Elizabeth Kirkpatrick. *The Red Network: A "Who's Who" and Handbook of Radicalism for Patriots*. Kenilworth, IL: Published by the author, 1934.

Dudman, Richard. *Men of the Far Right*. New York: Pyramid Books, 1962.

Ehrlichman, John. *Witness to Power: The Nixon Years*. New York: Simon & Schuster, 1982.

Elson, Edward L. R. *America's Spiritual Recovery*. Westwood, NJ: Fleming H. Revell Company, 1954.

Ernst, Morris L. *The Best Is Yet . . .* New York: Harper & Brothers, 1945.

Faulk, John Henry. *Fear on Trial*. New York: Simon & Schuster, 1964.

Felt, Mark. *The FBI Pyramid: From the Inside*. New York: Putnam, 1979.

Felt, Mark, and John O'Connor. *Felt: The Man Who Brought Down the White House*. New York: PublicAffairs, 2017.

———. *A G-Man's Life: The FBI, Being "Deep Throat," and the Struggle for Honor in Washington*. New York: PublicAffairs, 2006.

Ferrell, Robert H. *Off the Record: The Private Papers of Harry S. Truman*. Columbia: University of Missouri Press, 1980.

Floherty, John J. *Inside the FBI*. Philadelphia: J. B. Lippincott, 1943.

Forbush, William. *The Boy Problem: A Study in Social Pedagogy*. New York: Pilgrim Press, 1902.

Ford, Gerald R., and John R. Stiles. *Portrait of the Assassin*. New York: Simon & Schuster, 1965.

Friedly, Michael, and Gallen, David. *Martin Luther King, Jr.: The FBI File*. New York: Carroll & Graf, 1993.

George, Harrison. *The Red Dawn*. Chicago: I.W.W. Publishing Bureau, 1918.

Germany, Kent B., and David C. Carter, eds. *Presidential Recordings: Lyndon B. Johnson: Mississippi Burning and the Passage of the Civil Rights Act, June 23, 1964–July 4, 1964*, vol. 8. New York: W. W. Norton & Company, 2011.

Giancana, Sam, Chuck Giancana, and Bettina Giancana. *Double Cross: The Explosive Inside Story of the Mobster Who Controlled America*. New York: Skyhorse, 2014.

Goldman, Emma. *Living My Life*. New York: Alfred A. Knopf, 1931.

Gouzenko, Igor. *The Iron Curtain*. New York: E. P. Dutton, 1948.

Gray, L. Patrick III, and Ed Gray. *In Nixon's Web: A Year in the Crosshairs of Watergate*. New York: Times Books, 2008.

Green, Gil. *Cold War Fugitive: A Personal Story of the McCarthy Years*. New York: International, 1984.

Guthman, Edwin. *We Band of Brothers: A Memoir of Robert F. Kennedy*. New York: Harper & Row, 1964.

Haig, Alexander M. Jr. *Inner Circles: How America Changed the World: A Memoir*. New York: Warner Books, 1992.

Haldeman, H. R. *The Haldeman Diaries: Inside the Nixon White House*. New York: G. P. Putnam's Sons, 1994.

Hathaway, Henry, dir. *The House on 92nd Street*. Los Angeles: 20th Century Fox, 1945.

Healey, Dorothy Ray, and Maurice Isserman. *California Red: A Life in the American Communist Party*. Urbana: University of Illinois Press, 1993.

Hiss, Alger. *In the Court of Public Opinion*. New York: Alfred A. Knopf, 1957.

Holland, Max. *The Kennedy Assassination Tapes*. New York: Alfred A. Knopf, 2004.

Hoover, Herbert. *American Individualism*. Stanford, CA: Hoover Institution Press, 2016. First published 1922.

Hoover, J. Edgar. *J. Edgar Hoover on Communism*. New York: Random House, 1962.

———. *J. Edgar Hoover Speaks Concerning Communism*. Washington, DC: Capitol Hill Press, 1970.

———. *Masters of Deceit: The Story of Communism in America and How to Fight It*. New York: Holt, Rinehart and Winston, 1958.

———. *Persons in Hiding*. Boston: Little, Brown and Company, 1938.

———. *A Study of Communism*. New York: Holt, Rinehart and Winston, 1962.

Horney, Karen. *Our Inner Conflicts: A Constructive Theory of Neurosis*. New York: W. W. Norton & Company, 1945.

———. *Self-Analysis*. New York: W. W. Norton & Company, 1942.

Hosty, James. *Assignment: Oswald*. New York: Arcade, 1996.

Hurd, Henry M., ed. *The Institutional Care of the Insane in the United States and Canada*, vol. 2. Baltimore: Johns Hopkins University Press, 1916.

Hynd, Alan. *Passport to Treason: The Inside Story of Spies in America*. New York: National Travel Club, 1943.

Jackson, Robert. *That Man: An Insider's Portrait of Franklin D. Roosevelt*. Edited by John Q. Barrett. New York: Oxford University Press, 2003.

Johnson, Lyndon. *The Vantage Point: Perspectives of the Presidency, 1963–1969*. New York: Holt, Rinehart and Winston, 1971.

Karpis, Alvin, and Bill Trent. *The Alvin Karpis Story*. New York: Coward, McCann & Geoghegan, 1971.

Katzenbach, Nicholas deB. *Some of It Was Fun: Working with RFK and LBJ*. New York: W. W. Norton & Company, 2008.

Keighley, William, dir. *G Men*. Burbank, CA: Warner Bros. Pictures, 1935.

Kelley, Clarence M., and James Kirkpatrick Davis. *Kelley: The Story of an FBI Director*. New York: Andrews McMeel, 1987.

Kennedy, Robert F. *The Enemy Within*. New York: Harper & Brothers, 1960.

King, Martin Luther Jr. *Why We Can't Wait*. New York: New American Library, 1964.

Kutler, Stanley I., ed. *Abuse of Power: The New Nixon Tapes*. New York: Free Press, 1997.

Lait, Jack, and Lee Mortimer. *Washington Confidential*. New York: Crown, 1951.

Lamphere, Robert J., and Tom Schachtman. *The FBI-KGB War: A Special Agent's Story*. Macon, GA: Mercer University Press, 1995.

Lawson, Steven F., ed. *To Secure These Rights: The Report of President Harry S Truman's Committee on Civil Rights*. Boston: Bedford/St. Martin's, 2004.

Lee, Robert E., and John Shosky. *In the Public Interest: The Life of Robert Emmet Lee from the FBI to the FCC*. Lanham, MD: University Press of America, 1996.

Lenin, Vladimir. "A Letter to American Workers." New York: International Publishers, 1934. First published August 22, 1918.

LeRoy, Mervyn, dir. *The FBI Story*. Burbank, CA: Warner Bros. Pictures, 1959.

LeRoy, Mervyn, and Dick Kleiner. *Mervyn LeRoy: Take One*. New York: Hawthorn Books, 1974.

Letersky, Paul, and Gordon Dillow. *The Director: My Years Assisting J. Edgar Hoover*. New York: Scribner, 2021.

Liddy, G. Gordon. *Will: The Autobiography of G. Gordon Liddy*. New York: St. Martin's Press, 1980.

Link, Arthur S., ed. *The Papers of Woodrow Wilson*, vols. 1–69. Princeton, NJ: Princeton University Press, 1966–1994.

Lowenthal, Max. *The Federal Bureau of Investigation*. New York: William Sloane Associates, 1950.

Maheu, Robert, and Richard Hack. *Next to Hughes: Behind the Power and Tragic Downfall of Howard Hughes by His Closest Advisor*. New York: HarperCollins, 1992.

Mallett, William E. *The Reuther Memorandum: Its Applications and Implications*. Washington, D.C.: Liberty Lobby, 1963.

Manchester, William. *The Death of a President: November 20–November 25, 1963*. New York: Harper & Row, 1967.

Martin, Olga. *Hollywood's Movie Commandments: A Handbook for Motion Picture Writers and Reviewers*. New York: H. W. Wilson Company, 1937.

McGhee, Millie L. *Secrets Uncovered: J. Edgar Hoover, Passing For White?* Rancho Cucamonga, CA: Allen-Morris, 2000.

McJimsey, George, ed. *Documentary History of the Franklin D. Roosevelt Presidency*, vol. 32: *Roosevelt, J. Edgar Hoover, and Domestic Surveillance, 1939–1942,*. Bethesda, MD: University Publications of America, 2006.

Means, Gaston B. *The Strange Death of President Harding: From the Diaries of Gaston B. Means, As Told to May Dixon Thacker*. New York: Guild, 1930.

Meeropol, Robert, and Michael Meeropol. *We Are Your Sons*. Boston: Houghton Mifflin, 1975.

Merman, Ethel, and George Eells. *Merman: An Autobiography*. New York: Simon & Schuster, 1978.

Messick, Hank. *John Edgar Hoover: An Inquiry into the Life and Times of John Edgar Hoover and His Relationship to the Continuing Partnership of Crime, Business, and Politics*. New York: David McKay, 1972.

Milan, Michael. *The Squad: The Shocking True Story of J. Edgar Hoover's Private Hit Team—and the U.S. Government's Secret Alliance with Organized Crime!* New York: Berkley, 1992.

Miller, Kelly. *An Appeal to Reason: An Open Letter to John Temple Graves*. Washington, DC: Hayworth Pub. House, 1906.

Miller, Marion. *I Was a Spy: The Story of a Brave Housewife*. Indianapolis: Bobbs-Merrill, 1960.

Moley, Raymond. *The Hays Office*. Indianapolis: Bobbs-Merrill, 1945.

Myrdal, Gunnar. *An American Dilemma: The Negro Problem and Modern Democracy*. New York: Harper, 1944.

Nash, Jay Robert. *Citizen Hoover: A Critical Study of the Life and Times of J. Edgar Hoover*. Lanham, MD: Rowman & Littlefield, 1972.

Nelson, Jack. *Scoop: The Evolution of a Southern Reporter*. Jackson: University of Mississippi Press, 2013.

Nelson, Jack, and Jack Bass. *The Orangeburg Massacre*. New York: World Publishing, 1970.

Nelson, Jack, and Ronald J. Ostrow. *The FBI and the Berrigans: The Making of a Conspiracy*. New York: Coward, McCann & Geoghegan, 1972.

Nicolay, Helen. *Our Capital on the Potomac*. New York: Century Co., 1924.

Nixon, Richard. *RN: The Memoirs of Richard Nixon*. New York: Grosset & Dunlap, 1978.

O'Connor, John D. "I'm the Guy They Call Deep Throat." *Vanity Fair*, July 2005.

Ollestad, Norman. *Inside the FBI*. New York: Lyle Stuart, 1967.

Organized Sunday School Work in America, 1908–1911. Chicago: Executive Committee of the National Sunday School Association, 1911.

Ottenberg, Miriam. *The Federal Investigators*. Englewood Cliffs, NJ: Prentice-Hall, 1962.

Oudes, Bruce, ed. *From: The President: Richard Nixon's Secret Files*. New York: Harper & Row, 1989.

Oursler, Fulton. *The Greatest Story Ever Told: A Tale of the Greatest Life Ever Lived*. Garden City, NY: Doubleday, 1949.

Overstreet, Harry, and Bonaro Overstreet. *The FBI in Our Open Society*. New York: Norton, 1969.

Painter, Nell Irvin. *The Narrative of Hosea Hudson: The Life and Times of a Black Radical*. New York: W. W. Norton & Company, 1993.

Pearson, Drew. *Washington Merry-Go-Round: The Drew Pearson Diaries, 1960–1969*. Edited by Peter Hannaford. Lincoln: Potomac Books/University of Nebraska Press, 2015.

Perlstein, Rick, ed. *Richard Nixon: Speeches, Writings, Documents*. Princeton, NJ: Princeton University Press, 2008.

Philbrick, Herbert. *I Led Three Lives: Citizen, "Communist," Counterspy*. New York: McGraw-Hill Book Company, Inc., 1952.

Philby, Kim. *My Silent War*. London: Panther, 1969.

Popov, Dusko. *Spy/Counterspy*. New York: Grosset & Dunlap, 1974.

Post, Louis F. *The Deportations Delirium of Nineteen-Twenty: A Personal Narrative of an Historic Official Experience*. Chicago: Charles H. Kerr & Company, 1923.

Purvis, Melvin. *American Agent*. Garden City, NY: Doubleday, Doran & Co., 1936.

Race Problems of the South; Report of the Proceedings of the First Annual Conference Held under the Auspices of the Southern Society for the Promotion of the Study of Race Conditions and Problems in the South, at Montgomery, Alabama, May 8, 9, 10, A.D. 1900. Richmond, VA: B. F. Johnson Publishing Company, 1900.

Report of the National Advisory Commission on Civil Disorders. New York: E. P. Dutton, 1968.

Reynolds, Quentin. *The FBI*. New York: Random House, 1963.

Roemer, William F. *Roemer: Man against the Mob*. New York: Donald Fine, 1989.

Rogers, Ginger. *Ginger: My Story*. New York: Easton Press, 1991.

Roosevelt, Elliott, and James Brough. *A Rendezvous with Destiny: The Roosevelts of the White House*. New York: G. P. Putnam's Sons, 1975.

Rowe, Gary Thomas. *My Undercover Years with the Ku Klux Klan*. New York: Bantam Books, 1976.

Scammon, Richard M., and Ben J. Wattenberg. *The Real Majority: An Extraordinary Examination of the American Electorate*. New York: Primus, 1970.

Sheridan, Walter. *The Fall and Rise of Jimmy Hoffa*. New York: Saturday Review Press, 1972.

Skousen, W. Cleon. *The Naked Communist*. Salt Lake City: Ensign, 1958.

Smoot, Dan. *People along the Way: The Autobiography of Dan Smoot*. Tyler, TX: Tyler Press, 1996.

Spolansky, Jacob. *The Communist Trail in America*. New York: MacMillan Company, 1951.

Strober, Deborah Hart, and Gerald S. Strober. *"Let Us Begin Anew": An Oral History of the Presidency of John F. Kennedy*. New York: HarperCollins, 1993.

Sullivan, William C., and Bill Brown. *The Bureau: My Thirty Years in Hoover's FBI*. New York: W. W. Norton & Company, 1979.

Swan, Patrick A., ed. *Alger Hiss, Whittaker Chambers, and the Schism in the American Soul*. Wilmington, DE: ISI Books, 2003.

Theoharis, Athan, ed. *From the Secret Files of J. Edgar Hoover*. Chicago: Ivan R. Dee, 1993.

Tully, Andrew. *The FBI's Most Famous Cases*. New York: William Morrow, 1965.

Turner, William W. *Hoover's FBI: The Men and the Myth*. Los Angeles: Sherbourne Press, 1970.

Turrou, Leon G. *Nazi Spies in America*. New York: Random House, 1939.

———. *Where My Shadow Falls: Two Decades of Crime Detection*. Garden City, NY: Doubleday, 1949.

von Hoffman, Nicholas. *Mississippi Notebook*. New York: David White Company, 1964.

Wannall, Ray. *The Real J. Edgar Hoover, for the Record*. Paducah, KY: Turner, 2000.

Warren, Earl. *Memoirs of Chief Justice Earl Warren*. New York: Madison Books, 2001 (1977).

Washington Alumni Association of Central High School. *Centennial History of Central High School, 1876–1976*. Washington, D.C.: 1976.

Washington, D.C.: A Guide to the Nation's Capital: Compiled by Workers of the Writers Program of the Works Projects Administration for the District of Columbia. New York: Hastings House, 1942.

Watters, Pat, and Steve Gillers, ed. *Investigating the FBI*. New York: Doubleday & Co., 1973.

Welch, Neil J., and David W. Marston. *Inside Hoover's FBI: The Top Field Chief Reports*. Garden City, NY: Doubleday, 1984.

West, Nigel, ed. *British Security Coordination: The Secret History of British Intelligence in the Americas, 1940–45*. London: St. Ermin's Press, 1998.

Weyl, Walter. *The New Democracy: An Essay on Certain Political and Economic Tendencies in the United States*. New York: Macmillan Company, 1912.

Wheeler, Burton K. *Yankee from the West: The Candid, Turbulent Life Story of the Yankee-Born U.S. Senator from Montana*. Garden City, NY: Doubleday, 1962.

Whitehead, Don. *The FBI Story: A Report to the People*. New York: Random House, 1956.

White, Walter Francis. *A Man Called White: The Autobiography of Walter White*. New York: Viking, 1948.

Willens, Howard P. *History Will Prove Us Right: Inside the Warren Commission Report*. New York: Overlook Press, 2013.

Woodward, Bob. *The Secret Man: The Story of Watergate's Deep Throat*. New York: Simon & Schuster, 2005.

Young, Andrew. *An Easy Burden: The Civil Rights Movement and the Transformation of America*. New York: Harper-Collins, 1996.

Zion, Sidney. *Autobiography of Roy Cohn*. New York: St. Martin's Press, 1988.

Secondary Sources

Ackerman, Kenneth D. *Young J. Edgar: Hoover, the Red Scare, and the Assault on Civil Liberties*. New York: Carroll & Graf, 2007.

Adams, Samuel Hopkins. *Incredible Era: The Life and Times of Warren Gamaliel Harding*. Boston: Houghton Mifflin Company, 1939.

Aitken, Jonathan. *Nixon: A Life*. London: Weidenfeld and Nicolson, 1993.

Albright, Joseph, and Marcia Kunstel. *Bombshell: The Secret Story of America's Unknown Atomic Spy Conspiracy*. New York: Times Books, 1997.

Anderson, Devery S. *Emmett Till: The Murder That Shocked the World and Propelled the Civil Rights Movement*. Jackson: University Press of Mississippi, 2015.

Anderson, Jervis. *Bayard Rustin: Troubles I've Seen*. New York: HarperCollins, 1997.

Anderson, Karen. *Little Rock: Race and Resistance at Central High School*. Princeton, NJ: Princeton University Press, 2010.

Anderson, Scott. *The Quiet Americans: Four CIA Spies at the Dawn of the Cold War—A Tragedy in Three Acts*. New York: Knopf Doubleday, 2020.

Andrew, Christopher. *The Secret World: A History of Intelligence*. New Haven, CT: Yale University Press, 2018.

Andrew, Christopher, and Vasili Mitrokhin. *The Sword and the Shield: The Mitrokhin Archive and the Secret History of the KGB*. New York: Basic Books, 2000.

Aronson, Mark. *Master of Deceit: J. Edgar Hoover and America in the Age of Lies*. New York: Candlewick, 2012.

Arsenault, Raymond. *Freedom Riders: 1961 and the Struggle for Racial Justice*. New York: Oxford University Press, 2006 (unabridged); 2011 (abridged).

Asch, Chris Myers. *The Senator and the Sharecropper: The Freedom Struggles of James O. Eastland and Fannie Lou Hamer*. New York: New Press, 2008.

Asch, Chris Myers, and George Derek Musgrove. *Chocolate City: A History of Race and Democracy in the Nation's Capital*. Chapel Hill: University of North Carolina Press, 2017.

Avrich, Paul. *Sacco and Vanzetti: The Anarchist Background*. Princeton, NJ: Princeton University Press, 1991.

Avrich, Paul, and Karen Avrich. *Sasha and Emma*. Cambridge, MA: Belknap Press/Harvard University Press, 2012.

Bakke, Kit. *Protest on Trial: The Seattle 7 Conspiracy*. Pullman: Washington State University Press, 2018.

Balogh, Brian. *The Associational State: American Governance in the Twentieth Century*. Philadelphia: University of Pennsylvania Press, 2015.

Barbas, Samantha. *The Rise and Fall of Morris Ernst, Free Speech Renegade*. Chicago: University of Chicago Press, 2021.

Barrett, James R. *William Z. Foster and the Tragedy of American Radicalism*. Urbana: University of Illinois Press, 1999.

Barron, John. *Operation SOLO: The FBI's Man in the Kremlin*. Washington, D.C.: Regnery, 1996.

Bartley, Numan V. *The Rise of Massive Resistance: Race and Politics in the South During the 1950s*. Baton Rouge: Louisiana State University Press, 1969.

Bass, Jack, and Marilyn W. Thompson. *Strom: The Complicated Personal and Political Life of Strom Thurmond*. New York: PublicAffairs, 2005.

Batvinis, Raymond J. *Hoover's Secret War against Axis Spies: FBI Counterespionage during World War II*. Lawrence: University Press of Kansas, 2014.

———. *The Origins of FBI Counterintelligence*. Lawrence: University Press of Kansas, 2007.

Becker, Marc. *The FBI in Latin America: The Ecuador Files*. Durham, NC: Duke University Press, 2017.

Bederman, Gail. *Manliness and Civilization: A Cultural History of Gender and Race in the United States, 1880–1917*. Chicago: University of Chicago Press, 1996.

———. "'The Women Have Had Charge of the Church Work Long Enough': The Men and Religion Forward Movement of 1911–1912 and the Masculinization of Middle-Class Protestantism." *American Quarterly* 41, no. 3 (1989): 432–65.

Beito, David T., and Linda Royster Beito. *Black Maverick: T. R. M. Howard's Fight for Civil Rights and Economic Power*. Urbana: University of Illinois Press, 2009.

———. *T. R. M. Howard: Doctor, Entrepreneur, Civil Rights Pioneer*. Oakland, CA: Independent Institute, 2018.

Belknap, Michael R. *Cold War Political Justice: The Smith Act, the Communist Party, and American Civil Liberties*. Westport, CT: Greenwood Press, 1978.

Bellows, Susan, dir. *American Experience*. Season 30, episode 4, "The Bombing of Wall Street." Aired February 13, 2018, on PBS.

Benbow, Mark E. "Birth of a Quotation: Woodrow Wilson and 'Like Writing History with Lightning.'" *Journal of the Gilded Age and Progressive Era* 9, no. 4 (2010): 509–33.

Benson, Robert L. *The Venona Story*. Fort Meade, MD: National Security Agency Center for Cryptologic History, 2001.

Benson, Robert L., and Michael Warner, eds. *Venona: Soviet Espionage and the American Response, 1939–1957*. Washington, D.C.: National Security Agency, 1996.

Berg, Manfred. "Black Civil Rights and Liberal Anticommunism: The NAACP in the Early Cold War." *Journal of American History* 94, no. 1 (2007): 75–96.

Bérubé, Allan. *Coming Out under Fire: The History of Gay Men and Women in World War II*. Chapel Hill: University of North Carolina Press, 2010.

Beverly, William. *On the Lam: Narratives of Flight in J. Edgar Hoover's America*. Jackson: University Press of Mississippi, 2003.

Bird, Kai, and Martin J. Sherwin. *American Prometheus: The Triumph and Tragedy of J. Robert Oppenheimer*. New York: Alfred A. Knopf, 2006.

Blain, Keisha N. *Until I Am Free: Fannie Lou Hamer's Enduring Message to America*. Boston: Beacon Press, 2021.

Blight, David. *Race and Reunion: The Civil War in American Memory.* Cambridge, MA: Belknap Press, 2001.

Bloom, Joshua. *Black against Empire: The History and Politics of the Black Panther Party.* Berkeley: University of California Press, 2016.

Blumenthal, Ralph. *Stork Club: America's Most Famous Nightspot and the Lost World of Café Society.* Boston: Little, Brown and Company, 2000.

Blum, Howard. *In the Enemy's House: The Secret Saga of the FBI Agent and the Code Breaker Who Caught the Russian Spies.* New York: HarperCollins, 2018.

Bogus, Carl T. *Buckley: William F. Buckley Jr. and the Rise of American Conservatism.* New York: Bloomsbury Press, 2011.

Borne, Ronald F. *Troutmouth: The Two Careers of Hugh Clegg.* Jackson: University Press of Mississippi, 2015.

Bradley, Mark A. *A Very Principled Boy: The Life of Duncan Lee, Red Spy and Cold Warrior.* New York: Basic Books, 2014.

Branan, Karen. *The Family Tree: A Lynching in Georgia, a Legacy of Secrets, and My Search for the Truth.* New York: Atria, 2016.

Branch, Taylor. *At Canaan's Edge: America in the King Years, 1965–68.* New York: Simon & Schuster, 2006.

———. *Parting the Waters: America in the King Years, 1954–63.* New York: Simon & Schuster, 1988.

———. *Pillar of Fire: America in the King Years, 1963–65.* New York: Simon & Schuster, 1998.

Brandes, Stuart D. *American Welfare Capitalism, 1880–1940.* Chicago: University of Chicago Press, 1976.

Braslow, Joel. *Mental Ills and Bodily Cures: Psychiatric Treatment in the First Half of the Twentieth Century.* Berkeley: University of California Press, 1997.

Bratzell, John T. and Leslie B. Rout Jr. "Pearl Harbor, Microdots, and J. Edgar Hoover." *American Historical Review* 87, no. 5 (1982): 1342–51.

Breu, Christopher. *Hard Boiled Masculinities.* Minneapolis: University of Minnesota Press, 2005.

Bridges, Linda, and John R. Coyne Jr. *Strictly Right: William F. Buckley and the American Conservative Movement.* Hoboken, NJ: John Wiley & Sons, 2007.

Brinkley, Alan. *Voices of Protest: Huey Long, Father Coughlin, and the Great Depression.* New York: Alfred A. Knopf, 1982.

Brody, David. "The Rise and Decline of Welfare Capitalism," in *Workers in Industrial America: Essays on the Twentieth-Century Struggle.* New York: Oxford University Press, 1980.

Brown, Lonnie T. *Defending the Public's Enemy: The Life and Legacy of Ramsey Clark.* Stanford, CA: Stanford University Press, 2019.

Brown, Michael et al., eds. *New Studies in the Politics and Culture of U.S. Communism.* New York: Monthly Review Press, 1993.

Buckley, Kerry W. "A President for the 'Great Silent Majority': Bruce Barton's Construction of Calvin Coolidge." *New England Quarterly* 76, no. 4 (2003): 593–626.

Burrough, Bryan. *The Big Rich: The Rise and Fall of the Greatest Texas Oil Fortunes.* New York: Penguin Press, 2009.

———. *Days of Rage: America's Radical Underground, the FBI, and the Forgotten Age of Revolutionary Violence.* New York: Penguin Press, 2015.

———. *Public Enemies: America's Greatest Crime Wave and the Birth of the FBI, 1933–34.* New York: Penguin Press, 2004.

Caesar, Gene. *Incredible Detective: The Biography of William J. Burns.* Englewood Cliffs, NJ: Prentice-Hall, 1968.

Cagin, Seth, and Philip Dray. *We Are Not Afraid: The Story of Goodman, Schwerner, and Chaney and the Civil Rights Campaign for Mississippi.* New York: Macmillan, 1988.

Calder, James D. *The Origins and Development of Federal Crime Control Policy: Herbert Hoover's Initiatives.* Westport, CT: Praeger, 1993.

Camp, Jordan T. *Incarcerating the Crisis: Freedom Struggles and the Rise of the Neoliberal State.* Berkeley: University of California Press, 2016.

Canaday, Margot. *The Straight State: Sexuality and Citizenship in Twentieth-Century America.* Princeton, NJ: Princeton University Press, 2009.

Canaday, Margot, Nancy F. Cott, and Robert O. Self, eds. *Intimate States: Gender, Sexuality, and Governance in Modern U.S. History.* Chicago: University of Chicago Press, 2021.

Candeloro, Dominic. "Louis F. Post and the Red Scare of 1920." *Prologue* 11, no. 1 (1979): 41–55.

Canedy, Susan. *America's Nazis: A Democratic Dilemma: A History of the German American Bund.* Menlo Park, CA: Markgraf Publications Group, 1990.

Capozzola, Christopher. *Uncle Sam Wants You: World War I and the Making of the Modern American Citizen.* New York: Oxford University Press, 2008.

Carlson, Peter. *Roughneck: The Life and Times of Big Bill Haywood.* New York: W. W. Norton & Company, 1983.

Carnes, Mark C. *Secret Ritual and Manhood in Victorian America.* New Haven, CT: Yale University Press, 1989.

Caro, Robert A. *The Power Broker: Robert Moses and the Fall of New York.* New York: Vintage, 1975.

———. *The Years of Lyndon Johnson: Master of the Senate.* New York: Vintage, 2003.

———. *The Years of Lyndon Johnson: Means of Ascent.* New York: Vintage, 1990.

———. *The Years of Lyndon Johnson: The Passage of Power.* New York: Alfred A. Knopf, 2012.

Carpenter, Daniel P. *The Forging of Bureaucratic Autonomy: Reputations, Networks, and Policy Innovation in Executive Agencies, 1862–1928.* Princeton, NJ: Princeton University Press, 2001.

———. *Reputation and Power: Organizational Image and Pharmaceutical Regulation at the FDA.* Princeton, NJ: Princeton University Press, 2010.

Carr, Barnes. *Operation Whisper: The Capture of Soviet Spies Morris and Lona Cohen.* ForeEdge, 2016.

Carr, Robert K. *House Committee on Un-American Activities, 1945–1950.* Ithaca, NY: Cornell University Press, 1952.

Carson, Clayborne. *In Struggle: SNCC and the Black Awakening of the 1960s.* Cambridge, MA: Harvard University Press, 1995.

———. *Malcolm X: The FBI File.* New York: Carroll & Graf, 1991.

Carter, Dan. *The Politics of Rage: George Wallace, the Origins of the New Conservatism, and the Transformation of American Politics.* New York: Simon & Schuster, 1995.

Casto, William R. *Advising the President: Attorney General Robert H. Jackson and Franklin D. Roosevelt.* Lawrence: University Press of Kansas, 2018.

Caute, David. *The Great Fear: The Anti-Communist Purge under Truman and Eisenhower.* New York: Simon & Schuster, 1978.

Cecil, Matthew. *The Ballad of Ben and Stella Mae: Great*

Plains Outlaws Who Became FBI Public Enemies Nos. 1 and 2. Lawrence: University Press of Kansas, 2016.

———. *Branding Hoover's FBI: How the Boss's PR Men Sold the Bureau to America*. Lawrence: University Press of Kansas, 2016.

———. *Hoover's FBI and the Fourth Estate: The Campaign to Control the Press and the Bureau's Image*. Lawrence: University Press of Kansas, 2014.

Cervini, Eric. *The Deviant's War: The Homosexual vs. the United States of America*. New York: Farrar, Straus and Giroux, 2020.

Chace, James. *1912: Wilson, Roosevelt, Taft & Debs—the Election That Changed the Country*. New York: Simon & Schuster, 2004.

Chard, Daniel. *Nixon's War at Home: The FBI, Leftist Guerrillas, and the Origins of Counterterrorism*. Chapel Hill: University of North Carolina Press, 2021.

Charles, Douglas M. *The FBI's Obscene File: J. Edgar Hoover and the Bureau's Crusade against Smut*. Lawrence: University Press of Kansas, 2012.

———. *Hoover's War on Gays: Exposing the FBI's "Sex Deviates" Program*. Lawrence: University Press of Kansas, 2015.

———. *J. Edgar Hoover and the Anti-Interventionists: FBI Political Surveillance and the Rise of the Domestic Security State, 1939–1945*. Columbus: Ohio State University Press, 2007.

Charns, Alexander. *Cloak and Gavel: FBI Wiretaps, Bugs, Informers, and the Supreme Court*. Urbana: University of Illinois Press, 1992.

Chauncey, George. *Gay New York: Gender, Urban Culture, and the Making of the Gay Male World, 1890–1940*. New York: Basic Books, 1994.

Chudacoff, Howard P. *The Age of the Bachelor: Creating an American Subculture*. Princeton, NJ: Princeton University Press, 1999.

Churchill, Ward, and Vander Wall, Jim. *Agents of Repression: The FBI's Secret Wars against the Black Panther Party and the American Indian Movement*. Boston: South End Press, 1988.

Clarke, Thurston. *The Last Campaign: Robert F. Kennedy and 82 Days That Inspired America*. New York: Henry Holt, 2008.

Cleaver, Kathleen, and George Katsiaficas, eds. *Liberation, Imagination, and the Black Panther Party: A New Look at the Panthers and Their Legacy*. New York: Routledge, 2001.

Clune, Lori. *Executing the Rosenbergs: Death and Diplomacy in a Cold War World*. New York: Oxford University Press, 2016.

Coben, Stanley. *A. Mitchell Palmer: Politician*. New York: Columbia University Press, 1963.

Cohen, Lizabeth. *Making a New Deal: Industrial Workers in Chicago, 1919–1939*. New York: Cambridge University Press, 1990.

Cole, Simon A. *Suspect Identities: A History of Fingerprinting and Criminal Identification*. Cambridge, MA: Harvard University Press, 2002.

Conaway, James. *America's Library: The Story of the Library of Congress 1800–2000*. New Haven, CT: Yale University Press, 2000.

Cook, Blanche Wiesen. *Eleanor Roosevelt: The War Years and After, 1939–1962*. New York: Viking, 1962.

Cook, Brian J. *Bureaucracy and Self-Government: Reconsidering the Role of Public Administration in American Politics*. Baltimore: Johns Hopkins University Press, 1996.

———. *Democracy and Administration: Woodrow Wilson's Ideas and the Challenges of Public Management*. Baltimore: Johns Hopkins University Press, 2007.

Cook, Fred J. *Nightmare Decade: The Life and Times of Senator Joe McCarthy*. New York: Random House, 1971.

Cooper, John Milton. *The Warrior and the Priest: Woodrow Wilson and Theodore Roosevelt*. Cambridge, MA: Belknap Press/Harvard University Press, 1983.

———. *Woodrow Wilson: A Biography*. New York: Alfred A. Knopf, 2009.

Cottrell, Robert C. *Roger Nash Baldwin and the American Civil Liberties Union*. New York: Columbia University Press, 2000.

Cox, Carolyn. *The Snatch Racket: The Kidnapping Epidemic That Terrorized 1930s America*. Lincoln, NE: Potomac Books, 2021.

Craig, R. Bruce. *Treasonable Doubt: The Harry Dexter White Spy Case*. Lawrence: University Press of Kansas, 2004.

Crespino, Joseph. *In Search of Another Country: Mississippi and the Conservative Counterrevolution*. Princeton, NJ: Princeton University Press, 2007.

———. *Strom Thurmond's America*. New York: Hill and Wang, 2012.

Critchlow, Donald. *Phyllis Schlafly and Grassroots Conservatism: A Woman's Crusade*. Princeton, NJ: Princeton University Press, 2008.

Culleton, Claire A. *Joyce and the G-Men: J. Edgar Hoover's Manipulation of Modernism*. New York: Palgrave Macmillan, 2004.

Cunningham, David. *There's Something Happening Here: The New Left, the Klan, and FBI Counterintelligence*. Berkeley: University of California Press, 2004.

Cuordileone, K. A. *Manhood and American Political Culture in the Cold War*. New York: Routledge, 2002.

———. "The Torment of Secrecy: Reckoning with American Communism and Anticommunism after Venona." *Diplomatic History* 35, no. 4 (2011), 615–42.

Dallek, Matthew. *Defenseless under the Night: The Roosevelt Years and the Origins of Homeland Security*. New York: Oxford University Press, 2016.

Dallek, Robert. *Camelot's Court: Inside the Kennedy White House*. New York: HarperCollins, 2013.

———. *Flawed Giant: Lyndon Johnson and His Times, 1961–1973*. New York: Oxford University Press, 1998.

Dalton, Kathleen. *Theodore Roosevelt: A Strenuous Life*. New York: Alfred A. Knopf, 2002.

Davidson, Roger H. "The Advent of the Modern Congress: The Legislative Reorganization Act of 1946." *Legislative Studies Quarterly* 15, no. 3 (1990): 357–73.

Davis, Colin J. *Power at Odds: The 1922 National Railroad Shopmen's Strike*. Champaign: University of Illinois Press, 1997.

Davis, James Kirkpatrick. *Assault on the Left: The FBI and the Sixties Anti-war Movement*. Westport, CT: Praeger, 1997.

———. *Spying on America: The FBI's Domestic Counterintelligence Program*. New York: Praeger, 1992.

Davis, John H. *Mafia Kingfish: Carlos Marcello and the Assassination of John F. Kennedy*. New York: Signet, 1989.

Demaris, Ovid. *The Director: An Oral Biography of J. Edgar Hoover*. New York: Harper's Magazine Press, 1975.

DeLillo, Don. *Underworld*. New York: Scribner, 1997.

D'Emilio, John. *Lost Prophet: The Life and Times of Bayard Rustin*. New York: Free Press, 2003.

Denney, Matthew G. T. "'To Wage a War': Crime, Race, and State Making in the Age of FDR." *Studies in American Political Development* 35, no. 1 (2021): 16–56.

Destefano, Anthony M. *Top Hoodlum: Frank Costello, Prime Minister of the Mafia.* New York: Citadel Press, 2018.

Diamond, Sander. *The Nazi Movement in the United States, 1924–1941.* Ithaca: Cornell University Press, 1974.

Dobbs, Michael. *Saboteurs: The Nazi Raid on America.* New York: Vintage, 2007.

Doherty, Thomas. *Hollywood's Censor: Joseph I. Breen and the Production Code Administration.* New York: Columbia University Press, 2007.

———. *Pre-Code Hollywood: Sex, Immorality, and Insurrection in American Cinema, 1930–1934.* New York: Columbia University Press, 1999.

———. *Show Trial: Hollywood, HUAC, and the Birth of the Blacklist.* New York: Columbia University Press, 2018.

Doig, James W., and Erwin C. Hargrove. *Leadership and Innovation: A Biographical Perspective on Entrepreneurs in Government.* Baltimore: Johns Hopkins University Press, 1987.

Donner, Frank. *The Age of Surveillance: The Aims and Methods of America's Political Intelligence System.* New York: Vintage, 1981.

———. *Protectors of Privilege: Red Squads and Police Repression in Urban America.* Berkeley: University of California Press, 1990.

Drabble, John. "To Ensure Domestic Tranquility: The FBI, COINTELPRO-WHITE HATE and Political Discourse, 1964–1971," *Journal of American Studies* 38, no. 2 (2004), 297–328.

———. "The FBI, COINTELPRO-WHITE HATE, and the Decline of Ku Klux Klan Organizations in Alabama, 1964–1971." *Alabama Review* 61, no. 1 (2008): 3–47.

———. "From White Supremacy to White Power: The FBI, COINTELPRO WHITE HATE, and the Nazification of the Ku Klux Klan in the 1970s." *American Studies* 48, no. 3 (2007), 49–74.

Draper, Theodore. *American Communism and Soviet Russia: The Formative Period.* New York: Viking, 1960.

———. *The Roots of American Communism.* New York: Routledge, 2017. First published 1957.

Dray, Philip. *At the Hands of Persons Unknown: The Lynching of Black America.* New York: Modern Library, 2002.

Dubofsky, Melvyn. *We Shall Be All: A History of the Industrial Workers of the World.* Chicago: Quadrangle Books, 1969.

Dudziak, Mary. *Cold War Civil Rights: Race and the Image of American Democracy.* Princeton, NJ: Princeton University Press, 2000.

Duffy, Peter. *Double Agent: The First Hero of World War II and How the FBI Outwitted and Destroyed a Nazi Spy Ring.* New York: Scribner, 2014.

Dumenil, Lynn. *Freemasonry and American Culture, 1880–1930.* Princeton, NJ: Princeton University Press, 1984.

Eckstein, Arthur M. *Bad Moon Rising: How the Weather Underground Beat the FBI and Lost the Revolution.* New Haven, CT: Yale University Press, 2016.

Egerton, John. *Speak Now Against the Day: The Generation before the Civil Rights Movement in the South.* New York: Alfred A. Knopf, 1994.

Eig, Jonathan. *Get Capone: The Secret Plot That Captured America's Most Wanted Gangster.* New York: Simon & Schuster, 2010.

Elias, Christopher M. *Gossip Men: J. Edgar Hoover, Joe McCarthy, Roy Cohn, and the Politics of Insinuation.* Chicago: University of Chicago Press, 2021.

Ellis, Edward Robb. *A Nation in Torment: The Great American Depression, 1929–1939.* New York: Kodansha International, 1995. First published 1970.

Ellis, Mark. "J. Edgar Hoover and the 'Red Summer' of 1919." *Journal of American Studies* 28, no. 1 (1994): 39–59.

———. *Race, War, and Surveillance: African Americans and the United States Government During World War I.* Bloomington: Indiana University Press, 2001.

Eskew, Glenn T. *But for Birmingham: The Local and National Movements in the Civil Rights Struggle.* Chapel Hill: University of North Carolina Press, 1997.

Ewing, Adam. *The Age of Garvey: How a Jamaican Activist Created a Mass Movement and Changed Global Black Politics.* Princeton, NJ: Princeton University Press, 2014.

Farrell, John A. *Richard Nixon: The Life.* New York: Doubleday, 2017.

Felber, Garrett. *Those Who Know Don't Say: The Nation of Islam, the Black Freedom Movement, and the Carceral State.* Chapel Hill: University of North Carolina Press, 2020.

Feldstein, Mark. *Poisoning the Press: Richard Nixon, Jack Anderson, and the Rise of Washington's Scandal Culture.* New York: Farrar, Straus and Giroux, 2010.

Felzenberg, Alvin. *A Man and His Presidents: The Political Odyssey of William F. Buckley Jr.* New Haven, CT: Yale University Press, 2017.

Fernández, Johanna. *The Young Lords: A Radical History.* Chapel Hill: University of North Carolina Press, 2020.

Ferrell, Robert H. *The Presidency of Calvin Coolidge.* Lawrence: University Press of Kansas, 1998.

———. *The Strange Deaths of President Harding.* Columbia: University of Missouri Press, 1996.

———. *Truman and Pendergast.* Columbia: University of Missouri Press, 1999.

Fischer, Nick. *Spider Web: The Birth of American Anticommunism.* Urbana: University of Illinois Press, 2016.

Fisher, Jim. *The Ghosts of Hopewell: Setting the Record Straight in the Lindbergh Case.* Carbondale: Southern Illinois University Press, 1999.

Fisher, Louis. *Nazi Saboteurs on Trial: A Military Tribunal and American Law.* Lawrence: University Press of Kansas, 2003.

Flamm, Michael. *In the Heat of Summer: The New York Riots of 1964 and the War on Crime.* Philadelphia: University of Pennsylvania Press, 2017.

———. *Law and Order: Street Crime, Civil Unrest, and the Crisis of Liberalism in the 1960s.* New York: Columbia University Press, 2005.

Forman, James. *Locking Up Our Own: Crime and Punishment in Black America.* New York: Farrar, Straus and Giroux, 2017.

Fox, John. "Intelligence Analysis and the Bureau: The Evolution of Analysis and the Analyst Position in the FBI, 1908–2013." *Journal of Strategic Security* 6, no. 3 suppl. (2013): 114–23.

Fox, Renée C., and Mike Forrest Keen. *Stalking Sociologists: J. Edgar Hoover's FBI Surveillance of American Sociology.* New York: Routledge, 2017.

Fox, Stephen. *America's Invisible Gulag: A Biography of German American Internment & Exclusion in World War II.* New York: Peter Lang, 2000.

Francis, Megan Ming. *Civil Rights and the Making of the Modern American State.* New York: Cambridge University Press, 2014.

Frank, Jeffrey. *The Trials of Harry Truman: The Extraordinary Presidency of an Ordinary Man, 1945–1953*. New York: Simon & Schuster, 2022.

Frederickson, Kari. *The Dixiecrat Revolt and the End of the Solid South, 1932–1968*. Chapel Hill: University of North Carolina Press, 2001.

Fried, Albert, ed. *Communism in America: A History in Documents*. New York: Columbia University Press, 1997.

Friedman, Andrea. "The Strange Career of Annie Lee Moss: Rethinking Race, Gender, and McCarthyism." *Journal of American History* 94, no. 2 (2007): 445–68.

Friedman, Lawrence M. *Crime and Punishment in American History*. New York: Basic Books, 1993.

Fronczak, Joseph. "The Fascist Game: Transnational Political Transmission and the Genesis of the U.S. Modern Right." *Journal of American History* 105, no. 3 (2018): 563–88.

Frydl, Kathleen J. "Kidnapping and State Development in the United States." *Studies in American Political Development* 20, no. 1 (2006): 18–44.

Fujino, Diane C. *Samurai among Panthers: Richard Aoki on Race, Resistance, and a Paradoxical Life*. Minneapolis: University of Minnesota Press, 2012.

Fursenko, Aleksandr, and Timothy Naftali. *"One Hell of a Gamble": Khrushchev, Castro, and Kennedy, 1958–1964*. New York: W. W. Norton & Company, 1997.

Gabler, Neal: *Winchell: Gossip, Power and the Culture of Celebrity*. New York: Alfred A. Knopf, 1994.

Gaddis, John. *The United States and the Origins of the Cold War, 1941–1947*. New York: Columbia University Press, 1972.

Gage, Beverly. *The Day Wall Street Exploded: A Story of America in Its First Age of Terror*. New York: Oxford University Press, 2009.

———. "Deep Throat, Watergate, and the Bureaucratic Politics of the FBI." *Journal of Policy History*. 24, no. 2 (2012), 157–83.

———. "What an Uncensored Letter to M.L.K. Reveals." *New York Times Magazine*, November 11, 2014.

Gardner, Lloyd C. *The Case That Never Dies: The Lindbergh Kidnapping*. New Brunswick, NJ: Rutgers University Press, 2004.

Garraty, John A., and Mark C. Carnes, eds. *American National Biography*, vols. 1–24. New York: Oxford University Press, 1999.

Garrow, David J. *Bearing the Cross: Martin Luther King, Jr., and the Southern Christian Leadership Conference*. New York: Perennial, 1986.

———. "The FBI and Martin Luther King." *Atlantic,* July/August 2002.

———. *The FBI and Martin Luther King, Jr.: From "SOLO" to Memphis*. New York: W. W. Norton & Company, 1981.

———. "The Troubling Legacy of Martin Luther King." *Standpoint*, June 2019.

Geary, Rick. *J. Edgar Hoover: A Graphic Biography*. New York: Hill and Wang, 2008.

Gellman, Erik S. *Death Blow to Jim Crow: The National Negro Congress and the Rise of Militant Civil Rights*. Chapel Hill: University of North Carolina Press, 2012.

Gellman, Irwin F. *The Contender: Richard Nixon, The Congress Years, 1946–1952*. New York: Free Press, 1999.

———. *The President and the Apprentice: Eisenhower and Nixon, 1952–1961*. New Haven, CT: Yale University Press, 2015.

———. *Secret Affairs: Franklin Roosevelt, Cordell Hull, and Sumner Welles*. Baltimore: Johns Hopkins University Press, 1995.

Gentry, Curt. *J. Edgar Hoover: The Man and the Secrets*. New York: W. W. Norton & Company, 1991.

George, Carol V. R. *God's Salesman: Norman Vincent Peale and the Power of Positive Thinking*. New York: Oxford University Press, 1993.

Gerard, Christopher John. "'A Program of Cooperation': The FBI, the Senate Internal Security Subcommittee, and the Communist Issue, 1950–1956." PhD diss., Marquette University, 1993.

Gergel, Richard. *Unexampled Courage: The Blinding of Sgt. Isaac Woodard and the Awakening of President Harry S. Truman and Judge J. Waties Waring*. New York: Sarah Crichton, 2019.

Gerstle, Gary. *Liberty and Coercion: The Paradox of American Government from the Founding to the Present*. Princeton: Princeton University Press, 2015.

Gillon, Steven M. *Separate and Unequal: The Kerner Commission and the Unraveling of American Liberalism*. New York: Basic Books, 2018.

Gilmore, Glenda Elizabeth. *Defying Dixie: The Radical Roots of Civil Rights, 1919–1950*. New York: W. W. Norton & Company, 2008.

Girardin, G. Russell, and William J. Helmer. *Dillinger: The Untold Story*. Bloomington: Indiana University Press, 2009.

Godshalk, David Fort. *Veiled Visions: The 1906 Atlanta Race Riot and the Reshaping of American Race Relations*. Chapel Hill: University of North Carolina Press, 2005.

Goldstein, Robert Justin, ed. *Little "Red Scares": Anti-Communism and Political Repression in the United States, 1921–1946*. Burlington, VT: Ashgate, 2014.

Goluboff, Risa. *The Lost Promise of Civil Rights*. Cambridge, MA: Harvard University Press, 2007.

Goodall, Alex. *Loyalty and Liberty: American Countersubversion from World War I to the McCarthy Era*. Urbana: University of Illinois Press, 2013.

Goodman, Michael S. "Who Is Trying to Keep What Secret from Whom and Why? MI5-FBI Relations and the Klaus Fuchs Case." *Journal of Cold War Studies* 7, no. 3 (2005): 124–46.

Goodwin, Doris Kearns. *The Bully Pulpit: Theodore Roosevelt, William Howard Taft, and the Golden Age of Journalism*. New York: Simon and Schuster, 2013.

———. *Lyndon Johnson and the American Dream*. New York: St. Martin's Press, 1991.

Gordon, Linda. *The Second Coming of the KKK: The Ku Klux Klan of the 1920s and the American Political Tradition*. New York: Liveright, 2017.

Gorn, Elliott J. *Dillinger's Wild Ride: The Year That Made America's Public Enemy Number One*. New York: Oxford University Press, 2009.

———. *Let the People See: The Story of Emmett Till*. New York: Oxford University Press, 2018.

Graff, Garrett. *Watergate: A New History*. New York: Simon and Schuster, 2022.

Grams, Martin Jr. *I Led 3 Lives: The True Story of Herbert A. Philbrick's Television Program*. Albany, GA: BearManor Media, 2007.

Grann, David. *Killers of the Flower Moon: The Osage Murders and the Birth of the FBI*. New York: Doubleday, 2017.

Grant, Colin. *Negro with a Hat: The Rise and Fall of Marcus Garvey and His Dream of Mother Africa*. New York: Oxford University Press, 2008.

Gravely, William B. *They Stole Him out of Jail: Willie Earle,*

South Carolina's Last Lynching Victim. Columbia: University of South Carolina Press, 2019.

Graves, Melissa. *Nixon's FBI: Hoover, Watergate, and a Bureau in Crisis.* Boulder, CO: Lynne Rienner, 2020.

Greenberg, David. *Calvin Coolidge.* New York: Times Books, 2007.

Greenberg, Ivan. *The Dangers of Dissent: The FBI and Civil Liberties since 1965.* Lanham, MD: Lexington, 2010.

———. *Surveillance in America: Critical Analysis of the FBI, 1920 to the Present.* Lanham, MD: Lexington, 2012.

Green, Constance McLaughlin. *Secret City: A History of Race Relations in the Nation's Capital.* Princeton, NJ: Princeton University Press, 1967.

———. *Washington: Capital City, 1879–1950,* vol. 2. Princeton, NJ: Princeton University Press, 1963.

———. *Washington: Village and Capital, 1800–1878,* vol. 1. Princeton, NJ: Princeton University Press, 1962.

Greenidge, Kerri K. *Black Radical: The Life and Times of William Monroe Trotter.* New York: Liveright, 2019.

Green, Sam, and Bill Siegel, dirs. *The Weather Underground.* San Francisco: Free History Project, 2002.

Gregory, Anthony. *Building Law and Order: How New Deal Liberals Made the Security State.* Cambridge, MA: Harvard University Press, forthcoming.

Grimberg, Sharon, dir. *American Experience.* Season 32, episode 1, "McCarthy." Aired January 6, 2020, on PBS.

Grueter, Mark. "Red Scare Scholarship, Class Conflict, and the Case of the Anarchist Union of Russian Workers, 1919." *Journal for the Study of Radicalism* 11, no. 1 (2017): 53–82.

Guariglia, Matthew. "Wrench in the Deportation Machine: Louis F. Post's Objection to Mechanized Red Scare Bureaucracy." *Journal of American Ethnic History* 38, no. 1 (2018): 62–77.

Gustav-Wrathall, John Donald. *Take the Young Stranger by the Hand: Same-Sex Relations and the YMCA.* Chicago: University of Chicago Press, 1998.

Gutiérrez, J. Á. *The Eagle Has Eyes: The FBI Surveillance of César Estrada Chávez of the United Farm Workers Union of America, 1965–1975.* Baltimore: MSU Press, 2019.

Haas, Jeffrey. *Assassination of Fred Hampton: How the FBI and the Chicago Police Murdered a Black Panther.* Chicago: Lawrence Hill Books, 2019.

Hack, Richard. *Puppetmaster: The Secret Life of J. Edgar Hoover.* Beverly Hills, CA: New Millennium Press, 2004.

Hajdu, David. *The Ten-Cent Plague: The Great Comic-Book Scare and How It Changed America.* New York: Farrar, Straus and Giroux, 2008.

Hamilton, Johanna, dir. *1971.* New York: First Run Features, 2014.

Hamrick, S. J. *Deceiving the Deceivers: Kim Philby, Donald Maclean, and Guy Burgess.* New Haven, CT: Yale University Press, 2004.

Harmon, Rebecca Bouterie. "Hydrotherapy in State Mental Hospitals in the First Half of the Mid-Twentieth Century." *Issues in Mental Health Nursing* 30, no. 8 (2009): 491–4.

Hartmann, Rudolph. *The Kansas City Investigation: Pendergast's Downfall, 1938–1939.* Columbia: University of Missouri Press, 1999.

Hartshorn, Lewis. *Alger Hiss, Whittaker Chambers and the Case That Ignited McCarthyism.* Jefferson, NC: McFarland, 2013.

Haverty-Stacke, Donna. *Trotskyists on Trial: Free Speech and Political Persecution since the Age of FDR.* New York: New York University Press, 2015.

Hawley, Ellis Wayne. *The Great War and the Search for a Modern Order: A History of the American People and Their Institutions, 1917–1993.* New York: St. Martin's Press, 1979.

Haynes, John Earl, and Harvey Klehr. *Early Cold War Spies: The Espionage Trials That Shaped American Politics.* New York: Cambridge University Press, 2006.

———. *Venona: Decoding Soviet Espionage in America.* New Haven, CT: Yale University Press, 1999.

Haynes, John Earl, Harvey Klehr, and Alexander Vassiliev. *Spies: The Rise and Fall of the KGB in America.* New Haven, CT: Yale University Press, 2009.

Heale, M. J. *American Anticommunism: Combating the Enemy Within, 1830–1970.* Baltimore: Johns Hopkins University Press, 1990.

Hendershot, Heather. *What's Fair on the Air? Cold War Right-Wing Broadcasting and the Public Interest.* Chicago: University of Chicago Press, 2011.

Herken, Gregg. *The Georgetown Set: Friends and Rivals in Cold War Washington.* New York: Knopf, 2014.

Hernández, Kelly Lytle. *Migra! A History of the U.S. Border Patrol.* Berkeley: University of California Press, 2010.

Hersh, Burton. *Bobby and J. Edgar: The Historic Face-Off Between the Kennedys and J. Edgar Hoover That Transformed America.* New York: Carroll & Graf, 2007.

Hersh, Seymour M. *The Dark Side of Camelot.* New York: Little Brown, 1997.

Hill, Rebecca N. *Men, Mobs, and Law: Anti-Lynching and Labor Defense in U.S. Radical History.* Durham, NC: Duke University Press, 2008.

Hilkey, Judy. *Character Is Capital: Success Manuals and Manhood in Gilded Age America.* Chapel Hill: University of North Carolina Press, 1997.

Hinton, Elizabeth. *America on Fire: The Untold History of Police Violence and Black Rebellion since the 1960s.* New York: Norton, 2021.

———. *From the War on Poverty to the War on Crime: The Making of Mass Incarceration in America.* Cambridge, MA: Harvard University Press, 2016.

Hirshbein, Laura D. *American Melancholy: Constructions of Depression in the Twentieth Century.* New Brunswick, NJ: Rutgers University Press, 2009.

"Historians and the Carceral State," *Journal of American History* 102:1 (June 2015).

Hochman, Brian. *The Listeners: A History of Wiretapping in the United States.* Cambridge, MA: Harvard University Press, 2022.

Hogan, Michael J. *A Cross of Iron: Harry S. Truman and the Origins of the National Security State 1945–1954.* Cambridge, UK: Cambridge University Press, 1998.

Holland, Max. *Leak: Why Mark Felt Became Deep Throat.* Lawrence: University Press of Kansas, 2012.

Honey, Michael K. *Going Down Jericho Road: The Memphis Strike, Martin Luther King's Last Campaign.* New York: W. W. Norton & Company, 2008.

———. *To the Promised Land: Martin Luther King and the Fight for Economic Justice.* New York: W. W. Norton & Company, 2018.

Horne, Gerald. *Fire This Time: The Watts Uprising and the 1960s.* New York: Da Capo Press, 1997.

Hosokawa, Bill. *Nisei: The Quiet Americans.* Niwot: University Press of Colorado, 1992. First published 1969.

Howard, Josh, dir. *The Lavender Scare.* New York: Full Exposure Films, 2019.

Hughes, Ken. *Chasing Shadows: The Nixon Tapes, the Chen-*

nault Affair, and the Origins of Watergate. Charlottesville: University of Virginia Press, 2014.

Huie, William Bradford. *He Slew the Dreamer: My Search
for the Truth about James Earl Ray and the Murder of Martin Luther King.* Jackson: University Press of Mississippi,
2018.

Huntington, John S. *Far-Right Vanguard: The Radical
Roots of Modern Conservatism.* Philadelphia: University
of Pennsylvania Press, 2021.

Hurewitz, Daniel. *Bohemian Los Angeles and the Making of
Modern Politics.* Berkeley: University of California Press,
2007.

Hurt, Harry III. *Texas Rich: The Hunt Dynasty from the
Early Oil Days through the Silver Crash.* New York: W. W.
Norton & Company, 1981.

Ingalls, Robert P. *Point of Order: A Profile of Senator Joe Mc-
Carthy.* New York: Putnam, 1981.

Isserman, Maurice. *Which Side Were You On? The American
Communist Party during the Second World War.* Middletown, CT: Wesleyan University Press, 1982.

Ives, Steven, dir. *American Experience.* Season 22, episode 7,
"Roads to Memphis." Aired May 3, 2010, on PBS.

Jacobs, Nicholas, King, Desmond, and Milkis, Sidney M.
"Building a Conservative State: Partisan Polarization and
the Redeployment of Administration Power," *Perspectives
on Politics* 17:2 (June 2019), 453-69.

Jacobsen, Annie. *Operation Paperclip: The Secret Intelligence
Program That Brought Nazi Scientists to America.* New
York: Little Brown, 2014.

Jacoby, Susan. *Alger Hiss and the Battle for History.* New
Haven: Yale University Press, 2009.

Janken, Kenneth Robert. *Walter White: Mr. NAACP.* Chapel Hill: University of North Carolina Press, 2006.

Jansen, Axel. *Alexander Dallas Bache: Building the American Nation through Science and Education in the Nineteenth
Century.* Frankfurt, Germany: Campus Verlag, 2011.

Jeffreys-Jones, Rhodri. *The FBI: A History.* New Haven,
CT: Yale University Press, 2007.

———. *The Nazi Spy Ring in America: Hitler's Agents, the
FBI, and the Case That Stirred the Nation.* Washington,
DC: Georgetown University Press, 2020.

Jensen, Joan M. *The Price of Vigilance.* New York: Rand Mc-
Nally, 1968.

Johanningsmeier, Edward P. *Forging American Communism: The Life of William Z. Foster.* Princeton, NJ: Princeton University Press, 1994.

Johnson, David Alan. *Betrayal: The True Story of J. Edgar
Hoover and the Nazi Saboteurs Captured during WWII.*
New York: Hippocrene Books, 2007.

Johnson, David K. *The Lavender Scare: The Cold War Persecution of Gays and Lesbians in the Federal Government.*
Chicago: University of Chicago Press, 2004.

Johnson, Donald Leslie. *The Fountainheads: Wright, Rand,
the FBI and Hollywood.* Jefferson, NC: McFarland, 2005.

Johnson, Sylvester A., and Steven Weitzman, eds. *The FBI
and Religion: Faith and National Security before and after
9/11.* Oakland: University of California Press, 2017.

Jones, James H. *Alfred C. Kinsey: A Public/Private Life.*
New York: W. W. Norton & Company, 1997.

Joseph, Peniel E. *Stokely: A Life.* New York: Basic Civitas
Books, 2016.

———. *The Sword and the Shield: The Revolutionary Lives of
Malcolm X and Martin Luther King Jr.* New York: Basic,
2020.

———. *Waiting 'til the Midnight Hour: A Narrative History*
of Black Power in America. New York: Henry Holt and
Company, 2006.

Judis, John B. *William F. Buckley, Jr.: Patron Saint of the
Conservatives.* New York: Simon & Schuster, 1998.

Jung, Moon-Ho, ed. *The Rising Tide of Color: Race, State
Violence, and Radical Movements across the Pacific.* Seattle: University of Washington Press, 2014.

Kamin, Ben. *Dangerous Friendship: Stanley Levison, Martin Luther King Jr., and the Kennedy Brothers.* East Lansing: Michigan State University Press, 2014.

Katagiri, Yasuhiro. *The Mississippi State Sovereignty Commission: Civil Rights and States' Rights.* Jackson: University Press of Mississippi, 2001.

Kazin, Michael. *War against War: The American Fight for
Peace, 1914-1918.* New York: Simon & Schuster, 2017.

Keller, William W. *The Liberals and J. Edgar Hoover: Rise
and Fall of a Domestic Intelligence State.* Princeton, NJ:
Princeton University Press, 1989.

Kelley, Robin D. G. *Hammer and Hoe: Alabama Communists during the Great Depression.* Chapel Hill: University
of North Carolina Press, 1990.

Kendall, Joshua. *America's Obsessives: The Compulsive Energy That Built a Nation.* New York: Grand Central, 2013.

Kennedy, David M. *Freedom from Fear: The American People in Depression and War, 1929-1945.* New York: Oxford
University Press, 1999.

———. *Over Here: The First World War and American Society.* New York: Oxford University Press, 2004. First published 1980.

Kessler, Lauren, *Clever Girl: Elizabeth Bentley, the Spy Who
Ushered in the McCarthy Era.* New York: Perennial, 2003.

Kessler, Ronald. *The Bureau: The Secret History of the FBI.*
New York: St. Martin's Press, 2002.

———. *The Secrets of the FBI.* New York: Crown, 2011.

Kevles, Daniel J. "Not a Hundred Millionaires: The National Academy and the Expansion of Federal Science in
the Gilded Age." *Issues in Science and Technology* 29, no. 2
(2013): 37-46.

Kiel, R. Andrew. *J. Edgar Hoover: The Father of the Cold
War.* Lanham, MD: University Press of America, 2000.

Kimmel, Michael S., ed. *Changing Men: New Directions in
Research on Men and Masculinity.* Newbury Park, CA: Sage
Publications, 1987.

Klaber, William, and Philip Melanson. *Shadow Play: The
Unsolved Murder of Robert F. Kennedy.* New York: St.
Martin's Griffin, 2018.

Klehr, Harvey. *The Heyday of American Communism: The
Depression Decade.* New York: Basic Books, 1984.

———. *The Secret World of American Communism.* New
Haven: Yale University Press, 1995.

Klehr, Harvey, and Ronald Radosh. *The Amerasia Spy Case:
Prelude to McCarthyism.* Chapel Hill: University of
North Carolina Press, 1996.

Knight, Amy. *How the Cold War Began: The Igor Gouzenko
Affair and the Hunt for Soviet Spies.* New York: Carroll &
Graf, 2005.

Knightley, Phillip. *The Master Spy: The Story of Kim Philby.*
New York: Knopf, 1989.

Kornweibel, Theodore. *"Investigate Everything": Federal Efforts to Compel Black Loyalty During World War I.*
Bloomington: Indiana University Press, 2002.

———. *Seeing Red: Federal Campaigns Against Black Militancy, 1919-1925.* Bloomington: Indiana University Press,
1998.

Kovel, Joel. *Red Hunting in the Promised Land: Anticommu-*

nism and the Making of America. New York: Basic Books, 1994.

Kramer, Jacob. *The New Freedom and the Radicals: Woodrow Wilson, Progressive Views of Radicalism, and the Origins of Repressive Tolerance*. Philadelphia: Temple University Press, 2015.

Kramer, Paul A. *The Blood of Government: Race, Empire, the United States, & the Philippines*. Chapel Hill: University of North Carolina Press, 2006.

Kruse, Kevin M. *One Nation under God: How Corporate America Invented Christian America*. New York: Basic Books, 2015.

Kutler, Stanley I. *Wars of Watergate: The Last Crisis of Richard Nixon*. New York: W. W. Norton & Company, 1990.

Lane, Christopher. *Surge of Piety: Norman Vincent Peale and the Remaking of American Religious Life*. New Haven, CT: Yale University Press, 2016.

Lane, Mark. *Rush to Judgment: A Critique of the Warren Commission's Inquiry into the Murders of President John F. Kennedy, Officer J.D. Tippit and Lee Harvey Oswald*. New York: Holt, Rinehart & Winston, 1966.

Lane, Mark, and Dick Gregory. *Murder in Memphis: The FBI and the Assassination of Martin Luther King*. Charlottesville, VA: Lane Group, 2015.

Lauterbach, Preston. *Bluff City: The Secret Life of Photographer Ernest Withers*. New York: W. W. Norton & Company, 2019.

Lears, Jackson. *Rebirth of a Nation: The Making of Modern America, 1877–1920*. New York: HarperCollins, 2009.

Leonard, Aaron J., and Conor A. Gallagher. *Heavy Radicals: The FBI's Secret War on America's Maoists*. Winchester, UK: Zero Books, 2014.

———. *A Threat of the First Magnitude: FBI Counterintelligence & Infiltration From the Communist Party to the Revolutionary Union, 1962-1974*. Repeater Books, 2018.

Levin, Murray B. *Political Hysteria in America: The Democratic Capacity for Repression*. New York: Basic, 1971.

Lewis, David Levering. *W.E.B. Du Bois: A Biography*. New York: Holt, 2009.

Lewis, Eugene. *Public Entrepreneurship: Toward a Theory of Bureaucratic Political Power: The Organizational Lives of Hyman Rickover, J. Edgar Hoover, and Robert Moses*. Bloomington: Indiana University Press, 1980.

Lewis, Tom. *Washington: A History of Our National City*. New York: Basic Books, 2015.

Lichtblau, Eric. *The Nazis Next Door: How America Became a Safe Haven for Hitler's Men*. Boston: Mariner, 2014.

Lichtman, Allan J. *White Protestant Nation: The Rise of the American Conservative Movement*. New York: Grove Press, 2008.

Lichtman, Robert M. *The Supreme Court and McCarthy-Era Repression: One Hundred Decisions*. Urbana: University of Illinois Press, 2012.

Lichtman, Robert M., and Ronald D. Cohen. *Deadly Farce: Harvey Matusow and the Informer System in the McCarthy Era*. Urbana: University of Illinois Press, 2004.

Locker, Ray. *Nixon's Gamble: How a President's Own Secret Government Destroyed His Administration*. Guilford, CT: Lyons Press, 2016.

Logevall, Fredrik. *JFK: Coming of Age in the American Century, 1917–1956*. New York: Random House, 2020.

Lowitt, Richard. *George W. Norris: The Persistence of a Progressive, 1913–1933*, vol. 2. Urbana: University of Illinois Press, 1971.

———. *George W. Norris: The Triumph of a Progressive, 1933–1944*, vol. 3. Urbana: University of Illinois Press, 1978.

Luff, Jennifer. *Commonsense Anticommunism: Labor and Civil Liberties Between the World Wars*. Chapel Hill: University of North Carolina Press, 2012.

Lukas, J. Anthony. *Nightmare: The Underside of the Nixon Years*. Athens: Ohio University Press, 1999.

Lumpkins, Charles L. *American Pogrom: The East St. Louis Race Riot and Black Politics*. Athens: Ohio University Press, 2008.

Lvovsky, Anna. *Vice Patrol: Cops, Courts, and the Struggle over Urban Gay Life before Stonewall*. Chicago: University of Chicago Press, 2021.

Macintyre, Ben. *A Spy among Friends: Kim Philby and the Great Betrayal*. New York: Crown, 2014.

Mahoney, Richard D. *Sons & Brothers: The Days of Jack and Bobby Kennedy*. New York: Arcade, 1999.

Maier, Thomas. *Mafia Spies: The Inside Story of the CIA, Gangsters, JFK, and Castro*. New York: Skyhorse, 2019.

Malloy, Sean. *Out of Oakland: Black Panther Party Internationalism during the Cold War*. Ithaca: Cornell University Press, 2017.

Marable, Manning. *Malcolm X: A Life of Reinvention*. New York: Viking, 2011.

Maraniss, David. *A Good American Family: The Red Scare and My Father*. New York: Simon & Schuster, 2019.

Martelle, Scott. *The Fear Within: Spies, Commies, and American Democracy on Trial*. New Brunswick, NJ: Rutgers University Press, 2011.

Martin, David C. *Wilderness of Mirrors*. New York: Harper & Row, 1980.

Martin, Lerone. "Bureau Clergyman: How the FBI Colluded with an African American Televangelist to Destroy Dr. Martin Luther King, Jr." *Religion and American Culture* 28, no.1 (2018): 1–51.

———. *The Gospel of J. Edgar Hoover: How the FBI Aided and Abetted the Rise of White Christian Nationalism*. Princeton: Princeton University Press, forthcoming.

Martin, Ruth. "Operation Abolition: Defending the Civil Liberties of the 'Un-American,' 1957–1961." *Journal of American Studies* 47, no. 4 (2013), 1043–63.

Marton, Kati. *True Believer: Stalin's Last American Spy*. New York: Simon & Schuster, 2016.

Mason, Alpheus Thomas. *Harlan Fiske Stone: Pillar of the Law*. New York: Viking, 1956.

Maxwell, William J. *F.B. Eyes: How J. Edgar Hoover's Ghostreaders Framed African American Literature*. Princeton, NJ: Princeton University Press, 2015.

Mayer, Michael S. "The Eisenhower Administration and the Desegregation of Washington, D.C." *Journal of Policy History* 3, no. 1 (1991): 24–41.

May, Gary. *The Informant: The FBI, the Ku Klux Klan, and the Murder of Viola Liuzzo*. New Haven, CT: Yale University Press, 2005.

———. *Un-American Activities: The Trials of William Remington*. New York: Oxford University Press, 1994.

McAuliffe, Mary S. "Liberals and the Communist Control Act of 1954." *Journal of American History* 63, no. 2 (1976): 351–67.

McCartney, Laton. *The Teapot Dome Scandal: How Big Oil Bought the Harding White House and Tried to Steal the Country*. New York: Random House, 2008.

McCullough, David. *Truman*. New York: Simon & Schuster, 1992.

McDaniel, Rodger. *Dying for Joe McCarthy's Sins: The Sui-

cide of Wyoming Senator Lester Hunt. Cody, WY: Words-Worth, 2013.

McGirr, Lisa. *Suburban Warriors: The Origins of the New American Right*. Princeton, NJ: Princeton University Press, 2001.

———. *The War on Alcohol: Prohibition and the Rise of the American State*. New York: W. W. Norton & Company, 2016.

McIlhany, William H. II. *Klandestine: The Untold Story of Delmar Dennis and His Role in the FBI's War against the Ku Klux Klan*. New Rochelle, NY: Arlington House, 1975.

McKnight, Gerald D. *Breach of Trust: How the Warren Commission Failed the Nation and Why*. Lawrence: University Press of Kansas, 2005.

———. *The Last Crusade: Martin Luther King, Jr., the FBI, and the Poor People's Campaign*. Boulder, CO: Westview, 1998.

McMillan, George. *The Making of an Assassin: The Life of James Earl Ray*. New York: Little, Brown, 1976.

McRae, Elizabeth Gillespie. *Mothers of Massive Resistance: White Women and the Politics of White Supremacy*. New York: Oxford University Press, 2018.

McWhirter, Cameron. *Red Summer: The Summer of 1919 and the Awakening of Black America*. New York: Henry Holt and Company, 2011.

McWhorter, Diane. *Carry Me Home: Birmingham, Alabama: The Climactic Battle of the Civil Rights Revolution*. New York: Simon & Schuster, 2001.

Medsger, Betty. *The Burglary: The Discovery of J. Edgar Hoover's Secret FBI*. New York: Alfred A. Knopf, 2014.

Mee, Charles L. *The Ohio Gang: The World of Warren G. Harding*. New York: M. Evans, 1981.

Meier, Heinz K. *The United States and Switzerland in the Nineteenth Century*. The Hague, Netherlands: Mouton & Co., 1963.

Michaeli, Ethan. *The Defender: How the Legendary Black Newspaper Changed America*. Boston: Houghton Mifflin Harcourt, 2016.

Miller, Merle. *Plain Speaking: An Oral Biography of Harry S. Truman*. New York: Berkeley Publishing, 1974.

Miller, Vivien M. L. "Family Tragedy and FBI Triumph in the South: The 1938 Kidnapping and Murder of James Bailey 'Skeegie' Cash Jr." *Journal of Southern History* 79, no. 4 (2013): 841–78.

Mills, Bill. *The League: The True Story of Average Americans on the Hunt for WWI Spies*. New York: Skyhorse, 2013.

Mitchell, Jerry. *Race against Time: A Reporter Reopens the Unsolved Murder Cases of the Civil Rights Era*. New York: Simon & Schuster, 2020.

Mitchell, Marcia, and Thomas Mitchell. *The Spy Who Seduced America: Lies and Betrayal in the Heat of the Cold War: The Judith Coplon Story*. Montpelier, VT: Invisible Cities Press, 2002.

Morgan, Ted. *Reds: McCarthyism in Twentieth-Century America*. New York: Random House, 2003.

Moss, Norman. *Klaus Fuchs: The Man Who Stole the Atom Bomb*. London: Grafton, 1987.

Moynihan, Daniel Patrick. *Secrecy: The American Experience*. New Haven: Yale University Press, 1998.

Muhammad, Kahlil Gibran. *The Condemnation of Blackness: Race, Crime, and the Making of Modern Urban America*. Cambridge, MA: Harvard University Press, 2010.

Mulloy, D.J. *The World of the John Birch Society: Conspiracy, Conservatism, and the Cold War*. Nashville: Vanderbilt University Press, 2014.

Murakawa, Naomi. *The First Civil Right: How Liberals Built Prison America*. New York: Oxford University Press, 2014.

Murch, Donna Jean. *Living for the City: Migration, Education, and the Rise of the Black Panther Party in Oakland, California*. Chapel Hill: University of North Carolina Press, 2010.

Murchison, Kenneth M. *Federal Criminal Law Doctrines: The Forgotten Influence of National Prohibition*. Durham, NC: Duke University Press, 1994.

Murphy, Kevin P. *Political Manhood: Red Bloods, Mollycoddles, and the Politics of Progressive Era Reform*. New York: Columbia University Press, 2010.

Murphy, Paul L. *World War I and the Origins of Civil Liberties in the United States*. New York: W. W. Norton & Company, 1979.

Murray, Robert K. *The Harding Era: Warren G. Harding and His Administration*. Minneapolis: University of Minnesota Press, 1969.

———. *Red Scare: A Study in National Hysteria, 1919–1920*. Minneapolis: University of Minnesota Press, 1955.

Naftali, Timothy, and Fursenko, Aleksandr. *One Hell of a Gamble: Khrushchev, Castro, and Kennedy, 1958-1964*. New York: Norton, 1998.

Nasaw, David. *The Patriarch: The Remarkable Life and Turbulent Times of Joseph P. Kennedy*. New York: Penguin Press, 2012.

Nash, George H. *The Conservative Intellectual Movement in America Since 1945*. Wilmington, DE: ISI Books, 1976.

National Research Council and Institute of Medicine of the National Academies. *Depression in Parents, Parenting, and Children*. Washington, DC: National Academies Press, 2009.

Navasky, Victor S. *Kennedy Justice*. New York: Harper & Row, 1971.

———. *Naming Names*. New York: Viking, 1980.

———. *The O'Dell File*. Kindle Single, 2014.

Neiberg, Michael S. *The Path to War: How the First World War Created Modern America*. New York: Oxford University Press, 2016.

Nelson, Phillip F. *Who REALLY Killed Martin Luther King, Jr.? The Case Against Lyndon B. Johnson and J. Edgar Hoover*. New York: Skyhorse, 2018.

Nelson, Stanley, Jr., dir. *The Black Panthers: Vanguard of the Revolution*. New York: Firelight Films, 2015.

———. *Freedom Riders*. New York: Firelight Films, 2010.

Newton, Jim. *Eisenhower: The White House Years*. New York: Doubleday, 2011.

———. *Justice for All: Earl Warren and the Nation He Made*. New York: Riverhead, 2006.

Newton, Michael. *"Don't Shoot, G-Men!" The FBI Crime War, 1933–1939*. Jefferson, NC: McFarland, 2021.

———. *The FBI and KKK: A Critical History*. Jefferson, NC: McFarland, 2005.

———. *The Mafia at Apalachin, 1957*. Jefferson, NC: McFarland, 2012.

Newton, Verne W. *The Cambridge Spies: The Untold Story of Maclean, Philby, and Burgess in America*. Lanham, MD: Madison Books, 1991.

Nichols, David A. *Ike and McCarthy: Dwight Eisenhower's Secret Campaign against Joseph McCarthy*. New York: Simon & Schuster, 2017.

———. "'The Showpiece of Our Nation': Dwight D. Eisenhower and the Desegregation of the District of Columbia." *Washington History* 16, no. 2 (2004): 44–65.

Nickerson, Michelle M. *Mothers of Conservatism: Women and the Postwar Right.* Princeton, NJ: Princeton University Press, 2012.

North, Mark. *Act of Treason: The Role of J. Edgar Hoover in the Assassination of President Kennedy.* New York: Carroll & Graf, 1991.

Novak, Andrew. "The Desegregation of George Washington University and the District of Columbia in Transition, 1946–1954." *Washington History* 24, no. 1 (2012): 22–44.

Nunnelley, William A. *Bull Connor.* Tuscaloosa: University of Alabama Press, 1991.

Odgers, Merle M. *Alexander Dallas Bache: Scientist and Educator, 1806–1867.* Philadelphia: University of Pennsylvania Press, 1947.

O'Donnell, Pierce. *In Time of War: Hitler's Terrorist Attack on America.* New York: New Press, 2005.

Oliver, Willard M. *The Birth of the FBI: Teddy Roosevelt, the Secret Service, and the Fight over America's Premier Law Enforcement Agency.* Lanham, MD: Rowman & Littlefield, 2019.

Olmsted, Kathryn S. *Challenging the Secret Government: The Post-Watergate Investigations of the CIA and FBI.* Chapel Hill: University of North Carolina Press, 1996.

———. *Red Spy Queen: A Biography of Elizabeth Bentley.* Chapel Hill: University of North Carolina Press, 2002.

Olson, Lynne. *Those Angry Days: Roosevelt, Lindbergh, and America's Fight over World War II, 1939–1941.* New York: Random House, 2013.

O'Reilly, Kenneth, "Adlai E. Stevenson, McCarthyism, and the FBI." *Illinois Historical Journal* 81, no. 1 (1988), 45–60.

———. *Black Americans: The FBI Files.* New York: Carroll & Graf, 1994.

———. "The FBI and the Origins of McCarthyism." *Historian* 45, no. 3 (1983): 372–93.

———. "The FBI and the Politics of the Riots, 1964–1968." *Journal of American History* 75, no. 1 (1988): 91–114.

———. *Hoover and the Un-Americans: The FBI, HUAC, and the Red Menace.* Philadelphia: Temple University Press, 1983.

———. "A New Deal for the FBI: The Roosevelt Administration, Crime Control, and National Security." *Journal of American History* 69, no. 3 (1982): 638–58.

———. *"Racial Matters": The FBI's Secret File on Black America, 1960–1972.* New York: Free Press, 1989.

Orren, Karen and Skowronek, Stephen. *The Search for American Political Development.* Cambridge: Cambridge University Press, 2004.

Oshinsky, David M. *A Conspiracy So Immense: The World of Joe McCarthy.* New York: Oxford University Press, 2005.

Palella, Andrew G. "The Black Legion: J. Edgar Hoover and Fascism in the Depression Era." *Journal for the Study of Radicalism* 12, no. 2 (2018): 81–106.

Pavia, Peter. *The Cuba Project: Castro, Kennedy, and the FBI's Tamale Squad.* New York: Palgrave Macmillan, 2006.

Payne, Phillip G. *Dead Last: The Public Memory of Warren G. Harding's Scandalous Legacy.* Athens: Ohio University Press, 2009.

Pendergast, Tom. *Creating the Modern Man: American Magazines and Consumer Culture, 1900–1950.* Columbia: University of Missouri Press, 2000.

Pepper, William F. *The Plot to Kill King: The Truth Behind the Assassination of Martin Luther King Jr.* New York: Skyhorse, 2018.

Perlstein, Rick. *Before the Storm: Barry Goldwater and the Unmaking of the American Consensus.* New York: Nation Books, 2001.

———. *The Invisible Bridge: The Fall of Nixon and the Rise of Reagan.* New York: Simon & Schuster, 2014.

———. *Nixonland: The Rise of a President and the Fracturing of America.* New York: Simon & Schuster, 2008.

Perrusquia, Marc. *A Spy in Canaan: How the FBI Used a Famous Civil Rights Photographer to Infiltrate the Movement.* Brooklyn, NY: Melville House, 2017.

Persico, Joseph E. *Roosevelt's Secret War: FDR and World War II Espionage.* New York: Random House, 2002.

Pettegrew, John. *Brutes in Suits: Male Sensibility in America, 1890–1920.* Baltimore: Johns Hopkins University Press, 2007.

Phillips-Fein, Kim. "Conservatism: A State of the Field." *Journal of American History* 98, no. 3 (2011): 723–43.

———. *Invisible Hands: The Businessmen's Crusade against the New Deal.* New York: W. W. Norton & Company, 2009.

Pietrusza, David. *1960: LBJ vs. JFK vs. Nixon: The Epic Campaign That Forged Three Presidencies.* New York: Union Square Press, 2008.

Pitch, Anthony S. *The Last Lynching: How a Gruesome Mass Murder Rocked a Small Georgia Town.* New York: Skyhorse, 2016.

Pliley, Jessica. *Policing Sexuality: The Mann Act and the Making of the FBI.* Cambridge, MA: Harvard University Press, 2014.

———. "Vice Queens and White Slaves: The FBI's Crackdown on Elite Brothel Madams in 1930s New York City." *Journal of the History of Sexuality* 25, no. 1 (2016): 137–67.

Podair, Jerald E. *Bayard Rustin: American Dreamer.* Lanham, MD: Rowman & Littlefield, 2009.

Polenberg, Richard. *Fighting Faiths: The Abrams Case, the Supreme Court, and Free Speech.* Ithaca, NY: Cornell University Press, 1987.

Pollard, Sam, dir. *MLK/FBI.* New York: IFC Films, 2020.

Porter, Darwin. *J. Edgar Hoover and Clyde Tolson: Investigating the Sexual Secrets of America's Most Famous Men and Women.* New York: Blood Moon Productions, 2012.

Porter, Dawn, dir. *Spies of Mississippi.* New York: Trilogy Films, 2014.

Posner, Gerald L. *Case Closed: Lee Harvey Oswald and the Assassination of JFK.* New York: Random House, 1993.

Potter, Claire Bond. "Queer Hoover: Sex, Lies, and Political History." *Journal of the History of Sexuality* 15, no. 3 (2006): 355–81.

———. *War on Crime: Bandits, G-Men, and the Politics of Mass Culture.* New Brunswick, NJ: Rutgers University Press, 1998.

Powers, Richard Gid. *Broken: The Troubled Past and Uncertain Future of the FBI.* New York: Free Press, 2004.

———. *G-Men: Hoover's FBI in American Popular Culture.* Carbondale: Southern Illinois University Press, 1983.

———. *Not without Honor: The History of American Anticommunism.* New Haven, CT: Yale University Press, 1998.

———. *Secrecy and Power: The Life of J. Edgar Hoover.* New York: Free Press, 1987.

Preston, William Jr. *Aliens and Dissenters: Federal Suppression of Radicals, 1903–1933.* Cambridge, MA: Harvard University Press, 1963.

Price, David H. *Threatening Anthropology: McCarthyism and the FBI's Surveillance of Activist Anthropologists.* Durham, NC: Duke University Press, 2004.

Purvis, Alston, and Alex Tresniowski. *The Vendetta: Special Agent Melvin Purvis, John Dillinger, and Hoover's FBI in the Age of Gangsters.* New York: PublicAffairs, 2005.

Putney, Clifford. *Muscular Christianity: Manhood and Sports in Protestant America, 1880–1920.* Cambridge, MA: Harvard University Press, 2001.

Quigley, Joan. *Just Another Southern Town: Mary Church Terrell and the Struggle for Racial Justice in the Nation's Capital.* New York: Oxford University Press, 2019.

Rabban, David M. *Free Speech in Its Forgotten Years.* Cambridge, UK: Cambridge University Press, 1997.

Rachlis, Eugene. *They Came to Kill: The Story of Eight Nazi Saboteurs in America.* New York: Random House, 1971.

Radosh, Ronald, and Joyce Milton. *The Rosenberg File.* New Haven, CT: Yale University Press, 1997.

Randolph, Justin. "Civil Rights Arrested: Black Freedom Movements and Mass Incarceration in Rural Mississippi, 1938 to 1980." PhD diss., Yale University, 2020.

Ransby, Barbara. *Ella Baker and the Black Freedom Movement: A Radical Democratic Vision.* Chapel Hill: University of North Carolina Press, 2003.

Rasenberger, Jim. *The Brilliant Disaster: JFK, Castro, and America's Doomed Invasion of Cuba's Bay of Pigs.* New York: Scribner, 2011.

Rauchway, Eric. *Murdering McKinley: The Making of Theodore Roosevelt's America.* New York: Hill and Wang, 2003.

Reavill, Gil. *Mafia Summit: J. Edgar Hoover, the Kennedy Brothers, and the Meeting That Unmasked the Mob.* New York: Thomas Dunne, 2013.

Reeves, Richard. *Infamy: The Shocking Story of the Japanese American Internment in World War II.* New York: Henry Holt, 2015.

Reeves, Thomas C. *America's Bishop: The Life and Times of Fulton J. Sheen.* San Francisco: Encounter Books, 2001.

———. *The Life and Times of Joe McCarthy: A Biography.* New York: Stein and Day, 1982.

Rhodes, Jane. *Framing the Black Panthers; The Spectacular Rise of a Black Power Icon.* New York: New Press, 2007.

Richman, Daniel C., and Sarah Seo. "How Federalism Built the FBI, Sustained Local Police, and Left Out the States." Columbia Public Law Research Paper No. 14-679, 2020. *Stanford Journal of Civil Rights and Civil Liberties,* forthcoming.

Riebling, Mark. *Wedge: The Secret War between the FBI and CIA.* New York: Alfred A. Knopf, 1994.

Ritchie, Donald A. *The Columnist: Leaks, Lies, and Libel in Drew Pearson's Washington.* New York: Oxford University Press, 2021.

Roberts, Sam. *The Brother: The Untold Story of Atomic Spy David Greenglass and How He Sent His Sister, Ethel Rosenberg, to the Electric Chair.* New York: Random House, 2001.

Robin, Corey. *Fear: The History of a Political Idea.* New York: Oxford University Press, 2004.

Robinson, Greg. *By Order of the President: FDR and the Internment of Japanese Americans.* Cambridge, MA: Harvard University Press, 2011.

Rodden, John. *Of G-Men and Eggheads: The FBI and the New York Intellectuals.* Urbana: University of Illinois Press, 2017.

Romerstein, Herbert, and Eric Breindel. *The Venona Secrets: The Definitive Exposé of Soviet Espionage in America.* Washington, DC: Regnery History, 2000.

Rosenberg, Jane Aikin. *The Nation's Great Library: Herbert Putnam and the Library of Congress, 1899-1939.* Chicago: University of Illinois Press, 1993.

Rosenfeld, Seth. *Subversives: The FBI's War on Student Radicals, and Reagan's Rise to Power.* New York: Farrar, Straus and Giroux, 2012.

Ross, Jack. *The Socialist Party of America: A Complete History.* Lincoln: University of Nebraska Press, 2015.

Rosswurm, Steve. *The FBI and the Catholic Church, 1935–1962.* Amherst: University of Massachusetts Press, 2009.

Rotundo, E. Anthony. *American Manhood: Transformations in Masculinity from the Revolution to the Modern Era.* New York: Basic Books, 1993.

Rovere, Richard H. *Senator Joe McCarthy.* New York: Harcourt, Brace, Jovanovich, 1959.

Russell, Francis. *The Shadow of Blooming Grove: Warren G. Harding in His Times.* New York: McGraw-Hill, 1968.

Ruth, David E. *Inventing the Public Enemy: The Gangster in American Culture, 1918-1934.* Chicago: University of Chicago Press, 1996.

Sabin, Arthur J. *In Calmer Times: The Supreme Court and Red Monday.* Philadelphia: University of Pennsylvania Press, 1999.

Salisbury, Harrison E. "The Strange Correspondence of Morris Ernst and J. Edgar Hoover." *Nation,* January 25, 2007.

Savodnik, Peter. *The Interloper: Lee Harvey Oswald inside the Soviet Union.* New York: Basic Books, 2013.

Sbardellati, John. *J. Edgar Hoover Goes to the Movies: The FBI and the Origins of Hollywood's Cold War.* Ithaca, NY: Cornell University Press, 2012.

Schaffer, Sam. "New South Nation: Woodrow Wilson's Generation and the Rise of the South, 1884–1920." PhD diss., Yale University, 2010.

Schecter, Jerrold, and Leona Schecter. *Sacred Secrets: How Soviet Intelligence Operations Changed American History.* Washington, DC: Brassey's, 2002.

Scheiber, Harry N. *The Wilson Administration and Civil Liberties, 1917–1921.* Ithaca, NY: Cornell University Press, 1960.

Schlesinger, Arthur M. Jr. *The Age of Roosevelt, vol. 1: Crisis of the Old Order, 1919–1933.* Boston: Houghton Mifflin Company, 1957.

———. *Robert Kennedy and His Times.* Boston: Houghton Mifflin, 1978.

Schmidt, Regin. *Red Scare: FBI and the Origins of Anticommunism in the United States, 1919–1943.* Denmark: Museum Tusculanum Press, University of Copenhagen, 2000.

Schneir, Walter. *Final Verdict: What Really Happened in the Rosenberg Case.* Brooklyn, NY: Melville House, 2010.

Schneir, Walter, and Miriam Schneir. *Invitation to an Inquest.* Garden City, NY: Doubleday, 1965.

Schoenwald, Jonathan M. *A Time for Choosing: The Rise of Modern American Conservatism.* New York: Oxford University Press, 2001.

Schott, Joseph. *No Left Turns.* New York: Praeger, 1975.

Schrader, Stuart. *Badges without Borders: How Global Counterinsurgency Transformed American Policing.* Berkeley: University of California Press, 2019.

Schrecker, Ellen, ed. *Cold War Triumphalism: The Misuse of History after the Fall of Communism.* New York: New Press, 2004.

———. *Many Are the Crimes: McCarthyism in America.* Princeton, NJ: Princeton University Press, 1998.

Scott, Katherine A. *Reining in the State: Civil Society and Congress in the Vietnam and Watergate Eras.* Lawrence: University Press of Kansas, 2013.

Sebba, Anne. *Ethel Rosenberg: An American Tragedy.* New York: St. Martin's Press, 2021.

Seigel, Micol. *Violence Work: State Power and the Limits of Police.* Durham: Duke University Press, 2018.

Self, Robert. *American Babylon: Race and the Struggle for Postwar Oakland.* Princeton: Princeton University Press, 2003.

Seo, Sarah A. *Policing the Open Road: How Cars Transformed American Freedom.* Cambridge, MA: Harvard University Press, 2019.

Server, Lee. *Handsome Johnny: The Life and Death of Johnny Rosselli: Gentleman Gangster, Hollywood Producer, CIA Assassin.* New York: St. Martin's Griffin, 2018.

Shannon, David A. *The Socialist Party of America: A History.* New York: MacMillan Company, 1955.

Shenon, Philip. *A Cruel and Shocking Act: The Secret History of the Kennedy Assassination.* New York: Henry Holt and Company, 2013.

Sherwood, Timothy H. *The Rhetorical Leadership of Fulton J. Sheen, Norman Vincent Peale and Billy Graham in the Age of Extremes.* Lanham, MD: Lexington Books, 2013.

Shinkle, Peter. *Ike's Mystery Man: The Secret Lives of Robert Cutler.* Hanover, NH: Steerforth, 2018.

Shipp, Bill. *Murder at Broad River Bridge: The Slaying of Lemuel Penn by Members of the Ku Klux Klan.* Atlanta: Peachtree, 1981.

Sides, Hampton. *Hellhound on His Trail: The Stalking of Martin Luther King Jr. and the International Hunt for His Assassin.* New York: Doubleday, 2010.

Sinclair, Andrew. *The Available Man: The Life behind the Masks of Warren G. Harding.* New York: MacMillan, 1965.

Skowronek, Stephen with Stephen M. Engel, Bruce Ackerman. *The Progressives' Century: Political Reform, Constitutional Government, and the Modern American State.* New Haven. Yale University Press, 2016.

Slide, Anthony. *American Racist: The Life and Films of Thomas Dixon.* Lexington: University Press of Kentucky, 2004.

Slotten, Hugh. *Patronage, Practice, and the Culture of American Science: Alexander Dallas Bache and the U.S. Coast Survey.* New York: Cambridge University Press, 1994.

Smead, Howard. *Blood Justice: The Lynching of Mack Charles Parker.* New York: Oxford University Press, 1986.

Souter, Gerry. *Selling Americans on America: Journey into a Troubled Nation.* Metro-Jackson, MS: Sartoris Literary Group, 2019.

Sparrow, James T. *Warfare State: World War II Americans and the Age of Big Government.* New York: Oxford University Press, 2011.

Stafford, David. *Camp X: OSS, "Intrepid," and the Allies' North American Training Camp for Secret Agents, 1941–1945.* New York: Dodd, Mead, 1987.

Steinberg, Peter L. *The Great "Red Menace": United States Prosecution of American Communists, 1947–1952.* Westport, CT: Greenwood Press, 1984.

Stephan, Alexander. *"Communazis": FBI Surveillance of German Emigre Writers.* Translated by Jan van Heurck. New Haven, CT: Yale University Press, 2000.

Stevenson, William. *A Man Called Intrepid: The Secret War.* New York: Harcourt, Brace, Jovanovich, 1976.

Stewart, Alison. *First Class: The Legacy of Dunbar, America's First Black Public High School.* Chicago: Lawrence Hill Books, 2013.

Stockham, Aaron. "Lack of Oversight: The Relationship between Congress and the FBI, 1907–1975." PhD diss., Marquette University, 2011.

Stone, Geoffrey R. *Perilous Times: Free Speech in Wartime.* New York: W. W. Norton & Company, 2004.

Storrs, Landon. *The Second Red Scare and the Unmaking of the New Deal Left.* Princeton, NJ: Princeton University Press, 2013.

Stowe, David W. "The Politics of Café Society." *Journal of American History* 84, no. 4 (1998): 1384–406.

Strang, Dean. *Keep the Wretches in Order: America's Biggest Mass Trial, the Rise of the Justice Department, and the Fall of the IWW.* Madison: University of Wisconsin Press, 2019.

———. *Worse Than the Devil: Anarchists, Clarence Darrow, and Justice in a Time of Terror.* Madison: University of Wisconsin Press, 2016.

Streifer, Bill. "The Investigation: J. Edgar Hoover and the Manhattan Project." *American Intelligence Journal* 33, no. 2 (2016): 54–62.

Strunk, Mary Elizabeth. *Wanted Women: An American Obsession in the Reign of J. Edgar Hoover.* Lawrence: University Press of Kansas, 2010.

Stuart, Lyle. *The Secret Life of Walter Winchell.* New York: Boar's Head Books, 1953.

Sugrue, Thomas J. *The Origins of the Urban Crisis: Race and Inequality in Postwar Detroit.* Princeton, NJ: Princeton University Press, 1996.

Sullivan, Patricia. *Lift Every Voice: The NAACP and the Making of the Civil Rights Movement.* New York: New Press, 2009.

Summers, Anthony. *The Arrogance of Power: The Secret World of Richard Nixon.* New York: Viking, 2000.

———. *Goddess: The Secret Lives of Marilyn Monroe.* New York: Macmillan, 1985.

———. *Not in Your Lifetime: The Defining Book on the J.F.K. Assassination.* New York: Open Road Integrated Media, 2014.

———. *Official and Confidential: The Secret Life of J. Edgar Hoover.* New York: G. P. Putnam's Sons, 1993.

"Symposium: Wickersham Commission." *Marquette Law Review* 96, no. 4 (2013).

Syrett, Nicholas L. *The Company He Keeps: A History of White College Fraternities.* Chapel Hill: University of North Carolina Press, 2009.

Talbot, David. *The Devil's Chessboard: Allen Dulles, the CIA, and the Rise of America's Secret Government.* New York: HarperCollins, 2015.

Tanenhaus, Sam. *Whittaker Chambers: A Biography.* New York: Random House, 1997.

Theoharis, Athan, ed. *Beyond the Hiss Case: The FBI, Congress, and the Cold War.* Philadelphia: Temple University Press, 1982.

———. *Chasing Spies: How the FBI Failed in Counter-Intelligence but Promoted the Politics of McCarthyism in the Cold War.* Chicago: Ivan R. Dee, 2002.

———. *The FBI and American Democracy: A Brief Critical History.* Lawrence: University Press of Kansas, 2004.

———. "The FBI and the American Legion Contact Program, 1940–1966," *Political Science Quarterly* 100, no. 2 (1985): 271–86.

———. *J. Edgar Hoover, Sex, and Crime: An Historical Antidote.* Chicago: Ivan R. Dee, 1995.

———. *The Quest for Absolute Security: The Failed Relations among U.S. Intelligence Agencies.* Chicago: Ivan R. Dee, 2007.

———. *Seeds of Repression: Harry S. Truman and the Origins of McCarthyism*. Chicago: Quadrangle Books, 1971.

———. *The Truman Presidency: The Origins of the Imperial Presidency and the National Security State*. New York: E. M. Coleman, 1979.

Theoharis, Athan et al., eds. *The FBI: A Comprehensive Reference Guide*. Phoenix: Oryx Press, 1999.

Theoharis, Athan, and John Stuart Cox. *The Boss: J. Edgar Hoover and the Great American Inquisition*. Philadelphia: Temple University Press, 1988.

Thomas, Evan. *Robert Kennedy: His Life*. New York: Simon & Schuster, 2000.

———. *The Very Best Men: Four Who Dared: The Early Years of the CIA*. New York: Touchstone, 1995.

Thom, Cathleen, and Patrick Jung. "The Responsibilities Program of the FBI, 1951–1955." *Historian* 59, no. 2 (1997): 347–70.

Thompson, Heather Ann. *Blood in the Water: The Attica Prison Uprising of 1971 and its Legacy*. New York: Pantheon, 2016.

Toland, John. *The Dillinger Days*. New York: Da Capo Press, 1995. First published 1963.

———. *Infamy: Pearl Harbor and Its Aftermath*. New York: Doubleday & Company, 1982.

Toledano, Ralph de. *J. Edgar Hoover: The Man in His Time*. New Rochelle, NY: Arlington House, 1973.

Tompkins, Sally Kress. *A Quest for Grandeur: Charles Moore and the Federal Triangle*. Washington, DC: Smithsonian Institution Press, 1993.

Trelease, Allen W. *White Terror: The Ku Klux Klan Conspiracy and Southern Reconstruction*. New York: Harper and Row, 1971.

Turner, William, and Jonn Christian. *The Assassination of Robert F. Kennedy: The Conspiracy and Coverup*. New York: Carroll & Graf, 1993.

Tushnet, Mark V. *Making Civil Rights Law: Thurgood Marshall and the Supreme Court, 1936-1961*. New York: Oxford University Press, 1996.

Tye, Larry. *Demagogue: The Life and Long Shadow of Senator Joe McCarthy*. Boston: Houghton Mifflin Harcourt, 2020.

Tyrnauer, Matt, dir. *Where's My Roy Cohn?* Los Angeles: Altimeter Films, 2019.

Tyson, Timothy. *The Blood of Emmett Till*. New York: Simon & Schuster, 2017.

Underhill, Stephen M. *The Manufacture of Consent: J. Edgar Hoover and the Rhetorical Rise of the FBI*. East Lansing: Michigan State University Press, 2020.

Ungar, Sanford J. *FBI: An Uncensored Look behind the Walls*. Boston: Little, Brown, 1976.

Unger, Robert. *The Union Station Massacre: The Original Sin of J. Edgar Hoover's FBI*. Kansas City, MO: Andrews McMeel, 1997.

Usdin, Steven T. *Bureau of Spies: The Secret Connections between Espionage and Journalism in Washington*. Amherst, MA: Prometheus, 2018.

Varon, Jeremy. *Bringing the War Home: The Weather Underground, the Red Army Faction, and Revolutionary Violence in the Sixties and Seventies*. Berkeley: University of California Press, 2004.

von Hoffman, Nicholas. *Citizen Cohn: The Life and Times of Roy Cohn*. New York: Bantam, 1988.

Wacker, Grant. *America's Pastor: Billy Graham and the Shaping of a Nation*. Cambridge, MA: Belknap Press/Harvard University Press, 2014.

Waldrep, Christopher. *African Americans Confront Lynching: Strategies of Resistance from the Civil War to the Civil Rights Era*. Lanham, MD: Rowman & Littlefield, 2009.

———. "National Policing, Lynching, and Constitutional Change." *Journal of Southern History* 74, no. 3 (2008): 589–626.

———. *Popular Justice: A History of American Criminal Justice*. New York: Oxford University Press, 1980.

Walker, Samuel. *A Critical History of Police Reform: The Emergence of Professionalism*. Lexington, MA: Lexington Books, 1977.

———. *In Defense of American Liberties: A History of the ACLU*. New York: Oxford University Press, 1990.

Waller, Douglas. *Wild Bill Donovan: The Spymaster Who Created the OSS and Modern American Espionage*. New York: Free Press, 2011.

Ward, Jason Morgan. *Defending White Democracy: The Making of a Segregationist Movement and the Remaking of Racial Politics, 1936–1965*. Chapel Hill: University of North Carolina Press, 2011.

———. *Hanging Bridge: Racial Violence and America's Civil Rights Century*. New York: Oxford University Press, 2016.

Wasserman, Jacob. "Internal Affairs: Untold Case Studies of World War I German Internment." Senior thesis, Yale University, 2016.

Waters, Robert Alvin, and Zack C. Waters. *The Kidnapping and Murder of Little Skeegie Cash: J. Edgar Hoover and Florida's Lindbergh Case*. Tuscaloosa: University of Alabama Press, 2014.

Watson, Bruce. *Freedom Summer: The Savage Season of 1964 That Made Mississippi Burn and Made America a Democracy*. New York: Viking, 2010.

Weaver, Vesla M. "Frontlash: Race and the Development of Punitive Crime Policy." *Studies in American Political Development* 21, no. 2 (2007): 230–65.

Webb, Clive. *Rabble Rousers: The American Far Right in the Civil Rights Era*. Athens: University of Georgia Press, 2010.

Weiner, Ed. *Let's Go to Press: A Profile of Walter Winchell, America's Most Controversial Newsman*. New York: G. P. Putnam's Sons, 1955.

Weiner, Tim. *Enemies: A History of the FBI*. New York: Random House, 2012.

———. *Legacy of Ashes: The History of the CIA*. New York: Doubleday, 2007.

———. *One Man against the World: The Tragedy of Richard Nixon*. New York: Henry Holt, 2015.

Weinstein, Allen. *Perjury: The Hiss-Chambers Case*. Stanford, CA: Hoover Institution Press, 2013.

Weinstein, Allen, and Alexander Vassiliev. *The Haunted Wood: Soviet Espionage in America—the Stalin Era*. New York: Random House, 1999.

Weinstein, James. *The Decline of Socialism in America, 1912–1925*. New York: Monthly Review Press, 1967.

Weisberg, Harold. *Frame-Up: The Martin Luther King/James Earl Ray Case Containing Suppressed Evidence*. New York: Outerbridge & Dienstfrey, 1971.

———. *Whitewash II: The FBI-Secret Service Cover-Up*. New York: Skyhorse, 1966.

Weiss, Nancy J. *Farewell to the Party of Lincoln: Black Politics in the Age of FDR*. Princeton, NJ: Princeton University Press, 1983.

Welsome, Eileen. *Cold War Secrets: A Vanished Professor, A Suspected Killer, and Hoover's FBI*. Kent, OH: Kent State University Press, 2021.

West, Nigel. *Venona: The Greatest Secret of the Cold War.* New York: HarperCollins, 2000.

Wexler, Laura. *Fire in a Canebrake: The Last Mass Lynching in America.* New York: Scribner, 2003.

Whalan, Mark. *World War One, American Literature, and the Federal State.* New York: Cambridge University Press, 2018.

Whitehead, Don. *Attack on Terror: The FBI against the Ku Klux Klan in Mississippi.* New York: Funk & Wagnalls, 1970.

White, William Allen. *A Puritan in Babylon: The Story of Calvin Coolidge.* New York: Macmillan Company, 1938.

Whitfield, Stephen. *The Culture of the Cold War.* Baltimore: Johns Hopkins University Press, 1996.

Wiebe, Robert H. *The Search for Order, 1877–1920.* New York: Hill and Wang, 1967.

Williams, Jakobi. *From the Bullet to the Ballot: The Illinois Chapter of the Black Panther Party and Racial Coalition Politics in Chicago.* Chapel Hill: University of North Carolina Press, 2013.

Williams, Robert Chadwell. *Klaus Fuchs, Atom Spy.* Cambridge, MA: Harvard University Press, 1987.

Wilson, Veronica A. "'Now You Are Alone:' Anticommunism, Gender, and the Cold War Myths of Hede Massing and Whittaker Chambers." *Diplomatic History* 36, no. 4 (2012), 699–722.

Winks, Robin W. *Cloak & Gown: Scholars in the Secret War, 1939–1961.* New York: William Morrow & Company, 1987.

Witcover, Jules. *Sabotage at Black Tom: Imperial Germany's Secret War in America, 1914–1917.* Chapel Hill, NC: Algonquin Books of Chapel Hill, 1989.

Wohl, Alexander. *Father, Son, and Constitution: How Justice Tom Clark and Attorney General Ramsey Clark Shaped American Democracy.* Lawrence: University Press of Kansas, 2013.

Woods, Jeff. *Black Struggle, Red Scare: Segregation and Anti-Communism in the South, 1948–1968.* Baton Rouge: Louisiana State University Press, 2004.

Ybarra, Michael J. *Washington Gone Crazy: Senator Pat McCarran and the Great American Communist Hunt.* Hanover, NH: Steerforth, 2004.

Yellin, Eric Steven. *Racism in the Nation's Service: Government Workers and the Color Line in Woodrow Wilson's America.* Chapel Hill: University of North Carolina Press, 2013.

Zieger, Robert H. *The CIO, 1935–1955.* Chapel Hill: University of North Carolina Press, 1995.

Zipes, Greg. *Justice and Faith: The Frank Murphy Story.* Ann Arbor: University of Michigan Press, 2021.

Zwiers, Maarten. *Senator James Eastland: Mississippi's Jim Crow Democrat.* Baton Rouge: Louisiana State University Press, 2015.

INDEX